3 9077 06165 5042
W9-CKI-613

Cyclopedia of WORLD AUTHORS

Cyclopedia of WORLD AUTHORS

Fourth Revised Edition

Volume 5
Scot-Z
Indexes

Edited by
FRANK N. MAGILL

Associate Editors, Revised Edition
Dayton Kohler *and* Tench Francis Tilghman

Associate Editors, Revised Third Edition
McCrea Adams *and* Juliane Brand

Associate Editor, Fourth Revised Edition
Tracy Irons-Georges

SALEM PRESS
Pasadena, California Hackensack, New Jersey

Editor in Chief: Dawn P. Dawson
Editorial Director: Christina J. Moose
Project Editor: Tracy Irons-Georges
Copy Editors: Elizabeth Slocum, Leslie Ellen Jones
Assistant Editor: Andrea E. Miller
Acquisitions Editor: Mark Rehn
Research Supervisor: Jeffry Jensen
Research Assistant: Michelle Murphy
Production Editor: Joyce I. Buchea
Page Design: James Hutson
Layout: William Zimmerman

Fourth Revised Edition includes: *Cyclopedia of World Authors*, 1958 (first edition); *Cyclopedia of World Authors, Revised Edition*, 1974 (second edition); *Cyclopedia of World Authors II*, 1989; *Cyclopedia of World Authors, Revised Third Edition*, 1997; and material new to this edition.

∞ The paper used in these volumes conforms to the American National Standard for Permanence of Paper for Printed Library Materials, Z39.48-1992 (R1997).

Library of Congress Cataloging-in-Publication Data

Cyclopedia of world authors / edited by Frank N. Magill ; associate editor, Tracy Irons-Georges.— 4th rev. ed.

p. cm.

Includes bibliographical references and index.

ISBN 1-58765-122-X (set : alk. paper) — ISBN 1-58765-123-8 (vol. 1 : alk. paper) — ISBN 1-58765-124-6 (vol. 2 : alk. paper) — ISBN 1-58765-125-4 (vol. 3 : alk. paper) — ISBN 1-58765-126-2 (vol. 4 : alk. paper) — ISBN 1-58765-127-0 (vol. 5 : alk. paper)

1. Literature—Bio-bibliography. I. Magill, Frank Northen, 1907-1997. II. Irons-Georges, Tracy.

PN451 .M36 2003
809—dc22

2003017382

First Printing

PRINTED IN THE UNITED STATES OF AMERICA

LIST OF AUTHORS IN VOLUME 5

COMPLETE LIST OF AUTHORS

Volume 1

Volume 2

Volume 3

Volume 4

Volume 5

PRONUNCIATION KEY

Foreign and unusual or ambiguous English-language names of profiled authors may be unfamiliar to some users of the *Cyclopedia of World Authors*. To help readers pronounce such names correctly, phonetic spellings using the character symbols listed below have been added within parentheses, immediately after the first mention of the author's last name in the narrative text. Stressed syllables are indicated in capital letters, and syllables are separated by hyphens.

VOWEL SOUNDS

Symbol: Spelled (Pronounced)

a: answer (AN-sihr), laugh (laf), sample (SAM-pul), that (that)
ah: father (FAH-thur), hospital (HAHS-pih-tul)
aw: awful (AW-ful), caught (kawt)
ay: blaze (blayz), fade (fayd), waiter (WAYT-ur), weigh (way)
eh: bed (behd), head (hehd), said (sehd)
ee: believe (bee-LEEV), cedar (SEE-dur), leader (LEED-ur), liter (LEE-tur)
ew: boot (bewt), lose (lews)
i: buy (bi), height (hit), lie (li), surprise (sur-PRIZ)
ih: bitter (BIH-tur), pill (pihl)
o: cotton (CO-tuhn), hot (hot)
oh: below (bee-LOH), coat (coht), note (noht), wholesome (HOHL-suhm)
oo: good (good), look (look)
ow: couch (kowch), how (how)
oy: boy (boy), coin (koyn)
uh: about (uh-BOWT), butter (BUH-tur), enough (ee-NUHF), other (UH-thur)

CONSONANT SOUNDS

Symbol: Spelled (Pronounced)

ch: beach (beech), chimp (chihmp)
g: beg (behg), disguise (dihs-GIZ), get (geht)
j: digit (DIH-jiht), edge (ehj), jet (jeht)
k: cat (kat), kitten (KIH-tehn), hex (hehks)
s: cellar (SEHL-ur), save (sayv), scent (sehnt)
sh: champagne (sham-PAYN), issue (IH-shew), shop (shop)
ur: birth (burth), disturb (dihs-TURB), earth (urth), letter (LEH-tur)
y: useful (YEWS-ful), young (yuhng)
z: business (BIHZ-ness), zest (zehst)
zh: vision (VIH-zhuhn)

Cyclopedia
of
WORLD AUTHORS

Robert Falcon Scott

English explorer and memoirist

Born: Devonport, England; June 6, 1868
Died: Antarctica; c. March 29, 1912

NONFICTION: *The Voyage of the Discovery*, 1905; *Scott's Last Expedition*, 1913.

Robert Falcon Scott's early education was acquired at Stoke Damerel and Stubbington House, Fareham; at twelve years of age he entered service on HMS *Britannia*, and in 1882 he became a midshipman. He served on various ships, rising steadily in rank, and was promoted to first lieutenant in 1897. In 1899 he was offered, and accepted, the command of the National Antarctic Expedition. The party, consisting mostly of naval personnel but sailing under the merchant flag, embarked aboard the ship *Discovery* in 1901. They explored the Antarctic ice barrier, discovered King Edward VII Land, and established a camp in McMurdo Sound that remained the expedition base for approximately two years. Various scientific activities were carried out during this period, and Scott made two notable sledge journeys southward into the interior of the continent.

On his return from Antarctica in 1904 Scott was promoted to captain; his achievements were acclaimed, and publication of his journal in two volumes the following year assured his international reputation. In 1909 he was appointed naval assistant to the second sea lord of the Admiralty. At this time he was engaged in planning a second Antarctic expedition, which tried to reach the South Pole.

His party sailed aboard the *Terra Nova* in June, 1910, and upon arrival at McMurdo Sound a number of supply depots were established along the overland route Scott planned to follow. A similar expedition headed by the Norwegian Roald Amundsen arrived at the Bay of Whales during this time. Scott and four companions set out for the South Pole on November 1, 1911; after severe hardships and the longest sledge journey ever undertaken—1,842 miles—they reached their destination on January 18, 1912, only to find that Amundsen had been there on December 14. Scott's return journey was an unremitting series of disasters. Blizzards, frostbite, and exhaustion took their toll. Scott was the last of the five men to succumb. He made the final entry in his journal on March 29. The other tasks of the expedition were pursued by the members who had remained at the base camp. Much valuable exploration and scientific work was carried out by this group.

When the expedition returned to civilization in 1913, Scott's achievements and the circumstances of his death became generally known. His journal, published posthumously the same year, has remained a classic in the literature of exploration. It is an account of epic struggle and tenacity, of indomitable spirit, and of quiet courage when the end becomes inevitable. The concluding pages, which consist of messages to his own family and friends and those of his companions, betray only a deep concern for others. The sincerity and nobility expressed in his words have ensured his hold upon the public imagination.

Bibliography

Baughman, T. H. *Pilgrims on the Ice: Robert Falcon Scott's First Antarctic Expedition*. Lincoln: University of Nebraska Press, 1997.

Huntford, Roland. *Scott and Amundsen*. New York: Putnam, 1980.

Johnson, Anthony M. *Scott of the Antarctic and Cardiff*. Cardiff, Wales: University College Cardiff Press, 1984.

Lashly, William. *Under Scott's Command: Lashly's Antarctic Diaries*. New York: Taplinger, 1969.

Mear, Roger, and Robert Swan. *A Walk to the Pole: To the Heart of Antarctica in the Footsteps of Scott*. New York: Crown, 1987.

Preston, Diana. *A First Rate Tragedy: Robert Falcon Scott and the Race to the South Pole*. Boston: Houghton Mifflin, 1998.

Sir Walter Scott

Scottish novelist

Born: Edinburgh, Scotland; August 15, 1771
Died: Abbotsford, Scotland; September 21, 1832

LONG FICTION: *Waverley: Or, 'Tis Sixty Years Since*, 1814; *Guy Mannering*, 1815; *The Antiquary*, 1816; *The Black Dwarf*, 1816; *Old Mortality*, 1816; *Rob Roy*, 1817; *The Heart of Midlothian*, 1818; *The Bride of Lammermoor*, 1819; *A Legend of Montrose*, 1819; *Ivanhoe*, 1819; *The Monastery*, 1820; *The Abbot*, 1820; *Kenilworth*, 1821; *The Pirate*, 1821; *The Fortunes of Nigel*, 1822; *Peveril of the Peak*, 1823; *Quentin Durward*, 1823; *St. Ronan's Well*, 1823; *Redgauntlet*, 1824; *The Betrothed*, 1825; *The Talisman*, 1825; *Woodstock*, 1826; *The*

Highland Widow, 1827; *The Two Drovers*, 1827; *The Surgeon's Daughter*, 1827; *The Fair Maid of Perth*, 1828; *Anne of Geierstein*, 1829; *Count Robert of Paris*, 1831; *Castle Dangerous*, 1831; *The Siege of Malta*, 1976.

DRAMA: *Halidon Hill*, pb. 1822; *Macduff's Cross*, pb. 1823; *The House of Aspen*, pb. 1829; *The Doom of Devorgoil*, pb. 1830; *Auchindrane: Or, The Ayrshire Tragedy*, pr., pb. 1830.

POETRY: *The Eve of Saint John: A Border Ballad*, 1800; *The Lay of the Last Minstrel*, 1805; *Ballads and Lyrical Pieces*, 1806; *Marmion: A Tale of Flodden Field*, 1808; *The Lady of the Lake*, 1810; *The Vision of Don Roderick*, 1811; *Rokeby*, 1813; *The Bridal of Triermain: Or, The Vale of St. John, in Three Cantos*, 1813; *The Lord of the Isles*, 1815; *The Field of Waterloo*, 1815; *The Ettrick Garland: Being Two Excellent New Songs*, 1815 (with James Hogg); *Harold the Dauntless*, 1817.

NONFICTION: *The Life and Works of John Dryden*, 1808; *The Life of Jonathan Swift*, 1814; *Lives of the Novelists*, 1825; *Provincial Antiquities of Scotland*, 1826; *The Life of Napoleon Buonaparte: Emperor of the French, with a Preliminary View of the French Revolution*, 1827; *Religious Discourses by a Layman*, 1828; *The History of Scotland*, 1829-1830; *Letters on Demonology and Witchcraft*, 1830.

TRANSLATIONS: *"The Chase" and "William and Helen": Two Ballads from the German of Gottfried Augustus Bürger*, 1796; *Goetz of Berlichingen, with the Iron Hand*, 1799 (of Johann Wolfgang von Goethe).

EDITED TEXTS: *Minstrelsy of the Scottish Border*, 1802-1803 (3 volumes); *A Collection of Scarce and Valuable Tracts*, 1809-1815 (13 volumes); *Chronological Notes of Scottish Affairs from the Diary of Lord Fountainhall*, 1822.

In spite of physical handicaps Walter Scott lived a full, varied life and created an impressive body of writings. Stricken with infantile paralysis before he was two years old, and alternating between periods of physical vigor and serious ailments throughout his life, he loved and practiced outdoor sports for most of his sixty-one years.

Born in Edinburgh on August 15, 1771, he was a product of the eighteenth century as well as of the Romantic nineteenth. As a child he was a voracious reader and avid listener to tales and legends, particularly those of his native Scotland. His copious reading was stored in a retentive memory and used to advantage in his writings, and his interest in folklore led to his collection and publication of Scottish ballads. Although not a brilliant student, he was praised for his ability to enjoy and understand the Latin poets. He entered the University of Edinburgh in 1783, but after a year or so at college he suffered one of his severe illnesses. He completed his convalescence with a sympathetic uncle, Captain Robert Scott, who encouraged his literary interests.

He studied law in his father's office; in spite of a disinclination for the profession, he was admitted to the bar in 1792. He made use of his legal experiences in his novels, especially *Redgauntlet*, in which his friend William Clerk served as model for Darsie Latimer, and Scott himself for Alan Fairford. When he was about twenty, Scott cast his eye on a lovely fifteen-year-old girl, Williamina Belsches, who was his social superior. After an unsuccessful courtship of five years he lost her to a rival and indulged his sorrow for a time with melancholy self-dramatization out of keeping with his usual behavior.

In 1797, when the fear of a Napoleonic invasion seized Great Britain, Scott was the moving force in forming a volunteer home-guard unit in which he held the position of quartermaster. In spite of his disabled leg he was a bold and expert horseman, and apparently he was disappointed at not engaging Napoleon's forces. In the late summer of the same year, on a tour of the Lake Country with his brother John and his friend Adam Ferguson, he met Charlotte Carpenter, supposedly the daughter of a French royalist and ward of an English nobleman. This time his courtship was both short and successful, and he married Charlotte on Christmas Eve, 1797. Their first child died in infancy, but four children reached maturity, two sons and two daughters.

In 1799 Scott was appointed sheriff-deputy of Selkirkshire; the position brought him a steady income and not-too-onerous duties. Seven years later he became clerk of the session in Edinburgh, adding to his steady income and increasing his routine labors considerably.

Although he translated for publication Johann Wolfgang von Goethe's *Götz von Berlichingen mit der eisernen Hand* (pb. 1773) and collected and edited (and often revised) ballads in his *Minstrelsy of the Scottish Border*, he won his first recognition as a poet in 1805 with *The Lay of the Last Minstrel* and became a major literary figure in England with *Marmion* and *The Lady of the Lake*. His subsequent long poems added little to his reputation. Shortly after the publication of *The Lay of the Last Minstrel* he formed a partnership (as a silent partner) with the printer James Ballantyne, an old school friend. During his poetic career Scott also completed two major works of scholarship, an eighteen-volume edition of John Dryden and a nineteen-volume edition of Jonathan Swift, either of which would have made a reputation for a professional scholar.

In 1814, with the anonymous publication of *Waverley*, Scott began a new literary career and his most illustrious, for he is now considered primarily a historical novelist rather than a poet or scholar. Scott gave reasons for not acknowledging the authorship of his novels, but at least one reason was a childish delight in mystification, a puckish joy in throwing dust into the public eye. Between 1814 and his death in 1832, he completed about thirty novels and novellas, several long poems, a large mass of miscellaneous writings, and the nine-volume *The Life of Napoleon Buonaparte*.

In 1820 Scott was the first baronet created by George IV. By this time he had bought acres of land and was sinking a fortune in Abbotsford. One friend who helped furnish Abbotsford was Daniel Terry, the actor-manager who produced dramatic versions of several of Scott's works. Scott's publishing ventures were in bad circumstances which grew worse; in 1826 Constable and Ballantyne failed. Instead of taking refuge in bankruptcy, Scott undertook to write himself and his colleagues out of debt. Few people have displayed more fortitude under adversity. To cap the material loss, he suffered the death of his beloved wife. His grief was profound, but he continued to write. In 1830, apparently as a result of his Herculean labors under stress, he suffered his first stroke. He recovered and continued work until recurring strokes paralyzed him and practically destroyed his mind. He died September 21, 1832, still in debt. His son-in-law, John Gibson Lockhart, helped clear the debts with the proceeds of his superb biography of the baronet.

One of Scott's contemporary admirers called him a combination of William Shakespeare and Samuel Johnson. Those who think of him only as a cloak-and-sword romancer overlook his remarkable gift of creating comic characters and his broad view of human nature in all walks of life. He was greatly admired by Honoré de Balzac and Alexandre Dumas, and wise critics from Goethe to the present have been impressed with his humane wisdom.

William Baker

Bibliography

Bold, Alan, ed. *Sir Walter Scott: The Long-Forgotten Melody.* London: Vision Press, 1983. Nine essays cover such subjects in Scott's works as the image of Scotland, politics, and folk tradition and draw upon Scott's poetry for illustration. The essay by Iain Crichton Smith, "Poetry in Scott's Narrative Verse," shows appreciation for the art of the poetry. Includes endnotes and an index.

Chandler, Alice. "Origins of Medievalism: Scott." In *A Dream of Order: The Medieval Ideal in Nineteenth-Century English Literature.* Lincoln: University of Nebraska Press, 1970. Examines the role of Scott's poems in the popularity of medievalism in the writing of the era. His poetry derived from his scholarly research in medieval literature, and his novels would derive from his success as a poet. Supplemented by footnotes, a bibliography, and an index.

Crawford, Thomas. *Scott.* Rev. ed. Edinburgh: Scottish Academic Press, 1982. A revision and elaboration of Crawford's widely acclaimed study of Scott. Examines Scott's work as a poet, balladist, and novelist.

Johnson, Edgar. *Sir Walter Scott: The Great Unknown.* 2 vols. New York: Macmillan, 1970. Considered a definitive biography of Scott. Johnson has used the many sources and information available on Scott to present an accurate portrayal of the author. A must for the serious Scott scholar.

Lauber, John. *Sir Walter Scott.* Rev. ed. Boston: Twayne, 1989. Following a survey of Scott's poetry and his turn to fiction, seven chapters analyze major narratives: *Waverly*, *Guy Mannering*, *The Antiquary*, *Old Mortality*, *Rob Roy*, *The Heart of Midlothian*, *The Bride of Lammermoor*, and *Ivanhoe*. The final chapter assesses the reputation of the Waverly novels. Complemented by a chronology, notes, an annotated bibliography, and an index.

Todd, William B., and Ann Bowden. *Sir Walter Scott: A Bibliographical History, 1796-1832.* New Castle, Del.: Oak Knoll Press, 1998. Lists variant editions of the verse as well as the fiction, and casts light on Scott's occupations as advocate, sheriff, antiquarian, biographer, editor, historian, and reviewer.

Zimmerman, Everett. "Extreme Events: Scott's Novels and Traumatic History." *Eighteenth-Century Fiction* 10 (October, 1997): 63-78. Discussion of extreme events in history and fiction; argues that such descriptions of extreme events are a rhetorical device to assert a perspective that remains unanalyzed, implying that analysis would erode the clear boundaries that divide humanity from the inhumane.

Madeleine de Scudéry

French novelist

Born: Le Havre, France; 1607
Died: Paris, France; June 2, 1701

LONG FICTION: *Ibrahim: Ou, L'Illustre bassa*, 1641 (*Ibrahim: Or, The Illustrious Bassa*, 1652); *Artamène: Ou, Le Grand Cyrus*, 1649-1653 (*Artamenes: Or, The Grand Cyrus*, 1653-1655); *Clélie*, 1654-1660 (*Clelia*, 1656-1661); *Almahide: Ou, L'Esclave reine*, 1660-1663 (*Almahide: Or, The Captive Queen*, 1677).
NONFICTION: *Le Discours de la gloire*, 1671 (*An Essay upon Glory*, 1708).

Madeleine de Scudéry (skew-day-ree) was the sister of Georges de Scudéry, a famous dramatist and poet of seventeenth century France. After growing up in Le Havre, she went to Paris to live with her brother and soon became well known in French literary circles as a member of the Rambouillet coterie. Being a forceful personality, she became a person of consequence in Paris and succeeded Mme de Rambouillet as the leading hostess of literary Paris in the late 1640's. De Scudéry enjoyed the friendship of Louis XIV and other royalty as well as that of many prominent literary figures. The salon she established was called the *Société du Samedi*, the Saturday Club. She also became known for her vigorous and eloquent defense of the equality between men and women.

With *Ibrahim: Or, The Illustrious Bassa* in 1641 she began to publish prose romances. In an age when French romances earned notoriety for their length, hers were longer than most; *Artamenes: Or, The Grand Cyrus*, appeared in ten volumes. It was followed by *Clelia* and *Almahide: Or, The Captive Queen*. Though they ostensibly presented so-called Oriental settings and characters, these romances used the language and action of seventeenth century France. The characters were often recognizable figures from the writer's fashionable circle. Although love is the major theme in de Scudéry's historical romances, they continue to please readers because of the depth of her insights into the complex motivation for human behavior. Because of prejudice against women writers in seventeenth century France, her novels were published under her brother's name, but her contemporaries knew that Georges de Scudéry had written only the episodes in these novels dealing with war.

Although her novels fell into relative oblivion after her death, they began to attract renewed attention in the 1970's, partly because she expressed so eloquently the inalienable rights of women and the need for equality between the sexes. A writer of essays and other prose studies as well as fiction, de Scudéry was the first winner of the prize for French eloquence with her *An Essay upon Glory* in 1671.

Edmund J. Campion

Bibliography

Aronson, Nicole. *Mademoiselle de Scudéry.* Translated by Stuart Aronson. Boston: Twayne, 1978. This excellent biography explains de Scudéry's importance in the development of the novel in seventeenth century France and includes an annotated bibliography of critical studies.

Horowitz, Louise K. *Love and Language: A Study of the Classical French Moralist Writers.* Columbus: Ohio State University Press, 1977. The representation of love in Scudéry's novels is examined.

McDougall, Dorothy. *Madeleine de Scudéry: Her Romantic Life and Death.* 1938. Reprint. New York: B. Blom, 1972. A somewhat fanciful biography; includes bibliography.

Moriarity, Michael. *Taste and Ideology in Seventeenth-Century France.* New York: Cambridge University Press, 1988. Social and feminist aspects of de Scudéry's writings are studied.

W. G. Sebald

German literary scholar, novelist, and poet

Born: Wertach im Allgäu, Bavaria, Germany; May 18, 1944
Died: Norwich, Norfolk, England; December 14, 2001

LONG FICTION: *Schwindel: Gefühle*, 1990 (*Vertigo*, 1999); *Die Ausgewanderten*, 1992 (*The Emigrants*, 1996); *Die Ringe des Saturn*, 1995 (*The Rings of Saturn*, 1998); *Austerlitz*, 2001 (English translation, 2001).
POETRY: *Nach der Natur: Ein Elementargedicht*, 1988 (*After Nature*, 2002); *For Years Now*, 2001.
NONFICTION: *Die Beschreibung des Unglücks: Zurösterreichischen Literatur von Stifter bis Handke*, 1985; *A Radical Stage: Theatre in Germany in the 1970's and 1980's*, 1988; *Unheimliche Heimat: Essays zur österreichischen Literatur*, 1990 ; *Logis in einem Landhaus*, 1998; *Luftkrieg und Literatur*, 1999 (*On the Natural History of Destruction*, 2003).

Winfried Georg Maximilian Sebald (ZAY-bahlt) was an accomplished German literary scholar who first began writing poetry and fiction in his forties. In the last decade of the twentieth century he succeeded in creating what many regard as a new genre, combining fact, fiction, travelogue, hallucinatory imagery, cultural criticism, art history, diary, and memoir in a prose form that was both highly referential and stunningly original. A hallmark of his prose is the use of captionless photographs and other images.

The attempt to come to terms with his native country's destructive past is the impulse behind much of Sebald's fiction as well as his academic writing. He was born in the remote Alpine village of Wertach in Bavaria and grew up knowing little of what his fellow Germans (including his father, a soldier who served on several fronts) had participated in during World War II. The first in his family to pursue an academic career, Sebald matriculated at the University of Freiburg in 1963. The period of his studies coincided with the first Auschwitz trials and the emergence of a radical form of German theater aimed at exposing the institutionalized crimes of the German past and the survival of many Nazi Party members in positions of wealth and power in West Germany. In this atmosphere, Sebald became disenchanted with the German academic scene, which was characterized by congested lecture halls and a faculty composed of scholars who had received their degrees during Adolf Hitler's rule. Pursuing his interest in French literature, Sebald transferred to the University of Fribourg in Switzerland, where he received a Licence des Lettres in 1966. Emboldened by his Swiss sojourn to venture even further afield, he accepted a temporary teaching position in England, at the University of Manchester, even though his knowledge of English was rudimentary. In Manchester he obtained a master's degree in German literature and then returned to Switzerland in 1968. He taught at a grammar school for a year in St. Gallen but became disillusioned with elementary school teaching as well as life in Switzerland, which he regarded as too comfortable and too complacent. In 1969 he returned to England and taught another year at the University of Manchester. In 1970 he accepted a position in Norwich at the University of East Anglia, where he remained, with the exception of a year at the Goethe Institute in Munich in the mid-1970's, until his death in 2001.

Sebald developed a professional interest in Jewish writers early in his career, and he wrote a number of articles and books on authors such as Alfred Döblin, Joseph Roth, Franz Kafka, Elias

Canetti, and Jean Améry. He was especially interested in those writers' experiences as outsiders and exiles, being himself an expatriate. Sebald was also intrigued by what he viewed as a particularly Austrian form of melancholy in the works of Adalbert Stifter, Hugo von Hofmannsthal, Gerhard Roth, Thomas Bernhard, and Peter Handke. By 1986 he was in possession of both British and German doctoral degrees, and had established himself as an original and provocative scholar. In 1988 he was promoted to professor of Modern German Literature at the University of East Anglia and also became director of the British Centre for Literary Translation. Sebald became increasingly dissatisfied with university conditions during the regime of Prime Minister Margaret Thatcher, whose educational policies he considered meddlesome and ill-advised. He turned to nonacademic writing. In the same year as his promotion to full professor, he produced a volume of poetry titled *After Nature*. Sebald would not truly make his mark on the German literary scene until some time later, when the well-known writer Hans Magnus Enzensberger selected his first novel, *Vertigo*, for publication in 1990. The book comprises four distinct sections, two on literary figures and two on separate journeys to Italy and to Sebald's native Wertach. Despite its variety of subjects, the novel exhibits a thematic unity rooted in Sebald's preoccupation with artistic creativity, the nature of identity, the uncanny in everyday life, and the dynamics of memory.

The Emigrants appeared in German in 1992 and in English (Sebald took part in this and all other translations) in 1996. The novel, also in four distinct parts, signaled his emergence as a writer of international stature. It concerns four personalities, all affected in one way or another by exile, depression, and European anti-Semitism in the first half of the twentieth century. The novel met with unanimous critical acclaim and won numerous literary prizes. In 1995, even before the appearance of *The Emigrants* in English, Sebald published a third novel in German, *The Rings of Saturn*. The title alludes to the crushing forces of nature that produced Saturn's rings; the book is a lengthy meditation on Walter Benjamin's assertion that history is really an ongoing calamity, piling wreckage upon wreckage. In *The Rings of Saturn*, Sebald's first-person protagonist explores the "wreckage" of East Anglia, visiting country houses, heaths, churches, and various other sites, all the while indulging in diverse biographical, literary, historical, and cultural digressions which blend to form an eclectic narrative unity. The English translation followed closely on the heels of the success of *The Emigrants*, appearing less than two years later, in 1998. In the same year the novel was awarded Best Fiction Book by the *Los Angeles Times*.

In the meantime, Sebald had stirred up considerable scholarly controversy with a series of lectures at the University of Zurich in 1997. Elaborating on a theme he introduced in *The Rings of Saturn*, he used these lectures, which appeared later in book form, to illustrate how German postwar literature had remained mostly silent on the horror and mayhem of the massive aerial bombardment of German cities and had thereby failed to do justice to the human cost of the Allied bombing efforts. While some objected that Sebald had overlooked certain writers and texts, the rarity or obscurity of such exceptions only served to prove the rule.

Sebald's last novel was his most mature and in some ways most conventional narrative. *Austerlitz*, which appeared both in German and in English in 2001, is a sensitive study of a Czech exile's attempt to reconstruct his past after discovering that he was one of the Jewish children evacuated to Britain in the "Kindertransport" of 1938. Like most of Sebald's portraits, it is a composite, combining not only fact and fiction but also several individual identities. Not long after returning from a book tour of the United States in the autumn of 2001, Sebald died in a car crash near his home in Norwich on December 14, 2001.

Outwardly, Sebald's life was unexceptional; he went to work every day, taught his classes, helped raise a daughter, and was married to the same woman for more than thirty years. His inner life, as revealed in his erudite, allusive, and keenly inventive prose and poetry, was hardly ordinary. His perspective and methods were rightly recognized as highly original; not only was his writing unlike that of any other writer's, but his compositions were also in large part prompted by myriad visual cues in the form of collected drawings, paintings, and photographs, many of which he provided in his texts. Because of his status as a German expatriate who was fully at home neither in his native land nor in England, Sebald's oeuvre does not fit easily into the canon of either national literature. He occupies a place beside a number of modern international predecessors, however, including the Argentine Jorge Luis Borges, the Austrian Thomas Bernhard, and the Italian Claudio Magris. Sebald is admired as a "writer's writer" and is considered by many to be one of the most important European novelists of the last decade of the twentieth century.

Mark R. McCulloh

Bibliography

Iyer, Pico. "The Strange, Haunted World of W. G. Sebald." *Harper's Magazine*, October, 2000, 86-90. This stylistic analysis focuses on the restlessness and unease that drives Sebald's prose, attributing the uncanny, dreamlike mood of his work largely to the influence of Franz Kafka.

Lane, Anthony. "Higher Ground: Adventures in Fact and Fiction from W. G. Sebald." *The New Yorker*, May 29, 2000, 128-136. While Lane notes that Sebald's narratives all begin with typically "Sebaldian" prose, he nonetheless considers the author one of the most important novelists of the late twentieth century, with few English-speaking rivals in scope and imaginative power.

Lewis, Tess. "W. G. Sebald: The Past Is Another Country." *The New Criterion*, December, 2001, 85-90. This article, which appeared shortly before Sebald's death, is a good introduction for newcomers to the author's work. Lewis assesses Sebald's four novels, praising the last one, *Austerlitz*, as the most emotionally powerful and the most "unobtrusively constructed." She also discusses Sebald's theme of German "willful amnesia," not only in regard to the Holocaust but also in terms of the physical damage and psychological trauma inflicted by the Allied bombing raids in World War II.

Williams, Arthur. "The Elusive First-Person Plural: Real Absences in Reiner Kunze, Bernd-Dieter Hüge, and W. G. Sebald." In

Whose Story? Continuities in Contemporary German-Language Literature, edited by Williams, Stuart Parkes, and Julian Preece. New York: Peter Lang, 1998. Williams focuses on *The Emigrants* in his comparative treatment of Sebald and two other contemporary German writers who also treat German history within the framework of memoir and autobiography.

________. "W. G. Sebald: A Holistic Approach to Borders, Texts, and Perspectives." In *German-Language Literature Today: International and Popular?*, edited by Williams, Stuart Parkes, and Julian Preece. New York: Peter Lang, 2000. This chapter describes astutely the aesthetic principles behind Sebald's prose, emphasizing the author's eclectic but unifying blend of forms, sources, and literary allusions.

Woods, James. "Sebald's Uncertainty." In *The Broken Estate: Essays on Literature and Belief.* New York: Random House, 1999. Woods recognizes Sebald's debt to the nineteenth century Austrian writer Adalbert Stifter, whose writings possess a quiet poignancy and an almost fastidious attention to detail similar to Sebald's.

Eve Kosofsky Sedgwick

American critic

Born: Dayton, Ohio; May 2, 1950
Identity: Gay or bisexual

NONFICTION: *The Coherence of Gothic Conventions*, 1980; *Between Men: English Literature and Male Homosocial Desire*, 1985; *Epistemology of the Closet*, 1990; *Tendencies*, 1993; *A Dialogue on Love*, 1999; *Touching Feeling: Affect, Pedagogy, Performativity*, 2002.
POETRY: *Fat Art, Thin Art*, 1994.
EDITED TEXTS: *Performativity and Performance*, 1995 (with Andrew Parker); *Shame and Its Sisters: A Silvan Tomkins Reader*, 1995 (with Adam Frank); *Gary in Your Pocket: Stories and Notebooks of Gary Fisher*, 1996; *Novel Gazing: Queer Readings in Fiction*, 1997.

Eve Kosofsky Sedgwick (SEHJ-wihk) was born in 1950, the daughter of Leon Sedgwick, an engineer, and Rita Goldstein, a high school teacher. She received her bachelor's degree summa cum laude at Cornell University in 1971 and went on to earn a master's in philosophy in 1974 and a Ph.D. in 1975 at Yale University. From 1975 to 1976 she was an instructor in English at Hamilton College in Clinton, New York. From 1978 to 1981 she served as an assistant professor of English and creative writing at Boston University, where she also cofounded the Women's Studies Committee, the Faculty for Women's Concerns, and the Rousseau and Wollstonecraft Seminars.

From 1981 to 1983 she was on the faculty at Harvard University's Radcliffe College and a faculty fellow at the Mary Ingraham Bunting Institute. She joined the faculty of Duke University as an associate professor of English and women's studies in 1984, where she founded the lecture series "Sex, Gender, Representation." In 1987 Sedgwick was the Mrs. William Beckman Visiting Professor at the University of California, Berkeley, and in 1992 she was a professor at Dartmouth College; from 1991 to 1992 she was a research fellow at the National Humanities Center. She has judged literary awards for the Modern Language Association of America, including the James Russell Lowell Prize, the Crompton-Noll Award in Gay and Lesbian Studies, and the Michael Lynch Service Award. She has served on the Board of Trustees of The English Institute and the Dickens Society, and from 1985 to 1986 she was the co-chairperson of the Modern Language Association's Commission on the Status of Women in the Profession.

Sedgwick has been the recipient of a number of awards, honors, and prizes, including a Mellon fellowship (1976 to 1978) and a Kirkland Endowment (1980 and 1981); she was corecipient of the Crompton-Noll Award in Gay and Lesbian Studies from the Gay and Lesbian Caucus of the Modern Language Association for her article "Homophobia, Misogyny, and Capital: The Example of *Our Mutual Friend*" (1984). From 1987 to 1988 she was a Guggenheim Fellow.

In addition to her books, Sedgwick has published articles in such distinguished literary journals as *South Atlantic Quarterly*, *Critical Inquiry*, *Epoch*, *Massachusetts Review*, *Salmagundi*, and *Poetry Miscellany*. She was coeditor of the journal *Genders* from 1988 to 1991 and has been a member of the advisory board of the *Yale Journal of Law and the Humanities*, *Journal of the History of Sexuality*, and *Gay and Lesbian Quarterly*.

It was with the 1985 publication of her book *Between Men: English Literature and Male Homosocial Desire* that Sedgwick began the work that would make her one of the leading figures in the development of lesbian and gay studies in the literary academy. *Between Men* is a literary study of works including William Shakespeare's sonnets, William Wycherley's play *The Country Wife* (pr., pb. 1675), James Hogg's novel *The Private Memoirs and Confessions of a Justified Sinner* (1824), Alfred, Lord Tennyson's *The Princess* (1847), George Eliot's *Adam Bede* (1859), William Makepeace Thackeray's *Henry Esmond* (1852), Charles Dickens's *Our Mutual Friend* (1864-1865) and *The Mystery of Edwin Drood* (1870), and Walt Whitman's poetry. Intended for an audience of other feminist scholars as an antihomophobia, antiseparatist text, Sedgwick hypothesizes in this book that there is an unbroken continuum between the "homosocial"—that is, the normative and visible, relations—between men, and the "homosexual"—prohibited, hidden—relations between men. Building on the theories of René Girard, Sigmund Freud, Claude Lévi-Strauss, and Gayle Rubin, Sedgwick unifies her readings of these disparate texts with the underlying thematic paradigm of the "male traffic in women."

Epistemology of the Closet, another landmark in the development of what has been called "queer theory," further challenges assumptions about sexuality and gender. Through readings of Herman Melville, Marcel Proust, Friedrich Nietzsche, Oscar Wilde, and Henry James, Sedgwick persuasively argues that issues of sexual identities are central to every important form of knowledge in the twentieth century. *Tendencies* is a collection of many of Sedgwick's essays previously published in scholarly journals. In this book the essays range from discussions of Denis Diderot, Wilde, and James to her controversial article "Jane Austen and the Masturbating Girl," her discussion of bringing up gay children, an essay on poetry and spanking, a performance piece on the artist Divine (coauthored with Michael Moon), and an article about her own experience with breast cancer in the context of the acquired immunodeficiency syndrome (AIDS) crisis and its imperative to rethink the politics of sexualities.

Fat Art, Thin Art is a collection of her poetry. Sedgwick maintains a connection between her reputation as a literary critic and queer theorist and her poetic writing when she speaks of her desire to write poetry: "Part of my motive as a poet was that the most writerly writing I could do, and the most thinkerly thinking, be shown not to be generically alien to each other."

The collection of essays she edited with Andrew Parker, *Performativity and Performance*, further investigates the relationships between conventional forms of academic criticism and creative genres such as drama and poetry. *A Dialogue on Love* is a memoir of her experiences in therapy after surviving breast cancer, which was reviewed as being either thoughtful and enlightening or self-indulgent. *Touching Feeling* collects her articles on emotion, based on close readings of a number of different, and different types of, authors. Sedgwick became a leading literary critic not only because of her vast contributions to the field of gay and lesbian studies but also because of her experiments with stretching, expanding, and multiplying the forms that the genre of criticism can accommodate.

Lynda Hart

Bibliography

Fraiman, Susan. "Geometries of Race and Gender: Eve Sedgwick, Spike Lee, Charlayne Hunter-Gault." *Feminist Studies* 20, no. 1 (Spring, 1994): 67-84. Begins with Sedgwick's premise of a three-sided relationship in which two men bond over a woman and amplifies the triangle to include race, as well as gender and sexuality.

Loftus, Brian. "Speaking Silence: The Strategies and Structures of Queer Autobiography." *College Literature* 24 (February, 1997): 28-44. Discusses Sedgwick's autobiographical work along with that of Gertrude Stein.

Payne, W. Douglas. "Resisting Normalization: Queer Theory in an Interval." *College Literature* 26 (Spring, 1999): 200-209. *Novel Gazing* is reviewed along with two other works in an overview of the state of the field of queer theory.

Simerka, Barbara. "Homosociality and Dramatic Conflict: A Reconsideration of Early Modern Spanish Comedy." *Hispanic Review* 70 (Autumn, 2002): 521-534. Applies Sedgwick's theories of homosociality.

George Seferis
(Giorgos Stylianou Seferiades)

Greek poet

Born: Smyrna, Ottoman Empire (now İzmir, Turkey); March 13, 1900 (old style February 29, 1900)
Died: Athens, Greece; September 20, 1971

POETRY: *Strophe*, 1931 (*Turning Point*, 1967); *E sterna*, 1932 (*The Cistern*, 1967); *Mythistorema*, 1935 (English translation, 1960); *Gymnopaidia*, 1936 (English translation, 1967); *Emerologio katastromatos I*, 1940 (*Logbook I*, 1960); *Tetradio gymnasmaton*, 1940 (*Book of Exercises*, 1967); *Emerologio katastromatos II*, 1944 (*Logbook II*, 1960); *Kichle*, 1947 (*Thrush*, 1967); *Emerologio katastromatos III*, 1955 (*Logbook III*, 1960); *Poems*, 1960 (includes *Mythistorema*, *Logbook I*, *II*, and *III*); *Tria krypha poiemata*, 1966 (*Three Secret Poems*, 1969); *Collected Poems*, 1967, 1981, 1995 (includes *Turning Point*, *The Cistern*, *Gymnopaidia*, *Book of Exercises*, *Thrush*, and others).

TRANSLATIONS: *Phoniko stèn ekklesia*, pb. 1935 (of T. S. Eliot's *Murder in the Cathedral*); *T. S. Eliot*, 1936; *Asma asmaton*, 1966 (of *The Song of Songs*); *E Apokalypse tou Ioanne*, 1966 (of *The Apocalypse of St. John*).

NONFICTION: *Dokimes*, 1947; *Treis meres sta monasteria tes Kappadokias*, 1953; *Delphi*, 1962 (English translation, 1963); *Discours de Stockholm*, 1964; *'E glossa sten poiese mas*, 1965; *On the Greek Style: Selected Essays in Poetry and Hellenism*, 1966; *A Poet's Journal: Days of 1945-1951*, 1974.

Giorgos Stylianou Seferiades, who would later take the pen name George Seferis (seh-FEHR-ees), was born into a Greek community in Smyrna, Ottoman Empire (now İzmir, Turkey), at the start of the twentieth century. Interested in poetry even as a child, Seferis moved with his family to Athens at the beginning of World War I. In 1917, Seferis graduated from the First Classical Gymnasium and shortly thereafter went to Paris to study at the Sorbonne. Although technically a student of law, Seferis continued to write poetry, and he came under the influence of the French Symbolists, including such leading figures as Charles Baudelaire, Jules Laforge, Stéphane Mallarmé, Paul Verlaine, and, most notably, Paul Valéry.

After receiving his degree and traveling widely throughout the early 1920's, Seferis took a position with the Greek Ministry of Foreign Affairs in 1926. His service as a diplomat would eventually take him to Athens, London, and Korçë (Koritsa), Albania. While working as vice consul for the Greek diplomatic service in 1931, Seferis was exposed to the poetry of T. S. Eliot and Ezra Pound, two of the most influential poets writing in English during the early and mid-twentieth century. Seferis was particularly attracted to the dramatic voice of Eliot, and he published Greek translations of *The Waste Land* (1922) and *Murder in the Cathedral* (1935); these works were collected into Seferis's volume *T. S. Eliot* in 1936. At about the same time, Seferis also began publishing poetry of his own, releasing *Turning Point* in 1931 and *The Cistern* in 1932.

The Cistern, a lyric poem of twenty-five five-line stanzas (one of them containing nothing but dots), already reflects the profound influence of Eliot. Rhythms are more typical of English pentameter lines than traditional Greek pendecasyllables (fifteen-syllable lines that had been common in Greek poetry since the Byzantine period), and both the poem's free verse and its imagery appear to be closely modeled upon the works of Eliot. The theme of *The Cistern* is that the artist's vision arises out of human suffering and contemplation rather than an objective depiction of the world. The cistern that gives the poem its title is both a repository for the collected sorrow of humanity and a source of sustenance for those who thirst for passion or art.

In the mid-1930's Seferis returned to Athens, where he published two more volumes of poetry, *Mythistorema* in 1935 and *Gymnopaidia* in 1936. He began the poems in *Mythistorema* even as he continued to translate Eliot's poetry, and he again adopted a narrative style similar to that of *The Waste Land*. At the same time, however, Seferis was borrowing freely from ancient Greek images and mythology, often combining classical elements with settings or allusions familiar to those who lived in modern Greece. The result is a poetic world in which past and present are united. In *Mythistorema*, allusions to such classical figures as the Argonauts, Orestes, and Astyanax appear repeatedly—even as Seferis prefaces the collection with a couplet by the French Symbolist poet Arthur Rimbaud, dedicates another to the modern composer Maurice Ravel, and includes in a third allusions to the wedding ceremony of the Orthodox church. Another major work, *Book of Exercises*, published in 1940, contains the first appearance of Stratis Thalassinos (Stratis the Sailor), a literary persona that Seferis would adopt a number of times in his later poetry.

In 1941 Seferis married Maria Zannou. Shortly thereafter, Greece surrendered to Nazi Germany, and Seferis joined the Greek government-in-exile. He spent the war years in Egypt, Africa, and Italy, returning to Greece in 1946. He again went to London as consul to the Greek embassy in 1951, a trip that gave Seferis the opportunity to form a lasting friendship with Eliot. While ambassador to Great Britain from 1957 to 1962, Seferis played a major role in negotiating the independence of the island of Cyprus.

In 1963, Seferis became the first Greek to be awarded the Nobel Prize in Literature. His reputation grew among the international community as his works were translated into numerous languages. In the last two decades of his life, he was awarded honorary degrees by Cambridge, Oxford, and Princeton Universities as well as by the University of Thessaloniki (Salonica) in northeastern Greece. He returned to Athens, where he became an outspoken opponent of the military dictatorship of George Papadopoulos. Seferis died in 1971 from complications following stomach surgery.

George Seferis left behind works that combined clarity of style with the rich imagery that he borrowed from Eliot and the French Symbolists. Embracing all of Greek history at once, his poems take their inspiration equally from classical legend, Byzantine folk literature, and the modern Greek landscape.

Jeffrey L. Buller

Bibliography

Beaton, Roderick. *George Seferis*. Bristol, England: Bristol Classical, 1991. A critical study of selected works by Seferis. Includes bibliographic references.

Hadas, Rachel. *Form, Cycle, Infinity: Landscape Imagery in the Poetry of Robert Frost and George Seferis*. Lewisburg, Pa.: Bucknell University Press, 1985. Compares the literary style and similarities of Robert Frost and Seferis. Includes a bibliography and an index.

Kapre-Karka, K. *Love and the Symbolic Journey in the Poetry of Cavafy, Eliot, and Seferis: An Interpretation with Detailed Poem-by-Poem Analysis*. New York: Pella, 1982. A critical study of selected works by three poets. Includes an index and bibliography.

_______. *War in the Poetry of George Seferis: A Poem-by-Poem Analysis*. New York: Pella, 1985. A critical study of selected works by Seferis. Includes an index and bibliography.

Thaniel, George. *Seferis and Friends*. Toronto, Ont.: Mercury Press, 1994. Entertaining and informative correspondence from Seferis's wide circle of friends and acquaintances, including Henry Miller, T. S. Eliot, and Lawrence Durrell.

Tsatsou, Ioanna, and Jean Demos, trans. *My Brother George Seferis*. St. Paul, Minn.: North Central, 1982. An in-depth biography. Includes index.

Jaroslav Seifert

Czech poet

Born: Prague, Bohemia, Austro-Hungarian Empire (now Czech Republic); September 23, 1901
Died: Prague, Czechoslovakia (now Czech Republic); January 10, 1986

POETRY: *Město v slzách*, 1921; *Samá láska*, 1923; *Svatební cesta*, 1925; *Na vlnách TSF*, 1925; *Slavík zpívá špatně*, 1926; *Poštovní holub*, 1929; *Jablko z klína*, 1933; *Ruce Venušiny*, 1936; *Zpíváno do rotačky*, 1936; *Osm dní*, 1937; *Jaro sbohem*, 1937, 1942; *Zhasněte světla*, 1938; *Světlem oděná*, 1940; *Kamenný most*, 1944; *Přilba hlíny*, 1945; *Chlapec a hvezdy: Verse k obrazum a obrázkum Josefa Lady*, 1956; *Verse o Praze*, 1962; *Koncert na ostrově*, 1965; *Halleyova kometa*, 1967; *Odlévání zvonů*, 1967 (*The Casting of Bells*, 1983); *Zpevy o Praze*, 1968; *Morový sloup*, 1977 (*The Plague Column*, 1979; also known as *The Plague Monument*, 1980); *Deštník z Piccadilly*, 1979 (*An Umbrella from Piccadilly*, 1983); *Zápas s andelem*, 1981; *Býti Básníkem*, 1983; *The Selected Poetry of Jaroslav Seifert*, 1986; *The Early Poetry of Jaroslav Seifert*, 1997; *A sbohem*, 1999; *Treba vám nesu ruze*, 1999.
NONFICTION: *Hvězdy nad rajskou zahradou*, 1929; *Všecky krásy světa*, 1981 (autobiography).
CHILDREN'S/YOUNG ADULT LITERATURE: *Maminka: Yybor básni*, 1954.
MISCELLANEOUS: *Dílo*, 1953-1970 (collected works).

Jaroslav Seifert (SI-furt), 1984 winner of the Nobel Prize in Literature and the only Czech Nobel laureate in the twentieth century, slowly grew into the standard-bearer of Czech culture during his lifetime. Born on Riegrově Street in the colorful, working-class, partly Jewish Žižka suburb of Prague to a radical Socialist father and conservative Catholic mother, Seifert embraced life in an eager and open way. Indeed, he was so open to the color and excitement of his neighborhood and of greater Prague that he often played hooky from school, and he failed to enter Charles University, which most of his peers attended. Nonetheless, from the age of nineteen, the well-read young man who wished for no other profession than poetry was part of a stellar generation of Czech writers who began their careers in the first third of the twentieth century. His friends included the critics Antonín Piša and F. X. Šalda, the novelists Jaroslav Hašek and Vladislav Vančura, the multitalented artist and poet Karel Teige, the avant-garde poets Josef Hora, František Halas, and Vítězslav Nezval, and the Communist poets Stanislav Kostka Neumann and Jiří Wolker. Many of them come to life in Seifert's memoir, *Všecky krásy světa*. Seifert and Teige, serious students of both the Western and the Soviet avant-garde, traveled to Paris and Moscow in the 1920's. Seifert married in 1928; he and Marie Seifert had one daughter, Jana.

The exuberant creativity of the young Czech artists and poets led by Seifert and Teige flourished under the banner *Devětsil* (Nine-Powers). They dubbed their eclectic principles *Poetismus*. As youth and the modish influences of Futurism, Surrealism, and Dadaism waned, however, *Devětsil* disbanded in 1929.

From the beginning, Seifert had reached for a popular audience. With his liberation from youthful "isms," he developed his witty, yet accessible, and very direct style. He was aided by a poetry-loving public and a long-standing Czech tradition of discarding all pretense. As he remarked in his memoir, the poet should not turn away from his readers, because his work lives only through them: "There is no point to writing with black ink on black paper for the fleeting clouds."

Seifert's first book of poetry was *Město v slzách* (city in tears), followed by *Samá láska* (only love). While his stylistic mastery developed and dazzled in such collections as *Jablko z klína* (an apple from the lap) and *Ruce Venušiny* (the hands of Venus), he remained true to basic humanistic themes, balanced with a hedonistic delight in love as the greatest beauty in life. The titles, as well as the content, of his works reflect his shift from the playful, gentle, and hedonistic to a firm and steadying stance that made his works loved by his fellow Czechs during the dark days of World War II: *Zhasněte světla* (douse the lights), *Světlem oděná* (robed in light), *Kamenný most* (stone bridge), *Přilba hlíny* (a helmetful of clay). His devotion to his country's traditions and to the cultural resonance of Prague saturated his work and, in his last three decades, this took another form: the heroic public behavior of a man who protested that he was completely lacking in heroism.

Seifert was considered too subversive to be published at home during most of the Nazi occupation of Czechoslovakia and again during the initial Communist years, when he survived financially by writing books of children's poetry; *Maminka* (mother) has become a classic. In 1956 he spoke out passionately on behalf of imprisoned and harassed colleagues at the Second Congress of Czechoslovak Writers, a public act almost unheard of during the reign of totalitarian repression. The desire of Czech intellectuals to reassert themselves, under the guise of "Socialism with a human face," culminated in the rebellious Prague Spring of 1968. In the midst of the crackdown that followed, Seifert became president of the Union of Czechoslovak Writers (UCW) and remained a rock of protection for writers' liberties for almost two years. His role ended only when the UCW was disbanded late in 1969. For the decade that followed, publication of Seifert's work and mention of his name in the press was banned in his native country.

The year 1977 saw the appearance of *Charter 77*, a defiant petition for freedom, signed by seven hundred members of the Czech intelligentsia, with Seifert among those leading the way. In the same year, he broke another taboo by publishing a major new work abroad, *The Plague Monument*. This was his first book to be translated into English, thereby bringing him to international attention. What the world saw was the complexity of life expressed by a Czech master in simple, ironic, accessible terms. The Baroque "plague column" (which stood in Prague from 1648 until 1918, a symbol of deliverance from war and plague) is both a universal symbol and a special, oblique symbol of Czech renewal after plagues that included disastrous political and moral situations. The poet, even in old age and haunted by the death of millions, renews himself and his reader by evoking both death and life through naked feelings and exquisite imagery.

D. Gosselin Nakeeb

Bibliography

French, Alfred. *The Poets of Prague: Czech Poetry Between the Wars*. New York: Oxford University Press, 1969. Provides the larger context for Seifert's work in its formative phase, including poems by all the major poets of his generation in translation and the original Czech for comparison.

Gibian, George. "The Lyrical Voice of Czechoslovakia." In *The Selected Poetry of Jaroslav Seifert*. New York: Macmillan, 1986. Concise, insightful essay on Seifert's life and work by the dedicated editor who created one of the best anthologies of Seifert in English. Includes vivid description of Gibian's face-to-face meetings with Seifert in Prague. Seifert's poetry translated by Ewald Osers, prose by Gibian.

Iggers, Wilma A. "The World of Jaroslav Seifert." *World Literature Today* 60 (Spring, 1985): 8-12. Scholarly interpretation of Seifert's career, filling in some of Seifert's lesser-known literary associations.

Parrott, Sir Cecil. Introduction to *The Plague Column*, by Jaroslav Seifert. Translated by Ewald Osers. London: Terra Nova Editions, 1979. Appreciative essay on Seifert's career, by a journalist who was an eyewitness to much of it, with particular awareness of the political subtleties.

Škvorecký, Josef. "Czech Mate: Meet Jaroslav Seifert, Nobel Laureate." *The New Republic* 192 (February 18, 1985): 27-31. Insightful comments by a peer of Seifert, a major Czech novelist. Skvorecky explains why Seifert is popular among a broad Czech readership and why important aspects of his work are untranslatable.

Hubert Selby, Jr.

American novelist

Born: Brooklyn, New York; July 23, 1928

LONG FICTION: *Last Exit to Brooklyn*, 1964; *The Room*, 1971; *The Demon*, 1976; *Requiem for a Dream*, 1978; *The Willow Tree*, 1998; *Waiting Period*, 2002.
SHORT FICTION: *Song of the Silent Snow*, 1986.
SCREENPLAY: *Requiem for a Dream*, 2000 (adaptation of his novel; with Darren Aronofsky).

Hubert Selby, Jr., is one of the more controversial (and arguably the most pessimistic) of postwar American authors, generally more appreciated in Europe than in his home country. His early life was marked by serious physical illness and a chronic addiction to drugs and alcohol that he managed to overcome in his later years. His first novel, *Last Exit to Brooklyn*, was banned in Italy and underwent obscenity trials in both England and the United States. It contains six interrelated and deeply depressing stories that focus on the sordid lives of the prostitutes, transvestite homosexuals, drug addicts, and alcoholics whom Selby knew from his youth in Brooklyn. Its narrative style flows with the rhythms of jazz. The characters—the hooker Tralala, the transvestite Georgette, the union boss Harry Black—all suffer from obsessive, self-destructive behaviors that Selby believes result from a simple inability or refusal to love. The rejection of this narcissistic self-obsession in the characters represents the moral and spiritual theme that underlies all of Selby's naturalistic texts and is the touchstone of his critique of the materialism of American society. The book was filmed in 1989.

The novels *The Room* and *The Demon* also focus on individuals whose lives are destroyed by the obsessions and addictions that emerge from their damaged souls. The former text presents a disturbing portrait of an unnamed man who is awaiting trial in a police holding cell. The narrative moves between monologic first- and omniscient third-person viewpoints. The deranged man indulges in pathological paranoid visions of violent revenge against those who have wronged him and in grandiose fantasies of self-justification and of his own omnipotence. Many critics, including the author, feel that *The Room* is his masterpiece. It stands as one of the most disturbing books ever written about a human being. The theme of inner demons in Selby's writing comes to the fore in *The Demon*. Harry White is obsessed with the American dream of success and, driven by the demons of narcissistic sexual addictions, has lost all self-control. The tensions of his psychological conflicts result in his eventual descent into emotional and spiritual numbness. Both novels received a more positive critical reception in Europe than in the United States.

The novel *Requiem for a Dream* deals with the theme of addiction in the United States, from the blatant horrors of heroin and diet pill abuse to the subtler ones of food obsessions and the self-hypnosis of television. With an uncompromising look at the lives of four addicts—a mother, her son, and two of his friends—who live in Brooklyn's Brighton Beach, the narrative paints a devastating portrait of the world of drug addiction. The book was made into a well-received film in 2000 with a screenplay written by Selby.

Selby's later texts *The Willow Tree* and *Waiting Period* strike a more positive note than his earlier works. Although the brutal portrait of reality is still present, the characters of these two later novels—for example, Werner in *The Willow Tree*—are able to show love and empathy and to experience moments of blissful transcendence or enlightenment in which they feel in harmony with existence. The image of the willow tree represents a spiritual vision of human existence: the protected or sheltered condition of the individual within the universe. Selby appeared in the documentaries *Drug-Taking and the Arts* (1994), *Hubert Selby Jr., 2 ou 3 choses . . .* (2000), and *Lost Angeles* (2000).

Thomas F. Barry

Bibliography

Giles, James Richard. *Understanding Hubert Selby, Jr.* Columbia: University of South Carolina Press, 1998. This collection of essays provides an excellent introduction to the thematic and stylistic concerns of the author.

Peavy, Charles D. "The Sin of Pride and Selby's *Last Exit to Brooklyn*." *Critique* 11, no. 3 (1969): 35-42. A concise examination of the moral themes that underlie the relentlessly brutal vision of this novel.

Review of Contemporary Fiction 1, no. 2 (1981). Issue devoted to Paul Metcalf and Selby. An excellent collection of essays on the writings up to *Requiem for a Dream*. There is also an interview with Selby.

Sorrentino, Gilbert. "The Art of Hubert Selby." *Kulcher* 13 (Spring, 1964): 27-43. Selby considered Sorrentino to be one of his most astute readers and critics.

Will Self

English novelist and short-story writer

Born: London, England; September 26, 1961

LONG FICTION: *"Cock" and "Bull,"* 1992 (2 novellas); *My Idea of Fun: A Cautionary Tale*, 1993; *Great Apes*, 1997; *How the Dead Live*, 2000; *Dorian: An Imitation*, 2002.

SHORT FICTION: *The Quantity Theory of Insanity*, 1991; *Grey Area, and Other Stories*, 1994; *The Sweet Smell of Psychosis*, 1996; *Tough, Tough Toys for Tough, Tough Boys*, 1998.

NONFICTION: *Junk Mail*, 1995; *Sore Sites*, 2000; *Perfidious Man*, 2000 (with David Gamble); *Feeding Frenzy*, 2001.

Included in *Granta* magazine's influential "Best of the Young British Novelists" 1993 issue before he had even published his first novel, William Woodard Self would become one of Great Britain's quirkiest and most high-profile writers. Eschewing the self-effacing demeanor and style of, for example, Kazuo Ishiguro and going well beyond the personal and literary flamboyance of, say, Martin Amis, Self quickly became the "bad boy" of British literature, whose cocaine-fueled lifestyle in London's trendiest literary circles was consonant with his belief that the artist must have "the courage of his own perversions." However, the writer, who seems the very personification of cool Britannia and the literary equivalent of shock artists such as Damien Hirst, has been highly critical of the cultural sensibility with which he has been identified, as is evident in his disdain for the sophisticated but facile and merely fashionable nihilism of American filmmaker Quentin Tarantino. It is this seeming paradox that is at the heart of Will Self's important and distinctive writing.

Self grew up in the Hampstead Garden suburb, the kind of eminently safe but deadening North London neighborhood in which much of his fiction is set. His father, a professor of urban planning at the London School of Economics, and his neurotic American Jewish mother divorced when he was nine. Self's early drug use had blossomed into heroin addiction by the time he completed his degree in philosophy at Oxford. After brief stays in Australia and India, he returned to London, working as a cartoonist before turning to writing. Even as his fame and celebrity grew, the negative aspects of his addictive personality became more pronounced. The low point came in 1997 when, just embarked on a new marriage (to Deborah Orr) and with a child on the way, reports that he had used drugs aboard John Major's campaign jet led to his being fired by *The Observer.* Soon after, he gave up drugs and alcohol and settled down to a more domestic life, continuing to write fiction that has kept its satirical and stylistic edge while taking on a greater emotional intensity.

"I don't write fiction for people to identify with," Self has said, "and I don't write a picture of the world they recognize. I write to astonish people." Astonish the six-foot, five-inch Self has, in fiction that is extravagant, excessive, unruly, and irreverent. He is often criticized for being self-indulgent with his verbal pyrotechnics, but his scabrous, blackly humorous writing is furiously funny, as full of energy and outrage as it is devoid of plot and character development. As a self-professed writer of surrealist fiction, Self specializes in the deadpan delivery of the bizarre and sudden swerves into the fantastic as women grow penises, men vaginas; humans and apes, doctors and patients change places; fantasies become reality while reality becomes a grotesque distortion; and the dead live. The fiction may be idiosyncratic, but it is certainly not unprecedented. Jonathan Swift, Voltaire, François Rabelais, Lewis Carroll, William S. Burroughs, Hunter S. Thompson, Woody Allen, Joseph Heller, Oscar Wilde (Self's "hero"), and especially master of urban apocalypse J. G. Ballard have played their parts in the making of Self's satiric genius and dark vision. All satire, Self believes, betrays "a certain instability and tension" between mere cleverness and "deep compassion," between "outright cynicism, anomie and amorality" and "the equal and countervailing pressure towards objective truth, religion, and morality." In Self's fiction, this conflict manifests itself in the urge to satirize and thereby reform and in the competing urge to create an art of pure performance that has as much to do with deep-seated psychological insecurities and his self-described and self-destructive personality as with the postmodern times as he grinds his world down to word, spleen, and style.

Self's dilemma as an English satirist is complicated in the twenty-first century in much the same way that Philip Roth felt that American writers were in 1960 as they struggled "to understand, describe, and then make credible" a reality that stupefies, sickens, infuriates, and finally "embarrasses one's own meager resources." Utopian plans to improve the individual and the built environment—the theories of psychiatrists and urban planners in particular—are Self's most frequent targets. Self's characters (who either have too little will or too much) struggle to situate themselves in relation to their outsized environment. Feeling "decoupled," they often gravitate to grotesquely inadequate beliefs and explanatory systems, such as hypercapitalism or fashionable psychological theories.

Self's short stories—several of them interrelated—focus most intensely on the problems of adjusting to one's environment and of inhuman "theory in the face of real human distress." The linked novellas of *"Cock" and "Bull"* deal comically and grotesquely with gender issues and evidence the author at his most stylistically disciplined and imaginatively outrageous. *The Sweet Smell of Psychosis* is a wickedly funny send-up of the London literary scene in which Self was a featured player. His first novel, *My Idea of Fun*, is a much more diffuse and intermittently (if, again, grotesquely) brilliant satire of its time (the late 1980's and early 1990's), when, thanks to Margaret Thatcher's economic policies, "people had begun to feel less ashamed about being greedy" and the lines between fantasy and reality, desire and action, became much less clear. While the effectiveness of *My Idea of Fun* is mitigated, as satire, by Self's tendency to digress, that of *Great Apes* is undermined by Self's working so doggedly at a single idea over its 404 pages, while putting his literary sources (Franz Kafka's 1917 story "A Report to an Academy," Swift's 1726 novel *Gulliver's Travels*, and the 1968 film *Planet of the Apes*) to little advantage. The largely critical reviews of *Great Apes*, in which noted psychiatrist (and frequent Self target) Dr. Zack Busner investigates the strange case of fellow chimp Simon Dykes, a famous artist who believes he is a human, were just part of Self's *annus horribilis*.

Having been upstaged as the "bad boy of British fiction" by Irvine Welsh shortly before Self lost his position as special campaign reporter for *The Observer*, and finding little encouragement in reviews of his most recent novella, novel, and story collection, *Tough, Tough Toys for Tough, Tough Boys*, Self seemed a writer whose meteoric rise had come to a spluttering end as he took the necessary steps to put his personal life in order. If his next novel, *How the Dead Live*, was a struggle to complete, it was also to be his best to date. Returning to the subject of the lead story of his first book, "The North London Book of the Dead," Self writes wittily, energetically, and affectingly, about "the awful karmic outcome of having lived"—as his mother did—"a materialist, self-conscious, self-obsessed life." If *How the Dead Live* is more focused than any of his earlier long fictions and much more emotionally engaging than any of his work, the reason is that Self found in his mother's voice the most effective vehicle for venting his own spleen while gaining some distance from it: a way to recapitulate his major concerns as a satirist while coming to terms with many of his personal demons and thereby finding a way to move past them. Ever the observant, acerbic culture critic as well as pyrotechnic fiction writer, Self updates Wilde's *The Picture of Dorian Gray* (1891) in his fourth novel, *Dorian*, set in the age of acquired immunodeficiency syndrome (AIDS).

Robert A. Morace

Bibliography

Heller, Zoe. "Self-Examination." *Vanity Fair*, June, 1993, 125-127, 148-151. A lengthy, interview-based essay introducing Self to an American audience.

Lyall, Sarah. "Tale of Recovery from a Bad Boy of Letters." *The New York Times*, October 16, 2000, pp. B1, B6. Along with Barber's interview (below), explains the autobiographical basis of *How the Dead Live* and Self's long struggle with his "addictive personality."

Self, Jonathan. *Self-Abuse: Love, Loss, and Fatherhood*. London: John Murray, 2001. This memoir by Self's elder brother sheds light on Will Self, his parents, and his fiction (*My Idea of Fun* and *How the Dead Live* in particular).

Self, Will. "Self Control." Interview by Lynn Barber. *Guardian* 11 (June, 2000). An important interview occasioned by the publication of *How the Dead Live*.

Samuel Selvon

Trinidadian novelist

Born: San Fernando, Trinidad; May 20, 1923
Died: Port of Spain, Trinidad; April 16, 1994
Identity: East Indian descent

LONG FICTION: *A Brighter Sun*, 1952; *An Island Is a World*, 1955; *The Lonely Londoners*, 1956; *Turn Again Tiger*, 1958; *I Hear Thunder*, 1963; *The Housing Lark*, 1965; *A Drink of Water*, 1968; *The Plains of Caroni*, 1970; *Those Who Eat the Cascadura*, 1972; *Moses Ascending*, 1975; *Moses Migrating*, 1983.
SHORT FICTION: *Ways of Sunlight*, 1957.
DRAMA: *Eldorado West One*, pb. 1988 (collection); *Highway in the Sun, and Other Plays*, pb. 1991.
NONFICTION: *Foreday Morning: Selected Prose, 1946-1986*, 1989.

Samuel Dickson Selvon's contribution to Caribbean letters is manifold. He was a prolific novelist who created some of the most memorable characters in Caribbean writing; he was also a venturesome innovator in the use of folk idioms and folk language of such sophistication and sheer virtuosity that his influence is consistently apparent in the works of many fiction writers who have followed him. Above all, Selvon wrote with a rare combination of empathy and humor that managed, consistently, to capture the qualities of inventiveness and energy that have come to characterize the best of West Indian writing.

Selvon was born of East Indian parents in rural Trinidad, and he experienced the distinctly Trinidadian multicultural ethos through an immersion in the East Indian creole culture, which entailed the intermingling of cultures as disparate as Spanish, Dutch, French, African, and native Caribbean. Described by many, including poet Derek Walcott, as one of the most multicultural countries in the world, Trinidad became a remarkably fecund place for the generation of literature that, by its mere adherence to the project of speaking to a diverse and dynamic populace, always seemed to avoid parochialism and to achieve a certain humanity.

Selvon's experience growing up among peasant farmers on sugar plantations in rural Trinidad played a significant role in the creation of many of his stories and most of his novels. His first novel, *A Brighter Sun*, and consequent novels explored themes that related to the dignity inherent in the peasant and largely East Indian culture of rural Trinidadian society. Selvon's imagination, however, was never restricted to the East Indian experience; it expanded to include sensitive portrayals of African Trinidadians in such critically successful works as the comic trilogy *The Lonely Londoners*, *Moses Ascending*, and *Moses Migrating*.

After completing his secondary education at Naparima College, Selvon worked as a telegraph operator with the West Indian branch of the Royal Naval Reserve during World War II. During this time he began writing verse and short stories, many of which were published and earned him significant popularity as a fledgling author. He joined the staff of the *Trinidad Guardian* soon after the war, and while he worked as a journalist he continued to write and publish his poetry and stories in Caribbean journals.

His move to London in 1950 precipitated his shift to more ambitious writing projects. He began to work on novels and to develop his skills as a writer of radio plays; a compilation of his dramatic works was organized and published in 1991 as *Highway in the Sun, and Other Plays*. *A Brighter Sun*, published in 1952, explored the processes of maturation in the context of a rural Indian community. Set during World War II, the novel follows the movement to manhood of sixteen-year-old Tiger, who has just gotten married and faces the challenges of becoming a man.

By the time Selvon came to publish his most popular novel, *The Lonely Londoners*, in 1956, he had lived for six years in England and had developed a vivid sense of both the pathos and dynamism of the lives of West Indians in Britain. The novel, told as a "ballad," or a Calypso tale, by the main character, Moses, is a sophisticatedly constructed series of episodes that handle with humor the lives of the new wave of black immigrants in London. Written in Trinidadian dialect, Selvon's novel confirmed that the idioms of the West Indies could work effectively at conveying not only character-defined humor but also deep emotion and philosophical introspection. The success and popularity of the Moses saga would lead to two later sequels that observed the return of a longtime London West Indian to the Caribbean to contend with issues of alienation and loss.

In his fourth novel, *Turn Again Tiger*, Selvon returned to the protagonist of his first novel, looking more closely at the processes of "creolization." Selvon's short-story writing, like his novels, demonstrates his embrace of a multicultural aesthetic as well as his complete immersion in the business of telling a story for its entertaining qualities. His collection of short stories, *Ways of Sunlight*, reveals Selvon's capacity for wit, trickery (as a writer), and poetic sensibility.

In 1954, he was given a Guggenheim Fellowship, an award he was again granted in 1968. In 1958, he won a Travelling Scholarship from the Society of Authors; in 1960, he received two Arts Council of Great Britain grants, and he was given a Trinidad government scholarship in 1962. In 1969, on the weight of his already impressive publications, he was awarded the Hummingbird Medal, a significant Trinidadian national honor, for his contribution to Caribbean literature.

Selvon continued to write novels in the 1970's, including *The Plains of Caroni*, *Those Who Eat the Cascadura*, and *Moses Ascending*. In 1978, he left England for Canada; he settled in Calgary, Alberta, forging an existence out of his reputation as a writer and a highly respected West Indian voice. He served as writer-in-residence of the universities of Alberta, Calgary, Victoria, Winnipeg, and Dundee.

His writing in the "Moses" trilogy offers perhaps one of the most telling demonstrations of his preoccupation with issues of identity and belonging. Moses, the black character, finally musters the courage to return to Trinidad and to cope with the difficulty of recognizing that he has become thoroughly and yet peculiarly English in his values, his sense of the world, and his perception of himself. The self-deprecating discomfort felt by Moses epitomizes Selvon's own preoccupation with the struggle to remain relevant to his history and social context. In this sense, Selvon never truly left the Caribbean but sought always, in his fiction, to discover the quintessential West Indianness of people from that region, wherever they found themselves. Selvon was awarded honorary doctorates at the University of the West Indies and Warwick University.

In 1994, during a visit to Trinidad, Selvon died. His legacy as an author is a vital one in contextualizing the complexities of the colonial and postcolonial experience. At the time of his death, he was working on an unfinished novel entitled "A High of Zero," set in Trinidad and Canada, while also writing an autobiography. He had finished a film script for *The Lonely Londoners* while concluding negotiations on adaptations of *Moses Ascending* and *Those Who Eat the Cascadura*.

Kwame S. N. Dawes

Bibliography

Joseph, Margaret Paul. *Caliban in Exile: The Outsider in Caribbean Fiction*. Westport, Conn.: Greenwood Press, 1992. Looks at the image of Caliban as a symbol of colonialist alienation in the London-based works of Selvon, Jean Rhys, and George Lamming.

Looker, Mark. *Atlantic Passages: History, Community, and Language in the Fiction of Sam Selvon*. New York: P. Lang, 1996. Places Selvon's fiction at the center of postcolonial theoretical debates, measuring it against its social and cultural contexts and gauging its productive counterpoise with ideas of history and community.

Nasta, Sushiela, ed. *Critical Perspectives on Sam Selvon*. Washington, D.C.: Three Continents Press, 1988. A collection of essays on Selvon's work, especially focused on his place as a Trinidadian writer.

Salick, Roydon. *The Novels of Samuel Selvon: A Critical Study*. Westport, Conn.: Greenwood Press, 2001. Examines Selvon's novels within their historical, sociological, and ideological contexts and offers a fresh assessment of his works.

Wyke, Clement H. *Sam Selvon's Dialectal Style and Fictional Strategy*. Vancouver: University of British Columbia Press, 1991. Concentrates on Selvon's use of dialect for both literary and philosophical effect.

Ousmane Sembène

Senegalese novelist and filmmaker

Born: Ziguinchor, Senegal; January 1, 1923

LONG FICTION: *Le Docker noir*, 1956 (*Black Docker*, 1987); *Ô pays, mon beau peuple!*, 1957; *Les Bouts de bois de Dieu*, 1960 (*God's Bits of Wood*, 1962); *L'Harmattan, livre I: Référendum*, 1964; *"Vehi-Ciosane: Ou, Blanche-Genèse," suivi du "Mandat,"* 1965 (novellas; *"The Money-Order," with "White Genesis,"* 1972); *Xala*, 1973 (novella; English translation, 1976); *Le Dernier de l'Empire*, 1981 (*The Last of the Empire*, 1983); *"Niiwam," suivi de "Taaw,"* 1987 (*"Niiwam" and "Taaw": Two Novellas*, 1991).
SHORT FICTION: *Voltaïque*, 1962 (*Tribal Scars, and Other Stories*, 1974).
SCREENPLAYS: *Borom-Sarret*, 1962; *Niaye*, 1964; *La Noire de . . .* , 1966 (also known as *Black Girl*); *Mandabi*, 1968 (adaptation of his novella; also known as *Le Mandat* and *The Money Order*); *Taaw*, 1970; *Emitaï*, 1972; *Xala*, 1974 (adaptation of his novella; also known as *Impotence*); *Ceddo*, 1977; *Camp de Thiaroye*, 1987; *Guelwaar*, 1992; *Faat Kiné*, 2000.

The fiction of Ousmane Sembène (suhm-BEH-neh) treats the tensions in a society attempting to break with tradition and colonialism simultaneously. He was born at Ziguinchor, Casamance, in the south of Senegal, on January 1, 1923. (Some sources reverse the order of his given name and surname and indicate January 8 as his date of birth.) His family of fishermen spoke the Wolof language, but he would eventually begin to write in French. Therefore, the complex problems associated with tradition and colonialism arose early in his own life: French was the language of whites, but to write in Wolof would deprive his work of a significant audience. Sembène spent three years at a technical school at Marsassoum, near the place of his birth. He then worked at a variety of trades and was laying brick at Dakar when World War II began. He joined the Free French forces and participated in the invasion of Italy. He later served in France, working as a stevedore at the port of Marseilles, and in Germany. After his discharge in 1946, he returned to Dakar to work as a fisherman but was soon back on the docks of Marseilles, working this time as a civilian stevedore. He read widely and became active in his trade union, soon rising to a position of authority. His years as a laborer and a union representative gave him a sympathy for the working people, which is evident throughout his fiction. Sembène's first novel, *Le Docker noir* (the black docker), grew out of his waterfront years. It is the story of a black stevedore who writes a novel, only to have the manuscript stolen by a white woman who publishes it under her name. The problems of race, class, and expatriation are intermingled in the novel.

Sembène's next novel, *Ô pays, mon beau peuple!* (oh my country, my beautiful people), further explores these themes. A young expatriate Senegalese returns to his homeland with a white wife and ideas about modernized, cooperative farming. He is quickly estranged from both black and white societies, even from his own family, and is eventually murdered. Sembène traveled throughout Africa and Europe, and his proletarian sympathies and anticapitalist views soon led him to the Soviet Union, China, and Cuba as well. He studied at Moscow's Gorki Film Studios for a year. His third novel, *God's Bits of Wood*, is larger in scope and more optimistic in tone than the first two. It is based on the successful strike of railroad workers on the Dakar-Niger line in 1947-1948.

Tribal Scars is a collection of twelve stories emphasizing the plight of the common man and, especially, the common woman. *L'Harmattan, livre I* (the storm, book 1) treats Charles de Gaulle's referendum on French rule in colonial West Africa. The novel is the first in a projected trilogy. Sembène next published two novellas together under the title *"The Money-Order," with "White Genesis."* These won for Sembène the literature prize of the 1966 Festival of Negro Arts in Dakar. In the early 1960's, Sembène had embarked upon his second artistic career, that of filmmaker. His short films *Borom-Sarret* and *La Noire d . . .* (black girl) were followed by *Mandabi*, his first full-length film, an adaptation of *The Money-Order. Mandabi* portrays the bourgeoisie's exploitation of the poor, in the form of educated civil servants who cheat a simple Muslim out of the proceeds of a large money order he has received from Paris. The film was a significant turning point for Sembène. It employed his native language of Wolof in an attempt to reach an African audience never exposed to his written works. In addition, it was a great critical success, winning for Sembène the special jury prize at the 1968 Venice Film Festival and the award as the best foreign film at the 1970 Atlanta Film Festival.

From the 1970's onward, Sembène concentrated primarily on filmmaking. The film *Emitaï*, set in his native Casamance, dramatizes the clash of tribal customs and colonial military power. Sembène wrote *Xala* as a novella and as a film at virtually the same time. It satirizes the colonial attitudes that persist in independent Senegal, through the story of an acquisitive Senegalese businessman who suffers from the *xala*, impotence, immediately after adding a third wife to his household. *Ceddo* (the common people) is Sembène's most ambitious and controversial film. The history of the film's difficulties with the censors reads like a satire of Sembène's own devising. It has been banned in Senegal—not because it criticizes African complicity in the slave trade, the subjugation of women, and Islamic colonialism, but because the government balked at the spelling of the title. The official government position is that the Wolof term should be spelled *cedo*. Sembène, who had earlier returned to make his permanent home at Dakar, argued that African filmmakers must be free to express their own vision of their native land. Sembène founded and edits *Kaddu*, the first Wolof monthly. His satires, marked by a realistic presentation, show that he rejects both the rationalizations for colonialism and the sentimentality and chauvinism of *négritude*, a "black is beautiful" movement launched in Senegal during the 1930's. He is widely regarded as the finest film director Africa has produced.

Patrick Adcock

Bibliography

Murphy, David. *Sembène: Imagining Alternatives in Film and Fiction*. Trenton, N.J.: Africa World Press, 2000. A study that addresses all of Sembène's work in all media, stressing the thematic issues common to each.

Petty, Sheila, ed. *A Call to Action: The Films of Ousmane Sembène*. Westport, Conn.: Praeger, 1996. A collection of essays assessing Sembène's film career; includes a substantial bibliography.

Pfaff, Françoise. *The Cinema of Ousmane Sembène, a Pioneer of African Film*. Westport, Conn.: Greenwood Press, 1984. Sembène's film career is profiled.

Tsabedze, Clara. *African Independence from Francophone and Anglophone Voices: A Comparative Study of the Post-Independence Novels by Ngugi and Sembène*. New York: P. Lang, 1994. A scholarly comparative study of his fiction.

Seneca the Younger

Roman playwright

Born: Corduba (now Córdoba, Spain); c. 4 B.C.E.
Died: Rome (now in Italy); April, 65 C.E.

DRAMA: The dating of Seneca's plays is approximate; the following were written c. 40-55 C.E.: *Agamemnon* (English translation, 1581); *Hercules furens* (*Mad Hercules*, 1581); *Hercules Oetaeus* (*Hercules on Oeta*, 1581); *Medea* (English translation, 1581); *Oedipus* (English translation, 1581); *Phaedra* (English translation, 1581); *Phoenissae* (*The Phoenician Women*, 1581); *Thyestes* (English translation, 1581); *Troades* (*The Trojan Women*, 1581).

NONFICTION: *Ad Marciam de consolatione*, c. 40-41 C.E. (*To Marcia, on Consolation*, 1614); *Ad Helviam matrem de consolatione*, c. 41-42 (*To My Mother Helvia, on Consolation*, 1614); *De ira libri tres*, c. 41-49 (*Three Essays on Anger*, 1614); *Epigrammata super exilio*, c. 41-49; *Ad Polybium de consolatione*, c. 43-44 (*To Polybius, on Consolation*, 1614); *De brevitate vitae*, c. 49 (*On the Shortness of Life*, 1614); *Apocolocyntosis divi Claudii*, c. 54 (*The Deification of Claudius*, 1614); *De constantia sapientis*, c. 55-56 (*On the Constancy of the Wise Man*, 1614); *De clementia*, c. 55-56 (*On Clemency*, 1614); *De beneficiis*, c. 58-63 (*On Benefits*, 1614); *De tranquillitate animi*, c. 59-61 (*On the Tranquility of the Soul*, 1614); *De otio*, c. 62 (*On Leisure*, 1614); *Quaestiones naturales*, c. 62-64 (*Natural Questions*, 1614); *Epistulae morales ad Lucilium*, c. 62-65 (*Letters to Lucilius*, 1917-1925); *De providentia*, c. 63-64 (*On Providence*, 1614); *Workes: Both Morall and Naturall*, 1614; *Ad Lucilium epistulae morales*, 1917-1925 (3 volumes); *Seneca, Moral Essays*, 1928-1935 (3 volumes).

Seneca (SEHN-ih-kuh) was the son of Annaeus Seneca, a famous rhetorician of Corduba known as Seneca the Elder, whose own contributions to literary history had a profound influence on his son. Seneca the Younger, in his writings, lavished praise on both of his parents. Helvia, his mother, was a strong woman of character who is specifically honored in *To My Mother Helvia, on Consolation*. The family possessed wealth and high rank, and at an early age Seneca was sent to Rome to be educated. As a student of rhetoric and philosophy, the young man came to the notice of Emperor Caligula, under whose patronage he entered the Roman senate and gained fame as an orator. Accused by Empress Messalina of conducting a love affair with Caligula's sister, Seneca was banished to Corsica by Emperor Claudius. Many of Seneca's philosophical writings were written during his exile, but his conduct while in Corsica apparently exhibited little of the Stoicism he advocated. Unhappy in his banishment, he begged to be recalled to Rome. In the year 49 C.E. Agrippina, the new wife of Claudius, procured his return and made him a tutor to her eleven-year-old son Domitius, later Emperor Nero.

Seneca and Sextus Afranius Burrus, prefect of the Praetorian guard, exercised great influence over Nero and were, according to Tacitus, responsible for the mildness that marked the early years of that monarch's reign. In his writings, Seneca attributes words to Nero that perhaps reflect Seneca's own aspirations for peace and tolerance. Through Nero, Seneca was for a time virtually the ruler of Rome, but after the death of Burrus in 62 C.E., his position as an adviser became dangerous because of the restraints he tried to impose on his debauched and brutal master. New advisers to Nero, who cared little for good government or justice, were at the emperor's ear. Nero was constantly in need of money, and Seneca was wealthy, enormously so. Moreover, enemies had pointed out to the emperor that Seneca was Nero's greatest rival at oratory and poetry, that Seneca was very popular with the Romans, and that he had disparaged Nero's poetry and horsemanship. Seneca, learning of the dangerous situation, went to Nero and asked permission to retire from public life. Tacitus declares that Seneca knew that retirement from Nero was not an option and that his request would ultimately lead to his death. The request was denied, and although he was not immediately condemned, Seneca spent far less time at the court.

In 65 C.E. Seneca was accused of plotting against Nero. Ordered by the emperor to commit suicide, Seneca cut the veins of his wrists and, while entertaining friends at his villa near Rome, allowed himself to bleed to death. The fact that Seneca's death occurred about the time of Nero's attack on Christians has led some historians to suggest that Seneca may have himself become a Christian, but no evidence exists to support that possibility.

It is difficult to associate Seneca's writings with his life, for too little information has been saved that relates the two. In his philosophical writings Seneca delineated a Stoicism that he himself apparently failed to practice. In addition to his philosophical writings Seneca left nine tragedies, probably designed to be read rather than to be viewed on the stage. During the period between 1580 and 1640 Seneca's plays greatly influenced Elizabethan and Jacobean dramatists; stage devices such as ghosts, murders, and long-winded harangues by the chief characters were borrowed directly from Senecan drama. Some authorities have maintained that the Senecan plays are an adjunct to his philosophical writings, each play illustrating a point of Stoic doctrine—*Thyestes*, for example, dealing with retribution. Precise dating of the plays is next to impossible.

Glenn L. Swygart

Bibliography

Boyle, A. J. *Tragic Seneca: An Essay in the Theatrical Tradition*. New York: Routledge, 1997. A study of Seneca's tragedies and his influence on Renaissance dramatists. Includes bibliography and index.

Davis, Peter J. *Shifting Song: The Chorus in Seneca's Tragedies*. New York: Olms-Weidmann, 1993. An examination of Seneca's tragedies and Latin drama, with emphasis on the use of the chorus. Includes bibliography.

Griffin, Miriam T. *Seneca: A Philosopher in Politics*. 1976. Reprint. Oxford, England: Clarendon Press, 1992. A biography of Seneca that examines his political viewpoints and his participation in government. Includes bibliography and index.

Harrison, George W. M., ed. *Seneca in Performance*. London: Duckworth with the Classical Press of Wales, 2000. An analysis of Seneca's dramas that looks at production and staging issues. Includes bibliography and index.

Motto, Anna Lydia. *Further Essays on Seneca*. New York: Peter Lang, 2001. A collection of essays presenting interpretation and critical analysis of the works of Seneca. Includes bibliography and index.

Motto, Anna Lydia, and John R. Clark. *Essays on Seneca*. New York: Peter Lang, 1993. A collection of articles on the Roman dramatist and his literary works. Includes bibliography and index.

Tietze Larson, Victoria. *The Role of Description in Senecan Tragedy*. New York: Peter Lang, 1994. A study of the tragedies of Seneca with emphasis on the role of description in these plays. Includes bibliography.

Léopold Senghor

Senegalese statesman, poet, and political philosopher

Born: Joal, Senegal; October 9, 1906
Died: Verson, France; December 20, 2001

POETRY: *Chants d'ombre*, 1945; *Hosties noires*, 1948; *Chants pour Naëtt*, 1949; *Chants d'ombre—Hosties noires*, 1956; *Éthiopiques*, 1956; *Nocturnes*, 1961 (English translation, 1969); *Poèmes*, 1964; *Selected Poems*, 1964; *Élégie des Alizés*, 1969; *Selected Poems of Léopold Sédar Senghor*, 1977; *Oeuvre poétique*, 1990 (*The Collected Poetry*, 1991).

NONFICTION: *Congrès constitutif du P.F.A.: Rapport sur la doctrine et le programme du parti*, 1959 (*Report on the Principles and Programme of the Party*, 1959); *La Préhistoire et les groupes éthniques*, 1960; *Nation et voie africaine du socialisme*, 1961 (as volume 2 of *Liberté*, 1971; *Nationhood and the African Road to Socialism*, 1962; abridged as *On African Socialism*, 1964); *Pierre Teilhard de Chardin et la politique africaine*, 1962; *Liberté: Négritude et humanisme*, 1964 (*Freedom I: Negritude and Humanism*, 1974); *Théorie et pratique du socialisme sénégalais*, 1964; *Les Fondements de l'Africanité: Ou, Négritude et arabité*, 1967 (as *Négritude, arabisme, et francité: Réflexions sur le problème de la culture*, 1967; *The Foundations of "Africanité": Or, Négritude and "Arabité,"* 1971); *La Parole chez Paul Claudel et chez les négro-africains*, 1973; *Pour une relecture africaine de Marx et d'Engels*, 1976; *Liberté: Négritude et civilisation de l'universel*, 1977; *Liberté: Socialisme et planification*, 1983; *Liberté: Le Dialogue des cultures*, 1993.

EDITED TEXT: *Anthologie de la nouvelle poésie nègre et malgache de langue française*, 1948.

MISCELLANEOUS: *Prose and Poetry*, 1965.

Even though the three strands are intimately intertwined, it is appropriate to focus separately on the personal, artistic, and political lives of Léopold Sédar Senghor (SAYN-gor). He was born the son of a prosperous cattle breeder and peanut grower in Senegal. Senghor belonged to a Christian minority in a predominantly Muslim country. His early childhood exposed him to traditional customs and beliefs, indigenous poetry, and Senegal's natural setting. He was to return to these nostalgic, idyllic themes in his poetry.

Senghor went to a Catholic elementary school in a country still colonized by France. In 1914 he was admitted to a Catholic boarding school at Ngazobil, where, in addition to French, Senghor studied the native Wolof vernacular. He was also exposed to the French policy of assimilating gifted natives—in language and attitudes, the French tried to turn them into African Frenchmen through a curriculum based entirely on European civilization. Senghor proved to be a brilliant student, and he was so devout that he resolved to become a Catholic priest.

But at the seminary in Dakar, which he entered in 1922, the French principal exhibited racist attitudes which clashed with Senghor's outspokenness. In 1926 he moved to the secular French *lycée* (academic secondary school) in Dakar, from which he graduated in 1928. His outstanding record won him prizes and a scholarship to the elite Lycée Louis-le-Grand in Paris. There, Senghor met the Martinican poet Aimé Césaire and the French Guianan poet Léon Gontran Damas—two men who were later to help Senghor form his philosophy of Négritude. In 1931 Senghor earned his bachelor's degree from the University of Paris, receiving its highest degree—*agrégation de grammaire*—in 1935. After a year of military service, he began teaching at various *lycées* in France. The outbreak of World War II in 1939 saw him enrolled in the French colonial infantry.

Senghor's entire unit was captured by the advancing German army in 1940, but he was released in 1941 for health reasons. He resumed his teaching career at increasingly prestigious institutions in 1942 while engaging in French Resistance activities. Even though his themes ranged from love poems inspired by his first wife (*Nocturnes*), to poems about the Senegalese landscape such as *Chants pour Naëtt* (songs for Naëtt), to elegies for the dead (*Élégie des Alizés*, literally "elegy of the trade winds"), to the plight of Senegalese soldiers during World War II (*Chants d'ombre*, or "songs of shadow"), there is no question that Senghor's name is most closely associated with Négritude, a movement that influenced black culture worldwide. The term was coined by Aimé Césaire, but the concept had some vague antecedents in earlier African American literature. Négritude strives to seek out and rehabilitate the roots of black culture, drawing upon African history and anthropology along the way.

Senghor agreed with Césaire that African values are in some cases preferable to Western ones and that the African mind was more intuitive but less inclined to rational thought and science than that of the European. But he was less strident than others as he tried to define the differences between the black and the white worlds and especially as he strived to show how an African could remain comfortable partaking of French culture without denying his African roots (*Éthiopiques*, 1956). In 1964 Senghor's major verse became accessible to English speakers through translation in the volume *Selected Poems*.

Senghor's political ascent was as meteoric as his literary one, also partly because of his ease at working in both a French and a Senegalese milieu. After being elected representative from Senegal to the French Constituent Assembly in 1945, he moved up, through a number of elective and appointed positions in both France and Senegal, to become his country's first president in 1960. He was re-elected several times but finally resigned as of January 1, 1981.

Senghor's record as chief of state was not an unblemished one. Political power struggles and his occasional suppression of opposition parties, a huge and wasteful bureaucracy that accumulated because of patronage, a faltering economy, and Senghor's inability to galvanize the masses with his philosophy of Négritude were some of the reasons. To the end of his political career, Senghor continued to advocate an African road to socialism, which he explained as a middle position between individualism and collectivism, one promoting universal humanism.

Following his retirement, Senghor traveled, especially in Africa, but he settled in France. There, in 1984, he was invested as the first African member of the French Academy—the forty "immortals." He had already served as the official grammarian in the drafting of the French constitutions of 1946 and 1958.

Senghor's divorce from Ginette Eboué in 1956 and marriage to Colette Hubert in 1957 and the premature death of two of his three sons indicate that his private life, like his political life, also witnessed ups and downs. Nevertheless, he received universal accolades as a great poet and as the author of significant critical and political prose, and in 1996 France and Senegal joined together to celebrate his ninetieth birthday.

Peter B. Heller

Bibliography

Bâ, Sylvia W. *The Concept of Negritude in the Poetry of Léopold Sédar Senghor.* Princeton, N.J.: Princeton University Press, 1973. Examines issues of race identity in Senghor's works. Includes translations of selected poems. Bibliography.

Hymans, Jacques. *Leopold Sédar Senghor: An Intellectual Biography.* Edinburgh: Edinburgh University Press, 1971. This full biography pays particular attention to Senghor's philosophical and literary development. Considers, among other things, the influence of Pierre Teilhard de Chardin, Paul Claudel, Marc Chagall, and Jacques Maritain. Bibliography.

Kluback, William. *Léopold Sédar Senghor: From Politics to Poetry.* New York: P. Lang, 1997. A book of imagined conversations based on Senghor's philosophy regarding humanity's moral evolution.

Markovitz, Irving Leonard. *Leopold Sédar Senghor and the Politics of Négritude.* New York: Atheneum, 1969. A penetrating consideration of Senghor's philosophy of leadership and issues of race identity.

Mezu, Sebastian Okechukwu. *The Poetry of Leopold Sédar Senghor.* Rutherford, N.J.: Fairleigh Dickinson University Press, 1973. A rare monograph focusing on Senghor's poetry.

Rasmussen, R. Kent. *Modern African Political Leaders.* New York: Facts on File, 1998. Covers leaders, including Senghor, representative of the major regions of Africa during a period when many African nations moved from colonial rule to independence.

Spleth, Janice. *Léopold Sédar Senghor.* New York: Macmillan Library Reference, 1985. A detailed overview of Senghor's poetry, his development as poet and statesman, and the conflicts of those two roles. This discussion involves the author in extending her coverage beyond Senghor to examine the relationship between French and francophone African literature in general.

_______, ed. *Critical Perspectives on Léopold Sédar Senghor.* Washington, D.C.: Three Continents Press, 1993. A collection of critical essays on Senghor's writings.

Vaillant, Janet G. *Black, French, and African: A Life of Leopold Sédar Senghor.* Cambridge, Mass.: Harvard University Press, 1990. A biography that adds to previous literature an extended examination of Senghor's childhood, including interviews with his extended Senegalese family. More material on his poetry than on his presidency of Senegal. The first major biography in English.

Vikram Seth

Indian novelist and poet

Born: Calcutta, India; June 20, 1952

LONG FICTION: *The Golden Gate: A Novel in Verse*, 1986; *A Suitable Boy*, 1993; *An Equal Music*, 1999.

POETRY: *Mappings*, 1981; *The Humble Administrator's Garden*, 1985; *All You Who Sleep Tonight*, 1990; *Beastly Tales from Here to There*, 1992; *The Poems, 1981-1994*, 1995.

TRANSLATION: *Three Chinese Poets: Translations of Poems by Wang Wei, Li Bai, and Du Fu*, 1992.

NONFICTION: *From Heaven Lake: Travels Through Sinkiang and Tibet*, 1983.

CHILDREN'S/YOUNG ADULT LITERATURE: *Arion and the Dolphin*, 1994.

Vikram Seth (sayt) is a versatile writer who is at ease in a variety of genres. He has made a place for himself as an Indian writing in the English language. Seth was born in Calcutta, India, in 1952. He left India to study at Oxford University in England, where he earned degrees in philosophy, economics, and politics. He then enrolled at Stanford University for advanced study in economics. While at Stanford, Seth was a Wallace Stegner Fellow in creative writing. He wrote the poetry collected in *Mappings* during this time.

From 1980 to 1982, Seth went to China for economic research and to travel. He studied classical Chinese poetry and language at

Nanjing University. His account of a hitchhiking journey from China through Tibet to India was published as *From Heaven Lake*, which won the Thomas Cook Travel Book Award in 1983.

Returning to California, Seth published several books of poetry. *The Humble Administrator's Garden*, which won the Commonwealth Poetry Prize, is divided into three sections that identify their influences, Chinese, Indian, and Californian. *The Golden Gate: A Novel in Verse* was widely reviewed and critically well received. It established Seth's reputation as a poet and popular writer. The novel is a 307-page series of nearly six hundred sonnets of iambic tetrameter, loosely modeled on Russian poet Alexander Pushkin's *Eugene Onegin* (1825-1832). The narrative is driven by the lives and entanglements of its characters. Each character is part of a subculture of San Francisco life, and through them Seth demonstrates his thorough familiarity with his setting, San Francisco in the 1980's. *The Golden Gate* won the Quality Paperback Book Club New Voice Award and the Commonwealth Poetry Prize in 1986.

After the publication of *The Golden Gate*, Seth returned to India to live with his family and work on his major epic, *A Suitable Boy*. Three additional books of poetry were published between the two novels: *All You Who Sleep Tonight*, *Beastly Tales from Here to There*, and *Three Chinese Poets*, all of which demonstrate Seth's diversity of material and multicultural background.

A Suitable Boy, published in 1993, is Seth's best-known work. The book is a thirteen-hundred-page epic of Indian culture, religion, family life, and postcolonial politics. This novel propelled Seth into the public spotlight, launching a series of interviews, talk-show appearances, and book signings. Critical reviews were mixed, however, and the public and his publishers were disappointed when the book was not considered for the Booker Prize in 1993. It did win the W. H. Smith Award and earned Seth the Commonwealth Writer's Prize.

After *A Suitable Boy*, Seth returned to London, where he was commissioned by the English National Opera to write a libretto based on the Greek legend of Arion and the dolphin. This material was also published as a children's book. His 1999 novel, *An Equal Music*, is set in London and the Continent and is a love story about the members of a string quartet. Seth was awarded the Order of the British Empire in 2001 for his achievements.

Seth's work is noted for its versatility and variety of setting and form. His settings reflect the multicultural and geographic variety of his life experiences, with major works set in India, China, London and the European continent, and the United States. Translation has played a role in his life and work as well, expanding his multicultural influences.

Seth has written successful and prizewinning work in a variety of genres: poetry, nonfiction, and fiction as well as opera libretti and children's tales. He is noted for his technical mastery of traditional forms in poetry, using rhyme and meter unusual in a poet of the late twentieth century. *A Suitable Boy* has been described as having the style of a nineteenth century novel, and critics have compared its scope and some of its themes to the works of Jane Austen, Charles Dickens, and Leo Tolstoy. Seth's introductions to some of his own work suggest that as his academic training was in economics rather than English, he followed his own eclectic inclinations and tastes in his reading and writing.

While Seth's forms tend toward the traditional, his themes and sensibilities suggest the difficulty of forming relationships, the ultimate failure of love as a bond, and the loneliness of late twentieth century life, no matter where in the world the tale is set. Vikram Seth's importance is as a world writer, a writer in English who embraces the language, culture, and influence of the English-speaking world, the non-English Western world, and the Eastern regions of India and China as well. He is also important as a writer who unites the traditional forms of the nineteenth century and earlier with the themes and sensibilities of the late twentieth century.

Susan Butterworth

Bibliography

Agarwalla, Shyam S. *Vikram Seth's "A Suitable Boy": Search for an Indian Identity*. New Delhi: Prestige Books, 1995. A scholarly, book-length source on Seth. Employing the techniques of literary criticism, the book includes general cultural information and discussion of Seth's role as an Indian writer.

King, Bruce. "World Literature in Review: India." *World Literature Today* 68, no. 2 (Spring, 1994): 431-432. A review of *A Suitable Boy*. Places the novel in the context of the nineteenth century European novel, while describing it as a guide to the "intricacies of Indian society and politics." Discusses Seth's place in the literary canon and names him "a major writer."

Perloff, Marjorie. "Homeward Ho! Silicon Valley Pushkin." *The American Poetry Review* 15, no. 6 (November/December, 1986): 37-46. Critical review of *The Golden Gate*. Perloff asserts that Seth's concern with rhyme weakens the novel's characterization, plot, and satirical force. A scholarly article, with detailed analysis and extensive references to poetic form and poets in history.

Seth, Vikram. *The Poems, 1981-1994*. New York: Viking Penguin, 1995. In his introduction and forewords, Seth discusses his poetry and influences and reveals themes and insight into his priorities and thought process.

Woodward, Richard B. "Vikram's Seth's Big Book." *The New York Times Magazine* 142, no. 49319 (May 2, 1993): 32-36. A profile of Seth, written at the time of the release of *A Suitable Boy*. Biographical and background information on the author, his writing, and his career.

Mary Lee Settle

American novelist

Born: Charleston, West Virgina; July 29, 1918
Pseudonym: Mrs. Charles Palmer

LONG FICTION: *The Love Eaters*, 1954; *The Kiss of Kin*, 1955; *O Beulah Land*, 1956; *Know Nothing*, 1960; *Fight Night on a Sweet Saturday*, 1964; *The Clam Shell*, 1971; *Prisons*, 1973; *Blood Tie*, 1977; *The Scapegoat*, 1980; *The Killing Ground*, 1982 (revision of *Fight Night on a Sweet Saturday*); *Celebration*, 1986; *Charley Bland*, 1989; *Choices*, 1995; *I, Roger Williams: A Fragment of Autobiography*, 2001.
NONFICTION: *All the Brave Promises: Memories of Aircraft Woman Second Class 2146391*, 1966; *The Scopes Trial: The State of Tennessee vs. John Thomas Scopes*, 1972; *Turkish Reflections: A Biography of a Place*, 1991 (with an introduction by Jan Morris); *Addie*, 1998.
CHILDREN'S/YOUNG ADULT LITERATURE: *The Story of Flight*, 1967; *Water World*, 1984.

Mary Lee Settle is a distinguished American writer who has had to be periodically rediscovered; both her life and her career exhibit a series of ups and downs. Her father and mother, Joseph Edward and Rachel Tompkins Settle, were from the small circle of enterprising West Virginia families who helped establish industry and coal mining. When Settle was about two years old the family moved deeper into the Appalachian hinterlands, to Pineville, Kentucky, near where her father owned a coal mine on Straight Creek in Harlan County. When Settle was about seven years old, the coal business failed and the family moved to Orlando, Florida. There her father, a civil engineer, worked in the land boom, designing, among other things, the layout of Venice, Florida. When the Florida boom fizzled in 1928, the family returned to live with Settle's maternal grandmother in Cedar Grove, West Virginia. Eventually they settled in Charleston, where the family struggled through the Depression. Despite hard times, there was money for Settle's elocution lessons and, later, college.

After two years at Sweet Briar College from 1936 to 1938 Settle rebelled and left school. On the basis of her acting credentials—a summer at Virginia's Barter Theater and an audition for the film role of Scarlett O'Hara—she went to New York. There, after working as a model, she married an Englishman, Rodney Weathersbee, in 1939. They moved to Canada, where Weathersbee enlisted in the Canadian army and their son Christopher was born. Settle herself joined the World War II struggle in 1941: Leaving her son with her parents in West Virginia, she traveled to Great Britain and enlisted in the Women's Auxiliary Air Force (WAAF) branch of the Royal Air Force (RAF). Her service with the WAAF, recounted in *All the Brave Promises*, was a watershed period in her life during which she was forced to confront the British class system. She was on control tower duty for thirteen months until she began to be overcome by "signals shock" from constantly listening for radioed pilots' voices through enemy jamming. Settle then transferred to the Office of War Information in London; there she became friends with a group of excellent writers and editors, which motivated her to begin writing herself.

After World War II Settle faced a major decision. She had obtained a good editing job with *Harper's Bazaar* magazine in New York, but after a brief time there she decided to devote herself to her own writing. In 1946, divorced from Weathersbee, Settle returned to England with her son and married the British poet Douglas Newton. They embarked on the precarious existence of struggling writers in England and in Paris. Settle took on freelance journalistic assignments, writing, for example, an etiquette column for *Woman's Day* under the pseudonym Mrs. Charles Palmer and serving as English correspondent for *Flair* magazine. At the same time she wrote six plays and four film scripts, though without finding either a producer or a publisher. Finally, in 1954, she published her first novel, *The Love Eaters*, about an amateur play production in a West Virginia town. Her second novel, *The Kiss of Kin*, a reworking of one of her earlier plays and also set in West Virginia, soon followed and was received with enthusiasm; critics praised Settle as a sophisticated novelist of small-town manners.

Her marriage soon showed the strain of her newfound success, and in 1955 she left her husband (they were divorced in 1956) and returned to Charleston with her son. Here her situation gradually deteriorated, though she published *O Beulah Land* and *Know Nothing*, two volumes in the Beulah Quintet, considered by some to be her major work. A third volume, *Fight Night on a Sweet Saturday*, suffered so much editorial cutting that she later rewrote it as *The Killing Ground*. In 1961 she worked in New York as an editor for *American Heritage*; between 1965 and 1969 she taught one semester a year at Bard College until, in 1969, she moved abroad to protest Richard Nixon's election as president. Two of her novels—*The Clam Shell*, an autobiographical work based on her Sweet Briar years, and *Prisons*, another volume in the Beulah Quintet—appeared without benefit of New York reviews. She had trouble finding a publisher for her next novel, *Blood Tie*, which drew on her three-year stay in Turkey, but when that work was eventually published, it was awarded the 1978 National Book Award in Fiction, which marked a dramatic upswing in her career. Her subsequent novels, including *The Scapegoat* (considered the best volume in the Beulah Quintet), *The Killing Ground*, and *Celebration*, were published to major reviews. Settle returned to the United States in 1974 to live in Charlottesville, Virginia, and in 1978 she married the journalist and historian William Littleton Tazewell. They both taught writing at the University of Virginia until retiring to their home in Norfolk, Virginia, to concentrate on their own work.

The mixed response to Settle's fiction in part reflects her association with the South, particularly southern Appalachia. She has been sometimes scornfully dismissed, sometimes proudly claimed as a regional writer. No writer, however, more easily exposes the limited meaning of such labels; for her, "regional" in effect means "international." She lived abroad for long periods, and the two novels usually considered her best, *Blood Tie* and *Celebration*, have international settings. Even her monumental Beulah Quintet, with its great theme of the search for freedom, begins in seventeenth century Great Britain with the symbolically entitled *Prisons* (*O Beulah Land*, *Know Nothing*, *The Scapegoat*, and *The Killing Ground* follow in chronological order). Her novel *I, Roger Williams*, also returns to the seventeenth century roots of independence, creating a fictional autobiography of the founder of Rhode Island. Critical reception of Settle's work has also been shaped by prevailing attitudes toward historical fiction, which has at times been dismissed as a genre tainted by association with popular sagas. Critical fashions change, however, and Settle is one of a number of writers—including figures as diverse as Larry McMurtry and Thomas Flanagan—who have contributed to a modest renaissance of the historical novel.

Harold Branam

Bibliography

Bach, Peggy. "The Searching Voice and Vision of Mary Lee Settle." *Southern Review* 20 (October, 1984): 842-850. After outlining the various critical assessments of Settle's work, Bach supports her own insistence that it can hardly be rated too highly. In the Beulah Quintet, Settle has traced a family through three hundred years of history, showing how desperately even people beginning fresh in a new land need to have a sense of their past.

Galligan, Edward L. "The Novels of Mary Lee Settle." *The Sewanee Review* 104 (Summer, 1996): 413-422. Galligan offers a general view of Settle's fiction, focusing on her variety and unpredictability in order to undergird his argument that she is worthy of a serious place in American letters.

Garrett, George. *Understanding Mary Lee Settle*. Columbia: University of South Carolina Press, 1988. Garrett is one of Settle's most prolific analysts; in this work he offers an overview of her oeuvre, including sympathetic discussions of her major fiction, with special attention to the Beulah Quintet. He also devotes chapters to *Blood Tie*, *Celebration*, and some of her nonfiction.

Joyner, Nancy Carol. "Mary Lee Settle's Connections: Class and Clothes in the Beulah Quintet." In *Women Writers of the Contemporary South*, edited by Peggy Whitman Prenshaw. Jackson: University Press of Mississippi, 1984. Stresses the theme of social rigidity and social injustice in Settle's Beulah Quintet.

Rosenberg, Brian. *Mary Lee Settle's Beulah Quintet: The Price of Freedom*. Baton Rouge: Louisiana State University Press, 1991. Rosenberg examines the Quintet as a single fiction instead of a series of related novels, seeing it as a grand-scale work which uses the history of West Virginia as a paradigm of the history of the United States.

Speer, Jean Haskell. "Montani Semper Liberi: Mary Lee Settle and the Myths of Appalachia." In *Southern Women Writers: The New Generation*. Tuscaloosa: University of Alabama Press, 1990. Speer contends that in the Beulah Quintet one of Settle's purposes was to debunk such myths as the assumption that there is a single, easily defined Appalachian culture whose people are both ignorant and innocent.

Madame de Sévigné
(Marie de Rabutin-Chantal)

French letter writer

Born: Paris, France; February 5, 1626
Died: Grignan, Provence, France; April 17, 1696

NONFICTION: *Lettres*, 1696, 1725, 1726, 1734-1737 (6 volumes); 1862-1868 (14 volumes); 1953-1957 (3 volumes; *Letters*, 1727, 1764 [10 volumes]; 1811 [9 volumes]; 1927 [7 volumes]).

Madame de Sévigné (say-veen-yay) was born Marie de Rabutin-Chantal in Paris on February 5, 1626. Her father was Celse-Bénigne de Rabutin, Baron de Chantal, the son of a noble family whose titles went back at least to the twelfth century. Her paternal grandmother, Jeanne-Françoise, who as a widow had given the care of her family to her own parents, had withdrawn from the world in 1610 to embrace the religious life under the direction of the man who was to become one day Saint-François de Sales. She was canonized in 1767 for her exemplary life and work in establishing the Order of the Visitation of Saint Mary. Now known as St. Jeanne de Chantal, her extensive correspondence with St. François de Sales has been published and reveals her profound literary talent. De Sévigné's mother, Marie de Coulanges, was the daughter of a noble but somewhat less illustrious family.

In 1627, only a year after her birth, de Sévigné's father was killed in battle against the English. Six years later, in 1633, her mother also died, and the seven-year-old girl was sent to be cared for by her maternal grandparents. The child's misfortunes were not yet over. Her grandmother died in 1635, and her grandfather died the following year. The ten-year-old girl was then sent to her maternal uncle, Christophe de Coulanges, abbé of Livry. There at last she found security.

The abbé took the girl's upbringing and education quite seriously. He gave her the best teachers, from whom she learned, among other things, Latin, Spanish, and Italian, and he gave her a firm Christian education, by the tenets of which she lived her entire life, a respected and virtuous woman. Throughout the rest of his life (until 1687) the abbé, whom de Sévigné called "Kindness Itself," was a faithful friend and counselor of his niece.

In 1644, at the age of eighteen, de Sévigné married Henri Marquis de Sévigné. It was a "good" but unhappy match. The young marquis was a gambler, a fighter, and a rake. After badly damaging his own and his wife's fortunes, he was killed in 1651 in a duel over another woman. He left his widow with two small children, a daughter born in 1646 and a son born in 1648. De Sévigné, who, as she said, loved but did not esteem her husband, never remarried. She was much sought after for her person and her wit.

After her husband's death, de Sévigné spent several years on her estates reorganizing her children's patrimony. That task accomplished, she returned to Paris in 1654 and made a brilliant showing in the high society of the capital. She often appeared at the Hôtel de Rambouillet as well as at other aristocratic salons, and she was one of the most illustrious of the circle of cultured women who set the intellectual fashions of Paris. Among her many friends and admirers were François de La Rochefoucauld, Madame de La Fayette, and the great finance minister, Nicolas Fouquet (who sought to make her his mistress). Nevertheless, for the most part she devoted herself to the upbringing and education of her two children, the elder of whom, her daughter Françoise-Marguerite, she idolized.

In 1669 de Sévigné arranged the marriage of her daughter to the Comte de Grignan, who, much to the doting mother's distress, was soon appointed governor of Provence. The enforced separation of de Sévigné and her beloved daughter was the reason for the majority of the more than fifteen hundred letters about the life and society of Paris on which de Sévigné's literary reputation rests. She had begun writing characteristically vivid and brilliant letters to her friends before her marriage, and her circle of correspondence always remained wide. In all, she wrote more than three thousand well-crafted letters to her daughter, Madame de Grignan, and many other correspondents, including her cousin, the novelist Bussy-Rabutin, during the last three decades of her life. For these letters she has remained famous. The often tense mother-daughter relationship is the most fascinating aspect of her correspondence.

Her letters to her daughter were first published after the deaths of both de Sévigné and Madame de Grignan by de Sévigné's granddaughter Madame de Simiane, who destroyed de Grignan's letters but made public those of her grandmother. De Sévigné, who was visiting her daughter for only the third time since 1671, died of smallpox at her daughter's château in Provence on April 17, 1696.

Edmund J. Campion

Bibliography

Farrell, Michèle Longino. *Performing Motherhood: The Sévigné Correspondence*. Hanover, N.H.: University Press of New England, 1991. A feminist analysis of Sévigné's worldview.

Mossiker, Frances. *Madame de Sévigné: A Life and Letters*. New York: Knopf, 1983. A meticulously researched biography.

Ojala, Jeanne A. *Madame de Sévigné: A Seventeenth Century Life*. New York: St. Martin's Press, 1990. A biography that covers the events of Madame de Sévigné's life and assesses her place in her social world.

Recker, Jo Ann Marie. *Appelle-moi Pierrot: Wit and Irony in the Letters of Madame de Sévigné*. Philadelphia: J. Benjamins, 1986. A study of Madame de Sévigné's literary style.

Williams, Charles G. S. *Madame de Sévigné*. Boston: Twayne, 1981. A literary biography that contains a very useful bibliography.

Anne Sexton

American poet

Born: Newton, Massachusetts; November 9, 1928
Died: Weston, Massachusetts; October 4, 1974

POETRY: *To Bedlam and Part Way Back*, 1960; *All My Pretty Ones*, 1962; *Selected Poems*, 1964; *Live or Die*, 1966; *Poems*, 1968 (with Thomas Kinsella and Douglas Livingston); *Love Poems*, 1969; *Transformations*, 1971; *The Book of Folly*, 1972; *The Death Notebooks*, 1974; *The Awful Rowing Toward God*, 1975; *Forty-five Mercy Street*, 1976; *Words for Dr. Y.: Uncollected Poems with Three Stories*, 1978; *The Complete Poems*, 1981; *Selected Poems of Anne Sexton*, 1988.

DRAMA: *Forty-five Mercy Street*, pr. 1969.

NONFICTION: *Anne Sexton: A Self-Portrait in Letters*, 1977; *No Evil Star: Selected Essays, Interviews, and Prose*, 1985.

CHILDREN'S LITERATURE (with Maxine Kumin): *Eggs of Things*, 1963; *More Eggs of Things*, 1964; *Joey and the Birthday Present*, 1971; *The Wizard's Tears*, 1975.

Anne Sexton was born Anne Gray Harvey. After attending public school in Wellesley, Massachusetts, she went to a prep school and then, for a year, to Garland Junior College. She married Alfred Muller Sexton and worked briefly as a model. Her daughter Linda was born when Sexton was twenty-five. Sexton is often called a "confessional" poet (as are W. D. Snodgrass, Robert Lowell, and Sylvia Plath, who were her friends). Many of her poems indeed include the word "confession" or comparable religious language, yet the label is somewhat misleading. Despite displaying moments of remorse, her verse more often celebrates than bemoans unconventional behavior. Readers have admired her courage in breaking taboos, in struggling "part way back" from madness, and in admitting all that she did. Rather than furnishing accurate confessions, she changes details skillfully for dramatic effect.

Many of her best poems tailor autobiography to accentuate similarities between herself and literary characters or historical figures. For example, she began all her public readings with her poem "Her Kind," which identifies her with persecuted witches. In an interview with Barbara Kevles, Sexton explained that she thought of herself as being "many people," including the "Christ" (of another of her poems), whose pain she felt as she wrote it. She spoke of mystical visions accompanied by the same sensations she felt when composing poetry.

The salvation she sought may have been momentarily attained through the poetic experience of adopting a persona or role. It distanced her from daily problems and permitted her to look at herself from new vantage points. She longed to be a character living in an imaginary place of forgiveness and reconciliation that she termed "Mercy Street" (in her more pious moments she fervently prayed for it to be real). Assuming poses also seemed to gratify a lifelong craving for stardom.

Hungry for attention, Anne, during her childhood, felt less close to her parents than to the doting great-aunt after whom she was named (Anna Ladd Dingley, called "Nana," who became mentally ill late in life). Once an official at Sexton's grade school recommended psychoanalysis for Anne, but she did not begin therapy until 1954, when depression after the birth of her daughter Linda kept growing worse. In 1956 came Sexton's first suicide attempt—the culmination of a massive episode of depression after the birth of her second daughter, Joyce, nicknamed "Joy."

Sexton's analyst encouraged her to begin creative writing; for the first time since high school, she started to compose poetry. The next year brought a second suicide attempt but also a creative-writing seminar with John Holmes. There she met writer Maxine Kumin. In lengthy telephone conversations, they discussed each other's works, and they later collaborated on four children's books.

Sexton continued studying with Holmes until his death in 1962. In 1958 she also enrolled in a Boston University seminar taught by Robert Lowell. Another writer in that class was the poet most often compared with Sexton, Sylvia Plath. That year Sexton met W. D. Snodgrass at the Antioch Writers' Conference.

Professional success came rapidly, but it was never enough to satisfy Sexton. There were also negative reviews, including one by the poet James Dickey that she carried with her in her wallet. By 1964 she was taking the prescription drug thorazine, but neither therapy nor drugs could free her from debilitating depression. There were further suicide attempts. On an autumn day in 1974, she lunched with Kumin, finished proofreading *The Awful Rowing Toward God*, went home, shut herself in her garage, and killed herself by breathing carbon monoxide.

She had by that time garnered many honors, including prizes from *Audience* and *Poetry*; fellowships or grants from Bread Loaf, the Radcliffe Institute, the Congress for Cultural Freedom, the American Academy of Arts and Sciences, the Ford Foundation, and the Guggenheim Foundation; honorary doctorates from Tufts University, Regis College, and Fairfield University; a professorship from Boston University; the Crashaw Chair in Literature at Colgate University; membership in Phi Beta Kappa; a Shelley Memorial Award; and, most prestigious of all, the 1967 Pulitzer Prize in poetry.

Nonetheless, after her first two books, critics increasingly complained of unevenness in her work. She had in fact begun revising less obsessively, but the middle of her career was graced with the most unified of her volumes, *Transformations*, an interweaving of her life with fairy tales. Her play *Forty-five Mercy Street* (fictionalized autobiography organized in terms of an Episcopalian High Mass) appeared Off-Broadway in 1969. Throughout her career, her public readings remained popular, and she succeeded in promoting musical adaptations of her works, ranging from what she called "chamber rock" to an opera.

James S. Whitlark

Bibliography

Furst, Arthur. *Anne Sexton: The Last Summer.* New York: St. Martin's Press, 2000. A collection of Furst's photos of Sexton with letters and unpublished drafts of Sexton's poems written during the last months of her life, as well as previously unpublished letters to her daughters.

Hall, Caroline King Barnard. *Anne Sexton*. Boston: Twayne, 1989. This useful introduction to Sexton examines her poetry and its chronological development. Worth noting is the chapter "*Transformations:* Fairy Tales Revisited."

McClatchy, J. D. *Anne Sexton: The Artist and Her Critics*. Bloomington: Indiana University Press, 1978. A collection of documentary and interpretative material—overviews, reviews, and reflections—on Sexton, including what are thought to be three of her best interviews. The volume sets out to establish a balanced critical perspective on this poet's work and includes reprints of journals.

Middlebrook, Diane Wood. *Anne Sexton: A Biography*. Boston: Houghton Mifflin, 1991. Middlebrook's biography of Sexton is based on tapes from Sexton's therapy sessions and the intimate revelations of Sexton's family. Middlebrook explores Sexton's creativity and the relationship between art and mental disorder.

Sexton, Linda Gray, and Lois Ames, eds. *Anne Sexton: A Self-Portrait in Letters*. Boston: Houghton Mifflin, 1977. A compilation of the best and most representative letters written by Sexton, who was an exceptional correspondent. Contains a wonderful collection of letters, arranged chronologically and interspersed with biographical details, and providing much insight about this poet's imagination.

Wagner-Martin, Linda, ed. *Critical Essays on Anne Sexton*. Boston: G. K. Hall, 1989. A volume of selected critical essays, gathering early reviews and modern scholarship, including essays on Sexton's poems and her life. All the essays offer significant secondary material on Sexton; the introduction by Wagner-Martin is helpful, giving an overview of Sexton's poems.

Michael Shaara

American novelist and short-story writer

Born: Jersey City, New Jersey; June 23, 1928
Died: Tallahassee, Florida; May 5, 1988

LONG FICTION: *The Broken Place*, 1968; *The Killer Angels*, 1974; *The Herald*, 1981 (also known as *The Noah Conspiracy*, 1994); *For Love of the Game*, 1991.
SHORT FICTION: *Soldier Boy*, 1982.
SCREENPLAY: *Billy Boy*, 1980.

The father of writer Michael Shaara (SHAR-uh) was five years old when in 1904 he was brought to the United States from Italy by his parents, Giuseppe and Anna Russo Sciarra, whose Old World family name was altered by an Ellis Island immigration clerk. He was twenty-nine and married to Alleen Maxwell of Texas when his son Michael Joseph Shaara, Jr., was born in Jersey City on June 23, 1928.

Educated at Rutgers University, Michael, Jr., early became obsessed with writing, and he began turning out magazine stories even before his graduation in 1951 and more feverishly during his postgraduate studies at Columbia University (1952-1953) and at the University of Vermont (1953-1954). He had served as a merchant seaman and also as a paratrooper (in the Eighty-second Airborne Division, 1946-1949). While a student at Rutgers, he married Helen Krumwiede, the daughter of Howard and Elizabeth Krumwiede of Highland Park, New Jersey. At the close of his graduate studies he took his family (which now included his son, Jeffrey, who had been born February 21, 1952, in New Brunswick) to Florida. There he served as an officer in the St. Petersburg Police Department (1954-1955). Shortly after his second child, a daughter named Lila Elise, was born in 1958, he accepted a position teaching English at Florida State University, where he was to serve for the years 1961-1973.

Through all of this hectic time he continued to produce science fiction for the pulps and eventually prizewinning imaginative short stories for such prestigious magazines as *The Saturday Evening Post*, *Redbook*, *Cosmopolitan*, and *McCall's*. Over the thirty years from 1952 to 1982, he sold some seventy tales under titles such as "Beast in the House," "Grenville's Planet," "Man of Distinction," and "The Vanisher." These stories are much reprinted in science-fiction and short-story anthologies; sixteen appear, with Shaara's introduction and afterword, in his 1982 collection *Soldier Boy*.

Shaara's first novel, *The Broken Place*, is a moving tale of Tom McClain, a Korean War veteran at loose ends on his return to the United States. It was published in 1968 and, though noted favorably by critics, was scarcely read. Even *The Killer Angels*, today perhaps the most popular and highly regarded of all battlefield novels set during the Civil War, was rejected by the first fifteen publishers to whom Shaara dispatched it. An absorbing psychological study of Colonel Joshua Chamberlain and the central military figures of the four days at Gettysburg, it was seven years in composition. It was finally published in 1974 by the David McKay Company and issued in paperback by Ballantine Books in 1975, when it was awarded the Pulitzer Prize in fiction and began to attract a steady and enthusiastic readership. It contributed greatly to Ken Burns's 1990 television documentary of the Civil War and was also the basis for Ronald Maxwell's motion picture *Gettysburg* (1993), one of the most powerfully moving of all war films. Today the novel remains in print, a best-seller at all Civil War battlefields and at bookstores everywhere.

An active, adventurous man (who even tried his hand at boxing), Shaara lived three years in South Africa and two in Italy. In 1965 he suffered a serious heart attack, and it has been suggested that the nearly fatal motorcycle crash he later experienced in Florence, Italy, in April of 1972, may have been caused by a related stroke. In any case the accident left him brain-damaged and in such poor health that he was able to write little. He did complete a third novel, a science-fiction nail-biter titled first *The Herald* and later *The Noah Conspiracy*, which appeared in 1981. Although his failing health had led him into discouragement and bitterness, he was able to ready for publication one additional beautiful book. He died of cardiac arrest on May 5, 1988, at his home in Tallahassee, Florida.

He did not live to see the publication of his last novel, *For Love of the Game*, a touching story of a baseball pitcher in the twilight of his career (discovered among his papers by son, Jeff), nor would he see the popular 1999 motion-picture version starring Kevin Costner as Billy Chapel. He did not live to see his Union and Confederate heroes take to the stage in the motion picture *Gettysburg*. He did not live to read the books produced by his son, Jeff, which would have made him proud: *Gods and Generals* (1996), a prequel to *The Killer Angels*; *The Last Full Measure* (1998), a sequel to *The Killer Angels*; *Gone for Soldiers* (2000), a novel of the Mexican War; and *Rise to Rebellion* (2001), with its Revolutionary War sequel, *The Glorious Cause* (2002). The Michael Shaara Award for Excellence in Civil War Fiction is presented annually by the United States Civil War Center at Louisiana State University. Madison Jones, author of *Nashville 1864*, was the first writer to be so honored, in 1997.

William W. Betts, Jr.

Bibliography

Adams, Phoebe. "Short Reviews." *The Atlantic Monthly* 234 (October, 1974). Review speaks of "a novelist's liberty of invention" but finds in the narrative excitement and plausibility.

Brashler, Bill. Review of *For Love of the Game*, by Michael Shaara. *Chicago Tribune*, April 7, 1991, sec. 14, p. 5. Notes that "Shaara obviously had a love of the game, of its tradition and natural grace, and he left it this lovely token."

Leak, Thomas. "High Tide of the Confederacy." *The New York Times*, May 10, 1975, p. 27. Quotes author Shaara on his intent in composing *The Killer Angels*.

Le Clair, Thomas. Review of *The Killer Angels*, by Michael Shaara. *The New York Times Book Review*, October 20, 1974. Praises the narrative for its recording of "the terror and the bravery."

Pine, John C. Review of *The Broken Place*, by Michael Shaara. *Library Journal*, February 15, 1968. Praises the book for "a natural rhythm that is unmistakable."

Rhodes, Richard. "Boxer Gone Berserk." *The New York Times*, April 7, 1968, sec. 7, p. 36. Notes and explains the element of violence in *The Broken Place*.

Smith, L. C. Review of *The Killer Angels*, by Michael Shaara. *Best Seller* 34 (September 5, 1974). Laments the absence of the common soldier but lauds the book for its "particularly good description."

Stoppel, E. K. Review of *The Killer Angels*, by Michael Shaara. *Library Journal* 99 (September 1, 1974). Praises the novel for its vividness and fast-moving pace.

Weeks, Edward. "The Peripatetic Reviewer: *The Killer Angels*." *The Atlantic Monthly* 235 (April, 1975). Declares that "the best way to write about a battle is to tell it as the men who went through it saw it and felt it—and that is what Michael Shaara has done in this stirring, brilliantly interpretive novel."

Anthony Shaffer

English playwright, screenwriter, and novelist

Born: Liverpool, England; May 15, 1926
Died: London, England; November 6, 2001
Pseudonym: Peter Antony

DRAMA: *The Savage Parade*, pr. 1963, revised pr. 1987 (as *This Savage Parade*); *Sleuth*, pr., pb. 1970; *Murderer*, pr. 1975; *The Case of the Oily Levantine*, pr. 1977, pr. 1982 as *Whodunnit*; *Widow's Weeds: Or, For Years I Couldn't Wear My Black*, pr. 1977.

LONG FICTION: *The Woman in the Wardrobe*, 1951 (as Peter Antony; with Peter Shaffer); *How Doth the Little Crocodile?*, 1952 (as Peter Antony; with Peter Shaffer); *Withered Murder*, 1955 (with Peter Shaffer); *The Wicker Man*, 1978 (with Robin Hardy; adaptation of his screenplay); *Absolution*, 1979.

NONFICTION: *So What Did You Expect? A Memoir*, 2001.

SCREENPLAYS: *Mr. Forbush and the Penguins*, 1971; *Frenzy*, 1972; *Sleuth*, 1973 (adaptation of his play); *The Wicker Man*, 1974; *Masada*, 1974; *The Moonstone*, 1975; *Death on the Nile*, 1978 (adaptation of Agatha Christie's novel); *Absolution*, 1982 (adaptation of his novel); *Evil Under the Sun*, 1982 (adaptation of Christie's novel); *Appointment with Death*, 1988 (adaptation of Christie's novel); *Sommersby*, 1993 (with others).

Anthony Joshua Shaffer (SHAF-ur) is best known for his play *Sleuth*, which reinvented the murder mystery by creating a new genre: the comedy thriller. He was born five minutes before his twin brother, dramatist Peter Shaffer. Their parents, Jack and Reka Shaffer, moved to London in 1936 where Jack's real estate business was successful enough to fund the brothers' enrollment in St. Paul's School. During World War II, the twins were conscripted as "Bevin boys" to work in the coal mines of Kent and Yorkshire. After the war they entered Trinity College, Cambridge University, where they coedited the school newspaper, *Granta*. While Peter decided to become a writer, Anthony became a barrister, a profession that stimulated his interest in murder mystery. Peter, who had already written one mystery, *The Woman in the Wardrobe* (under the name Peter Antony in 1951), convinced Anthony to coauthor two murder mysteries, *How Doth the Little Crocodile?* and *Withered Murder*. The distinguishing trait of these novels is that from the discovery of the murder to the moment of revelation, the stories are told almost exclusively in dialogue. As Peter became established as a playwright, the brothers embarked on separate professional paths. Anthony was working in advertising and film production, but at his brother's prodding he decided to try to earn his living as a writer. His first play, *This Savage Parade*, a thriller about the trial of Nazi Adolf Eichmann, closed after only one performance.

Shaffer had been studying classic English mysteries by such greats as Agatha Christie and Dorothy L. Sayers; however, he viewed these as amusing puzzles and erudite games for intellectuals. The murders were never believable, but there was great pleasure in the extreme characterizations, clever clues, false leads, and the experience of solving "who done it." His enjoyment of, but irreverent attitude toward, the suspense thriller, and his belief that television had destroyed their viability, became major influences on his writing.

Shaffer decided to satirize the murder mystery while using its form—"having my cake and eating it too," he said. The result was *Sleuth*, considered by many to be the greatest murder mystery of the modern theater. *Sleuth* has all the trappings of the English murder mystery, but the audience soon discovers that it cannot trust the viability of anything they see or hear, down to and including the printed program. The entire confrontation between an older, outrageous mystery writer and a younger, outraged emigrant whose wife is having an affair with the older man is presented as a series of humiliating games that keeps the audience laughing while trying to figure out who (if anyone) has actually been murdered. By starting with the premise that the form of the thriller is artificial, Shaffer ignores the depiction of reality and focuses on artifice, satire, wit, and suspense.

The play's impact was such that murder mysteries can be categorized as "before *Sleuth*" or "after *Sleuth*." Writers of these new comedy thrillers, such as Ira Levin (*Deathtrap*, 1980) and Gerald Moon (*Corpse*, 1985), devise theatrical trickery in blatant attempts to hoodwink their audiences. Shaffer's own later attempts to combine satire and suspense have not fared so well on the stage. *Murderer* tells of a man obsessed with historical murders. Audiences found it too difficult to move from gore to satire in this play's exploration of the relationship between murderer and victim, while playing the playwright's game of "right murderer/wrong corpse, wrong murderer/right corpse." *Whodunnit* is an attempt to satirize Christie, but the amusing and clever plot twist in the second act does not compensate for the tedious setup of the entire first act.

Shaffer found more success as a screenwriter. His combination of wit and suspense provided the framework for Alfred Hitchcock's "comeback" film *Frenzy* in 1972. This was followed by the successful screen adaptation of *Sleuth*. *The Wicker Man*, a modern horror story, became a cult classic. His stylish adaptations of Christie's *Death on the Nile* and *Evil Under the Sun* found widespread popularity.

For more than a decade, Shaffer dropped out of sight, producing nothing for either stage or screen. Peter Shaffer, at a 1990 press conference for his play *Lettice and Lovage*, remarked that Anthony had been living in Australia. In 1995 Anthony Shaffer surfaced in an article in *Sight and Sound*, saying that he was head of script development at Ealing Studios. He announced that he was writing a Goya-esque film for a Spanish studio based on a novel by Arturo Perez as well as a script for a film set in Australia (the working title was "Tell Me Lies"), based on a novel by John Gordon Davis. Even though Shaffer appears to have moved entirely to the genre of film, his literary reputation rests primarily upon *Sleuth* and the establishment of the modern comedy thriller.

Gerald S. Argetsinger

Bibliography

Glen, Jules. "Anthony and Peter Shaffer's Plays: The Influence of Twinship in Creativity." *American Imago* 31 (1974). Considers the phenomenon of twin writers.

_______. "Twins in Disguise, II: Content, Form, and Style in Plays by Anthony and Peter Shaffer." In *Blood Brothers: Siblings as Writers*, edited by Norman Kiell. New York: International Universities Press, 1983. Considers the phenomenon of twin writers.

Klein, Dennis A. *Peter and Anthony Shaffer: A Reference Guide*. Boston: G. K. Hall, 1982. Although in need of updating, this guide covers most of Anthony Shaffer's career as a playwright and novelist.

Shaffer, Anthony. "Death of a Bloodsport." *Harper's Bazaar*, November, 1970. The most insightful articles on Shaffer are those written by himself. Here he pronounces the traditional murder mystery dead.

_______. *So What Did You Expect? A Memoir*. London: Picador, 2001. Published shortly after Shaffer's sudden death to a heart attack, this autobiography is a richly anecdotal work that reveals much about his writing career.

_______. "Wicker Man and Others." *Sight and Sound* 5 (August, 1995). Shaffer examines his own mysteries for the cinema.

Peter Shaffer

English playwright, screenwriter, and novelist

Born: Liverpool, England; May 15, 1926
Pseudonym: Peter Antony

DRAMA: *Five Finger Exercise*, pr., pb. 1958; *The Private Ear*, pr., pb. 1962 (one act); *The Public Eye*, pr., pb. 1962 (one act); *The Merry Roosters Panto*, pr. 1963 (music by Stanley Myers, lyrics by Lionel Bart); *The Royal Hunt of the Sun*, pr., pb. 1964; *Black Comedy*, pr. 1965 (one act); *The White Liars*, pb. 1967, 1968 (one act; originally as *White Lies*, pr., pb. 1967); *Shrivings*, pb. 1973 (with *Equus*; originally as *The Battle of Shrivings*, pr. 1970); *Equus*, pr., pb. 1973; *Amadeus*, pr. 1979; *The Collected Plays of Peter Shaffer*, pb. 1982; *Yonadab: The Watcher*, pr. 1985; *Lettice and Lovage*, pr., pb. 1987; *The Gift of the Gorgon*, pr. 1992.

LONG FICTION: *The Woman in the Wardrobe*, 1951 (as Peter Antony; with Anthony Shaffer); *How Doth the Little Crocodile?*, 1952 (as Peter Antony; with Anthony Shaffer); *Withered Murder*, 1955 (with Anthony Shaffer).

SCREENPLAYS: *The Public Eye*, 1972 (adaptation of his play); *Equus*, 1977 (adaptation of his play); *Amadeus*, 1984 (adaptation of his play).

TELEPLAYS: *The Salt Land*, 1955; *Balance of Terror*, 1957.

RADIO PLAYS: *The Prodigal Father*, 1955; *Whom Do I Have the Honour of Addressing?*, 1989.

Peter Levin Shaffer (SHAF-ur) is one of the most important playwrights of the twentieth century. He is the son of Jack Shaffer, a realtor, and his wife, Reka Fredman Shaffer. He was educated at St. Paul's School, London. In wartime he was conscripted for service in the coal mines, where he served from 1944 to 1947. He then completed his education, receiving a B.A. from Trinity College, Cambridge, in 1950. Shaffer then began to write mystery novels, beginning with *The Woman in the Wardrobe* under the pseudonym Peter Antony. The next year he collaborated with his twin brother Anthony to write *How Doth the Little Crocodile?* After living in New York, where he worked in the New York Public Library from 1951 to 1954, Shaffer returned to England and got a job with a firm of music publishers in London, where he worked for a year. In 1955 the British Broadcasting Corporation (BBC) produced his radio play, *The Prodigal Father*; that same year, an independent television company produced his first television play, *The Salt Land*. In 1955 the Shaffer brothers published one more mystery, *Withered Murder.*

It was clear to Shaffer, however, that his genre was dramatic writing, whether for stage or screen. After writing another teleplay, *Balance of Terror*, produced in 1957 by the BBC, Shaffer wrote his first stage play, *Five Finger Exercise*, which opened at the Comedy Theatre in London's West End on July 16, 1958, where it ran for a year before moving to New York in December, 1959. Although the play was conventional in form, in it Shaffer's fascination with psychology was already evident: The story traces the effects that a German tutor has on various members of a household. From 1961 to 1962 Shaffer served as a music critic for *Time and Tide*, while continuing to explore various possibilities in drama. In 1962 Shaffer moved toward comedy of the absurd with two one-act plays performed together, *The Private Ear* and *The Public Eye*. The following year, Shaffer collaborated with Peter Brook on a screenplay for William Golding's *Lord of the Flies* (1954). It was not used for Brook's film, but Shaffer gained valuable experience for later adaptations of his own plays.

Shaffer's first major success was the historical play *The Royal Hunt of the Sun*, a highly stylized play with elements of the Japanese Kabuki theater. Although critics differed about the effectiveness of Shaffer's dialogue and his realization of character, no one questioned the high quality of the play as spectacular theater. With *Equus* in 1973 Shaffer proved his quality as a thinker, as well as his ability in theatrical invention. The play is the story of a psychiatrist, Martin Dysart, who is attempting to treat a boy named Alan Strang by discovering why he blinded several horses in a north England stable. As the play proceeds, Dysart concludes that curing the boy means depriving him of his contact with divinity, which Alan had found in the horses. At the end of the play, the tragedy is not only Alan's, but Dysart's as well, and probably that of the whole modern world, which cannot reconcile sanity and faith. *Equus* brought Shaffer the Tony Award, the Outer Critics Circle Award, and the New York Drama Critics Circle Award. When the play was made into a film in 1977, Shaffer wrote the screenplay.

Two years later came the play which many consider Shaffer's masterpiece. *Amadeus* is the story of the composer Antonio Salieri's obsessive jealousy of the young musical genius Wolfgang Amadeus Mozart. Shaffer based his play on a rumor that Salieri had poisoned Mozart. Using that story, he writes of a second-rate artist whose anger is directed at the God who denied him genius, to bestow it upon a foolish boy; in order to revenge himself upon God, he turns his fury on Mozart, vowing to destroy him. *Amadeus* was acclaimed by the critics and embraced by the public. It won for Shaffer the Tony Award and the Best Play of the Year award from *Plays and Players*. When it was made into a film in 1984, with Shaffer writing the screenplay, it received the New York Film Critics Circle Award, the Los Angeles Film Critics Association Award, and the 1985 Academy Award for Best Picture. Shaffer also received the Academy Award for Best Screenplay Adaptation. Although none of Shaffer's later plays has shared the critical or popular success of *Amadeus*, the intellectual comedy *Lettice and Lovage* attracted a following in both London and New York. Shaffer continues to hold his place as one of the most interesting playwrights and filmwriters of the twentieth century. In 1987 the British government recognized his achievements by naming him a Commander of the British Empire.

Although some of Shaffer's best plays have been set in the past, for example, *The Royal Hunt of the Sun*, placed in the sixteenth century, and *Amadeus*, in the eighteenth, his themes arise from what he sees as the tragic elements in modern life. In *The Royal Hunt of the Sun*, for example, the central character, Martin Ruiz, is portrayed by two actors, who split the role between them, one playing the young Martin, who sees the conqueror of Peru, Francisco Pizarro, as a hero, and the other assuming the role of the older Martin, who realizes that when Pizarro brought Christianity and civilization to Peru, he brought the infidelity and the uncertainty of modern life. In *Equus* the loss of faith is again a central theme. The rational psychiatrist Dysart, appalled by Alan's seemingly senseless cruelty to the horses, comes to realize that even though Alan's religion is allied to madness, the boy has experienced a contact with divinity that Dysart himself has never known. For all his rationality, Dysart feels a terrible sense of emptiness.

The mystery of genius is one of the themes of *Amadeus*, yet it is related to the believer's eternal quest for some understanding of God's actions. Shaffer explores the character of Salieri, a Job without God's favor, who dies as miserably as he lived. If Salieri had not had faith, he could have endured the blind judgments of fate, which denied him genius; because he does believe in God, he is tortured by the evidence of God's injustice. Ironically, the only gift God gives Salieri is the power to perceive the genius of his rival. In the play *Yonadab* Shaffer went to the Old Testament for the story of Amnon's rape of his sister Tamar, which eventually led to Absalom's murder of Amnon and his rebellion against his father David. In Shaffer's version of the story he has the rape orchestrated by a court hanger-on, the title character of the play, who honestly believes a legend that incest in the royal family is good, rather than evil. Here once again Shaffer poses a question that is essentially religious: How does one decide among competing systems, whether of faith or of ethics based on faith? Shaffer's success is based on the fact that, as he himself has said, he does not repeat himself, in setting, in theatrical technique, or in theme. Certainly his audiences are spellbound by his plays. The literal-minded are delighted by the pure spectacle; the thoughtful find that Shaffer's plays, in the tradition of the best drama from Aeschylus on, pose more questions than they answer.

Rosemary M. Canfield Reisman
Gerald S. Argetsinger

Bibliography

Beckerman, Bernard. "The Dynamics of Peter Shaffer's Drama." In *The Play and Its Critic: Essays for Eric Bentley*, edited by Michael Bertin. Lanham, Md.: University Press of America, 1986. A structural study, especially of *Equus*, by an important dramatic critic.

Cooke, Virginia, and Malcolm Page, comps. *File on Shaffer.* London: Methuen, 1987. An indispensable source with brief comments, play by play, and Shaffer's own comments on his methods of work, rewrites, film adaptations, and more.

Gianakaris, C. J. *Peter Shaffer: A Casebook.* New York: Garland, 1991. Volume 10 in the Casebooks on Modern Dramatists series. Consists of a collection of essays on Shaffer's work.

Klein, Dennis A. *Peter Shaffer.* Rev. ed. New York: Twayne, 1993. A combination of biographical and critical information.

Plunka, Gene A. *Peter Shaffer: Roles, Rites, and Rituals in the Theatre.* Rutherford, N.J.: Fairleigh Dickinson University Press, 1988. Disappointing in the absence of coverage of later plays but strong on *The Royal Hunt of the Sun*, *Equus*, and *Amadeus*. This work is part sociology and part mythology, and it is fed by an interview with the playwright in 1986. It contains occasional insights but is generally too scholarly to get at the essence of Shaffer's examination of the ways of God to humankind.

Taylor, John Russell. *Peter Shaffer.* London: Longman, 1974. Provocative essay on Shaffer's contributions through *Equus* that sees detachment in the play and "a tendency to analyze emotions without too far engaging himself in them as a dramatist."

Thomas, Eberle. *Peter Shaffer: An Annotated Bibliography.* New York: Garland, 1991. Detailed checklist of works on Shaffer, from four full-length studies to six dissertations and theses, to individual studies of plays through *Lettice and Lovage*. Includes a general chronology.

William Shakespeare

English playwright and poet

Born: Stratford-upon-Avon, England; April 23, 1564
Died: Stratford-upon-Avon, England; April 23, 1616

DRAMA: *Henry VI, Part I*, wr. 1589-1590, pr. 1592; *Edward III*, pr. c. 1589-1595; *Henry VI, Part II*, pr. c. 1590-1591; *Henry VI, Part III*, pr. c. 1590-1591; *Richard III*, pr. c. 1592-1593 (revised 1623); *The Comedy of Errors*, pr. c. 1592-1594; *The Taming of the Shrew*, pr. c. 1593-1594; *Titus Andronicus*, pr., pb. 1594; *The Two Gentlemen of Verona*, pr. c. 1594-1595; *Love's Labour's Lost*, pr. c. 1594-1595, revised 1597 for court performance; *Romeo and Juliet*, pr. c. 1595-1596; *Richard II*, pr. c. 1595-1596; *A Midsummer Night's Dream*, pr. c. 1595-1596; *King John*, pr. c. 1596-1597; *The Merchant of Venice*, pr. c. 1596-1597; *Henry IV, Part I*, pr. c. 1597-1598; *The Merry Wives of Windsor*, pr. 1597, revised c. 1600-1601; *Henry IV, Part II*, pr. 1598; *Much Ado About Nothing*, pr. c. 1598-1599; *Henry V*, pr. c. 1598-1599; *Julius Caesar*, pr. c. 1599-1600; *As You Like It*, pr. c. 1599-1600; *Hamlet, Prince of Denmark*, pr. c. 1600-1601; *Twelfth Night: Or, What You Will*, pr. c. 1600-1602; *Troilus and Cressida*, pr. c. 1601-1602; *All's Well That Ends Well*, pr. c. 1602-1603; *Othello, the Moor of Venice*, pr. 1604, revised 1623; *Measure for Measure*, pr. 1604; *King Lear*, pr. c. 1605-1606; *Macbeth*, pr. 1606; *Antony and Cleopatra*, pr. c. 1606-1607; *Coriolanus*, pr. c. 1607-1608; *Timon of Athens*, pr. c. 1607-1608; *Pericles, Prince of Tyre*, pr. c. 1607-1608; *Cymbeline*, pr. c. 1609-1610; *The Winter's Tale*, pr. c. 1610-1611; *The Tempest*, pr. 1611; *The Two Noble Kinsmen*, pr. c. 1612-1613 (with John Fletcher); *Henry VIII*, pr. 1613 (with Fletcher).

POETRY: *Venus and Adonis*, 1593; *The Rape of Lucrece*, 1594; *The Passionate Pilgrim*, 1599 (miscellany with poems by Shakespeare and others); *The Phoenix and the Turtle*, 1601; *A Lover's Complaint*, 1609; *Sonnets*, 1609.

William Shakespeare, greatest of English poets and dramatists, was born at Stratford-upon-Avon in 1564 and died there in 1616. Biographical information about him is scant, and much must be inferred from brief references to him by his contemporaries and from various church and civil records and documents regarding performance of his plays. His parents were John and Mary Arden; his father was a respectable middle-class businessman. Young William Shakespeare probably attended grammar school in Stratford (a small city in western England), where he apparently received a fundamental education in Christian ethics, rhetoric, and classical literature. Although he did not attend a university, his plays indicate his familiarity with ancient and modern history, many English and European writers, and philosophers such as Michel de Montaigne. Little else is known of his activities prior to 1590, save that in 1582 he married Anne Hathaway, eight years older than he, and had three children with her: a daughter named Susanna and twins named Hamnet and Judith. At some point during the 1580's he moved to London.

Most of Shakespeare's working life was spent in London, and allusions in the writings of others, friendly and otherwise, show that by 1592 he was a dramatist of recognized achievement. Francis Meres, in *Palladis Tamia* (1598), virtually establishes that his supremacy in comedy, tragedy, and narrative poetry was generally acknowledged, and this view is endorsed by later testimony, notably that of Ben Jonson. From 1594 on, Shakespeare was associated exclusively with the Lord Chamberlain's Company, which became the King's Company in 1603 on James I's accession. This was the most stable and prosperous of the Elizabethan dramatic companies. It built the Globe Theatre in 1599 and acquired the Blackfriars private theater in 1608.

So far as can be ascertained, Shakespeare's career as a dramatist covers the period from about 1590 to about 1612, after which he apparently moved back to Stratford. His early years show him working in all categories. Chronicle histories are a conspicuous feature of the years from 1590 to 1599, and these reflect England's self-awareness at a time when the threat from Spain was still acutely felt. The same period saw the maturing of his comic genius, through such minor masterpieces as *Love's Labour's Lost* and *A Midsummer Night's Dream*, to the four great middle comedies, *The Merchant of Venice*, *Much Ado About Nothing*, *As You Like It*, and *Twelfth Night*.

After 1600 Shakespeare's drama takes a darker and deeper direction with the so-called "problem plays": *Troilus and Cressida*, *All's Well That Ends Well*, and *Measure for Measure*. As a group, they have led to the greatest critical disagreement. His great tragedies, *Hamlet*, *Othello*, *King Lear*, and *Macbeth*, are also from this period. In these titanic masterpieces the human response to the workings of a relentless and malign destiny is explored and exploited to the fullest, and the terrible logic of the action is communicated in language of ever-increasing urgency and intensity. *Antony and Cleopatra*, which is valued for its superlative poetry and the transcendent aspirations of its heroine, looks forward to the regenerative pattern of the late romances. *Timon of Athens* is excessive in its pessimism and was left unfinished, but *Coriolanus* is a triumphant, original accomplishment. Though outwardly uninviting in both matter and manner, its emotional impact proves terrific, and its psychology is penetrating.

The plays of Shakespeare's final period are dramatic romances which present improbable persons and incidents and draw freely upon the musical and spectacular elements popular in the Court masques of the period. Here the themes of atonement and reconciliation, earlier treated in *All's Well That Ends Well* and *Measure for Measure*, are coordinated in a general pattern of regeneration symbolized by the heroines. *Pericles, Prince of Tyre* and *Cymbeline* are uncertain in their handling of complicated plot material, but *The Winter's Tale* is magnificent and intense, and *The Tempest* confers perfection on these endeavors.

Henry VIII, last of the canonical plays, is thought to have been written in collaboration with John Fletcher. *The Two Noble Kinsmen* purports to be the product of the same partnership, but the alleged Shakespearean scenes have been denounced by many competent critics. Attempts to claim other dramatic works of the period for Shakespeare have, in the main, proved abortive, though it has now been established beyond reasonable doubt that *The Book of Sir Thomas More* (British Museum MS. Harley 7368) contains three pages of his work in autograph.

John Dryden justly claimed that Shakespeare "was the man who of all Modern, and perhaps Ancient Poets, had the largest and most comprehensive soul." He is the supreme interpreter of human relationships, the supreme percipient of human frailties and potentialities. It is often alleged that he is no philosopher, that his mind is neither mystical nor prophetic, that the beatific vision of Dante Alighieri is beyond his scope. Even so, his thought, governed by the Christian neo-Platonism of his day, is earnest and profound. The comedies move ultimately to an acute awareness of the mutability of human affairs, and this sense of time's implacability is crystallized in the *Sonnets* and communicated with poignancy in *Twelfth Night*.

In the historical plays the curse which falls upon the commonwealth through the deposition and murder of an anointed king is pursued through successive manifestations of violence and anarchy, of which Falstaff is made finally the most potent symbol, until expiation is complete in Henry Tudor. Here the manipulation of history is determined by a clearly ordered conception of political morality no less than by an artistic conscience. The same outlook is more flexibly presented in *Hamlet, Prince of Denmark*, and Ulysses' great exposition of degree in *Troilus and Cressida* summarizes the acquired political wisdom of a decade.

Cognate with the doctrine of degree, and informing the histories and tragedies at all stages, is the concept of absolute justice. Portia, in *The Merchant of Venice*, pleads that mercy is above justice, and this is exemplified, in strenuous and practical terms, in *Measure for Measure*. The conflict between justice and mercy is a conspicuous feature of the great tragedies, notably *King Lear*, and is ultimately resolved, in its tragic context, in *Coriolanus*, when the hero spares Rome and gains his greatest victory—that over himself.

Cymbeline and *The Winter's Tale* plunge (albeit artificially) into chaos comparable to the chaos of the tragedies, but the resolution now is in terms of reconciliation and regeneration instead of sacrifice and waste. The Platonic vision of the Many and the One, which informs these plays and carries them nearly into mysticism, though dramatically new, is something which Shakespeare had earlier achieved in certain of the *Sonnets* and in the concentrated intricacy of *The Phoenix and the Turtle*, published in Robert Chester's *Love's Martyr* in 1601.

Criticism has often erred in emphasizing particular aspects of Shakespeare's art. In his work, action, thought, character, and language are not separable elements, and the reader's response must be to a complex unity in which dramatic conceptions are simultaneously natural and poetic and language is unique and infinitely creative. The greatest Shakespeare critics—Dryden, Samuel Johnson, Samuel Taylor Coleridge, and A. C. Bradley—can always be read with profit and delight. The enormous mass of twentieth century criticism contains much that is of value, but if one has ears to hear and a heart to understand, one shall always find that Shakespeare is his own best interpreter.

James J. Balakier

Bibliography

De Grazia, Margreta, and Stanley Wells, eds. *The Cambridge Companion to Shakespeare*. New York: Cambridge University Press, 2001. This work provides an extensive guide to Shakespeare's life and works.

Dobson, Michael, and Stanley Wells, eds. *The Oxford Companion to Shakespeare*. Oxford, England: Oxford University Press, 2001. An encyclopedic treatment of the life and works of Shakespeare.

Duncan-Jones, Katherine. *Ungentle Shakespeare: Scenes from His Life*. London: Arden Shakespeare, 2001. Duncan-Jones portrays Shakespeare as a man influenced by the political, social, and literary climate in which he found himself. She also examines speculative stories such as his love for a Dark Lady. Includes bibliography and index.

Honan, Park. *Shakespeare: A Life*. 1999. Reprint. New York: Oxford University Press, 1999. Honan's life of Shakespeare shuns the mythology that has grown up around the playwright and places him in the context of his age.

Kermode, Frank. *Shakespeare's Language*. New York: Farrar Straus & Giroux, 2000. Between 1594 and 1608, Kermode argues, the language of Shakespeare's plays was transformed, acquiring a new complexity that arose out of the playwright's increasingly successful attempts to represent dramatically the excitement and confusion of thought under stress.

McConnell, Louise. *Dictionary of Shakespeare*. Chicago: Fitzroy Dearborn, 2000. A basic reference companion.

Southworth, John. *Shakespeare, the Player: A Life in the Theatre*. Stroud, Gloucestershire, England: Sutton, 2000. A biography that focuses on the dramatist as a member of the theater, writing for the theater in collaboration with the theater company.

Thomson, Peter. *Shakespeare's Professional Career*. New York: Cambridge University Press, 1992. Thomson examines the theatrical world of Elizabethan England to illuminate Shakespeare's life and writings.

Wells, Stanley. *Shakespeare: A Life in Drama*. New York: W. W. Norton, 1995. A critical introduction to Shakespeare's life and work.

Wilson, Ian. *Shakespeare: The Evidence: Unlocking the Mysteries of the Man and His Work*. London: Headline, 1993. Wilson draws on documents discovered during the excavation of the site of the Globe Theatre to delve into the mysteries surrounding Shakespeare's life, including authorship of his plays, his sexuality, his religion, and the curse he set on his own grave.

Varlam Shalamov

Russian short-story writer, poet, and essayist

Born: Vologda, Russia; July 1, 1907
Died: Moscow, Soviet Union (now in Russia); January 17, 1982

SHORT FICTION: *Kolymskie rasskazy*, 1978 (*Kolyma Tales*, 1980, and *Graphite*, 1981).
POETRY: *Shelest List'ev*, 1964; *Tochka kipeniia: Stikhi*, 1977.
NONFICTION: *Ocherki prestupnogo mira*, n.d.

Varlam Tikhonovich Shalamov (SHAH-lahm-uhf) was a prose writer, poet, and essayist whose seventeen-year imprisonment in Soviet labor camps provided him with the material for a remarkable set of short stories, known collectively as *Kolyma Tales*. He was born on July 1, 1907 (June 18, according to the Julian calendar used in prerevolutionary Russia), the fifth child of a Russian Orthodox priest. Vologda, Shalamov's hometown, is a provincial city some 250 miles northeast of Moscow. Shalamov continued to live in Vologda through World War I and the revolution that brought the Bolsheviks to power; soon afterward, though, his family began to come apart. The first blow was material: Under the new, officially atheist government, Shalamov's father lost his pension. Then in 1920 one of Shalamov's brothers was killed in the civil war between the regime and its opponents, and his father went blind from glaucoma.

In 1924 Shalamov left Vologda for Moscow, where he first worked as a tanner at a leather factory. In 1926 he enrolled in the law department of Moscow State University. Throughout the late 1920's he was very much caught up in Moscow's cultural life, with its rapidly evolving literary groups and the fierce polemics that raged in the press. While a student, he came into contact with circles that opposed the emerging Stalinist direction in the Soviet Union's political life. In February of 1929, he was arrested during a raid on an underground printing press and was sentenced to three years of hard labor in the northern Ural Mountains.

He was freed a year early, in 1931, and by 1932 he had returned to Moscow, where he worked for the next five years as a journalist, critic, and writer, publishing several articles and stories in some of the more prestigious literary journals. He was rearrested in 1937, at the beginning of the purges, and that year he was sent to hard labor in the Kolyma region, one of the coldest inhabited places on earth. In 1942, when his original five-year sentence should have ended, his term was extended until the end of the war, and in 1943, after having been denounced for remarking upon the quality of German armaments, he was sentenced to ten more years. (According to one story, he was also condemned for referring to Ivan Bunin, the 1933 Nobel laureate who had emigrated from the Soviet Union, as a classic Russian writer.) On several occasions Shalamov narrowly escaped execution, and he was often close to death from cold, hunger, and exhaustion. Somehow he survived, and during the 1950's he returned once more to Moscow to resume his literary career.

Shalamov's subsequent writings can be grouped into four categories. He wrote a handful of essays on literature, primarily on poetry; to the general Soviet reader, though, he was best known as a poet of moderate talent, with five collections of poetry appearing between 1961 and 1977. He had begun to publish his poems in 1957, but before that—beginning in the late 1930's and continuing until 1956—he wrote the poems that made up the unpublished collection "Kolymskie tetradi" (the Kolyma notebooks). These works represented a first attempt to detail the horrors of Kolyma and to reflect upon his experience. The third type of work, and that for which he is most likely to be remembered, comprises the more than one hundred short prose pieces that deal with his imprisonment. He appears to have written the vast majority of them during the late 1950's and early 1960's. Some were smuggled out to the West and published abroad, but even during the relatively liberal Khrushchev years, his writing on Kolyma was too graphic to be printed in the Soviet Union. In 1972 Shalamov was forced to denounce the publication of his works abroad, though the statement he issued was not without its ambiguities. Even under the policy of *glasnost* instituted by Mikhail Gorbachev, Shalamov's stories were not published immediately; only in June, 1988, did the highly regarded literary journal *Novy mir* print a major selection of the *Kolyma Tales*. The fourth category of Shalamov's writing, his memoirs, remained unpublished during his lifetime. During the 1970's, his health gradually began to fail. He died on January 17, 1982, with his major achievements yet to be recognized in his homeland.

For many years the Soviet public knew Shalamov only through the verse that he could publish openly. Much of it deals with nature; some of it is about poetry itself. Running through nearly all of his poems is a reflective mood. He seems less interested in capturing a moment than in conveying ideas that have been given time to mature. On the surface the poems seem simple and direct, and they are often classical in their form. Yet their quiet exterior conceals a second meaning that no doubt escaped readers unfamiliar with Shalamov's life or with his other works. Thus in the poem "Stlannik" (dwarf cedar) he describes how that tree grasps the earth and seeks only a drop of warmth, how it nurtures life though seemingly dead, and how it rises from the snow in the spring. Readers of *Kolyma Tales* would readily see the poem as an allegory of the survival of prisoners in the far north.

Shalamov's greatest achievement is clearly *Kolyma Tales*. The stories' power derives in part from their understatedness: Their form is laconic and often seemingly artless, their emotional tone neutral. Shalamov wants to convey a physical suffering and spiritual despair so great that at times his characters are beyond feeling anything at all except perhaps an animal instinct to survive or a blind desire to end their misery. While some writers—Aleksandr Solzhenitsyn, for example—have remarked that people could grow stronger as a result of their experiences in the camps, Shalamov has stated that nothing good ever came to anybody from Kolyma, and his stories illustrate that conviction. However, he also believed that human qualities can survive in the camps, even if they must remain dormant.

Shalamov manages to remove the usual narrative distance between the reader and the events that he describes; thus, his audience comes into direct contact with a world in which the usual values have been turned upside down or have lost their meaning entirely. His brief pieces powerfully condemn the modern totalitarian state's oppression of the individual.

Barry P. Scherr

Bibliography

Conquest, Robert. *Kolyma: The Arctic Death Camps*. New York: Viking Press, 1978. An excellent source of background information about the Kolyma concentration camp, facilitating better understanding of Shalamov's stories. Contains frequent references to, and quotes from, Shalamov.

Glad, John. "Art Out of Hell: Shalamov of Kolyma." *Survey* 107 (1979): 45-50. Seeing Shalamov's stories in the Chekhovian tradition, Glad discusses his struggle with the authorities and his contribution to the camp literature as a lasting document of human courage.

_______. Foreword to *Graphite*, by Varlam Shalamov. New York: W. W. Norton, 1981. Glad describes the conditions in Kolyma and the Soviet penal system. He sees the uniqueness of Shalamov's stories in their being a bridge between fact and fiction. Their artistic quality, however, especially their pantheistic surrealism, makes them true works of art.

_______. Foreword to *Kolyma Tales*, by Varlam Shalamov. New York: W. W. Norton, 1980. Similar to Glad's article in *Survey*.

Hosking, Geoffrey. "The Ultimate Circle of the Stalinist Inferno." *New Universities Quarterly* 34 (1980): 161-168. In this review of the Russian edition of *Kolyma Tales*, Hosking discusses several stories and the overall significance of Shalamov as a witness of crimes against humanity. He also compares Shalamov to Aleksandr Solzhenitsyn as writers of camp literature.

Toker, Leona. "A Tale Untold: Verlam Shalamov's 'A Day Off.'" *Studies in Short Fiction* 28 (Winter, 1991): 1-8. A discussion of some aspects of Shalamov's modernist techniques, comparable to the works of Ernest Hemingway and Vladimir Nabokov, as embodied in his story "A Day Off."

_______. "Toward a Poetics of Documentary Prose: From the Perspective of Gulag Testimonies." *Poetics Today* 18 (Summer, 1997): 187-222. Discusses the clash between the rhetorical principles of "defamiliarization" and the "economy of effort" in documentary prose by a brief analysis of Shalamov's story "Berries."

Ntozake Shange

(Paulette Williams)

American playwright, novelist, and poet

Born: Trenton, New Jersey; October 18, 1948
Identity: African American

DRAMA: *for colored girls who have considered suicide/ when the rainbow is enuf*, pr., pb. 1975; *A Photograph: Still Life with Shadows; A Photograph: A Study in Cruelty*, pr. 1977, revised pr. 1979 (as *A Photograph: Lovers in Motion*); *Where the Mississippi Meets the Amazon*, pr. 1977 (with Thulani Nkabinde and Jessica Hagedorn); *From Okra to Greens: A Different Kinda Love Story*, pr. 1978; *Spell # 7: Geechee Jibara Quik Magic Trance Manual for Technologically Stressed Third World People*, pr. 1979; *Boogie Woogie Landscapes*, pr. 1979; *Mother Courage and Her Children*, pr. 1980 (adaptation of Bertolt Brecht's play *Mutter Courage und ihre Kinder*); *Three Pieces*, pb. 1981; *Betsey Brown*, pr. 1991 (adaptation of her novel); *The Love Space Demands: A Continuing Saga*, pb. 1991; *Plays: One*, pb. 1992; *Three Pieces*, pb. 1992.

LONG FICTION: *Sassafras: A Novella*, 1976; *Sassafras, Cypress, and Indigo*, 1982; *Betsey Brown*, 1985; *Liliane: Resurrection of the Daughter*, 1994.

POETRY: *Nappy Edges*, 1978; *Natural Disasters and Other Festive Occasions*, 1979; *A Daughter's Geography*, 1983, 1991; *From Okra to Greens: Poems*, 1984; *Ridin' the Moon in Texas: Word Paintings*, 1987; *I Live in Music*, 1994.

NONFICTION: *See No Evil: Prefaces, Essays, and Accounts, 1976-1983*, 1984; *If I Can Cook, You Know God Can*, 1998.

CHILDREN'S/YOUNG ADULT LITERATURE: *Whitewash*, 1997; *Ellington Was Not a Street*, 2002; *Muhammad Ali: The Man Who Could Float Like a Butterfly and Sting Like a Bee*, 2002; *Daddy Says*, 2003.

EDITED TEXT: *The Beacon Best of 1999: Creative Writing by Women and Men of All Colors*, 2000.

The works of poet, playwright, and novelist Ntozake Shange (SHAHN-gay) are an essential part of modern African American literature. Her first successful work, *for colored girls who have considered suicide/ when the rainbow is enuf*, is poetry brought to the stage and expressed through dance and music. This work was Shange's initial step toward a prolific and innovative literary career.

Shange's intellectual and cultural environment as a child affected her artistic development. She was born Paulette Williams, the daughter of Paul T. Williams, a surgeon, and Eloise Williams, a psychiatric social worker and educator. An eclectic combination of popular music and various types of literature shaped her artistic development. In a self-interview in her poetry *Nappy Edges* Shange said that her mother read to her from such diverse writers as the Scottish poet William Dunbar, William Shakespeare, T. S. Eliot, and the American poet Countée Cullen. Her musical sense was influenced by Dizzy Gillespie, Chuck Berry, Charlie Parker, Miles Davis, and Josephine Baker, who were frequent guests at her parents' home.

Although the combination of diverse literary and musical influences nourished her literary aspirations, Shange felt oppressed by society because of her race and gender. While she was an undergraduate, she attempted suicide and struggled with the reality of life as a black and a woman. She attempted to resolve her feelings of oppression by changing her name while working toward her master's degree at the University of Southern California. She changed her name to Ntozake Shange, Zulu words for "she who comes with her own things" and "she who walks like a lion." By changing her name, Shange replaced a name that had nothing to do with her sense of her own reality (Paulette is derived from a man's name, Paul, and Williams is an Anglo-Saxon name) with a name that clarified her identity as a black woman.

Shange's creative goals became clearer and more productive during her teaching years. She taught humanities, women's studies, and African American studies at Sonoma State College, the all-woman Mills College, and at University of California extension classes between 1972 and 1975. During this period she created interdisciplinary and improvisational works performed in bars from San Francisco to New York. These were poetry readings accompanied by dance and music. Shange strives to create a sense of movement in her poetry, and music and dance are the elements by which she attempts to bring the written word to life.

After moving to New York in 1975, Shange's creative integration of music, dance, and poetry moved from the bar to the stage. Seven women dressed as the colors of the rainbow enacted Shange's poetry in what she calls a choreopoem: *for colored girls who have considered suicide/ when the rainbow is enuf. The New York Times* praised Shange's effort, noting that it was "a play to be seen, savored, and treasured." Official recognition is evidenced by its many subsequent productions in the United States, England, Brazil, and the West Indies, and Shange was awarded the Obie Award, the Outer Critics Circle Award, and the *Mademoiselle* Award.

Shange's success with poetry and play-forms led her to experiment with other genres of literature. In a prose piece entitled *Sassafras, Cypress, and Indigo* she explores the aspirations, beliefs, and personal turmoil of three black girls from Charleston, South Carolina, and follows their dreams to different American cities. Shange's continual stress on the importance of the black female voice is evident in her poetry in *Nappy Edges*. She discusses the responsibility of the black poet in "things i wd say," of black heritage, and of the subjugation of women by men. In *See No Evil* Shange explains her creative and political voice. Shange's travels to the Caribbean, South and Central America, and the South Pacific exposed her to different theater communities. In her collection of poems *A Daughter's Geography* Shange poetically describes her travels "from the indigo moods of Harlem streets to the sun-drenched colors of the Caribbean," and she emphasizes her belief in the power of women to improve and revolutionize societies.

Shange has experimented with language and form in her works. *Ridin' the Moon in Texas* is a book of "word paintings." Her poetry is combined with visual aids such as photographs and paintings by other artists. The subject of the black woman and the style of implementing and combining different art forms are characteristic of Shange's work. Shange celebrates the black woman in poetry, novels, and performance pieces. She uses music, dance, psychology, sociology, and politics to exercise her voice. In addition to her experiments combining poetry and drama and her collaborative work with other writers, Shange has been on the cutting edge of multimedia performance poetry, adding music to her spoken word performances and releasing audio and video tapes of her work. Although Shange has been criticized for her "worn-out feminist clichés" and her failure to develop her characters adequately, she expresses an honesty and sincerity in her work. Her works are woman-centered: She presents vulnerability, fear, and joy by using dance and music to capture the vitality of women and by using politics and oppressive aspects of society to capture thoughts and attitudes of women.

Her experiments far outweigh the criticisms her work has elicited, and she continues to be an important voice in contemporary literature. During the late 1990's, she turned her attention toward children's books, including biographies of jazz musician Duke Ellington and heavyweight boxing champion Muhammad Ali. *Daddy Says* is a children's novel about two African American girls whose father is a rodeo performer.

Kathleen M. Ermitage
John Jacob

Bibliography

Brown-Guillory, Elizabeth. *Their Place on the Stage: Black Women Playwrights in America*. New York: Greenwood Press, 1988. A good study of Shange, along with Alice Childress and Lorraine Hansberry. Focuses on *for colored girls who have considered suicide/ when the rainbow is enuf* and the 1979 trilogy *Spell No. 7, Boogie Woogie Landscapes*, and *A Photograph: Lovers in Motion*.

Effiong, Philip Uko. *In Search of a Model for African American Drama: A Study of Selected Plays by Lorraine Hansberry, Amiri Baraka, and Ntozake Shange*. New York: University Press of America, 2000. Analyzes the historical and sociopolitical considerations that determine the choices made by each dramatist.

King, Anne Mills, Thomas J. Taylor, and Judith K. Taylor. "Ntozake Shange." In *Critical Survey of Drama*, edited by Carl Rollyson. 2d rev. ed. Pasadena, Calif.: Salem Press, 2003. A thorough overview of Shange's life and career through 2002, emphasizing her plays. A good starting point.

Lester, Neal A. *Ntozake Shange: A Critical Study of the Plays*. New York: Garland, 1995. Lester examines critically Shange's contributions to the American stage, suggests aspects of her work for further study, and contextualizes Shange's drama within appropriate literary traditions.

Olaniyan, Tejumala. *Scars of Conquest/Masks of Resistance: The Invention of Cultural Identities in African, African-American, and Caribbean Drama*. New York: Oxford University Press, 1995. Study of English-speaking dramatists that gives special attention to Amiri Baraka, Wole Soyinka, Derek Walcott, and Ntozake Shange.

Russell, Sandi. *Render Me My Song: African American Women Writers from Slavery to the Present*. New York: St. Martin's Press, 1990. Covers Shange's work through *Betsey Brown*, whose stage version was written with Emily Mann. Good biography and comments on the "choreopoem" format. Discusses the trilogy of plays ending with *A Photograph: Lovers in Motion* and compares Shange's work with Bertolt Brecht's *Mutter Courage und ihre Kinder* (pr. 1941, pb. 1949; *Mother Courage and Her Children*, 1941). Places Shange in context with Alexis DeVeaux, Rita Dove, and Toni Cade Bambara, women trying blues styles fed by oral traditions

Shange, Ntozake. Interview. In *Interviews with Contemporary Women Playwrights*, edited by Kathleen Betsko. New York: Beech Tree Books, 1987. A candid interview with Shange.

Shange, Ntozake, and Emily Mann. "The Birth of an R&B Musical." Interview by Douglas J. Keating. *The Philadelphia Inquirer*, March 26, 1989. Follows the story of how Emily Mann and Shange took Shange's *Betsey Brown* from book to stage, in a long interview with both playwrights to mark the opening of the play at the Forum Theater in Philadelphia, as part of the American Music Theater Festival. Shange says of Mann, "Emily is one of the few American playwrights who understands the drama of the blending of voices."

Alan Shapiro

American poet

Born: Boston, Massachusetts; February 18, 1952
Identity: Jewish

POETRY: *After the Digging*, 1981; *The Courtesy*, 1983; *Happy Hour*, 1987; *Covenant*, 1991; *Mixed Company*, 1996; *The Dead Alive and Busy*, 2000; *Selected Poems, 1974-1996*, 2000; *Song and Dance*, 2002.

NONFICTION: *In Praise of the Impure, Poetry and the Ethical Imagination: Essays, 1980-1991*, 1993; *The Last Happy Occasion*, 1996 (memoir); *Vigil*, 1997 (memoir).

Alan Shapiro was born in 1952 of Jewish parents, and being Jewish has played a large part in his development as a writer and a poet. He found himself both appreciating and despising his Jewish heritage, wanting to escape from it at the same time that he saw his life thoroughly formed by it. From his earliest years he wanted to be a poet, finally informing his parents of his decision while he was in college.

One of the most significant periods of his life was his sojourn in Ireland during his college years. He knew that Ireland was a country that honored storytellers and poets, and he thrived on being in such a place. There he met and married an Irish Catholic woman, Carol Ann, to the surprise of his parents, who eventually accepted her. Still, the marriage was brief. Shapiro received a scholarship to Stanford University in California, and the transition proved disastrous to the marriage. In 1984 he remarried, this time to Della, a Jewish woman; their marriage endured for sixteen years before it, too, ended in divorce.

Shapiro found a way to make use of his poetry to examine his life and his experiences. His first book, *After the Digging*, appeared in 1981. The influence of Shapiro's years in Ireland is evident in this book, as it deals with the potato famine, which devastated Ireland in the nineteenth century and which exists today in the minds and collective memories of the Irish. His next book, *The Courtesy*, dealt with the Puritans in seventeenth century America.

Shapiro was named a fellow of the National Endowment for the Arts in 1984 and a Guggenheim Fellow in 1986. His book *Happy Hour* was nominated for a National Book Critics Circle Award in 1987. In 1991 Shapiro won the Lila Wallace-Reader's Digest Writer's Award. Later *Mixed Company* won the 1996 *Los Angeles Times* award for poetry and was nominated for the National Book Critics Circle Award. In 2000 *The Dead Alive and Busy* won the Kingsley Tufts Award.

However, as Shapiro himself pointed out, if one wants a larger readership, one must write prose, and so he did, in the award-winning *The Last Happy Occasion*. In this book he tried to come to terms with the way that all human beings have been influenced and changed by the art in their lives, especially literature in the form of poetry. Poetry not only is written about life and as a reflection on life but also intensifies and informs life.

In *The Last Happy Occasion*, which was a finalist for the 1996 National Book Critics Circle for biography/autobiography, Shapiro wrote of his coming of age, including much about his family and the others who influenced him. In *Vigil*, published the next year, he wrote of the death of his sister, Beth. Through it all, Shapiro handled his world with words. He also managed to find compassion and feeling for others beneath their sometimes despicable acts, as well as through their thoughtlessness and misunderstanding.

Shapiro's poetry is modern in the sense that it lacks formal form and structure, but it has its own form and structure, not rhyming but rhythmic, and its subjects are the ordinary things of life. His concrete, often sensual, images force the reader to delve deeper into what is happening in the poem so that what the poet experiences becomes the universal experience. In addition, Shapiro makes use of Greek myths in his search for meaning in life, sometimes devastated by gods or God.

Although Shapiro handled his sister's death with his *Vigil*, a narrative of her actual dying experiences, he rounded out that book with poems. When his brother David died three years later, at the same time that his own marriage fell apart and the health of his parents began to deteriorate badly, he worked through his grief with more poetry, *Song and Dance*, which, ironically, is less sorrowful than it is celebratory.

Regardless of his Jewish identity, Shapiro sees himself as a quintessentially American poet. He carries with him his ethnic heritage and memories of the Old World passed on by his grandparents, as well as his experiences of twentieth century America. His marriage to an Irish Catholic was a source of disappointment in his family, but when his sister married an African American, he learned more deeply what family alienation meant. Watching his brother-in-law gave him strong insights into dealing with prejudice. Shapiro never became the businessman his parents would have preferred, choosing the difficult life of a poet. Eventually, his work took him to North Carolina as professor of English and creative writing at the University of North Carolina at Chapel Hill.

Lucy Fuchs

Bibliography

Daniels, Kate. "Human Voices." *The Southern Review* 36, no. 1 (Winter, 2000): 165-178. This is an analysis of Shapiro's poetry, particularly his book *Song and Dance*. The author places Shapiro with the best of the modern poets, able to write both lyrically and concretely.

Harp, Jerry. "Alan Shapiro's Song and Dance: Postcard from Gambier, Ohio." *Poets and Writers Magazine*, February 15, 2002. This is a report of a presentation Shapiro gave in Gambier, Ohio, in which he explained some of his philosophy of poetry.

Shapiro, Alan. "An Aesthetics of Inadequacy." Interview by Eric McHenry. *The Atlantic Monthly*, May, 2002. An extended interview of Shapiro in which he speaks of his life, his work, and particularly his family and how they influenced his poetry.

Karl Shapiro

American poet

Born: Baltimore, Maryland; November 10, 1913
Died: New York, New York; May 14, 2000

POETRY: *Poems*, 1935; *Person, Place, and Thing*, 1942; *The Place of Love*, 1942; *V-Letter, and Other Poems*, 1944; *Trial of a Poet, and Other Poems*, 1947; *Poems, 1942-1953*, 1953; *Poems of a Jew*, 1958; *The Bourgeois Poet*, 1964; *The White-Haired Lover*, 1968; *Selected Poems*, 1968; *Adult Bookstore*, 1976; *Collected Poems, 1940-1978*, 1978; *Love and War, Art and God*, 1984; *Adam and Eve*, 1986; *New and Selected Poems, 1940-1986*, 1987; *The Old Horsefly*, 1992; *The Wild Card: Selected Poems, Early and Late*, 1998 (Stanley Kunitz and David Ignatow, editors).

LONG FICTION: *Edsel*, 1971.

DRAMA: *The Tenor*, pr. 1952 (libretto); *The Soldier's Tale*, pr. 1968 (libretto).

NONFICTION: *Essay on Rime*, 1945; *English Prosody and Modern Poetry*, 1947; *A Bibliography of Modern Prosody*, 1948; *Beyond Criticism*, 1953; *In Defense of Ignorance*, 1960; *Start with the Sun: Studies in Cosmic Poetry*, 1960 (with James E. Miller, Jr., and Bernice Slote); *Prose Keys to Modern Poetry*, 1962; *A Prosody Handbook*, 1965 (with Robert Beum); *To Abolish Children, and Other Essays*, 1968; *The Poetry Wreck: Selected Essays, 1950-1970*, 1975; *The Younger Son*, 1988; *Reports of My Death*, 1990; *Poet: An Autobiography in Three Parts*, 1988-1990 (includes *The Younger Son* and *Reports of My Death*).

EDITED TEXTS: *Poets at Work*, 1948 (with W. H. Auden); *The Writer's Experience*, 1964 (with Ralph Ellison).

Karl Jay Shapiro was born in Baltimore, Maryland, and attended the University of Virginia, The Johns Hopkins University, and Enoch Pratt Library School. In World War II he served in the U.S. Army for three years in the South Pacific. During this absence from the United States his fiancé, Evelyn Katz, saw two of his books through the presses, including *V-Letter, and Other Poems*, which won the Pulitzer Prize in poetry in 1945. In 1946 and 1947 he served as Consultant in Poetry to the Library of Congress; for the next three years he taught as a professor of writing at Johns Hopkins. From 1950 until 1956 he edited *Poetry* magazine in Chicago; he then went to the University of Nebraska and edited *Prairie Schooner* until 1968, when he joined the English faculty of the University of California at Davis.

Shapiro's early poetry established him firmly among the best poets of his generation. *Person, Place, and Thing* contains such familiar poems as "Haircut" and "Auto Wreck"; "Elegy for a Dead Soldier" and "The Leg" appeared in *V-Letter, and Other Poems*. Poems in these volumes are characterized by an immediacy of experience and an indebtedness to traditionalist poetry. Having written some of the best war poems of the decade, Shapiro found himself out of the army and in the midst of the literary "establishment"; despite the success of his earlier work, Shapiro seemed to doubt the significance of the "established" tradition. Consequently, in his essays, he attacked the lack of newness in the poetry of his contemporaries and embraced the "open" prosodies of Walt Whitman and William Carlos Williams. Convinced that emotion or feeling should take precedence over traditional form, Shapiro began to explore the broader applications of the Whitman tradition.

Some of these explorations, such as *In Defense of Ignorance* and *The Bourgeois Poet*, constitute extreme reactions against the intellectual tradition fostered by T. S. Eliot and W. H. Auden; others, like *Poems of a Jew*, are attempts to establish a positive state of sociopolitical consciousness from which to speak.

Later, as in *The White-Haired Lover* and *The Old Horsefly*, Shapiro's poetry became more personal and reflective. Most significant to Shapiro's later work, however, is neither poetry nor criticism. *The Younger Son* and *Reports of My Death* are candid, third-person autobiographies that examine the poet's involvement in World War II, his years as editor of *Poetry*, and controversies involving Ezra Pound and the editing of *Prairie Schooner*. While his most memorable poems are perhaps the war poems of *V-Letter, and Other Poems*, the prose poetry of *The Bourgeois Poet* and the exacting essays of *The Poetry Wreck* account also for the greatness and diversity of Shapiro's work.

Mark Sanders

Bibliography

Bartlett, Lee. *Karl Shapiro: A Descriptive Bibliography, 1933-1937*. New York: Garden, 1979. A bibliographic record of Shapiro's work up to 1977. Includes articles and poems in periodicals, translations of his works, and contributions to anthologies.

Engels, Tim. "Shapiro's 'The Fly.'" *Explicator* 55, no. 1 (1991): 41-43. A close reading of one of Shapiro's better-known poems.

Oostdijl, Diederick. "'Someplace Called Poetry': Karl Shapiro, *Poetry* Magazine, and Postwar American Poetry." *English Studies* 81 (August, 2000): 346-357. Reviews Shapiro's influence and accomplishments as editor of *Poetry*.

Reino, Joseph. *Karl Shapiro*. Boston: Twayne, 1981. Although dated, this overview study offers biographical information, critical assessment, and a bibliography of primary and secondary sources.

Richman, Robert. "The Trials of a Poet." *The New Centurion* 6 (April, 1988): 74-81. This review of Shapiro's *New and Selected Poems, 1940-1986* provides quick observations of a number of poems, as well as a commentary on development and theme. Richman also pulls from Shapiro's nonpoetic writing for elaboration.

Shapiro, Karl. "Poetry and Family: An Interview with Karl Shapiro." Interview by Andrea Gale Hammer. *Prairie Schooner* 55 (Fall, 1981): 3-31. A long, very personal, and intriguing interview with the poet, interesting for the insight it sheds on the man and his thought. An excellent portrait of Shapiro.

Shapiro, Karl, and Ralph Ellison. *The Writer's Experience*. Washington, D.C.: Library of Congress, 1964. Included in this pamphlet is an essay by Shapiro entitled "American Poet?" that is autobiographical in part. Shapiro shares a retrospective of his career and his personal struggles and mentions his influences and colleagues. He also comments on the state of poetry in America and around the world. An excellent and revealing essay.

George Bernard Shaw

Irish playwright and essayist

Born: Dublin, Ireland; July 26, 1856
Died: Ayot St. Lawrence, Hertfordshire, England; November 2, 1950
Pseudonym: Corno di Bassetto

DRAMA: *Widowers' Houses*, wr. 1885-1892, pr. 1892; *Mrs. Warren's Profession*, wr. 1893, pb. 1898; *The Philanderer*, wr. 1893, pb. 1898; *Arms and the Man*, pr. 1894; *Candida: A Mystery*, pr. 1897; *The Devil's Disciple*, pr. 1897; *The Man of Destiny*, pr. 1897; *You Never Can Tell*, pb. 1898; *Captain Brassbound's Conversion*, pr. 1900; *Caesar and Cleopatra*, pb. 1901; *The Admirable Bashville*, pr. 1903 (based on his novel *Cashel Byron's Profession*); *Man and Superman*, pb. 1903; *How He Lied to Her Husband*, pr. 1904; *John Bull's Other Island*, pr. 1904; *Major Barbara*, pr. 1905; *Passion, Poison, and Petrifaction*, pr., pb. 1905; *The Doctor's Dilemma*, pr. 1906; *The Interlude at the Playhouse*, pr., pb. 1907 (playlet); *Getting Married*, pr. 1908; *Press Cuttings*, pr., pb. 1909; *The Shewing up of Blanco Posnet*, pr. 1909; *The Fascinating Foundling*, wr. 1909, pb. 1926; *The Glimpse of Reality*, wr. 1909, pb. 1926; *The Dark Lady of the Sonnets*, pr. 1910; *Misalliance*, pr. 1910; *Fanny's First Play*, pr. 1911; *Androcles and the Lion*, pr. 1912 (in German), pr. 1913 (in English); *Overruled*, pr. 1912; *Pygmalion*, pb. 1912; *Beauty's Duty*, wr. 1913, pb. 1932 (playlet); *Great Catherine*, pr. 1913; *Heartbreak House*, wr. 1913-1919, pb. 1919; *The Music Cure*, pr. 1914; *The Inca of Perusalem*, pr. 1916; *O'Flaherty, V.C.*, pr. 1917; *Augustus Does His Bit*, pr. 1917; *Annajanska, the Bolshevik Empress*, pr. 1918; *Back to Methuselah*, pb. 1921; *Jitta's Atonement*, pr. 1923; *Saint Joan*, pr. 1923; *The Apple Cart*, pr. 1929; *Too True to Be Good*, pr. 1932; *How These Doctors Love One Another!*, pb. 1932 (playlet); *On the Rocks*, pr. 1933; *Village Wooing*, pr., pb. 1934; *The Six Men of Calais*, pr. 1934; *The Simpleton of the Unexpected Isles*, pr., pb. 1935; *Arthur and Acetone*, pb. 1936; *The Millionairess*, pr., pb. 1936; *Cymbeline Refinished*, pr. 1937 (adaptation of William Shakespeare's *Cymbeline*, act 5); *Geneva*, pr. 1938; *In Good King Charles's Golden Days*, pr., pb. 1939; "The British Party System," wr. 1944 (playlet); *Buoyant Billions*, pb. 1947; *Shakes Versus Shaw*, pr. 1949; *Far-Fetched Fables*, pr., pb. 1950; *The Bodley Head Bernard Shaw: Collected Plays with Their Prefaces*, pb. 1970-1974 (7 volumes).

LONG FICTION: *Cashel Byron's Profession*, 1886; *An Unsocial Socialist*, 1887; *Love Among the Artists*, 1900; *The Irrational Knot*, 1905; *Immaturity*, 1930.

SHORT FICTION: *The Adventures of the Black Girl in Her Search for God*, 1932.

NONFICTION: *The Quintessence of Ibsenism*, 1891; *The Perfect Wagnerite*, 1898; *The Common Sense of Municipal Trading*, 1904; *Dramatic Opinions and Essays*, 1907; *The Sanity of Art*, 1908 (revised from 1895 serial publication); *Letters to Miss Alma Murray*, 1927; *The Intelligent Woman's Guide to Socialism and Capitalism*, 1928; *Ellen Terry and Shaw*, 1931; *Everybody's Political What's What*, 1944; *Sixteen Self Sketches*, 1949; *Correspondence Between George Bernard Shaw and Mrs. Patrick Campbell*, 1952; *The Matter with Ireland*, 1961; *Platform and Pulpit*, 1961 (Dan H. Laurence, editor); *Collected Letters*, 1965-1988 (4 volumes; Laurence, editor); *An Autobiography, 1856-1898*, 1969; *An Autobiography, 1898-1950*, 1970; *The Nondramatic Literary Criticism of Bernard Shaw*, 1972 (Stanley Weintraub, editor); *Shaw: Interviews and Recollections*, 1990 (A. M. Gibbs, editor); *Bernard Shaw's Book Reviews*, 1991 (Brian Tyson, editor).

EDITED TEXT: *Fabian Essays in Socialism*, 1889.

MISCELLANEOUS: *Works*, 1930-1938 (33 volumes); *Short Stories, Scraps, and Shavings*, 1932; *Works*, 1947-1952 (36 volumes).

One of the greatest British dramatists, perhaps the greatest dramatist of his generation, George Bernard Shaw revitalized the moribund English stage with a body of work that continues to entertain and challenge audiences around the world. Born in Dublin, Ireland, on July 26, 1856, to a family in financial decline, he was raised in a household that might have come from one of his plays. His father, George Carr Shaw, was a good-natured drunkard somewhat in the manner of Alfred Doolittle in *Pygmalion*, while his mother, the former Lucinda Elizabeth Gurly, was a strong-willed woman who in 1874 abandoned her family to go to London with her voice teacher, George John Vandeleur Lee, to pursue a musical career. Largely self-taught, Shaw left school early. From 1874 to 1876 he worked as an office boy, cashier, and rent collector for Charles Townsend, a Dublin real estate agent. There, as well as at home, he saw the evil effects of poverty and social injustice that he would repeatedly attack in his plays.

In 1876 Shaw joined his mother in London. After a brief stint with the Edison Telegraph Company (1879-1880), he devoted himself entirely to literature, writing five mediocre novels (he once observed that anyone who would read *An Unsocial Socialist* would read anything). A lecture by Henry George in 1882 converted Shaw to socialism; two years later he helped Beatrice and Sidney Webb found the Fabian Society, an organization of bourgeois socialists who favored gradual reform. Shaw's "desperate days," as he called this period, ended when William Archer asked him to become a music critic for the *Star.* Under the pseudonym Corno di Bassetto, he wrote readable, astute analyses of performances, always advocating innovation and excellence. These qualities also characterize his art and music criticism for the *World* and his theater criticism for the *Saturday Review.*

His 1890 lecture to the Fabian Society on Henrik Ibsen led to his book *The Quintessence of Ibsenism.* The Independent Theatre Company then asked Shaw for a play of his own. He revised *Widowers' Houses*, an attack on slumlords, which he had begun in 1885 with Archer. By 1901 he had written nine more plays, the best of them mingling wit with social criticism. His first major success, *The Devil's Disciple*, came not in London but in New York. Not until Harley Granville-Barker produced eleven of his plays at the Royal Court Theatre, largely funded by Shaw himself (he had married the Irish heiress Charlotte Payne Townsend in 1898), did his reputation become secure. Awarded the Nobel Prize in Literature in 1925, largely for his brilliant *Saint Joan*, he continued to write until his death at age ninety-four.

Like Ibsen, and like many English playwrights of the seventeenth and eighteenth centuries, Shaw wanted to use the stage as a pulpit to reform society by forcing audiences to see the disparity between reality and conventional wisdom. In *Major Barbara* it is the munitions factory owner, Andrew Undershaft, not the Salvation Army, who helps the poor. *Pygmalion* points to the folly of class distinctions, as accent—not character or merit—determines one's station. Joan of Arc is canonized, but if she returned to earth she would once again be executed for her refusal to accept any authority beyond personal revelation.

Shaw was less concerned with specific political or social reforms, though he did want these, than with the evolution of humankind from its present state of weak imperfection to a condition approaching the divine. Like the serpent in *Back to Methuselah*, Shaw did not examine present conditions and ask why things were that way; rather, he imagined a different future and asked why things could not be so ordered. He believed in an irresistible "life force" that would lead to a better world if only people linked their wills to its power. Significantly, Shaw's women characters are more aware of this evolutionary force, more in harmony with it, than his men characters; Major Barbara, Candida, and, most clearly, Saint Joan come immediately to mind.

Rejecting the notion of his contemporary Oscar Wilde that art should exist solely for its own sake, Shaw sometimes went to the opposite extreme of writing tracts rather than plays. The early dramas are especially didactic. Act 3 of *Man and Superman* is little more than a Platonic discourse on the life force. However, Shaw realized that to educate he first had to entertain, and his best comedies both delight and instruct. *Major Barbara*'s wit rivals that of Wilde in *The Importance of Being Earnest* (pr. 1895); the exposure of the hypocrisy of organizations dedicated to doing good is at once pointed and funny. *John Bull's Other Island*, Shaw's exploration of the Irish question (the issue of Irish self-determination), made King Edward VII laugh so hard that he broke his chair. *Pygmalion* is highly enjoyable, but audiences cannot miss the implied criticism of England's class system. Always a gadfly, often a butterfly, Shaw created among his fifty plays at least a dozen that will remain staples of the dramatic repertoire, inviting spectators to laugh at the same time that they compel them to think.

Joseph Rosenblum

Bibliography

Davis, Tracy C. *George Bernard Shaw and the Socialist Theatre.* Westport, Conn.: Greenwood Press, 1994. Davis examines Shaw's belief in socialism and how it affected and was demonstrated in his dramatic works. Includes bibliography and index.

Dukore, Bernard Frank. *Shaw's Theater.* Gainesville: University Press of Florida, 2000. Explores the production of Shaw's dramatic works. Includes bibliography and index.

Holroyd, Michael. *The Search for Love: 1856-1898.* Vol. 1 in *Bernard Shaw.* New York: Random House, 1988. In this superb beginning to his authoritative biography, Holroyd describes Shaw's Irish origins and trials of following his mother to London. His journalistic and musical career is interwoven with various love affairs, culminating in marriage in 1898. Sensitive analyses of political and aesthetic ideas are balanced with insights into early drama. Includes illustrations, a bibliographic note, and an index.

_______. *The Pursuit of Power: 1898-1918.* Vol. 2 in *Bernard Shaw.* New York: Random House, 1989. Describes the complicated interrelationships of Shaw's middle plays (from *Caesar and Cleopatra* to *Heartbreak House*) with ethics, politics, economics, medicine, religion, and war. The popularity of his drama is explained and analyzed, while the sophistication of his personality is narrated through his friendships with such persons as G. K. Chesterton, H. G. Wells, and Mrs. Patrick Campbell. Includes illustrations and index.

_______. *The Lure of Fantasy: 1918-1950.* Vol. 3 in *Bernard Shaw.* New York: Random House, 1991. The final volume covers Shaw's drama from *Saint Joan*, with late plays such as *Geneva* and *In Good King Charles's Golden Days* receiving balanced attention. Also surveys Shaw's films from his plays, including *Pygmalion* and *Major Barbara.* Shaw's interest in Communism and the Soviet Union receives attention, as does his criticism of American culture. Includes illustrations, bibliographic note, and index.

Innes, Christopher, ed. *The Cambridge Companion to George Bernard Shaw.* New York: Cambridge University Press, 1998. Provides an in-depth look at Shaw's life, works, and philosophy. Includes bibliography and index.

Larson, Gale K., ed. *Shaw: The Annual Bernard Shaw Studies.*

Vol. 21. University Park: Pennsylvania State University Press, 2001. This collection of essays is part of an annual series that examines various aspects of Shaw. This volume contains essays on Shaw's stagecraft, Shaw's and Mark Twain's revisions of Genesis, and Shaw in Sinclair Lewis's writings. Includes bibliography.

Lenker, Lagretta Tallent. *Fathers and Daughters in Shakespeare and Shaw.* Westport, Conn.: Greenwood Press, 2001. Lenker examines the fathers and daughters portrayed in the plays of William Shakespeare and of Shaw. Includes bibliography and index.

Irwin Shaw

American short-story writer and novelist

Born: New York, New York; February 27, 1913
Died: Davos, Switzerland; May 16, 1984
Identity: Jewish

SHORT FICTION: *Sailor off the Bremen, and Other Stories*, 1939; *Welcome to the City, and Other Stories*, 1942; *Act of Faith, and Other Stories*, 1946; *Mixed Company*, 1950; *Tip on a Dead Jockey, and Other Stories*, 1957; *Love on a Dark Street*, 1965; *Retreat, and Other Stories*, 1970; *God Was Here, but He Left Early*, 1973; *Short Stories: Five Decades*, 1978.

LONG FICTION: *The Young Lions*, 1948; *The Troubled Air*, 1951; *Lucy Crown*, 1956; *Two Weeks in Another Town*, 1960; *Voices of a Summer Day*, 1965; *Rich Man, Poor Man*, 1970; *Evening in Byzantium*, 1973; *Nightwork*, 1975; *Beggarman, Thief*, 1977; *The Top of the Hill*, 1979; *Bread upon the Waters*, 1981; *Acceptable Losses*, 1982.

DRAMA: *Bury the Dead*, pr., pb. 1936; *Siege*, pr. 1937; *The Gentle People: A Brooklyn Fable*, pr., pb. 1939; *Quiet City*, pr. 1939; *Retreat to Pleasure*, pr. 1940; *Sons and Soldiers*, pr. 1943; *The Assassin*, pr. 1945; *The Survivors*, pr., pb. 1948 (with Peter Viertel); *Children from Their Games*, pb. 1962; *A Choice of Wars*, pr. 1967; *I, Shaw*, pr. 1986 (two one-act plays; *The Shy and Lonely* and *Sailor off the Bremen*).

SCREENPLAYS: *The Big Game*, 1936; *Commandos Strike at Dawn*, 1942; *The Hard Way*, 1942 (with Daniel Fuchs and Jerry Wald); *Talk of the Town*, 1942 (with Sidney Buchman); *Take One False Step*, 1949 (with Chester Erskine and David Shaw); *I Want You*, 1951; *Act of Love*, 1953; *Fire down Below*, 1957; *Desire Under the Elms*, 1958; *This Angry Age*, 1958 (with Rene Clement); *The Big Gamble*, 1961; *In the French Style*, 1963; *Survival*, 1968.

TELEPLAY: *The Top of the Hill*, 1980.

NONFICTION: *Report on Israel*, 1950 (with Robert Capa); *In the Company of Dolphins*, 1964; *Paris! Paris!*, 1977; *Paris/Magnum: Photographs, 1935-1981*, 1981.

Irwin Gilbert Shamforoff (his father changed the family name to Shaw) has been most widely acclaimed as a writer of ironically urbane short stories, which helped to define what many think of as "*The New Yorker* story," and for *The Young Lions*, which remains one of the most noteworthy American novels about World War II. Shaw was born in New York City on February 27, 1913, to William Shaw and Rose (Tompkins) Shaw. He attended public schools in Brooklyn before enrolling in Brooklyn College. After his freshman year, however, he was forced to withdraw from college because of academic difficulties. For the next several years, he worked in a variety of jobs in local factories and retail stores in order to make his reenrollment financially feasible. In 1934 he graduated from Brooklyn College with a B.A. degree, having distinguished himself by writing several plays for the college dramatic society and a regular column for the college newspaper. He also played quarterback for the varsity football team.

After graduation, Shaw helped to support his family by writing radio scripts for the serials *Dick Tracy* and *The Gumps*. In 1936 he submitted *Bury the Dead* to the New Theater League, and after several Off-Broadway performances, it was produced on Broadway, establishing Shaw as an important new voice in the American theater. The play concerns the refusal of six ordinary soldiers to be buried after they have been killed in battle. In technique, it owes much to the experimental German theater of the 1920's; in tone and theme, it is distinctly American, resembling much of the antiwar literature that followed World War I.

The success of *Bury the Dead* led to a Hollywood contract. Shaw's second stage play, *The Gentle People*, was produced on Broadway by the Group Theater. Also during this time he published his first collection of short stories, *Sailor off the Bremen, and Other Stories*. *The Gentle People* had more commercial success than *Bury the Dead*, but the critical response was more lukewarm. When *The Assassin* was dismissed for its fairly conventional technique and structure and for its seemingly propagandist acceptance of conventional views of the war, Shaw responded bitterly in the 1946 preface to the published play, denouncing the narrow ideological range afforded by the major Broadway critics to political plays and, in effect, ending his career as a dramatist.

Still, Shaw's reputation as a writer of short stories became firmly established, with his stories being included regularly in the

O. Henry Prize collections and with several, such as "Walking Wounded" in 1944, being awarded first prize. This war story appeared in *Act of Faith, and Other Stories*, which, along with *Sailor off the Bremen, and Other Stories* and *Welcome to the City, and Other Stories*, established Shaw's range as a writer of short stories. The much-anthologized "The Girls in Their Summer Dresses" and "The Eighty-Yard Run" deftly treat the sexual and social ironies that undercut the success seemingly inherent in upper-middle-class American life. "Second Mortgage" and "Main Currents of American Thought" are notable explorations of the effects of economic turmoil on the urban family struggling to avoid poverty. "Residents of Other Cities," "Act of Faith," and "Medal from Jerusalem" are notable for their treatments of Jewish issues.

In 1948 Shaw published *The Young Lions*, his first and still most highly regarded novel. The first American novel to attempt a panoramic treatment of the European theater of World War II (and still generally acknowledged as the most successful of all such treatments), *The Young Lions* presents the eventually interconnected experiences of three soldiers, two Americans and one German. The structure of the novel depends on very elaborate parallels between events and characters and on a subtle pattern of interrelated symbols. It has been criticized for being structurally too contrived, but it has been praised for its precise depiction of incidents and its memorable characterizations.

Shaw subsequently published many other works of both short and long fiction. In general, the short stories have been much more highly regarded than the novels, which have been seen as relying too much on melodramatic structural devices. This impression of the novels has been reinforced by the publication of "entertainments" such as *Nightwork* and *The Top of the Hill*. In addition, the television adaptation of the Jordache novels, *Rich Man, Poor Man* and *Beggerman, Thief*, did much to increase Shaw's commercial success at the expense of his critical reputation.

In almost all Shaw's work, there is an underlying pessimism about the horrors of experience, represented as "accidents" that dramatically alter a character's circumstances and attitudes. This pessimism is balanced only by a restrained faith in the basic goodness of some individuals who can by their actions somewhat mitigate the effects of those horrors. The critical consensus is that the balance is maintained effectively by the ironic detachment in Shaw's short stories but is undercut in the novels by the melodramatic structuring. Nevertheless, the response to Shaw's last two novels, *Bread upon the Waters* and *Acceptable Losses*, has suggested to some critics that a serious reevaluation of Shaw's importance is necessary.

Martin Kich

Bibliography

Giles, James R. *Irwin Shaw.* Boston: Twayne, 1983. This book is one volume in an expanding series of literary biographies. Includes index and bibliography.

_______. *Irwin Shaw: A Study of the Short Fiction*. Boston: Twayne, 1991. An excellent review of Shaw's short stories.

Reynolds, Fred. "Irwin Shaw's 'The Eighty-Yard Run.'" *The Explicator* 49 (Winter, 1991): 121-123. Interprets the story as a case study in psychoneurosis in which the protagonist exhibits three symptoms of arrested development: sexual confusion, Oedipal relationships, and neurotic fixation on the past.

Shaw, Irwin. "Interview with Irwin Shaw." Interview by James R. Giles. *Resources for American Literary Study* 18 (1992): 1-21. Shaw discusses his experiences writing for movies and his reaction to being a "popular" writer.

Shnayerson, Michael. *Irwin Shaw: A Biography.* New York: Putnam, 1989. A good look at Shaw's life and times. Includes bibliography and index.

Wallace Shawn

American playwright, screenwriter, and actor

Born: New York, New York; November 12, 1943

DRAMA: *The Hotel Play*, wr. 1970, pr. 1981; *Play in Seven Scenes*, pr. 1974; *Our Late Night*, pr. 1974; *In the Dark*, pr. 1976 (libretto); *Three Short Plays: Summer Evening, The Youth Hostel, Mr. Frivolous*, pr. 1976, pr. 1977 (as *A Thought in Three Parts*); *The Mandrake*, pr. 1977 (adaptation of Niccolò Machiavelli's play *La mandragola*); *The Family Play*, pr. 1978; *Marie and Bruce*, pr. 1979; *My Dinner with André*, pr. 1980 (with André Gregory); *The Music Teacher*, pr. 1982 (libretto); *Aunt Dan and Lemon*, pr., pb. 1985; *The Fever*, pr. 1990; *The Designated Mourner*, pr., pb. 1996; *Four Plays*, pb. 1998.

SCREENPLAY: *My Dinner with André*, 1981 (with André Gregory); *The Designated Mourner*, 1997 (adaptation of his play).

Playwright, screenwriter, and actor Wallace Shawn was born in New York City, the elder son of William Shawn, noted editor of *The New Yorker*, and Cecille Shawn. After attending Dalton School, a private high school in New York, and Putney, a preparatory school in Vermont, he studied history at Harvard University, from which he graduated in 1965, and philosophy, politics, and economics at Magdalen College of Oxford University, from which he received a bachelor's degree in 1968 and a master's degree in

1975. In 1965 and 1966, he taught English at Indore Christian College in India as a Fulbright fellow.

Shawn's work as a playwright led him to study acting, in order to sharpen his skills in creating and developing characters for the stage. Like many who pursue careers in the theater, he has held numerous jobs unrelated to the practice of his art, such as clerking in New York's garment district, teaching Latin, and photocopying documents. For many years, Shawn has lived with the writer Deborah Eisenberg in a Manhattan loft.

Shawn's interest in the theater and the performing arts dates back to childhood productions that he and his brother, the composer Allen Shawn, would create and produce for the family's enjoyment. As a young man, he considered a career as a diplomat; however, while attending Oxford University in 1967, he wrote a script, *Four Meals in May*, and entered it in a competition for playwrights. The script did not win, but its author discovered his calling in the theater and continued to write plays. In 1975, he won an Obie Award from *The Village Voice* for the Off-Broadway staging of *Our Late Night*, directed by André Gregory. Shawn subsequently received a Guggenheim Fellowship in 1978.

Shawn began acting in 1977, more than ten years after he started writing plays. Professional acting, like clerking, teaching, and photocopying, was initially merely a source of income, more remunerative and less time-consuming than other jobs. Yet he expanded his range with a diversity of remarkable performances on stage and in films, and his talent has circumvented the typecasting that his puckish appearance invites. He began acting by performing in his own plays, first in *The Mandrake*. This performance brought him to the attention of Woody Allen, who cast him in his first film role. Shawn's most noted film appearances include roles as the ex-husband of Diane Keaton's character in *Manhattan* (1979), directed by Allen; as Wally in *My Dinner with André* (1981), directed by Louis Malle; as the wicked Vizzini in *The Princess Bride* (1987), directed by Rob Reiner; as a doctor in *Scenes from the Class Struggle in Beverly Hills* (1989), directed by Paul Bartel; and as Vanya in *Vanya on Forty-Second Street* (1994), directed by Malle. He has also appeared in *All That Jazz* (1979), *Atlantic City* (1980), *Strange Invaders* (1983), *The Hotel New Hampshire* (1984), *Prick Up Your Ears* (1987), *The Princess Bride* (1987), and other films.

Shawn's playwriting is noted for its shockingly explicit yet realistic language and for the conversational interactions among characters. Plot takes a back seat to character, and action is subordinated to words. The quintessential setting in a play by Wallace Shawn is a public place such as a restaurant, a cocktail party, or a hotel, and the quintessential purpose of the characters is to socialize and interact with others. Countering this public and social element in Shawn's work is an opposing tendency toward isolation and soliloquy: Characters in public places sometimes fall into prolonged disquisitions that silence (and not infrequently shock) everyone else present. The most positive of these self-absorbed speeches is perhaps André's lengthy and fascinating exposition of his worldwide quest for reality in *My Dinner with André*. At the extreme, direct address to the audience may replace meaningful interaction with other characters onstage; in fact, *The Fever* is a monologue spoken by one character and designed for performance in living rooms for small groups of guests. In this case, the play itself becomes the pretext for public interactions among people in the audience, who can reasonably be expected to socialize before and after viewing the play that has brought them together.

Victoria Gaydosik

Bibliography

Billington, Michael. "A Play of Ideas Stirs Political Passions." *The New York Times*, October 27, 1985, p. B1. Billington discusses with Shawn the controversy over the political implications of *Aunt Dan and Lemon*. Shawn explains his dialogic theory of audience communication.

King, W. D., John Lahr, and Wallace Shawn. *Writing Wrongs: The Work of Wallace Shawn*. Philadelphia: Temple University Press, 1997. The first comprehensive study of Shawn' s life and literary output, analyzing each play and placing it in the context of drama from the Greeks to the present.

Posnock, Ross. "New York Phantasmagoria." *Raritan* 11 (Fall, 1991): 142-159. Shawn's concerns in *The Fever* are cleverly juxtaposed with those of New York intellectual Richard Sennett. Both writers are concerned with the contemporary crisis of human values in urban culture.

Rees, Jasper. "A Life in Two Halves." *The Daily Telegraph*, May 3, 1999, p. 18. Discusses the disparity between Shawn's challenging plays and his roles in films he describes as "silly," such as *Toy Story* and *Toy Story 2*. Shawn says that his fifty or so film and television roles pay for his writing.

Savran, David. "Wally Shawn." In *In Their Own Words: Contemporary American Playwrights*. New York: Theatre Communications Group, 1988. This long interview covers Shawn's career up to 1986. Shawn talks specifically about his processes of composition and revision for production.

Shewey, Don. "The Secret Life of Wally Shawn." *Esquire* 100 (October, 1983): 90-94. This personal portrait, undertaken in conjunction with the release of *My Dinner with André*, outlines several of the playwright's basic beliefs.

Wetzsteon, Ross. "The Holy Fool of the American Theater." *The Village Voice*, April 2, 1991, pp. 35-37. Wetzsteon explains the critical reception of *The Fever*, and Shawn responds to criticisms of his politics and his use of alternative dramatic forms with some explanations of his intentions.

_______. "Wallace Shawn, Subversive Moralist." *American Theater* 14, no. 7 (September, 1999): 12. Argues that Shawn's later plays not only challenge the audience's sense of morality but also question assumptions about the meaning of theater itself. Includes comments from Shawn, including his assertion that the audience is the main character in his plays.

Gail Sheehy

American journalist

Born: Mamaroneck, New York; November 27, 1937

NONFICTION: *Speed Is the Essence*, 1971; *Panthermania: The Clash of Black Against Black in One American City*, 1971; *Hustling: Prostitution in Our Wide Open Society*, 1973; *Passages: Predictable Crises of Adult Life*, 1976; *Pathfinders*, 1981; *Spirit of Survival*, 1986; *Character: America's Search for Leadership*, 1988; *The Man Who Changed the World: The Lives of Mikhail S. Gorbachev*, 1990; *The Silent Passage: Menopause*, 1992; *New Passages: Mapping Your Life Across Time*, 1995; *Understanding Men's Passages: Discovering the New Map of Men's Lives*, 1998; *Hillary's Choice*, 1999.
LONG FICTION: *Lovesounds*, 1970.

Gail Sheehy (SHEE-hee), born Gail Henion, is a journalist and nonfiction writer who specializes in psychological biographies and studies of life span and developmental psychology. Born to Harold Merritt and Lillian Rainey Henion, Sheehy grew up and attended high school in Mamaroneck, New York. A 1958 graduate of the University of Vermont, she pursued a dual major in English and home economics. After college, her first employment was as a consumer representative for the J. C. Penney Company. In 1960, she married Albert Francis Sheehy, and they moved to Rochester, New York, where he attended medical school and she became the fashion editor for the *Rochester Democrat and Chronicle*. Their daughter, Maura, was born during this time; later the family moved to New York City. Gail and Albert Sheehy divorced in 1969.

In New York City, Sheehy began an active career writing, first for the women's department of the *Herald Tribune* and a few years later as a freelancer and contributing editor for *New York* magazine, where she met her second husband, Clay Felker, founder and editor of the magazine. In 1969-1970, she attended Columbia University on a fellowship, studying with anthropologist Margaret Mead. Sheehy's first book, *Lovesounds*, appeared in 1970. It was followed in 1971 with two more: *Speed Is the Essence* and *Panthermania*, a study of the rise of the Black Panthers movement in New Haven, Connecticut, which received mixed reviews. Some critics praised her powerful reporting, while others noted the book's confusing organization and faddish rhetoric. Continuing her studies of provocative topics, Sheehy wrote *Hustling* in 1973, a book that had started as a series of exposés in *New York* magazine. The book was controversial and hard-hitting, exposing to society the pornography palaces and their owners on New York City's Forty-second Street.

Passages, published in 1976, propelled Sheehy into national prominence when it sold more than ten million copies and remained on *The New York Times* best-seller list for more than three years. Readers recognized themselves in "The Trying Twenties," "The Catch Thirties," "The Forlorn Forties," and "The Refreshed (or Resigned) Fifties." In this book, Sheehy first presented her unusual style of journalism that interwove 115 anecdotal case studies, a style that has been described as a psychobiographical approach. The storytelling style appealed to readers. The book also drew attention when psychologist Roger Gould, a pioneer in the new social science of adult development, claimed plagiarism of his work. It was his understanding that he was to be the coauthor of *Passages*. The case was settled out of court.

In 1981, *Pathfinders* succeeded *Passages* and also became a best-seller. Based on years of research, this book unfolded the stories of men and women who had confronted adversity, taken significant risks, and created new and fulfilling lives.

Sheehy successfully used the theme of passages in subsequent books, such as *The Silent Passage* in 1992, *New Passages* in 1995, and *Understanding Men's Passages* in 1998. In *New Passages*, Sheehy extended her original study of adulthood that had ended with the fifties, an age beyond which earlier she could not imagine living. In the new book, she proclaimed that the stereotype of middle age was now obsolete, that there was another adulthood after age fifty. Her conclusion was that adults have the ability to customize their own life cycles. In *Understanding Men's Passages*, she attempted to help men understand their life development, much in the way women had already been enlightened.

To underscore the resilience of Mohm, the twelve-year-old daughter she and lay Felker had adopted, Sheehy wrote the biographical *Spirit of Survival* in 1986. Mohm had lived through the regime of Pol Pot in Cambodia, during which her family was almost totally extinguished. In 1988, Sheehy wrote *Character: America's Search for Leadership*, a series of biographical sketches of 1988 presidential candidates, including George H. W. Bush, Robert Dole, Al Gore, and Jesse Jackson. This book, with its theme of character as destiny, drew its share of attention with criticisms of psychobabble, simplicity, and inaccuracy of quoted material. This collection of biographical essays was followed in 1990 with a biography of Mikhail Gorbachev, titled *The Man Who Changed the World*. In 1999, at the height of the congressional investigation of Bill Clinton, Sheehy wrote *Hillary's Choice*, an examination of Hillary Rodham Clinton and Bill Clinton's marriage and the challenging situations Hillary had encountered.

As a journalistic writer, Sheehy has six times received the Newswomen's Club of New York Front Page Award for distinguished journalism. She has also received the National Magazine Award, the Penny-Missouri Journalism Award, and the Anisfield-Wolf Book Award. Sheehy became an editor of *New York* magazine, a contributing editor of *Vanity Fair*, reader of her books on tape, frequent lecturer, and author of essays that serve as forewords for new books about adult development and health issues.

Deborah Elwell Arfken

Bibliography

Bronson, Tammy J. "Gail Sheehy: An Overview." In *Contemporary Popular Writers*, edited by Dave Mote. Detroit: St. James Press, 1996. A concise entry on Sheehy.

Jones, Anne Hudson. "Gail Sheehy." In *American Women Writers: A Critical Reference Guide from Colonial Times to the Present*, edited by Lina Mainiero. Vol. 4. New York: Frederick Ungar, 1982. A profile of Sheehy and her early works.

Prose, Francine. Review of *Hillary's Choice*, by Gail Sheehy. *People* 53, no. 1 (January 1, 2000): 41. A brief review that labels the book "dishy and satisfying."

_______. Review of *Understanding Men's Passages*, by Gail Sheehy. *People* 49, no. 19 (May 18, 1998): 45. A brief review defending the usefulness of Sheehy's "exemplary bits of wisdom" against charges that the work is simplistic.

Mary Wollstonecraft Shelley

English novelist

Born: London, England; August 30, 1797
Died: London, England; February 1, 1851

LONG FICTION: *Frankenstein: Or, The Modern Prometheus*, 1818; *Valperga: Or, The Life of Castruccio, Prince of Lucca*, 1823; *The Last Man*, 1826; *The Fortunes of Perkin Warbeck*, 1830; *Lodore*, 1835; *Falkner*, 1837.

SHORT FICTION: *Mary Shelley: Collected Tales and Stories*, 1976.

DRAMA: *Proserpine*, pb. 1922; *Midas*, pb. 1922.

NONFICTION: *History of a Six Weeks' Tour Through a Part of France, Switzerland, Germany, and Holland*, 1817 (with Percy Bysshe Shelley); *Lardner's Cabinet Cyclopaedia*, 1838 (numbers 63, 71, 96); *Rambles in Germany and Italy*, 1844; *The Letters of Mary Shelley*, 1980 (2 volumes; Betty T. Bennett, editor).

Authorship of *Frankenstein* was not the only claim to distinction possessed by Mary Wollstonecraft Shelley. The daughter of a radical philosopher and an early feminist and the wife of an unconventional genius, she early came to know life as something of a roller coaster. Her writing of the masterpiece of fictional horror was only one of the important incidents in an existence heavily underscored with drama.

The future novelist was born in London on August 30, 1797, the child of William Godwin and Mary Wollstonecraft. Bereft of her mother almost immediately, she was raised in a complex family which included a stepmother, a stepbrother, a stepsister, a half brother, and a half sister. As Mary Godwin grew up she increasingly idolized her dead mother, for whose loss she was inclined to blame herself. The depth of this feeling was one of the important factors in her girlhood, the other being the atmosphere of intellectual discussion and debate which enveloped her father and his many visitors.

One of these visitors, Percy Bysshe Shelley, was a twenty-one-year-old youth whose accomplishments had made quite an impression upon William Godwin. The impression darkened when, a month before her seventeenth birthday, his daughter eloped with Shelley, despite the fact that he was already married. More than two years passed before the suicide of Harriet Shelley allowed Percy Shelley and Mary Godwin to legalize their union. All evidence available points to a happy marriage, though Mary, whose mind was clear and penetrating, experienced times of bafflement in dealing with the unpredictable Shelley. On the other hand, she sometimes succumbed to periods of melancholy, which the death of her first three children did much to deepen.

Frankenstein was written in the Shelleys' first Italian days, during their initial companionship with George Gordon, Lord Byron. It is a remarkable achievement, especially for a woman of twenty, and it undoubtedly owes much of its sustained quality to the intellectual stimulation provided by the Shelley circle. The author's only novel to attain lasting fame, it is an appealing combination of strangeness and reality, skillful in its plot structure and enlivened by sharp character contrasts. Published in 1818, *Frankenstein* was an immediate sensation. Its repeated dramatizations have given its title the familiarity of a household word.

Percy Shelley's drowning on July 8, 1922, radically changed Mary Shelley's life. She faced immediate penury because her husband's annuity ceased with his death, and she could not inherit his estate until the death of her father-in-law, Sir Timothy Shelley, who also made it clear that he would not support his grandson, Percy Florence, unless Mary gave him up to guardians in England. Returning to England in August of 1823, Mary Shelley was determined to support herself, her father, and her son by her literary output. During this prolific period in her life, she wrote six novels and revised her first novel, *Frankenstein*; authored two dramas; penned numerous short stories, poems, and semifictional essays; translated and adapted several foreign works; published travel works, biographies, articles, and reviews; and edited Percy Shelley's poetical and prose works. Forbidden by Sir Timothy Shelley to write a biography of her late husband, she broke new critical ground in her editions by including pertinent biographical information about the composition of Shelley's works, thus integrating his life and his works. Most of her works, especially her novels, did not receive the critical or popular acclaim of *Frankenstein*. Nevertheless, *The Last Man* is interesting for its expression of Mary Shelley's liberal social and political views, and *Lodore* has the fascination of a veiled autobiography.

Though Mary Shelley, without compromising her own ideals, sought acceptance in the society of the day, she refused various offers of marriage. Among her suitors were Percy Shelley's friend Edward John Trelawny, John Howard Payne, and, reportedly, Washington Irving. After the death of Sir Timothy Shelley in 1844, her financial situation became somewhat easier. One of the disappointments of her later years was the discovery that she lacked the strength to complete a long-planned biography of her husband. She died on February 1, 1851, at the age of fifty-three, and was buried at Bournemouth, Dorset, England.

Christine R. Catron

Bibliography

Baldick, Chris. *In Frankenstein's Shadow: Myth, Monstrosity, and Nineteenth-Century Writing*. Oxford, England: Clarendon Press, 1987. Baldick analyzes the structure of modern myth as it has adapted and misread Shelley's novel until the film version of 1931. Focuses on *Frankenstein* as itself a monster, which is assembled, speaks, and escapes like its protagonist. Includes footnotes, five illustrations, an appendix summarizing the novel's plot, and an index.

Bennett, Betty T., and Stuart Curran, eds. *Mary Shelley in Her Times*. Baltimore: The Johns Hopkins University Press, 2000. An examination of Shelley in the full context of her life and times; delves into all her writings rather than concentrating on her best-known novel.

Forry, Steven Earl. *Hideous Progenies: Dramatizations of "Frankenstein" from Mary Shelley to the Present*. Philadelphia: University of Pennsylvania Press, 1990. Examines the influence of Shelley's novel on the history of theater and cinema from 1832 to 1930. Provides the texts of seven dramatic adaptations of *Frankenstein*. Contains thirty-one illustrations, a list of ninety-six dramatizations from 1821 to 1986, an appendix with the music from *Vampire's Victim* (1887), a bibliography, and an index.

Mellor, Anne K. *Mary Shelley: Her Life, Her Fiction, Her Monsters*. London: Methuen, 1988. Argues against trends of analysis which subordinate Shelley to her husband, Percy Bysshe Shelley. Extends feminist and psychoanalytic criticism of *Frankenstein* to include all of Shelley's life and work, arguing that her stories are creations of the family she never enjoyed. Includes eight illustrative plates, a chronology, ample notes, a bibliography, and an index.

Seymour, Miranda. *Mary Shelley*. New York: Grove Press, 2001. A biography of the novelist that sheds much of the mythology that has hung around her since her time.

Smith, Johanna M. *Mary Shelley*. New York: Twayne, 1996. This good introductory volume on Shelley opens with a chapter devoted to her biography, then divides her works into categories. More descriptive than analytical, this is an accessible overview of Shelley's career. Includes selected bibliography.

Spark, Muriel. *Mary Shelley*. London: Constable, 1988. A revision of Spark's *Child of Light* (1951) which reassesses the view that Shelley craved respectability after her husband's death. Spark skillfully narrates Shelley's life and then analyzes her writings. Contains eight pages of illustrations, a selected bibliography, and an index.

Percy Bysshe Shelley

English poet

Born: Field Place, Sussex, England; August 4, 1792
Died: Off Viareggio, Italy; July 8, 1822

POETRY: *Original Poetry by Victor and Cazire*, 1810 (with Elizabeth Shelley); *Posthumous Fragments of Margaret Nicholson*, 1810; *Queen Mab: A Philosophical Poem*, 1813, revised 1816 (as *The Daemon of the World*); *Alastor: Or, The Spirit of Solitude, and Other Poems*, 1816; *Mont Blanc*, 1817; *The Revolt of Islam*, 1818; *Rosalind and Helen: A Modern Eclogue, with Other Poems*, 1819; *Letter to Maria Gisborne*, 1820; *Epipsychidion*, 1821; *Adonais: An Elegy on the Death of John Keats*, 1821; *Posthumous Poems of Percy Bysshe Shelley*, 1824 (includes *Prince Athanase*, *Julian and Maddalo: A Conversation*, *The Witch of Atlas*, *The Triumph of Life*, *The Cyclops*, and *Charles the First*); *The Mask of Anarchy*, 1832; *Peter Bell the Third*, 1839; *The Poetical Works of Percy Bysshe Shelley*, 1839; *The Wandering Jew*, 1887; *The Complete Poetical Works of Shelley*, 1904 (Thomas Hutchinson, editor); *The Esdaile Notebook: A Volume of Early Poems*, 1964 (K. N. Cameron, editor).

LONG FICTION: *Zastrozzi: A Romance*, 1810; *St. Irvyne: Or, The Rosicrucian*, 1810.

DRAMA: *The Cenci*, pb. 1819; *Prometheus Unbound: A Lyrical Drama in Four Acts*, pb. 1820; *Oedipus Tyrannus: Or, Swellfoot the Tyrant*, pb. 1820; *Hellas: A Lyrical Drama*, pb. 1822; *Charles the First*, pb. 1824 (fragment).

NONFICTION: *The Necessity of Atheism*, 1811 (with Thomas Jefferson Hogg); *An Address to the Irish People*, 1812; *Declaration of Rights*, 1812; *A Letter to Lord Ellenborough*, 1812; *Proposals for an Association of . . . Philanthropists*, 1812; *A Refutation of Deism, in a Dialogue*, 1814; *History of a Six Weeks' Tour Through a Part of France, Switzerland, Germany, and Holland*, 1817 (with Mary Shelley); *A Proposal for Putting Reform to the Vote Throughout the Kingdom*, 1817; *An Address to the People on the Death of the Princess Charlotte*, 1817(?); *Essays, Letters from Abroad, Translations, and Fragments*, 1840; *A Defence of Poetry*, 1840; *Shelley Memorials*, 1859; *Shelley's Prose in the Bodleian Manuscripts*, 1910; *Note Books of Shelley*, 1911; *A Philosophical View of Reform*, 1920; *The Letters of Percy Bysshe Shelley*, 1964 (2 volumes; Frederick L. Jones, editor).

TRANSLATIONS: *The Cyclops*, 1824 (of Euripides' play); *Ion*, 1840 (of Plato's dialogue); "The Banquet Translated from Plato," 1931 (of Plato's dialogue *Symposium*).

MISCELLANEOUS: *The Complete Works of Percy Bysshe Shelley*, 1926-1930 (10 volumes; Roger Ingpen and Walter E. Peck, editors); *Shelley's Poetry and Prose: Authoritative Texts and Criticism*, 1977 (Donald H. Reiman and Sharon B. Powers, editors).

Percy Bysshe Shelley, English poet, was born at Field Place, near Horsham, Sussex, on August 4, 1792, the eldest son of a landed country squire. After some tutoring he was sent to Syon House Academy, where his shyness exposed him to brutal bullying. Entering Eton in 1804, he lived as much apart from the other students as possible, a moody, sensitive, and precocious boy with the nickname "mad Shelley." There he wrote *Zastrozzi*, a wild gothic romance, *Original Poetry by Victor and Cazire*, and another inferior gothic romance, *St. Irvyne*, all published in 1810.

Shelley matriculated at University College, Oxford, in 1810. He and Thomas Jefferson Hogg were expelled during their second term for publishing and sending to bishops and heads of colleges a pamphlet called *The Necessity of Atheism*. At this time Shelley fell in love with Harriet Westbrook, daughter of a retired hotel keeper. They eloped and, despite Shelley's open break with the conventions of the Christian religion and particular scorn for the marriage ceremony, they were married in Edinburgh in August, 1811. Both fathers contributed to their support for the next three years, which the couple spent pursuing political reforms in southern England, Ireland, and Wales.

In 1813 their first child was born in London, and Shelley's first long poem, *Queen Mab*, was published. Meanwhile, marriage with Harriet was proving a failure. In May, 1814, Shelley met Mary Godwin, the daughter of William and Mary Wollstonecraft Godwin, radical reformers. Mary shared his belief that marriage was only a voluntary contract. Harriet left for her father's home, and Shelley and seventeen-year-old Mary eloped to Switzerland, accompanied by Claire Clairmont, Mary's stepsister. When they returned to England in September, Shelley proposed to Harriet that she come live with Mary and him; however, there was no reconciliation.

Mary and Shelley had a son in 1816 (the year of *Alastor*). They, with Claire, spent the summer in Switzerland and became close friends of George Gordon, Lord Byron. Soon after they returned to England in the autumn, they heard that Harriet had drowned herself. Shelley was then free to marry Mary Godwin, and they wed on December 30, 1816. A court order denied him the custody of his two children by Harriet.

After he had completed *The Revolt of Islam*, the Shelleys and Claire Clairmont, with her child by Byron, went to Italy. There Shelley remained the rest of his life, wandering from Lake Como, Milan, Venice, Este, Rome, Florence, and Pisa to other places. He spent much time with Byron. *Julian and Maddalo* is a poem in the form of a conversation between Shelley (Julian) and Byron (Maddalo). Next followed *The Mask of Anarchy*, a revolutionary propaganda poem; *The Cenci*, a realistic tragedy; and *Prometheus Unbound*, a lyric tragedy completed in 1819 and published in 1820. Earlier in the same year, at Pisa, he wrote some of his most famous lyrics, in "The Cloud," "Ode to the West Wind," and "Ode to a Skylark."

The chief productions of 1821 were *Epipsychidion*, a result of his platonic relationship with Countess Emilia Viviani; an uncompleted prose work, *A Defence of Poetry*, published after his death, and *Adonais*, an elegy inspired by the death of John Keats. From his wide reading, Shelley was most greatly influenced by Plato, Lucretius, Baruch Spinoza, Jean-Jacques Rousseau, David Hume, and Robert Southey. Godwin's influence lasted until Shelley's death. His final poem, *The Triumph of Life*, was incomplete at the time he was drowned, July 8, 1822, while sailing off Viareggio. His body was first buried in the sand, then cremated. The ashes were buried in the Protestant cemetery at Rome, January 21, 1823.

The nineteenth century notion of the sensitive poetic soul owes a great deal to the ideal young man (Alastor, "the brave, the beautiful the child of grace and genius") built up largely by Shelley of Shelley. Yet in the history of English literature, Shelley is not as important as William Wordsworth or as influential as Byron or Keats. Today he has many admirers, but for those who dislike Romantic poetry in general, Shelley is a particularly vulnerable target. Unquestionably he could give a songlike character to his verse, and he was a lover of unusual colors, blurred outlines, and large effects. He was also a lover of startling and frank realism and had an obvious passion for the mysterious. In technique he illustrated something more concrete by the less concrete. What Shelley starts to define often results in vague though pretty images. He offers emotion in itself, unattached, in the void.

Shelley was at war with the conventions of society from childhood. As a political dreamer he was filled with the hope of transforming the real world into an Arcadia through revolutionary reform. As a disciple of Godwin he directed *Queen Mab* against organized religion. The queen shows the human spirit that evil times in the past and present are attributable to the authority of church and state. In the future, however, when love reigns supreme, the chains of the human spirit will dissolve; humankind will be boundlessly self-assertive and will temper this self-assertion by a boundless sympathy for others. Then a world will be realized in which there are no inferior or superior classes or beings. The end of *Prometheus Unbound* expresses this vision of humanity released from all evil artificially imposed from without, a humanity "where all things flow to all, as rivers to the sea," and "whose nature is its own divine control."

The moral law that evolved with Shelley's thought was an insistence on the duty and the right of all individuals to rule their own destinies. This right was not arbitrary but devolved from the high standard of universal love which linked the seeking of individual liberty with the obligation to do all in one's power to secure a like freedom from tyranny for all. The reign of love when no authority is necessary was his millennium.

Christine R. Catron

Bibliography

Bloom, Harold, ed. *Percy Bysshe Shelley.* New York: Chelsea House, 1985. An excellent selection of some of the most important works on Shelley published since 1950. Bloom's introduction, an overview of Shelley's poetry, is highly recommended.

Cronin, Richard. *Shelley's Poetic Thoughts.* New York: St. Martin's Press, 1981. An incisive study of Shelley's thought within his poems and his manner of handling language. Cronin scrutinizes poetic forms as they manage realism and fantasy, elegy and dream. Contains notes and an index.

Everest, Kelvin, ed. *Percy Bysshe Shelley: Bicentenary Essays.* Cambridge, England: D. S. Brewer, 1992. A collection of biographical and critical essays on the life and works of Shelley. Includes bibliographical references.

Höhne, Horst. *In Pursuit of Love: The Short and Troublesome Life and Work of Percy Bysshe Shelley.* New York: Peter Lang, 2000. A biography of Shelley offering insights into his life and work. Includes bibliographical references and index.

Holmes, Richard. *Shelley: The Pursuit.* New York: E. P. Dutton, 1975. This major biography presents Shelley as a sinister and sometimes cruel artist of immense talent. Holmes claims new answers to questions about Shelley's Welsh experiences and about his paternity of a child born in Naples. Critical readings of Shelley's writings are less valuable than their biographical context. Contains illustrations, bibliography, notes, and an index.

Sperry, Stuart M. *Shelley's Major Verse: The Narrative and Dramatic Poetry.* Cambridge, Mass.: Harvard University Press, 1988. This excellent study of *Queen Mab*, *Alastor*, *The Revolt of Islam*, *Prometheus Unbound*, *The Cenci*, *The Witch of Atlas*, *Epipsychidion*, and *The Triumph of Life* attempts to synthesize philosophical, psychological, and biographical approaches to Shelley.

Wasserman, Earl R. *Shelley: A Critical Reading.* Baltimore: The Johns Hopkins University Press, 1971. Wasserman's massive, detailed readings of virtually all Shelley's major poems have been extremely influential. Wasserman emphasizes Shelley's metaphysical skepticism and discusses his conceptions of existence, selfhood, reality, causation, and their relation to transcendence. Some of the readings are very dense and may be intimidating for the beginning student, but no serious student of Shelley can ignore them.

Wheatley, Kim. *Shelley and His Readers: Beyond Paranoid Politics.* Columbia: University of Missouri Press, 1999. Examines Shelley's reception in major British periodicals and the poet's idealistic passion for reforming the world.

Sam Shepard

(Samuel Shepard Rogers VII)

American playwright and screenwriter

Born: Fort Sheridan, Illinois; November 5, 1943

DRAMA: *Cowboys*, pr. 1964 (one act); *The Rock Garden*, pr. 1964 (one act); *Up to Thursday*, pr. 1964; *Chicago*, pr. 1965; *Dog*, pr. 1965; *Icarus's Mother*, pr. 1965; *4-H Club*, pr. 1965; *Rocking Chair*, pr. 1965; *Fourteen Hundred Thousand*, pr. 1966; *Melodrama Play*, pr. 1966; *Red Cross*, pr. 1966; *La Turista*, pr. 1966; *Cowboys #2*, pr. 1967; *Forensic and the Navigators*, pr. 1967; *The Unseen Hand*, pr., pb. 1969; *Operation Sidewinder*, pb. 1969; *Shaved Splits*, pr. 1969; *The Holy Ghostly*, pr. 1970; *Back Bog Beast Bait*, pr., pb. 1971; *Cowboy Mouth*, pr., pb. 1971 (with Patti Smith); *The Mad Dog Blues*, pr. 1971; *Nightwalk*, pr., pb. 1972 (with Megan Terry and Jean-Claude van Itallie); *The Tooth of Crime*, pr. 1972; *Action*, pr. 1974; *Geography of a Horse Dreamer*, pr., pb. 1974; *Little Ocean*, pr. 1974; *Killer's Head*, pr. 1975; *The Sad Lament of Pecos Bill on the Eve of Killing His Wife*, pr. 1975; *Angel City*, pr., pb. 1976; *Curse of the Starving Class*, pb. 1976; *Suicide in B Flat*, pr. 1976; *Buried Child*, pr. 1978; *Seduced*, pr. 1978; *Tongues*, pr. 1978; *Savage/Love*, pr. 1979; *True West*, pr. 1980; *Seven Plays*, pb. 1981; *Fool for Love*, pr., pb. 1983; *A Lie of the Mind*, pr. 1985; *States of Shock*, pr. 1991; *Simpatico*, pr. 1994; *Plays*, pb. 1996-1997 (3 volumes); *When the World Was Green*, pr. 1996 (with Joseph Chaikin); *Eyes for Consuela*, pr. 1998; *The Late Henry Moss*, pr. 2000.

SHORT FICTION: *Cruising Paradise*, 1996; *Great Dream of Heaven*, 2002.

SCREENPLAYS: *Me and My Brother*, 1967 (with Robert Frank); *Zabriskie Point*, 1969; *Ringaleevio*, 1971; *Paris, Texas*, 1984 (with L. M. Kit Carson); *Far North*, 1988; *Silent Tongue*, 1993.

NONFICTION: *Rolling Thunder Logbook*, 1977.

MISCELLANEOUS: *Hawk Moon: A Book of Short Stories, Poems, and Monologues*, 1973; *Motel Chronicles*, 1982 (poetry and short fiction); *Joseph Chaikin and Sam Shepard: Letters and Texts, 1972-1984*, 1989.

Samuel Shepard Rogers VII has been compared to Eugene O'Neill in theatrical range and power. He is the son of Army Air Force bomber pilot Samuel Shepard Rogers and Jane Schook Rogers. Between 1943 and 1955, the family moved often from army post to army post, including a stay in Guam. They finally settled in California, residing during Shepard's teenage years on an avocado and sheep ranch in Duarte. Shepard found some aspects of the ranching life attractive but chafed against the ordinariness of his relationship with his parents and the tedium of rural society. He became enamored of motion pictures and their heroes, took up jazz drumming, and read Beat poets Lawrence Ferlinghetti and Gregory Corso. In 1962 he auditioned for the Bishop's Company Repertory Players and began a six-month tour as an itinerant actor, ending up in New York City's East Village in 1963. There he secured a job at the Village Gate, which introduced him to the country's best jazz musicians and to Ralph Cook, who launched the Theatre Genesis, as well as Sam Shepard's career, in the 1960's.

The atmosphere of East Village and the impetus of Off-Off-Broadway theater perfectly nurtured Shepard's eclectic talent. In 1964 he made his debut as a playwright with *Cowboys* and *The Rock Garden*, two one-act plays that introduced several of his themes and stylistic techniques. In *The Rock Garden* he presents a father who revels in his lifeless arrangement of rocks, whereas the son builds a counterpointed description of his sexual techniques with women until it subsumes the father's drone in an explosion of metaphors. This conflict of generations, brought forth through metaphorical language that rises from a dark, nearly bare stage, is typical of Shepard's early plays. The open stage requires audience members to exercise their imaginations in order to "complete" Shepard's dramatic scenes.

Taking his lead from the Beat generation and from jazz improvisation, Shepard creates "transformational" characters, who act themselves out through disruptions, explosions, contradictions, and shifting realities. Often they fear the loss of their individuality because of some unnameable force, and they move and talk rapidly in an attempt to invent themselves as larger-than-life figures. As a member of the first generation of playwrights to grow up under the influence of rock music and television, Shepard is preoccupied with various mythic models of the mass media—the cowboy, the Indian, the rock star, the gangster, the film star, the gothic monster, the business magnate—and with the desire to escape the traps of body, geography, or system.

Many of Shepard's characters do escape or transform themselves on the stage. For example, several in *Operation Sidewinder* emerge to a "fifth world" of Hopi legend, as the corrupt "fourth world" comes to final destruction. The mythical figures of *The Mad Dog Blues* join hands and exit dancing through the audience. In *La Turista* Kent ends the play by swinging from a rope at the back of the theater, crashing through the set, and leaving only his outline behind. These attempts at escape stem from the playwright's serious concern that America was "cracking open and crashing into the sea"—an outlook that led him to rely on apocalyptic endings, not necessarily motivated or prepared for by the dramatic plot. They also reflect his personal restlessness.

Eventually, however, Shepard began to recognize that escape is not always possible. Many of his mature plays rely on bankrupt myths of the frontier and the old West. In *The Tooth of Crime*, for example, an established rock star, Hoss, dreams of shucking off his responsibilities and his retinue to strike out like a "gypsy killer" into open territory. Instead, his personality and reputation are usurped by Crow, a young challenger, and he finally kills himself as a last act of independence. *Curse of the Starving Class* portrays a family one member describes as having "nitroglycerine in the blood"—a condition that leads to their destruction and the loss of their ranch. *Buried Child*, for which Shepard won the Pulitzer Prize in 1979, is a dramatization of blighted family relationships, brought forth by incest between mother and son. So long as the dead child of that union remains buried on their property, no crops grow, and the family members are mentally or physically crippled. Only a violent intrusion by an outsider can unearth their secret and make their farm, as well as their lives, productive again.

Eyes for Consuela is based on the Mexican writer Octavio Paz's short story "The Blue Bouquet." In it, Henry, a middle-class American whose marriage has disintegrated, flees to a decrepit hotel in a Mexican jungle. There he meets a philosophical Mexican bandit Amado, who threatens to cut out Henry's blue eyes as a gift to his wife, Consuela. Henry insists that his eyes are brown, not blue, but this does not impress Amado. Throughout two acts the men argue, drink tequila, and trade life histories, as Amado contends that Henry's despair is an example of anxiety caused by the complexity of American civilization.

A major concern in Shepard's work, hinted at in the plays discussed above, is that the nuclear family may also be a bankrupt myth—that power struggles, conflicts, and obligatory role-playing destroy most family relationships. *True West*, *Fool for Love*, and *A Lie of the Mind* all illustrate the playwright's preoccupation with the family's decay and the fragility of modern love. In Shepard's family conflicts, women appear to have the lesser voice, seeming only to support the males in their macho strivings. Yet as Florence Falk points out, Shepard's women are resilient survivors, whereas the men often remain empty inside their macho images. Later plays, such as *Fool for Love* and *A Lie of the Mind*, have countered critics' complaints about his female characters by presenting women who work through their debilities and establish themselves as equal or even superior to their men.

Shepard's dramatic imagination and power have been widely recognized, but opinion is unsettled as to his eventual stature in American drama. While his plays have not been produced on

Broadway, the sheer volume of his work commands attention. Besides writing plays, Shepard has acted in many films, including *Days of Heaven* (1978), *Resurrection* (1980), *Raggedy Man* (1981), *Frances* (1982), *Country* (1984), *Fool for Love* (1985), *Crimes of the Heart* (1986), and *The Right Stuff* (1983), for which he won the Academy Award for Best Supporting Actor. He has received the Pulitzer Prize, the Golden Palm Award at the Cannes Film Festival for the screenplay of *Paris, Texas*, and a New York Drama Critics Circle Award for *A Lie of the Mind*, as well as more than a dozen Obie awards for dramatic excellence. In 1998 the Public Broadcasting Service's (PBS) *Great Performances* devoted an hour-long TV program to Shepard's life and plays. All these achievements and honors make him, at the very least, one of the leading lights in American arts and letters.

Perry D. Luckett
Trey Strecker

Bibliography

Auerbach, Doris. *Shepard, Kopit, and the Off Broadway Theater.* Boston: Twayne, 1982. One of the first important academic analyses of Shepard's plays, this book provides a valuable analysis of Shepard's work as Off-Broadway drama.

Bottoms, Stephen J. *The Theatre of Sam Shepard: States of Crisis.* Cambridge, England: Cambridge University Press, 1998. Along with a thorough examination of Shepard's plays, Bottoms compares Shepard's work to that of other leading contemporary dramatists.

DeRose, David J. *Sam Shepard.* New York: Twayne, 1992. This book offers a brief overview of Shepard's life and work, analyzing his theatrical and thematic goals. Includes an annotated bibliography of secondary sources and a detailed list of important play reviews.

Hart, Lynda. *Sam Shepard's Metaphorical Stages.* Westport, Conn.: Greenwood Press, 1987. Hart argues that Shepard's plays from *Cowboys #2* to *A Lie of the Mind* are influenced by techniques developed by the Theater of the Absurd, particularly by the work of Samuel Beckett, Antonin Artaud, and Eugène Ionesco. The book also has a brief chapter on Shepard's television and film work.

Howard, Patricia, ed. "Special Issue: Sam Shepard and Contemporary American Drama." *Modern Drama* 36, no. 1 (1993). An excellent collection of critical essays.

King, Kimball, ed. *Sam Shepard: A Casebook.* New York: Garland, 1988. This collection of essays written mostly by academics approaches Shepard's work from many angles and demonstrates the range of responses his plays evoke.

Lanier, Gregory W., and Milton Berman. "Sam Shepard." In *Critical Survey of Drama*, edited by Carl Rollyson. 2d rev. ed. Pasadena, Calif.: Salem Press, 2003. A thorough overview of Shepard's life and career as a playwright and screenwriter.

Marranca, Bonnie, ed. *American Dreams: The Imagination of Sam Shepard.* New York: Performing Arts Journal, 1981. A compendium of essays written by academics, directors, and actors, this volume is a good introduction to Shepard's early work for the Off-Broadway theater. Short pieces by Shepard himself round out the volume, including his influential essay "Language, Visualization, and the Inner Library."

Mottram, Ron. *Inner Landscapes: The Theater of Sam Shepard.* Columbia: University of Missouri Press, 1984. Perhaps the best sustained examination of Shepard's plays, Mottram's biographical analysis offers many insightful readings of Shepard's work by comparing incidents in the plays to parallel episodes from Shepard's life or to stories from *Hawk Moon* or *Motel Chronicles* with similar characters or incidents. Mottram also includes a brief chronology of Shepard's work to 1985.

Oumano, Ellen. *Sam Shepard: The Life and Work of an American Dreamer.* New York: St. Martin's Press, 1986. Although a popular biography, this book is eminently readable and contains most of the important details about Shepard's professional and personal life. Includes a complete and accurate performance record of the plays.

Wilcox, Leonard, ed. *Rereading Shepard: Contemporary Critical Essays on the Plays of Sam Shepard.* New York: St. Martin's Press, 1993. An excellent collection of critical essays.

Richard Brinsley Sheridan

Irish playwright

Born: Dublin, Ireland; October 30, 1751
Died: London, England; July 7, 1816

DRAMA: *The Rivals*, pr., pb. 1775; *St. Patrick's Day: Or, The Scheming Lieutenant*, pr. 1775; *The Duenna: Or, The Double Elopement*, pr. 1775 (libretto; music by Thomas Linley the elder, Thomas Linley the younger, and others); *A Trip to Scarborough*, pr. 1777 (adaptation of Sir John Vanbrugh's *The Relapse*); *The School for Scandal*, pr. 1777; *The Critic: Or, A Tragedy Rehearsed*, pr. 1779; *Pizarro: A Tragedy in Five Acts*, pr., pb. 1799 (adaptation of August von Kotzebue's *Die Spanier in Peru*); *Complete Plays*, pb. 1930; *Plays*, pb. 1956 (L. Gibbs, editor); *The School for Scandal, and Other Plays*, pb. 1998 (Michael Cordner, editor).

POETRY: "Clio's Protest," 1771; "The Ridotto of Bath," 1771; *A Familiar Epistle to the Author of the Heroic Epistle to Sir William Chambers*, 1774; "Epilogue to *The Rivals*," 1775; "Epilogue to *Semiramis*," 1776; "Verses to the Memory of Garrick, Spoken as a Monody," 1779; "Epilogue to *The Fatal Falsehood*," 1779; "Prologue to *Pizarro*," 1799; "Lines by a Lady of Fashion," 1825.

NONFICTION: *Speeches of the Late Right Honourable Richard Brinsley Sheridan (Several Corrected by Himself)*, 1816 (5 volumes); *The Letters of Richard Brinsley Sheridan*, 1966 (3 volumes; C. J. L. Price, editor).

MISCELLANEOUS: *The Plays and Poems of Richard Brinsley Sheridan*, 1928, 1962 (3 volumes; R. Compton Rhodes, editor).

Between 1775 and 1779, Richard Brinsley Sheridan wrote five plays, two of which remain popular theater pieces. Indeed, among the many comic plays of the eighteenth and much of the nineteenth centuries, *The Rivals* and *The School for Scandal* are the only ones still being produced, except for Oliver Goldsmith's *She Stoops to Conquer* (1773). Having achieved such successes while still in his twenties, Sheridan forsook a promising career as playwright and turned to other pursuits: theater management and politics.

Sheridan's paternal grandfather, Thomas Sheridan, had distinguished himself in the classics at Trinity College in Dublin, taken holy orders, and become an educational reformer as head of a school in Dublin. The future playwright's father, also named Thomas Sheridan, took his M.A. at Trinity College. Though prepared for a clerical career, he preferred the stage, becoming manager of Dublin's Smock-Alley Theatre and the country's leading actor. Sheridan's mother, Frances, not only was the author of three popular romantic novels but also wrote three comic plays, two of which were produced at London's Drury Lane.

Frances Sheridan was her younger son's tutor until 1757, when he was enrolled in Samuel Whyte's grammar school; however, a year later the Sheridans moved to England. In 1762 Richard was sent to Harrow, where he remained until about 1768, gaining a reputation for pranks, indolence, and carelessness but at the same time enjoying the esteem of his schoolfellows and the admiring attention of his masters. He was, in fact, unhappy there and felt deserted by his parents, who had moved to France, where his mother died in 1766.

When he was seventeen, Sheridan left Harrow for London, where his father again was living. For a time he was tutored by a physician, the owner of a fencing and riding school, and his father. In 1770 Thomas Sheridan again moved his family, this time to Bath. Though his father's entertainment and educational ventures were unsuccessful, the move was propitious for young Sheridan, for in Bath he met seventeen-year-old Elizabeth Ann Linley, a celebrated soprano known for her beauty. So she could escape an unwanted admirer, a family friend named Thomas Matthews, she and Sheridan eloped to France in March, 1772. There they went through a marriage ceremony but lived apart until they returned to England two months later, when Sheridan faced Matthews in two duels. Seriously wounded in the second encounter, Sheridan had a long recuperation, following which, on April 6, 1773, he entered the Middle Temple, London. A week later, against their families' wishes, he and Linley were married at London's Marylebone Church.

His law studies notwithstanding, Sheridan had already taken steps toward a literary career. At Harrow he had written a stage adaptation of Oliver Goldsmith's *Vicar of Wakefield* (1766) and political satires, and at Bath he published light satiric verse and collaborated on a burlesque and translations of Greek love epistles. In London after his marriage, he wrote political and social tracts as well as his first full-length play.

When *The Rivals* premiered at Covent Garden on January 17, 1775, audience reaction was so negative that Sheridan withdrew it, extensively rewrote it, and presented the play anew eleven days later. His primary source for *The Rivals* was his own experience: living in a resort town, dealing with recalcitrant parents, falling in love, coping with rivals, and engaging in duels. Lacking a substantive plot, this comedy of character succeeds because of the deft handling of farce, imaginative disguises and deceptions, and clever dialogue, mainly that spoken by Mrs. Malaprop, whose mangling of English has given a word—malapropism—to the language. With its mockery of sentiment and prevalence of sheer fun, *The Rivals* is closer to William Congreve's witty comedies of seventy-five years earlier than to those by some eighteenth century contemporaries. Whereas Sheridan disdained "the sentimental Muse" (in a prologue to *The Rivals*), he did not crusade to change the comic drama. Like Goldsmith—with *She Stoops to Conquer*—Sheridan demonstrated the vitality of old conventions in skillful new hands.

His second play opened at Covent Garden on May 2, 1775. *St. Patrick's Day* was a farcical "afterpiece" that ran for six performances. Sheridan's third play, a comic opera titled *The Duenna*, was his second major success. *The Duenna* premiered at Covent Garden on November 21, 1775, and broke all previous records for full-length plays, with seventy-five performances in its first season. Sheridan's elopement with Linley and his mother's romance *Eugenia and Adelaide* (1791) probably served as sources.

The following year Sheridan and two partners bought David Garrick's interest in the Drury Lane Theatre and took over its management, a role he filled for more than thirty years. The first of his Drury Lane plays opened on February 24, 1777, a transformation of Sir John Vanbrugh's bawdy *The Relapse* (1696) into the more decorous *A Trip to Scarborough*. It was followed, on May 8, 1777, by *The School for Scandal*, whose intricate plot with parallel intrigues is complemented by farce and social criticism. It has endured on the stage partly because of its universal theme: the contrast between reality and appearance, depth and superficiality, and truth and delusion. Stereotypical though they are, Sir Peter and Lady Teazle, Snake and Lady Sneerwell, and the Surface brothers are among the most memorable characters in English comedy, and the auction and screen scenes are comic masterpieces. *The Critic*, which opened at Drury Lane on October 30, 1779, is a topical burlesque of stage absurdities in the tradition of the duke of Buckingham's *The Rehearsal* (1672) and Henry Fielding's *The Tragedy of Tragedies: Or, The Life and Death of Tom Thumb the Great* (1731). The timelessness of Sheridan's hilarious satire of theatrical banalities accounts for its continued stage life.

Though he continued to manage the Drury Lane Theatre into the next century and did a few translations and adaptations for the stage, *The Critic* was Sheridan's last original play, and in 1780 he embarked on a political career. Elected to Parliament, where he gained renown as an orator, he also served in cabinet and other government posts. While enjoying public successes, he had private troubles. His wife and an infant daughter died in 1792 (he remarried, to Hester Jane Ogle, in 1795, and a son was born the next year. In 1802 creditors took him to court (his eloquently delivered defense won the day), the Drury Lane Theatre burned down in 1809, and in 1813 he was imprisoned briefly for debt. He died in 1816 and was buried in the Poets' Corner of Westminster Abbey.

Gerald H. Strauss

Bibliography

Hare, Arnold. *Richard Brinsley Sheridan*. Windsor, England: Profile Books, 1981. This thin volume sketches the major details of Sheridan's life, family, and career. Pays brief attention to the theatrical milieu but analyzes the plays, including some relatively minor ones. Includes a select bibliography.

Loftis, John. *Sheridan and the Drama of Georgian England*. Cambridge, Mass.: Harvard University Press, 1977. This authoritative volume examines Sheridan's relationships with his dramatic predecessors, then analyzes extensively Sheridan's plays. The bibliography is divided into editions, biographies, critical studies, and background studies. Includes a lengthy index.

Norwood, James. *The Life and Works of Richard Brinsley Sheridan*. Edinburgh: Scottish Academic Press, 1985. Norwood attempts a lengthy biographical study in which extensive discussion of the writing career appears. Makes an effort to evaluate Sheridan's political career and to create a balanced assessment of his thirty-two years as manager of the Drury Lane. Includes several illustrations, a bibliography, and an index.

Smith, Dane F., and M. L. Lawhon. *Plays About the Theatre in England, 1737-1800*. Lewisburg, Pa.: Bucknell University Press, 1979. Interprets *The Critic* as an attack on the sentimentalism of the contemporary comedy and of the writers and critics who supported it. Also sees parts of *The School for Scandal* and *The Rivals* as attacks on sentimentalism. Some comparisons are made with Oliver Goldsmith's comedies.

Worth, Katharine. *Sheridan and Goldsmith*. New York: St. Martin's Press, 1992. The commentary emphasizes performance and dramaturgy.

R. C. Sherriff

English playwright and screenwriter

Born: Kingston-on-Thames, England; June 6, 1896
Died: London, England; November 13, 1975

DRAMA: *Journey's End*, pr. 1928; *Badger's Green*, pr., pb. 1930; *St. Helena*, pb. 1934 (with Jeanne de Casalis); *Miss Mabel*, pr. 1948; *Home at Seven*, pr., pb. 1950; *The White Carnation*, pr., pb. 1953; *The Long Sunset*, pr., pb. 1955; *The Telescope*, pr., pb. 1957; *A Shred of Evidence*, pr. 1960.

LONG FICTION: *Journey's End*, 1930 (with Vernon Bartlett; adaptation of his play); *The Fortnight in September*, 1931; *Greengates*, 1936; *The Hopkins Manuscript*, 1939; *King John's Treasure*, 1954.

SCREENPLAYS: *The Invisible Man*, 1933 (with Philip Wylie; adaptation of H. G. Wells's novel); *The Road Back*, 1937 (with Charles Kenyon; adaptation of Erich Maria Remarque's novel); *Goodbye, Mr. Chips*, 1939 (with Claudine West and Erich Maschwitz; adaptation of James Hilton's novel); *The Four Feathers*, 1939 (adaptation of A. E. W. Mason's novel); *That Hamilton Woman*, 1941 (with Walter Reisch); *This Above All*, 1942 (adaptation of Eric Knight's novel); *Forever and a Day*, 1943 (with others); *Odd Man Out*, 1947 (with F. L. Green; adaptation of Green's novel); *Quartet*, 1949 (adaptation of W. Somerset Maugham's stories); *Trio*, 1950 (adaptation of Maugham's stories); *No Highway in the Sky*, 1951 (with Oscar Millard and Alec Coppel; adaptation of Nevil Shute's novel); *The Dam Busters*, 1954; *The Night My Number Came Up*, 1955 (based on an article by Air Marshal Sir Victor Goddard).

NONFICTION: *No Leading Lady: An Autobiography*, 1968; *The Siege of Swayne Castle*, 1973.

Robert Cedric Sherriff was born on June 6, 1896, at Kingston-on-Thames, near London. His father, Herbert Hankin Sherriff, worked for the Sun Insurance Company; his mother was Constance Winder Sherriff. Robert grew up in Kingston-on-Thames, where he attended the local grammar school. He graduated at age seventeen, after which he followed his father into the insurance business, but his career was interrupted after nine months by the outbreak of World War I. Sherriff volunteered for service and became a second lieutenant in the Ninth East Surrey Regiment. He was wounded so severely at Ypres (where four-fifths of the original British Expeditionary Force died) that he was hospitalized for six months. At war's end he was mustered out as a captain.

Back in civilian life, Sherriff returned to the Sun Insurance Company, where he worked for the next ten years as a claims adjuster. For recreation, he joined the Kingston rowing club, and to raise funds for the organization, he and some fellow members wrote and produced plays. Sherriff took to playwriting with zeal and studied William Archer's *Play-Making* (1912) so thoroughly that he claimed to have memorized it. In addition, he began to read modern plays systematically and commuted to London to see the latest productions. Returning home on the train, he sometimes developed dialogue for a play he had in mind.

After writing plays for six years for amateur productions, Sherriff turned to a more serious project: a drama based upon his firsthand knowledge of trench warfare. His parents had saved the letters he had written to them from the trenches, and these helped him revive the immediacy of the experience, its realistic details, and his friendships and feelings at the time. Throughout 1928 he worked alone on the play. Gradually the drama, at first called "Suspense" and then "Waiting," took final shape as *Journey's End*.

Realizing that this drama was not the stuff of amateur theatricals, Sherriff sent it to the Curtis Brown theatrical agency. Impressed but unable to see the play's commercial possibilities, Brown sent it on to Geoffrey Dearmer at the Incorporated Stage Society. Dearmer advised Sherriff to send a copy to George Bernard Shaw, who sent it back with the comment that it was "a document, not a drama," and that as a slice of "horribly abnormal life" it should be "performed by all means, even at the disadvantage of being the newspaper of the day before yesterday." Even so, all the London theatrical managements rejected *Journey's End*; they were strongly opposed to war plays, and this one lacked all the standard ingredients for a popular success. It had no leading lady, no romance, and no conventional heroics, and all the action took place offstage. Though this was the author's seventh play, the first six were all amateur productions, and the insurance agent earning six pounds a week was utterly obscure.

Nevertheless, Dearmer arranged for a production by the noncommercial Incorporated Stage Society. To direct, he picked a minor actor named James Whale. Whale, in turn, looked for a leading actor to play Captain Stanhope. All the eminent London actors had declined the role, but twenty-one-year-old Laurence Olivier, who was hoping to win the lead in a stage version of *Beau Geste* that director Basil Dean was then casting, saw the role of Stanhope as a chance to prove that he could play a soldier and thus handle the lead in the Foreign Legion drama.

The first performance, on the evening of Sunday, December 9, 1928, went off flawlessly but received only moderate applause, though Barry Jackson commended the play's honest realism. The critics did not appear en masse until the second and final performance at the Monday matinee. The play and production so overwhelmed them that Hannen Swaffer, London's most scathing critic, hailed *Journey's End* as "the greatest of all war plays." James Agate devoted his entire weekly radio talk show to praising it, concluding, "But you will never see this play. I have spoken with several managers, urging them to give you the opportunity of judging it for yourselves, but they are adamant in their belief that war plays have no audience in the theater."

Six weeks passed with no sign that the play might be revived by a commercial producer, and Olivier accepted the lead in *Beau Geste*. Then a fan persuaded a millionaire friend to put up the money. The new production opened on January 21, 1929, at the Savoy Theatre. The first performance received nineteen curtain calls, and the success of *Journey's End* became a theatrical legend. It went on to play 594 performances in London. A second production opened at the Henry Miller Theater in New York on March 22, 1929, and ran for 485 performances. Translated into twenty-seven languages, *Journey's End* played around the world.

Sherriff's friends urged him to write another play. At the moment, he had no ideas for one and instead, collaborating with Vernon Bartlett, turned *Journey's End* into a novel. It did not have the overwhelming success of the play and film versions, and Sherriff turned back to playwriting with his next venture, a problem comedy called *Badger's Green*, about the conflict between developers trying to exploit the imaginary village of the title and the conservationists opposing them. Perhaps the problem, now a vital one, was ahead of its time, for the 1930 production fared poorly.

Discouraged, Sherriff feared that he might not be able to continue supporting himself by his pen, and being unwilling to return to the insurance business, he entered New College at Oxford University to earn a degree in history and become a schoolmaster. While a student, he wrote another novel, *The Fortnight in September*, about a middle-class family's annual vacation at a seaside resort. Favorably reviewed, it sold well in England and abroad. Still at Oxford, Sherriff joined an undergraduate rowing crew, though he was then thirty-five years old. Before he could participate in the annual races or earn his degree, he received an invitation from James Whale to collaborate with Philip Wylie on a screenplay of H. G. Wells's 1897 novel *The Invisible Man*. The scenarios for Whale's *Frankenstein* films had departed drastically from the novel, but the script for *The Invisible Man* followed Wells with reasonable fidelity. Released in 1933, *The Invisible Man* was one of the year's most memorable films, and its literate script helped make it one of the most successful film adaptations of a Wells novel.

The Invisible Man was important in Sherriff's career, introducing him to screenwriting, a genre in which he was to do some of his most memorable work. Immediately after it, however, he first returned to the stage, collaborating with actress Jeanne de Casalis on *St. Helena*, a play about the exiled and imprisoned Napoleon. Written and published in 1934, it was not produced until 1936, when it had a faltering start until Winston Churchill wrote to *The Times* (London) in its defense, calling it "a work of art of a very high order." Churchill added, "I was among the very first to acclaim the quality of *Journey's End*. Here is the end of the most astonishing journey ever made by mortal man." The letter boosted ticket sales from fewer than one hundred for a performance to overflow houses; when the demand held for almost two months, the management moved the production to a larger theater in the West End. Possibly the house was wrong for the show; the move was a disaster, and attendance plunged precipitously.

Fortunately for Sherriff, Whale once more invited him to write a screenplay for him, this time an adaptation of Erich Maria Remarque's novel *The Road Back*. Though the 1937 film was only moderately successful, it was important in Sherriff's career in that it returned him to screenwriting. During the next eighteen years, he wrote the scripts for an impressive number of outstanding films, among them *Goodbye, Mr. Chips*, *The Four Feathers*, *That Hamilton Woman*, *This Above All*, *Odd Man Out*, *Quartet*, and *Trio*.

Sherriff did not return to playwriting until 1948, with *Miss Mabel*, a popular comedy-mystery. From 1950 to 1960, he wrote five more plays: *Home at Seven*, *The White Carnation*, *The Long Sunset*, *The Telescope*, and *A Shred of Evidence*. The last two were not successful, and after 1960, Sherriff went into semiretirement. In 1968, he published an autobiography, *No Leading Lady*, the title of which refers to complaints about *Journey's End* before its unexpected triumph. It is valuable as a lively account not only of Sherriff's life and career but also of forty years in the history of British theater and cinema. In those forty years, Sherriff played a prominent part.

Robert E. Morsberger

Bibliography

Bracco, Rosa Maria. *Merchants of Hope: British Middlebrow Writers and the First World War, 1919-1939*. Providence, R.I.: Berg, 1993. Bracco examines British literature written about World War I, focusing on Sherriff's *Journey's End*. Includes bibliography and index.

Cottrell, John. *Laurence Olivier*. Englewood Cliffs, N.J.: Prentice-Hall, 1975. Laurence Olivier, in 1928, was the star of the first production of *Journey's End*, which was staged by the Incorporated Stage Society before it reopened in London. Cottrell gives a detailed account of the play's first two stagings.

Darlington, William A. "'Keying Down': The Secret of *Journey's End*." Review of *Journey's End*, by R. C. Sherriff. *Theatre Arts Monthly* 13 (July, 1929): 493-497. A critic who had seen all the performances of *Journey's End* compares the play's first two productions to the New York production.

Hill, Eldon C. "R. C. Sherriff." In *Modern British Dramatists, 1900-1945*, edited by Stanley Weintraub. Vol. 10 in *Dictionary of Literary Biography*. Detroit: Gale Research, 1982. Hill goes into detail in his discussion of *Journey's End*, quoting G. Wilson Knight's 1962 statement that it is "the greatest war play of the century." He gives a briefer account of the other plays and novels and says little about the screenplays. Includes two photographs of the author, a reproduction of the program, and a photograph of the 1929 production of *Journey's End*.

Robert E. Sherwood

American playwright and screenwriter

Born: New Rochelle, New York; April 4, 1896
Died: New York, New York; November 14, 1955

DRAMA: *The Road to Rome*, pr., pb. 1927; *The Love Nest*, pr. 1927 (adaptation of Ring Lardner's story); *The Queen's Husband*, pr., pb. 1928; *Waterloo Bridge*, pr., pb. 1930; *This Is New York*, pr. 1930; *Reunion in Vienna*, pr. 1931; *Acropolis*, pr. 1933; *The Petrified Forest*, pr., pb. 1935; *Idiot's Delight*, pr., pb. 1936; *Tovarich*, pr., pb. 1936 (adaptation of Jacques Deval's comedy); *Abe Lincoln in Illinois*, pr. 1938; *There Shall Be No Night*, pr., pb. 1940; *The Rugged Path*, pr. 1945; *Miss Liberty*, pr. 1949 (libretto; music by Irving Berlin); *Small War on Murray Hill*, pr., pb. 1957.

LONG FICTION: *The Virtuous Knight*, 1931.

SCREENPLAYS: *Cock of the Air*, 1932 (with Charles Lederer); *The Scarlet Pimpernel*, 1935 (with Arthur Wimperis; adaptation of Baroness Orczy's novel); *The Ghost Goes West*, 1936; *Thunder in the City*, 1937 (with Aben Kandel); *The Adventures of Marco Polo*, 1938; *The Divorce of Lady X*, 1938 (with Lajos Biro; adaptation of Biro's play *Counsel's Opinion*); *Abe Lincoln in Illinois*, 1939 (adaptation of his play); *Idiot's Delight*, 1939 (adaptation of his play); *Rebecca*, 1940 (with Joan Harrison; adaptation of Daphne du Maurier's novel); *The Best Years of Our Lives*, 1946; *The Bishop's Wife*, 1947 (with Leonardo Bercovici); *Man on a Tightrope*, 1953.

NONFICTION: *Roosevelt and Hopkins*, 1948 (also known as *The White House Papers of Harry Hopkins*, 1949).

EDITED TEXT: *The Best Moving Pictures of 1922-1923*, 1923.

Robert Emmet Sherwood was the product of an affluent and artistic family. His mother, the former Rosina Emmet, was sufficiently well known as an artist to be listed in *Who's Who*. His father, Arthur Murray Sherwood, was a prominent investment broker and held a seat on the New York Stock Exchange. Arthur Sherwood was a frustrated actor and had been an active member of the Hasty Pudding Club during his student days at Harvard University, where he was also the first president of the Harvard *Lampoon*. Robert Sherwood followed in his father's footsteps at Harvard, both as a member of the Hasty Pudding Club and as editor of the *Lampoon*.

Sherwood was named for the Irish patriot Robert Emmet, brother of his mother's great-grandfather, who led an attack on Dublin Castle and was hanged in 1803. Sherwood was proud of his renegade namesake. Mary Elizabeth Wilson Sherwood, mother of Sherwood's father, had been honored both by the French government and by Queen Victoria of Britain. She was active in literary and artistic circles and in her lifetime wrote more than twenty books and hundreds of articles.

Thus, Robert Sherwood, the next to the youngest of five Sherwood children, was born into an artistically active family of considerable means. Shortly after his birth, the family moved to a house on Lexington Avenue in New York City. The family also maintained a forty-room Georgian mansion, Skene Wood, set on three hundred acres bordering Lake Champlain. It was there that Sherwood spent most of his childhood summers.

During the summers at Skene Wood, Sherwood and his siblings put on amateur dramatic productions, and Sherwood produced a handwritten newspaper, *Children's Life*. At eight, he wrote an ending for Charles Dickens's unfinished novel *The Mystery of Edwin Drood*, and two years later he wrote his first original play.

When he was nine years old, Sherwood was sent to the Fay School in Southborough, Massachusetts, and at thirteen he was sent to the Milton Academy near Boston to begin his preparatory studies for Harvard. Both in preparatory school and later at Harvard, Sherwood's energies were to be directed more toward literary matters than toward academic ones. He was managing editor of Milton's monthly magazine, *Orange and Blue*, for much of his final year at Milton; he was deeply in trouble with his studies, however, and in April the school forced his withdrawal from this post. Ultimately, his grades were so low that Milton Academy refused him a diploma, giving him instead a certificate of attendance. Despite this, Sherwood was elected valedictorian by his classmates, and he gave the valedictory address.

Sherwood's academic career at Harvard was no more distinguished than his career at Milton Academy had been, although his contributions to Harvard's dramatic and literary clubs were substantial. On the brink of expulsion three times during his freshman year alone, Sherwood did not make it to graduation.

In July of 1917, having been rejected (on account of his great height) by the various branches of the United States armed forces in which he attempted to enlist, Sherwood became a member of the Canadian Expeditionary Force, serving in the Forty-second Battalion of the Fifth Royal Highlanders and achieving the distinction of being probably the tallest serviceman in World War I to wear kilts. At six feet, seven inches, he towered over his fellow combatants. He served six months in France, where he was gassed on Vimy Ridge. In 1918, Harvard awarded him a bachelor's degree in absentia, although he had not met the academic standards for this degree.

On his return from the war, Sherwood was offered a position at *Vanity Fair*, a magazine that the *Lampoon* under Sherwood's editorship had burlesqued so effectively that its editor wanted Sherwood on his staff. At *Vanity Fair*, Sherwood shared an office with Robert Benchley and Dorothy Parker; the three were fired in 1920 for rebelling against *Vanity Fair*'s editorial staff, but soon they were all hired by *Life* magazine, to whose editorship Sherwood rose in 1924. During this period, Sherwood was a regular participant in the Round Table which met at the Algonquin Hotel.

Sherwood married Mary Brandon in 1922. Their turbulent marriage lasted until 1934, when they were divorced. The following year, Sherwood married playwright Marc Connelly's former wife, actress Madeline Hurlock Connelly. Sherwood's extravagant lifestyle during the early years of his marriage to Mary Brandon had caused him to sink deeply into debt, from which he extricated himself in 1926 by writing *The Road to Rome* in three weeks' time. When the play opened on Broadway the following year, it was an immediate success and ran for 392 performances. Throughout his career, Sherwood frequently relied on his gift for rapid composition to free himself from debts.

The activism that had led Sherwood to serve in the armed forces during the war and to speak his mind at *Vanity Fair* shifted its focus to the problems of actors and writers as well as national affairs. In 1935, he became secretary of the Dramatists' Guild, and he rose to the presidency of that organization in 1937. In that year he combined forces with Maxwell Anderson, S. N. Behrman, Sidney Howard, and Elmer Rice to form the Playwrights' Company, which was incorporated in 1938 for the purpose of permitting playwrights to stage their own plays, either directing the plays themselves or appointing directors of their own choosing. Sherwood was elected president of the American National Theatre and Academy in 1939.

Although Sherwood had been a strident pacifist, Adolf Hitler's ascendancy in Germany forced him to rethink his stand. A political idealist, Sherwood was finally forced to recognize the impossibility of allowing a dictator to run roughshod over Europe. *There Shall Be No Night* calls for action against aggressors of Hitler's ilk and represents an important turning point in Sherwood's thinking. In his presidential address to the Dramatists' Guild in 1939, Sherwood called upon writers to turn their talents to writing in support of freedom. *There Shall Be No Night* is in line with this imperative.

Long a friend and political supporter of Franklin D. Roosevelt, Sherwood was asked by the Roosevelt Administration to write war propaganda. He did so willingly, and in time he became not only a confidant of the president, visiting him often at the White House, but also one of his chief speech writers. In 1940 Sherwood was appointed a special assistant to the secretary of war, and in 1942 he was appointed director of the overseas branch of the office of war information. In 1945 he served as a special assistant to the secretary of the navy.

Sherwood was also active as a screenwriter. As early as 1932, he had collaborated with Charles Lederer on *Cock of the Air* for United Artists, followed in 1935 by *The Scarlet Pimpernel*, a collaboration with Arthur Wimperis, and many others followed. His finest Hollywood effort was *The Best Years of Our Lives*, in 1946.

Sherwood received Pulitzer Prizes in drama in 1936 for *Idiot's Delight*, in 1939 for *Abe Lincoln in Illinois*, and in 1941 for *There Shall Be No Night*. The historical work *Roosevelt and Hopkins* won for Sherwood a fourth Pulitzer Prize in 1949. His film script *The Best Years of Our Lives* took an Academy Award for Best Screenplay of 1946, one of nine Academy Awards garnered by the film. Sherwood also received the Gold Medal for Drama of the National Institute of Arts and Letters in 1941, the Gutenberg Award in 1949, and the Bancroft Prize for Distinguished Writing in American History in 1949. He was awarded honorary doctorates by Dartmouth College (1940), Yale University (1941), Harvard University (1949), and Bishop's University (1950).

Always a man of the world, Sherwood's insights were deepened by his direct contact with high levels of government during the war. His work with the Hopkins papers was meticulously researched, although some scholars think that Sidney Hyman deserves more credit than he was given for the high level of research apparent in *Roosevelt and Hopkins*. The quality and effectiveness of Sherwood's dramatic writing declined after the war. He died in 1955 at age fifty-nine.

R. Baird Shuman
Christian H. Moe

Bibliography

Brown, John Mason. *The Ordeal of a Playwright: Robert E. Sherwood and the Challenge of War.* Edited by Norman Cousins. New York: Harper & Row, 1970. Brown's uncompleted second biography furnishes a fragmentary but telling portrait of Sherwood as being wrenched away from devout pacifism to become aroused by world affairs. Includes an index and a complete text of *There Shall Be No Night.*

_______. *The Worlds of Robert E. Sherwood: Mirror to His Times, 1897-1939.* 1965. Reprint. Westport, Conn.: Greenwood Press, 1979. This thoroughly documented and admiring biography extends from Sherwood's early childhood and up through his career as a critic and playwright to include the writing of *Abe Lincoln in Illinois.* Contains a list of Sherwood's work and an index, in addition to twenty-eight illustrations of Sherwood, his family and friends, and several productions.

Meserve, Walter J. *Robert E. Sherwood: Reluctant Moralist.* New York: Pegasus, 1970. In addition to examining Sherwood as a dramatist, Meserve considers the playwright's role as an adviser and speech writer for Franklin D. Roosevelt, as a prominent member of the Author's League, and as a founding partner in the Playwright's Company. The book offers a detailed analysis of all Sherwood's plays and includes a bibliography and an index.

Mishra, Kshamanidhi. *American Leftist Playwrights of the 1930's: A Study of Ideology and Technique in the Plays of Odets, Lawson, and Sherwood.* New Delhi, India: Classical, 1991. The author looks at the political and social views of Sherwood, Clifford Odets, and John Lawson. Includes bibliography.

Shuman, R. Baird. *Robert E. Sherwood.* New York: Twayne, 1964. An accessible and comprehensive biographical and critical treatment of the playwright and his work. It contains a chronology, a detailed examination of Sherwood's plays within the context of his life and career, and an annotated listing of secondary sources.

Shi Naian

Chinese novelist

Born: China; c. 1290
Died: China; 1365

LONG FICTION: *Shuihu zhuan*, possibly the fourteenth century (*All Men Are Brothers*, 1933; also known as *Water Margin*).

Nothing is definitely known about Shi Naian (shee nah-ee-ahn), the man who has been generally accepted as the author of *All Men Are Brothers* ever since 1644, when Jin Shengtan wrote his seventy-chapter version of the novel with a preface of his own composition and forged Shi's name to it; an equally good claim can, however, be made for Luo Guanzhong. Until the early 1930's all that could be said of Shi was that he probably flourished in the middle decades of the fourteenth century and was perhaps an older contemporary of Luo. Then a researcher named Zha Yuting reported that he had found evidence to support the claim that Shi was a native of Huai'an in Jiangsu, that he was the teacher of Luo, and that Jiangyin was the place where he wrote the novel. A census taker reported that he had come upon two documents in the archives of a clan in the Dongtai district of Jiangsu. These give the information that Shi Naian's real name was Er, that he was born in 1296 and died in 1370, that he passed his *jinshi* examinations in 1331, and that after serving two years as a magistrate of Qiantang in Zhejiang, he resigned because of disagreements with his superiors and devoted the rest of his life to writing. A list of his writings is given, which include not only the *Shuihu zhuan* (under a slightly different title) but also several additional historical romances generally attributed to Luo, with the remark that he was helped in his work by his pupil Luo Guanzhong. At first these reports gained wide circulation, but soon doubts began to be voiced and the dispute over authorship of the novel resumed.

Actually neither Shi nor Luo could be the only author of the extant versions of the novel, of which there are at least five (in 100, 110, 115, 120, and 124 chapters respectively) that antedate Jin's version. Historical and legendary romances such as *Shuihu zhuan* and *Sanguo zhi yanyi* lived first in the oral tradition of professional storytellers. After a time some of them were set down in crude, sketchy form and were used largely as promptbooks. Shi and Luo, who lived under the oppressive rule of the Yuan dynasty, were the first two authors who rewrote some of these romances and arranged them into a novel about 108 brave men and women banded together in their fight against tyranny. When literary hacks began to make up more elaborate reading versions of these romances from about the middle of the sixteenth century on, they appropriated the Shi-Luo names rather than give their own, since it was not to one's credit in those days to be responsible for such light literature.

Chenliang Sheng

Bibliography

Bartell, Shirley Miller. "The Chinese Bandit Novel and the American Gangster Film." *New Orleans Review* 8, no. 1 (Winter, 1981).

Irwin, Richard G. *The Evolution of a Chinese Novel: "Shui-hu chuan."* Cambridge, Mass.: Harvard University Press, 1953.

Sheng-t'an, Chin. "On How to Read the *Shihu Chuan*." In *How to Read the Chinese Novel*, edited by David L. Rolston. Princeton, N.J.: Princeton University Press, 1990.

Wu, Hua-Laura. "The Structuring of Fictional Worlds of Western and Chinese Romance." *Style* 25, no. 2 (Summer, 1991).

Carol Shields

American-born Canadian novelist

Born: Oak Park, Illinois; June 2, 1935
Died: Victoria, British Columbia, Canada; July 16, 2003

LONG FICTION: *Small Ceremonies*, 1976; *The Box Garden*, 1977; *Happenstance*, 1980; *A Fairly Conventional Woman*, 1982; *Swann: A Mystery*, 1987; *A Celibate Season*, 1991 (with Blanche Howard); *The Republic of Love*, 1992; *The Stone Diaries*, 1993; *Larry's Party*, 1997; *Unless*, 2002.

SHORT FICTION: *Various Miracles*, 1985; *The Orange Fish*, 1989; *Dressing Up for the Carnival*, 2000.

DRAMA: *Departures and Arrivals*, pr., pb. 1990; *Thirteen Hands*, pr., pb. 1993; *Fashion, Power, Guilt, and the Charity of Families*, pr., pb. 1995 (with Catherine Shields); *Anniversary: A Comedy*, pr., pb. 1998 (with Dave Williamson); *Thirteen Hands, and Other Plays*, pb. 2002.

POETRY: *Others*, 1972; *Intersect*, 1974; *Coming to Canada*, 1992.

NONFICTION: *Susanna Moodie: Voice and Vision*, 1976; *Jane Austen*, 2001.

Carol Shields's novels have been lauded for their deft exploration of marriage, parenthood, and the battle between the sexes. Shields was a perceptive, and sometimes humorous, observer of social trends whose work is more serious in tone than it may initially appear. "Because she's a comic writer and genuinely funny, early on, she was put in the 'sweet' box, where she does not belong," Canadian novelist Margaret Atwood once said. "The fact is, there's a dark thread in everything she writes." Critics have often commented on Shields's descriptive prose, comparing her work with that of British novelist A. S. Byatt and Canadian short-story writer Alice Munro.

The author was born Carol Warner on June 2, 1935, in Oak Park, Illinois, a prosperous suburb of Chicago which is also the birthplace of Ernest Hemingway. Her father managed a candy factory, and her mother was a schoolteacher. The author has described her childhood as bookish and happy. As a student at Hanover College in Hanover, Indiana, she was participating in a study abroad program in England when she met Canadian engineering student Donald Shields. They were married in 1957, six weeks after her college graduation. A week after their wedding, Shields followed her husband to Canada, never to live in the United States again.

While her husband pursued an academic career, ultimately becoming a professor of engineering at the University of Manitoba, Shields was a devoted wife and mother. She gave birth to five children within a span of ten years. While her children were in school, Shields kept busy, writing poetry and fiction. During this time she studied at the University of Ottawa, where she received an M.A. Her thesis was on nineteenth century writer Susanna Moodie. Moodie was an Englishwoman who, like Shields, established her literary career after emigrating to Canada.

Small Ceremonies, Shields's first novel, was published in 1976, when she was forty. Her early books, which portrayed ordinary people in everyday situations, gained a popular following in Canada, but critics generally dismissed her work as too naturalistic. It was not until her fifth book, *Swann*, that Shields began to draw attention from outside Canada. With this novel, she experimented with form by using four different voices to tell the story. *Swann*, which Shields said was her favorite book, depicts a scholar's quest to establish the reputation of an obscure woman poet as an overlooked genius.

Shields experimented again when writing *The Republic of Love*, emulating the structure of a romance novel. The book that firmly cemented her reputation with critics around the world was *The Stone Diaries*. Written in the first and third person, this book is the fictional biography of a woman whose life spanned eight decades and who lived in both Canada and the United States. With this groundbreaking novel, Shields won acclaim for her deft examination of loneliness and lost opportunities and for writing movingly about the lives that women lead. *The Stone Diaries* was lauded for its exploration of the relationships among fiction, biography, and autobiography. This novel won the Pulitzer Prize in fiction and the Canadian Governor-General's Award. It was also short-listed for Britain's Booker Prize.

After the publication of *The Stone Diaries*, Shields was named chancellor of the University of Winnipeg. She had been teaching literature courses for years at the University of Manitoba. She found time to write despite a hectic schedule. Her next novel, *Larry's Party*, grappled with, as she put it, "what life was like for a man in the second half of the 20th century." *Larry's Party* won the National Book Critics Circle Award in the United States and the Orange Prize for Fiction in Britain. In 2000, the government of France appointed Shields a Chevalier de l'Ordre des Arts et des Lettres.

Shortly after *Larry's Party* was published, Shields was diagnosed with an aggressive form of breast cancer. She underwent chemotherapy and radiation, but the cancer did not respond to treatment. Faced with the fatal nature of her disease, Shields wrote what she knew would be her final book, *Unless*, which documents a year in the life of a writer and deals more directly with loss, suffering, and unhappiness than any of her previous books.

Shields said that she was grateful she was able to live in Winnipeg during the early years of her writing career, a city that kept her isolated from the pressures of book publishing. In 1999 she and her husband relocated to Victoria, British Columbia. She died there in 2003.

Scott D. Johnston

Bibliography

Russo, Maria. "Final Chapter." *The New York Times Magazine*, April 14, 2002, 32-35. A personal profile of Shields.

Shields, Carol. "An Interview with Carol Shields." Interview by Donna Krolik Hollenberg. *Contemporary Literature* 39, no. 3 (Fall, 1998): 339-355. Discusses the writer and her craft.

Slethaug, Gordon E. "'The Coded Dots of Life': Carol Shields's Diaries and Stones." *Canadian Literature* 156 (Spring, 1998): 59-81. A useful critical study.

Trozzi, Adriana. *Carol Shields' Magic Wand: Turning the Ordinary into the Extraordinary.* Rome: Bulzoni, 2001. Examines Shields's writings at length.

James Shirley

English playwright

Born: London, England; September 7, 1596 (baptized)
Died: London, England; October 29, 1666

DRAMA: *The School of Compliment*, pr. 1625 (also known as *Love Tricks: Or, The School of Compliments*); *The Brothers*, pr. 1626; *The Maid's Revenge*, pr. 1626; *The Wedding*, pr. 1626(?); *The Witty Fair One*, pr. 1628; *The Grateful Servant*, pr. 1629 (also known as *The Faithful Servant*); *The Traitor*, pr. 1631; *Love's Cruelty*, pr. 1631; *The Duke*, pr. 1631; *The Changes: Or, Love in a Maze*, pr. 1631; *Hyde Park*, pr. 1632; *The Ball*, pr. 1632 (with George Chapman); *The Bird in a Cage*, pr. 1632 (also known as *The Beauties*); *The Young Admiral*, pr. 1633; *The Gamester*, pr. 1633; *The Triumph of Peace*, pr., pb. 1634 (masque); *The Coronation*, pr. 1635; *The Lady of Pleasure*, pr. 1635; *Chabot, Admiral of France*, pr. 1635 (with Chapman); *The Duke's Mistress*, pr. 1636; *The Constant Maid*, pr. 1636-1640(?); *The Royal Master*, pr. 1637; *The Doubtful Heir*, pr. c. 1638 (also known as *Rosania: Or, Love's Victory*); *The Politician*, pr. 1639(?); *The Gentleman of Venice*, pr. 1639; *Patrick for Ireland*, pr. 1639(?); *The Humorous Courtier*, pr., pb. 1640 (revision of *The Duke*); *The Imposture*, pr. 1640; *The Cardinal*, pr. 1641; *The Sisters*, pr. 1642; *The Court Secret*, wr. 1642, pb. 1653; *The Contention of Ajax and Ulysses for the Armour of Achilles*, pr. c. 1645 (masque); *Dramatic Works and Poems*, pb. 1833 (6 volumes).

POETRY: *Eccho: Or, The Infortunate Lovers*, 1618; *Poems &c. by James Shirley*, 1646 (includes *Narcissus: Or, The Self-Lover*).

NONFICTION: *Via ad Latinam Linguam Complanata: The Way Made Plain to the Latin Tongues*, 1649 (also known as *Grammatica anglolatina*, 1651); *The Rudiments of Grammar*, 1656 (enlarged as *Manductio*, 1660); *An Essay Towards an Universal and Rational Grammar*, 1726 (Jenkin Thomas Philipps, compiler and editor; from Shirley's writings on grammar).

James Shirley was born in London in September, 1596. He received a standard classical education at the Merchant Taylors' School from 1608 to 1612, and he may have attended St. John's College, Oxford. He matriculated at St. Catherine's College, Cambridge, in 1615, received the bachelor of arts degree in 1617, and continued working for his master of arts at Cambridge. After receiving his M.A., he was ordained in the Anglican church, married Elizabeth Gilmet, with whom he had two daughters and a son, and took a curacy in Lincolnshire. He left this post to become headmaster of a grammar school in St. Albans, about which time he converted to Catholicism. Among the fruits of Shirley's work as a schoolmaster, which preceded and followed his career as a dramatist, are several grammar texts. His first published work was the 1618 narrative poem *Eccho*, and his 1646 *Poems &c. by James Shirley* includes both witty verse and poetry in the Ovidian tradition. Shirley is remembered, however, primarily as a prolific playwright who dominated the Caroline stage.

In 1625, Shirley came to London and took up lodging in Gray's Inn. A favorite of Queen Henrietta Maria, he wrote during the next decade twenty-two of his thirty-one extant plays for Queen Henrietta's Men, Christopher Beeton's company at the Phoenix. When the theaters were closed in 1636 because of the plague, Shirley went to Ireland and stayed until 1640, writing plays and managing John Ogilby's St. Werburgh Street playhouse in Dublin.

This self-exile may have cost him the poet laureateship, which became vacant when Ben Jonson died in 1637 and was awarded the following year to William Davenant. Shirley returned to England in 1640 and succeeded Philip Massinger as principal playwright of the King's Men at Blackfriars. Only three of his plays for the company had been produced when the Puritans closed the theaters in 1642 and effectively ended his career as a dramatist. During his seventeen-year career he wrote more than forty comedies, tragedies, tragicomedies, and masques, primarily for the privileged audiences of London's private stages. Soon after the civil war began, Shirley fled with a patron, William Cavendish (later the duke of Newcastle), and fought against Oliver Cromwell for two years. When he came back to London about 1645, he resumed teaching, married for a second time (his first wife apparently having died), and continued to write occasional masques, grammar texts, and poetry. In the Great Fire of London, he and his wife, Frances, were severely burned and fled to St. Giles in the Fields, Middlesex, where they died on October 29, 1666.

Coming late in the golden age of Renaissance drama, Shirley was no innovator but wrote in the manner of his Elizabethan predecessors: the revenge tragedy of Thomas Kyd and John Webster, the city comedy of Thomas Dekker and Philip Massinger, the humors comedy of Ben Jonson, and the tragicomedy of Francis Beaumont and John Fletcher. His tragedies reflect the decadence of the serious drama of the period. His comedies, on the other hand, not only recall the past but also look forward to Restoration comedies of manners by George Etherege, William Wycherley, and William Congreve. Exploiting proven themes, devices, and character types of others while creating dramas uniquely his own, Shirley was largely responsible for the continued vitality of the Renaissance drama into the 1640's. His antilicentiousness links him to the Elizabethans more closely than to the Restoration playwrights, for though his plays are not homiletic, he rewards virtue and encourages reformation. In his realistic and urbane comedies of manners, which are peopled by recognizable types, he usually dramatizes the contrasting values of town, country, and court.

The Cardinal is one of his memorable works, a revenge tragedy echoing Webster's *The Duchess of Malfi* (pr. 1614), Kyd's *The Spanish Tragedy* (pr. c. 1585-1589), John Ford's *The Broken Heart* (pr. c. 1627-1631), and even William Shakespeare's *Hamlet, Prince of Denmark* (pr. c. 1600-1601). Like these antecedents, it includes the murder of a rival, support for the murderer by a Machiavellian villain, madness (feigned or real) as a result of grief, a play-within-a-play, and revenge as an obsessive motive.

His other noteworthy plays are the comedies *Hyde Park* and *The Lady of Pleasure*. The former probably premiered to coincide with the seasonal opening of Hyde Park, a favorite London gathering place and sporting center which recently had become a public facility. The three plots have a common device: A woman is pursued by two rivals, within the triangle her position changes unexpectedly, and the suitor surprisingly is unsuccessful. With its Enoch Arden motif, termagant woman, verbal sparring, and conversion of a lecher, *Hyde Park* is a lively portrait of Cavalier London. *The Lady of Pleasure* also is a highly entertaining, fast-paced comedy of manners about London's upper classes and their pastimes. Shirley develops in it variations on the theme of honor, and the play may be a commentary upon a Platonic love cult in the Caroline court. Perhaps because of its satire, the play was not popular with contemporary audiences, but later playwrights adapted plot elements, characters, and even dialogue from it for their use. Most notable is Richard Brinsley Sheridan's indebtedness in his 1777 *The School for Scandal*, whose Sir Peter and Lady Teazle are descendants of Shirley's Sir Thomas Bornwell and his wife, Aretina; the conceit of the scandal school also owes something to Shirley.

Perhaps the most telling measure of his success as a dramatist is the fact that Shirley, unlike most of his Renaissance predecessors and contemporaries, had the satisfaction of seeing his works revived successfully in the 1660's, though occasionally adapted and presented as if by current playwrights.

Gerald H. Strauss

Bibliography

Burner, Sandra A. *James Shirley: A Study of Literary Coteries and Patronage in Seventeenth Century England*. Lanham, Md.: University Press of America, 1988. This biography of Shirley focuses on the literary circles and patrons of the theater in seventeenth century England. Includes bibliography and index.

Clark, Ira. *Professional Playwrights: Massinger, Ford, Shirley, and Brome*. Lexington: University Press of Kentucky, 1992. Clark looks at English drama in the seventeenth century, focusing on Shirley, Philip Massinger, John Ford, and Richard Brome. Includes bibliography and index.

Lucow, Ben. *James Shirley*. New York: Twayne, 1981. Opening chapters on the dramatist's biography, masques, and nondramatic verse are followed by a chronological discussion of the plays. An excellent introduction to Shirley's drama combines plot summaries with pertinent background material and critical analyses. Contains a chronology of the author's life and a select bibliography of primary and secondary sources.

Sanders, Julie. *Caroline Drama: The Plays of Massinger, Ford, Shirley, and Brome*. Plymouth, England: Northcote House, in association with the British Council, 1999. Sanders examines the plays of Shirley as well as those of Philip Massinger, John Ford, and Richard Brome. Includes bibliography and index.

Zimmer, Ruth K. *James Shirley: A Reference Guide*. Boston: G. K. Hall, 1980. Zimmer annotates works by and about Shirley published through 1978. The secondary sources include bibliographies, books and articles, commentaries on Shirley within larger works, theses and dissertations, and poems in praise of the dramatist. Also includes a brief sketch of Shirley's life, a chronology of his extant works, and an overview of his dramatic career.

Viktor Shklovsky

Russian critic

Born: St. Petersburg, Russia; January 24, 1893
Died: Moscow, Soviet Union (now in Russia); December 8, 1984

NONFICTION: *Voskreshenie slova*, 1914 (criticism; *Resurrection of the Word*, 1972); *Svintsovyi zhrebii*, 1914 (criticism); *Rozanov*, 1921 (criticism; English translation, 1982); *Khod konia*, 1923 (criticism); *Literatura i kinematograf*, 1923 (criticism); *O teorii prozy*, 1925 (criticism; *Theory of Prose*, 1990); *Udachi i porazheniia Maksima Gorkogo*, 1926 (criticism); *Ikh nastoiashchee*, 1927 (criticism); *Motalka, knizhka ne dlia kinematografov*, 1927 (criticism); *Piat chelovek znakomykh*, 1927 (criticism); *Tekhnika pisatelskogo remesla*, 1927 (criticism); *Gamburgskii sche*, 1928 (criticism); *Material i stil v romane Lva Tolstogo "Voina i mir,"* 1928 (criticism); *Matvei Komarov, zhitel goroda Moskvy*, 1929 (biography); *Room, zhizn i rabota*, 1929 (biography); *Gornaia Gruziia: Pshaviia, Khevsuretiia, Mukheviia*, 1930 (travel sketch); *Podenshchina*, 1930 (criticism); *Poiski optimizma*, 1931 (criticism); *Kak pisat stsenarii*, 1931 (criticism); *Chulkov i Levshin*, 1933 (criticism); *Zametki o proze Pushkina*, 1937 (criticism); *Dnevnik*, 1939 (criticism); *O Maiakovskom*, 1940 (biography; *Mayakovsky and His Circle*, 1972); *Vstrechi*, 1944 (journalism); *Zametki o proze russkikh klassikov*, 1953 (criticism); *Za i protiv: Zametki o Dostoevskom*, 1957 (criticism); *Khudozhestvennaia proza: Razmyshleniia i razbory*, 1959 (criticism); *Lev Tolstoi*, 1963 (biography; *Lev Tolstoy*, 1978); *Zhili-byli*, 1964 (memoir); *Za sorok let: Stati o kino*, 1965 (criticism); *Staroe i novoe*, 1966 (criticism); *Povesti o proze: Razmyshleniia i razbory*, 1966 (criticism); *Tetiva: O neskhodstve skhodnogo*, 1970 (criticism); *Eizenshtein*, 1973 (biography); *Energiia zabliuzhdeniia: Kniga o siuzhete*, 1981 (criticism); *Za 60 let*, 1985 (criticism).

LONG FICTION: *Sentimentalnoe puteshestvie: Vospominaniia, 1917-1922*, 1923 (*A Sentimental Journey: Memoirs, 1917-1922*, 1970); *Zoo: Ili, Pisma ne o liubvi*, 1923 (*Zoo: Or, Letters Not About Love*, 1971); *Tretia fabrika*, 1926 (*Third Factory*, 1977); *Kratkaia no dostovernaia povest o dvorianine Bolotove*, 1930; *Zhitie arkhiereiskogo sluzhi*, 1931; *Kapitan Fedotov*, 1936; *Marko Polo*, 1936; *Povest o khudozhnike Fedotove*, 1955.

SHORT FICTION: *Minin i Pozharskii*, 1940; *O masterakh starinnykh, 1714-1812*, 1951; *Istoricheskie povesti i rasskazy*, 1958.

SCREENPLAYS: *Bukhta smerti*, 1926; *Krylia kholopa*, 1926; *Po zakonu*, 1926; *Predatel*, 1926 (with Lev Nikulin); *Prostitutka*, 1927; *Schastlivye cherepki*, 1927 (libretto); *Tretia meshchanskaia*, 1927 (with Abram Room); *Dva bronevika*, 1928; *Dom na trubnoi*, 1928 (with others); *Ivan da Maria*, 1928 (with Blanche Altshuler and V. Sirokov); *Kazaki*, 1928 (with Vladimir Barskii); *Kapitanskaia dochka*, 1928; *Ledianoi dom*, 1928 (with Georgiy Grebner and Boris Leonidov); *Ovod*, 1928 (with Konstantin Marzhanov); *Ukhaby*, 1928; *Poslednii attraktsion*, 1929; *Turksib*, 1929 (with Aleksandr Macheret, E. Aron, and V. Turin); *Ochen prosto*, 1931; *Mertvyi dom*, 1932; *Gorizont*, 1933; *Zhit*, 1933; *Zolotye ruki*, 1933; *Minin i Pozharskii*, 1939; *Alisher Navoi*, 1947; *Dalekaia nevesta*, 1948 (with E. Pomeshchikov and N. Rozhkov); *Chuk i Gek*, 1953; *Dokhunda*, 1957; *Kazaki*, 1961.

CHILDREN'S/YOUNG ADULT LITERATURE: *Puteshestvie v stranu kino*, 1926; *Nandu II*, 1928; *Turksib*, 1930; *Marko Polo, razvedchik*, 1931; *Skazka o teniakh*, 1931; *Zhizn khudozhnika Fedotova*, 1936; *Rasskaz o Pushkine*, 1937.

MISCELLANEOUS: *Sobranie sochinenii*, 1973-1974 (3 volumes); *Izbrannoe v dvukh tomakh*, 1983.

Because of the energy, imagination, and versatility manifested in his numerous writings, Viktor Borisovich Shklovsky (SHKLAWF-skee) won recognition as the most durable and possibly the most prominent critic and writer affiliated with the Russian Formalist movement. His father was a mathematics teacher of Jewish ancestry, and his mother was of Latvian descent; he was born in St. Petersburg on January 24, 1893, and was raised in a household which included an older half brother and a sister. Apparently even during his adolescent years, Shklovsky had a proclivity for literary disputation. He published a short article in 1908, and while he was enrolled at the University of St. Petersburg in 1913, problems of critical theory evidently interested him more than academic matters. In 1914, an important essay, *Resurrection of the Word*, appeared, which presented his assessment of the challenging new ideas advanced by Russian Futurist writers. In order to promote innovative approaches to art and literary style, he took a leading part in the formation of Opoyaz, a society for the study of poetic language.

During World War I Shklovsky enlisted in the army and served with Russian forces stationed in Galicia and Ukraine. For a time he also was employed in the capital as an instructor for armored car personnel. His political leanings led to complications after the Russian Revolution of 1917. In connection with his official duties, he spent time on the Austrian front and also in Iran; while in Petrograd, he took part in a plot to restore parliamentary government at the expense of the Bolshevik regime. Afterward, he escaped to Kiev, and upon his return he was exonerated of political charges.

In Petrograd, Shklovsky married Vasilisa Georgievna Kordi, who became the mother of his two children, Varvara and Nikita. Shklovsky assisted young writers, such as the Serapion brothers, and he became a member of Lef, an association of Futurist and Formalist authors. Once more to avoid arrest on political grounds, he emigrated and remained abroad for more than a year, first in Finland and then in Germany. In the autumn of 1923, under the terms of a general amnesty, he returned to his native country and settled in Moscow.

Highly idiosyncratic views of his personal travails during this period were presented in semiautobiographical works such as *A Sentimental Journey*, *Zoo*, and *Third Factory*, which have the appearance of novels but, because of their unusual patterns of narration and odd ways of designating the author's point of view, elude precise classification. Shklovsky's penchant for experimentation also was demonstrated in curious traits, such as the frequent use of one-sentence paragraphs. In places he employed an erratic mixture of high-sounding phrases and colloquial expressions.

In such major theoretical efforts as *Theory of Prose*, Shklovsky formulated distinctions which posed the criteria that he thought were important for literary analysis. Contending that fictional works should be understood in terms of form rather than content, he maintained that devices such as obstruction, parallelism, retardation, and contact were the essential elements of narrative writing. In arguing that the sum total of such means determined the nature and quality of literary works, Shklovsky posited an approach to criticism that, although supported by many examples, struck some readers as extreme and was viewed by others as a bold and innovative method. The notion of estrangement (*ostranenie*), which later was cited by many others in a variety of contexts, was probably the most influential of the conceptions that Shklovsky developed.

A sizable part of Shklovsky's writing had to do with the cinema, and he wrote many screenplays; his views about film were presented in theoretical works and biographical studies. Among the exemplars he cited as vital in the development of modern cultural ideas was Sergei Eisenstein, the director whose seemingly plotless techniques in some ways resembled Shklovsky's prose conceptions. At times he discussed other literary figures, both major and relatively little known, in the course of critical investigations that were meant to illustrate the interdependence of genres. Works dealing with historical figures were followed by fictional narratives that were set in past centuries.

During periods when, under Soviet premier Joseph Stalin, ideological constraints imposed severe limitations on the nature and scope of creative activity, Shklovsky turned to outwardly more innocuous forms of writing. In a 1930 newspaper article he renounced his earlier views in an effort to mollify critics in official circles. Nevertheless, when subsequently his memoir *Mayakovsky and His Circle* appeared, Shklovsky was taken to task for his positive stance toward Futurism. Concerns of a different sort also affected his life; during World War II, he served as a correspondent and furnished reports from areas where fighting had taken place. In February, 1945, his son Nikita was killed in action. Some time later, Shklovsky was divorced from his wife and was married to Serafima Gustavovna Narbut.

Although further difficulties with his literary efforts arose during the later years of Stalin's government, Shklovsky subsequently was honored as an important Soviet author. His biographical study *Lev Tolstoi*, which presented an extensive though somewhat uneven interpretation of the great writer, was well received. He was awarded the State Prize of the Soviet Union for his work on Sergei Eisenstein. The continuing vitality of Formalist conceptions in his thought was demonstrated in *Tetiva*, where he enlarged upon his earlier views to set forth a balanced version of his theories. Even during the last years of his life, further works as well as new editions of his writings appeared. At the time of Shklovsky's death, at the age of ninety-one, he was generally regarded as one of the most significant literary theorists of the twentieth century.

J. R. Broadus

Bibliography

Avins, Carol. "Emigration and Metaphor: Viktor Shklovsky, *Zoo: Or, Letters Not About Love* (1923)." In *Border Crossings: The West and Russian Identity in Soviet Literature, 1917-1934*. Berkeley: University of California Press, 1983. Historical and critical study; contains index and bibliography.

Crawford, Lawrence. "Viktor Shklovskii: *Différance* in Defamiliarization." *Comparative Literature* 36 (1984). One of the most celebrated tenets of Shklovsky's theories is considered.

Jackson, Robert Louis, and Stephen Rudy, eds. *Russian Formalism, a Retrospective Glance: A Festschrift in Honor of Victor Erlich*. New Haven, Conn.: Yale Center for International and Area Studies, 1985. Shklovsky's position in relation to that of other writers is discussed in several of the contributions.

Lary, N. M. *Dostoevsky and Soviet Film: Visions of Demonic Realism*. Ithaca, N.Y.: Cornell University Press, 1986. The relationship among fiction, criticism, and film in some of Shklovsky's endeavors is discussed in the first part of this work.

Ognev, Vladimir. "Viktor Shklovskii Teaches Us to Think." *Soviet Studies in Literature* 20, no. 1 (1983/1984). Sympathetic comments by a Soviet observer.

Riccomini, Donald R. "Defamiliarization, Reflexive Reference, and Modernism." *Bucknell Review* 25, no. 2 (1980). One of the most celebrated tenets of Shklovsky's theories is considered.

Smart, Robert Augustin. "Viktor Shklovsky and *Sentimental Journey*." In *The Nonfiction Novel*. Lanham, Md.: University Press of America, 1985. The unusual hybrid genre developed in Shklovsky's autobiographical novels is dealt with from the standpoint of this well-known work.

Steiner, Peter. *Russian Formalism: A Metapoetics*. Ithaca, N.Y.: Cornell University Press, 1984. Deals with theoretical issues.

Mikhail Sholokhov

Russian novelist

Born: Kruzhilino, Russia; May 24, 1905
Died: Kruzhilino, Soviet Union (now in Russia); February 21, 1984

LONG FICTION: *Tikhii Don*, 1928-1940 (partial translation as *And Quiet Flows the Don*, 1934, also known as *The Don Flows Home to the Sea*, 1940; complete translation as *The Silent Don*, 1942, also known as *And Quiet Flows the Don*, 1967); *Podnyataya tselina*, 1932, 1960 (translation of volume 1, *Virgin Soil Upturned*, 1935, also known as *Seeds of Tomorrow*, 1935; translation of volume 2, *Harvest on the Don*, 1960; complete translation as *Virgin Soil Upturned*, 1979); *Oni srazhalis za rodinu*, 1943-1944 (serial), 1971 (book; *They Fought for Their Country*, 1959); *Sud'ba cheloveka*, 1956-1957 (novella; *The Fate of a Man*, 1958).

SHORT FICTION: *Donskiye rasskazy*, 1926; *Lazorevaya Step*, 1926, 1931 (1931 edition includes *Donskiye rasskazy; Tales from the Don*, 1961); *Early Stories*, 1966.

MISCELLANEOUS: *Sobranie sochinenii*, 1956-1960 (8 volumes; *Collected Works in Eight Volumes*, 1984); *One Man's Destiny, and Other Stories, Articles, and Sketches, 1923-1963*, 1967; *At the Bidding of the Heart: Essays, Sketches, Speeches, Papers*, 1973.

Mikhail Aleksandrovich Sholokhov (SHOH-loh-kof), epic novelist of the Cossacks, was born in Kruzhilino, a small village near Veshenskaya on the river Don; he was the eighth child in the family. His father was a farmer, a cattle buyer, a clerk, and later the owner of a power mill. The family was of modest means, but the parents nevertheless managed to send the boy to school near Moscow. Sholokhov's mother, half Turkish and half Cossack, was an illiterate woman of strong determination; she learned to read and write in order to be able to correspond with her son while he was away at school.

Sholokhov, forced to leave his school at Voronezh because of the German invasion, returned to his home when he was fifteen. His plans to teach school upset by the revolution, he was assigned by the Bolsheviks to various jobs, among them assignments in a statistical bureau, as a freight handler, as a food inspector, and as a mason. In 1922, during bandit raids in the region, he participated in some of the fighting.

When he was eighteen he began to write for various newspapers and magazines, and he wrote some short fiction before beginning his long novel and eventual masterpiece, the Don Cossack tetralogy, which was translated into English as *And Quiet Flows the Don* and *The Don Flows Home to the Sea* before the whole was combined as *The Silent Don* in 1942. This monumental work, composed over a ten-year period, appeared in Russia in four separate volumes in 1928, 1929, 1933, and 1940. With the first volume of the novel, the author became famous. His analysis of the lives of the Cossacks, showing how history was forcing them into new social roles, became popular because it was an intimate portrait of realistic regional life. The novel expresses something of the power and dignity of the human beings whose lives it portrays. Ivan Dzerzhinsky, the Soviet composer, used the Don novels as the basis of a highly popular opera, and it was a successful film as well. Largely on the basis of this work, Sholokhov received the Stalin Prize in 1941. More than a million copies of the book were sold in the Soviet Union during its first year of publication, and before the fourth appeared, the novel had gone through seventy-nine editions, had been translated into thirty-eight languages, and had sold more than four and a half million copies.

Sholokhov's work on *The Silent Don* was not continuous. In 1932 he completed the first volume of a two-volume work, *Seeds of Tomorrow*; the second volume appeared in 1960. This novel, dealing with the building of a *kholkoz*, or collective farm, was also a great success in Russia and in other countries. Like the Don novel, it was filmed and made into an opera by Dzerzhinsky. It was also presented as a four-act play at the Simonov Studio Theatre. Until 1941, Sholokhov lived a quiet life in the Veshenskaya region, where he wrote, farmed, hunted, fished, and entertained his friends. When the Nazis invaded Russia in 1941, he became one of Russia's "fighting correspondents," settling in Moscow, where he lived until his death in 1984.

In 1937 he was elected a deputy to the Supreme Soviet. He was a member of the Academy of Sciences of the U.S.S.R. and of the Praesidium Union of Soviet Writers. In 1955, during an official state celebration of his fiftieth birthday, he received the Order of Lenin. He was married to Maria Petrovna and had four children. Sholokhov has been criticized as a Communist apologist, but most readers of his works agree in regarding him as an artist who managed to triumph over the propagandist. He is valued as an epical writer who portrayed a significant aspect of contemporary Russian life.

Vasa D. Mihailovich

Bibliography

Ermolaev, Herman. *Mikhail Sholokhov and His Art*. Princeton, N.J.: Princeton University Press, 1982. A study of Sholokhov's life and art, philosophy of life, and handling of style and structure, with a separate chapter on the historical sources of *The Quiet Don* and another on the question of plagiarism. Includes maps, tables (of similes), notes, and bibliography.

Klimenko, Michael. *The World of Young Sholokhov: Vision of Violence*. North Quincy, Mass.: Christopher Publishing House, 1972. The introduction discusses the Sholokhov canon as well as the man and his critics. Other chapters explore the genesis of his novels, his vision of life, his heroes, and his treatment of revolution. Includes a bibliography.

Medvedev, Roy. *Problems in the Literary Biography of Mikhail Sholokhov*. Cambridge, England: Cambridge University Press, 1977. A piercing examining of *The Quiet Don*, exploring the issue of Sholokhov's authorship and how it poses problems for his literary biography.

Muherjee, G. *Mikhail Sholokhov: A Critical Introduction*. New Delhi: Northern Book Center, 1992. A useful discussion of Sholokhov's work and critical reactions to it.

Murphy, A. B., V. P. Butt, and H. Ermolaev. *Sholokhov's "Tikhii Don": A Commentary in Two Volumes*. Birmingham, England: Department of Russian Language and Literature, the University of Birmingham, 1997. An excellent study of *The Silent Don*.

Stewart, David Hugh. *Mikhail Sholokov: A Critical Introduction*. Ann Arbor: University of Michigan Press, 1967. Found in most university libraries, this accessible, 250-page overview of the man and his works includes bibliographical references.

Joseph Henry Shorthouse

English novelist

Born: Birmingham, England; September 9, 1834
Died: Egbaston, near Birmingham, England; March 4, 1903

LONG FICTION: *John Inglesant*, 1880; *The Little Schoolmaster Mark*, 1883-1884; *Sir Percival*, 1886; *The Countess Eve*, 1888; *Blanche, Lady Falaise*, 1891.
SHORT FICTION: *A Teacher of the Violin, and Other Tales*, 1888.
NONFICTION: *On the Platonism of Wordsworth*, 1881.

As a child Joseph Henry Shorthouse, born into a Quaker family, developed a stammer that embarrassed him all his life. Because of that speech impediment he was, except for a brief stay at Tottenham College at the age of fifteen, educated by tutors at home. At the age of sixteen he entered his father's business, a manufacturing concern in Birmingham, where he proved quite successful. Although born a Quaker, he apparently had less sympathy for his parents' religion than for others. Throughout his life he evidenced an interest in spiritualism, and after his marriage to Sarah Scott in 1857 he became a convert to the Church of England.

An attack of epilepsy in 1862, while Shorthouse was still in his twenties, forced him to turn to literary study and writing, which afforded him the quiet, restful existence he needed. For ten years, from 1866 to 1876, Shorthouse worked on the novel *John Inglesant*. It lay in manuscript for three years before Shorthouse had it privately printed in 1880 for distribution to friends. At the suggestion of the writer Mrs. Humphry Ward, the work was published for the trade in 1881 and became very popular. Shorthouse went on to write other novels, though none was as successful as the first. He also wrote an essay, *On the Platonism of Wordsworth*, and a volume of stories, *A Teacher of the Violin, and Other Tales*. Shorthouse's *John Inglesant* aroused surprise at the time it first appeared, and it has remained an amazing work because of its vivid descriptions of Italy, a land the author did not know at first hand, and the quality of mysticism not ordinarily associated with writings by men of business.

Irene Struthers

Bibliography

Baker, Joseph Ellis. "Joseph Henry Shorthouse." In *The Novel and the Oxford Movement*. Reprint. New York: Russell & Russell, 1965.

Hutchinson, Joanne. "John Inglesant, Victorian Cavalier: History as Faith in the 1880's." *University of Hartford Studies in Literature* 13, no. 1 (1981).

Ryan, J. S. "Those Birmingham Quietists: J. R. R. Tolkien and J. H. Shorthouse (1834-1903)." *Minas Tirith Evening Star: Journal of the American Tolkien Society* 17, no. 3 (Fall, 1988).

Shorthouse, Sarah, ed. *The Life, Letters, and Literary Remains*. 2 vols. 1905. Reprint. London: Macmillan, 1976.

Wagner, F. J. *J. H. Shorthouse*. Boston: Twayne, 1979.

Dmitri Shostakovich

Soviet composer and memoirist

Born: St. Petersburg, Russia; September 25, 1906
Died: Moscow, Soviet Union (now in Russia); August 9, 1975

NONFICTION: *Testimony: The Memoirs of Dmitri Shostakovich*, 1979 (Solomon Volkov, editor; Antonia W. Bouis, translator); *Pisma k drugu*, 1993 (*Story of a Friendship: The Letters of Dmitry Shostakovich to Isaak Glikman, 1941-1975*, 2001).

Dmitri Dmitrievich Shostakovich (shahs-tuh-KOH-vihch) was one of the foremost Soviet composers of the twentieth century. His musical works include fifteen symphonies, three operas, eight string quartets, twenty-four preludes and fugues for piano, and sonatas and concertos for violin, viola, cello, and piano. This composer's prolificacy and genius survived Vladimir Lenin's October Revolution, Joseph Stalin's purges, a civil war, and two world wars. In his memoirs, dictated to and edited by Solomon Volkov, Shostakovich tells the story of his struggle between artistic pursuits and obligations to the Soviet state.

Shostakovich's father, Dmitri Boleslavovich, was a successful engineer and a talented amateur musician; his mother, Sofia Vasilyevna, was a pianist. The young Shostakovich spent many a musical evening with his parents and two sisters, and at the age of nine he began taking piano lessons from his mother. In 1919, in the midst of the Civil War, he began to attend the Petrograd Conservatory and to compose pieces for piano, strings, and orchestra. He wrote his first symphony when he was nineteen years old, in 1925, as his graduation composition from the conservatory, but his studies had been interrupted when his father died in 1922, at which point Shostakovich had helped support his family by playing the piano in silent-movie cinemas.

In *Testimony*, Shostakovich reminisces less about his family than about his teachers and moments spent at the conservatory. He recounts anecdotes about his involvements with such prominent members of the intelligentsia in the 1920's as the composer Sergei Prokofiev, the satirical writer Mikhail Zoshchenko, the famous avant-garde theater director Vsevolod Meyerhold, and Alexander Glazunov, the director of the conservatory and Shostakovich's beloved composition teacher. These artists were inspiring influences on the young composer, and they contributed to the vitality and relative freedom of artistic expression that marked the first half of that decade.

After Stalin's rise to power in 1924, the Communist Party ideologist Andrei Zhdanov began to impose increasing pressure on artists. As a result the 1930's and 1940's were years filled with hardship, fear, and political persecution for Shostakovich. He married Nina Varzar, a physicist, in 1932, and their first child, Galya, was born in 1936. That was also the year that Stalin attended a performance of Shostakovich's opera *Lady MacBeth*. The Soviet leader was incensed by the production, which recalled prison camps and portrayed characters with no hope or future. A damaging article titled "Muddle Instead of Music" immediately thereafter appeared in the official party newspaper, *Pravda*, through which Stalin denounced the composer's creation. Though Shostakovich, unlike many of his contemporaries, was never arrested, this event established the political and social climate that defined his artistic production. His entire career was ruled by the threat of arrest and the fear of displeasing the state leader. The composer tells of Stalin's anger with the praise that his Symphonies 7 and 8, his "war symphonies," attracted from the West. The Stalinist epithet used to condemn artists to life in the gulag was "formalist," and Shostakovich strove to compose music that would be invulnerable to this attack. At the same time, he realized the need to remain true to his musical self.

Shostakovich begins his memoirs by noting that they are less about him than about others; he ends his 277-page testimony by declaring that all public and political acts are lies and by observing that his life and those of his friends were sad and gray. By telling his story, he hopes to save young people from the disillusionment he suffered.

Shostakovich's official image was that of a proud Leninist who strove to meet the needs of socialist realism through his work. His work reflects ambiguity and duality: The Communist Party called upon him to represent the Soviet state with his musical compositions. However, he tried to survive in the deceptive, duplicitous, and unpredictable political system and also to maintain professional integrity, be true to his talents, and uphold his ideas on art. In *Testimony* Shostakovich contests his official conformist image and reveals scorn for the Soviet horrors and bitterness because of his personal ideological defeat. Although some critics have questioned the authenticity of these memoirs for being too much at variance with Shostakovich's previous words and deeds, others interpret what he dictated to Solomon Volkov as reflecting at least some of the composer's discouragement with the system in which he lived and worked.

Nirmala Singh

Bibliography

Bartlett, Rosamund, ed. *Shostakovich in Context*. New York: Oxford University Press, 2000. This volume presents research into Shostakovich's life and work by leading scholars and aims to place the composer in a variety of different contexts: musical, literary, and historical. The contributors are musicologists, Russian literature specialists, biographers, and cultural historians.

Fay, Laurel E. *Shostakovich: A Life*. New York: Oxford University Press, 2000. Life history of the composer includes a chronicle of his works.

Ho, Allan Benedict, and Dmitry Feofanov. *Shostakovich Reconsidered*. London: Toccata Press, 1998. Shostakovich's memoirs, *Testimony*, have been the subject of fierce debate since their 1979 publication. Ho and Feofanov systematically address the questions about *Testimony*'s authenticity, amassing much information about Shostakovich and his position in Soviet society and burying forever the picture of Shostakovich as a willing participant in the Communist charade. Includes a number of other essays.

MacDonald, Ian. *The New Shostakovich*. Boston: Northeastern University Press, 1990. A thorough biography with a chronology of the composer's life and political events of the time.

Norris, Christopher, ed. *Shostakovich: The Man and His Music*. Boston: M. Boyars, 1982. A set of essays that cover not only Shostakovich's music but also the mix of politics and creative expression that dominated his life.

Sollertinsky, Dmitri, and Ludmilla Sollertinsky. *Pages from the Life of Dmitri Shostakovich*. Translated by Graham Hobbs and Charles Midgley. New York: Harcourt Brace Jovanovich, 1980. Offers an intimate look at Shostakovich's life.

Elaine C. Showalter

American critic

Born: Cambridge, Massachusetts; January 21, 1941

NONFICTION: *A Literature of Their Own: British Women Novelists from Brontë to Lessing*, 1977, revised 1982; "Towards a Feminist Poetics," 1979; "Women's Time, Women's Space: Writing the History of Feminist Criticism," 1984; *The Female Malady: Women, Madness, and English Culture, 1830-1980*, 1985; *Sexual Anarchy: Gender and Culture at the Fin de Siècle*, 1990; *Sister's Choice: Tradition and Change in American Women's Writing*, 1991; *Hysteria Beyond Freud*, 1993 (with others); *Hystories: Hysterical Epidemics and Modern Culture*, 1997; *Inventing Herself: Claiming a Feminist Intellectual Heritage*, 2001; *Teaching Literature*, 2003.

EDITED TEXTS: *Women's Liberation and Literature*, 1971; *These Modern Women: Autobiographical Essays from the Twenties*, 1978; *The New Feminist Criticism: Essays on Women, Literature, and Theory*, 1985; *Alternative Alcott*, 1988; *Speaking of Gender*, 1989; *Little Women*, 1989 (Louisa May Alcott); *Modern American Women Writers*, 1993; *Daughters of Decadence: Women Writers of the Fin-de-Siècle*, 1993; *Where Are You Going, Where Have You Been*, 1994 (Joyce Carol Oates); *Ethan Frome*, 1996 (Edith Wharton); *Scribbling Women: Short Stories by Nineteenth Century American Women*, 1997.

Elaine Showalter's scholarship in literary criticism, history, Victorian literature, the English novel, and women's studies intersects to inform the sociocultural texts that have made her a key figure in the resurrection of forgotten women writers. Showalter has struggled to redefine literary periods and the recognized literary canon to include the contributions of women.

She was born Elaine Cottler to a father who had only an elementary-level education and a mother who was a frustrated housewife. Her eventual ideology was both an outgrowth of and reaction to her family background. She has cited her mother's empty, unhappy life as a source of her own feminism. Although her parents protested against her intellectual pursuits, Elaine attended and graduated Phi Beta Kappa from Bryn Mawr College in 1962. When she went on to earn her M.A. at Brandeis and announced her intention to marry English Showalter, who was not Jewish, her parents disowned her; Elaine married in 1963 and received her graduate degree in 1964. She went on to pursue a Ph.D. at the University of California, Davis, under the feminist Gwendolyn Needham, but she took time out to bear her first child, Vinca, in July, 1965. Her second child, Michael, was born in June, 1970, just after she had received her Ph.D.

Showalter's career began as a teaching assistant at the University of California, 1964-1966. When her husband was appointed assistant professor of French at Princeton University, Showalter became one of the first women to teach at Douglass College, the women's branch of Rutgers College. While there, between 1969 and 1978, she progressed from instructor to associate professor of English; in 1978 she was awarded full professorship and in 1983 distinguished professorship. In 1984 she left Douglass to become the Avalon Foundation Professor of English and Humanities at Princeton. Over the years, Showalter also served as visiting professor at a variety of institutions, including the University of Delaware, Dartmouth College, and Oxford University in England.

Showalter is a pioneer in women's studies and revisionist scholarship. In 1968 she became an active voice in the Princeton chapter of the National Organization for Women, whose presidency she assumed the following year. With her groundbreaking courses and scholarship, Douglass College became a center of women's studies and feminist scholarship.

Showalter's influence began to be felt most profoundly in the late 1970's with her publication of *A Literature of Their Own: British Women Novelists from Brontë to Lessing*, which identifies and analyzes the double standards applied to women's writing, and her 1979 article, "Towards a Feminist Poetics," wherein she coined the term "gynocritics" to refer to a way of bringing women's writings out of the periphery and into the center of literary study. She makes a clear distinction between woman-centered gynocritics and the political implications of feminist theory, which she sees as operating within a male-created paradigm. In revising literary history and notions of canonicity Showalter continues the momentum that begins with gynocritics and proceeds to the stage she identifies, using poststructuralist theories, as gynesic criticism (this term is drawn from Alice Jardin's 1985 book *Gynesis*). Showalter's alignment is with a French, feminist-inspired version of womanist thought; she suggests that, instead of creating an aesthetic in response to a male norm, a separate-but-equal tradition of women's writing be created. Showalter sees the beginning of such a tradition in learning to reread and subsequently value women's styles and forms as their own.

Showalter edited the first textbook on women in literature, the 1971 *Women's Liberation and Literature*; her book *A Literature of Their Own* is the first to chronicle a separate tradition of British women's writing; and her 1985 anthology *The New Feminist Criticism* compiles for the first time a collection of essays (from African American, lesbian, and French feminism points of view) that sketches the roots of feminist scholarship.

In *The Female Malady: Women, Madness, and English Culture, 1830-1980* Showalter examines the way in which women were diagnosed and treated throughout psychiatric history. In this analysis she unveils the gender biases of psychiatry and analyzes the resulting social and cultural implications. In her 1990 *Sexual Anarchy: Gender and Culture at the Fin de Siècle* she explores a theory she terms "endism" to critique those cultural and sexual crises that recur in the end of both the nineteenth and twentieth centuries. With her 1991 *Sister's Choice: Tradition and Change in American Women's Writing* Showalter shifts her focus to American literature, offering the metaphor of a "literary quilt" to discuss the common threads that make up a tradition of American women's writing and culture. In *Hysteria Beyond Freud* she offers a feminist response to the psychoanalytical theory. Showalter continues to be a formative voice in the study of women's literature, and her criticism has become a guide to the development of contemporary feminist theories. However, she did arouse enormous controversy with her 1997 work *Hystories*, a commentary on the mind-body relationship and psychosomatic illness, when she suggested that Gulf War syndrome, a diffuse collection of ailments plaguing veterans of the 1991 Gulf War, chronic fatigue syndrome, recovered memories of Satanic ritual abuse and alien abduction, and multiple personality disorder are psychosomatic reactions to Freudian hysteria rather than organic in origin. Chronic fatigue and Gulf War syndrome sufferers were particularly vocal, some going so far as to issue threats against Showalter. She, for her part, noted that this reaction merely proved her point that physiological disease is still "less demeaning" than psychological disorder.

Jill Hufnagel

Bibliography

Button, Warren. Review of *Hystories*, by Elaine C. Showalter. *Urban Education* 45 (March, 2000): 126-132. A review of Showalter's controversial work that summarizes the reaction to it as well as assessing the strengths and weaknesses of its arguments.

Davidson, Cathy N., and Linda Wagner-Martin, eds. *The Oxford Companion to Women's Writing in the United States*. New York: Oxford University Press, 1995. Showalter's wide-ranging impact on the study of literature is mentioned throughout this work.

Moi, Toril. *Sexual/Textual Politics: Feminist Literary Theory*. 2d ed. New York: Routledge, 2002. Positions Showalter's critical stance.

Myslobodsky, Michael S. "*Grand Hysterie* as Grand Mentor." *American Journal of Psychology* 112 (Spring, 1999): 158-166. A thorough review of *Hystories* by a psychologist.

Bapsi Sidhwa

American novelist

Born: Karachi, India (now in Pakistan); August 11, 1938
Identity: Pakistani American

LONG FICTION: *The Crow-Eaters*, 1978; *The Bride*, 1983; *Ice-Candy-Man*, 1988 (pb. in U.S. as *Cracking India*); *An American Brat*, 1993.

Bapsi Sidhwa (SIH-dwuh) invented English-language fiction in Pakistan. Unlike India, from which Pakistan was carved, the country had no established literary tradition in English. Urdu was the official language, and many would have preferred that the former colonizers' language disappear altogether.

Born into a wealthy family, Sidhwa spent her first seven years as an Indian citizen in the plains city of Lahore. In 1945, after India was divided, she became a Pakistani. The tremendous turmoil and bloodshed she observed as a child left its mark on Sidhwa, and later in her fiction she revived those powerful memories of Partition (as the division of India has come to be known). That she was born a Parsee also affected her writing. A Zoroastrian religious group of fewer than 200,000, the Parsees had long exerted enormous influence on the subcontinent through their business and professional standing. They also tended to be more Westernized than most of their fellow countrymen.

At age two, Sidhwa contracted polio, and she did not attend school until she was fourteen. Tutored at home in English, she read

British literature extensively, a practice that encouraged her to become a writer. Her parents, however, had other ideas, and at nineteen she entered an arranged marriage and soon bore three children. As an upper-class wife and mother, Sidhwa broke tradition by starting to write, even though she admitted in an interview that at first she wrote in secret. Otherwise her friends would have thought her "pretentious," she said: "After all, I was only a businessman's wife."

Her first novel, *The Bride*, was initiated by a story she heard during a family vacation in Pakistan's tribal regions in the Himalayas. A young woman had made an arranged marriage with a tribal man. Unable to cope with the harsh treatment accorded women in that society, she ran away, only to be pursued, then murdered by her husband and his relatives. Sidhwa felt compelled to tell this story, which to her symbolized the plight of many women on the subcontinent. A friend helped her to place the manuscript with an agent, who tried for seven years to find a publisher.

In the meantime Sidhwa wrote *The Crow-Eaters*, a boisterous and earthy account of the Parsee community in pre-Partition India. Although warned that Pakistan was too remote for international audiences to consider it interesting, Sidhwa eventually found a British publisher for the book. In 1983, *The Bride* was published in London, followed by American editions. While both novels were well received overseas and on the subcontinent, the closely knit Parsee community at first objected to *The Crow-Eaters*, condemning it as an irreverent portrayal of their customs, religious beliefs, and attitudes. Once Sidhwa had established herself internationally as an important writer, the Parsees, proud of one of their own, forgave her for treating them in a comic manner.

Divorced and remarried, Sidhwa moved to the United States during the early 1980's. In 1992 she became an American citizen and settled in Houston, Texas. Although far removed from the world of her childhood, soon after her arrival in America she began writing one of her finest works, *Ice-Candy-Man*. Sidhwa was seven when Partition came about, and violence erupted once millions of Muslims and Hindus were uprooted to turn Pakistan into an Islamic nation, India into a Hindu nation. The number of deaths has never been determined, but it is estimated that several hundred thousand died. Lahore, which had been assigned to Pakistan, witnessed some of the fiercest battles during this struggle for territory and possessions. In *Ice-Candy-Man* a seven-year-old female narrator recalls Lahore on the eve of Partition, then reveals the bloody aftermath of the political acts that brought about what she calls the "cracking" of India. Even though many Indian novelists in English have focused on Partition, Sidhwa's novel carries a greater immediacy—perhaps because she was there and was able four decades later to re-create that tumultuous period through a singular act of memory. In 1991 Sidhwa received the *Liberatur* Prize for *Ice-Candy-Man*, a yearly award given by Germany to a distinguished writer from a non-Western country.

In her next novel, *An American Brat*, Sidhwa depicts the Pakistani immigrant in America. She noted in an interview that she was partially attempting to define her own experiences and reactions as she herself worked to know a new country. The narrative follows Feroza, a Parsee girl from Lahore, through her uncertain start in the United States and her adjustments as a college student. Partially set in Pakistan, the novel also introduces Feroza's colorful family—her mother, in particular, who visits Colorado to break up a romance between Feroza and a non-Parsee. At the novel's conclusion, Feroza realizes there is no going back, and she accepts that even while retaining her roots in the Parsee community she has become the product of two cultures.

Sidhwa received in 1994 the Lila Wallace-Reader's Digest Fund Award of $105,000 for her fiction. This recognition proves that the Pakistani-Parsee experience, remote and foreign though it may be to the Western reader, carries universal significance when viewed through the eyes of a perceptive writer.

Robert L. Ross

Bibliography

Afzal-Khan, Fawzia. "Women in History." In *International Literature in English: Essays on the Major Writers*, edited by Robert L. Ross. New York: Garland, 1991. Examines the feminist stance in Sidhwa's work.

Daiya, Kavita. "'Honorable Resolutions': Gendered Violence, Ethnicity, and the Nation." *Alternatives: Global, Local, Political* 27 (April, 2002): 219-247. Looks at questions of gender, nationalism, and violence in the work of Sidhwa and Salman Rushdie.

Dhawan, R. K., and Novy Kapadia, eds. *The Novels of Bapsi Sidhwa*. New Delhi: Prestige Books, 1996. A collection of essays exploring Sidhwa's work.

Hai, Ambreen. "Border Work, Border Trouble: Postcolonial Feminism and the Ayah in Bapsi Sidhwa's *Cracking India*." *Modern Fiction Studies* 46 (Summer, 2000): 379-427. Focusing on feminisms in Sidhwa's novel, offers ways of reading the text and the problems it faces.

Jussawalla, Feroza, and Reed Way Dasenbrock. *Interviews with Writers of the Post-Colonial World*. Jackson: University Press of Mississippi, 1992. Contains an interview in which Sidhwa discusses, among other matters, the treatment of women in Pakistan and the role of the postcolonial novelist.

Sir Philip Sidney

English poet

Born: Penshurst, Kent, England; November 30, 1554
Died: Arnhem, the Netherlands; October 7, 1586

POETRY: *Astrophel and Stella*, 1591 (pirated edition printed by Thomas Newman), 1598 (first authorized edition); *Certaine Sonnets*, 1598; *The Psalmes of David, Translated into Divers and Sundry Kindes of Verse*, 1823 (with Mary Sidney Herbert, Countess of Pembroke); *The Complete Poems of Sir Philip Sidney*, 1873 (2 volumes); *The Poems of Sir Philip Sidney*, 1962 (William A. Ringler, Jr., editor); *The Psalms of Sir Philip Sidney and the Countess of Pembroke*, 1963 (J. C. A. Rathmell, editor).
LONG FICTION: *Arcadia*, 1590, 1593, 1598 (originally titled *The Countess of Pembroke's Arcadia*).
DRAMA: *The Lady of May*, pr. 1578 (masque); *Fortress of Perfect Beauty*, pr. 1581 (with Fulke Greville, Lord Brooke; Phillip Howard, the earl of Arundel; and Baron Windsor of Stanwell).
NONFICTION: *Defence of Poesie*, 1595 (also published as *An Apologie for Poetry*).
MISCELLANEOUS: *Miscellaneous Prose of Sir Philip Sidney*, 1973.

Philip Sidney's father, Sir Henry Sidney, was a member of a high-born family, and most of his near relatives were titled, but Sidney was poor throughout his life. He was a man of steadfast character, and his influence on English literature was that of a chivalrous, courtly poet, critic, and patron.

Sydney entered Shrewsbury School, near Ludlow Castle, in 1564 and from there was sent to Oxford in 1568; he also studied at Cambridge. Throughout his life Sidney was intensely interested in learning, and in 1572 he capped his formal education with an extended tour of Europe. By his peers he was generally recognized as a young man of charm, intelligence, and good judgment.

After his return to England in 1575 he remained at court until he was sent to Austria and Germany in 1577. While in England, he labored sedulously to defend his father's policies and position. By 1578 he was becoming known in the world of letters. In that year he wrote *The Lady of May*, a masque performed before Queen Elizabeth I, but his success at court was short-lived; he was forced to share the disgrace of the earl of Leicester, in whose affairs he had become involved. His virtual banishment to the home of his sister, the countess of Pembroke, may well have been a blessing, for it was there that he began writing *Arcadia* for his sister's amusement. This work, begun in 1580, was later revised and expanded.

After being permitted to return to court, Sidney wrote the great sonnet sequence *Astrophel and Stella*. The "Stella" in this largely autobiographical poetic narrative was Penelope Devereux, the daughter of the earl of Essex, who had intended her for Sidney. In 1581 she instead married Lord Rich, and, in serious play, Sidney's sonnets equate unfulfilled sexual desire with frustrated political ambition.

In 1583 Sidney was knighted, and in the same year he married Frances, the daughter of Sir Francis Walsingham. Before and during these events Sidney had been working on what was probably his most influential piece of writing, his *Defence of Poesie*, which set an almost wholly new set of standards for English poetry. By poesie Sidney meant any form of imaginative writing that inspired virtue by example.

Sidney was more than a courtier or literary figure; he was also a man of affairs. A champion of the Protestant cause in Europe, with his primary animosity directed against Spain, in 1585 he was given a command in Holland and made governor of Flushing. He engaged valiantly in several battles during that year. On September 22, 1586, he was severely wounded in a cavalry charge. The famous story is often told, as an example of Sidney's fine sense of humanity and chivalry, of how he refused a cup of water and ordered it to be given to a soldier near him on the battlefield. Sidney died of his wound on October 7, 1586. Following his death he was widely mourned and elegized.

Because none of his writing was actually published during his lifetime, most of Sidney's widespread influence was posthumous; nevertheless, it was considerable. The proto-novel *Arcadia*, although essentially a romance, achieves epic qualities and contains some richly developed passages. *Astrophel and Stella*, perhaps the most fully written sonnet sequence in English, rivals the subsequent sonnets of Edmund Spenser and William Shakespeare. With the writing of *Defence of Poesie* he injected moral and artistic standards into English literature. The influence of his genius was felt throughout English writing in the centuries that followed.

Gayle Gaskill

Bibliography

Berry, Edward I. *The Making of Sir Philip Sidney*. Toronto: University of Toronto Press, 1998. Explores how Sidney created himself as a poet by making representations of himself in the roles of some of his most literary creations, including *Astrophel and Stella* and the intrusive persona of *Defence of Poesie*.

Connell, Dorothy. *Sir Philip Sidney: The Maker's Mind*. Oxford, England: Clarendon Press, 1977. Considers Sidney's life and art in a biographical and historical context. Connell discusses in detail important historical influences on Sidney. Includes maps, a bibliography, and an index.

Garrett, Martin, ed. *Sidney: The Critical Heritage*. New York: Routledge, 1996. A collection of essays that gather a large body of critical sources on Sidney. Includes bibliographical references and index.

Hamilton, A. C. *Sir Philip Sidney: A Study of His Life and Works*. New York: Cambridge University Press, 1977. A study of Sidney's life, poetics, and selected works. General survey places his work in a biographical context. Includes an appendix, notes, a bibliography, and an index.

Kay, Dennis, ed. *Sir Philip Sidney: An Anthology of Modern Criticism.* Oxford, England: Clarendon Press, 1987. A collection of scholarly criticism. Kay's introduction places Sidney in a cultural heritage and surveys the changes that have occurred in the critical approaches to Sidney's work. Includes a chronology, a bibliography, an index, and a list of early editions.

Kinney, Arthur F., ed. *Essential Articles for the Study of Sir Philip Sidney.* Hamden, Conn.: Archon Books, 1986. A collection of twenty-five articles with a wide range of critical approaches. Topics include Sidney's biography, *The Lady of May*, *Defence of Poesie*, *Astrophel and Stella*, and *Arcadia*. Includes bibliography.

Sidney, Philip, Sir. *Sir Philip Sidney: Selected Prose and Poetry.* Edited by Robert Kimbrough. Madison: University of Wisconsin Press, 1983. Kimbrough gives detailed attention to *Defence of Poesie*, *Astrophel and Stella*, and *Arcadia.* Also surveys the critical approaches to Sidney. Contains a chronology and a select bibliography.

Sir Robert Sidney

English poet

Born: Penshurst Place, Kent, England; November 19, 1563
Died: Penshurst Place, Kent, England; July 13, 1626

POETRY: *The Poems of Robert Sidney*, 1984 (P. J. Croft, editor).

Sir Robert Sidney was the fifth of six children born to Sir Henry Sidney, of whom only three survived. The children's father was lord deputy of Ireland, and their uncle was Robert Dudley, earl of Leicester, who may have given his name to his nephew. His older brother, Sir Philip (1554-1586), and sister, Mary, countess of Pembroke (1561-1621), both distinguished themselves in letters and politics. The fertile ground that led to this productive mix was the family home at Penshurst Place.

Robert grew up with his father away much of the time attending to business in Ireland. He followed his elder brother to Christ Church, Oxford, where he studied classics, letters, mathematics, and sciences. After graduating, he traveled throughout Europe, again following Philip's lead. In each of these cases, the younger brother was the focused target of his brother's developing interest in education and the promotion of Protestantism. During his time at Oxford, Robert, along with all the Sidneys, made regular trips to the court of Queen Elizabeth I. The elder brother's politics became too extreme for the queen and had a moderately negative effect on the reception of both siblings at court for a time.

Robert Sidney married Barbara Gamage in 1584. The marriage was a largely strategic affair, much like that of his younger sister, Mary, who at fifteen married Henry Herbert, earl of Pembroke, who was then forty. Both marriages were seen as positive moves for the family. In Robert's case, this involved twelve children, all but two of whom survived. One of his daughters, Lady Mary Wroth, continued the family tradition of literary production.

One of the most significant factors in Robert's life was his father's support of his career. At the time, it was usual for family monies to go to the eldest son's pursuits, but Henry Sidney seems to have been committed to the education of both of his surviving sons. Robert's trip through Europe was part of a necessary training for a life in politics. During his time abroad, Robert became familiar with the new movements in Renaissance humanist thought and gained knowledge of several foreign languages. Upon his return, Robert entered Parliament in 1585.

Later that same year both Robert and Philip went to Flushing, Holland, where they fought against Spain. At the Battle of Zutphen, Sir Philip received injuries that led to his death ten days later. His younger brother, Robert, was knighted for his performance during the same battle and became head of the Sidney household at Penshurst Place upon his brother's passing. Owing partly to his and his brother's performance on the battlefield in Holland, Sir Robert was named governor of Flushing (1589-1616). From that point, Robert Sidney's career continued to develop. He later became Baron Sidney (1603), Viscount De L'Isle (1605), and earl of Leicester (1618). Much of his work in the world of politics would involve the careful negotiation of the tensions surrounding various forms of Protestant factionalism and its rejection or acceptance at home and abroad. A highlight of this work came when he acted as an ambassador to Henri IV of France in ensuring proper treatment of Protestants under Henri's rule. Sidney died at Penshurst in Kent on July 13, 1626.

Sir Robert Sidney's body of work is small in one respect and large in another. He did not publish any of his poetry during his lifetime, though it did circulate among family and friends. However, the discovery in 1973 of his notebook has provided scholars with the single largest collection of poetry from the Elizabethan period. This ninety-page book is in the form of a sonnet cycle, with thirty-five numbered sonnets, twenty-four separately numbered poems or songs, and seven unnumbered poems. The manuscript is dedicated to his sister, the countess of Pembroke. Given the state of the manuscript, with its author's notes and corrections, scholars believe it is most likely an incomplete draft, which would later have been sent out for publication.

Patrick Finn

Bibliography

Croft, P. J., ed. *Autograph Poetry in the English Language: Facsimiles of Original Manuscripts from the Fourteenth to the Twentieth Century.* 2 vols. New York: McGraw-Hill, 1973. Includes Croft's introduction, commentary, and transcripts.

_______. *The Poems of Robert Sidney.* New York: Oxford University Press, 1984. This volume is edited from the poet's autograph notebook, found by Croft in 1973. It is the largest single collection of original Tudor poetry in existence. Includes an introduction and commentary by Croft.

Hay, Millicent V. *The Life of Robert Sidney, Earl of Leicester (1563-1626).* London: Associated University Presses, 1984. Hay's biography of the poet includes genealogical tables, a bibliography, index, and an interesting account of Sidney's life as poet and politician.

Jonson, Ben. "To Penhurst." In *The Complete Poems*, by Ben Jonson. Edited by George Parfitt. New York: Penguin Books, 1996. In this tribute, Jonson acknowledges Robert Sidney's contribution as poet and patron of the arts through an examination of Penshurst Place. This form of tribute based on a physical place went on to become a popular literary form. For more on this see Parker (below).

Kelliher, W. Hilton, and Katherine Duncan-Jones. "A Manuscript of Poems by Robert Sidney: Some Early Impressions." *British Library Journal* 1 (1975): 107-144. A textual and bibliographic analysis of the find made by Croft (see above).

Parker, Tom W. N. *Proportional Form in the Sonnets of the Sidney Circle: Loving in Truth.* Oxford, England: Clarendon Press, 1998. Parker traces the relationship of poetic form to contemporary thinking about astrological matters in the love poetry of Robert and Philip Sidney as well as several of their contemporaries.

Warkentin, Germaine. "Robert Sidney's 'Darcke Offrings': The Making of a Late Tudor Manuscript *Canzoniere*." *Spenser Studies* 12 (1992): 37-73. An aesthetic appreciation of the work of Robert Sidney that argues against the characterization of the poems as "Darcke Offrings" and for their consideration alongside the works of his famous brother.

Henryk Sienkiewicz

Polish novelist

Born: Wola Okrzejska, Poland; May 5, 1846
Died: Vevey, Switzerland; November 15, 1916

LONG FICTION: *Na marne*, 1872 (*In Vain*, 1899); *Szkice węglem*, 1877; *Ogniem i mieczem*, 1884 (*With Fire and Sword: An Historical Novel of Poland and Russia*, 1890); *Potop*, 1886 (*The Deluge: An Historical Novel of Poland, Sweden, and Russia*, 1891); *Pan Wołodyjowski*, 1887-1888 (*Pan Michael: An Historical Novel of Poland, the Ukraine, and Turkey*, 1893); *Bez dogmatu*, 1891 (*Without Dogma*, 1893); *Rodzina Połanieckich*, 1895 (*Children of the Soil*, 1895); *Quo vadis*, 1896 (*Quo Vadis: A Narrative of the Time of Nero*, 1896); *Krzyżacy*, 1900 (*The Knights of the Cross*, 1900; also known as *The Teutonic Knights*, 1943); *Na polu chwały*, 1903-1905 (*On the Field of Glory*, 1906); *W pustyni i w puszczy*, 1911 (*In Desert and Wilderness*, 1912); *Dzieła*, 1948-1955 (60 volumes).

SHORT FICTION: *Yanko the Musician, and Other Stories*, 1893 (includes "Yanko the Musician" and "The Lighthouse Keeper of Aspinwall"); *Lillian Morris, and Other Stories*, 1894; *Hania*, 1897 (includes "Tartar Captivity"); *Let Us Follow Him, and Other Stories*, 1898; *For Daily Bread, and Other Stories*, 1898; *Sielanka: A Forest Picture, and Other Stories*, 1898; *Life and Death, and Other Stories*, 1904; *Tales*, 1931; *Western Septet: Seven Stories of the American West*, 1973; *The Little Trilogy*, 1995.

NONFICTION: *Listy z podróży do Ameryki*, 1876-1878 (serial), 1896 (book; *Portrait of America: Letters*, 1959); *Listy z Afryki*, 1891.

Poland's greatest novelist was born on May 5, 1846, near Lukow, in Russian Poland, of a family that belonged to the country gentry. Educated by a tutor who shared his interest in history with his charge, Henryk Adam Alexander Pius Sienkiewicz (shehn-KYEHV-eech) attended the University of Warsaw. There, as one of the Young Positivist admirers of Auguste Comte, he became convinced that all knowledge can be observed through the human senses, including not only colors and sounds but also their interrelationship. Although he and the other Positivists did not follow their master in scorning the microscope as an attempt to peer beyond human observation, they were interested in the how, rather than the why, of changes. This group largely revolutionized Poland's literary life following the 1863 revolt against Russia. Then, and throughout his life, Sienkiewicz was noted for his hatred of Russia.

Motivated by his anti-Russian feelings as well as by a spirit of adventure, he emigrated from Poland as a member of a socialistic colony that settled at Anaheim, near Los Angeles. He remained in the United States until 1878, studying the life of Polish immigrants and sending articles back to newspapers in Warsaw. The differences in culture between Poland and the United States, as well as the unwillingness of his fellow colonists to cooperate, brought failure to the project. Sienkiewicz returned to Warsaw to make his living as a journalist.

Reading Sir Walter Scott and Alexandre Dumas inspired him to do something similar for his own land. Discarding his Positivist theories, he began a trilogy dealing with seventeenth century Poland as it tried to establish national unity through wars with the Swedes, Turks, and Cossacks. In *With Fire and Sword*, *The Deluge*, and *Pan Michael*, the central character, Zagloba, has been likened to Falstaff and to Ulysses because of his combination of heroism and buffoonery.

Interested also in psychology and modern social problems, Sienkiewicz wrote about contemporary Poland in *Without Dogma* and *Children of the Soil*. After these works he apparently realized that his real talent lay in the romantic field, for he returned to the manner of his earlier successes and in *Quo Vadis* re-created in colorful detail Roman life under Nero. The most well-developed character in the novel is the epicure Petronius Arbiter. Since one of the purposes of Sienkiewicz's writing was "to strengthen the heart and to help maintain the Polish national spirit," he included in his Roman picture two Polish countrymen, the heroine Lygia and the giant Ursus. The popularity of the novel was enormous. Translated into thirty languages, it is undoubtedly the best-known work of Polish literature, far better known than the same author's four-volume *The Knights of the Cross* (also known as *The Teutonic Knights*). The narrowness of Sienkiewicz's intellectual sympathies is frequently blamed for some of the flaws in this and his other novels, yet his ability to write with dash and fire has never been questioned; his award of the Nobel Prize in Literature in 1905 was universally acclaimed.

Because of his literary status and his anti-Russian sentiments, Sienkiewicz was frequently sought by patriots to lead them in their movement for the liberation of Poland. During World War I, he and the pianist Ignacy Paderewski organized a committee to help Polish war victims. While working for the Polish Red Cross in Switzerland, Sienkiewicz died at Vevey on November 15, 1916. In 1924 his body was taken to Cracow, former capital of Poland, for burial in the ancient cathedral.

Bibliography

Coleman, Arthur Prudden, and Marion Moore Coleman. *Wanderers Twain: Modjeska and Sienkiewicz—A View from California*. Cheshire, Conn.: Cherry Hill Books, 1964. A study of the trip Sienkiewicz and Helena Modjeska made to Anaheim, California, in 1876. Most useful for the student of Sienkiewicz's fiction are the chapters on his early years in Poland.

Giergielewicz, Mieczyslaw. *Henryk Sienkiewicz*. New York: Twayne, 1968. This introductory volume begins with a section on historical background, as Sienkiewicz's fiction is tied so closely to the fate of Poland and of Central Europe in the eighteenth and nineteenth centuries. There are also chapters on his life, his experience as a journalist, his tales, and his epic novels. Includes a chronology, notes, and an annotated bibliography.

_______. *Henryk Sienkiewicz: A Biography*. New York: Hippocrene, 1991. An excellent source for information on Sienkiewicz's life and times.

Krzyanowski, Jerzy R. "Sienkiewicz's Trilogy in America." *The Polish Review* 41 (1996): 337-49. A good example of well-informed scholarship on Sienkiewicz's fiction.

Leslie Marmon Silko

American poet and novelist

Born: Albuquerque, New Mexico; March 5, 1948
Identity: American Indian (Laguna and Plains)

POETRY: *Laguna Woman: Poems*, 1974.
LONG FICTION: *Ceremony*, 1977; *Almanac of the Dead*, 1991; *Gardens in the Dunes*, 1999.
SHORT FICTION: *Yellow Woman*, 1993.
DRAMA: *Lullaby*, pr. 1976 (with Frank Chin).
NONFICTION: *The Delicacy and Strength of Lace: Letters Between Leslie Marmon Silko and James Wright*, 1986; *Sacred Water: Narratives and Pictures*, 1993; *Yellow Woman and a Beauty of the Spirit: Essays on Native American Life Today*, 1996; *Conversations with Leslie Marmon Silko*, 2000 (Ellen L. Arnold, editor).
MISCELLANEOUS: *Storyteller*, 1981 (includes poetry and prose).

Leslie Marmon Silko, one of the most acclaimed writers of the American Indian literary renaissance of the 1970's, was reared on the Laguna Pueblo Reservation, in the house where her father, Lee H. Marmon, had been born. During her childhood she spent much time with her great-grandmother, A'mooh, who lived next door. A'mooh and Silko's Aunt Susie, Mrs. Walter K. Marmon, were among the people who taught her the Laguna traditions and stories that became the principal resource for her poetry and fiction. Silko's family background included Laguna, Mexican, Plains Indian, and white ancestors. Her great-grandfather, Robert Gunn Marmon, was a trader who had been elected to one term as governor of the pueblo. Nevertheless, the family, which lived at the edge of the village, occupied a marginal place in the community. After attending schools in Laguna and Albuquerque, she went on to the University of New Mexico, where she graduated in 1969 with a B.A. magna cum laude in English. She entered law school and attended three semesters before deciding to devote herself to writing. Silko taught at Navajo Community College, Many Farms, Arizona; at the University of New Mexico; and at the University of Arizona. For a time she was married to an attorney, John Silko, with whom she had two sons, Robert and Cazimir.

In Silko's first book, *Laguna Woman*, she set out many of the themes she developed in her later work. Laguna myth, culture, and ceremony are embodied in the contemporary experience of these poems, as in "Prayer to the Pacific," where she refers to one of the Laguna creation myths: "Thirty thousand years ago/ Indians came riding across the ocean/ carried by giant sea-turtles." The poem conveys a cyclic concept of nature, in which the ocean separates, but also connects, the landmass of North America and China. In her novel *Ceremony* the central character, Tayo, a veteran of World War II, remembers refusing to kill a Japanese soldier, who looked like his uncle, Josiah. Weather patterns in the Philippine jungles and at Laguna are also shown to be related to one another and to the people living in these places. Other poems, such as "When Sun Came to River Woman," reveal nature as both the setting and the result of copulation. Human intercourse, the rain and sun, and the ceremonial songs are all necessary in the bringing of new life; they are interconnected and interdependent. An essential part of Tayo's recovery in *Ceremony* is his relationship with T'seh Montano, a medicine woman who revives his sexuality and teaches him how to use and protect medicinal plants growing in the natural locale.

In *Ceremony* the prose narrative, set in the aftermath of World War II, is juxtaposed with ancient myths, told in centered verse. The nonchronological prose narrative is told in segments with many flashbacks, similar to the structure of N. Scott Momaday's *House Made of Dawn* (1969). The nearly five-hundred-year existence of Laguna at its present location has made it possible for Silko to write out of a cultural tradition intricately tied to the natural environment. Yet it is a place that suffered severe trauma in the second half of the twentieth century. The atom bomb was developed at nearby Los Alamos, and the first atom bomb exploded just 150 miles from Laguna. In the early 1950's the Anaconda Company opened a large, open-pit uranium mine on Laguna land. The danger of nuclear war is a central concern in *Ceremony*. Tayo comes to understand that this threat could have the effect of uniting all the world's people into one clan again.

Silko collected her short fiction, nonfiction prose, and poetry, including the poems from *Laguna Woman* and the centered verse in *Ceremony*, in *Storyteller*. The selections in the book vary greatly in content and form, from the directly autobiographical poetry at the beginning to the title piece, "Storyteller," which is set in Alaska, and "Lullaby," the story of a Navajo woman who, like most Native Americans, has suffered cultural and personal losses. Out of these diverse selections emerges the central idea that all live in relation to the earth, and that the individual's physical, mental, and spiritual survival depends on an awareness of that relationship.

In 1991 Silko published the novel *Almanac of the Dead*, which she had begun with a MacArthur Foundation grant awarded in 1983. This sprawling, complicated work is a combination of revisionist history and fiction. Unlike *Ceremony*, with its limited setting, *Almanac of the Dead* takes place throughout the New World; the many characters roam over four hundred years and thousands of miles. As does all of her work, however, this one explores connectedness in the midst of fragmentation, both among people and with the earth.

Gardens in the Dunes takes place at the turn of the twentieth century and contrasts the lives and cultures of Native Americans and Europeans. It also, however, illustrates the planting of the seeds that produce the culture of late twentieth century Americans of all ethnic backgrounds, especially of feminism. Her main character, Indigo, a Sand Lizard Indian, begins at her birthplace on the California-Arizona border and travels throughout Europe as the companion to an upper-class Victorian family.

After the poet James Wright wrote a letter to Silko in August, 1978, praising *Ceremony* as "one of the four or five best books" he had read about America, a correspondence ensued between them that lasted until Wright's death in March, 1980, and which was published in 1986 as *The Delicacy and Strength of Lace*. These letters reveal Silko's spontaneity and talent; perhaps more important, they chronicle a literary friendship between a white, male, mainstream poet and a Native American female writer. Dialogues such as theirs prepare the way for the long overdue acceptance of the Native American contributions to American literature.

Norma C. Wilson
Kelly C. Walter

Bibliography

Allen, Paula Gunn. "The Feminine Landscape of Leslie Marmon Silko's *Ceremony*." In *Studies in American Indian Literature: Critical Essays and Course Design*. New York: Modern Language Association of America, 1983. Analyzes the main characters of *Ceremony* and the causes for Tayo's illness from a Jungian perspective. Gives a brief and helpful bibliography of Silko's work and of criticism about her fiction. Also discusses her poetry and the storyteller tradition that underpins her fiction.

Barnett, Louise K., and James L. Thorson, eds. *Leslie Marmon Silko*. Albuquerque: University of New Mexico Press, 1999. A collection of critical essays on the entire range of Silko's work through *Almanac of the Dead*, this text offers biographical information on Silko as well as an extensive bibliography of primary and secondary sources complete with a helpful bibliographical essay.

Chavkin, Allan, ed. *Leslie Marmon Silko's "Ceremony": A Casebook*. New York: Oxford University Press, 2002. Fourteen essays offer readings of Silko's novel from a variety of theoretical perspectives and provide background information on Native American culture.

Graulich, Melody, ed. *"Yellow Woman": Leslie Marmon Silko*. New Brunswick, N.J.: Rutgers University Press, 1993. An important addition to Silko scholarship, this collection of critical essays contains a great deal of useful background information on the Yellow Woman myth so central to Silko's *Storyteller* collection. In addition, it gathers some of the most influential Silko scholarship.

Jaskoski, Helen. *Leslie Marmon Silko: A Study of the Short Fiction*. New York: Twayne, 1998. A thorough critical study of Silko's short fiction, touching upon the roles of women, Native Americans, and the Southwest as they figure in her work. Includes a bibliography and an index.

Palmer, Linda. "Healing Ceremonies: Native American Stories of Cultural Survival." In *Ethnicity and the American Short Story*, edited by Julie Brown. New York: Garland Publishing, 1997. Shows how the structure, image, and theme of Silko's story "Lullaby," from *Storyteller*, exemplifies the recurring Native American theme of ceremony, song, story, and memory as a means of cultural survival against the dominant society.

Ramirez, Susan Berry Brill de. "Storytellers and Their Listener-Readers in Silko's 'Storytelling' and 'Storyteller.'" *The American Indian Quarterly* 21 (Summer, 1997): 333-335. Discusses the role of the listener-reader in American Indian literature; discusses the "transformational" relationship between a storyteller and listener-readers in Silko's stories "Storyteller" and "Storytelling."

Salyer, Greg. *Leslie Marmon Silko*. New York: Twayne, 1997. A useful overview of Silko's life and work prior to *Gardens in the Dunes*. Good chronology and bibliography.

Seyersted, Per. *Leslie Marmon Silko*. Boise, Idaho: Boise State University Press, 1980. A good critical study of Silko's work; includes a bibliography.

Studies in American Indian Literatures (SAIL) 2, no. 10 (Fall, 1998). Special issue on *Almanac of the Dead*. Includes excellent essays as well as Ellen Arnold's interview, in which Silko discusses *Gardens in the Dunes*.

Wiget, Andrew. *Native American Literature*. Boston: Twayne, 1985. Offers an overview analysis of *Ceremony* and *Storyteller*.

Frans Eemil Sillanpää

Finnish novelist

Born: Hämeenkyrö, Finland, Russian Empire (now in Finland); September 16, 1888
Died: Helsinki, Finland; June 3, 1964

LONG FICTION: *Elämä ja aurinko*, 1916; *Hurskas kurjuus*, 1919 (*Meek Heritage*, 1938); *Nuorena nukkunut*, 1931 (*The Maid Silja*, 1933; also known as *Fallen Asleep While Young*, 1939); *Miehen tie*, 1932; *Ihmiset suviyössä*, 1934 (*People in the Summer Night*, 1966); *Elokuu*, 1941; *Ihmiselon ihanuus ja kurjuus*, 1945.

SHORT FICTION: *Ihmislapsia elämän saatossa*, 1917; *Rakas isänmaani*, 1919; *Enkelten suojatit*, 1923; *Hiltu ja Ragnar*, 1923 (novelette); *Maan tasalta*, 1924; *Töllinmäki*, 1925; *Rippi*, 1928; *Kiitos hetkistä, Herra*, 1930; *Virran pohjalta*, 1933; *Viidestoista*, 1936; *Erään elämän satoa*, 1948.

NONFICTION: *Poika eli elämäänsä*, 1953; *Kerron ja kuvailen*, 1955; *Päivä korkeimmillaan*, 1956.

Frans Eemil Sillanpää (SIHL-ahn-pah), winner of the Nobel Prize in Literature in 1939, began life as a peasant's son in the Finnish town of Hämeenkyrö, September 16, 1888. As a child he displayed a great aptitude for science; consequently he was sent to the Imperial Alexander University at Helsingfors. There he found more excitement in the company of writers, artists, and musicians (including the composer Jean Sibelius) than he did in the laboratory. As a result of this new interest, he faced a great emotional crisis. Having decided that his vocation was writing, he left the university without taking his examinations for a degree and returned home on Christmas Eve of 1913. After that time his interests followed no other course.

He published his first novel in 1916 and in that same year married a servant girl with whom he would have seven children. His second novel, *Meek Heritage*, concerned with the clash of the Reds and the Whites in the Finnish Revolution, won him fame in his country and a government pension for life. Translated into a number of languages, the novel also helped to establish his international reputation. *The Maid Silja*, published in 1931, was equally popular at home and abroad. In 1936 Sillanpää was made an honorary doctor of philosophy by the Finnish government. Three years later he became the first Finn to be awarded a Nobel Prize.

Bibliography

Ahokas, Jaakko. *A History of Finnish Literature*. Bloomington: Indiana University, Research Center for the Language Sciences, 1973.

Crouse, Timothy. "Past Present." *The Nation*, October 1, 1990.

Kinneavy, Gerald. "Sillanpää." *Scandinavica: An International Journal of Scandinavian Studies* 20 (November, 1981).

Laitinen, Kai. "F. E. Sillanpää, Life and Sun: The Writer and His Time." *Books from Finland* 22, no. 2 (1988).

Paddon, Seija. "The De-Centered Subject in F. E. Sillanpää's Short Fiction." *Scandinavica: An International Journal of Scandinavian Studies* 29 (November, 1990).

Stark, Tuula. "Frans Eemil Sillanpää." In *The Nobel Prize Winners: Literature*, edited by Frank N. Magill. Vol. 2. Englewood Cliffs, N.J.: Salem Press, 1987.

Alan Sillitoe

English novelist, playwright, and poet

Born: Nottingham, England; March 4, 1928

LONG FICTION: *Saturday Night and Sunday Morning*, 1958; *The Loneliness of the Long-Distance Runner*, 1959 (novella); *The General*, 1960; *Key to the Door*, 1961; *The Death of William Posters*, 1965; *A Tree on Fire*, 1967; *A Start in Life*, 1970; *Travels in Nihilon*, 1971; *The Flame of Life*, 1974; *The Widower's Son*, 1976; *The Storyteller*, 1979; *Her Victory*, 1982; *The Lost Flying Boat*, 1983; *Down from the Hill*, 1984; *Life Goes On*, 1985; *Out of the Whirlpool*, 1987; *The Open Door*, 1989; *Last Loves*, 1990; *Leonard's War*, 1991; *Snowstop*, 1993; *The German Numbers Woman*, 1999; *Birthday*, 2001.

SHORT FICTION: *The Ragman's Daughter*, 1963; *A Sillitoe Selection*, 1968; *Guzman Go Home, and Other Stories*, 1968; *Men, Women, and Children*, 1973; *The Second Chance, and Other Stories*, 1981; *The Far Side of the Street*, 1988; *Collected Stories*, 1995; *Alligator Playground: A Collection of Short Stories*, 1997.

DRAMA: *All Citizens Are Soldiers*, pr. 1967 (adaptation of Lope de Vega; with Ruth Fainlight); *Three Plays*, pb. 1978.

SCREENPLAYS: *Saturday Night and Sunday Morning*, 1960 (adaptation of his novel); *The Loneliness of the Long-Distance Runner*, 1961 (adaptation of his novella); *Che Guevara*, 1968; *The Ragman's Daughter*, 1974 (adaptation of his novel).

POETRY: *Without Beer or Bread*, 1957; *The Rats, and Other Poems*, 1960; *A Falling out of Love, and Other Poems*, 1964; *Shaman, and Other Poems*, 1968; *Love in the Environs of Voronezh, and Other Poems*, 1968; *Poems*, 1971 (with Ted Hughes and Ruth Fainlight); *Barbarians, and Other Poems*, 1974; *Storm: New Poems*, 1974; *Snow on the North Side of Lucifer*, 1979; *More Lucifer*, 1980; *Sun Before Departure*, 1984; *Tides and Stone Walls*, 1986; *Collected Poems*, 1993.

NONFICTION: *The Road to Volgograd*, 1964; *Raw Material*, 1972; *Mountains and Caverns: Selected Essays*, 1975; *The Saxon Shore Way: From Gravesend to Rye*, 1983 (with Fay Weldon); *Nottinghamshire*, 1986 (with David Sillitoe); *Every Day of the Week*, 1987; *Leading the Blind: A Century of Guidebook Travel, 1815-1914*, 1996; *Life Without Armor*, 1996.

CHILDREN'S/YOUNG ADULT LITERATURE: *The City Adventures of Marmalade Jim*, 1967; *Big John and the Stars*, 1977; *The Incredible Fencing Fleas*, 1978; *Marmalade Jim at the Farm*, 1980; *Marmalade Jim and the Fox*, 1984.

Alan Sillitoe (SIHL-ih-toh) is one of England's best writers of proletarian fiction and the spokesperson for the English working class of the 1950's and 1960's. He was born in Nottingham, England, the setting for much of his fiction. The son of Sylvia and Christopher Sillitoe, the latter a tannery worker, he grew up in the slums. Through his family's struggle for survival during the economic depression of the 1930's, he gained the subject matter and the political beliefs that found expression in his work. Though an avid student, he left school at fourteen and between 1942 and 1946 worked in a bicycle plant, then in a plywood mill, and later as a lathe operator. He worked as a controller at the Langar Airfield in Nottingham before serving with the Royal Air Force (RAF) in Malaya in 1947 and 1948. After his stint with the RAF, he married an American woman.

While in Malaya, Sillitoe began writing, but he destroyed the poems, short stories, and first draft of a novel that he completed while recuperating from tuberculosis. In 1949, following his convalescence, he returned to Nottingham and then traveled to France and Majorca, where he met and became friends with the influential British poet and mythologist Robert Graves, who urged him to write about what he knew best: Nottingham. *Saturday Night and Sunday Morning* was awarded the Authors' Club Prize as the best English first novel of 1958; the following year, Sillitoe won the Hawthornden Prize for *The Loneliness of the Long-Distance Runner*. The Nottingham novels and books of poetry that followed his initial success reflect his leftist political views, which were also the subject of *The Road to Volgograd*, a topographical and ideological journey to Russia.

After 1970, Sillitoe completed his Nottingham trilogy and, while returning sporadically to his Nottingham settings, would use more diverse settings (including Antarctica in *The Lost Flying Boat*). He has also experimented with narrative strategies (as in *The Storyteller* and *Down from the Hill*). He is one of the first British stylists to use "metafiction." Despite the change in setting and style, Sillitoe's fiction has remained consistent in his criticism of the English establishment and of capitalism generally, though increasingly his focus has been on the individual rather than society. *The Widower's Son*, for example, attests the failure of the human heart to survive society's conditioning and to sustain human relationships.

Sillitoe's reputation rests on his Nottingham novels and short stories, with their proletarian protagonists, their struggle between the authority figures and the working class, and their condemnation of social and political institutions. Sillitoe's early protagonists, Smith in *The Loneliness of the Long-Distance Runner* and Arthur Seaton of *Saturday Night and Sunday Morning*, embrace their working-class status and refuse to bow to a coercive and alienating society. Their behavior is at odds with the ambitious social climbing of Joe Lampton, the working-class hero of *Room at the Top* (1957), by John Braine, with whom Sillitoe is often compared. With *Key to the Door*, however, Sillitoe's switch of protagonists meant a new focus—the plight of the working-class intellectual with literary interests in a repressive society (the tie to Sillitoe is obvious). When Brian Seaton refuses to fire on the Malayan communists, his action is overtly political. Similarly, Frank Dawley, the protagonist of Sillitoe's trilogy (*The Death of William Posters*, *A Tree on Fire*, and *The Flame of Life*), joins the struggle to free Algeria from colonialism and learns to channel his anger into a worthwhile course of action. These decisions are both personal and political.

Some of Sillitoe's later fiction (*Out of the Whirlpool* and a few of the stories included in *The Second Chance, and Other Stories*) are set in Nottingham and do involve the working class, but Sillitoe has extended his range and become more concerned with style. *Life Goes On*, a sequel to *A Start in Life*, continues the earlier novel's account of the improbable adventures of lower-class outcasts, but it becomes more focused on literary technique and incorporates a novel-within-a-novel. The same concern with metafiction occurred earlier in *The Storyteller*, which depicts a working-class protagonist who tells stories to survive. As the protagonist's stories begin to merge with his life, Sillitoe allegorically poses questions about the nature and motivation of the writer/creator. *Down from the Hill*, a memory novel, depicts the storyteller-protagonist first as an apolitical youth, then as a politicized screenwriter. *The Widower's Son*, on the other hand, concerns a more mainstream subject, the institutionalizing of the human heart.

Though *The Widower's Son* and *Her Victory* seem closely related to the work of D. H. Lawrence, another Nottingham writer with an underprivileged background, it is only in the later novels that Sillitoe has been able to get any Lawrentian distance from his subject, so closely has he been tied to his characters in the past. In fact, he has been associated with the "angry young men" of the generation of John Osborne. Despite his movement from the Nottingham working-class jungle to a more inclusive English society, a more detached stance, and a less overtly political subject matter, Sillitoe will be remembered as the proletarian novelist of the 1950's and the 1960's, the spokesperson whose career parallels the rise of the New Left in England. His style is poetic, and had he not written fiction so appropriate to his time, he certainly would be remembered for his several books of poems.

Thomas L. Erskine
John Jacob

Bibliography

Atherton, Stanley S. *Alan Sillitoe: A Critical Assessment.* London: W. H. Allen, 1979. This study approaches Sillitoe as primarily a political novelist interesting for his diagnosis of British society's ills and his vision of revolution.

Hanson, Gillian Mary. *Understanding Alan Sillitoe.* Columbia: University of South Carolina Press, 1999. A useful volume of Sillitoe criticism and appreciation.

Hitchcock, Peter. *Working-Class Fiction in Theory and Practice: A Reading of Alan Sillitoe.* Ann Arbor, Mich.: UMI Research Press, 1989. A good examination of the writer's themes and execution.

Kalliney, Peter. "Cities of Affluence: Masculinity, Class, and the Angry Young Man." *Modern Fiction Studies* 47 (Spring, 2001): 92-117. Studies the class element in Sillitoe's work and the way in which gender dynamics illustrate class dynamics.

Leonardi, Susan J. "The Long-Distance Runner (the Loneliness, Loveliness, Nunliness of)." *Tulsa Studies in Women's Literature* 13 (Spring, 1994): 57-66. An intertextual examination of how Grace Paley's "The Long-Distance Runner" and Sara Maitland's "The Loveliness of the Long-Distance Runner" rewrite Sillitoe's "The Loneliness of the Long-Distance Runner."

Penner, Allen Richard. *Alan Sillitoe.* Boston: Twayne, 1972. A useful midcareer overview of Sillitoe's work. Penner offers a short biography and a helpful bibliography. The discussion covers Sillitoe's poetry and fiction.

Sawkins, John. *The Long Apprenticeship: Alienation in the Early Work of Alan Sillitoe.* New York: P. Lang, 2001. A semiotic reading of Silltoe's work.

Ignazio Silone
(Secondo Tranquilli)

Italian novelist

Born: Pescina dei Marsi, Italy; May 1, 1900
Died: Geneva, Switzerland; August 22, 1978

LONG FICTION: *Fontamara*, 1930, 1933, revised 1958 (English translation, 1934, revised 1960); *Pane e vino*, 1937, revised 1955 (as *Vino e pane*; first pb. as *Brot und Wein*, 1936; *Bread and Wine*, 1936, revised 1962); *Il seme sotto la neve*, 1942 (first pb. as *Der Samen unterm Schnee*, 1941; *The Seed Beneath the Snow*, 1942); *Una manciata di more*, 1952 (*A Handful of Blackberries*, 1953); *Il segreto di Luca*, 1956 (*The Secret of Luca*, 1958); *La volpe e le camelie*, 1960 (*The Fox and the Camellias*, 1961).
SHORT FICTION: *Viaggio a Parigi: Novelle*, 1993 (first pb. as *Die Reise nach Paris*, 1934; *Mr. Aristotle*, 1935).
DRAMA: *La scuola dei dittatori*, pb. 1938 (*The School for Dictators*, 1938); *Ed egli si nascose*, pb. 1944 (*And He Did Hide Himself*, 1946); *L'avventura di un povero cristiano*, pb. 1968 (*The Story of a Humble Christian*, 1971).
NONFICTION: *Uscita di sicurezza*, 1965 (essays; *Emergency Exit*, 1968).
MISCELLANEOUS: *Romanzi e saggi*, 1998-1999 (2 volumes).

Ignazio Silone (see-LOH-nay), who was born in the Appenine Mountains of the Abruzzi district, dropped his real name, Secondo Tranquilli, to save his family from Fascist persecution. Born the son of a small landowner, he became active in the labor movement as a young boy. In 1917, as secretary for the land workers of the Abruzzi district, he was charged with organizing an antiwar demonstration. In 1921 he joined and became secretary of the Italian Communist Party, and in 1922 he began to contribute, with Antonio Gramsci, to the paper *L'Unita*. He was also the editor of a daily newspaper in Trieste. Even after Benito Mussolini's rise to power, Silone continued to print illegal newspapers and carry out other assignments. After his trip to Moscow in 1927 he became disillusioned with Communism and broke with the Communist Party in 1930. By 1932 one of his brothers had died in a Fascist prison, and Silone had been imprisoned and then expelled from various European countries.

Taking up residence in Switzerland in 1930, he set to work on his first novel, *Fontamara*, in which he describes the systematic destruction by the Black Shirts of a small Italian town that has attempted to resist the Fascists. A propagandistic novel that is nevertheless powerful and affecting, it ends with a plea for action against the scourge. *Bread and Wine*, perhaps Silone's finest book, tells the story of Pietro Spina, a revolutionist who returns to his native Abruzzi district for refuge while trying to regain his health. Disguised as a priest, he finds the best aspects of his youthful religiousness returning. In carrying out his undercover work he achieves a kind of regeneration as he attempts to fuse the best of Christianity and Marxism. *The School for Dictators* was a book of satiric dialogues against Fascism. His third novel, *The Seed Beneath the Snow*, followed the further activities of Pietro Spina among the peasants and small landowners of Silone's native district. (In 1944 Silone published a drama based on the activities of Pietro Spina, *And He Did Hide Himself.*) With the Allied invasion of Italy, Silone slipped back into Italy disguised as a priest and spent the remainder of the war as a member of the underground.

At the war's end he became manager of the newspaper *Avanti!* and, as a member of the Constituent Assembly, he participated in drawing up the new Italian constitution. In 1952, two years after retiring from political life to devote himself to literature, Silone published *A Handful of Blackberries*. This powerful novel, set in postwar Italy, was the story of a former Communist's attempt to break with the Party, despite its retributory attempts against him and his sweetheart, and to resume his work for the peasants against the great landowners. During his final years Silone was active in Italian and international writers' associations while continuing to write. His last writings include a philosophical tale, *The Secret of Luca*; a political tale, *The Fox and the Camellias*; and a play, *The Story of a Humble Christian*, which deals with the life of Celestine V, who abdicated the papacy in 1294.

Sandra Carletti

Bibliography

Krieger, Murray. "Ignazio Silone: The Failure of the Secular Christ." In *The Tragic Vision: Variations on a Theme in Literary Interpretation*. New York: Holt, Rinehart and Winston, 1960. This is a probing study of *Bread and Wine*.

Mooney, Harry J., Jr., and Thomas F. Staley, eds. *The Shapeless God: Essays on Modern Fiction*. Pittsburgh: University of Pittsburgh Press, 1968. See chapter 2, "Ignazio Silone and the Pseudonyms of God." This is chiefly a study of *Bread and Wine*, but there are illuminating references to Silone's other novels as well.

Origo, Iris. *A Need to Testify: Portraits of Lauro de Bosis, Ruth Draper, Gaetano Salvemini, Ignazio Silone and an Essay on Biography*. New York: Books & Company/Helen Marx Books, 2002. A penetrating portrait of the writer by a distinguished biographer. Includes notes but no bibliography.

Paynter, Maria Nicolai. *Ignazio Silone: Beyond the Tragic Vision*. Buffalo, N.Y.: University of Toronto Press, 2000. Critical study focuses on Silone's use of symbolism. Includes bibliography and index.

Scott, Nathan A., Jr. "Ignazio Silone: Novelist of the Revolutionary Sensibility." In *Rehearsals of Discomposure: Alienation and Reconciliation in Modern Literature: Franz Kafka, Ignazio Silone, D. H. Lawrence, T. S. Eliot*. New York: Columbia University Press, 1952. Scott offers a wide-ranging overview of Silone's fiction in the context of European literature.

Slonim, Marc. Afterword to *Bread and Wine*, by Ignazio Silone. New York: New American Library, 1963. A useful introduction to the novel, explaining the circumstances in which it was written, analyzing its characters, the author's politics, and Silone's artistic achievement.

Georges Simenon

Belgian novelist and short-story writer

Born: Liège, Belgium; February 13, 1903
Died: Lausanne, Switzerland; September 4, 1989

LONG FICTION: *Pietr-le-Letton*, 1931 (*The Strange Case of Peter the Lett*, 1933; also known as *Maigret and the Enigmatic Lett*, 1963); *M. Gallet, décédé*, 1931 (*The Death of Monsieur Gallet*, 1932; also known as *Maigret Stonewalled*, 1963); *Le Pendu de Saint-Pholien*, 1931 (*The Crime of Inspector Maigret*, 1933; also known as *Maigret and the Hundred Gibbets*, 1963); *Le Charretier de la "Providence,"* 1931 (*The Crime at Lock 14*, 1934; also known as *Maigret Meets a Milord*, 1963); *La Tête d'un homme*, 1931 (*A Battle of Nerves*, 1939); *Le Chien jaune*, 1931 (*A Face for a Clue*, 1939; also known as *Maigret and the Yellow Dog*, 1987); *La Nuit du carrefour*, 1931 (*The Crossroad Murders*, 1933; also known as *Maigret at the Crossroads*, 1964); *Un Crime en Hollande*, 1931 (*A Crime in Holland*, 1940); *Au rendez-vous des terreneuves*, 1931 (*The Sailors' Rendezvous*, 1940); *La Danseuse du Gai-Moulin*, 1931 (*At the "Gai-Moulin,"* 1940); *La Guinguette à deux sous*, 1931 (*The Guinguette by the Seine*, 1940); *Le Relais d'Alsace*, 1931 (*The Man from Everywhere*, 1941); *Le Passager du "Polarlys,"* 1932 (*The Mystery of the "Polarlys,"* 1942; also known as *Danger at Sea*, 1954); *Le Port des brumes*, 1932 (*Death of a Harbour Master*, 1941); *L'Ombre chinoise*, 1932 (*The Shadow in the Courtyard*, 1934; also known as *Maigret Mystified*, 1964); *L'Affaire Saint-Fiacre*, 1932 (*The Saint-Fiacre Affair*, 1940; also known as *Maigret Goes Home*, 1967); *Chez les Flamands*, 1932 (*The Flemish Shop*, 1940); *Le Fou de Bergerac*, 1932 (*The Madman of Bergerac*, 1940); *Liberty Bar*, 1932 (English translation, 1940); *L'Écluse numéro un*, 1932 (*The Lock at Charenton*, 1941); *Les Gens d'en face*, 1933 (*The Window over the Way*, 1951); *La Maison du canal*, 1933 (*The House by the Canal*, 1948); *Les Fiançailles de M. Hire*, 1933 (*Mr. Hire's Engagement*, 1956); *Le Coup de lune*, 1933 (*Tropic Moon*, 1942); *Le Haut Mal*, 1933 (*The Woman in the Gray House*, 1942); *L'Homme de Londres*, 1934 (*Newhaven-Dieppe*, 1942); *Le Locataire*, 1934 (*The Lodger*, 1943); *Les Suicidés*, 1934 (*One Way Out*, 1943); *Maigret*, 1934 (*Maigret Returns*, 1941); *Quartier Nègre*, 1935; *Les Demoiselles de Concarneau*, 1936 (*The Breton Sisters*, 1943); *Faubourg*, 1937 (*Home Town*, 1944); *Le Blanc à lunettes*, 1937 (*Talatala*, 1943); *L'Assassin*, 1937 (*The Murderer*, 1949); *Chemin sans issue*, 1938 (*Blind Alley*, 1946); *L'Homme qui regardait passer les trains*, 1938 (*The Man Who Watched the Trains Go By*, 1945); *Monsieur la Souris*, 1938 (*The Mouse*, 1950); *Les Inconnus dans la maison*, 1940 (*Strangers in the House*, 1951); *Il pleut, bergère . . .*, 1941 (*Black Rain*, 1949); *Le Voyageur de la Toussaint*, 1941 (*Strange Inheritance*, 1950); *La Veuve Couderc*, 1942 (*Ticket of Leave*, 1954; also known as *The Widow*, 1955); *Oncle Charles s'est enfermé*, 1942 (*Uncle Charles Has Locked Himself In*, 1987); *L'aîné des Ferchaux*, 1945 (*Magnet of Doom*, 1948); *La Fuite de Monsieur Monde*, 1945 (*Monsieur Monde Vanishes*, 1967); *Le Clan des Ostendais*, 1947 (*The Ostenders*, 1952); *Lettre à mon juge*, 1947 (*Act of Passion*, 1952); *Maigret à New York*, 1947 (*Maigret in New York's Underworld*, 1955); *La Neige était sale*, 1948 (*The Snow Was Black*, 1950; also known as *The Stain in the Snow*, 1953); *Les Vacances de Maigret*, 1948 (*Maigret on Holiday*, 1950; also known as *No Vacation for Maigret*, 1953); *Maigret et son mort*, 1948 (*Maigret's Special Murder*, 1964); *Pedigree*, 1948 (English translation, 1962); *La Première Enquête de Maigret*, 1949 (*Maigret's First Case*, 1958); *Mon Ami Maigret*, 1949 (*My Friend Maigret*, 1956); *Le Fond de la bouteille*, 1949 (*The Bottom of the Bottle*, 1954); *Les Fantômes du chapelier*, 1949 (*The Hatter's Ghosts*, 1956); *Les Quatre Jours du pauvre homme*, 1949 (*Four Days in a Lifetime*, 1953); *Les Volets verts*, 1950 (*The Heart of a Man*, 1951); *Maigret et la vieille dame*, 1950 (*Maigret and the Old Lady*, 1958); *L'Amie de Mme Maigret*, 1950 (*Madame Maigret's Own Case*, 1959; also known as *Madame Maigret's Friend*, 1960); *Les Mémores de Maigret*, 1951 (*Maigret's Memoirs*, 1963); *Maigret au "Picratt's,"* 1951 (*Maigret in Montmartre*, 1954); *Maigret en meublé*, 1951 (*Maigret Takes a Room*, 1960); *Maigret et la grande perche*, 1951 (*Maigret and the Burglar's Wife*, 1969); *Une Vie comme neuve*, 1951 (*A New Lease on Life*, 1963); *Maigret, Lognon, et les gangsters*, 1952 (*Inspector Maigret and the Killers*, 1954; also known as *Maigret and the Gangsters*, 1974); *Le Revolver de Maigret*, 1952 (*Maigret's Revolver*, 1956); *Maigret et l'homme du banc*, 1953 (*Maigret and the Man on the Bench*, 1975); *Maigret a peur*, 1953 (*Maigret Afraid*, 1961); *Maigret se trompe*, 1953 (*Maigret's Mistake*, 1954); *Antoine et Julie*, 1953 (*The Magician*, 1955); *Feux rouges*, 1953 (*The Hitchhiker*, 1955); *Crime impuni*, 1954 (*The Fugitive*, 1955); *Le Grand Bob*, 1954 (*Big Bob*, 1954); *Les Témoins*, 1954 (*The Witnesses*, 1956); *Maigret à l'école*, 1954 (*Maigret Goes to School*, 1957); *Maigret et la jeune morte*, 1954 (*Maigret and the Dead Girl*, 1955); *Maigret chez le ministre*, 1954 (*Maigret and the Calame Report*,

1969); *Maigret et le corps sans tête*, 1955 (*Maigret and the Headless Corpse*, 1967); *Maigret tend un piège*, 1955 (*Maigret Sets a Trap*, 1965); *Les Complices*, 1955 (*The Accomplices*, 1964); *En cas de malheur*, 1956 (*In Case of Emergency*, 1958); *Un Échec de Maigret*, 1956 (*Maigret's Failure*, 1962); *Maigret s'amuse*, 1957 (*Maigret's Little Joke*, 1957); *Maigret voyage*, 1958 (*Maigret and the Millionaires*, 1974); *Les Scrupules de Maigret*, 1958 (*Maigret Has Scruples*, 1959); *Dimanche*, 1958 (*Sunday*, 1960); *Maigret et les témoins récalcitrants*, 1959 (*Maigret and the Reluctant Witnesses*, 1959); *Une Confidence de Maigret*, 1959 (*Maigret Has Doubts*, 1968); *Maigret aux assises*, 1960 (*Maigret in Court*, 1961); *Maigret et les vieillards*, 1960 (*Maigret in Society*, 1962); *L'Ours en peluche*, 1960 (*Teddy Bear*, 1971); *Betty*, 1961 (English translation, 1975); *Le Train*, 1961 (*The Train*, 1964); *Maigret et le voleur paresseux*, 1961 (*Maigret and the Lazy Burglar*, 1963); *Maigret et les braves gens*, 1962 (*Maigret and the Black Sheep*, 1976); *Maigret et le client du samedi*, 1962 (*Maigret and the Saturday Caller*, 1964); *La Porte*, 1962 (*The Door*, 1964); *Les Anneaux de Bicêtre*, 1963 (*The Patient*, 1963; also known as *The Bells of Bicêtre*, 1964); *Maigret et le clochard*, 1963 (*Maigret and the Bum*, 1973); *La Colère de Maigret*, 1963 (*Maigret Loses His Temper*, 1964); *Maigret et le fantôme*, 1964 (*Maigret and the Apparition*, 1975); *Maigret se défend*, 1964 (*Maigret on the Defensive*, 1966); *La Chambre bleue*, 1964 (*The Blue Room*, 1964); *Le Petit Saint*, 1965 (*The Little Saint*, 1965); *La Patience de Maigret*, 1965 (*The Patience of Maigret*, 1966); *Maigret et l'affaire Nahour*, 1966 (*Maigret and the Nahour Case*, 1967); *Le Confessional*, 1966 (*The Confessional*, 1968); *La Mort d'Auguste*, 1966 (*The Old Man Dies*, 1967); *Le Chat*, 1967 (*The Cat*, 1967); *Le Voleur de Maigret*, 1967 (*Maigret's Pickpocket*, 1968); *Maigret à Vichy*, 1968 (*Maigret in Vichy*, 1969); *Maigret hésite*, 1968 (*Maigret Hesitates*, 1970); *L'Ami de l'enfance de Maigret*, 1968 (*Maigret's Boyhood Friend*, 1970); *La Prison*, 1968 (*The Prison*, 1969); *La Main*, 1968 (*The Man on the Bench in the Barn*, 1970); *Novembre*, 1969 (*November*, 1970); *Maigret et le tueur*, 1969 (*Maigret and the Killer*, 1971); *Maigret et le marchand de vin*, 1970 (*Maigret and the Wine Merchant*, 1971); *La Folle de Maigret*, 1970 (*Maigret and the Madwoman*, 1972); *Maigret et l'homme tout seul*, 1971 (*Maigret and the Loner*, 1975); *Maigret et l'indicateur*, 1971 (*Maigret and the Informer*, 1972); *La Disparition d'Odile*, 1971 (*The Disappearance of Odile*, 1972); *La Cage de verre*, 1971 (*The Glass Cage*, 1973); *Les Innocents*, 1972 (*The Innocents*, 1973); *Maigret et Monsieur Charles*, 1972 (*Maigret and Monsieur Charles*, 1973).

SHORT FICTION: *Les 13 coupables*, 1932 (*The Thirteen Culprits*, 2002); *Les Dossiers de L'Agence O*, 1943; *Nouvelles exotiques*, 1944; *Les Nouvelles Enquêtes de Maigret*, 1944 (*The Short Cases of Inspector Maigret*, 1959).

NONFICTION: *Le Roman de l'homme*, 1958 (*The Novel of Man*, 1964); *Quand j'étais vieux*, 1970 (*When I Was Old*, 1971); *Lettre à ma mère*, 1974 (*Letter to My Mother*, 1976); *Mémoires intimes*, 1981 (*Intimate Memoirs*, 1984); *Mes Apprentissages: Reportages, 1931-1946*, 2001.

Georges Joseph Christian Simenon (see-muhn-awn), the master of the contemporary psychological novel, is perhaps best known for his detective stories featuring Inspector Maigret, but he also became internationally celebrated for his other novels, which—like the Maigret works—deal with guilt and innocence, flight and return, and the search for home.

Simenon's parents were a mismatched couple; his father was a petit bourgeois accountant whose values were at complete variance with those of his wife. The contrast between his parents' values is reflected in Simenon's stories, which often depict the narrowness and hypocrisy of middle-class values and the appeal of working-class honesty. Simenon dropped out of school at the age of sixteen to help augment the family income. After finding that he was inept at manual work, he became a successful reporter. His writing career was fully launched by the time he was seventeen years old, when he wrote his first novel. At this time he also began writing fiction pieces for Paris journals. Although Simenon himself was not certain of the extent of his enormous body of fiction, it has been estimated to be more than four hundred books and more than two thousand short stories.

Simenon began writing thrillers and romances for an audience of shop girls and secretaries, but he soon found that his greatest strength lay in the detective story. Inspector Jules Maigret made his debut in *Maigret and the Enigmatic Lett* in 1931. Intuitive, fatherly, as much against the inhumane criminal justice system as against crime itself, Maigret proved an instant success. Over the next four years, Simenon produced about twenty novels featuring this popular pipe-smoking detective before turning to "straight" novels, many of which were also well received. By the late 1930's, Maigret fans were mourning the lack of new Maigret novels, and Simenon felt compelled to satisfy the public. In 1939, he began a new series of Maigret stories, and he continued writing them along with other novels for the rest of his career. At about the time he began the new series, he was divorced from his first wife and married Denise Ouimet, a French Canadian. The second group of Maigret novels features Simenon's experiences in the United States and even includes episodes in which Maigret collaborates with the American police. In the early 1970's, Simenon gave up writing novels entirely; one of his late works, *Intimate Memoirs*, is an account of the events that led to the suicide of his daughter, Mary-Georges, in 1978.

Like Graham Greene, Simenon divided his works into two categories, the "Maigrets" and the serious novels. Although the author declared that novels should be short enough to be read in one sitting, his serious "romans durs" often run to three or four hundred pages of action, reflections, and careful settings for his social "dropouts." Violent action is central to Simenon's fiction and is brought on by revolt against an intolerable situation. Both the author and his detective, Maigret, realize that the seeds of violence are within all human beings and need only a fatal moment to be triggered. Simenon tended to work by closeting himself for a week or more and living "inside the skin" of his main character until the tale was complete.

Maigret is a very human detective, subject to error; in fact, he is most often blinded by his own desire to believe in innocence and Eden. In *Maigret and the Old Lady*, for example, he is deceived by the woman's childlike femininity; in *Maigret at the Crossroads*, he at first sees openness and innocence, and his unwillingness or inability to look past the surface causes damage. He escapes the dark world of crime by returning to an ideal wife, an orderly and familiar Paris apartment, and the comforting aroma of a French kitchen.

What makes the novels memorable is not their characters, which are sometimes sketchily developed, or their themes, which lack variety, but Simenon's detailed observation, which makes these novels so realistic that they could easily serve the sociologist as well as the fiction reader. Nearly every conceivable milieu within the French social structure is reproduced in most minute detail—the details of ordinary houses of prostitution, furniture factories, shipping firms, petit bourgeois and haute bourgeois households, fishing vessels, and boardinghouses. Many novels take place in exotic settings, and Simenon prepared himself for his descriptions of Africa, Central America, and Asia by traveling around the world. He believed that people are essentially the same but that their lives and destinies are determined by their environments. The evocative use of the concrete permeates all the novels, giving Simenon the reputation of a novelist of ambience. Simenon's major contribution to literature may well be in the detective field. He has joined the hard-boiled American school of detective fiction with the more descriptive British school to create an enactment of the ritual of crime and investigation that is both realistic and mythic.

Janet McCann
Lucy Golsan

Bibliography

Assouline, Pierre. *Simenon: A Biography.* Translated by Jon Rothschild. New York: Knopf, 1997. A good reference for biographical information on Simenon.

Becker, Lucille Frackman. *Georges Simenon.* Boston: Twayne, 1977. An informative introductory study, with chapters on Simenon's family background, the creation of Maigret, his handling of such basic themes as solitude and alienation, and his understanding of the art of the novel. Includes a chronology, notes, and an annotated bibliography.

Bresler, Fenton. *The Mystery of Georges Simenon.* Toronto: General, 1983. A well-written biography that gives a strong sense of Simenon's roots and the development of his career. Includes conversations between Bresler and Simenon.

Eskin, Stanley. *Simenon: A Critical Biography.* Jefferson, N.C.: McFarland, 1987. Eskin provides a meticulous narrative and analysis of Simenon's work. His notes and bibliography are very detailed and helpful.

Franck, Frederick. *Simenon's Paris.* New York: Dial, 1970. While this is basically a book of illustrations of Paris, a good deal is revealed about the way Simenon chose locations for his fiction.

Gill, Brendan. "Profiles: Out of the Dark." *The New Yorker,* January 24, 1953, 35-45. A succinct biographical and critical profile by an astute essayist.

Marnham, Patrick. *The Man Who Wasn't Maigret: A Portrait of Georges Simenon.* London: Bloomsbury, 1992. An excellent study of Simenon's life and times. Includes bibliographical references and an index.

Raymond, John. *Simenon in Court.* New York: Harcourt Brace and World, 1968. An excellent overview of Simenon's fiction, as valuable as Becker's introductory study.

Simenon, Georges. "The Art of Fiction IX: Georges Simenon." Interview by Carvel Collins. *The Paris Review* 9 (Summer, 1993): 71-90. A comprehensive interview with the author about his career and his fictional methods.

Charles Simic

American poet

Born: Belgrade, Yugoslavia (now in Serbia and Montenegro); May 9, 1938

POETRY: *What the Grass Says*, 1967; *Somewhere Among Us a Stone Is Taking Notes*, 1969; *Dismantling the Silence*, 1971; *White*, 1972, revised 1980; *Return to a Place Lit by a Glass of Milk*, 1974; *Biography and a Lament: Poems, 1961-1967*, 1976; *Charon's Cosmology*, 1977; *Brooms: Selected Poems*, 1978; *Classic Ballroom Dances*, 1980; *Austerities*, 1982; *Shaving at Night*, 1982; *The Chicken Without a Head*, 1983; *Weather Forecast for Utopia and Vicinity: Poems, 1967-1982*, 1983; *Selected Poems, 1963-1983*, 1985, revised 1990, expanded as *Selected Early Poems*, 1999; *Unending Blues*, 1986; *The World Doesn't End: Prose Poems*, 1989; *The Book of Gods and Devils*, 1990; *In the Room We Share*, 1990; *Hotel Insomnia*, 1992; *A Wedding in Hell*, 1994; *Frightening Toys*, 1995; *Walking the Black Cat*, 1996; *Looking for Trouble*, 1997; *Jackstraws*, 1999; *Night Picnic*, 2001.

TRANSLATIONS: *Four Yugoslav Poets: Ivan V. Lalic, Brank Miljkovic, Milorad Pavic, Ljubomir Simovic*, 1970; *The Little Box: Poems*, 1970 (of Vasko Popa); *Homage to the Lame Wolf: Selected Poems, 1956-1975*, 1979, enlarged 1987 (of Popa); *Roll Call of Mirrors: Selected Poems*, 1988 (of Ivan V. Lalic); *Some Other Wine and Light*, 1989 (of Aleksandar Ristovic); *The Bandit Wind*, 1991 (of Slavko Janevski); *The Horse Has Six Legs: An Anthology of Serbian Poetry*, 1992; *Night Mail: Selected Poems*, 1992 (of Novica Tadic); *Devil's Lunch: Selected Poems*, 2000 (of Ristovic).

NONFICTION: *The Uncertain Certainty: Interviews, Essays, and Notes on Poetry*, 1985; *Wonderful Words, Silent Truth: Essays on Poetry and a Memoir*, 1990; *Dime-Store Alchemy: The Art of Joseph Cornell*, 1992; *The Unemployed Fortune-Teller: Essays and Memoirs*, 1994; *Orphan Factory: Essays and Memoirs*, 1997; *A Fly in the Soup: Memoirs*, 2000.

EDITED TEXTS: *Another Republic*, 1976 (with Mark Strand); *The Essential Campion*, 1988 (Thomas Campion); *The Best American Poetry, 1992*, 1992; *Mermaids Explained: Poems*, 2001.

Charles Simic (SEEM-ihch) is a Pulitzer Prize-winning poet. Naturalized as an American citizen in 1971, Simic was born in Belgrade, then located in Yugoslavia. With black humor he recalls his childhood during World War II, marked by bombings and waves of advancing and retreating soldiers, as "a three-ring circus." He describes how, from the summer of 1944 to mid-1945, he "ran around the streets of Belgrade with other half-abandoned kids." Critics have speculated that the peculiar blend of horror and whimsy in Simic's work can be traced to those days. Simic admits to still being "haunted by images" of the war.

In 1949 Simic and his mother moved to Chicago to join his father, an engineer who had found employment there with the telephone company for which he had worked in Yugoslavia. His father took him to hear jazz, which Simic credits with making him "both an American and a poet."

Beginning in 1957, Simic attended the University of Chicago at night and worked during the day as a proofreader at the *Chicago Sun Times*. He eventually transferred to New York University, from which he received a B.A. in 1967. From 1966 to 1969 Simic, who initially studied to be an artist, worked as an editorial assistant for *Aperture*, a photography magazine. He began teaching at California State College, Hayward, in 1970. He left that position in 1973, when he was hired as an associate professor of English at the University of New Hampshire.

While a student at the University of Chicago, Simic had audited a poetry workshop taught by John Logan. Logan's workshops and seminars were associated with Surrealist experimentation, and many of Simic's early poems appeared in the magazine *kayak*, an organ for American Surrealist verse. The impulse of Surrealism, which appealed to poets coming of age during and after the unleashing of tribalism's dark side in World War II, was to draw on an archetypal voice inside oneself that transcended national borders. The influence of Surrealism has been noted by critics in the visionary and dreamlike structure of Simic's poems.

The concentrated effort of attention on an object in Simic's early verse more specifically links him to a group of American poets known as the Deep Imagists, which included Robert Bly and W. S. Merwin. From Simic's first published collection, *What the Grass Says*, to his second, *Somewhere Among Us a Stone Is Taking Notes*, critic Victor Contoski finds the poet receding in the poems, becoming "more absorbed in objects." Silence becomes a means of communication, as in it the poet hears the "tiny voices of things." In Simic's next collection, *Dismantling the Silence*, Simic offers instruction for deconstructing silence in order to discover its nature. In the three-part *White* the narrative voice perceptively shifts to that of the object, here, the color white. *White* has been read by critics as a deliberate dispossession, freeing the poet to re-create himself. Subsequent poetry finds Simic exploring the self, though less as a subject than as a verb—that is, the self in action and in flux.

Critic Peter Schmidt, noting references to Walt Whitman's poetry throughout *White*, sees in it Simic confronting his American poetic origins. Simic claims that, because all his serious reading had been in English and American literature when he started writing poetry in high school, he has never been capable of writing a poem in Serbian, his native language. Nevertheless, critics invariably characterize his work as European in its mordant playfulness and primitive, folkloric elements. Simic has been a prolific English-language translator of Serbian poets, including Vasko Popa, Ivan Lalic, and Aleksandar Ristovic. In both 1970 and 1980 Simic received the translation award given by the International Association of Poets, Playwrights, Editors, Essayists, and Novelists (PEN).

The Third Balkan War echoes in much of Simic's work starting in the 1990's. In an essay first published in *The New Republic*, the father of two unflinchingly condemned his fellow Serbs for their aggression. "Lyric poets," he has said, "assert the individual's experience against that of the tribe."

Amy Allison

Bibliography

Nash, Susan Smith. Review of *Walking the Black Cat*, by Charles Simic. *World Literature Today* 71, no. 4 (Autumn, 1997): 793-794. This is an enthusiastic appraisal that views this collection as a cohesive and focused expression of Simic's major themes.

Orlich, Ileana. "The Poet on a Roll: Charles Simic's 'The Tomb of Stéphane Mallarmé.'" *Centennial Review* 36, no. 2 (Spring, 1992): 413-428. Orlich examines Simic's relationship to the Surrealists, and in particular the role of chance, through a close reading of a key poem. Orlich considers the poem to be an aesthetic manifesto.

Stitt, Peter. "Charles Simic: Poetry in a Time of Madness." In *Uncertainty and Plenitude: Five Contemporary Poets*. Iowa City: University of Iowa Press, 1997. Though Simic's imagery suggests a surrealist orientation, he is essentially a realist who reflects his Eastern European heritage. A close reading of several poems establishes the archetypal nature of Simic's speakers and the displacement of the poet's own ego.

Vendler, Helen. "A World of Foreboding: Charles Simic." In *Soul Says: On Recent Poetry*. Cambridge, Mass.: Harvard University Press, 1995. Focusing on *Hotel Insomnia*, Vendler provides a comprehensive overview of Simic's themes and methods. She charts a "master list" of key words that run through this collection. Astute analysis by a major critic.

Weigl, Bruce. *Charles Simic*. Ann Arbor: University of Michigan Press, 1996. Traces the critical reception of Simic's poetry across a quarter century, in an effort to delineate Simic's aesthetic. Bibliography.

William Gilmore Simms

American novelist

Born: Charleston, South Carolina; April 17, 1806
Died: Charleston, South Carolina; June 11, 1870

LONG FICTION: *Martin Faber: The Story of a Criminal*, 1833; *Guy Rivers: A Tale of Georgia*, 1834; *The Yemassee: A Romance of Carolina*, 1835; *The Partisan: A Tale of the Revolution*, 1835; *Mellichampe: A Legend of the Santee*, 1836; *Richard Hurdis: Or, The Avenger of Blood, a Tale of Alabama*, 1838; *Pelayo: A Story of the Goth*, 1838; *The Damsel of Darien*, 1839; *Border Beagles: A Tale of Mississippi*, 1840; *The Kinsmen: Or, The Black Riders of the Congaree*, 1841 (revised as *The Scout*, 1854); *Confession: Or, The Blind Heart*, 1841; *Beauchampe: Or, The Kentucky Tragedy, a Tale of Passion*, 1842; *Helen Halsey: Or, The Swamp State of Conelachita, a Tale of the Borders*, 1845; *Count Julian: Or, The Last Days of the Goth, a Historical Romance*, 1845; *Katharine Walton: Or, The Rebel of Dorchester*, 1851; *The Sword and the Distaff: Or, "Fair, Fat and Forty,"* 1852 (revised as *Woodcraft*, 1854); *Vasconselos: A Romance of the New World*, 1853; *The Forayers: Or, The Raid of the Dog-Days*, 1855; *Eutaw: A Sequel to the Forayers*, 1856; *Charlemont: Or, The Pride of the Village*, 1856; *The Cassique of Kiawah: A Colonial Romance*, 1859.

SHORT FICTION: *The Book of My Lady*, 1833; *Carl Werner*, 1838; *The Wigwam and the Cabin*, 1845; *Southward Ho!*, 1854.

DRAMA: *Michael Bonham: Or, The Fall of Bexar, a Tale of Texas*, pb. 1852.

POETRY: *Monody on the Death of Gen. Charles Cotesworth Pinckney*, 1825; *Early Lays*, 1827; *Lyrical and Other Poems*, 1827; *The Vision of Cortes*, 1829; *The Tri-Color*, 1830; *Atalantis: A Story of the Sea*, 1832; *Areytos: Or, Songs of the South*, 1846; *Poems Descriptive, Dramatic, Legendary, and Contemplative*, 1853.

NONFICTION: *The History of South Carolina*, 1840; *The Geography of South Carolina*, 1843; *The Life of Francis Marion*, 1844; *Views and Reviews in American Literature, History, and Fiction*, 1845; *The Life of Captain John Smith*, 1846; *The Life of Chevalier Bayard*, 1847; *The Life of Nathanael Greene*, 1849; *The Lily and the Totem: Or, The Huguenots in Florida*, 1850; *South-Carolina in the Revolutionary War*, 1853; *Sack and Destruction of the City of Columbia, S.C.*, 1865; *The Letters of William Gilmore Simms*, 1952-1956 (5 volumes; Mary C. Simms Oliphant, editor).

MISCELLANEOUS: *The Centennial Edition of the Writings of William Gilmore Simms*, 1969-1975 (16 volumes; John C. Guilds and James B. Meriwether, editors).

William Gilmore Simms was known in his lifetime as a novelist, short-story writer, poet, historian, and journalist; today his reputation rests on his novels. Simms's childhood was an unusual one. His mother died while he was still an infant, and his father left the baby William in the care of his maternal grandmother. He seems to have had only casual schooling, but he read widely and listened intently to his grandmother's stories of the American Revolution as it had occurred in the South. When the boy was ten years old, his father, a frontiersman who had gone westward toward the Mississippi River, paid a visit to Charleston, and at eighteen William went to visit his father on his plantation in what is now Mississippi.

During this visit he observed frontier life and American Indian tribes. Upon his return to Charleston, Simms published some poems, most of them with a Byronic flavor. In 1828 he entered upon the editorship of a short-lived magazine titled *The Tablet*. After its failure he became editor of the *Charleston City Gazette*, which opposed the election of John C. Calhoun. Because of the political animosity he incurred as a result, plus the deaths of his wife, grandmother, and father, Simms left for the North, where he found friends and a future.

Some early work was published shortly after he left Charleston, but his first important success came with the publication of *Guy Rivers* in 1834. A story of gold mining in northern Georgia, the novel, packed with action, is a romantic piece of writing with a realistic American theme. His next work was *The Partisan*, which was probably inspired by his grandmother's accounts of the revolution. In the same year, 1835, *The Yemassee* appeared; it was destined to remain his most popular book. It is an exciting tale of early days in South Carolina, notable for its realistic portrayal of Native Americans. Simms's portrayal of American Indians has been judged by scholars to be more accurate than the more popular, idealized pictures presented by James Fenimore Cooper in his novels. Simms's realism, in fact, was a little too much for his own day. Two of his novels, *Beauchampe* and *Charlemont*, both about a celebrated Kentucky murder case, were considered in his lifetime too realistic to be within the bounds of good taste, although they seem tame enough today.

Following his second marriage in 1836, Simms's life began to change. Filling the position of a wealthy planter on his wife's plantation and raising a family of fifteen children made him a prominent spokesman for the southern notion of Greek democracy in the United States, a concept which implied a defense of slavery. Simms's theories on slavery were found in his *The History of South Carolina*. His viewpoint and his reputation as an author made him a great man in the South, but they caused him to be unpopular in the North. While his works were in vogue before the Civil War, they were neglected afterward. All Simms's important writing came before the war, which both ruined his reputation in the North and destroyed his home and way of life in the South.

Simms's reputation has been slow in returning. For a half century his books were out of print, except for *The Yemassee*. His novels were influenced by his reading of Sir Walter Scott, and his work has frequently been compared with that of Cooper. He wrote about South Carolina during the eighteenth century and about the pre-Civil War frontier, then east of the Mississippi River. He celebrated little-known elements of American history and culture. He excelled at three kinds of fiction: the border romance, of which *Guy Rivers* is his best; the novel of Indian warfare, of which *The Yemassee* is a classic; and the romance about the American Revolution, of which *The Partisan* is a good example. In addition to fiction, poetry, and history, Simms wrote biographies of Francis Marion, Captain John Smith, and Nathanael Greene.

Jonathan S. Cullick

Bibliography

Butterworth, Keen, and James E. Kibler, Jr. *William Gilmore Simms: A Reference Guide*. Boston: G. K. Hall, 1980. This bibliography lists all writings about Simms in chronological order, from 1825 to 1979. The lengthy introduction gives general background information. Includes an index.

Guilds, John Caldwell. *Simms: A Literary Life*. Fayetteville: University of Arkansas Press, 1992. The first critical biography of Simms to appear in one hundred years, Guilds's book proceeds in a chronological fashion and emphasizes Simms's accomplishments as a novelist. Five appendices include a chart of birth and death dates for Simms's fifteen children; the will of Nash Roach, Simms's father-in-law, bequeathing the bulk of his estate to Simms and Chevillette Roach Simms, his wife; a letter written by Simms to the United States Congress in support of an international copyright bill; two elegies published in Charleston periodicals after Simms's death; and a list of Simms's writings appearing in book form.

_______, ed. *Long Years of Neglect: The Work and Reputation of William Gilmore Simms*. Fayetteville: University of Arkansas Press, 1988. This collection brings together a dozen essays, some rather scholarly, though many suitable for the high school student. Includes a portrait of Simms.

Guilds, John Caldwell, and Caroline Collins, eds. *William Gilmore Simms and the American Frontier.* Athens: University of Georgia Press, 1997. A good look at Simms's use of the frontier in his works.

Johanyak, Debra. "William Gilmore Simms: Deviant Paradigms of Southern Womanhood?" *The Mississippi Quarterly* 46 (Fall, 1993): 573-588. Discusses the portrayal of women in Simms's fiction; claims that just as intellectual, independent, or masculinized women are repeatedly destroyed by seducers in Simms's work, readers are encouraged to view them as deviant and as contributing to their own downfall.

Mayfield, John. "'The Soul of a Man': William Gilmore Simms and the Myths of Southern Manhood." *Journal of the Early Republic* 15 (Fall, 1995): 477-500. An examination of southern men in Simms's fiction; argues that both as literary figures and as paradigms Simms's characters are failures, being stereotypes with little to offer.

Watson, Charles S. *From Nationalism to Secessionism: The Changing Fiction of William Gilmore Simms*. Westport, Conn.: Greenwood Press, 1993. Examines the political and social views of this Southern author. Includes bibliographical references and an index.

Wimsatt, Mary Ann. *The Major Fiction of William Gilmore Simms: Cultural Traditions and Literary Forms*. Baton Rouge: Louisiana State University Press, 1989. Although Wimsatt focuses primarily on Simms's novels, this study is a useful discussion of Simms's work, as it reevaluates many of the misconceptions and dismissive attitudes about his fiction.

Claude Simon

French novelist

Born: Tananarive, Madagascar; October 10, 1913

LONG FICTION: *Le Tricheur*, 1945; *Gulliver*, 1952; *Le Sacre du printemps*, 1954; *Le Vent: Tentative de restitution d'un rétable baroque*, 1957 (*The Wind: Attempted Restoration of a Baroque Altarpiece*, 1959); *L'Herbe*, 1958 (*The Grass*, 1960); *La Route des Flandres*, 1960 (*The Flanders Road*, 1961); *Le Palace*, 1962 (*The Palace*, 1963); *Histoire*, 1967 (English translation, 1968); *La Bataille de Pharsale*, 1969 (*The Battle of Pharsalus*, 1971); *Les Corps conducteurs*, 1971 (*Conducting Bodies*, 1974); *Triptyque*, 1973 (*Triptych*, 1976); *Leçon de choses*, 1975 (*The World About Us*, 1983); *Les Géorgiques*, 1981 (*The Georgics*, 1989); *L'Invitation*, 1987 (*The Invitation*, 1991); *L'Acacia*, 1989 (*The Acacia*, 1991); *Le Jardin des plantes*, 1997 (*The Jardin des Plantes*, 2001); *Le Tramway*, 2001 (*The Trolley*, 2002).

DRAMA: *La Séparation*, pr. 1963.

NONFICTION: *La Corde raide*, 1947 (journal); *Femmes*, 1966 (commentaries on painting by Joan Miró); *Orion aveugle*, 1970 (portions of *Conducting Bodies* and paintings); *La Chevelure de Bérénice*, 1983 (*Bérénice's Golden Mane*, 1998).

One of the principal French writers of the New Novel, Claude-Eugène-Henri Simon (see-mohn) has combined the exploration of new modes of novelistic discourse with a trenchant view of the human condition to create a unique fictional universe. He was born in Tananarive, Madagascar (then a French possession), on October 10, 1913. He left the African island one year later when, with the onset of World War I, his father, an army officer, was called up for active military service. After his father was killed in the war, Simon spent his childhood in Perpignan, a small town in the eastern Pyrenees. Simon received his secondary education at the Collège Stanislas in Paris and later studied at both Oxford and Cambridge universities. He then began to train as a painter with André Lhote, who had been one of the early cubist painters. Paintings of various kinds appear in several of Simon's novels. Simon spent the years 1936 to 1939 traveling in Europe. His peregrinations included a brief stay in Spain, where he participated in the Civil War on the Republican side. When World War II started, Simon was drafted into a cavalry regiment. After the French defeat at the Battle of the Meuse, he was captured by the Germans but managed to escape from his prison camp. Simon's reflections on the two wars in which he took part appear in *La Corde raide* (the tightrope), a journal that he published in 1947. War is a major theme in many of Simon's novels, for, in addition to its specific devastation, it exposes the chaos underlying the apparent order of existence as well as emphasizing humankind's lack of progress. After the war, Simon returned to the Pyrenees region, settling in the village of Salses and becoming a vintner. He later moved to Paris, where he stayed.

Simon's first novel, *Le Tricheur* (the cheater), was published in 1945. The works that he produced during the 1940's and 1950's, which constitute his first phase, present many of the themes that appeared in later, better-known novels but are largely traditional in form. Yet *The Wind* and, to a lesser extent, *The Grass* already point toward the more innovative fictions of Simon's second period with respect to such matters as narrative perspective, temporality, and the nature of representation. The anonymous narrator of *The Wind* attempts to restore the reality of a series of incidents in a small town in southern France. The ceaselessly blowing wind is a metaphor of the destructive passage of time that blurs events and characters. The narrator succeeds in establishing a pattern of criminal activities but begins to suspect that his discovery is an invention created by his desire to give meaning to the events he is investigating, by language that has imposed its own particular order. What is baroque in this novel and in so many of the later novels is the tension between the work of art as an illusion and the self-consciousness of the processes that engendered it.

Simon's first recognition as a novelist came with the publication of *The Flanders Road* in 1960, which won for him the Prix de l'Express and placed its author among the foremost practitioners of the New Novel. These writers, among them Alain Robbe-Grillet, Nathalie Sarraute, and Michel Butor, were attempting to elaborate a new poetics of the novel by calling into question its traditional structures. In *The Flanders Road*, considered by many to be Simon's best work, the protagonist Georges had been a soldier in World War II and was captured by the Germans after most of his unit had been killed. After the war, Georges spends a night with Corinne, his dead captain's wife, about whom he had fantasized while a prisoner. In the course of this night Georges pursues his memories of the war, in the hope of determining the true nature of the events with which he was involved and thereby seizing his own identity. Georges discovers that he cannot adequately separate fact from imagination, however, and that his memories have become mental images, re-presentations that have lost their spatiotemporal coordinates as they have combined with one another in associative patterns. The self, fragmented in proliferating language, becomes a fictional construct.

Triptych ushered in the third phase of Simon's novelistic production. Simon eliminates the central narrative consciousness of his earlier works in order to emphasize further the novel as text. Like a piece of cloth, a textile, the work becomes an interweaving of many strands. As its title implies, the novel consists of three principal stories, which become progressively interconnected through various processes of association and generation. A particular element may function in a variety of contexts, within one or several stories. For example, a couple making love in a barn is linked to a nude woman in another story. She resembles a woman on a strip of film in the possession of two boys spying on the couple in the barn—and that figure is linked to a film being shown locally and, in another story, to a film being made. *The Georgics* creates a complex polyphony through its interweaving of three historical events—the French Revolution, the Spanish Civil War, and the defeat of France in 1940. Yet given Simon's concept of the cyclical nature of history, the convergence of these moments tends to restore the unifying narrative consciousness more typical of Simon's earlier works.

The awarding of the Nobel Prize in Literature to Simon in 1985 was met with some opposition in both France and the United States. Simon's detractors felt that his experimental writing had impoverished the novel instead of enriching it. Unlike the works of some of the writers with which he is associated, however, Simon's novels are never arid intellectual exercises reflecting solipsistically on their own elaboration. For Simon, the activity of writing is inseparable from an exploration of the human condition. Simon's vision of the human condition is, admittedly, a relatively pessimistic one. The specious order of everyday existence is easily shattered by war, crime, and passion. History is cyclical, belying apparent progress and imposing predetermined roles on the actors who occupy its stage. The demarcation between the real and the imaginary is illusory. Enmeshed in the labyrinthine web of language, the pursuit of identity and meaning generates other fictions. Although Simon continued to break down differences between the real and the imaginary, his work took an increasingly autobiographical turn with *The Acacia*, continuing in *The Jardin des Plantes* and *The Trolley*. He also told the story of a trip to the Soviet Union in *The Invitation*. Yet this apprehension of reality is coextensive with the creation of new novelistic forms and with the assumption by Simon's readers of a greater share in the creative process.

Philip H. Solomon
Margaret Wade Krausse

Bibliography

Birn, Randi, and Karen Gould, eds. *Orion Blinded: Essays on Claude Simon*. London: Associated University Presses, 1981. Brings together fifteen critics on Simon, plus an interview with the novelist. Concentrates on groupings of essays on Simon's worldview, different critical approaches, studies of evil, and links between Simon and Latin American fiction in the 1970's.

Britton, Celia, ed. *Claude Simon*. New York: Longman, 1993. A collection of articles, from 1959 to 1982. Britton has selected diverse critics who address questions of perception and memory, textual space, bricolage, intertextuality, the subject, and the problem of the referent; she covers all approaches in an extended introduction to the articles.

Duffy, Jean H. *Reading Between the Lines: Claude Simon and the Visual Arts*. Liverpool, England: Liverpool University Press, 1998. An illustrated study that explores and analyzes the relation between Simon's fiction and the visual and plastic arts. Duffy analyzes such artists as Jean Dubuffet and Paul Cézanne in connection with Simon's frequent statements about painting and the role of art in his novels. Excellent bibliography of both works on the visual arts and on Simon, including extended list of interviews and short pieces by him for newspapers.

Duffy, Jean, and Alistair Duncan, eds. *Claude Simon: A Retrospective*. Liverpool: Liverpool University Press, 2002. A collection of essays edited by two prominent Simon scholars, offering an overview of responses to Simon's work.

Duncan, Alistair. *Claude Simon: Adventures in Words*. 2d ed. Manchester, England: Manchester University Press, 2003. Designed to introduce new readers to Simon's work by placing them within the context of French literary theory and debate of the second half of the twentieth century.

Gould, Karen. *Claude Simon's Mythic Muse*. Columbia, S.C.: French Literature, 1979. Gould provides an exhaustive study of mythic and mythological themes as inspiration for Simon's novels.

Jimenez-Fajardo, Salvador. *Claude Simon*. Boston: Twayne, 1975. This early study examines Simon's novels through *Triptych*. Situates the novelist in the tradition of Marcel Proust and William Faulkner; examines the themes of Eros, death, memory, and representation.

Loubère, J. A. E. *The Novels of Claude Simon*. Ithaca, N.Y.: Cornell University Press, 1975. Eclectic, broadly based introduction to Simon's fiction that focuses on formal approach; Loubère relies frequently on Simon's statements about his fiction.

Neil Simon

American playwright and screenwriter

Born: Bronx, New York; July 4, 1927
Identity: Jewish

DRAMA: *Come Blow Your Horn*, pr. 1960; *Little Me*, pr. 1962, revised pr. 1982 (music by Cy Coleman, lyrics by Carol Leigh; adaptation of Patrick Dennis's novel); *Barefoot in the Park*, pr. 1963; *The Odd Couple*, pr. 1965; *Sweet Charity*, pr., pb. 1966 (music and lyrics by Coleman and Dorothy Fields; adaptation of Federico Fellini's film *Nights of Cabiria*); *The Star-Spangled Girl*, pr. 1966; *Plaza Suite*, pr. 1968; *Promises, Promises*, pr. 1968 (music and lyrics by Hal David and Burt Bacharach; adaptation of Billy Wilder and I. A. L. Diamond's film *The Apartment*); *Last of the Red Hot Lovers*, pr. 1969; *The Gingerbread Lady*, pr. 1970; *The Comedy of Neil Simon*, pb. 1971 (volume 1 in *The Collected Plays of Neil Simon*); *The Prisoner of Second Avenue*, pr., pb. 1971; *The Sunshine Boys*, pr. 1972; *The Good Doctor*, pr. 1973 (adaptation of Anton Chekhov's stories); *God's Favorite*, pr. 1974 (adaptation of the story of Job); *California Suite*, pr. 1976; *Chapter Two*, pr. 1977; *They're Playing Our Song*, pr. 1978 (music by Marvin Hamlisch, lyrics by Carole Bayer Sager; adaptation of Dennis's novel); *The Collected Plays of Neil Simon*, pb. 1979 (volume 2); *I Ought to Be in Pictures*, pr. 1980; *Fools*, pr., pb. 1981; *Brighton Beach Memoirs*, pr. 1982; *Biloxi Blues*, pr. 1984; *Broadway Bound*, pr. 1986; *The Odd Couple*, pr. 1985 (female version); *Rumors*, pr. 1988; *Jake's Women*, pr. 1990; *Lost in Yonkers*, pr., pb. 1991; *The Collected Plays of Neil Simon*, pb. 1991 (volume 3); *Laughter on the 23rd Floor*, pr. 1993; *London Suite*, pr. 1994; *Three from the Stage*, pb. 1995; *Proposals*, pr. 1997; *The Dinner Party*, pr. 2000; *45 Seconds from Broadway*, pr. 2001.

SCREENPLAYS: *After the Fox*, 1966 (with Cesare Zavattini); *Barefoot in the Park*, 1967; *The Odd Couple*, 1968; *The Out-of-Towners*, 1970; *Plaza Suite*, 1971; *The Last of the Red Hot Lovers*, 1972; *The Heartbreak Kid*, 1972; *The Prisoner of Second Avenue*, 1975; *The Sunshine Boys*, 1975; *Murder by Death*, 1976; *The Goodbye Girl*, 1977; *California Suite*, 1978; *The Cheap Detective*, 1978; *Chapter Two*, 1979; *Seems Like Old Times*, 1980; *Only When I Laugh*, 1981; *I Ought to Be in Pictures*, 1982; *Max Dugan Returns*, 1983; *The Lonely Guy*, 1984; *The Slugger's Wife*, 1985; *Brighton Beach Memoirs*, 1987; *Biloxi Blues*, 1988; *The Marrying Man*, 1991; *Lost in Yonkers*, 1993; *The Odd Couple II*, 1998.

TELEPLAYS: *Broadway Bound*, 1992; *Jake's Women*, 1996; *London Suite*, 1996; *The Sunshine Boys*, 1997.

NONFICTION: *Rewrites: A Memoir*, 1996; *The Play Goes On: A Memoir*, 1999.

From the early 1960's into the early twenty-first century, Neil Simon has dominated the popular theater in America. His seemingly endless string of well-made comedies has provided him with both popular recognition and tremendous wealth. He is the son of Irving Simon, a garment salesman, and Mamie Simon. As a young child, Simon remembers sitting on a stone ledge watching a Charlie Chaplin film. He laughed so hard that he fell off the ledge and had to be taken to the doctor's office. This incident would define for Simon the true meaning of comedy: "to make a whole audience fall onto the floor." Simon graduated from DeWitt Clinton High School in 1943 and entered New York University as an engineering student under the U.S. Army Air Force Reserve training program. Leaving the service in 1946, Simon went to work in the mailroom of the New York office of Warner Brothers. Then, Goodman Ace, a veteran Columbia Broadcasting System (CBS) comedy writer, asked Simon and his brother, Daniel Simon, to submit a comic sketch. Ace read their work and hired the pair immediately. For the next fifteen years, the Simon duo wrote for a variety of radio and television shows, including *The Phil Silvers Arrow Show* (1948), Tallulah Bankhead's *The Big Show* (1951), *Caesar's Hour* (1956-1957), and *The Garry Moore Show* (1959-1960).

After his brother ended their collaboration to become a television director, Simon turned his attention to writing full-length plays. *Come Blow Your Horn* premiered on Broadway in 1960. Based on his own experiences as a young man leaving the Bronx to live with his brother in Manhattan, this autobiographical work contains many of the now well-recognized Simon hallmarks: quick, witty dialogue, vivid characterizations, and plot complications. After writing the book for the musical *Little Me*, Simon wrote *Barefoot in the Park*, a play that enjoyed 1,532 performances on Broadway. One of Simon's most popular plays, its theme, that relationships can succeed only if individuals learn to be tolerant and to compromise, became another central feature of the playwright's work.

Simon followed this success with a series of Broadway hits. *The Odd Couple* was a humorous look at the attempt of two opposites, the now-famous Oscar and Felix, to live together. *The Star-Spangled Girl*, a rare Simon flop, was the story of radical protest in the late 1960's. In *Plaza Suite* Simon abandoned strict comedy and engineered three delicate one-act segments around more serious themes. This tragicomic blend worked well both on the stage and for the audience, and Simon continued to incorporate these poignant moments of pathos in his future work. Simon followed *Plaza Suite* with *Last of the Red Hot Lovers*. A dark work, the play marked an advance in Simon's writing from the polite comedy of his early plays to a more harsh, black humor.

Simon's next play, *The Gingerbread Lady*, almost closed before its Broadway opening. A drama focusing on the career of an alcoholic cabaret singer, the play failed to attract the same enthusiastic reviews and large audiences that his earlier plays had enjoyed; however, Simon's next two comedies, *The Prisoner of Second Avenue* and *The Sunshine Boys*, were extremely successful. Simon's next project was *The Good Doctor*, a series of dramatic vignettes based on Anton Chekhov's short stories. That same year Simon's wife, Joan Baim, a former dancer, died, and the playwright married actress Marsha Mason. Simon wrote about this period of his life in *Chapter Two*, perhaps his most autobiographical work and one of his most acclaimed plays. After the failure of *God's Favorite*, Simon returned to the one-act structure of *Plaza Suite* to write *California Suite*. The four playlets in this work examine both the comic and serious consequences of life's difficulties. In the following years Simon wrote two musicals, *They're Playing Our Song* and a revision of the 1962 musical comedy *Little Me*, and two more comedies, *I Ought to Be in Pictures* and *Fools*. Simon's most fully realized work in later years has been the highly autobiographical trilogy that began with *Brighton Beach Memoirs*, first produced in 1982. Treating Simon's own childhood and family, the play traces the painful transition of a young Jewish adolescent, Eugene, into confusing manhood. The second play, *Biloxi Blues*, follows Eugene as he undergoes basic training in Biloxi, Mississippi, in 1943. The cycle is completed by *Broadway Bound*, which establishes Eugene as a Broadway playwright, first to his family's delight and then to their horror as they see the private details of their lives mirrored on stage.

Simon's stature among theater critics was greatly enhanced by his autobiographical trilogy, and he has continued to become more respected as a serious writer. Simon next began to experiment with form and produced *Rumors*, his only farce. *Lost in Yonkers*, the tale of young brothers sent to live with relatives while their father tries to establish a career, was honored with the 1991 Pulitzer Prize in drama. Other later plays include *Jake's Women*, an autobiographical examination of destroyed relationships, and *Laughter on the 23rd Floor*, in which Simon re-creates the writers' room of *Caesar's Hour*, which starred Sid Caesar. He later surprised the New York theater establishment with a protest against the current way of doing business by opening his third collection of hotel-based one acts, *London Suite*, Off-Broadway in 1994.

Simon's later plays include *Proposals*, set in the 1950's at a summer cottage in a resort area of eastern Pennsylvania. It revolves around the disagreements between a retired businessman, his former wife, his daughter, and his daughter's various boyfriends, one of whom is the son of a Mafia baron. *The Dinner Party* is set in a private room at an expensive Parisian restaurant as six diners explore the various reasons their marriages have failed. *45 Seconds from Broadway* takes its title from the time needed to walk from the theaters to a coffee shop, familiarly known as the Polish Tea Room, that is a favorite hangout of theater folk. There, ten actors exchange banter and good-natured insults with each other and the restaurant's owners.

Despite the variety of Simon's comedies, several recurring themes and features remain at the heart of each work. Simon tends to write about the close and often difficult relationships between husbands and wives and within families. Beyond the witty dialogue and the masterful comic episodes, Simon captures, with both sensitivity and depth, the many conflicts that characterize these groupings. His finely drawn characters are middle class, sometimes Jewish, but always searching for balance in their lives. Simon's central message is a plea for moderation and for people to make meaningful commitments and to learn to adapt to the needs and insecurities of others. Perhaps because of his tremendous commercial success, critical opinion about Simon's work is divided.

Some critics argue that Simon is a superficial playwright, that his plays are mere "vehicles" for gags and one-liners. Others have identified a growing maturity in his work and have effectively challenged those who are dismissive of Simon's work. Whatever the case, Simon enjoys a popularity with audiences that no other contemporary American playwright can match.

Michael John McDonough
Gerald S. Argetsinger

Bibliography

Henry, William A., III. "Reliving a Poignant Past." *Time*, December 15, 1986, 72-78. Henry describes the success of the play *Broadway Bound* and its biographical sources, and includes details about Simon's marriages, lifestyle, writing habits, and older brother Danny. Compares Simon's life with its fictional parallels, especially in *Broadway Bound.*

Johnson, Robert K. *Neil Simon*. Boston: G. K. Hall, 1983. In this thoughtful and penetrating study, Johnson examines Simon's career and output through 1982, providing thorough synopses, analysis, and criticism of both plays and screenplays. Includes a chronology, a select bibliography, notes, and an index.

Konas, Gary, ed. *Neil Simon: A Casebook*. New York: Garland, 1997. Seven scholarly articles examine the influence of Simon's Jewish heritage and compare his work with that of other dramatists. Four essays discuss recurrent patterns in Simon's plays. The volume includes two Simon interviews.

Koprince, Susan. *Understanding Neil Simon*. Columbia: University of South Carolina Press, 2002. Offering a guide to Simon's work, Koprince provides an overview of Simon's career and an in-depth analysis of his major plays. Includes bibliography and index.

McGovern, Edythe. *Not-So-Simple Neil Simon: A Critical Study.* Van Nuys, Calif.: Perivale Press, 1978. McGovern examines twelve of Simon's early plays with an even, theoretical, scholarly tone, occasionally tending toward unqualified praise. The slim volume includes a preface by the playwright, a list of characters from the plays, production photographs, and illustrations by Broadway caricaturist Al Hirschfeld.

Simon, Neil. "The Art of Theater X." Interview by James Lipton. *The Paris Review* 34 (Winter, 1992): 166-213. A chatty, revealing interview that covers how Simon became a playwright and the strong autobiographical elements in his work. Other topics include the "almost invisible line" between comedy and tragedy and the gradually darkening vision of Simon's plays, which he sees as a movement toward greater truthfulness.

_______. "Simon Says." Interview by David Kaufman. *Horizon* 28 (June, 1985): 55-60. In this smooth, candid interview with the playwright, Simon talks openly about the autobiographical impulses in his plays, the critical response, and his popular and critical success. Through his own words, Simon's humility, directness, and commitment to craft are evident.

Louis Simpson

Jamaican-born American poet

Born: Kingston, Jamaica; March 27, 1923

POETRY: *The Arrivistes: Poems, 1940-1949*, 1949; *Good News of Death, and Other Poems*, 1955; *A Dream of Governors*, 1959; *At the End of the Open Road*, 1963; *Selected Poems*, 1965; *Adventures of the Letter I*, 1971; *Searching for the Ox*, 1976; *Caviare at the Funeral*, 1980; *The Best Hour of the Night*, 1983; *People Live Here: Selected Poems, 1949-1983*, 1983; *Collected Poems*, 1988; *In the Room We Share*, 1990; *Jamaica Poems*, 1993; *There You Are*, 1995.

LONG FICTION: *Riverside Drive*, 1962.

NONFICTION: *James Hogg: A Critical Study*, 1962; *North of Jamaica*, 1972; *Three on the Tower: The Lives and Works of Ezra Pound, T. S. Eliot, and William Carlos Williams*, 1975; *A Revolution in Taste: Studies of Dylan Thomas, Allen Ginsberg, Sylvia Plath, and Robert Lowell*, 1978; *A Company of Poets*, 1981; *The Character of the Poet*, 1986; *Ships Going into the Blue: Essays and Notes on Poetry*, 1994; *The King My Father's Wreck*, 1995 (autobiography).

EDITED TEXTS: *The New Poets of England and America*, 1957 (with Donald Hall and Robert Pack); *An Introduction to Poetry*, 1967.

TRANSLATIONS: *Modern Poets of France: A Bilingual Anthology*, 1997; *"The Legacy" and "The Testament,"* 2000 (of François Villon).

MISCELLANEOUS: *Selected Prose*, 1989.

Louis Aston Marantz Simpson was born in Jamaica, where his father was a lawyer. His parents were divorced when he was young, and his father remarried. When Simpson traveled to New York to attend Columbia University, he learned for the first time that his mother was Jewish—"and therefore, according to Jewish law, so was I." He served in the army during World War II. When the war ended, he returned to Columbia to complete his studies. After working in publishing, he returned to Columbia to earn a doctorate and began an academic career that led him first to the University of California at Berkeley and then to the State University of New York at Stony Brook, where he taught from 1967 to 1993.

Simpson's early poems were metrical and rhymed. His style underwent two major changes, the first (in *At the End of the Open Road*, which won the Pulitzer Prize) a breaking away from elegant metrics into hard-edged, imagistic free verse, the second (begun in *Searching for the Ox*) a delving into narrative, in spare lines stripped of most artifice. Yet his interest in storytelling was there from the beginning, in poems such as "Carentan O Carentan," which recounts a bloody ambush in ironic ballad stanzas, contrasting the pastoral beauty of a "shady lane" with the "watchers in leopard suits" who "aimed between the belt and boot/ And let the barrel climb."

One of the sections of Simpson's second volume of selected poems, *People Live Here*, is devoted to "The Fighting in Europe." In "The Battle" the speaker recalls most vividly "how hands looked thin/ Around a cigarette, and the bright ember/ Would pulse with all the life there was within." These lines suggest that even though Simpson's manner changed dramatically, he remained interested in the telling detail (the ember) and the life within people. The other sections of *People Live Here* show the range of Simpson's thematic interests: "Songs and Lyrics," "The Discovery of America," "Modern Lives," and "Tales of Volhynia" (poems about Russia, where his mother's family had lived). Some of Simpson's lyric poems, such as "Birch" and "As Birds Are Fitted to the Boughs," are sonorous and neatly articulated, but others tell stories in their musical forms. "My Father in the Night Commanding No," for example, uses rhymed quatrains to recount life with his practical father and romantic mother.

Many of Simpson's poems deal with American life, both his own immigrant discovery and astonishment (as in "The Pawnshop") and his close observation of neighbors in the suburbs. In "The Tenant" Simpson mentions a kind of investigation similar, perhaps, to his own practice: "Behind the Perry Masons and Agatha Christies/ I came across a packet of letters./ It was like being a detective." Behind the commonplace mysteries lie the greater mysteries of the commonplace.

Simpson continues peering into other lives and examining his own mind—because he is still trying to figure out America. An outsider in a constantly strange land, he has remained an insider, from early childhood, within the world of books. Perhaps his great facility with the poetic tradition has allowed him to give up prosodic virtuosity in the pursuit of the pure, bare story, transformed into poetry because it was not embellished but cut into nononsense lines.

Simpson is, at heart, a visionary poet, much of whose power comes from the plainspokenness of his narrative probings. His vision owes much to two writers in particular, Walt Whitman and Anton Chekhov. The two great changes in his work correspond to his close reading of these masters. Several poems in *At the End of the Open Road*, Simpson's first breakthrough, pay homage to Whitman and speak to him. Simpson concludes that "[a]t the end of the open road we come to ourselves." His own vision of America is dark and foreboding: "the heart misplaced, and seeds/ As black as death, emitting a strange odor."

The second breakthrough began with *Searching for the Ox* and was confirmed by *Caviare at the Funeral*, whose title poem is based on a story by Chekhov. A later poem, "Another Boring Story," begins with a Chekhov story about one professor and then adds a story about another, apparently drawn from Simpson's own experiences of university life. The similarity, like a good metaphor, is rooted in contrast, the distance between the two parts.

Simpson's vision is based in irony, the sense of a discrepancy between how things were and now are, between dreams and lives, between beauty and ugliness, between clamor and quiet. In "Ed," for example, a drunken man whose family, years ago, disapproved of his former girlfriend, a cocktail waitress, wishes that he had married her instead of the "respectable woman" who eventually left him: "'Well,' they said, 'why didn't you?'"

John Drury

Bibliography

Lazer, Hank. "Louis Simpson and Walt Whitman: Destroying the Teacher." *Walt Whitman Quarterly Review* 1 (December, 1983): 1-21. Lazer believes that Simpson's poetic development since 1963 has been shaped by Simpson's "dialogue" with Whitman.

_______, ed. *On Louis Simpson: Depths Beyond Happiness*. Ann Arbor: University of Michigan Press, 1988. Simpson himself said that one "should definitely have" this book. Lazer's introduction surveys the criticism of Simpson's work. The book itself offers shorter reviews and longer essays.

Mason, David. "Louis Simpson's Singular Charm." *The Hudson Review* 48, no. 3 (Autumn, 1995): 499-507. Mason examines Simpson's literary theories and ideas as they are revealed in his poetry, criticism, and memoirs, particularly his latest publications.

Moran, Ronald. *Louis Simpson*. New York: Twayne, 1972. A book-length study of Simpson's literary career. Opens with a brief biography and then examines the first five collections of poems and Simpson's novel *Riverside Drive*. Moran discusses critical response to each of the publications and places many of the poems in the larger context of Simpson's thought, emphasizing the development of the "emotive imagination" in his poetry.

Roberson, William H. *Louis Simpson: A Reference Guide*. Boston: G. K. Hall, 1980. Hank Lazer describes this work as "an invaluable book for anyone interested in Louis Simpson's writing and in critical reactions to that body of writing." Begins with a survey of Simpson's poetic career and critical reputation. Part 1 lists writings by Simpson, and part 2 lists writings about him.

Simpson, Louis. "Louis Simpson: An Interview." Interview by Ronald Moran. *Five Points* 1, no. 1 (Fall, 1996): 45-63. Moran's questions lead Simpson through a wide range of subjects, including his views on other poets, such as Sylvia Plath, themes in his own poetry, some favorites of his own poems, and contemporary poetry.

Stitt, Peter. "Louis Simpson: In Search of the American Self." In *The World's Hieroglyphic Beauty: Five American Poets*. Athens: University of Georgia Press, 1985. Stitt follows Simpson's development through "three distinct phases" and traces the unifying sensibility in the poetry, looking closely at a number of the poems along the way. One of the longer essays on Simpson, this is one of the most illuminating as well.

Mona Simpson

American novelist

Born: Green Bay, Wisconsin; June 14, 1957

LONG FICTION: *Anywhere but Here*, 1986; *The Lost Father*, 1991; *A Regular Guy*, 1996; *Off Keck Road*, 2000.
SHORT FICTION: "What My Mother Knew," 1982; "Approximations," 1983; "The Day He Left," 1983; "Lawns," 1984; "You Leave Them," 1985; "Victory Mills," 1989; "I Am Here to Tell You It Can Be Done," 1990.

Although she has published several short stories, Mona Elizabeth Simpson is best known for her critically acclaimed novels. Her books are lengthy, lyrical explorations of the search for identity in America at the end of the twentieth century. Simpson's narrators are lonely people, most often women, who as children were continuously betrayed by adults, physically and emotionally abused, and left to assemble an identity out of the fragments of their lives. Wounded and deprived of the rituals and processes of a daily family life, they survive by taking sometimes courageous, often desperate control of events: they steal, develop eating disorders, and put themselves at risk in dangerous situations and unfulfilling relationships.

Simpson, born to Syrian immigrants from Homs, grew up in Green Bay, Wisconsin, a landscape that figures prominently in her fiction. She received her B.A. from the University of California, Berkeley, in 1979 and an M.F.A. from Columbia University in 1983. Her fiction has been supported by several literary grants and awards, including the Whiting Writer's Award, a National Endowment for the Arts grant, and a Guggenheim Fellowship, and by foundations such as the Corporation of Yaddo and the MacDowell Colony. Simpson was an editor at *The Paris Review* during the 1980's. Beginning in 1988 she was a Bard Center Fellow and a teacher at Bard College. She has also spent time in New York and Los Angeles.

Simpson's first two novels, *Anywhere but Here* and *The Lost Father*, share the same narrator, although they have different names. *Anywhere but Here* chronicles the journey west of Ann August and her mother, Adele August Diamond. Although the voices of Ann's grandmother Lillian, her aunt Carol, and her mother are interspersed between Ann's chapters, the daughter's narrative makes up the bulk of the novel, and she is the central consciousness. In *The Lost Father* Mayan Atassi, a medical student at Columbia University, embarks on a search for her father who left home when she was a child. The shared histories of Ann August and Mayan Atassi, and their similar voices, let the reader know that she is the same person, each novel detailing a different part of her life and her family history.

Adele August Diamond is a selfish, narcissistic person who convinces her daughter Ann that she has the potential to be a child star. She uproots Ann from home and family in Wisconsin and heads for Hollywood in a Lincoln that she essentially steals from her second husband. Adele becomes increasingly deluded, believing that she and Ann belong to the wealthy Beverly Hills neighborhood in which they settle, while she passes bad checks, pretends to be in the market for houses she cannot afford, and prepares for marriage to lovers who have no intention of marrying her. As Ann negotiates her complex relationship with Adele, the reader sees the frightening dependence of the mother/daughter bond, with its moments of beauty and terror.

Ann learns to wield what power she has, often playing the maternal role. Eventually, she lands a role on a television situation comedy, a part she wins by mimicking her mother. Ironically, the work allows her to make enough money to attend college on the East Coast and finally leave her mother. Although she never returns, her life with her mother has deeply affected the way she perceives the world.

In *The Lost Father* Mayan Atassi's knowledge that she was unwanted by her father haunts her, preventing her from establishing enduring relationships with men, constructing a career, and creating an adult life. Convinced that she will remain emotionally crippled until she finds her father, she hires a detective, but eventually she takes up the search herself. As Mayan retraces her father's steps and imagines his life, she reconstructs her own past, finding again and again the painful places inside where her father's abandonment affects her. Both Ann August and Mayan Atassi's journeys are inward voyages juxtaposed against their road trips in search of an ideal that ultimately does not exist. Once Mayan's goal is reached and she finds her father, she realizes that it changes little. Finding him does not heal the wound of his absence. As she ultimately concludes, "I used to think, before I found him, that the sun or the moon had to be my father. And now I'm kind of back to that. I still haven't found what I'm looking for. But I am more like anybody else."

A Regular Guy is another story of coming to terms with an absent father; however, while the father is literally absent at the beginning of the novel, he is soon found, but remains emotionally absent. The protagonist, Jane di Natali, is the daughter of mentally unstable Mary, who drags her daughter around the Pacific Northwest. When Jane is ten, her mother decides that she should go live with her father, Tom Owens, now a multimillionare biotechnology entrepreneur (critics noted that he bears a resemblance to Simpson's older half brother Steve Jobs, founder of Apple Computers, who had been put up for adoption as an infant and did not know his birth family until he was in his late twenties). Owens, however, will take financial responsibility for his daughter but nothing more; he gives Mary and Jane a house and an allowance, but his attention remains on his businesses. His relationship with his daughter does not begin to develop until his business fortunes begin to decline.

Off Keck Road, which won the *Chicago Tribune* Heartland Award and was nominated for the PEN/Faulkner Award, focuses on Bea Maxwell, an upper-class woman who never quite fits into the world, and her friendships with two women from Keck Road, which constitutes the wrong side of the tracks in Green Bay, Wisconsin. June Umberhum, a college friend, has come home to raise her young daughter, while Shelley is the last person in town to have ever contracted polio.

Anne M. Downey

Bibliography

Heller, Dana. "Shifting Gears: Transmission and Flight in Mona Simpson's *Anywhere but Here*." *University of Hartford Studies in Literature* 21 (1989). A creative reading of Ann's and Adele's desire for each other's love versus an equally strong need for independence. Heller argues that the novel redefines the relationship between the polarized spheres of home (traditionally considered a female realm) and the world (regarded as a male realm, full of adventure and independence).

Morse, Deborah Denenholz. "The Difficult Journey Home: Mona Simpson's *Anywhere but Here*." In *Mother Puzzles: Daughters and Mothers in Contemporary American Literature*, edited by Mickey Pearlman. Westport, Conn.: Greenwood Press, 1989. Discusses Adele and Ann's ultimately divergent definitions of "home." Morse examines the many images of abandonment in the novel and looks at Lillian's well-ordered domesticity in contrast to Adele's inability to create, or disinterest in creating, a home.

Rogers, Kim Lacy. "The Autobiographical Anna." In *The Anna Book: Searching for Anna in Literary History*, edited by Mickey Pearlman. Westport, Conn.: Greenwood Press, 1992. Connects Simpson's novel with Susanna Moore's *My Old Sweetheart* (1982). Rogers argues that the fictional daughters in both novels are "victims of their mothers' narcissism" and finds Ann August strong enough to break the ties that bind her to her mother.

Smyth, Jacqui."Getaway Cars and Broken Homes: Searching for the American Dream in *Anywhere but Here*." *Frontiers* 20, no. 2 (1999): 115-132. Discusses symbols of female identity and the image of the mother-outlaw.

May Sinclair

English novelist

Born: Rock Ferry, Cheshire, England; August 24, 1863
Died: Aylesbury, Buckinghamshire, England; November 14, 1946

LONG FICTION: *Audrey Craven*, 1897; *Two Sides of a Question*, 1901; *The Divine Fire*, 1904; *The Helpmate*, 1907; *The Creators*, 1910; *The Three Sisters*, 1914; *Tasker Jevons*, 1916 (pb. in U.S. as *The Belfry*, 1914); *The Tree of Heaven*, 1917; *Mary Olivier: A Life*, 1919; *Mr. Waddington of Wyck*, 1921; *Anne Severn and the Fieldings*, 1922; *The Life and Death of Harriet Frean*, 1922; *A Cure of Souls*, 1924; *The Rector of Wyck*, 1925.

SHORT FICTION: *The Judgment of Eve*, 1908 (pb. in U.S. as *The Return of the Prodigal*, 1914); *Uncanny Stories*, 1923; *The Intercessor, and Other Stories*, 1931.

POETRY: *The Dark Night*, 1924.

NONFICTION: *The Three Brontës*, 1912; *The New Idealism*, 1922.

May Amelia St. Clair Sinclair was an unusual British author in that her work found a wider, more enthusiastic audience in the United States than it did in her native England. Born in Cheshire in 1863, she was educated at home and at Ladies' College, Cheltenham. As a girl she wrote poetry and philosophical criticism, some of which was published. Her first published short story appeared in 1895, and her first novel, *Audrey Craven*, in 1897. Real fame as a novelist waited for almost a decade, until the publication of *The Divine Fire* in 1904. A biography, *The Three Brontës*, published in 1912, was followed by another successful novel, *The Three Sisters*, which showed the influence of her Brontë studies.

During World War I Sinclair, who was then and throughout her life unmarried, served with an ambulance unit on the front in Belgium and worked with the Hoover Relief Commission. After the war she lived a quiet life that was unbroken except for several visits to the United States. Sinclair worked steadily, producing more than a dozen books, until physical problems (she was an invalid in her later life) made writing impossible. Outstanding among her later books are *Mary Olivier* and *Anne Severn and the Fieldings*. *Uncanny Stories* is a volume of short fiction reflecting her interest in the supernatural and spiritualism. Her lifelong interest in philosophy, especially idealism, resulted in the study *The New Idealism*. In the 1920's she wrote several light satirical comedies of manners; *Mr. Waddington of Wyck* and *A Cure of Souls* belong to this genre. *The Dark Night* is a long narrative poem.

As early as the writing of *Mary Olivier*, Sinclair had begun using the subconscious in her fiction, very much in the manner of Dorothy Richardson, and she has been termed one of the pioneers in the stream-of-consciousness technique. As a young woman she was a suffragist, and throughout her life she maintained an interest in feminist movements.

Bibliography

Kemp, Sandra. "'But How Describe a World Seen Without a Self?'—Feminism, Fiction, and Modernism." *Critical Quarterly* 32, no. 1 (Spring, 1990). Compares the ideas and techniques of Sinclair to those of Dorothy Richardson and Elizabeth Bowen.

Mumford, Laura Stempel. "May Sinclair's *The Tree of Heaven:* The Vortex of Feminism, the Community of War." In *Arms and the Woman: War, Gender, and Literary Representation*, edited by Susan Merrill Squier et al. Chapel Hill: University of North Carolina Press, 1989. Feminist critic Mumford takes a new approach to Sinclair's work.

Neff, Rebecca Kinnamon. "May Sinclair's Uncanny Stories as Metaphysical Quest." *English Literature in Transition (1880-1920)* 26, no. 3 (1983). Considers the author's interest in the supernatural and spiritualism.

Raitt, Suzanne. *May Sinclair: A Modern Victorian*. New York: Oxford University Press, 2000. Draws on previously undiscovered manuscripts to tell the story of Sinclair, whose emotional isolation bears witness to the price Victorian women had to pay for their intellectual freedom.

Stark, Susanne. "Overcoming Butlerian Obstacles: May Sinclair and the Problem of Biological Determinism." *Women's Studies: An Interdisciplinary Journal* 21, no. 3 (1992). Samuel Butler's theories of determinism and their relationship to feminism is the subject.

Upton Sinclair

American novelist

Born: Baltimore, Maryland; September 20, 1878
Died: Bound Brook, New Jersey; November 25, 1968
Pseudonyms: Clarke Fitch, Frederick Garrison, Arthur Stirling

LONG FICTION: *Springtime and Harvest*, 1901; *Prince Hagen*, 1903; *The Journal of Arthur Stirling*, 1903; *Manassas*, 1904 (revised as *Theirs Be the Guilt*, 1959); *The Jungle*, 1906; *A Captain of Industry*, 1906; *The Overman*, 1907; *The Metropolis*, 1908; *The Moneychangers*, 1908; *Samuel the Seeker*, 1910; *Love's Pilgrimage*, 1911; *Sylvia*, 1913; *Sylvia's Marriage*, 1914; *King Coal*, 1917; *Jimmie Higgins*, 1919; *100%*, 1920; *They Call Me Carpenter*, 1922; *Oil! A Novel*, 1927; *Boston*, 1928; *Mountain City*, 1930; *Roman Holiday*, 1931; *The Wet Parade*, 1931; *Co-op*, 1936; *The Flivver King*, 1937; *No Pasaran!*, 1937; *Little Steel*, 1938; *Our Lady*, 1938; *World's End*, 1940; *Between Two Worlds*, 1941; *Dragon's Teeth*, 1942; *Wide Is the Gate*, 1943; *Presidential Agent*, 1944; *Dragon Harvest*, 1945; *A World to Win*, 1946; *Presidential Mission*, 1947; *One Clear Call*, 1948; *O Shepherd, Speak!*, 1949; *Another Pamela: Or, Virtue Still Rewarded*, 1950; *The Return of Lanny Budd*, 1953; *What Didymus Did*, 1954; *It Happened to Didymus*, 1958; *Affectionately Eve*, 1961.

DRAMA: *Plays of Protest*, pb. 1912; *Hell: A Verse Drama and Photo-Play*, pb. 1923; *The Millennium*, pb. 1924; *The Pot Boiler*, pb. 1924; *Singing Jailbirds*, pb. 1924; *Bill Porter*, pb. 1925; *Wally for Queen!*, pb. 1936; *Marie Antoinette*, pb. 1939; *A Giant's Strength*, pr., pb. 1948.

NONFICTION: *Our Bourgeois Literature*, 1904; *The Industrial Republic*, 1907; *The Fasting Cure*, 1911; *The Profits of Religion*, 1918; *The Brass Check: A Study in American Journalism*, 1919; *The Book of Life, Mind, and Body*, 1921; *The Goose-Step: A Study of American Education*, 1923; *The Goslings: A Study of the American Schools*, 1924; *Mammonart*, 1925; *Letters to Judd*, 1925; *Money Writes!*, 1927; *Mental Radio*, 1930; *American Outpost: A Book of Reminiscences*, 1932; *I, Governor of California and How I Ended Poverty*, 1933; *The Way Out—What Lies Ahead for America?*, 1933; *The EPIC Plan for California*, 1934; *What God Means to Me*, 1936; *Terror in Russia: Two Views*, 1938; *Expect No Peace!*, 1939; *A Personal Jesus*, 1952; *The Cup of Fury*, 1956; *My Lifetime in Letters*, 1960; *The Autobiography of Upton Sinclair*, 1962.

CHILDREN'S/YOUNG ADULT LITERATURE: *The Gnomobile: A Gnice Gnew Gnarrative with Gnonsense, but Gnothing Gnaughty*, 1936.

Born in Baltimore, Maryland, on September 20, 1878, Upton Sinclair moved with his family to New York City in 1888 and began his career as a prodigy. He finished secondary school when he was twelve and became a student at the City College of New York at the age of fourteen. From the age of fifteen he supported himself in part by writing stories for the pulp magazines. After graduating from City College in the middle of his class, Sinclair attended Columbia University from 1897 to 1900. He had intended to become a lawyer but became interested in literature and left Columbia without a graduate degree. He married Meta Fuller in 1900 and began to write novels. His first five books, published between 1901 and 1906, gave him little encouragement, for they produced together less than a thousand dollars.

Before leaving college Sinclair had become a socialist, and his political views influenced his writing. His first fame came in 1906 with the publication of *The Jungle*, an exposé of the Chicago stockyards. Originally serialized in the socialist newspaper *Appeal to Reason, The Jungle* attracted immediate worldwide attention and is said to have hastened the passing of the 1906 Pure Food and Drug Act. With his profits from the book, Sinclair founded Helicon Hall, a cooperative community near Englewood Cliffs, New Jersey; it burned down in March, 1907.

Sinclair continued to write at a furious pace, also becoming a publisher during 1918-1919 with *Upton Sinclair's Magazine* and the Jungle Publishing firm in Pasadena, California. Beginning with *The Profits of Religion* in 1918, he wrote a series of nonfictional works on the effects of capitalism in the United States from a socialist viewpoint. The series, which has the collective title *The Dead Hand*, reviewed such phases of American culture as schools, colleges, newspapers, publishing, art, and literature.

Sinclair had difficulties in both his private and public life. He was divorced in 1911 and remarried in 1913. In 1915 he and his second wife, poet Mary Craig Kimbrough, moved to California. In 1923 Sinclair founded the California chapter of the American Civil Liberties Union. In the 1930's he led the movement End Poverty in California (EPIC). Several times he ran for political office, seeking seats in the U.S. House of Representatives and the Senate. He also ran for the governorship of California, twice as a Socialist Party candidate and once, in 1934, as a Democratic nominee.

In his novels of the period 1917-1940, Sinclair explored many areas of contemporary life. *King Coal* described conditions in the Colorado coal fields. *Oil!* described life in the oil fields of California, with looks also at the young motion picture industry. *Boston*, his fictionalized response to the Sacco-Vanzetti case, was published in 1928, a year after the men were executed. *Little Steel* described conditions and strikes in the steel mills during the 1930's. Concerned with issues of poverty, pure food, population control, and prostitution, Sinclair corresponded with several influential reformers, including Jane Addams, Margaret Sanger, and Theodore Dreiser.

During the years between 1940 and 1953, Sinclair labored at a series of novels relating world events from 1913 to 1950, including World War I, the peace negotiations after that war, the rise to power of Adolf Hitler and Benito Mussolini, the Spanish Civil War, the Munich debacle, Franklin D. Roosevelt's election and reelections, World War II, and the aftermath of World War II. The whole series is tied together picaresquely and romantically by the character of Lanny Budd, son of a wealthy munitions manufacturer. Lanny Budd, a young man with socialist leanings, travels far and wide, meets many people, and happens usually to be at the right spot at the right time (he even serves as a special agent for Roosevelt). *Dragon's Teeth*, which portrayed Lanny in Germany from 1929 to 1934, won the Pulitzer Prize in 1942.

Works published by Sinclair in the 1950's include *Another Pamela*, a twentieth century version of Samuel Richardson's novel about virtue rewarded, and *A Personal Jesus*, Sinclair's own interpretation of Jesus. *The Cup of Fury*, published in 1956, is an analysis of the effects of alcohol, with the conclusion that other writers, had they abstained from liquor as Sinclair did, would have been greater writers and would have written much more. The book is, in effect, an old-fashioned temperance tract, an attempt to reform.

After his second wife's death on April 26, 1961, Sinclair married May Hard on October 15, 1961, in Milwaukee. She died in December, 1967. Sinclair died a year later on November 25, 1968, in a New Jersey nursing home; he was ninety years old.

Sinclair's works have been translated into dozens of languages and were often more popular abroad than in the United States because of their political content. At times Sinclair employed pseudonyms, among them Clarke Fitch, Frederick Garrison, and Arthur Stirling.

Geralyn Strecker

Bibliography

Colburn, David R., and George E. Pozzetta, eds. *Reform and Reformers in the Progressive Era.* Westport, Conn.: Greenwood Press, 1983. Examines Sinclair's position as a muckraker and his role in inspiring Progressive reforms. Unlike other journalistic writers, Sinclair was personally and ideologically committed.

Dell, Floyd. *Upton Sinclair: A Study in Social Protest.* New York: AMS Press, 1970. Dell's treatment of Sinclair's career analyzes the apparent discrepancy between his literary position in the United States and throughout the rest of the world. Personal incidents and psychological insights are intertwined with evaluations and interpretations of specific works. Contains a bibliography of out-of-print books and an index.

Harris, Leon. *Upton Sinclair: American Rebel.* New York: Thomas Y. Crowell, 1975. Traces Sinclair's rise from obscurity to fame, with his subsequent decline in popularity. The text provides interesting information regarding source materials for some of his novels. A section of photographs, extensive notes, a list of Sinclair's books, and an index complete the book.

Herms, Dieter, ed. *Upton Sinclair: Literature and Social Reform.* New York: Peter Lang, 1990. This is a collection of papers from the Upton Sinclair World Conference of July, 1988, at the University of Bremen. Includes bibliographical references.

Mookerjee, R. N. *Art for Social Justice: The Major Novels of Upton Sinclair.* Metuchen, N.J.: Scarecrow Press, 1988. Mookerjee, a critic of writers of the 1930's, provides a reevaluation of *The Jungle*, *King Coal*, *Oil! A Novel*, *Boston*, and the Lanny Budd series. This slender volume is a reminder of the pioneering role of Sinclair in the "documentary novel." Contains a selected bibliography.

Scott, Ivan. *Upton Sinclair: The Forgotten Socialist.* Lewiston, N.Y.: Edwin Mellen Press, 1997. See especially chapters 1 and 2, "The Formation of Genius" and "*The Jungle*." In his introduction, Scott makes a good case for Sinclair's importance. A sound scholarly biography, drawing extensively on the Sinclair collection at Lilly Library, the University of Indiana.

Yoder, Jon A. *Upton Sinclair.* New York: Frederick Ungar, 1975. Like some other critics, Yoder attributes Sinclair's "meager reputation" in part to his socialistic views. Five chapters in this volume examine various facets of the novelist's life and career. Includes a chronology, notes, a bibliography, and an index.

Isaac Bashevis Singer

Polish-born American novelist, short-story writer, and playwright

Born: Leoncin, Poland; July 14 or November 21, 1904
Died: Surfside, Florida; July 24, 1991
Identity: Jewish

LONG FICTION: *Der Sotn in Gorey*, 1935 (*Satan in Goray*, 1955); *Di Familye Mushkat*, 1950 (*The Family Moskat*, 1950); *Der Hoyf*, 1953-1955 (*The Manor*, 1967, and *The Estate*, 1969); *Shotns baym Hodson*, 1957-1958 (*Shadows on the Hudson*, 1998); *Der Kuntsnmakher fun Lublin*, 1958-1959 (*The Magician of Lublin*, 1960); *Der Knekht*, 1961 (*The Slave*, 1962); *Sonim, de Geshichte fun a Liebe*, 1966 (*Enemies: A Love Story*, 1972); *Neshome Ekspeditsyes*, 1974 (*Shosha*, 1978); *Der Bal-Tshuve*, 1974 (*The Penitent*, 1983); *Reaches of Heaven: A Story of the Baal Shem Tov*, 1980; *Der Kenig vun di Felder*, 1988 (*The King of the Fields*, 1988); *Scum*, 1991; *The Certificate*, 1992; *Meshugah*, 1994.

SHORT FICTION: *Gimpel the Fool, and Other Stories*, 1957; *The Spinoza of Market Street*, 1961; *Short Friday, and Other Stories*, 1964; *The Séance, and Other Stories*, 1968; *A Friend of Kafka, and Other Stories*, 1970; *A Crown of Feathers, and Other Stories*, 1973; *Passions, and Other Stories*, 1975; *Old Love*, 1979; *The Collected Stories*, 1982; *The Image, and Other Stories*, 1985; *The Death of Methuselah, and Other Stories*, 1988.

DRAMA: *The Mirror*, pr. 1973; *Yentl, the Yeshiva Boy*, pr. 1974 (with Leah Napolin); *Shlemiel the First*, pr. 1974; *Teibele and Her Demon*, pr. 1978.

NONFICTION: *Mayn Tatn's Bes-din Shtub*, 1956 (*In My Father's Court*, 1966); *The Hasidim*, 1973 (with Ira Moskowitz); *A Little Boy in Search of God: Mysticism in a Personal Light*, 1976; *A Young Man in Search of Love*, 1978; *Isaac Bashevis Singer on Literature and Life*, 1979 (with Paul Rosenblatt and Gene Koppel); *Lost in America*, 1980; *Love and Exile*, 1984; *Conversations with Isaac Bashevis Singer*, 1985 (with Richard Burgin); *More Stories from My Father's Court*, 2000.

CHILDREN'S/YOUNG ADULT LITERATURE: *Zlateh the Goat, and Other Stories*, 1966; *The Fearsome Inn*, 1967; *Mazel and Shlimazel: Or, The Milk of a Lioness*, 1967; *When Shlemiel Went to Warsaw, and Other Stories*, 1968; *A Day of Pleasure: Stories of a Boy Growing Up in Warsaw*, 1969; *Elijah the Slave*, 1970; *Joseph and Koza: Or, The Sacrifice to the Vistula*, 1970; *Alone in the Wild Forest*, 1971; *The Topsy-Turvy Emperor of China*, 1971; *The Wicked City*, 1972; *The Fools of Chelm and Their History*, 1973; *Why Noah Chose the Dove*, 1974; *A Tale of Three Wishes*, 1975; *Naftali the Storyteller and His Horse, Sus, and Other Stories*, 1976; *The Power of Light: Eight Stories*, 1980; *The Golem*, 1982; *Stories for Children*, 1984.

TRANSLATIONS: *Romain Rolland*, 1927 (of Stefan Zweig); *Die Volger*, 1928 (of Knut Hamsun); *Victoria*, 1929 (of Hamsun); *All Quiet on the Western Front*, 1930 (of Erich Remarque); *Pan*, 1931 (of Hamsun); *The Way Back*, 1931 (of Remarque); *The Magic Mountain*, 1932 (of Thomas Mann); *From Moscow to Jerusalem*, 1938 (of Leon Glaser).

Isaac Bashevis Singer, the Yiddish writer who transcended his ethnic category, skillfully employs modernist fictional techniques to pose questions about human beings, God, and existence. In his writing Singer reveals the conflicting elements of his upbringing. His father, Pinchas Mendel Singer, was a Hasidic rabbi who told his son stories of demons and spirits. His mother, Bathsheba Zylberman Singer, whose first name he eventually adopted in its Yiddish form, was on the contrary a rationalist who talked of their Biłgoraj relatives. This difference in temperament between his parents is evident in "Why the Geese Shrieked," one of the tales in *A Day of Pleasure*. When a woman brings two dead geese to Rabbi Singer because they have continued to make strange noises, he seeks a supernatural explanation; his wife remarks that the sound is merely air passing through the severed windpipe and that if the woman removes the windpipe, the shrieking will cease, as indeed it does.

Singer's two older siblings also influenced him. His sister Hende Esther, thirteen years his senior, enjoyed telling him love stories. Most important to his literary growth was his brother, Israel Joshua Singer, who also became an important author; for many years Singer was better known as Israel's brother than as a writer himself. When Singer was four, the family moved to 10 Krochmalna Street, Warsaw, which serves as the setting for *Shosha* and some of Singer's best short fiction. In 1917 he and his mother left the Polish capital for Biłgoraj to escape the hunger and disease caused by World War I. During the four years he remained in the hamlet, he observed the rural Jewish life that later played so large a role in his writing.

After a brief attempt at rabbinical training at the Tachkemoni Seminary, Warsaw (1921-1922), he returned to Biłgoraj, then went to Dzikow, where his father was serving as rabbi. In this village he found the Hasidic tales of Rabbi Nachman of Bratzlav. One may regard Singer's fiction as the inverse of Rabbi Nachman's: Both are haunted by the supernatural, but while Rabbi Nachman's always have a happy ending directed by God, Singer's reveal a more ambivalent attitude toward Divine Providence.

In 1923 Singer's literary career began when his brother invited him to become proofreader for the Yiddish magazine he was coediting in Warsaw, *Literarische Bletter*. To supplement his income, Singer also translated popular works into Yiddish, and he began to write himself, publishing his first story in 1925 in his brother's periodical. When Israel Joshua left for America, Singer worked for a time as associate editor of *Globus* magazine. In 1935, convinced that Nazism posed real dangers, he followed his brother to New York, where he began his long and fruitful association with the *Jewish Daily Forward*.

Singer's first significant recognition in the United States came in 1950, with the English-language publication of *The Family Moskat*, a family saga modeled on his brother's work. Saul Bellow's translation of "Gimpl Tam" as "Gimpel the Fool" in the *Partisan Review* three years later added to a reputation that has continued to grow. Singer went on to win Newbery Awards for his children's stories (which he did not begin writing until he was sixty-two years old), National Book Awards, and the Nobel Prize in Literature in 1978.

In presenting the Nobel Prize to Singer, Lars Gyllensten of the Swedish Academy remarked that in his works "the Middle Ages seem to spring to life again, . . . the daily round is interwoven with wonders, reality is spun from dreams, the blood of the past pulsates in the present." Seven of Singer's novels and most of his successful short stories are set in the vanished world of Eastern European Jewry, a world he neither sentimentalizes nor romanticizes. His chief critics have been Yiddishists who see him as pessimistic and irreligious, but Singer countered that he is merely realistic: Not all Polish Jews were honest, God-fearing, and chaste, and tragedy was their lot at least as often as comedy. Singer mingles his mother's rationalism with the surrealistic realm of demons, dybbuks, and other supernatural beings that he had learned from his father and through whom he explores the unfathomable nature of the universe.

One of the reasons Singer has given for his delight in writing for children is that young readers want a good story, not a message. His writing instead highlights the unfathomable nature of the world. How can the existentially isolated individual survive? How should he live? How can he relate to the rest of suffering humanity? "If God is wisdom," Haiml Chentshiner asks in *Shosha*, "how can there be foolishness? And if God is life, how can there be death?" Cybula in *The King of the Fields* wonders why any creature must suffer. As puzzling as these questions are, they must be faced. Characters such as Jacob and Wanda/Sarah (*The Slave*) or Gimpel the Fool are saved because they are willing to believe in a Providence they cannot see. Recognizing their estrangement from God, the source of wisdom, they still reveal a sense of compassion for his creation, a compassion that ultimately redeems all foolishness. Whether set in upper West Side Manhattan or primitive Poland, Singer's fiction portrays the ongoing struggle between the forces of good and evil, between humankind's highest aspirations and deepest sensuality.

Joseph Rosenblum
Richard A. Hill

Bibliography

Alexander, Edward. *Isaac Bashevis Singer.* New York: Twayne, 1980. An incisive book-length introduction to Singer's life and work that provides a useful starting point for further study.

_______. *Isaac Bashevis Singer: A Study of the Short Fiction*. Boston: Twayne, 1990. An introduction to Singer's stories in terms of their themes, types, and motifs. Focuses on Singer's universal appeal rather than his Jewish appeal. Includes a section of quotations from Singer about his work, as well as essays on Singer by Irving Howe and two other critics.

Allison, Alida. *Isaac Bashevis Singer: Children's Stories and Memoirs*. New York: Twayne, 1996. Focuses on Singer's children's work and nonfiction, providing close readings of selected pieces, biographic information, and a useful bibliography of both primary and secondary sources.

Farrell, Grace. *From Exile to Redemption: The Fiction of Isaac Bashevis Singer.* Carbondale: Southern Illinois University Press, 1987. A study of the Kabbalic subtexts of Singer's fiction, especially its concern with the linguistic nature of reality and its connection with humankind's yearning for wholeness and exile from meaning.

_______, ed. *Critical Essays on Isaac Bashevis Singer.* New York: G. K. Hall, 1996. An extensive introduction on Singer's critical reception and the issues that have preoccupied him and his critics. Collects both contemporary reviews and a wide range of essays, including Leslie Fiedler's "I. B. Singer: Or, The American-ness of the American Jewish Writer."

Hadda, Janet. *Isaac Bashevis Singer: A Life*. New York: Oxford University Press, 1997. Focusing on both the forces of family and that social environment that influenced Singer, Hadda uncovers the public persona to reveal a more complex man than heretofore understood.

Kresh, Paul. *Isaac Bashevis Singer: The Magician of West 86th Street*. New York: Dial Press, 1979. A biography that includes many quotations and anecdotes, some relayed in a seemingly day-by-day manner. Kresh attempts to clarify details of the publishing history of Singer's work. Photographs, index, and bibliography.

Saltzman, Roberta. *Isaac Bashevis Singer: A Bibliography of His Works in Yiddish and English, 1960-1991*. Lanham, Md.: Scarecrow Press, 2002. A useful resource.

Sinclair, Clive. *The Brothers Singer.* London: Allison and Busby, 1983. A fascinating examination of Singer and his work in the context of one of the most important personal and literary relationships of the author's life. Sinclair effectively interweaves biography and literary analysis, conveying a deep understanding of the lives and works of Isaac and Joshua Singer.

Wolitz, Seth L., ed. *The Hidden Isaac Bashevis Singer.* Austin: University of Texas Press, 2001. A collection of essays focusing on Singer's use of Yiddish language and cultural experience, themes that persist through his writing, his interface with other times and cultures, his autobiographical work, and a translation of a previously unpublished "gangster" novel.

Zamir, Israel. *Journey to My Father, Isaac Bashevis Singer.* New York: Arcade, 1995. A lively memoir by Singer's only child that paints a complex portrait of the writer.

Israel Joshua Singer

Polish-born American novelist

Born: Biłgoraj, Poland, Russian Empire (now in Poland); November 30, 1893
Died: New York, New York; February 10, 1944
Identity: Jewish

LONG FICTION: *Shtol un ayzh*, 1927 (*Blood Harvest*, 1935; also known as *Steel and Iron*, 1969); *Yoshe Kalb*, 1932 (*The Sinner*, 1933); *Di brider Ashkenazi*, 1936 (*The Brothers Ashkenazi*, 1936); *Khaver Nakhman*, 1938 (*East of Eden*, 1939); *Di mishpokha Karnovsky*, 1943 (*The Family Carnovsky*, 1943).
SHORT FICTION: *Perl, un andere dertseylungen*, 1922; *The River Breaks Up: A Volume of Stories*, 1938.
NONFICTION: *Fun a velt vos iz nishto mer*, 1946 (*Of a World That Is No More*, 1970).

Israel Joshua Singer, Yiddish writer, was born on November 30, 1893, in Biłgoraj, Poland. The son of a rabbi, he studied the Talmud as a boy, but at seventeen he developed more worldly interests that led him finally to newspaper work. In 1922 he became the Warsaw representative of the *Jewish Daily Forward*. The paper sent him to Russia in 1926 and made him an editor when he emigrated to the United States in 1934.

Perl, un andere dertseylungen, his first volume of stories, was highly successful in Europe, and it was followed by more stories and a book about Russia, but Singer's reputation rests on three novels: *Yoshe Kalb*, published in English first as *The Sinner* and reissued as *Yoshe Kalb* in 1965; *The Brothers Ashkenazi*, translated in 1936 and sent through eleven editions before 1939; and *East of Eden*, translated in 1939. *The Brothers Ashkenazi* shows the social, economic, and political forces that affect an industrial town in Poland in the course of the nineteenth century and focuses on the contrasting fortunes of twin brothers. The more somber *East of Eden* traces the desperate careers of the members of a poor, dispossessed family and particularly of the son who turns hopefully to communism, only to be bitterly disillusioned. Often hailed as Singer's greatest work, *Yoshe Kalb* treats a homeless wanderer who appears to have two distinctly different personalities. Maurice Schwartz, the great Yiddish actor, wrote and starred in a stage version of the novel. In terms of critical reception and audience reaction, the play was one of the most successful Yiddish dramas ever produced.

Until his death, I. J. Singer was one of the most popular Yiddish writers in America, but after his death, he was overshadowed by his younger brother, Isaac Bashevis Singer, who won the Nobel Prize in Literature in 1978.

Richard Tuerk

Bibliography

Landis, Joseph C. "The Brothers Singer: Faith and Doubt." In *Blood Brothers: Siblings as Writers*, edited by Norman Kiell. New York: International Universities Press, 1983. Examines autobiographical writing of the two brothers to contrast the ways in which their loss of faith affected them.

Madison, Charles A. *Yiddish Literature: Its Scope and Major Writers*. New York: F. Ungar, 1968. Madison briefly traces Singer's movement from the Orthodoxy of his childhood toward the secularism of his adult years at the same time that he places him in the context of Yiddish literature and Yiddish authors.

Norich, Anita. *The Homeless Imagination in the Fiction of Israel Joshua Singer.* Bloomington: Indiana University Press, 1991. Treats the cultural tensions that Norich feels inform Singer's works, placing him in the contexts of Yiddish and American literature and culture.

Novak, Estelle Gergoren, and Maximilian E. Novak. "Savinkov: History, Revolution, and the Alienated Hero." *Yiddish* 8, no. 2 (1992). Treats one of Singer's plays as Singer's reaction to the way in which he felt the Russian Revolution failed to connect its ideals and its methods.

Sinclair, Clive. *The Brothers Singer.* New York: Schocken Books, 1983. Examines the lives of Israel Joshua Singer and his brother Isaac Bashevis Singer.

Elsie Singmaster

American novelist and short-story writer

Born: Schuylkill Haven, Pennsylvania; August 29, 1879
Died: Gettysburg, Pennsylvania; September 30, 1958

LONG FICTION: *Katy Gaumer*, 1915; *Basil Everman*, 1920; *Ellen Levis*, 1921; *Bennett Malin*, 1922; *The Hidden Road*, 1923; *Keller's Anna Ruth*, 1926; *What Everybody Wanted*, 1928; *The Magic Mirror*, 1934; *The Loving Heart*, 1937; *A High Wind Rising*, 1942; *I Speak for Thaddeus Stevens*, 1947; *I Heard of a River*, 1948.

SHORT FICTION: *Gettysburg*, 1913; *Bred in the Bone*, 1925; *Stories to Read at Christmas*, 1940.

NONFICTION: *Pennsylvania's Susquehanna*, 1950.

CHILDREN'S/YOUNG ADULT LITERATURE: *When Sarah Saved the Day*, 1909; *Emmeline*, 1916; *John Baring's House*, 1920; *A Boy at Gettysburg*, 1924; *"Sewing Susie,"* 1927; *Virginia's Bandit*, 1929; *You Make Your Own Luck*, 1929; *Swords of Steel*, 1933; *Stories of Pennsylvania*, 1937-1940 (4 volumes); *Rifles for Washington*, 1938; *The Isle of Que*, 1948.

The fiction of Elsie Singmaster may be clearly charted in geography and time. She is the novelist of Pennsylvania, more particularly of the Pennsylvania German region from the colonial period to the present. First in time are her stories of the early settlements in *A High Wind Rising* and *I Heard of a River*, set against the years when French and Indian raiders swept over the Warrior Road and Carlisle and Lancaster stood on a disputed frontier between the French lands on the Ohio and English territory along the Schuylkill and the Delaware. Later the history of the state widens into the history of the nation in her Revolutionary War novel, *Rifles for Washington*, and in *I Speak for Thaddeus Stevens* and in her stories of the three bloody days at Gettysburg in 1863. For a later time she wrote novels and tales of small-town and country life. These are regional rather than historical, for in them she makes vivid and real the Pennsylvania German countryside of red barns and fieldstone houses, the landscape of the sturdy, patriarchal Mennonites, Dunkers, and Amish, with their religious dress and slow unchanging ways of conduct and belief. This was her own region as well, and she brought to it her vision and understanding as a writer.

Singmaster was born in the Lutheran parsonage at Schuylkill Haven, Pennsylvania. Her father, the Reverend John Alden Singmaster, had among his ancestors one who studied under Martin Luther and another who was the first Lutheran minister ordained in the United States. Part of her childhood was spent at Macungie, the Millerstown of her fiction, where her father had been called to a pastorate of six churches between Allentown and Reading. She gathered impressions of this locality as she drove about with him when he went to preach to the different congregations in his charge. English was always spoken in the Singmaster home, as her mother was a Quaker of English descent, but from playmates and neighbors the children learned the hybrid mixture of English and German known as Pennsylvania Dutch. This was the only language known to the first teacher who taught her rhetoric.

If her early education was at best rudimentary, there were always good books to read in her father's library. By the time she was eleven she had begun to write stories of her own. Later, at Cornell University and Radcliffe College, she continued to write sketches of Pennsylvania life and character, partly to set down her observations and partly to explain a group of people she thought were misunderstood. She sold her first story in 1905. By the time she graduated from Radcliffe in 1907 she had already contributed to *Scribner's*, *Century*, and *The Atlantic Monthly*. In 1912 she married Harold Lewars, a musician, and went to live in Harrisburg. After his death in 1915 she made her permanent home in Gettysburg, where her father was the president of the Lutheran theological seminary.

Singmaster had already written a number of stories and several books for children when in 1915 she published her first novel, *Katy Gaumer*. Katy is one of Singmaster's typical heroines, a Pennsylvania German girl eager to acquire the learning that will prepare her for life in a larger world. *Basil Everman*, which is set in a college town that may be identified as Gettysburg, deals with the influence a young writer of genius has on a group of people of the college and the town many years after his death. *Ellen Levis* and *Keller's Anna Ruth* are stories of gentle, self-sacrificing young women, handicapped by environment, who ultimately have a better future. *Bennett Malin*, darker in mood and implications, tells of a man who builds a false, bright world about himself on a shaky foundation of literary theft. In *What Everybody Wanted*, Singmaster shifts the scene to Maryland to present a light and amusing account of human vanity and desire. *The Magic Mirror* returns to a more familiar Pennsylvania setting and brings to life a community, a countryside, and a strange but rich way of life through the experiences of Jesse Hummer, whose ambition it is to tell the story of his people after he becomes a writer.

Singmaster's later novels reveal a renewed interest in historical themes. In *Rifles for Washington* she presents the events and battles of seven years of war from a boy's point of view because she wanted to stress the element of action that would make the deepest impression on a boy's mind. Like many of her stories, this book is juvenile fiction only in the sense that it deals with a youthful hero. *A High Wind Rising* is a regional chronicle dealing with the early settlements and the part played by the Pennsylvania Germans under Conrad Weiser in holding the land for the English during the French and Indian wars. *I Speak for Thaddeus Stevens* is a biographical novel throwing new light on the powerful political figure of the Civil War period. *I Heard of a River* is another story of the early settlements. Of Singmaster's short stories, the most vivid and moving are the Civil War tales in *Gettysburg*, the most amusing her stories of the Mennonite Shindledecker sisters in *Bred in the Bone*. Much of her magazine fiction remains to be collected.

A writer of quiet but satisfying richness and depth within her chosen field, Singmaster never attracted a wide reading public or the attention of popular criticism. One reason may be that as examples of work done within a clearly defined regional tradition, her books have owed almost nothing to literary fashion.

Bibliography

Hart, James David, ed. *The Oxford Companion to American Literature*. 4th ed. New York: Oxford University Press, 1965. Singmaster has an entry devoted to her in this reference work.

Kohler, Dayton. "Elsie Singmaster and the Regional Tradition." *Commonwealth* 1 (September, 1947). Singmaster's place in the nineteenth century regional tradition is explored.

Kribbs, Jayne K. "Elsie Singmaster." In *American Novelists, 1910-1945*, edited by James J. Martine. Vol. 9 in *Dictionary of Literary Biography*, edited by Matthew Bruccoli. Detroit: Gale Group, 1981. Contains biography and short critical analysis.

Wagenknecht, Edward. *Cavalcade of the American Novel*. New York: Holt, 1952. Singmaster is mentioned.

Warfel, Harry R. *American Novelists of Today*. 1951. Reprint. Westport, Conn.: Greenwood Press, 1972. Contains a short profile of Singmaster.

Andrei Sinyavsky

Russian novelist

Born: Moscow, Soviet Union (now in Russia); October 8, 1925
Died: Fontenay-aux-Roses, France; February 25, 1997
Pseudonym: Abram Tertz

LONG FICTION: *Sud idyot*, 1959 (in Polish), 1960 (in Russian; as Abram Tertz; *The Trial Begins*, 1960); *Lyubimov*, 1963 (in Polish), 1964 (in Russian; as Tertz; *The Makepeace Experiment*, 1965); *Kroshka Tsores*, 1980 (novella; *Little Jinx*, 1992); *Spokoynoy nochi*, 1984 (*Goodnight!*, 1989).

SHORT FICTION: *Fantasticheskie povesti*, 1961 (*Fantastic Stories*, 1963; also known as *The Icicle, and Other Stories*).

NONFICTION: *Istoriya russkoy sovetsky literatury*, 1958, 1961; *Chto takoe sotsialisticheskii realizm*, 1959 (as Abram Tertz; *On Socialist Realism*, 1960); *Pikasso*, 1960 (with I. N. Golomshtok); *Poeziya pervykh let revolyutsii, 1917-1920*, 1964 (with A. Menshutin); *Mysli vrasplokh*, 1966 (as Tertz; *Unguarded Thoughts*, 1972); *For Freedom of Imagination*, 1971 (essays); *Golos iz khora*, 1973 (*A Voice from the Chorus*, 1976); *Progulki s Pushkinym*, 1975 (*Strolls with Pushkin*, 1993); *V teni Gogolya*, 1975; *"Opavshie list'ya" V. V. Rozanova*, 1982; *Soviet Civilization: A Cultural History*, 1990; *The Russian Intelligentsia*, 1997.

Andrei Donatovich Sinyavsky (sihn-YOV-skee) was the godfather of the post-Stalin renaissance in Russian literature. Born on October 8, 1925, into the family of an ineffectual radical idealist, Sinyavsky was reared as a true believer in the Communist system. Although well-educated, his parents held menial white-collar jobs. In his late teens Sinyavsky served in the Soviet army. Demobilized, he entered Moscow University in 1947, where he defended his dissertation on Maxim Gorky, the father of Socialist Realism, in 1952. Two friendships of his student years would have enormous consequences for Sinyavsky: Hélène Pelletier, the daughter of the French naval attaché who was permitted to attend Moscow University, and Yuli Daniel, whose bohemian apartment became a center for young intellectuals. Soon after graduation Sinyavsky was married to Mariya Rozanova, a student of art history. Although Sinyavsky had acquired some exposure to Western literature and art, he remained a fervent believer in the moral integrity of the Communist system. The first doubt arose when his father was arrested in 1951 on preposterous charges. In the early 1950's Sinyavsky worked as a lecturer at Moscow University and then as a researcher at the Institute of World Literature. His articles were bringing him a degree of renown, but he wished to write fiction as well. Sinyavsky's first story, "At the Circus" (1955), already reflects his love of the phantasmagoric and his persistent identification of the artist with the criminal.

Nikita Khrushchev's historic 1956 denunciation of Stalin's twenty-year reign of terror shattered Sinyavsky's illusions. His new friendship with Boris Pasternak, who had sent his suppressed novel, *Doctor Zhivago* (1957), abroad, perhaps inspired him to ask Pelletier to smuggle his work abroad for publication. Under the pseudonym Abram Tertz, two long works appeared in France in 1959: a theoretical essay, *On Socialist Realism*, decrying the sterility of Socialist Realism and calling for a new "phantasmagoric" literature, and a novella, *The Trial Begins*, which illustrated the essay's literary thesis and was a powerful indictment of the Stalinist dictum that the end justifies the means. In 1961, his story collection *Fantastic Stories* appeared in the West, followed two years later by *The Makepeace Experiment*, an antiutopian political fantasy. Sinyavsky's reflections on many themes, especially religious ones, appeared in a collection of aphoristic notes entitled *Unguarded Thoughts*. These Western publications created a sensation and endless speculation about the identity of their author. Sinyavsky/Tertz successfully led his double life for nearly six years. Pressure mounted after the fall of the relatively liberal Khrushchev in 1964. In late 1965, the Soviet government learned the identity of "Tertz," and Sinyavsky and his fellow writer Yuli Daniel were arrested. Wishing to preserve the appearance of legality in the eyes of Western public opinion, Soviet officials orchestrated a show trial in February, 1966. Although the trial was closed to the Western press, the defendants' wives smuggled out their own handwritten transcripts, which were published abroad. Sinyavsky was sentenced to seven years.

Sinyavsky was released in June of 1971, and two years later he was permitted to emigrate to France with his wife and child. The camp years had not been wasted. During his sentence he had utilized his bimonthly letters to his wife to pour out his thoughts on many subjects. Once in Paris, these letters, totaling some fifteen hundred pages, became the nuclei of three books. *A Voice from the Chorus* is a gathering of reflections inspired both by camp life and by the author's philosophical and artistic interests. The other two volumes, *V teni Gogolya* (in the shadow of Gogol) and *Strolls with Pushkin*, are irreverent and highly personal meditations on two giants of Russian literature. Sinyavsky resumed his career as a creative writer with *Kroshka Tsores* (little Tsores), a brief novella exploring the theme of guilt and the artist. The major work of the emigration is *Goodnight!*, a long, highly fragmented, phantasmagoric memoir-novel about Sinyavsky's life as a Soviet intellectual and secret dissident writer, his betrayal, his trial, and his years in a labor camp.

Sinyavsky, who secured a teaching position at the Sorbonne, was widely known and translated into many languages, but his life in emigration was not easy. Just as he found himself in conflict with Soviet society, he also found himself odd man out in émigré circles. Émigré journals at first welcomed Sinyavsky to their pages, where he published penetrating essays on the Soviet scene. His brilliantly eccentric views proved unacceptable to opinionated editors, however, and he soon found himself without an outlet for his writings. Partially in response, Sinyavsky and his wife established their own small journal. Beginning in 1978, *Sintaksis* served as a forum for the views of Sinyavsky and other émigré writers who urge a "pluralist" outlook in opposition to those who favor more traditional, if not authoritarian approaches to art and society.

Goodnight! is a distillation of Sinyavsky's approach to fiction. Densely metaphoric and richly allusive, it makes heavy demands on the reader's knowledge of culture and history (especially Russian), as well as of the author's own life. Each of the memoir-novel's five chapters centers on the events of a particular night. The biographic fact serves as a point of departure for numerous seemingly unrelated vignettes that ultimately form a sort of ornate, surrealist mosaic depicting one man's life during the nightmare of Stalinism.

In spite of the structural and stylistic complexity of Sinyavsky's writings, his themes are simple: Stalinist tyranny and the nature of art and the artist. Stalinism very nearly destroyed a nation and its culture—all in the name of an ideal, Communism. The means perverted the goal. So bizarre was that world that it could be rendered only by an equally bizarre, phantasmagoric art. Sinyavsky's other theme was the transcending power of art and the inherently subversive character of the free artist. These two interconnected themes unite Sinyavsky's oeuvre from *The Trial Begins* through *Goodnight!* and his critical and journalistic writings.

Andrei Sinyavsky introduced a fantastic, modernist, aesthetically oriented prose into a literature which had been stifled by a primitive, dogmatic Socialist Realism. Although the realistic strain remains dominant in Russian letters, Sinyavsky's seminal essay *On Socialist Realism* and his subsequent fiction blazed a path for the revival of the fantastic. Both Vassily Aksyonov and Sasha Sokolov, the most important younger writers to emerge in the 1960's and 1970's (and later both émigrés), heeded Sinyavsky/Tertz's phantasmagoric imperative.

D. Barton Johnson

Bibliography

Dalton, Margaret. *Andrei Siniavskii and Julii Daniel: Two Soviet "Heretical" Writers*. Würzburg: Jal-verlag, 1973. Along with a discussion of the other works that Sinyavsky wrote prior to his arrest, this study contains a detailed story-by-story analysis of the six stories from that period. Throughout, Dalton pays special attention to the unusual literary devices that often make the works difficult to interpret. Contains notes and a bibliography.

Durkin, Andrew R. "Narrator, Metaphor, and Theme in Sinjavskij's *Fantastic Tales*." *Slavic and East European Journal* 24 (1980): 133-144. Durkin divides the six early stories into three pairs for the purposes of analysis, but his goal is to discern the thematic concerns and formal devices that link all the stories. He emphasizes the role of art and of the artist, as well as the theme of escape, or liberation.

Fenander, Sara. "Author and Autocrat: Tertz's Stalin and the Ruse of Charisma." *The Russian Review* 58 (April, 1999): 286-297. Discusses Sinyavsky in his role as both cultural critic and provocateur, Abram Tertz; claims that by turning the discredited Joseph Stalin into a double for himself, Sinyavsky/Tertz reveals both the artistry of Stalinism and the mythical privileged place of the writer in Russian culture.

Haber, Erika. "In Search of the Fantastic in Tertz's Fantastic Realism." *Slavic and East European Journal* 42 (Summer, 1998): 254-267. Shows how the presence of an eccentric narrator who often plays a double role as both character and narrator, creating a highly self-conscious text is a basic feature of Tertz's fantastic realism.

Kolonosky, Walter. "Andrei Sinyavsky: Puzzle Maker." *Slavic and East European Journal* 42 (Fall, 1998): 385-388. Compares Sinyavsky's works to puzzles; his pieces are not simply read, but contain historical references, allegorical links, language peculiarities, grotesque allusions, and autobiographical asides that require interpretation.

Lourie, Richard. *Letters to the Future: An Approach to Sinyavsky-Tertz*. Ithaca, N.Y.: Cornell University Press, 1975. Lourie's analyses are distinctive both for his critiques of certain stories and for his efforts to show their relationship to other works in Russian literature. Includes notes, bibliography, and an index.

Nepomnyashchy, Catharine Theimer. "Andrei Donatovich Sinyavsky (1925-1997)." *Slavic and East European Journal* 42 (Fall, 1998): 367-371. Claims that Sinyavsky's works have been misunderstood; challenges the characterization of him as a political dissident and argues for a view of his texts as works that engage fantasy and encourage the fanciful.

_______. "Sinyavsky/Tertz: The Evolution of the Writer in Exile." *Humanities in Society* 7, no. 314 (1984): 123-142. After providing a brief overview of Sinyavsky's career during his first decade in the West, the author goes on to detail Sinyavsky's concerns with the role of the writer in relationship to reality and society at large. Concludes with a discussion of *Kroshka Tsores*.

Pevear, Richard. "Sinyavsky in Two Worlds: Two Brothers Named Chénier." *The Hudson Review* 25 (1972): 375-402. Pevear contrasts Sinyavsky and Yevgeny Yevtushenko in an effort to elucidate Sinyavsky's views about the tasks of the writer. Contains a thoughtful analysis of "The Icicle."

Edith Sitwell

English poet

Born: Scarborough, Yorkshire, England; September 7, 1887
Died: London, England; December 9, 1964

POETRY: *The Mother, and Other Poems*, 1915; *Twentieth Century Harlequinade, and Other Poems*, 1916 (with Osbert Sitwell); *Clown's Houses*, 1918; *The Wooden Pegasus*, 1920; *Facade*, 1922; *Bucolic Comedies*, 1923; *The Sleeping Beauty*, 1924; *Troy Park*, 1925; *Poor Young People*, 1925 (with Osbert Sitwell and Sacheverell Sitwell); *Elegy on Dead Fashion*, 1926; *Rustic Elegies*, 1927; *Popular Song*, 1928; *Five Poems*, 1928; *Gold Coast Customs*, 1929; *Collected Poems*, 1930; *In Spring*, 1931; *Epithalamium*, 1931; *Five Variations on a Theme*, 1933; *Selected Poems*, 1936; *Poems New and Old*, 1940; *Street Songs*, 1942; *Green Song, and Other Poems*, 1944; *The Weeping Babe*, 1945; *The Song of the Cold*, 1945; *The Shadow of Cain*, 1947; *The Canticle of the Rose*, 1949; *Facade, and Other Poems*, 1950; *Gardeners and Astronomers*, 1953; *Collected Poems*, 1954; *The Outcasts*, 1962; *Music and Ceremonies*, 1963; *Selected Poems*, 1965; *The Early Unpublished Poems of Edith Sitwell*, 1994.

LONG FICTION: *I Live Under a Black Sun*, 1937.

NONFICTION: *Poetry and Criticism*, 1925; *Alexander Pope*, 1930; *Bath*, 1932; *The English Eccentrics*, 1933; *Aspects of Modern Poetry*, 1934; *Victoria of England*, 1936; *Trio*, 1938 (with Osbert Sitwell and Sacheverell Sitwell); *A Poet's Notebook*, 1943; *Fanfare for Elizabeth*, 1946; *A Notebook on William Shakespeare*, 1948; *The Queens and the Hive*, 1962; *Taken Care Of*, 1965; *Selected Letters of Edith Sitwell*, 1997 (Richard Greene, editor).

EDITED TEXTS: *Wheels*, 1916-1921; *The Pleasures of Poetry*, 1930-1932, 1934; *Planet and Glow Worm*, 1944; *A Book of Winter*, 1950; *The American Genius*, 1951; *A Book of Flowers*, 1952; *The Atlantic Book of British and American Poetry*, 1958.

Edith Sitwell, one of the twentieth century's foremost poets and a flamboyant exponent of experimentation in verse, was the oldest child of Sir George Sitwell, fourth baronet of Renishaw Park, the family seat for six hundred years. Much of the extravagant personality of Edith and her brothers, Osbert and Sacheverell, is readily understandable to the reader of Sir Osbert Sitwell's memoirs of their outrageous father, *Left Hand, Right Hand*.

Educated in secret (as she said), Edith Sitwell first became known in 1916 as the editor of an anthology, *Wheels*, which stridently featured for six years her own work, that of her brothers, and other authors whose voices were to be heard frequently in the 1920's. One of the highlights of the 1925 theater season in London was the premiere of Sitwell's *Facade*, in which she chanted her early fanciful and rhythmical verse to similarly exciting musical settings provided by William Walton. For the performance Sitwell spoke through an amplifying mask behind a screen, a device to provide artificiality for the exotic occasion. The London Hall was an uproar of Sitwell's admirers and detractors. Twenty-five years later, the work was similarly performed in New York's Museum of Modern Art, but so far had modern taste and Sitwell's reputation advanced that the last occasion was almost regal in dignity, as befitted its central performer—Sitwell had been given the accolade of Grand Dame of the Cross of the British Empire in 1954.

Her flair for self-dramatization made students of literature uneasy about the seriousness of her poetry for a long time. Standing six feet in height, she always appeared in extravagant and archaic costumes and headgear, often medieval, spangled with ostentatious rings and necklaces. "I have always had a great affinity for Queen Elizabeth [I]," she said once. "We were born on the same day of the month and about the same hour of the day."

Although her Dadaist stunts were calculated to express her love of being flamboyant and of irritating the stuffy ("Good taste," she claimed, "is the worst vice ever invented"), her interest in poetry was serious, as was her talent. Her keenness for verbal experimentation found a fit subject in the extraordinary *Gold Coast Customs*, her own version of T. S. Eliot's *The Waste Land* (1922) and one of the remarkable poems of the remarkable decade of the 1920's.

For ten years after *Gold Coast Customs* Sitwell wrote little poetry, devoting herself to critical essays and nonfiction, including a biography of Alexander Pope, but mainly taking care of a friend, Helen Rootham, through her fatal illness. With the coming of World War II, Sitwell returned to poetry, still with her dazzling technical equipment but now with a rich store of traditional Christian imagery, having become a Roman Catholic in 1955. The agonies of the bombardment of London and the terror of the atomic bomb evoked from Sitwell some of the most moving poetry ever written about the cruelty of war.

Along with her delight in self-dramatization, Sitwell was renowned, from the publication of *Wheels* all through her life, for her championship of younger writers. Dylan Thomas is but one of the best known of the writers whose verbal experimentation she praised and championed early in their careers.

Bibliography

Brophy, James D. *Edith Sitwell: The Symbolist Order.* Carbondale: Southern Illinois University Press, 1968. Brophy examines the themes and techniques of Sitwell's admittedly difficult poetry. He finds in her work a coherent use of modernist symbolism. A valuable study for close analysis of her poems and critical views. Supplemented by a select bibliography and an index.

Cevasco, G. A. *The Sitwells: Edith, Osbert, and Sacheverell.* Boston: Twayne, 1987. Edith and her younger brothers, all writers and famous personalities, are brought together in an excellent, compact survey of their writings and family life. Their texts are shown to respond to the major events that shaped the twentieth century: two world wars, an economic depression, and the opening of the atomic age. Contains a chronology, notes, a select bibliography, and an index.

Elborn, Geoffrey. *Edith Sitwell: A Biography.* London: Sheldon Press, 1981. Traces Sitwell's life, from her birth as an unwanted female to her solitary death (by her own command). Includes photographs that illustrate her life, twelve half-plates, two plates, notes, a bibliography, and an index.

Glendinning, Victoria. *Edith Sitwell: A Unicorn Among Lions.* London: Phoenix, 1993. Revisionary appraisal separates the myths from the newer status of Sitwell's work. Glendinning discusses Sitwell's poetry, her criticism, and her literary relationships. Includes six plates, seventeen half-plates, notes, and an index.

Pearson, John. *Facades: Edith, Osbert, and Sacheverell Sitwell.* London: Macmillan, 1978. A detailed, year-by-year account of the literary activities, travels, and relationships of the famous sister and her brothers, which places Sitwell in her literary environment. Photographs are placed throughout the text. Contains seventeen plates, notes, and an index.

Sitwell, Edith. *Selected Letters of Edith Sitwell.* Edited by Richard Greene. Rev. ed. London: Virago, 1998. A collection including previously unpublished letters to a remarkable array of notables, including Bertrand Russell, Gertrude Stein, Cecil Beaton, Kingsley Amis, T. S. Eliot, and Virginia Woolf.

John Skelton

English poet

Born: Northern England, possibly Yorkshire; c. 1460
Died: London, England; June 21, 1529

POETRY: *The Bowge of Court*, 1499; *Phyllyp Sparowe*, c. 1508; *Ware the Hawk*, c. 1508; *The Tunnyng of Elynour Rummyng*, 1508; *Speke, Parrot*, 1521; *Collyn Clout*, 1522; *Why Come Ye Nat to Courte*, 1522; *The Garlande of Laurell*, 1523; *Pithy, Pleasaunt, and Profitable Workes of Maister Skelton, Poete Laureate*, 1568; *The Complete Poems of John Skelton, Laureate*, 1931 (Philip Henderson, editor).
DRAMA: *Magnyfycence*, pb. 1516.
NONFICTION: *Speculum Principis*, 1501 (also known as *A Mirror for Princes*).

John Skelton was born about 1460. The facts about his early life are few. He seems to have attended Cambridge University when quite young, but there is no record of his receiving a degree. When the noted printer William Caxton spoke of him in 1490, Skelton had already established his position as writer and scholar. He was "laureated" by the universities of Oxford, Cambridge, and Louvain; the precise nature of this honor is still being debated.

He won royal favor for his accomplishment and was made tutor to Prince Henry, later King Henry VIII, about 1496. He was ordained to the priesthood in 1498. During this period Skelton struck up an acquaintance with the visiting Dutch scholar Erasmus, who later honored Skelton by calling him "England's Homer." His observations on the life around him inspired his satire on royal hangers-on, *The Bowge of Court*.

The death of Arthur, prince of Wales, in 1502 brought an abrupt end to Skelton's career as tutor. While his gifts were considered suitable for the education of a future archbishop of Canterbury, they were apparently not what Henry VII thought fitting for the heir to the throne. Skelton was made rector of Diss in Norfolk, presumably as a reward for his services, and he lived there for several years, performing the duties of parish priest. It is reasonably conjectured that many of his poems were composed during this period, though during his life he was more known for his polemical and sometimes heated debates.

After Henry VIII's accession to the throne in 1509, Skelton sent him several gifts, hoping to remind him of their past association and thereby win his patronage. His efforts were eventually successful, and in 1512 he returned to Westminster as *orator regius*. As court poet he commemorated notable events in both Latin and English verse, writing elegies for Henry VII and his mother, Lady Margaret Beaufort, who had been Skelton's patron when he was tutor to Prince Henry, and celebrating the English victory over James IV of Scotland at Flodden.

Skelton soon exceeded his responsibility as *orator regius* by attacking Cardinal Wolsey, who was rapidly becoming the most powerful man in England. Skelton's play *Magnyfycence* uses the traditional form of the Tudor interlude, the contest between figures representing virtues and vices for the possession of a hero, to attack the influence of the cardinal on the young king. It was perhaps fortunate for the poet that he was then residing on the grounds of Westminster Abbey and therefore in sanctuary, for he faced sure arrest for his satire. Some accord between the two men was apparently reached about 1522, for Skelton felt free to spend Christmas at the home of the countess of Surrey in York that year. He dedicated *The Garlande of Laurell* to Wolsey in 1523, and yet even then he would not spare Wolsey from his criticisms, for in the previous year he had written "Speke, Parot," and in 1522 he wrote "Why Come Ye Not to Court?"—both poems attacking the cardinal for many abuses.

As Skelton's quasi-allegorical morality play indicates his advocacy of traditional values, so does his position during the so-named grammarian's war that divided scholars and Latin pedagogues in 1519 and 1520. Skelton's debates, apparently acrimonious, with those in favor of a progressive educational agenda is a clear manifestation of his medieval heritage. Thus Skelton is truly a transitional figure, philosophically aligned with the doctrines of conservatism but increasingly embattled by the dawning of Renaissance humanism. Skelton lived and wrote in Westminster for the last years of his life and died there on June 21, 1529.

Scott D. Vander Ploeg

Bibliography

Carpenter, Nan Cooke. *John Skelton*. New York: Twayne, 1968. This overview contains a preface, a chronology, and an outline of Skelton's life. Carpenter discusses all of his important poetic works and highlights the poet's intimate technical knowledge of music, dance songs, and popular song tags. Skelton's reputation and influence is also discussed. Includes notes and references.

Kinney, Arthur F. *John Skelton, Priest as Poet: Seasons of Discovery*. Chapel Hill: University of North Carolina Press, 1987. Maintaining that Skelton's primary vocation, the priesthood, was fundamental to his literary work, Kinney attempts to give a comprehensive evaluation of his poetry. Includes notes and an index.

Scattergood, V. J. *Reading the Past: Essays on Medieval and Renaissance Literature*. Portland, Oreg.: Four Courts Press, 1996. Includes a critical essay on the works of Skelton, bibliographical references, and an index.

Spinrad, Phoebe S. "Too Much Liberty: *Measure for Measure* and Skelton's *Magnyfycence*." *Modern Language Quarterly* 60, no. 4 (December, 1999): 431-449. Spinrad explores the themes of liberty and restraint in William Shakespeare's *Measure for Measure* and John Skelton's early sixteenth century *Magnyfycence*, a "governance" play. Skelton's drama remained in print well into Shakespeare's lifetime and may have influenced *Measure for Measure* and other plays.

Walker, Greg. *John Skelton and the Politics of the 1520's*. New York: Cambridge University Press, 1988. Discusses the political and social views of Skelton and gives a history of English political satire as well as a view of the politics and government in England during the first half of the sixteenth century.

B. F. Skinner

American psychologist

Born: Susquehanna, Pennsylvania; March 20, 1904
Died: Cambridge, Massachusetts; August 18, 1990

NONFICTION: *The Behavior of Organisms: An Experimental Analysis*, 1938; *Science and Human Behavior*, 1953; *Verbal Behavior*, 1957; *Schedules of Reinforcement*, 1957 (with Charles. B. Ferster); *Cumulative Record*, 1959, enlarged 1961, 3d edition 1972; *The Analysis of Behavior*, 1961 (with James G. Holland); *The Technology of Teaching*, 1968; *Contingencies of Reinforcement: A Theoretical Analysis*, 1969; *Beyond Freedom and Dignity*, 1971; *About Behaviorism*, 1974; *Particulars of My Life*, 1976; *Reflections on Behaviorism and Society*, 1978; *The Shaping of a Behaviorist*, 1979; *Notebooks*, 1980 (Robert Epstein, editor); *Skinner for the Classroom*, 1982 (Epstein, editor); *Enjoy Old Age*, 1983 (with Margaret E. Vaughan); *A Matter of Consequences*, 1983; *Upon Further Reflection*, 1987; *Recent Issues in the Analysis of Behavior*, 1989;
LONG FICTION: *Walden Two*, 1948.

Burrhus Frederic Skinner, known as "Fred" to his friends and as "B. F." to most others, was born in the railroad town of Susquehanna, Pennsylvania (population about 2,500) and lived there until leaving for college at eighteen. Skinner's family was middle-class. His father, William Arthur Skinner, was a lawyer for the railroad and ran for political office several times without ever winning an election. Fred's mother, Grace Madge Skinner, was a homemaker known for her beauty, her singing voice, and her community service. Burrhus was her maiden name.

Skinner's mother nearly died in childbirth, a fact Fred was to be reminded of occasionally as he grew older. Skinner had one sibling, a younger brother named Ebbe who died tragically at sixteen of a brain hemorrhage. Fred Skinner was a college freshman when Ebbe died and never spoke much of the event.

Skinner attended the local high school, making good grades and graduating second in a class of seven. (His mother and father also graduated second in their classes.) He then attended Hamilton College in Clinton, New York, a small liberal arts school, where he majored in English. He took no psychology courses.

Although Will Skinner wanted his son to go into law, Fred had no taste for the field. He was interested in writing, and after graduating from Hamilton, Skinner proposed to his parents, who had relocated to Scranton, Pennsylvania, that he live back at home while writing a novel. Skinner's father, who had himself tried unsuccessfully to write stories, agreed reluctantly to support Fred for a year. One year turned into two, although only the first was spent actually writing. Skinner had published poetry, essays, and news articles in local or college papers and even in some national magazines, and he had received encouragement from poet Robert Frost for his writing. However, he decided after what he later referred to as his "Dark Year" that he would never be a literary success. In fact, he began to doubt literature's worth to anyone. According to *Particulars of My Life*, the first of Skinner's autobiographical trilogy, this is when he began to consider science as a future.

Although Skinner had never taken psychology courses, he had always observed the behavior of humans and animals. He also realized that many of his stories had dealt with psychological issues. Perhaps the biggest catalyst for Skinner's decision to focus on behavioral psychology came when he read Bertrand Russell's *An Outline of Philosophy* (1927). From Russell he discovered the work of John Watson, the founder of the school of psychology called behaviorism. In the fall of 1928 Skinner started graduate school at Harvard University. There, he found kindred spirits in behaviorism, most notably Fred Keller, an early influence who also became Skinner's lifelong friend.

Skinner obtained his Ph.D. from Harvard in 1931 and then stayed for five more years to study animal behavior. When his fellowships ended in 1936, he accepted a teaching job at the University of Minnesota. Although never having taught before, he was apparently a good teacher. In addition to accepting new job, in 1936 Skinner married Yvonne Blue (called Eve), who had also been an English major. They had two daughters, Julie and Deborah. A persistent myth concerning Skinner is that he raised his second daughter, Deborah, in a "Skinner box" and that she became psychotic and either committed suicide or was institutionalized. This is untrue. Skinner, a talented inventor since childhood, developed a specialized crib for Deborah, sometimes called an "Aircrib," which had an enclosed space with a glass front in which the temperature and lighting could be carefully controlled. Toys were available to Deborah, and although she slept in the crib, she was taken out frequently during the day to be cuddled. It was not, as so often reported, a cold and unfeeling approach to child rearing. Skinner's daughters both adored him and spoke of him as a loving and involved father.

While at Minnesota, Skinner wrote his first two major books. One established his reputation as an innovative researcher and behaviorist; the other created controversy that made Skinner infamous to the public. The first book was *The Behavior of Organisms*, in which Skinner reported the results from years of research into rat behavior, using what is widely known as the Skinner box. (Skinner hated that term.) The second book, *Walden Two*, was a work of fiction written in the summer of 1945, just before Skinner left Minnesota to become departmental chairman at Indiana University. Skinner's one-time dream of writing a novel had come true, though it was to be the only one he ever wrote and he had to promise the publisher a psychology textbook to get it accepted. Skinner waited three years to see *Walden Two* published, but, though it sold slowly at first, sales were in the millions by the time he died.

Although *Walden Two* became his best-known book, *The Behavior of Organisms* established Skinner's reputation in psychology. It laid out the scientific basis for all of his later work, including *Walden Two*. Skinner presented six important concepts, as follows. First, psychologists should study behavior alone, not internal states such as thoughts or feelings. Second, behavior is determined by genetic and environmental factors, with environmental factors being of greater interest because they are more easily manipulated to change behavior. Third, organisms are active, and the behaviors they "emit" are primarily determined by environmental conditions. Fourth, when organisms act, they experience consequences; reinforcing consequences make behaviors more likely to reoccur, and punishing consequences make them less likely to reoccur. Fifth, animals such as rats and pigeons behave in ways that are essentially the same as in humans, which means that an understanding of animal behavior can be applied to understanding human behavior. Sixth, human problems, from abnormal behavior to criminality, can be corrected using behavioral concepts such as positive reinforcement. His later writings, including numerous articles and such books as *Schedules of Reinforcement*, *Science and Human Behavior*, and *About Behaviorism*, rendered Skinner the primary "behaviorist" in the world.

After only a few years as departmental chairman at Indiana, a position at which Skinner worked hard but for which he was not truly suited, he was invited in 1947 to give some lectures at Harvard. A position was offered him for the following year, and he accepted. He remained associated with Harvard for the rest of his life. There, his work varied even more widely among fields that interested him. He wrote a theoretical book titled *Verbal Behavior* and practical books about teaching that laid out basic principles that have strongly influenced American education. Among these principles were, first, that reinforcement is better than punishment for motivating students; second, that feedback on correct or incorrect student responses should be given as quickly as possible—preferably immediately; and third, that students should be allowed to learn at their own pace. He felt that many of these principles could be realized through technology.

While at Harvard, Skinner also became, increasingly, a social critic. He argued that humankind had made great strides in physical technology but that what was needed more was a "behavioral technology." His best known work of social criticism was *Beyond Freedom and Dignity*. Skinner believed that his book explained and extended the concepts of freedom and dignity. His detractors saw his views as cold and inhuman and argued that Skinner treated people as little more than machines.

Skinner retired officially in 1974 at age seventy, but his was a working retirement. He visited his Harvard office frequently and continued his writing and correspondence without fail in his basement home office. He added three autobiographies to his resume: *Particulars of My Life*, *The Shaping of a Behaviorist*, and *A Matter of Consequences*, and he became increasingly in demand as a speaker. He received honorary degrees from many colleges and universities, including the University of Chicago, the University of Exeter (England), and McGill University (Canada). He received such awards as the National Medal of Science and the Humanist of the Year Award, and he became the first to receive the Citation for Outstanding Lifetime Contribution to Psychology. Next to Sigmund Freud, B. F. Skinner became the best-known psychologist of the twentieth century. His critics complained that his concepts dehumanized people, but many others have hailed him as a scientific innovator who developed novel and effective ways of dealing with human problems through the study and control of behavior. In 1989 Skinner was diagnosed with leukemia. He died the following year.

Charles A. Gramlich

Bibliography

Bjork, Daniel W. *B. F. Skinner: A Life*. Washington, D.C.: American Psychological Association, 1997. Presents views from both supporters and detractors of Skinner and tries to place Skinner in the larger context of American intellectual life.

Nye, Robert D. *The Legacy of B. F. Skinner.* Belmont, Calif.: Wadsworth, 1992. An excellent short introduction to Skinner's life and thoughts.

_______. *Three Psychologies: Perspectives from Freud, Skinner, and Rogers*. 6th ed. Pacific Grove, Calif.: Brooks/Cole, 2000. The most important section contrasts Skinner's views with those of Sigmund Freud and Carl Rogers.

Smith, Laurence D., and William R. Woodward, eds. *B. F. Skinner and Behaviorism in American Culture*. Bethlehem, Pa.: Lehigh University Press, 1996. Meant mostly for scholars.

Wiener, Daniel N. *B. F. Skinner: Benign Anarchist*. Needham Heights, Mass.: Allyn and Bacon, 1996. One of the most complete biographies of Skinner. Examines the unpleasant aspects of Skinner's personality.

Josef Škvorecký

Czech novelist

Born: Náchod, Czechoslovakia (now in Czech Republic); September 27, 1924

LONG FICTION: *Zbabělci*, 1958 (*The Cowards*, 1970); *Legenda Emöke*, 1963 (*Emöke*, 1977); *Bassaxofon*, 1967 (*The Bass Saxophone*, 1977); *Konec nylonoveho véku*, 1967; *Farářův konec*, 1969 (with Evald Schorm); *Lvíče*, 1969 (*Miss Silver's Past*, 1974); *Tankový prapor*, 1969 (*The Republic of Whores: A Fragment from the Time of the Cults*, 1993); *Mirákl: Politická detectivka*, 1972 (*The Miracle Game*,1991); *Prima sezóna*, 1975 (*The Swell Season: A Text on the Most Important Things in Life*, 1982); *Konec poručíka Borůvky*, 1975 (*The End of Lieutenant Boruvka*, 1989); *Příběh inženýra lidských duší*, 1977 (*The Engineer of Human Souls: An Entertainment on the Old Themes of Life, Women, Fate, Dreams, the Working Class, Secret Agents, Love, and Death*, 1984); *Návrat poručíka Borůvky*, 1981 (*The Return of Lieutenant Boruvka*, 1990); *Scherzo capriccioso: Veselý sen o Dvořákovi*, 1983 (*Dvořák in Love: A Light-Hearted Dream*, 1986); *Nevěsta z Texasu*, 1992 (*The Bride of Texas*, 1995); *Nevysvšetlitelny pšríbšeh: Aneb, Vyprávšení Questa Firma Sicula*, 1998 (*An Inexplicable Story: Or, The Narrative of Questus*, 2002); *Two Murders in My Double Life*, 1999.

SHORT FICTION: *Smutek poručíka Borůvky*, 1966 (*The Mournful Demeanour of Lieutenant Boruvka*, 1973); *Hříchy pro pátera Knoxe*, 1973 (*Sins for Father Knox*, 1988); *Povídky tenorsaxofonisty*, 1993 (*The Tenor Saxophonist's Story*, 1997).

NONFICTION: *O nich'o nás*, 1968; *All the Bright Young Men and Women: A Personal History of the Czech Cinema*, 1971; *Jiří Menzel and the History of the "Closely Watched Trains,"* 1982; *Talkin' Moscow Blues*, 1988; *When Eve Was Naked: A Journey Through Life*, 2000 (also known as *When Eve Was Naked: Stories of a Life's Journey*, 2002).

MISCELLANEOUS: *Headed for the Blues: A Memoir with Ten Stories*, 1997.

Josef Václav Škvorecký (SHKWOR-eht-skee), long one of the best-known Czech novelists, has established a distinguished international literary reputation since his exile in 1968. He was born to Josef Škvorecký, a bank clerk, and Anna Kurazova Škvorecký, an actress. Between 1943 and 1945, after having graduated from high school during the Nazi occupation of his homeland, Škvorecký was impressed into labor at Messerschmitt factories, first in Náchod and then in Nové Mesto. These experiences are vividly depicted in several of his major novels. During the final months of the war he spent time digging trenches and working in a cotton mill. In 1945 he began studying medicine at Prague's Charles University, but after beginning to write fiction he transferred to the Faculty of Philosophy, graduated in 1949, and received his Ph.D. in 1951. During this time he became an active member of the Prague underground community of writers and artists resisting the censorship imposed by the postwar Communist regime. After being drafted Škvorecký served in the elite tank division at a military post near Prague from 1951 to 1953.

During the next decade Škvorecký built a substantial literary reputation as a translator and editor of such American writers as Stephen Crane, Ernest Hemingway, and Edgar Allan Poe. His early short stories and an early novel, however, were censored before publication. Although written in 1948, when he was twenty-four, Škvorecký's first published novel, *The Cowards*, did not appear until 1958. In this work Daniel Smiricky, who became the protagonist of several other Škvorecký novels, is full of youthful preoccupation with self, jazz, and girls as he moves through eight days at the beginning of the dramatic May, 1945, transition from German occupation to Soviet occupation of Czechoslovakia. The book was banned and confiscated for its depictions of German and Soviet military men, and the author was removed from his post as editor of the journal *Světová Literatura*. Suppression made the book even more popular, and Škvorecký became a national literary figure. Subsequent fluctuations in political climate permitted occasional publication of some of his shorter fictions, among them *Emöke*, but the greater part of Škvorecký's work during this period was film and television screenplays. Two books in English on the history of Czech cinema and Škvorecký's associations with the director Jiři Menzel and other luminaries of the screen attest Škvorecký's passion for film.

In spite of continued censorship of his work, Škvorecký published several short-story collections between 1964 and 1968, as well as a detective novel, *The Mournful Demeanor of Lieutenant Boruvka*. He won several awards for translation and fiction and served actively in film, television, and literary organizations. August 21, 1968, the date of the Soviet invasion of Czechoslovakia, marked a radical break in Škvorecký's career. He and his wife of ten years, Zdena Salivarová, a singer, actress, and novelist, emigrated to Toronto, Canada, where Škvorecký became a professor in the English department at Erindale College of the University of Toronto. There he and his wife established Sixty-Eight Publishers, which they dedicated to distributing the works of Czechoslovakian writers both in Czechoslovakia and in exile. With the fall of communism in Czechoslovakia the publishing enterprise was brought to an end, having fulfilled its task.

In 1970 a translation of *The Cowards* first made Škvorecký's work available to English-speaking audiences. Other notable translations followed, including *Miss Silver's Past* and *The Bass Saxophone*. Contributions to the literary community as political commentator, critic, editor, publisher, and translator brought Škvorecký international visibility, and in 1980 he was awarded the Neustadt International Prize for Literature. One of the most notable of Škvorecký's novels, *The Engineer of Human Souls*, was published in 1984 and received the Canadian Governor General's Literary Award in the same year. In *The Engineer of Human Souls* Daniel Smiricky, the semiautobiographical young protagonist of *The Cowards*, *Tankovy prapor* (the tank corps), *The Miracle Game*, and *The Swell Season*, appears once more. Smiricky's adventures as he matures, from girl chasing to teaching English at a Canadian college, are chronicled in these novels. He seems to have been the inspiration for Škvorecký's protagonists in *The Bass Saxophone*, *Miss Silver's Past*, and *Dvořák in Love*.

Škvorecký's foray into mystery and detective fiction produced a continuing series of novels with Lieutenant Boruvka as their central character. In a context of ever alert and powerful political and social censors, mystery fiction allowed a writer to continue his profession. At the same time, he could, perhaps, incorporate subtle commentary on politics and society, as Škvorecký does in *Miss Silver's Past*. Škvorecký ranks among such distinguished Eastern European post-World War II, exiled writers as his fellow countryman Milan Kundera, Polish Nobel Prize winner Czesław Miłosz, and the Russian writers Joseph Brodsky and Aleksandr Solzhenitsyn. *The Engineer of Human Souls* and *The Cowards* have met with great critical acclaim. Škvorecký's works transcend national borders and ideologies to address a truly international audience. In 1999, the Czech Republic honored his contribution to Czech letters during his years of exile with the State Prize for Literature.

Virginia Crane
Vasa D. Mihailovich

Bibliography

Kalish, Jana. *Josef Škvorecký: A Checklist*. Toronto: University of Toronto Library, 1986. Extremely helpful but limited to pre-1986 subject matter.

O'Brien, John, ed. "Special Issue: Mario Vargas Llosa and Josef Škvorecký." *The Review of Contemporary Fiction* 17, no. 1 (Spring, 1997): 78-158. Contains brief but perceptive essays, a limited select bibliography, an interview with and a previously unpublished short story by Škvorecký, and two essays on *The Bride of Texas*.

Solecki, Sam, ed. *The Achievement of Josef Škvorecký*. Toronto: University of Toronto Press, 1994. Concentrates on the major works and includes an essay on the literary scandal surrounding the publication of *The Cowards*. Extensive bibliography.

_______. *Prague Blues: The Fiction of Josef Škvorecký*. Toronto: ECW Press, 1990. The best starting point for a study of Škvorecký. Solecki has an appreciation of Škvorecký's work and is extremely perceptive. Includes a good bibliography.

Trensky, Paul I. *The Fiction of Josef Škvorecký*. New York: St. Martin's Press, 1991. A good perspective on the earlier works, with additional comments on the detective stories.

David Slavitt

American novelist, poet, and translator

Born: White Plains, New York; March 23, 1935
Pseudonyms: Henry Sutton, Henry Lazarus, David Benjamin

LONG FICTION: *Rochelle: Or, Virtue Rewarded*, 1966; *The Exhibitionist*, 1967 (as Henry Sutton); *Feel Free*, 1968; *The Voyeur*, 1969 (as Sutton); *Anagrams*, 1970; *Vector*, 1971 (as Sutton); *A B C D*, 1972; *The Liberated*, 1973 (as Sutton); *The Outer Mongolian*, 1973; *The Killing of the King*, 1974; *King of Hearts*, 1976; *That Golden Woman*, 1976 (as Henry Lazarus); *Jo Stern*, 1978; *The Sacrifice*, 1978 (as Sutton); *The Idol*, 1979 (as David Benjamin); *The Proposal*, 1980 (as Sutton); *Cold Comfort*, 1980; *Ringer*, 1982; *Alice at 80*, 1984; *The Agent*, 1986 (with Bill Adler); *The Hussar*, 1987; *Salazar Blinks*, 1988; *Lives of the Saints*, 1989; *Turkish Delights*, 1993; *The Cliff*, 1994, *Bank Holiday Monday*, 1996 (as Sutton).
SHORT FICTION: *Short Stories Are Not Real Life*, 1991.
POETRY: *Suits for the Dead*, 1961; *The Carnivore*, 1965; *Day Sailing*, 1969; *Child's Play*, 1972; *Vital Signs: New and Selected Poems*, 1975; *Rounding the Horn*, 1978; *Dozens*, 1981; *Big Nose*, 1983; *The Walls of Thebes*, 1986; *Equinox, and Other Poems*, 1989; *Eight Longer Poems*, 1990; *Crossroads*, 1994; *A Gift: The Life of Da Ponte, a Poem*, 1996; *PS3569.L3: Poems*, 1998; *Falling from Silence*, 2001.
NONFICTION: *Understanding Social Life*, 1976 (with Paul F. Secord and Carl W. Backman); *Physicians Observed*, 1987; *Virgil*, 1991.
TRANSLATIONS: *The Eclogues of Virgil*, 1971; *The Eclogues and the Georgics of Virgil*, 1972; *The Tristia of Ovid*, 1986; *Ovid's Poetry of Exile*, 1990; *Five Plays of Seneca*, 1991; *The Metamorphoses of Ovid*, 1994; *Sixty-one Psalms of David*, 1996; *Hymns of Prudentius*, 1996; *Epic and Epigram: Two Elizabethan Entertainments*, 1997 (of John Owen's *Epigrammata*); *A Crown for the King*, 1998 (of Ibn Gabirol); *The Oresteia*, 1998 (of Aeschylus); *The Poem of Queen Esther*, 1999 (of João Pinto Delgado); *The Voyage of the Argo: The Argonautica of Gaius Valerius Flaccus*, 1999; *The Book of the Twelve Prophets*, 2000; *The Latin Odes of Jean Dorat*, 2000; *Sonnets of Love and Death*, 2001 (of Jean de Sponde).
EDITED TEXTS: *Land of Superior Mirages: New and Selected Poems*, 1986 (by Adrien Stoutenburg); *Aristophanes*, 1998-1999 (with Palmer Bovie); *Euripides*, 1998-1999 (with Bovie); *Menander*, 1998 (with Bovie); *Sophocles*, 1998-1999 (with Bovie); *Aeschylus*, 1998-1999; *Plautus: The Comedies*, 1995 (with Bovie).

David Rytman Slavitt has had four writing careers: as a poet, as a translator of Latin poetry, as a respected (if not widely read) novelist, and (briefly and pseudonymously) as a best-selling pop trash writer in the 1960's.

Slavitt was born in 1935, the son of attorney Samuel Saul Slavitt and the former Adele Beatrice Rytman. From childhood, David was told it was his duty to fulfill a failed dream of his father's: Samuel Slavitt had been admitted to Yale University and spent two happy years there, then was forced to withdraw because his parents could no longer afford the tuition. Samuel persevered, attending New York University at night while working, and became a successful lawyer. He vowed, however, that his son would follow the path he had wanted: prep school at Phillips Andover, undergraduate study at Yale, followed by Harvard Law School.

David Slavitt followed orders, graduating from Andover in 1952 and proceeding to Yale, which he found, to his surprise, he actually enjoyed, despite the aspects of filial duty. He graduated magna cum laude in 1956 but refused to go on to law school and took a job in the personnel department at *Reader's Digest*. He stayed there long enough to buy two ship tickets, then, on August 27, 1956, he married Lynn Nita Meyer, and they sailed on the *Queen Elizabeth*. The trip ended badly, however: After they had been on their honeymoon for only a week, they learned that Lynn's mother had died, and they had to return home immediately.

Slavitt returned to school, gaining an M.A. in English from Columbia University in 1956 for a dissertation on the poetry of Dudley Fitts. His son, Evan Meyer Slavitt, was born that year. (Slavitt and his wife later had two more children, Sarah Rebecca and Joshua Rytman.) Slavitt accepted a teaching job at Georgia Institute of Technology. He hated his year there, blaming the low level of educational development of his students and the lack of esteem for literary studies.

He returned to New York in 1958 and was hired by *Newsweek*, where he worked in various editorial capacities, including book and film reviewing, and was given the title of associate editor. His wife suffered a debilitating attack of mononucleosis, and he began staying at his parents' house in his native city, White Plains, New York.

His first book of poetry, *Suits for the Dead*, was published in Scribner's prestigious Poets of Today series in 1961. Series editor John Hall Wheelock praised him for his virtuosity, his mastery of a variety of forms, and his use of tone.

In 1965 Slavitt left *Newsweek* to become a full-time writer. Like Robert Graves, he set out to support the poetry that he loved to create by the writing of novels. In 1966 he published *Rochelle: Or Virtue Rewarded*, a serious novel. At this point Bernard Geis, notorious as the publisher of Jacqueline Susann's *Valley of the Dolls* (1966) and other fiction for the mass market, suggested that Slavitt could make a lot of money writing that sort of book. Slavitt yielded, producing *The Exhibitionist*, a showbiz *roman à clef* he allowed Geis to publish under the pseudonym Henry Sutton. The book reached the best-seller lists, and the revelation that its actual author was a serious writer and poet probably supplied a frisson that helped its sales.

The second Sutton book, *The Voyeur*, whose protagonist resembled publisher Hugh Hefner, sold less well; perhaps readers were tiring of the joke. *Vector* represented an effort at socially conscious mass-market pop, warning of the dangers of biological warfare experiments. It made little splash, as did four succeeding Sutton novels and three other pseudonymous popular books.

Meanwhile, Sutton was writing under his own name, with poetry collections appearing from university presses every three years or so. As Slavitt, he wrote a wide variety of literary novels, including *Anagrams*, a university novel enriched by Joycean word play, and *The Outer Mongolian*, an imaginative tale in which a child with Down syndrome, his intellect briefly and freakishly enhanced to superhuman levels, plays havoc with the American politics of the 1960's.

In 1971 he began yet another literary career, as a Latin translator, with his rendition of *The Eclogues of Virgil*. In 1975 his poetry received notice, with a major publisher, Doubleday, issuing *Vital Signs*.

On December 20, 1977, Slavitt divorced his first wife; the next year he married physician Janet Lee Abrahm. Also in 1978 he published *Jo Stern*, a surprisingly sympathetic fictionalized account of Jacqueline Susann's courageous struggle with terminal cancer. *Alice at 80* was a fictional treatment of the old age of the woman who, as a child, had inspired Lewis Carroll's *Alice's Adventures in Wonderland* (1865). *The Agent*, published as "Created by" book packager Bill Adler and written by Slavitt, returned to the territory of *The Exhibitionist* but with a new wit and irony. In the 1990's, Slavitt continued to publish poetry and fiction, usually with university presses. He also worked more as a Latin translator, publishing more than a dozen translations and adaptations of poetry, plays, and fables.

Arthur D. Hlavaty

Bibliography

Bizzaro, Patrick, and Philip K. Jason. "David Slavitt." In *Critical Survey of Poetry*, edited by Philip K. Jason. 2d rev. ed. Pasadena, Calif.: Salem Press, 2003. A thorough overview of Slavitt's life and career as a poet.

Garrett, George. "David Slavitt." In *American Poets Since World War II*, edited by James E. Kibler, Jr. Vol. 5 in *Dictionary of Literary Biography*. Detroit: Gale, 1980. Thorough outline of Slavitt's career.

_______. *My Silk Purse and Yours*. Columbia: University of Missouri Press, 1992. Discusses Slavitt's career in depth as an aspect of the contemporary publishing scene.

O'Neil, Paul. "Calculating Poet Behind a Very Gamy Book." *Life* 64 (January 26, 1968): 64-68. A contemporaneous look at the revelation of Henry Sutton's identity.

Christopher Smart

English poet

Born: Shipbourne, Kent, England; April 11, 1722
Died: King's Bench Prison, London, England; May 2, 1771
Pseudonym: Mary Midnight

POETRY: *On the Eternity of the Supreme Being*, 1750; *On the Immensity of the Supreme Being*, 1751; *On the Omniscience of the Supreme Being*, 1752; *Poems on Several Occasions*, 1752; *The Hilliad*, 1753; *On the Power of the Supreme Being*, 1754; *On the Goodness of the Supreme Being*, 1755; *Hymn to the Supreme Being, on Recovery from a Dangerous Fit of Illness*, 1756; *A Song to David*, 1763; *Poems*, 1763; *Ode to the Earl of Northumberland*, 1764; *Hymns for the Amusement of Children*, 1772; *Jubilate Agno*, 1939 (also known as *Rejoice in the Lamb*, 1954); *Collected Poems*, 1950 (2 volumes; Norman Callan, editor).

DRAMA: *Hannah: An Oratorio*, pb. 1764 (libretto); *Abimelech: An Oratorio*, pb. 1768 (libretto); *Providence: An Oratorio*, pb. 1777 (libretto).

NONFICTION: *Mother Midnight's Miscellany*, 1751 (as Mary Midnight); *The Nonpareil: Or, The Quintessence of Wit and Humor*, 1757 (as Midnight).

TRANSLATIONS: *The Works of Horace, Translated Literally into English*, 1756; *A Poetical Translation of the Fables of Phaedrus*, 1765; *A Translation of the Psalms of David Attempted in the Spirit of Christianity, and Adapted to the Divine Service, with Hymns and Spiritual Songs for the Fasts and Festivals of the Church of England*, 1765; *The Works of Horace Translated into Verse*, 1767.

Christopher Smart's life is the record of a very considerable talent profoundly affected by personal misfortunes. He was frail as a child, and, according to the rules of eighteenth century medicine, he was treated with "cordials," which probably began his lifelong alcoholism. From what witnesses such as Samuel Johnson said, it would appear that Smart sometimes suffered from delirium tremens and later from a form of mental illness which manifested itself in religious mania. Smart's earlier life did not presage so tragic an ending. He began writing as a child, attracted some literary attention as a young man, and was sent to Pembroke Hall, Cambridge. At the university both his talents and his troubles seem to have had their maturation. He won a reputation as a poet, but his personal difficulties, including a habit of running into debt that was to become perennial, forced him to leave the university.

The next events of Smart's career took place in London, where he spent his time writing, composing music, and publishing his own and others' literary work. Smart was married in 1752 and enjoyed a short period of happiness and health. Within a few years, however, his troubles began in earnest. He was unable to face up to the problems of his domestic life, his literary life, and the business affairs into which he had entered. In his middle thirties he became increasingly liable to attacks of madness, many of them violent, and all of them, at least by the treatment of his time, incurable. As one might expect, much of Smart's poetry seems to reflect a disengagement from reality. It also shows his quest for spiritual and psychological security. If his deep emotions found no cure, they did find impressive expression in the hymns and in *A Song to David*.

Smart's mental illness did not necessitate his complete confinement; after some years of treatment (1757-1763) he was able to emerge and take his place in the literary society of London. His talents won important friends such as Samuel Johnson and Thomas Gray, men who recognized his ability and made allowances for his condition. He was aided by Fanny Burney and her father, who did what they could, personally and financially, to ease his life. Smart, although far from the totally insane man he is often incorrectly pictured as being, was also far from being able to lead a life even remotely normal. His financial condition was as precarious as it had been years before at Cambridge, and the last months of his life witnessed his confinement in debtor's prison. Although he was what may too easily be called a failure, Smart's very weakness enabled him to reach his own form of success. His religious poetry, written in an age of dominant rationalism, was imbued with a strong and valuable sense of the mystical. He reinvigorated the English tradition of holy poetry, a tradition which had been allowed to wither for many years.

George F. Horneker

Bibliography

Dillingham, Thomas F. "'Blest Light': Christopher Smart's Myth of David." In *The David Myth in Western Literature*, edited by Raymond-Jean Frontain and Jan Wojick. West Lafayette, Ind.: Purdue University Press, 1980. The biblical David is central to Smart's highest poetic achievements, says Dillingham, whether used as subject, as in *A Song to David*, or as a model for imitation, as in the translations and biblical paraphrases. Smart combines the Old Testament figure with the Greek Orpheus and Christian theology in seeking a unified vision for his faith.

Havens, Raymond D. "The Structure of Smart's *Song to David*." Review of English Studies 14 (1938): 178-182. This work is old but not outdated, and it is a highly regarded source with which to begin a study of Smart's major work. The poem's structure is analyzed from a mathematical and a mystical point of view.

Hawes, Clement, ed. *Christopher Smart and the Enlightenment*. New York: St. Martin's Press, 1999. A reappraisal of Smart's legacy and his remarkable impact on twentieth century poetry. Analyzes the generative impact of Smart on modern poetry and music, demonstrating the reach of his contemporary resonance.

Mounsey, Chris. *Christopher Smart: Clown of God*. Cranbury, N.J.: Associated University Presses, 2001. A biography of the poet, detailing his confinement for mental illness. Includes bibliographical references and index.

Sherbo, Arthur. *Christopher Smart: Scholar of the University*. East Lansing: Michigan State University Press, 1967. Concentrates on biographical material interpreted through a detailed look at eighteenth century history. The poems are discussed in their contemporary setting without extensive analysis.

Agnes Smedley

American journalist and biographer

Born: Campground, Missouri; February 23, 1892
Died: Oxford, England; May 6, 1950

NONFICTION: *Chinese Destinies: Sketches of Present-Day China*, 1933 (journalism); *China's Red Army Marches*, 1934 (journalism); *China Fights Back: An American Woman with the Eighth Route Army*, 1938 (journalism); *Battle Hymn of China*, 1943 (journalism); *The Great Road: The Life and Times of Chu Teh*, 1956 (biography).
LONG FICTION: *Daughter of Earth*, 1929.

Agnes Smedley wanted to be known, and primarily is known, as an independent American radical, a working-class feminist, and a writer who served the causes in which she believed. She was born in Campground, Missouri, on February 23, 1892, the daughter of a farmer and jack-of-all-trades, Charles Smedley, and his wife, Sarah Ralls. Smedley's lifelong commitment to the causes of the poor and to feminism were fueled by the wretched life she experienced as a child. Her family moved constantly. Their constant financial instability caused both parents to suffer, something they, at times, passed on to their children. Her mother died at an early age from the cumulative effects of poverty and overwork.

With the help of relatives, Smedley escaped from this life by getting an eighth-grade education and becoming a schoolteacher. At one of her jobs she met the sister of Ernest Brundin, who would later become Smedley's first husband, and she moved with the two of them to California, where they all became involved in radical political movements. Smedley learned about the anti-imperialist Indian national independence movement, about anarchism and socialism from Emma Goldman, and about Margaret Sanger's birth control movement. While she admired the cultural sophistication of the Brundins, transplanted New Yorkers, she remained throughout her life a rough, earthy, outspoken person. Eventually she married Ernest Brundin, but they were temperamentally unsuited to each other. After their divorce, Smedley moved to New York City, where she lived among a generation of radicals and artists that made Greenwich Village famous.

In New York, Smedley became deeply involved in politics. She helped to establish birth control clinics, studied Indian culture, and worked at establishing herself as a journalist. There she met Virendranath Chattopadhyaya, who was to become her teacher and, later, her common-law husband. With him she traveled to Germany and the Soviet Union and worked in exile for Indian independence from England.

In 1927 Smedley left "Chatto" for good, taking refuge in Denmark, where she wrote her first book, *Daughter of Earth*, a thinly disguised autobiographical novel. It summarizes her life powerfully and melodramatically but in unsophisticated language. (She continues this story in her later book *Battle Hymn of China*.) Smedley reoriented her life, shifting her attention from India to China. In 1928 she went to China as a special correspondent for the *Frankfurter Zeitung*, and it was there that she did her most important work between 1929 and 1942.

During this time Smedley was one of a few foreign visitors who recognized the power, popularity, and, consequently, the importance of the Chinese Communist forces in the war against Japan. In China, Smedley, always an independent leftist in politics, immediately identified with the causes of the poor industrial workers in Shanghai and with the even poorer peasants in the countryside. She believed that the Communist revolutionaries were nationalists who fought against Western and Japanese imperialism and for agrarian land reform and democracy.

Like most Western journalists in China, Smedley spent most of her early years in Shanghai and other cities controlled by the Nationalist government. Unlike many journalists, however, she was immediately and continuously involved in social and political work. Her first book on China, *Chinese Destinies*, is a collection of articles which has Shanghai for its background. Her next, *China's Red Army Marches*, depicts the struggles of the Communist forces in Jiangxi province to regroup after their early defeats by the Nationalists. Although Smedley never visted Jiangxi, her description of this battle between good and evil forces is based on information she gathered from refugees whom she sheltered and helped.

After a visit to Moscow and a brief stay in the United States, Smedley returned to China and gained fame as the reporter who broadcast news of the Xian incident, when Chiang Kai-shek was kidnapped and forced to agree to a united front with the Communist forces against the Japanese. Living in Hankow (now the city of Wu-han), Smedley also helped to smuggle medical supplies through Japanese territory to Communist forces at their headquarters in Yen-an.

During this period, Smedley (along with the more famous Edgar Snow) spent long periods of time with Communist forces. She was able to interview leaders of the revolutionary armies, especially Mao Zedong and Chu Teh. These experiences formed the basis for her last three books. *China Fights Back* and *Battle Hymn of China* are eyewitness reports designed to tell Americans about China's struggles against the Japanese, especially about the Red Army—its leaders, its organization and tactics—and China's attempts to shed the feudal culture with which China had, so to speak, bound its own feet.

Smedley's last book, a biography of Chu Teh, was an attempt to introduce the West to China's most important military figure. It was published posthumously, and, like all Smedley's books, it was highly partisan and a bit oversimplified. Nevertheless, Smedley was a highly respected authority on the Chinese situation who advised both the civilian and military arms of the American government on Chinese matters.

With the end of World War II and the onset of the Cold War, Smedley quickly became, like other journalists, military personnel, and diplomats who did not support Chiang Kai-shek, a victim of smear campaigns and political witch-hunts. At the time of her death, Smedley had been accused of spying for the Soviet Union and being a member of the Communist Party. Neither of these accusations proved to be true. Smedley was always an independent radical, and her major writings belong to that tradition of opinionated journalism, popular in the nineteenth century, which was practiced by writers as diverse as Horace Greeley, Jack London, Upton Sinclair, John Reed, and H. L. Mencken.

Michael Helfand

Bibliography

Ickes, Harold L. "Agnes Smedley's 'Cell-Mates.'" *Signs* 3 (Winter, 1977). A feminist reading of Smedley's life and work.

MacKinnon, Janice R., and Stephen R. MacKinnon. *Agnes Smedley: The Life and Times of an American Radical*. Berkeley: University of California Press, 1988. A biography.

Milton, Joyce. *A Friend of China*. New York: Hastings House, 1980. A biography written for younger readers.

Jane Smiley

American novelist

Born: Los Angeles, California; September 26, 1949

LONG FICTION: *Barn Blind*, 1980; *At Paradise Gate*, 1981; *Duplicate Keys*, 1984; *The Greenlanders*, 1988; *A Thousand Acres*, 1991; *Moo*, 1995; *The All-True Travels and Adventures of Lidie Newton*, 1998; *Horse Heaven*, 2000; *Good Faith*, 2003.
SHORT FICTION: *The Age of Grief: A Novella and Stories*, 1987; *"Ordinary Love" and "Good Will": Two Novellas*, 1989.
NONFICTION: *Catskill Crafts: Artisans of the Catskill Mountains*, 1988; *Charles Dickens*, 2002.

Jane Graves Smiley has distinguished herself as a trenchant observer of the disruptive workings of human desire within middle-class American families in the late twentieth century. Born in Los Angeles in 1949 to James La Verne Smiley and Frances Graves Nuelle during her father's military posting to California, she was reared in St. Louis. Although she never lived on a working farm, Smiley regards the Midwest, where both her parents had deep family ties, as having imprinted a decidedly rural stamp upon her imagination. She also credits her two principal themes, self-identified as "sex and apocalypse," to her youthful attention to a culture simultaneously preoccupied with the twin threats of nuclear war and the newly available contraceptive pill.

Smiley's proclivities as a budding writer began early. She completed her B.A. in English from Vassar College in 1971 by presenting a novel as her senior thesis. Later she undertook graduate work at the University of Iowa, securing not only a master's in fine arts in 1976 but also an M.A. (in 1975) and Ph.D. (in 1978), both in medieval literature. This blend of interests and training is perhaps best evidenced in *The Greenlanders*, Smiley's exhaustively researched 1988 epic novel about fourteenth century Scandinavian pioneers. It is based upon Norse sagas she had studied during a Fulbright Fellowship to Iceland in 1976 to 1977. *The Greenlanders* dramatizes Smiley's affinities with the worldview of those medieval settlers. Their tragic vision of existence is as a grim round of harsh physical travail alleviated by contradictory human impulses toward both the intense, unpredictable pleasures of the body and the spiritual consolations of self-abnegation and transcendence.

Smiley's Greenlanders resemble her more contemporaneous midwesterners in the degree to which their sense of place deeply infuses their sense of self. Moreover, characters in both worlds demonstrate a capacity to absorb disaster, commit themselves to the burdens of daily toil, and stumble toward personal responsibility and communal obligation at moments of stark moral crisis.

Smiley's publishing career officially began with the appearance of *Barn Blind* in 1980. She joined the faculty at Iowa State University in Ames in 1981 and subsequently earned the rank of full professor, teaching classes in creative writing and literature. Smiley's writing earned her grants from the National Endowment for the Arts in 1978 and 1987; she also served as a visiting professor at the University of Iowa in 1981 and 1987. Her familiarity with academe was put to excellent use in the mordant satirical novel *Moo*, a contemporary fiction that skewers the careerist vanities of the professoriat alongside the moral evasions of university administrators and the anti-intellectualism of the student body. *Moo*'s most salient target, however, is America's pervasive culture of consumption, which changes all human desire into specialized market-niche appetites worthy of endless (and highly profitable) gratification. Higher education itself is shown to pander shamelessly to corporate sponsors and classroom "customers" alike. At the heart of Moo U. sits an eight-hundred-pound pig named Earl Butz, an eating machine that, like the mortals who have genetically programmed him, inexplicably yearns for an Edenic past he vaguely recalls but is powerless to recover.

Smiley's marital history suggests that here, too, personal experience informs her literary investigations into the politics of love, friendship, and family. Her 1970 marriage to John Whiston, while she was still an undergraduate, ended in 1975. A second marriage, to editor William Silag, produced two daughters, Phoebe and Lucy, but in 1986 also ended in divorce. In 1987 Smiley married screenwriter Stephen Mark Mortensen; they had a son, Axel, and were divorced in 1997. She has credited motherhood with having dramatically realigned her literary priorities. Upon finding herself pregnant for the first time, Smiley the alienated modernist enamored of existential anomie abruptly became a more tolerant humanist intent on illuminating the hard-fought moments of grace that buffer the follies and griefs of daily existence. She subsequently set out to demonstrate that women can be procreative and creative at the same time, centuries of literary prejudice to the contrary. In the process she found her true subject: the intricate dance of need, love, retribution, and loss produced by the forever competing, occasionally reconciled, subjectivities jostling one another in every family.

She has proved especially adept at writing the maternal experience into literature, challenging both idealizations and caricatures by rendering the mother as an irreducibly complex subject rather than as the loved/loathed object of the disillusioned child-cum-writer. Accordingly, Smiley's fiction boasts a wide array of women with varying aptitudes for the role. *Barn Blind*'s Kate Karlson demonstrates how a strong parental personality can become the central force holding other family members in her orbit even as she inflicts deep wounds with her unflinching expectations, unyielding standards, and unquestioning exploitation. Only a year later, *At Paradise Gate* demystified the Catheresque earth mother in the person of Anna Robinson, whose grandmotherly demeanor masks deep ambivalences about the choices she has made at considerable cost to her own sense of self. In *The Age of Grief* and *Ordinary Love*, two superbly crafted novellas—a form whose economy Smiley regards as fostering a "more meditative" result than the novel—she creates female characters whose seeming domestic idylls (the former as a professional partner as well as wife to her dentist husband, the latter as a traditional housewife in the midst of a hive of young children) are ripped asunder by their respective adulteries.

Smiley does not, however, follow the predictable course in having the career woman heedlessly follow through on her desires; rather, the painful dismantling of the idealized familial myth falls to her homemaker counterpart. Throughout her work, Smiley portrays the female psychological imperative coming to terms with the woman's procreative energies: while one woman cold-bloodedly pursues a likely male simply to ensure her biological destiny as childbearer ("Jeffrey, Believe Me" in *The Age of Grief*), for example, another (the narrator of *A Thousand Acres*) is denied fertility in a bitter symbolic evocation of the larger environmental contamination that figures prominently throughout Smiley's fiction.

An avowed feminist, Smiley has nonetheless made clear her interest in mapping the emotional terrain of men as well as women, children as well as parents. An entire work might unfold from a single point of view, as in the novella *Good Will*, where she assumes the first-person voice of an aging Vietnam War veteran trapped by his own desperate effort to isolate his family from the corrupting influences of the broader culture. On the other hand, she might move the reader through a kaleidoscope of perspectives, as in *Barn Blind*, where each family member is accorded an independent point of view on the steadily unfolding tragedy of the Karlsons. In a more lighthearted vein, in *Moo*, even the hapless pig Earl Butz is accorded his own ruminations on his lot.

Smiley proves equally adept at handling disparate genres. Her skill as a writer of short fiction earned the collection *The Age of Grief* a nomination for the National Book Critics Circle Award. In *Duplicate Keys* she turned the conventions of the murder mystery to her own thematic ends. She violently destabilized the ordered world of the protagonist to prompt her to move beyond her illusions about life, love, and friendship. The sheer abundance of characters and plotlines in *Moo*, as well as the comic exuberance with which they are woven together, recalls nineteenth century masters of the genre such as William Makepeace Thackeray, Charles Dickens, and Mark Twain, not to mention her own contemporary Tom Wolfe. Its playfulness seemed all the more pronounced in coming on the heels of Smiley's Pulitzer Prize- and National Book Critics Circle Award-winning novel *A Thousand Acres*. In *Horse Heaven*, however, she returned to the Dickensian sprawl of characters and locales.

In *A Thousand Acres*, Smiley transplanted William Shakespeare's *King Lear* into the Iowa countryside and reimagined it as a tragedy of primal violation and unrelenting vengeance at the very heart of the American nuclear family. Here she boldly enunciates the links between her feminism and environmentalism by tracing the institutional networks of power that render all nature, be it within the female body or abroad in the landscape, passively subject to the male will to dominate. Yet in the face of such hierarchies Smiley nonetheless insists that her women characters take themselves seriously as moral beings responsible for their own self-definition even as she elucidates the circumstances that foster their economic and emotional dependencies.

Jane Smiley has the rare distinction of being both a best-selling and critically acclaimed author. Her point of view is always fresh and her characters are fully realized and recognizable while also being surprising.

Barbara Kitt Seidman

Bibliography

Farrell, Susan Elizabeth. *Jane Smiley's "A Thousand Acres": A Reader's Guide*. New York: Continuum, 2001. A good, close look at Smiley's award-winning novel. It addresses such subjects as father and daughter relationships, King Lear as a legendary character, and rural families and farm life in the work. Includes bibliographical references.

Nakadate, Neil. "Jane Smiley." In *American Novelists Since World War II, Sixth Series*, edited by James H. Giles and Wanda R. Giles. Vol. 227 in *Dictionary of Literary Biography*. Detroit: Gale Group, 2000. A good general overview of Smiley's career and writing.

_______. *Understanding Jane Smiley*. Columbia: University of South Carolina Press, 1999. A volume in the series Understanding Contemporary American Literature. Takes a close look at most of Smiley's titles through *The All-True Travels and Adventures of Lidie Newton*. Includes a bibliography and an index.

Sheldon, Barbara H. *Daughters and Fathers in Feminist Novels*. New York: P. Lang, 1997. Examines *A Thousand Acres* and novels by Gail Godwin, Mary Gordon, and other feminist writers.

Smiley, Jane. "The Adventures of Jane Smiley." Interview by Katie Bacon. *Atlantic Unbound*, May 28, 1998. In this interview about the influences shaping *The All-True Travels and Adventures of Lidie Newton*, Smiley discusses her controversial 1996 *Harper's* essay comparing Mark Twain's *Adventures of Huckleberry Finn* (1884) unfavorably to Harriet Beecher Stowe's *Uncle Tom's Cabin* (1852), her interest in the unresolved question of race in American life, her belief that all of her writing is on some level historical fiction, and her continually evolving perspective on the family drama as literary subject.

_______. "A Conversation with Jane Smiley." Interview by Lewis Burke Frumkes. *The Writer* 112 (May, 1999): 20-22. Smiley discusses her work, her favorite contemporary writers, and her own writing habits.

_______. Interview by Marcelle Thiebaux. *Publishers Weekly* 233 (April 1, 1988): 65-66. Notes that in all of her books, Smiley focuses on the theme of family life. Smiley discusses the research that goes into her writing.

Adam Smith

Scottish economist

Born: Kirkcaldy, Fifeshire, Scotland; June 5, 1723 (baptized)
Died: Edinburgh, Scotland; July 17, 1790

NONFICTION: *The Theory of Moral Sentiments*, 1759; *An Inquiry into the Nature and Causes of the Wealth of Nations*, 1776 (commonly known as *The Wealth of Nations*); *Essays on Philosophical Subjects*, 1795.

Adam Smith studied at the University of Glasgow, where he came under the influence of the famous professor of moral philosophy Francis Hutcheson (1694-1746). Smith then studied at Balliol College, Oxford, for six years before returning to Scotland to lecture in rhetoric and polite literature at the University of Edinburgh. His lectures were popular and, unlike those of many of his contemporaries, attracted listeners from the town as well as from the university.

Smith returned to the University of Glasgow in 1751 as professor of logic, and that same year he was appointed to the chair in moral philosophy. At this time Smith was strongly under the influence of his close friend the historian and philosopher David Hume (1711-1776) and shared in a milder form much of Hume's skepticism. Smith never took holy orders, for example, an unusual circumstance for a professor of moral philosophy in Scotland at that time. In 1759 Smith published *The Theory of Moral Sentiments*, in which he claimed that sympathy or feeling was the foundation for all moral sentiments or judgments. He felt that evil or wrongdoing was punished by remorse in the individual and that certainly remorse was the most painful of the human sentiments. His position was not very far from that of later philosophers who claim that ethical principles are merely statements of human emotions.

Even at this early date Smith was highly interested in economics. He often talked of trade and political economy in his lectures, and he urged both students and young businessmen from the growing commercial city and port of Glasgow to attend his lectures. Many criticized him, and one of his colleagues later sneered that "he had converted the chair of moral philosophy into a professorship of trade and finance."

Late in 1762 the wealthy duke of Buccleuch became interested in Smith and hired him as his private tutor. Smith left the university and traveled with his patron to France, where he lived for more than two years and met physiocratic economic philosophers such as Anne-Robert-Jacques Turgot, Claude-Adrien Helvétius, and François Quesnay. Becoming more and more convinced of the need for coherent study of the principles of political economy, Smith returned from France and spent ten years studying and writing *An Inquiry into the Nature and Causes of the Wealth of Nations*. This book, the first complete work on political economy, established the author as the founder of classical economics. Smith defined the doctrine of laissez faire, or noninterference, and declared that labor is the real source of a nation's wealth. Therefore the individuals who perform the labor know what is best for them and should have the rights of private initiative and free enterprise, as well as the right to produce the products that society demands. In this way only can self-interest be harnessed to the common good. Although a good deal of Smith's theorizing was borrowed from his French associates, his copious illustrations and his applications of his principles to contemporary problems in England and Scotland ensured him a wide and interested audience.

Smith wrote little after *The Wealth of Nations*, but both the book and its author had become famous. Smith made frequent trips to London, where he had a good deal of influence on the prime minister, William Pitt (1708-1778), and his opinion was sought on almost all tax legislation passed by Parliament after the disastrous Stamp Act of 1765. Widely honored, he was made commissioner of customs for Scotland in 1777 and in 1787 was elected rector of the University of Glasgow.

In later life Adam Smith came to represent a kind of calm, rational, principled Augustan. He was intimate with many of the great of his age, including Hume, Edward Gibbon (1737-1794), and Samuel Johnson (1709-1784)—although the last apparently never forgave him for an unkind review of Johnson's famous dictionary in the *Edinburgh Review*; and he enjoyed discussing philosophy, semantics, history, politics, and economics in the various London clubs. He was a man apparently without fanaticism or a doctrinaire approach. Despite his advocacy of free trade and unrestricted operation of the law of supply and demand, he did acknowledge the necessity for government control in such matters as education and the public highways. Interested in many phases of the intellect, he was the first to synthesize and articulate many of the economic principles and problems that grew out of the rapid industrial and commercial expansion of his age.

Glenn L. Swygart

Bibliography

Brown, Maurice. *Adam Smith's Economics: Its Place in the Development of Economic Thought*. New York: Routledge, 1992. Scholarly but approachable work sets forth the economic and historical contexts of Smith's theories.

Brown, Vivienne. *Adam Smith's Discourse: Canonicity, Commerce, and Conscience*. New York: Routledge, 1994. Discusses inconsistency between *The Wealth of Nations* and Smith's *Theory of Moral Sentiments*.

Dwyer, John. *The Age of the Passions: An Interpretation of Adam Smith and Scottish Enlightenment Culture*. East Linton, East Lothian, Scotland: Tuckwell Press, 1998. Approaches Smith as an Enlightenment writer and analyzes the philosophy of passion as it emerges from his work.

Lai, Cheng-chung, ed. *Adam Smith Across Nations: Translations and Receptions of "The Wealth of Nations."* New York: Oxford University Press, 2000. Twenty-nine essays address the translation of Smith's important work into other languages.

Lindgren, J. Ralph. The *Social Philosophy of Adam Smith*. The Hague, the Netherlands: Martinus Nijhoff, 1973. Undertakes to survey the full breadth of Smith's philosophy, including moral judgment, psychology, religion, and science.

Motooka, Wendy. *The Age of Reasons: Quixotism, Sentimentalism and Political Economy in Eighteenth-Century Britain*. New York: Routledge, 1998. Compares the "reason" of Smith's economics with the "sentimentalism" of novelists such as Laurence Sterne and Henry Fielding, concluding that contemporary social sciences are the legacy of sentimentalism. An interesting view of Smith's work as literature.

Muller, Jerry Z. *Adam Smith in His Time and Ours: Designing the Decent Society*. New York: Free Press, 1993. Broad, relatively nontechnical view of Smith's analysis and philosophy, defending his relevance for modern society.

Raphael, D. D. *Adam Smith*. New York: Oxford University Press, 1985. A brief intellectual biography written for the general reader.

Vivenza, Gloria. *Adam Smith and the Classics: The Classical Heritage in Adam Smith's Thought*. New York: Oxford University Press, 2002. Analyzes the influence of classical thought—the cornerstone of the Enlightenment—on Smith's work.

Wood, John Cunningham, ed. *Adam Smith: Critical Assessments*. 4 vols. London: Croom Helm, 1983. Presents 150 articles and excerpts, many of which extend beyond Smith's economic analysis.

Betty Smith

American novelist

Born: Brooklyn, New York; December 15, 1896
Died: Shelton, Connecticut; January 17, 1972

LONG FICTION: *A Tree Grows in Brooklyn*, 1943; *Maggie-Now*, 1958; *Joy in the Morning*, 1963.
DRAMA: *A Tree Grows in Brooklyn*, pr., pb. 1951 (musical; with George Abbott; adaptation of her novel).

Betty Smith was born in Brooklyn and went to college in Michigan. Enrolled as a part-time student at the University of Michigan, she studied writing, particularly playwriting, almost exclusively. In 1930 she published two short plays in a volume written by drama students at Michigan, and in 1931 she won the first prize of one thousand dollars in the Avery Hopwood competition, mainly for her work in fiction. Even then she was developing the material she used later in her novels; one of her winning stories was called "Death of a Singing Waiter."

She continued her studies at the Yale School of Drama and was awarded playwriting fellowships by the Rockefeller Foundation and the Dramatists' Guild. Although she published or produced more than seventy one-act plays, it was not until the publication of *A Tree Grows in Brooklyn* that she received widespread public recognition. The novel was praised mainly for its lyrical treatment of naturalistic subject matter and for its realistic dialogue. She collaborated with George Abbott to write a musical version for the stage.

She again turned from her interest in drama to writing novels, returning to the Irish section of Brooklyn for her settings. Yet she never equaled her first success, which, many critics believe, overshadowed her subsequent books.

Bibliography

Gelfant, Blanche H. "Sister to Faust: The City's 'Hungry' Woman as Heroine." In *Women Writers and the City: Essays in Feminist Literary Criticism*, edited by Susan Merrill Squier. Knoxville: University of Tennessee Press, 1984.

Ginsberg, Elaine K. "Betty Wehner Smith." In *American Women Writers: A Critical Reference Guide from Colonial Times to the Present*, edited by Lina Mainiero. 4 vols. New York: Frederick Ungar, 1982.

Pearlman, Mickey. "Betty Smith." In *Biographical Dictionary of Contemporary Catholic Writing*, edited by Daniel J. Tynan. Westport, Conn.: Greenwood Press, 1989.

Dave Smith

American poet

Born: Portsmouth, Virginia; December 19, 1942

POETRY: *Bull Island*, 1970; *Mean Rufus Throw Down*, 1973; *The Fisherman's Whore*, 1974; *Drunks*, 1975; *Cumberland Station*, 1976; *In Dark, Sudden with Light*, 1977; *Goshawk, Antelope*, 1979; *Blue Spruce*, 1981; *Dream Flights*, 1981; *Homage to Edgar Allan Poe*, 1981; *In the House of the Judge*, 1983; *Gray Soldiers*, 1983; *The Roundhouse Voices: Selected and New Poems*, 1985; *Cuba Night*, 1990; *Night Pleasures: New and Selected Poems*, 1991; *Fate's Kite: Poems, 1991-1995*, 1995; *Floating on Solitude: Three Volumes of Poetry*, 1996; *The Wick of Memory: New and Selected Poems, 1974-2000*, 2000.

LONG FICTION: *Onliness*, 1981.

NONFICTION: *Local Assays: On Contemporary American Poetry*, 1985.

EDITED TEXTS: *The Pure Clear Word: Essays on the Poetry of James Wright*, 1982; *The Morrow Anthology of Younger American Poets*, 1985 (with David Bottoms); *The Essential Poe*, 1991.

MISCELLANEOUS: *Southern Delights: Poems and Stories*, 1984.

Dave Smith's parents, Ralph Gerald Smith and Catherine Mary Cornwell, were both from working-class families, their ancestors the farmers and coal miners of Virginia and Maryland. The work ethic by which Ralph Smith was able to lift his family into the suburban middle class undoubtedly left its impression on the son, but there was no precedent for the boy's future in poetry. Dave Smith read widely as a teenager, but he cites *Hot Rod* magazine and rock and roll, especially rhythm and blues, as influences on his sense of language that were no less significant than the classics of English and American literature. The fishermen and laborers of the tidewater region around Chesapeake Bay, near his home in Portsmouth, Virginia, also imbued his imagination with scenes and characters that would begin to appear in the poems he wrote in early adulthood.

In 1960 his father was killed in a car accident at the age of thirty-nine. Shortly afterward, at the University of Virginia, Smith made his first serious commitment to literature. After graduating with a B.A. in 1965, he took up teaching and coaching football at Poquoson (Virginia) High School, and he married Dolores Weaver (they would eventually have three children—Jeddie, Lael, and Mary Catherine). At Poquoson, a fishing village known to the natives as Bull Island, Smith began to hone his skill as a poet, finding in the local watermen the heroic subjects that would often inspire his most characteristic verse. In 1967 he entered a master's program at Southern Illinois University, where he wrote a thesis on the poetry of James Dickey and edited *Sou'wester*, the student literary magazine. He received his M.A. in 1969, the year he was drafted into the Air Force. He served most of his tour of duty in Langley, Virginia, just a few miles from his sources of inspiration in Poquoson, and was able to continue to write and teach in the evenings. With his wife, he edited and published *Back Door*, a small magazine, and operated a chapbook press. After his discharge, Smith entered a doctoral program in creative writing at Ohio University, though he interrupted his studies to teach in Michigan and Missouri. By 1973 he was publishing regularly in literary journals and was seeing *Mean Rufus Throw Down* into print, the first in a steady stream of books. He quickly established a reputation with his second book, *The Fisherman's Whore*, published by Ohio University Press, and with the first of his poems to appear in *The New Yorker*.

The year 1976 proved to be a turning point in Smith's career: He completed his Ph.D., attracted national attention with the publication of *Cumberland Station*, and was appointed director of creative writing at the University of Utah in Salt Lake City. Smith thrived in the unfamiliar but invigorating landscape of the West, and during the following five years, while in his late thirties, his output was extraordinary—in quality as well as volume. The poems of *Goshawk, Antelope* (a finalist for both the Pulitzer Prize and the National Book Critics Circle Award) and *Blue Spruce* reflect the interplay of landscape, imagination, and memory that his new situation made possible, and they aroused considerable excitement among reviewers who found their complex images and energetic Anglo-Saxon cadences, together with their stubborn search for the truth of experience, both challenging and refreshing.

In 1980, wanting to bring his family back east, Smith took a position at the State University of New York in Binghamton. In nearby Montrose, Pennsylvania, he and Dee found a Victorian home that had formerly belonged to Judge Edward Little; here he wrote the poems for *In the House of the Judge*. Although frequently linked to the Southern gothic tradition, Smith's work could no longer be identified with one or even two regions. He had become a regionalist in the best sense, a poet who discovers the universal in the local and particular. With his itinerant career, it is hardly surprising that "home"—ancestral or suburban, lost or tentatively found—became a central theme in his poems, and that narrative structures became thickly layered with memory and reflection. A year later, he returned to the South, first to the University of Florida, Gainesville, then back to his roots, taking a position at Virginia Commonwealth University in Richmond, Virginia.

The 1985 publication of *The Roundhouse Voices: Selected and New Poems* met with a favorable reception, though some critics wondered if Smith was publishing too much too quickly. Nevertheless, it encouraged retrospective assessments of Smith's substantial body of work at this point of early maturity, and these reviews widely recognized him as one of America's most accomplished and influential poets. Subsequently, Smith's output has been smaller, with the dark, unsettling *Cuba Night* appearing in 1990, after a relatively long silence, to critical acclaim. In that year he began teaching at Louisiana State University in Baton Rouge, and coediting the influential literary journal *Southern Review* with James Olney. His anthology *The Wick of Memory* was praised for its well-rounded representation of Smith's work. Despite living and working in academic settings, he resists the abstract and systematic, exploring instead the intricate dramas that spring from common objects and common lives.

Matthew Parfitt

Bibliography

Christensen, Paul. "Malignant Innocence." *Parnassus: Poetry in Review* 12 (Fall/Winter, 1984): 154-182. Christensen's article is one of the most comprehensive examinations of Smith's work, discovering in the poet's voice a version of an American and Southern archetype mediating between youth and age, initiate and elder. Christensen provides a rich understanding of the mythic taproots of Smith's career and of his major themes.

DeMott, Robert J. *Dave Smith: A Literary Archive*. Athens: Ohio University Libraries, 2000. Important for biographical and bibliographical research. The introduction, which traces DeMott's relationship to Smith, sheds a highly personal light on Smith's life and art. DeMott also describes the Ohio University Alden Library's Foundational Dave Smith Collection.

Millichap, Joseph K. "Dave Smith." In *Contemporary Southern Writers*. Detroit: St. James Press, 1999. This brief overview of Smith's career stresses the "trend toward variety and diversity" in style and subject. Comments on each major volume through *Fate's Kite*.

Smith, Dave. "An Interview with Dave Smith." Interview by Ernest Suarez. *Contemporary Literature* 37, no. 3 (Fall, 1996): 348-369. This excellent interview begins with an intelligent overview of Smith's art and an examination of a representative poem. Suarez's questions bring forth comments on influences, writing habits, the creative process, Smith's sense of the poet's role, and his own particular ambitions as a writer. Intriguing comments as well on form and on the term "confessional" poetry.

Swiss, Thomas. "'Unfold the Fullness': Dave Smith's Poetry and Fiction." *The Sewanee Review* 91 (Summer, 1983): 483-490. Swiss examines the architecture of *Dream Flights*, *Homage to Edgar Allan Poe*, and *In the House of the Judge*, collections that mark Smith's imaginative homecoming.

Vendler, Helen. "Dave Smith." In *The Music of What Happens: Poems, Poets, Critics*. Cambridge, Mass.: Harvard University Press, 1988. Vendler here modifies her original view that Smith is a regional Southern writer. She now argues, on the basis of *Goshawk, Antelope*, that he is "a distinguished allegorist of human experience."

_______. "'Oh I Admire and Sorrow.'" In *Part of Nature, Part of Us: Modern American Poets*. Cambridge, Mass.: Harvard University Press, 1980. The first extended statement by a major critic on Smith's work. Vendler enjoys the momentous energy in Smith's style, the range of his subjects, and his ambition. Praises especially his poems about the Civil War and fishing.

Weigl, Bruce. "Forms of History and Self in Dave Smith's *Cuba Night*." *Poet Lore* 85 (Winter, 1990/1991): 37-48. In examining the long poem "To Isle of Wight," Weigl stresses Smith's mythmaking ability and his ongoing struggle with his Southern heritage.

_______, ed. *The Giver of Morning: On the Poetry of Dave Smith*. Birmingham, Ala.: Thunder City Press, 1982. This first slender collection of comment on Smith's work fittingly assesses the amazing first dozen years of his career.

Homer W. Smith

American novelist and physiologist

Born: Denver, Colorado; January 2, 1895
Died: New York, New York; March 25, 1962

LONG FICTION: *Kamongo*, 1932 (revised paperback edition 1956); *The End of Illusion*, 1935.
NONFICTION: *The Kidney: Structure and Function in Health and Disease*, 1951; *Man and His Gods*, 1952 (with foreword by Albert Einstein); *From Fish to Philosopher*, 1953; *Principles of Renal Physiology*, 1956.

For thirty-four years Homer W. Smith was associated with the New York University Medical School, both in teaching and administrative capacities, and he served as chairman of its Department of Physiology. He had an eminent career as a physiologist, and his major work on the kidney is regarded as an important contribution to the literature on that subject.

He wrote two novels. The second, *The End of Illusion*, which many critics considered rather contrived—even mechanical—in its formulations of plot and ideas, deals with a young man who goes to Malaya to enjoy complete freedom and discovers that the freedom he seeks is nothing but an illusion. The first novel, *Kamongo*, is more successful in its handling of theme. It has a slender story line; its chief interest lies in the detailed account by an American naturalist to an Anglican priest—as they journey homeward on a French steamer through the Red Sea and the Suez Canal—of his capture of the African lungfish, a relic of the Devonian Age when it unsuccessfully sought to sustain itself on land. The naturalist's narrative, graphic and vivid in the telling, forms only a section of the novel; the remaining portion is the long debate between the two men on various issues of skepticism and faith, with Joel, the scientist, triumphantly demolishing the beliefs of the priest.

The novel, though without formal plot, contains excellent descriptive passages, and Smith's style, even when it deals with scientific matters that generally are of interest only to the specialist, is always lively and colorful. Upon its initial publication, *Kamongo* attracted wide popular attention and was a selection of the Book-of-the-Month Club in 1932. In 1935 Alexander Woollcott included it in one of his anthologies of current literary favorites, and in 1950, eighteen years after publication, it was a Natural History Book Club choice for its readers.

Two other works by Smith are worthy of notice. *Man and His Gods* is a vigorous discussion of religion, in which the author, after examining its origin in myth and superstition, decides that human beings' sense of scientific truth cannot permit them to embrace a belief in supernatural authority. They must find within their own resources the will to bring about "fulfillment." The book has been compared to Sir James George Frazer's *The Golden Bough* (1890-1915) and has been praised as a suitable condensation of that multivolume study. *From Fish to Philosopher* is an original examination of human beings' origin and physical development, told largely in terms of the kidney's growing adaptability to varying qualities of environment. Both books are characterized by engaging, at times brilliant, prose; not the least of Smith's virtues as a writer is his ability to maintain the interest of his readers.

Bibliography

Bing, Richard J. "Recollections of an Eyewitness." *Perspectives in Biology and Medicine* 39, no. 2 (Winter, 1996). Discusses the signs of creativity in artists and scientists, among them Homer Smith, Charles Lindbergh, and the surgeon Alfred Blalock.

Chasis, Herbert, and William Goldring, eds. *Homer William Smith: His Scientific and Literary Achievements*. New York: New York University Press, 1965.

Pitts, R. F. "Homer William Smith." *National Academy of Sciences, Biographical Memoirs* 39 (1967).

Martin Cruz Smith

American novelist

Born: Reading, Pennsylvania; November 3, 1942
Pseudonyms: Jake Logan, Nick Carter, Martin Quinn, Simon Quinn

LONG FICTION: *The Indians Won*, 1970; *Gypsy in Amber*, 1971; *The Analog Bullet*, 1972; *Canto for a Gypsy*, 1972; *The Inca Death Squad*, 1972; *Code Name: Werewolf*, 1973; *The Devil's Dozen*, 1973; *The Devil in Kansas*, 1974; *His Eminence, Death*, 1974; *The Last Time I Saw Hell*, 1974; *Nuplex Red*, 1974; *The Human Factor*, 1975; *Last Rites for the Vulture*, 1975; *The Midas Coffin*, 1975; *The Adventures of the Wilderness Family*, 1976; *North to Dakota*, 1976; *Nightwing*, 1977; *Ride for Revenge*, 1977; *Gorky Park*, 1981; *Stallion Gate*, 1986; *Polar Star*, 1989; *Red Square*, 1992; *Rose*, 1996; *Havana Bay*, 1999; *December 6*, 2002.
EDITED TEXT: *Death by Espionage: Intriguing Stories of Betrayal and Deception*, 1999.

Martin Cruz Smith's books are exemplars of well-crafted police procedurals—mysteries written from the point of view of the police investigating a crime. With the appearance of his *Gorky Park* in 1981, after eleven years as a prolific novelist, Smith moved into the ranks of America's best-selling authors. Although nominated for a Mystery Writers of America Edgar Allan Poe Award for *Nightwing* in 1978, a sign of professional recognition from fellow authors, Smith achieved national recognition only after his books set in the Soviet Union that depict tense but engaging partnerships between Russian and American detectives. Smith's *Gorky Park* and additional novels that appeared by the early twenty-first century evoked critical evaluations that ranked these works above ordinary mystery genre writing, if somewhat below the best novels of Eric Ambler, Len Deighton, and John le Carré. Smith's readers, voting with their pocketbooks, made him a wealthy man.

Born Martin William Smith on November 3, 1942, in Reading, Pennsylvania, Smith was the son of musician John Calhoun and American Indian rights activist Louise Lopez Smith. Only after the success of *Nightwing* in 1977 did he change his middle name from William to Cruz, the name of his maternal grandmother. Entering the University of Pennsylvania in 1960, his initial interests were in sociology, but, defeated by the discipline's statistics, he switched to creative writing and graduated with a bachelor of arts degree in 1964. Smith spent the next year as a reporter for the *Philadelphia Daily News* and then took a job with Magazine Management, publishers of popular "macho" magazines. This position lasted until 1969, when his "bad attitude" led to his departure. In the interim, he married chef Emily Arnold and began a family that eventually included three children. Following publication of his first novel, *The Indians Won*, in 1970—a work reviewed as science fiction—Smith wrote pseudonymously as Jake Logan, Nick Carter, Martin Quinn, and Simon Quinn, producing a variety of Western adventure and mystery novels. The relative success of *Nightwing* persuaded him to drop his pseudonyms entirely in the mid-1970's.

As critics and readers alike have noted, Smith's novels possess several distinctions that set them apart from pedestrian popular literature. His prose is terse; his sentences are compact, heavily reliant on well-chosen nouns and verbs and unencumbered by adjectives or the wordy demands of metaphors. Thus his better works are fast-paced. Moreover, within the mystery genre, Smith has managed to create several plausible and memorable characters. In his so-called Roman Grey novels published in the early 1970's, for example, the protagonist, New York City Gypsy antique dealer Roman Grey, is preeminently the marginal man, steering a precarious emotional course between Gypsy and non-Gypsy societies. Romantically Grey is linked to a *gaja*, or non-Gypsy, woman, an association uncongenial to the close-knit Gypsy community, while in his crime-solving efforts, which he pursues to uphold the Gypsy code of honor, he relies on his collaboration with Harry Isadore, a *gaja* policeman, one of a breed seldom perceived as friends to the Gypsy.

Similarly, in Smith's Inquisitor series, a few characters, notably Francis Xavier Killy, a former Central Intelligence Agency operative who serves as a lay brother in the Vatican's Militia Christi, emerges as a plausible sleuth who adeptly navigates the shoals of church politics and international crises to expose corruption and murder. *Gorky Park*'s Russian detective, Arkady Renko, and his American collaborator, James Kirwill, along with the American villain of the piece, John Osborne, are among Smith's most widely known characters. A deeply patriotic Russian, Renko reveals the three-dimensional qualities of his character confronting the venal and cynical bureaucracy within which he works, as well as coping with an adulterous wife, a dissenting girlfriend, and his combative American partner. Renko, ever the vulnerable patriot, reappears in several of Smith's subsequent novels, including *Polar Star*, *Red Square*, and *Havana Bay*, again battling political and bureaucratic disfavor, coping with cantankerous partners, trying to differentiate sex from love, and pursuing his own innate version of justice. As in the Renko novels, Smith not only excels in developing characters with real, multidimensional relationships with one another but also skillfully integrates them into convincing plots that are devoid of gratuitous sex and violence. In addition, in his best novels Smith catches the ambience of different cultures, whether Russian or Native American, with his spare but carefully selected details. His protagonists, while marked by commonplace modern cynicism (whether the setting is contemporary or historical), nevertheless evince a strong sense of justice that leaves his novels generally hopeful at their conclusions.

Clifton K. Yearley

Bibliography

"Martin Cruz Smith." *Current Biography* 51 (November, 1990). A well-informed article on Smith as a personality, on the progression of his work, and on the distinctions of his writings.

Smith, Martin Cruz. "Martin Cruz Smith." Interview by Christian Amodeo. *Geographical Magazine* 74, no. 12 (December, 2002): 1. Smith addresses his work and approach to *Rose* and "Tokyo Station," which was published as *December 6*.

_______. "PW Talks with Martin Cruz Smith." Interview by Dorman T. Shindler. *Publishers Weekly* 249, no. 31 (August 5, 2002): 51. Smith discusses the writing of *December 6*.

Swann, Christopher. "Martin Cruz Smith." In *Contemporary Popular Writers*, edited by Dave Mote. Detroit: St. James Press, 1997. A brief entry that provides an overview of Smith's work from *Gorky Park* to *Red Square*.

Van Dover, J. K. "Martin Cruz Smith." In *St. James Guide to Crime and Mystery Writers*, edited by Jay P. Pederson. 4th ed. Detroit: St. James Press, 1996. A brief overview of Smith's career, ending with *Red Square*.

Stevie Smith
(Florence Margaret Smith)

English poet and novelist

Born: Hull, Yorkshire, England; September 20, 1902
Died: Ashburton, England; March 7, 1971

POETRY: *A Good Time Was Had by All*, 1937; *Tender Only to One*, 1938; *Mother, What Is Man?*, 1942; *Harold's Leap*, 1950; *Not Waving but Drowning*, 1957; *Selected Poems*, 1962; *The Frog Prince, and Other Poems*, 1966; *The Best Beast*, 1969; *Two in One: Selected Poems and The Frog Prince, and Other Poems*, 1971; *Scorpion, and Other Poems*, 1972; *The Collected Poems of Stevie Smith*, 1975; *Selected Poems*, 1978; *Cats, Friends, and Lovers: For Women's Chorus*, 1987 (music by Stephen Paulus); *New Selected Poems of Stevie Smith*, 1988; *Stevie's Tunes: An Anthology of Nine Songs for Mezzo-soprano and Piano*, 1988 (music by Peter Dickinson); *Two Stevie Smith Songs: For Voice and Piano*, 1990 (music by Geoffrey Bush).

LONG FICTION: *Novel on Yellow Paper: Or, Work It Out for Yourself*, 1936; *Over the Frontier*, 1938; *The Holiday*, 1949.

NONFICTION: *Some Are More Human than Others: Sketch-Book by Stevie Smith*, 1958, 1990.

MISCELLANEOUS: *Me Again: Uncollected Writings of Stevie Smith*, 1981; *Stevie Smith: A Selection*, 1985; *A Very Pleasant Evening with Stevie Smith: Selected Short Prose*, 1995.

Stevie Smith is a complicated, often controversial, poet who dazzles readers with her variety of styles, moods, voices, and literary references. She is considered simple and naïve by some critics, yet others find her one of the most intellectual and sophisticated of modern poets. Her work was first popular in the 1930's, then made a resurgence in the 1960's. Since then many readers have been fascinated by Smith's unique blend of humor and despair.

Smith was born Florence Margaret Smith in Hull. After her father abandoned the family, her mother was financially unable to support herself and her two daughters. Her mother's sister, Aunt Maggie, moved in with them, offering financial and emotional support. She located a house at 1 Avondale Road in Palmer's Green, a suburb north of London, and sent for her sister and the two children, Molly and Florence Margaret. This was to be Smith's home throughout her life.

Smith liked the neighborhood around Palmer's Green, but childhood illnesses forced the family to send her, at age five, to a children's rest home. She stayed there for three years, coming home only briefly for holidays. The rigidity of life there caused her to consider suicide when she was eight. This thought, however, freed her; she realized that accepting death gave her ultimate control over her life. After her mother's death in 1919, she again had to accept death. This idea of an understanding with death would become a key theme in her writing.

Smith initially did well in school, but later she rebelled under the harsh disciplinary regulations at London Collegiate. After secretarial training, she worked for the publishing firm C. Arthur Pearson as secretary to Sir Neville Pearson; she remained there until 1953. Since her job was not taxing, Smith had spare time and she used it to read voraciously. She began to keep notebooks recording her ideas and thoughts. During the 1920's she began to write poetry.

Smith attempted to have her poems published in the early 1930's but was unable to do so. In 1935, however, David Garnett of the *New Statesman* accepted several poems. The same year, Ian Parsons of Chatto and Windus encouraged her to write a novel. She quickly responded. Although his company ultimately refused to publish it, Jonathan Cape did. The book, *Novel on Yellow Paper*, had a generally enthusiastic reception: Smith was compared with such diverse writers as Virginia Woolf (1882-1941), James Joyce (1882-1941), Marcel Proust (1871-1922), and Dorothy Parker (1893-1967). The book was strongly autobiographical, however, and many of her friends were angered by their portraits.

The success of her novel led to publication of her first poetry collection, *A Good Time Was Had by All*. Smith was now sought by magazines for poems and reviews. She enjoyed the literary scene but always returned to her Aunt Maggie at 1 Avondale for solace. The personal impression Smith made on others seems as varied as the response to her poetry. Although some found her witty and assured, others saw her as lonely and childlike. Her poetry reflects the fact that, although she had many friends and an active social life, she felt a sense of isolation and separation from others.

In 1938 she published *Over the Frontier*, the sequel to *Novel on Yellow Paper*, and another poetry collection, *Tender Only to One*. The collection sold poorly and Jonathan Cape was not anxious to publish further volumes. Only when she threatened to go to another publisher did they put out *Mother, What Is Man?*, a collection that explores mother-child relationships, isolation, and loneliness. Smith continued writing, but it was more difficult for her to get published after the war.

In the summer of 1953 Smith began to withdraw from social activities, and on July 1 she attempted suicide. Treated for depression and forced to retire, she began concentrating on her writing again. She wrote more reviews and had poetry published in magazines. Then, in 1957, *Not Waving but Drowning*, perhaps her best-known book, was published. It had taken several years to arrange publication because Smith insisted that her sketches illustrate the poems, an arrangement which many publishers rejected. The next year, she published a book of her sketches; it was not a success.

In the late 1950's she started giving poetry readings. In the 1960's her career took an upswing as new collections of her works were issued. James Laughlin of New Directions Press introduced her to the United States audience. Unfortunately, in 1962, her aunt's ill health confined her to the upstairs of their house. Smith became her full-time caretaker, with only brief escapes, until her aunt died in 1967. Smith won the Cholomondeloy Prize for Poetry in 1966 and the Queen's Gold Medal for Poetry in 1969. After months of hospitalization, she died on March 7, 1971.

Mary Mahony

Bibliography

Barbera, Jack, and William McBrien. *Stevie: A Biography of Stevie Smith*. New York: Oxford University Press, 1987. Barbera and McBrien's literary biography is well researched and very readable.

Bedient, Calvin. "Stevie Smith." In *Eight Contemporary Poets*. New York: Oxford University Press, 1974. Bedient's study is useful for its discussion of individual poems.

Civello, Catherine A. *Patterns of Ambivalence: The Fiction and Poetry of Stevie Smith*. Columbia, S.C.: Camden House, 1997. An analysis of Smith's work using feminist theory.

Pumphrey, Martin. "Play, Fantasy, and Strange Laughter: Stevie Smith's Uncomfortable Poetry." *Critical Quarterly* 28 (Autumn, 1986): 85-96. Pumphrey uses some of the basic assumptions of play theory to approach Smith's poems. He discusses her use of fairy-tale elements and describes her as an "anticonfessional" poet.

Rankin, Arthur. *The Poetry of Stevie Smith, "Little Girl Lost."* Totowa, N.J.: Barnes and Noble, 1985. Clearly analyzes Smith's poetic styles, themes, and attitudes.

Severin, Laura. *Stevie Smith's Resistant Antics*. Madison: University of Wisconsin Press, 1997. Severin's extensive study challenges the notions of Smith as an apolitical and eccentric poet, instead portraying her as a well-connected literary insider who used many genres to resist domestic ideology in Britain.

Spalding, Frances. *Stevie Smith: A Biography*. Updated ed. New York: Sutton House, 2002. A classic biography of Smith that challenges the notion that the writer was a recluse.

Sternlicht, Sanford. *Stevie Smith*. Boston: Twayne, 1990. Sternlicht's book is a good introduction to Smith's work. It includes chapters on her novels and nonfiction as well as chronological descriptions of Smith's development. The book contains a chronology of Smith's life and a selected bibliography.

_______, ed. *In Search of Stevie Smith*. Syracuse, N.Y.: Syracuse University Press, 1991. A collection of biographical and critical essays on the life and works of Smith. Includes bibliographical references and index.

Williams, Jonathan. "Much Further Out than You Thought." *Parnassus: Poetry in Review* 2 (Spring/Summer, 1974): 105-127. This article is a meditation by a personal friend of Smith, most interesting for its quotations from a 1963 interview.

Tobias Smollett

Scottish novelist

Born: Dalquhurn, Scotland; March 19, 1721 (baptized)
Died: Antignano (now in Italy); September 17, 1771

LONG FICTION: *The Adventures of Roderick Random*, 1748; *The Adventures of Peregrine Pickle: In Which Are Included Memoirs of a Lady of Quality*, 1751; *The Adventures of Ferdinand, Count Fathom*, 1753; *The Adventures of Sir Launcelot Greaves*, 1760-1761; *The Expedition of Humphry Clinker*, 1771.

DRAMA: *The Regicide: Or, James the First of Scotland, a Tragedy*, pb. 1749; *The Reprisal: Or, The Tars of Old England*, pr. 1757.

NONFICTION: *The History and Adventures of an Atom*, 1749, 1769; *An Essay on the External Use of Water*, 1752; *A Compendium of Authentic and Entertaining Voyages*, 1756; *A Complete History of England*, 1757-1758; *Continuation of the Complete History of England*, 1760-1765; *Travels Through France and Italy*, 1766; *The Present State of All Nations*, 1768-1769; *Letters of Tobias Smollett*, 1970 (Lewis M. Knapp, editor).

TRANSLATIONS: *The Adventures of Gil Blas of Santillane*, 1748 (of Alain-René Lesage); *The History and Adventures of the Renowned Don Quixote*, 1755 (of Miguel de Cervantes); *The Works of M. de Voltaire*, 1761-1774 (35 volumes); *The Adventures of Telemachus, the Son of Ulysses*, 1776 (of François de Salignac de La Mothe-Fénelon).

Tobias Smollett (SMAHL-uht), born in 1721 at Dalquhurn near Bonhill, Scotland, was the most prolific and venturesome of the eighteenth century's novelists. After 1754, the year Henry Fielding died and Samuel Richardson published his last work, Smollett was often praised as the most talented novelist in the language. He was at the same time one of England's foremost political journalists and, after David Hume, its most influential historian; in the 1750's and 1760's he wrote or edited some seventy volumes of nonfiction.

A poor and hot-tempered Scot, Smollett was a real-life replica of one of his own literary creations. After study at Glasgow University, he went to London to seek his fortune. After a stint in the navy as surgeon's mate, he remained for a time in the West Indies, where he fell in love with Nancy Lascelles, daughter of a Jamaica planter, whom he later married. In 1744 he was back in London, doctoring and writing.

His first novel, *The Adventures of Roderick Random*, was a picaresque work that strung together a series of episodes through which the hero ultimately finds love and wealth. In all Smollett's novels, there is a plenitude of delight to be found in the minor characters, who are treated as humor types. Lieutenant Tom Bowling, eccentric sea dog, and Morgan, a Welsh surgeon, are two such figures. Because of his interest in naval life, Smollett has been called the father of the nautical novel. The picture of shipboard life and the account of the disastrous attack on Cartagena in *The Adventures of Roderick Random* are among the earliest literary protests against naval abuses.

The Adventures of Peregrine Pickle, his next novel, mined the vein of *The Adventures of Roderick Random*. Again, a young man with roguish tendencies achieves security after a series of adventures and amours. Commodore Hawser Trunnion, Smollett's finest picture of an old salt, graces this novel. *The Adventures of Ferdinand, Count Fathom*, published in 1753, is a novel remarkable chiefly for the baseness of its hero, a thoroughly villainous ingrate who is made to undergo an unconvincing reformation. This was followed by *The Adventures of Sir Launcelot Greaves*, a lackluster imitation of *Don Quixote*.

In the year of his death Smollett published *The Expedition of Humphry Clinker*, at once his masterpiece and his happiest book. This epistolary novel employs a trip through the British Isles as the framework for the exhibition of a brilliant set of humorous characters. Chief among them is Matthew Bramble, a kindhearted man who unsuccessfully tries to hide his goodness behind a gruff manner. Bramble is accompanied by his sister Tabitha, a virago who finally succeeds in marrying Lieutenant Obadiah Lismahago, a terrible-tempered Scot. The novel takes its title from a starveling whom Bramble befriends and who turns out to be Bramble's natural son. The episode of the discovery of Humphry's identity is unsurpassed in the English novel.

In addition to his novels, Smollett labored prodigiously at a number of literary projects in which he was sometimes the coordinator of the work of several hack writers. His translations include *The Adventures of Gil Blas of Santillane*, *The History and Adven-*

tures of the Renowned Don Quixote, and *The Works of M. de Voltaire*. He edited *The Critical Review* (1756-1763), *The British Magazine* (1760-1767), and *The Briton* (1762-1763). He also wrote or edited a group of multiple-volume works, including *A Complete History of England*, *A Compendium of Authentic and Entertaining Voyages*, and *The Present State of All Nations*. In the field of poetry he wrote "The Tears of Scotland" (1746?, 1753), "Advice, a Satire" (1746), "Reproof, a Satire" (1747), and "Ode to Independence" (1773). Smollett was very ambitious for a stage success; after the failure of his tragedy *The Regicide*, he enjoyed a small hit with a farce, *The Reprisal*.

Ill health sent Smollett abroad, and out of his trips came *Travels Through France and Italy*, a curious mixture of laughter and anger. *The History and Adventures of an Atom* is a scurrilous political satire in which events attributed to Japan stand for occurrences in England.

John Sekora

Bibliography

Bold, Alan, ed. *Smollett: Author of the First Distinction*. New York: Barnes & Noble Books, 1982. Contains four essays dealing with general issues and five concentrating on each of Smollett's major novels. Includes index.

Bulckaen, Denise. *A Dictionary of Characters in Tobias Smollett*. Nancy, France: Presses Universitaires de Nancy, 1993. A useful way of keeping track of the plethora of characters in Smollett's fiction. Each character is identified; chapter and page number of the character's first appearance are also cited. There is also an index of the main categories of characters.

Rousseau, G. S. *Tobias Smollett: Essays of Two Decades*. Edinburgh, Scotland: T. and T. Clark, 1982. Collects fifteen previously published essays and reviews on such topics as Smollett as letter writer and his role in various medical controversies of his day. Makes a good case for not regarding Smollett's novels as picaresque.

Spector, Robert D. *Smollett's Women: A Study in an Eighteenth-Century Masculine Sensibility*. Westport, Conn.: Greenwood Press, 1994. Organized differently from most books on Smollett, with chapters on society, personality, and literary tradition; heroines, fallen women, and women as victims; and the comic and the grotesque. Includes notes and bibliography.

_______. *Tobias George Smollett*. 1968. Rev. ed. Boston: Twayne, 1989. The first chapter of the book quickly surveys Smollett's minor works. The rest of the book is a consideration of his novels. Contains an annotated bibliography of secondary criticism.

Wagoner, Mary. *Tobias Smollett*. New York: Garland, 1984. Provides an extensive list of editions of Smollett's works as well as an annotated bibliography of secondary material. Arranged by subject (for example, "Biographies and Biographical Material" and "The Expedition of Humphry Clinker") and therefore easy to use for locating criticism on a specific topic.

W. D. Snodgrass

American poet

Born: Wilkinsburg, Pennsylvania; January 5, 1926
Pseudonym: S. S. Gardons

POETRY: *Heart's Needle*, 1959; *After Experience: Poems and Translations*, 1968; *Remains: Poems*, 1970 (as S. S. Gardons), revised 1985 (as Snodgrass); *The Führer Bunker: A Cycle of Poems in Progress*, 1977; *If Birds Build with Your Hair*, 1979; *The Boy Made of Meat*, 1983; *Magda Goebbels*, 1983; *D. D. Byrde Callyng Jennie Wrenn*, 1984; *A Locked House*, 1986; *The Kinder Capers*, 1986; *Selected Poems, 1957-1987*, 1987; *W. D.'s Midnight Carnival*, 1988 (with paintings by DeLoss McGraw); *The Death of Cock Robin*, 1989 (with paintings by McGraw); *Each in His Season*, 1993; *The Fuehrer Bunker: The Complete Cycle*, 1995.

TRANSLATIONS: *Gallows Songs*, 1967 (with Lore Segal; of Christian Morgenstern); *Miorita*, 1975 (of Romanian ballads); *Six Troubadour Songs*, 1977; *Traditional Hungarian Songs*, 1978; *Six Minnesinger Songs*, 1983 (of high middle German poems); *The Four Seasons*, 1984 (of sonnets including Antonio Vivaldi's music score).

NONFICTION: *In Radical Pursuit: Critical Essays and Lectures*, 1975; *W. D. Snodgrass in Conversation with Philip Hoy*, 1998; *After-Images: Autobiographical Sketches*, 1999; *De/Compositions: 101 Good Poems Gone Wrong*, 2001.

Along with Robert Lowell and Sylvia Plath, William DeWitt Snodgrass is one of the most important of the so-called confessional poets who heavily influenced American poetry in the 1960's and 1970's. Snodgrass grew up in Beaver Falls, a small town in western Pennsylvania, and began his college career at Geneva College, located in his hometown. His studies were interrupted by a term in the Navy near the end of World War II, and when he returned he spent one more year at Geneva before transferring to the University of Iowa, where he earned his B.A. degree in 1949. He stayed at Iowa to complete the M.A. in 1951 and the M.F.A. in 1953. At Iowa one of Snodgrass's teachers was Robert Lowell, who significantly influenced the young poet's early work.

Like many mid-twentieth century American poets, Snodgrass made his living teaching at universities, beginning as an instructor at Cornell University in 1955, then moving on to the University of Rochester, Wayne State University, Syracuse University, Old Dominion University, and the University of Delaware, where he began teaching in 1979.

Without question Snodgrass's most important and influential volume of poetry has been his first, *Heart's Needle*, for which he won the Pulitzer Prize in 1960 and the British Guinness Award in 1961. Both Robert Lowell and Anne Sexton have referred to *Heart's Needle* as an important influence on their poetry. The title poem is a ten-part sequence addressed to his daughter, Cynthia, on the subject of Snodgrass's divorce in 1953 and remarriage in 1954. Part of the poem's epigraph, from an Irish romance, reads, "And an only daughter is the needle of the heart." Each of the poem's ten parts is set in one of the four seasons, from the winter of 1952 to the spring of 1955, and each concerns the speaker's overpowering emotions of guilt and suffering revolving around the loss of his daughter. Sometimes these are directly expressed; at other times they are expressed indirectly by means of everyday images—the day's newspaper headlines, helping his wife to lift their daughter over a puddle, or pushing Cynthia on a swing. Although at times the poem grows sentimental or nostalgic, for the most part it is a moving depiction of heartbreaking, even violent, emotional pain.

Several critics have professed disappointment with both the quality and quantity of Snodgrass's later poetry. His second volume, apart from some translations, did not appear until 1968, and although its reviews were not nearly as enthusiastic as were those of *Heart's Needle*, the book showed Snodgrass's characteristic diversity: It included several poems in the "confessional" mode of *Heart's Needle* but also contained translations of such poets as Arthur Rimbaud (1854-1891) and Rainer Maria Rilke (1875-1926), an excellent satire called "The Examination" (in which a university is depicted as an operating room in which surgeons shape the beliefs of the patient into dull conformity), several poems about specific Impressionist paintings, and a remarkable dialogue poem called "After Experience Taught Me," in which excerpts from the philosopher Baruch Spinoza (1632-1677) are interspersed with a military drill instructor explaining very graphically how to kill an opponent with one's bare hands.

Snodgrass's diverse interests, and his repeated contention that his poetry is not "confessional," are clearly reflected in his next major book, *The Fuehrer Bunker*, a series of dramatic monologues in which the speakers are prominent Nazis who were living in Hitler's Berlin bunker in April, 1945. Each poem's title names its speaker—Joseph Goebbels, Hermann Göring, Heinrich Himmler, Adolf Hitler, Eva Braun, Magda Goebbels—and the sequence is chronological, so that the reader knows the date and sometimes the hour of each monologue. The form of the poems varies with the speakers; for example, Goebbels speaks in rhymed couplets, whereas Braun's monologue is interspersed with lyrics from her favorite American song, "Tea for Two." Like Robert Browning in "My Last Duchess" (1842), Snodgrass focuses attention on the speaker's character. Whereas Browning's villain is a fictional character, however, Snodgrass's are historical figures. The poems have been criticized for humanizing the Nazis, for depicting them too sympathetically. The speakers come across not as war criminals or ethical monsters but as psychological case histories. Two limited-edition additions to the cycle appeared in 1983, and the complete cycle was published in 1995.

Shifting course dramatically once more in the 1980's, Snodgrass published *The Death of Cock Robin* and *W. D.'s Midnight Carnival*, two volumes in which his poems are paired with paintings by DeLoss McGraw—often a poem and painting will have an identical or very similar title, and a poem will serve as comment on a painting, or vice versa. Both paintings and poems are comic, whimsical, childlike—very close in spirit to folk art—but that playfulness is balanced by serious concerns: in *The Death of Cock Robin*, the problematic connection between art (and the artist) and freedom, and in *W. D.'s Midnight Carnival*, the ways in which the light and dark, the comic and tragic, enfold one another. Although in some readers' minds Snodgrass has failed to live up to the early promise of *Heart's Needle*, he is widely acknowledged to be a central figure of mid-twentieth century American poetry, especially within that vein in which the poet's self serves as both object and subject. His critical eye has also been recognized: his book of criticism *De/Compositions: 101 Good Poems Gone Wrong*, won the National Book Critics Circle Award for literary criticism in 2001. In it, he rewrites well-known "good" poems to make them "bad" and uses the comparison as a tool to understanding the subtleties of good poetic writing.

Gary Grieve-Carlson

Bibliography

Gatson, Paul L. *W. D. Snodgrass*. Boston: Twayne, 1978. The first book-length study of Snodgrass, this volume is the fullest available introduction to his life and works. It offers insightful studies of the major poems in Snodgrass's first three volumes. The text is supplemented by a chronology, notes, a select bibliography, and an index.

Goldstein, Laurence. "*The Führer Bunker* and the New Discourse About Nazism." *The Southern Review* 24 (Winter, 1988): 100-114. This article raises a concern that poems about Hitler might elevate him to the stature of a charismatic figure because of the absoluteness of his power. A review of the form and content of the most important poems, however, shows how completely Snodgrass has revealed the twisted nature of Hitler and his supporters.

Haven, Stephen, ed. *The Poetry of W. D. Snodgrass: Everything Human*. Ann Arbor: University of Michigan Press, 1993. Gathers reviews and criticism on Snodgrass and his major collections, by poets and critics such as John Hollander, Hayden Carruth, J. D. McClatchy, Harold Bloom, Hugh Kenner, and Dana Gioia. Haven includes a chronology of the poet's life and work, as well as a bibliography. The first major book-length work on Snodgrass.

McClatchy, J. D. *White Paper on Contemporary American Poetry*. New York: Columbia University Press, 1989. A fellow poet writes a long chapter about the lyricism in Snodgrass's poetry. He sees the confessional mode as dominant in his early poems and then modified in the later works, but never abandoned.

Phillips, Robert. *The Confessional Poets*. Carbondale: Southern Illinois University Press, 1973. Phillips defines the confessional mode in modern American poetry and discusses the six major poets in the movement. Snodgrass's central role is shown through a close study of the poems in *Heart's Needle* and *Remains*. His success results from his sincerity and his ability to communicate personal loss while avoiding sentimentality.

Raisor, Philip, ed. *Tuned and Under Tension: The Recent Poetry of W. D. Snodgrass*. Newark: University of Delaware Press, 1998. Essays examine Snodgrass's "poetic musics," his use of history, and his standing along with Walt Whitman as a constructor of the American consciousness. Index.

Snorri Sturluson

Icelandic historian

Born: Hvamm, Iceland; 1178 or 1179
Died: Reykjaholt, Iceland; September 22, 1241

NONFICTION: *Snorra Edda*, c. 1220-1230 (*The Prose Edda*, partial translations 1916, 1954; full translation 1987); *Heimskringla*, c. 1230-1235 (English translation, 1844).

Scion of a family of powerful Icelandic chiefs, Snorri Sturluson (SNAWR-ee STUR-luh-suhn) was Iceland's most widely influential medieval writer, an adviser to and historian of the Norse kings, and the author of the most coherent Scandinavian cosmography composed in the Middle Ages. When he was three years of age, a legal settlement between his father (a forceful arbitrator) and Jón Loptsson (Iceland's single most powerful citizen) caused Snorri to become Loptsson's foster son. Snorri's benefits from this fosterage cannot be underestimated. Loptsson's home was a center of learning, and he had connections to continental cultural centers. Snorri was trained not only in ecclesiastical curricula but also in law, history, and Iceland's rich tradition of saga literature and skaldic poetry.

Snorri became a lawyer, eventually rising to the position of president of the Icelandic legislative assembly and of the highest court of the land. Still seeking power and adventure, he journeyed to Norway, where he curried favor from Norwegian rulers by composing his own skaldic poetry, nearly all of which has been lost. The young King Hákon Hákonarson (1217-1263) appointed him *skutilsveinn* (page or chamberlain) and later titled him a baron. Returning to Iceland as Hákon's vassal, Snorri became embroiled in the *sturlungaöld*, a long period of political turmoil that culminated (in 1262, after Snorri's death) in Iceland's subjugation to Norway. He ended a second stay in Norway by returning to Iceland in open defiance of the Norwegian king's order. Although it is not entirely clear whether the king ordered Snorri to be executed, Snorri was killed by the king's emissaries at Reykjaholt in 1241.

For all his ambition and avarice, Snorri was apparently regarded by his contemporaries as pious and patriotic. Certainly the *Heimskringla* indicates his diligent striving after historical accuracy and his desire to immortalize the deeds and characters of the great Norse kings, beginning in the days of the legendary migration of the æsir (descendants of survivors of the Trojan war) to Scandinavia. Following an account of this folk legend, *Heimskringla* becomes a compendium of saga material, concluding with the reign of Sverri, which ended in 1177. Snorri's history is set forth in the form of a series of brilliant biographies, from which every irrelevant detail that does not contribute to the characterization has been carefully rejected. He borrows from Thucydides and Plutarch the device of putting into his characters' mouths speeches, not as they were actually spoken, but as they might have been. Snorri's sources are many, including the writings of the priest-historian Ari Torgelson the Wise, the orally transmitted traditions handed down in ballad form, and the legendary biographies of Norway's two King Olafs.

The degree of influence of continental European sources on Snorri's work remains a divisive issue in scholarship on this period. Many are convinced that the neo-Platonism underlying the twelfth century Chartres school strongly affected Snorri's historiographical vision, while other scholars reject such ideas. No one denies, however, that *Heimskringla* is a masterpiece, one that has been somewhat neglected because Iceland's literary heritage lies at the margins of European traditions. Although Snorri was Christian, he does not condescend to or condemn the pagan elements of his work. The work as a whole has a patchwork quality, but the individual portraits of royal rulers are coherent and witty, offering insight into the kings' psychologies. Probably the most famous section (sometimes titled *The Separate Saga of St. Óláfr*) describes the life and death of Norway's most famous historical figure, King Óláfr, who ruled from 1015-1030. Already in Snorri's time, the saint's fame had spread as far east as Constantinople. Possibly this caused Snorri to abandon his scientific approach to history only in his account of miracles attributed to the saint. In addition to forming the zenith of *Heimskringla*, Snorri's biographical saga is the greatest work of literature dedicated to Óláfr produced in world literature.

A minority of scholars credits Snorri with the famous *Egils Saga*, but the only other work universally attributed to Snorri is *The Prose Edda*. Primarily a primer for young poets, the *Edda* is the first work of its kind to be produced in medieval Western Europe: a study of vernacular poetics written in a vernacular European language. It is divided into four parts: Prologue, *Gylfaginning* (the deluding of Gylfi), *Skáldskaparmál* (poetic diction), and *Háttatál* (list of poetic meters). The last two of these sections are studied almost exclusively by scholars fluent in Old Icelandic, but *Gylfaginning*, like *Heimskringla*, has a much broader appeal. In the form of an extended dialogue, Snorri tells how Gylfi, a pagan ruler of Sweden, was tricked into accepting pagan gods as genuine. Marked with humor and irony, this entertaining story represents the most coherent account of Norse mythology that dates from the Middle Ages, forming an admirable complement to *Heimskringla.* Written in prose, the language of the entire *Edda* is highly poetic, reflecting Snorri's gifts as a creative poet in his own right.

Willard J. Rusch

Bibliography

Andersson, Theodore M. "The Politics of Snorri Sturluson." *Journal of English and Germanic Philology* 93 (1994). Useful for understanding the political turmoil through which Snorri wrote and led his public career.

Bagge, Sverre. *Society and Politics in Snorri Sturluson's Heimskringla.* Berkeley: University of California Press, 1991. An outstanding analysis of *Heimskringla.* This book is more intended for specialists than Whaley's (see below) but is just as accessible.

Byock, Jesse. *Medieval Iceland: Societies, Sagas, and Power.* Berkeley: University of California Press, 1990. Helpful introduction to medieval Icelandic literature, with a good section on Snorri.

Clover, Carol, and John Lindow, eds. *Old Norse-Icelandic Literature: A Critical Guide.* Ithaca, N.Y.: Cornell University Press, 1985. Introductory volume; includes bibliographies and indexes.

Faulkes, Anthony, trans. Prologue to *Edda*, by Snorri Sturluson. London: Dent, 1987. Gives the Icelandic texts of the prologue and *Gylfaginning*. This translation also has a fine English glossary and notes.

Glendinning, R. J., and Haraldur Bessason, eds. *Edda: A Collection of Essays.* Winnipeg, Man.: University of Manitoba Press, 1983. Essays analyze *The Prose Edda*.

Lindow, John, Lars Lönnroth, and Gerd W. Weber, eds. *Structure and Meaning in Old Norse Literature: New Approaches to Textual Analysis and Literary Criticism.* Odense, Denmark: Odense University Press, 1986. Critical guide introduces medieval Icelandic literature, including the works of Snorri.

Ross, Margaret Clunies. *Skáldskaparmál: Snorri Sturluson's ars poetica and Medieval Theories of Language.* Odense, Denmark: Odense University Press, 1987. Contains an excellent discussion of *The Prose Edda.*

Whaley, Diana. *Heimskringla: An Introduction.* London: Viking Society for Northern Research, University College, 1991. An outstanding analysis of *Heimskringla*. More for the general reader than Bagge's work, but both are accessible.

C. P. Snow

English novelist and critic

Born: Leicester, England; October 15, 1905
Died: London, England; July 1, 1980

LONG FICTION: *Death Under Sail*, 1932, 1959; *New Lives for Old*, 1933; *The Search*, 1934, 1958; *Strangers and Brothers*, 1940-1970 (collective title for the following 11 novels); *Strangers and Brothers*, 1940 (reissued as *George Passant*, 1972); *The Light and the Dark*, 1947; *Time of Hope*, 1949; *The Masters*, 1951; *The New Men*, 1954; *Homecomings*, 1956 (pb. in U.S. as *Homecoming*); *The Conscience of the Rich*, 1958; *The Affair*, 1960; *Corridors of Power*, 1964; *The Sleep of Reason*, 1968; *Last Things*, 1970; *The Malcontents*, 1972; *In Their Wisdom*, 1974; *A Coat of Varnish*, 1979.

DRAMA: *A View over the Bridge*, pr. 1950; *The Supper Dance*, pb. 1951 (with Pamela Hansford Johnson); *Family Party*, pb. 1951 (with Johnson); *Spare the Rod*, pb. 1951 (with Johnson); *To Murder Mrs. Mortimer*, pb. 1951 (with Johnson); *The Pigeon with the Silver Foot*, pb. 1951 (with Johnson); *Her Best Foot Forward*, pb. 1951 (with Johnson); *The Public Prosecutor*, pr. 1967 (with Johnson; adaptation).

NONFICTION: *Richard Aldington: An Appreciation*, 1938; *Writers and Readers of the Soviet Union*, 1943; *The Two Cultures and the Scientific Revolution*, 1959 (revised as *Two Cultures and a Second Look*, 1964); *The Moral Un-neutrality of Science*, 1961; *Science and Government*, 1961; *A Postscript to Science and Government*, 1962; *Magnanimity*, 1962; *C. P. Snow: A Spectrum, Science, Criticism, Fiction*, 1963; *Variety of Men*, 1967; *The State of Siege*, 1969; *Public Affairs*, 1971; *Trollope: His Life and Art*, 1975; *The Realists*, 1978; *The Physicists*, 1981.

Charles Percy Snow, British novelist, scientist, and literary critic, is notable for both his realistic fiction and his commentaries about the "two cultures" of science and literature. He was born on October 15, 1905, in the lower-middle-class district of Leicester. His father, William Edward Snow, a clerk in a shoe factory, was an amiable but remote figure in Snow's early life, who seems to have neither helped nor hindered his son's intellectual growth. Snow's doting mother, Ada Sophia Robinson, on the other hand, encouraged her son's precocity and, despite the family's poverty, sent Snow to private grammar schools until the age of sixteen.

In 1925 he entered Leicester University College, where he received his B.S. in chemistry in 1927 and master's degree in physics in 1928. Having determined from his youth to become a novelist, Snow nevertheless chose science for a career, following his own pragmatic instincts and aversion to poverty. In 1928 he gained acceptance into the Ph.D. program in physics at Christ's College, Cambridge, and its prestigious research core, the Cavendish Laboratory. This pivotal event in Snow's life marked his entry into the "corridors of power" (a phrase he coined), as the University of Cambridge was clearly the exuberant center of a new "heroic age" of scientific discovery, where men such as Lord Ernest Rutherford, J. D. Bernal, John Cockroft, and P. M. S. Blackett were revolutionizing physics and biochemistry. Upon completing his doctorate in 1930 Snow, who wore thick horn-rimmed glasses and looked well beyond his twenty-five years, was elected a fellow at Christ's College. Now comfortable in science, he turned his attentions to his first interest, fiction writing.

Snow began writing in deliberate reaction against the purely aesthetic mode of fiction typified by writers such as James Joyce and Virginia Woolf. This antirealistic trend, he believed, was self-indulgent and pernicious, and it threatened the breakdown in society of morality and individual responsibility. His early novels are apprentice works: *Death Under Sail*, an intriguing detective story intended for a popular audience; *New Lives for Old*, a story about rejuvenation, for which he was compared with H. G. Wells; and *The Search*, a weightier novel about the ambitions of research scientists, the fruit of Snow's close observations of the academic power structure and the brilliant, temperamental scientists who controlled it.

On holiday in Marseilles in 1935, Snow was suddenly struck by the idea of a *roman-fleuve*, a series of novels to be connected by a central protagonist (Lewis Eliot) whose private pursuits would intertwine, and often clash, with his public actions. Snow's objective was to examine the actions of man alone and man in society, and his inner design was to create a "resonance" between what Lewis Eliot sees in observing people and events outside himself and what he feels as similar experiences enter his own life. The novel *Strangers and Brothers* was completed in 1940; however, between 1940 and 1944, Snow's war job as technical director for the Ministry of Labour retarded his progress on the series. *The Light and the Dark* and *Time of Hope* earned for Snow wider recognition. *The Masters*, by consensus his most exquisitely constructed novel, intrigued many with its behind-the-scenes analysis of committee politics and personal ambition. *The New Men*, *Homecomings*, *The Conscience of the Rich*, and *The Affair* all helped to establish Snow's international reputation as the preeminent novelist of the individual in society.

In 1959 Snow delivered the time-honored Rede Lecture at the University of Cambridge, an event that sparked one of the most heated debates of the decade between scientific and literary intellectuals. In the lecture, titled *The Two Cultures and the Scientific Revolution*, Snow warned that a "gulf of mutual incomprehension" between the literary culture and scientific community threatened Western society and implied that this ignorance of science by nonscientists was irresponsible. Rebuttals followed, the most scathing of which came from Cambridge professor of English and literary critic F. R. Leavis. Snow weathered these attacks as well as bouts of ill health in the 1960's. He produced one of his most widely admired novels, *Corridors of Power*, and finished his series with *Last Things* in 1970.

Like his literary predecessors Anthony Trollope and Matthew Arnold, Snow assumed a humanitarian stance with an insistence upon the moral function of art. His thematic landscape is marked by polarities that create the central tension in the novels, for example, power and responsibility, private ambition and social ethics, personal suffering and public performance, and redemptive love and possessive love. Underlying the series is the moral directive that a person should do what he or she can to improve the human condition, that even though the individual life may be tragic, the social life need not be so. Most readers detect a darkening of moral vision in *The Sleep of Reason* and *Last Things*. An aging protagonist here records the effects wrought by a permissive, affluent society in which individual social responsibility has been abdicated.

Snow was once anachronistically referred to as the greatest living nineteenth century novelist. When the mood of the time was predominantly antiexperimental, Snow's literary reputation soared. All tallied, however, the critical reception of Snow's novels has never been strongly positive, there being several persistent complaints, such as a failure to integrate the personal and external experiences of the protagonist from one novel to the next, the plain and functional prose style that many find dull, and the lack of empathy for the protagonists.

Caroline Nobile Gryta

Bibliography

De la Mothe, John. *C. P. Snow and the Struggle of Modernity*. Austin: University of Texas Press, 1992. Chapters on Snow's view of literature, science, and the modern mind and on his career as writer and public intellectual. Includes extensive notes and bibliography.

Ramanathan, Suguna. *The Novels of C. P. Snow: A Critical Introduction*. London: Macmillan, 1978. A sympathetic assessment of Snow which discusses all of his novels save his two earliest works, *Death Under Sail* and *New Lives for Old*. Notes Snow's "imaginative impulse," his understanding of the changing social scene in England over a span of fifty years, and the gradual change in his outlook from hopefulness to doom. Upholds Snow as being free from fanaticism. A recommended reading.

Shusterman, David. *C. P. Snow*. Rev. ed. Boston: Twayne, 1991. A competent, compact study of Snow, including his early life, the controversies surrounding his nonfiction, and his literary output. Contains an in-depth analysis of the *Strangers and Brothers* series of novels, noting their interest apart from their literary value. Includes a chronology and a select bibliography.

Snow, Philip. *A Time of Renewal: Clusters of Characters, C. P. Snow, and Coups*. New York: Radcliffe Press, 1998. Written by C. P. Snow's brother. Includes plates, index, and bibliography.

Gary Snyder

American poet

Born: San Francisco, California; May 8, 1930

POETRY: *Riprap*, 1959; *Myths and Texts*, 1960; *Hop, Skip, and Jump*, 1964; *Nanao Knows*, 1964; *The Firing*, 1964; *Riprap, and Cold Mountain Poems*, 1965; *Six Sections from Mountains and Rivers Without End*, 1965; *A Range of Poems*, 1966; *Three Worlds, Three Realms, Six Roads*, 1966; *The Back Country*, 1967; *The Blue Sky*, 1969; *Sours of the Hills*, 1969; *Regarding Wave*, 1969, enlarged 1970; *Manzanita*, 1972; *The Fudo Trilogy: Spel Against Demons, Smokey the Bear Sutra, The California Water Plan*, 1973; *Turtle Island*, 1974; *All in the Family*, 1975; *Axe Handles: Poems*, 1983; *Left Out in the Rain: New Poems, 1947-1986*, 1986; *No Nature: New and Selected Poems*, 1992; *Mountains and Rivers Without End*, 1996.

NONFICTION: *Earth House Hold: Technical Notes and Queries to Fellow Dharma Revolutionaries*, 1969; *The Old Ways*, 1977; *He Who Hunted Birds in His Father's Village: The Dimensions of a Haida Myth*, 1979; *The Real Work: Interviews and Talks, 1964-1979*, 1980; *Passage Through India*, 1983; *The Practice of the Wild*, 1990; *Gary Snyder Papers*, 1995; *A Place in Space: Ethics, Aesthetics, and Watersheds*, 1995.

MISCELLANEOUS: *The Gary Snyder Reader: Prose, Poetry, and Translations, 1952-1998*, 2000.

Poet, translator, essayist, and educator Gary Sherman Snyder grew up in the state of Washington and later moved to Portland, Oregon, where he gained an appreciation for the wilderness and mountain trails that became interests dominating his future writings. In 1947 he attended Reed College, studying literature and anthropology with a special interest in Native American myth. At Reed he gained a lifelong interest in Chinese calligraphy and began a lifelong friendship with fellow Buddhist poet Philip Whalen. He pursued graduate work at Indiana University, then studied classical Chinese at the University of California at Berkeley.

In the mid-1950's he became associated with poets Kenneth Rexroth, Lawrence Ferlinghetti, Allen Ginsberg, and especially Jack Kerouac. These were all central figures in the "San Francisco renaissance" poetry movement, of which Snyder would later be described as the pivotal "renaissance man." During this period he participated in the historic 1955 Six Gallery poetry reading that launched the Beat Generation, translated the "Cold Mountain Poems" by Zen poet Han-Shan, and climbed the Matterhorn with Kerouac. Kerouac wrote of their experiences in his autobiographical novel *The Dharma Bums* (1958), in which Snyder is fictionalized as the central character, Japhy Ryder.

During the 1960's, Snyder lived primarily in Kyoto, Japan, until 1968. There he took Buddhist instructions from Zen masters, traveled extensively, began his communal lifestyle, kept journals (that were compiled in *Earth House Hold*), and wrote the poems of *Regarding Wave* as well as numerous broadsides, which included criticism of America's Vietnam policy. Since 1969 he has worked primarily in the Yuba River country of the Sierra Nevada in Northern California, where he built his own house and became involved in civic affairs. In 1983 he began a formal relationship with the University of California at Davis, where he teaches and where his papers are kept for researchers.

His poetic work, which frequently combines reading and study with physical outdoor activity, reflects his various jobs as timber scaler, forest-fire lookout, logger, and hand on a tanker in the South Pacific. His themes and style reflect his interests in the natural world, mythology, the discipline of Eastern religions, and the living oral traditions of Native American cultures—themes he summarizes in the phrase "wilderness, wildness, and wisdom." Snyder describes poetry as healing, a Native American concept in which the poet is a shaman, or medicine man, nourishing the welfare of the community and environment, both of which Snyder sees as interconnected and interdependent.

His verse and essays are moral, didactic, political, and cultural criticisms of contemporary Western dominant values, particularly the excesses of capitalism, industry, technology, and the exploitation of both human and natural resources. His views are evident in his 1974 Pulitzer Prize-winning *Turtle Island*, which expresses the ideas that American history goes back much further than white settlement, that time and matter are relative concepts, and that modern values must change to avoid ecological destruction of the planet. These views are repeated throughout his collections of essays. The essays, in particular "Poetry and the Primitive" (1967), provide the reader with insights for understanding the background of his verse.

In 1992 Snyder's *No Nature: New and Selected Poems* both reviewed Snyder's career by republishing poems from his previous eight volumes and introduced new verse that demonstrates his evolution from apocalyptic visionary to his more optimistic contentment with his family, community, and region. Yet his recurring emphasis on nature, especially in western United States settings, and his use of Asian and Native American sources emphasize the Buddhist concept that the self cannot be separated from the world around it. Also of Buddhist influence are Snyder's repeated ideas that both identity in the mind and cultural background should be negated in favor of a spiritual transformation, and that humans should be aware of and linked to both physical reality and the knowledge that all is impermanent and transitory. In much of his verse Snyder attempts to make these Buddhist precepts accessible to Western readers, bringing the religion into everyday practices and readily understandable language. However, readers unfamiliar with Asian poetic forms may need reference works to help them understand and appreciate his non-Western poetic structures and artistic designs, especially in his earlier verse.

Snyder's work is often compared to that of American poets

Henry David Thoreau, Robert Duncan, Carl Sandburg, William Carlos Williams, and particularly Ezra Pound, whose 1920's poetic school of Imagism profoundly affected Snyder's verse structure and aesthetics, notably in *Riprap* and *Myths and Texts*. Snyder has won numerous awards for his poetry and has earned considerable praise from critics and fellow poets for his work and his principles, and he is widely regarded as both an important poet and influential spokesman for his culture. In 1963 he began working on a long poem called *Mountains and Rivers Without End*, portions of which have appeared in various journals, and which was finally published whole in 1996. Most critics felt it had been worth the wait.

Wesley Britton

Bibliography

Dean, Tim. *Gary Snyder and the American Unconscious*. New York: St. Martin's Press, 1991. An intelligent and careful reading of Snyder's work, somewhat limited by an academic style and perspective.

Murphy, Patrick, ed. *Critical Essays on Gary Snyder.* Boston: G. K. Hall, 1990. A comprehensive, well-chosen collection of critical essays by one of Snyder's most intelligent critics. Ranging from the earliest responses to the poet's work through three decades of criticism, this book is evidence of the variety of perspectives Snyder's work has brought forth.

_______. *A Place for Wayfaring: The Poetry and Prose of Gary Snyder.* Corvallis: Oregon State University Press, 2000. After three introductory chapters on themes in Snyder's work, especially mythological themes, Murphy offers close readings of a number of individual poems.

_______. *Understanding Gary Snyder.* Columbia: University of South Carolina Press, 1992. A useful overview, written for students and general readers, of Snyder's work and influences with detailed explications of his work.

Phillips, Rod. *"Forest Beatniks" and "Urban Thoreaus": Gary Snyder, Jack Kerouac, Lew Welch, and Michael McClure*. New York: P. Lang, 2000. Examines the attitudes toward nature, ecology, and conservationism in the Beats' poetry, countering the notion that Beat poetry was a purely urban phenomenon.

Schuler, Robert Jordan. *Journeys Toward the Original Mind: The Long Poems of Gary Snyder.* New York: P. Lang, 1994. Close readings of *Myths and Texts* and *Mountains and Rivers Without End*, focusing on Snyder's concept of "original mind," in which the mind is purified of all its cultural baggage in order to comprehend the universe directly.

Sciagaj, Leonard M. *Sustainable Poetry: Four American Ecopoets*. Lexington: University Press of Kentucky, 1999. Along with Snyder, discusses and compares A. R. Ammons, Wendell Berry, and W. S. Merwin and their treatment of nature and environmental concerns in their works. Bibliographical references, index.

Smith, Eric Todd. *Reading Gary Snyder's "Mountains and Rivers Without End."* Boise, Idaho: Boise State University Press, 2000. An extended close reading of Snyder's long-awaited poem.

Suiter, John. *Poets on the Peaks: Gary Snyder, Philip Whalen, and Jack Kerouac in the North Cascades*. Washington, D.C.: Counterpoint, 2002. Examines the environmental influences on Snyder and other Beat poets that occurred through living in the Pacific Northwest mountains. Includes thirty-five photographs of places where Snyder and others lived.

Socrates

Greek philosopher

Born: Athens, Greece; c. 470 B.C.E.
Died: Athens, Greece; 399 B.C.E.

Socrates (SAHK-ruh-teez) did not make a written record of his teachings. What is known of his philosophy comes from the *Dialogues* of Plato, in which Socrates is the central figure.

What is known of Socrates, the great Greek philosopher, comes primarily from two of his pupils, Xenophon and Plato. The account of Socrates by Plato in the *Dialogues* is generally taken as being, on the whole, the more reliable report, both of the character and of the teachings of Socrates.

Socrates was the son of Sophroniscus, a sculptor, and Phænarete, a nonprofessional midwife. The family was neither poor nor wealthy, and Socrates received the usual elementary education in gymnastics and music, to train the body and the mind. He may have planned to follow his father's occupation, and there are some reports that he actually did produce some works of sculpture; but he apparently decided that he was more at ease with ideas than with stone. He had a reflective, almost mystical temperament at times, and throughout his life had the habit of assuming immobile positions, or trancelike states, during which he sometimes thought he heard a supernatural voice that warned him against certain acts he was considering. He claimed that he always regretted it when he disregarded the voice.

Socrates has been pictured as a short, snub-nosed person with widely spaced, perhaps protruding eyes and broad nostrils. The comic dramatists of the time, Aristophanes, Amipsias, and Eupolis, made him the subject of satirical dramas in which his physical traits as well as his dialectical habits were exaggerated. He lived simply, wearing the same garment winter and summer and traveling barefoot in all seasons. He ate and drank moderately, although he could drink more wine than most men without being affected. He was married to Xanthippe, who is reputed to have been a virago, and they had two children.

Socrates began his philosophical studies with the ideas of Pythagoras, Parmenides, Heraclitus, Anaxagoras, Anaximander, Zeno, and others. Because of the conflicting and sometimes fantastic ideas he found in these philosophies concerning the nature of the universe, he came to the conviction that more was to be gained by a study of justice and goodness. He combined his interest in ethics and the philosophy of politics with a faith in the capacity of the mind to clarify itself by working out the inconsistencies in various notions through a conversational technique that has come to be known as the Socratic method. He claimed that if there were any truth in the report that the Oracle at Delphi had called him the wisest man in Greece, it was only because, unlike others, he recognized his own ignorance. He believed that he had a mission in life to make people aware of the limitations and defects in their beliefs and thus, by knowing themselves, to prepare for knowledge.

He wandered the streets and marketplaces of Athens, and when young men, politicians, or other bystanders became involved in conversation with him about justice, honor, courage, or some other philosophical matter, Socrates would adroitly question them, leading them to an awareness of the inadequacy or falsity of their ideas. Because his ability was obvious and his insight undeniable, those who knew his method began to regard his profession of ignorance as either ironic or sophistical, and opinion was divided as to whether he was a beneficial genius or a dangerous nuisance.

Before he was forty Socrates had established himself as a remarkable teacher and philosopher; he was known and respected by many of the leading philosophers, politicians, and sophists of his time, including Protagoras, with whom he had one of his most famous debates. Others who at various times came to be companions of Socrates during his conversational tours of Athens were Crito, Charmides (Plato's uncle), Critias (Plato's mother's cousin), Plato, Xenophon, Alcibiades, Adimantus and Glaucon (Plato's brothers), Callias (son of the wealthiest Athenian of the time), and Nicias (an outstanding Athenian democrat).

Socrates' role as "gadfly" (his own term) to the Athenian people irritated the democratic leaders, particularly because he was closely associated with Alcibiades, who in 415 B.C.E. led the Sicilian expedition that ended in defeat for Athens, and with Critias, leader of the Thirty Tyrants imposed on the city by the Spartans after the defeat of the Athenians ended the Peloponnesian War in 404 B.C.E. That defeat was blamed in part on the new ideas with which, so it was charged, Socrates had corrupted the youth of the city. In 399 B.C.E., after the democracy had been restored, and despite the commendable military record he had made during the war, Socrates was brought to trial on the charges of impiety and corrupting the young. In an eloquent and dignified defense he argued that he had been fulfilling a mission to goad the Athenians into searching for truth, that he was no man's master, and that he would accept acquittal only if it could be had without a sacrifice of his principles. When he was found guilty and was asked to propose a punishment, he claimed that he deserved to be rewarded for his services to Athens, but that he would agree to pay a fine. Condemned to death, he died after drinking hemlock, having refused the opportunity to escape and go into exile.

Plato's dialogues about Socrates' trial and death, the *Apology* (c. 399-390 B.C.E.), the *Crito* (c. 399-390 B.C.E.), and the *Phaedo* (c. 388-368 B.C.E.), together constitute one of the most moving portraits of all dramatic literature and are probably fairly reliable historically. *The Symposium* (c. 388-368 B.C.E.) presents an intensely interesting portrait of Socrates as a man of great powers of intellect and of physical endurance.

Believing that the "unexamined life is not worth living" and that knowledge leads to virtue, Socrates developed a method of questioning others in which he relied on inductive reasoning, proceeding from particular facts to general principles. In his dialectical questioning his dialogists were brought to see the error of their initial beliefs and to become wiser and better people. This dialectical exchange is known as the Socratic method, and it remains a viable education strategy to this day. Socrates is famous for his theory of knowledge as the recollection of ideas, for his conception of the soul and his attempted proofs of the soul's immortality, and for the theory of Ideas or universal forms, which Plato adopted and expanded. He is remembered as much for his personal courage and his clear idealism as for his philosophy, and he remains one of the towering figures of the Western world.

Robert G. Blake

Bibliography

Colaiaco, James A. *Socrates Against Athens: Philosophy on Trial*. New York: Routledge, 2001. Provides historical and cultural context to a modern understanding of Socrates' trial.

Gottlieb, Anthony. *Socrates*. New York: Routledge, 1999. Short introductory volume places the philosopher and his ideas in historical perspective. An explanation of Socrates' basic concepts of thought is accompanied by biographical details.

May, Hope. *On Socrates*. Belmont, Calif.: Wadsworth/Thomson Learning, 2000. Brief text is meant to assist students in understanding Socrates' philosophy and thinking.

Ranasinghe, Nalin. *The Soul of Socrates*. Ithaca, N.Y.: Cornell University Press, 2000. Traces Plato's struggle, in his *Dialogues*, to understand and convey the presence of Socrates. Claims that the dialogues reflect Plato's awe and frustration before his teacher.

Rudebusche, George. *Socrates, Pleasure, and Value*. New York: Oxford University Press, 1999. Addresses whether Socrates believed pleasurable activities to be virtuous activities.

Smith, Nicholas D., and Paul B. Woodruff, eds. *Reason and Religion in Socratic Philosophy*. New York: Oxford University Press, 2000. Examines Socratic pedagogy to ascertain why Plato portrays Socrates as a failure in his attempts to purge his fellow citizens of their unfounded beliefs.

Taylor, C. C. W. *Socrates: A Very Short Introduction*. Oxford, England: Oxford University Press, 2000. Explores the relationship between the historical Socrates and the Platonic character.

Sasha Sokolov

Russian novelist

Born: Ottawa, Ontario, Canada; November 6, 1943

LONG FICTION: *Shkola dlia durakov*, 1976 (*A School for Fools*, 1977); *Mezhdu sobakoi i volkom*, 1980; *Palisandriia*, 1984 (*Astrophobia*, 1989).

Sasha Aleksandr Vsevolodovich Sokolov (SUH-kohl-uhv) was the most critically acclaimed writer to appear on the Russian literary scene during the 1970's and 1980's. He was born in Ottawa, Canada, where his father was a Soviet military diplomat until forced to return to Moscow following an espionage scandal. There the young Sokolov drifted through an unsatisfactory career in the public schools before, in 1962, entering the Military Institute of Foreign Languages. Army life was not to his liking, and he ended first in jail for being absent without leave and then in a mental hospital as part of a ploy to gain his military discharge.

After a period living on the fringes of Moscow's literary bohemia, Sokolov entered the journalism department at Moscow State University. Upon completing an internship on a provincial newspaper, he returned to the capital, where he worked for *Literary Russia*. When he received his university degree in 1971, Sokolov left Moscow for a job as a gamekeeper on the remote upper Volga. Here, over a two-year period, he completed *A School for Fools*, a modernist tour de force that then had little chance of appearing in the Soviet Union. Smuggled abroad with the help of an Austrian friend whom Sokolov subsequently married, the novella appeared in the United States in 1976. Growing out of Sokolov's youthful encounters with Soviet institutions and the sheer dreariness and duplicity of Soviet life, the work depicts that world through the innocent eyes of its schizophrenic narrator, a student at a "special" school. Translated into several languages, *A School for Fools* became the only novel by a living Russian author to win the praise of Vladimir Nabokov.

While the novel was making its way toward publication abroad, Sokolov launched a campaign to emigrate, which brought him into conflict with the government. Following a hunger strike and extensive publicity, he was allowed to join his bride-to-be in Vienna in late 1975. One year later he arrived in North America, where he was able to claim his Canadian citizenship. While still in Russia, Sokolov had started a novel based upon an unsolved murder he had heard about during his years as a gamekeeper. Many critics considered *Mezhdu sobakoi i volkom* (between dog and wolf) a novel of startling originality and daring. Its metaphorical title refers to twilight, when the normally distinct becomes blurred. The plot emerges from the drunken narrator's inability to distinguish between a real dog and wolf—a failure that results in his murder for the killing of a hunting dog. As a result of its structural and stylistic complexity, the novel gained much critical acclaim but few readers. The unofficial Leningrad journal *Chasy* awarded it its 1981 Andrey Bely Prize.

Sokolov has been peripatetic during his years in the United States and Canada. He held a variety of short-term jobs ranging from language teacher and radio writer to ski instructor in Vermont. He has also held grants from the Canadian government and has been Regents' Lecturer at the University of California, as well as giving many literary readings and conference lectures, which are highly polished essays of great wit and charm.

Sokolov's work was banned in the Soviet Union under Leonid Brezhnev, although it was known to literary cognoscenti through smuggled copies and radio broadcasts. With the rise of Mikhail Gorbachev's *glasnost* and after the dissolution of the Soviet Union, Sokolov became recognized as a major literary figure in his homeland.

Sokolov's third novel, *Astrophobia*, a radical departure from his earlier, more involuted work, is a comic, picaresque work that lampoons many popular genres: the sensational memoir, the political espionage thriller, the futurological fantasy, and the pornographic novel. Its hero(ine), the bizarre Palisander/Palisandra, recounts his/her life story from privileged Kremlin orphan to penniless exile, ending with a triumphant return to his/her rightful position as the ruler of Russia. The novel is parody raised to the level of high art.

A School for Fools is representative of Sokolov's work. It is a first-person account of the mental landscape of a nameless, schizophrenic adolescent. There is little or no plot, and the work is composed of a small number of scenes that occur and recur in evolving variants. It is difficult to determine whether events occur in the past, present, or future, or whether they are real or imaginary. The boy's disordered perceptions literally shape the language, the manner, and the content of the story, which deals with his attempts to come to terms with the elemental experiences of love, sex, and death in his small, oppressive universe. The novella progresses largely through a complex pattern of phonetic associations and recurrent images. The language is of great wit and beauty.

The central theme that runs throughout Sokolov's novels is ambiguity. Traditional fiction, like life, rests on certain unconscious and unquestioned assumptions. Time is linear and is divided into past, present, and unknown future; it is constant for all. Memory recalls the past, not the future. People are either male or female, not both. Personal identity is fixed. Incest is avoided. One is either dead or alive. These assumptions are implicitly called into question in Sokolov's novels. Everything takes place in a twilight zone where nothing is certain. Sokolov replaces the usual coordinates of existence with a richly woven web of words which arises from the world of the subconscious and replaces mundane reality. Sound texture and wordplay are the heart of his lyrical style, which tends to displace content. One critic has aptly remarked that Sokolov's prose is not merely a stream of consciousness, but rather an inundation of consciousness.

The mainstream of Russian literature in both the nineteenth and twentieth centuries has been realistic in form, socially and morally committed in content. Sokolov belongs to a brilliant, minor line in Russian literary history which was inaugurated by the modernist Andrey Bely in the early years of the twentieth century. That tradition, suppressed in the early years of the revolution in favor of a sturdy, simple-minded Socialist Realism, was reinvoked by Andrei Sinyavsky (as Abram Tertz), whose 1956 samizdat essay "On Socialist Realism" called for a "phantasmagoric art." Sokolov's work is the most brilliant response to Sinyavsky's modernist imperative.

D. Barton Johnson

Bibliography

Beraha, Laura. "The Last Rogue of History: Picaresque Elements in Sasha Sokolov's *Palisandriia*." *Canadian Slavonic Papers* 35, nos. 3/4 (1993). Discusses Sokolov's attack on historical and self-referential narrative through the structure of his novel.

Boguslawski, Alexander. "Sokolov's *A School for Fools:* An Escape from Socialist Realism." *Slavic and East European Journal* 27 (1983). A good discussion of *A School for Fools*.

Canadian-American Slavic Studies 22, nos. 1/2 (1988). A special Sokolov issue. An extensive literary biography and a bibliography of works by and about Sokolov, as well as essays on many aspects of Sokolov's work.

Johnson, D. Barton. "Sasha Sokolov: The New Russian Avant-Garde." *Critique: Studies in Contemporary Fiction* 30 (1989). An excellent introductory survey.

_______. "Sasha Sokolov's *Between Dog and Wolf* and the Modernist Tradition." In *Russian Literature in Emigration: The Third Wave*, edited by Olga Matich and Michael Heim. Ann Arbor, Mich.: Ardis, 1984. On the untranslated *Mezhdu sobakoi i volkom*.

_______. "A Structural Analysis of Sasha Sokolov's *School for Fools:* A Paradigmatic Novel." In *Fiction and Drama in Eastern and Southeastern Europe: Evolution and Experiment in the Postwar Period*, edited by Henrik Birnbaum and Thomas Eekman. Columbus, Ohio: Slavonica, 1980. A theoretically oriented discussion.

Kolb, Hannah. "The Dissolution of Reality in Sasha Sokolov's *Mezhdu sobakoi i volkom*." In *Reconstructing the Canon: Russian Writing in the 1980's*, edited by Arnold McMillin. Amsterdam: Harwood Academic, 2000. Discusses Sokolov's untranslated novel as an example of the unprecedented turn in Russian literature in the late twentieth century.

McMillin, Arnold. "Aberration or the Future: The Avant-Garde Novels of Sasha Sokolov." In *From Pushkin to "Palisandriia": Essays on the Russian Novel in Honor of Richard Freeborn*, edited by McMillin. New York: St. Martin's Press, 1990. Assesses Sokolov's position in influencing the direction of contemporary Russian fiction.

Matich, Olga. "Sasha Sokolov's *Palisandriia:* History and Myth." *The Russian Review* 45 (1986). *Astrophobia* is treated.

Porter, Robert. *Russia's Alternative Prose*. Providence, R.I.: Berg, 1994. Sokolov is one of several writers discussed.

Simmons, Cynthia. *Their Father's Voice: Vassily Aksyonov, Venedikt Erofeev, Eduard Limonov, and Sasha Sokolov*. New York: P. Lang, 1993. Focuses on Sokolov's oppositional relationship to traditional Russian novel form.

Aleksandr Solzhenitsyn

Russian novelist, playwright, and poet

Born: Kislovodsk, Soviet Union (now in Russia); December 11, 1918

LONG FICTION: *Odin den' Ivana Denisovicha*, 1962 (novella; *One Day in the Life of Ivan Denisovich*, 1963); *Rakovy korpus*, 1968 (*Cancer Ward*, 1968); *V kruge pervom*, 1968 (*The First Circle*, 1968); *Avgust chetyrnadtsatogo*, 1971 (*August 1914*, 1972); *Lenin v Tsyurikhe*, 1975 (*Lenin in Zurich*, 1976); *Krasnoe koleso*, 1983-1991 (includes *Avgust chetyrnadtsatogo*, expanded version, 1983 [*The Red Wheel*, 1989]; *Oktiabr' shestnadtsatogo*, 1984 [*November 1916*, 1999]; *Mart semnadtsatogo*, 1986-1988; *Aprel' semnadtsatogo*, 1991).

SHORT FICTION: *Dlya pol'zy dela*, 1963 (*For the Good of the Cause*, 1964); *Dva rasskaza: Sluchay na stantsii Krechetovka i Matryonin dvor*, 1963 (*We Never Make Mistakes*, 1963); *Krokhotnye Rasskazy*, 1970; *Rasskazy*, 1990.

DRAMA: *Olen'i shalashovka*, pb. 1968 (*The Love Girl and the Innocent*, 1969; also known as *Respublika truda*); *Svecha na vetru*, pb. 1968 (*Candle in the Wind*, 1973); *Dramaticheskaya trilogiya-1945: Pir Pobediteley*, pb. 1981 (*Victory Celebrations*, 1983); *Plenniki*, pb. 1981 (*Prisoners*, 1983).

SCREENPLAYS: *Znayut istinu tanki*, 1981; *Tuneyadets*, 1981.

POETRY: *Etyudy i krokhotnye rasskazy*, 1964 (translated in *Stories and Prose Poems by Alexander Solzhenitsyn*, 1971); *Prusskie nochi*, 1974 (*Prussian Nights*, 1977).

NONFICTION: *Les Droits de l'écrivain*, 1969; *Nobelevskaya lektsiya po literature 1970 goda*, 1972 (*The Nobel Lecture*, 1973); *A Lenten Letter to Pimen, Patriarch of All Russia*, 1972; *Solzhenitsyn: A Pictorial Autobiography*, 1972; *Arkhipelag GULag, 1918-1956: Opyt khudozhestvennogo issledovaniya*, 1973-1975 (*The Gulag Archipelago, 1918-1956: An Experiment in Literary Investigation*, 1974-1978); *Iz-pod glyb*, 1974 (*From Under the Rubble*, 1975); *Pis'mo vozhdyam Sovetskogo Soyuza*, 1974 (*Letter to Soviet Leaders*, 1974);

Bodalsya telyonok s dubom, 1975 (*The Oak and the Calf*, 1980); *Amerikanskiye rechi*, 1975; *Warning to the West*, 1976; *East and West*, 1980; *The Mortal Danger: How Misconceptions About Russia Imperil America*, 1980; *Kak nam obustroit' Rossiiu?: Posil'nye soobrazheniia*, 1990 (*Rebuilding Russia: Reflections and Tentative Proposals*, 1991); *Russkii vopros*, 1994 (*The Russian Question: At the End of the Twentieth Century*, 1994); *Invisible Allies*, 1995; *Dvesti let vmeste, 1795-1995*, 2001.

MISCELLANEOUS: *Sochineniya*, 1966; *Stories and Prose Poems by Alexander Solzhenitsyn*, 1971; *Six Etudes by Aleksandr Solzhenitsyn*, 1971; *Mir i nasiliye*, 1974; *Sobranie sochinenii*, 1978-1983 (10 volumes); *Izbrannoe*, 1991.

Aleksandr Isayevich Solzhenitsyn (sohl-zeh-NEET-sihn) is widely regarded as the most significant Russian writer of the twentieth century. Many critics see in his writings a revival of nineteenth century Russian realist literature. He was born on December 11, 1918, in Kislovodsk, Soviet Union. His father, an artillery officer in the Russian army, died six months before Aleksandr's birth. His mother worked as a typist and stenographer. As a youth, Solzhenitsyn felt a desire to become a writer but did not receive any encouragement. From 1939 to 1941 he studied mathematics at the University of Rostov. He was drafted into the army in 1941, where he served with distinction. In February, 1945, the Soviet secret police (KGB) intercepted a letter from Solzhenitsyn to a friend. The letter allegedly contained comments critical of Soviet premier Joseph Stalin. Solzhenitsyn was promptly arrested on February 9, and he was sentenced to eight years of imprisonment. From 1945 to 1953 he was confined in several prisons and labor camps. Solzhenitsyn's experiences during those years provided the inspiration for the bulk of his subsequent literary output.

Following his release from prison in 1953 Solzhenitsyn was sentenced to internal exile in Kazakhstan in the Asian portion of the Soviet Union. In 1956 he was declared "rehabilitated" and allowed to settle in Riazan, not far from Moscow. Nikita Khrushchev's rise to power in 1956 and his subsequent de-Stalinization program (1962-1963) created a climate in which Solzhenitsyn was able to experience his first success as a writer. *One Day in the Life of Ivan Denisovich*, Solzhenitsyn's first novel, appeared in the November 20, 1962, issue of *Novy mir.* It was an immediate success. Its portrayal of the horrors of a labor camp during Stalin's tenure in power complemented Khrushchev's criticism of the former dictator. Two short stories were published by *Novy mir* in January, 1963. With Khrushchev's fall from power, individuals less willing to condemn Stalin's memory publicly came to power and with them, a return to stricter censorship. After 1963, Solzhenitsyn was unable to have any more of his writings approved for publication. He soon became known as one of the Soviet Union's leading dissidents. His works circulated in the Soviet Union in handwritten or typed samizdat copies; in the West, they appeared in print, although unauthorized.

The publication abroad of *The First Circle* and *Cancer Ward* in 1968, his being awarded the Nobel Prize in Literature in 1970, and the publication of *August 1914* in 1971 all intensified his problems with the state. In 1973 the KGB discovered a manuscript of *The Gulag Archipelago*, Solzhenitsyn's exposé of the origins and nature of the Soviet labor camp system. The discovery prompted him to authorize its publication abroad. The immediate popularity of *The Gulag Archipelago* in the West led to Solzhenitsyn's arrest on February 12, 1974. The following day, he was stripped of his citizenship and expelled from the Soviet Union.

Solzhenitsyn's fictional works are both historical and autobiographical. Common themes are the basic injustice of the Soviet system that purports to liberate, while enslaving the Russian people; the heroic struggle of the individual to keep a sense of human dignity while being subjected to the injustice and brutality of the prison or labor camp; and the ironic fact that the police state succeeds in creating a socialist society in the prison or labor camp, while failing to do so in society at large.

Solzhenitsyn's first novel, *One Day in the Life of Ivan Denisovich*, is set in a Siberian labor camp during January, 1951. It chronicles a single day in the life of Ivan Denisovich Shukov, sentenced to ten years for having survived a German prisoner-of-war camp. His life consists of a struggle for survival, in which individual cunning and teamwork are the means to that end. For those who felt that *One Day in the Life of Ivan Denisovich* was only a recollection of Solzhenitsyn's own nightmare, he later wrote the massive documentary *The Gulag Archipelago.* Solzhenitsyn used the letters, memoirs, and oral testimony of 227 survivors to demonstrate that the prison camp system was an intrinsic part of the Soviet system dating back to the 1917 Revolution. The brutality and dehumanization of the gulag is not an aberration but an inevitable byproduct of Marxism-Leninism.

Using imagery from Dante's *Inferno* (c. 1320), Solzhenitsyn in *The First Circle* depicts the Soviet system as a series of increasingly tight circles of Hell. Marvino Prison, on the outskirts of Moscow, is a model in miniature of the Soviet state. Stalin and his immediate lieutenants, like the "privileged" prisoners in Marvino, occupy the first circle. With one false move, anyone can slip down to the next circle in a spiraling descent into Hell. In *Cancer Ward* the locale is the cancer ward of a hospital somewhere in a central Asian city. There, a group of people from all walks of life, including both opponents and proponents of the Soviet system, are brought together by a common enemy, cancer. The ever-present threat of death gives to each of them the freedom to discuss frankly otherwise forbidden subjects, such as the individual and the state, ideology, morality, and humaneness. Despite a feeling of gloom and despair in Solzhenitsyn's novels, a glimmer of hope seems to shine through. It is evident in the indestructible spirit of the individual, like Ivan Denisovich, who refuses to give up hope or to surrender his human dignity and be crushed by the system. It also appears in the person of the Baptist, Alyoshka, in *One Day in the Life of Ivan Denisovich*, who sees Jesus Christ as the lord of all situations, or the Christian woman among the patients in *Cancer Ward.* Both possess an inner peace that those around them cannot comprehend.

After his expulsion in 1974, Solzhenitsyn went first to West Germany, where he was received by Germany's leading postwar writer, Heinrich Böll. Solzhenitsyn then resided briefly in Zurich, Switzerland, where he was joined by his second wife, Natalya

Svetlova, and their children. After 1976, he made his home in Vermont. To his continued criticism of the Soviet system, Solzhenitsyn added an equally harsh criticism of Western materialism. Some Western intellectuals were disillusioned and disappointed to find that Solzhenitsyn's struggle for freedom was rooted in his love for Russia and his deep Christian faith, rather than Western liberalism and rugged individualism. He returned to Russia in May, 1994, after twenty years of exile and assumed the role of a moral authority and reformer.

Paul R. Waibel
Vasa D. Mihailovich

Bibliography

Bloom, Harold, ed. *Aleksandr Solzhenitsyn*. Philadelphia: Chelsea House, 2001. A collection of critical essays representing the spectrum of opinion on Solzhenitsyn's work.

Ericson, Edward E., Jr. *Solzhenitsyn and the Modern World*. Washington, D.C.: Regnery Gateway, 1993. An examination of the reputation of Solzhenitsyn in the West that tries to clear up previous misunderstandings. Argues that Solzhenitsyn has never been antidemocratic and that his criticisms of the West have been made in the spirit of love, not animosity.

Klimoff, Alexis. *"One Day in the Life of Ivan Denisovich": A Critical Companion*. Evanston, Ill.: Northwestern University Press, 1997. A guide for readers encountering Solzhenitsyn's novel for the first time; provides contextual background and critical appraisal.

Lakshin, Vladislav. *Solzhenitsyn, Tvardovsky, and "Novyi Mir."* New York: Oxford University Press, 1980. Lakshin presents an insider's view of the publication history of *A Day in the Life of Ivan Denisovich*, involving Aleksandr Tvardovsky, a poet and the editor of the journal *Novyi Mir.*

Mahoney, Daniel J. *Aleksandr Solzhenitsyn: The Ascent from Ideology*. Lanham, Md.: Rowman and Littlefield, 2001. Focuses on Solzhenitsyn's political philosophy.

Medina, Loreta, ed. *Readings on "One Day in the Life of Ivan Denisovich."* San Diego, Calif.: Greenhaven Press, 2001. A compendium of critical essays.

Moody, Christopher. *Solzhenitsyn*. 2d rev. ed. New York: Barnes & Noble Books, 1976. Moody provides an essentially negative view of Solzhenitsyn's literary works to 1975 that represents an alternative to the generally favorable reception of his early work.

Pearce, Joseph. *Solzhenitsyn: A Soul in Exile*. London: HarperCollins, 1999. A biography that focuses on the writer's faith. Features exclusive personal interviews with Solzhenitsyn, previously unpublished poetry, and rare photographs.

Scammell, Michael. *Solzhenitsyn*. New York: W. W. Norton, 1984. This exhaustive but lively biography deals with practically all important aspects of Solzhenitsyn's life. Unfortunately, his works are not discussed at great length.

_______, ed. *The Solzhenitsyn Files*. Chicago: Edition q, 1995. A carefully edited documentation of Solzhenitsyn's struggles with Soviet literary and political authorities.

Thomas, D. M. *Alexander Solzhenitsyn: A Century in His Life*. New York: St. Martin's Press, 1998. An imaginative, well-documented, and at times combative biography of Solzhenitsyn. It includes discussion of his return to Russia in 1994.

Stephen Sondheim

American composer and lyricist

Born: New York, New York; March 22, 1930

DRAMA: *West Side Story*, pr. 1957 (lyrics; music by Leonard Bernstein; book by Arthur Laurents); *Gypsy*, pr. 1959 (lyrics; music by Jule Styne; book by Laurents); *A Funny Thing Happened on the Way to the Forum*, pr., pb. 1962 (lyrics and music; book by Larry Gelbart and Burt Shevelove); *Anyone Can Whistle*, pr. 1964 (lyrics and music; book by Laurents); *Do I Hear A Waltz?*, pr. 1965 (lyrics; music by Richard Rodgers; book by Laurents); *Company*, pr., pb. 1970 (lyrics and music; book by George Furth); *Follies*, pr., pb. 1971 (lyrics and music; book by James Goldman); *A Little Night Music*, pr., pb. 1973 (lyrics and music; book by Wheeler); *Candide*, pr. 1974 (lyrics with Richard Wilbur and John Latouche; music by Bernstein; book by Hugh Wheeler); *The Frogs*, pr. 1974 (lyrics and music; book by Shevelove); *Pacific Overtures*, pr. 1976 (lyrics and music; book by John Weidman); *Sweeney Todd: The Demon Barber of Fleet Street*, pr., pb. 1979 (lyrics and music; book by Wheeler); *Marry Me a Little*, pr. 1980 (lyrics and music; book by Craig Lucas and Norman René); *Merrily We Roll Along*, pr. 1981 (lyrics and music; book by Furth); *Sunday in the Park with George*, pr. 1983 (lyrics and music; book by James Lapine); *Into the Woods*, pr. 1987 (lyrics and music; book by Lapine); *Assassins*, pr. 1990 (lyrics and music; book by Weidman); *Passion*, pr., pb. 1994 (lyrics and music; book by Lapine); *Getting Away with Murder*, pr. 1995 (with Furth); *Gold!*, pr. 2002 (lyrics and music; book by Weidman; originally pr. 1999 as *Wise Guys*).

SCREENPLAY: *The Last of Sheila*, 1973 (with Anthony Perkins).

TELEPLAY: *Evening Primrose*, 1966 (lyrics and music).

Stephen Joshua Sondheim (SOND-him) extended the art of theater beyond the class of sentimental musicals that dominated the stage during the mid-twentieth century. Sondheim's honors include a Grammy Award for "Sooner or Later" from the 1990 film *Dick Tracy*, Tony Awards for several Broadway productions, and a Pulitzer Prize for *Sunday in the Park with George*, an artistic examination of pointillist painter George Seurat. Sondheim was born in New York City. His family resided in a Manhattan high-rise overlooking Central Park. His father, Herbert Sondheim, owned a successful clothing business, and his mother, Janet (Fox) Sondheim, was a fashion designer.

Sondheim was precocious, learning to read well before his classmates and advancing from sixth grade to eighth grade in one year. He studied piano during his elementary school years but did not pursue music as a vocation until college. Sondheim's father often played show tunes on the family piano and frequently took his son along with business clients to Broadway productions. When Sondheim was ten, his parents divorced. His mother, Janet (nicknamed "Foxy"), retained custody of her son. She sent him to the New York Military Academy for two years (1940-1942), where he learned to play the academy pipe organ. Sondheim later recalled that the orderly regimen at the academy was a welcome contrast to the disorder brought by his parents' separation. Family acquaintances often described him as a child of affluence and neglect. After the divorce, he experienced troubled relationships with family members, especially his mother.

In 1942, Janet Sondheim moved to Pennsylvania and enrolled her son in the George School. They lived near Mrs. Sondheim's friend Dorothy Hammerstein, whose husband, Oscar, was the notable Broadway lyricist. The Hammersteins' home became a refuge for Sondheim, providing an escape from his stormy relationship with his mother. This family connection profoundly influenced his musical training when Oscar Hammerstein II began tutoring him in the art of musical theater.

At Williams College in Massachusetts, Sondheim studied music with Robert Barrow, learning composition as craft. The theoretical study appealed to his mathematical aptitudes and confirmed his pursuit of a musical career. After graduating magna cum laude in 1950, he received a graduate fellowship to study composition with Milton Babbitt, an avant-garde composer and music professor at Princeton and Columbia Universities.

Sondheim wrote and performed in theater productions during high school and college and continually sought Hammerstein's instruction. His early professional opportunities included television scriptwriting, but he gained early success when he wrote lyrics for Leonard Bernstein's *West Side Story*. By the 1960's, he was writing both lyrics and music for productions such as *A Funny Thing Happened on the Way to the Forum* and *Anyone Can Whistle*.

During the second stage of his career in the 1970's, Sondheim collaborated with Hal Prince to develop five major productions with diverse themes such as marriage and divorce in the "plotless" show *Company*, age and life choices in *Follies*, and love and sex in *A Little Night Music*. After 1981, once the Prince-Sondheim collaboration ended, Sondheim coproduced experimental works with various theater artists. *Sunday in the Park with George*, inspired by the George Seurat painting *A Sunday Afternoon on the Island of La Grande Jatte*, examines the relationship between art and the alienated artist. In contrast, *Into the Woods* intertwines various fairy tales into a complex plot, illustrating that fulfilled wishes may bring unwelcome consequences. Later 1990's works such as *Assassins* and *Getting Away with Murder* explored issues of moral responsibility,

In 1990, Oxford University appointed Sondheim as its first visiting professor of contemporary theater, and his musicals enjoyed successful revivals in England, reflecting his British appeal. In 2000, the music division of the Library of Congress honored Sondheim on his seventieth birthday. The celebratory concert acknowledged his contribution to American musical theater by presenting *The Frogs* (an adaptation of Aristophanes' play *Batrachoi*, 405 B.C.E.; *The Frogs*, 1780) and included performances of popular Sondheim tunes, along with his favorite songs by composers such as Irving Berlin, Cole Porter, and DuBose Heyward.

Sondheim's works reflect the influence of literary and musical masters. The themes arising in *Company* and *Assassins*, in which human beings seem unable to connect with one another, are reminiscent of the works of Anton Chekhov. The complexity of his rhyme schemes resembles the poetic forms of William Shakespeare or Alexander Pope. His use of internal rhyme and alliteration advance the verbal intricacy of his lyrics. The complex chords that infuse his musical scores are influenced by impressionistic composer Maurice Ravel and mirror the twentieth-century modes of Igor Stravinsky, Benjamin Britten, and George Gershwin.

"Send in the Clowns" has endured as one of Sondheim's best-known songs from *A Little Night Music*. He has earned a place in the tradition of popular composers and lyricists such as George Gershwin and Lorenz Hart. His art is often experimental, hinging on a central metaphor rather than a structured plot. The elements of his productions—lyrics, music, dialogue, and dance—present idea rather than story, creating timeless portraits that artfully communicate human experience.

Paula M. Miller

Bibliography

Banfield, Steve. *Sondheim's Broadway Musicals*. Ann Arbor: University of Michigan Press, 1993. The work focuses on Sondheim's background and career. The volume contains a song index and source list. The chapter discussions feature musicals from *A Funny Thing Happened on the Way to the Forum* to *Into the Woods*.

Gordon, Joanne. *Art Isn't Easy: The Achievement of Stephen Sondheim*. Carbondale: Southern Illinois University Press, 1990. Gordon's academic study of Sondheim's works through *Into the Woods* includes production photographs, extensive endnotes, and a bibliography.

_______, ed. *Stephen Sondheim: A Casebook*. New York: Garland, 1997. A compilation of fourteen essays, assessing various Sondheim musicals.

Gottfried, Martin. *Sondheim*. New York: Harry N. Abrams, 1993. This large-page album features full-color photographs and a sampling of Sondheim lyrics. Gottfried discusses beginning works through *Assassins*.

Lipton, James. "The Art of the Musical." *The Paris Review* 39 (Spring, 1997): 258-278. The article excerpts Lipton's interview with Sondheim at the New School in New York City, which aired as an *Inside the Actors' Studio* episode on Bravo Network.

Secrest, Meryle. *Stephen Sondheim: A Life*. New York: Alfred A. Knopf, 1998. Secrest's detailed biography explores the influential forces in the composer's life and career.

Zadan, Craig. *Sondheim and Co*. 2d ed. New York: Harper and Row, 1986. Zadan examines Sondheim's career and includes photographs and testimonials from collaborators and colleagues.

Monica Sone

American memoirist

Born: Seattle, Washington; 1919
Identity: Japanese American

NONFICTION: *Nisei Daughter*, 1953.

Monica Sone is primarily known for her autobiography, *Nisei Daughter*, an account of her years of growing up in the waterfront area of Seattle. The Japanese word *nisei* means second generation, and Sone's autobiography thus reflects the experiences of a second-generation Japanese American.

Sone's father, who immigrated to the United States in 1904, initially worked as a farmhand and then as a cook on ships sailing between Seattle and Alaska before acquiring a small business. Because of the immigration laws then restricting Asians, there were few unattached young Japanese women, but he was fortunate to meet the daughter of a visiting Japanese Christian minister. Kazuko Monica Itoi was their second child.

Kazuko, as Sone was known in her childhood, spent her early years in the hotel managed by her parents. Surrounded by people of many different ethnic backgrounds, Kazuko did not become aware of her Japanese ancestry until, at the age of five, she and her older brother were sent to Nihon Gakko, a Japanese school they attended for one and a half hours every day after public school. They were taught the proper way to talk and walk and sit and bow in the Japanese tradition and they learned the language.

In her autobiography Sone captures the excitements and the tranquillity of her early years. Her life was in many ways similar to the lives of her "yellow-haired, red-haired, and brown-haired friends at grammar school," but in her family there were occasional special events in the Japanese community. During a family visit to Japan when she was about seven years old, she enjoyed meeting her relatives and seeing new places but felt like an alien; she was relieved to be back in Seattle.

As she was growing up Sone noticed the repercussions of world events on her community. After Japan attacked Shanghai, the Chinese in the neighborhood became openly hostile toward the local Japanese residents. Some first-generation Japanese, who by law could not become American citizens, considered returning to their homeland, but most decided to stay for the sake of their children, who had been born in the United States and would have no future in Japan.

Sone had planned to go to the university after high school but, following her parents' advice, she completed the business program first. Before she could enroll at a university, she was stricken by tuberculosis, and the subsequent nine-month stay at the sanatorium provided her an education of a different sort. Away from her family and on her own for the first time, she learned to shed her submissive attitude and become more assertive.

After recuperating in the sanatorium, Sone came back to a new house her family had purchased. Life changed abruptly, however, on December 7, 1941, when Japan attacked Pearl Harbor. Sone describes the confusion, uncertainty, and fear in her community when the authorities began questioning Japanese and Japanese American citizens. She recalls how the families systematically destroyed any Japanese books, papers, or objects that could create the slightest suspicion.

In February, 1942, Executive Order 9066 decreed the mass evacuation of individuals of Japanese ancestry from the West Coast. Those in the Seattle area were asked to report to the state fairground from where they were eventually sent to inland camps. Each person was allowed one seabag of bedding and two suitcases of clothing. Families lost their houses, businesses, and belongings.

Sone and her family reported to a fenced camp that was named Camp Harmony, where she remembers feeling like a criminal who had been convicted without a trial. From May to August they lived in the temporary camp before being moved to Minidoka Camp in Idaho, which was still under construction and lacked even the basic amenities. To make matters worse, there were dust storms in the fall and intense cold in the winter. Life was hard, but the Japanese American community faced the adversity calmly in the hope that their loyalty would eventually be recognized. In 1943 the authorities granted permanent leave to those who had job offers or who had been accepted in colleges and universities. Sone was able to leave for Chicago and later go to college in southern Indiana.

Although *Nisei Daughter* ends at this point, Sone in a new preface to a 1979 edition provides an addendum. Her brother and sister also left the camp, but her parents were not allowed to return to Seattle until 1946. Sone continued her education at Case Western University, where she earned a degree in clinical psychology. She married Geary Sone, settled in Canton, Ohio, and brought up four children.

Nisei Daughter is a valuable historical document, for it provides a moving account of the manner in which the relocation policy disrupted the lives of ordinary citizens of Japanese origin.

Leela Kapai

Bibliography

Lim, Shirley Geok-lin. "Japanese American Women's Life Stories: Maternality in Monica Sone's *Nisei Daughter* and Joy Kogawa's *Obasan*." *Feminist Studies* 16 (Summer, 1990): 289-314. Lim gives a feminist reading of *Nisei Daughter* in an attempt to refute assertions that major Asian American writers are women because they cater to stereotypical views of Asian American men.

Sumida, Stephen H. "Protest and Accommodation, Self-Satire and Self-Effacement, and Monica Sone's *Nisei Daughter*." In *Multicultural Autobiography: American Lives*, edited by James Robert Payne. Knoxville: University of Tennessee Press, 1992. Presents a perceptive analysis of the work, suggesting that Sone presents "subversive antiracist themes."

Yamamoto, Traise. *Masking Selves, Making Subjects: Japanese American Women, Identity, and the Body*. Berkeley: University of California Press, 1999. Sone's autobiography is one of many works considered in this study of gender-specific and ethnicity-specific strategies of subverting Anglo-American racism and patriarchalism.

Cathy Song

American poet

Born: Honolulu, Hawaii; August 20, 1955
Identity: Korean American

POETRY: *Picture Bride*, 1983; *Frameless Windows, Squares of Light*, 1988; *School Figures*, 1994; *The Land of Bliss*, 2001.
EDITED TEXT: *Sister Stew: Fiction and Poetry by Women*, 1991 (with Juliet S. Kono).

A chronological examination of the poems of Cathy Song's books would result, among other things, in an intimate autobiography and memoir. The title poem of the first collection, *Picture Bride*, winner of the Yale Younger Poets award for 1982, sets the tone and thematic direction for most of Song's writing. Meditations and reflections on her family dominate her poems, and she celebrates the self with sensitivity and precision.

After receiving her B.A. from Wellesley College in 1977, Song graduated with an M.A. in creative writing from Boston University in 1981. After teaching at various colleges and universities, she returned to her home in Honolulu with her husband, a physician, and her two children.

Song's fascination with her own domestic history begins with the title poem of her first book, in which more than two-thirds of the poems pertain to her grandparents, parents, and siblings, as well as her husband and children and herself. The poems are recognizably autobiographical and recognizably written from a female perspective. The first lines of "Picture Bride" refer to the poet's Korean grandmother, who came to Hawaii and married a Korean immigrant thirteen years older than herself, with whom she had been matched by photograph. Song also inserts herself: "She was a year younger/ than I,/ twenty-three when she left Korea." At the age of twenty-four Cathy Song was working on her master's degree in Boston and living in a world very different from that of the Hawaiian sugarcane fields.

Her proposed title for the first book was "From the White Place," a reference to the art of Georgia O'Keeffe, which significantly influenced her imagery after she encountered the book *Georgia O'Keeffe* (1976). The five sectional headings in *Picture Bride*, beginning with "Black Iris," are drawn from the world of art, but the title of the book selected by the publisher directs the reader toward Song's ethnic interests.

Song was twenty-seven when *Picture Bride* was selected for the Yale Younger Poets award. In 1987, following a stay in Colorado, she moved back to Hawaii with her family. Her second book, *Frameless Windows, Squares of Light*, contains poems in which snow falls (in contrast with the majority of her poems, which are set in Hawaii), and the title returns to the language of art. Song has observed, "These are poems about the window and the field," about the window one occupies every day and the field beyond the glass into which one looks. She is concerned with perspective in both space and time, and the title poem is about the relationship between a mother and child (referred to as "you" throughout) in the summer during which the child's sister was born. In conclusion, Song asserts that the child's heart is not in its smile in the photographs because the child has given it to the boy "who sits under the trees/ . . . waiting for the words to come in." Parenthetically she states, "(frameless windows, squares of light/ float upward in the dark like luminous kites)."

Song's collection *School Figures* sustains her focus on her family. "Old Story" concerns her daughter, "the family truth-teller," and "A Conservative View" begins with the line "Money, my mother/ never had much." "Mooring" depicts her daughter and infant son bathing together, and in "Tangerines and Rain" Song portrays her father picking the "Green and neon globes of orange" as her children call up to him. In this and other poems, ethnic identity is suggested but it is not the thematic focus. In "The Grammar of Silk," for example, Song recalls going to sewing school at Mrs. Umemoto's house, which is located near Kaimuki Dry Goods, but the poem itself has little to do with ethnic issues; instead it concerns the mother's offering of the sewing school as a "sanctuary" in which the speaker has learned the "charitable oblivion/ of hand and mind as one—/ a refuge such music affords the maker—/ the pleasure of notes in perfectly measured time." The poem becomes an *ars poetica*.

The last four poems of *School Figures* indicate Song's prevailing tendencies as she entered middle age. As in earlier work, she is concerned with her family, and the references to artists (John Constable, Piet Mondrian, Jean-Auguste-Dominique Ingres, Paul Cezanne, Pieter Brueghel) suggest her "painterly" concerns. Her poems often depend for their effects on color and perspective. The only allusion in this collection to an ethnic context is passing but significant: "*Views of Mt. Fuji* our devotion might have seemed,/ persistent as Hokusai's fine gradations of seeing,/ intent on exactitude, replication, students of nature uncovering/ the mineral world, the invisible fire beneath the ice." That may be said to be the aim of nearly all serious poets.

The Land of Bliss, while not as well received as Song's previous collections, marks another stage in the poet's exploration of family as her parents age. Several of the most moving poems deal with her mother's hospitalizations for depression. Others draw on Song's ancestral Korean vision of the afterlife.

Ron McFarland

Bibliography

Bloyd, Rebekah. "Cultural Convergences in Cathy Song's Poetry." *Peace Review* 10 (September, 1998): 393-400. Looks at the way Song's poetry expresses the tensions felt by women existing with one foot each in contemporary and traditional cultures.

Fujita-Sato, Gayle K. "'Third World' as Place and Paradigm in Cathy Song's *Picture Bride*." *MELUS* 15, no. 1 (Spring, 1988): 49-72. Fujita-Sato analyzes *Picture Bride* in terms of its examination of "relationships among ethnicity, culture, and writing." She defines "third world" in two ways: as place and as paradigm. She sees these two senses of the third world as interconnected and asserts that both are illustrated in *Picture Bride*.

Kyhan, Lee. "Korean-American Literature: The Next Generation." *Korean Journal* 34, no. 1 (Spring, 1994): 20-35. Kyhan reviews the history of Korean American literature and devotes the third section of his article to Song, the most widely known of those he considers the "next" or third generation of Korean American writers.

Song, Cathy. "Cathy Song: Secret Spaces of Childhood Part 2: A Symposium on Secret Spaces." *Michigan Quarterly Review* 39, no. 3 (Summer, 2000): 506-508. In response to an invitation from editors of this *MQR* special issue to "[d]escribe a private realm of your own early life that has left vivid images in your memory," Song reflects on her fascination with singing. In saying, "In singing I found my true voice," she makes the implicit connection between this lifelong love of singing and her dedication to her voice, her poetry.

Sumida, Stephen H. "Hawaii's Local Literary Tradition." In *And the View from the Shore: Literary Traditions of Hawai'i*. Seattle: University of Washington Press, 1991. In the final chapter of his book, Sumida focuses on two poems by Song to support his contention that her work has broken the "critical stranglehold" on local Hawaiian literature that considered it "insular, provincial, not universal."

Wallace, Patricia. "Divided Loyalties: Literal and Literary in the Poetry of Lorna Dee Cervantes, Cathy Song, and Rita Dove." *MELUS* 18, no. 3 (Fall, 1993): 3-20. Wallace examines the work of three contemporary American women poets and women of color from the perspective of their struggle to reconcile the presentation of a literal, historical, and often personal world with the wish to incorporate the literary elements necessary to poetry.

Susan Sontag

American essayist, novelist, and political activist

Born: New York, New York; January 16, 1933

NONFICTION: *Against Interpretation and Other Essays*, 1966; *Trip to Hanoi*, 1968 (journalism); *Styles of Radical Will*, 1969; *On Photography*, 1977; *Illness as Metaphor*, 1978; *Under the Sign of Saturn*, 1980; *AIDS and Its Metaphors*, 1989; *Conversations with Susan Sontag*, 1995 (Leland Poague, editor); *Where the Stress Falls*, 2001; *Regarding the Pain of Others*, 2003.

LONG FICTION: *The Benefactor*, 1963; *Death Kit*, 1967; *The Volcano Lover*, 1992; *In America*, 1999.

SHORT FICTION: *I, Etcetera*, 1978.

DRAMA: *Alice in Bed: A Play in Eight Scenes*, pb. 1993.

SCREENPLAYS: *Duet for Cannibals*, 1969; *Brother Carl*, 1972; *Promised Lands*, 1974; *Unguided Tour*, 1983.
EDITED TEXTS: *Selected Writings*, 1976 (by Antonin Artaud); *A Barthes Reader*, 1982; *Homo Poeticus: Essays and Interviews*, 1995 (by Danilo Kiš).
MISCELLANEOUS: *A Susan Sontag Reader*, 1982.

Although Susan Sontag has written novels and short fiction and considers herself a creative writer, her work as a critic is what has established her as one of the most important American writers of her time. She was born in New York City but grew up in Tucson, Arizona, and Los Angeles, California. She was a precocious student, thinking herself a writer at the age of eight, reading the *Partisan Review* in high school, and attending college by the time she was fifteen years old. Her bachelor's degree in philosophy at the University of Chicago and her master's degrees in English literature and philosophy from Harvard University are reflective of her desire to understand the principles behind the subjects she studies. At Chicago, she met and married sociologist Philip Rieff; their son, David, was born in 1952. Susan and Philip were divorced in 1958.

Sontag's forte is the extended essay, in which she examines her subject as a phenomenon around which her perceptions and insights arrange themselves. *On Photography* is a characteristic title. Neither a history of photography nor an interpretation of specific photographs, the book is an inquiry into what photography means. What is the significance of the medium as an art form? What are photographs supposed to prove or to show? Such questions are epistemological; that is, they are about ways of knowing. Sontag asks how photography knows the world, focusing on the subject as it relates to the nature of art and the representation of reality.

Similarly, when Sontag investigates the way cancer has been used as metaphor, her attention is drawn to the integrity of the disease and to what it means to have cancer. Sontag herself was hospitalized for cancer treatment in 1976. She has hard words for writers who simply use the cancer metaphor to describe various species of corruption. To do so, she argues, is to cloud what it means to have an illness—to insert a moral factor in the metaphor of disease. Thus, she protests the widespread use of military metaphors to justify the authoritarian social war against acquired immunodeficiency syndrome (AIDS).

When Sontag says in a famous essay that she is "against interpretation," she has in mind the kind of criticism that dissects a subject and robs it of its vitality. The critic or commentator has to grasp a subject in its entirety, seeing it as a living totality, in order to convey its intricate structure and style. One of the reasons she has favored films and made some of her own is that people still seem to be able to respond to them in a holistic way and are willing to take this art form in all of its immediacy by surrendering themselves to it. She has been inspired by the French New Novel and has patterned her own fiction after its destruction of logical plots and psychological characterization. She aims, instead, for sensory pleasure, an erotics of art that destroys hard categorizations. She favors suggestiveness over precision.

In virtually all of her writing, Sontag has presented herself as a cutting-edge intellectual, deeply engaged with the politics and aesthetics of her time. Numerous honors, including a National Book Award nomination for *Against Interpretation*, the National Book Critics Circle Award for *On Photography* and *Illness as Metaphor*, a position as PEN president in 1987, and a MacArthur Foundation Fellowship in 1990, testify to her enduring importance. Her work appears in influential periodicals such as the *Partisan Review* and *The New York Review of Books*, and she travels widely, appearing at many important public forums and lecture series. Whether it is a new trend in world history (such as the advent of Solidarity in Poland), a new illness (such as AIDS), or a trendy term (such as "camp"), Sontag is likely to be the critic who will articulate public consciousness of these developments. Many of her essays have become classics. In the 1990's, Sontag redirected her energy to creative projects. She wrote *The Volcano Lover: A Romance*, her first novel in twenty-five years, and *Alice in Bed*, a play about Alice James. In 1993, she brought a production of Samuel Beckett's *Waiting for Godot* to Sarajevo.

Sontag has spent much time in Europe and has been heavily influenced by such thinkers as Roland Barthes and Walter Benjamin. Like them, she has been interdisciplinary, drawing upon art history, literary theory, and political philosophy. Like Barthes, she reflects on a society's signs, on the language that is elaborated to describe phenomena. Like Benjamin, she is enough of a historian to want to know the conditions out of which art arises. Although she writes as an intellectual, her criticism is insistent on the primacy of feeling, on a form of knowing that transcends analysis of particular elements. If she can examine only aspects of her subjects, she nevertheless implies that they must be seen as no more than representative parts of a larger whole.

Carl Rollyson
Trey Strecker

Bibliography

Boyers, Robert. "Women, the Arts, and the Politics of Culture: An Interview with Susan Sontag." *Salmagundi* 31/32 (1975). An invaluable introduction to Sontag's life and work.

Bruss, Elizabeth W. *Beautiful Theories: The Spectacle of Discourse in Contemporary Criticism*. Baltimore: The Johns Hopkins University Press, 1982. A thorough exploration of Sontag's essays and screenplays, with discussions of her theory of literature that contribute to understanding her short fiction.

Kennedy, Liam. *Susan Sontag: Mind as Passion*. Manchester, England: Manchester University Press, 1995. A detailed study of Sontag's career that is especially insightful about the intellectual influences on her writing. Includes discussions of individual stories.

Nelson, Cary. "Soliciting Self-Knowledge: The Rhetoric of Susan Sontag's Criticism." *Critical Inquiry* 6 (Summer, 1980). Provides insights into Sontag's critical essays.

Poague, Leland, ed. *Conversations with Susan Sontag*. Jackson:

University Press of Mississippi, 1995. An indispensable guide to Sontag's writing. Not only do her interviews contain many illuminating remarks about her short fiction, but also Poague's introduction and chronology provide the best introduction to Sontag's work as a whole.

Rollyson, Carl. "Susan Sontag." In *Critical Survey of Short Fiction*, edited by Charles E. May. 2d rev. ed. Pasadena, Calif.: Salem Press, 2001. Overview of Sontag's life and career, emphasizing the short stories in *I, Etcetera*.

Rollyson, Carl, and Lisa O. Paddock. *Susan Sontag: The Making of an Icon*. New York: W. W. Norton, 2000. The first, and unauthorized, biography of Sontag.

Sayres, Sohnya. *Susan Sontag: The Elegiac Modernist*. New York: Routledge, 1990. Sayres's introduction and biographical chapter provide significant insight into the background of Sontag's short fiction. Sayres also discusses individual stories, but her jargon will prove difficult to the beginning student of Sontag's work.

Vidal, Gore. *United States Essays, 1952-1992*. New York: Random House, 1993. Contains essays on the French New Novel and on Sontag's second novel, *Death Kit*. Although Vidal does not discuss Sontag's short fiction, his lucid explanation of the New Novel and of Sontag's theory of fiction provide an excellent framework for studying the stories in *I, Etcetera*.

Sophocles

Greek playwright

Born: Colonus, near Athens, Greece; c. 496 B.C.E.
Died: Athens, Greece; 406 B.C.E.

DRAMA: *Aias*, early 440's B.C.E. (*Ajax*, 1729); *Antigonē*, 441 B.C.E. (*Antigone*, 1729); *Trachinai*, 435-429 B.C.E. (*The Women of Trachis*, 1729); *Oidipous Tyrannos*, c. 429 B.C.E. (*Oedipus Tyrannus*, 1715); *Ēlektra*, 418-410 B.C.E. (*Electra*, 1649); *Philoktētēs*, 409 B.C.E. (*Philoctetes*, 1729); *Oidipous epi Kolōnōi*, 401 B.C.E. (*Oedipus at Colonus*, 1729); *Sophocles: The Plays and Fragments with Critical Notes, Commentary, and Translation in English Prose*, pb. 1897 (7 volumes).

Few facts about Sophocles (SAHF-uh-kleez) are known. He was born about 496 B.C.E. at Colonus in Attica, near Athens, and his father, Sophillus, was said by tradition to have been a carpenter, a blacksmith, or a sword-cutler. Perhaps he owned slaves skilled in these trades. At any rate, Sophocles apparently moved in the best society and was not lampooned by the comic writers for low birth, as was his rival Euripides. He married a woman named Nicostrate, with whom he had a son, Iophon. His second wife, a woman of Sicyon, was, according to Athenian law, not legally a wife. Together they had several illegitimate children, including a son named Ariston, whose son Sophocles was legitimized, wrote tragedies, and staged his grandfather's *Oedipus at Colonus* immediately after the latter's death. In his old age the playwright kept a mistress, Archippe, whom he named his heiress, but she was cheated of her legacy.

It is reported that as a boy Sophocles was handsome and well educated in the conventional music and gymnastics, and that he was chosen to lead the chorus that celebrated the victory of Salamis in 480 B.C.E. He studied music under Lampros, an outstanding professional musician (the term is broader than today), and he learned the art of writing tragedy from Aeschylus, with whom he was eventually to compete and whom he sometimes defeated. His first production was offered in 468 B.C.E., but the names of the tragedies then presented are not known with certainty. It is generally agreed that *Antigone* was the first of his surviving plays to be produced. This is dated by the fact that its popularity is credited with getting him elected to the board of ten generals (another of whom was Pericles), whose term of office occurred during the Samian war of 441-439 B.C.E.

Sophocles was already a public figure. He had been elected to the board of Hellenotamiai, the treasurers of the Athenian League, in 443 B.C.E. This was the year in which the tribute list was revised, and therefore the office was exceptionally responsible.

It is likely that he held the generalship during the Peloponnesian War. Presumably Pericles held a low opinion of Sophocles' military ability, as he once said to the dramatist, "You may know how to write poetry, but you certainly don't know how to command an army." Sophocles was one of the ten commissioners in 413-411 B.C.E. that governed Athens after the failure of the Sicilian campaign. His direct involvement in public affairs extended over a period of some thirty years even as he was writing his plays—which eventually numbered more than 120.

An uncertain tradition connects Sophocles with the introduction of the worship of Asclepius, the god of healing, at Athens, makes him a priest of a mysterious healer god Alon (or Alkon), and has the Athenians decree him heroic honors under the name Dexion (Receiver) after his death. This tradition may reflect his interest in Ionian medicine. He certainly knew the historian Herodotus, and from the language of his plays, as well as from other sources, it is fairly certain that he was aware of the growing interest in the technical aspects of language, from which the sciences of grammar, rhetoric, and logic took their start.

Sophocles' personality impressed his contemporaries with its even temper and gentleness. He lived through the great Periclean Age of Athens—until 406 or 405 B.C.E.—and came to symbolize to a later generation the largeness, serenity, and idealism of that time. His dramas reflect these qualities in the idealized aspect of their heroes, the ease and skill of their dramatic construction, and the calm beauty of many of their choral odes. They have, however, something more than these qualities. The hero of a Sophoclean tragedy is at bottom intransigent. He is destroyed by circumstances only partly, if at all, of his own making, which would crush into nothingness a lesser man. Yet, though destroyed, he is not crushed. For the spectators, he retains in his ruin the integrity of his nature. Sophocles' dramatic skill consists in his ability to reveal this quality through speeches of the characters and songs by the chorus. His heroes are intelligent. Though they do not foresee their approaching doom, they recognize it when it is at hand for what it is. The action of most of the tragedies consists in showing by dialogue or monologue the steps by which this awareness is achieved. Sophocles uses the chorus well to heighten this effect. The chorus sympathizes with the hero but feels terror at his suffering. The chorus often gives expression to pessimism about life as a result of being close observers of the tragic fate of the hero. This pessimism is often wrongly attributed to Sophocles himself.

Not all of his seven extant tragedies exactly fit this pattern. Sophocles had a variety of things to say, but he is most Sophoclean in the plays that do fit it to a greater or lesser degree. Antigone, the daughter of Oedipus, is the starkest tragic figure in her self-isolation in the cause of her brother's burial. *Oedipus Tyrannus* shows the hero weaving for himself an involuntary net of dire circumstance to discover his own undoing. In his last play, *Oedipus at Colonus*, Sophocles shows the same hero, still maintaining his integrity and ending in the awe-filled isolation of a mysterious death. *Ajax* is a variation on this theme. The hero has in madness disgraced himself. Suicide and its consequences in regard to his burial raise the problem of the place of the hero in a world of politicians and small-minded people. Herakles in *The Women of Trachis* literally goes through fire to purge his human weakness. Only the *Philoctetes* mutes the theme. Though the hero suffers and stands firm, a happy ending is brought about by the intervention of a god. *Electra*, dealing with the old theme of the punishment of the murderers of Agamemnon, is more a melodrama than a tragedy. Orestes and Electra do the bloody deed and rejoice at the end. They, too, preserve their integrity but at the cost, for the spectators, of appearing devoid of human feeling. This statement could not be made of any other known Sophoclean heroes.

Aristotle in the *Poetics* (334-323 B.C.E.) credits Sophocles with adding a third actor, inventing scene-painting, and increasing the size of the chorus from twelve to fifteen members. These innovations increased the complexity of the dramatic action and heightened the sense of realism. Sophocles lacks Aeschylus's cosmic grandeur and his grim, majestic gods that intervene directly in human affairs. In Sophocles the gods are more hidden, manifesting themselves in oracles and in humankind's inner nature. If Sophocles' characters are less human than those of Euripides, they are more recognizable as fellow creatures and therefore more sympathetic than the personages of Aeschlyus. Sophocles' language is tenser and more ironic than that of Aeschylus, his poetry more metaphoric, allusive, and supple. Sophocles was the most influential of the great Greek dramatists. His emphasis on a single tragic hero set the pattern for Western tragedy which prevails to this day.

Robert G. Blake

Bibliography

Budelmann, Felix. *The Language of Sophocles: Communality, Communication, and Involvement*. New York: Cambridge University Press, 2000. A wide-ranging study of Sophoclean language. From a detailed analysis of sentence structure in the first chapter, it moves on to discuss in subsequent chapters how language shapes the perception of characters, of myths, of gods, and of choruses. All chapters are united by a shared concern: how Sophoclean language engages readers and spectators.

Edinger, Edward F. *The Psyche on Stage: Individuation Motifs in Shakespeare and Sophocles*. Toronto: Inner City Books, 2001. Analyzes Sophocles' plays *Oedipus Tyrannus* and *Oedipus at Colonus* with a focus on the archetypal tragic hero and human beings' search for wholeness.

Griffin, Jasper. *Sophocles Revisited: Essays Presented to Sir Hugh Lloyd-Jones*. New York: Oxford University Press, 1999. Papers in this volume give varied approaches to Sophocles, his work, and his influence.

Ormand, Kirk. *Exchange and the Maiden: Marriage in Sophoclean Tragedy*. Austin: University of Texas Press, 1999. Marriage is a central concern in five of the seven extant plays of Sophocles. In this study, Ormand discusses the ways in which these plays represent and problematize marriage, thus finding insights into how Athenians thought about the institution of marriage.

Segal, Charles. *Tragedy and Civilization: An Interpretation of Sophocles*. Norman: University of Oklahoma Press, 1999. Segal's study attempts to show how Sophoclean tragedy reflects the human condition in its constant struggle for order and civilized life.

Gilbert Sorrentino

American novelist and poet

Born: Brooklyn, New York; April 27, 1929

LONG FICTION: *The Sky Changes*, 1966; *Steelwork*, 1970; *Imaginative Qualities of Actual Things*, 1971; *Splendide-Hotel*, 1973; *Mulligan Stew*, 1979; *Aberration of Starlight*, 1980; *Crystal Vision*, 1981; *Blue Pastoral*, 1983; *Odd Number*, 1985; *Rose Theatre*, 1987; *Misterioso*, 1989; *Under the Shadow*, 1991; *Red the Fiend*, 1995; *Pack of Lies*, 1997; *Gold Fools*, 1999; *Little Casino*, 2002.

POETRY: *The Darkness Surrounds Us*, 1960; *Black and White*, 1964; *The Perfect Fiction*, 1968; *Corrosive Sublimate*, 1971; *A Dozen Oranges*, 1976; *White Sail*, 1977; *The Orangery*, 1978; *Selected Poems, 1958-1980*, 1981; *A Beehive Arranged on Humane Principles*, 1986.

DRAMA: *Flawless Play Restored: The Masque of Fungo*, pb. 1974.

NONFICTION: *Something Said*, 1984 (essays).

TRANSLATION: *Suspiciae Elegidia/Elegies of Sulpicia*, 1977.

Gilbert Sorrentino (saw-rehn-TEE-noh) was a central figure in the literary avant-garde of the 1960's and 1970's, which was centered in New York but had artistic ties to other communities in the United States. His work displays fictional devices and techniques that are now associated with postmodernism. The child of a Sicilian-born father and a third-generation Irish mother, he grew up among Roman Catholics in a working-class Brooklyn neighborhood. Sorrentino used this milieu, which he considered deadening, in his second novel, *Steelwork*. A precocious boy, he began his migratory travels by moving across the river to the cultural centers of Manhattan when he was eighteen.

In 1950 Sorrentino enrolled in Brooklyn College and began to write fiction, but he attended classes only one year before his education was interrupted by his being drafted into the Army Medical Corps. When he was released in 1953, he attempted to write a novel that was unsuccessful, then returned to Brooklyn College in 1955. While there, he founded a magazine, *Neon*, with some of his friends. From 1956 to 1960 Sorrentino edited the magazine and published the works of many prominent writers, including William Carlos Williams, LeRoi Jones (Amiri Baraka), Hubert Selby, Jr., and Joel Oppenheimer. Although its readership was small, Sorrentino believed that an audience of two hundred was sufficient because in the late 1950's the New York community of poets and writers was so close. With novelist James Joyce and poet William Carlos Wiilliams, Sorrentino shared faith in the power of the word and in its multiple technical possibilities, the motif for much of his work.

Together with LeRoi Jones, Sorrentino shared the editorship of another significant magazine of the 1960's, *Kulchur* (1960-1965), whose contributors included members of the Beats, the Black Mountain School, and the New School. Sorrentino wrote numerous critical, iconoclastic pieces for *Kulchur* and during these years published two poetry collections: *The Darkness Surrounds Us* and *Black and White*. From 1965 to 1970 he worked at Grove Press, rising from assistant to editor. His first editing assignment was Alex Haley's edited text, *The Autobiography of Malcolm X* (1965). In these years Sorrentino published his first novel, *The Sky Changes*, which ignores time sequence by scrambling the past, present, and future. He also began his teaching career with a course at Columbia University.

Although critics held him in high esteem, his work was always avant-garde and experimental, and he did not gain popular attention until the publication of his novel *Mulligan Stew* in 1979. Literary parody is the major device of *Mulligan Stew*, which is considered Sorrentino's masterpiece. It was published to rave reviews, gained popularity, and led to Sorrentino's appointment to the faculty of Stanford University in 1982, where he taught creative writing until his retirement in 1999. In an interview with Alexander Laurence in 1994, Sorrentino spoke of his opinion about the Northern California culture in which he lived during the Stanford years. He found it antithetical and struggled with its "cuteness, its apathy, its general air of paralysis, its relentless small-townishness . . . " San Francisco, he said, "has the air of an amateur stage production set in sinister natural surroundings." In the same interview he castigated publishers, popular culture, the reading public, and the denigration of Italian Americans.

For all of his cavils, Sorrentino has been the recipient of many awards, including Guggenheim Fellow in Fiction in 1973 and 1987, John Dos Passos Prize for Literature in 1981, American Academy of Arts and Letters Award for Literature in 1985, and the Lannan Literary Award for Fiction in 1992.

Sorrentino has spent his life pursuing his ideal of art. He believes that as the artist works, the vision is changed, reformed, and corrupted, so that all artistic effort is essentially a drive to reach an ideal that is unattainable. Within these limitations, however, Sorrentino is an artist of unusual drive and ability and has provided his readers with new ways to think about language and literature.

Sheila Golburgh Johnson

Bibliography

Greiner, Donald J. "Antony Lamont in Search of Gilbert Sorrentino: Character and *Mulligan Stew*." *The Review of Contemporary Fiction* 1 (Spring, 1981): 104-112. This article analyzes the ways Sorrentino enlarges the traditional role of character.

Klinkowitz, Jerome. *The Life of Fiction*. Urbana: University of Illinois Press, 1977. Explores major developments in American fiction, with an emphasis on modernism and its nucleus in New York. Contains a chapter on Sorrentino.

Mackey, Louis. *Fact, Fiction, and Representation: Four Novels by Gilbert Sorrentino*. Columbia, S.C.: Camden House, 1997. A critical study of *Crystal Vision*, *Odd Number*, *Rose Theatre*, and *Misterioso*. Includes bibliographical references and an index.

McPheron, William. *Gilbert Sorrentino: A Descriptive Bibliography*. Elmwood Park, Ill.: Dalkey Archive Press, 1991. Traces Sorrentino's career from his first short story in 1956 to early 1990. Treats writings both by and about Sorrentino. Includes an index.

Gary Soto

American poet and memoirist

Born: Fresno, California; April 12, 1952
Identity: Mexican American

POETRY: *The Elements of San Joaquin*, 1977; *The Tale of Sunlight*, 1978; *Where Sparrows Work Hard*, 1981; *Black Hair*, 1985; *Who Will Know Us?*, 1990; *Home Course in Religion*, 1991; *New and Selected Poems*, 1995; *A Natural Man*, 1999.

LONG FICTION: *Nickel and Dime*, 2000; *Poetry Lover*, 2001.

NONFICTION: *Living up the Street: Narrative Recollections*, 1985; *Small Faces*, 1986; *Lesser Evils: Ten Quartets*, 1988; *A Summer Life*, 1991; *The Effects of Knut Hamsun on a Fresno Boy*, 2000.

CHILDREN'S/YOUNG ADULT LITERATURE: *Baseball in April, and Other Stories*, 1990; *Taking Sides*, 1991; *Neighborhood Odes*, 1992 (poetry); *Pacific Crossing*, 1992; *The Skirt*, 1992; *Too Many Tamales*, 1993; *Local News*, 1993; *Crazy Weekend*, 1994; *Jesse*, 1994; *Boys at Work*, 1995; *Canto Familiar*, 1995 (poetry); *The Cat's Meow*, 1995; *Chato's Kitchen*, 1995; *Off and Running*, 1996; *Buried Onions*, 1997; *Novio Boy*, 1997 (play); *Petty Crimes*, 1998; *Big Bushy Mustache*, 1998; *Chato Throws a Pachanga*, 1999; *Chato and the Party Animals*, 1999; *Nerdlania*, 1999 (play); *Jesse De La Cruz: A Profile of a United Farm Worker*, 2000; *My Little Car*, 2000; *Body Parts in Rebellion: Hanging Out with Fernie and Me*, 2002 (poetry); *If the Shoe Fits*, 2002.

EDITED TEXTS: *California Childhood: Recollections and Stories of the Golden State*, 1988; *Pieces of the Heart: New Chicano Fiction*, 1993.

Gary Soto (SOH-toh), who has been called one of the finest natural talents among Mexican American writers, was born on April 12, 1952, to Manuel and Angie (Trevino) Soto. Although his parents were born in the United States, Soto's grandfather, Frank Soto, immigrated there to escape economic and political instability in Mexico. He met his future wife, Paola, in Fresno. Soto's parents and grandparents were members of the working class. Every day, the Soto family would join other Mexican American families from their barrio in Fresno and travel to the lush San Joaquin Valley to pick grapes and oranges. At a young age, Gary experienced the grimness of working in mind-deadening, physically exhausting labor, picking cotton in the fields, collecting aluminum cans, all to help his family survive. The lushness of the valley juxtaposed with the backbreaking labor his family had to endure because of their poverty would figure prominently in Soto's poetry and fiction.

When Soto was five years old, tragedy struck his family; Manuel Soto died as a result of a factory accident at the age of twenty-seven. The father's death left Soto's mother to raise him, his older brother, Rick, and his younger sister Debra. Manuel's death created financial and emotional hardships for the family. They never discussed his death, never dealt with their individual or communal grief. The silence created an emotional chasm for Gary. The effects of Soto's father's death have become a key issue in Soto's writings as he attempts to reconcile his love for his father and his feelings of abandonment with the numbing effects of silence.

Soto grew up in a Catholic family and attended Catholic and private schools. However, his family never stressed the importance of obtaining an education or had books in the house or encouraged him to read. His mother and father left high school to get married when they were eighteen. Even though Soto received no encouragement at home to work hard in school, he did graduate from high school in 1970 and enrolled in Fresno City College to avoid the draft.

A key event occurred in Soto's life after enrolling in college. While browsing through the college library, he discovered a collection of poems titled *The New American Poetry*. After reading several of the poems, he immediately began writing poetry and discovered his poetic voice. He had found his niche.

Seeking the companionship and intellectualism of other writers, Soto transferred to California State University, Fresno, and enrolled in Philip Levine's creative writing class. This decision was life-altering. From 1972 to 1973, Levine nurtured and encouraged Soto's talent as a poet. As he created more poetry under the tutelage of Levine, Soto began to discover his own sense of aloneness, a feeling of being alienated from two cultures, his own because of his education and the Anglo world, which both encouraged and rejected him. Through his writings, he delves into the theme of alienation and learns that it is a human, universal emotion that is not particular to him.

In 1974, Soto graduated magna cum laude from California State University, Fresno. In 1975 he married Carolyn Oda, a native of Fresno and the daughter of Japanese-American farmers who had been imprisoned in internment camps during World War II. At first, his family opposed their marriage, hoping he would marry a good Mexican American girl. Soto discusses their initial reaction and eventual consent in one of his prose memoirs, *Small Faces*. Five years after they were married, Carolyn gave birth to their daughter, Mariko.

Soto earned a master's degree in creative writing from the University of California, Irvine in 1976. He then became writer-in-residence at San Diego State University but left to become a lecturer in the Chicano studies department at the University of California at Berkeley. There, in 1977 he received an associate professorship in both Chicano studies and English. In 1992 he became a senior lecturer in the English department.

While fulfilling his teaching responsibilities, Soto continued to write poetry. In 1977 his first volume of poetry, *The Elements of San Joaquin*, a book he dedicated in part to his grandmother, was published and earned several literary awards. In this volume, Soto gives voice to the grim, impoverished, violent, and soul-deadening world of his childhood: a world that was often filled with human suffering caused by his family's poverty and their inability to become upwardly mobile. He conveys his feelings by using a street as a major motif. Although the street implies movement and a journey, Soto uses the street to imply a dead-end existence on the mean streets of his neighborhood.

In his next two volumes of poetry, *The Tale of Sunlight* and *Where Sparrows Work Hard*, Soto seems to have exorcised his demons because he tempers his social commentary on the poverty his family endured and instead focuses on the human suffering poverty causes. The street motif still exists in these works, but it is used to show that mobility is possible. Creatively, 1985 proved to be a very important year for Soto: He published his fourth volume of poetry, *Black Hair*, in which he fondly remembers his family and friends. He also attempted a new genre, autobiographical prose, when his *Living up the Street: Narrative Recollections* was published and earned for him an American Book Award. In this memoir and the one that immediately followed it, *Small Faces*, Soto vividly re-creates the racially mixed, laboring-class neighborhood in which he was raised, the struggles his family endured to provide the children with a safe environment, and the central dilemma of a life continually lived on the margins as a product of two cultures.

After writing poems and autobiographical memoirs, Soto ventured into children's literature with the publication of *Baseball in April, and Other Stories*. It immediately earned critical recognition, including the Best Book For Young Adults award from the American Library Association. The eleven short stories focus on Mexican American boys and girls and their fears, aspirations, angst, and desires as they enter adolescence. In this collection and his other fiction for children, *Jesse*, *Taking Sides*, and *Pacific Crossing*, Soto depicts real-life situations. Even though his writings are set in ethnic neighborhoods, the conflicts and situations in which he places his characters are universal. To depict these situations, he uses a quiet, often humorous and empathetic tone.

Soto's consistent attention to his craft has earned him the respect of critics and readers. His numerous awards and fellowships, among which include the Guggenheim Fellowship and being nominated for a Pulitzer Prize, attest to his literary genius and his versatility. Gary Soto is a gifted writer who transcends the particular he knew and re-creates a universalized world that touches all of his readers.

Sharon K. Wilson

Bibliography

De La Fuente, Patricia. "Entropy in the Poetry of Gary Soto: The Dialectics of Violence." *Discurso Literario* 5, no. 1 (Autumn, 1987): 111-120. De La Fuente examines the use of entropy and how it reinforces the structure of Soto's poetry.

Erben, Rudolf, and Ute Erben. "Popular Culture, Mass Media, and Chicano Identity in Gary Soto's *Living up the Street* and *Small Faces*." *MELUS* 17, no. 3 (Fall, 1991/1992): 43-52. The authors explore the conflict of dual consciousness and social problems that Soto examines.

Olivares, Julian. "The Streets of Gary Soto." *Latin America Literary Review* 18, no. 35 (January-June, 1990): 32-49. Olivares explores Soto's ability to universalize the situations his characters face.

Robert Southey

English poet

Born: Bristol, England; August 12, 1774
Died: Greta Hall, Keswick, England; March 21, 1843

POETRY: *Poems*, 1795 (with Robert Lovell); *Joan of Arc: An Epic Poem*, 1796, 1798, 1806, 1812; *Poems*, 1797-1799; *Thalaba the Destroyer*, 1801; *Madoc*, 1805; *Metrical Tales, and Other Poems*, 1805; *The Curse of Kehama*, 1810; *Roderick, the Last of the Goths*, 1814; *Odes to His Royal Highness the Prince Regent, His Imperial Majesty the Emperor of Russia, and His Majesty the King of Prussia*, 1814; *Minor Poems*, 1815; *The Poet's Pilgrimage to Waterloo*, 1816; *The Lay of the Laureate: Carmen Nuptiale*, 1816; *Wat Tyler: A Dramatic Poem*,

1817; *A Vision of Judgement*, 1821; *A Tale of Paraguay*, 1825; *All for Love, and the Pilgrim to Compostella*, 1829; *Poetical Works*, 1829; *The Devil's Walk*, 1830 (with Samuel Taylor Coleridge); *Selections from the Poems*, 1831, 1833; *Poetical Works*, 1839; *Oliver Newman: A New-England Tale (Unfinished), with Other Poetical Remains*, 1845; *Robin Hood: A Fragment*, 1847 (with Caroline Southey).

LONG FICTION: *The Doctor*, 1834-1847 (7 volumes).

DRAMA: *The Fall of Robespierre*, pb. 1794 (with Samuel Taylor Coleridge).

NONFICTION: *Letters from England by Don Manuel Espriella*, 1807; *Letters in Spain and Portugal*, 1808; *The History of Europe*, 1810-1813; *History of Brazil*, 1810-1819; *The Origin, Nature, and Object of the New System of Education*, 1812; *Life of Nelson*, 1813; *A Summary of the Life of Arthur, Duke of Wellington*, 1816; *Life of Wesley and the Rise and Progress of Methodism*, 1820; *History of the Expedition of Orsua and Crimes of Aguirre*, 1821; *Life of John, Duke of Marlborough*, 1822; *History of the Peninsular War*, 1823-1832; *The Book of the Church*, 1824; *Vindiciae Ecclesiae Anglicanae*, 1826; *Sir Thomas More*, 1829; *Essays Moral and Political*, 1832; *Lives of the British Admirals*, 1833-1840; *The Life of the Rev. Andrew Bell*, 1844.

TRANSLATIONS: *On the French Revolution*, 1797 (of Jacques Necker); *Amadis de Gaul*, 1805 (of Vasco Lobeira); *Chronicle of the Cid*, 1808 (of *Crónica del famoso cavallero Cid Ruy Diaz Campeador*, *La crónica de España*, and *Poema del Cid*); *The Geographical, Natural, and Civil History of Chili*, 1808 (of Abbe Don Ignatius Molina).

EDITED TEXTS: *The Annual Anthology*, 1700-1800; *The Works of Chatterton*, 1803 (with Joseph Cottle); *Palmerin of England*, 1807; *Horae Lyricae*, 1834 (by Isaac Watts); *The Works of William Cowper*, 1835-1837.

One of the hardiest of English poet laureates, Robert Southey (SOW-thee) held that post for the last thirty years of his life, from 1813 to 1843. During that time he also held a firm grip on the attention of the English reading public, though modern criticism has removed him from the pedestal that it still allows William Wordsworth and Samuel Taylor Coleridge to rest upon. Nevertheless, even today it is impossible to dismiss him as a factor in the literary scene of the Romantic era.

Southey was the son of a Bristol linen draper. At the age of three he was surrendered to the care of a maternal aunt, Elizabeth Tyler, who lived in Bath. He attended Westminster, from which he was expelled for writing an article about flogging for the school paper. Another sympathetic relative, the Reverend Herbert Hill, sent him on to Oxford, where, after Christ Church rejected him because of the Westminster incident, he was accepted at Balliol in November, 1792.

At Oxford, according to Southey, his chief interests turned out to be boating and swimming; he did, however, briefly espouse the cause of the French Revolution. It was also at Oxford that he met Coleridge, who promptly converted him to Unitarianism and pantisocracy. The two youths jointly sponsored an idealistic scheme to establish a perfect community in America on the banks of the Susquehanna River in Pennsylvania, a venture that died for lack of funds. Southey's aunt, learning of the utopian project, promptly dismissed him from her house and her affections.

After various temporary employments, Southey settled at Keswick in 1803, where his family shared a double house with the Coleridges. There he devoted himself completely to literature, forming a connection with the *Quarterly Review* and turning out a steady stream of books, poems, and articles. Of these, comparatively few are read today, and those that still receive attention are mostly his shorter poems, such as "The Battle of Blenheim" and "The Inchcape Rock." Modern taste does not respond to the ambitious epic poems that were Southey's chief stock in trade, though *Thalaba the Destroyer*, *Madoc*, and *The Curse of Kehama* achieved considerable contemporary success. Efforts were made in the late twentieth century, notably by Marilyn Butler, to reinstate Southey to the canon, but modern criticism prefers the author's prose to his verse, particularly his outstanding biographies *Life of Nelson* and *Life of Wesley and the Rise and Progress of Methodism*. Southey was also the original author of the popular children's story "Tale of Three Bears."

Though the laureateship in 1813 brought added recognition to Southey, its effect was offset by a series of family tragedies. The deaths of his much-loved son and a daughter were followed by an additional blow, the loss of his wife's mental health. Mrs. Southey died in 1837. Two years later Southey married Caroline Bowles, and he died four years later; his mental faculties had been gradually failing, and contemporary accounts say that he died of "brain fever." Wordsworth attended his funeral, and memorials were placed in Westminster Abbey and Bristol Cathedral.

Paul Varner

Bibliography

Bernhardt-Kabisch, Ernest. *Robert Southey*. Boston: Twayne, 1977. A study of *Joan of Arc* follows a sketch of Southey's early life. Chapter 3 assesses his personality and lyrical poetry. The central chapters analyze his epics and the verse of his laureate years. The last chapter is a survey of Southey's prose. Contains chronology, notes, select bibliography, and index.

Curry, Kenneth. *Southey*. London: Routledge & Kegan Paul, 1975. Reviews Southey's life, prose, and poetry. Includes bibliography and index.

Smith, Christopher J. P. *A Quest for Home: Reading Robert Southey*. Liverpool, England: Liverpool University Press, 1997. A historical and critical study of the works of Southey. Includes bibliographical references and index.

Storey, Mark. *Robert Southey: A Life*. New York: Oxford University Press, 1997. Storey tells the fascinating story of a complex and contradictory man, the mirror of his age, and provides a different perspective on familiar events and figures of the Romantic period.

Robert Southwell

English poet

Born: Horsham St. Faith, Norfolk, England; 1561
Died: London, England; March 4, 1595
Identity: Catholic

POETRY: *Saint Peter's Complaint, with Other Poems*, 1595; *Moeoniae*, 1595; *A Foure-Fould Meditation of the Foure Last Things*, 1605; *The Complete Poems of Robert Southwell*, 1872 (Alexander B. Grosart, editor); *The Poems of Robert Southwell*, 1967 (James H. McDonald and Nancy Pollard Brown, editors).

NONFICTION: *A Hundred Meditations on the Love of God*, wr. c. 1585, pb. 1873; *Epistle of a Robert Southwell to His Father, Exhorting Him to the Perfect Forsaking of the World*, 1589; *Mary Magdalens Funerall Teares*, 1591; *An Humble Supplication to Her Majestie*, wr. 1591, pb. 1595; *The Triumphs over Death: Or, A Consolatory Epistle for Afflicted Minds, in the Affects of Dying Friends*, wr. 1591, pb. 1596; *An Epistle of Comfort*, wr. 1591, pb. 1605; *His Letter to Sir Robert Cecil*, 1593; *A Short Rule of Good Life: To Direct the Devout Christian in a Regular and Orderly Course*, 1596; *Two Letters and Short Rules of a Good Life*, 1973 (Nancy Pollard Brown, editor).

Robert Southwell, while now known mostly for the highly anthologized lyric "The Burning Babe," is important in the history of English poetry for anticipating the mode of religious poetry that would prevail in the following century. A Jesuit priest in Elizabethan England, where practicing Catholicism was a capital crime, Southwell expressed his faith in prose and poetry until the queen's pursuivants made him a martyr to that faith.

Southwell's early education was in Douai, where many English Catholics found refuge and trained for the priesthood. His later studies at Paris (probably after 1575) placed him under the tutelage of the English Jesuit Thomas Darbyshire, in whose footsteps Southwell followed by joining the Jesuit order in 1580. He was sent to Rome as prefect of studies, a precocious appointment for a young man still in his teens. He was ordained in 1584. Because his early education took place on the Continent, the young Southwell had trouble remembering his English, and it has been suggested that his earliest poetry, which consists of translations from Spanish religious verse, was undertaken at least partly to strengthen his command of English.

During this time in Rome, or perhaps shortly after in England, Southwell wrote one of his most famous prose works, *Mary Magdalens Funerall Teares*, although the work was not published until 1591. Its prose style is very rich, almost poetic in its rhythmic effects. Many modern critics have a pronounced distaste for such a style, known as euphuistic. It is marked by heavy use of balance and parallelism, rhythmic repetitions, elaborate conceits, and appeals to emotion.

In the summer of 1586 Southwell was sent to England to be part of the "English mission" of the Jesuit order. Southwell remained in disguise and often stayed only a step or two ahead of the authorities, called pursuivants, sent to apprehend Catholic priests. While on the run in this way Southwell composed a second euphuistic prose piece, *An Epistle of Comfort*. This emotional appeal to the persecuted Catholic priests in England urged them to bear up under their hardships; Southwell's own example was as eloquent as his prose.

The formal epistle became Southwell's most effective mode of writing during his English mission. A letter to his brother, and a later one to his father, dated October 22, 1589, show some of Southwell's most effective prose, abandoning the elaborate baroque style of the *Epistle of Comfort* and adopting a more direct style that made them worth publishing in seventeenth century editions of Southwell's works. He kept this simpler style in order to speak directly to those who considered him their enemy in what is probably the last prose work written before his capture by the pursuivants, *An Humble Supplication to Her Majestie*, written before the end of 1591. The *Humble Supplication* was just that: a heartfelt plea for justice, asserting that it was possible to be a Roman Catholic without being a traitor to England and her queen.

Finally, on June 24, 1592, the pursuivant Richard Topcliffe captured Southwell. He was subjected to torture repeatedly in order to force from him information about other Catholics in England. He refused to divulge any, and so on March 4, 1595, he was hanged, and then drawn and quartered, publicly in London. Eyewitnesses recorded that the crowd, which usually shouted "Traitor!" when the heads of the executed prisoners were raised, was silent at the sight of Southwell's.

In the year of his death, London booksellers sold many editions of Southwell's work, and his poetry appeared in print for the first time. It was immediately and sensationally popular. There is no way to date the composition of these poems accurately, but many were clearly early works dating from his priestly formation in Rome, and many were no doubt written in prison. A preface, which takes the form of a euphuistic epistle to the author's cousin (identity unknown), describes Southwell's poetic goal as reclaiming poetry from the service of profane love and bringing it back to the service of God. In this aim Southwell anticipates some of the Metaphysical poets of the following century. George Herbert's famous letter to his mother in 1610 announcing similar aims of turning secular love poetry to the love of God inaugurated two generations of devotional poetry in England, but Southwell's anticipation of this trend twenty years earlier is not always acknowledged.

One work that illustrated Southwell's principle is his longest poem, *Saint Peter's Complaint*, a 792-line exploration of the storms of emotion experienced by Peter after denying Christ. The "complaint" was a popular genre in sixteenth century love poetry, based on the fourteenth century love poetry of Petrarch, in which the speaker "complained" about the way in which his beloved ignored or did not return his love. The secular love poetry of Southwell's era had been largely of this type; Southwell adapted the form to religious poetry. In doing so, he anticipated forms of devotional, meditative poetry that would usher in the most prolific era of English religious poetry ever.

John R. Holmes

Bibliography

Brownlow, F. W. *Robert Southwell*. New York: Twayne, 1996. An introductory biography and critical study of selected works by Southwell. Includes bibliographic references and an index.

Caraman, Philip. *A Study in Friendship: Saint Robert Southwell and Henry Garnet*. St. Louis: Institute of Jesuit Sources, 1995. This slim volume from religion scholar Caraman contains a bibliography and an index.

Janelle, Pierre. *Robert Southwell the Writer: A Study in Religious Inspiration*. 1935. Reprint. Mamaroneck, N.Y.: Paul J. Appel, 1971. Though a relatively "old" book, Janelle's biography—the first three chapters of the book—remains the standard account of the life of Southwell. The other chapters concerning Jesuit influence, Petrarchan origins, and Southwell's place among his contemporaries have stood the test of time. Contains an extensive bibliography.

Scallon, Joseph D. *The Poetry of Robert Southwell, S.J.* Salzburg, Austria: Institut für Englische Sprache und Literatur, 1975. Scallon's monograph provides chapters on Southwell's biography, his short poems (particularly those concerning Christ and the Virgin Mary), and the poems on repentance. *St. Peter's Complaint*, Southwell's best poem, receives extensive analysis. Contains a substantial bibliography.

Wole Soyinka

Nigerian playwright, poet, and essayist

Born: Ijebu Isara, near Abeokuta, Nigeria; July 13, 1934

DRAMA: *The Swamp Dwellers*, pr. 1958; *The Invention*, pr. 1959 (one act); *The Lion and the Jewel*, pr. 1959; *A Dance of the Forests*, pr. 1960; *The Trials of Brother Jero*, pr. 1960; *The Strong Breed*, pb. 1963; *Three Plays*, pb. 1963; *Five Plays*, pb. 1964; *Kongi's Harvest*, pr. 1964; *The Road*, pr., pb. 1965; *Madmen and Specialists*, pr. 1970, revised pr., pb. 1971; *The Bacchae*, pr., pb. 1973 (adaptation of Euripides' play); *Jero's Metamorphosis*, pb. 1973; *Collected Plays*, pb. 1973-1974 (2 volumes); *Death and the King's Horseman*, pb. 1975; *Opera Wonyosi*, pr. 1977 (adaptation of Bertolt Brecht's play *The Three-Penny Opera*); *Requiem for a Futurologist*, pr. 1983; *A Play of Giants*, pr., pb. 1984; *Six Plays*, pb. 1984; *From Zia, with Love*, pr., pb. 1992; *The Beatification of Area Boy: A Lagosian Kaleidoscope*, pb. 1995; *Plays: Two*, pb. 1999.

LONG FICTION: *The Interpreters*, 1965; *Season of Anomy*, 1973.

POETRY: *Idanre, and Other Poems*, 1967; *Poems from Prison*, 1969; *A Shuttle in the Crypt*, 1972; *Ogun Abibiman*, 1976; *Mandela's Earth, and Other Poems*, 1988; *Early Poems*, 1997.

RADIO PLAYS: *Camwood on the Leaves*, pr. 1960; *A Scourge of Hyacinths*, pr. 1990, pb. 1992.

NONFICTION: *"The Man Died": Prison Notes of Wole Soyinka*, 1972 (autobiography); *Myth, Literature, and the African World*, 1976; *Aké: The Years of Childhood*, 1981 (autobiography); *Art, Dialogue, and Outrage*, 1988; *Ìsarà: A Voyage Around "Essay,"* 1989; *The Credo of Being and Nothingness*, 1991; *Wole Soyinka on "Identity,"* 1992; *Orisha Liberated the Mind: Wole Soyinka in Conversation with Ulli Beier on Yoruba Religion*, 1992; *"Death and the Kings' Horseman": A Conversation Between Wole Soyinka and Ulli Beier*, 1993; *Ibadan: The Penkelemes Years: A Memoir, 1946-1965*, 1994; *The Open Sore of a Continent: A Personal Narrative of the Nigerian Crisis*, 1996; *The Burden of Memory, the Muse of Forgiveness*, 1999; *Seven Signposts of Existence: Knowledge, Honour, Justice, and Other Virtues*, 1999; *Conversations with Wole Soyinka*, 2001 (Biodun Jeyifo, editor).

TRANSLATION: *Forest of a Thousand Daemons: A Hunter's Saga*, 1968 (of D. O. Fagunwa's novel *Ogboju Ode Ninu Igbo Irunmale*).

One of Africa's most important writers, Akinwande Oluwole Soyinka (shoy-IHNG-kuh) became the first African to be awarded the Nobel Prize in Literature, in 1986. His extraordinary work exemplifies his vision as a Yoruba, an African, and a world citizen. His knowledge of oral and written literature is a fusion of his traditional Yoruba and his Western and world literary heritage. He was born of mixed Ijebu and Egba parentage in western Nigeria. His father was a catechist elementary school principal; his mother, a businesswoman, provided the stimulating home environment that Soyinka describes in *Aké*. Both of his parents were Christians, and on both sides of the family were three generations of distinguished relatives. He attended St. Peter's School, Abeokuta Grammar School, and, later, Ibadan Government College forty-five miles away. Although he was not permitted to be initiated into manhood in the traditional Yoruba manner until after years of family discussions with Isara relatives, he overheard relatives speak of *òrò* uncles as well as British rule; in his youth Soyinka also observed the rise of the women's movement begun by his mother and women friends to help inform illiterate young women about children, family, health, and business care. When yet another market tax was imposed, the women marched on the Alake until the District Officer secured a withdrawal of the tax. Early observation of leadership by family women enabled Soyinka to portray women with independence, whether urban professionals and businesswomen, village traditionalists, or earth-mothers. The importance of the earth or fertility is central to Soyinka's cyclical view of the past, present, and future, wherein those living are in touch with ancestors and are the vehicles for spirits to be reborn, ensuring the future.

From 1954 to 1957 Soyinka studied English literature at Leeds University in West Yorkshire, England, where he earned a B.A. Soyinka began his drama career as a play reader at London's Royal Court Theatre, 1957 to 1959. In 1958 he married Barbara Dickson, and that same year he produced his first play, *The Swamp Dwellers*, at the London Students' Drama Festival. During these years he also taught, wrote, acted, and finally directed for the Royal Court Theatre, which, in 1959, produced his first play about South Africa, *The Invention*, and then the comedy *The Lion and the Jewel* (which was also performed in Lagos with *The Swamp Dwellers*, which is considered one of his most important works). In 1960 Soyinka formed the Masks drama group in Lagos and traveled widely in Nigeria on a Rockefeller grant before writing the commissioned play *A Dance of the Forests*; he also wrote *Madmen and Specialists* for Nigerian Independence Day on October 1.

Nearly every year for more than two decades, Soyinka prodigiously produced poetry, drama, prose, and criticism, each work always showing a clear moral pattern. All works in each genre have proved to be significant. His views have ranged from traditional (*The Strong Breed*; *Idanre, and Other Poems*; *Ogun Abibiman*; *The Road*; and *A Dance of the Forests*) to colonial (*The Interpreters* and *Death and the King's Horseman*) to postcolonial ("October Poems" in *Idanre, and Other Poems*; *Madmen and Specialists*; *A Shuttle in the Crypt*; and *Season of Anomy*) to international (*Opera Wonyosi*, *Ogun Abibiman*, and *A Play of Giants*) to pro-black diaspora (*Ogun Abibiman*; *Myth, Literature, and the African World*; and most of his literary criticism). His plays have been produced worldwide, and he has lectured on campuses in Nigeria, Europe, and the United States. Always he has spoken out against apartheid and affirmed African life; for Soyinka, to write is to be both political and religious as part of the African character. To be an artist, and to perform dramatically and verbally, is to be like Ogun, whom Soyinka considers the most admirable god in the Yoruba pantheon. He chose to emulate Ogun because to act physically, which includes speech, is to cross the abyss of transition between the visible and invisible worlds. Each of Soyinka's works, as he explains in *Myth, Literature, and the African World*, reflects his devotion to Ogun.

Soyinka's *The Man Died*, the autobiography in which he recounts his treatment in isolation during the Nigerian Civil War, stridently criticizes the atrocities he witnessed during that time. Denunciation of leaders who abuse their power runs throughout Soyinka's canon, from *The Swamp Dwellers* through *Season of Anomy* and beyond: The purpose of art is as much a moral one, to denounce the perpetrators of oppression, as it is a celebratory one in service of the Dionysian qualities embodied in Ogun.

After the mid-1960's Soyinka's writing was often attacked by anti-democracy Nigerian political leaders. In October, 1965, he was arrested in connection with a pirate radio broadcast protesting a rigged election; he was acquitted two months later. Two years later he was arrested for campaigning against the Nigerian Civil War and spent two years in prison. Fighting against censorship of pro-democratic literature, he became secretary-general of the Union of Writers of African Peoples in 1975. In 1979 he joined the People's Redemption Party (which collapsed soon afterward). During a more favorable political climate he was awarded the Order of Commander of the Federal Republic of Nigeria in conjunction with his 1986 Nobel Prize. However, after the militarist government annulled an election in June, 1993, Soyinka again found himself the target of government suppression. In November, 1994, fearing arrest, he fled Nigeria after the government raided his office, banned two books about him, and seized his passport. Since then, he has been in exile, traveling mainly between London and the United States. In December, 1994, he asked the United States government to impose sanctions against the military government in Nigeria for civil rights violations. Because of his strident support of democracy, Soyinka has been called "the conscience of Nigeria."

Three plays that Soyinka wrote during the 1990's—*From Zia, with Love*; *A Scourge of Hyacinths*; and *The Beatification of Area Boy: A Lagosian Kaleidoscope*—are his responses to the military dictators and irresponsible governments of Nigeria. For his critical portrayals, Soyinka paid an additional four years (1993 to 1998) of self-imposed exile. During that period, he taught and traveled in the United States and England. Both *From Zia, with Love* and *A Scourge of Hyacinths* were originally written as radio plays. Each grew out of real situations. Whether parodying the dictatorship of General Sani Abachu by comparing life under him to living in a prison in *From Zia, with Love* or likening the destruction of civil liberties to an invasion of water hyacinths in *A Scourge of Hyacinths*, Soyinka used his position as a world-respected writer to protest and was charged with treason for his efforts.

Greta McCormick Coger
Geralyn Strecker

Bibliography

Adelugba, Dapo, ed. *Before Our Very Eyes: Tribute to Wole Soyinka*. Ibadan, Nigeria: Spectrum, 1987. Collection of sixteen essays divided into two parts. The first part consists of ten personal tributes, and the second of six analytical essays. Brian Crow's essay on Soyinka's romanticism is particularly useful.

Banks, Thomas, and Judith Steininger. "Wole Soyinka." In *Critical Survey of Drama*, edited by Carl Rollyson. 2d rev. ed. Pasadena, Calif.: Salem Press, 2003. A thorough overview of Soyinka's life and career, emphasizing the plays.

Gates, Henry Louis, Jr., ed. *In the House of Oshugbo: Critical Essays on Wole Soyinka*. London: Oxford University Press, 2002. Large collection of essays that includes analyses of individual plays, biographical information, comparative studies involving contemporary writers such as Bertolt Brecht and James Joyce, and discussions of literary theory, the art of writing, and Yoruba culture.

Gibbs, James, ed. *Critical Perspectives on Wole Soyinka*. Washington, D.C.: Three Continents Press, 1980. Contains introductory essays by Bernth Lindfors and Abiola Irele; fifteen essays on individual plays and such subjects as popular theater, tragedy, Third World drama, and dramatic theory. Other essays cover Soyinka's poetry and prose.

Jeyifo, Biodun, ed. *Conversations with Wole Soyinka*. Jackson: University Press of Mississippi, 2001. The first book to feature recorded interviews of Soyinka. Interviewers include Henry Louis Gates, Jr., Anthony Appiah, and Biodun Jeyifo. These interviews help clarify obscure aspects of Soyinka's most difficult plays.

_______. *Perspectives on Wole Soyinka*. Jackson: University Press of Mississippi, 2001. This collection of critical essays covers three decades. Its major contribution is its analysis of Soyinka's work using several schools of critical theory, from feminism to recuperated phenomenology. Also discussed are his postcolonial politics and aestheticism.

Jones, Eldred Durosimi. *The Writing of Wole Soyinka*. Rev. ed. London: Heinemann, 1988. For years, the standard general introduction to Soyinka's work and still a useful resource. Contains lucid analysis of all the major works and helpful information about Soyinka's background.

Lindfors, Bernth, and James Gibbs, eds. *Research on Wole Soyinka*. Lawrenceville, N.J.: Africa World Press, 1992. Essays representing a wide variety of critical methodologies applied to Soyinka's works, including linguistics and structural, textual, and cultural interpretations.

Maduakor, Obi. *Wole Soyinka: An Introduction to His Writing*. New York: Garland, 1986. A helpful, critical study designed to clarify difficult aspects of Soyinka's works. Its four parts include "The Poems," "Fictional and Autobiographical Prose," "Five Metaphysical Plays," and "The Literary Essays."

Maja-Pearce, Adewale. *Wole Soyinka: An Appraisal*. Portsmouth, N.H.: Heinemann, 1994. This book is a collection of essays primarily by African writers. Topics include Soyinka's fiction, poetry, and drama, as well as the African culture from which he writes. His Nobel lecture is the lead entry. An interview with Soyinka is also presented.

Moore, Gerald. *Wole Soyinka*. 2d ed. London: Evans Brothers, 1978. This expanded new edition of Moore's chronological study devotes most of its pages to the plays. It begins with a biographical introduction that helps explain "the foundations of Soyinka's dramatic career." "Early Work in the Theatre," "A Dance in the Forests," and "The Tragedies" treat the plays before Soyinka's imprisonment, and later chapters look at postwar plays through *Death and the King's Horseman*.

Okome, Onookome. *Ogun's Children: The Literature and Politics of Wole Soyinka Since the Nobel Prize*. Lawrenceville, N.J.: Africa World Press, 2002. An analysis of Soyinka that focuses on his work since receiving the Nobel Prize.

Wright, Derek. *Wole Soyinka Revisited*. New York: Twayne, 1992. This introductory study of Soyinka includes critical studies of his works, biographical information, and a chronology of his life and works.

Muriel Spark

Scottish novelist, short-story writer, and biographer

Born: Edinburgh, Scotland; February 1, 1918

LONG FICTION: *The Comforters*, 1957; *Robinson*, 1958; *Memento Mori*, 1959; *The Ballad of Peckham Rye*, 1960; *The Bachelors*, 1960; *The Prime of Miss Jean Brodie*, 1961; *The Girls of Slender Means*, 1963; *The Mandelbaum Gate*, 1965; *The Public Image*, 1968; *The Driver's Seat*, 1970; *Not to Disturb*, 1971; *The Hothouse by the East River*, 1973; *The Abbess of Crewe: A Modern Morality Tale*, 1974; *The Takeover*, 1976; *Territorial Rights*, 1979; *Loitering with Intent*, 1981; *The Only Problem*, 1984; *A Far Cry from Kensington*, 1988; *Symposium*, 1990; *The Novels of Muriel Spark*, 1995; *Reality and Dreams*, 1996; *Aiding and Abetting*, 2000.

SHORT FICTION: *The Go-Away Bird, and Other Stories*, 1958; *Voices at Play*, 1961 (with radio plays); *Collected Stories I*, 1967; *The Stories of Muriel Spark*, 1985; *Open to the Public: New and Collected Stories*, 1997; *All the Stories*, 2001 (also pb. as *The Complete Short Stories*).

DRAMA: *Doctors of Philosophy*, pr. 1962.

POETRY: *The Fanfarlo, and Other Verse*, 1952; *Collected Poems I*, 1967; *Going Up to Sotheby's, and Other Poems*, 1982.

NONFICTION: *Child of Light: A Reassessment of Mary Wollstonecraft Shelley*, 1951 (revised as *Mary Shelley*, 1987); *Emily Brontë: Her Life and Work*, 1953 (with Derek Stanford); *John Masefield*, 1953; *Curriculum Vitae*, 1992 (autobiography).

CHILDREN'S/YOUNG ADULT LITERATURE: *The Very Fine Clock*, 1968.

EDITED TEXTS: *Tribute to Wordsworth*, 1950 (with Derek Stanford); *My Best Mary: The Selected Letters of Mary Shelley*, 1953 (with Stanford); *The Brontë Letters*, 1954 (pb. in U.S. as *The Letters of the Brontës: A Selection*, 1954); *Letters of John Henry Newman*, 1957 (with Stanford).

Muriel Spark is one of the most critically acclaimed of contemporary novelists. Born Muriel Sarah Camberg, Spark was educated at James Gillespie's School for Girls (which appears fictionally as the Marcia Blaine School in *The Prime of Miss Jean Brodie*) and wrote poetry from the age of nine. At the age of nineteen she moved to Rhodesia and married S. O. Spark; they had one son, Robin. Many of Spark's short stories (such as "Bang-Bang You're Dead," "The Go-Away Bird," and "The Curtain Blown by the Breeze") can be linked to this period of her life.

In 1944, divorced from her husband and having returned to England, Spark began work with the Political Intelligence Office of the British Foreign Office, which was concerned with anti-Nazi propaganda. There, she gained an appreciation for the paradoxes of fact made into fiction and fiction presented as fact that figure in many of her novels. After the war, Spark was appointed General Secretary of the Poetry Society in London, and between 1948 and 1949 she served not only as editor of *Poetry Review* but also as coeditor and cofounder (with Derek Stanford) of *Forum Stories and Poems*. In the early 1950's Spark's interests turned to biography with her studies of Mary Shelley and John Masefield.

Although a critic, poet, and short fiction writer (she has also written radio plays, a full-length drama, and a children's book), Spark's primary genre is the novel. Acknowledging no religious faith between her Presbyterian school days and 1952, Spark converted to Roman Catholicism in 1954 and began her career as a novelist when Macmillan and Company commissioned her to write a novel the same year. Spark has said that her conversion, which was preceded by an illness and followed by several months of Jungian therapy, enabled her to write longer fiction, which she has published consistently ever since. Although her novels during the 1970's (particularly *Not to Disturb, The Driver's Seat*, and *The Abbess of Crewe*) reflect a bleaker view of the human condition, Spark's work is generally satiric, focusing on the frauds, murders, blackmailings, and terrorism that representatives of the modern secular world practice upon one another. Drawing from the techniques of the Metaphysical poets, Spark forces the reader to join disparate ideas with a resulting effect that is close to what T. S. Eliot calls, in his 1921 essay "The Metaphysical Poets," a "dissociation of sensibility." That is, one is never quite certain in a Spark novel where the reality ends and the illusion begins.

The themes with which Spark is concerned have remained consistent since the publication of her first novel in 1957. A modern woman and a Roman Catholic, Spark demonstrates an ambivalence toward the contemporary secular world in general and the Roman Catholic community in particular. Her novels are filled with lies and deceptions and those who scheme and blackmail through their use. As a novelist, Spark is herself a plotter, and her stories place the reader in a position not unlike that occupied by her characters. In *The Comforters*, for example, Caroline Rose finds herself manipulated by an agency outside the frame of the novel (a "typing ghost"), which is, like the novelist herself, a manipulator of plot. Fond of conjoining seen and unseen worlds, Spark often forces her characters (and readers) to accept the inexplicable: messages from Death (*Memento Mori*), novels coming to life (*Loitering with Intent*), and the existence of malevolent spirits (*The Ballad of Peckham Rye, A Far Cry from Kensington*, and *The Bachelors*). These examples allude to one of Spark's primary themes: an acceptance of the existence of evil and the problem of human suffering (a theme explicitly treated in *The Only Problem*). Later novels also explore political themes such as terrorism (*Territorial Rights*) and the media industry (*The Public Image*). *The Hothouse by the East River* returns Spark to her year in publishing in New York, and *A Far Cry from Kensington* returns to early years in literary London. Soon after this novel, she published her indispensable autobiography, *Curriculum Vitae*. Her most successful book remains *The Prime of Miss Jean Brodie*. Standing with Selina Redwood (*The Girls of Slender Means*), Margaret Murchison (*Symposium*), and Maggie Radcliffe (*The Takeover*), Miss Brodie is Spark's most memorable "woman of power."

Spark's later work includes *Aiding and Abetting*, a novel speculating on what was behind the scandal that occurred when the earl of Lucan disappeared in 1974. By contrast, *Reality and Dreams* is a comedy of manners revolving around the family of a famous film director.

Alan Bold has said that Spark's "singular achievement as a novelist" has been "to synthesize the linguistic cunning of poetry with the seeming credibility of prose." In general, critics have agreed, praising Spark for her wit and the economy of her prose style. While some reviewers believe Spark's concerns as a Catholic interfere with her aims as a novelist, most see a connection between her faith and satiric vision, considering her one of the most important novelists of the second half of the twentieth century. In 1993 Spark was created a dame of the British Empire.

Jennifer L. Randisi
Margaret Boe Birns

Bibliography

Bold, Alan. *Muriel Spark*. London: Methuen, 1986. Bold is concerned with the relationship between Spark's personal background and the development of her characters, particularly links between Spark's religious experience and the religious facets of her fiction. He includes biographical information and discusses Spark's works in chronological order, specifically the novels.

_______, ed. *Muriel Spark: An Odd Capacity for Vision*. Totowa, N.J.: Barnes and Noble Books, 1984. Bold has compiled a collection of nine essays from different contributors, regarding various aspects of Spark's fiction.

Edgecombe, Rodney Stenning. *Vocation and Identity in the Fiction of Muriel Spark*. Columbia: University of Missouri Press, 1990. A critical and historical study of the psychological in Scottish literature. Includes a bibliography and index.

Hynes, Joseph, ed. *Critical Essays on Muriel Spark*. New York: G. K. Hall, 1992. A comprehensive collection of reviews, essays, and excerpts from books on Spark's fiction, by both her detractors and her admirers. Includes autobiographical essays and a survey and critique of past criticism.

Little, Judy. "Muriel Spark's Grammars of Assent." In *The British and Irish Novel Since 1960*, edited by James Acheson. New York: St. Martin's Press, 1991. Argues that in Spark's fiction, characters often reject the steadying control of a notional assent and allow their personal obsessions to turn their lives to the freely imaginative.

Montgomery, Benilde. "Spark and Newman: Jean Brodie Reconsidered." *Twentieth Century Literature* 43 (Spring, 1997): 94-106. An insightful study of the influence of John Henry Newman on the tension between Jean Brodie and Sandy Stranger in *The Prime of Miss Jean Brodie*, arguably Spark's most enduring novel.

Page, Norman. *Muriel Spark*. New York: St. Martin's Press, 1990. Part of the Modern Novelists series, this book contains biographical information, criticism, and interpretation of Spark and her works. Includes bibliography and index.

Randisi, Jennifer Lynn. *On Her Way Rejoicing: The Fiction of Muriel Spark*. Washington, D.C.: Catholic University of America Press, 1991. Argues that Spark's vision is metaphysical, combining piety and satire, deception and anagogical truth. Discusses the tension between mysticism and satire in Spark's novels and stories.

Richmond, Velma B. *Muriel Spark*. New York: Frederick Ungar, 1984. Richmond explores Spark's writing in terms of content and emphasis. Spark's novels, poetry, and short stories are discussed in relation to their themes rather than their chronology.

Spark, Muriel. *Curriculum Vitae*. Boston: Houghton Mifflin, 1993. Spark examines her life and literary career.

Sproxton, Judy. *The Women of Muriel Spark*. New York: St. Martin's Press, 1992. Looks at the female characters in Sparks's fiction. Includes an index.

Stubbs, Patricia. *Muriel Spark*. Essex: Longman, 1973. Stubbs deals with theme in Spark's novels, from *The Comforters* through *Not to Disturb*, tracing the development of Spark's work, range, and attempts at experimentation.

Walker, Dorothea. *Muriel Spark*. Boston: Twayne, 1988. An informative study on the main themes of Spark's work, with emphasis given to the wit and humor of her characters. The extensive bibliography is particularly helpful.

Whittaker, Ruth. *The Faith and Fiction of Muriel Spark*. New York: St. Martin's Press, 1982. Whittaker's work elaborates on the diversity of Spark's themes, meanings, and purpose.

Elizabeth Spencer

American novelist and short-story writer

Born: Carrollton, Mississippi; July 19, 1921

LONG FICTION: *Fire in the Morning*, 1948; *This Crooked Way*, 1952; *The Voice at the Back Door*, 1956; *The Light in the Piazza*, 1960; *Knights and Dragons*, 1965; *No Place for an Angel*, 1967; *The Snare*, 1972; *The Salt Line*, 1984; *The Night Travellers*, 1991.

SHORT FICTION: *Ship Island, and Other Stories*, 1968; *Marilee: Three Stories*, 1981; *The Stories of Elizabeth Spencer*, 1981; *Jack of Diamonds, and Other Stories*, 1988; *On the Gulf*, 1991; *The Southern Woman: New and Selected Fiction*, 2001.

NONFICTION: *Conversations with Elizabeth Spencer*, 1991 (Peggy Whitman Prenshaw); *Landscapes of the Heart: A Memoir*, 1998.

Elizabeth Spencer, a major fiction writer of the second half of the twentieth century, is often classified as an important figure in the later Southern Renaissance, but she does not limit herself in setting, subject, and theme. She was the daughter of a businessman, James L. Spencer, and Mary J. McCain Spencer, whose families had lived in northern Mississippi for almost a century. Elizabeth spent her childhood roaming the countryside, reading, and avidly listening to local stories about the past.

After graduating from high school, Spencer attended Belhaven College in Jackson, Mississippi. During that period, she became acquainted with the writer Eudora Welty, who later contributed the foreword to *The Stories of Elizabeth Spencer.* After earning her B.A., Spencer continued her studies at Vanderbilt University in Nashville, Tennessee. There one of her mentors was the scholar and writer Donald Davidson. After completing her M.A., Spencer taught in Senatobia, Mississippi, and in Nashville, and also spent a year working on the Nashville *Tennessean*. With Davidson's help she obtained a contract to publish her first novel, *Fire in the Morning*. The year it appeared, she began to teach at the University of Mississippi in Oxford.

By this time she was regularly publishing her short stories. She was also working hard on her second novel, *This Crooked Way*, which appeared in 1952 and led to an award from the National Institute of Arts and Letters that enabled her to spend a summer in New York. In 1953 a Guggenheim Fellowship enabled her to travel to Italy. There she met John Arthur Blackwood Rusher, an Englishman from Cornwall who was the director of a language school. In 1956, shortly after the publication of her third novel, Spencer and Rusher were married. Two years later they moved to Montreal, where they lived for more than twenty-five years.

Spencer's new experiences began to be reflected in her works. Whereas her first three novels had been set in the South, the novellas that followed, *The Light in the Piazza* and *Knights and Dragons*, were set in Italy. Spencer continued to write about life in rural Mississippi, as in the "Marilee stories," but she set *The Snare* in New Orleans, *The Salt Line* on the Mississippi Gulf Coast, and the novel

The Night Travellers and a number of short stories in Canada. Though the settings may vary, however, her themes do not. She writes about the sense of place, the power of the past, the need for community, the quest for a personal identity, and the eternal struggle between good and evil.

In the 1960's, however, a change of focus can be detected. Often a woman searching for her identity is blocked in her efforts either by a man or by the assumptions of a male-dominated society. In *Knights and Dragons*, for example, when harassed by her former spouse, Spencer's heroine reacts traditionally: She looks for a knight to slay her dragon. Though the men who come to her aid are well intentioned, they are no more willing to let her be herself than her husband was. Similarly, in *The Night Travellers*, Spencer's focus is not on the male antiwar activists but on the women whose lives they affect.

Spencer uses a wide range of techniques to reveal the full complexity of her vision of life. She moves rapidly in and out of her characters' minds, leaps into the past, imagines the future, and incorporates other fictions, such as legends and dreams, into her own. Though her patterns are complicated, however, she never leaves her readers stranded.

In 1976 Spencer began teaching creative writing at Concordia University in Montreal. Periodically she also appeared on American university campuses, and she regularly visited the South. In 1986 she and John Rusher moved to Chapel Hill, North Carolina, and she began teaching at the University of North Carolina, a position she held until her retirement in 1992. She received the Dos Passos Award for Fiction and the Salem Award for Literature in 1992, the North Carolina Governor's Award for Literature in 1994, and the Richard Wright Award for fiction in 1997.

Rosemary M. Canfield Reisman

Bibliography

Entzminger, Betina. "Emotional Distance as Narrative Strategy in Elizabeth Spencer's Fiction." *The Mississippi Quarterly* 49 (Winter, 1995/1996): 73-87. Discusses emotional detachment in Spencer's fiction. Argues that Spencer's female characters become separate and autonomous by repressing the emotion that traditionally binds them to their confining domestic roles.

Greene, Sally. "Mending Webs: The Challenge of Childhood in Elizabeth Spencer's Short Fiction." *Mississippi Quarterly* 49 (Winter, 1995/1996): 89-98. Argues that, as human relationships become more fragile in her fiction, Spencer repeatedly turns to the imaginative perspective of a child to mend and protect these relationships. However, because of social fragmentation, Spencer's children face increasingly difficult challenges in holding their world together.

Nettels, Elsa. "Elizabeth Spencer." In *Southern Women Writers: The New Generation*, edited by Tonette Bond Inge. Tuscaloosa: University of Alabama Press, 1990. This insightful essay draws on biographical details, as well as on comments in a number of published interviews with Spencer, in order to trace the development of her art and thought. The extensive annotations and the list of interviews in the bibliography are particularly helpful.

Prenshaw, Peggy Whitman. *Elizabeth Spencer.* Boston: Twayne, 1985. An authoritative book-length study based on numerous interviews with the author and checked by her for factual accuracy. Contains a chronology and a helpful selected bibliography.

Roberts, Terry. *Self and Community in the Fiction of Elizabeth Spencer.* Baton Rouge: Louisiana State University Press, 1994. Discusses a wide range of themes appearing in Spencer's fiction. Includes a bibliography and an index.

Welty, Eudora. Foreword to *The Stories of Elizabeth Spencer.* Garden City, N.Y.: Doubleday, 1981. Welty offers a brief but significant description of her first meeting with Spencer and the friendship that developed between the two writers. Welty's succinct evaluation of Spencer as a writer who is both part of the southern tradition and uniquely herself is essential reading for students.

Winchell, Mark Royden. "A Golden Ball of Thread: The Achievement of Elizabeth Spencer." *The Sewanee Review* 97 (Fall, 1989): 581-586. In this overview of Spencer's fiction, Winchell argues that its excellence can be explained, at least in part, by two facts: that moral issues and moral decisions are inherently complex and that real independence can be attained only by someone who recognizes and accepts every human being's need for a memory of home.

Stephen Spender

English poet, critic, and essayist

Born: London, England; February 28, 1909
Died: London, England; July 16, 1995

POETRY: *Nine Experiments, by S. H. S.: Being Poems Written at the Age of Eighteen*, 1928; *Twenty Poems*, 1930; *Poems*, 1933, 1934; *Vienna*, 1935; *The Still Centre*, 1939; *Selected Poems*, 1940; *Ruins and Visions*, 1942; *Spiritual Exercises (To Cecil Day Lewis)*, 1943; *Poems of Dedication*, 1947; *Returning to Vienna 1947: Nine Sketches*, 1947; *The Edge of Being*, 1949; *Collected Poems, 1928-1953*, 1955; *Inscriptions*, 1958; *Selected Poems*, 1964; *The Generous Days*, 1971; *Recent Poems*, 1978; *Collected Poems, 1928-1985*, 1985; *Dolphins*, 1994.
LONG FICTION: *The Backward Son*, 1940; *The Temple*, 1988.

SHORT FICTION: *The Burning Cactus*, 1936; *"Engaged in Writing" and "The Fool and the Princess,"* 1958.
DRAMA: *Trial of a Judge*, pr. 1938; *Danton's Death*, pr. 1939 (with Goronwy Rees); *To the Island*, pr. 1951; *Mary Stuart*, pr. 1957; *Lulu*, pr. 1958; *Rasputin's End*, pb. 1963; *Oedipus Trilogy: A Play in Three Acts Based on the Oedipus Plays of Sophocles*, pr. 1983.
NONFICTION: *The Destructive Element: A Study of Modern Writers and Beliefs*, 1935; *Forward from Liberalism*, 1937; *Citizens in War and After*, 1945; *European Witness*, 1946; *Poetry Since 1939*, 1946; *World Within World: The Autobiography of Stephen Spender*, 1951; *Shelley*, 1952; *The Creative Element: A Study of Vision, Despair, and Orthodoxy Among Some Modern Writers*, 1953; *The Making of a Poem*, 1955; *The Struggle of the Modern*, 1963; *Love-Hate Relations: A Study of Anglo-American Sensibilities*, 1974; *Eliot*, 1975; *The Thirties and After*, 1978; *Journals, 1939-1983*, 1985.

Stephen Harold Spender, one of the best lyrical poets and most ardent political writers of the 1930's, later became an important literary critic, essayist, and journalist. He was born in London on February 28, 1909, the second of four children. Because both of his parents, Edward Harold Spender and Violet Hilda Schuster Spender, died when he was a teenager, his maternal grandmother, Hilda Schuster, played a significant role in his upbringing. In his perceptive autobiography, *World Within World*, Spender characterized his unhappy youth as a "humorless adolescence." In 1928, Spender published his first volume of poetry, *Nine Experiments, by S. H. S.*, and entered University College, Oxford. There he felt like an outsider, cut off from the "hearties and aesthetes" who populated his college. He fell in love with one of the "hearties," I. A. R. Hyndman. Perhaps because of Spender's unhappy youth, his work is characterized by its onlooker's viewpoint and its sympathy for the underdog.

The verses that Spender wrote between 1928 and 1930 (published under the title *Twenty Poems* in 1930) show the influence of his Oxford environment, especially that of his friend W. H. Auden and the members of his literary circle, which included Cecil Day Lewis, Louis MacNeice, Christopher Isherwood, and Edward Upward. Because Spender had an inherited income of three hundred pounds a year, he was financially independent and, therefore, able to travel and write without the awkward necessity of earning a living. In the summer of 1930, he left Oxford without a degree in order to join Isherwood in Germany. Spender's talent blossomed in the politically explosive, *Sturmfrei* (permissive) atmosphere of Berlin, where he wrote some of his best verse, collected in the 1933 volume *Poems*. He then moved to Austria, where he attempted to blend poetry with political ideology in *Vienna*, a long poem about the savage suppression of the February, 1934, socialist insurrection by the right-wing Dollfuss government. In 1936, after publishing *The Burning Cactus*, a volume of carefully crafted short stories, and ending long affairs with Hyndman and an Austrian woman, Spender met and married Agnes (Inez) Pearn, an Oxford student.

Like many of his generation, Spender thought that Marxism was the only viable alternative to fascism. Because the Communists were aiding the Republicans in the Spanish Civil War, Spender joined the Communist Party in order to take a personal stand against fascism. The Spenders went to Spain in 1937, an odyssey Spender described in his autobiography and in an important volume of his poetry, *The Still Centre*. In Spain, he broke with the Communists over the question of the atrocities committed by both sides. The same year that *The Still Centre* was published, Spender's childless marriage to Pearn was dissolved. In April, 1941, he married the well-known pianist Natasha Litvin, with whom he would have a son and a daughter. During World War II, from 1941 to 1944, Spender served with the London Auxiliary Fire Service.

In the postwar era, Spender had almost abandoned poetry to concentrate on prose. In 1953, he published *The Creative Element*, a work of criticism which, along with *The Destructive Element* and *The Struggle of the Modern*, represents his finest critical work. From 1953 to 1967, he coedited *Encounter* magazine, but when he learned that the Central Intelligence Agency (CIA) was helping to fund it, he immediately resigned his position. Although Spender wrote in a variety of literary forms, several themes permeate his literary canon. The most important of these is the proper relationship of the individual to society and its corollary concept, the merger of the public self with the private soul. Other topics emphasized by Spender include the nature of sexuality, the role of belief in the modern world, and the relationship of poetry and the poet to politics. In *Trial of a Judge*, Spender's struggle to merge poetry and politics is expressed through the moral and legal dilemmas faced by a liberal judge (representing Spender's authorial voice) who realizes that both Communism and fascism, though ideologically antithetical, will ultimately strangle individual freedom. Much of Spender's poetry and some of his most important prose (for example, *The Destructive Element*) are concerned with the nature of faith in the modern world. In *The Creative Element*, he argued that poetry was the proper vehicle to provide a connection between people's private and public lives by using it to transform the realities of the external world into symbols representing the individual's inner experience.

Spender's many public and literary honors included being named a Companion in The Order of the British Empire (C.B.E.) in 1962, receiving the Queen's Gold Medal for Poetry in 1971, and being given an honorary fellowship to University College, Oxford, in 1973. While his works have a remarkable lyrical quality, Spender cannot be considered either a great poet or a great prose writer. He is, nevertheless, an important figure in both genres. His works express the concerns of a self-critical and compassionate man, uncompromisingly honest and dedicated to truth, attempting to reconcile his natural inclination for individualism with his social concerns.

Nancy E. Rupprecht

Bibliography

Blamires, Harry. *Twentieth Century English Literature*. Rev. ed. New York: Schocken Books, 1985. This standard account of the development of English literature devotes only four pages to Spender, but it represents the judgment of the last quarter of the century and places the poet well in his generation and cultural context. Includes an index, a list for further reading, and a chronology.

Leeming, David Adams. *Stephen Spender: A Life in Modernism*. New York: Henry Holt, 1999. Leeming's friendship with his subject began in 1970 and lasted until Spender's death; it is a relationship that, coupled with Spender's eloquent self-disclosure in his journals, autobiography, critical writings, and poetry, makes for a fluent narrative. Leeming sees Spender as a key witness to and participant in the rise of modernism.

Sternlicht, Sanford V. *Stephen Spender*. New York: Twayne, 1992. A study of the entire Spender canon that discusses all genres of the author's work. Sternlicht begins by providing the reader with a well researched, biographical sketch of the poet's development over several decades. He also includes a discussion of Spender's influential role as literary and political critic.

Thurley, Geoffrey. "A Kind of Scapegoat: A Retrospect on Stephen Spender." In *The Ironic Harvest: English Poetry in the Twentieth Century*. London: Edward Arnold, 1974. Provides a good synthesis of the changing estimate of the enduring value of Spender's poetry. This account places Spender in the context of the 1930's.

Weatherhead, A. Kingsley. *Stephen Spender and the Thirties*. Lewisburg, Pa.: Bucknell University Press, 1975. Covers most aspects of interest in Spender's work and life and is a comprehensive source. Weatherhead's bibliography is still useful.

Edmund Spenser

English poet

Born: London, England; c. 1552
Died: London, England; January 13, 1599

POETRY: *The Shepheardes Calender*, 1579; *The Faerie Queene*, 1590, 1596; *Complaints*, 1591; *Daphnaïda*, 1591; *Colin Clouts Come Home Againe*, 1595; *Astrophel*, 1595; *Amoretti*, 1595; *Epithalamion*, 1595; *Fowre Hymnes*, 1596; *Prothalamion*, 1596; *The Poetical Works of Edmund Spenser*, 1912 (J. C. Smith and Ernest de Selincourt, editors).

NONFICTION: *Three Proper, and Wittie, Familiar Letters*, 1580; *Foure Letters and Certaine Sonnets*, 1586; *A View of the Present State of Ireland*, wr. 1596, pb. 1633.

MISCELLANEOUS: *The Works of Edmund Spenser: A Variorum Edition*, 1932-1949 (Edwin Greenlaw et al., editors).

Edmund Spenser was one of three children born to John and Elizabeth Spenser. He wrote in *Prothalamion* that London was his birthplace. With his brother he attended the Merchant Taylors' School under the famous progressive educator Richard Mulcaster. Under Mulcaster the principal studies were Hebrew, Greek, Latin, French, English, and music; the students also practiced acting, which the master believed to be of considerable educational value.

When Spenser was still in his teens, his first published poetry appeared in *A Theatre wherein be represented . . . the miseries & calamities that follow voluptuous Worldlings* (1569). In the same year he entered Pembroke College, Cambridge. At college he was apparently a wide reader rather than a profound scholar. Among his favorite classical authors were Plato, Aristotle, and Vergil; his later favorites included Geoffrey Chaucer and Ludovico Ariosto. At Cambridge began his lasting friendship with Gabriel Harvey, the pedantic target of much Elizabethan wit and barbed satire. Also at Cambridge Spenser imbibed Puritan leanings. As both Mulcaster and Harvey were staunch advocates of English composition rather than Latin specialization, Spenser was a worthy protégé of both men. He received his M.A. degree from Cambridge in 1576 after an undistinguished academic career and left to visit some of his family in Lancashire.

He probably made his first trip to Ireland, the scene of much of his mature life, in 1577. In 1578 he worked in London as secretary of Dr. John Young, bishop of Rochester. In 1579 the first major event of his literary career took place, the publication of *The Shepheardes Calender*. Looking back over the great peaks of Elizabethan drama, the modern reader can hardly realize the impact *The Shepheardes Calender* must have had on the poetic circle of its day. *The Shepheardes Calender*, published anonymously, was dedicated to Sir Philip Sidney and was furnished with notes by a mysterious E. K.—supposedly a close friend of the author—with great inside knowledge but with very convenient ignorance about any matter that might have political repercussions. In general, scholars assume that E. K. was Spenser's friend Edward Kirke but that Spenser himself furnished or inspired most of the notes. The pastoral names of the characters sometimes cloak actual individuals, but some may have been entirely fictitious. *The Shepheardes Calender* contains twelve eclogues (which Spenser wrote to establish his reputation as a poet and acquire patronage) concerning love, the pastoral, and the role of the poet.

As the dedication of *The Shepheardes Calender* indicates, by 1579 Spenser was acquainted with Sir Philip Sidney and knew Sidney's uncle, the earl of Leicester, who had a distinguished career as a patron. For some reason the earl did not take the interest in Spenser that the latter hoped for—or, indeed, that his ability justified. It is ironic that today Leicester is more remembered for his halfhearted patronage of Spenser than for his wholehearted patronage of many others.

In 1580 Spenser ventured to Ireland as a secretary of Lord Grey de Wilton, the lord deputy of Ireland, whose policies he defended in verse and prose for many years to come. For about eight years he lived in or near Dublin. During this period the friendship between Spenser and Lodowick Bryskett developed. Bryskett's *Discourse of Civil Life* (1606) contains an account of a courtly conversation with Spenser in a literary company. Bryskett also contributed poems to Spenser's *Astrophel*, the memorial volume on the death of Sir Philip Sidney. Spenser served as clerk of the Council of Munster, in which province he lived from 1588 to 1598, serving for part of that time as Bryskett's deputy.

In 1589 Sir Walter Ralegh visited Spenser in Munster. The visit was recorded in *Colin Clouts Come Home Againe*, the dedicatory letter of which is dated 1591. Spenser returned Ralegh's visit and took with him to London three books of *The Faerie Queene*, on which he had been working for about a decade. (Although conceived to be twelve books, Spencer would finish only these six.) To his great disappointment the visit did not lead to an eminent position in court, but he did gain a pension of fifty pounds, by no means a negligible amount if the poet ever collected it. The first three books of *The Faerie Queene* were published in 1590. The next six years proved productive, climaxed by the publication in 1596 of the first six books of the masterpiece, bringing it to the halfway point. *The Faerie Queene* dramatizes in each book a virtue that a knight (or in Spenser's time, a courtier) should embody. The first six books cover the virtues of holiness, temperance, chastity, friendship, justice, and courtesy. Spenser's seventh and uncompleted book, called "The Mutabilitie Cantos," concerns constancy. The poem employs allegory to illuminate the aforementioned virtues and offer the poet's social and political commentary. Spenser's poem "Mother Hubberds Tale" satirizes the Elizabethan court. These productive years of writing and publishing, however, were filled with turmoil and disappointment. For ten years Spenser was harassed by lawsuits instigated by Lord Roche of Fermoy.

The final decade of Spenser's life was not, however, a period of unmitigated gloom: In 1594 he married Elizabeth Boyle and celebrated his love and marriage by publishing his sonnets, *Amoretti*, and his magnificent marriage hymn, *Epithalamion*. Some skeptics believe the sonnets were originally written to another woman, but the general view is that the sequence is unique in the Tudor period in being written and addressed to the poet's wife. The couple had three children.

In 1598, in Tyrone's rebellion, Spenser's Irish home, Kilcolman Castle, was sacked. He and his family escaped first to Cork and then to England, but within a month after his return to his native land Spenser died. He was buried near Chaucer's tomb in what is now known as the Poets' Corner in Westminster Abbey.

Eric Sterling

Bibliography

Berry, Phillipa. *Of Chastity and Power: Elizabethan Literature and the Unmarried Queen*. London: Routledge & Kegan Paul, 1989. This example of feminist critical theory supplies a fascinating analysis of Elizabeth I and her relationships with the male writers who sought to make her fame immortal. Berry analyzes the works of Edmund Spenser in relation to those of John Lyly, Sir Walter Ralegh, George Chapman, and William Shakespeare.

Bieman, Elizabeth. *Plato Baptized: Towards the Interpretation of Spenser's Mimetic Fictions*. Toronto: University of Toronto Press, 1988. Offers a clear and insightful reading of Spenser in relation to the Christian and Platonic sources that inform his thought. Bieman offers subtle and rich readings of the *Fowre Hymnes* and the "Mutabilitie Cantos."

Hamilton, A. C., et al., eds. *The Spenser Encyclopedia*. Toronto: University of Toronto Press, 1990. This 858-page volume represents the cooperative efforts of Spenserian scholars to compile a series of articles on every aspect of Spenser's life and work. Also offers many articles on the history of England and on literary theory and practice. With index.

Heale, Elizabeth. *The Faerie Queene: A Reader's Guide*. Cambridge, England: Cambridge University Press, 1987. Offers an up-to-date guide to Spenser's *The Faerie Queene*, the first great epic poem in English. Emphasizes the religious and political context for each episode. One chapter is devoted to each book of *The Faerie Queene*. Contains an index for characters and episodes.

Morrison, Jennifer Klein, and Matthew Greenfield Aldershot, eds. *Edmund Spenser: Essays on Culture and Allegory*. Burlington, Vt.: Ashgate, 2000. A collection of critical essays dealing with the works of Spenser. Includes bibliographical references and an index.

Oram, William A. *Edmund Spenser*. New York: Twayne, 1997. An introductory biography and critical study of selected works by Spencer. Includes bibliographic references and an index.

Patterson, Annabel. *Pastoral and Ideology: Virgil to Valery*. Berkeley: University of California Press, 1987. Offers an introduction to the three great types of poems given authority in classical tradition: the pastoral, the georgic, and the epic. Patterson's reading of Spenser's *The Shepheardes Calender* illustrates its political commentary on the church and state.

Wells, Robin Headlam. *Spenser's "Faerie Queene" and the Cult of Elizabeth*. Totowa, N.J.: Barnes & Noble Books, 1983. This study of Spenser concentrates on the ways in which the moral and political allegory in the poem are parts of a continuous pattern of meaning. Wells contends that the idea of praise is fundamental to the poem and that for the first time it gives voice to the national myth.

Jack Spicer

American poet

Born: Los Angeles, California; January 30, 1925
Died: San Francisco, California; August 17, 1965
Identity: Gay or bisexual

POETRY: *After Lorca*, 1957, reprint 1974; *Billy the Kid*, 1959; *The Heads of the Town up to the Aether*, 1962; *Lament for the Makers*, 1962; *The Holy Grail*, 1964; *Book of Magazine Verse*, 1966; *A Book of Music*, 1969; *The Red Wheelbarrow*, 1971; *Admonitions*, 1974; *Fifteen False Propositions About God*, 1974; *The Collected Books of Jack Spicer*, 1975 (Robin Blaser, editor); *One-Night Stand, and Other Poems*, 1980.

LONG FICTION: *The Tower of Babel*, 1994.

NONFICTION: *The House That Jack Built: The Collected Lectures of Jack Spicer*, 1998 (Peter Gizzi, editor).

California poet Jack Spicer attended the University of Redlands from 1943 to 1944, transferring to the University of California at Berkeley, where he earned his B.A. in 1947. His first poems appeared in *The Occident* (1946) and *Contour 1* (1947), in which he introduced his oft-repeated imagery of chess, cards, baseball, and other games. While earning his M.A., which he received in 1950, he formed important friendships with fellow poets Robert Duncan and Robin Blaser, whom Spicer dubbed the core of the "Berkeley renaissance," each poet contributing much to the others' subsequent poetic careers. At Berkeley, Spicer studied linguistics and poetic history, contributing to the *Linguistic Atlas of the Pacific Coast* from 1958 to his death. His linguistic studies led to many other scholarly works and influenced his poetic doctrine that the meanings of words are arbitrary and changeable.

From 1940 to 1950 Spicer also worked as a radio announcer for KPFA in San Francisco. His work there provided the imagery for *Billy the Kid*, considered an allegory on death and homosexuality representing Spicer's early interest in writing imaginary elegies. His refusal to sign a loyalty oath at Berkeley effectively ended Spicer's mainstream academic career. Dividing his life between academic studies and poetic concerns, he became a local poet in bars and helped form the historic Six Gallery. This small art gallery hosted poetry readings and would become the setting for the launch of the Beat generation, of which Spicer was a marginal member, although he later became the leader of the "anti-Beat" poets in the San Francisco Bay Area.

In 1957, a pivotal year for Spicer, his poems appeared in the important *Evergreen Review*. He formed the influential "Magic Workshop" teaching sessions in San Francisco, and he prompted poet and publisher Joe Dunn to establish the White Rabbit Press, a small press that became noted for its publication of works by Spicer and others in his circle. In 1958 Spicer briefly took over as editor of the press. After his death, it would evolve into a major printing house, Black Sparrow Press.

Spicer wrote prolifically over the next several years, employing a difficult and discontinuous style. His books frequently were in epistle form, with titles that indicated the thematic content. Beginning with *After Lorca*, Spicer wrote what he called "serial poetry," which included translations and fake translations of the work of Federico García Lorca and other past poets. The "Fake Biography of Arthur Rimbaud" appears in *The Heads of the Town up to the Aether*. Regarded as his most important work, this book is often compared to Dante's *Inferno* (c. 1320). Spicer claimed that, in this three-part descent into the underworld, each poem was a ghost speaking to other ghosts, living and dead. This work was an important turning point for Spicer, who began using poetic dictation or "automatic writing," influenced by poets William Blake, William Butler Yeats, and friend Robert Duncan. Spicer's gnostic religious beliefs and independent poetic philosophy also helped shape the poems that he claimed were mysterious codes or messages received from an outside force. In lectures addressed to other poets, Spicer advocated that, instead of exerting control as authors, they allow alien and ghostlike languages to enter them.

Admonitions, written in 1958 but not published until 1974, is a book on music. Its poems act as mirrors reflecting personal allusions in what Spicer called "false connections." Throughout his career, his themes often focused on love and the dialectic between language or poetry and experience, exploring the relationship between the self and the outside world in surreal forms and imagery. *Fifteen False Propositions About God* reflects Spicer's Calvinist debate with "big huge loneness," a God that he felt was an absolute gamemaker detached from human life. *Book of Magazine Verse* shows a decline in Spicer's powers; for example, he attacks T. S. Eliot, as he had done in earlier works, but here he uses techniques that are no longer innovative.

During the late 1960's, Spicer published frequently in *Open Space*, a Bay-Area magazine published by White Rabbit. During his lifetime, Spicer was well known only in his home region. After alcoholism led to his death, he gained a larger audience through *The Collected Books of Jack Spicer*, published posthumously by his friend Robin Blaser. Spicer is regarded as an important influence on poets Richard Brautigan, Lew Welch, Michael McClure, and Bob Kaufman, who were students in Spicer's "Magic Workshops." Poet Thomas Parkinson published *Homage to Jack Spicer, and Other Poems* in 1970, and in 1974 Robert Duncan published "An Ode and Arcadia," a poem cowritten with Spicer. Still, Spicer has been largely ignored by mainstream scholars and is rarely anthologized.

Wesley Britton

Bibliography

Duncan, Robert. Preface to *One-Night Stand, and Other Poems*, by Jack Spicer. San Francisco: Grey Fox Press, 1980. In his lengthy preface, Duncan discusses his relationship with Spicer, points to Spicer's poetic influences, and analyzes his poetic career. In a note to this volume, the poet and editor Donald Allen surveys Spicer's poetic theory, technique, and publishing history.

Ellingham, Lewis. *Poet Be Like God: Jack Spicer and the San Francisco Renaissance*. Hanover, N.H.: University Press of New England for Wesleyan University Press, 1998. Describes how Spicer spent most of his time disdaining the publishing world and making enemies. This portrait depicts a brilliant, difficult, and largely unlikable man whose talent for writing equaled his inability to function in the world.

Foster, Edward Halsey. *Jack Spicer.* Boise, Idaho: Boise State University Press, 1991. A short critical biography juxtaposing Spicer with poets in the Walt Whitman tradition.

Herndon, James. *Everything as Expected*. San Francisco: Author, 1973. Published by a friend of his, this short personal reminiscence of Spicer includes some photographs by Isadore Klein.

Johnston, Alastair. *A Bibliography of the White Rabbit Press*. Berkeley, Calif.: Poltroon Press in association with Anacapa Books, 1985. Gives the history of Bay Area publishing and discusses Spicer's contributions to publishing history.

Spicer, Jack. *The Collected Books of Jack Spicer.* Edited by Robin Blaser. Los Angeles: Black Sparrow, 1975. Blaser's commentary provides valuable insights.

Mickey Spillane

American novelist and short-story writer

Born: Brooklyn, New York; March 9, 1918

LONG FICTION: *I, the Jury*, 1947; *My Gun Is Quick*, 1950; *Vengeance Is Mine!*, 1950; *The Big Kill*, 1951; *The Long Wait*, 1951; *One Lonely Night*, 1951; *Kiss Me, Deadly*, 1952; *The Deep*, 1961; *The Girl Hunters*, 1962; *Day of the Guns*, 1964; *The Snake*, 1964; *Bloody Sunrise*, 1965; *The Death Dealers*, 1965; *The By-Pass Control*, 1966; *The Twisted Thing*, 1966; *The Body Lovers*, 1967; *The Delta Factor*, 1967; *Survival . . . Zero!*, 1970; *The Erection Set*, 1972; *The Last Cop Out*, 1973; *The Killing Man*, 1989; *Black Alley*, 1996.

SHORT FICTION: *Me, Hood!*, 1963; *The Flier*, 1964; *Return of the Hood*, 1964; *Killer Mine*, 1965; *The Tough Guys*, 1969; *Tomorrow I Die*, 1984; *Together We Kill: The Uncollected Stories of Mickey Spillane*, 2001.

SCREENPLAY: *The Girl Hunters*, 1963 (adaptation of his novel; with Roy Rowland and Robert Fellows).

CHILDREN'S/YOUNG ADULT LITERATURE: *The Day the Sea Rolled Back*, 1979; *The Ship That Never Was*, 1982.

MISCELLANEOUS: *Mike Hammer: The Comic Strip 1*, 1982; *Mike Hammer: The Comic Strip 2*, 1984.

Mickey Spillane (spuh-LAYN) is one of the best-selling detective fiction writers in the history of world literature. He was once listed as the author of seven of the ten best-sellers in the United States. He was born Frank Morrison Spillane in Brooklyn, the only child of an Irish Catholic bartender and a Presbyterian mother. His father nicknamed him Mickey. An inveterate reader, Spillane boasted that by age eleven he had read all the works of Alexandre Dumas, *père*, and Herman Melville. Spillane attended Brooklyn's Erasmus High School (1935-1939) and briefly studied (1939-1940) at Kansas State Teachers College (now Fort Hays State University).

While working at Gimbel's Department Store during the 1940 Christmas season, Spillane met Joe Gill, whose brother, Ray, was a comic-book editor. He hired Spillane to be a scriptwriter and assistant editor. After the Japanese attacked Pearl Harbor and the United States entered World War II, Spillane enlisted in the Army Air Forces, earned his pilot's wings, and trained fighter pilots in Florida and Mississippi. He was honorably discharged as a captain in 1945.

In 1945 Spillane married Mary Ann Pearce; the couple would have four children. Back in Brooklyn, he and the Gill brothers started a comic-book factory. For money to build a block house and garage on land he owned outside Newburgh, New York, he wrote *I, the Jury*, in—he boasted—nine days. He received one thousand dollars as initial payment. Mike Hammer, its brutal private-eye hero, was based on Mike Danger, Spillane's comic-book creation. The novel, combining sadistic violence and easy sex, became a postwar best-seller, and Spillane's career was launched. Five more Hammer novels soon followed, ending with *Kiss Me, Deadly* and interrupted by *The Long Wait*, Spillane's first non-Hammer novel. In it, Spillane employed a plot chestnut: amnesia. In these thrillers, as well as in his later fiction, the hero outwits communists; the Mafia; sneaky Asians and Middle Easterners; inept United Nations, Central Intelligence Agency, and Federal Bureau of Investigation agents; crooked politicians and policemen; and homegrown criminals and deviants. Velda, Hammer's gorgeous, pistol-packing, brunette secretary, helps professionally but never sexually.

In 1952 Spillane, persuaded that the theory of evolution was incorrect, became a Jehovah's Witness. In 1953 a British filmmaker paid him $250,000 for permission to produce *I, the Jury*, *The Long Wait*, *Kiss Me, Deadly*, and *My Gun Is Quick*, based on his novels. Spillane wrote new comic strips, stories for magazines catering to male readers, and the (uncredited) script for the 1954 film

Ring of Fear, in which he played a circus detective. It was produced by actor John Wayne, who was so pleased he gave Spillane a Jaguar. In 1954 Spillane moved to Murrell's Inlet, south of Myrtle Beach, South Carolina. In 1958 to 1959 he authorized a seventy-eight-episode television series titled *Mickey Spillane's Mike Hammer*, starring Darren McGavin. In 1962 Spillane published *The Girl Hunters*, in which Hammer resumes work stalled by a seven-year alcoholic binge; flew his own P-51 Mustang from South Carolina to New York and Florida to supervise the filming of his novels; and got divorced. In 1963, he starred as Hammer in his own screen adaptation of *The Girl Hunters*.

Spillane married Sherri Malinou, an actress, in 1964 and continued writing Hammer novels as well as those featuring heroes who were more sophisticated versions of Hammer. Tiger Mann, foolishly named, was Spillane's overt response to the popularity of James Bond, hero of British spy-story writer Ian Fleming's novels. Tiger, who appears in Spillane's *Day of the Guns*, *Bloody Sunrise*, *The Death Dealers*, and *The By-Pass Control*, is smoother than Hammer but less suave than Bond. Spillane capitalized on his own macho photogenic qualities by appearing in television commercials for Miller Lite beer from 1973 to 1989.

For *The Killing Man* and *Black Alley*, Hammer blockbusters, Bantam paid Spillane $1,500,000 each. *The Erection Set* and *The Last Cop Out* are noteworthy as Spillane's offerings that come closest to pornography. The first, provocatively titled, concentrates on sadistic depravity. The second sympathetically portrays a dirty police officer, obviously a product of Spillane's disgust at leftists' alleged hamstringing of law enforcement agencies in the early 1970's.

Spillane responded to persistent criticism of his violent plots by writing two children's novels. *The Day the Sea Rolled Back* involves two young boys' search for exposed treasures on the ocean floor. It won a Junior Literary Guild Award. In *The Ship That Never Was*, the same boys outwit murderous adults and rescue a princess. Beginning in 1982 Spillane resumed his sporadic relationship with comic-strip publishers.

In 1983 Spillane divorced again and married Jane Rodgers Johnson, a former Miss South Carolina twenty-eight years his junior. That same year he received long overdue recognition when his peers honored him with the Private Eye Writers of America's Lifetime Achievement Award. Television audiences welcomed the return of *Mickey Spillane's Mike Hammer* (1984-1987), starring Stacy Keach. In 1995 Spillane received the Mystery Writers of America's Short Story Award. Mickey Spillane, uniquely popular with the masses as one of the most significant developers of tough-guy crime fiction, proved to be uniquely popular, with 200,000,000-plus copies of his works in print.

Robert L. Gale

Bibliography

Collins, Max Allan, and James L. Traylor. *One Lonely Knight: Mickey Spillane's Mike Hammer*. Bowling Green, Ohio: Bowling Green State University Popular Press, 1984. Discusses Hammer's controversial appeal in detail.

Fetterley, Juddith. "Beauty as the Beast: Fantasy and Fear in *I, the Jury*." *Journal of Popular Culture* 8 (1975): 775-782. Psychoanalyzes Hammer's dilemma upon discovering that a sadistic murderer is a sexy woman.

Haut, Woody. *Pulp Culture: Hardboiled Fiction and the Cold War*. New York: Serpent's Tail, 1995. Discusses Spillane's antileftist appeal.

Johnson, Richard W. "Death's Fair-Haired Boy." *Life*, June 23, 1952, 79ff. Presents Spillane's personality.

La Farge, Christopher. "Mickey Spillane and His Bloody Hammer." In *Mass Culture: The Popular Arts in America*. Glencoe, Ill.: Free Press, 1957. Vicious early criticism of Spillane.

McCann, Sean. *Gumshoe America: Hard-Boiled Crime Fiction and the Rise and Fall of New Deal Liberalism*. Durham, N.C.: Duke University Press, 2000. Places Spillane amid sociopolitical movements democratizing but degenerating American culture.

Silet, Charles L. P. "The First Angry White Male: Mickey Spillane's Mike Hammer." *Armchair Detective* 29 (Spring, 1996): 194-199. Reevaluates Spillane by reviewing his social background.

Baruch Spinoza

Dutch philosopher

Born: Amsterdam, United Provinces (now the Netherlands); November 24, 1632
Died: The Hague, United Provinces (now the Netherlands); February 21, 1677
Identity: Jewish

NONFICTION: *Renati des Cartes principia philosophiae*, 1663 (*Principles of Descartes' Philosophy*, 1905); *Tractatus theologico-politicus*, 1670 (*A Theologico-Political Treatise*, 1862); *Opera posthuma*, 1677; *Ethica*, 1677 (*Ethics*, 1870); *Tractatus politicus*, 1677 (*A Political Treatise*, 1883); *De intellectus emendatione*, 1677 (*On the Improvement of the Understanding*, 1884); *Epistolae doctorum quorundam virorum ad B.D.S. et auctoris responsiones*, 1677 (*Letters to Friend and Foe*, 1966); *Compendium grammatices linguae hebraeae*, 1677

(*Hebrew Grammar*, 1962); *Tractatus de deo et homine eiusque felicitate*, 1862 (*A Short Treatise on God, Man, and His Well-Being*, 1963); *The Chief Works of Benedict de Spinoza*, 1883-1884 (2 volumes); *The Collected Works of Spinoza*, 1985 (Edwin Curley, editor); *A Spinoza Reader: The Ethics, and Other Works*, 1994 (Curley, editor).

Baruch Spinoza (spuh-NOH-zuh), the great Dutch philosopher who tried to demonstrate the existence and nature of God in a geometrically precise fashion, was christened Baruch, the son of Michael and Hannah Deborah de Spinoza. His parents were descendants of Jews who, having been forced into the Catholic faith and having practiced their Jewish religion in secret, fled from Spain and Portugal during the Inquisition. Michael Spinoza was a merchant, only moderately prosperous, and Baruch, born in Amsterdam on November 24, 1632, was the third child of his second wife. Baruch's mother died when he was six years old, and Baruch was probably left in the care of Rebecca, the remaining child of Michael Spinoza's first marriage.

He attended a local Hebrew school, where his education began with the Hebrew alphabet and proceeded through the Old Testament and the Talmud. His early education can be characterized as Orthodox Jewish. When he was eight years old his father married for the third time, and the family soon moved to better quarters as the father's business improved. The boy's studies continued; his work was so promising that he went on to advanced studies at a Hebrew academy, Etz Hayim, and remained there from 1645 to 1652. He studied Latin and Greek and had a thorough grounding in Scholastic theology and philosophy as well as the philosophies of René Descartes and Thomas Hobbes.

Sometime in the course of his studies Spinoza began to doubt the truth of what he was being taught. Although he followed the Hebrew tradition, he also began to study philosophy and gradually realized that he was not interested in being a rabbi. His questioning attitude became apparent to his fellow students, and in 1656, two years after his father's death, he was excommunicated by the Jews. Feeling against him was intense; at one time before the excommunication someone had tried to assassinate him. Spinoza, believing himself to be right in his doubts, quietly settled in Amsterdam and took up the trade of grinding lenses; it was said that he was an excellent craftsman. The work was arduous and painstaking, and the dust irritated his lungs, but he was able to devote his nights to study, particularly to reading Descartes. Fascinated with Descartes's method of constructing proofs from ideas that could not be doubted, he began to consider constructing an account of reality that would have geometrical exactness. Euclidian geometry in Spinoza's time was considered *a priori* knowledge, representing a system of immutable truth. Spinoza was fascinated by geometry and the way Descartes utilized geometrical models in philosophical and scientific investigations.

He changed his name from Baruch to Benedictus, the Latin form of Baruch, which means "blessed," and thereby completed his liberation from the traditions of his fathers. He studied Latin with the Dutch scholar Van den Enden, and there were rumors that he was attracted to his tutor's daughter. If he was, nothing came of it, and Spinoza finally left Amsterdam and moved to the village of Rijnsburg. While he was there he wrote his first philosophical work, *Principles of Descartes' Philosophy*, an attempt to put into geometric form the philosophy of Descartes. At the same time he was working on other projects, the most important being his *Ethics*, and he was spending a considerable amount of time corresponding and helping visiting students who came to him from Amsterdam. He moved to The Hague, and in 1670 his second book, *A Theologico-Political Treatise*, appeared. It caused a furor, for the philosopher's conception of God and reality was quite different from both the orthodox Christian and Jewish views. The Dutch Synod prohibited the work, and its anonymous author was condemned as the devil. When Spinoza became known as the author, the criticism abated to some extent because of his quiet manner and scholarly reputation, but it never wholly died down during his lifetime.

Offered the chair of philosophy at the University of Heidelberg, he refused the post in order to be free both in his opinions and in his time to write. He continued to grind lenses during the day and to write philosophy at night. It is not clear why he continued grinding lenses for the rest of his life. Some contend that he needed the money, others that he did it for diversion. He lived a modest, frugal, and simple life. Pleasant in his personal relationships, he had many good friends. In spite of his retiring way of life, he was well known. He engaged in wide correspondence, and numerous philosophers came to visit him. His death came at The Hague on February 21, 1677, from tuberculosis, probably aggravated by having breathed glass dust over the years. As he had planned it, his principal works were published after his death.

Many religious leaders of Spinoza's day wrongly accused him of pantheism. His system, as spelled out in his *Ethics*, is monistic in nature. Unlike Descartes, who started his system of knowledge from the foundation of self (Cogito) and argued his way to the existence of God, Spinoza began his monistic journey with the existence of God and constructed his system around it.

Chogollah Maroufi

Bibliography

Chappell, Vere, ed. *Baruch de Spinoza*. New York: Garland, 1992. A very short biography of Spinoza accompanied by a series of essays explaining and discussing his ideas.

Deleuze, Gilles. *Spinoza: Practical Philosophy*. San Francisco: City Lights Books, 1988. Brief volume offers a biography of Spinoza and discusses his work succinctly.

Garrett, Don, ed. *The Cambridge Companion to Spinoza*. New York: Cambridge University Press, 1996. Spinoza was a mass of conflicting ideas. In the introduction, Garrett tries to place Spinoza's work in the tradition of philosophy, and in the opening essay, W. N. A. Klever offers a biography of Spinoza and a discussion of his works in general. Following is a series of essays examining specific parts of Spinoza's thought.

Gullan-Whur, Margaret. *Within Reason: A Life of Spinoza*. London: Jonathan Cape, 1998. A feminist account of Spinoza's life that contrasts his acceptance of the male domination of society with his egalitarian republican ideals. Contains a bibliography and an index.

Harris, Errol F. *Spinoza's Philosophy: An Outline*. Atlantic Highlands, N.J.: Humanities Press, 1992. A book for beginners, discussing Spinoza's life and style, his principal works, and a means of understanding his methods and his writings.

Hunter, Graeme, ed. *Spinoza: The Enduring Questions*. Toronto: University of Toronto Press, 1994. A series of essays that attempt to define Spinoza's place in the history of philosophy.

Scruton, Roger. *Spinoza*. New York: Routledge, 1999. A biographical introduction to the thoughts of the philosopher, clearly presented and requiring no special background. Includes bibliography.

Woolhouse, R. S. *Descartes, Spinoza, Leibniz*. London: Routledge, 1993. The three seventeenth century philosophers are examined in relation one to another. René Descartes is recognized as the father of the modern shape of philosophy (not of all of its twists and turns), and Spinoza and Gottfried Wilhelm Leibniz are examined as to their agreements and disagreements with Descartes.

Carl Spitteler

Swiss novelist and poet

Born: Liestal, Switzerland; April 24, 1845
Died: Lucerne, Switzerland; December 29, 1924
Pseudonym: Carl Felix Tandem

LONG FICTION: *Conrad der Leutnant*, 1898; *Imago*, 1906; *Die Mädchenfeinde*, 1907 (*Two Little Misogynists*, 1922).

POETRY: *Prometheus und Epimetheus*, 1881 (as Carl Felix Tandem; *Prometheus and Epimetheus*, 1931); *Extramundana*, 1883 (as Tandem); *Schmetterlinge*, 1889 (as Tandem); *Olympischer Frühling*, 1900-1905 (4 volumes); *Glockinlieder*, 1906; *Meine frühesten Erlebnisse*, 1914; *Prometheus der Dulder*, 1924; *Selected Poems*, 1928.

NONFICTION: *Lachende Wahrheiten*, 1898 (*Laughing Truths*, 1927); *Meine Beziehungen zu Nietzsche*, 1908.

Carl Friedrich Georg Spitteler (SHPIHT-uh-lur), Swiss novelist, epic poet, short-story writer, essayist, and Nobel Prize winner, was born in Liestal, near Basel. He moved with his family to Bern four years later, when his father was appointed treasurer of the Swiss Confederacy. Spitteler returned to Basel in 1856, living with his aunt and attending first the *Gymnasium* and later the *Obergymnasium* called Pädagogium. To please his father, he studied law at the University of Zürich in 1863 and branched into the study of theology. With theology his primary focus, by 1867 Spitteler was preparing himself for a future as a Protestant minister. A crisis of faith turned him from that direction, however, and by 1870 he no longer hoped for a religious career. Having no means of earning a living, he managed to secure an invitation from Russian General Standertskjöld to tutor his young children in St. Petersburg, Russia. Spitteler spent the years from 1871 to 1879 in Russia and Finland, during that time writing his first major literary work, the verse epic *Prometheus and Epimetheus*. Under the pseudonym Carl Felix Tandem, he self-published the piece, which he had conceived during his university years, but its lack of commercial success proved disheartening to Spitteler, who moved back to Switzerland and resigned himself to earning his living as a schoolteacher rather than as a poet.

In 1883, Spitteler married his former student Marie op der Hoff, and together they had two daughters. Supplementing his income with newspaper work, he wrote for *Grenzpost* in Basel from 1885 to 1886 and *Neue Zürcher Zeitung* in Zürich from 1890 to 1892. When in 1892 his wife received a substantial inheritance from her parents, Spitteler used his new financial independence to retire from teaching and newspaper writing, moving his family to Lucerne and concentrating full-time on his writing. Preferring to live and work in near-seclusion, he produced novels and several collections of poems, short stories, and critical essays.

Two incidents briefly marred an otherwise peaceful literary life for Spitteler. Upon republishing *Prometheus and Epimetheus* in the early 1890's, this time under his own name, Spitteler was accused of plagiarizing some of German philosopher Friedrich Nietzsche's ideas, despite the fact that Spitteler's original publication of his epic predated Nietzsche's ideas. Eventually, Spitteler felt compelled to defend himself against plagiarism charges in *Meine Beziehungen zu Nietzsche* (my relation to Nietzsche) in 1908. The second troubling incident occurred in 1914 when Spitteler publicly voiced support for Swiss neutrality amid World War I-era Europe and opposed the increasingly popular view that German-speaking Swiss citizens should ally themselves with Germany. In contrast to earning the disdain of many Swiss for his views, he earned praise from the French and was awarded the Medal of the Society of French Men of Letters, 1916.

Spitteler's most noteworthy epic poem, *Olympischer Frühling*, appeared between 1900 and 1905 in installments and was revised in 1910. The culmination of a lifetime of work, this six-hundred-page work combines many facets of his ideas, including religion, philosophy, mythology, and allegory. Books 1 and 2 of the piece were relatively unnoticed, but famous composer Felix Weingartner endorsed the work in a special pamphlet, *Carl Spitteler, ein künstlerisches Erlebnis* (1904), bringing widespread recognition to those first two books, along with the other three yet to come. The 1919 Nobel Prize in Literature was awarded to Spitteler at age seventy-five for *Olympischer Frühling*; however, too ill to travel to Stockholm, he received the award from the Swiss Minister of Foreign Affairs, who had accepted it on Spitteler's behalf.

Four years later, Spitteler died in Lucerne, shortly after producing *Prometheus der Dulder*, a new rhyming version of his first epic. Following his death, much praise was accorded Spitteler's life and work; the most notable was given by Romain Rolland, who called Spitteler "Our Homer, the greatest German poet since Goethe, the only master of the epic since Milton died three centuries ago. But a more solitary figure amid the art of his day than either the one or the other of these."

Cherie Castillo

Bibliography

Jantz, Harold S. "The Factor of Generation in German Literary History." *Modern Language Notes* 52, no. 5 (May, 1937): 324-330. A "generational" approach to literature, examining how writers of an era assimilate contemporary culture. Spitteler is included in the "idealistic, anti-realistic" generation.

Muirhead, James F. Introduction to *Selected Poems of Carl Spitteler*. Translated by Ethel Colburn Mayne and James F. Muirhead. London: G. P. Putnam's Sons, 1928. Muirhead shows the poems to represent Spitteler's deepest convictions. Biographical material also presented.

Robertson, John George. *Essays and Addresses on Literature*. 1935. Reprint. Freeport, N.Y.: Books for Libraries Press, 1968. Connections between classical and romantic in German literature. Spitteler and other writers are studied.

Carol B. Stack

American anthropologist

Born: Bronx, New York; 1940

NONFICTION: *All Our Kin: Strategies for Survival in a Black Community*, 1974; *Call to Home: African Americans Reclaim the Rural South*, 1996.

EDITED TEXT: *Holding on to the Land and the Lord: Kinship, Ritual, Land Tenure, and Social Policy in the Rural South*, 1982 (with Robert Hall).

Carol B. Stack is an urban anthropologist whose studies of African American family networks, minority women, and youth have become modern classics in several social science disciplines. Born to Russian Jewish immigrant parents, she grew up in New York City, Albuquerque, New Mexico, and Los Angeles. For most of her childhood, her father worked as a bread truck driver. Every summer he took Carol along on his route, explaining, "I want her to learn how to work!"

She did learn to work, tirelessly, although in a different vocation. Graduating from the University of California at Berkeley with a degree in philosophy in 1961, she went on to get teaching credentials and then taught social studies at Berkeley High School from 1962 to 1965. Her participation in an M.A. program was only temporarily interrupted when she married John Stack, a physicist, and moved with him to Urbana, Illinois; she continued graduate study in anthropology at the University of Illinois, receiving a master's degree in 1968 and a Ph.D. in 1972.

For her doctoral research, she spent almost three years living in the black community of a small midwestern city, participating in and observing the activities of daily life. During this time, racial issues were constantly in the news. As a white woman studying the community's interpersonal networks, Stack expected resistance or resentment, but she was accepted fairly readily. She attributes this partly to entering the community as a friend of a woman who had lived there, rather than with an introduction by more distant sponsors from the black establishment. It also helped that her small son Kevin, born in 1968, lived with her there, so she shared child-rearing problems with other single mothers in the community.

This study resulted in her first book, *All Our Kin*, which has become an integral part of the research canon on the African American family. Her respondents were interviewed informally, in the context of daily life and usually on several occasions over a period of time. Stack found that, although her subjects' actions and family structure may have appeared chaotic from outside, many aspects of their lifestyles emerged out of the limited resources available to them. For example, what had been described simplistically as a disorganized "black matriarchal family" structure was actually an intricately functioning network of kin, mates, and friends providing mutual aid, a successful coping strategy for survival under the constraints of poverty.

In 1975 Stack accepted a faculty position in the School of Public Policy at Duke University, with a joint appointment in anthropology. Among her accomplishments there were establishing the Family Policy Center and carrying out the research for her second book, *Call to Home*. This work looks at the return of African Americans in large numbers to family lands or home counties in North and South Carolina between 1975 and 1990, often after many years spent living in the North. The phenomenon was less reported than was the earlier migration to northern urban centers. Nevertheless, many people were involved, and they brought back with them certain skills and a determination to change the face of the rural South, even though they as individuals were struggling with limited job opportunities and the lagging pace of social change in the region. Their reasons for moving back varied but often were based on the call of the land and of extended family ties.

One notable feature of *Call to Home* is its stylistic difference from *All Our Kin*. The earlier work, while trailblazing and quite accessible, is written in the careful, objective prose expected from graduate students and young scholars. *Call to Home* uses a variety of literary techniques, along with straight exposition. There are long quotations which read like internal monologues, question-and-answer interview passages, and tales of mortgage foreclosures and other crises. In addition, the stories of outward and return migration often reflect, if not consciously, the hero's-journey pattern found in many myths, oral traditions, and literary epics.

In 1985 Carol Stack returned to Berkeley as a professor of social and cultural studies in education. Her professional involvements begun at Duke have expanded, adding to a hectic schedule with its central demands of teaching, research, and committee work. She has won many awards and research grants and serves on boards for a variety of national organizations.

Her planned book "Coming of Age at Minimum Wage" studies the efforts of minority young people—African American, Latino, and Asian—to participate in the American Dream through the entry gate of employment in the fast-food industry.

Emily Alward

Bibliography

Dickerson, Debra. "Going Back Down Home." *The Nation* 262, no. 15 (April 15, 1996). Long review supporting Stack's premise in *Call to Home* about the powerful pull of the rural South. Praises the author's style and insight.

McCarthy, Peggy, and Jo An Loren, eds. *Breast Cancer? Let Me Check My Schedule*. Boulder, Colo.: Westview Press, 1997. Testimony by Stack and other high-achieving professional women on the impact of breast cancer on their lives.

Publishers Weekly. Review of *Call to Home: African Americans Reclaim the Rural South*, by Carol B. Stack. 243, no. 18 (February 19, 1996): 198. Calls Stack's book a "sensitive portrayal of a little-studied phenomenon."

Madame de Staël

(Anne Louise Germaine Necker)

French critic and novelist

Born: Paris, France; April 22, 1766
Died: Paris, France; July 14, 1817

NONFICTION: *Essai sur les fictions*, 1795 (*Essay on Fiction*, 1795); *De l'influence des passions sur le bonheur des individus et des nations*, 1796 (*A Treatise on the Influence of the Passions upon the Happiness of Individuals and Nations*, 1798); *De la littérature considérée dans ses rapports avec les institutions sociales*, 1800 (*A Treatise on Ancient and Modern Literature*, 1803; also known as *The Influence of Literature upon Society*, 1813); *De l'Allemagne*, 1813 (*Germany*, 1813); *Considérations sur les principaux événemens de la Revolution française*, 1818 (*Considerations on the Principal Events of the French Revolution*, 1818); *Dix années d'exil*, 1821 (*Ten Years' Exile*, 1821); *Madame de Staël on Politics, Literature, and National Character*, 1964 (Morroe Berger, editor); *Selected Correspondence*, 2000 (Kathleen Jameson-Cemper, editor).
LONG FICTION: *Delphine*, 1802 (English translation, 1803); *Corinne: Ou, L'Italie*, 1807 (*Corinne: Or, Italy*, 1807).
MISCELLANEOUS: *Œuvres complètes*, 1820-1821 (17 volumes); *An Extraordinary Woman: Selected Writings of Germaine de Staël*, 1987.

Madame de Staël (stahl) was born Anne Louise Germaine Necker in Paris on April 22, 1766, and was the only child of Jacques Necker and the former Suzanne Cuchod from Geneva. A wealthy Swiss banker who became the minister of finance to Louis XVI, Jacques Necker was idolized by his daughter. Ostensibly because the king had dismissed Necker from his ministry, the French people stormed the Bastille in 1789, carrying its seven prisoners away in triumph; as a result, the king was forced to ask Necker to return. Necker returned but was ineffective and resigned in September of 1790; he retired to Coppet, leaving two million francs of his own in the state treasury. One trait that Germaine shared with her indulgent father was her ability to preserve the Necker fortune and to pass it on, undiminished, to her children.

She received an Enlightenment education. Taught by her Calvinist mother until the age of thirteen, she was subjected to a rigorous course of study that included Latin and English. The writings of Baron de Montesquieu, the Marquis de Condorcet, Voltaire, and Jean-Jacques Rousseau were major and early influences on her. More important, before she could walk, she became part of her mother's salon, which was frequented by the philosophes, including Denis Diderot, Jean Le Rond d'Alembert, and the Comte de Buffon. It was clear to the young girl that public attention from men for brilliant conversation was not only to be expected but was her birthright as well.

Her arranged marriage to Eric Magnus, Baron de Staël-Holstein, was bereft of emotional and intellectual ties. Nevertheless, his position as the Swedish ambassador to the French court led to an increased sphere of political influence for his wife. Her passionate need for intellectual dialogue and her temperament, which readily subscribed to Rousseau's damnation of human institutions such as marriage, led her into a number of intense love affairs. She and her husband were divorced in 1797. Although her biographers often discuss her faults, no one questions her courage and generosity. Her loyalty to friends and former lovers was unfailing, and even her enemies received her support.

To escape the Reign of Terror she fled to Coppet, Switzerland, where she and the Comte de Narbonne had a son together. She visited England and returned to Paris, where she began her famous love affair with Benjamin Constant. Napoleon exiled her for her political activities in 1803, and she set up her salon at Coppet. Although her Parisian salon was extremely important to her (Napoleon knew that exile from Paris was the worst torture he could inflict on her), Madame de Staël had less need for a home than for dialogue. Truly cosmopolitan at a time when nationalism was becoming increasingly fanatical, she traveled throughout Europe, from England to Italy, Scandinavia, Germany, and Russia, and planned to go to the United States as well. She was accustomed to dealing with royalty and heads of state. No beauty by contemporary standards, she was criticized not only for her liaisons and devouring intellect but also for her outlandish costumes. She nevertheless fascinated men with her candor, her guileless curiosity, and her brilliant gift for conversation.

In 1811 she married Albert de la Rocca, who would survive her by one year. After her years of exile she returned to Paris in 1814 and reopened her salon, gathering about her the leading young republicans of France, who were to overthrow the Bourbon dynasty in 1830. Even after her death on July 14, 1817, her ideas lived on, reflected in the members of her last and greatest salon.

Apart from her books on literature and society, de Staël wrote two romantic novels, *Delphine* and *Corinne*, and introduced the popular figure of the misunderstood heroine into French literature. A believer in the inevitability of progress, she set the themes for much of the literature of nineteenth century France and England.

Carol Bishop

Bibliography

Balayé, Simone. *Madame de Staël et les Français*. New York: Oxford University Press, 1996. In English; includes bibliographical references.

Besser, Gretchen R. *Germaine de Staël Revisited*. New York: Twayne, 1994. A comprehensive biographical study.

Gutwirth, Madelyn, Avriel Goldberger, and Karyna Szmurlo, eds. *Germaine de Staël: Crossing the Borders*. New Brunswick, N.J.: Rutgers University Press, 1991. Critical study includes bibliographical references and index.

Herold, J. Christopher. *Mistress to an Age: A Life of Madame de Staël*. 1958. Reprint. Alexandria, Va.: Time-Life Books, 1981. Biography places Madame de Staël within the context of her time.

Hogsett, Charlotte. *The Literary Existence of Germaine de Staël*. Carbondale: Southern Illinois University Press, 1987. Critical and biographical study includes index and bibliography.

Isbell, John Claiborne. *The Birth of European Romanticism: Truth and Propaganda in Staël's "De l'Allemagne," 1810-1813*. New York: Cambridge University Press, 1994. Includes index and bibliography.

Larg, David G. *Madame de Staël: Her Life as Revealed in Her Work, 1766-1880*. Translated from the French by Veronica Lucas. New York: Alfred A. Knopf, 1926. Comprehensive biographical study.

Marso, Lori Jo. *(Un)Manly Citizens: Jean-Jacques Rousseau's and Germaine de Staël's Subversive Women*. Baltimore: The Johns Hopkins University Press, 1999. Study of de Staël's use of characterization; includes bibliographical references and index.

Jean Stafford

American short-story writer and novelist

Born: Covina, California; July 1, 1915
Died: White Plains, New York; March 26, 1979

SHORT FICTION: *Children Are Bored on Sunday*, 1953; *Bad Characters*, 1964; *Selected Stories of Jean Stafford*, 1966; *The Collected Stories of Jean Stafford*, 1969.

LONG FICTION: *Boston Adventure*, 1944; *The Mountain Lion*, 1947; *The Catherine Wheel*, 1952; *A Winter's Tale*, 1954.

NONFICTION: *A Mother in History*, 1966.

CHILDREN'S/YOUNG ADULT LITERATURE: *Arabian Nights: The Lion and the Carpenter, and Other Tales from the Arabian Nights, Retold*, 1959; *Elephi: The Cat with the High I.Q.*, 1962.

Jean Stafford was a novelist and short-story writer of considerable distinction. Born to John and Mary McKillop Stafford on July 1, 1915, in Covina, California, Jean was the youngest of four children in a family beset by poverty. Her father, who held many jobs, also wrote stories and opinionated essays which he regularly read aloud to his children. The Stafford family moved from Covina to San Diego, then to a succession of small towns in Colorado, finally settling in Boulder in 1925. At age six, Jean began to write poems and stories, and she completed her first novel by age eleven. She also began to read the dictionary simply for pleasure and, even as a child, displayed an incredible command of language. From 1925 to 1932, Stafford attended University Hill School and State Preparatory School in Boulder. In 1932 she enrolled in the University of Colorado, Boulder, financing her education by scholarships and part-time work; she graduated with both B.A. and M.A. degrees in 1936. After graduation, she studied philology at the University of Heidelberg on a one-year fellowship.

Shy and intellectual, Stafford was a misfit in both high school and college. Returning from Germany, she attended a writing school in Boulder and was introduced to poet Robert Lowell (1917-1977), a man with a very different background from her own, whom she would later marry. She spent one unhappy year as an instructor at Stephens College and in 1938 taught briefly at the Writers' Workshop in Iowa. There she decided to write, not teach, and left abruptly in midsemester for Boston, arriving with one-third of a manuscript under her arm. In Boston, Stafford renewed her acquaintance with Robert Lowell. One night, returning home from an evening of drinking at a Boston nightclub, Lowell lost control of the car in which they were driving and Stafford was seriously injured. Despite the accident and the lawsuit which followed, a courtship blossomed and the two were married on April 2, 1940, in New York City.

Stafford's first novel, published in 1944, was a best-seller and was praised by reviewers for its traces of Marcel Proust (1871-1922) and Henry James (1843-1916). *Boston Adventure* deals with a young woman's realization that discovery of self requires rejection of society's limitations and introduces concerns that would reoccur in Stafford's later work: human motivations, instincts, relationships, and the complexities and incongruities of being alive, especially of being alive as a woman. In 1945 Stafford received a Guggenheim Fellowship for fiction and a National Institute of Arts and Letters grant. In that year, she also bought her first home in the small village of Damariscotta Mills, Maine, and she was at work on her second novel, *The Mountain Lion*.

Stafford and Lowell's marriage had always been stormy, even violent, and they were separated in 1946. The subsequent months were difficult for Stafford. She traveled, spent a few days in a mental hospital, then stayed in a run-down Greenwich Village hotel. In 1947 she committed herself to the Payne Whitney Clinic in New York and spent a year there under treatment for hysteria and deep depression. Also in 1947 Stafford's masterpiece second novel was published. Unlike the first, *The Mountain Lion* was written out of her own experience in the West rather than her imaginings of an East she hardly knew. It explored this geographical dichotomy as well as the complexities of childhood, themes that appear in many of Stafford's stories. The style was also more naturally her own in this work, reflecting her ability to find the most appropriate word for her creative expression, no matter how unusual it might be.

In 1948 Stafford obtained a divorce from Lowell. In that same year, she was awarded another Guggenheim Fellowship for fiction and the National Book Club Award. In 1950 Stafford married Oliver Jensen, a second unhappy marriage that lasted only a few months. In 1952 Stafford's third novel, *The Catherine Wheel*, was published. In what is considered her most carefully structured novel, Stafford again deals with psychological motivation and alienation and explores the major theme of her work: women and their situation in society. In 1953 Stafford was divorced from Jensen and, as before, experienced psychological collapse, this time complicated by physical ill health. While recuperating with friends in the Virgin Islands, she wrote "In the Zoo," which received the First Prize O. Henry Award in 1955.

Stafford is best known for her more than fifty short stories, which, like her novels, are largely autobiographical. Almost all of her characters are girls and women; many are orphans, aged, or ill. Stafford deals with the powerlessness of women caught in social roles; for those who assert themselves in an attempt to develop identity, her stories suggest, the result is often madness. Her first collection, *Children Are Bored on Sunday*, appeared in 1953. In 1959 Stafford married A. J. Liebling, critic and columnist for *The New Yorker*. During this four-year marriage, she published no fiction, except for two juvenile books, and explained that perhaps it was because she was happy for the first time in her life. Nevertheless, Stafford and Liebling began to drift apart before Liebling's death. They quarreled over Stafford's drinking, which was a problem throughout her life, and they were frequently separated.

Although very much a part of the New York literary world, Stafford had often felt ill at ease with the New York intellectuals. Thus, after Liebling's death in 1963, she made her home in Springs, Long Island. There, known locally as the Widow Liebling and in failing health, Stafford became increasingly reclusive. Her second collection of short stories, *Bad Characters*, was published in 1964. In 1965 she contracted for an autobiographical novel, "The Parliament of Women," which remained unpublished at her death. Another collection, *Selected Stories of Jean Stafford*, was published in 1966. During the 1960's and 1970's Stafford wrote nonfiction for popular magazines and in 1969 her *Collected Stories* was published. In 1970 Stafford received the Pulitzer Prize for *Collected Stories* and was also made a member of the National Academy of Arts and Letters. As she aged, Stafford grew more and more to resemble the ill-tempered old women in her fiction. Her life—beset by physical and mental illness, unhappiness, lack of deserved recognition for her work, and lessening creativity—was further debilitated in 1977 when she suffered a stroke resulting in aphasia. The Jean Stafford who had read the dictionary for pleasure then found it difficult to speak even the simplest of thoughts. She died on March 26, 1979, at the Burke Rehabilitation Center in White Plains, New York.

Critics have suggested that Stafford's ironic vision allows for no clear-cut perspective on her work. Her preoccupation with language is reflected in a rich and complex style, rooted both in the formal, rhetorical tradition of Henry James and the more informal and colloquial of Mark Twain, and she has been compared with both. Stafford has been praised for her nonsentimental approach but perhaps more often criticized for emotional detachment from her characters, who are seldom able to resolve feelings of alienation. Ironically, this same detachment seems to suggest that the objective, intellectual viewpoint is the only way for individuals to rise above the inevitable difficulties of life to experience realization or knowledge, however short-lived.

Most critical analyses tend to view Stafford's treatment of women as a metaphor for the universal alienation in modern society, rather than as a commentary on the lives of women. Stafford would probably approve of the lack of attention she has received from the feminist perspective, because she expressed strong disapproval of the feminist movement in articles written toward the end of her life. At the time of Stafford's death, her name was not familiar to most readers. Although she has to some extent been "rediscovered"—*The Catherine Wheel* was reissued in 1981 in a series called Neglected Books of the Twentieth Century—critics still suggest that she deserves more attention.

William S. Haney II

Bibliography

Avila, Wanda. *Jean Stafford: A Comprehensive Bibliography.* New York: Garland, 1983. This reference contains short summaries of 220 publications by Stafford (books, stories, articles, essays, book and movie reviews) and 428 critical works about her.

Goodman, Charlotte Margolis. *Jean Stafford: The Savage Heart.* Austin: University of Texas Press, 1990. Delineating the connections between Jean Stafford's life and her fiction, this literary biography presents a portrait of Stafford as an extremely talented but troubled individual. Drawing heavily from Jean Stafford's letters, it is well researched and makes interesting reading.

Hulbert, Ann. *The Interior Castle: The Art and Life of Jean Stafford.* New York: Alfred A. Knopf, 1992. Rigorously focused on Stafford's literary work and on the development of her ambivalent literary sensibility, this superbly written biography nevertheless scants a depiction of the full range of her life.

Roberts, David. *Jean Stafford: A Biography.* Boston: Little, Brown, 1988. This comprehensive, 494-page biography includes photographs and a select bibliography of primary and secondary sources.

Ryan, Maureen. *Innocence and Estrangement in the Fiction of Jean Stafford.* Baton Rouge: Louisiana State University Press, 1987. This detailed study of Stafford's themes and technique includes two chapters that focus on the feminine situations Stafford creates in her short fiction. Supplemented by a bibliography.

Walsh, Mary Ellen Williams. *Jean Stafford.* Boston: Twayne, 1985. This extended critique examines Stafford's fiction from the perspective of the stages in women's lives: childhood, adolescence, young womanhood, maturity, and old age. It gives considerable attention to her stories, both collected and uncollected, and includes a chronology and select bibliography.

Wilson, Mary Ann. *Jean Stafford: A Study of the Short Fiction.* New York: Twayne, 1996. Discusses a representative sample of Stafford's stories under Stafford's own regional headings. Includes several critical comments about fiction writing by Stafford and brief critical comments on her fiction by a number of critics, including Joyce Carol Oates and Peter Taylor. Discusses such stories as "A Country Love Story" and "The Interior Castle," as well as many lesser-known stories.

William Stafford

American poet

Born: Hutchinson, Kansas; January 17, 1914
Died: Lake Oswego, Oregon; August 28, 1993

POETRY: *West of Your City*, 1960; *Traveling Through the Dark*, 1962; *The Rescued Year*, 1966; *Eleven Untitled Poems*, 1968; *Weather: Poems*, 1969; *Allegiances*, 1970; *Temporary Facts*, 1970; *Poems for Tennessee*, 1971 (with Robert Bly and William Matthews); *Someday, Maybe*, 1973; *That Other Alone*, 1973; *In the Clock of Reason*, 1973; *Going Places: Poems*, 1974; *North by West*, 1975 (with John Haines); *Braided Apart*, 1976 (with Kim Robert Stafford); *Stories That Could Be True: New and Collected Poems*, 1977; *The Design in the Oriole*, 1977; *Two About Music*, 1978; *All About Light*, 1978; *Things That Happen Where There Aren't Any People*, 1980; *Sometimes Like a Legend*, 1981; *A Glass Face in the Rain: New Poems*, 1982; *Smoke's Way: Poems from Limited Editions, 1968-1981*, 1983; *Roving Across Fields: A Conversation and Uncollected Poems, 1942-1982*, 1983; *Segues: A Correspondence in Poetry*, 1983 (with Marvin Bell); *Stories and Storms and Strangers*, 1984; *Listening Deep*, 1984; *Wyoming*, 1985; *Brother Wind*, 1986; *An Oregon Message*, 1987; *Fin, Feather, Fur*, 1989; *A Scripture of Leaves*, 1989; *How to Hold Your Arms When It Rains: Poems*, 1990; *Passwords*, 1991; *My Name Is William Tell*, 1992; *The Darkness Around Us Is Deep*, 1993 (selected by Robert Bly).

NONFICTION: *Down in My Heart*, 1947, 2d edition 1985; *Friends to This Ground: A Statement for Readers, Teachers, and Writers of Literature*, 1967; *Leftovers, A Care Package: Two Lectures*, 1973; *Writing the Australian Crawl: Views on the Writer's Vocation*, 1978; *You Must Revise Your Life*, 1986; *Writing the World*, 1988.

EDITED TEXTS: *The Voices of Prose*, 1966 (with Frederick Caudelaria); *The Achievement of Brother Antonius: A Comprehensive Selection of His Poems with a Critical Introduction*, 1967; *Poems and Perspectives*, 1971 (with Robert H. Ross); *Modern Poetry of Western America*, 1975 (with Clinton F. Larson).

William Stafford was one of the most prolific and best-loved of American poets in an age when it is often said that hardly anyone reads poetry, that more people write it than read it, and that there are no "major" American poets. After receiving his B.A. at the University of Kansas in 1937, Stafford acted as a conscientious objector during World War II in Arkansas, Illinois, and California, then returned to Kansas to complete his master's degree in 1946. *Down in My Heart*, the memoir of his experiences as a conscientious objector, includes a half dozen of his earliest published poems. He taught at Lewis and Clark College near Portland, Oregon, for two years before attending the University of Iowa, where he completed his Ph.D. in 1954. After brief teaching stints elsewhere, he returned to Lewis and Clark, where he taught from 1956 until his retirement in 1980. His specialty was Romantic poetry; although he taught short-term workshops in poetry writing elsewhere, he did not teach creative writing at Lewis and Clark.

In "Mountain Conscription," a poem included in *Down in My Heart*, Stafford portrays himself standing "suddenly alone" in "small shoes upon the sand," hearing "the end of things," and "not knowing what to say." The ambiguous "they" tell him that nostalgia is "a feeling men have" and that he "will know it, later," all of his life. Although no admirer of Stafford's poems would likely cite that poem as one of his best, it captures much of his vision and of the image he portrays of himself. Critics, scholars, and fellow poets described Stafford as quietistic, tentative, passive, Indian-like, Quaker-like, low-key, congenial, pastoral, nostalgic, regional, and paternal (but not "patriarchal").

Stafford was interviewed frequently, and he wrote extensively about his practices as a poet. In *Writing the Australian Crawl* he defines poetry as "the kind of thing you have to see from the corner of your eye," and in *You Must Revise Your Life* he writes, "A poem is a lucky piece of talk." Throughout Stafford's work one may detect a somewhat oblique angle on life.

Stafford's second collection, *Traveling Through the Dark*, gained him broad recognition when it won the National Book Award for poetry in 1962, and the title poem has been widely anthologized. In this collection, Stafford speaks for the random people of the world, including himself, as opposed to the heroes or notorious villains. Stafford's third book of poems, *The Rescued Year*, includes "Fifteen," a poem frequently anthologized in secondary school texts, and "Passing Remark," which opens with a terse couplet that some readers regard as indicative of both his own reticence and the understated nature of his poems: "In scenery I like flat country./ In life I don't like much to happen." Yet things do happen in Stafford's poems, and in "The Animal That Drank Up Sound" he offers a narrative poem of nearly fifty lines after the fashion of Native American myth.

In *Allegiances*, Stafford ranges freely from Kansas to Oregon, and his family continues to figure prominently. As he says in the opening line of the title poem, "It is time for all the heroes to go home." He aligns himself with "us common ones" who "locate ourselves by the real things/ we live by." Mundane diction, avoidance of flashy imagery, and a flatly conversational tone are his stylistic trademarks. *Someday, Maybe*, a title suggestive of Stafford's playful evasiveness, includes such powerful poems as "Report to Crazy Horse" and "Report from a Far Place." *Stories That Could Be True* includes "Accountability" and "Whispered into the Ground," which concludes, "Even far things are real."

Because Stafford was so prolific, readers might find Robert Bly's edition of one hundred selected poems, *The Darkness Around Us Is Deep*, especially valuable. These poems vary from such apparently artless short pieces as "First Grade," from *An Oregon Message*, to "Stories to Live in the World With," from *Someday, Maybe*. Stafford's poems are renowned for their accessibility, but he compels his readers to look at the things, events, places, and people of this world from a peculiar slant.

Ron McFarland

Bibliography

Andrews, Tom, ed. *On William Stafford: The Worth of Local Things*. Ann Arbor: University of Michigan Press, 1993. Presents an assortment of over fifty mostly (but not wholly) complimentary essays on Stafford's poetry and prose. Overall, they rank Stafford among the best American poets. Important historical analogies are proposed, favorably comparing his subject matter, voice, and vision to those of poets such as Whitman and Frost. There is enough hard criticism, especially regarding the occasional flatness of Stafford's style, to allow the reader to share in the debate.

Holden, Jonathan. *The Mark to Turn*. Lawrence: University Press of Kansas, 1976. This volume, the first book-length study of Stafford's work, is a useful overview of his major themes and technique. Holden focuses his close readings on poems from Stafford's first published collection and the four collections with his major publisher that followed. The ninety-one-page study includes a biography.

Kitchen, Judith. *Writing the World: Understanding William Stafford*. Corvallis: Oregon State University Press, 1999. This comprehensive volume is accessible for the student as well as the good nonacademic reader. In addition to a short biography and overview of Stafford's work, it presents detailed analysis of seven of Stafford's major collections and also considers his chapbooks and distinguished small-press editions. This 175-page work concludes with a detailed bibliography of primary and secondary sources.

Pinsker, Sanford. "William Stafford: 'The Real Things We Live

By.'" In *Three Pacific Northwest Poets*. Boston: Twayne, 1987. This chapter begins with a biographical sketch and then unfolds a book-by-book analysis of six of Stafford's collections, offering close readings of representative poems to support more general conclusions. It includes a selected bibliography.

Stitt, Peter. "William Stafford's Wilderness Quest." In *The World: Hieroglyphic Beauty: Five American Poets*. Athens: University of Georgia Press, 1985. This excellent chapter develops Stafford as a "wisdom poet" and explores his process-rather-than-substance view of writing. It includes an interview with Stafford originally conducted at his home in 1976 and updated in 1981 at the Bread Loaf Writers' Conference.

Laurence Stallings

American playwright and screenwriter

Born: Macon, Georgia; November 25, 1894
Died: Pacific Palisades, California; February 28, 1968

DRAMA: *What Price Glory?*, pr. 1924 (with Maxwell Anderson); *First Flight*, pr. 1925 (with Anderson); *The Buccaneer*, pr. 1925 (with Anderson); *Three American Plays*, pb. 1926 (includes previous 3 titles); *Deep River*, pr. 1926 (libretto and lyrics, music by W. F. Harling); *Rainbow*, pr. 1928 (with Oscar Hammerstein II); *A Farewell to Arms*, pr. 1930 (adaptation of Ernest Hemingway's novel); *Virginia*, pr. 1937 (with Owen Davis); *The Streets Are Guarded*, pr. 1944.

LONG FICTION: *Plumes*, 1924.

SHORT FICTION: "Vale of Tears," (in *Men at War: The Best War Stories of All Time*, 1942; Ernest Hemingway, editor).

SCREENPLAYS: *The Big Parade*, 1925; *What Price Glory?*, 1926; *Old Ironsides*, 1926; *Song of the West*, 1930; *Billy the Kid*, 1930; *Way for a Sailor*, 1930; *Big Executive*, 1933; *So Red the Rose*, 1935; *After Office Hours*, 1935; *Too Hot to Handle*, 1938; *Northwest Passage*, 1940; *Thunder Birds*, 1942; *The Jungle Book*, 1942 (adaptation of Rudyard Kipling's book of stories); *Salome: Where She Danced*, 1945; *Christmas Eve*, 1947; *A Miracle Can Happen*, 1948; *Three Godfathers*, 1948; *She Wore a Yellow Ribbon*, 1949; *The Sun Shines Bright*, 1954.

NONFICTION: *The First World War: A Photographic History*, 1933; *The Doughboys: A History of the A.E.F. 1917-1918*, 1963.

An important early influence on Laurence Tucker Stallings's development was his mother, Aurora Brooks Stallings, who had a flair for music and literature. As a boy Stallings also developed a fascination for Civil War heroes. He earned his B.A. at Wake Forest University in North Carolina in 1916, and after a short stint as a reporter for the *Atlanta Journal*, he enlisted in the Marines in 1917 after the United States entered World War I. In France he saw action on the last day of battle at Belleau Wood. In the course of a charge he was seriously wounded, an injury that led to the amputation of one leg in 1922. (In 1963 the other leg also had to be amputated). Following the war he earned an M.A. at Georgetown University in 1922, after which he worked as a reporter first for *The Washington Times* and then for *The New York World*, where playwright Maxwell Anderson was also employed; in 1931 he joined *The New York Sun*. During these years in New York, Stallings met many literary figures of the day at the legendary Algonquin Hotel.

Unquestionably Stallings's first play, *What Price Glory?*, written in collaboration with Maxwell Anderson, became his most celebrated, even though he wrote only one of the three acts of this dramatic comedy. In this act, however, Stallings documents his response to his war experience. In the cellar of an embattled French town on the Western Front, two longtime friendly enemies, Captain Flagg and Sergeant Quirt, quarrel about the bloody business of war. Stallings mixes bawdy humor with a more subtle message about war's futility. He also spiced up Anderson's language with the kind of talk he had heard at the Front, profanities Broadway had not previously witnessed. With its language and its representation of men in the trenches, the play brought realism to the stage in an unprecedented manner.

The war continued to permeate both Stallings's fiction and nonfiction, and that is where his strength lay. He was less successful when he attempted to write about other topics. Both *First Flight*, which tells the romantic adventures of a young President Andrew Jackson, and *The Buccaneer*, which is about a seventeenth century British adventurer, were failures and in fact brought about the end of Stallings's collaboration with Maxwell Anderson. By contrast, *The Big Parade*, in which an officer wearily appreciates the brutal irony that in war some soldiers are chosen to live and some to die, was made into a successful film in 1925. The same is true of Stallings's stage adaptation of Ernest Hemingway's *A Farewell to Arms* (1929) in 1930. After *What Price Glory?*, however, Stallings's career as a dramatist deteriorated, and as a novelist and short-story writer he remained essentially a single-topic author. He admitted: "Like a lot of writers, I had just one thing to say and I said it."

In 1934 Stallings became editor of the Fox newsreel series *Movietones*. In that capacity he toured Ethiopia to film the Italian conquest of that country (1935-1936). In 1936 he was divorced from Helen Poteat, with whom he had had two daughters, and one year later he married Louise St. Leger Vance, with whom he had one son and one daughter. He moved to California and became a scriptwriter for various Hollywood film studios. During World War II he reenlisted in the U.S. Marines, was given a desk assignment in Washington, and finally retired as a lieutenant-colonel.

In 1963 Stallings's expansion of an earlier essay titled "The War to End War" led to the publication of *The Doughboys*, which dealt with the military tactics and campaigns of the American Expeditionary Force in France during World War I. It was his last work.

Stallings died of a heart attack on February 28, 1968. His name will always be associated with the trauma and alienation suffered by individuals at war as well as with his biting portrayal of those fighting and dying in a world of political confusion and insanity, a world in which war is futile and incomprehensible.

Peter B. Heller

Bibliography

Brittain, Joan T. *Laurence Stallings*. Boston: Twayne, 1975. A brief and simple treatment of Stallings's life and work. Includes a selected bibliography.

Flexner, Eleanor. *American Playwrights, 1918-1938: The Theatre Retreats from Reality*. Freeport, N.Y.: Books for Libraries Press, 1969. Provides a good philosophical critique of *What Price Glory?*

Krutch, Joseph Wood. *The American Drama Since 1918: An Informal History*. Rev. ed. New York: G. Braziller, 1957. Insightful in contrasting the romantic dash and vivid portrayal of emotions in *What Price Glory?* with the unexceptional qualities of *First Flight* and *The Buccaneer*, which both feature more routine kinds of cloak-and-dagger melodrama.

Elizabeth Cady Stanton

American political reformer and journalist

Born: Johnstown, New York; November 12, 1815
Died: New York, New York; October 26, 1902

NONFICTION: *The Woman's Bible*, 1895 (volume 1), 1898 (volume 2); *Eighty Years and More*, 1898; *The Selected Papers of Elizabeth Cady Stanton and Susan B. Anthony*, 1997-2000 (2 volumes; Ann D. Gordon, editor).

EDITED TEXT: *History of Woman Suffrage*, 1881-1922 (6 volumes; with Susan B. Anthony and Matilda Joslyn Gage).

Elizabeth Cady Stanton is considered the mother of woman suffrage in the United States. Her father, Daniel Cady, was a federal judge, and Elizabeth spent many childhood hours listening to him interpret the law. Angered by the injustice of the law toward women, she vowed to work for changes. Having attended secondary school with her brothers to learn Latin, Greek, and algebra, she was astounded when refused admission to Union College on the basis of her sex. She attended Troy Female Seminary in Troy, New York, where she unhappily studied French, music, and dancing.

She spent the next seven years reading and studying law, painting, riding horses, and generally developing her mind and body. Disturbed by her own lack of purpose, she was heartened to meet Henry Brewster Stanton, the famous antislavery orator, journalist, and author. The injustice against which he fought for African American slaves she found similar to the inequality women faced under the law. Against family objections, she married Stanton and left immediately with him for England to attend the World's Anti-Slavery Convention as delegates. There she met Lucretia Mott, the great Quaker women's rights activist, and took up the banner officially for the cause of women's equality.

The Stantons went home to Seneca Falls, New York. A year later, Stanton met with Mott and some of her Quaker friends to propose a convention for women at which the proper steps could be drawn up to improve their status. They called for women to attend a Women's Rights Convention in the United States. It was in 1848 at the first convention in Seneca Falls Wesleyan Chapel that Stanton read her document called the "Declaration of Sentiments." Based on the Declaration of Independence, it called for equality in all areas—education, economic issues, marriage property laws, and, for the first time in the history of the nation, the right to vote. The subject of suffrage drew fire from many protesters; however, after much debate, the declaration was signed by more than one hundred men and women, and the first official stance on suffrage for women was recorded. Two weeks later at a meeting in Rochester, New York, the document was again endorsed.

Stanton continued, along with Mott and others, to work toward women's equality. Delivering speeches and writing articles were as much a part of her life as her family. In 1851, fortuitous circumstances brought Elizabeth Cady Stanton and Susan B. Anthony together, and an alliance was formed that lasted until Stanton's death. Anthony's work up to that point had mainly been in the area of temperance; however, she quickly added Stanton's agenda to her own, and the two women steered the course of the fight for American women's rights during the second half of the nineteenth century. Working together delivering speeches (with Susan helping Elizabeth with her seven children when Henry was in the legislature), leading protests, and banding with others to plead their cause in other cities, the two were formidable.

In 1854 Stanton was invited to address the joint judiciary committees of the New York legislature on the legal disabilities of women. Although the speech was warmly received, no laws were immediately effected. In 1869 the Fifteenth Amendment to the

U.S. Constitution was ratified, removing all racial barriers to the right to vote. Despite activists' efforts to include woman suffrage in the amendment, it had not been mentioned. That same year Stanton was elected president of the National Woman Suffrage Association, a post she held for twenty-one years. She and a group of women's leaders drafted a proposal for a sixteenth amendment enfranchising women. The struggle was not to be over for many years; it was not until 1920 and the Nineteenth Amendment that all women in the United States were finally granted the right to vote. During the intervening years, the proposal became known as the Susan B. Anthony amendment because of Anthony's long association with the fight which continued almost twenty years after Stanton's death.

Stanton joined with Anthony and Matilda Joslyn Gage in 1876 to begin writing *History of Woman Suffrage*. Three volumes were published by 1886, covering the history up to that date. The document's contribution to the literature has been invaluable, providing information on the suffrage movement from those who were centrally involved. It was a collaborative effort in which the women were both editors and writers, writing chapters for the book and collecting other documents to include. In the first volumes, Stanton was responsible for most of the connecting narrative, while Anthony supervised the collection of documents. Three more volumes appeared after 1886, but Stanton's role was much smaller, the work being supervised by Ida Husted Harper.

Although Anthony's efforts for women continued to center on suffrage, Stanton was not satisfied to limit her own activity to a single cause. The inequality in many areas disturbed her, and she pursued issues such as women's career choices, impractical restrictions on women's fashions, women's rights to abortion and fair divorce laws, and taboos and folk wisdom associated with women's health issues such as childbearing. Aspects of theology, as well, had disturbed Stanton since her youth. After much study, she wrote a two-volume commentary addressing the false teachings against women which some theologians claimed were biblically based. The two volumes of *The Woman's Bible* were published in 1895 and 1898 and were well received. In 1898 Stanton published a set of memoirs entitled *Eighty Years and More*. In conversational style, the book provides personal information that complements the facts about her professional life found in *History of Woman Suffrage*.

Elizabeth Cady Stanton remained a voice for women until her death. When no longer able to attend conventions, she wrote speeches to be delivered by her friends. She died in 1902, the day after she had drafted a letter to President Theodore Roosevelt urging his support for the emancipation of women. At her funeral she was called the "great statesman of the woman's rights movement," having sparked the revolution which ultimately changed women's lives in the twentieth century.

Sandra C. McClain

Bibliography

Banner, Lois W. *Elizabeth Cady Stanton: A Radical for Women's Rights*. Boston: Little, Brown, 1988. An accessible biography.

Cott, Nancy. *The Grounding of Modern Feminism*. New Haven, Conn.: Yale University Press, 1987. Discusses Stanton's work in context of the women's movement as a whole.

DuBois, Ellen Carol, ed. *Elizabeth Cady Stanton, Susan B. Anthony: Correspondence, Writings, Speeches*. New York: Schocken Books, 1981. Includes critical comments by DuBois and gives an inside look at Stanton's work in conjunction with Susan B. Anthony.

Griffin, Elisabeth. *In Her Own Right: The Life of Elizabeth Cady Stanton*. New York: Oxford University Press, 1984. A scholarly biography.

Kern, Kathi. *Mrs. Stanton's Bible*. Ithaca, N.Y.: Cornell University Press, 2001. Traces the impact of Stanton's religious dissent on the suffrage movement and presents the first book-length reading of her radical text *The Woman's Bible*.

Loos, Pamela. *Elizabeth Cady Stanton*. Philadelphia: Chelsea House, 2001. Drawing largely on Stanton's autobiography as well as a few other sources, Loos presents a surprisingly detailed psychological and emotional portrait of the revolutionary. Intended for middle school students but useful for older readers as well.

Ward, Geoffrey C., and Ken Burns. *Not for Ourselves Alone: The Story of Elizabeth Cady Stanton and Susan B. Anthony, an Illustrated History*. New York: Alfred A. Knopf, 1999. With contributions by historians and dozens of contemporary photographs, this book provides a view of the suffrage movement through the eyes of the women who fought for it.

Olaf Stapledon

English novelist and philosopher

Born: Wirral Peninsula, near Liverpool, Merseyside, England; May 10, 1886
Died: Caldy, Cheshire, England; September 6, 1950

LONG FICTION: *Last and First Men*, 1930; *Last Men in London*, 1932; *Odd John: A Story Between Jest and Earnest*, 1935; *Star Maker*, 1937; *Darkness and the Light*, 1942; *Sirius: A Fantasy of Love and Discord*, 1944; *Death into Life*, 1946; *The Flames*, 1947; *A Man Divided*, 1950; *Nebula Maker*, 1976.

SHORT FICTION: *Old Man in New World*, 1944; *Far Future Calling: Uncollected Science Fiction and Fantasies of Olaf Stapledon*, 1979 (Sam Moskowitz, editor).

NONFICTION: *A Modern Theory of Ethics*, 1929; *Waking World*, 1934; *Philosophy and Living*, 1939 (2 volumes); *Beyond the "Isms,"* 1942; *The Opening of the Eyes*, 1954 (Agnes Z. Stapledon, editor).

MISCELLANEOUS: *An Olaf Stapledon Reader*, 1997.

Born into a moderately wealthy family, William Olaf Stapledon had sufficient private income to free him from any pressing need to work for a living, and he elected to become a philosopher. He never held a university post, although he did a good deal of teaching for the Workers Educational Association. He was a pacifist but served in World War I with the Friends' Ambulance Unit, and his worldview was permanently colored by his experiences at the front. His inability to believe in a god who was at all interested in the day-to-day affairs of humankind sent him forth in search of a humanistic basis for hope and charity, a preliminary sketch of which he presents in *A Modern Theory of Ethics*.

Stapledon attempted to extrapolate this search in an unprecedentedly ambitious way in *Last and First Men*. This speculative history follows eighteen descendant species of *Homo sapiens* over a period of two billion years. Although these beings remain bound to Earth's solar system, they migrate to various other planets therein, eventually taking up residence on Neptune when the evolution of the Sun renders the inner planets uninhabitable. The book carries forward a tradition of "ecstatic visions" that began with Edgar Allan Poe's 1848 prose poem *Eureka* and the fictional works of the French astronomer Camille Flammarion, but it is far more detailed than any of its predecessors. Its focus on the Socratic problem of how human beings should live is intensified in the sequel, *Last Men in London*, which attempts to incorporate its perspectives and moral lessons within the life of a contemporary man (whose biography borrows extensively from Stapledon's own experiences). *Odd John* retains a similarly narrow focus in its examination of the career of a man born ahead of his time into the twentieth century, moving inexorably to a bleak conclusion that reflects little optimism about contemporary humanity's ability to adapt to changing circumstances.

Stapledon's ecstatic vision resumed its outward momentum in *Star Maker*, which expanded its scope to take in the entire universe. A crudely allegorical false start—published posthumously as *Nebula Maker*—was wisely forsaken, making way for a careful, hierarchical series of visions that constitutes one of the masterpieces of modern imaginative fiction. *Last and First Men* labors under the slight handicap of an unorthodox theory of evolution, but this becomes irrelevant in *Star Maker*, which attempts to set the everyday moral problems of human beings in their "true" context—in this case, the sublime but sobering discoveries of modern science. The protagonist, who experiences a vision after leaving his house because of a bitter argument with his wife, perceives the fundamental patterns of creation on a series of escalating scales, until at last he glimpses the intelligence seemingly at work in the business of creation: a "god" who, while not merely uncaring, is not yet fully practiced in his art. The novel concludes with a desperate but nevertheless hopeful prescription for psychological survival in the new world war that Stapledon could already see looming on the horizon.

Darkness and the Light is a scrupulous examination of two of the possible futures open to human civilization, one supposedly representing the best case and the other the worst. A deep pessimism is evident in Stapledon's dour view of the possibility of progress. *Sirius: A Fantasy of Love and Discord* is a powerful tale of a dog experimentally gifted with human intelligence, who serves as an objective observer of humankind's failings. The love affair between Sirius and his creator's daughter, Plaxy, constitutes an implicit criticism of almost all existing relationships between human beings. The visionary fantasy *Death into Life* tries hard to recover some uplifting lesson from the wreckage of World War II, but its failure is made acutely obvious by the bleak parable of *The Flames*, in which luminous refugees from the Sun are denied a home on Earth, banished instead to dark inertia.

Stapledon's last novel, *A Man Divided*, returns to the intimate and highly personal perspective of *Last Men in London*. It portrays with painful intensity the plight of a man who alternates between superhuman wisdom and dull conformity, not merely in intellectual terms but in moral terms as well. Its hero tries to move as Stapledon did in his philosophical work—"beyond the 'isms,'" but the task is continually confounded by his extreme emotional swings. Stapledon presumably experienced his own internal struggles with an unusual intensity and could never resolve them, but they were the spur that drove his vaulting imagination to limits no one else had reached. Although his work can be uncomfortable to read, the discomfort is of a kind that nourishes the intellect. His writing continually gravitates toward despair, yet it never ceases to rage against that end.

Brian Stableford

Bibliography

Crossley, Robert. *Olaf Stapledon: Speaking for the Future*. Syracuse, N.Y.: Syracuse University Press, 1994. A detailed and scrupulously scholarly biography. Includes bibliography and index.

Fiedler, Leslie A. *Olaf Stapledon: A Man Divided*. New York: Oxford University Press, 1983. A rather combative commentary on the moral import of Stapledon's novels.

McCarthy, Patrick A., et al., eds. *The Legacy of Olaf Stapledon: Critical Essays and an Unpublished Manuscript*. New York: Greenwood Press, 1989. A good collection of essays that includes several previously unpublished "Letters to the Future" by Stapledon.

Satty, Harvey, and Curtis C. Smith. *Olaf Stapledon: A Bibliography*. Westport, Conn.: Greenwood Press, 1984. Admirably comprehensive bibliography. Includes index.

Statius

Roman poet

Born: Neapolis, Campania (now Naples, Italy); c. 45 C.E.
Died: Neapolis, Campania (now Naples, Italy); c. 96 C.E.

POETRY: *Thebais*, c. 90 (*Thebaid*, 1767); *Silvae*, c. 91-95 (English translation, 1908); *Achilleid*, c. 95-96 (English translation, 1660).

Publius Papinius Statius (STAY-shuhs) was a poet of the court of the Emperor Domitian (81-96) and wrote adulatory poetry for that ruler, who had no taste for verse. Statius's father had been a poet, and the son began early and competed frequently, and usually successfully, in poetic contests in Naples. One clue to his success may be that the public never saw his verse until it had been approved by the Divine Emperor.

Victor at Domitian's festival at Alba, where he was awarded the coveted gold wreath from Domitian's hands, he entered the quinquennial Capitoline competition in 94, but failed to win the oakleaf crown. Discouraged, he returned to Naples, where he died in about 96.

It took Statius twelve years to complete the twelve books of his Vergilian poem *Thebais*, which tells of the battle between the sons of Oedipus, Eteocles and Polynices, for the throne of Thebes. Although it is at times marked by a certain turgidity, *Thebais* is a rich tapestry of the dark side of human ambition, murderous violence, and the mutability of fate. Only fragments remain of his epic about the early life of Achilles. *Silvae* is a collection of pleasant occasional verse about his friends, the emperor, and his wife, Claudia. He also wrote a birthday ode to Lucan, which is valuable because of its comments on earlier writers.

David H. J. Larmour

Bibliography

Dominik, William J. *The Mythic Voice of Statius: Power and Politics in the "Thebaid."* New York: E. J. Brill, 1994. Examines in detail the thematic design of the *Thebaid* and explores the poem's political undercurrents.

_______. *Speech and Rhetoric in Statius's "Thebaid."* New York: Olms-Weidmann, 1994. Presents a critical analysis of the stylistic, narrative, and thematic functions of the characters' speeches in the *Thebaid*.

Geyssen, John W. *Imperial Panegyric in Statius: A Literary Commentary on "Silvae."* New York: Peter Lang, 1996. Examines Statius as a panegyrist working within an accepted poetic tradition, focusing on the first of the *Silvae*.

Hardie, Alex. *Statius and the "Silvae": Poets, Patrons, and Epideixis in the Graeco-Roman World.* Liverpool, England: Francis Cairns, 1983. Considers Statius's performance as a Latin poet against the context of contemporary social and literary history.

Vessey, David. *Statius and the "Thebaid."* Cambridge, England: Cambridge University Press, 1973. Provides a critical analysis and evaluation of Statius's epic, placing the work in its historical and literary context and surveying its form, style, and content.

_______. *Statius: "Thebaid."* Translated by A. D. Melville. Oxford, England: Clarendon Press, 1992. Provides a general introduction to the *Thebaid* as well as a summary of the poem and a list of principal characters.

Christina Stead

Australian novelist and short-story writer

Born: Rockdale, Australia; July 17, 1902
Died: Sydney, Australia; March 31, 1983

LONG FICTION: *Seven Poor Men of Sydney*, 1934; *The Beauties and Furies*, 1936; *House of All Nations*, 1938; *The Man Who Loved Children*, 1940, 1965; *For Love Alone*, 1944; *Letty Fox: Her Luck*, 1946; *A Little Tea, a Little Chat*, 1948; *The People with the Dogs*, 1952; *Dark Places of the Heart*, 1966 (pb. in England as *Cotters' England*, 1966); *The Little Hotel*, 1973; *Miss Herbert: The Suburban Wife*, 1976; *I'm Dying Laughing: The Humourist*, 1986.

SHORT FICTION: *The Salzburg Tales*, 1934; *The Puzzleheaded Girl*, 1967; *Ocean of Story: The Uncollected Short Stories of Christina Stead*, 1985.

TRANSLATIONS: *Colour of Asia*, 1955 (of Fernand Gignon); *The Candid Killer*, 1956 (of Jean Giltène); *In Balloon and Bathyscaphe*, 1956 (of August Piccard).

EDITED TEXTS: *Modern Women in Love*, 1945 (with William Blake); *Great Stories of the South Sea Islands*, 1956.

Until the 1960's, Christina Stead was either unmentioned in Australian literary histories or briefly alluded to as an expatriate writer who had inexplicably attracted the attention of British and American readers and critics. Her work had never been published in her own country. By 1990, however, she was regarded as the most important writer of fiction in the history of Australia after Patrick White.

Christina Stead was born in Rockdale, a working-class suburb of Sydney, and attended first St. George High School and then the academically selective Sydney Girls' High School; subsequently, she went to Sydney Teachers' College and later became a demonstrator in psychology at the university. She developed an interest in modern fiction and in writing at college, and her novels and short stories all attest a keen perception and understanding of psychological problems and their subtle manifestations. In this respect she has been compared with Russian writers Leo Tolstoy and Fyodor Dostoevski, not without justification.

Seven Poor Men of Sydney was written in Europe, after Stead had left Australia in 1928. It is a study of poverty in an urban environment but (like almost all of her later writing) is directed at an understanding of interpersonal relationships rather than of political and social phenomena. Especially compelling is the treatment of the latent incestuous feelings of Catherine Bagenault and her illegitimate half brother Michael, a veteran who is unable to take action. The descriptions of various locations in Sydney are impressive both in natural detail and in evocation of atmosphere supportive of the story. *The Salzburg Tales* (which includes four stories written while Stead was training to be a teacher) and *The Beauties and Furies* (about a married Englishwoman who goes to live with a younger man, a student in Paris) cannot be said to have advanced Stead's art, though they do demonstrate her interest in certain character types: the prevaricator, the charmer, the domineering father, the doctrinaire, and the nascent feminist.

With *House of All Nations*, Stead entered a new area of fiction: the world of international finance, centered in Paris, and an almost journal-like narration of events. What results is a prolix account of the machinations of Jules Bertillon and his Banque Mercure that result in his personal wealth and the bank's failure. The novel uses as its epigraph Bertillon's observation, "No one ever made enough money," and a Balzacian array of minor characters shows humankind's attempt to overcome the shortfall with the aid of the charming confidence-man banker. Because the House of All Nations is a chic Parisian brothel, the novel's title suggests Stead's satiric intent. (Her husband, William Blake, was a stockbroker and banker, so the details of financial manipulations are presumably reliable.) If the Great Depression made *House of All Nations* a contemporary success, its interest has since diminished; its length and overcrowded canvas of minor characters are clear weaknesses.

Stead's next two books, *The Man Who Loved Children* and *For Love Alone*, are certainly her greatest achievements, though the former was not recognized fully until its republication in 1965 with a long and detailed appreciation by the respected critic Randall Jarrell. In many ways, *The Man Who Loved Children*, which is set in Washington, D.C., is a brutal picture of family life: Sam Pollitt, "a subaltern bureaucrat," and his second wife, Henrietta (Henny), a scion of a wealthy Baltimore family, yet one who could be "beautifully, wholeheartedly vile," have grown apart, and their children are the stakes in their bitter battles. The oldest child, Louisa (by Sam's first wife, now dead), aged twelve, is swept into the vortex of the parental conflict and exhibits extraordinary perceptiveness of the psychological forces at work. Yet she plans her parents' murder. Because of its study of family relationships, emotional shortcomings, and personal priorities, *The Man Who Loved Children* is an acute and meaningful study of modern bourgeois life.

Hardly less compelling and authoritative is *For Love Alone*, Stead's best exposition of the theme of personal discovery through casting off of family, unworthy models, and lovers. Teresa Hawkins (like Stead, a teacher trainee) seeks self-fulfillment—first through adoration of Jonathan Crow, a minor university teacher in Australia, then through attachment to James Quick, an American businessman in England—and escape from her insensitive father, who personifies the belief that women must accept a role of social and sexual dependency. Many readers assumed that this was an overtly feminist novel, but the author vehemently denied this, asserting that it was yet another exploration of the forces that motivate individuals to think and act. Indeed, Stead excels in the analysis of motivation, the description of passions, and the differentiation of male and female speech, particularly in dialogue. In almost every respect, Stead's art is advanced in *For Love Alone*: There is greater economy of plot and characters, the prose is more beautifully textured, and the theme is more clearly and effectively developed.

In Stead's next novel, *Letty Fox: Her Luck*, a study of free love, the texture of the prose and the pace of narration seem inharmonious with the subject and theme. Detail often buries interest and obscures the view. Some critics think this Stead's weakest novel, though others reserve that place for *A Little Tea, a Little Chat*, a quite untypical work that takes as its subject matter the search for money and the pursuit of sex of a middle-aged Wall Street manipulator, Robbie Grant.

The People with the Dogs is a book about an American family. The Massines, New York descendants of nineteenth century Russian liberals, live in a typical brownstone and yet own a thousand-acre unproductive farm. They accommodate their European culture and refinement to the haste and materialism of their immediate environment. As Stead commented, "The Massines have joy and they love each other and live for each other." They personify, somewhat ironically, rootedness in transience, democracy in an aristocratic tradition, and rural simplicity amid urban sophistication. It is a compassionate study.

Dark Places of the Heart purports to be a proletarian novel about Nellie Cotter, a London journalist and bohemian from a Tyneside family who has incestuous impulses (like those of Catherine Bagenault in *Seven Poor Men of Sydney*) and who is married to and deserted by George Cook. Again, Stead details a search for love and friendship, for self. *The Little Hotel*, with its wider range of eccentrics and poseurs, is a more satisfactory fiction set in a nondescript Swiss pension: the genteel poor and their vanities are subjected to Horatian satiric study, and the examination is livened by an almost uncharacteristic levity.

One posthumous work, *I'm Dying Laughing: The Humourist*,

set in the milieu of the American Left in the 1930's and 1940's, draws on the basic elements of all Stead's earlier works: political and social commitments, family feuds, sexual fantasies, political and personal infidelities, betrayals, and the search for love and self-realization. It suggests the impossibility of being both morally upright and rich. Stead's novels have established her as a major modern writer in English and not merely a major Australian author, and *The Man Who Loved Children* and *For Love Alone* remain her most successful fictions.

Marian B. McLeod

Bibliography

Blake, Ann. *Christina Stead's Politics of Place*. Nedlands: University of Western Australia Press, 1999. A political reading of Stead's work, focusing on her social views.

Harris, Margaret, ed. *The Magic Phrase: Critical Essays on Christina Stead*. St. Lucia: University of Queensland Press, 2000. A collection of sixteen essays, some of which review Stead's entire career and other of which concentrate on individual works.

Jarrell, Randall. "An Unread Book." Introduction to *The Man Who Loved Children*, by Christina Stead. New York: Holt, Rinehart and Winston, 1965. This first serious and thorough critical examination of Stead's work incorporates many of the themes on which subsequent critics enlarge.

Lidoff, Joan. *Christina Stead*. New York: Frederick Ungar, 1982. The earliest full reading of Stead's fiction from a feminist perspective, this book concentrates on *The Man Who Loved Children* and *For Love Alone*. Includes an interview, a chronology, and an extensive secondary bibliography.

Pender, Anne. *Christina Stead: Satirist*. Altoona, Victoria, Australia: Common Ground Publishing, 2002. Focuses on Stead's attempt to interpret the history of her own period through satire. Shows the ways in which Stead both uses and reinterprets the conventions of the genre.

Peterson, Teresa. *The Enigmatic Christina Stead*. Melbourne: Melbourne University Press, 2001. Argues that there is a latent subtext of lesbianism and male homosexuality in Stead's work.

Rowley, Hazel. *Christina Stead: A Biography*. New York: Henry Holt, 1994. A good study of Stead's life and times. Includes bibliographical references and an index.

Sheridan, Susan. *Christina Stead*. Bloomington: Indiana University Press, 1988. Intends not to argue that Stead's work is feminist, but to uncover feminist themes in it. The study rejects other critical approaches that place the novels in the naturalistic or international tradition.

Williams, Chris. *Christina Stead: A Life of Letters*. Melbourne: McPhee Gribble, 1989. This admirable and first full-length biography of Stead depends in large part on unpublished materials, including Stead's letters and early drafts of stories, and on interviews with friends and family members.

Yelin, Louise. *From the Margins of Empire: Christina Stead, Doris Lessing, Nadine Gordimer*. Ithaca, N.Y.: Cornell University Press, 1998. Examines the political and social views of the three authors and the themes of imperialism and decolonization.

Sir Richard Steele

British playwright and essayist

Born: Dublin, Ireland; March, 1672
Died: Carmarthen, Wales; September 1, 1729

DRAMA: *The Funeral: Or, Grief-à-la-Mode*, pr. 1701; *The Lying Lover: Or, The Ladies' Friendship*, pr. 1703 (adaptation of Pierre Corneille's play *Le Menteur*); *The Tender Husband: Or, The Accomplished Fools*, pr., pb. 1705 (adaptation of Molière's play *Le Sicilien*); *The Conscious Lovers*, pr. 1722 (adaptation of Terence's play *Andria*); *The Plays of Richard Steele*, pb. 1971 (Shirley Strum Kenny, editor).

POETRY: *The Procession*, 1695; *Prologue to the University of Oxford*, 1706; *Epilogue to the Town*, 1721; *The Occasional Verse of Richard Steele*, 1952 (Rae Blanchard, editor).

NONFICTION: *The Christian Hero*, 1701; *The Tatler*, 1709-1711 (with Joseph Addison; periodical essays); *The Spectator*, 1711-1712, 1714 (with Addison; periodical essays); *The Importance of Dunkirk Reconsidered*, 1713; *The Guardian*, 1713 (with Addison; periodical essays); *The Englishman*, 1713-1714, 1715 (periodical essays); *The Reader*, 1714 (with Addison); *The Lover*, 1714 (with Addison; periodical essays); *The Plebiean*, 1718; *The Theatre*, 1720 (later pb. as *Richard Steele's "The Theatre,"* 1920, 1962; John Loftis, editor); *The Correspondence of Richard Steele*, 1941 (Rae Blanchard, editor); *Tracts and Pamphlets by Richard Steele*, 1944 (Blanchard, editor).

Sir Richard Steele was born in Dublin in March, 1672, the son of an attorney. Both his parents died when he was a child, and he became the ward of a prominent uncle, Henry Gascoigne. Through his uncle's influence he entered the Charterhouse School in 1684, where he met and became the lifelong friend of Joseph Addison (1672-1719). In 1689 he followed Addison to Oxford University, but while Addison remained to take his M.A. and to become a fellow, Steele left without a degree in 1694 to enlist as a private in a regiment of guards under the command of his uncle's employer, the duke of Ormond. On the strength of a poem which he published anonymously, he became in the following year an ensign in Lord Cutts's regiment.

By 1700 he was Captain Steele, stationed at the Tower, and the friend of Sir Charles Sedley (1639-1701), Sir John Vanbrugh (1664-1726), William Congreve (1670-1729), and other wits and writers of the day. In that same year John Dryden died, and Congreve published his last important play, these two latter events marking the sunset of Restoration comedy.

Steele's life as a soldier stationed at the Tower led him into excesses of which he repented, and which caused him to publish in 1701 a small book, *The Christian Hero*, to prove "that no principles but those of religion are sufficient to make a great man." The sentiments expressed in this little volume lost him his popularity among his fellow soldiers, and to regain that popularity he wrote his first comedy, *The Funeral: Or, Grief-à-la-Mode*, for "nothing can make the town so fond of a man as a successful play."

This play, which met with "more than expected success," illustrates the tendency of the age to react against libertine elegance and to return to bourgeois respectability. In it Steele attacks the mockery of grief in the person of Sable the undertaker, the mockery of justice in Puzzle the lawyer, and the popular dramatic disregard for women in the persons of Lady Sharlot and Lady Hariot. This staunch stand for morality is readily seen as unusual when compared with that in the plays of Sir George Etherege (c. 1635-c. 1692), Congreve, and even Vanbrugh. The success of this play led Steele to write *The Lying Lover* in 1703; this work was, however, "dam'd for its piety," as Steele himself said. Steele tried again in 1705 with *The Tender Husband*, which had somewhat more success than its predecessor, but even so, Steele wrote no more plays for seventeen years.

He entered, instead, into politics (quite actively from 1707 to 1710) and began to write periodical essays, most significantly in collaboration with his old friend Addison. These two men, with some little help from other writers now forgotten except by scholars, published first *The Tatler*, which appeared three times weekly from 1709 to 1711, and later *The Spectator*, which appeared daily from 1711 to 1712. Of both papers Steele was the fathering genius. Having served the government's cause through his writing, he was knighted in 1714.

In both these forerunners of the modern newspaper, Steele, writing on subjects ranging from descriptions of London and of life in the country to articles on dueling and the question of immortality, preached the gospel of reformed gentility and true gentle manliness to oppose the artificial elegance symbolized by Etherege's Dorimant (the protagonist of Etherege's comedy *The Man of Mode*, 1676), and he preached in a style supple and precise, warm and penetrating, a style later used by Benjamin Franklin (1706-1790) as a model when he was teaching himself to write. In the dedication to the first collected volume of *The Tatler* (1710), Steele wrote, "The general purpose of this paper, is to expose the false arts of life, to pull off the disguises of cunning, vanity, and affectation, and to recommend a general simplicity in our dress, our discourse, and our behavior."

It is indicative of the trend toward "rational conduct" that these papers were eminently successful in an age when journals, like the lilies of the field, bloomed today and were cast tomorrow into the fire. It is moreover indicative of the influence they had—or the trend they reflected—that when Steele's last play, *The Conscious Lovers*, appeared at Drury Lane in 1722, it ran for eighteen nights and was a great success.

In this play, the contrast with the Restoration is complete. The characters are not fine ladies and gentlemen, but frankly middle class. The lovers do not fence verbally through four acts about their affection before they dare to confess it in the fifth; their mutual love is clear throughout the play, though no amorous words pass between them. Young Bevil, the hero, is not even tainted with rakishness but is thoroughly upright and worthy. The solution to the plot which occurs in the last act, just in time to show virtue rewarded with wealth and consequent lifelong happiness, appears not at all incongruous but achieves its purpose of moving the audience to compassion.

Though the play has a well-knit structure—even the startling denouement is handled with sureness and restraint—and though the expression is easy and natural, it celebrated the funeral of Restoration comedy and the coming-of-age of sentimental comedy. True dramatic comedy was dead; whatever the faults of Restoration comedy, and they were many, it was dramatic, it was funny, and it was sometimes brilliant. *The Conscious Lovers* banished vice and, for a time at least, theatrical immorality was dead. One imagines that Steele would have been pleased, not offended, at William Hazlitt's remark: "It is almost a misnomer to call them comedies; they are rather homilies in dialogues." In any case, Sir Richard Steele had temporarily achieved the purpose he set forth in *The Tatler*. In that respect, he must have gone peacefully to his death. He died September 1, 1729. He lies buried in St. Peter's Church, Carmarthen, Wales.

Bibliography

Bloom, Edward A., and Lillian D. Bloom, eds. *Addison and Steele: The Critical Heritage*. New York: Routledge, 1996. A collection of critical analyses of the works of Steele and Joseph Addison. Bibliography and index.

_______. *Educating the Audience: Addison, Steele, and Eighteenth Century Culture: Papers Presented at a Clark Library Seminar, 15 November 1980*. Los Angeles: William Andrews Clark Memorial Library, University of California, Los Angeles, 1984. A collection of essays presenting critical analysis of the works of Steele and Addison as well as essays on the theater of their time.

Calhoun, Wineton. *Captain Steele: The Early Career*. Baltimore: The Johns Hopkins University Press, 1964. Primarily a biographical study, this book discusses *The Tatler* and *The Spectator* but focuses mostly on the circumstances surrounding them rather than on actual analysis.

Connely, Willard. *Sir Richard Steele*. New York: Charles Scribner's Sons, 1934. This volume is the standard biography on Steele. While it is old, it is relatively useful. The chapters on *The Tatler* and *The Spectator* are helpful, including information on the business aspects of producing the two papers.

Dammers, Richard H. *Richard Steele*. Boston: Twayne, 1982. A good overview of Steele's work. This study discusses Steele's essays, dramas, and includes two excellent chapters on his short fiction in *The Tatler* and *The Spectator.* Contains a chronology and a select bibliography.

Kenny, Shirley S. *The Plays of Richard Steele.* Oxford, England: Clarendon Press, 1971. Contains a substantial introduction to each Steele play, providing information on the sources, the manner of composition, the stage history, and the fame and influence of the play, with notes on the text.

Ketcham, Michael G. *Transparent Designs: Reading, Performance, and Form in the Spectator Papers.* Athens: University of Georgia Press, 1985. This study takes apart *The Spectator* by examining its readers, its treatment of time, family, and language, and the social and historical context. A good, closely detailed examination of *The Spectator.*

Knight, Charles A. *Joseph Addison and Richard Steele: A Reference Guide, 1730-1991.* New York: G. K. Hall, 1994. Annotated bibliographies of works about and by Steele and Addison. Indexes.

_______. "The Spectator's Moral Economy." *Modern Philology* 91 (November, 1993): 161-179. Examines principles of moral economy presented by Joseph Addison and Steele in *The Spectator* to control dreams of endless gains. Argues that Addison and Steele found in the economic order a secular basis for moral behavior that emphasized the common good over individual gain. Suggests that they connected commercial values to values of politeness and restraint.

Loftis, John. *Steele at Drury Lane.* 1952. Reprint. Westport, Conn.: Greenwood Press, 1973. The book details Steele's theatrical career and provides a good understanding of the eighteenth century stage and business management. Includes a useful appendix.

McCrea, Brian. *Addison and Steele Are Dead: The English Department, Its Canon, and the Professionalization of Literary Criticism.* Newark: University of Delaware Press, 1990. Examines the legacy of Steele and Joseph Addison.

Schneider, Ben Ross, Jr. *The Ethos of Restoration Comedy.* Urbana: University of Illinois Press, 1971. Schneider discusses Steele passim but provides a commentary related to major elements in late seventeenth century comedy: satire, the plain-dealing versus the double-dealing characters, criticism of characters who show self-love, and others.

Shelby Steele

American sociologist

Born: Chicago, Illinois; January 1, 1946
Identity: African American

NONFICTION: *The Content of Our Character: A New Vision of Race in America*, 1990; *A Dream Deferred: The Second Betrayal of Black Freedom in America*, 1998.

Shelby Steele's first book, *The Content of Our Character: A New Vision of Race in America*, which contained several of his essays on social issues primarily affecting African Americans, was a bombshell. The book was denounced by many African American leaders, and despite Steele's harsh criticism of nonblacks for their attitude in racial situations, his book was applauded by millions, both black and white, and earned for its author numerous honors and much critical acclaim.

Steele grew up in an all-black community south of Chicago. His father, who left school in the third grade, believed in education as the route to success and pushed his children in that direction. This strong parental influence contributed to Steele's philosophy about how African Americans should gain equality. Steele contended that too many African Americans have come to rely on the preferences demanded by affirmative action programs or on the leverage provided by allegations of racial prejudice rather than on individual initiative. His criticism of racial quotas in the job market and in college admissions, his contention that preference programs such as affirmative action are enslaving, and his call for African Americans to examine their own prejudices put him at odds with many who labeled him a traitor to his race. He was angrily accused of providing comfort to whites, of being an "Uncle Tom," and of being simplistic.

Steele's philosophy was formed, in part, by a strong family that included a twin brother, two sisters, and interracial parents. His father grew up in the South before eventually making his way to Chicago, where he married a white social worker. As a child, Steele attended an all-black elementary school; in high school, he excelled in an integrated environment, and as a senior, he was student council president. His parents involved Steele in the Civil Rights movement in the 1960's, and he became a follower of both Martin Luther King, Jr., and Malcolm X. His early affection was for King. As a student at Coe College in Cedar Rapids, Iowa, he became involved in student civil rights groups adhering to King's philosophy. Later in his college experience, he adopted a more militant stance in keeping with his new role model, Malcolm X, who preached Black Power. During this period, he wore African-style clothing and led campus protests. He also began to identify with what he later called "victimized black Americans"—a condition that he came to rail strongly against and that he views as a weakness in African Americans who claim to be victims as a way of avoiding individual responsibility and initiative.

After receiving his degree from Coe in 1968, Steele entered Southern Illinois University and received a degree in sociology in 1971. He then earned a Ph.D. in English literature in 1974 from the University of Utah. Before completing his education, he married Rita Steele, a white student who eventually became a clinical psychologist. Following his graduation from the University of Utah, Steele began teaching literature at San Jose State University in California. The birth of his two children, Steele contends, gave him another look at his racial identity, and he began to have different ideas about the opportunities that were available to African Americans. This led to several thoughtful essays that appeared in such highly regarded magazines as *Harper's*, *American Scholar*, and *Commentary*. In 1989, he won a National Magazine Award, and one of his essays was named in "The Best American Essays 1989." In 1990, several of his previously published essays were combined with new material in *The Content of Our Character: A New Vision of Race in America*. This book, the title of which echoed a phrase used by Martin Luther King, made Steele a literary and philosophical celebrity. He became the subject of numerous articles and interviews that appeared in such publications as *Time* and *The New York Times*. He also hosted a Public Broadcasting Service documentary on the murder of a young African American boy by a group of whites in the Bensonhurst section of Brooklyn, New York.

Steele's book was named a Book-of-the-Month Club alternate selection and was honored with a National Book Critics Circle Award. The book caused a heated debate, primarily between scholars and leaders in the African American community, and opened up new thoughts and new ideas about how racial equality might be fully achieved. Those who disagreed with Steele accused him of not fully understanding the depth of racism in America and claimed he was too far removed from those on the lower social rungs of the community to understand the reality of their situation. Yet supporters, many labeled as "new black conservatives," defended Steele's philosophy and called for individual achievements as a way for African Americans to gain full acceptance in the larger society and to remove their own feelings of inferiority. In 1994, Steele was appointed a senior fellow of the Hoover Institute at Stanford University, a public policy research institution devoted to the study of politics and economics founded by President Herbert Hoover in 1919.

A Dream Deferred, Steele's second book, expanded his critique of black victimization and affirmative action, likening government intervention in racial relations, no matter how well-intentioned, to the worst practices of slavery, segregation, and even Nazi Germany and Soviet Communism. Steele makes a distinction between civil rights—the rights owed to any person in the United States, regardless of color—and affirmative action, which singles out color and ethnicity to give one group rights not shared by all. Such racial preference programs, he argues, serve more to assuage white guilt over racism than to assist blacks in bettering their lives, and leave the roles of victimizer and victim intact and dysfunctionally codependant. Steele's writings thus served to open up a new debate that continued to affect the discussion of American racial problems into the twenty-first century.

Kay Hively

Bibliography

Cooper, Matthew. "Inside Racism." *The Washington Monthly* 23, no. 9 (October, 1990). Takes some issue with Steele's comments about affirmative action but generally supports his ideas.

Loury, Glenn C. "Why Steele Demands More of Blacks than of Whites." *Academic Questions* 5 (Fall, 1992): 19-23. Provides an overview and analysis of the controversy aroused by *The Content of Our Character*.

Prager, Jeffrey. "Self Reflection(s): Subjectivity and Racial Subordination in the Contemporary African American Writer." *Social Identities* 1 (August, 1995): 355-371. Compares Steele's *The Content of Our Character* and John Wideman's *Philadelphia Fire* (1990) to reveal these authors' confrontation with self-expression and self-definition in the American society which denies African American individuality.

Vassallo, Phillip. "Guarantees of a Promised Land: Language and Images of Race Relations in Shelby Steele's *The Content of Our Character*." *ETC: A Review of General Semantics* 49 (Spring, 1992): 36-42. Analyzes the language Steele uses to make his case in his book, especially his coinage of phrases such as "race-holding" and "harangue-flagellation ritual" to frame his argument.

Lincoln Steffens

American journalist

Born: San Francisco, California; April 6, 1866
Died: Carmel, California; August 9, 1936

NONFICTION: *The Shame of the Cities*, 1904 (journalism); *The Struggle for Self-Government*, 1906 (journalism); *Upbuilders*, 1909 (journalism); *Moses in Red*, 1926 (philosophy); *The Autobiography of Lincoln Steffens*, 1931; *Lincoln Steffens Speaking*, 1936 (journalism); *The Letters of Lincoln Steffens*, 1938.

Joseph Lincoln Steffens, the most notable of the early twentieth century muckrakers and one of the most important journalists of his time, was born in San Francisco on April 6, 1866. The son of Joseph Steffens, a prominent businessman, and his wife, English-born Elizabeth Symes, he grew up in Sacramento, where the family moved in 1870. Childhood explorations took precedence over schooling and discipline until his parents seized the initiative and enrolled him in a military academy. After an additional year with a private tutor, Steffens entered the University of California at Berkeley and earned his degree in 1889. Declining his father's offer to join his business, he decided to pursue a general interest in philosophy and began graduate study in Germany. There, his interests broadened to include ethics and psychology. When Steffens finally returned to New York City in 1892, his father discontinued financial support and forced him to seek work.

Steffens's first job was covering Wall Street as a reporter for the *New York Evening Post*. He quickly became disillusioned with big business. Steffens also worked as a police reporter. He soon discovered that police, criminals, politicians, and businessmen often worked together for mutual benefit—with the public usually the loser. He was beginning to piece together an understanding of interdependence among various social elements that he would later describe as a "System."

After a brief stint as a city editor, Steffens moved to *McClure's* magazine in 1901. There he gave his fascination with civic corruption a national scope. His "Tweed Days in St. Louis," which appeared in the October, 1902, *McClure's*, gave him the distinction of being the first "muckraker" and made him an influential figure in the emerging Progressive movement. Steffens continued his systematic research into the causes of municipal corruption and broadened his study to include other municipalities. He found a cycle of corruption that was pervasive and consistent. His articles, collected in *The Shame of the Cities*, confirmed his earlier suspicion that politics and business were inseparable. Yet Steffens was optimistic, hoping that an informed public would become righteously indignant, abandon its moral apathy, and work to make government more democratic.

As Progressivism moved from the city to the state level, Steffens followed. He soon published *The Struggle for Self-Government*, a series of investigative articles on state politics. Certain that corruption had become institutionalized and that a "System" did in fact exist, Steffens believed that civic awareness in itself would be insufficient to bring about meaningful reform unless coupled with strong progressive leadership. As his interest in the role of leadership in the cause of national reform grew, he completed *Upbuilders*. The book presented chapters on five individuals who had successfully applied the Golden Rule as a means of solving social and political problems. Steffens hoped to illustrate the potential of applied Christianity as an ethical basis for human relationships, but the Golden Rule appeared to be unobtainable for society as a whole. Middle-class hypocrisy prevented it.

Steffens became increasingly disillusioned. He suggested that perhaps the greatest evil in society was "privilege"—special legislation, "pull," and "protection." He analyzed this point in a series of articles he wrote in 1910 and 1911 entitled "It: An Exposition of the Sovereign Political Power of Organized Business." His knowledge of the workings of the political economy was increasing, but so too was his belief that changes far more drastic than those sought by most Progressives were necessary. Steffens's pessimism increased after the death of his wife in 1911. Seeking rejuvenation, he moved to New York's Greenwich Village and joined the circle of writers, artists, and socialists gathered by Mabel Dodge (1879-1962). The Mexican and Russian revolutions provided him with opportunities to observe violent social upheavals, and he began to flirt with the idea of historical determinism. In Russia, Steffens thought he had truly witnessed the future. Finally, the "System" had been destroyed. As a defender of the goals of the Russian Revolution and as an admirer of Vladimir Ilich Lenin (1870-1924), Steffens wrote *Moses in Red*. In comparing modern revolutions with the story of Moses in the Old Testament, Steffens hoped to show that revolution was a scientifically determinable phenomenon. If humankind chose to ignore the laws of nature and maintain outdated forms of economy (capitalism), then revolution was inevitable.

In the mid-1920's, Steffens began writing his autobiography. He thought that he could use his life as an instructive example of a process of "unlearning" the ingrained political and social processes of his society. He wanted to share his wisdom with a younger generation, in which he placed hope for the future. His last book, *Lincoln Steffens Speaking*, published after his death in 1936, was a collection of newspaper articles in which he attempted to explain the collapse of the economic system during the Great Depression.

Steffens's importance rests with his talent as a journalist and social thinker. His muckraking books provide insights into business, politics, and human nature that embody the liberal prescription for a truly democratic society. His autobiography is a classic recounting of a lifetime spent in search of a democratic-humanistic ideal. Steffens has been criticized for being superficial and for lacking an ideological center. The charges are somewhat unfair. He offered a fundamental critique of capitalism and the profit motive. He challenged the legitimacy of corporate and political elites and helped to generate a mass reaction to injustice. He appeared to wander intellectually because he never stopped asking questions; political analysis always seemed to take precedence over political commitment.

Steven L. Piott

Bibliography

Filler, Louis. *Muckraking and Progressivism in the American Tradition*. Somerset, N.J.: Transaction, 1996. Places Steffens in the context of the larger muckraking movement.

Horton, Russell M. *Lincoln Steffens*. New York: Twayne, 1974. An excellent, short, intellectual biography.

Kaplan, Justin. *Lincoln Steffens*. New York: Simon & Schuster, 1974. A detailed, popular account.

Palermo, P. F. *Lincoln Steffens*. Boston: Twayne, 1978. A brief analysis of Steffens's writings and career.

Stinson, Robert. *Lincoln Steffens*. New York: F. Ungar, 1979. An account of Steffens as writer and journalist.

Winter, Ella. *And Not to Yield: An Autobiography*. New York: Harcourt, Brace, and World, 1963. An excellent source for personal information on Steffens's later years written by his widow.

Winter, Ella, and Herbert Shapiro, eds. *The World of Lincoln Steffens*. New York: Hill and Wang, 1962. A collection of articles from Steffens's post-muckraking years.

Wright, Melanie Jane. *Moses in America: The Cultural Uses of Biblical Narrative*. New York: Oxford University Press, 2002. An analysis of three retellings of Moses's life, including Steffens's *Moses in Red*.

Wallace Stegner

American novelist, short-story writer, essayist, historian, and biographer

Born: Lake Mills, Iowa; February 18, 1909
Died: Santa Fe, New Mexico; April 13, 1993

LONG FICTION: *Remembering Laughter*, 1937; *The Potter's House*, 1938; *On a Darkling Plain*, 1940; *Fire and Ice*, 1941; *The Big Rock Candy Mountain*, 1943; *Second Growth*, 1947; *The Preacher and the Slave*, 1950; *A Shooting Star*, 1961; *All the Little Live Things*, 1967; *Angle of Repose*, 1971; *The Spectator Bird*, 1976; *Recapitulation*, 1979; *Joe Hill*, 1980; *Crossing to Safety*, 1987.

SHORT FICTION: *The Women on the Wall*, 1950; *The City of the Living, and Other Stories*, 1956; *Collected Stories of Wallace Stegner*, 1990.

NONFICTION: *Mormon Country*, 1942; *One Nation*, 1945 (with the editors of *Look*); *Look at America: The Central Northwest*, 1947; *The Writer in America*, 1951; *Beyond the Hundredth Meridian: John Wesley Powell and the Second Opening of the West*, 1954; *Wolf Willow: A History, a Story, and a Memory of the Last Plains Frontier*, 1962; *The Gathering of Zion: The Story of the Mormon Trail*, 1964; *The Sound of Mountain Water*, 1969; *The Uneasy Chair: A Biography of Bernard DeVoto*, 1974; *Ansel Adams: Images, 1923-1974*, 1974; *One Way to Spell Man*, 1982; *American Places*, 1983; *Conversations with Wallace Stegner on Western History and Literature*, 1983; *The American West as Living Space*, 1987; *On the Teaching of Creative Writing: Responses to a Series of Questions*, 1988 (Edward Connery Lathem, editor); *Where the Bluebird Sings to the Lemonade Springs: Living and Writing in the West*, 1992; *Marking the Sparrow's Fall: Wallace Stegner's American West*, 1998 (Page Stegner, editor); *Stealing Glances: Three Interviews with Wallace Stegner*, 1998 (James R. Hepworth, editor); *On Teaching and Writing Fiction*, 2002 (Lynn Stegner, editor).

EDITED TEXTS: *An Exposition Workshop*, 1939; *Readings for Citizens at War*, 1941; *Stanford Short Stories, 1946*, 1947 (with Richard Scowcroft); *The Writer's Art: A Collection of Short Stories*, 1950 (with Scowcroft and Boris Ilyin); *This Is Dinosaur: The Echo Park and Its Magic Rivers*, 1955; *The Exploration of the Colorado River of the West*, 1957; *Great American Short Stories*, 1957 (with Mary Stegner); *Selected American Prose: The Realistic Movement*, 1958; *Report on the Lands of the Arid Region of the United States*, 1962; *Modern Composition*, 1964 (4 volumes); *The American Novel: From Cooper to Faulkner*, 1965; *Twenty Years of Stanford Short Stories*, 1966; *The Letters of Bernard DeVoto*, 1975.

In a varied career of more than half a century, Wallace Earle Stegner (STEHG-nehr) has earned an honored place in American letters and is one of the foremost authors to have been closely associated with western North American themes. He was born in Lake Mills, Iowa, to George H. Stegner and his wife, Hilda (Paulson) Stegner, but his family soon moved from the Midwest to live in a succession of western locales ranging from southern Saskatchewan to Salt Lake City, Utah, where he entered the University of Utah in 1925. Stegner was a shy, quiet child, but he became both a fine athlete and scholar despite a domineering father and the displacements of his early family life. At the university, he became a student of the noted writer Vardis Fisher, whose work was an early influence upon him. Completing a B.A. there in 1930, Stegner then attended the University of Iowa, from which he received an M.A. in 1932 and a Ph.D. in 1935.

In his mid-twenties, Stegner was poised for a career either as a teacher or as a writer, but by 1937, he had chosen both, for in that year he gained the first of several university appointments and his first major fiction work, *Remembering Laughter*, was published. This novella is the story of an Iowa farmer, Alec Stuart, and his prim wife, Margaret, whose vital younger sister is drawn into an affair with Alec. The heart of the tale describes the affair's somber legacy of pregnancy, alienation, and death, relieved only at the end by the courageous departure of the fourteen-year-old son/nephew to find a new life. While *Remembering Laughter* is far surpassed by most of Stegner's later fiction, it is a well-wrought statement of many themes he would later explore, particularly that of conflicts within families.

From 1937 to 1945, Stegner taught creative writing at the University of Utah, University of Wisconsin, and Harvard University. Stegner's next three novels describe other varieties of social, emotional, and physical isolation. *The Potter's House*, set in California, concerns a deaf-mute artisan and his family, whose life is upset by the meddling of the potter's brother. *On a Darkling Plain* is the story of a young Canadian soldier who, wounded by gas in World War I, seeks recuperative isolation by homesteading in Saskatchewan, only to be brought back to a sense of community in joining with his neighbors to combat the deadly influenza epidemic of

1918. *Fire and Ice* forgoes the connection with the land seen in Stegner's first novels and concerns the struggles of a midwestern college student caught in conflicts of ideology and personal conduct.

In these few years, Stegner had completed his novelist's apprenticeship, and in 1943 he achieved his first critical and popular success with *The Big Rock Candy Mountain*. This semiautobiographical novel is dominated by the character of the ambitious but erratic Bo Mason, a seeker after the American Dream whose search for prosperity pushes the limits of the law and family cohesion alike. The events of the novel closely parallel the Stegner family's years in Saskatchewan, Montana, Washington, and Utah as Wallace's father pursued a futile series of money-making schemes. In large measure, this first longer novel set the tone of Stegner's future writing, particularly in suggesting that the restless individualism of Bo Mason is the disabling, if not destructive, expression of an outworn frontier mythology.

In 1945 he accepted a position at Stanford University, where he stayed for the remainder of his academic career, until 1971. After *The Big Rock Candy Mountain*, Stegner might conceivably have become identified exclusively with the West (and in fact he remained, throughout his career, a spokesman for the West both as a writer and as a conservationist), but he chose New England as the locale of his next novel, *Second Growth*, a study of change and renewal in social values following World War II. Almost all the author's subsequent books have had western locales, but Stegner has resisted easy classification as a "regional" writer by diversifying his themes and by examining their widest cultural implications. Stegner's 1972 Pulitzer Prize-winning novel *Angle of Repose*, perhaps the best known of all of his books, is a key example of his wish to examine major issues such as the relationship of the West and the East in American culture and the significance of history in personal and social life. The novel's narrator, Lyman Ward, is an ailing professor of history engaged in distilling the letters and diaries of his grandparents, whose married life in the nineteenth century West Lyman discovers to have been a web of misunderstanding. Susan Ward, his grandmother, regarded her marriage as an undeserved exile from the genteel East, while her husband, a visionary and idealistic mining engineer, suffered professional failure and Susan's incomprehension. The geological term "angle of repose," denoting the incline at which a landslide or talus slope achieves stability, serves as a metaphor for the uneasy stability of relationships maintained at cross-purposes. Stegner achieved a new level of thematic and structural richness in *Angle of Repose* by mingling past and present while maintaining control of the narrative through his alter ego Lyman Ward, who expresses Stegner's belief in "life chronological, not life existential."

In the short story "Field Guide to the Western Birds" and in the novel *All the Little Live Things*, Stegner developed the character Joe Allston, who, like Lyman Ward, is a vigorously ironic dissenter from contemporary American social and moral values. Allston reappeared in *The Spectator Bird*, a National Book Award winner in 1977 that was well received by the public, though some critics found the older Allston tedious, if believable. *The Spectator Bird* is another retrospective novel but uses European locales and themes (surprisingly, the Danish writer Isak Dinesen is a minor character). The theme of remembrance was further explored in *Recapitulation*, which reintroduces the character of Bruce Mason of *The Big Rock Candy Mountain*, and a novel set in the Midwest and New England, *Crossing to Safety*. An account of Stegner's career as a novelist reveals chronological gaps that were largely taken up with work on short fiction and nonfiction writing. In his short stories, Stegner often rehearses material that he later explores in novels. For example, both "The Blue-Winged Teal" (perhaps his best short story) and "Maiden in a Tower" make an appearance, in altered form, in *Recapitulation* two decades after their publication in the collection *The City of the Living, and Other Stories*. Similarly, within the body of his nonfiction, the commissioned documentary study *One Nation* anticipates *Second Growth*, and more indirectly, Stegner's scholarly historical study *Beyond the Hundredth Meridian* precedes *Angle of Repose* in its attention to the conflict between myth and reality in western development.

While his acclaimed book on John Wesley Powell is straight history, Stegner's *Wolf Willow*, subtitled *A History, a Story, and a Memory of the Last Plains Frontier*, combines autobiography, history, and two short stories, "Genesis" and "Carrion Spring." Widely admired in Canada as well as the United States, *Wolf Willow* is centered on the author's reminiscence of the part of his childhood spent in East End, Saskatchewan, at the foot of the Cypress Hills. Notwithstanding the fact that it was written before the midpoint of his literary career, the book draws together so many of Stegner's strengths as a writer, including his mastery of the short story, his use of evocative family chronicle, and his appreciation of the role of history and environment in daily life, that it may be taken as a paradigm of the work of this unusually versatile man of letters. Stegner died in 1993 from injuries sustained in an automobile accident.

C. S. McConnell

Bibliography

Arthur, Anthony, ed. *Critical Essays on Wallace Stegner.* Boston: G. K. Hall, 1982. Although not an exhaustive discussion of Stegner's works, these essays cover much of his most important writing, including his novels and short fiction. Includes an interview with Stegner and an introductory essay.

Benson, Jackson J. *Wallace Stegner: His Life and Work.* New York: Viking Press, 1996. A biography that argues against pigeonholing Stegner as a Western writer. Focuses on the people and events that most influenced Stegner's art, including Robert Frost and Bernard DeVoto. Covers Stegner's teaching career and his influence on such writers as Ken Kesey, Edward Abbey, Wendell Berry, and Larry McMurtry.

Burrows, Russell. "Wallace Stegner's Version of Pastoral." *Western American Literature* 25 (May, 1990): 15-25. Burrows discusses the importance of the topic of ecology in Stegner's fiction. The article includes some discussion of *Crossing to Safety.* A more penetrating review of that book, by Jackson J. Benson, follows Burrows's article.

Colberg, Nancy. *Wallace Stegner: A Descriptive Bibliography.* Lewiston, Idaho: Confluence Press, 1990. This text contains detailed descriptions of Stegner's works, from his very early writing to *The American West as Living Space*. Colberg also provides sections for other Stegner material, such as contributions to books and edited works. A short appendix that also serves as a secondary bibliography is a good resource for the original publication information for Stegner's individual short stories.

Cook-Lynn, Elizabeth. *Why I Can't Read Wallace Stegner, and Other Essays*. Madison: University of Wisconsin Press, 1996. In the title essay of this collection, Cook-Lynn, a Native American, challenges Stegner's view of Native American culture, particularly his claim that Western history ended in 1890, the year of the massacre at Wounded Knee, and his statement that the Plains Indians are gone forever.

Dillman, Richard H. "Wallace Stegner." In *Critical Survey of Long Fiction*, edited by Carl Rollyson. 2d rev. ed. Pasadena, Calif.: Salem Press, 2000. An overview of Stegner's life and analysis of his novels.

Meine, Curt, ed. *Wallace Stegner and the Continental Vision: Essays on Literature, History, and Landscape*. Washington, D.C.: Island Press, 1997. A collection of papers presented at a 1996 symposium in Madison, Wisconsin. Includes essays on Stegner and the shaping of the modern West, the art of storytelling, history, environmentalism, politics, and bioregionalism.

Mosher, Howard Frank. "The Mastery of Wallace Stegner." *The Washington Post*, October 4, 1987. This review of *Crossing to Safety* includes some biographical information on Stegner as well as an in-depth discussion of the novel.

Nelson, Nancy Owne. "Land Lessons in an 'Unhistoried' West: Wallace Stegner's California." In *San Francisco in Fiction: Essays in a Regional Literature*, edited by David Fine and Paul Skenazy. Albuquerque: University of New Mexico Press, 1995. Argues that Stegner's California experience from the 1940's to the 1970's helped to shape the environmental philosophy of his work. Discusses Stegner's preservationist position in several fictional and nonfictional works.

Peden, William, and Jo-Ellen Lipman Boon. "Wallace Stegner." In *Critical Survey of Short Fiction*, edited by Charles E. May. 2d rev. ed. Pasadena, Calif.: Salem Press, 2001. A thorough overview of Stegner's life and career, emphasizing his short stories.

Rankin, Charles E., ed. *Wallace Stegner: Man and Writer.* Albuquerque: University of New Mexico Press, 1996. Essays by various critics on Stegner's life and art.

Robinson, Forrest Glen, and Margaret G. Robinson. *Wallace Stegner.* Boston: Twayne, 1977. Part of Twayne's United States Authors series, this volume provides a brief chronology of personal and professional events in Stegner's life and general biographical information.

Stegner, Wallace. "The Art of Fiction: An Interview with Wallace Stegner." Interview by James R. Hepworth. *The Paris Review* 115 (Summer, 1990): 58-90. In this interview, Stegner talks about how he became a writer, as well as about writing in general. Although no references are included, this article is useful for the firsthand information it provides about Stegner through the interview process.

_______. "Back to Work After Bora-Bora." Interview by Eden Ross Lipson. *The New York Times Book Review* 92 (September 20, 1987): 14. This interview with Stegner includes his reflections on writing *Crossing to Safety* as well as a discussion of that novel.

Stegner, Wallace, and Richard Etulain. *Conversations with Wallace Stegner.* Rev. ed. Salt Lake City: University of Utah Press, 1990. Expanded edition of a book that first came out in 1983; a later interview section has been added to the first part of the book. In it, Stegner talks about all of his work up to *Crossing to Safety.* Includes biographical information in the form of answers to interview questions and also covers Stegner's view of the American literary West as well as the West itself.

Willrich, Patricia Rowe. "A Perspective on Wallace Stegner." *The Virginia Quarterly Review* 67 (Spring, 1991): 240-258. This article covers the high points of Stegner's long career as a writer and scholar, giving both biographical details and information about his work.

Gertrude Stein

American poet, playwright, and novelist

Born: Allegheny, Pennsylvania; February 3, 1874
Died: Neuilly-sur-Seine, France; July 27, 1946
Identity: Gay or bisexual

LONG FICTION: *Three Lives*, 1909; *The Making of Americans*, 1925; *Lucy Church Amiably*, 1930; *A Long Gay Book*, 1932; *Ida, a Novel*, 1941; *Brewsie and Willie*, 1946; *Blood on the Dining-Room Floor*, 1948; *Things as They Are*, 1950 (originally known as *Q. E. D.*); *Mrs. Reynolds and Five Earlier Novelettes, 1931-1942*, 1952; *A Novel of Thank You*, 1958.

DRAMA: *Geography and Plays*, pb. 1922; *Operas and Plays*, pb. 1932; *Four Saints in Three Acts*, pr., pb. 1934; *In Savoy: Or, Yes Is for a Very Young Man (A Play of the Resistance in France)*, pr., pb. 1946; *The Mother of Us All*, pr. 1947; *Last Operas and Plays*, pb. 1949; *In a Garden: An Opera in One Act*, pb. 1951; *Lucretia Borgia*, pb. 1968; *Selected Operas and Plays*, pb. 1970.

POETRY: *Tender Buttons: Objects, Food, Rooms*, 1914; *Before the Flowers of Friendship Faded Friendship Faded*, 1931; *Two (Hitherto Unpublished) Poems*, 1948; *Bee Time Vine, and Other Pieces, 1913-1927*, 1953; *Stanzas in Meditation, and Other Poems, 1929-1933*, 1956.

NONFICTION: *Composition as Explanation*, 1926; *How to Write*, 1931; *The Autobiography of Alice B. Toklas*, 1933; *Matisse, Picasso, and Gertrude Stein, with Two Shorter Stories*, 1933; *Portraits and Prayers*, 1934; *Lectures in America*, 1935; *Narration: Four Lectures*, 1935; *The Geographical History of America*, 1936; *Everybody's Autobiography*, 1937; *Picasso*, 1938; *Paris, France*, 1940; *What Are Masterpieces?*, 1940; *Wars I Have Seen*, 1945; *Four in America*, 1947; *Reflections on the Atomic Bomb*, 1973; *How Writing Is Written*, 1974; *The Letters of Gertrude Stein and Thornton Wilder*, 1996 (Edward Burns and Ulla E. Dydo, editors); *Baby Precious Always Shines: Selected Love Notes Between Gertrude Stein and Alice B. Toklas*, 1999 (Kay Turner, editor).

CHILDREN'S/YOUNG ADULT LITERATURE: *The World Is Round*, 1939.

MISCELLANEOUS: *The Gertrude Stein First Reader and Three Plays*, 1946; *The Yale Edition of the Unpublished Writings of Gertrude Stein*, 1951-1958 (8 volumes; Carl Van Vechten, editor); *Selected Writings of Gertrude Stein*, 1962.

Gertrude Stein, who studied psychology under William James (1842-1910) at Harvard University and went to medical school at The Johns Hopkins University, became one of the United States' most celebrated expatriates. Abandoning her medical studies just months short of graduation, Stein moved to Paris in 1903 and, except for occasional brief visits, she never returned to the United States.

Stein spent her childhood in Europe and until her teens was more comfortable speaking French and German than English. Her parents—Daniel Stein, a businessman who became vice president of the Omnibus Cable Company in San Francisco, and Amelia Keyser Stein—were both dead before Gertrude Stein went east in 1893. Stein left Oakland, California, where the family had lived, to enter Harvard's annex, later Radcliffe College. Stein's oldest brother, Michael, set up trust funds that assured Gertrude and her siblings life incomes sufficient to sustain them. Gertrude's closest family connection was with her brother Leo, two years her junior, whom she joined in Paris, where he lived, in 1903.

Stein was always interested in the essence of how people communicate. At Harvard, she had conducted experiments in automatic writing, and she was struck by the poetry and repetitiveness of what her subjects produced. In France, she came under the spell of novelist Gustave Flaubert (1821-1880), whom she translated, and of the impressionist artist Paul Cézanne (1839-1906). From Cézanne, she imbibed the notion that everything in an artistic composition is as important as every other thing in the composition. Working with words, she began to transpose this idea into her writing, first in *Three Lives*, then in the rambling novel *The Making of Americans.* Such emerging cubists as Pablo Picasso (1881-1973), Henri Matisse (1869-1954), and Marcel Duchamp (1887-1968)—frequent callers at 27 rue de Fleurus, where Gertrude lived from 1903 until 1938— gave Stein the idea of applying to writing principles with which the cubists were experimenting in art.

Just as cubists used paint and form as their building blocks, so did Stein consciously strive to strip writing—which she approached as the universal poetry—to its essences: words, surfaces, rhythms, repetitions, and finally, entities. The last of these, her most significant literary achievement, is exemplified by her oft-quoted but little understood utterance that "Rose is a rose is a rose is a rose. . . ," a categorical statement of her concept of absolute quintessence, which harks back to the interest in discovering universals with which William James had challenged her at Harvard. Stein, like the pre-Socratic philosophers, embarked on a quest for essences, seeking to discover them in words, the building blocks of thought.

Sitting for Picasso some ninety times in 1906 while he was painting her portrait, Stein talked extensively about cubism, with which Picasso was then experimenting, and about her notions that words have equal value and that people think continuously in seemingly chaotic and repetitive ways. She was beginning to formulate standards and methods of verbal portraiture that would defy current literary conventions and would result in such stylistically controversial works as *Three Lives* and "Portrait of Mabel Dodge at the Villa Curonia," as well as to such subsequent works as *Matisse, Picasso, and Gertrude Stein*; *Picasso*; and *Mrs. Reynolds and Five Earlier Novelettes, 1931-1942*.

From 1907 until her death, Gertrude Stein lived with her friend and lover Alice B. Toklas (1877-1967). Stein's close relationship with her brother Leo deteriorated and came to an end around 1914, near the start of her literary career, which Leo disparaged. Stimulated by the composers, artists, and writers with whom she was regularly surrounded, Stein wrote profusely in every possible creative medium. During her lifetime, few academicians took Stein's work seriously.

Stein was, however, writing at the beginning of an age when literary theorists such as Jacques Derrida, Roland Barthes, Harold Bloom, Norman Holland, Helen Vendler, Jane Tompkins, Fredric Jameson, Jacques Lacan, and others would begin to examine writing in the light of sophisticated theoretical constructs derived from psychology, linguistics, and rhetoric. Clearly Stein was a monumental pioneer in language whose contributions to the understanding of literature have not yet been wholly appreciated.

R. Baird Shuman

Bibliography

Bloom, Harold, ed. *Modern Critical Views: Gertrude Stein*. New York: Chelsea House, 1986. Essays written by leading Stein scholars deal with biographical as well as feminist, intellectual, and physical issues. Concludes with a useful chronology of Stein's life and work.

Bowers, Jane Palatini. *Gertrude Stein*. New York: St. Martin's Press, 1993. A succinct, feminist-oriented introduction to Stein, with separate chapters on the short fiction, novels, and plays. Includes notes and bibliography.

Brinnin, John Malcom. *The Third Rose: Gertrude Stein and Her World*. Boston: Little, Brown, 1959. Aside from its significant biographical value, this study contains provocative comments on Stein's writing, twentieth century painting, and modern intellectual and artistic movements. Includes a useful bibliography.

Curnutt, Kirk, ed. *The Critical Response to Gertrude Stein*. Westport, Conn.: Greenwood Press, 2000. While including quintessential pieces on Stein by Carl Van Vechten, William Carlos Williams, and Katherine Anne Porter, this guide to her critical reception also includes previously obscure estimations from contemporaries such as H. L. Mencken, Mina Loy, and Conrad Aiken.

DeKoven, Marianne. *A Different Language: Gertrude Stein's Experimental Writing*. Madison: University of Wisconsin Press, 1983. Viewing the incoherence and unrestrictive play in the writing as essentially positive forces, DeKoven argues that Stein's writing successfully overcame conventional expectations of meaning and form. Contains notes and an index.

Dubnick, Randa. *The Structure of Obscurity: Gertrude Stein, Language, and Cubism*. Urbana: University of Illinois Press, 1984. Dubnick's interdisciplinary study deals not only with Gertrude Stein but also with cubism, structuralism, and semiotics. The author distinguishes between Stein's prose (genuine cubism), which exaggerates syntax and minimizes vocabulary, and poetry (synthetic cubism), which abbreviates syntax and extends vocabulary. Includes a bibliography.

Hoffman, Michael J. *Gertrude Stein*. Boston: Twayne, 1976. A useful book with strong analyses of Stein's writing and interesting sidelights on its production and its relationship to the avant-garde movements of the period. Especially strong on cubist influences.

Kellner, Bruce, ed. *A Gertrude Stein Companion*. New York: Greenwood Press, 1988. Kellner supplies a helpful introduction on how to read Stein. The volume includes a study of Stein and literary tradition, her manuscripts, and her various styles, and biographical sketches of her friends and enemies. Provides an annotated bibliography of criticism.

Knapp, Bettina. *Gertrude Stein*. New York: Continuum, 1990. A general introduction to Stein's life and art. Discusses her stylistic breakthrough in the stories in *Three Lives*, focusing on repetition and the use of the continuous present. Devotes a long chapter to *Tender Buttons* as one of Stein's most innovative and esoteric works; discusses the nonreferential nature of language in the fragments.

Pierpont, Claudia Roth. *Passionate Minds: Women Rewriting the World*. New York: Alfred A. Knopf, 2000. Evocative, interpretive essays on the life paths and works of twelve women, including Stein, connecting the circumstances of their lives with the shapes, styles, subjects, and situations of their art.

Ruddick, Lisa. *Reading Gertrude Stein: Body, Text, Gnosis*. Ithaca, N.Y.: Cornell University Press, 1990. Ruddick's study combines poststructuralism with a humanist understanding of the artistic process; she sees *Tender Buttons* as Stein's work of genius because it orients the reader ethically rather than disorienting the reader in the play of language.

Simon, Linda. *Gertrude Stein Remembered*. Lincoln: University of Nebraska Press, 1994. Consists of short memoirs of the modernist writer by her colleagues and contemporaries. Selections include pieces by Daniel-Henri Kahnweiler, Sylvia Beach, Sherwood Anderson, Cecil Beaton, and Eric Sevareid, who offer intimate and often informal views of Stein.

Will, Barbara. *Gertrude Stein, Modernism, and the Problem of "Genius."* Edinburgh: Edinburgh University Press, 2000. A chronological study of Stein's development of her concept of "genius" with much historical context.

John Steinbeck

American novelist and short-story writer

Born: Salinas, California; February 27, 1902
Died: New York, New York; December 20, 1968

LONG FICTION: *Cup of Gold*, 1929; *The Pastures of Heaven*, 1932; *To a God Unknown*, 1933; *Tortilla Flat*, 1935; *In Dubious Battle*, 1936; *The Red Pony*, 1937, 1938, 1945; *Of Mice and Men*, 1937; *The Grapes of Wrath*, 1939; *The Moon Is Down*, 1942; *Cannery Row*, 1945; *The Pearl*, 1945 (serial), 1947 (book); *The Wayward Bus*, 1947; *Burning Bright*, 1950; *East of Eden*, 1952; *Sweet Thursday*, 1954; *The Short Reign of Pippen IV*, 1957; *The Winter of Our Discontent*, 1961.

SHORT FICTION: *Saint Katy the Virgin*, 1936; *The Long Valley*, 1938.

DRAMA: *Of Mice and Men*, pr., pb. 1937; *The Moon Is Down*, pr. 1942; *Burning Bright*, pb. 1951.

SCREENPLAYS: *The Forgotten Village*, 1941; *Lifeboat*, 1944; *A Medal for Benny*, 1945; *The Pearl*, 1945; *The Red Pony*, 1949; *Viva Zapata!*, 1952.

NONFICTION: *Their Blood Is Strong*, 1938; *The Forgotten Village*, 1941; *Sea of Cortez*, 1941 (with Edward F. Ricketts); *Bombs Away*, 1942; *A Russian Journal*, 1948 (with Robert Capa); *Once There Was a War*, 1958; *Travels with Charley: In Search of America*, 1962; *Letters to Alicia*, 1965; *America and Americans*, 1966; *Journal of a Novel*, 1969; *Steinbeck: A Life in Letters*, 1975 (Elaine Steinbeck and Robert Wallsten, editors); *America and Americans, and Selected Nonfiction*, 2002 (Susan Shillinglaw and Jackson J. Benson, editors).

TRANSLATION: *The Acts of King Arthur and His Noble Knights*, 1976.

Winner of the Nobel Prize in Literature for 1962, John Ernst Steinbeck secured his place in American literature largely on the basis of his inimitable novel *The Grapes of Wrath*, which defined an epoch in American life by brilliantly combining the documentary quality of journalism with the superior insight of highly imaginative fiction. Steinbeck grew up in California, close to itinerant farm laborers and to the economic struggles brought on by the Depression. Although Steinbeck attended Stanford University intermittently in the early 1920's and supported himself with odd jobs, his earliest stories reflect his interest in the nature-oriented lives of simple workers and peasants, not intellectual matters. Based on his acute perceptions, this early fiction has a directness and immediacy that is sometimes lacking in his later work, where his prose is unduly burdened by his theories of nature.

By 1936, Steinbeck's focus shifted to incorporate the political conditions in which his proletarians lived. *In Dubious Battle*, published that year, centered on a strike of migratory fruit pickers who were identified as an exploited class of people. *Of Mice and Men* is one of his fullest explorations of biological determinism, the notion that men and women are shaped by nature in ways that practically ensure their fate. Lenny is a retarded giant of a man who depends on his friend, the smaller and smarter George, to protect him. Yet Lenny does not know his own strength. He crushes puppies when he means only to pet them; he breaks Curly's wife's neck when he means only to stroke her lovely blonde hair.

The Grapes of Wrath, Steinbeck's masterpiece, follows the fate of the Joad family, who are evicted from their foreclosed farm in Oklahoma and make their way to the "promised land" of California. Slowly they lose their illusions as they are forced to work for starvation wages and are treated as riffraff by the police and the landowners. Tom Joad becomes a labor organizer when he realizes that his family cannot survive by itself. Steinbeck does not take a specifically socialist point of view—although he does provide an admiring glimpse of a government camp where the Joads and their fellow workers are able to establish a harmonious community based on equality of opportunity and responsibility.

What makes *The Grapes of Wrath* such an impressive work is its panoramic view of society. While the Joads' story particularizes the events of an epoch, the novel contains beautifully written passages that evoke the spirit of the times and create large-scale pictures of the displacement felt by people who lose their jobs and their farms. Steinbeck's remarkable accomplishment is that he not only makes readers empathize with a single family but also makes them identify with whole classes of people who are thrust into chaotic conditions as the result of a devastated economy.

None of Steinbeck's subsequent work equals the breadth and the depth of *The Grapes of Wrath*. *East of Eden*, his next major novel, is turgid and overly allegorical. Set in Southern California, from the Civil War to World War I, this family saga about two brothers and their stern father is a reenactment of the story of Cain and Abel with an overlay of psychologizing that attempts to explain the genesis of good and evil.

Except for *The Winter of Our Discontent*, a fine novel tracing the moral collapse of a descendant of an old New England family who cannot cope with the twentieth century, Steinbeck's best work as a writer in the postwar years is to be found in his lighthearted travel book *Travels with Charley*, an account of his forty-state tour with his poodle.

Carl Rollyson

Bibliography

Astro, Richard. *John Steinbeck and Edward F. Ricketts: The Shaping of a Novelist*. Hemet, Calif.: Western Flyer, 2002. Examines the relationship between Steinbeck and Ricketts, a marine biologist who was a close friend and who greatly influenced Steinbeck's views on nature.

Benson, Jackson D. *The True Adventures of John Steinbeck, Writer*. New York: Viking Press, 1984. This biography emphasizes Steinbeck's rebellion against critical conventions and his attempts to keep his private life separate from his role as public figure. Benson sees Steinbeck as a critical anomaly, embarrassed and frustrated by his growing critical and popular success.

French, Warren. *John Steinbeck's Fiction Revisited*. New York: Twayne, 1994. Thoroughly revises French's two other books in this Twayne series. Chapters on Steinbeck's becoming a novelist, his relationship to modernism, his short fiction, his wartime fiction, and his final fiction. Includes chronology, notes, and annotated bibliography.

George, Stephen K., ed. *John Steinbeck: A Centennial Tribute*. New York: Praeger, 2002. A collection of reminiscences from Steinbeck's family and friends as well as wide-ranging critical assessments of his works.

Hayashi, Tetsumaro, ed. *A New Study Guide to Steinbeck's Major Works, with Critical Explications*. Metuchen, N.J.: Scarecrow Press, 1993. Hayashi's third collection of essays published under this title (the others appeared in 1974 and 1979). Offers analyses of the Steinbeck works most often taught in college classes.

Hughes, R. S. *John Steinbeck: A Study of the Short Fiction*. New York: Twayne, 1989. A general introduction to Steinbeck's short fiction, focusing primarily on critical reception to the stories. Also includes some autobiographical statements on short-story writing, as well as four essays on Steinbeck's stories by other critics.

Johnson, Claudia Durst, ed. *Understanding "Of Mice and Men," "The Red Pony," and "The Pearl": A Student Casebook to Issues, Sources, and Historical Documents*. Westport, Conn.: Greenwood Press, 1997. This casebook contains historical, social, and political materials as a context for Steinbeck's three novellas. Contexts included are California and the West, land ownership, the male worker, homelessness, and oppression of the poor in Mexico.

McElrath, Joseph R., Jr., Jesse S. Crisler, and Susan Shillinglaw, eds. *John Steinbeck: The Contemporary Reviews*. New York: Cambridge University Press, 1996. A fine selection of reviews of Steinbeck's work.

Parini, Jay. *John Steinbeck: A Biography*. New York: Henry Holt, 1995. This biography suggests psychological interpretations of the effect of Steinbeck's childhood and sociological interpretations of his fiction. Criticizes Steinbeck for his politically incorrect gender and social views; also takes Steinbeck to task to what he calls his blindness to the political reality of the Vietnam War.

Timmerman, John H. *The Dramatic Landscape of Steinbeck's Short Stories*. Norman: University of Oklahoma Press, 1990. A formalist interpretation of Steinbeck's stories, focusing on style, tone, imagery, and character. Provides close readings of such frequently anthologized stories as "The Chrysanthemums" and "Flight," as well as such stories as "Johnny Bear" and "The Short-Short Story of Mankind."

Gloria Steinem

American critic

Born: Toledo, Ohio; March 25, 1934

NONFICTION: *Outrageous Acts and Everyday Rebellions*, 1983; *Marilyn: Norma Jean*, 1986; *Revolution from Within*, 1992; *Moving Beyond Words*, 1994.

Gloria Steinem, founder of the National Women's Political Caucus, is one of the leading spokespersons for the feminist movement in the United States, and her witty, cogent, and vivid writing style exemplifies the vitality of the women's movement. When she was eleven, her parents were divorced, and Steinem had to care for her mother, who apparently had a nervous breakdown. Steinem wrote of her mother in "Ruth's Song," in *Outrageous Acts and Everyday Rebellions*, viewing her as a victim of a patriarchal society. Steinem graduated Phi Beta Kappa from Smith College and pursued a career in journalism. Despite her popularity as a "feminist," Steinem was never actually a member of any active group fighting for women's rights.

Beginning in the 1960's, while writing and editing for magazines and newspapers, Steinem traveled extensively, campaigning for civil rights. She also went "under cover" as a Playboy bunny to investigate the treatment and lifestyle of Hugh Hefner's employees; his Playboy Clubs were nightclubs in which female employees dressed in bunny ears, leotards, and fuzzy tails to entertain male customers. Likewise, Steinem's light-hearted look at the way life would change "If Men Could Menstruate" indicates her ability to poke fun at cultural stereotypes. However, she also raises questions about patriarchal religions, traditional marriage, and negative images of women.

Although Steinem never joined an active women's rights group, she was accepted readily as a spokesperson for women's liberation because her relatively conservative views were palatable to the mainstream media. Her article in *New York* magazine entitled "After Black Power, Women's Liberation" and her money-raising talents caused the popular press to embrace her as a "voice of reason" in the women's rights debate. *McCall's* named her "Woman of the Year" in 1971. Steinem's activism is humane, altruistic, and focused on inclusion, as she urges radical feminists to welcome more conservative, traditional women into the fold, arguing logically that the women's movement is not only for career women or man-haters.

In her first book, *Outrageous Acts and Everyday Rebellions*, Steinem issued a collection of the best of her early columns and some provocative new articles, including "In Praise of Women's Bodies," "If Hitler Was Alive, Whose Side Would He Be On?" and "The International Crime of Genital Mutilation." The collection profiles everyone from Pat Nixon (wife of President Richard M. Nixon) to Linda Lovelace (a one-time pornography star who was a victim both of male desire and sadistic abuse) as well as Alice Walker (the African American writer famous for *The Color Purple*, detailing the treatment of black women by black men).

To Steinem, writing "produces a sense of accomplishment and, once in a while, pride," but she also says it can be "frightening." She served as editor and columnist for *New York* magazine and *Ms.* (the first feminist magazine, which she established) until she relinquished control in the 1980's. She has written prolifically from the 1960's on for *Ladies' Home Journal*, *Life*, *Look*, *Esquire*, *Glamour*, *McCall's*, and others, all of which put her in the midst of the firestorm begun over the demand for civil rights and pay equity for women. Like other feminist activists, Steinem supports women's choice in issues relating to reproduction. She surprised many feminists in 2000 when she married businessman and activist David Bale.

Considered a visionary by some and a predictable apologist for women's causes by others, Steinem identifies with those oppressed by a sexist system that views all women as mere objects of desire or conquest. Thus, her biography of 1950's movie star Marilyn Monroe, *Marilyn: Norma Jean*, was met with some dismay, since Monroe's "dumb blonde" persona angers female critics for fueling a world order based on superficial traits such as beauty, affability, and passivity. Denied recognition for her acting and singing abilities, Monroe was a victim of the very social order that had made her a star. Steinem's engaging tribute to a flawed but gentle spirit is one of the kinder biographies of this gifted actress, seen as vulnerable and as an unmothered child. Steinem asks what might have occurred had Monroe lived to see the dawn of the women's rights revolution.

In the era of self-help, Steinem's *Revolution from Within* allows readers to survey old and new pathways to self-esteem for women, drawing upon the words and ideas of experts in anthropology, religion, philosophy, art, and literature. This effort was seen by critics as a reasonable but predictable montage of the self-help genre. In 1994 Steinem published a new collection of essays entitled *Moving Beyond Words*, which met with mixed reviews. Some critics complained that she fails to listen to anyone—male or female—unless they share her life view, one conviction of which is her famous saying, "the personal is the political." As with *Outrageous Acts and Everyday Rebellions*, the book perhaps tries to be too much to too many, lacking a comprehensive overview. Nonetheless, in 2002 Steinem was awarded the PEN Center West Literary Award of Honor.

Linda L. Labin

Bibliography

Brown, Spencer. "Outrageous Acts and Everyday Rebellions." *Sewanee Review* 92 (Fall, 1984). Praises Steinem's courage in speaking out against genital mutilation of girls in Arab and African countries yet dismisses her portrayal of women as more decent than men.

Cohen, Marcia. *The Sisterhood: The True Story of the Women Who Changed the World*. New York: Simon & Schuster, 1988. Offers a look at the lives of Betty Friedan and other feminists, including Germaine Greer, Susan Brownmiller, and Gloria Steinem, and their positions and struggles in the women's rights movement.

Fritz, Leah. "Rebel with a Cause." *The Woman's Review of Books* 1 (December, 1983). Argues that *Outrageous Acts and Everyday Rebellions* is thought-provoking and vital.

Heilbrun, Carolyn G. *The Education of a Woman: The Life of Gloria Steinem*. New York: Dial Press, 1995. A biography written by the feminist literary critic who was to academic women what Steinem was to American women as a whole.

Stern, Sydney Ladensohn. *Gloria Steinem: Her Passion, Politics, and Mystique*. Secaucus, N.J.: Carol, 1997. A biography that addresses many of the contradictions in Steinem's character and life.

George Steiner

American critic and philosopher

Born: Paris, France; April 23, 1929
Identity: Jewish

NONFICTION: *Tolstoy or Dostoevsky: An Essay in the Old Criticism*, 1959; *The Death of Tragedy*, 1960; *Language and Silence: Essays on Language, Literature, and the Inhuman*, 1967; *Extraterritorial: Papers on Literature and the Language Revolution*, 1971; *In Bluebeard's Castle: Some Notes Toward the Redefinition of Culture*, 1971; *Fields of Force: Fischer and Spassky at Reykjavik*, 1974; *Nostalgia for the Absolute*, 1974; *After Babel: Aspects of Language and Translation*, 1975; *On Difficulty, and Other Essays*, 1978; *Heidegger*, 1978, revised and expanded 1992 (also known as *Martin Heidegger*); *Antigones*, 1979; *Real Presences: Is There Anything in What We Say?*, 1986; *What Is Comparative Literature?*, 1995; *No Passion Spent: Essays, 1978-1996*, 1996; *Errata: An Examined Life*, 1997; *Grammars of Creation: Originating in the Gifford Lectures for 1990*, 2001.
LONG FICTION: *The Portage to San Cristóbal of A. H.*, 1979.
SHORT FICTION: *Anno Domini*, 1964; *Proofs and Three Parables*, 1992; *The Deeps of the Sea, and Other Fiction*, 1996.
EDITED TEXTS: *Homer: A Collection of Critical Essays*, 1962 (with Robert Fagles); *The Penguin Book of Modern Verse Translation*, 1966 (also known as *Poem into Poem: World Poetry in Modern Verse Translation*, 1970); *Homer in English*, 1996.
MISCELLANEOUS: *George Steiner: A Reader*, 1984.

George Steiner (SHTI-nur), one of the most influential comparatists, critics, and translation theorists of the late twentieth century, was born on April 23, 1929, in Paris. His parents, Austrian émigrés, were both university professors, and, as the author notes in *After Babel*, his early youth was spent in multilingual surroundings—so much so that some critics consider him equally a native speaker of English, French, and German. He studied at various universities and subsequently filled professorial positions at universities in Europe and the United States. Steiner became a United States citizen in 1944 and is generally considered an American critic, although he has spent considerable time in Europe. After some time at Yale University, Steiner accepted a professorship in English and comparative literature at the University of Geneva, where he later became head of the comparative literature department.

Steiner emerged as a critical force before his thirtieth birthday with his first long work, *Tolstoy or Dostoevsky*, published in 1959. This work is based on the premise that the function of the critic differs from that of the reviewer in that the critic distinguishes not between the good and the bad but between the good and the excellent. *Tolstoy or Dostoevsky*, as a gauntlet thrown in the face of the then-prevailing critical current of New Criticism, also proved that there was still much to say about literary greats through the employ of "old" critical methods, centering on the various nontextual forces that mold the literary work and that aid in its interpretation.

The Death of Tragedy appeared two years later. In this book the author locates the tragic tradition solely in the classical world (and in truly classically oriented works), which regard the forces that govern the fate of human beings as blind. The decline of the dramatic tradition is necessarily paralleled by the waxing of the Christian worldview of justice and redemption, as well as by the artistic heritage of Romanticism, with its cult of genius. This interesting volume ends with the (optimistic?) hint that the twentieth century world, with its unspeakable cruelty and totalitarian systems, might see the rebirth of this ancient dramatic genre. Steiner's next book was a collection of essays entitled *Language and Silence*. This volume is an attempt to understand the scope, importance, and future of language and linguistic culture in the face of the antihumanistic history of twentieth century totalitarianism. Steiner speaks of a certain "retreat from the word"—the inability of modern language to function in the face of bestiality as well as of the necessary role of the spoken and written word faced with inhumanity.

Steiner was also working on his theories as editor of *The Penguin Book of Modern Verse Translation*. This anthology, with its enlightening introduction (published later as the essay "Poem into Poem"), became one of the most important texts in verse translation theory, and set translation into verse—the re-creation of a poem in one given language into another poem in another tongue—as the only viable and honest method of translating verse. The magisterial study *After Babel* derived from this preliminary essay. Like the foregoing, it battles the notion that "what remains untranslated in verse translation is the poem itself." In *After Babel* Steiner suggests that all linguistic interpretation—even in everyday conversation—is a type of translation and delineates the re-creative process of the verse translator as a hermeneutic method, which he considers literary criticism of the highest caliber. (This idea is connected with Steiner's conviction that literary criticism should be vivid, engaging, and text- rather than theory-centered).

Steiner's volume entitled *Extraterritorial* continues in the vein of *Language and Silence*. Again, he speaks of the "lost center" of linguistic expression of the mid- and late-twentieth century. This collection of essays reexamines Steiner's earlier thesis of the deep relationship between poetry and linguistics and deals with various linguists and their theories, including Roman Jakobson and Noam Chomsky. *On Difficulty, and Other Essays* was published in 1978. By Steiner's own admission, the essays collected in this volume are "working papers" or "position papers," designed to provoke a response from his colleagues. *On Difficulty, and Other Essays* addresses many of the same questions discussed in *After Babel*, though here the linguistic element is more pronounced. Among others, there may be found articles dealing with linguistics theorists Noam Chomsky and Benjamin Lee Whorf and their relationship to literature.

Steiner's work of short fiction "A Conversation Piece" concerns the arguments of Talmudic scholars in response to Abraham's dilemma regarding the sacrifice of Isaac at God's command. Eleazer, son of Eleazer of Cracow, insists that Abraham was forced by God to offer his beloved son Isaac to God as a sacrifice, for God had issued a command. Baruch of Vilna counters that Abraham had free will and possessed the opportunity to question God's word. The scholars next consider whether God had foreknowledge that Abraham would obey, thus possibly rendering the first question moot. The argument then involves the concomitant question as to whether God had complete faith in Abraham. The scholars ponder whether God could have allowed the sacrifice, since he had promised Abraham that his lineage would create a new people; thus, Isaac had to survive. The work illuminates several important questions regarding Jewish theology.

Steiner's novella *Proofs* concerns one man's reaction to the fall of communism in Europe. The protagonist faces the decline of communism as he loses his eyesight. Because he neglected to visit an ophthalmologist earlier, has cataracts, and possibly has some congenital defects, he may go blind. One way to save what remains of his eyesight is to avoid the strain on his eyes, which would entail quitting his job as a proofreader and text editor—an occupation that he enjoys because of his devotion to Marxism. In fact, the protagonist correlates communism with precision, with the exactness that proofreading entails.

Holocaust scholars often quote from Steiner, who has become an integral critic regarding the subject of the Holocaust language and art. In *Language and Silence*, Steiner claims that because the Nazis employed the German language to justify genocide, a new harshness has infiltrated the language: The Holocaust created a new sadism and deception that have become part of the language. As for the language of the survivors who write about the Holocaust, Steiner claims that their words speak for themselves and should be "review[ed]" but not embellished by writers. In his work *In Bluebeard's Castle*, Steiner claims that the Holocaust was like art because the Nazis attempted to stage—literally—a living hell on earth for Jews. Steiner states in *Language and Silence* that the Holocaust is so tragic that it defies words, that language cannot do justice to the sufferings of those in Auschwitz. He asserts that the most effective and powerful response to the Holocaust is not art but suffering.

Unlike many contemporary critics, Steiner has always emphatically insisted on the distinction between creative work and the criticism, commentary, and theorizing that feeds on it. He has spoken frankly of the critic's envy of the great writer (with the implication that to be anything less than great is not worth the game). In 1964 Steiner published a collection of three long stories or novellas, *Anno Domini*; the book was respectfully received but created no stir. His only other venture into fiction was both more substantial and more controversial. *The Portage to San Cristóbal of A. H.*, a short novel first published in *The Kenyon Review* in 1979 and later issued in book form, tells of the capture of Adolf Hitler (who is supposed to have survived the war and who is in his nineties as the story takes place) in a South American jungle. Controversy over Steiner's portrait of Hitler dominated critical responses to the novel, which is in fact an engaging work written in a clean, poetic style with striking imagery. In this novel Steiner dramatizes the almost magical power of the Word, which in the hands of an evil master can invest ghastly cruelty with a seductive charm.

In 1984 Steiner published *Antigones*, a wide-ranging critical study of the metamorphoses of Antigone in Western literature from Sophocles to the twentieth century. In 1985 Steiner was invited to deliver the annual Leslie Stephen Memorial Lecture at the University of Cambridge. That lecture, published in pamphlet form in 1986 under the title *Real Presences*, argues the thesis developed at greater length in Steiner's 1989 book of the same title. The title alludes to the "real presence" of the divine that has permeated world literature for thousands of years. In recent memory, Steiner suggests, modernism has denied the existence of God, and in doing so has left literature prey to the meaning-destructive methods of deconstruction. Although he does not foresee any large-scale reacceptance of the divine as an informing presence, Steiner defends this "outdated" approach to literature as a valid manifestation of the ideal toward which art strives, and he offers a hopeful prediction for the regeneration of art. However, his conclusions on much the same topics in *Grammars of Creation*, published twelve years later, are considerably more pessimistic. *No Passion Spent* collects essays on a wide range of literary topics, ranging from the Hebrew Bible and the Greek poet Homer to Sigmund Freud, Franz Kafka, and Søren Kierkegaard. The subtitle of Steiner's 1997 autobiographical essays, *Errata: An Examined Life*, refers to the remark attributed to the classical Greek philosopher Socrates: An unexamined life is not worth living. Steiner's life, recounted in episodes rather than a continuous narrative, is the starting point for a series of meditations on literature, language, music, and scholarship.

Charles Kraszewski
Eric Sterling

Bibliography

Chayette, Bryan. "Between Repulsion and Attraction: George Steiner's Post-Holocaust Fiction." *Jewish Social Studies* 5 (Spring/Summer, 1999): 67-81. Discusses the dramatization of Steiner's academic concerns in his fiction.

Lojek, Helen. "Brian Friel's Plays and George Steiner's Linguistics: Translating the Irish." *Contemporary Literature* 35, no. 1 (1994): 83-100. Uses Steiner's literary theories to analyze the works of Irish playwright Brian Friel, focusing on the playwright as both the product of and shaper of his culture.

Sharp, Ronald A., and Nathan A. Scott, Jr., eds. *Reading George Steiner.* Baltimore: The Johns Hopkins University Press, 1994. Several important articles on Steiner appear; the book includes essays on Steiner as a cultural critic, as a literary journalist, as an interpreter of literature and scholarship, as a Jewish critical moralist, as a theologian, as a writer of fiction, and as a thinker influenced by Martin Heidegger.

Young, Michael. "Real Presence and the Conscience of Words: Language and Repetition in George Steiner's *Portage to San Cristóbal of A. H.*" *Style* 26 (Spring, 1992): 114-128. Analyzes the way in which Steiner sees the relationship between language and the Holocaust in his novel.

Stendhal

(Marie-Henri Beyle)

French novelist, historian, and critic

Born: Grenoble, France; January 23, 1783
Died: Paris, France; March 23, 1842

LONG FICTION: *Armance*, 1827 (English translation, 1928); *Le Rouge et le noir*, 1830 (*The Red and the Black*, 1898); *Lucien Leuwen*, wr. 1834-1835, pb. 1855, 1894, 1926-1927 (English translation, 1950); *La Chartreuse de Parme*, 1839 (*The Charterhouse of Parma*, 1895); *Lamiel*, wr. 1839-1842, pb. 1889, 1971 (English translation, 1929).

SHORT FICTION: *Chroniques italiennes*, 1839, 1855 (*The Abbess of Castro, and Other Tales*, 1926).

NONFICTION: *Vies de Haydn, de Mozart et de Métastase*, 1815 (*The Lives of Haydn and Mozart, with Observations on Métastase*, 1817); *Histoire de la peinture en Italie*, 1817; *Rome, Naples et Florence en 1817*, 1817, 1826 (*Rome, Naples, and Florence, in 1817*, 1818); *De l'amour*, 1822 (*Maxims of Love*, 1906); *Vie de Rossini*, 1823 (*Memoirs of Rossini*, 1824; also known as *Life of Rossini*, 1956); *Racine et Shakespeare*, part 1, 1823; part 2, 1825 (*Racine and Shakespeare*, 1962); *Notes d'un dilettante*, 1824-1827; *Promenades dans Rome*, 1829 (*A Roman Journal*, 1957); *Souvenirs d'égotisme*, wr. 1832, pb. 1892 (*Memoirs of an Egotist*, 1949); *Vie de Henry Brulard*, wr. 1835-1836, pb. 1890 (*The Life of Henry Brulard*, 1925); *Mémoires d'un touriste*, 1838 (*Memoirs of a Tourist*, 1962); *Voyage dans le midi de la France*, 1838 (*Travels in the South of France*, 1971); *Journal*, 1888; *Pensées, filosofia nova*, 1931; *Correspondance*, 1933-1934.

MISCELLANEOUS: *The Works*, 1925-1928 (6 volumes).

Stendhal (stehn-dahl), the most "unromantic" figure of France's Romantic period (1830-1848), ranks with Victor Hugo, Honoré de Balzac, Gustave Flaubert, and Émile Zola as one of the greatest French novelists of the nineteenth century. He was born Marie-Henri Beyle in Grenoble, France, on January 23, 1783. Always of an independent nature, he left his birthplace at an early age to seek his fortune in Paris. Despite ambitions as a playwright, Stendhal obtained a position in the Ministry of War and, in 1800, became a dragoon in the army of Napoleon. As an aide-de-camp and later an imperial commissioner, he accompanied the army in the Italian, Prussian, and Russian campaigns, serving with distinction until the fall of Napoleon in 1814. Still a young man, he spent the next seven years in Milan, scene of *The Charterhouse of Parma*, one of his two masterpieces. The rest of his life was spent as an independent and stubborn consular officer of France, mainly in Civitavecchia. Tempestuous, and usually disastrous, love affairs occupied a considerable amount of his time, and some of the events connected with these are to be found in his writings. He died in Paris on March 23, 1842.

Stendhal's writing career began in 1814 in Milan. There he produced two studies, *The Lives of Haydn and Mozart, with Observations on Métastase* and *Rome, Naples, and Florence, in 1817*. He also contributed several critical essays to British literary journals during this period, and his name was better known in England then than it was in France. Stendhal's first novel, *Armance*, appeared in 1827. Five years earlier, he had written a searching study of one of his own love affairs titled *Maxims of Love* (1822). None of these early writings received significant attention. In 1830 appeared the first of Stendhal's two unquestioned masterpieces, *The Red and the Black*. The title indicates the strife between the Napoleonic spirit of the military and the power of the clergy, whom Stendhal detested. The protagonist of the novel, Julien Sorel, has come to typify the post-Revolutionary arriviste in France. Much of Stendhal himself is in this character. Sorel is a poor tutor who makes love to the children's mother in order to further his own ambitions. When this woman, his first mistress, betrays him to a second, he attempts to kill her and is condemned to die. In addition to giving a profound psychological study of Sorel, *The Red and the Black* furnishes an excellent representation of the social upheaval France had undergone during the years since the Revolution. Sorel epitomizes the uprooted peasant, the man of mediocre talent who is intelligent enough to wish above all to avail himself of the limitless opportunities offered those like him under the Republic.

During the years 1831 to 1838, Stendhal wrote two autobiographical works, *Memoirs of an Egotist* and *The Life of Henry Brulard*, and one novel, *Lucien Leuwen*, which were not published until later. Stendhal's greatest novel, *The Charterhouse of Parma*, was published in 1839. This is the story of Fabrice del Dongo (roughly the equivalent of Julien Sorel) and his relations with a duchess and a highwayman. The story is laid in nineteenth century Italy, although the most famous passage is a realistic description of the Battle of Waterloo as seen through the young hero's eyes. Stendhal, who professed to love Italy more than France, succeeds admirably in painting a vivid picture of life in a petty Italian principality. His study of the loves and intrigues of his characters is especially brilliant. This work, like *The Red and the Black*, shows Stendhal at his best: careless of form but willing to put his brilliant energy and his stubborn and egotistical mind to the task of recording, with effective economy of detail, the minutiae and grandeur of life. Stendhal is not above using improbable characters and situations, but his study of both is brutally exact. Thus he is called both romantic and realist.

In his own day Stendhal was not appreciated; only Balzac saw much worth to his novels. But in the late 1880's the appearance of his unpublished works produced a curious literary revival; he was praised by both the naturalists and the psychologists. Stendhal, it has been said, went further than any other writer of France in reconciling the two great literary traditions of that country, classical simplicity and romantic imagination.

Philip McDermott

Bibliography

Adams, Robert M. *Stendhal: Notes on a Novelist*. New York: Funk and Wagnalls, 1959. Still one of the best critical introductions, written lucidly, with a biographical chapter and discussions of Stendhal's major works. Adams includes an appendix identifying the "major slips, inconsistencies, oversights, and verbal faults" in Stendhal's two major novels.

Alter, Robert. *A Lion for Love: A Critical Biography of Stendhal*. New York: Basic Books, 1979. A biography that well integrates an analysis of Stendhal's fiction into the story of his life.

Bell, David F. *Circumstances: Chance in the Literary Text*. Lincoln: University of Nebraska Press, 1993. Examines the realistic writing of Stendhal and Honoré de Balzac.

Bloom, Harold, ed. *Stendhal*. New York: Chelsea House, 1989. Essays by distinguished critics on women in Stendhal's oeuvre, his use of autobiography, and his love plots. Includes introduction, chronology, and bibliography.

Bolster, Richard. *Stendhal: "Le Rouge et le noir."* London: Grant and Cutler, 1994. A critical guide to *The Red and the Black*.

Keates, Jonathan. *Stendhal*. New York: Carroll and Graf, 1998. A lucid and shrewd biography, emphasizing the events of Stendhal's life over exegesis of his works.

Richardson, Joanna. *Stendhal*. New York: Coward, McCann and Geoghegan, 1974. A sound narrative biography with excellent documentation. Includes a bibliography.

Talbot, Emile J. *Stendhal Revisited*. New York: Twayne, 1993. A revision of a useful introductory work, with a chapter on the man and the writer and separate chapters on Stendhal's major novels. Contains a chronology, notes, and an annotated bibliography.

Wood, Michael. *Stendhal*. Ithaca, N.Y.: Cornell University Press, 1971. A meticulous, scholarly study of Stendhal's style and structure. Includes notes and brief bibliography. One of the standard works of Stendhal criticism in English.

James Stephens

Irish poet, novelist, and short-story writer

Born: Dublin, Ireland; February 9, 1880, or February 2, 1882
Died: London, England; December 26, 1950

POETRY: *Insurrections*, 1909; *The Lonely God, and Other Poems*, 1909; *The Hill of Vision*, 1912; *The Rocky Road to Dublin*, 1915; *Songs from the Clay*, 1915; *Green Branches*, 1916; *Reincarnations*, 1918; *Collected Poems*, 1926, revised 1954; *The Outcast*, 1929; *Theme and Variations*, 1930; *Strict Joy*, 1931.

LONG FICTION: *The Charwoman's Daughter*, 1912 (also known as *Mary, Mary*); *The Crock of Gold*, 1912; *The Demi-gods*, 1914; *Deirdre*, 1923; *In the Land of Youth*, 1924.

SHORT FICTION: *Here Are Ladies*, 1913; *Irish Fairy Tales*, 1920; *Etched in Moonlight*, 1928.

DRAMA: *Julia Elizabeth*, pb. 1929.

NONFICTION: *On Prose and Verse*, 1928; *Letters of James Stephens*, 1974 (Richard J. Finneran, editor).

EDITED TEXTS: *English Romantic Poets*, 1933 (with E. L. Beck and R. H. Snow); *Victorian and Later English Poets*, 1934 (with Beck and Snow).

James Stephens grew up in the slums of Dublin and for the most part educated himself by reading widely. To earn a living he taught himself stenography, and while working as a stenographer he began to write poems and stories, some of which were praised by George W. Russell (Æ; 1867-1935), who read them in manuscript. Even the praise of an established writer was, however, insufficient to secure publication, and Stephens's first success did not come until he was thirty, with the publication of *The Crock of Gold*. A contemporary fantasy involving two philosophers, leprechauns, and Irish gods, *The Crock of Gold* achieved the status of a minor classic and won the Polignac Prize for 1912. This was followed by another fantasy set in the present, *The Demi-gods*, about three angels who come to earth to accompany an engaging Irish vagabond. After that Stephens set out to retell Irish legends. *Irish Fairy Tales* offered stories from the legend cycle revolving around Finn MacCumhal, and Stephens planned a five-volume series of stories from the Táin Bó Cuailnge cycle but only completed two volumes: *Deirdre*, which was awarded the Tailteann Gold Medal, and *In the Land of Youth*.

Stephens was married and had two children. Among his lifelong interests was almost every phase of Gaelic culture, language, art, and literature. As an authority on Gaelic art, he served for some years as an assistant curator of the Dublin National Gallery. Among his amusements was singing Irish folk songs, playing an accompaniment on the concertina.

As an adult Stephens spent much time away from his native city and land. After a first visit to the United States in 1925, he returned a number of times, once spending almost a year on the West Coast lecturing on literature and Gaelic culture at the University of California. Stephens left another imprint on American higher education with two anthologies he edited with E. L. Beck and R. H. Snow which became standard college textbooks: *English Romantic Poets* and *Victorian and Later English Poets*. Between the two world wars Stephens also spent a great deal of time in France, especially Paris. In spite of his travels abroad, Stephens remained an ardent Irish nationalist, belonged to the Sinn Féin movement, and ardently supported Eamon De Valera (1882-1975), the Irish political leader and president of Éire. During World War II, however, he felt obliged to go against Irish neutrality and declare himself a supporter of the Allies. The British government granted him a pension in 1942.

In addition to his novels and poetry, none of which achieved wide popularity in America, Stephens tried his hand at other literary forms: *Here Are Ladies* and *Etched in Moonlight*, collections of short stories; *Julia Elizabeth*, an attempt at drama; and *On Prose and Verse*, a critical study of literature. He forged a strong friendship with the Irish expatriate James Joyce (1882-1941) and at one point formally agreed to complete *Finnegans Wake* in the event of Joyce's untimely death.

Gary Westfahl

Bibliography

Bramsbäck, Birgit. *James Stephens: A Literary and Bibliographical Study*. Cambridge, Mass.: Harvard University Press, 1959.

Douglas, Claire. "'Oisin's Mother': Because I Would Not Give My Love to the Druid Named Dark." In *Psyche's Stories: Modern Jungian Interpretations of Fairy Tales*, edited by Murray Stein and Lionel Corbett. Vol. 2. Wilmette, Ill.: Chiron, 1992.

McFate, Patricia. *The Writings of James Stephens: Variations on a Theme of Love*. New York: St. Martin's Press, 1979.

Martin, Augustine. *James Stephens: A Critical Study*. Totowa, N.J.: Rowman and Littlefield, 1977.

Pyle, Hilary. *James Stephens: His Work and an Account of His Life*. New York: Barnes and Noble, 1965.

Sayers, William. "Molly's Monologue and the Old Woman's Complaint in James Stephens's *The Crock of Gold*." *James Joyce Quarterly* 36, no. 3 (1999).

Tallone, Giovanna. "James Stephens' *Deirdre:* The Determining Word." *Canadian Journal of Irish Studies* 16 (July, 1990).

Richard G. Stern

American novelist and short-story writer

Born: New York, New York; February 25, 1928

LONG FICTION: *Golk*, 1960; *Europe: Or, Up and Down with Schreiber and Baggish*, 1961; *In Any Case*, 1962 (also known as *The Chaleur Network*, 1981); *Stitch*, 1965; *Other Men's Daughters*, 1973; *Natural Shocks*, 1978; *A Father's Words*, 1986; *Pacific Tremors*, 2001.
SHORT FICTION: *Teeth, Dying, and Other Matters*, 1964; *1968: A Short Novel, an Urban Idyll, Five Stories, and Two Trade Notes*, 1970; *Packages*, 1980; *Noble Rot: Stories, 1949-1988*, 1989; *Shares, and Other Fictions*, 1992.
DRAMA: *The Gamesman's Island*, pb. 1964.
NONFICTION: *One Person and Another: On Writers and Writing*, 1993; *A Sistermony*, 1995.
EDITED TEXTS: *Honey and Wax: The Powers and Pleasures of Narrative*, 1966; *American Poetry of the Fifties*, 1967.
MISCELLANEOUS: *The Books in Fred Hampton's Apartment*, 1973; *The Invention of the Real*, 1982; *The Position of the Body*, 1986; *What Is What Was*, 2002.

Richard Stern is often referred to as a writer's writer, much honored by his peers but relatively neglected by the critics and (with one or two exceptions) by the reading public. He was born Richard Gustave Stern on February 25, 1928, in New York City, the son of a dentist; both his parents were of German Jewish descent. A brilliant and precocious student, Stern entered the University of North Carolina at the age of sixteen; he graduated in 1947. He received an M.A. from Harvard University in 1949 and a Ph.D. from the University of Iowa in 1954. In 1955 he began teaching at the University of Chicago, where he would remain, with visiting stints at other universities. In 1950 Stern and Gay Clark were married; they had four children. The marriage ended in divorce; in 1985 Stern married the poet Alane Rollings.

With *Golk*, Stern made a strong debut as a novelist. Centering on a fictitious television program based on the then-popular *Candid Camera*, the 1960 work came at a time when television, though already all-pervasive in American life, had received little serious attention. The program, called *You're On Camera*, catches people unawares, exposing them to the laughter of viewers all over the country. The novel's protagonist, Herbert Hondorp, becomes involved in the program, but when he himself is trapped in embarrassing behavior, he decides to betray his employer. Involved in the plot is Hondorp's marriage, in which fidelity and betrayal become equally entwined—as in the television program. Fidelity and betrayal are recurring themes in Stern's fiction. *In Any Case*, his third novel, is based on a historical incident during World War II. The protagonist seeks to prove that his son, who was killed during the war and who has been branded as a traitor, was in fact innocent. As a "spy novel," *In Any Case* is above the usual run of thrills-and-secrets fiction; its main intent is to focus on the father's unswerving loyalty to his son's memory. Ultimately, the father manages to prove that his son indeed was not a traitor; this discovery brings a modicum of fulfillment.

Fidelity and betrayal are also central to the autobiographical novel *Other Men's Daughters*, Stern's greatest popular success, which enjoyed a brief run on the best-seller list. The protagonist, a professor of biology at Harvard, is deeply unhappy in his marriage yet reluctant to leave his family. His hesitations are overcome when he forms a relationship with a student. *Other Men's Daughters* illustrates another defining characteristic of Stern's fiction: his intellectual curiosity. In *Other Men's Daughters*, one sees the world as a biologist sees it; the protagonist's profession is not mere window-dressing. Similarly, in *Natural Shocks* both style and theme are related to the profession of the protagonist, a globe-trotting journalist accustomed to the company of people who make things happen. In the course of the novel he must confront the unyielding reality of death.

After a long hiatus, Stern published *Pacific Tremors* in 2001. It is the story of two aging friends, but it is set in the milieu of the youth-obsessed film industry. The tremors of the title refer both to the constantly shifting earth in Southern California and the tremors running through each man's life as he accommodates to growing older and losing touch with his creativity and profession.

The range and variousness of Stern's fiction—and his relative lack of self-absorption (compare his friend and fellow novelist Philip Roth)—have no doubt cost him readers, yet these are the very qualities that make his work stand out. His achievements have been recognized with Fulbright, Guggenheim, and Rockefeller fellowships; in addition, he has been honored by the American Academy of Arts and Letters.

Philip Brantingham

Bibliography

Bergonzi, Bernard. "Herzog in Venice, I." *The New York Review of Books* 5 (December 9, 1965): 26. Bergonzi claims that the hero of *Stitch* is modeled on Ezra Pound. He likes the novel but is uneasy about Stern's evocation of literary myths.

Cavell, Marsha. "Visions of Battlements." *Partisan Review* 38, no. 1 (1971): 117-121. Cavell reviews four books in this article, including *1968*, by Stern. She discusses "Veni, Vidi . . . Wendt" and "East, West . . . Midwest" from Stern's collection, seeing him as a satirist whose writing is "at once gentle and biting."

Harris, Mark. *Saul Bellow: Drumlin Woodchuck*. Athens: University of Georgia Press, 1980. This book is primarily a study of Stern's friend Bellow. It is dedicated to Stern and repeatedly mentions him, especially in connection with his friendships with Harris and Bellow. Also discusses his friendship with Philip Roth and recognizes the difficulty most readers have with

Stern's work. Although Harris treats Stern throughout the book, the treatment is especially intensive in chapters 2 and 3.

Izzo, David Garrett. *The Writings of Richard Stern: The Education of an Intellectual Everyman*. Jefferson, N.C.: McFarland, 2001. A literary biography, discussing the major themes in his fiction and his use of fictionalized autobiography. Analyzes all of his novels and short stories through 2001.

Kenner, Hugh. "*Stitch:* The Master's Voice." Review of *Stitch*, by Richard G. Stern. *Chicago Review* 18 (Summer, 1966): 177-180. A very favorable review, in which Kenner praises Stern's originality and his ability to construct a novel out of discrete parts. Kenner also calls the book an act of homage to Ezra Pound.

Rogers, Bernard. Foreword to *Golk*, by Richard G. Stern. Chicago: University of Chicago Press, 1987. This introduction to the Phoenix reprint of Stern's first novel treats his fiction in general, especially his novels. It traces through Stern's novels four of his major themes: adapting to change, handling moral responsibility, dealing with problems of fatherhood and domestic life, and handling power. It also discusses his distinctive narrative voice.

Schiffler, James. *Richard Stern*. New York: Twayne, 1993. The first book-length critical study of Stern; includes a brief overview of his life, a survey of his novels and short stories, and discussions of his style and themes; chapter 5 is primarily on the theme of the "comedy of failure" in his short stories.

Laurence Sterne

British novelist and essayist

Born: Clonmel, Ireland; November 24, 1713
Died: London, England; March 18, 1768

LONG FICTION: *The Life and Opinions of Tristram Shandy, Gent.*, 1759-1767; *A Sentimental Journey Through France and Italy*, 1768.
NONFICTION: *A Political Romance*, 1759; *The Sermons of Mr. Yorick*, 1760 (volumes 1-2), 1766 (volumes 3-4); *Sermons by the Late Rev. Mr. Sterne*, 1769 (volumes 5-7); *Letters from Yorick to Eliza*, 1773; *Sterne's Letters to His Friends on Various Occasions, to Which Is Added His History of a Watch Coat*, 1775; *Letters of the Late Rev. Mr. L. Sterne to His Most Intimate Friends*, 1775 (3 volumes); *In Elegant Epistles*, 1790; *Journal to Eliza*, 1904.

Laurence Sterne, one of the most delightfully eccentric of English novelists, was born in Clonmel, Ireland, on November 24, 1713, the son of an Irish woman and an ensign in the English army whose regiment had just been transferred to Ireland from Dunkirk. Though his parentage was undistinguished, Sterne's father came from an old family in Yorkshire, where a great-grandfather had been an archbishop. A childhood spent in the rigors of camp-following undoubtedly had a harmful effect on the novelist's frail constitution, but the experience provided him with details of barracks life and campaign reminiscences that ultimately enriched his great novel with such authentic creations as Uncle Toby and Corporal Trim.

Between 1723 and 1731, the year of his father's death, Sterne was in school at Halifax, Yorkshire. In 1733, after two years of idleness at Elvington, he was enrolled as a sizar in Jesus College, Cambridge, through the grudging benevolence of relatives. At Cambridge he indulged in the easy, convivial university life of the time. He discovered an incapacity for mathematics and a contempt for formal logic. Nevertheless, he did considerable reading, developing a deep admiration for John Locke (1632-1704), whose philosophy was to be the most important single influence on his thinking. He also formed a close friendship with John Hall-Stevenson, later the hypochondriac author of *Crazy Tales* (1762). Cambridge granted Sterne a B.A. in 1737 and an M.A. in 1740.

As a matter of expediency rather than religious conviction, he took holy orders. He was ordained deacon in 1737 and inducted into the vicarage of Sutton on the Forest in 1738. Two years later he received a prebendal stall in the York Cathedral. In 1744 he acquired the parish of Stillington, near Sutton.

In 1741, after a sentimental courtship, he married Elizabeth Lumley. A daughter, Lydia, was born in 1747. The Sternes, however, were never really compatible. Elizabeth was said to be ill-tempered, a condition certainly not improved by her husband's interests in other women. Yet, although Sterne was not averse to paying attention to other women, his philandering was probably chiefly sentimental—as was, for example, his affair with Catherine ("Kitty") Fourmantelle, a singer from London who came to York in 1759.

In Sutton, Sterne spent twenty years of relative obscurity, serving two parishes with some conscientiousness, unsuccessfully farming his glebe, and making occasional trips to York to preach his turn in the cathedral or to dabble in diocesan politics. He found amusement in hunting, skating, fiddling, and painting, as well as in social gatherings at Newburgh Priory, the seat of Lord Fauconberg, and in the ribald carousals of the "Demoniacks" at Hall-Stevenson's Skelton Castle. He later immortalized his role of "heteroclite parson" in his portrait of Yorick.

In 1759 his participation in local church politics produced a satire called *A Political Romance* (later renamed *The History of a Good Warm Watch-Coat*). Though all but a few copies were burned to prevent embarrassment to the diocese, its success among Sterne's friends gave him the impetus to embark on *Tristram Shandy*, the first two volumes of which came out in York in December of the same year. Introduced to London through the enthusiasm of the actor David Garrick, the novel so impressed the capital with its whimsicality, eccentric humor, and indecorum that it was immediately successful. In fact, when Sterne journeyed to London in the spring of 1760, he found himself a social lion. Never had the city seen such a witty, hedonistic priest, whose lustrous eyes and ebulliently secular conversation so enchantingly belied his black garb, pale face, thin body, and hollow chest.

However, disapprobation soon followed success. Literary men such as Horace Walpole (1717-1797), Oliver Goldsmith (1730-1774), and Samuel Richardson (1689-1761) condemned the book for various evils ranging from tediousness to indecency, and a flood of hostile articles, pamphlets, and bad imitations poured from the press. When the author brought out the first two volumes of *The Sermons of Mr. Yorick* in 1760, the comminatory chorus grew.

Returning to Yorkshire, Sterne received from Lord Fauconberg the living of Coxwold, to which "sweet retirement" he moved his family. Here for the rest of his life his home was a rambling gabled house that he called Shandy Hall. In January, 1761, he was again in London to see two more volumes of *Tristram Shandy* published. Though the critical reception was now unfavorable, the books sold well. Sterne returned to Coxwold, completed two more volumes, and was back in November for their publication. This time his reputation soared again. The story of Le Fever, Trim's animadversions on death, and Uncle Toby's campaigns had won near-universal applause.

Weakened by a serious hemorrhage from chronically weak lungs, Sterne set out for France in 1762 in a "race with death." Recovering in Paris, he was lionized by the cream of French intellectual society. He later settled with his family in Toulouse. Back in Coxwold in 1764, he completed volumes seven and eight of *Tristram Shandy*, including an account of his tour through France and the affair of Uncle Toby and the Widow Wadman. These came out in January, 1765. Two more volumes of sermons followed in January, 1766.

Once again on the Continent in 1766, Sterne had a "joyous" winter in France and Italy. Though hemorrhages were becoming more frequent, he returned during the year to his desk in Coxwold, and by January, 1767, he was on hand in London for the appearance of the ninth volume of *Tristram Shandy*. During this winter he indulged in his famous sentimental affair with Eliza Draper, the young wife of an official of the East India Company, for whom he kept the *Journal to Eliza* after her departure for Bombay.

Late in February, 1768, Sterne brought out *A Sentimental Journey Through France and Italy*. He could enjoy its triumphant reception only briefly, however. An attack of influenza that developed into pleurisy proved more than his disease-wracked body could bear. He died in London on March 18, 1768, and was buried at St. George's, Hanover Square.

Sterne's work, like his life, is marked with a refreshing unconventionality. Though the *Sermons* (1760-1769) lack religious conviction and originality of material, they preach a warm benevolence and a comfortable morality in a style that can be at once graceful and dramatic. *A Sentimental Journey Through France and Italy*—in which Sterne substituted his traveler's sentimental adventures for the conventional accounts of nations, peoples, and memorable sights in travel books—is a nearly perfect small masterpiece.

The humor of *Tristram Shandy* is plainly in the tradition of François Rabelais (c. 1483-1553), Miguel de Cervantes (1547-1616), and Jonathan Swift (1667-1745); and its borrowings range from Robert Burton (1577-1640) to miscellaneous curiosa. Superficially, the novel may seem merely like an engaging hodgepodge full of tricks, including black, marbled, and blank pages, omitted chapters, unorthodox punctuation and typography, and numerous digressions. But *Tristram Shandy* is far from planless. By insisting on the importance of opinions about action rather than on that of action itself Sterne opened unexplored avenues into the inner lives of his characters and achieved a new architectonic principle based on the mind as Locke had illuminated it in *An Essay on Human Understanding* (1690). At the same time he achieved a new concept of time in fiction, a fascinating awareness of the life process itself, and a fresh concept of comedy based on the idea of individual isolation in a world where each person is a product of his own peculiar association of ideas.

Ann D. Garbett

Bibliography

Cash, Arthur Hill. *Laurence Sterne*. 2 vols. London: Methuen, 1975-1986. The definitive biography. The first volume follows Sterne's life to early 1760 and offers many details about his role in the religious and political affairs of York. The second volume treats Sterne the author. Presents a realistic picture freed from Victorian strictures and romantic glosses. The appendices provide a series of portraits and of letters never before published.

Cash, Arthur Hill, and John M. Stedmond, eds. *The Winged Skull: Papers from the Laurence Sterne Bicentenary Conference*. Kent, Ohio: Kent State University Press, 1971. A collection of essays on a range of subjects, including Sterne's style, his reputation outside England, and his fictional devices. Includes some helpful illustrations.

Kraft, Elizabeth. *Laurence Sterne Revisited*. New York: Twayne, 1996. Gives a short biography, and then devotes individual chapters to specific works. Also includes a final chapter on Sterne's changing critical reputation as well as a selected bibliography.

Myer, Valerie Grosvenor, ed. *Laurence Sterne: Riddles and Mysteries*. New York: Barnes and Noble Books, 1984. Contains eleven essays on *The Life and Opinions of Tristram Shandy, Gent.*, covering such matters as the nature of Sterne's comedy, the intellectual background of the novel, and Sterne's influence on the work of Jane Austen. Includes a brief annotated bibliography.

New, Melvin. *"Tristram Shandy": A Book for Free Spirits*. New York: Twayne, 1994. After providing a literary and historical milieu for Stern's most famous work, New explores five different methods of approaching *Tristram Shandy:* "Satire," "Heads" (that is, intellectually), "Hearts" (that is, emotionally), "Joy," and "Tartuffery" (as a humorous attack on hypocrisy).

Ross, Ian Campbell. *Laurence Sterne: A Life*. New York: Oxford University Press, 2001. A well-researched biography that concentrates on the events of Sterne's life rather than literary analysis of the works.

Stedmond, John M. *The Comic Art of Laurence Sterne: Convention and Innovation in "Tristram Shandy" and "A Sentimental Journey."* Toronto: University of Toronto Press, 1967. Sterne's novels highlight the comic distance between aspiration and attainment that is endemic in human existence. Provides helpful readings of the novels and an appendix recording Sterne's direct borrowings.

Walsh, Marcus, ed. *Laurence Sterne*. New York: Longman, 2002. Sterne's works are particularly amenable to post-structuralist interpretation; this collection pulls together a stimulating group of essays that take theoretical approaches to the work.

James Stevens

American short-story writer and novelist

Born: Albia, Iowa; November 15, 1892
Died: Seattle, Washington; December 30, 1971

SHORT FICTION: *Paul Bunyan*, 1925; *Homer in the Sagebrush*, 1928; *The Saginaw Paul Bunyan*, 1932; *Paul Bunyan's Bears*, 1947.
LONG FICTION: *Brawny-man*, 1926; *Mattock*, 1927; *Big Jim Turner*, 1948.
NONFICTION: *Green Power: The Story of Public Law 273*, 1958.

James Floyd Stevens, born in Monroe County, Iowa, on November 15, 1892, was drawn to the great outdoors, the rivers and forests of America. His novels, short stories, and journalistic writings constitute, on the whole, a partial autobiography and an account of the realistic and mythic heroes of the lumberman, fisherman, and pioneer laborer.

Stevens's strongest claim to a place in literary history is his first book, *Paul Bunyan*, published in 1925. Although one reviewer said that it "converted folklore to farce," most critics were laudatory: "James Stevens merits to be known by his epical work as the prose Homer of American mythology"; "No one but Mark Twain has been able to set down tall tales with such winning conviction." By 1948, the book had sold more than 200,000 copies, and Stevens issued a new edition, adding a chapter that described a fabulous log run up the Columbia River with tame whales doing the work.

Paul Bunyan was followed by *Brawny-man*, which describes in a ragged, raw style the life of a hobo laborer, Jim Turner, who hops freights from job to job. *Mattock* is based on Stevens's fourteen months in France as an infantryman in World War I. It is Private Parvin Mattock's vernacular account of a farm boy's shocking experiences during the war; it closes with the first convention of the American Legion.

Homer in the Sagebrush, a collection of magazine stories of the Northwest frontier, was criticized for being too raw, lacking artistic form. His next collection, *The Saginaw Paul Bunyan*, seemed, on the other hand, "too prosy and correct . . . a saga in pseudo-literary style." Stevens, however, continued to produce novels and stories, the most significant being *Big Jim Turner*, an autobiographical social chronicle of the early 1900's: railroading and lumber, labor agitation, the International Workers of the World (IWW), Eugene V. Debs (1855-1926). Although picturesque and often forceful, his later books did not fulfill the expectations aroused by *Paul Bunyan*.

Bibliography

Clare, Warren L. "James Stevens: The Laborer and Literature." *Research Studies* 32 (1964).

Hoffman, Daniel. *Paul Bunyan: Last of the Frontier Demi-gods*. 1952. Reprint. East Lansing: Michigan State University Press, 1999.

Montgomery, Elizabeth. *The Story Behind Modern Books*. New York: Dodd, Mead, 1949.

Sherman, Stuart. *The Main Stream*. New York: Charles Scribner's Sons, 1927.

Warfel, Harry R. *American Novelists of Today*. 1951. Reprint. Westport, Conn.: Greenwood Press, 1972.

Wallace Stevens

American poet

Born: Reading, Pennsylvania; October 2, 1879
Died: Hartford, Connecticut; August 2, 1955
Pseudonym: Peter Parasol

POETRY: *Harmonium*, 1923, expanded 1931 (with 14 additional poems); *Ideas of Order*, 1935; *Owl's Clover*, 1936; *The Man with the Blue Guitar, and Other Poems*, 1937; *Parts of a World*, 1942; *Notes Toward a Supreme Fiction*, 1942; *Esthétique du Mal*, 1945; *Transport to Summer*, 1947; *The Auroras of Autumn*, 1950; *Selected Poems*, 1953; *The Collected Poems of Wallace Stevens*, 1954.
DRAMA: *Three Travelers Watch a Sunrise*, pb. 1916; *Carlos Among the Candles*, pr. 1917; *Bowl, Cat, and Broomstick*, pr. 1917.
NONFICTION: *Three Academic Pieces*, 1947; *The Necessary Angel: Essays on Reality and the Imagination*, 1951; *Letters of Wallace Stevens*, 1966; *Souvenirs and Prophecies: The Young Wallace Stevens*, 1977.
MISCELLANEOUS: *Opus Posthumous*, 1957 (Samuel French Morse, editor).

Wallace Stevens's life has been called a "double life," split between the seemingly antithetical professions of poet and insurance lawyer. However, as critic Frank Kermode notes, "Stevens did not find that he must choose between the careers of insurance lawyer and poet. The fork in the road where he took the wrong turning is a critic's invention." Rather, Stevens became one of America's most respected poets. He was an accomplished stylist whose power over language and intense imagination wrought exhilarating and complex poems.

Stevens was born in Reading, Pennsylvania, in 1879, of Pennsylvania Dutch ancestry, a fact important in some of his verse, notably "Dutch Graves in Bucks County." However, Stevens does not approach autobiographical writing; his symbols are impersonal, and comprehension of his work does not depend closely on a knowledge of his life.

Stevens attended Harvard University from 1897 until 1900, and there his first poems appeared in *The Harvard Advocate*. He left Harvard before graduating due to a shortage of family finances and planned to go to Paris to write. Instead, Stevens took a job as reporter on the *New York Herald Tribune*. Later, he entered New York Law School. He received his law degree in 1903 and was admitted to the New York Bar Association, practicing law in New York City from 1904 until 1916. During this period, Stevens continued to write poetry and made friends among Greenwich Village writers, including William Carlos Williams (1883-1963), Marianne Moore (1887-1972), and Harriet Monroe (1860-1936). According to Williams, who, like Stevens, devoted himself to two professions, Stevens was always reserved, shy, "unwilling to be active or vocal. . . . He was always the well-dressed one, diffident about letting down his hair. Precise when we were sloppy. Drank little. . . . But we all knew, liked, and admired him."

During his New York sojourn, Stevens published in Monroe's *Poetry* as well as in Alfred Kreymborg's *Others*, at first under the pseudonym Peter Parasol. Two plays appeared in *Poetry*, including *Three Travellers Watch a Sunrise*, which won a verse-play competition; however, more important, the journals of Monroe and Kreymborg offered an outlet for some of Stevens's best early verse—for example, "Sunday Morning" and "Peter Quince."

In 1916, Stevens joined the legal staff of the Hartford Accident and Indemnity Company, becoming vice president of the firm in 1934. Like Crispin in "The Comedian as the Letter C," Stevens in Hartford seemed to find the end of his journey, establishing "a nice shady home" and raising a "daughter with curls"—Holly Bright Stevens, offspring of Stevens and his wife Elsie. As a "romantic poet," Stevens made Hartford his "ivory tower," looking down on a reality made up of insurance law, Key West, Connecticut, and, at times, "an exceptional view of the public dump," which any public man must face. Nevertheless, neither business, family life, self-scrutiny, nor social scrutiny seem important keys to Stevens's verse. They function merely as "parts of a world"—three more "porpoises" and "apricots" in an "inscrutable" reality.

Stevens's first volume of verse was *Harmonium*; it appeared in 1923 and was not widely noticed. There followed twelve years in which he published little, but then came *Ideas of Order* and *The Man with the Blue Guitar.* Subsequent volumes include *Parts of a World*, *Transport to Summer*, *Three Academic Pieces*, *The Auroras of Autumn*, *The Necessary Angel*, *The Collected Poems*, and *Opus Posthumous*. While Stevens did not relish public appearances and readings, later in his career he lectured in verse and read prose lectures that sounded like poetry—as *The Necessary Angel*, containing both prose and verse, testifies. When asked to be Charles Eliot Norton Professor at Harvard for 1955 to 1956, Stevens declined the offer, feeling, as he was well on in years, that acceptance of the position would entail his retirement from Hartford Accident.

For *The Auroras of Autumn*, Stevens won the National Book Award in 1951, winning it again, along with a Pulitzer Prize in poetry, in 1955 for *The Collected Poems of Wallace Stevens*. Stevens was also recipient of the Yale Library Bollingen Prize in poetry in 1949. Following the publication of *The Collected Poems*, Stevens suffered from recurrent bouts with cancer and was often hospitalized. He died in August, 1955, after an operation.

Mark Sanders

Bibliography

Bates, Milton J. *Wallace Stevens: A Mythology of Self.* Berkeley: University of California Press, 1985. A readable, biographical approach to studying the poems. Discusses the familial, philosophical, and aesthetic background of the poet. Family papers and letters are used extensively. The parallels between Stevens's life and poetry are excellent in the account of the poet's growth and development.

Bloom, Harold. *Wallace Stevens: The Poems of Our Climate*. Ithaca, N.Y.: Cornell University Press, 1977. A full commentary on almost all Stevens's poetry. A chapter on American poetics from Emerson to Stevens explores the prevalent themes of fate, freedom, and power. Includes an index of Stevens's work.

Cleghorn, Angus J. *Wallace Stevens' Poetics: The Neglected Rhetoric*. New York: Palgrave, 2000. A study responding to critical misapprehension about *Owl's Clover*, argues that the poem's rhetorical poetics are crucial to understanding Stevens's complete poetry as an ethical challenge to the destructive and rigidly repetitive routes of history.

Ford, Sara J. *Gertrude Stein and Wallace Stevens: The Performance of Modern Consciousness*. New York: Routledge, 2002. Compares the conceptions of consciousness revealed in the poetry of Stein and Stevens.

Morse, Samuel F. *Wallace Stevens: Poetry as Life*. New York: Pegasus, 1970. This study relates Stevens's life to his poetry and introduces his poetic ideas, theories, and methods. This is the authorized critical biography commissioned by Stevens's widow and daughter. Supplemented by a short select bibliography.

Santilli, Kristine S. *Poetic Gesture: Myth, Wallace Stevens, and the Motions of Poetic Language*. New York: Routledge, 2002. A study of the role of myth in Stevens's poetry.

Sharpe, Tony. *Wallace Stevens: A Literary Life*. New York: St. Martin's Press, 2000. Sharpe explores the symbiotic and antagonistic relations between Stevens's literary life and his working life as a senior executive, outlining the personal, historical, and publishing contexts which shaped his writing career, and suggesting how awareness of these contexts throws new light on the poems.

Robert Louis Stevenson

Scottish novelist, short-story writer, poet, and essayist

Born: Edinburgh, Scotland; November 13, 1850
Died: Vailima, near Apia, Samoa; December 3, 1894

LONG FICTION: *Treasure Island*, 1881-1882 (serial), 1883 (book); *Prince Otto*, 1885; *The Strange Case of Dr. Jekyll and Mr. Hyde*, 1886; *Kidnapped*, 1886; *The Black Arrow*, 1888; *The Master of Ballantrae*, 1889; *The Wrong Box*, 1889; *The Wrecker*, 1892 (with Lloyd Osbourne); *Catriona*, 1893; *The Ebb-Tide*, 1894 (with Osbourne); *Weir of Hermiston*, 1896 (unfinished); *St. Ives*, 1897 (completed by Arthur Quiller-Couch).

SHORT FICTION: *The New Arabian Nights*, 1882; *More New Arabian Nights*, 1885; *The Merry Men, and Other Tales and Fables*, 1887; *Island Nights' Entertainments*, 1893.

DRAMA: *Deacon Brodie*, pb. 1880 (with William Ernest Henley); *Admiral Guinea*, pb. 1884 (with Henley); *Beau Austin*, pb. 1884 (with Henley); *Macaire*, pb. 1885 (with Henley); *The Hanging Judge*, pb. 1887 (with Fanny Van de Grift Stevenson).

POETRY: *Moral Emblems*, 1882; *A Child's Garden of Verses*, 1885; *Underwoods*, 1887; *Ballads*, 1890; *Songs of Travel, and Other Verses*, 1896.

NONFICTION: *An Inland Voyage*, 1878; *Edinburgh: Picturesque Notes*, 1878; *Travels with a Donkey in the Cévennes*, 1879; *Virginibus Puerisque*, 1881; *Familiar Studies of Men and Books*, 1882; *The Silverado Squatters, Sketches from a Californian Mountain*, 1883; *Memories and Portraits*, 1887; *The South Seas: A Record of Three Cruises*, 1890; *Across the Plains*, 1892; *A Footnote to History*, 1892; *Amateur Emigrant*, 1895; *Vailima Letters*, 1895; *In the South Seas*, 1896; *The Letters of Robert Louis Stevenson to His Family and Friends*, 1899 (2 volumes), 1911 (4 volumes); *The Lantern-Bearers, and Other Essays*, 1988.

Robert Louis Balfour Stevenson, born in Edinburgh in 1850, achieved fame because of his romantic life nearly as much as because of his romantic fiction. His life displays the same split between romantic adventure and grim reality that the discerning reader finds in much of his writing. Stevenson's brief life was a nearly constant journey in search of adventure and relief from the agonies of tuberculosis, with which he was afflicted from early childhood. His father, Thomas Stevenson, a successful Edinburgh lighthouse engineer, hoped for a law career for his only son. Robert did study to be a barrister, but he soon commenced a life of traveling that took him to Switzerland, France, the United States, and, finally, the South Seas. In each place Stevenson found adventure; when he did not find it ready-made, he created it for himself out of his teeming imagination.

Although Stevenson is best known for his fiction, he was a prodigious essayist. The vivid impressions made by the places he visited are recorded in such brilliant travel sketches and essays as *An Inland Voyage*, which tells of a canoeing trip through Belgium and France, and *Travels with a Donkey in the Cévennes*, which records his journeys in southern France. In these books Stevenson shows the sharp eye and sensitivity that were to add so much to the popularity of his fiction.

He had always been ambitious to write and had prepared himself laboriously for a literary career. His famous statements about how he copied the style of great writers such as Charles Lamb (1775-1834), William Hazlitt (1778-1830), Daniel Defoe (1660-1731), and Nathaniel Hawthorne (1804-1864) and about how he was always writing, polishing, and correcting are evidence of this ambition. So, too, is the delicate, precise, but rich style that his fiction achieves.

In France, Stevenson fell in love with Fanny Osbourne, a married woman. He went to California in 1879 to marry her after she had secured a divorce from her husband. This trip caused a break with Stevenson's family, who were opposed to the match, and he suffered many hardships until he acquired a measure of fame and prosperity with the publication of his first major work, *Treasure Island*, written chiefly for the entertainment of his stepson, Lloyd Osbourne. This most famous of adventure stories demonstrated Stevenson's colorful narration and his technique of using a relatively minor character as observer and narrator. *Kidnapped* was immediately popular, but it never attained the following of *Treasure Island*. A striking contrast to these tales of romantic adventure is *The Strange Case of Dr. Jekyll and Mr. Hyde*, perhaps the most famous of all Stevenson's fiction; this grim story of dual personality is filled with Stevenson's concern with ethical problems.

Again in search of improved health, Stevenson left California and traveled in the United States, his longest stay being at Saranac Lake, a health resort in the Adirondacks. He lived there in 1887 and 1888, writing *The Master of Ballantrae*, a tale of the Jacobite struggle, the same subject dealt with in the earlier *Kidnapped*. In *The Black Arrow* he went further back in time to the Wars of the Roses; this book contains a lively picture of late medieval times.

In a final desperate effort to regain his health, Stevenson moved to the South Seas and settled on the island of Samoa. There he found a serenity that encouraged his literary efforts. He was considered a great man by the islanders, and he took an active interest in Samoan politics. In his last years Stevenson was very productive, turning out *The Wrecker* with Lloyd Osbourne and *Catriona*, a sequel to *Kidnapped* but a more able literary performance.

Stevenson died suddenly on December 3, 1894, leaving unfinished his *Weir of Hermiston*, the work that is generally regarded as his masterpiece. In this fragment Stevenson displays again his conviction that the romance of life is, to the individual, more real than what critics and other materialistic novelists of his period were praising as detached objectivity. Criticism has been sharply divided over his work, but he holds a firm place in the favor of all children and adults who believe that adventure is—or at least should be—a part of life.

Victoria Gaydosik

Bibliography

Bathurst, Bella. *The Lighthouse Stevensons*. New York: HarperPerennial, 2000. A history of Stevenson's family, who built fourteen lighthouses along the Scottish coast during the nineteenth century. A fascinating insight into Stevenson's family background.

Bell, Ian. *Dreams of Exile: Robert Louis Stevenson—a Biography*. New York: Henry Holt, 1992. Bell, a journalist rather than an academic, writes evocatively of Stevenson the dreamer and exile. This brief study of Stevenson's short but dramatic life does a fine job of evoking the man and the places he inhabited. It is less accomplished in its approach to the work.

Calder, Jenni. *Robert Louis Stevenson: A Life Study*. New York: Oxford University Press, 1980. A richly detailed, engaging biography of "Tusitala"—the teller of tales, as the Samoan natives called Stevenson. Calder concentrates on the personal history, leaving literary criticism to other writers. She sympathetically presents Fanny Van de Grift Osbourne, Stevenson's wife, who travelled on many journeys with her popular husband. Includes thirty-three photographs, notes, and an index.

Callow, Philip. *Louis: A Life of Robert Louis Stevenson*. Chicago: Ivan R. Dee, 2001. An engaging biography that draws on the work of other biographers to present for the general reader a cohesive life of the novelist.

Chesterton, G. K. *Robert Louis Stevenson*. London: Hodder and Stoughton, 1927. An older but distinguished critical study of Stevenson that is still highly regarded for its insights as well as for its wit and lucidity.

Davies, Hunter. *The Teller of Tales: In Search of Robert Louis Stevenson*. New York: Interlink Books, 1996. Davies recounts Stevenson's life as well as the author's own visits to places where Stevenson lived. Neither conventional scholarly biography nor a book for the armchair traveler, this work is strictly for cultists and would be ideal for someone who, like Davies, wants to tread every corner of the earth, from England to California to Samoa, trod by Stevenson himself.

Furnas, J. C. *Voyage to Windward*. New York: William Sloane, 1951. Furnas, who briefly lived in Stevenson's home in Samoa, traced the author's steps backward to his native Scotland. The work is a popular and sympathetic biography documented with unpublished letters. It contains an elaborate works-consulted bibliography.

Hammond, J. R. *A Robert Louis Stevenson Companion: A Guide to the Novels, Essays, and Short Stories*. London: Macmillan, 1984. The first three sections cover the life and literary achievements of Stevenson and contain a brief dictionary which lists and describes his short stories, essays, and smaller works. The fourth section critiques his novels and romances, and the fifth is a key to the people and places of Stevenson's novels and stories.

McLynn, Frank. *Robert Louis Stevenson: A Biography*. New York: Random House, 1993. The author traces Robert Louis Stevenson's career, noting the malignant influence of his wife and stepson and concluding that Stevenson "is Scotland's greatest writer of English prose."

Saposnik, Irving S. *Robert Louis Stevenson*. New York: Twayne, 1974. A useful critical survey of Stevenson's major works. Saposnik's volume is the best starting point for serious study of Stevenson's fiction. Supplemented by a helpful annotated bibliography.

Adalbert Stifter

Austrian novelist

Born: Oberplan, Bohemia, Austro-Hungarian Empire (now Horní Planá, Czech Republic); October 23, 1805
Died: Linz, Austria; January 28, 1868

LONG FICTION: *Der Condor,* serial 1840, book 1844, 1896; *Die Mappe meines Urgrossvaters*, serial 1841, book 1847, 1939 (*My Great-Grandfather's Note-book*, 1851); *Der Hochwald*, serial 1842, book 1844, 1852 (*Hochwald: A Story of the Thirty Years War,* 1851); *Die Narrenburg*, serial 1843, book 1844, 1855; *Wirkungen eines weissen Mantels*, serial 1843, book 1922 (also known as *Bergmilch* in *Bunte Steine*); *Brigitta*, serial 1844, book 1847, 1899 (English translation, 1957); *Der Hagestolz*, serial 1844, book 1850, 1852 (*The Recluse*, 1968); *Studien*, 1844-1850 (6 volumes; includes *Der Condor, Die Mappe meines Urgrossvaters, Der Hochwald, Die Narrenburg, Brigitta*, and *Der Hagestolz*); *Abdias*, serial 1845, book 1847, 1852 (*Abdias the Jew*, 1851); *Der heilige Abend*, serial 1845, book 1940 (also known as *Bergkristall* in *Bunte Steine*; *Rock Crystal*, 1945); *Der arme Wohltäter,* serial 1848 (also known as *Kalkstein* in *Bunte Steine*; *Limestone*, 1968); *Die Pechbrenner,* serial 1849 (also known as *Granit* in *Bunte Steine*); *Der Pförtner im Herrenhause*, serial 1852 (also known as *Turmalin* in *Bunte Steine*; *Tourmaline*, 1968); *Bunte Steine*, 1853 (2 volumes; includes *Bergmilch, Bergkristall, Kalkstein, Granit, Turmalin*); *Der Nachsommer,* 1857 (*Indian Summer,* 1985); *Witiko*, 1865-1867 (3 volumes; English translation, 1999); *Erzählungen*, 1869 (2 volumes; novellas and short stories); *Julius*, 1950; *Limestone, and Other Stories*, 1968 (includes *The Recluse, Limestone, Tourmaline*).

NONFICTION: *Wien und die Wiener in Bildern aus dem Leuen*, 1844 (with C. E. Langer and C. F. Langer); *Über den geschnitzten Hochaltar in der Kirche zu Kefermarkt*, 1853; *Briefe . . . Herausgegeben von Johannes Aprent*, 1869 (3 volumes); *Vermischte Schriften*, 1870 (2 volumes).

MISCELLANEOUS: *Sämtliche Werke*, 1908-1940 (25 volumes); *Selections*, 1952.

The literary fortunes of Adalbert Stifter (SHTIHF-tur) have risen and fallen several times in the German-speaking world, but in the United States he has remained nearly unknown outside the circle of scholars of German literature. Born October 23, 1805, in the village of Oberplan, in the Czech Republic (then a part of the Austrian Empire), he was the son of a linen trader and small-scale farmer. His mother was the daughter of a butcher. After his father died in an accident in 1817, Stifter's maternal grandfather took him to the well-respected school of the Benedictine monastery of Kremsmünster, where he succeeded admirably. He left Kremsmünster in 1826 and entered the University of Vienna as a student of law. In Vienna, partly because he was often in financial difficulties, he experienced the sadness of being rejected as the suitor of Fanny Greipl, whose parents thought that he was beneath her. Supporting himself as a private tutor, often tutoring the children of prominent families, and occasionally selling a painting he had done, he married Amalia Mohaupt on November 15, 1837, even though he was still in love with Fanny.

In the 1840's he began to succeed as a writer, but his gifts as a painter served him well in the moving descriptions of his native Austrian landscape found in his prose. The first novella he published, *Der Condor* (the condor), was well received, and it was soon followed by a number of others during a period of unusual creative activity. *Abdias* and *Brigitta* in particular secured for him great fame. By 1850, six volumes of his works, each volume appearing under the title *Studien*, had been published. In 1849 Stifter moved from Vienna to Linz, and in 1850 he was appointed as an inspector of schools for that part of Austria, a task that took away precious time from his writing. The revolution of 1848 caused him to become disenchanted with political action, and he sought in education a means of ennobling humankind.

His most cogent statement of aesthetic, moral, and philosophical principles is found in the preface to his 1853 collection of novellas, *Bunte Steine* (colorful stones). In his view it is not the dramatic, cataclysmic events and emotions of life that are actually powerful, but rather the quiet, steady working of rational conduct. This philosophy, which he called the "gentle law," is reflected in the best-known novella from *Bunte Steine*, *Rock Crystal*, and in his most widely appreciated novel, *Indian Summer.* The latter work especially has been faulted for dwelling too much on the details of the scenes and characters portrayed, but for Stifter, the general is seen through the particular and the discrete is an embodiment of overarching principles. By means of the serene word, he hoped to embody the ideals of classical German humanism, although in his personal life he was not able, in an age of revolution and social change, to achieve the ideal to which his prose tends. After an unfortunate series of deaths of individuals who were close to him and after suffering from illnesses himself, he committed suicide in January of 1868.

His admirers have included such famous writers as Friedrich Nietzsche, Rainer Maria Rilke, Hugo von Hofmannsthall, Thomas Mann, and W. H. Auden. Since at least the 1850's, however, opinion has been divided in regard to Stifter's stature, with the earliest and most notorious attacks on him led by the German playwright Friedrich Hebbel. Stifter's supporters admit that his prose is one of loving devotion to the seemingly unspectacular, but they find in this devotion an atmosphere of rarest beauty and profundity.

Thomas P. Baldwin

Bibliography

Buckley, Thomas L. *Nature, Science, Realism: A Re-examination of Programmatic Realism and the Works of Adalbert Stifter and Gottfried Keller.* New York: P. Lang, 1995.

Danford, Karen Pawluk. *The Family in Adalbert Stifter's Moral and Aesthetic Universe: A Rarified Vision*. New York: P. Lang, 1991.

Gump, Margaret. *Adalbert Stifter.* Boston: Twayne, 1974.

Haines, Brigid. *Dialogue and Narrative Design in the Works of Adalbert Stifter.* London: Modern Humanities Research Association for the Institute of Germanic Studies, University of London, 1991.

Jeter, Joseph Carroll. *Adalbert Stifter's "Bunte Steine": An Analysis of Theme, Style, and Structure in Three Novellas*. New York: P. Lang, 1996.

Mason, Eve. *Stifter: "Bunte Steine."* Wolfeboro, N.H.: Grant and Cutler, 1986.

Ragg-Kirkby, Helena. *Adalbert Stifter's Late Prose: The Mania for Moderation*. Rochester, N.Y.: Camden House, 2000.

Sjögren, Christine O., ed. *The Marble Statue as Idea: Collected Essays on Adalbert Stifter's "Der Nachsommer."* Chapel Hill: University of North Carolina Press, 1972.

Stone, Barbara S. Grossmann. *Adalbert Stifter and the Idyll: A Study of "Witiko."* New York: P. Lang, 1990.

Swale, Martin, and Erika Swale. *Adalbert Stifter: A Critical Study.* New York: Cambridge University Press, 1984.

James Still

American poet, novelist, and short-story writer

Born: Double Creek, Alabama; July 16, 1906
Died: Hindman, Kentucky; April 28, 2001

LONG FICTION: *River of Earth*, 1940, 1968, 1978; *Sporty Creek*, 1977.

SHORT FICTION: *On Troublesome Creek*, 1941; *The Wolfpen Rusties: Appalachian Riddles and Gee-Haw Whimmy-Diddles*, 1975; *Pattern of a Man*, 1976; *The Run for the Elbertas*, 1983.

POETRY: *Hounds on the Mountain*, 1937; *River of Earth*, 1983; *The Wolfpen Poems*, 1986; *From the Mountain, from the Valley: New and Collected Poems*, 2001 (Ted Olson, editor).

NONFICTION: *The Man in the Bushes: The Notebooks of James Still, 1935-1987*, 1988; *The Wolfpen Notebooks: A Record of Appalachian Life*, 1991.

CHILDREN'S/YOUNG ADULT LITERATURE: *Way Down Yonder on Troublesome Creek*, 1974; *Jack and the Wonder Beans*, 1977; *An Appalachian Mother Goose*, 1998.

A Kentuckian by adoption, James Still was born in Alabama. His boyhood ambition was to be a veterinarian like his father, and among his earliest recollections were the nights they spent together while nursing a sick animal on some neighbor's farm. At the age of seventeen, he entered Lincoln Memorial University at Harrogate, Tennessee, paying his expenses by working in a rock quarry and in the school library. After his graduation in 1929, he completed work for his M.A. degree at Vanderbilt University in 1930 and spent a year at the University of Illinois Library School. For the six years following, he was librarian at the Hindman Settlement School in Knott County, Kentucky. One of his duties was to carry boxes of books, twenty to the carton, over mountain trails to supply one-room schools that did not have libraries of their own. During those years, he tramped over every ridge and hollow mentioned in his books, which he sets in the region of hill farms and coal camps scattered along the branch waters of Little Carr and Troublesome Creeks.

In 1937 he published *Hounds on the Mountain*, a book of poems that were highly praised for their regional freshness and the lyric beauty of their style. By that time he had gone to live in a log cabin between Deadmare Branch and Wolfpen Creek, where he worked on his first novel, *River of Earth*. Covering two years in the life of a mountain family, it is a simple but moving chronicle of Appalachian mountain life presented through the eyes of a boy growing into a realization of the strange, bewildering world of human relationships and of human responsibilities within that world. The story loses nothing in the episodic manner of its telling, and the whole is tuned to a clear colloquial style that holds echoes of old proverbs and hill-born wisdom as well as of the occasional incorrectness of idiomatic folk speech. *River of Earth* was selected for the Southern Authors' Award in 1941. *On Troublesome Creek* is a collection of short stories in much the same pattern and mood, set against a landscape where the lives of men and women follow the round of the seasons in an almost timeless cycle of birth, growth, seed-time, and death.

During World War II, Still served with the U.S. Army Air Force in Africa and the Middle East. He received a Guggenheim Fellowship in 1946, and in 1947, in recognition of "his gift of style and mastery of character and scene," he received a special award from the Academy of Arts and Letters and the National Institute of Arts and Letters. He subsequently became the librarian at the Hindman School again, as well as a member of the faculty at the annual writers' conference sponsored by Morehead State University.

In the 1970's James Still began publishing a series of "Wolfpen" works, beginning with *The Wolfpen Rusties: Appalachian Riddles and Gee-Haw Whimmy-Diddles*, a collection of folk sayings and riddles from the eastern Kentucky mountains. He continued the series with *The Wolfpen Poems* and *The Wolfpen Notebooks: A Record of Appalachian Life*, a collection of journal entries from twenty-one notebooks covering half a century. One of his most popular works and one he often reads aloud to audiences is *Jack and the Wonder Beans*, a retelling of the Jack and the Beanstalk fairy tale in the Appalachian idiom. Still was recognized for his contributions to literature at the 1994 South Atlantic Modern Language Association convention, and in April, 1995, at the age of eighty-nine, he was appointed to a two-year term as poet laureate of Kentucky. During the 1990's, he also served as a commentator on National Public Radio's *All Things Considered*. He died in Hindman at the age of ninety-four.

Danny L. Miller

Bibliography

Berry, Wendell. "A Master Language." *Sewanee Review* 105, no. 3 (Summer, 1997): 419-422. Berry discusses the works of James Still and their masterful use of dialect and language.

Cadle, Dean. "Pattern of a Writer: Attitudes of James Still." *Appalachian Journal* 15 (Winter, 1988): 104-143. Cadle presents notes from conversations he had with Still between December, 1958, and December, 1959. Includes Still's views on writing; also has photographs of Still, his house, and neighbors and friends.

Dickey, James. Review of *The Wolfpen Poems*, by James Still. *Los Angeles Times Book Review* 1 (December 7, 1986): 19. Dickey states that these poems establish Still as the "truest and most remarkable poet of mountain culture." Notes his sincerity and modesty and commends him for the feel of the country in his poems. Sees the strength of *The Wolfpen Poems* collection in that it underscores the necessity of Appalachian culture and its values.

Foxfire 22 (Fall, 1988). This special issue on Still concentrates on *The Wolfpen Notebooks*; it contains an interview and selections from the book (not yet published at the time of the issue).

The Iron Mountain Review 2 (Summer, 1984). This issue devoted to Still contains an interview with Still as well as essays on his poetry ("James Still's Poetry: 'The Journey of a Worldly Wonder,' " by Jeff Daniel Marion) and short fiction and a Still bibliography.

Miller, Jim Wayne. "James Still." In *Critical Survey of Poetry*, edited by Philip K. Jason. 2d rev. ed. Pasadena, Calif.: Salem Press, 2003. A good starting point for a solid analysis of Still's poetry. Includes a brief biography.

Turner, Martha Billips. "A Vision of Change: Appalachia in James Still's *River of Earth*." *Southern Literary Journal* 24, no. 2 (Spring, 1992): 11. James Still's writings have established his reputation as a serious, talented writer of the Appalachian region. Still's portrayal of Appalachia in *River of Earth* is discussed.

Frank R. Stockton

American short-story writer and novelist

Born: Philadelphia, Pennsylvania; April 5, 1834
Died: Washington, D.C.; April 20, 1902
Pseudonyms: Paul Fort, John Lewes

SHORT FICTION: *The Floating Prince, and Other Fairy Tales*, 1881; *Ting-a-Ling Tales*, 1882; *The Lady, or the Tiger?, and Other Stories*, 1884; *A Christmas Wreck, and Other Stories*, 1886; *Amos Kilbright: His Adscititious Experiences, with Other Stories*, 1888; *The Stories of the Three Burglars*, 1889; *The Rudder Grangers Abroad, and Other Stories*, 1891; *The Clock of Rondaine, and Other Stories*, 1892; *The Watchmaker's Wife, and Other Stories*, 1893; *Fanciful Tales*, 1894; *A Chosen Few*, 1895; *New Jersey: From the Discovery of the Scheyichbi to Recent Times*, 1896; *Stories of New Jersey*, 1896 (also known as *New Jersey*); *A Story-Teller's Pack*, 1897; *Afield and Afloat*, 1900; *John Gayther's Garden and the Stories Told Therein*, 1902; *The Magic Egg, and Other Stories*, 1907; *Stories of the Spanish Main*, 1913; *Best Short Stories*, 1957.

LONG FICTION: *What Might Have Been Expected*, 1874; *Rudder Grange*, 1879; *A Jolly Fellowship*, 1880; *The Story of Viteau*, 1884; *The Transferred Ghost*, 1884; *The Late Mrs. Null*, 1886; *The Casting Away of Mrs. Lecks and Mrs. Aleshine*, 1886; *The Hundredth Man*, 1887; *The Dusantes: A Sequel to "The Casting Away of Mrs. Lecks and Mrs. Aleshine,"* 1888; *The Great War Syndicate*, 1889; *Personally Conducted*, 1889; *Ardis Claverden*, 1890; *The Squirrel Inn*, 1891; *The House of Martha*, 1891; *Pomona's Travels*, 1894; *The Adventures of Captain Horn*, 1895; *Mrs. Cliff's Yacht*, 1896; *Captain Chap: Or, The Rolling Stones*, 1896; *The Great Stone of Sardis: A Novel*, 1898; *The Girl at Cobhurst*, 1898; *The Buccaneers and Pirates of Our Coasts*, 1898; *The Associate Hermits*, 1899; *The Vizier of the Two-Horned Alexander*, 1899; *The Young Master of Hyson Hall*, 1899; *A Bicycle of Cathay: A Novel*, 1900; *Kate Bonnet: The Romance of a Pirate's Daughter*, 1902; *The Captain's Toll-Gate*, 1903; *The Lost Dryad*, 1912; *The Poor Count's Christmas*, 1927.

NONFICTION: *A Northern Voice Calling for the Dissolution of the Union of the United States of America*, 1860; *The Home: Where It Should Be and What to Put in It*, 1872.

CHILDREN'S/YOUNG ADULT LITERATURE: *Ting-a-Ling*, 1870; *Roundabout Rambles in Lands of Fact and Fancy*, 1872; *Tales Out of School*, 1875; *The Bee-Man of Orn, and Other Fanciful Tales*, 1887; *The Queen's Museum*, 1887.

MISCELLANEOUS: *The Novels and Stories of Frank R. Stockton*, 1899-1904 (23 volumes).

Francis Richard Stockton was one of the most popular American humorists of the late nineteenth century, excelling in stories of whimsical fancy, in episodic novels of domestic comedy, and in tales of the occult and supernatural. A descendant of one of the signers of the Declaration of Independence, Stockton was the third son of William Smith Stockton and his second wife, Emily Drean Stockton. Because his physique was generally frail and because he had been born with one leg shorter than the other, young Frank was severely limited in his childhood activities. On his daily walks to school, however, he began to develop his imaginative faculties by orchestrating dramas in his mind, plotting serial tales for his personal diversion. He later noted, "I caused the fanciful creatures who inhabited the world of fairy-land to act . . . as if they were inhabitants of the real world." Such creative strategy later came to characterize Stockton's most successful children's literature and science fiction.

At Central High School in Philadelphia, Stockton won a short-story contest, an achievement which encouraged his aspirations toward an eventual career in writing. In 1852, though, when he graduated, Stockton was apprenticed to a wood engraver and for the next fourteen years worked for a living at this craft, accumulating rejection slips for his occasional forays into fiction. By 1859, he had published only two short stories. In 1860, Stockton married Mary Anne (or Marianne) Edwards Tuttle (her first name has also been spelled without the *e*). He then began to apply himself more vigorously to his writing, and he soon had a serialized tale accepted for publication in the prestigious *Southern Literary Messenger*, a journal at one time partially written and edited by Edgar Allan Poe (1809-1849). A brief, uncharacteristic political posture manifested itself at this time in Stockton's life: He published a pamphlet supporting the right of the South to secede from the Union. When Fort Sumter fell, however, Stockton, a genial, amiable gentleman who actually abhorred controversy, withdrew the slender publication and, for the rest of his life, happily avoided any social or political dispute.

When Stockton published "Ting-a-Ling," a fairy tale about a giant and a dwarf, in *Riverside Magazine* in 1867, he came to the attention of Mary Mapes Dodge (1831-1905), soon to be recognized as a significant force in children's literature. Dodge hired Stockton as her assistant editor on *Hearth and Home*, a periodical for the juvenile market. He was now able to focus his complete attention on the literary arena, and when five years later Dodge assumed the editorship of the classic *St. Nicholas* magazine, she took Stockton along to continue as her assistant editor. Stockton not only helped edit *St. Nicholas* but also contributed tales under his own name and under the pseudonyms Paul Fort and John Lewes.

In 1876, Stockton began experiencing eye difficulties, problems exacerbated by his increasingly heavy load of editorial work and his demanding writing schedule; by 1878, he was forced to resign his post at *St. Nicholas*. From then on, with his wife often acting as his amanuensis and reader, Stockton devoted himself to his own creative writing, with humor constituting his major orientation. He observed, "The discovery that humorous compositions could be used in journals other than those termed comic marked a new era in my life." Sitting comfortably in his New Jersey home, Stockton dictated stories and novels which, he insisted, were without hidden philosophic meaning or deep, critical implications. Success as an entertainer was his simple aim.

His best-known works now began to appear in book form as well as in such popular magazines of the day as *Cosmopolitan*, *Scribner's*, and the *Ladies' Home Journal*. A resounding success was the episodic novel *Rudder Grange*, vignettes chronicling the misadventures of a newly married couple who, with their shrewd but often miscalculating maid Pomona, settle on a houseboat. The audience demanded sequels, and Stockton delivered more sketches of the hapless group in *The Rudder Grangers Abroad, and Other Stories* and *Pomona's Travels*.

Financial success afforded the Stocktons opportunity to travel, and voyages abroad continued to energize the abundant imagination of the acclaimed humorist, particularly directing him to compose another renowned success, *The Casting Away of Mrs. Lecks and Mrs. Aleshine*, a tale of two widows from a small town in Pennsylvania who, along with a formal gentleman, are shipwrecked but, nevertheless, find themselves in enviable circumstances: They are castaways on a tropical island, yet living in a charming home with a full larder. *The Dusantes* became the sequel demanded by Stockton's readership.

Stockton's most memorable piece, however, the one for which succeeding generations of readers have remembered and will continue to remember his name is "The Lady, or the Tiger?" a tale originally appearing in *Century's Magazine* for November, 1882. The story's challenging conclusion spawned much speculation as intrigued readers endeavored to disentangle the verbal clues in pursuit of a solution to this literary cipher that is timelessly intriguing. From time to time, Stockton exploited occultist worlds and other spiritualist manifestations in his imaginative prose. "The Lady in the Box," for example, a tale from *John Gayther's Garden and Stories Told Therein*, is strongly reminiscent of Poe and the elements of gothic mystery as a woman's cataleptic trance is controlled in history, a phenomenon enabling her to transcend forty years without aging. *The Great Stone of Sardis*, set in the New York of 1947, deals with materials virtually foreign to the pre-twentieth century sensibility: submarines, sophisticated communications systems, and the existence of a mammoth diamond located in the very center of the earth. The influence of Jules Verne (1828-1905) on Stockton's science-fiction work is most clearly noticeable in this story.

The Stocktons retired to an estate they had purchased in West

Virginia. In mid-April, 1902, Stockton attended the banquet of the National Academy of Sciences in Washington, D.C. While there, he was taken ill and carried to his hotel room, where he died of a cerebral hemorrhage. Stockton was buried in Woodland Cemetery, Philadelphia, not far from the spot where he had been born.

Abe C. Ravitz

Bibliography

Golemba, Henry L. *Frank R. Stockton*. Boston: Twayne, 1981. This extended examination of Stockton and his art includes an introductory bibliography and chronological investigation of Stockton's works. Golemba also suggests reasons for Stockton's neglect, in relation not only to the works themselves but also to the history of publishing and literary criticism over the last hundred years.

Griffin, Martin I. J. *Frank R. Stockton*. Philadelphia: University of Pennsylvania Press, 1939. This biography gathers together details of Stockton's life—many taken from original sources—and shows the relationship between his life and his works. In the discussion of Stockton's work, however, plot summary dominates over critical interpretation. Includes a bibliography.

Johnson, Robert U. *Remembered Yesterdays*. Boston: Little, Brown, 1923. This memoir by a former editor in chief of *The Century Illustrated Monthly Magazine* includes information about many men and women memorable in the fields of letters and publishing. His short chapter on Stockton, entitled "A Joyful Humorist," gives a feeling for the man through personal recollections and anecdotes.

May, Charles. *The Short Story: The Reality of Artifice*. New York: Twayne, 1995. Brief comment on Stockton's best-known story, "The Lady, or the Tiger?" as a so-called trick-ending story; suggests the story is not as open-ended as it is often claimed to be.

Bram Stoker

Irish novelist

Born: Dublin, Ireland; November 8, 1847
Died: London, England; April 20, 1912

LONG FICTION: *The Snake's Pass*, 1890; *Dracula*, 1897; *The Mystery of the Sea*, 1902; *The Jewel of Seven Stars*, 1904; *The Lady of the Shroud*, 1909; *The Lair of the White Worm*, 1911.
NONFICTION: *Personal Reminiscences of Henry Irving*, 1906.

Abraham "Bram" Stoker, famous for his sensational novel, *Dracula*, was a sickly child, so weak that he was unable to stand up unaided until the age of seven. He outgrew his childhood weakness, however, and became a champion athlete while at Dublin University, from which he graduated in 1867. For the next ten years he worked as an Irish civil servant. From 1871 to 1876 Stoker served as an unpaid drama critic for the Dublin *Mail*, work which won for him the friendship of the actor Henry Irving (1838-1905). As a result of their friendship, Stoker served as Irving's manager for many years.

After touring America with Irving, Stoker wrote a series of lectures about life in the United States to deliver to English audiences. The success of the lectures when printed in pamphlet form caused Stoker to consider other kinds of writing. *Dracula* appeared in 1897. The novel, written in the form of journal entries and letters, tells of the vampire Count Dracula's attempt to spread his evil to London and his eventual defeat. The tale has been produced on stage and in several film versions. The work represents a late nineteenth century development of the earlier gothic novel, and its marked success stimulated other authors to imitate the type. Other works by Stoker worth noting are *The Jewel of Seven Stars* and *The Lair of the White Worm*, both novels, and *Personal Reminiscences of Henry Irving*, which recounts Stoker's life with Irving and with the Lyceum Theatre. During his last years Stoker was also on the literary staff of the *London Telegraph*.

Elisabeth Anne Leonard

Bibliography

Bedford, Barbara. *Bram Stoker: A Biography of the Author of "Dracula."* New York: Alfred A. Knopf, 1996.

Hughes, William. *Beyond "Dracula": Bram Stoker's Fiction and Its Cultural Context*. New York: St. Martin's Press, 2000.

Hughes, William, and Andrew Smith, eds. *Bram Stoker: History, Psychoanalysis, and the Gothic*. New York: St. Martin's Press, 1998.

Senf, Carol A. *Dracula: Between Tradition and Modernism*. New York: Twayne, 1998.

_______, ed. *The Critical Response to Bram Stoker*. Westport, Conn.: Greenwood Press, 1993.

Valente, Joseph. *Dracula's Crypt: Bram Stoker, Irishness, and the Question of Blood*. Urbana: University of Illinois Press, 2002.

Irving Stone

American novelist

Born: San Francisco, California; July 14, 1903
Died: Los Angeles, California; August 26, 1989

LONG FICTION: *Pageant of Youth*, 1933; *Lust for Life*, 1934; *Sailor on Horseback*, 1938; *The President's Lady*, 1951; *Love Is Eternal*, 1954; *The Agony and the Ecstasy*, 1961; *The Passions of the Mind*, 1971; *The Greek Treasure*, 1975; *The Origin*, 1980; *Depths of Glory*, 1985.
NONFICTION: *Clarence Darrow for the Defense*, 1941; *They Also Ran: The Story of the Men Who Were Defeated for the Presidency*, 1945; *Earl Warren: A Great American Story*, 1948; *Men to Match My Mountains: The Opening of the Far West, 1840-1900*, 1956; *The Story of Michelangelo's Pietà*, 1964.
EDITED TEXT: *I, Michelangelo, Sculptor: An Autobiography Through Letters*, 1962 (with Jean Stone).

Irving Stone was born July 14, 1903, in San Francisco, California, son of Charles Tennenbaum and Pauline Rosenberg Tennenbaum Stone. He legalized the surname of his stepfather. Educated at the University of California at Berkeley, Stone received his B.A. in 1923, taught economics at the University of Southern California from 1923 to 1924, when he was awarded his M.A., and then did postgraduate work at the University of California for two more years. In 1934 Stone married Jean Factor, who was to become his editor and researcher. They had a daughter and a son, Paula and Kenneth.

Although Stone's *Pageant of Youth* was published in 1933, he first scored heavily with the "biographical novel" format in 1934, when he dramatically re-created the life of artist Vincent van Gogh. Spirited, colorful, and fact-filled, *Lust for Life* attracted a wide audience who wanted both livelier biographies and rewarding, factual novels. (The nature of this and Stone's similar works—fact-based but imaginatively re-created biography—makes it somewhat inadequate to categorize them as either fiction or nonfiction.) Traveling across Holland, Belgium, and France to recapture the life of the shy and awkward but compassionate artist driven to madness by his less feeling peers, Stone developed a special method of characterization by writing as if he were the character himself. The success of *Lust for Life* was enough to inspire a Hollywood film in 1956 starring Kirk Douglas.

In 1938 Stone won high praise from critics for *Sailor on Horseback*, which detailed the life of American novelist Jack London. Armed with London's correspondence, family documents, and autobiographical writings, Stone produced a seamless amalgam, leaving the reader to wonder where London left off and Stone began. Vivid scenes that account for both London's actions and his dreams caused critics to hail Stone's portrait as full, skillful, and honest. Preferring to write about artists, authors, and political leaders, Stone moved close to the realm of romantic suspense when he chose Rachel Jackson, the wife of Andrew Jackson, as the center of *The President's Lady*. Scorned by the public because of doubt about her divorce from her first husband, Rachel was crafted as an undeniably appealing victim by the author, especially in those scenes where she was used as a political weapon against her husband. The couple's deep love and her untimely death before his presidency greatly moved women readers. The story was filmed in 1953.

In Mary Todd Lincoln, the protagonist of *Love Is Eternal*, Stone found an ideal subject, for he could merge an account of her vilification by the public with a solidly researched narrative of the Civil War period to deliver a heady mixture. Taking his title from the romantic inscription inside Mary Todd Lincoln's wedding band, Stone wrote some of his most moving prose about the deepening love that comes to a couple—in this case, a most unusual couple—who must grow and rebuild after defeat and remorse. *Love Is Eternal* was a popular success, broadening Stone's audience.

Stone's next subject was the great sculptor Michelangelo. Although some critics regarded *The Agony and the Ecstasy* as simply a bad novel and believed the author to be better suited to historical nonfiction, an eager public pushed the work up the best-seller list. The story became a major motion picture in 1965. The four and a half years of research, including Stone's apprenticeship to a sculptor, the book's mix of letters, diaries, histories, and observations, as well as extensive editing by his wife, brought forth an accessible Michelangelo "purged not only of ambisexuality, but of egotism, fault-finding, harsh irony, and ill temper," as one reviewer noted, describing the book as a simplistic view for a popular audience. Stone followed this popular triumph with nonfiction spin-offs such as *I, Michelangelo, Sculptor*; *The Story of Michelangelo's Pietà*; and his introduction to *The Drawings of Michelangelo*.

By the time *The Passions of the Mind* was written, Stone was even more smitten with research. Sigmund Freud's psychoanalytical studies, his friends, and their milieu—all this took Stone six and a half years of research and writing, only to produce a work considered ponderous and indiscriminate by most critics. Similarly, *The Greek Treasure*, the story of Heinrich and Sophia Schliemann and the discovery of ancient Troy, was poorly received by the critics and failed to attain the popular success of its predecessors. *The Origin*, about Charles Darwin's life and writings, garnered higher praise for Stone from most critics. Redmon O'Hanlon termed it "Stone's best researched and best written book to date." Stone compressed Darwin's early life in order to concentrate on the voyage of the *Beagle*, and he is especially fine at rendering the scientist's familial surroundings.

Stone's account of the Impressionist painter Camille Pissarro—*Depths of Glory*—received the most damning critiques of the author's career, ranging from one critic's comment on the less than ideal subject and the "arch drivel" of its dialogue to another's reflection that "it is filled with information—but so is the almanac," adding that "no one comes to life." The more Stone wrote, the more he was criticized for offering too much history and not enough life. Nevertheless, two of his books—*Lust for Life* and *The Agony and the Ecstasy*—were among the most widely read biographical novels of the twentieth century.

Clifton L. Warren

Bibliography

Andrews, Thomas F. *Van Gogh and Stone*. Van Nuys, Calif.: Richard J. Hoffman, 1987. A study of *Lust for Life*.

Isaacs, Susan. "Painter and the Maid." *The New York Times Book Review*, October 20, 1985. Review of *Depths of Glory*.

Jackson, Joseph Henry. *Irving Stone and the Biographical Novel*. Garden City, N.Y.: Country Life Press, 1954. A literary study.

O'Hanlon, Redmon. "Tracking Down the *Beagle*." *The Times Literary Supplement*, June 19, 1981. Review of *The Origin*.

Plagens, Peter. "Artist Novel." *Art in America*, February, 1986. Stone's fictions of artistic life are profiled.

Stieg, Lewis. *Irving Stone: A Bibliography*. Los Angeles: Friends of the Libraries, University of Southern California, 1973. A useful guide for further study.

Robert Stone

American novelist and short-story writer

Born: Brooklyn, New York; August 21, 1937

LONG FICTION: *A Hall of Mirrors*, 1967; *Dog Soldiers*, 1974; *A Flag for Sunrise*, 1981; *Children of Light*, 1986; *Outerbridge Reach*, 1992; *Damascus Gate*, 1998; *Bay of Souls*, 2003.
SHORT FICTION: *Bear and His Daughter: Stories*, 1997.
SCREENPLAYS: *WUSA*, 1970; *Who'll Stop the Rain*, 1978 (with Judith Roscoe).

Robert Anthony Stone is one of the most important novelists of his generation. The son of C. Homer Stone and his wife, Gladys Catherine Grant, Stone was reared almost entirely by his mother in rather economically difficult circumstances. Because of his mother's emotional problems, Stone spent a number of years in a Catholic orphanage and attended Catholic schools. He left high school before his graduation and joined the U.S. Navy, serving from 1955 to 1958. He attended New York University from 1958 to 1959 while also working as an editorial assistant for the New York *Daily News*. In 1959, he married Janice G. Burr, with whom he had two children. In 1962, he was a Stegner Fellow at Stanford University, where he met Ken Kesey and became involved with Kesey's Merry Pranksters and the drug-oriented counterculture, which Tom Wolfe describes in his book *The Electric Kool-Aid Acid Test* (1968). Stone taught writing courses at a number of colleges and universities, including Princeton, Amherst, Stanford, Harvard, and New York Universities.

His first novel, *A Hall of Mirrors*, won for Stone the Faulkner Award for best first novel. His second novel, *Dog Soldiers*, won for Stone the National Book Award in 1975. *A Flag for Sunrise*, his third novel, won the John Dos Passos Prize for literature as well as the American Academy of Arts and Literature Award in 1982. He was a Guggenheim Fellow in 1971 and a National Endowment for the Humanities Fellow in 1983. He became a member of the International Association of Poets, Playwrights, Editors, Essayists, and Novelists (PEN). In addition to novels, Stone writes reviews, essays, and occasional stories for such periodicals as *Harper's Magazine*, *Esquire*, and *The Atlantic Monthly*.

Stone's fiction is deeply engaged with the complex issues and forces of the age. His fiction has virtually Tolstoyan ambitions: to show ideas and morality in action in darkly extreme circumstances and to probe the spiritual depths of the American experience. If Stone receives criticism for the unrelieved harshness of his portrayal of the human condition, he nevertheless earns praise for his uncompromising honesty and artistic integrity. "As a young man," Stone has noted, "I made it a point to be where things were happening." This concern is reflected in his fiction, to which he gives a strong sense of place. In his essay "The Reason for Stories: Toward a Moral Fiction," Stone writes, "I think the key is to establish the connection between political forces and individual lives." Accordingly, in his works, Stone casts rather beleaguered selves into situations of social and political crisis—New Orleans in a time of racial strife and right-wing plots for *A Hall of Mirrors*, California at the end of the Vietnam War for *Dog Soldiers*, Central America in the late 1970's for *A Flag for Sunrise*, Hollywood and a Mexican filmmaking location for *Children of Light*, Jerusalem in the early 1990's for *Damascus Gate*.

Stone's novels are chronicles of survivors, although often rather unfit and undeserving ones. His protagonists are failed and lost pilgrims in a world dominated by corruption and betrayal. For Stone, modern American history is the history of moral failure and moral enfeeblement. At the heart of the moral failure is betrayal—of self, of others, of ideals, and of beliefs. Stone lets his wounded characters work out their destinies in starkly extreme circumstances, portrayals offering only slim grounds for hope. The cynical Rheinhart, the protagonist of *A Hall of Mirrors*, betraying his artistic and humane sensibilities, comes to New Orleans and works as an announcer for a right-wing radio station spewing forth racism and jingoism. He barely survives an elaborate right-wing plot to foment racial conflict. John and Marge Converse are the feckless and reckless survivors of *Dog Soldiers*, who try to cash in on the moral corruption of the Vietnam War by trying to smuggle three kilograms of heroin out of Vietnam for a quick score in the States. Another moral burnout, encapsulated by his cynicism, is anthropologist and former Central Intelligence Agency operative Frank Holliwell of *A Flag for Sunrise*, who betrays any sense of goodness to survive the murky political corruption of Central America in the late 1970's. In *Children of Light*, the actor and screenwriter Gordon Walker fails miserably to recover a lost dream on a film set in Mexico. Recovering from his excesses, Walker ultimately decides to stop going with the flow, a decision which offers some hope for moral renewal. Owen Browne, the hero of *Outerbridge Reach*, attempts to redeem what he considers a shallow middle-class life by entering a yacht race. Browne discovers that neither he nor the boats he has spent his life selling can withstand the crucible of the sea. Unlike Stone's other protagonists, Browne does not survive. In *Damascus Gate*, Christopher Lucas, an American journalist, seeks religious truth in Jerusalem only to be drawn into a plot by Christian fundamentalists and Jewish radicals to bomb the mosques on Jerusalem's Temple Mount. He finds love with Sonia Barnes, an African American Jew, but they part ways in the knowledge that their relationship would never work. *Bay of Souls* features Michael Ahearn, an English professor from the Midwest who leaves his wife and son for Lara Purcell, a political science professor from the Caribbean island of St. Trinity. He follows her there and becomes embroiled in political violence and voodoo.

Along with the survival of the morally unfit in Stone's fiction is often defeat and death for the morally decent. The actions of those characters who bear the burden of decency and caring are rendered futile and ineffectual by the corrupt social and political forces swirling about them. Thus, in *A Hall of Mirrors*, Morgan Rainy and Geraldine, Rheinhart's lover, are defeated, with Geraldine dying in jail. Ray Hicks, the Nietzsche-reading samurai figure of *Dog Soldiers*, suffers death at the hands of corrupt American drug officials. The idealism of Sister Justin Feeney is exploited in *A Flag for Sunrise*, and she faces rape, torture, and death in the aftermath of a failed coup. In *Children of Light*, the lovely but schizophrenic actress Lu Anne Bourgeois commits suicide like the character Edna Pontellier from Kate Chopin's *The Awakening* (1899), whose role she is portraying. In each case, the moral weaknesses and failures of the protagonists directly or indirectly contribute to the defeat and death of the decent and morally sensitive. Stone's work shows great depth and insight in its treatment of the American experience.

Following in the tradition of such writers as Theodore Dreiser and John Dos Passos, Stone is a realist who yet takes full advantage of modernist techniques in such things as point of view and narrative variety. He locates his stories in recognizable social and political contexts to probe a condition beyond politics—the moral and spiritual tenor of the twentieth century. The high critical success of his work is a tribute to the honesty and seriousness of his artistic commitments.

John G. Parks
Steven R. Luebke

Bibliography

Bonetti, Kay, et al., eds. *Conversations with American Novelists*. Columbia: University of Missouri Press, 1997. Stone talks about his early stories in a far-ranging 1982 interview.

Edwards, Thomas R. Review of *Bear and His Daughter: Stories*, by Robert Stone. *The New York Review of Books*, October 9, 1997, 36-38. A favorable review arguing that Stone's stories make more clear his metaphysical bent. Edwards calls the collection "remarkable" for depicting the characters' cries of pain.

Epstein, Jason. "Robert Stone: American Nightmares." In *Plausible Prejudices: Essays on American Writing*. New York: W. W. Norton, 1985. Epstein delineates the violence and destruction in Stone's works and attacks Stone's pessimism.

Finn, James. "The Moral Vision of Robert Stone: Transcendent in the Muck of History." *Commonweal* 119 (November 5, 1993): 9-14. This article in a *Commonweal* series on contemporary Catholic writers of fiction identifies the peculiarly moral strain of Stone's writing.

Gardner, James. "Apocalypse Now." *National Review*, June 1, 1998, 53-54. Gardner reviews *Damascus Gate* favorably, saying that it is informed by a "luminous spiritualism." He comments, however, that the character of Christopher Lucas is somewhat bland for a main character in such a substantive book.

Hower, Edward. "A Parable for the Millennium." *World and I* 13, no. 9 (September, 1998): 255-262. This unreservedly positive review of *Damascus Gate* finds Christopher Lucas a credible world-weary hero who finds his redemption in seeking to understand the conflicts in the Middle East.

Jones, Robert. "The Other Side of Soullessness." *Commonweal* 113 (May 23, 1986): 305-306, 308. Jones shows how Stone chronicles, with cinematic vividness, the country's decay through the voices of its burnt-out cases, always in distant locales, and shows how dangerous and careless people are with one another. In *Children of Light*, Stone tries to mirror the American cultural breakdown but provides only meaningless choices.

Moore, L. Hugh. "The Undersea World of Robert Stone." *Critique: Studies in Modern Fiction* 11, no. 3 (1969): 43-56. Moore argues that Stone's recurring images and metaphors of fish-seafloor-evolution are vital to theme and character. They capture a movement toward a new person who can cope with a nightmarish environment, cold and immoral. In this hostile world, to survive is immoral, but there is no other choice but despair and death.

O'Brien, Tim, and Robert Stone. "Two Interviews: Talks with Tim O'Brien and Robert Stone." Interview by Eric James Schroeder. *Modern Fiction Studies* 30 (Spring, 1984): 135-164. In this interview Stone talks about the background and research for his books, his sense of American values, his personal interpretation of some of his characters, and the changes in his own perceptions.

Parks, John G. "Unfit Survivors: The Failed and Lost Pilgrims in the Fiction of Robert Stone." *CEA Critic* 53 (Fall, 1990): 52-57. Examines the characters of Stone's fiction.

Solotaroff, Robert. *Robert Stone*. New York: Twayne, 1994. The first full-length study of Stone's fiction. Solotaroff's final chapter, "The Stories and the Nonfiction," is a trenchant treatment of Stone's work with analyses of "Helping" and "Absence of Mercy," as well as two other stories from *Bear and His Daughter*, "Porque No Tiene, Porque Le Falta," and "Aquarius Obscured."

Stone, Robert. "Robert Stone." Interview by Charles Ruas. In *Conversations with American Writers*. New York: Alfred A. Knopf, 1984. An intriguing interview in which Stone discusses his early influences, the drug culture, the counterculture movement, his writing process, his goals and values, and his characters and plots.

Phil Stong

American novelist

Born: Keosauqua, Iowa; January 27, 1899
Died: Washington, Connecticut; April 26, 1957

LONG FICTION: *State Fair*, 1932; *Stranger's Return*, 1933; *Village Tale*, 1934; *Week-end*, 1935; *Farmer in the Dell*, 1935; *Buckskin Breeches*, 1937; *The Long Lane*, 1939; *The Iron Mountain*, 1942; *Our Destiny*, 1942; *Jessamy John*, 1947; *Return in August*, 1953.
NONFICTION: *Horses and Americans*, 1939; *Hawkeyes*, 1940; *If School Keeps*, 1940 (autobiography); *Marta of Muscovy*, 1947.
CHILDREN'S/YOUNG ADULT LITERATURE: *The Hired Man's Elephant*, 1939.

Following graduation from the public schools of Keosauqua, Iowa, where he was born in 1899, Philip Duffield Stong went to Drake University, from which he graduated in 1919. After some graduate study at Columbia University (1920-1921) and at the University of Kansas (1923-1924), Stong wrote editorials for the *Des Moines Register* and later taught courses in journalism and speech at Drake University. In 1925 he went to New York City, working successively for the Associated Press, the North American Newspaper Alliance, *Liberty*, *Editor and Publisher*, and the New York *World*. In 1931 he began to devote all his time to creative writing.

Stong's first published novel, *State Fair*, was an immediate success, bringing him economic security and a strong reputation. The novel was made into a motion picture, with Will Rogers in one of the lead roles; after World War II the story was again filmed, this time in color. One of the immediate results of the first motion picture version was that the author was able to repurchase the farmstead which had belonged to his maternal grandfather. After 1932 Stong published a number of novels, but none achieved the popularity of his first. Most of his fiction is about Iowa and the people from the rural areas and small towns of that state. Stong presents midwestern farm life as a full and pleasant existence. *Stranger's Return* relates the return to happy farm life of a young woman who went east to marry a newspaperman. *Village Tale* depicts life, and an episode of unusual violence, in a small Iowa railroad town. *Week-end* exposes the shams of supposedly sophisticated New Yorkers. *Farmer in the Dell* drew upon Stong's experience in Hollywood and presents an Iowa farmer's brief experience as a Hollywood actor. In 1937 Stong reached back into history for *Buckskin Breeches*, which tells of a family's migration from Ohio to Iowa early in the nineteenth century.

Later novels draw upon different kinds of materials. *The Iron Mountain*, a study of a Finnish woman's impact on a Scandinavian and Balkan community in the Mesabi country of Minnesota, makes skillful use of dialects. *Our Destiny* is a topical novel describing the effect of the Pearl Harbor attack and World War II on an Iowa farm family and their way of life. *Jessamy John* is a fictional presentation of John Law. None of these later novels, all well-done pieces of fiction, achieved great popularity or won critical acclaim; Stong has remained for most readers the author of a single novel, *State Fair*.

In addition to these novels, Stong turned out a host of other volumes, including a number of books for children. One of them, *The Hired Man's Elephant*, won the New York Herald Tribune prize for juvenile fiction in that year. Also in 1939 appeared Stong's study of the horse in the United States, *Horses and Americans*. Other nonfictional items include *Hawkeyes*, a history of Iowa; *If School Keeps*, an autobiographical volume; and *Marta of Muscovy*, a biography of the wife of Peter the Great. Stong's last novel was *Return in August*, a sequel to *State Fair* which resumes the story of Margy Drake twenty years after the first volume left her and her romance.

Bibliography

Andrews, Clarence A. *A Literary History of Iowa*. Iowa City: University of Iowa Press, 1972.

Mills, George. "Phil Stong's Legacy." *Des Moines Register*, August 11, 1974.

Paluka, Frank. *Iowa Authors: A Bio-Bibliography of Sixty Native Writers*. Iowa City: Friends of the University of Iowa Libraries, 1967.

"Phil Stong." In *Dictionary of American Biography, Supplement 6: 1956-1960*. New York: Charles Scribner's Sons, 1980.

Tom Stoppard
(Tomas Straussler)

English playwright and screenwriter

Born: Zlín, Czechoslovakia (now in Czech Republic); July 3, 1937

DRAMA: *A Walk on the Water*, pr. 1964 (televised; revised and televised as *The Preservation of George Riley*, pr. 1964; revised and staged as *Enter a Free Man*, pr., pb. 1968); *The Gamblers*, pr. 1965; *Rosencrantz and Guildenstern Are Dead*, pr. 1966; *Tango*, pr. 1966 (adaptation of Sławomir Mrożek's play); *Albert's Bridge*, pr. 1967 (radio play), pr. 1969 (staged); *The Real Inspector Hound*, pr., pb. 1968 (one act); *After Magritte*, pr. 1970, pb. 1993 (one act); *Dogg's Our Pet*, pr. 1971 (one act); *Jumpers*, pr., pb. 1972; *Travesties*, pr. 1974; *Dirty Linen and New-Found-Land*, pr., pb. 1976; *The Fifteen-Minute Hamlet*, pr. 1976; *Every Good Boy Deserves Favour*, pr. 1977 (music by André Previn); *Night and Day*, pr., pb. 1978; *Dogg's Hamlet, Cahoot's Macbeth*, pr. 1979; *Undiscovered Country*, pr. 1979 (adaptation of Arthur Schnitzler's play *Das weite Land*); *On the Razzle*, pr., pb. 1981 (adaptation of Johann Nestroy's play *Einen Jux will er sich machen*); *The Real Thing*, pr., pb. 1982; *The Dog It Was That Died, and Other Plays*, pb. 1983; *The Love for Three Oranges*, pr. 1983 (adaptation of Sergei Prokofiev's opera); *Rough Crossing*, pr. 1984 (adaptation of Ferenc Molnár's play *Play at the Castle*); *Dalliance*, pr., pb. 1986 (adaptation of Schnitzler's play *Liebelei*); *Hapgood*, pr., pb. 1988; *The Boundary*, pb. 1991 (with Clive Exton); *Arcadia*, pr., pb. 1993; *The Real Inspector Hound and Other Entertainments*, pb. 1993; *Indian Ink*, pr., pb. 1995; *The Invention of Love*, pr., pb. 1997; *The Seagull*, pr., pb. 1997 (adaptation of Anton Chekhov's play); *Plays: Four*, pb. 1999; *Plays: Five*, pb. 1999; *The Coast of Utopia*, pr., pb. 2002 (includes *Voyage*, *Shipwreck*, and *Salvage*).

LONG FICTION: *Lord Malquist and Mr. Moon*, 1966.

SCREENPLAYS: *The Engagement*, 1970; *The Romantic Englishwoman*, 1975 (with Thomas Wiseman); *Despair*, 1978 (adaptation of Vladimir Nabokov's novel); *The Human Factor*, 1979 (adaptation of Graham Greene's novel); *Brazil*, 1986; *Empire of the Sun*, 1987 (adaptation of J. G. Ballard's novel); *The Russia House*, 1990 (adaptation of John le Carré's novel); *Rosencrantz and Guildenstern Are Dead*, 1990; *Billy Bathgate*, 1991 (adaptation of E. L. Doctorow's novel); *Medicine Man*, 1992; *Vatel*, 1997 (translation and adaptation of Jeanne LaBrunne's screenplay); *Shakespeare in Love*, 1998; *Enigma*, 1999.

TELEPLAYS: *A Separate Peace*, 1966; *Teeth*, 1967; *Another Moon Called Earth*, 1967; *Neutral Ground*, 1968; *The Engagement*, 1970; *One Pair of Eyes*, 1972 (documentary); *Boundaries*, 1975 (with Clive Exton); *Three Men in a Boat*, 1975 (adaptation of Jerome K. Jerome's novel); *Professional Foul*, 1977; *Squaring the Circle*, 1984; *The Television Plays, 1965-1984*, 1993; *Poodle Springs*, 1998.

RADIO PLAYS: *The Dissolution of Dominic Boot*, 1964; *M Is for Moon Among Other Things*, 1964; *If You're Glad I'll Be Frank*, 1965; *Where Are They Now?*, 1970; *Artist Descending a Staircase*, 1972; *In the Native State*, 1991; *Stoppard: The Plays for Radio, 1964-1991*, 1994.

NONFICTION: *Conversations with Stoppard*, 1995.

TRANSLATION: *Largo Desolato*, 1986 (of Václav Havel's play).

Catapulted to fame in 1967 with the National Theatre's production of *Rosencrantz and Guildenstern Are Dead* (it was first produced in Edinburgh), Tom Stoppard (STOP-ahrd) emerged as a leading dramatist in the second of the two waves of new drama that arrived on the London stage in the mid-1950's and the mid-1960's. Writing high comedies of ideas with what critic Kenneth Tynan described as a hypnotized brilliance, Stoppard established a reputation almost immediately with dazzling displays of linguistic fireworks that evoked comparisons with Oscar Wilde, George Bernard Shaw, and James Joyce. His reinventions of William Shakespeare's *Hamlet* (pr. c. 1600-1601) in *Rosencrantz and Guildenstern Are Dead*, Wilde's *The Importance of Being Earnest* (pr. 1895) in *Travesties*, and August Strindberg's *Fröken Julie* (pb. 1888; *Miss Julie*, 1912) in *The Real Thing* are considered masterpieces. His linguistic caprices and his creative plagiarisms join forces with a love of ideas with which his characters play as much as they do with language.

Born Tomas Straussler to Eugene and Martha Straussler of Zlín (later Gottwaldov), Czechoslovakia, Stoppard was two years old when his father, the company doctor for an international shoe company, was transferred to Singapore on the eve of Germany's annexation of Czechoslovakia. Shortly before the Japanese invasion of Singapore—during which his father was killed—he, his mother, and his brother were moved to Darjeeling, India. There Martha Straussler managed a company shoe shop; she later married Major Kenneth Stoppard, who moved the family to England in 1946. Bored by school, the young Stoppard chose not to go to a university and, instead, became a news reporter in Bristol and later a drama critic for the short-lived magazine *Scene*. His early writing included a novel, some short stories, and a series of short radio plays.

His major early plays (*Rosencrantz and Guildenstern Are Dead*, *Jumpers*, *Travesties*, *Night and Day*, *The Real Thing*, and *Hapgood*), although scintillating in their language, ideas, and plots, have frequently been criticized for the absence of emotionally credible characters and for their lack of social or political commitment. In other plays for stage and television—*Every Good Boy Deserves Favour*, which is about political prisoners in central Europe, *Professional Foul*, about freedoms in Czechoslovakia, and *Squaring the Circle*, about Poland's Solidarity movement—Stoppard entered the political arena. Although active in the anticommunist human rights movement, he kept his distance from the many new playwrights whose political orientation was leftist, who protested economic injustices at home, and who opposed strongly the English class system and the effects of England's colonial past.

In *Rosencrantz and Guildenstern Are Dead* Shakespeare's two most insignificant characters take center stage and become metaphysicians of sorts as they ponder philosophical questions of existence and choice. Like Vladimir and Estragon in Samuel Beckett's *En attendant Godot* (pb. 1952; *Waiting for Godot*, 1954), Ros and Guil debate with each other and with the leader of the traveling players some of the same problems that plague Hamlet in Shakespeare's play. In *Jumpers*, debates on ethics take place between the traditional philosopher George Moore (after G. E. Moore, the author of *Principia Ethica*, 1903), and a modern logical positivist, Archibald Jumper (patterned after the Oxford philosopher Sir Frederick Ayer). Theories of art are debated in *Travesties* by Lenin, James Joyce, and the dadaist Tristan Tzara. Since all three are said to have lived in Zurich about the time of the Russian Revolution, Stoppard pictures their meeting in a library in Zurich. The ingenious plot includes secretaries to Joyce and Lenin named Gwendolyn and Cecily and is structured on the kinds of confusion of identities found in Wilde's *The Importance of Being Earnest*.

The debate of ideas continues in *The Real Thing*, in which the subject of the debate is art as well as love. In *Hapgood* Stoppard fuses debates on modern scientific theories of waves, a spy mystery, and romance; the play shows his usual brilliance of ideas, plot inventiveness, and character identities that remain confusing even at the play's conclusion. Stoppard is a self-educated student of physics, an interest that is reflected in both *Hapgood* and *Arcadia*. *Arcadia* moves back and forth in time as he explores the vast shifts in thinking that humankind has undergone in its shift from Romanticism to scientific theory. Stoppard has also written several screenplays—most notably for Terry Gilliam's film *Brazil*—and he adapted and directed the film version of *Rosencrantz and Guildenstern Are Dead*.

Perhaps one of Stoppard's best works is the 1991 radio play *In the Native State*, which he later adapted for the stage as *Indian Ink*. Stoppard deals here with the theme of India gaining its independence (or losing its status as a British territory). It also addresses the cultural taboo of sexual relations between British women and Indian men. *The Invention of Love* is a memory play again based on the life of A. E. Housman, a poet and classics scholar of the late nineteenth and early twentieth century.

The title of Irving Wardle's review of *The Real Thing*, "Cleverness with Its Back to the Wall," is a description that in varying degrees can be applied to all of Stoppard's plays. To the critic, however, who applies Stoppard's own description of his plays as "ambushes for the audience" and his own rejection of "yes" and "no" answers to questions, the literate high comedies of ideas provide a refreshing contrast to the plays of the so-called committed dramatist.

Stoppard admires Beckett, who "picks up a proposition and then dismantles and qualifies each part of its structure as he goes along, until he nullifies what he started out with." Characterizing his play debates as a "series of conflicting statements made by conflicting characters who tend to play an infinite leapfrog," Stoppard divides his characters into two types: Moons and Boots. The former lose themselves in their arguments, while the latter emerge victorious by means of their style, the controlling factor in their survival. Many of his early plays contain characters with the names Moon and Boot. Stoppard himself, who derives the name Boot from a character in Evelyn Waugh's novel *Scoop* (1938), can, by virtue of his own identity as inventive stylist, be categorized as a Boot character.

Stoppard is not a philosopher, however; he is definitely a playwright. He uses the world and the thought he finds around him in something of the wild, dizzy, and exhilarating manner of a metaphysical poet. With Harold Pinter, Stoppard shares a reputation as the most inventive stylist of the two waves of revolution that swept the English stage in the second half of the twentieth century.

Susan Rusinko
Janet Lorenz

Bibliography

Billington, Michael. *Stoppard the Playwright*. London: Methuen, 1987. Long the drama critic of *The Guardian*, Billington, who writes from a leftist perspective, admires Stoppard's eloquence but mistrusts his conservative ideas. Still, Billington praises *The Real Thing* and expresses his hopes that Stoppard will increase his passion for both people and causes.

Brassell, Tim. *Tom Stoppard: An Assessment*. New York: St. Martin's Press, 1985. Brassell's study is detailed, elegantly written, and learned. He applies a considerable knowledge of modern drama as well as philosophy.

Cahn, Victor. *Beyond Absurdity: The Plays of Tom Stoppard*. Rutherford, N.J.: Fairleigh Dickinson University Press, 1979. Traces absurdist techniques through Stoppard's plays.

Gusso, Mel. *Conversations with Stoppard*. New York: Limelight Editions, 1995. A collection of interviews between *New York Times* drama critic Gusso and the playwright that covers the time from 1972 to 1995 when the playwright's *Indian Ink* was about to open in London. Presents Stoppard's own erudite thoughts on his work.

Hayman, Ronald. *Tom Stoppard*. London: Heinemann, 1977. Hayman's compact text is chiefly valuable for two highly revealing interviews conducted in 1974 and 1976.

Kelly, Katherine E., ed. *The Cambridge Companion to Tom Stoppard*. Cambridge, England: Cambridge University Press, 2001. Provides essays on all things Stoppard, including an in-depth biography, as well as scholarly criticism on his plays, radio plays, and screenplays. Also contains a very extensive bibliography.

Londré, Felicia Hardison. *Tom Stoppard*. New York: Frederick Ungar, 1981. Especially good in tracing the sources of the abundant allusions in Stoppard's writing.

Rusinko, Susan. *Tom Stoppard*. Boston: Twayne, 1986. Mainly summarizes the views of other critics and reviewers. Its chief service is an extended bibliography of secondary as well as primary sources.

Sammells, Neil. *Tom Stoppard: The Artist as Critic*. New York: St. Martin's Press, 1988. Examines the playwright's exploration of literary forms and contrasts his artistic freedom with his political conservatism.

Whitaker, Thomas. *Tom Stoppard*. New York: Grove Press, 1983. Whitaker's text is succinct, perceptive, and smoothly worded. He stresses the performance aspects of Stoppard's plays, often commenting on particular productions that he has seen.

David Storey

English playwright and novelist

Born: Wakefield, England; July 13, 1933

DRAMA: *The Restoration of Arnold Middleton*, wr. 1959, pr. 1966; *In Celebration*, pr., pb. 1969; *The Contractor*, pr. 1969; *Home*, pr., pb. 1970; *The Changing Room*, pr. 1971; *Cromwell*, pr., pb. 1973; *The Farm*, pr., pb. 1973; *Life Class*, pr. 1974; *Mother's Day*, pr. 1976; *Sisters*, pr. 1978; *Early Days*, pr., pb. 1980; *Phoenix*, pr. 1984; *The March on Russia*, pr., pb. 1989; *Stages*, pr., pb. 1992; *Caring*, pb. 1992; *Plays: One*, pb. 1992; *Plays: Two*, pb. 1994; *Plays: Three*, pb. 1998.
LONG FICTION: *This Sporting Life*, 1960; *Flight into Camden*, 1960; *Radcliffe*, 1963; *Pasmore*, 1972; *A Temporary Life*, 1973; *Saville*, 1976; *A Prodigal Child*, 1982; *Present Times*, 1984; *A Serious Man*, 1998; *As It Happened*, 2002.
SCREENPLAYS: *This Sporting Life*, 1963 (adaptation of his novel); *In Celebration*, 1975 (adaptation of his play).
POETRY: *Storey's Lives: Poems, 1951-1991*, 1992.
CHILDREN'S/YOUNG ADULT LITERATURE: *Edward*, 1973.

David Malcolm Storey is renowned as both a novelist and a playwright. His works are awaited in Great Britain as major statements on his times by a writer whom many consider to be the best of his generation. Born the third son of a coal miner, Storey was reared on a large urban housing estate in the provincial north of England. His life was complicated from the first by the fact that an elder brother died before his birth, leaving his mother in the grips of a suicidal grief. (Another brother, Anthony, is a minor novelist known for his melodramatic mixing of theology and eroticism.)

The young Storey's sense of being an outsider was exacerbated by his being educated out of his class at Wakefield's Queen Elizabeth Grammar School and by his decision, at age seventeen, to become an artist. This determination involved him in a class and family struggle. Two years at Wakefield College of Art were made more desolate by his teachers' pressuring him to become a commercial artist. Next, disappointed by his failure to train for a professional life, his parents refused to sign his application form to the Slade School of Fine Art in London. Then, in order to support himself fully while in school, Storey played professionally for Leeds Rugby League Club for four seasons. In a 1982 interview he commented on the psychological strain of living in two opposing worlds: "When I played football the other players thought I was homosexual, and at the Slade, they thought I was a yob [hooligan]." Storey's move to London was final; his marriage to Barbara Rudd Hamilton in 1956 produced two sons and two daughters. His painting won for him several prizes, but it was to writing that Storey dedicated himself after leaving art school.

Storey's Leeds experiences are evident in *This Sporting Life*, the story of professional rugby footballer Arthur Machin's tender but abortive affair with his downtrodden landlady, and his discovery that material "success" (as defined by both the working and the middle classes of England in the newly prosperous late 1950's) cannot bring a sense of wholeness of belonging. The novel was the eighth that Storey had written (he has continued to write far more than he publishes) and went the rounds of more than a dozen publishers over a four-year period before it was finally accepted. Similarly, Storey's first play, *The Restoration of Arthur Middleton*, was written nine years before its first production. The difficulties of Storey's early years ended when in 1960 *This Sporting Life* won for him the Macmillan Fiction Award, the icing on the cake of widespread critical acclaim. Numerous other awards have included Great Britain's most prestigious literary award, the Booker-McConnell Prize, for his autobiographical *Saville* in 1976. Awards for his dramas, above all *The Contractor*, *Home* (set in an insane asylum), and *The Changing Room*, have included the *Evening Standard* Award in 1967, and the New York Drama Critics Circle Award in 1971, 1973, and 1974.

This Sporting Life also led to an intense and fruitful working friendship with film and play director Lindsay Anderson, for whom Storey wrote screen versions of both his first novel and his play *In Celebration*, in which three "successful" sons briefly return home to their working-class family. (*A Prodigal Child* is one of Storey's later explorations of this autobiographical theme of the return.) *In Celebration* exemplifies how Storey's work balances on a knife-edge between black melodrama and stoic satire: The film, he has said, "came out as very remorseless, . . . whereas the audiences always laughed heartily at the live production." (*Mother's Day*, by way of analogy, is a farce about incest.) Over the course of his career, Storey has moved away from the schematizing and allegorizing of his first three novels toward letting his material dictate his form. His hugely ambitious third novel, *Radcliffe* (compared by critics to Emily Brontë's *Wuthering Heights*, 1847; though also condemned as morbid gothic fantasy), had been predicated on what Storey sees as the original sin of decadent Western society—the division between soul and body, which in *Radcliffe* is paralleled by the division between an enfeebled upper class and a vigorous but philistine lower class, figured in the destructive homosexual relationship of Leonard Radcliffe and "Vic" Tolson, a working-class giant drawn with demoniac energy. A similar decadence of society breeds the breakdowns of the central characters in *Pasmore* and *A Temporary Life*.

Storey's plays, unlike his novels, are loosely plotted, poetic evocations of situations and relationships, far more psychological in method and intent than the novels, although frequently intimately related to them: *The Contractor*, for example, dramatizes and expands one episode from *Radcliffe*, the erecting of a huge show marquee for a wedding; *The Changing Room* picks up on the last scene of *This Sporting Life* (a climactic rugby match), focusing on what Storey has called the "rituals" of men gathered into groups, where their individual personalities, as well as their clothes, may undergo "change"; *In Celebration* dramatizes psychological material Storey decided mostly to leave out of *Saville* and was written during a period when work on the novel had ground to a halt.

Storey's slowly written novels and his swiftly written plays also share a quality of distance: The dialogue of both often has a very British quality of unemotional understatement, difficult to read for some Americans; indeed, all communication in *Home* takes place in evasive euphemisms. A similar distance informs Storey's use of autobiographical material: Clearly, his work depends on it, but his imagination transforms it. Finally, both plays and novels are powerfully visual. Storey has said that he envisages his plays as moving paintings, with the proscenium arch as a "picture frame." Similarly, much of the enormous and disturbing energy of his novels is stored in their imagery and descriptions: Landscapes can become Kafkaesque states of mind.

Joss Marsh

Bibliography

Hutchings, William. *The Plays of David Storey: A Thematic Study.* Carbondale: Southern Illinois University Press, 1988. The first full-length study devoted solely to Storey's work for the theater, Hutchings's valuable book provides detailed critical analyses of each drama. Hutchings sees Storey as stressing the importance of physical work and daily rituals to help the individual achieve a sense of community in a modern society that has been radically desacralized by industrialism and technology. Contains an extensive bibliography.

_______, ed. *David Storey: A Casebook.* New York: Garland, 1992. The essays on Storey's plays concern the role of the artist, the depiction of women, the relationship between family and madness, and the use of comedy. Hutchings provides an introduction, a chronology, and an extensive bibliography dealing with Storey's dramas. One of the only collections devoted exclusively to Storey's dramatic output.

Kerensky, Oleg. *The New British Drama: Fourteen Playwrights Since Osborne and Pinter.* New York: Taplinger, 1977. Kerensky focuses on the conflict between working-class parents and well-educated middle-class sons in Storey's plays, wherein fidelity to naturalistic detail often takes precedence over plot. He devotes his lengthiest comments to *Mother's Day*, Storey's negatively reviewed farce about English domestic life.

Liebman, Herbert. *The Dramatic Art of David Storey: The Journey of a Playwright.* Westport, Conn.: Greenwood Press, 1996. Liebman provides some biographical information, comments on the ties between Storey's novels and his films, and groups the plays into three categories for purposes of analysis: plays of madness, plays of work, and family plays. He also provides a selected bibliography.

Quigley, Austin E. "The Emblematic Structure and Setting of David Storey's Plays." *Modern Drama* 22, no. 3 (1979): 259-276. In response to conflicting assessments over whether Storey should be regarded as a traditional or an experimental playwright, Quigley probes the basis for Storey's originality as a dramatist. He proposes that it rests in his uncanny ability to reconceive conventional theatrical devices as "structuring images" that contain the plays' themes.

Randall, Phyllis R. "Division and Unity in David Storey." In *Essays on Contemporary British Drama*, edited by Hedwig Bock and Albert Wertheim. Munich: Max Hueber Verlag, 1981. Randall sees as major themes in Storey's writing the disintegration of both the individual and the family or social unit, and "the struggle to make life work on both the external and internal levels." The dramas, she argues, accept the impossibility of full integration, often ironically undercutting the spiritual values. Concludes with a useful chart indicating the interrelationships between Storey's novels and plays.

Taylor, John Russell. *David Storey.* London: Longman, 1974. This pamphlet, written by one of the principal authorities on contemporary British drama as part of the British council's Writers and Their Work series, charts the connections between Storey's novels and plays up through 1973. Taylor emphasizes the tension between the physical and the spiritual in the fiction and the blending of realistic with symbolic or allegorical levels in the dramas. Includes a photograph of Storey as a frontispiece.

Worth, Katharine J. *Revolutions in Modern English Drama.* London: G. Bell and Sons, 1972. In brief yet sensitive remarks, Worth explores Storey's use of physical objects as a focal point and his expert handling of space (stage space in *The Contractor* and screen space in the television adaptation of *Home*). Worth believes that audiences relish the process through which space is transformed, and the characters too, as they participate in fleeting moments of communion.

Theodor Storm

German novelist

Born: Husum, Schleswig (now in Germany); September 14, 1817
Died: Hademarschen, Holstein, Germany; July 4, 1888

LONG FICTION: *Immensee*, 1849 (*Immensee: Or, The Old Man's Reverie*, 1858); *Sommer-Geschichten und Lieder*, 1851 (novellas and poetry); *Im Sonnenschein*, 1854 (*In the Great Hall*, 1923); *Ein grünes Blatt*, 1855 (*A Green Leaf*, 1964); *Hinzelmeier*, 1857; *In der Sommer-Mondnacht*, 1860; *Drei Novellen*, 1861 (includes *Veronika* [English translation, 1964]); *Auf der Universität*, 1863; *Im Schloss*, 1863; *Lenore*, 1865; *Zwei Weihnachtsidyllen*, 1865; *Drei Märchen*, 1866; *Von Jenseits des Meeres*, 1867; *In St. Jürgen*, 1868 (*In St. Jurgen*, 1964); *Novellen*, 1868; *Sämtliche Schriften*, 1868-1889 (19 volumes); *Eine Halligfahrt*, 1871 (*Journey to a Hallig*, 1999); *Geschichten aus der Tonne*, 1873; *Zerstreute Kapitel*, 1873; *Novellen und Gedenkblätter*, 1874; *Viola tricolor*, 1874 (English translation, 1956); *Pole Poppenspäler*, 1874 (*Paul the Puppeteer*, 2003); *Waldwinkel*, 1874; *"Ein stiller Musikant," "Psyche," "Im Nachbarhaus links,"* 1876 (three novellas); *Aquis submersus*, 1877 (English translation, 1910; also known as *Beneath the Flood*, 1962); *Carsten Curator*, 1878 (*Curator Carsten*, 1956); *Neue Novellen*, 1878; *Renate*, 1878 (English translation, 1909); *Drei neue Novellen*, 1880; *Eekenhof*, 1880 (novella; English translation, 1908); *Zur "Wald- und Wasserfreude,"* 1880; *Die Söhne des Senators*, 1881 (*The Senator's Sons*, 1947); *Der Herr Etatsrath*, 1881; *Hans und Heinz Kirch*, 1883 (*Hans and Heinz Kirch*, 1999); *Zwei Novellen*, 1883; *Zur Chronik von Grieshuus*, 1884 (*A Chapter in the History of Grieshuus*, 1908); *Ein Fest auf Haderslevhuus*, 1885 (novella; *A Festival at Haderslevhuus*, 1909); *Vor Zeiten*, 1886; *Bei kleinen Leuten*, 1887; *Bötjer Basch*, 1887; *Ein Doppelgänger*, 1887; *Ein Bekenntniss*, 1888; *"Es waren zwei Königskinder,"* 1888; *Der Schimmelreiter*, 1888 (novella; *The Rider on the White Horse*, 1915); *The Rider on the White Horse, and Selected Stories*, 1964 (includes *In the Great Hall*, *Immensee*, *A Green Leaf*, *In the Sunlight*, *Veronika*, *In St. Jurgen*, *Aquis submersus*, and *The Rider on the White Horse*).

POETRY: *Liederbuch dreier Freunde*, 1843 (with Theodor Mommsen and Tycho Mommsen); *Sommer-Geschichten und Lieder*, 1851; *Gedichte*, 1852, 1856, 1864, 1885.

NONFICTION: *Der Mörike-Storm Briefwechsel*, 1891; *Briefe an Friedrich Eggers*, 1911; *Briefe an seine Frau*, 1915; *Briefe an seine Freunde*, 1917; *Heyse-Storm Briefwechsel*, 1917-1918.

MISCELLANEOUS: *Theodor Storms Sämtliche Werke*, 1919-1924.

Hans Theodor Woldsen Storm (shtawrm) was one of Germany's greatest writers of the Age of Realism. In addition to his well-constructed novellas, he also produced highly regarded lyric poetry. Storm was born in Husum, a small coastal town in the province of Schleswig, and much of his writing is closely associated with the area. After completing law school, he settled in his hometown, expecting to live there for the rest of his life. The Danish occupation of Schleswig-Holstein (1853-1864) and his outspokenness against Danish oppression forced him into unhappy exile to Potsdam in 1853 and, in 1856, to Heiligenstadt, where he worked as the district judge. After the Prussians defeated the Danes, the author was again able to return to his beloved Husum in 1864.

Storm was married twice. He married his first cousin, Constanze Esmarch, in 1846; she died in 1865. Constanze was a major inspiration for Storm's writing, and her sensitive critique of his work helped the author to achieve stylistic perfection. Even during his marriage to Constanze, however, the author was attracted to Dorothea Jensen, who loved him passionately even though he was already married. After Constanze's death, Storm was free to marry Dorothea. The turbulent and sometimes tragic relationship with Dorothea and their search for happiness are the background to Storm's 1874 novella *Viola tricolor.*

After Storm's return to Husum, he was elected to various high judicial and administrative positions that he held until 1880, when he retired to nearby Hademarschen. The author remained preoccupied with his writing, which was closely connected to his personal experiences, the local environment, and local history. His lyric poetry was influenced primarily by folklore and by the poet Joseph von Eichendorff. The poems are, variously, joyful, restrained, descriptive of the native landscape, politically patriotic, impressionistic, and—later—mostly melancholy and tragic. They reach a high point of creativity in the poems written after his first wife's death, works that reflect solitude, love, and death.

Storm corresponded with a number of other contemporary literary figures, including Theodor Fontane, Paul Heyse, Gottfried Keller, Eduard Mörike, and the Russian novelist Ivan Turgenev. By the middle of the 1860's, he began to write almost exclusively realistic prose, primarily novellas. His more than fifty novellas reflect a variety of subjects and moods. They deal with themes of solitude and isolation, lack of communication, superstition and religious bigotry, social problems such as alcoholism, family life, the dilemmas of artists, and love. Many of the novellas are based on ancient chronicles or local history, and although they are realistic, they are characterized by subtle lyricism and subjectivism. They give the reader insight into a human existence in which one sometimes finds joy or humor but mostly tragedy and despair.

Storm's life and art are deeply connected to his native town of Husum, a small trade center on the North Sea, which he affectionately referred to as "the gray town of the sea." The patriotism reflected frequently in the author's works derives from his deep love for his people, his town, and the native landscape. Storm's nostalgic longing for the past and a vanished glorious history is based on the fact that Husum had lost its economic significance and, with the Danish occupation, even its political independence.

The transformation in Storm's artistry is best exemplified by a comparison between his first novella, *Immensee*, and his last, *The Rider on the White Horse*. The former combines a deep joy of life with a gentle melancholy and resignation that can also be found in the works of many late Romantics. The nostalgic longing for the past combines joy and suffering; the present will never reach the beauty of the past. In contrast, the tone of *The Rider on the White Horse*, a story about an ambitious dike master who is destroyed by nature and a lack of support by his fellow men, is much harsher. The hero's valiant battle against nature and superstition is powerfully and graphically described. There is little room for digressions in this realistically gripping tragedy.

It is somewhat surprising that Storm never tried to write a full-length novel or a drama. Most of his novellas are set in his native environment, which may be the reason for his image as a regional or provincial writer; it may also be why his work is not well known internationally and relatively little translated.

Rado Pribic

Bibliography

Alt, A. Tilo. *Theodor Storm*. New York: Twayne, 1973. Contains biography, literary analysis, a chronology, and a bibliography of primary and secondary sources.

Artiss, David. *Theodor Storm: Studies in Ambivalence—Symbol and Myth in His Narrative Fiction*. Amsterdam: Benjamins, 1978. A study of Storm's literary technique.

Burns, Barbara. *Theory and Patterns of Tragedy in the Later Novellen of Theodor Storm*. Stuttgart, Germany: Heinz, 1996. Storm's position as a tragedian is analyzed.

Dysart, David L. *The Role of Painting in the Works of Theodor Storm*. New York: P. Lang, 1992. The visual aspect of Storm's work is addressed.

Jackson, David A. *Theodor Storm: The Life and Works of a Democratic Humanitarian*. New York: St. Martin's Press, 1992. A useful bibliography.

Strehl, Wiebke. *Theodor Storm's "Immensee": A Critical Overview*. Rochester, N.Y.: Camden House, 2000. A study of Storm's novel.

Rex Stout

American novelist

Born: Noblesville, Indiana; December 1, 1886
Died: Danbury, Connecticut; October 27, 1975

LONG FICTION: *Her Forbidden Knight*, 1913; *A Prize for Princes*, 1914; *Under the Andes*, 1914; *The Great Legend*, 1916; *How Like a God*, 1929; *Seed on the Wind*, 1930; *Golden Remedy*, 1931; *Forest Fire*, 1933; *Fer-de-Lance*, 1934; *The President Vanishes*, 1934; *O Careless Love*, 1935; *The League of Frightened Men*, 1935; *The Rubber Band*, 1936; *The Hand in the Glove*, 1937; *The Red Box*, 1937; *Mr. Cinderella*, 1938; *Too Many Cooks*, 1938; *Double for Death*, 1939; *Mountain Cat*, 1939; *Red Threads*, 1939; *Some Buried Caesar*, 1939; *Bad for Business*, 1940; *Bitter End*, 1940 (novella); *Over My Dead Body*, 1940; *Where There's a Will*, 1940; *Alphabet Hicks*, 1941; *The Broken Vase*, 1941; *Black Orchids*, 1944 (2 novellas; includes *Black Orchids* and *Cordially Invited to Meet Death*); *Not Quite Dead Enough*, 1944 (2 novellas; includes *Not Quite Dead Enough* and *Booby Trap*); *The Silent Speaker*, 1946; *Too Many Women*, 1947; *And Be a Villain*, 1948; *The Second Confession*, 1949; *Trouble in Triplicate*, 1949 (3 novellas; includes *Help Wanted, Male*, *Instead of Evidence*, and *Before I Die*); *Curtains for Three*, 1950 (3 novellas; includes *Bullet for One*, *The Gun with Wings*, and *Disguise for Murder*); *In the Best Families*, 1950; *Three Doors to Death*, 1950 (3 novellas; includes *Man Alive*, *Omit Flowers*, and *Door to Death*); *Murder by the Book*, 1951; *Prisoner's Base*, 1952; *Triple Jeopardy*, 1952 (3 novellas; includes *The Cop-Killer*, *The Squirt and the Monkey*, and *Home to Roost*); *The Golden Spiders*, 1953; *The Black Mountain*, 1954; *Three Men Out*, 1954 (3 novellas; includes *This Won't Kill You*, *Invitation to Murder*, and *The Zero Clue*); *Before Midnight*, 1955; *Might as Well Be Dead*, 1956; *Three Witnesses*, 1956 (3 novellas; includes *When a Man Murders*, *Die Like a Dog*, and *The Next Witnesses*); *If Death Ever Slept*, 1957; *Three for the Chair*, 1957 (3 novellas; includes *Immune to Murder*, *A Window for Death*, and *Too Many Detectives*); *And Four to Go*, 1958 (4 novellas; includes *Christmas Party*, *Easter Parade*, *Fourth of July Picnic*, and *Murder Is No Joke*); *Champagne for One*, 1958; *Plot It Yourself*, 1959; *Three at Wolfe's Door*, 1960 (3 novellas; includes *Poison à la Carte*, *Method Three for Murder*, and *The Rodeo Murder*); *Too Many Clients*, 1960; *The Final Deduction*, 1961; *Gambit*, 1962; *Homicide Trinity*, 1962 (3 novellas; includes *Death of a Demon*, *Eeny Meeny Murder Mo*, and *Counterfeit for Murder*); *The Mother Hunt*, 1963; *A Right to Die*, 1964; *Trio for Blunt Instruments*, 1964 (3 novellas; includes *Kill Now—Pay Later*, *Murder Is Corny*, and *Blood Will Tell*); *The Doorbell Rang*, 1965; *Death of a Doxy*, 1966; *The Father Hunt*, 1968; *Death of a Dude*, 1969; *Please Pass the Guilt*, 1973; *A Family Affair*, 1975; *Death Times Three*, 1985 (3 novellas; includes *Bitter End*, *Frame-Up for Murder*, and *Assault on a Brownstone*).

EDITED TEXTS: *The Illustrious Dunderheads*, 1942; *Rue Morgue No. 1*, 1946 (with Louis Greenfield); *Eat, Drink, and Be Buried*, 1956; *The Nero Wolfe Cookbook*, 1973 (with others).

Rex Todhunter Stout, perhaps the most prolific of American mystery authors, was born in Noblesville, Indiana, on December 1, 1886. The son of John Wallace Stout and Lucetta Todhunter Stout, he descended from five generations of Quakers and had an impressive legacy of ancestors, including Mary Franklin, Benjamin Franklin's sister, and Joshua Hoopes, a member of the Pennsylvania Colonial Assembly. His father, known as a disciplined and exacting man, worked as a teacher and educational administrator as well as publisher and traveling salesman, never truly finding a vocation that could provide him a professional home. John Stout's success was often marginal, causing numerous upheavals and moves during Rex Stout's boyhood. His mother, one of nine children, completed college along with seven of her siblings, a rare accomplishment before the turn of the twentieth century. Lucetta Todhunter Stout encouraged her children to aspire to exceptional achievement and self-reliance.

In 1887 the Stout family relocated to Wakarusa, Kansas, where Stout would spend his early childhood years. His accomplishments during his early childhood made him known as a phenomenon throughout the state of Kansas, as he began to read at the age of eighteen months, had read the Bible in its entirety by the age of five, and by ten was touring the state of Kansas, giving mathematical demonstrations as a prodigy. The family later relocated to Topeka, Kansas, where Stout attended and graduated from Topeka High School at the age of sixteen and considered and rejected the idea of attending college at the University of Kansas, Lawrence, before enlisting in the United States Navy, where he worked as a yeoman on President Theodore Roosevelt's yacht.

Shortly thereafter, Stout began writing poetry and then short stories and novels, presented serially in magazines. By the age of twenty-six, he had already received respectable reviews as an author. In 1916 Stout met and married Fay Kennedy, the sister of a high school classmate. Concerned that his work as an author was hampered because of financial need, Stout teamed with his brother in developing a banking system designed for children. The development of this banking system gave Stout the financial freedom to allow for a period of European travel during which time he began his writing in earnest, no longer feeling compelled to write because of financial necessity.

After the stock market crash, Stout settled in Brewster, New York, and began the building of his estate, High Meadow. During this time, a change in lifestyle and personal direction undermined and eventually ended his first marriage. Shortly after his divorce in 1932, Stout married Pola Weinbach Hoffmann, a textile designer, a second marriage for both parties. They had two daughters, Barbara and Rebecca.

In 1934, after the birth of his first daughter, Stout published his book *Fer-de-Lance*, in which the often-quoted and illustrious detective genius, Nero Wolfe, and his irascible sidekick, Archie, are introduced. Criticism of Stout's work frequently notes that by combining the more articulate and thinking man's character of Wolfe, reminiscent of Sir Arthur Conan Doyle's character Sherlock Holmes and of the British school of mystery writing, with the detective Archie, based on the mostly American school of "hard-boiled" detective novels, that Stout was able to assimilate the best qualities of both genres of mystery fiction. The result is a fascinating and often humorous blend of two very different characters working together to solve crimes. Wolfe, the master genius who chose almost never to leave his house, was a connoisseur of fine beer, a gourmet cook, and an orchid aficionado. Archie, on the other hand, besides providing the locomotion by which Wolfe could gain access to locations outside of his own famous West Thirty-fifth Street brownstone walk-up, also provided the romantic entanglements and the "man about town" attitude that made him the sort of charming rogue who could infiltrate the best houses of the city, finding women eager to share information with him.

John McAleer notes in his 1977 biography, *Rex Stout*, that Stout may have been using the characters of Wolfe and Archie to work though relationship issues with his own dictatorial and perfectionist father. McAleer also states that both Wolfe and Archie serve as vehicles for Stout to reveal his true self, with Stout aligning himself more greatly with Archie during the beginning novels of the series and gradually completing the metamorphosis to Wolfe as an expression of his own author's voice. Stout experimented with other detective characters in several novels, but these never gained the popular success or acceptance of the Wolfe mysteries.

Stout's work style was remarkable; he rarely worked on any book more than forty days. He did very little rewriting and preferred to spend his leisure time pursuing a variety of hobbies and causes, both personal and political. He was an accomplished gardener and constructed the furniture for his home in Brewster. He twice served as the president of the Author's Guild and continued throughout his life to champion a variety of causes; most notably he wrote United States propaganda materials during World War II as chairman of the War Writers' Board.

Rex Stout's contribution to the mystery novel may be second only to Doyle's contribution of Sherlock Holmes. Stout's death in 1975 at his estate in Danbury, Connecticut, silenced an important voice in American mystery writing.

Grace Jasmine

Bibliography

Baring-Gould, William S. *Nero Wolfe of West Thirty-fifth Street*. New York: Viking Press, 1969. The result of Baring-Gould's painstaking research of Rex Stout's Nero Wolfe series provides, in essence, a biography of Stout's fictional characters.

McAleer, John. *Rex Stout: A Biography*. Boston: Little, Brown, 1977. McAleer's authorized biography of Rex Stout is considered the definitive and inclusive information source regarding Stout's life.

Murphy, Bruce. *The Encyclopedia of Murder and Mystery*. New York: Saint Martin's Minotaur, 1999. Murphy's short biographical section on Stout provides a crisply written and succinct look at the most important facts of the author's life.

Randolph Stow

Australian novelist and poet

Born: Geraldton, Australia; November 28, 1935

LONG FICTION: *A Haunted Land*, 1956; *The Bystander*, 1957; *To the Islands*, 1958; *Tourmaline*, 1963; *The Merry-Go-Round in the Sea*, 1965; *Visitants*, 1979; *The Girl Green as Elderflower*, 1980; *The Suburbs of Hell*, 1984.

POETRY: *Act One*, 1957; *Outrider: Poems, 1956-1962*, 1962; *A Counterfeit Silence: Selected Poems*, 1969.

DRAMA: *Eight Songs for a Mad King*, pr. 1969 (libretto; music by Peter Maxwell Davies); *Miss Donnithorne's Maggot*, pr. 1974 (libretto; music by Davies).

CHILDREN'S/YOUNG ADULT LITERATURE: *Midnite: The Story of a Wild Colonial Boy*, 1967.

MISCELLANEOUS: *Randolph Stow: Visitants, Episodes from Other Novels, Poems, Stories, Interviews, and Essays*, 1990 (Anthony J. Hassall, editor).

Julian Randolph Stow was born in Western Australia, where his father was a lawyer. The largely autobiographical novel *The Merry-Go-Round in the Sea* gives an account of his childhood experiences there. His first novel, *A Haunted Land*, and most of the poems in *Act One* were written while he was an undergraduate at the University of Western Australia. He spent his years there studying English and French literature and avidly reading in other European literatures. The reading of these years shows in a number of his novels, but especially in the rich allusiveness of *To the Islands*. *The Bystander*, Stow's second novel, was written after he graduated. In 1957 Stow worked for some months on an Aboriginal mission in the northwestern corner of Australia, and from his experiences there was born what most critics consider to be his masterpiece and one of the best Australian novels of the twentieth century, *To the Islands*. *Tourmaline*, too, in the geographical isolation of its setting, reflects his sense at the mission of being at the world's end, as if he were at a remote settlement within the remote settlement of Western Australia.

After studying anthropology at the University of Sydney, Stow worked as an assistant anthropologist in the Trobriand Islands off northeastern New Guinea until he suffered a physical and emotional collapse there. *Visitants*, which he wrote twenty years later, is based upon these experiences. In 1960 Stow moved to England. Soon after first arriving in England he was awarded a Harkness Fellowship in the United States, where he wrote *The Merry-Go-Round in the Sea*, a fairly cheerful account of his childhood. The next fourteen years were unproductive, from a literary viewpoint, until after he finished *Visitants* in 1979, which was followed one year later by *The Girl Green as Elderflower* and in 1984 by *The Suburbs of Hell*. *Outrider*, Stow's second book of verse, was published after he moved to England. His main book of verse, however, is considered to be *A Counterfeit Silence*.

Stow is one of the earliest of a group of Australians—writers such as Bruce Beaver, David Malouf, Roger McDonald, and Rodney Hall—who during the period from the 1960's to the 1980's wrote both fiction and poetry. That association of genres is especially a phenomenon of this time, an expression perhaps of the breakdown of formal distinctions between genres. Few of these writers, however, have written novels strong in narrative content; their novels, like Stow's, tend to be elusive. Moreover, Stow, as a number of critics have remarked, has always had difficulty in harmonizing romantic and realistic elements in his novels. The works that are freest of that difficulty are *To the Islands*, in which the level of poetic intensity is steadily maintained, and *The Merry-Go-Round in the Sea*, a warm and relaxed record of childhood years.

It is difficult to generalize about Stow, for each of his novels is different from the others; change rather than development characterizes his literary career. His work shows not so much recurrent themes as areas of interest: a penchant for the romantic (whether medieval or nineteenth century Romantic), for the anthropological, and for the symbolism of the twentieth century French movement. Linear narrative and realism do not appeal to him. There are fewer restraints operating upon his poetry than upon his fiction, and the best of his poetry, especially his love poems, is more accessible than his novels. Stow's works, like the man himself, are elusive and, except in the case of the two novels mentioned, have a withheld quality about them. The events and personages of his novels are always seen at a distance and are obscured underneath technical experimentation. As early as in the epigraph to *A Counterfeit Silence*—a quotation from Thornton Wilder, "Even speech was for them a debased form of silence; how much more futile is poetry, which is a debased form of speech"—Stow betrayed an ambivalence toward writing, a reluctance to communicate in words.

John B. Beston

Bibliography

Hassall, Anthony J. "Randolph Stow." In *Australian Writers, 1915-1950*, edited by Selina Samuels. Vol. 260 in *Dictionary of Literary Biography*. Detroit: Gale Group, 2002. A solid overview of Stow's career.

_______. *Strange Country: A Study of Randolph Stow*. Rev. ed. St. Lucia, Queensland, Australia: University of Queensland Press, 1990. An academic study that covers Stow's later work.

Lear, Martin. "Mal du Pays: Symbolic Geography in the Work of Randolph Stow." *Australian Literary Studies* 15, no. 1 (May, 1991): 3-26. Examines geography in Stow's works, addressing it as both literal place and symbolic of feelings.

"Stow, Randolph." In *The Oxford Companion to Australian Literature*, edited by William H. Wilde, Joy Hooton, and Barry Andrews. New York: Oxford University Press, 1985. A brief but helpful essay.

_______. *Randolph Stow: "Visitants," Episodes from Other Novels, Poems, Stories, Interviews, and Essays*. Edited by Anthony J. Hassall. St. Lucia, Queensland, Australia: University of Queensland Press, 1990. Includes insightful and enlightening interviews with the author.

Willbanks, Ray. *Randolph Stow*. Boston: Twayne, 1978. A good introduction to Stow's career and major work.

Harriet Beecher Stowe

American novelist

Born: Litchfield, Connecticut; June 14, 1811
Died: Hartford, Connecticut; July 1, 1896
Pseudonym: Catharine Stowe

LONG FICTION: *Uncle Tom's Cabin: Or, Life Among the Lowly*, 1852; *Dred: A Tale of the Great Dismal Swamp*, 1856; *The Minister's Wooing*, 1859; *Agnes of Sorrento*, 1862; *The Pearl of Orr's Island*, 1862; *Oldtown Folks*, 1869; *Pink and White Tyranny*, 1871; *My Wife and I*, 1871; *We and Our Neighbors*, 1875; *Poganuc People*, 1878.
SHORT FICTION: *The Mayflower: Or, Sketches of Scenes and Characters of the Descendants of the Pilgrims*, 1843; *Sam Lawson's Oldtown Fireside Stories*, 1872.
POETRY: *Religious Poems*, 1867.
NONFICTION: *A Key to "Uncle Tom's Cabin,"* 1853; *Sunny Memories of Foreign Lands*, 1854; *Lady Byron Vindicated*, 1870; *Palmetto Leaves*, 1873.
CHILDREN'S/YOUNG ADULT LITERATURE: *First Geography for Children*, 1833 (as Catharine Stowe).
MISCELLANEOUS: *The Oxford Harriet Beecher Stowe Reader*, 1999 (Joan D. Hedrick, editor).

Harriet Elizabeth Beecher Stowe presented two regional backgrounds in her fiction: the South before the Civil War and the rural area of New England and Maine. Her novels of the antebellum South, were less authentic as well as more melodramatic in style. They were more popular, however, because of the timeliness of their theme and the antislavery feeling they created.

Harriet Elizabeth Beecher was the daughter of a famous minister, the Reverend Lyman Beecher, and the sister of Henry Ward Beecher. She was educated in the school of her older sister Catharine, who encouraged her inclination to write. The family moved to Cincinnati when Harriet was eighteen. There she married Calvin Ellis Stowe, a professor in the Lane Theological Seminary. The Stowes had seven children, including a set of twin daughters.

Uncle Tom's Cabin, written after the Stowes had moved to Maine, brought its author immediate and worldwide fame. The literature of the period generally was influenced by a humanitarian impulse, and Stowe had a ready audience for her romantic, even melodramatic history of the relations of a group of southern white families and their slaves. She said of her material, "Two nations, the types of two exactly opposite styles of existence, are here struggling; and from the intermingling of these two a third race has arisen, and the three are interlocked in wild and singular relations, that evolve every possible combination of romance." She added, "It is the moral bearings of the subject involved which have had the chief influence in its selection." To promote the antislavery cause, Stowe toured North America and England, and to convince skeptical readers of the truths behind her novel she published *A Key to "Uncle Tom's Cabin,"* a collection of firsthand narratives and information about slavery. The novel itself became the best-selling work of fiction in the nineteenth century United States.

The success of her first novel encouraged Stowe to write a second on the same theme. The Dred Scott decision, stating that African Americans did not have the rights of citizenship, served as the catalyst for the novel *Dred: A Tale of the Great Dismal Swamp*, in which she further expounded on her theme that slavery led to the general corruption of Christian principles. This book, like its predecessor, was faulted by critics for artificiality of language, contrived plotting, and sentimental characterizations, and it did not attain the popularity of her first novel.

Stowe next turned to her New England background, writing four novels—*The Minister's Wooing, The Pearl of Orr's Island, Oldtown Folks*, and *Poganuc People*—that are generally considered to be of greater literary merit than her first two. She also wrote society novels, and in *Agnes of Sorrento* produced a didactic historical romance. Stowe was the first writer to use New England dialect for the sake of realism and thus became a pioneer in the local-color tradition of Mary E. Wilkins Freeman and Sarah Orne Jewett. Her constant interpolation of Christian aphorisms, however, and her use of routine plots kept these novels on the level of conventional nineteenth century romance. Although Stowe's reputation faltered somewhat after the publication of *Lady Byron Vindicated*, which was considered scandalous, her short stories and nonfiction articles were in constant demand by periodicals such as *Independent*, *Christian Union*, and *The Atlantic Monthly*. A daughter of the transcendental period, she was the most famous sentimental novelist of her time.

Geralyn Strecker

Bibliography

Adams, John R. *Harriet Beecher Stowe*. Boston: Twayne, 1989. An introduction to the life and works of Stowe. Includes bibliographical references and an index.

Boydston, Jeanne, Mary Kelley, and Anne Margolis. *The Limits of Sisterhood: The Beecher Sisters on Women's Rights and Woman's Sphere*. Chapel Hill: University of North Carolina Press, 1988. A superb study of Stowe and her sisters, Catharine and Isabella. Brief but insightful essays address each woman as an individual and as a sister. Primary documents are appended to each chapter, providing excellent resources. Illustrations, careful documentation, and a detailed index make this an invaluable text.

Donovan, Josephine. *"Uncle Tom's Cabin": Evil, Affliction, and Redemptive Love*. Boston: Twayne, 1991. Places *Uncle Tom's Cabin* in literary and historical context. As her subtitle suggests, Donovan views Stowe's masterpiece as a book about evil and its redemption, taking it more or less at face value and reading it with the approach she believes Stowe intended—which has a decidedly feminist bent.

Hedrick, Joan D. *Harriet Beecher Stowe: A Life*. New York: Oxford University Press, 1994. Stowe's family kept a tight rein on her literary remains, and the only previous attempt at a full-scale independent biography, Forrest Wilson's *Crusader in Crinoline* (1941), is now very much out of date. Hedrick's book makes use of new materials, including letters and diaries, and takes fresh approaches to Stowe occasioned by the Civil Rights and women's movements.

Stowe, Charles Edward, comp. *Life of Harriet Beecher Stowe*. 1889. Reprint. Detroit: Gale Research, 1967. Compiled by her son, this is the first full-length biography of Stowe, drawn from her letters and her journal. Though not critical, it offers extensive excerpts of her personal writings and of correspondence from other renowned writers. An annotated primary bibliography and a detailed index are included.

Sundquist, Eric J., ed. *New Essays on "Uncle Tom's Cabin."* New York: Cambridge University Press, 1986. A collection of essays on Stowe's most famous novel. The introduction discusses changing literary theories as they relate to *Uncle Tom's Cabin*. The six diverse contributions by notable scholars include analyses of genre and gender issues. A selected bibliography also notes additional criticism.

Lytton Strachey

English biographer

Born: London, England; March 1, 1880
Died: Ham Spray House, near Hungerford, Berkshire, England; January 21, 1932

NONFICTION: *Landmarks in French Literature*, 1912; *Eminent Victorians*, 1918; *Queen Victoria*, 1921; *Books and Characters, French and English*, 1922; *Elizabeth and Essex*, 1928; *Portraits in Miniature*, 1931; *Characters and Commentaries*, 1933.

The new movement in biography as a literary form began in England with Giles Lytton Strachey (STRAY-chee) as World War I came to an end. Strachey came from a family distinguished in the army, the civil service, and literature. His mother, Lady Jane Strachey, was a respected essayist and an amateur student of French literature; Lionel Strachey, a cousin, had established a literary reputation in the United States; another cousin, John St. Loe Strachey, was the brilliant editor of the *Spectator* from 1898 to 1925, and his children, John Strachey and Mrs. Amabel Williams-Ellis, were both writers.

A delicate child of marked but rather special talents, Lytton Strachey was limited in his choice of profession. At Trinity College, Cambridge, he distinguished himself in his studies, composed verses, and won the Chancellor's Medal with his poem "Ely." Fearing that he lacked true creative power, however, he dallied with literature in the critical essays that he wrote while living with his mother on an independent income. He began writing sketches of the great and the near-great of the Victorian Age; some of these sketches were later published in *Eminent Victorians*. As biography, his style was new to the English public, but it caught their fancy, and the book sold well. Actually Strachey had been strongly influenced by French biographers, especially Sainte-Beuve—his first publication was *Landmarks in French Literature*—and their naturalistic approach suited his predilection for accentuating the negative in personal relations. Strachey laid emphasis on others' weak points, especially among the famous in politics or letters.

Consciously or not, he was effecting in his attitude a new realism to which his readers reacted not with scorn but rather with greater insight and sympathy. With flaws, the sacrosanct Victorian figures became more human and thus more lovable. This was true especially in the reaction to his *Queen Victoria*. While this biography was just as iconoclastic as the others in its portrait of the queen, the very style of the book, witty and concise, brought her to life as a woman as no similar work or public eulogy had ever done. Emphasizing personality, he brought his subject down to the human level. His greatest popular success, *Elizabeth and Essex*, strongly reflects the author's tendency to judge the world by what was within himself.

He moved with his mother to Bloomsbury, London, on a whim. By chance there were other literary people in the neighborhood, and they were welcomed at the Strachey home. Among them were Virginia Woolf and E. M. Forster. Though known later as the Bloomsbury Group, their only tie besides sociability was a desire to reveal the warm current of fallibility beneath the facade of conventionality in English life. Among the members of the so-called Bloomsbury Group Strachey found his spiritual home and his friends, who shared his interest in the exercise of clarity, restraint, and precision as the basis of literary style. These qualities are all apparent in the portrait gallery of minor, even obscure, figures whom Strachey presents in his *Portraits in Miniature*, perhaps the best book of his lifetime. He died in 1932, at a country residence he had bought with his royalties from *Queen Victoria*.

David H. J. Larmour

Bibliography

Hampton, Christopher. *Carrington*. Boston: Faber & Faber, 1995. Biography of Dora Carrington, Strachey's platonic lover.

Holroyd, Michael. *Lytton Strachey: The New Biography*. New York: Farrar, Straus and Giroux, 1995. An up-to-date biography.

Rosenbaum, S. P., ed. *The Bloomsbury Group: A Collection of Memoirs, Commentary, and Criticism*. Buffalo, N.Y.: University of Toronto Press, 1995. Provides information and background for Strachey's social milieu.

Taddeo, Julie Anne. *Lytton Strachey and the Search for Modern Sexual Identity: The Last Eminent Victorian*. New York: Harrington Park Press, 2002. A biography that brings contemporary queer studies to bear on Strachey's life.

Mark Strand

American poet

Born: Summerside, Prince Edward Island, Canada; April 11, 1934

POETRY: *Sleeping with One Eye Open*, 1964; *Reasons for Moving*, 1968; *Darker*, 1970; *The Story of Our Lives*, 1973; *The Sargeantville Notebook*, 1973; *Elegy for My Father*, 1973; *The Late Hour*, 1978; *Selected Poems*, 1980; *Prose: Four Poems*, 1987; *The Continuous Life*, 1990; *Dark Harbor*, 1993; *Blizzard of One*, 1998; *Chicken, Shadow, Moon, and More*, 1999.

TRANSLATIONS: *Eighteen Poems from the Quechua*, 1971; *The Owl's Insomnia: Poems by Rafael Alberti*, 1973; *Souvenir of the Ancient World*, 1976 (of Carlos Drummond de Andrade).

LONG FICTION: *The Monument*, 1978.

SHORT FICTION: *Mr. and Mrs. Baby, and Other Stories*, 1985.

NONFICTION: *William Bailey*, 1987; *Hopper*, 1994, rev. 2001; *The Weather of Words: Poetic Invention*, 2000.

CHILDREN'S/YOUNG ADULT LITERATURE: *The Planet of Lost Things*, 1982; *The Night Book*, 1985; *Rembrandt Takes a Walk*, 1986.

EDITED TEXTS: *The Contemporary American Poets: American Poetry Since 1940*, 1969; *New Poetry of Mexico*, 1970; *Another Republic: Seventeen European and South American Writers*, 1976 (with Charles Simic); *Art of the Real: Nine American Figurative Painters*, 1983; *The Best American Poetry, 1991*, 1991; *Stories and Poems*, 1995 (with Tim O'Brien); *The Making of a Poem: A Norton Anthology of Poetic Forms*, 2000 (with Eavan Boland).

Mark Strand began life on remote Prince Edward Island, Canada, and when he was four, he moved with his parents to the United States. Eventually he landed in Yellow Springs, Ohio, where he graduated with his B.A. from Antioch College in 1957. He earned his B.F.A. from Yale University in 1959, was a Fulbright Fellow at the University of Florence (1960-1961), and earned his M.A. from University of Iowa in Iowa City, Iowa, in 1962. As a visiting professor or instructor, Strand has taught at the University of Rio de Janeiro (1965-1966), Mount Holyoke College (1967), the University of Washington (1968), Columbia and Yale Universities (1968-1970), Princeton University (1972), Brandeis University (1973), the University of California at Irvine (1977), and Harvard University (1980). Strand eventually became a professor of English at the University of Utah in Salt Lake City.

He has received the Cook and Bergin prizes, a second Fulbright Fellowship, the Ingram-Merril Foundation grant, a National Endowment for the Arts grant, and a Rockefeller grant. He won the Academy of American Poets' Edgar Allan Poe Award (in 1974 for *The Story of Our Lives*), a Guggenheim Fellowship, and an award from the National Institute of Arts and Letters. He was honored to succeed Robert Penn Warren as the poet laureate of the United States Library of Congress (1990-1991). He was awarded the Bollingen Prize for Poetry from the Yale University Library in 1993. *Blizzard of One* won for Strand the Pulitzer Prize in poetry and the Boston Book Review Bingham Poetry Prize, 1999.

This professorial path supported his habit—creating poetry through impeccable and effortless technique. The graphic quality of Strand's poems results from his early training as a painter; eventually he chose poetry over painting. He is considered a minimalist with a knack for dark abstractions. His restlessness exposes a brooding, introspective, nearly terrifying environment. In his first book, *Sleeping with One Eye Open*, Strand introduced his controlled verse and surreal imagery and explored an unsettling series of contradictions and challenges. In this collection the stage was set for the mood and style of his subsequent work. Verse is stripped of non-essential attributes; simple actions, repeated at times, are worked into phrases of surprising strength.

Strand grabs themes and events and then contorts them to mysterious effect. In "Poem," from *Sleeping with One Eye Open*, a torturer with nail clippers slowly cuts his bedroom-bound victim into small pieces. Convinced that he has done enough, the villain expresses his gratitude to the victim for being dismissed, then leaves. Quintessential Strand, this poem responds to the nightmarish grotesquerie of life. These early works represent morbid concerns and realistic solutions; later, in *Darker*, Strand suggests that the best action may be no action at all.

From these earlier works of tombstone dread, the poet elevated his mood and his life's impressions in *The Continuous Life*, published in 1990. Critics recognized this new view and likenened it to a countryside view from the shadow of the mountain. These poems arrived after a ten-year hiatus from poetry publications and are considered to be idiosyncratic and searching. In *Dark Harbor*, the overarching plot appears to be the poet's counterlife in art, separation from family, and journey to darkness and then to the final safety of a harbor replete with poets.

Strand's 1998 Pulitzer Prize-winning collection, *Blizzard of One*, is classic Strand: stylish and lyrical, yet seemingly effortless as he oscillates between the ordinary and extraordinary.

Strand has written in genres other than poetry. His two biographical books on artists, one on William Bailey and one on Edward Hopper, possess the Strand brand of poetic critique. His affinity for the arts—in particular, painting—drew Strand to edit *Art of the Real*, a collection of essays on painters. Married twice, with a daughter from his first marriage, Strand may have written his children's books as a reflection on his family life. Even his children's tales are woven through darkened dreams and prophesies.

Craig Gilbert

Bibliography

Aaron, Jonathan. "About Mark Strand: A Profile." *Ploughshares* 21, no. 4 (Winter, 1995/1996): 202-205. This is an excellent short overview of Strand's career, accomplishments, and sense of himself as a writer. Strand is the guest editor of this issue of the magazine.

Bloom, Harold. "Dark and Radiant Peripheries: Mark Strand and A. R. Ammons." *Southern Review* 8 (Winter, 1972): 133-141. This article is formally divided into four main sections: The introduction and conclusion briefly compare the poetry of Strand and Ammons, while the second section is given to Strand and the third to Ammons. Critical commentary is provided for the title poems of Strand's first three volumes: *Sleeping with One Eye Open*, *Reasons for Moving*, and *Darker*. Bloom focuses upon the "dark" elements of Strand's work.

Gregorson, Linda. "Negative Capability." *Parnassus: Poetry in Review* 9 (1981): 90-114. Gregorson discusses poems selected from Strand's *Selected Poems*. She focuses on the rhymes and meters of the poetry, as well as the imagery. Also included are some critical analyses of the poet's use of prosody. Her overall effort is to trace the developing forms and formats of the recognizably better poems.

Howard, Richard. "Mark Strand." In *Alone with America: Essays on the Art of Poetry in the United States Since 1950*. New York: Atheneum, 1980. Howard writes critically of Strand's first two collections of poems, *Sleeping with One Eye Open* and *Reasons for Moving*. He sees the second volume as an outgrowth and continuation of the first one. Howard focuses on the duality of Strand's nature and his inability to reconcile the different aspects of his personality.

Kirby, David. *Mark Strand and the Poet's Place in Contemporary American Culture*. Columbia: University of Missouri Press, 1990. A fascinating exploration of the public roles and stances of the poet, with Strand as the central case in point. More a study in the sociology of literature than a work of literary criticism, yet important because Strand's public persona and his writing have a strange symbiotic relationship.

Olsen, Lance. "Entry to the Unaccounted For: Mark Strand's Fantastic Autism." In *The Poetic Fantastic: Studies in an Evolving Genre*, edited by Patrick D. Murphy and Vernon Hyles. New York: Greenwood Press, 1989. In this short article of some ten pages, Olsen interprets much of Strand's work in terms of fantasy. He deals specifically with poems taken from *Sleeping with One Eye Open* and *Reasons for Moving*. The critic sees many elements of science fiction in Strand's poems, as well as metafiction.

Singleton, Carl, and Philip K. Jason. "Mark Strand." In *Critical Survey of Poetry*, edited by Philip K. Jason. 2d rev. ed. Pasadena, Calif.: Salem Press, 2003. A solid and accessible overview of Strand's poetry. Includes a brief biography.

Strand, Mark. "Mark Strand: The Art of Poetry LXXVII." Interview by Wallace Shawn. *The Paris Review* 40, no. 148 (Fall, 1998): 146-179. Strand discusses his poetic themes and writing style.

Botho Strauss

German playwright and novelist

Born: Naumburg an der Saale, Germany; December 2, 1944

DRAMA: *Peer Gynt: Nach Henrik Ibsen*, pb. 1971; *Die Hypochonder*, pr., pb. 1972 (*The Hypochondriacs*, 1977); *Prinz Friedrich von Homburg: Nach Heinrich von Kleist*, pb. 1972; *Bekannte Gesichter, gemischte Gefühle*, pb. 1974 (*Familiar Faces, Confused Feelings*, 1976); *Sommergäste: Nach Maxim Gorky*, pb. 1974; *Trilogie des Wiedersehens*, pr. 1975 (*Three Acts of Recognition*, 1981); *Gross und Klein: Szenen*, pr., pb. 1978 (*Big and Little*, 1979); *Kalldewey: Farce*, pb. 1981; *Der Park*, pb. 1983 (*The Park*, 1988); *Die Fremdenführerin*, pr., pb. 1986 (*The Tour Guide*, 1995); *Besucher*, pr., pb. 1988; *Sieben Türen, Bagatellen*, pr., pb. 1988; *Die Zeit und das Zimmer*, pb. 1988 (*Time and the Room*, 1995); *Jeffers-Akt*, pr. 1989 (radio play); *Angelas Kleider*, pr., pb. 1991; *Schlusschor*, pr., pb. 1991; *Das Gleichgewicht: Stück in drei Akten*, pr., pb. 1993; *Ithaka: Schauspiel nach den Heimkehr-Gesängen der Odyssee*, pr., pb. 1996; *Jeffers: Akt I & II*, pr., pb. 1998; *Der Kuss des Vergessens*, pr., pb. 1998; *Die Ähnlichen*, pr., pb. 1998; *Der Narr und seine Frau heute abend in Pancomedia*, pr., pb. 2001; *Unerwartet Rückkehr*, pr., pb. 2002.

LONG FICTION: *Schützenehre*, 1974; *Marlenes Schwester*, 1975; *Die Widmung*, 1977 (*Devotion*, 1979); *Rumor*, 1980 (*Tumult*, 1984); *Paare, Passanten*, 1981 (*Couples, Passersby*, 1996); *Der junge Mann*, 1984 (*The Young Man*, 1989); *Niemand anderes*, 1987; *Kongress: Die Kette der Demütigungen*, 1989; *Beginnlosigkeit*, 1992; *Wohnen, Dämmern, Lügen*, 1994 (*Living, Glimmering, Lying*, 1999); *Die Fehler des Kopisten*, 1997; *Das Partikular*, 2000.

POETRY: *Unüberwindliche Nähe*, 1976; *Diese Erinnerung an einen, der nur einen Tag zu Gast war*, 1985.

NONFICTION: *Versuch, ästhetische und politische Ereignisse zusammenzudenken: Texte über Theater, 1967-1986*, 1987; *Der Gebärdensammler: Texte zum Theater*, 1999.

Botho Strauss (shtrows) was born on December 2, 1944, to middle-class parents in the Ruhr region of Germany. He attended school in that area and went on to study German literature, theater history, and sociology at the University of Cologne and the University of Munich during the early 1960's. From 1967 to 1970, he served as critic and editor of the well-known West German journal, *Theater heute*. In 1970, he began work as a producer with the theatrical group Schaubühne am Hallischen Ufer. Strauss has received a number of literary prizes and awards, and several of his works have been made into films.

Strauss's writings present examples of the style that has been termed the "new subjectivity," a trend that emerged in German literature during the early 1970's. The works of Peter Handke and Karin Struck are also included in this movement. Many of the writers of the 1960's had focused on political themes and had sought to promote a socially committed literature. Authors such as Strauss and Handke, however, began to write about the more personal themes of the individual's existential and psychological alienation. Strauss's texts seek to uncover not the political factors that shape the individual's existence but rather the unconscious and irrational forces that seem to determine so much of the conscious personality. This focus is motivated, in part at least, by the belief that true social change must first begin within the self.

Strauss's first major play, *The Hypochondriacs*, is set in Amsterdam in 1901 and involves a rather complicated murder-mystery plot. The traditional conventions of this genre—open questions concerning the identity of the murderer and the motivation for the act—make the concepts of interpretation, meaning, and a transcendent order to events problematic. Strauss's deliberately convoluted plot confounds notions of "reality" and forces the viewer to confront his subjectivity and the essential impenetrability of experience. *Three Acts of Recognition*, one of Strauss's better-known plays, presents a series of characters who are visiting an art exhibition and who, as they come and go on the stage, make observations on topics such as art, love and marriage, careers, and friendships. The plot serves as a vehicle for Strauss's comments on the complex and alienating nature of modern life and the various types of personalities that modern society has produced. Many of the characters suffer from a profound sense of isolation and an inability to establish true communication with others. The play moves along on a disturbing note of pessimism about the nature of human relationships.

The play *Big and Little* is written in the manner of many expressionist dramas such as the *Stationendramen* of Georg Kaiser. It consists of ten connected but not continuous scenes involving the life of a woman named Lotte. Her husband has left her for another woman, and, disillusioned, she tries to promote an idealistic message of love and forgiveness to those she sees. The people that she meets in the various scenes are all representative of the existential emptiness, the essential lack of spiritual significance, that Strauss sees as characteristic of modern life. Lotte becomes deeply emotionally disturbed by what she encounters and the play ends on this pessimistic note. The novel *Devotion* deals with a man, Richard Schroubek, who is writing a chronicle of his love affair with Hannah Beyl, who has recently left him. Such moments of loss, abandonment, and dislocation mark the experience of Strauss's characters and initiate their reflections upon the self and others. Schroubek's document of self-examination, which is at times ironic and rather morbid, has a therapeutic effect, and he believes that he has put his emotions in perspective. When he finally sees her again, however, he is disillusioned, and the whole affair no longer seems to make any sense.

Strauss's figures are all involved at some level in a quest to make sense of their feelings. *Tumult* is another novel in which the main character, Bekker, is extremely isolated from others and, as a result, prone to anger and violence. He reacts strongly against a world in which power games dictate the nature of relationships. Bekker's experience of himself and others becomes gradually more fragmented and frustrated.

The Young Man consists of several sections held together by the ironic reflections of the narrator, Leon Pracht. A somewhat autobiographical "novel of education," it bears a faint resemblance to the eighteenth century German novels of that same genre, Novalis's *Henry of Ofterdingen* (1802) and Johann Wolfgang von Goethe's *Wilhelm Meister's Apprenticeship* (1795-1796). As is common with Strauss's works, this text is an extended rumination on the quality of life in the depersonalized and anonymous modern world. The introduction contains the narrator's reflections on the romantic form of his novel and his "poetic" journey. In the first section Leon has left his work in the theater world and become a writer. He is obsessed with ideas about life in the nuclear era. In the novel's second section he observes an alternative society—the "Synkreas"—in which a person's creative and artistic faculties could be wholly utilized.

The third section deals with a businesswoman who has a profound spiritual experience after a series of horrible visions and nightmares. She commits herself to a life of love and unselfish activity. Strauss suggests that the compulsive pursuit of material goods so prevalent in Western culture is motivated by an existential fear of death. In the section entitled "The Tower" Leon meets with the film producer Ossia in a high-tech hotel, and they discuss theories of art. The novel ends with Leon alone, since his girlfriend, Yossica, has left him to pursue her own artistic career.

Strauss's writings present a critical view—an often ironic unmasking—of life in twentieth century postindustrial society. It is best understood as a counterpoint to the political and sociological preoccupations of German authors during the 1960's. Strauss produces a profound and rather bleak vision of the psychological stresses and existential alienation that define the modern individual's sense of self: People are plagued by a spiritual vacuum and crippling neuroses that limit their capacity for self-knowledge and stifle their ability to establish genuine intimacy with other human beings.

Thomas F. Barry

Bibliography

Calandra, Denis. *New German Dramatists: A Study of Peter Handke, Franz Xaver Kroetz, Rainer Werner Fassbinder, Heiner Müller, Thomas Brasch, Thomas Bernhard, and Botho Strauss.* New York: Grove Press, 1983. Includes a section on Strauss's plays of the 1970's with emphasis on characters and themes (isolation, relationships, shifting identities). Also discusses specific stage productions, especially premieres.

McGowan, Moray. "Past, Present, and Future: Myth in Three West German Dramas of the 1980's." *German Life and Letters* 43, no. 3 (April, 1990): 267-279. Looks at the growing interest in myth during the 1980's and places Strauss's use of Shakespeare's *Midsummer Night's Dream* in the context of other playwrights adapting Arthurian and Germanic myths. None of the authors uses myth as an escape from reality.

Stoehr, Ingo R. *German Literature of the Twentieth Century: From Aestheticism to Postmodernism.* Rochester, N.Y.: Camden House, 2001. Provides a broad survey of twentieth century German literature with brief sections on plays and novels by Strauss that allow the reader to see Strauss's contribution to literature.

August Strindberg

Swedish playwright

Born: Stockholm, Sweden; January 22, 1849
Died: Stockholm, Sweden; May 14, 1912

DRAMA: *Fritänkaren*, pb. 1870; *I Rom*, pr., pb. 1870; *Den fredlöse*, pr. 1871 (*The Outlaw*, 1912); *Hermione*, pb. 1871; *Anno fyrtioåtta*, wr. 1876, pb. 1881; *Mäster Olof*, pb. 1878 (*Master Olof*, 1915); *Gillets hemlighet*, pr., pb. 1880; *Herr Bengts hustru*, pr., pb. 1882; *Lycko-Pers resa*, pr., pb. 1883 (*Lucky Peter's Travels*, 1912); *Fadren*, pr., pb. 1887 (*The Father*, 1899); *Marodörer*, pr. 1887; *Fröken Julie*, pb. 1888 (*Miss Julie*, 1912); *Kamraterna*, pb. 1888 (with Axel Lundegård; *Comrades*, 1912); *Fordringsägare*, pb. 1888 (in Danish), pr. 1889 (*Creditors*, 1910); *Hemsöborna*, pr. 1889 (adaptation of his novel); *Paria*, pr. 1889 (*Pariah*, 1913); *Den starkare*, pr. 1889 (*The Stronger*, 1912); *Samum*, pr., pb. 1890 (*Simoom*, 1906); *Himmelrikets nycklar: Eller, Sankte Per vandrar på jorden*, pb. 1892 (*The Keys of Heaven*, 1965); *Moderskärlek*, pb. 1893 (*Mother Love*, 1910); *Bandet*, pb. 1893 (in German), pb. 1897 (*The Bond*, 1960); *Debet och kredit*, pb. 1893 (*Debit and Credit*, 1906); *Första varningen*, pr., pb. 1893 (*The First Warning*, 1915); *Inför döden*, pr., pb. 1893 (*In the Face of Death*, 1916); *Leka med elden*, pb. 1893 (*Playing with Fire*, 1930); *Till Damaskus, forsta delen*, pb. 1898 (*To Damascus I*, 1913); *Till Damaskus, andra delen*, pb. 1898 (*To Damascus II*, 1913); *Advent, ett mysterium*, pb. 1899 (*Advent*, 1912); *Brott och Brott*, pb. 1899 (*Crime and Crime*, 1913, also known as *There Are Crimes and Crimes*); *Erik XIV*, pr., pb. 1899 (English translation, 1931); *Folkungasagan*, pb. 1899 (*The Saga of the Folkungs*, 1931); *Gustav Vasa*, pr., pb. 1899 (English translation, 1916); *Gustav Adolf*, pb. 1900 (English translation,

1957); *Carl XII*, pb. 1901 (*Charles XII*, 1955); *Dödsdansen, första delen*, pb. 1901 (*The Dance of Death I*, 1912); *Dödsdansen, andra delen*, pb. 1901 (*The Dance of Death II*, 1912); *Engelbrekt*, pr., pb. 1901 (English translation, 1949); *Kaspers fet-tisdag*, pr. 1901; *Kristina*, pb. 1901 (*Queen Christina*, 1955); *Midsommar*, pr., pb. 1901 (*Midsummertide*, 1912); *Påsk*, pr., pb. 1901 (*Easter*, 1912); *Ett drömspel*, pb. 1902 (*A Dream Play*, 1912); *Halländarn*, wr. 1902, pb. 1918; *Kronbruden*, pb. 1902 (*The Bridal Crown*, 1916); *Svanevit*, pb. 1902 (*Swanwhite*, 1914); *Genom öknar till arvland: Eller, Moses*, wr. 1903, pb. 1918 (*Through Deserts to Ancestral Lands*, 1970); *Gustav III*, pb. 1903 (English translation, 1955); *Lammet och vilddjuret: Eller, Kristus*, wr. 1903, pb. 1918 (*The Lamb and the Beast*, 1970); *Näktergalen i Wittenberg*, pb. 1904 (*The Nightingale of Whittenberg*, 1970); *Till Damaskus, tredje delen*, pb. 1904 (*To Damascus III*, 1913); *Brända tomten*, pr., pb. 1907 (*After the Fire*, 1913); *Oväder*, pr., pb. 1907 (*Storm*, 1913); *Pelikanen*, pr., pb. 1907 (*The Pelican*, 1962); *Spöksonaten*, pb. 1907 (*The Ghost Sonata*, 1916); *Abu Casems tofflor*, pr., pb. 1908; *Bjälbo-Jarlen*, pr., pb. 1909 (*Earl Birger of Bjälbo*, 1956); *Riksföreståndaren*, pr. 1909 (*The Regent*, 1956); *Siste riddaren*, pr., pb. 1909 (*The Last of the Knights*, 1956); *Stora landsvägen*, pb. 1909 (*The Great Highway*, 1954); *Svarta handsken*, pb. 1909 (*The Black Glove*, 1916); *Hellas: Eller, Sokrates*, pb. 1918 (*Hellas*, 1970); *Toten-Insel: Eller, Hades*, pb. 1918 (*Isle of the Dead*, 1962); *Six Plays*, pb. 1955; *Eight Expressionist Plays*, pb. 1965.

LONG FICTION: *Från Fjärdingen och Svartbäcken*, 1877; *Röda rummet*, 1879 (*The Red Room*, 1913); *Jäsningstiden*, 1886 (*The Growth of the Soul*, 1914); *Hemsöborna*, 1887 (*The Natives of Hemsö*, 1965); *Tschandala*, 1889 (in Danish), 1897; *I havsbandet*, 1890 (*By the Open Sea*, 1913); *Le Plaidoyer d'un fou*, 1893 (in German), 1895; (*A Madman's Defense*, 1912; also known as *The Confessions of a Fool*); *Inferno*, 1897 (English translation, 1912); *Ensam*, 1903 (*Alone*, 1968); *Götiska rummen*, 1904; *Svarta fanor*, 1907; *Taklagsöl*, 1907; *Syndabocken*, 1907 (*The Scapegoat*, 1967); *Författaren*, 1909.

SHORT FICTION: *Giftas I*, 1881; *Svenska öden och äventyr*, 1882-1892; *Utopier i verkligheten*, 1885; *Giftas II*, 1886 (*Married*, 1913; also known as *Getting Married*, 1973; includes *Giftas I* and *Giftas II*); *Skärkarlsliv*, 1888; *Legender*, 1898 (*Legends*, 1912); *Fagervik och Skamsund*, 1902 (*Fair Haven and Foul Strand*, 1913); *Sagor*, 1903 (*Tales*, 1930); *Historiska miniatyrer*, 1905 (*Historical Miniatures*, 1913).

POETRY: *Dikter och verkligheter*, 1881; *Dikter på vers och prosa*, 1883; *Sömngångarnätter på vakna dagar*, 1884.

NONFICTION: *Gamla Stockholm*, 1880; *Det nya riket*, 1882; *Svenska folket i helg och söcken, krig och fred, hemma och ute: Eller, Ett tusen år av svenska bildningens och sedernas historia*, 1882; *Tjänstekvinnans son: En s äls utvecklingshistoria*, 1886 (4 volumes; *The Son of a Servant: The Story of the Evolution of a Human Being*, 1966, volume 1 only); *Vivisektioner*, 1887; *Blomstermalningar och djurstycken*, 1888; *Bland franska bönder*, 1889; *Antibarbarus*, 1896; *Jardin des plantes*, 1896; *Svensk natur*, 1897; *Världshistoriens mystik*, 1903; *Modersmålets anor*, 1910; *Religiös renässans*, 1910; *Världsspråkens rötter*, 1910; *Folkstaten*, 1910-1911; *Tal till svenska nationen*, 1910-1911; *Öppna brev till Intima Teatern*, 1911-1912 (*Open Letters to the Intimate Theater*, 1959); *Zones of the Spirit: A Book of Thoughts*, 1913.

Johan August Strindberg, greatest of Swedish writers and one of the few true geniuses among modern dramatists, was born in Stockholm on January 22, 1849. He barely escaped illegitimacy, for his father, a bankrupt shipping agent, married his servant-mistress just before August's birth; three boys had been born before the marriage, and of the numerous children born later, four survived to crowd the tiny flat of the impoverished family. The overly sensitive boy was unhappy at home and less happy at school. He felt himself tormented because of his origins, and he was exasperated by a school system geared to the most stupid children. Upon the death of August's mother, whom he idealized, his father married his young housekeeper, much to August's pain and humiliation.

At secondary school he was stimulated by the study of science, and to the end of his life he studied geology, astronomy, biology, and chemistry. He attended Uppsala University but was unhappy there; he was poor, lonely, and confused. Leaving the university without taking a degree, he engaged in a bewildering series of activities, becoming at various times a teacher, a tutor, an actor, a journalist, a political radical, a landscape painter, a medical student, a playwright, a librarian, a Sinologist, a poet, a chemist, a novelist, and an autobiographer.

Most of all, however, he was a dramatist who gradually attained fame all over Europe, though at home his genuine distinction proved difficult for his compatriots to discern through the clouds of scandal surrounding his melodramatically unsuccessful marriages, the shocking notoriety resulting from his frankly autobiographical books, subjective novels, and short stories, and his bizarre conduct during periods of near-insanity and frightening religious mania. Although few of the many studies of Strindberg have succeeded in making him a completely understandable human being, the "mad genius" strikes scholars of literature and drama increasingly as a genius, less as a madman. Strindberg spent much of his adult life abroad, but five years preceding his death he ended his continental exile and again lived in Stockholm, where he was associated with an intimate theater for the presentation of his plays and where he became a respected public figure. Nevertheless, he was still frustrated and tormented in his search for certainty, and his literary record of volcanic adventures of mind and spirit made him a violent and controversial figure to the end.

Critics consider Strindberg one of the most important and influential playwrights of the twentieth century. George Bernard Shaw and Eugene O'Neill are two of many dramatists who greatly admired his work. Strindberg wrote naturalistic plays such as *The Father*, *Miss Julie*, and *The Stronger* in the late 1880's but later penned expressionistic dramas such as *A Dream Play* and *The Ghost Sonata* in the first decade of the twentieth century.

The sweep of Strindberg's dramatic output is breathtaking: historical verse plays, fairy plays, romances, dozens of realistic and naturalistic plays, moralities, religious dramas, plays of complete cynicism and pessimism, and expressionistic plays. Not only was he far more versatile than any other modern playwright, but he also attained distinction in every genre he attempted. The reader is sharply conscious of the dynamic intellect on every page of Strindberg.

Strindberg's historical and religious dramas and his social-reform or crusading plays generally hold little interest for British and American critics, who believe that Strindberg reached his full stature in his revolutionary naturalistic and expressionistic plays. The former reflect, if not a pathological misogyny, at least the most ferocious antifeminism ever to appear in drama. *The Father*, *Comrades*, *The Dance of Death*, and *Creditors* have as their central theme the duel of the sexes, in each of which the woman is more unscrupulous, selfish, and conscienceless than the man. *The Father* is one of the most terrifying tragedies ever written, partly because Strindberg poured into it experience from his own shattered marriage, partly because there is no alleviation of hope, and partly because of the superb construction and swift tempo that sweep the playgoer or reader along in breathless horror to the tragic and cynical final curtain. This work includes echoes of Greek tragedy (the Omphale motif) and of William Shakespeare's works (Iago cleverly planting the seeds of doubt in *Othello*), but *The Father* is modern in its sharp study of a crumbling mind. *Comrades* is not a tragedy but is no less an intense expression of Strindberg's misogyny, his contempt for Henrik Ibsen's and Nora Helmer's ideal of marriage as a companionship of equals. To Strindberg, woman has neither the integrity nor the intelligence to succeed as a comrade or partner. *The Dance of Death* exploits the same theme: that the underside of love is hate and that only tragedy can result from their inseparableness.

Miss Julie is perhaps Strindberg's most popular play in the United States; the play involves an aristocratic young woman who sleeps with Jean, an impudent, attractive servant and who subsequently commits suicide. Miss Julie's problems derive from various sources, such as her mother's immorality, her father's failure to bring her up properly, and the rigid class system, but her dilemma arises predominantly from her own want of character. She is far wealthier than Jean, and her social class results in greater expectations for her and greater shame when Jean, the thirty-year-old valet, deflowers her. Julie mistakenly thinks that she loves Jean; her feelings prove to be an infatuation, and the significant difference between their social classes renders their relationship impossible. Perhaps the impossibility of their relationship makes Jean more attractive to Julie. Jean's power thus derives, ironically, from his lower social class; the twenty-five-year-old heroine has much more to lose than he. Gender roles also prove a factor in Strindberg's drama because of the sexual double standard, which increases Jean's reputation while destroying that of Julie. Strindberg effectively juxtaposes Julie's tragedy with the jocular festivities of Midsummer Eve.

Strindberg stands as the father of expressionistic drama, which was carried to its greatest success in Germany after World War I and then declined as a dramatic form in the 1930's. Echoes of expressionism still appear in modern plays, where its techniques have been used to some extent by O'Neill, Elmer Rice, Tennessee Williams, Arthur Miller, Jean Anouilh, J. B. Priestley, and others. *To Damascus* is the first real expressionistic drama. In it Strindberg abandoned traditional dramatic techniques in order to dramatize his own soul's inferno in his search for religious certainty. His other two great expressionistic dramas are *A Dream Play* and *The Ghost Sonata*. This latter play O'Neill much admired, and its influence may be seen in a number of his plays.

Eric Sterling

Bibliography

Carlson, Harry Gilbert. *Out of "Inferno": Strindberg's Reawakening as an Artist*. Seattle: University of Washington Press, 1996. A study of the change in Strindberg's literary works after his publication of *Inferno*. Includes bibliography and index.

Ekman, Hans-Göran. *Strindberg and the Five Senses: Studies in Strindberg's Chamber Plays*. Somerset, N.J.: Transaction, 2000. A critical analysis of Strindberg's chamber plays, with particular emphasis on the five senses. Includes bibliography and index.

Marker, Frederick J., and Christopher Innes, eds. *Modernism in European Drama: Ibsen, Strindberg, Pirandello, Beckett*. Buffalo: University of Toronto Press, 1998. A collection of essays from *Modern Drama* published between 1963 and 1994 on modernism in the dramatic works of Strindberg, Henrik Ibsen, Luigi Pirandello, and Samuel Beckett. Includes bibliography and index.

Martinus, Eivor. *Strindberg and Love*. Charlbury, Oxford, England: Amber Lane Press, 2001. A study of Strindberg's relations with women, including how they manifested in his literary works. Includes bibliography and index.

Robinson, Michael, and Sven Hakon Rossel, eds. *Expressionism and Modernism: New Approaches to August Strindberg*. Vienna: Edition Praesens, 1999. A collection of papers from the Thirteenth International Strindberg Conference, Linz Austria, October, 1997, and one essay from the Internationale Strindberg-Tage, Vienna, October, 1997, that examine the literary works of Strindberg. Includes bibliography and index.

Törnqvist, Egil. *Strindberg's "The Ghost Sonata": From Text to Performance*. Amsterdam: Amsterdam University Press, 2000. An in-depth analysis of Strindberg's *The Ghost Sonata*. Includes bibliography and index.

L. A. G. Strong

English novelist

Born: Near Plymouth, Devonshire, England; March 8, 1896
Died: Guilford, Surrey, England; August 17, 1958

LONG FICTION: *Dewer Rides*, 1929; *The Jealous Ghost*, 1930; *The Garden*, 1931; *The Brothers*, 1932; *Sea Wall*, 1933; *Corporal Tune*, 1934; *The Seven Arms*, 1935; *The Last Enemy*, 1936; *The Swift Shadow*, 1937; *Laughter in the West*, 1937; *The Open Sky*, 1939; *The Bay*, 1941; *The Directory*, 1944; *Trevannion*, 1948; *The Hill of Howth*, 1953; *Deliverance*, 1955.

SHORT FICTION: *Doyle's Rock, and Other Stories*, 1925; *The English Captain*, 1929; *The Big Man*, 1931; *Don Juan and the Wheelbarrow*, 1932; *Tuesday Afternoon, and Other Stories*, 1935; *Sun on the Water*, 1940; *Travellers*, 1945; *Darling Tom*, 1952.

POETRY: *Dallington Rhymes*, 1919; *Dublin Days*, 1921; *Twice Four*, 1921; *Says the Muse to Me, Says She*, 1922; *Eight Poems*, 1923; *The Lowery Road*, 1923; *Seven*, 1924; *Difficult Love*, 1927; *At Glenan Cross*, 1928; *Northern Light*, 1930; *Selected Poems*, 1931; *March Evening*, 1932; *Call to the Swans*, 1936; *The Body's Imperfection*, 1957.

NONFICTION: *Common Sense About Poetry*, 1932; *A Letter to W. B. Yeats*, 1932; *Life in English Literature*, 1932 (with Monica Redlich); *The Hansom Cab and the Pigeons*, 1935; *The Minstrel Boy*, 1937; *John McCormack*, 1941; *The Sacred River*, 1949; *Maude Cherrill*, 1950; *The Writer's Trade*, 1953; *Dr. Quicksilver*, 1955; *Green Memory*, 1961.

Leonard Alfred George Strong, of Irish descent, spent part of his childhood in the vicinity of Dublin and retained staunch ties with his Irish Protestant heritage, upon which he drew for much of his fiction. He was educated on scholarships at Brighton College and at Wadham College, Oxford. After being exempted from military service on account of disability, he began to teach at Summer Fields, a preparatory school near Oxford, in 1917. There he remained twelve years before moving to London in 1930 to devote himself to writing. Interested in speech and its development, he also taught oral interpretation of drama and broadcast for the British Broadcasting Corporation. His interest in regional dialects is reflected in his poems of rustic life.

Strong became known first for his poems, some of which show affinities with the work of Thomas Hardy. His succinct lyric portrayals of provincial life express satire, pathos, and laughter. Outstanding among his poems are "An Old Woman, Outside the Abbey Theatre," which is epigrammatically ironic in a manner worthy of William Butler Yeats, and "The Mad Woman of Punnet's Town," which depicts vitality and joy. After deciding to live by his writing, he concentrated on works of prose; most of his novels, short stories, and essays were published in rapid succession. As a novelist he is at his best in treatments of rural domestic scenes and in his realistic handling of conversation. In his late years he wrote several crime stories featuring the character of Ellis McKay, a Scotland Yard detective indifferently successful at solving cases by induction. In these short novels Strong, like his friend C. Day Lewis, who wrote under the pseudonym Nicholas Blake, holds to the British tradition of "playing fair" with the mystery-reading public.

With English readers he achieved great celebrity as the author of short stories. For the 1945 collection titled *Travellers* Strong was awarded the James Tait Black Memorial Prize. His other works include works for young readers and several penetrating critical studies, notably his study of James Joyce in *The Sacred River.*

Bibliography

Berger, Laura Standley, ed. *Twentieth-Century Children's Writers*. 4th ed. Detroit: St. James Press, 1995.

Kirkpatrick, D. L., ed. *Twentieth-Century Children's Writers*. New York: St. Martin's Press, 1978.

Seymour-Smith, Martin, ed. *Novels and Novelists: A Guide to the World of Fiction*. New York: St. Martin's Press, 1980.

Arkady and Boris Strugatsky

Russian novelists

Arkady Strugatsky

Born: Batumi, Georgia, Soviet Union (now in Republic of Georgia); August 28, 1925
Died: Moscow, Russia; October 14, 1991

Boris Strugatsky

Born: Leningrad, Soviet Union (now St. Petersburg, Russia); April 15, 1933

LONG FICTION: *Izvne*, 1960; *Strana bagrovykh tuch*, 1960 (*The Country of the Crimson Clouds*, n.d.); *Popytka k begstvu*, 1962 (*Escape Attempt*, 1982); *Dalekaya raduga*, 1964 (*Far Rainbow*, 1967); *Khishchnye veshchi veka*, 1965 (*The Final Circle of Paradise*, 1976); *Ponedel'nik nachinayetsya v subbotu*, 1965 (*Monday Begins on Saturday*, 1977); *Trudno byt' Bogom*, 1966 (*Hard to Be a God*, 1973); *Ulitka na sklone*, 1966-1968 (*The Snail on the Slope*, 1980); *Skazka o troyke*, 1968 (*Tale of the Troika*, 1977); *Vtoroe nashestvie Marsian*, 1968 (*The Second Martian Invasion*, 1970); *Obitayemyy ostrov*, 1969 (*Prisoners of Power*, 1977); *Malysh*, 1971; *Gadkie lebedi*, 1972 (*The Ugly Swans*, 1979); *Piknik na obochine*, 1972 (*Roadside Picnic*, 1977); *Za milliard let do knotsa sveta*, 1976-1977 (*Definitely Maybe: A Manuscript Discovered Under Unusual Circumstances*, 1978); *Zhuck v muraveinike*, 1979-1980 (*Beetle in the Anthill*, 1980); *Volny gasyat veter*, 1985-1986 (*The Time Wanderers*, 1987); *Khromaya sud'ba*, 1986; *Otyagoshchennye zlom*, 1989; *Grad obrechennyi*, 1991.
SHORT FICTION: *Put'na Amal'teyu*, 1960 (partial trans. as *Destination: Amaltheia*, 1962); *Vozvrashchenie (Polden', XXII vek)*, 1962 (*Noon: Twenty-second Century*, 1978); *Stazhery*, 1962 (*Space Apprentice*, 1982).
DRAMA: *Zhidy goroda Pitera*, pb. 1990, pr. 1991.

Arkady and Boris Strugatsky (strew-GAHT-skee) are among the best-known Russian science-fiction writers in America, and they were honored for their wit and imagination. Arkady, the elder brother, died on October 14, 1991, in Moscow. Arkady and Boris were sons of Nathan Strugatsky, a bibliographer, and Aleksandra Litvinchova, a teacher.

Arkady, the linguist of the writing team, received a degree from the Russian Institute of Foreign Languages in 1949. He worked as an editor and translator of English and Japanese until 1964. Arkady married Elena Oshanina, a Sinologist (a student of Chinese language, literature, and civilization), in 1955. Boris, the younger brother, earned an astronomy degree from Leningrad University in 1956 and became the team's scientist. In 1957 Boris married Adelaida Karpeliuk, another astronomer. Both brothers worked in their chosen fields until 1964, when they became full-time writers.

The Strugatskys began writing science fiction in 1955. Their first novel, presenting a flight to Venus, *The Country of the Crimson Clouds*, began an interplanetary cycle that included *Destination: Amaltheia* and *Space Apprentice*. Similar to space operas by Robert A. Heinlein and Arthur C. Clarke, these future histories presented classless societies on Earth and on the distant planets and stars, along with the death of capitalism and the universal acceptance of communism.

In the 1960's, the Strugatskys turned away from their earlier sociopolitical orthodoxy and developed their science fiction through witty parables, social satires, or folktales. *Far Rainbow*, *Hard to Be a God*, *Monday Begins on Saturday*, and *Tale of the Troika* evidence their growing concern and disillusionment with socialism. *Prisoners of Power* portrays a bewildered protagonist in a strange country clearly resembling Russia.

Such criticism brought the Strugatskys under censorship during the 1970's. Many of their writings were published only in magazines or outside Russia; some were withheld for future publication. During this dark cycle, the brothers wrote *The Snail on the Slope*, a caricature of Soviet bureaucracy, *The Ugly Swans* (published in Germany), and *Roadside Picnic*, a dystopian depiction of a nation as a concentration camp which became the basis for Andrei Tarkovsky's 1972 film *Stalker*. Banned in the Soviet Union, the film won a prize at the 1978 Cannes Film Festival.

During the Soviet thaw in the 1980's, the Strugatskys were awarded the prestigious Aelita Prize (1981) by the Union of Soviet Writers for *Beetle in the Anthill*. This work uses conventional science-fiction themes—alien encounters and the coming of supermen—to complete their future history series.

Three other Strugatsky books appeared in this period of *glasnost*. The protagonist of *Grad obrechennyi* (the doomed city) searches for salvation, progressing from blind faith in Communism through disillusionment to his final quasi-understanding of his moral, social, and spiritual responsibility. *Khromaya sud'ba* (crooked destiny) provides a fictional commentary on *The Ugly Swans*, a realistic portrayal of a Russian writer's life under state control. *Otyagoshchennye zlom* (burdened by evil) deals with a search for some value system, perhaps even a religious one, to replace the political control in human lives.

One last play, *Zhidy goroda Pitera* (Yids of the city of Peter), was performed in Leningrad during the 1991 spring season. The underlying premise, the play's fearful twist, is that despite Perestroika reforms, the country could suddenly revert to its old totalitarian methods. Within four months of the play's publication, just such a political coup by old Communists was overcome in Moscow on August 19, 1991.

One final honor was awarded to the Strugatskys on August 28, 1990. The Soviet Academy of Science announced that the Smithsonian astrophysical observatory had confirmed the naming of minor planet 3054 as "Strugatskaia."

R. C. Lutz
Betsy P. Harfst

Bibliography

Csicsery-Ronay, Istvan. "Towards the Last Fairy Tale: On the Fairy-Tale Paradigm in the Strugatskys' Science Fiction." *Science-Fiction Studies* 13 (March, 1986). Discusses the relationship between folktale and science fiction.

Gomel, Elana. "The Poetics of Censorship: Allegory as Form and Ideology in the Novels of Arkady and Boris Strugatsky." *Science-Fiction Studies* 22 (March, 1995). Focuses on the era during which the Strugatskys' work was out of official favor.

Howell, Yvonne. *Apocalyptic Realism: The Science Fiction of Arkady and Boris Strugatsky.* New York: P. Lang, 1994. A book-length study.

Pike, Christopher. "Change and the Individual in the Work of the Strugatskys." In *Science Fiction, Social Conflict, and War*, edited by Philip John Davies. New York: Manchester University Press, 1990. Discusses the cultural politics of the Strugatskys' work.

Potts, Stephen W. *The Second Marxian Invasion: The Fiction of the Strugatsky Brothers*. San Bernardino, Calif.: Borgo Press, 1991. An analysis of the Strugatskys' work; includes a complete bibliography of their works in English.

Salvestroni, Simonetta. "The Science-Fiction Films of Andrei Tarkovsky." *Science-Fiction Studies* 14 (November, 1987). The Strugatskys' novel *Roadside Picnic* is discussed as the basis of Tarkovsky's film *Stalker*.

Slusser, George E., ed. *Stalkers of the Infinite: The Science Fiction of Arkady and Boris Strugatsky—A Collection of Essays*. San Bernardino, Calif.: Borgo Press, 1991. Offers a variety of approaches to read the Strugatskys' work.

Suvin, Darko. "The Literary Opus of the Strugatskii Brothers." *Canadian-American Slavic Studies* 8 (1974). Early source.

Jesse Stuart

American short-story writer and novelist

Born: W-Hollow, Riverton, Kentucky; August 8, 1907
Died: Ironton, Ohio; February 17, 1984

SHORT FICTION: *Head o' W-Hollow*, 1936; *Men of the Mountains*, 1941; *Tales from the Plum Grove Hills*, 1946; *Clearing in the Sky, and Other Stories*, 1950; *Plowshare in Heaven: Tales True and Tall from the Kentucky Hills*, 1958; *Save Every Lamb*, 1964; *My Land Has a Voice*, 1966; *Come Gentle Spring*, 1969; *Come Back to the Farm*, 1971; *Votes Before Breakfast*, 1974; *The Best-Loved Short Stories of Jesse Stuart*, 1982.

LONG FICTION: *Trees of Heaven*, 1940; *Taps for Private Tussie*, 1943; *Foretaste of Glory*, 1946; *Hie to the Hunters*, 1950; *The Good Spirit of Laurel Ridge*, 1953; *Daughter of the Legend*, 1965; *Mr. Gallion's School*, 1967; *The Land Beyond the River*, 1973; *Cradle of the Copperheads*, 1988.

POETRY: *Harvest of Youth*, 1930; *Man with a Bull-Tongue Plow*, 1934; *Album of Destiny*, 1944; *Kentucky Is My Land*, 1952; *Hold April*, 1962; *The World of Jesse Stuart: Selected Poems*, 1975.

NONFICTION: *Beyond Dark Hills*, 1938; *The Thread That Runs So True*, 1949; *The Year of My Rebirth*, 1956; *God's Oddling*, 1960; *To Teach, to Love*, 1970; *My World*, 1975; *The Kingdom Within: A Spiritual Autobiography*, 1979; *Lost Sandstones and Lonely Skies, and Other Essays*, 1979; *If I Were Seventeen Again, and Other Essays*, 1980; *Jesse Stuart on Education*, 1992 (J. R. LeMaster, editor).

CHILDREN'S/YOUNG ADULT LITERATURE: *Mongrel Mettle: The Autobiography of a Dog*, 1944; *The Beatinest Boy*, 1953; *A Penny's Worth of Character*, 1954; *Red Mule*, 1955; *The Rightful Owner*, 1960; *Andy Finds a Way*, 1961.

Jesse Hilton Stuart was one of the more remarkable and original writers in American literature. Amazingly prolific, with more than sixty books in a variety of genres, Stuart produced work that was largely uneven. It has been as much admired by a broad popular audience as it has been maligned, or ignored, by the mainstream of literary opinion. Born in a log cabin in W-Hollow in the hills of eastern Kentucky, Stuart was the first in his family to finish high school. He worked his way through Lincoln Memorial University, a small mountain college in Tennessee, from which he graduated in 1929.

After two years of teaching and administrative experience in his native region, he attended Vanderbilt University, where he pursued but did not complete an M.A. in English. He was particularly drawn to Vanderbilt because of the presence there of the Fugitive-Agrarians, such poets, writers, and teachers as Donald Davidson, John Crowe Ransom, and Robert Penn Warren. Although Stuart sometimes seemed to confuse the moral, aesthetic, and philosophical bases of Nashville Agrarian thought with mere farming, he was certainly influenced profoundly by what he took to be the group's back-to-the-farm and anti-industrial arguments, as well as by its emphasis on the southern sense of place, family, community, and language. The best record of Stuart's vision of these years is found in his first and finest autobiographical volume, *Beyond Dark Hills*, which was originally submitted as a term paper at Vanderbilt.

Man with a Bull-Tongue Plow, Stuart's first important book, appeared in 1934. This rough collection of 703 sonnets is a work of genuine force and energy. Stuart begins the volume with an announcement: "I am a farmer singing at the plow." He then carries the reader through the cycles of the seasons, the land, and the lives, loves, and deaths of the mountain country and people. The stance he assumes here—the primitive mountain bard, the poet of Appalachia—would remain his typical persona and most effective voice throughout his career. He had been profoundly influenced by the work of Robert Burns, and, with the appearance of this volume, Stuart was hailed as the American Burns. His later volumes of poetry never lived up to the power and freshness of this work.

With the publication of *Head o' W-Hollow*, Stuart's first collection of stories, he was hailed as an important writer of fiction with substantial gifts of humor, observation, and creative use of language based on mountain dialect and idiom. Through many volumes over the next four decades Stuart's fiction evoked this hillbilly world, until W-Hollow seemed, to some observers, to have earned a place akin to William Faulkner's Yoknapatawpha County in the literary geography of the United States. *Trees of Heaven*, his first novel, renders this world fully as it works out a love story between a squatter's daughter, Subrinea Tussie, and a landowner's son, Tarvin Bushman, against the thematic background of the squatter-landowner conflict. Through the patriarchal landowner Anse Bushman, Stuart powerfully renders what may be his single great theme: love of land, of farming, of drawing strength from the earth. *Taps for Private Tussie*, Stuart's next novel, continues the hilarious chronicle of the Tussies, the indolent hill clan committed to avoiding work, to eating, drinking, and dancing all night long. Immensely popular, this comic novel was a best-seller and received the Thomas Jefferson Award for the best southern book of 1943.

Much of his life Stuart was a teacher, in the country schools of Kentucky and in colleges and universities as far afield as Egypt, where he taught for a year at the University of Cairo. Stuart thought teaching "the greatest profession under the sun," and in *The Thread That Runs So True* he paid tribute to the profession. This award-winning autobiographical hymn to teaching has at its center the dramatic presence of a man who walked twenty miles to carry a suitcase loaded with books to his poor mountain students. It was declared "the best book on education" written in the twentieth century by the president of the National Education Association, and it remains Stuart's most popular book.

In 1954 Stuart was named poet laureate of Kentucky. In the same year he suffered a severe heart attack. *The Year of My Rebirth* is his journal of the struggle back to life from that near-fatal incident. It is also a spiritual autobiography which weaves together his love of place and a motif of resurrection. Another strong presence in this meditation on life and death is his father, who had died shortly after Stuart's heart attack. A few years later, in *God's Oddling*, Stuart paid moving tribute to his father as farmer, earth poet, "giant of the earth."

Conservationist, farmer, teacher, and writer, Stuart lived a rich, eventful life. He imprinted W-Hollow deeply in the literary imagination of millions of readers. As a farmer-conservationist who eventually owned one thousand acres of his beloved valley, he planted thousands of trees, leaving his mark on the landscape of Kentucky. After his death in 1984 Stuart's bequest to the people established the Jesse Stuart Nature Preserve. Balanced assessment of Stuart's literary achievement was complicated during his lifetime by the uncritical enthusiasm of the popular press. His position as a major twentieth century local colorist is secure, but he may, with the passage of time, come to be seen in a more positive and less limited sense as a genuine voice of Appalachian consciousness and as one of the more important regional writers in American literature.

H. R. Stoneback

Bibliography

Foster, Ruel E. *Jesse Stuart*. New York: Twayne, 1968. One of the earliest and best critical studies. Contains biographical information as well as extensive critiques on Stuart's work up to the date of publication.

LeMaster, J. R. *Jesse Stuart: Kentucky's Chronicler-Poet*. Memphis, Tenn.: Memphis State University Press, 1980. This full-length book concentrates on Stuart as a poet, although he has more often been admired as a popular writer for his prose. LeMaster's definition of poet is an inclusive one, however, meaning more nearly a *Dichter* (a writer of fiction) than a versifier. Stuart has an ear for sounds and an eye for images, and ballads and stories are an essential ingredient of his art. Includes an index.

________, ed. *Jesse Stuart: Selected Criticism*. St. Petersburg, Fla.: Valkyrie Press, 1978. A good start to Stuart criticism, this volume includes previously published articles by different scholars. Excellent introduction to Stuart's work.

LeMaster, J. R., and Mary Washington Clark, eds. *Jesse Stuart: Essays on His Work*. Lexington: University Press of Kentucky, 1977. These essays (written specifically for this volume) provide critical perspectives on different facets and forms of Stuart's work, including poetry, short fiction, and novels, as well as his humor and use of folklore.

Lowe, Jimmy. *Jesse Stuart: The Boy from the Dark Hills*. Edited by Jerry A. Herndon, James M. Gifford, and Chuck D. Charles. Ashland, Ky.: Jesse Stuart Foundation, 1990. A good, updated biography of Stuart.

Thompson, Edgar H. "A Cure for the Malaise of the Dislocated Southerner: The Writing of Jesse Stuart." *Journal of the Appalachian Studies Association* 3 (1991): 146-151. A good survey of Stuart emphasizing his regional heritage.

Towles, Donald B. "Twenty Stories from Jesse Stuart." *The Courier-Journal*, September 20, 1998, p. O51. A review of *Tales from the Plum Grove Hills*; surveys the themes and subjects of the stories and comments on their use of Eastern Kentucky dialect.

Ward, William S. *A Literary History of Kentucky*. Knoxville: University of Tennessee Press, 1988. Includes a biographical-critical discussion of Stuart's work, pointing out that Stuart deals with people as individuals rather than in sociological terms. Claims that a principal source of his success with the short story was the zest with which he carried a story through in a flood of detail.

Theodore Sturgeon
(Edward Hamilton Waldo)

American novelist and short-story writer

Born: Staten Island, New York; February 26, 1918
Died: Eugene, Oregon; May 8, 1985
Pseudonyms: E. Waldo Hunter, E. Hunter Waldo, Frederick R. Ewing, Ellery Queen, Billy Watson

LONG FICTION: *The Dreaming Jewels*, 1950 (also known as *The Synthetic Man*); *More than Human*, 1953; *I, Libertine*, 1956 (as Frederick R. Ewing; with Jean Shepherd); *The King and Four Queens*, 1956; *The Cosmic Rape*, 1958; *Venus Plus X*, 1960; *Some of Your Blood*, 1961; *Voyage to the Bottom of the Sea*, 1961; *Alien Cargo*, 1984; *Godbody*, 1986.

SHORT FICTION: *Without Sorcery: Thirteen Tales*, 1948 (also known as *Not Without Sorcery*); *E Pluribus Unicorn*, 1953; *Caviar*, 1955; *A Way Home: Stories of Science Fiction and Fantasy*, 1955 (also known as *Thunder and Roses*); *A Touch of Strange*, 1958; *Aliens 4*, 1959; *Beyond*, 1960; *Sturgeon in Orbit*, 1964; *The Joyous Invasions*, 1965; *Starshine*, 1966; *Sturgeon Is Alive and Well*, 1971 (also known as *To Here and the Easel*); *The Worlds of Theodore Sturgeon*, 1972; *Sturgeon's West*, 1973 (with Don Ward); *Case and the Dreamer, and Other Stories*, 1974; *Visions and Venturers*, 1978; *Maturity: Three Stories*, 1979; *The Stars Are the Styx*, 1979; *The Golden Helix*, 1979; *Slow Sculpture*, 1982; *Alien Cargo*, 1984; *Pruzy's Pot*, 1986; *A Touch of Sturgeon*, 1987; *To Marry Medusa*, 1987; *The [Widget], the [Wadget], and Boff*, 1989; *The Complete Stories of Theodore Sturgeon*, 1994-2002 (8 volumes).

DRAMA: *It Should Be Beautiful*, pr. 1963; *Psychosis: Unclassified*, pr. 1977 (adaptation of his novel *Some of Your Blood*).

TELEPLAYS: *Mewhu's Jet*, 1950's; *The Adaptive Ultimate*, 1950's; *They Came to Bagdad*, 1950's; *Ordeal in Space*, 1950's; *The Sound Machine*, 1950's; *Dead Dames Don't Dial*, 1959; *Shore Leave*, 1966; *Amok Time*, 1967; *Killdozer!*, 1974; *The Pylon Express*, 1975-1976.

RADIO PLAYS: *Incident at Switchpath*, 1950; *The Stars Are the Styx*, 1953; *Mr. Costello, Hero*, 1956; *Saucer of Loneliness*, 1957; *More than Human*, 1967 (adaptation of his novel).

NONFICTION: *Argyll: A Memoir*, 1993.

Theodore Sturgeon (STUR-juhn) was one of the most important writers of short stories and novels within the American science-fiction and fantasy genres between about 1940 and 1960. His great concern for characters and emotions was unique at a time when most of the works in those genres were concerned with plots and settings. He was born Edward Hamilton Waldo; his name was changed when he was adopted in 1929. Because of a ruthlessly strict stepfather, Sturgeon's childhood was unhappy, a situation only made clear in the posthumously published *Argyll: A Memoir*. His childhood also provided much material for his fiction, in which characters feel compelled to be cruel with the best of intentions (in stories including "Cellmate" and novels such as *The Dreaming Jewels*).

Sturgeon attended high school in Philadelphia. In his early teens he showed great promise as a gymnast, winning a national title on the horizontal bar and having high hopes of becoming a circus performer. When he developed rheumatic fever, his stepfather would not allow him to be ill, insisting that he must go to school. This worsened the condition and ended his circus ambitions. He escaped from home by going to nautical school; there he observed and suffered from the misuse of authority, so that he developed the antiauthority stance which he maintained for the rest of his life. After running away from the school, he became a merchant seaman.

At the same time, in his late teens, he was writing stories. The first of these appeared in 1937 in newspapers owned by the McClure syndicate. This gave him the confidence to leave the merchant marine and, from about 1938, to live in New York as a full-time writer. His first science fiction story, "Ether Breather," was published in *Astounding Science Fiction* magazine in September, 1939. Many of the stories which followed it were fantasy-horror stories which appeared in *Unknown* magazine. Sturgeon worked hard at writing stories, but it was a poor living, and in 1940 he was afflicted by the first of a series of writer's blocks.

Trying to escape from these, and also needing more money because he had married in 1940, he tried a string of different jobs. He worked as a hotel manager in the West Indies, as a steward in the U.S. Army, and as a bulldozer operator in Puerto Rico. This last experience led to the writing of one of his most popular stories, "Killdozer" (published in *Astounding* in 1944) about a bulldozer which achieves sentience.

By the mid-1940's, Sturgeon was back in New York, working as an advertising copy editor, a literary agent, and as editor of *Tales of Tomorrow* magazine. One of his noted stories from this period, "Bianca's Hands," was considered too terrifying for publication in the United States, but it won a competition run by the British magazine *Argosy*, appearing there in 1947. At this time, Sturgeon was placing about a story a month, mostly science fiction and fantasy-horror but also crime and Western.

He married for a second time in 1949 and for a third in 1951. His first novel, *The Dreaming Jewels*, was published in 1950, originally as a magazine story in *Fantastic Adventures*. It features a young man who escapes from cruel stepparents by running away to join a circus, in part a wish-fulfillment version of his own life. The 1950's were a very fertile time for Sturgeon. He continued to produce stories prolifically, many of them being gathered together in several collections. His novel *More than Human*, about the forming of a gestalt by several talented but incomplete individuals with psychic powers, was well accepted by critics and readers; it won the International Fantasy Award in 1954.

By 1960 he had succumbed to another writer's block. Although he kept busy during the 1960's, editing, writing articles and reviews, and doing teleplays and novelizations of screenplays, he was never again to write fiction freely. He had built up a great following over the previous fifteen years and was widely regarded as the most important writer in his genre. The prestigious *The Magazine of Fantasy and Science Fiction* dedicated an issue to him (September 1962), an honor given to only a handful of writers.

In 1970 Sturgeon returned to the top of his form with the science fiction story "Brownshoes," which received the Hugo and Nebula awards. In 1980 he produced a fine horror story, "Vengeance Is." He worked spasmodically on a big, new science fiction novel (*Godbody*, only published after his death, and which proved disappointing). He married twice more, and he continued to write reviews and articles, some within the science-fiction genre but also for the men's magazine *Hustler.* His stories were frequently reprinted in new collections that overlapped with older ones. In his last few years he was a frequent attendee at science-fiction conventions, where his urbane conversation was always welcomed by large numbers of fans.

When Sturgeon died in May, 1985, with his fifth wife and six of his seven children in attendance, there was a great outpouring of grief from writers and readers alike. He was a very popular figure, charming all who met him and giving freely of his time and experience to anyone who asked. He was responsible for a useful definition of science fiction: a story built around humans, with a human problem, and a human solution, which would not have occurred without a scientific content. Sturgeon sometimes said that this was only meant to refer to a good example of the genre. He also originated Sturgeon's Rule, that 90 percent of everything is rubbish. Sturgeon showed that science fiction should look not so much at future hardware or at alien bogeymen but into the hearts of people.

Chris Morgan

Bibliography

Bleiler, Richard, ed. *Science Fiction Writers*. 2d ed. New York: Scribners, 1999. Contains a brief but usefully analytical article by Brian Stableford.

Diskin, Lahna F. *Theodore Sturgeon*. Mercer Island, Wash.: Starmont, 1981. The standard guide to Sturgeon's output.

Pringle, David, ed. *St. James Guide to Horror, Ghost, and Gothic Writers*. Detroit: St. James Press, 1998. Contains a comprehensive bibliography of Sturgeon's works.

William Styron

American novelist

Born: Newport News, Virginia; June 11, 1925

LONG FICTION: *Lie Down in Darkness*, 1951; *The Long March*, 1952 (serial), 1956 (book); *Set This House on Fire*, 1960; *The Confessions of Nat Turner*, 1967; *Sophie's Choice*, 1979.
SHORT FICTION: *A Tidewater Morning: Three Tales from Youth*, 1993.
DRAMA: *In the Clap Shack*, pr. 1972.
NONFICTION: *This Quiet Dust, and Other Writings*, 1982, expanded 1993; *Darkness Visible: A Memoir of Madness*, 1990.

William Styron (STI-ruhn) was born in Newport News, Virginia, which he later called "a very Southern part of the world." His mother, Pauline Margaret Abraham Styron, was from the North, but his father, William Clark Styron, a shipyard engineer, came from an old, if not aristocratic, land-poor Virginia family, and Styron remembers his grandmother telling him as a little boy of the days when the family owned slaves, a memory he incorporated years later into *Sophie's Choice*. Styron's father was a "Jeffersonian gentleman," liberal in his views for a Southerner, who implanted in his son much of the philosophical curiosity that characterized the young Styron's novels. His mother, a gentling influence, died when Styron was twelve after a long, painful siege with cancer, an experience that also left a mark on his fiction in the form of an almost obsessive concern with physical pain, suffering, and the vulnerability of the flesh. After his mother's death Styron began "going wild," and his father sent him to an Episcopal boys' school in Middlesex County, where he was an indifferent student but a voracious reader. After graduating, he enrolled in Davidson College during World War II but soon dropped out to enlist in the Marines.

Styron's service in Officers Candidate School marked the beginning of his writing career, for while there he enrolled in a creative writing course at Duke University under William Blackburn, whom Styron acknowledges as the most powerful formative influence on his work. One of his stories, about a Southern lynching, similar in tone and execution to William Faulkner's "Dry September," appeared in a student anthology, Styron's first published fiction. Toward the end of the war Styron was commissioned and sent to the Pacific, arriving on the island of Okinawa after the fighting was over. Styron spoke later of his sense of guilt at not having seen action, as well as his feeling of horror at the waste and destruction of the war and the terrible, almost casual way in which life could be lost. Back in the United States Styron resumed his studies at Duke and graduated in 1947. He took a job in New York as an associate editor in the book division at McGraw-Hill. His senior editor and immediate superior was Edward C. Aswell, the second editor of Thomas Wolfe and an éminence grise to rival Maxwell Perkins; Aswell was to appear grotesquely as "The Weasel" in an autobiographical passage in *Sophie's Choice* nearly thirty years later. Styron found McGraw-Hill humorless and confining, and after six months he was fired.

Living in a Brooklyn boardinghouse on a tiny legacy from his grandmother, Styron took another creative writing course, this time from Hiram Haydn at the New School for Social Research. He began work on his first novel, *Lie Down in Darkness*, the story of a star-crossed upper-middle-class Southern family whose failure to find love and meaning in life drives the sensitive daughter, Peyton Loftis, to insanity and suicide. The complex treatment of time in the novel and its high Southern rhetoric showed the influence of William Faulkner, whom Styron had been reading intensely, but *Lie Down in Darkness* was manifestly the work of a powerful and original talent. Styron found that the writing of the book, although exhausting, went surprisingly fast, and he finished it and saw it accepted for publication by Bobbs-Merrill before he was recalled by the Marines for service in the Korean War. The novel was published in 1951. Styron was then on active reserve duty, and his experiences during that time became the basis for his second novel, *The Long March*.

Lie Down in Darkness was an immediate critical success and a moderate popular one, winning the prestigious Prix de Rome in 1952. At that time Styron had decamped to Paris and fallen in with a young crowd of American expatriate intellectuals, many of whom would later make names for themselves in literature. George Plimpton and Peter Matthiessen were at the center the group, which also included Harold Humes, John P. C. Train, Donald Hall, and, on the fringe, writers such as James Baldwin, James Jones, and Irwin Shaw. In 1952 and 1953 the group began compiling a literary magazine, *The Paris Review*, which became one of the most influential literary periodicals of the postwar period. Plimpton became the first editor, Matthiessen became the fiction editor, and Styron wrote the statement of purpose for the first issue. He also gave the periodical one of the first of its famous "Writers at Work" interviews. It was recorded by Matthiessen and Plimpton at Patrick's, the *Paris Review* crowd's favorite bar, and in it Styron claimed that "this generation . . . will produce literature equal to that of any other generation . . ." and that "a great writer . . . will give substance to and perhaps even explain all the problems of the world. . . ." From the start his ambitions were large.

Although he later said he drank enough brandy in bistros to develop a *crise de foie* and that he spent months in the summer of 1952 on a sybaritic "Ovidian idyll" on the Riviera with Humes, Styron was also writing at top speed during this period. In just six weeks he wrote a novella based on his Marine Corps training-camp experience, *The Long March*, which was accepted for publication in the fall by *discovery*, a literary magazine (Knopf published it as a book four years later). In 1953 he used the money from his Prix de Rome to travel in Italy, an experience that laid the groundwork for his 1960 novel of expatriates, *Set This House on Fire*, and during this time he met Rose Burgunder, a Jewish poet with some family money from Baltimore, whom he soon married. They returned to America, to Roxbury, Connecticut, which thereupon became Styron's home. Here he began work on the "big novel" that he planned to follow up the success of *Lie Down in Darkness*.

This "big novel" was *Set This House on Fire*, a sprawling account of American intellectuals living a life of self-indulgence and self-destruction in postwar Italy. The book contains fine lyrical passages of description, particularly of the physical beauty of Italy and the horrifying squalor and suffering of its people, but as Styron later admitted, the novel is seriously flawed. The reviews were mixed, some of them savage. Styron's former friend Norman Mailer called *Set This House on Fire* "a bad, maggoty novel," suggesting that Styron could "write like an angel about landscape, but like an adolescent about people." The novel was better received by Styron's European critics—it is still highly regarded in France—but Styron was wounded by his first really bad press, and he retreated to Roxbury to work on his next book, a novel he resolved to make so thoroughly a work of craftsmanship as to defy criticism.

It took Styron years to research and write *The Confessions of Nat Turner*, and true to Styron's expectations it was immediately acclaimed as a masterpiece. Styron had long had his mind on Nat Turner's 1831 slave rebellion as a subject for fiction. It had taken place close to his own Tidewater Virginia home, and Styron saw the suffering, the violence, and the misunderstanding of the revolt as emblematic both of the South's guilt and pain and of his personal concerns as a writer. Styron claimed that reading Albert Camus's *The Stranger* (1942) furnished him with the technique he was to use in presenting Nat Turner's story—the narrative persona reflecting from jail—and there is no doubt that much of the novel's perspective on black people and black problems was derived from Styron's friend, the black writer James Baldwin, who was a guest of Styron for months while writing *Another Country* (1962), Baldwin's first major novel about black/white relations. Styron called *The Confessions of Nat Turner* "less a 'historical novel' than a meditation on history," but despite almost unanimous critical accolades, including the praise of Baldwin, who suggested that the novel might be considered the beginning of a black/white "mutual history," Styron became the target of a group of black critics who protested vehemently the right of a white man to consider himself qualified to interpret the black experience. Nat Turner, as Styron presented him, was a strong and sensitive character, unquestionably the hero of the novel, but so volatile was the political climate of America in the late 1960's that for some critics, any black character who was not a warrior saint was unacceptable as a fictional creation, particularly the creation of a white writer.

The critical assaults provoked by the *The Confessions of Nat Turner* left Styron bruised, but he was encouraged by the praise for the novel's powerful rhetoric and masterly structure, not to mention its enormous financial success. Of the controversy, he said, "It really had very little effect on me . . . largely because of the fact that I knew that it was politically motivated and hysterical, and that I had not violated any truth that a novelist is capable of doing." He turned to new work, first to a lengthy projected novel exploring the psyche of a career army officer, which he finally shelved, then to *Sophie's Choice*. The book began as an autobiographical reminiscence of his aimless days as a junior editor at McGraw-Hill, when he found himself frustrated artistically, philosophically, and sexually. As he worked through his memories in the character of his narrator, Stingo, whose fictional background is almost identical with Styron's own, he found his real theme: the life and eventual death by suicide of a woman who survived the Nazi concentration camps but emerged terribly scarred emotionally. This woman, the Sophie of the title, becomes the vehicle through which Stingo confronts the potential horror of life, and through whom he matures.

Sophie's Choice took five years to write, but Styron was richly rewarded when it was finally published in 1979. A few critics, notably John Gardner, raised questions about its structure, and about the sometimes jejune intrusions of the shallow Stingo, but for the most part the novel was accepted as a fine and satisfying offering by a major writer. "It has the feel of permanence," Peter Prescott wrote. The gratifying large sales were capped by a spectacular sale of the film rights. In 1983 Meryl Streep won an Academy Award for Best Actress for her portrayal of Sophie in the film version.

In 1985 Styron was hospitalized with acute clinical depression. His struggle to overcome his suicidal feelings and to return to health are recounted in his memoir *Darkness Visible*, published five years later. Styron credited the peaceful seclusion of his hospital stay and the loving patience of his wife and grown children (three daughters and a son) as the principal factors in his recovery.

John L. Cobbs

Bibliography

Casciato, Arthur D., and James L. W. West III, eds. *Critical Essays on William Styron*. Boston: G. K. Hall, 1982. Collection of critical essays that cover all of Styron's major novels and include bibliographical references.

Coale, Samuel. *William Styron Revisited*. Boston: Twayne, 1991. A brief biography and an analysis of Styron's novels. Coale devotes a chapter to each major work, including a selected bibliography.

Cobbs, John L., and Roark Mulligan. "Styron, William." In *Critical Survey of Long Fiction*, edited by Carl Rollyson. 2d rev. ed. Pasadena, Calif.: Salem Press, 2000. A thorough overview of Styron's life and career, with analyses of his individual novels.

Cologne-Brookes, Gavin. *The Novels of William Styron: From Harmony to History*. Baton Rouge: Louisiana State University Press, 1995. Study of the influence of the modernist movement on Styron, explores Styron's psychological themes, and analyzes his shifting patterns of discourse. Includes analysis of Styron's later work.

Hadaller, David. *Gynicide: Women in the Novels of William Styron*. Madison, N.J.: Fairleigh Dickinson University Press, 1996. Explores women in Styron's fiction, particularly the deaths of women and the meaning of these deaths. Hadaller argues that Styron's depictions force readers to question a society that victimizes women.

Morris, Robert K., and Irving Malin, eds. *The Achievement of William Styron*. Athens: University of Georgia Press, 1975. Provides essays by various critics on Styron's fiction up to *Sophie's Choice*. The essay by Morris and Malin on Styron's career as a visionary novelist is a good introduction to his work.

West, James L. W., III, ed. *Conversations with William Styron*. Jackson: University Press of Mississippi, 1985. Collected interviews with William Styron in which Styron attempts to "restore a little balance," giving his side to the many controversies that his books have caused.

_______. *William Styron: A Life*. New York: Random House, 1998. The first comprehensive biography of Styron, West's extraordinary work lucidly and cogently connects events in Styron's life to his fiction. This is an essential work for anyone who wishes to understand Styron and his writing.

Virgil Suárez

Cuban-born American novelist and poet

Born: Havana, Cuba; 1962
Identity: Cuban American

LONG FICTION: *Latin Jazz*, 1989; *The Cutter*, 1991; *Havana Thursdays*, 1995; *Going Under*, 1996.

SHORT FICTION: *Welcome to the Oasis, and Other Stories*, 1992.

POETRY: *You Come Singing*, 1998; *Garabato Poems*, 1999; *In the Republic of Longing*, 1999; *Palm Crows*, 2001; *Banyan*, 2001; *Guide to the Blue Tongue*, 2002.

EDITED TEXTS: *Iguana Dreams: New Latino Fiction*, 1992 (with Delia Poey); *Paper Dance: Fifty-five Latino Poets*, 1995 (with Victor Hernández and Leroy V. Quintana); *Little Havana Blues: A Cuban-American Literature Anthology*, 1996 (with Poey); *American Diaspora: Poetry of Displacement*, 2001 (with Ryan G. Van Cleave); *Like Thunder: Poets Respond to Violence in America*, 2002 (with Van Cleave).

MISCELLANEOUS: *Spared Angola: Memories from a Cuban-American Childhood*, 1997 (short stories, poetry, and essays); *Infinite Refuge*, 2002 (sketches, poetry, memories, and fragments of short stories).

Virgil Suárez (SWA-rays), the son of a pattern cutter and a piecemeal seamstress who worked in the sweatshops of Havana, left Cuba in 1970 with his family. After four years in Madrid, Spain, they went to Los Angeles. A man of many interests and prolific literary output, Suárez raised three daughters with his wife in Florida. His multitude of works in numerous genres deal with immigration, exile, and acclimatization to life and culture in the United States as well as the hopes and struggles of Cubans and Cuban Americans who had to abandon their island home under political duress.

A self-confessed obsessive, whether about his family, his hobbies, or his writing, Suárez is preoccupied by voice. He cites physical place as paramount in the process of finding and producing his voice, whether in prose or poetry. Initially recognized for his fiction, Suárez has written poetry since 1978, though he only began to publish it in the mid-1990's. He believes that voice is most important in poetry because of poetry's space limitations. He feels so strongly about maintaining the authenticity of his personal voice that he discards any poem he believes does not respect and represent his voice.

That voice is of an immigrant who, although he has spent the majority of his life in his adopted land and does not expect to return to Cuba, still does not feel completely acclimated. Suárez writes about what he knows: the nature and travails of exile. Appropriately, given his mixed feelings, Suárez writes in English and includes a sprinkling of Spanish, reiterated in English. Nonetheless, critics characterize Suárez's style as unwavering, definitive, and direct.

Suárez finished his secondary schooling in Los Angeles and received a B.A. in creative writing from California State University, Long Beach, in 1984. He studied at the University of Arizona and received an M.F.A. in creative writing from Louisiana State University in 1987. In addition to having been a visiting professor at the University of Texas in Austin in 1997, Suárez has taught at the University of Miami, Florida International University, Miami-Dade Community College, and Florida State University in Tallahassee.

Suárez's poems alone have appeared in more than 250 magazines and journals. He has also been a book reviewer for the *Los Angeles Times*, the *Miami Herald*, *The Philadelphia Inquirer*, and *The Tallahassee Democrat*. He is a member of PEN, the Academy of American Poets, the Associated Writing Programs, and the Modern Language Association.

Nominated for five Pushcart Prizes, Suárez was a featured lecturer at the Smithsonian Institution in 1997. He received a Florida State Individual Artist grant in 1998 and a National Endowment for the Arts Fellowship in 2001-2002 to write a poetry work. His volume *Garabato Poems* was named *Generation Ñ* magazine's Best Book of 1999. He served as a National Endowment for the Arts Fellowship panel judge in 1999 and a Mid-Atlantic Arts Foundation panelist in 2000.

Debra D. Andrist

Bibliography

Alvarez-Borland, Isabel. *Cuban-American Literature of Exile: From Person to Persona*. Charlottesville: University of Virginia Press, 1998.

_______. "Displacements and Autobiography in Cuban American Fiction." *World Literature Today* 68, no. 1 (1994): 43-49.

Cortina, Rodolfo. "A Perfect Hotspot." In *Hispanic American Literature*. Lincolnwood, Ill.: NTC, 1998.

Herrera, Andrea O'Reilly. "Song for the Royal Palms of Miami." In *ReMembering Cuba: Legacy of a Diaspora*. Austin: University of Texas Press, 2001.

Sir John Suckling

English poet and playwright

Born: Whitton, Twickenham, England; February, 1609
Died: Paris, France; 1642

POETRY: *Fragmenta Aurea*, 1646; *The Last Remains of Sir John Suckling*, 1659.

DRAMA: *Aglaura*, pr., pb. 1638; *The Goblins*, pr. 1638; *Brennoralt*, pr. 1646; *The Works of Sir John Suckling: The Plays*, pb. 1971 (L. A. Beaurline, editor).

MISCELLANEOUS: *The Works of Sir John Suckling: The Non-dramatic Works*, 1971 (Thomas Clayton, editor).

Sir John Suckling is typical of the Cavalier poets, who flourished at the court of Charles I and Queen Henrietta Maria during the decade before the outbreak of the English civil war. They served the king, wrote polished, witty verses, and entertained the court ladies with their gallantries. Suckling was born in 1609 in Twickenham, a suburb of London, into a family with close court connections. His father, Sir John Suckling, was a member of parliament, secretary of state, and comptroller of the household under James I, and he became a member of the Privy Council of Charles I. The poet's mother, who died when he was four, was the sister of Lionel Cranfield, James's lord treasurer from 1622 to 1626, the one man who almost succeeded in curbing the royal extravagances for a brief period.

Suckling may have attended the Westminster school before he

entered Trinity College, Cambridge, in 1623. He left the university without a degree and went on to London to Gray's Inn, ostensibly to study law. However, at this period the Inns of Court were as much a playground for rich young noblemen as institutions of learning, and Suckling probably sought amusement where he could find it. When his father died in 1627, he began at once to squander his newly acquired fortune, which was substantial.

The young nobleman left Gray's Inn in 1628 for a two-year tour of France and Italy. Knighted by Charles I at Theobalds when he came back to England in 1630, he soon joined a group of English soldiers who fought under King Gustavus Adolphus of Sweden in the following year. His extravagance on his return to London in 1632 was legendary; the story is told that his sisters wept for fear he would gamble away their dowries. He lived chiefly at court, where he was named gentleman of the privy chamber, and where he composed many of his clever, cynical lyrics addressed to mournful lovers and faithless ladies.

Suckling's interests were not exclusively frivolous; he numbered among his friends the noted philosopher Lucius Cary, Lord Falkland, and the scientist Robert Boyle as well as many of the poets of his time. He composed a philosophical tract, "An Account of Religion by Reason," which was published with his poetry in *Fragmenta Aurea* in 1646.

A number of Suckling's best works were written between 1635 and 1640; one of the wittiest of them, "A Session of the Poets," contains satirical portraits of his literary acquaintances. His play *Aglaura* was lavishly produced for the court at his own expense in 1637, and *Brennoralt*, a dramatic commentary on the Scottish rebellion, appeared a few years later.

When Charles I raised an army to invade Scotland in 1639, Suckling furnished a unit that was distinguished for its magnificent finery, if not for its military ability, an act which earned him considerable ridicule from his countrymen. He became a member of the Long Parliament in 1640, but his public career ended abruptly with his involvement in a plot to free Thomas Wentworth, Earl of Strafford, who had been sentenced to death by Parliament for treason. To escape arrest Suckling fled to France, where he died in 1642—according to the gossipy seventeenth century biographer John Aubrey, by a self-administered dose of poison. Another report says that a servant caused his death. While his death was untimely, the world in which he had delighted no longer existed: There was no place in Oliver Cromwell's Commonwealth for the dilettante man of letters who played at being a soldier when it suited his fancy.

Bibliography

Clayton, Thomas. "'At Bottom a Criticism of Life': Suckling and the Poetry of Low Seriousness." In *Classic and Cavalier: Essays on Jonson and the Sons of Ben*, edited by Claude J. Summers and Ted-Larry Pebworth. Pittsburgh: University of Pittsburgh Press, 1982. Clayton's essay provides an overview of Suckling criticism and proceeds to analyze four poems: the early "Upon St. Thomas's Unbelief," "An Answer to Some Verses Made in His Praise," "Why So Pale and Wan," and "Love's Clock." Places Suckling's work in its literary context.

Miner, Earl. *The Cavalier Mode from Jonson to Cotton*. Princeton, N.J.: Princeton University Press, 1971. Though he disapproves of Suckling the man, Miner often finds in him the poetic embodiment of Cavalier love poetry. In fact, Miner believes the "battle of the sexes" cliché was first given Cavalier expression in Suckling's "A Soldier" and "Loves Siege."

Squires, Charles L. *Sir John Suckling*. Boston: Twayne, 1978. Squires covers Suckling's life, plays, poems, prose, and literary reputation. He also provides careful readings of several poems, and his criticism of the four plays is detailed. Suckling emerges as the spokesman for the Cavalier era. Includes a chronology and bibliography.

Summer, Joseph H. *The Heirs of Donne and Jonson*. Oxford, England: Oxford University Press, 1970. Summers considers Suckling as an exemplar of the gentleman at court and finds in his verse debts to Ben Jonson and John Donne. Treating the narrative voice in poetry, Summers makes distinctions between the Donne originals and the Suckling responses, particularly in the cases of "The Indifferent" and "Love's Deity," which are answered in Suckling's Sonnets II and III.

Van Strien, Kees. "Sir John Suckling in Holland." *English Studies* 76, no. 5 (September, 1995): 443. Suckling traveled in the Low Countries in the early seventeenth century yet left no record of his journeys. A letter written by Suckling and additional material are pieced together to develop a picture of the writer during a little-known period of his life.

Ruth Suckow

American novelist

Born: Hawarden, Iowa; August 6, 1892
Died: Claremont, California; January 23, 1960

LONG FICTION: *Country People*, 1924; *The Bonney Family*, 1928; *The Kramer Girls*, 1930; *The Folks*, 1934; *New Hope*, 1942; *The John Wood Case*, 1959.
SHORT FICTION: *Iowa Interiors*, 1926; *Children and Other People*, 1931; *Some Others and Myself*, 1952.

Ruth Suckow (SEW-koh) was the grandchild of German immigrants on both sides of her family. Her father was a liberal Congregational minister whose work took his family to a number of Iowa communities during his daughter's childhood; at that time western Iowa was but recently settled.

After high school Suckow spent three years at Grinnell College and one year in Boston at the Curry Dramatic School. She received her A.B. degree in 1917 from the University of Denver. While in Colorado she learned beekeeping so as to have a way of earning a living, and after graduation from college she operated the Orchard Apiary at Earleville, Iowa. Her work allowed her to spend the winter months writing in Greenwich Village, New York. Her first published work, "Uprooted," appeared in *Midland*, a periodical for which she later became an associate editor. The editor of *Midland* encouraged her to submit some manuscripts to H. L. Mencken, who praised her work. During the 1920's she became a contributor to *Smart Set*, *American Mercury*, and other periodicals. Her *Country People* was first published by Carl Van Doren in the *Century* as a serialized novel.

Her stories, as well as her novels, of the 1920's set the pattern for all her subsequent work. As a regionalist she drew upon the people and the countryside and the towns of the Midwest, especially the families of German immigrants, thus using the region and the people she knew closely from her early life. *The Bonney Family*, a novel of life in a minister's home, reflects the experiences of Suckow's own family. In the early 1930's she began working on the novel *The Folks*, usually considered her most typical and best work. In it she describes the average midwestern small-town family, one that is a single generation removed from the farm and two generations removed from genuine pioneer experience.

Following her marriage to Ferner Nuhn in 1929, she lived at various times in New York City, Washington, D.C., California, Vermont, New Mexico, and Iowa. She considered Cedar Falls, Iowa, where she is buried, as home. During the 1940's and 1950's her literary fame and reputation dwindled, and she wrote less than she had earlier in life. Her last novel, *The John Wood Case*, appeared just a few months before she died in her sixty-eighth year.

Craig Gilbert

Bibliography

Andrews, Clarence A. *A Literary History of Iowa*. Iowa City: University of Iowa Press, 1988.

Casey, Roger. *Bulletin of Bibliography* 46, no. 4 (1989).

Martin, Abigail. *Ruth Suckow.* Boise, Idaho: Boise State University Press, 1978.

Oehlschlaeger, Fritz. "The Art of Ruth Suckow's 'A Start in Life.'" *Western America Literature* 15 (1980).

_______. "A Book of Resolutions: Ruth Suckow's *Some Others and Myself*." *Western American Literature* 21 (August, 1986).

Hermann Sudermann

German playwright and novelist

Born: Matziken, East Prussia (now Macikai, Lithuania); September 30, 1857
Died: Berlin, Germany; November 21, 1928

DRAMA: *Die Ehre*, pr., pb. 1889 (*Honor*, 1915); *Sodoms Ende*, pr. 1890 (*A Man and His Picture*, 1903); *Heimat*, pr., pb. 1893 (*Magda*, 1895); *Die Schmetterlingsschlacht*, pr. 1894; *Das Glück im Winkel*, pr. 1895 (*The Vale of Content*, 1915); *Teja*, pr., pb. 1896 (English translation, 1897); *Fritzchen*, pr., pb. 1896 (English translation, 1910); *Das ewig Männliche*, pr., pb. 1896 (*The Eternal Masculine*, 1910); *Morituri*, pr., pb. 1896 (includes *Teja*, *Fritzchen*, and *Das ewig Männliche*; English translation, 1910); *Johannes*, pr., pb. 1898 (*John the Baptist*, 1899); *Die drei Reiherfedern*, pr., pb. 1899 (*The Three Heron's Feathers*, 1900); *Johannisfeuer*, pr., pb. 1900 (*Fires of St. John*, 1904); *Es lebe das Leben!*, pr., pb. 1902 (*The Joy of Living*, 1902); *Der Sturmgeselle Sokrates*, pr., pb. 1903; *Stein unter Steinen*, pr., pb. 1905; *Das Blumenboot*, pr., pb. 1906; *Die Lichtbänder*, pr., pb. 1907 (*Streaks of Light*, 1909); *Margot*, pr., pb. 1907 (English translation, 1909); *Der letzte Besuch*, pr., pb. 1907 (*The Last Visit*, 1909); *Die ferne Prinzessin*, pr., pb. 1907 (*The Far-Away Princess*, 1909); *Rosen*, pr., pb. 1907 (includes *Streaks of Light*, *Margot*, *The Last Visit*, and *The Far-Away Princess*; *Roses*, 1909); *Strandkinder*, pr. 1909; *Der Bettler von Syrakus*, pr., pb. 1911; *Der gute Ruf*, pr., pb. 1913; *Die Lobgesänge des Claudian*, pr., pb. 1914; *Die Freundin*, pr., pb. 1916; *Die gutgeschnittene Ecke*, pr., pb. 1916; *Das höhere Leben*, pr., pb. 1916; *Die entgötterte Welt: Bilder aus kranker Zeit*, pr., pb. 1916 (includes *Die Freundin*, *Die gutgeschnittene Ecke*, and *Das höhere Leben*); *Regine*, pr. 1916; *Die Raschoffs*, pr., pb. 1919; *Heilige Zeit*, pb. 1921; *Opfer*, pb. 1921; *Das deutsche Schicksal*, pb. 1921 (includes *Heilige Zeit*, *Opfer*, and *Notruf*); *Wie die Träumenden*, pb. 1922; *Die Denkmalsweihe*, pb. 1923; *Dramatische Werke*, pb. 1923 (6 volumes); *Der Hasenfellhändler*, pb. 1927.

LONG FICTION: *Frau Sorge*, 1887 (*Dame Care*, 1891); *Der Katzensteg*, 1889 (*Regina*, 1894); *Es war*, 1894 (*The Undying Past*, 1906); *Das hohe Lied*, 1908 (*The Song of Songs*, 1909); *Der tolle Professor*, 1926 (*The Mad Professor*, 1928); *Die Frau des Steffen Tromholt*, 1927 (*The Wife of Steffen Tromholt*, 1929); *Purzelchen*, 1928 (*The Dance of Youth*, 1930).

SHORT FICTION: *Im Zwielicht: Zwanglose Geschichten*, 1887; *Iolanthes Hochzeit*, 1892 (*Iolantha's Wedding*, 1918); *Die indische Lilie*, 1911 (*The Indian Lily*, 1911); *Litauische Geschichten*, 1917 (*The Excursion to Tilsit*, 1930).
NONFICTION: *Die Verrohung in der Theaterkritik*, 1902; *Das Bilderbuch meiner Jugend*, 1922 (*The Book of My Youth*, 1923).
MISCELLANEOUS: *Romane und Novellen*, 1919 (6 volumes).

The novelist and playwright Hermann Sudermann (ZEWD-ur-mahn), regarded during his lifetime as one of Germany's great literary figures, was the son of a brewer who worked in the village of Heydekrug. The Sudermann family was Mennonite and from Holland; one of Sudermann's ancestors was the moralistic writer Daniel Sudermann. Hermann Sudermann's birthplace, the village Matziken in East Prussia, was characterized by a mixture of German and Lithuanian elements, and it was from the rich local strain of folk tales and customs that he drew late in his career in order to put new life into his work.

He received his early education at the Realschule in Elbing, but as a result of his family's near-poverty he was compelled to go to work at the age of fourteen as apprentice to a chemist. Later he entered the Realgymnasium in Tilsit, and he received his advanced education at the University of Königsberg, where he studied philology and history, and at the University of Berlin. While in Berlin, to which he came at the age of twenty, he was tutor of the children of Hans von Hopfen, a writer by whom Sudermann was to some extent influenced in his own creative work.

In 1881 and 1882 Sudermann worked as an editor of the political journal *Deutsches Reichsblatt*. At that time his political views were fairly liberal, but after leaving the editorship he became increasingly conservative; he was later charged with allowing considerations of royalties to affect his political convictions.

His literary career began with the writing of short stories, and a first collection, *Im Zwielicht*, appeared in 1887. The same year saw the publication of *Dame Care*, a sentimental example of German Romanticism, skillful enough in its portrayal of persons of various classes to make it one of Sudermann's most successful novels. Neither this book nor *Regina* achieved popular recognition until after the overwhelming reception accorded to his play *Honor*, which opened at the Lessing Theater in Berlin on November 27, 1889. Sudermann had originally intended the play as a tragedy, but following the advice of others he gave it a happy ending. *Honor* shows the influence of Nietzsche; the play is in effect a pseudointellectual attack on the morality of the lower classes. This play launched Sudermann's highly successful career as a dramatist, and as a result his novels, too, suddenly began to sell well. With the play *Magda*, Sudermann's name became known all over Europe, and the play became a favorite vehicle for the leading actresses of the day, among them Sarah Bernhardt, Mrs. Patrick Campbell, Eleonora Duse, and Helena Modjeska.

Sudermann lived in a villa at Grunewald, a suburb of Berlin, and at his castle at Blankensee, near Trebbin, which he was able to purchase with royalties from his plays. In 1891 he married Klara Schultz Lauckner, a writer. Sudermann wrote his plays at a fortunate time, and he was careful to give them the kind of technical finish that would make them popular. Although he enjoyed considerable fame for a number of years and was ranked with Gerhart Hauptmann, his plays lost favor when the fashion changed. Sudermann thereupon concentrated on the novel during the last few years of his life, and established himself as an important writer in that genre.

The play *A Man and His Picture*, like *Fires of St. John*, provided some critics with evidence to support their claim that Sudermann was a writer with an honest social conscience, that he was freeing German drama from the French influence and replacing Romanticism with naturalism. Sudermann's portrayals of the vicious social life of fashionable Berlin never quite succeeded in losing the drawing-room comedy touch, however; perhaps the very features that accounted for his quick success were also accountable for the decline of interest in his plays. Of his novels, *Dame Care* and *The Song of Songs* later came to be regarded as his best, and the short stories in *The Excursion to Tilsit*, which contain much of his best writing, remain highly regarded.

Irene Struthers

Bibliography

Friesen, Lauren. "Dramatic Arts and Mennonite Culture." *MELUS* 21, no. 3 (Fall, 1996): 107-124. In her essay about Mennonite plays, Friesen examines the role played by Sudermann, a Mennonite.

Leydecker, Karl. *Marriage and Divorce in the Plays of Hermann Sudermann*. New York: Peter Lang, 1996. Leydecker analyzes the concepts of marriage and divorce as they appear in the plays of Sudermann. Includes bibliography.

Matulis, Anatole C. *Lithuanian Culture in Modern German Prose Literature: Hermann Sudermann, Ernest Wiechert, Agnes Miegel*. Lafayette, Ind.: Purdue University, 1966. This study of the Lithuanian culture's presence in German literature focuses on prose, but it sheds light on Sudermann's plays as well. Includes bibliography.

Stroinigg, Cordelia E. *Sudermann's "Frau Sorge": Jugendstil, Archetype, Fairy Tale*. New York: Peter Lang, 1995. Although this work deals primarily with *Dame Care*, one of Sudermann's novels, it discusses the naturalism to be found in his plays. Includes bibliography and index.

Sudraka

Indian playwright

Born: India; fl. 100 B.C.E.
Died: India; Date unknown

DRAMA: *Mrcchakatika*, pr. between second century B.C.E. and sixth century C.E. (*The Little Clay Cart*, 1905).

Sudraka (SHEW-druh-kuh), also spelled Shudraka or Çudraka, is possibly a legendary prince who never really existed. Tradition has it that he lived in the first or second century before Christ, and *The Little Clay Cart*, a Sanskrit drama of political intrigue and romantic comedy, has been attributed to him by tradition. The *Sutradhara*, a later Sanskrit manuscript, ascribes the play to him and describes him as a student of the *Vedas*, a mathematician, and an expert on women and elephants. Sudraka's authorship of the play is disputed, however, and some scholars believe that its author was Dandin, a seventh century Sanskrit author best known for a picaresque narrative titled *Dasakumāracharita* (the adventures of the ten princes). It may be that neither Sudraka nor Dandin actually wrote the play; many scholars believe that it dates from the fifth century C.E., six or seven centuries after Sudraka's supposed dates and about two centuries before Dandin's lifetime. It seems likely that *The Little Clay Cart* was written at the beginnings of a golden age of Sanskrit drama under the Gupta kings of Kanauj, who ruled over the greater part of India during the fourth and fifth centuries. The play would belong then to that great age of Sanskrit drama which includes the anonymous *Mudrārāksasa* (the prime minister's ring) and Kālidāsa's famous *Sakuntala*.

Bibliography

Bernhard, Betty. *Taking a Ride on the Clay Cart: Dynamics of Sanskrit Theater, a Production Casebook of the Classic Natyashastra Style*. Claremont, Calif.: Pomona College, 1995.

Chakrabarti, Prakaschandra. *A Treatise on Sudraka's "Mrcchakatika."* Delhi: Pilgrim's Books, 1999.

Chattopadhya, Nisikanta. *Dr. Nishikanta Chattopadhyaya's "Mrcchakatika," or "The Toy-Cart" of King Sudrakak: A Study*. Reprint. Calcutta: Sanskrit Book Depot, 1984.

Devasarma, Visvanatha. *Shudraka*. New Delhi: Sahitya Akademi, 1999.

Naikar, Chandramouli S. *The "Mrcchakatika" and the Indian Laws*. Dharwad, India: Medha, 1994.

Eugène Sue

French novelist

Born: Paris, France; January 20, 1804
Died: Annecy, France; August 3, 1857

LONG FICTION: *Plik et Plok*, 1831; *Latréaumont*, 1838 (English translation, 1845); *Jean Cavalier*, 1840 (*The Protestant Leader*, 1849); *Les Mystères de Paris*, 1842-1843 (*The Mysteries of Paris*, 1843); *Le Juif errant*, 1844-1845 (*The Wandering Jew*, 1868).
SHORT FICTION: *Les Sept Péchés capitaux*, 1848-1852.

Born in Paris on January 20, 1804, Eugène Sue (sew), whose real name was Marie Joseph Sue, was the son of a distinguished surgeon who had served with Napoleon's armies. At his baptism, Sue's sponsors were Prince Eugène Beauharnais and the Empress Joséphine; it was his godfather's name that Sue adopted as part of his pseudonym. Educated at private schools in Paris, Sue later studied medicine and became a surgeon. From 1823 to 1829 he served aboard ships of the French navy as a naval surgeon, taking part in the French campaign against Spain in 1823 and in the battle of Navarino in 1828. At his father's death, Sue inherited a large fortune and retired from the navy. Returning to Paris, he became a fashionable young man-about-town, but the life bored him, and he turned to writing as an outlet for his energies.

Sue is reputed to have become a novelist by accident when an editor outlined a novel of the sea and suggested that Sue was the man to write the book because of his experience in the navy. *Plik et Plok* was the first of a series of sea novels that brought him critical praise as "the French James Fenimore Cooper." Charles-Augustin Sainte-Beuve, the eminent French critic, claimed that Sue was the first Frenchman to exploit the sea for French literature and the first author to make use of the Mediterranean Sea for literature. Eager to become a serious man of letters, Sue turned to writing historical works, including a history of the French navy (1837) in five volumes. He then wrote historical romances, the two best-known being *Jean Cavalier* and *Latréaumont*.

His most famous novels, *The Mysteries of Paris* and *The Wandering Jew*, resulted from his interest in social problems. The former, taking the reader through episodes of lower-class and underworld Paris, presented the social misery Sue saw in his city; his attempts at reform were comparable to those of Charles Dickens in England at the time. In *The Wandering Jew*, Sue used the wretched man doomed to wander for centuries as an allegory for the long, weary journey of humanity in its search for just social structures. Although both novels are long and rambling, they illustrate the writer's ability to combine dramatic episodes with moral earnestness. Extremely popular in France, the books were also circulated widely in translation. A later work of moral earnestness, although never popular, was *Les Sept Péchés capitaux* (the seven capital sins), a series of stories that illustrated each of the sins.

After the revolution of 1848, Sue stood for a seat in the French assembly representing Paris. He served in that chamber until the *coup d'état* of 1851 aroused his opposition, whereupon he went to live in exile in Haute-Savoie, dying six years later.

Irene Struthers

Bibliography

Brooks, Peter. "The Mark of the Beast: Prostitution, Melodrama, and Narrative." *New York Literary Forum* 7 (1980).

Leerssen, J. Th. "Outer and Inner Others: The Auto-image of French Identity from Madame de Staël to Eugène Sue." In *France—Europe*, edited by J. Th. Leerssen and M. van Montfrans. Atlanta: Rodopi, 1989.

Luce, Louise Fiber. "The Masked Avenger: Historical Analogue in Eugène Sue's *Les Mystères de Paris*." *French Forum* 1 (1976).

Pickup, Ian. "Eugène Sue." In *Nineteenth Century French Fiction Writers: Romanticism and Realism, 1800-1860*, edited by Catharine Savage Brosman. Vol. 119 in *Dictionary of Literary Biography*. Detroit: Gale Research, 1992.

Wright, Gordon. *Notable or Notorious? A Gallery of Parisians*. Stanford, Calif.: Stanford Alumni Association, 1989.

Suetonius

Roman biographer

Born: Possibly Rome (now in Italy); c. 69 C.E.
Died: Possibly Rome (now in Italy); after 122 C.E.

NONFICTION: *De viris illustribus urbis Romeo*, 106-113 C.E. (*The Lives of Illustrious Romans*, 1693); *De vita Caesarum*, c. 120 C.E. (*History of the Twelve Caesars*, 1606); *The Works*, 1914.

Because his father was military tribune of the XIII Legion, Gaius Suetonius (sew-TOH-nee-uhs) Tranquillus may have been born in Rome, Britain, or Africa; the year was around 69 C.E. He studied in Rome and became a lawyer and teacher of rhetoric. He also traveled widely. He accompanied Governor Pliny (Pliny the Younger) to Bithynia in 112. He also served for a time (119-121) as private secretary to Emperor Hadrian, but he lost favor, apparently for inattention to Empress Sabina while Hadrian was in Britain.

Suetonius's fame rests on his historical biographies of famous men. He collected anecdotes about figures in the public eye and set them down with more attention to their interest than to their accuracy. He eschewed a straight chronological method, grouping his material by subject and personality traits. He made little attempt at general assessment or psychological interpretation, but his stories about Horace and Terence, among others, and his private lives of the twelve caesars cover ground untouched by any contemporary except Tacitus and Dio Cassius. His approach is relatively free of bias and his tone one of detachment. Many later biographers took him as a model, including Einhard (in his ninth century biography of Charlemagne). Suetonius wrote about some of the most fascinating figures—as well as about one of the most important formative eras—in the Western tradition. His work therefore is an invaluable source for scholars of the Roman Imperial period. It is believed that he died in Rome sometime after 122, perhaps about 140.

David H. J. Larmour

Bibliography

Baldwin, Barry. *Suetonius: The Biographer of the Caesars*. Amsterdam: A. M. Hakkert, 1983.

Bradley, K. R. *Suetonius' Life of Nero: An Historical Commentary*. Brussels: Latorus, 1978.

Hurley, Donna W. *A Historical and Historiographical Commentary on Suetonius' Life of C. Caligula*. Atlanta: Scholars Press, 1993.

Jones, Brian W. "Suetonius." In *The Flavian Emperors: A Historical Commentary*. Bristol, England: Bristol Classical, 2002.

Kaster, Robert A. *Studies on the Text of Suetonius, "De grammaticis et rhetoribus*." Atlanta: Scholars Press, 1992.

Lounsbury, R. C. *The Arts of Suetonius: An Introduction*. New York: P. Lang, 1987.

Wallace-Hadrill, Andrew. *Suetonius: The Scholar and His Caesars*. New Haven: Yale University Press, 1984.

Wardle, D. *Suetonius' Life of Caligula: A Commentary*. Brussels: Latomus, 1994.

Sully Prudhomme
(René-François-Armand Prudhomme)

French poet

Born: Paris, France; March 16, 1839
Died: Châtenay, France; September 7, 1907

POETRY: *Stances et poèmes*, 1865; *Les Épreuves*, 1866; *Croquis italiens*, 1866-1868; *Les Solitudes*, 1869; *Impressions de la guerre*, 1870; *La France*, 1870; *Les Destins*, 1872; *La Révolte des fleurs*, 1874; *Les Vaines Tendresses*, 1875; *La Justice*, 1878; *Le Bonheur*, 1888; *Les Épaves*, 1908.

NONFICTION: *Préface à la Traduction du Premier Chant de Lucrèce*, 1869; *Discours de réception à l'Académie Française*, 1882; *L'Expression dans les beaux-arts*, 1883; *Réflexions sur l'art des vers*, 1892; *Sur l'origine de la vie terrestre*, 1893; *Que sais-je? Examen de conscience*, 1895; *Testament poétique*, 1897; *L'Histoire et l'état social*, 1899; *Le Problème des causes finales*, 1899; *Le Crédit de la science*, 1902; *Sur les liens nationaux et internationaux*, 1904; *La Vraie Religion selon Pascal*, 1905; *Psychologie du libre arbitre*, 1907; *Le Lien social*, 1909; *Fragments inédits: Notes pour servir à une physiologie de l'adultère*, 1910; *Lettres à une amie*, 1911; *Journal intime*, 1922.

TRANSLATION: *Lucrèce: De la nature des choses*, 1869 (of Lucretius's poem *De rerum natura*).

MISCELLANEOUS: *Œuvres de Sully Prudhomme*, 1908 (7 volumes).

René-François-Armand Prudhomme, later known as Sully Prudhomme (sewl-lee prew-dawm), was born in Paris in 1839, the son of a shopkeeper. When he was two, his father died, and thereafter he lived with his mother and an older sister in Paris and in Châtenay, a village south of Paris. In childhood he acquired the nickname "Sully," which would become his pseudonym.

Although Châtenay was noted as a center of intellectual activity, in his youth Sully Prudhomme was more interested in mathematics than in literature. However, his hopes for an engineering career were blasted when he developed an eye disease. After clerking briefly in a foundry, in 1860 he went to Paris to study law and began working in a solicitor's office. Meanwhile, encouraged by friends who were writers, he tried his hand at poetry. In 1863, his poem "L'Art" appeared in *La Revue Nationale et Étrangère*. By that time, Prudhomme confided in his journal, he wanted only to be a poet. When a bequest made him financially independent, he abandoned the law to devote his full time to writing. In 1865, one of his friends financed the publication of *Stances et poèmes*, his first collection. Another took the volume to Charles-Augustin Sainte-Beuve, France's most influential literary critic, whose favorable review established the young poet's reputation.

Among Sully Prudhomme's friends in Paris was Charles-Marie-René Leconte de Lisle, the leader of a group of poets who called themselves the "Parnassians," after Mount Parnassus in Greece, supposedly the home of the Muses. The Parnassians sought to replace Romanticism with poetry marked by classical formality and decorum.

Sully Prudhomme's lyrics reflected how much this aesthetic theory appealed to him. However, his intellectual interests also included philosophy, metaphysics, science, and technology. At the time he was producing some of his finest lyrics, he also published a metrical translation of *De rerum natura* (c. 60 B.C.E.; *On the Nature of Things*, 1682 C.E.), the philosophical poem by the Roman writer Lucretius. Moreover, his continuing interest in science was reflected in his poetic metaphors.

The melancholy tone of Sully Prudhomme's early poetry reflects both his disappointment when the woman he loved married another man and a shattering loss of religious faith. In 1870, three of his closest relatives died in a single month. His army service in the Franco-Prussian War left him in fragile health. Moreover, like most of his generation, he felt deeply his country's defeat and subsequent humiliation. After 1875, he turned from lyrical to philosophical poetry, then finally to prose.

During his later years, Sully Prudhomme won many honors, including election to the French Academy and appointment as a grand officer of the Legion of Honor. In 1901, he was awarded the first Nobel Prize in Literature. He spent his last fifteen years at his villa in Châtenay. Though he had long been troubled by insomnia, paralysis, and periods of anguish, his life ended peacefully. He died in his garden, his sister beside him, on September 7, 1907.

Though the long, didactic epics that he considered his most significant works were much admired when they were first published, it was his exquisitely crafted lyrics that most impressed the Nobel Prize Committee. Undoubtedly his scientific interests were a factor in his selection. Sadly, one hundred years later, Sully Prudhomme's works were out of print and his name largely forgotten. The man who was once considered one of the most important writers of his time was now considered merely a minor poet in a movement of slight significance.

Rosemary M. Canfield Reisman

Bibliography

Cornell, William Kenneth. *The Post-Symbolist Period: French Poetic Currents, 1900-1920*. New Haven, Conn.: Yale University Press, 1958. Includes a perceptive analysis of Sully Prudhomme's influence on Parnassian theory.

Hunt, Herbert James. *The Epic in Nineteenth-Century France*. Oxford, England: B. Blackwell, 1941. A thorough study of the epic form as adapted by Parnassian poets. Sully Prudhomme's epics are discussed at length.

Legge, James Granville. *Chanticleer: A Study of the French Muse*. New York: E. P. Dutton, 1935. Reprint. Port Washington, N.Y.:

Kennikat Press, 1969. Provides an excellent overview of the importance of the Parnassians in the history of French literature. Several of Sully Prudhomme's poems are analyzed.

Levy, Gayle A. "Refiguring the Muse." In *Currents in Comparative Romance Languages and Literature*. Vol. 59. New York: Peter Lang, 1999. Points out how changing attitudes toward gender are reflected in new definitions of the poetic muse. A segment of chapter 3, called "Sully Prudhomme and the Bergsonian Inspiration," focuses on the early poetry. By connecting chance and inspiration, Sully Prudhomme contributed toward a modern redefinition of the muse. Includes a bibliography.

Manns, James W. *Reid and His French Disciples: Aesthetics and Metaphysics*. Boston: Brill Academic, 1994. This study of Thomas Reid's influence on French intellectuals concludes with a discussion of Sully Prudhomme's works. Includes a bibliography and an index.

William Graham Sumner

American sociologist

Born: Paterson, New Jersey; October 30, 1840
Died: Englewood, New Jersey; April 12, 1910

NONFICTION: *A History of American Currency*, 1874; *Andrew Jackson as a Public Man*, 1882; *Discipline*, 1883; *What Social Classes Owe to Each Other*, 1883; *What Is the "Proletariat"?*, 1886; *What Is Free Trade?*, 1886; *Legislation by Clamor*, 1887; *Alexander Hamilton*, 1890; *Robert Morris*, 1892; *The Absurd Effort to Make the World Over*, 1894; *Earth Hunger: Or, The Philosophy of Land Grabbing*, 1896; *Advancing Social and Political Organization in the United States*, 1897; *The Conquest of the United States by Spain*, 1899; *The Bequests of the Nineteenth Century to the Twentieth*, wr. 1901, pb. 1933; *War*, 1903; *Economics and Politics*, 1905; *Folkways*, 1907; *Science of Society*, 1927 (with A. G. Keller).

William Graham Sumner's father, Thomas, a Lancashire artisan who came to Paterson, New Jersey, in 1836, was a self-educated man who acquired the lessons of the English classical economists through practical experience and became a railroad mechanic in Hartford, Connecticut. One of three children, William developed a profound respect for the man who worked, saved regularly, and expected nothing from the government but to be left in peace. After William's mother, Sarah Graham, died in 1848, his father married Eliza Van Alstein, whom William disliked even though she was greatly responsible for funding his college education. She died in 1859, and William got along better with his father's third wife, Catherine Mix.

Sumner entered Yale University in 1859. After graduating in 1863 he studied theology, languages, and scientific method in Geneva, Göttingen, and Oxford. In 1866 he returned to Yale as a tutor. Ordained as a deacon in the Episcopal church in 1867, Sumner was named assistant to the rector of Calvary Church in New York City in 1869. In July of that year he was ordained as priest, and the following year he was assigned to a pastorate in Morristown, New Jersey. On April 17, 1871, he married Jeannie Elliott.

Sumner's interests in social and economic questions outgrew his religious calling, so he left the clergy in 1872, returned to Connecticut, and accepted a position as professor in the Department of Political Economy at Yale. In 1873 he was elected as Republican alderman in New Haven. Yale administrators had expected Sumner to be an orthodox theologian, but he shocked them by attacking governmental subsidies in the form of protective tariffs and by converting to evolutionism in 1875. That same year he taught the first "sociology" course ever offered by a university. His textbook selection—Herbert Spencer's *The Study of Sociology* (1873)—was the subject of a major controversy about academic freedom in 1879. In 1890 Sumner became a member of the Connecticut State Board of Education. He began speaking against American imperialism abroad during and after the Spanish American War. A former student, Thomas Beer, remembered him as

> . . . a prodigious personality, something cold and massive and autocratic. He came stalking into the classroom with a sort of "Be damned to you" air. . . . We respected and admired him, however little we appreciated him. If he had been seriously threatened with expulsion from Yale in 1899, when he blew up imperialism, there would have been an academic revolution.

Sumner gradually began to focus less on theological concerns and to turn his attention to the public affairs of the post-Civil War period. His faith in his father's concept of the Protestant ethic led him to relate the successful middle-class property holder with a moral and natural superiority. He fortified his belief in classical economics with the writings of Spencer and Charles Darwin. It was Spencer who first used the phrase "survival of the fittest" and applied it to economics. Sumner accepted these conclusions and became an outspoken opponent of reform laws, protective tariffs, anti-trust legislation, and any form of socialism.

For Sumner the first prerequisite to an understanding of political economy is a willingness to look at the world the way it is, not the way it could or should be. According to Sumner, state interference is never justified. Social reformers and humanitarians take away honestly earned money from the thrifty, hardworking middle class and give it to those who pay the least and benefit the most: the poor and the unfit. He was convinced that catering to the poor and the weak would carry "society downward and favors its worst enemies."

Sumner was an avowed critic of American imperialism and war, mainly because they represented and required the inflexible and centrally controlled state he opposed. He denounced the Republican platform of 1900 as nonsense and predicted for the United States in the twentieth century "war, debt, taxation, diplomacy, a grand governmental system, pomp, glory, a big army and navy, lavish expenditures, political jobbery."

Sumner's sociological and anthropological study *Folkways* is considered to be his most significant and influential book. Its direct and honest approach had a great impact on the early twentieth century United States. His short, biting essays, however, also continue to be effective, relevant, and capable of provoking intelligent and rational debate. In 1909 Sumner retired from Yale, received an honorary Doctor of Laws degree, and became president of the American Sociological Society. In diminishing health after 1890, he suffered a major stroke on December 26, 1909, and died while giving a public lecture in Englewood, New Jersey, on April 12, 1910.

Geralyn Strecker

Bibliography

Curtis, Bruce. *William Graham Sumner.* Boston: Twayne, 1981. An intellectual biography with a good bibliography.

Garson, Robert, and Richard Maidment. "Social Darwinism and the Liberal Tradition: The Case of William Graham Sumner." *South Atlantic Quarterly* 80, no. 1 (1981). A study of the philosophical basis of Sumner's writing.

Healy, Mary Edward. *Society and Social Change in the Writings of St. Thomas, Ward, Sumner, and Cooley.* 1948. Reprint. Westport, Conn.: Greenwood Press, 1972. A comparative study.

Lee, Alfred McClung. "The Forgotten Sumner." *Journal of the History of Sociology* 3 (Fall/Winter, 1980/1981). A sociological profile.

Pickens, Donald K. "Westward Expansion and the End of American Exceptionalism: Sumner, Turner, and Webb." *Western Historical Quarterly* 12, no. 4 (1981). Discusses Sumner's influence on American self-image.

_______. "William Graham Sumner as a Critic of the Spanish American War." *Continuity* 11 (1987). Sumner's political views are analyzed.

Henry Howard, earl of Surrey

English poet

Born: Hunsdon, Hertfordshire, England; 1517
Died: London, England; January 19, 1547

POETRY: *An Excellent Epitaffe of Syr Thomas Wyat*, 1542; *Songes and Sonettes*, 1557 (also known as *Tottel's Miscellany*); *The Poems of Henry Howard, Earl of Surrey*, 1920, 1928 (Frederick Morgan Padelford, editor).
TRANSLATIONS: *The Fourth Boke of Virgill*, 1554; *Certain Bokes of Virgiles Aenaeis*, 1557.

Henry Howard, earl of Surrey (SUR-ee), was born about 1517 into one of the most powerful noble families of sixteenth century England. His father, Sir Thomas Howard, was made third duke of Norfolk in 1524 and served for many years as Henry VIII's earl marshal. Surrey was given a fine early education in Latin, French, Spanish, and Italian by his tutor, John Clerke. At thirteen he went to Windsor Castle to be the companion of Henry, duke of Richmond, the illegitimate son of King Henry VIII. Surrey recalled the pleasures of their life in a poem written many years later, after he had been imprisoned at Windsor.

The two young men accompanied King Henry to France in 1532, remaining at the court of Francis I for several months and traveling on the Continent with the sons of the French king. On their return Richmond married Surrey's sister; Surrey had wed the young Frances de Vere, daughter of the earl of Oxford, before his trip to France, but they did not begin living together until 1535, when he was eighteen.

Surrey was given many public responsibilities once he reached manhood. He took part in the coronation ceremonies of his first cousin Anne Boleyn and later acted as earl marshal at her trial, substituting for his father, who was presiding. In 1536, Surrey accompanied Norfolk on his mission to put an end to the Pilgrimage of Grace, a rebellion of men from the northern counties in opposition to the king's separation from the Church of Rome.

Surrey commanded forces against the French in 1539 and 1543; he was responsible for organizing the defense of Norfolk against invasion in 1539. Surrey's family reached the height of their power that year with the overthrow of Thomas Cromwell and the marriage of Henry VIII to Catherine Howard, and in 1541 the young earl was made knight of the garter and steward of Cambridge University. Catherine's execution in 1542 had no immediate effect on her relatives, but it contributed to the rise of the Seymours, uncles of the prince of Wales, who ultimately destroyed both Norfolk and Surrey.

Surrey's career had its less illustrious moments during this period: He was twice imprisoned for public quarrels, and he was arrested in 1543 with several other young men, among them the son of the poet Thomas Wyatt, for breaking windows and eating meat on the streets during Lent.

In spite of the fact that he was still in his twenties, Surrey served as marshal of the army at Montreuil in 1544 and as commander of Boulogne the following year. He was relieved of his command as lieutenant general of his foreign forces after losing a battle at St. Etienne, but his military failure was probably less the reason for his recall than political intriguing in London.

His fortunes changed swiftly during the last days of Henry VIII. Edward Seymour, who was to become regent for Edward VI, was jealous of the power of the Howards, his principal rivals for control of the young prince. He had Surrey arrested and charged with treason in 1546, accusing him of quartering the royal arms with his own in an attempt to claim the right of succession to the throne. Although the charges were clearly flimsy fabrications, Surrey was convicted and executed on Tower Hill in January, 1547, just eight days before Henry VIII's death. The duke of Norfolk, arrested with his son, survived the king, and Seymour, fearful of public anger, kept him imprisoned for the rest of his life rather than arouse enmity by executing him.

At intervals during his brief and active life Surrey wrote a number of sonnets, verse epistles, and lyrics, and he translated two books of Vergil's *Aeneid* into the first English blank verse. He was recognized as one of England's outstanding poets from the time his lyrics appeared with Wyatt's in Tottel's *Songes and Sonettes* in 1557, and his works served as lyric models for the great Elizabethans. His innovations in poetic diction and prosody had lasting significance.

Cynthia A. Bily

Bibliography

Heale, Elizabeth. *Wyatt, Surrey, and Early Tudor Poetry.* New York: Longman, 1998. An indispensable resource that brings together critical analysis of the early Tudor poets. Those who would study Edmund Spenser and William Shakespeare's sonnets will benefit from the reading of these wonderful authors.

Lever, J. W. *The Elizabethan Love Sonnet.* 1956. Reprint. London: Methuen, 1978. Through a comparison of Surrey's love poems with their Petrarchan originals, Lever demonstrates Surrey's experimentation and use of sensory images.

Mazzaro, Jerome. *Transformations in the Renaissance English Lyric.* Ithaca, N.Y.: Cornell University Press, 1970. Mazzaro regards Surrey's poetry as completing the process of humanizing the lyric, of preferring the literal to the metaphorical, and of describing a natural rather than a moral world.

Sessions, William A. *Henry Howard, the Poet Earl of Surrey: A Life.* New York: Oxford University Press, 1999. Sessions's narrative combines historical scholarship with close readings of poetic texts and Tudor paintings to reveal the unique life of the first Renaissance courtier and a poet who wrote and created radically new forms.

Spearing, A. C. *Medieval to Renaissance in English Poetry.* Cambridge, England: Cambridge University Press, 1985. After discussing Renaissance classicism in Surrey's poetry, Spearing proceeds to extended analyses of three poems: two epitaphs on Sir Thomas Wyatt and "So crewell prison," the poem about Surrey's imprisonment at Windsor.

Thomson, Patricia. "Wyatt and Surrey." In *English Poetry and Prose, 1540-1674*, edited by Christopher Ricks. 1970. Reprint. New York: Peter Bedrick Books, 1987. Thomson first compares Sir Thomas Wyatt and Surrey to John Skelton, whose poetry was primarily late medieval, then discusses Surrey and particularly Wyatt as inheritors of the Petrarchan tradition.

Robert Smith Surtees

English novelist

Born: The Riding, Northumberland, England; May 17, 1803
Died: Brighton, Sussex, England; March 16, 1864

LONG FICTION: *Jorrocks' Jaunts and Jollities*, 1838; *Handley Cross: Or, The Spa Hunt*, 1843, expanded 1854; *Hillingdon Hall: Or, The Cockney Squire*, 1845; *Hawbuck Grange: Or, The Sporting Adventures of Thomas Scott, Esq.*, 1847; *Mr. Sponge's Sporting Tour*, 1853; *"Ask Mamma": Or, The Richest Commoner in England*, 1858; *"Plain or Ringlets?,"* 1860; *Mr. Facey Romford's Hounds*, 1865.
NONFICTION: *The Horseman's Manual*, 1831; *The Analysis of the Hunting-Field*, 1846.

Like Anthony Trollope, Robert Smith Surtees (SURT-eez) recreated in his novels a limited but significant phase of the social milieu of his time. The world of his fiction, although small, is admirably self-contained and complete in every detail within its boundaries of the kennel and the stable, the hunting fields and the drawing rooms of the English "squirearchy." Against this background he presented a cross-section of Victorian society: The aristocracy entrenched behind barriers of caste and privilege, the new middle class trying to rise above its origins in trade, tuft-hunters and amiable blackguards aping the gentry and living at the expense of their social betters, sturdy yeoman farmers, the laboring tenantry, and comic yokels. These people fill a series of sporting novels lively with humor and pungent with that flavor of satire which was Surtees' strong point.

Descended from an ancient country family that took its name from the River Tees, Surtees was born at The Riding, Northumberland, on May 17, 1803. His boyhood was spent at Hamsterley Hall, near Durham, a seventeenth century manor bought by his father in

1810. A younger son without prospects of inheritance, he was educated at Ovingham School and at the Durham Grammar School, and in 1822 was articled to a solicitor at Newcastle-on-Tyne in preparation for a career in law. Three years later he transferred to the office of another solicitor in Bow Churchyard, London. Admitted in Chancery in 1828, he abandoned law for journalism a year later and became a hunting correspondent for *Sporting Magazine*.

His first book, combining his knowledge of law with his interest in sport, was *The Horseman's Manual*, published in 1831. In the same year his older brother died, and Surtees became the heir to Hamsterley, a change of fortune which probably influenced his decision to join Rudolph Ackermann in founding the *New Sporting Magazine*, which he edited until 1836. For the third issue of the magazine, in July, 1831, he wrote the first of the humorous sketches dealing with John Jorrocks, the sporting Cockney grocer of Great Coram Street. This series, continued until September, 1834, proved so popular that the publishing house of Chapman and Hall planned a similar miscellany which resulted in Charles Dickens's *Pickwick Papers* (1836-1837). Opposed to repeal of the Corn Laws, Surtees stood unsuccessfully for Parliament in 1837. Following his father's death in 1838, he returned to Hamsterley to lead the life of a country landlord and hunting squire. He married in 1841 and in the following year was appointed a justice of the peace and deputy lieutenant for Durham County. He was also for a time a major in the Durham Militia, an experience he later satirized in his account of the Heavysteed Dragoons. He became high sheriff of Durham County in 1856.

A shy, unsentimental, taciturn man, Surtees, after *The Horseman's Manual*, would not allow his name to be used in connection with his books. Published anonymously, the Jorrocks sketches were collected in 1838 as *Jorrocks' Jaunts and Jollities*. On its appearance the book was completely eclipsed by the greater popularity of *Pickwick Papers*, which had been published a year before, so much so that friendly critics were forced to defend the author of *Jorrocks' Jaunts and Jollities* against charges of plagiarism. The third edition of 1843 contained the fifteen colored plates by Henry Alken which have become the familiar illustrations of this humorous classic. The adventures of Jorrocks were continued in *Handley Cross*, also published in 1843 but not expanded to its full proportions until 1854. This book, now considered Surtees' masterpiece, received little attention at the time; the reappearance of Jorrocks as a Master of Fox Hounds gave Surtees every opportunity to ridicule social snobbery and the idea that fox hunting was a fashionable sport to be enjoyed only by the rich. A snobbish age repaid him with its neglect. Jorrocks made his last appearance in *Hillingdon Hall*, where as a country squire he was allowed to voice Surtees' own views on agriculture and reform. The election of his hero to Parliament at the end of the novel hints that Surtees may have intended to continue the series with an account of the Cockney grocer in politics. If so, the plan was abandoned. Instead, *Hillingdon Hall* was followed in 1846 by *The Analysis of the Hunting-Field*, a collection of sporting sketches of a rather technical nature, and in 1847 by *Hawbuck Grange*.

Surtees' first real success came in 1853 with *Mr. Sponge's Sporting Tour*. Here the ancient rogue story is transformed into a satirical comedy of manners, with a cast that includes aristocratic bores and wastrels, ambitious social climbers, dishonest horse dealers, patronizing masters of hounds, and the raggle-taggle of the army and the stage. This was the first of Surtees' books to be illustrated by John Leech, whose drawings for *Mr. Sponge's Sporting Tour* and later novels are almost as familiar as the author's text. The novel had been serialized in the *New Monthly Magazine*, edited by William Harrison Ainsworth. Ainsworth, eager to print another work by Surtees, had contracted for the publication of "Young Tom Hall, His Heartbreaks and Horses." Before many installments had appeared, however, Ainsworth printed an advertisement giving Surtees' name as the author of the new serial. Surtees was angry and Ainsworth tactless; as a result Surtees stopped work on the novel, which promised to be one of his best. Although the book was never completed, it was not a total loss: *"Ask Mamma"* and *"Plain or Ringlets?"* contain a few characters and several episodes he was able to salvage for later use. These novels are decidedly inferior to *Handley Cross* and *Mr. Sponge's Sporting Tour* and reveal too plainly the patchwork of their design. Surtees was once more at his best in *Mr. Facey Romford's Hounds*, a comic hunting novel and sly satire in which Mr. Sponge and Lucy Glitters, his actress wife, reappear. Surtees did not live to see his last novel in print. At work on an autobiographical work to be called "Sporting and Social Recollections," he and his wife went to Brighton for a short holiday. He died there on March 16, 1864.

Surtees is not one of the eminent Victorians. His field was limited, and he had no imagination for anything which lay outside his own experience. He knew the town as well as the country, however, and he had seen the agricultural England of his youth transformed by the development of the railway and the growth of factories. Writing of these things, he became what most of the major Victorians, except William Makepeace Thackeray, were not, a social historian and a novelist of manners. His true genius, however, was in creating the comic character; among English novelists he is second only to Dickens in this respect. Jorrocks, in the gallery of great humorous characters, stands only a few notches below Falstaff, Parson Adams, Mr. Pickwick, and Mr. Micawber. Mr. Sponge and Facey Romford are rogues, but their vulgarity and cunning point to the underlying spirit of an age.

Bibliography

Collison, Robert L. *A Jorrocks Handbook*. London: Coole Book Service, 1964. A guide to Surtees' comic invention.

Gash, Norman. *Robert Surtees and Early Victorian Society*. New York: Oxford University Press, 1993. Places Surtees in his historical and cultural context.

Neumann, Bonnie Rayford. *Robert Smith Surtees*. Boston: Twayne, 1978. An intellectual and literary biography.

Watson, Frederick. *Robert Smith Surtees: A Critical Study*. 1933. Reprint. Nunney, Somerset, England: Robert Smith Surtees Society, 1991. An overview study of the spectrum of Surtees' work.

Welcome, John. *The Sporting World of R. S. Surtees*. New York: Oxford University Press, 1982. Concentrates on Surtees' hunting writing.

Italo Svevo
(Ettore Schmitz)

Italian novelist

Born: Trieste, Austrian Empire (now in Italy); December 19, 1861
Died: Motta di Livenza, Italy; September 13, 1928

LONG FICTION: *Una vita*, 1892 (*A Life*, 1963); *Senilità*, 1898 (*As a Man Grows Older*, 1932); *La coscienza di Zeno*, 1923 (*Confessions of Zeno*, 1930).
SHORT FICTION: *Una burla riuseita*, 1929 (*The Hoax*, 1929); *La novella del buon vecchio e della bella fanciulla*, 1930 (*The Nice Old Man and the Pretty Girl, and Other Stories*, 1930); *Corto viaggio sentimentale e altri racconti inediti*, 1949 (*Short Sentimental Journey, and Other Stories*, 1966); *Further Confessions of Zeno*, 1969.
NONFICTION: *James Joyce*, 1950 (lecture given in 1927); *Corrispondenza*, 1953; *Saggi e pagini sparse*, 1954 (essays).
MISCELLANEOUS: *Opera omnia*, 1966-1969.

Italo Svevo (SVAY-voh) is an important author whose works have never quite achieved popular success. He was born Aron Hector Schmitz, in Trieste, in what was then Austria, in 1861, the fifth child of Jewish parents Francesco and Allegra Moravia Schmitz. The household was affluent, and Svevo, called Ettore Schmitz in those years, had a happy childhood. His father, more through diligence than astuteness, had become a prosperous businessman, a feat of which he was intensely proud. Hoping that his sons would follow in his footsteps, in 1873 he sent Ettore and his brother Adolfo to business school in Germany, where Ettore displayed utter indifference to commerce, preferring philosophy and literature. Several years later, however, he found himself forced into the business world when his father's business dealings suddenly failed, and Francesco, who had taken such pride in being self-made, spiraled into depression and senility. This event left a great mark on Svevo, who as a writer was to imbue his characters with a sort of self-induced senility. As a result of this catastrophe, Svevo went to work as a bank clerk to help support the family, and this job provided the inspiration for his first novel, *A Life*. Published in 1892 at his own expense, the book recounted, with the ironic character analysis that would be Svevo's stock-in-trade, the day-to-day existence of a daydreaming bank clerk. Six years later, he published a second novel, *As a Man Grows Older*, which describes a man's attempts to aggrandize his unremarkable love affair. Both books were ignored.

Svevo's marriage to his cousin Livia Veneziani in 1895 eventually afforded him a position in his father-in-law's very successful paint manufacturing company. Daydreaming and writing seemed inextricably bound for Svevo, so when he went to work for Livia's parents, he swore to abandon writing in order to concentrate on his job and, amazingly, kept his vow for more than two decades, indulging his creative desire only to the extent of producing an occasional article or short story for his own amusement.

During these years, however, at least one person provided encouragement. Svevo had engaged an English tutor, a struggling Irish writer named James Joyce, to whom he gave copies of his books. To Svevo's surprise, Joyce responded enthusiastically, yet the books remained in oblivion until the paint factory temporarily closed during World War I and, twenty years after the publication of his last novel, Svevo's thoughts again returned to serious literature. He began to compose what is today generally acknowledged as his masterpiece, *Confessions of Zeno*, which he had published, again at his own expense, in 1923. This third book fell as flat as its predecessors had, and Svevo, who had entertained great hopes for it, became very depressed. His depression was soon alleviated. Joyce, now a well-respected writer, admired the novel and was able to get it reviewed by several prominent European critics who were almost unanimous in their praise. To say that Svevo became the toast of Europe would be an exaggeration; however, he was feted by the Parisian literary society, and he returned to Italy to find himself something of a mentor to a new generation of Italian writers. After so many years of public indifference, he enjoyed his newfound recognition tremendously. He died as the result of an automobile crash two years later, in 1928.

It seems natural that Svevo, with his interest in character analysis, would be intrigued by psychology, and *Confessions of Zeno* is one of the first significant novels to incorporate Freudian analysis. Zeno's "confessions" begin when a psychoanalyst suggests that Zeno write his memoirs in order to understand his compulsive cigarette smoking. The ensuing memoirs reflect Zeno's daydreams, delusions, neuroses, and rationalizations, and the reader is thrust into the position of playing Zeno's therapist, trying to sort out the truth.

Svevo's novels are not primarily plotted works so much as slices of life designed to shed light upon the main character's unconscious motivations. His protagonists are willing victims of what Svevo called "senility"—habitual daydreaming leading to an inability to respond lucidly and directly to real life. Some of Svevo's early critics thought that his characters were weak and contemptible, implying that they did not represent the average person; yet the Svevian hero has emerged a successful portrait precisely because Svevo managed to depict a universal human tendency. Unlike his "healthy" characters, who take life in stride, Svevo's heroes seem to regard life as an immense project requiring much cerebral management. Even the smallest detail is absorbed and made self-conscious. When a man in a café tells Zeno how many muscles are used in the simple act of walking, Zeno finds, when he rises to leave, that he has acquired a slight limp. Emilio

Brentano, in *As a Man Grows Older,* cannot relax and enjoy his love affair because he is too busy neurotically trying to "improve" his dull but beautiful mistress. Far from being contemptible, Svevo's heroes actually elicit the empathy of the reader, who is given to understand that all this neurosis and anxiety merely add up to a strange kind of *joie de vivre*.

Svevo's early detractors criticized not only the insignificance of his heroes but the insignificance of his prose style as well. Accustomed to beautiful prose, Italian critics regarded Svevo's style as mundane and lacking in poetry. Most modern critics, while admitting Svevo's style lacks distinction, do not perceive this as a major failing (some find that it actually complements his subject matter) and cite as Svevo's strengths his irony, his accuracy and integrity of perception, and his originality. As a result of the recognition of *Confessions of Zeno* as a major literary contribution, Svevo's first two books were resurrected and reevaluated. Today, *As a Man Grows Older* is regarded as a brilliant but somewhat lesser novel than *Confessions of Zeno*, while *A Life* is viewed as a flawed but exceedingly innovative first attempt. Two volumes of short stories, *Short Sentimental Journey, and Other Stories* and *The Nice Old Man and the Pretty Girl, and Other Stories*, as well as a collection of essays, were published posthumously and were well received. However, Svevo has never reached the popular appeal it would seem he deserves, considering that many critics regard two of his books as literary milestones. In Italy he is very well known, more sporadically so in the rest of Europe, but in the United States he remains virtually unknown.

Susan Davis

Bibliography

Gatt-Rutter, John. *Italo Svevo: A Double Life*. Oxford, England: Clarendon Press, 1988. Gatt-Rutter stresses the duality of Svevo's life: a writer and businessman, an atheist who converted from Judaism to Catholicism, a socialist who was a successful capitalist. While it is short on literary criticism, this work covers the details of Svevo's life and is based on letters and other primary sources.

Lebowitz, Naomi. *Italo Svevo*. New Brunswick, N.J.: Rutgers University Press, 1978. In an excellent study that focuses on Svevo's writing rather than on his life, Lebowitz regards him as the father of modern Italian literature and as one of the great modernists, ranked with James Joyce, Franz Kafka, and William Faulkner.

Moloney, Brian. *Italo Svevo: A Critical Introduction*. Edinburgh, Scotland: Edinburgh University Press, 1974. An excellent short critical introduction to Svevo's work; includes chapters on his short fiction.

Svevo, Livia Veneziani. *Memoir of Italo Svevo*. Marlboro, Vt.: Marlboro Press, 1990. A loving memoir by Svevo's widow which captures his humor and his gentle nature. It includes many of his letters and an appendix that includes a 1927 lecture by Svevo on James Joyce.

Weiss, Beno. *Italo Svevo*. Boston: Twayne, 1987. Weiss considers Svevo to be one of the seminal figures in modern European literature. Weiss stresses the divided nature of Svevo's life and the importance of Judaism to his life and literature.

Glendon Swarthout

American novelist

Born: Pinckney, Michigan; April 8, 1918
Died: Scottsdale, Arizona; September 23, 1992

LONG FICTION: *Willow Run*, 1943; *They Came to Cordura*, 1958; *Where the Boys Are*, 1960; *Welcome to Thebes*, 1962; *The Cadillac Cowboys*, 1964; *The Eagle and the Iron Cross*, 1966; *Loveland*, 1968; *Bless the Beasts and Children*, 1970; *The Tin Lizzie Troop*, 1972; *Luck and Pluck*, 1973; *The Shootist*, 1975; *The Melodeon*, 1977; *Skeletons*, 1979; *Cadbury's Coffin*, 1982; *The Old Colts*, 1985; *The Homesman*, 1988; *Pinch Me, I Must Be Dreaming*, 1994.

SHORT FICTION: *Easterns and Westerns: Short Stories*, 2001 (Miles Hood Swarthout, editor).

Glendon Swarthout (SWORT-owt) was educated at the University of Michigan, where he received a baccalaureate in 1939. After his graduation he served in the U.S. Army as an infantryman from 1943 to 1945, rising to the rank of sergeant. He was twice decorated for his bravery in combat during World War II. In 1940 he married Kathryn Vaughan, who survived him after his death in 1992 following a long battle with emphysema. She would be not only his wife and the mother of their only child, Miles, but also his coauthor on a number of children's books. Miles, in turn, would share screenwriting credit with Scott Hale for the film adaptation of Glendon Swarthout's *The Shootist*, a story of the last days of a legendary gunfighter dying from cancer.

Following World War II, Swarthout returned to school on the G.I. Bill and pursued a literature curriculum. He earned a master's degree from Michigan State University in 1946, after which he earned his living as a teaching fellow there. He received his Ph.D. in 1955 and by 1959 had risen to the position of associate professor. That year he moved his family to the Phoenix, Arizona, area. He taught intermittently afterward, primarily at nearby Arizona State University. For the remainder of his life, his first love and major endeavor would be fiction writing rather than academics.

Of all his books, *Bless the Beasts and Children* earned for him the greatest critical recognition, remaining in print continuously for more than a quarter of a century. Arguably his best work, it is the book in which central concerns of his writing career seem to cohere and flower: the nature of the heroic act in an unheroic age, the frail possibility of a meaningful community in an era of isolation, the longing for ordered principles with which to make sense of disordered lives, and the need for sacred experience in a secular age.

Set in and around Flagstaff, Arizona, *Bless the Beasts and Children* tells of a summer in which six troubled adolescents are sent west by their parents to a camp that promises to set the boys straight on the path to manhood. The promise is only a come-on meant to milk their wealthy parents, the boys soon learn. However, they also learn of a seasonal hunt underwritten by the government to "thin" herds of buffalo in the state—actually a senseless, brutal slaughter put on for the amusement of wealthy sportsmen. On their own, the boys steal away in a truck and set out to free the remaining buffalo. Of the six liberators, Cotton and Teft receive Swarthout's fullest attention, but their stories are the others' stories as well. None have parents up to the task of raising and guiding them. At home, each has been left to his own devices; here, among others of their own kind, each finds a family of sorts for the first time in their lives, drawing strength and support from the group as they risk their personal interests in the name of something higher.

They Came to Cordura, Swarthout's second novel, is set near the Mexican border in 1916, following a U.S. Cavalry attempt to subdue Pancho Villa and his forces. It chronicles Major Thomas Thorne's six-day trek from Ojos Azules to an American outpost at Cordura. Having proven himself a coward before the Mexican marauders, Thorne, now assigned the humiliating position of awards officer, is ordered to select five candidates from the battle sites for Medal of Honor recognition, then bring them to Cordura while their paperwork is being processed. Thorne can see that, whether these men are heroes, murderers, or fools, they live beyond the immediate boundaries of normal human conduct. The author's broader concern was what heroism would mean, if anything, as the United States leaves behind its frontier mentality.

Although an acclaimed writer of popular books for many years, Swarthout probably reached the widest audience through the adaptations of his work for television and motion pictures. *The Shootist* was the fourth of Swarthout's novels to be made into a film (in 1976). Preceding it were *They Came to Cordura* (1959), *Where the Boys Are* (1960), and *Bless the Beasts and Children* (1971). Swarthout produced more than fifteen novels, in addition to plays, short stories, and children's books. There is much to be found in his novels that reflects his literary training and deft artistry. However, as his critics were quick to point out, Swarthout seldom sustains a high level of artistry throughout a novel. While his works are more than entertaining, marketable fiction, many critics saw Swarthout as unable or unwilling to elevate his work to their standards of literature as a higher art.

Jay Boyer

Bibliography

Contemporary Literary Criticism. Vol. 35. Detroit: Gale Research, 1985. An excellent critical work on Swarthout's writing, which offers thoughtful reactions to his work from *Willow Run* through *Skeletons* by some of his most consistent readers.

Corodimas, Peter. *Best Sellers* 37 (March, 1978): 325. The first article to attempt to locate Swarthout's place in the American literary canon.

Dear, Pamela S., ed. *Contemporary Authors*, New Revision Series. Vol. 47. Detroit: Gale Research, 1995. Offers a solid, if spare, critical-biographical treatment.

Schickel, Richard. *Harpers* 240 (April, 1970): 107. The most famous article about Swarthout, and the first to complain that Swarthout was being short-changed by the critics.

Emanuel Swedenborg

Swedish philosopher and theologian

Born: Stockholm, Sweden; January 29, 1688
Died: London, England; March 29, 1772

NONFICTION: *Opera philosophica et mineralia*, 1734; *Prodromus philosophiae ratiocinantis de infinito et causa finali creationis*, 1734; *Œconomia regni animalis*, 1740-1741 (*The Economy of the Animal Kingdom*, 1846); *Regnum animale*, 1744-1745 (*The Animal Kingdom*, 1843-1844); *Arcana coelestia quae in scriptura sacra seu verbo Domini sunt detecta*, 1749-1756 (8 volumes; *The Heavenly Arcana*, 1951-1956); *De coelo et ejus mirabilibus et de inferno*, 1758 (*Heaven and Its Wonders and Hell*, 1884; also known as *Heaven and Hell*); *De ultimo judicio*, 1758 (*The Last Judgment*, 1788-1791); *Sapientia angelica de divino amore et de divina sapientia*, 1763 (*The Wisdom of Angels Concerning Divine Love and Divine Wisdom*, 1788; also known as *The Divine Love and Wisdom*); *Vera Christiana religio*, 1771 (*True Christian Religion*, 1781); *Apocalypsis explicata*, 1785-1789 (4 volumes; *Apocalypse Explained*, 1846-1847).

Emanuel Swedenborg (SWEED-uhn-bawrg) was born Emanuel Swedberg at Stockholm on January 29, 1688. His father was Dr. Jesper Swedberg, professor of theology at the University of Uppsala and Bishop of Skara who, raised to the rank of the nobility for services to the Swedish crown, later changed his name to Swedenborg. By Swedenborg's own account, his childhood was unusual in that he spent much time in spiritual thought and in conversation with clergymen on matters of faith. He attended the University of Uppsala, taking his degree in 1709. He then traveled in England, Holland, France, and Germany before returning to Sweden in 1715. During his travels he studied wherever he went, and upon his return he entered Uppsala once again to study science and engineering. In 1716, Charles XII of Sweden, who had become a friend and admirer of Swedenborg, appointed him assessor on the Swedish board of mines, a post Swedenborg filled until 1747 (with some opposition between 1718 and 1723) and for which he received a salary for the rest of his life.

By 1720 Swedenborg had published a volume of Latin verse and more than twenty treatises on scientific and mechanical subjects. The scientific works before 1721 were largely in Swedish, but the later writings, regardless of subject, were written in Latin and were mostly published outside Sweden. His first major work in philosophy and theology was the *Principia*, which was one volume in the three-volume *Opera philosophica et mineralia* published in 1734. In the same year he published *Prodromus philosophiae ratiocinantis de infinito et causa finali creationis*, a work dealing with the relations of the finite to the infinite and the body to the soul. During the next few years Swedenborg turned his attention to anatomy, hoping to find the seat of the soul. Two works on anatomy resulted from his studies. These works, to which little attention was paid, anticipated many modern physiological theories.

In addition to being a scientist, Swedenborg was a mystic. According to his report, he experienced God on three occasions between 1743 and 1745. During the third of these spiritual experiences Swedenborg, according to his own account, was called upon to reveal what he called the "Doctrine of the New Jerusalem." He then turned his energies to religious inquiry, dividing his time among stays in Sweden, England, and Holland while he wrote works of biblical interpretation and oversaw their publication. Among the important books of this period was *The Heavenly Arcana*, an eight-volume work giving a revealed interpretation of the Bible, originally published anonymously. *Heaven and Its Wonders and Hell* describes the future of humankind after death. *The Last Judgment* tells of a mystical experience in which God revealed to Swedenborg a vision of doomsday. The last of many theological works from Swedenborg's hand was *True Christian Religion*, in which he set forth his New Church doctrines. Although he did not found a sect or attempt to do so, later adherents to his doctrines formed a sect of their own, the New Jerusalem Church.

Swedenborg died on March 29, 1772, while on one of his visits to England. Temporarily buried in London, his body was later removed and interred in a place of honor in the cathedral at Uppsala. Many major artists and thinkers were influenced by Swedenborg, most notably William Blake but also Ralph Waldo Emerson, Jorge Luis Borges, and even Helen Keller. In 1989 active Swedenborgian groups comprised sixty thousand people worldwide.

Bernadette Lynn Bosky

Bibliography

Benz, Ernst. *Emanuel Swedenborg: Visionary Savant in the Age of Reason*. West Chester, Pa.: Swedenborg Foundation, 2002.

Bishop, Paul. *Synchronicity and Intellectual Intuition in Kant, Swedenborg, and Jung*. Lewiston, N.Y.: E. Mellen Press, 2000.

Brock, Erland J., et al., eds. *Swedenborg and His Influence*. Bryn Athen, Pa.: Academy of the New Church, 1988.

Jonsson, Inge. *Emanuel Swedenborg*. New York: Twayne, 1971.

_______. *Visionary Scientist: The Effects of Science and Philosophy on Swedenborg's Cosmography*. West Chester, Pa.: Swedenborg Foundation, 1999.

Lagercrantz, Olof. *Epic of the Afterlife: A Literary Approach to Swedenborg*. Translated by Anders Hallengren. West Chester, Pa.: Swedenborg Foundation, 2002.

Lamm, Martin. *Emanuel Swedenborg: The Development of His Thought*. Translated by Tomas Spiers and Anders Hallengren. West Chester, Pa.: Swedenborg Foundation, 2000.

Larsen, Robin, ed. *Swedenborg: A Continuing Vision*. New York: Swedenborg Foundation, 1988.

Woofenden, William R. *Swedenborg Researcher's Manual: A Research Reference Manual for Writers of Academic Dissertations and For Other Scholars*. Bryn Athen, Pa.: Swedenborg Scientific Association, 1988.

May Swenson

American poet

Born: Logan, Utah; May 28, 1919
Died: Ocean View, Delaware; December 4, 1989

POETRY: *Another Animal: Poems*, 1954; *A Cage of Spines*, 1958; *To Mix with Time: New and Selected Poems*, 1963; *Half Sun Half Sleep*, 1967; *Iconographs*, 1970; *New and Selected Things Taking Place*, 1978; *In Other Words*, 1987; *The Love Poems of May Swenson*, 1991; *Nature: Poems Old and New*, 1994; *May Out West: Poems of May Swenson*, 1996.

CHILDREN'S/YOUNG ADULT LITERATURE: *Poems to Solve*, 1966; *More Poems to Solve*, 1971; *The Guess and Spell Coloring Book*, 1976; *The Complete Poems to Solve*, 1993.

DRAMA: *The Floor*, pr. 1966.

NONFICTION: *The Contemporary Poet as Artist and Critic*, 1964; "The Experience of Poetry in a Scientific Age" in *Poets on Poetry*, 1966.

TRANSLATION: *Windows and Stones: Selected Poems by Tomas Tranströmer*, 1972 (with Leif Sjöberg).

May Swenson, born and raised in Utah, graduated from Utah State University, where her father taught mechanical engineering. After working as a reporter in Salt Lake City, she moved to New York, where she was an editor for New Directions from 1959 to 1966. She resigned to devote more time to her writing.

In many ways, however, Swenson remained both reporter and editor throughout her writing life. Her poems observe the world closely and report back in detail. In "News from the Cabin" she describes a sequence of animal visitors (woodpecker, squirrel, jay, snake) in precise images and evocative sounds ("His nostril I saw, slit in a slate whistle"). But, characteristic of her playfulness, she gives the creatures nicknames ("Hairy," "Scurry," "Slicker," "Supple") and makes the poem a kind of easy riddle. In many other poems she presents nature through a field guide of the imagination.

Swenson's reporting ranges from travel ("Notes Made in the Piazza San Marco") to sports ("Analysis of Baseball") to space exploration ("August 19, Pad 19") to science ("The DNA Molecule"). Her interest in the topical suggests the importance of immediate experience to Swenson, and her volume of selected poems is titled *New and Selected Things Taking Place*. As Robert Frost sees each poem as a "performance," Swenson sees it as a "thing taking place."

Swenson does not limit her reporting to external facts. She is equally interested in her own subjective responses. After her death, a substantial volume of love poems was published, erotic in both language and sensibility. Swenson's eroticism takes in everything she loves, from people to animals to whatever she finds around her, from the Long Island Railroad to the Atlantic Ocean.

The editor in Swenson serves as a balance to the passionate reporter. Her writing is careful and precise in its language and metaphors. In "Choosing Craft," for example, she alternates descriptions of sailing with italicized comments on accuracy and the appearance of ease. She ends with a paradox: "*How close-hauled, canted, apt to capsize/ you keep, must be why you don't*." In the craft of her writing, Swenson prefers to sail precariously close to the edge, to be accurate through audacity, to make her turns by cutting them close.

Perhaps another outgrowth of Swenson's editing is her interest in shaped poems, which she called "iconographs." Some of her shapes are mimetic: a sun on the horizon ("Out of the Sea, Early"), the world seen from outer space ("Orbiter 5 Shows How Earth Looks from the Moon"), lightning represented by a diagonal streak of white space through the lines ("The Lightning"). Most of her iconographs, however, arrange their shapes abstractly or impressionistically; "Bleeding," for example, uses space breaks within most of its lines to give an audible pause and the visual appearance of a gash. Her poems do not tip over into the entirely visual domain of concrete poetry, as they sound wonderful read aloud. The visual arrangements represent a sculptor's chiseling of the composer's music: an extension of the sensory ways in which a poem affects the reader.

In "The Truth Is Forced" Swenson declares, "I wish/ to be honest in poetry." In her writing she can "say and cross out/ and say over" the truth she would hide in person; she can speak in symbols, riddles, and double meanings; she can remove masks and get under the skin—her own included. Poetry was a way for this private person to shed her protective layers. Even in a poem about a particular childhood memory, "The Centaur," Swenson makes passionate connections. She recalls going to a willow grove and cutting herself a stick horse to play with. Most of the poem describes the ten-year-old's wild ride. At the end, the mother notices green around the girl's mouth. The poem ends: "*Rob Roy, he pulled some clover/ as we crossed the field*, I told her." The horse may exist in the child's imagination, but the galloping is a physical sensation, and the clover's taste remains on the poet's tongue. Ezra Pound once remarked, "Poetry is a centaur," and for Swenson, too, the mind conjoins with the body in the act of the poem. Experience is multiple, both received and transmitted.

She is a poet open to experience, willing to strip down and be suffused by what she perceives, ready to try out anything as subject matter. In a poem about having her watch repaired, Swenson transforms something mundane into something comic ("'Watch out!' I/ almost said."), vivid ("two flicks of his/ tools like chopsticks"), and metaphorically personal ("my/ ticker going lickety-split").

John Drury

Bibliography

Doty, Mark. "Queen Sweet Thrills: Reading May Swenson." *The Yale Review* 88, no. 1 (January, 2000): 86-110. Doty discusses Swenson's work, describing how, over the course of her eleven books of poetry, Swenson developed a dramatic dialogue between revelation and concealment.

Gould, Jean. *Modern American Women Poets*. New York: Dodd, Mead, 1984. Account of Swenson's life includes details of her childhood, the influence—or lack of influence—of her parents' Mormon faith, and her associations with other writers, especially Robert Frost and Elizabeth Bishop. Gould also explores Swenson's longtime relationship with teacher and children's author Rozanne Knudson.

Hammond, Karla. "An Interview with May Swenson: July 14, 1978." *Parnassus: Poetry in Review* 7 (Fall/Winter, 1978): 60-75. In this piece, Swenson talks in some detail on a range of subjects, from her childhood and education to her writing habits, her approach to poetry, and her admiration for such poets as Elizabeth Bishop and E. E. Cummings. Throughout, she illustrates the discussion with examples from her work.

Salter, Mary Jo. "No Other Words." *The New Republic* 201 (March 7, 1988): 40-41. This review of Swenson's last volume of poems, *In Other Words*, offers a brief but perceptive discussion of Swenson's poetic strengths and limitations. Salter compares her work to that of poets as diverse as Elizabeth Bishop, Gerard Manley Hopkins, and George Herbert.

Stanford, Ann. "May Swenson: The Art of Perceiving." *The Southern Review* 5 (Winter, 1969): 58-75. This essay treats Swenson as a master of observation and perception. Through numerous examples—drawn mostly from the poet's nature poems—Stanford explores Swenson's ability to surprise and delight the reader by observing the world from unexpected angles or by simply noticing and recording the easily overlooked detail.

Zona, Kirstin Hotelling. "A 'Dangerous Game of Change': Images of Desire in the Love Poems of May Swenson." *Twentieth Century Literature* 44, no. 2 (Summer, 1998): 219-241. Zona argues that Swenson's strategy of employing blatantly heterosexual or stereotypically gendered tropes is central to the relationship between sexuality and subjectivity that shapes her larger poetic.

Graham Swift

English novelist

Born: London, England; May 4, 1949

LONG FICTION: *The Sweet Shop Owner*, 1980; *Shuttlecock*, 1981; *Waterland*, 1983; *Out of This World*, 1988; *Ever After*, 1992; *Last Orders*, 1996; *The Light of Day*, 2003.

SHORT FICTION: *Learning to Swim, and Other Stories*, 1982.

Graham Colin Swift is one of England's important contemporary novelists. Born in London in 1949, he did not directly experience the momentous events of the Depression-ridden 1930's, World War II, or the difficult postwar problems of social and economic recovery, but his work has consistently concerned itself with history and its subtle influences. Swift, whose father was a government civil servant, attended Dulwich College in London, where he had been preceded half a century before by two other noted writers, Raymond Chandler and P. G. Wodehouse. He graduated with a bachelor's degree from the University of Cambridge in 1970 and received his master's from the same university in 1975. He also attended the University of York. From the mid-1970's until the success of his third novel, *Waterland*, published in 1983, he was a part-time English instructor in London. His first novel, *The Sweet Shop Owner*, was published in 1980, and his subsequent work has won for Swift much praise and many awards. *Waterland* was one of the finalists for the prestigious Booker Prize and was named by *The Guardian* as the best English novel of 1983.

The Sweet Shop Owner contains a number of themes which have continued to occupy Swift. Willy Chapman, the protagonist, is the long-standing proprietor of a small London shop. His wife, now dead, married Willy to spite and to escape her family and provided the funds and the initial discipline that made the shop successful. The novel takes place on the last day of Chapman's life, and Swift illuminates Chapman's story by a series of flashbacks to his own history and to the relations with his wife and his estranged daughter, all governed by the long-established currents and rhythms of his ordered existence. On his last day, Willy—suffering from heart disease—rebels against those rhythms in the futile hope and expectation that his daughter will return. Personal history rather than the usual history of war and politics infuses the story; family relationships, or the lack of them, provide the story's focus; and alienation, personal and familial, and its unrequited quest for healing, is the overriding theme.

These concerns continue to dominate Swift's work. His second novel, *Shuttlecock*, published in 1981, is also a history of personal and familial alienation. Prentis, like Chapman, is a cog in society's machine, working as an archivist or researcher in the police bureaucracy; as Willy was dominated by his wife, so Prentis is subjected to his superior. Prentis's relations with his wife and son are also strained and convoluted. Again history and its permeability play a part in the story of Prentis's father, ostensibly a war hero who in reality was perhaps the opposite. There is no resolution to the problems raised in the novel, however, and the questions asked remain unanswered. In 1982 Swift published a series of short stories in *Learning to Swim, and Other Stories*. Swift wrote the stories before any of his novels, and they announce, in miniature, many of his characteristic themes. For example, "Learning to Swim" relates the tale of an unsatisfactory marriage, and in "The Watch" Swift tells a magical story of time and history.

Waterland was the novel that captured the attention of the critics. Swift's tale of Tom Crick, a history teacher, and Crick's story of his present life and past history—including the saga of his own ancestors—has been compared to the works of Charles Dickens, William Faulkner, and James Joyce. As often happens in Swift's writings, Crick's relationship with his childhood, his students, his wife, and the headmaster of the school where he teaches is difficult, consuming, and fated. Crick, in his fifties, is being made redundant: History is being cut back and merged with something called general studies. Yet the headmaster and the educational establishment are not being merely philistine; Crick himself has abandoned formal history—the history of the French Revolution—in order to relate the more intimate, personal history of himself, his ancestors, and the Fens, the waterlands of the title, of Eastern England. In addition, Crick's wife, unable to have a child of her own, had kidnapped an infant, was apprehended, and is in a mental institution. The Fens—flat but always changing from land to water and back again—become a metaphor for the convolutions between past and present, between sons and fathers, husbands and wives, reality and imagination, history and fiction. Crick and his worlds reflect the themes that Swift had earlier explored: the impact of an earlier time, the aloneness and alienation of the individual, and the difficulty if not impossibility of relating to others.

Swift followed *Waterland* with *Out of This World*, published in 1988. Here the author again works with generational relationships, this time between a sixtyish photographer, Harry Beech, who is currently photographing from the air the prehistoric remains of England, and his daughter Sophie, who is undergoing psychoanalysis in New York. Experiences, the past, and history itself have all come between them, and Swift explores the attempt to restitch the rift, to transcend, somehow, what has occurred before. The chapters generally alternate between the first-person narratives of Harry and Sophie, with other voices remaining muted in the background. In its stylistic austerity *Out of This World* is reminiscent of Swift's early work, but it carries forward his concerns with communication between generations, the interplay of public and personal histories, and the nature and functions of narrative.

In 1992 Swift published a fifth novel, *Ever After.* Beginning like *Waterland*'s Tom Crick with the impetus of a personal crisis—here the deaths of his wife, mother, and stepfather and his own attempted suicide—university lecturer Bill Unwin searches the past for a foundation on which to rebuild his life. He hopes to justify his tenuous academic standing by editing the notebooks of his ancestor Matthew Pearce, an associate of the famous nineteenth century engineer Isambard Kingdom Brunel; instead he finds himself in an exploration of the elusiveness of knowledge and the arbitrary nature of what we call "history." Like *Waterland*, *Ever After* offers a multilayered, evocative narrative that raises complex questions about the relations of art and life. Its uncharacteristically positive conclusion suggests that the very impulse to write—either fiction or history—is a foredoomed but eternally hopeful manifestation of the desire to defy mortality.

Like *The Sweet Shop Owner*, *Last Orders* and *The Light of Day* each takes place on a single day. *Last Orders*, which won the 1996 Booker Prize, recounts the journey made by a group of men, friends since World War II, to scatter the ashes of one of them who has died. The trip provides an opportunity for the friends to assess who they are and where their lives have led them. In *The Light of Day*, private investigator George Webb's interior monologue meditates on his childhood, his scandal-terminated police career, his failed marriage, and the case that led to the day's investigations, which ended with his client murdering her unfaithful husband.

In regard to his constant references to history and its echoes and its relationship to his novels and short stories, Swift has written, "Fiction is not fact, but it is not fraud. The imagination has the power of sheer, fictive invention, but it also has the power to carry us to truth, to make us arrive at knowledge we did not possess and even, looked at from a common point of view, thought we had no right to possess."

Eugene S. Larson
Del Ivan Janik

Bibliography

Broich, Ulrich. "Muted Postmodernism: The Contemporary British Short Story." *Zeitschrift für Anglistik und Amerikanistik* 41 (1993): 31-39. Discusses the market conditions of the contemporary British short story, surveys three major types of British short fiction: the feminist story, the cultural conflict story, and the experimental, postmodernist story. Discusses Swift's story "Seraglio" as a story in which postmodernist narrative strategies are used in a muted way.

Cooper, Pamela. *Graham Swift's "Last Orders."* New York: Continuum, 2002. A short guide for readers' groups, offering background and discussion topics.

Decoste, Damon Marcel. "Question and Apocalypse: The Endlessness of Historia in Graham Swift's *Waterland*." *Contemporary Literature* 43 (Summer, 2002): 377-399. Discusses the element of historical narrative in Swift's novel.

Higdon, David Leon. "Double Closures in Postmodern British Fiction: The Example of Graham Swift." *Critical Survey* 3 (1991): 88-95. A theoretical discussion of the lack of closure in British postmodern fiction, using Swift as an example of a writer who successfully combines the postmodern sense of lack of certainty with the aesthetic demands of some type of boundary; argues that Swift has created a kind of double closure, maintaining the ambiguity of postmodern narratology while at the same time providing a firm, clear response.

________. "'Unconfessed Confessions': The Narrators of Graham Swift and Julian Barnes." In *The British and Irish Novel Since 1960*, edited by James Acheson. New York: St. Martin's Press, 1991. Argues that the fiction of Swift and Barnes defines what is meant by British postmodernism. Claims they share themes of estrangement, obsession, and the power of the past.

Pedot, Richard. "Dead Lines in Graham Swift's *Last Orders*." *Critique* 44 (Fall, 2002): 60-71. A review of Swift's novel.

Powell, Ktrina M. "Mary Metcalf's Attempt at Reclamation: Maternal Representation in Graham Swift's *Waterland*." *Women's Studies* 32 (January/February, 2003): 59-77. Discusses Swift's narrative structure and representations of sexuality and history in his novel.

Widdowson, Peter. "Newstories: Fiction, History, and the Modern World." *Critical Survey* 7 (1995): 3-17. A theoretical discussion of the relationship between history and story in postmodernist fiction, using Swift as the most self-conscious and sophisticated British writer concerned with the interface between history and story. Although the essay focuses primarily on Swift's *Out of This World*, the focus is on a thematic/narrative tactic, which Swift uses in other fiction as well.

Jonathan Swift

Irish novelist and essayist

Born: Dublin, Ireland; November 30, 1667
Died: Dublin, Ireland; October 19, 1745

LONG FICTION: *A Tale of a Tub*, 1704; *Gulliver's Travels*, 1726 (originally titled *Travels into Several Remote Nations of the World, in Four Parts, by Lemuel Gulliver, First a Surgeon, and Then a Captain of Several Ships*).

POETRY: *Cadenus and Vanessa*, 1726; *On Poetry: A Rapsody*, 1733; *Verses on the Death of Dr. Swift, D.S.P.D.*, 1739; *The Poems of Jonathan Swift*, 1937, 1958 (3 volumes; Harold Williams, editor).

NONFICTION: *A Discourse of the Contests and Dissensions Between the Nobles and the Commons in Athens and Rome*, 1701; *The Battle of the Books*, 1704; *The Accomplishment of the First of Mr. Bickerstaff's Predictions*, 1708; *An Argument to Prove That the Abolishing of Christianity in England May, as Things Now Stand, Be Attended with Some Inconveniences, and Perhaps Not Produce Those Many Good Effects Proposed Thereby*, 1708; *Predictions for the Year 1708*, 1708; *A Project for the Advancement of Religion, and the Reformation of Manners By a Person of Quality*, 1709; *A Vindication of Isaac Bickerstaff, Esq.*, 1709; *The Conduct of the Allies*, 1711; *A Proposal for Correcting, Improving, and Ascertaining the English Tongue, in a Letter to the Most Honourable Robert Earl of Oxford and Mortimer, Lord High Treasurer of Great Britain*, 1712; *The Public Spirit of the Whigs, Set Forth in Their Generous Encouragement of the Author of the Crisis*, 1714; *A Letter to the Shop-Keepers*, 1724; *A Letter to Mr. Harding the Printer*, 1724; *A Letter to the Whole People of Ireland*, 1724; *A Letter to . . . Viscount Moleworth*, 1724; *Some Observations upon a Paper*, 1724; *A Modest Proposal for Preventing the Children of Poor People of Ireland from Being a Burden to Their Parents or the Country, and for Making Them Beneficial to the Public*, 1729; *Journal to Stella*, 1766, 1768; *Letters to a Very Young Lady on Her Marriage*, 1797; *The Drapier's Letters to the People of Ireland*, 1935; *The Correspondence of Jonathan Swift*, 1963-1965 (5 volumes; Harold Williams, editor).

MISCELLANEOUS: *Miscellanies in Prose and Verse*, 1711; *Miscellanies*, 1727-1733 (4 volumes; with Alexander Pope and other members of the Scriblerus Club); *A Complete Collection of Genteel and Ingenious Conversation*, 1738; *The Prose Works of Jonathan Swift*, 1939-1968 (14 volumes; Herbert Davis, editor); *Directions to Servants in General . . .*, 1745; *"A Tale of the Tub" to Which Is Added "The Battle of the Books" and the "Mechanical Operation of the Spirit,"* 1958 (A. C. Guthkelch and D. Nichol Smith, editors).

Jonathan Swift, with perhaps the keenest mind and sharpest wit in an age marked by intellectual brilliance, was a mass of contradictions. He was dedicated to the ideals of rationality and common sense, yet he approached the irrational in his contempt for humankind's failure to live up to his ideal. Profoundly distrustful of all "enthusiasm" or fanaticism, he was himself something of an enthusiast in his glorification of "pure reason." He was possessed of one of the clearest and most direct styles in the English language, but the subtleties of his irony were misunderstood in his own and later ages.

Although biographical details do not adequately explain either the genius or the contradictions of Swift, the combination of extreme pride and a position of dependence on the favors of the rich or powerful throws light on the persistent dissatisfaction with life that colors almost all his work. Born in Dublin on November 30, 1667, the son of an impecunious Englishman who had settled in Ireland, Swift was educated at Trinity College with the aid of a wealthy uncle. In 1688 he left Ireland and became secretary to Sir William Temple at Moor Park, Surrey. Temple was not a congenial master, and Swift chafed to be independent in the more exciting world of London. It was the cultured Sir William, however, who gave polish to the somewhat uncouth young man and introduced him to his own world of wit and polite learning, and it was on his behalf that Swift entered the controversy over the relative merits of the "ancients" and the "moderns" in *The Battle of the Books*. In this brilliant example of neoclassical mock-heroic prose, Swift pours out his contempt for the self-righteous complacency of modern criticism and poetry. In this battle between the "ancients" and "moderns," books by classical and modern authors war with one another. Swift attacks the hubris of moderns such as John Dryden. It was also at Moor Park that Swift first met Esther Johnson, possibly Temple's illegitimate daughter, the "Stella" of his later life.

During this same period, Swift wrote *A Tale of a Tub*, a burlesque history of the Church in which his genius first revealed itself in its full force. Just as important as his tale of the degradation of the Church through selfishness and fanaticism are the numerous digressions on moral, philosophical, and literary subjects.

In 1694, dissatisfied with Moor Park, Swift returned to Ireland, where he was ordained an Anglican priest, but after a dreary year in an Irish parish he returned to England. Between 1708 and 1714 he lived in London, and during that period he achieved his greatest triumphs—social, literary, and political. He quickly became familiar with the literary lights of the age, including Richard Steele, Joseph Addison, Alexander Pope, and John Gay. He wrote pieces for Steele's *Tatler* and entered Church controversies with such essays as the brilliantly ironic *An Argument to Prove That the Abolishing of Christianity in England, May, as Things Now Stand, Be Attended with Some Inconveniences, and Perhaps Not Produce Those Many Good Effects Proposed Thereby.*

In 1710, partly from hopes of personal advancement and partly through a passionate interest in defending the prerogatives of the Church, Swift switched his allegiance from the Whig to the Tory

Party. This move won for him the enmity of Whigs such as Addison and Steele but gained him even more powerful friends in Robert Harley and Henry St. John, leaders of the new Tory ministry. Swift's political writing, in the Tory *Examiner* (which he edited briefly, 1710-1711) and in pamphlets attacking Robert Walpole and the duke of Marlborough, proved a powerful aid to the Tory administration in its attempts to discredit the Whig "war party." For his untiring labors, Swift hoped, and expected, to be rewarded with ecclesiastical preferment, perhaps a bishopric, but the memories of those who have risen to high places are notoriously short. Finally, in 1713, Swift was made dean of St. Patrick's Cathedral, Dublin—virtually exiled from England. When the Tory ministry collapsed in 1714, all hope ended, and Swift returned to Ireland for good, disillusioned and bitter. Probably the best picture of his mind during this period of political writing, as well as of the behind-the-scenes intrigue of London politics, appears in the charming and frank letters that make up the *Journal to Stella*, his correspondence with his protégé and friend, Esther Johnson. Also during this period Esther Vanhomrigh, whom he had met in London, followed him to Ireland. The "Vanessa" of his poem *Cadenus and Vanessa*, she died in 1723.

Bitter as he was, Swift's energy and wit could not long be stifled, and he turned his talents to defending Irish political and economic interests against the English. In such pamphlets as *The Drapier's Letters to the People of Ireland*, in which he protests the circulation of debased coinage in Ireland, or his ironic masterpiece, *A Modest Proposal for Preventing the Children of Poor People of Ireland from Being a Burden to Their Parents or the Country, and for Making Them Beneficial to the Public*, in which he suggests that for the Irish to sell their infants as food is their only defense against economic starvation by England, Swift not only continued his war with the Whig administration but also won the love and respect of all Ireland. When England offered a substantial reward to anyone who would turn in the anonymous author, no one in Ireland did—even though many recognized Swift as the writer. Swift proudly recalls this fact in his poem, "Verses on the Death of Dr. Swift." During this period (1721-1725), he also worked intermittently on his greatest and best-known work, *Travels into Several Remote Nations of the World, in Four Parts, by Lemuel Gulliver, First a Surgeon, and Then a Captain of Several Ships*, better known today as *Gulliver's Travels*.

Gulliver's Travels, Swift's final word on humankind and human nature, is a witty and at times vitriolic comment on humanity's abuse and perversion of God-given reason. Books 1 and 2, the account of voyages to Lilliput and Brobdingnag, deal with the corruption of practical reason, as it operates in the social and political worlds. Books 3 and 4 concern theoretical reason, either in its misuse, as among the Laputans and in the Academy of Lagado, or in its excessive application among the Houyhnhnms. Swift's brutal characterization of humans as despicable Yahoos (book 4) has led many readers to feel that the intensity of his misanthropy destroys the validity of his work as satire. However, bitter as Swift was at humankind's failure to live up to ideals of rationality and common sense, the very fact that he wrote *Gulliver's Travels* suggests his recognition of the existence of such a goal and perhaps his hope that humankind could be stimulated to reach it. Although Gulliver becomes misanthropic in book 4, Swift clearly undercuts his protagonist, as when Gulliver distrusts the altruistic Pedro de Mendez.

Swift's health had never been good, and by 1740 mental decay had seriously weakened his mind. He also suffered from a painful inner ear infection. In 1742 guardians were appointed for him, as he was on the verge of mental illness. He died in Dublin on October 19, 1745.

Eric Sterling

Bibliography

Ehrenpreis, Irvin. *Swift: The Man, His Works, and the Age*. 3 vols. Cambridge, Mass.: Harvard University Press, 1962-1983. A monumental biography that rejects long-held myths, provides much new information about Swift and his works and relates him to the intellectual and political currents of his age.

Fox, Christopher, and Brenda Tooley, eds. *Walking Naboth's Vineyard: New Studies of Swift*. Notre Dame, Ind.: University of Notre Dame Press, 1995. The introduction discusses Swift and Irish studies, and the subsequent essays all consider aspects of Swift as an Irish writer. Individual essays have notes, but there is no bibliography.

Glendinning, Victoria. *Jonathan Swift: A Portrait*. New York: Henry Holt, 1998. Glendinning illuminates this proud and intractable man. She investigates the main events and relationships of Swift's life, providing a portrait set in a tapestry of controversy and paradox.

Hunting, Robert. *Jonathan Swift*. Boston: Twayne, 1989. While primarily useful as a source for biographical information, this volume does contain much insightful, if general, analysis of Swift's art. One chapter is devoted to *Gulliver's Travels*. Includes chronology, notes and references, bibliography, and index.

Nokes, David. *Jonathan Swift, A Hypocrite Reversed: A Critical Biography*. Oxford, England: Oxford University Press, 1985. Draws heavily on Swift's writings, offering a good introduction for the general reader seeking information about his life and works. Nokes views Swift as a conservative humanist.

Palmieri, Frank, ed. *Critical Essays on Jonathan Swift*. New York: G. K. Hall, 1993. Divided into sections on Swift's life and writings, *Gulliver's Travels*, *A Tale of a Tub* and eighteenth century literature, and his poetry and nonfiction prose. Includes index but no bibliography.

Quintana, Ricardo. *The Mind and Art of Jonathan Swift*. 1936. Reprint. London: Oxford University Press, 1953. One of the standards of Swift criticism, concentrating on the public Swift. Examines his political activities and writings, tracing the intellectual sources of his thought. Includes synopses of his major works and provides historical background. Reprint contains additional notes and an updated bibliography.

Rawson, Claude. *The Character of Swift's Satire: A Revised Focus*. Newark: University of Delaware Press, 1983. Presents eleven essays by Swift scholars, including John Traugatt's excellent reading of *A Tale of a Tub*, Irvin Ehrenpreis on Swift as a letter writer, and F. P. Lock on Swift's role in the political affairs of Queen Anne's reign.

Real, Hermann J., and Heinz J. Vienken, eds. *Proceedings of the First Münster Symposium on Jonathan Swift*. Munich: Wilhelm Fink, 1985. Includes twenty-four essays on all aspects of Swift's work, each preceded by an abstract. Includes index.

Swift, Jonathan. *The Correspondence of Jonathan Swift*. Edited by David Woolley. New York: Peter Lang, 1999. A collection of letters by Swift that offer insight into his life and work. Includes bibliographical references.

Algernon Charles Swinburne

English poet and playwright

Born: London, England; April 5, 1837
Died: Putney, London, England; April 10, 1909

POETRY: *Poems and Ballads*, 1866; *A Song of Italy*, 1867; *Ode on the Proclamation of the French Republic*, 1870; *Songs Before Sunrise*, 1871; *Songs of Two Nations*, 1875; *Poems and Ballads: Second Series*, 1878; *Songs of the Springtides*, 1880; *The Heptalogia*, 1880; *Tristram of Lyonesse, and Other Poems*, 1882; *A Century of Roundels*, 1883; *A Midsummer Holiday, and Other Poems*, 1884; *Gathered Songs*, 1887; *Poems and Ballads: Third Series*, 1889; *Astrophel, and Other Poems*, 1894; *The Tale of Balen*, 1896; *A Channel Passage, and Other Poems*, 1904; *Posthumous Poems*, 1917; *Rondeaux Parisiens*, 1917; *Ballads of the English Border*, 1925.

LONG FICTION: *Love's Cross-Currents*, 1901 (serialized as *A Year's Letters* in 1877); *Lesbia Brandon*, 1952.

DRAMA: *The Queen-Mother*, pb. 1860; *Rosamond*, pb. 1860; *Atalanta in Calydon*, pb. 1865; *Chastelard*, pb. 1865; *Bothwell*, pb. 1874; *Erechtheus*, pb. 1876; *Mary Stuart*, pb. 1881; *Marino Faliero*, pb. 1885; *Locrine*, pb. 1887; *The Sisters*, pb. 1892; *Rosamund, Queen of the Lombards*, pb. 1899; *The Duke of Gandia*, pb. 1908.

NONFICTION: *Byron*, 1866; *Notes on Poems and Reviews*, 1866; *William Blake: A Critical Essay*, 1868; *Under the Microscope*, 1872; *George Chapman*, 1875; *Essays and Studies*, 1875; *A Note on Charlotte Brontë*, 1877; *A Study of Shakespeare*, 1880; *Miscellanies*, 1886; *A Study of Victor Hugo*, 1886; *A Study of Ben Jonson*, 1889; *Studies in Prose and Poetry*, 1894; *The Age of Shakespeare*, 1908; *Three Plays of Shakespeare*, 1909; *Shakespeare*, 1909; *Contemporaries of Shakespeare*, 1919.

MISCELLANEOUS: *The Complete Works of Algernon Charles Swinburne*, 1925-1927 (20 volumes; reprinted 1968).

Algernon Charles Swinburne's fame as a poet rests on several claims: his dexterity in manipulation of verse; his subject matter, which often glorified the life of the senses or argued for the necessity of social change; and certain oddities in his actual career. In all of these claims, the man can be seen at odds with his age and yet drawing strength from it.

Swinburne was descended from English nobility. His mother was the daughter of the earl of Ashburnham, and his father was Admiral Charles Henry Swinburne. Algernon Charles Swinburne enjoyed fully the advantages of his background. From his mother he acquired a literary taste, a love of the French and Italian languages and literatures, and a thorough knowledge of the Bible. He was also allowed to read such critical writers as Victor Hugo and W. S. Landor, both advocates of republicanism and both objects of Swinburne's hero worship. From a grandfather in Northumberland Swinburne learned hatred of monarchy and disapproval of the hereditary privileges of the House of Lords.

Swinburne early discovered his poetic vocation. Acquaintance in childhood with William Wordsworth and Samuel Rogers confirmed his intent by the time he was fifteen. The next decade brought Swinburne the companionship and encouragement of some leading literary figures of the period, among them Alfred, Lord Tennyson, John Ruskin, and, among the Pre-Raphaelites, William Morris, Edward Burne-Jones, and Dante Gabriel Rossetti. Swinburne's youthful claims to attention led Burne-Jones to welcome him thus: "We have hitherto been three, and now there are four of us." Swinburne modeled for some of Rossetti's paintings and had the painter's personal direction in his writings. His affiliation with the Pre-Raphaelite movement drew attention to his own work, which early struck his contemporaries as clever, audacious, and erudite. From the time *Atalanta in Calydon* and *Chastelard* were published in 1865, Swinburne's place in the literary world was secure, and it remained so for about fifteen years.

Swinburne's themes—glorification of the senses and the assertion of human dignity—are but two aspects of his central impatience with restraint; the only restraint that Swinburne ever welcomed was that imposed by rather elaborate and even archaic poetical forms. In *Poems and Ballads* he scandalized his times with outspoken endorsement of sensuality; in *Songs Before Sunrise* he stirred them deeply with apostrophes to the insurgent republicans of Italy. In these years he was also a prose propagandist for the Pre-Raphaelites and a defender of his own literary practices. Against a charge made by *Saturday Review* that with colors intense and violent he effected an "audacious counterfeiting of strong and noble passion by mad, intoxicated sensuality," Swinburne protested against a literary age that "has room only for such as are content to write for children and girls."

The revolt in Swinburne's own life needed to be curbed, however. In 1879 Theodore Watts-Dunton took Swinburne from London to save him from the effects of acute alcoholic dysentery. Although the move to Putney and a simpler life restored Swinburne's health, it took the essential fire from his writings. He relinquished the idea of political freedom and increasingly turned from poetry to literary criticism. He became capable, as the young Swinburne with his impassioned seriousness would not have been, of composing parodies on the work of such prominent Victorian poets as Tennyson, Rossetti, and himself. The prose of his last years is far removed from his Pre-Raphaelite struggles and contemporary politics; he took up his early enthusiasm for the drama of Elizabethan England, of which he wrote brilliantly.

Swinburne was described as a man more "elf-like than human." He was just over five feet tall and thin; he had a massive head thatched with shaggy red hair. His bizarre appearance prevented his success in love and, it can be believed, underlay the heightened behavior that led to his removal from Eton and Oxford; he later refused a degree from the university that had ejected him. He welcomed the implications of Darwinism and rejected, on the other hand, Robert Browning's optimism and Tennyson's aspirations toward immortality. Here, too, he departed from contemporary canons of taste and created his own philosophy and forms.

George F. Horneker

Bibliography

Louis, Margot Kathleen. *Swinburne and His Gods: The Roots and Growth of an Agnostic Poetry.* Buffalo, N.Y.: McGill-Queen's University Press, 1990. Louis examines Swinburne's views on religion, as they were demonstrated in his writings.

Pease, Allison. *Modernism, Mass Culture, and the Aesthetics of Obscenity.* New York: Cambridge University Press, 2000. Pease's scholarly study of erotic literature and views of obscenity looks at the works of Swinburne and others. Includes bibliography and index.

Reide, David G. *Swinburne: A Study of Romantic Mythmaking.* Charlottesville: University Press of Virginia, 1978. Reide argues that Swinburne is the link between the first English Romantics and the modern Romantics.

Rooksby, Rikky. *A. C. Swinburne: A Poet's Life.* Brookfield, Vt.: Ashgate, 1997. This biography of Swinburne looks at his life and works, focusing on his poetry and his critical writings. Includes bibliography and index.

Rooksby, Rikky, and Nicholas Shrimpton, eds. *The Whole Music of Passion: New Essays on Swinburne.* Brookfield, Vt.: Ashgate, 1993. A collection of essays providing literary criticism of Swinburne's works. Includes bibliography and index.

Thomas, Donald Serrell. *Swinburne: The Poet in His World.* New York: Oxford University Press, 1979. This volume depicts Swinburne in relation to the society in which he lived. An insightful biography of what the author deems to be one of the most eccentric and original writers of the Victorian period. Contains illustrations and a select bibliography.

Frank Swinnerton

English novelist

Born: Wood Green, a suburb of London, England; August 12, 1884
Died: Guildford, Surrey, England; November 6, 1982

LONG FICTION: *The Merry Heart*, 1909; *The Casement*, 1911; *The Happy Family*, 1912; *Nocturne*, 1917; *September*, 1919; *Coquette*, 1921; *The Three Lovers*, 1922; *Young Felix*, 1923; *The Elder Sister*, 1925; *Summer Storm*, 1926; *A Brood of Ducklings*, 1928; *Sketch of a Sinner*, 1929; *The Georgian House*, 1932; *Elizabeth*, 1934; *Harvest Comedy*, 1937; *The Two Wives*, 1939; *The Fortunate Lady*, 1941; *Thankless Child*, 1942; *A Woman in Sunshine*, 1945; *A Flower for Catherine*, 1951; *A Month in Gordon Square*, 1953; *The Summer Intrigue*, 1955; *Woman from Sicily*, 1957; *Tigress in the Village*, 1959; *The Grace Divorce*, 1960; *Death of a Highbrow*, 1961; *Quadrille*, 1965; *Sanctuary*, 1966.

NONFICTION: *George Gissing*, 1912; *R. L. Stevenson*, 1914; *Tokefield Papers*, 1927; *A London Bookman*, 1928; *The Georgian Scene*, 1934 (pb. in Britain as *The Georgian Literary Scene*, 1935); *Swinnerton, an Autobiography*, 1936; *The Bookman's London*, 1951; *Background with Chorus*, 1956; *Authors I Never Met*, 1956; *Figures in the Foreground: Literary Reminiscences 1917-1940*, 1963; *Reflections from a Village*, 1969.

Frank Arthur Swinnerton, born in a London suburb on August 12, 1884, was a precocious boy who avowedly taught himself to read at the age of four. A series of illnesses as a child, including diphtheria, paralysis, and scarlet fever, caused poor health through most of his later boyhood. His family frequently endured straitened circumstances, especially after his father's death, when he and his brother became responsible for supporting the family.

He decided early to be a journalist and became an office boy for a Scottish newspaper publisher, Hay, Nisbet & Company, in 1898, at the age of fourteen. In 1900, having decided to become a man of letters rather than a journalist, he became a confidential clerk with publishers J. M. Dent. He worked there until 1907. In 1907 he joined Chatto & Windus, another British publisher, as a proofreader. In 1909, Chatto & Windus published his first novel, *The Merry Heart*, and made him an editor. He remained with Chatto & Windus through 1926, bringing novelists such as Aldous Huxley,

A. A. Milne, Arnold Bennett, and H. G. Wells to the firm. Before he was thirty Swinnerton had published several books, novels, and critical biographies. His first outstanding success came in 1917 with *Nocturne*, a short but almost perfect Cockney idyll. He went on publishing through his ninety-fourth year, completing sixty-one books, including forty-one novels. *A London Bookman*, *Tokefield Papers*, and *The Bookman's London* are volumes of essays. *The Georgian Scene* is a work of literary criticism; it is, with *Harvest Comedy*, one of the two books Swinnerton considered his best.

From 1937 to 1942 Swinnerton was chief reviewer of fiction for the *London Observer*. During World War II he served the British government as a civil servant in the Ministry of Information. His first wife was Helen Dircks, a poet. His second wife, whom he married in 1924, was Mary Dorothy Bennett; they had one daughter. Swinnerton was considered a competent novelist and a dependable storyteller. Critics rarely were enthusiastic, but they gave measured approval to many of his works, and he was accepted as a literary personality. His books sold well.

Ralph L. Langenheim, Jr.

Bibliography

Bennet, Arnold. *Frank Swinnerton*. 1920. Reprint. Plainview, N.Y.: Books for Libraries Press, 1975.

Catron, Douglas M. "Frank Swinnerton." In *British Novelists, 1890-1929: Traditionalists*, edited by Thomas F. Staley. Vol. 34 of *Dictionary of Literary Biography*. Detroit: Gale Research, 1984.

McKay, Ruth. *George Gissing and His Critic Frank Swinnerton*. 1933. Reprint. Folcroft, Pa.: Folcroft Press, 1969.

John Millington Synge

Irish playwright

Born: Rathfarnham, Ireland; April 16, 1871
Died: Dublin, Ireland; March 24, 1909

DRAMA: *When the Moon Has Set*, wr. 1900-1901, pb. 1968; *Luasnad, Capa, and Laine*, wr. 1902, pb. 1968; *A Vernal Play*, wr. 1902, pb. 1968; *The Tinker's Wedding*, wr. 1903, pb. 1908; *In the Shadow of the Glen*, pr. 1903 (one act); *Riders to the Sea*, pb. 1903 (one act); *The Well of the Saints*, pr., pb. 1905; *The Playboy of the Western World*, pr., pb. 1907; *Deirdre of the Sorrows*, pr., pb. 1910; *The Complete Plays*, pb. 1981.

NONFICTION: *The Aran Islands*, 1907; *In Wicklow*, 1910; *The Autobiography of J. M. Synge*, 1965; *Letters to Molly: John Millington Synge to Máire O'Neill, 1906-1909*, 1971 (Ann Saddlemyer, editor); *My Wallet of Photographs*, 1971 (Lilo Stephens, introducer and arranger); *Some Letters of John M. Synge to Lady Gregory and W. B. Yeats*, 1971 (Saddlemyer, editor); *The Collected Letters of John Millington Synge*, 1983-1984 (2 volumes; Saddlemyer, editor).

MISCELLANEOUS: *Plays, Poems, and Prose*, 1941; *Collected Works*, 1962-1968 (Ann Saddlemyer and Robin Skelton, editors).

John Millington Synge (sihng) was long considered the greatest Irish dramatist until his eminence was challenged by Sean O'Casey, who was not the superior of the older playwright in tragic or comic power, or in beauty of language, but who exhibited far greater versatility and productive powers. Synge's five completed plays all deal with the Irish peasant; about 1900 all literary Ireland was fascinated by the peasant and peasant culture—William Butler Yeats, Æ (George William Russell), Douglas Hyde, Padraic Colum, Lady Gregory, and others were recording stories and trying to capture the lilting poetry of peasant speech. Just before Synge died, however, he told Yeats that he was tired of the peasant on the stage and planned a play about Dublin slum life. Had he not died at such a young age, his dramatic work might have had the sweep of O'Casey's.

Synge was born near Dublin on April 16, 1871, the son of a barrister and grandson of the translator of Josephus. He attended private schools until he was fourteen, then studied for three years with a tutor. Later, while a student at Trinity College, Dublin, he also studied music at the Royal Irish Academy and became a more than competent pianist and violinist. After receiving his degree, he went to Germany to study music and the German language, then to Italy for further language study, and finally to Paris, where he wrote verse and studied French literature. With his small legacy he might have spent the rest of his life as a minor poet and critic if William Butler Yeats had not met him in Paris and urged him to go to Galway and the Aran Islands to study the peasants, whose rich, if primitive, life had never been treated in literature. Synge left his Latin Quarter hotel, went to Wicklow, Kerry, and the Aran Islands, and for some years lived among the peasants, carefully studying their life and speech. With his genius for companionship, this association bore rich rewards—articles in British weeklies, a book of great beauty, *The Aran Islands*, and finally his classic folk plays.

At the same time the Irish literary revival, which had started in the 1890's, was advancing with spectacular success, its happiest manifestation being the famed Abbey Theater, founded in 1904 for the production of native plays. Synge's devotion to the Abbey and his close friendship with its other literary advisers made the performance of his own plays there inevitable. Because he failed to idealize the Irish national character or concern himself with passionate nationalism, his plays provoked hostile demonstrations at the Abbey when first produced, but they were later accepted, even by the Irish, as the greatest classics of the Abbey Theater.

In the Shadow of the Glen, derived from an old folk tale, is sharp with satire and was at first resented as a slur on Irish womanhood. *Riders to the Sea*, considered by many critics the greatest short tragedy in modern drama, has as its themes the eternal conflict of humankind and nature and humankind's dignified submission to fate. Every line in the play has a solemn music, rhythmical and poetic, yet with genuine folk flavor. *The Well of the Saints* is a sardonic comedy, a tragic farce of the flavor of Jean Anouilh's *Waltz of the Toreadors* (1952). *The Playboy of the Western World* is one of the great modern comedies—satirical, boisterous, exquisitely beautiful in language. The crude humors of *The Tinker's Wedding* are in contrast to the legendary, poetic theme of *Deirdre of the Sorrows*, left unfinished at Synge's death. He died of Hodgkin's disease in a nursing home in Dublin, March 24, 1909.

Coílín D. Owens

Bibliography

Casey, Daniel J. *Critical Essays on John Millington Synge*. New York: G. K. Hall, 1994. These essays by Synge scholars covers topics such as Synge's use of language, his poems, and most of his plays, including *The Well of the Saints* and *The Tinker's Wedding* as well as the more famous *The Playboy of the Western World*. Includes bibliography and index.

Gerstenberger, Donna Lorine. *John Millington Synge*. Rev. ed. Boston: Twayne, 1990. A basic biography and critical evaluation of Synge's works. Includes bibliography.

Kiely, David M. *John Millington Synge: A Biography*. New York: St. Martin's Press, 1995. Kiely covers the life of this complex and difficult dramatist. Includes bibliography and index.

Krause, Joseph. *The Regeneration of Ireland: Essays*. Bethesda, Md.: Academica Press, 2001. This scholarly work focuses on the intellectual life of Ireland in the late nineteenth and early twentieth centuries, focusing on Synge's life and works. Includes bibliography and index.

McCormack, W. J. *Fool of the Family: A Life of J. M. Synge*. New York: New York University Press, 2000. McCormack draws on previously unpublished material in his depiction of Synge, which places the dramatist in the context of the cultural changes taking place around him.

McDonald, Ronan. *Tragedy and Irish Writing: Synge, O'Casey, Beckett*. New York: Palgrave, 2001. McDonald examines the treatment of tragedy in Irish literature, focusing on the works of Synge, Sean O'Casey, and Samuel Beckett. Includes bibliography and index.

Watson, George J. *Irish Identity and the Literary Revival: Synge, Yeats, Joyce, and O'Casey*. 2d ed. Washington, D.C.: Catholic University of America Press, 1994. Watson looks at the historical and sociological developments taking place in Ireland while Synge, W. B. Yeats, James Joyce, and Sean O'Casey were writing and the influence these events had on their works. Includes bibliography and index.

Wisława Szymborska

Polish poet

Born: Bnin (now Kórnick), Poland; July 2, 1923

POETRY: *Dlatego żyjemy*, 1952; *Pytania zadawane sobie*, 1954; *Wołanie do Yeti*, 1957; *Sól*, 1962; *Sto pociech*, 1967; *Poezje*, 1970; *Wszelki wypadek*, 1972; *Wielka liczba*, 1976; *Sounds, Feelings, Thoughts: Seventy Poems by Wisława Szymborska*, 1981; *Ludzie na moście*, 1986 (*People on a Bridge*, 1990); *Poems*, 1989; *Koniec i początek*, 1993; *View with a Grain of Sand: Selected Poems*, 1995; *Widok z ziarnkiem piasku*, 1996; *Nothing Twice: Selected Poems*, 1997; *Poems: New and Collected, 1957-1997*, 2000; *Miracle Fair: Selected Poems of Wisława Szymborska*, 2001.

NONFICTION: *Lektury nadobowiązkowe*, 1973; *Nonrequired Reading: Prose Pieces*, 2002.

MISCELLANEOUS: *Poczta literacka*, 2000.

Wisława Szymborska (shihm-BOHR-skah) is one of the most important Polish poets of the post-World War II period. During the second half of the twentieth century, there was a renaissance in Polish poetry, with a number of poets creating work of great breadth and power. Two poets of this era, in fact, were awarded the Nobel Prize in Literature: Czesław Miłosz in 1980 and Szymborska in 1996.

Wisława Szymborska was born in 1923 in the small town of Bnin, near the larger city of Poznan. She lived in Bnin (now part of Kórnick) for her early years and moved to the city of Cracow in 1931; she has lived in Cracow ever since. She was selected for university work and graduated from the prestigious Jagellonian University, where she studied literature and languages, in the midst of World War II. She published her first poem in a Cracow newspaper in 1945. By 1948, she had a collection of twenty-six poems and attempted to have them published as a book. However, Poland was at that time a satellite of Russia, and the communist influence and ideology was very strong. Her proposed book was rejected as presenting a "morbid" rather than heroic treatment of World War II. In addition, it did not celebrate the triumph of the proletariat as communist ideology demanded. She was branded a purveyor of decadent art, and communist leaders began a campaign to undermine her work.

In 1952 Szymborska tried again to publish a book of poems. These poems, in contrast to the aborted collection of 1948, were on themes—such as the need for peace and an anti-Western stance—that the communist establishment found agreeable. However, there was a good deal of criticism of the style of the book; it was described as "agitation-propaganda in a 'chamber music' style." *Dlatego żyjemy* (that's what we live for) was published in 1952, but Szymborska did not include any of the poems from that book in her collected works. She found a way to accommodate the authorities in this one instance, but it compromised her vision if not her literary technique.

In 1954 Szymborska published another book of poems, *Pytania zadawane sobie* (questions to put to myself). The poems of this collection directly reject the communist agenda and socialist poetics. The subjects of these poems include love and the consciousness of the self. Her typical wit, a quality for which communist ideology had little use, is always present.

Szymborska found her unique voice in the collection *Wołanie do Yeti* (calling out to Yeti), published in 1957; this collection brought her great popularity in Poland, although she was not well known outside that country. The poems reflect a broad range of subjects, and wit and the use of imaginary worlds are prominent in them. For example, in "From a Himalayan Expedition Not Made," the speaker contrasts the silence of the Himalayas to the ordinary world which has "ABC's, bread/ and two times two is four. . . ." She calls to the Yeti to come back to a world where "tears do not freeze," but he gives no sign of recognition. Another poem on a lost world is "Atlantis," which is a "plus minus" world made of contradictions. In the same collection is a poem that is closer to statement and social criticism, "Still." The poem portrays boxcars traveling across the land. They are inhabited by names, such as "The name Nathan" and "name David." These Jews of the Holocaust are given back their names and their identities by the poem. In addition to criticizing the inhumanity of the Nazis, the poem places blame on those many eastern Europeans who were silent. "Awakened in the night I hear/ cor-rect, cor-rect, crash of silence on silence."

Sól (salt) was published in 1962, and it continued the witty and ironic technique that Szymborska was making her own. For example, "Museum" looks at the objects in a museum and asks where the human feelings are that once made these objects valued. "Unexpected Meeting" is a love poem that deals with the loss of love. The former lovers meet, only to find that their passion, which is metaphorically represented by such wild animals as tigers and hawks, is now tame and has "nothing to say."

The poems in *Sto pociech* (a million laughs, a bright hope), published in 1967, are for the most part written in free verse and deal with such social issues as the Vietnam War. There is, however, also the theme of creation in "The Joys of Writing," and a poem on Thomas Mann sees him as an archetypal creator. *Wszelki wypadek* (there but for the grace) balances dreams and reality, as in "In Praise of Dreams." The poem portrays the speaker as one who can do wonders, such as discovering Atlantis. However, the last line returns the reader to reality as she sees "the day before yesterday a penguin./ With the utmost clarity." No matter how fanciful Szymborska's poems may become, there is always that "utmost clarity."

Wielka liczba (a great number) was published in 1976, and it has poems of sharp wit, a quality central to Szymborska's work. For example, "Review of an Unwritten Poem" has a harsh critic as a speaker. The critic condemns the "authoress" (itself an archaic and demeaning word) for the same qualities that have made Szymborska such an admired poet: The authoress is "lost in infinitude" and mixes "the lofty with the vernacular."

Szymborska values her privacy and has never sought the spotlight, although she is far from being a recluse. The announcement that she had been awarded the Nobel Prize in Literature in 1996 took the literary world by surprise. The award brought her poetry greater worldwide attention. This was very apparent to English-language readers by the number of her collections that were published in English after the mid-1990's. Most were received with almost unanimous critical acclaim. She continued to write on a variety of topics. In *People on a Bridge*, she addresses political questions for the first time since *Wołanie do Yeti*, and in *Koniec i początek* her poems are often very private, even elegiac in tone. In her work, readers find a singular contemporary poet who has created some of the most elegant and witty poems of the post-World War II period.

James Sullivan

Bibliography

Aaron, Jonathan. "In the Absence of Witnesses: The Poetry of Wisława Szymborska." *Parnassus: Poetry in Review* 11, no. 2 (1981/1982): 254-264. An insightful overview of the major themes in Szymborska's poetry based on the 1981 and 1982 English language collections of her poems.

Cavanagh, Clare. "Poetry and Ideology: The Example of Wisława Szymborska." *Literary Imagination* 2, no. 1 (1999): 174-190. An analysis of Szymborska's poetry written by its American translator. Cavanagh emphasizes the dialogical character of Szymborska's work, as well as its affinities with poststructuralist thought.

Czerniawski, Adam, ed. *The Mature Laurel: Essays on Modern Polish Poetry.* Chester Springs, Pa.: Dufour, 1991. A collection of essays dealing with twentieth century Polish poets. Two important articles on Szymborska appear in a collection: Adam Czerniawski, "Poets and Painters," and Edward Rogerson, "Anti-Romanticism: Distance."

Krynski, Magnus J., and Robert A. Maguire. Introduction to *Sounds, Feelings, Thoughts: Seventy Poems by Wisława Szymborska.* Princeton, N.J.: Princeton University Press, 1981. This good English-language collection of Szymborska's poetry contains an excellent introduction discussing the poet and her work.

Mączyńska, Magdalena. "Wisława Szymborska." In *Critical Survey of Poetry*, edited by Philip K. Jason. 2d rev. ed. Pasadena, Calif.: Salem Press, 2003. A good introduction to, and starting point for learning about, Szymborska's life and poetry.

Tacitus

Roman orator

Born: Place unknown; c. 56 C.E.
Died: Probably Rome (now in Italy); c. 120 C.E.

NONFICTION: *De vita Julii Agricolae*, c. 98 (*The Life of Agricola*, 1591); *De origine et situ Germanorum*, c. 98 (also known as *Germania*; *The Description of Germanie*, 1598); *Dialogus de oratoribus*, c. 98-102 (*A Dialogue Concerning Oratory*, 1754); *Historiae*, c. 109 (*Histories*, 1731); *Ab excessu divi Augusti*, c. 116 (also known as *Annales*; *Annals*, 1598).

The life of Publius (or Gaius) Cornelius Tacitus (TAS-uht-uhs) is known only from autobiographical allusions in the extant parts of his works and from eleven letters written to him by Pliny the Younger. This remarkable republican lived through the reign of ten emperors, from Nero to Hadrian. As a brilliant lawyer, senator, and consul, he was a close observer of public affairs, and his dismay at the degeneration of his age and his fear of tyranny are expressed in pithy language.

Tacitus was born into a prosperous provincial family. He studied rhetoric as an adolescent and came to public notice as a skilled orator. His career took a notable advance when he married the daughter of the future Roman governor of Britain, Julius Agricola. He was appointed to high offices by the cruel Emperor Domitian, then reached the pinnacle of his civil career when he was named to the important governorship of Asia by Emperor Trajan in 112.

His *A Dialogue Concerning Oratory* laments the decay of education and eloquence; *The Life of Agricola* is a fine biography of his father-in-law, with a sketch of Britain under the Romans; *The Description of Germanie* (also called *Concerning the Geography, the Customs and Manners, and the Tribes of Germany*), a valuable classic despite its errors, contrasts the free barbarians with the servile Romans; and the *Histories* includes an unforgettable account of rebellion and civil war throughout the vast Roman terrain as well as a fascinating, prejudiced account of the Jews. The *Annals* provides a rich, almost novelistic account of the pivotal reign of the emperors Tiberius and Claudius as well as a philosophy of history. Tacitus is memorable as a chronicler of what it is like to live under tyranny in a nation that still remembers its own freedom. His experience under the persecution launched by Domitian permitted him to take a moral reckoning of the ethics and responsibilities of individual behavior of people enduring such a regime.

Despite the "singularly blessed time" of his last years, Tacitus could never shake off the morbid effects of Domitian's reign of terror. Nevertheless, although convinced of Rome's corruption, he served loyally and well, receiving in 99 a special vote of thanks from the Roman Senate. He recorded the society more than he cured it, and his works collectively provide a vivid, panoramic view of the empire in the first century. Many modern historians still subscribe to his dictum that "history's highest function is to rescue merit from oblivion, and to hold up as a terror to base words and actions the reprobation of posterity."

Nicholas Birns

Bibliography

Ash, Rhiannon. *Ordering Anarchy: Armies and Leaders in Tacitus' Histories*. Ann Arbor: University of Michigan Press, 1999.

Kraus, Christina Shuttleworth. *Latin Historians*. New York: Oxford University Press, 1997.

Luce, T. J., and A. J. Woodman. *Tacitus and the Tacitean Tradition*. Princeton, N.J.: Princeton University Press, 1993.

Mellor, Ronald. *Tacitus*. New York: Routledge, 1993.

O'Gorman, Ellen. *Irony and Misreading in the Annals of Tacitus*. New York: Cambridge University Press, 2000.

Sinclair, Patrick. *Tacitus the Sententious Historian: A Sociology of Rhetoric in Annales*. University Park: Pennsylvania State University Press, 1995.

Woodman, A. J. *Tacitus Reviewed*. New York: Oxford University Press, 1998.

Rabindranath Tagore

Indian poet, playwright, novelist, and short-story writer

Born: Calcutta, India; May 7, 1861
Died: Calcutta, India; August 7, 1941

POETRY: *Saisab sangit*, 1881; *Sandhya sangit*, 1882; *Prabhat sangit*, 1883; *Chabi o gan*, 1884; *Kari o komal*, 1887; *Mānashi*, 1890; *Sonār tari*, 1893 (*The Golden Boat*, 1932); *Chitra*, 1895; *Chaitāli*, 1896; *Kanika*, 1899; *Kalpana*, 1900; *Katha o kahini*, 1900; *Kshanikā*, 1900; *Naivedya*, 1901; *Sisu*, 1903 (*The Crescent Moon*, 1913); *Smaran*, 1903; *Utsarga*, 1904; *Kheya*, 1905; *Gitānjali*, 1910 (*Gitanjali: Song Offerings*, 1912); *The Gardener*, 1913; *Gitali*, 1914; *Balāka*, 1916 (*A Flight of Swans*, 1955, 1962); *Fruit-Gathering*, 1916; *Gan*, 1916; *Stray Birds*, 1917; *Love's Gift, and Crossing*, 1918; *Palataka*, 1918 (*The Fugitive*, 1921); *Lipika*, 1922; *Poems*, 1922; *Sisu bholanath*, 1922; *The Curse at Farewell*, 1924; *Prabahini*, 1925; *Purabi*, 1925; *Fifteen Poems*, 1928; *Fireflies*, 1928; *Mahuya*, 1929; *Sheaves: Poems and Songs*, 1929; *Banabani*, 1931; *The Child*, 1931; *Parisesh*, 1932; *Punascha*, 1932; *Vicitrita*, 1933; *Bithika*, 1935; *Ses saptak*, 1935; *Patraput*, 1936, 1938 (English translation, 1969); *Syamali*, 1936 (English translation, 1955); *Khapchada*, 1937; *Prantik*, 1941; *Janmadine*, 1941; *Poems*, 1942; *Sesh lekha*, 1942; *The Herald of Spring*, 1957; *Wings of Death: The Last Poems*, 1960; *Devouring Love*, 1961; *A Bunch of Poems*, 1966; *One Hundred and One*, 1967; *Last Poems*, 1973; *Later Poems*, 1974.

LONG FICTION: *Bau-Thakuranir Hat*, 1883; *Rajarshi*, 1887; *Chokher bāli*, 1902 (*Binodini*, 1959); *Naukadubi*, 1906 (*The Wreck*, 1921); *Gora*, 1910 (English translation, 1924); *Chaturanga*, 1916 (English translation, 1963); *Ghare bāire*, 1916 (*Home and the World*, 1919); *Jogajog*, 1929; *Shesher kabita*, 1929 (*Farewell, My Friend*, 1946); *Dui bon*, 1933 (*Two Sisters*, 1945).

SHORT FICTION: *The Hungry Stones, and Other Stories*, 1916; *Mashi, and Other Stories*, 1918; *Stories from Tagore*, 1918; *Broken Ties, and Other Stories*, 1925; *The Runaway, and Other Stories*, 1959.

DRAMA: *Prakritir Pratishodh*, pb. 1884 (verse play; *Sanyasi: Or, The Ascetic*, 1917); *Rājā o Rāni*, pb. 1889 (verse play; *The King and the Queen*, 1918); *Chitrāngadā*, pb. 1892 (verse play; *Chitra*, 1913); *Prayaschitta*, pr. 1909 (based on his novel *Bau-Thakuranir Hat*); *Rājā*, pb. 1910 (*The King of the Dark Chamber*, 1914); *Dākghar*, pb. 1912 (*The Post Office*, 1914); *Phālguni*, pb. 1916 (*The Cycle of Spring*, 1917); *Arupratan*, pb. 1920 (revision of his play *Rājā*); *Muktadhārā*, pb. 1922 (English translation, 1950); *Raktakarabi*, pb. 1924 (*Red Oleanders*, 1925); *Chirakumār Sabhā*, pb. 1926; *Natir Pujā*, pb. 1926 (*Worship of the Dancing Girl*, 1950); *Paritrān*, pb. 1929 (revision of *Prayaschitta*); *Tapati*, pb. 1929 (revision of *Rājā o Rāni*); *Chandālikā*, pr., pb. 1933 (English translation, 1938); *Bānsari*, pb. 1933; *Nritya-natya Chitrāngadā*, pb. 1936 (revision of his play *Chitrāngadā*); *Nritya-natya Chandālikā*, pb. 1938 (revision of his play *Chandālikā*); *Three Plays*, pb. 1950.

NONFICTION: *Jivansmriti*, 1912 (*My Reminiscences*, 1917); *Sadhana*, 1913; *Personality*, 1917; *Nationalism*, 1919; *Greater India*, 1921; *Glimpses of Bengal*, 1921; *Creative Unity*, 1922; *Talks in China*, 1925; *Lectures and Addresses*, 1928; *Letters to a Friend*, 1928; *The Religion of Man*, 1931; *Mahatmaji and the Depressed Humanity*, 1932; *Man*, 1937; *Chhelebela*, 1940 (*My Boyhood Days*, 1940); *Sabhyatar Samkat*, 1941 (*Crisis in Civilization*, 1941); *Towards Universal Man*, 1961.

MISCELLANEOUS: *Collected Poems and Plays*, 1936; *A Tagore Reader*, 1961.

Rabindranath Tagore (tah-GOR), who won the Nobel Prize in Literature in 1913, is considered the founder and shaper of modern Bengali-language literature. He was the fourteenth of fifteen children born to Debendranath Tagore and Sarada Devi. His mother, Sarada, died when he was thirteen years old. His name Rabin means Lord of the Sun. Tagore's ancestors came from what is now Bangladesh to live in Calcutta, located in the eastern region of India known as Bengal. His immediate family was wealthy by Indian standards of the time; his grandfather, Dwarkanath Tagore, was referred to as a prince.

Tagore was a precocious child who was educated primarily at home by tutors. He wrote his first poem at the age of eight. The household of his family in Calcutta was like a small city, populated by immediate family, in-laws, servants of all sorts, and tutors. The family also owned vast agricultural estates in eastern Bengal, and they would prove to be a big influence on both the topics and the themes of much of his work. Tagore married Mrinalini Devi when she was eleven years old and he was twenty-two.

He first traveled to the family's rural estates, an area called Santiniketan, and North India, including the Himalayas, with his father in 1873. This trip was shortly after the investiture of the sacred thread, a Hindu religious rite-of-passage ceremony. This trip and his numerous returns to the area are much in evidence in his writings, particularly in his short stories, sensitive tales of the simple village life he observed, which was so different from the frenetic pace of the Tagore household and life in Calcutta. "The Postmaster" is a classic representation.

Tagore is first and foremost a lyric poet; in his lifetime he published fifty-four collections of Bengali poems, and six more were published posthumously. *Gitānjali* was the collection primarily responsible for his getting the attention that led to the Nobel Prize. Tagore began writing short stories in the 1890's and eventually published more than ninety of them. He wrote nearly fifty dramas, though only a fraction of them were translated into English. During the period 1883 to 1934, he published ten Bengali novels, one-third of them translated into English. Tagore's nonfiction prose, including songs, essays, lectures, sermons, and instructional writings, runs into the thousands of pages, but little of it has been translated. During his lifetime, Tagore translated many of his own works into English. His song "Our Golden Bengal" became the national anthem of Bangladesh. Near the end of his life, he became a prolific painter, producing twenty-five hundred pieces.

In addition to his well-to-do, intense family life and his ability to travel, other influences on Tagore were British colonialism, begun in India in 1690 with the establishment of the East India Company, and his family's adherence to the Vaishnava tradition of Hinduism. Because of colonialism, he was exposed early in life to the literature of William Shakespeare, John Milton, and George Gordon, Lord Byron, who became his particular favorites, as well as the philosophy of John Stuart Mill and Jeremy Bentham. Other literary influences (Tagore read them in their original languages) included Johann Wolfgang von Goethe and Guy de Maupassant. Tagore attended University College, London for one year. He was knighted by the British in 1915 but resigned his knighthood in 1919, after the Amritsar Massacre, when the British army slaughtered hundreds of innocent Indian men, women, and children.

Vaishnavism emphasizes worship of Vishnu, the Preserver. It puts no restrictions on caste, class, or gender, and central to its tenets is pursuit of the enigmatic, personal relationship between the Creator and humans. A major component of the faith is worshiping through songs. Themes that weave throughout Tagore's works, regardless of genre, have to do with the remoteness of nature and the human dimension, the world beyond India and attempts to coalesce or synthesize opposites, including Eastern and Western cultures or a search for the universal.

Throughout his life, beginning with his first trip to London in 1879, Tagore traveled widely and frequently. In addition to trips to Europe, he visited the United States several times as well as Japan and China. His travels brought him friendships and contacts with famous contemporary Western writers such as William Butler Yeats and Ezra Pound.

Physically, Tagore resembled the West's idea of what a poet and holy man from the East should look like. His appearance, in the flowing robes of traditional Bengali dress, with long hair and beard, and what some describe as the romantic quality of his writing, both helped and hurt the initial acceptance of and the legacy of his work.

Judith Steininger

Bibliography

Chatterjee, Bhabatosh. *Rabindranath Tagore and Modern Sensibility*. Delhi: Oxford University Press, 1996. A collection of the author's original essays about Tagore's writings, reanalyzed for this book.

Dutta, Krishna, and Andrew Robinson. *Rabindranath Tagore: The Myriad-Minded Man*. New York: St. Martin's Press, 1996. A complete biography of Tagore, with references to his works.

Kripalani, Krishna. *Tagore: A Life*. New Delhi: Malancha, 1961. Biography and works are closely interwoven in this text. The drawings and photographs of and by Tagore, his family, and his friends are extremely interesting.

Lago, Mary. *Rabindranath Tagore*. Boston: Twayne, 1976. The book includes an outline biography and an analysis of each of the major genres in which Tagore wrote.

Morash, Chris, ed. *Creativity and Its Contexts*. Dublin: Lilliput Press, 1995. A collection of essays about regionalism and creativity for several writers. Indian novelist Anita Desai wrote the essay on Tagore.

Nandy, Ashish. *Return from Exile*. New York: Oxford University Press, 1998. An analysis of Tagore's political writing which puts him in the context of India's move in the 1920's toward nationalism. This, in turn, illuminates some of the philosophy and themes in his other writing.

Hippolyte-Adolphe Taine

French essayist

Born: Vouziers, France; April 21, 1828
Died: Paris, France; March 5, 1893

NONFICTION: *Essai sur les fables de La Fontaine*, 1853 (revised as *La Fontaine et ses fables*, 1861); *Voyages aux eaux des Pyrénées*, 1855 (*A Tour Through the Pyrenees*, 1874); *Essai sur Tite-Live*, 1856; *Les Philosophes français du XIXe siècle*, 1857 (revised as *Les Philosophes classiques du XIX siècle en France*, 1868); *Essais de critique et d'histoire*, 1858; *Histoire de la littérature anglaise*, 1863-1864 (4 volumes; *History of English Literature*, 1871); *L'Idéalisme anglais: Étude sur Carlyle*, 1864; *Le Positivisme anglais: Étude sur Stuart Mill*, 1864 (*English Positivism: A Study on John Stuart Mill*, 1870); *Nouveaux Essais de critique et d'histoire*, 1865; *Philosophie de l'art: Leçons professées à l'École des Beaux-Arts*, 1865 (*Philosophy of Art*, 1865); *Philosophie de l'art en Italie*, 1866 (*The Philosophy of Art in Italy*, 1875); *Voyage en Italie*, 1866 (translated as *Italy: Naples and Rome*, 1867, and *Italy: Florence and Venice*, 1869); *Notes sur Paris: Vie et opinions de M. Frédéric-Thomas Graindorge*, 1867 (*Notes on Paris*, 1875); *De l'idéal dans l'art: Leçons professées à l'École des*

Beaux-Arts, 1867 (*The Ideal in Art*, 1868); *Philosophie de l'art en Grèce*, 1869 (*The Philosophy of Art in Greece*, 1871); *Philosophie de l'art dans les Pays-Bas*, 1869 (*The Philosophy of Art in The Netherlands*, 1871); *De l'intelligence*, 1870 (2 volumes; *On Intelligence*, 1871); *Notes sur l'Angleterre*, 1872 (*Notes on England*, 1872); *Les Origines de la France contemporaine*, 1876-1894 (6 volumes; *The Origins of Contemporary France*, 1876-1894); *Derniers Essais de critique et d'histoire*, 1894; *Carnets de voyage: Notes sur la province, 1863-1865*, 1897 (*Journeys Through France: Being Impressions of Provinces*, 1897); *H. Taine: Sa vie et sa correspondance*, 1902-1907 (4 volumes; *Life and Letters of H. Taine*, 1902-1908, 3 volumes); *Voyage en Allemagne*, 1920.

Hippolyte-Adolphe Taine (tehn), born at Vouziers, France, on April 21, 1828, was educated at the Collège Bourbon and the Normal School in Paris. By 1848 he had two baccalaureate degrees, one in science and one in letters. After leaving school he became a teacher at Toulon, but because of his political views he was appointed to successively poorer posts until he left teaching entirely in 1852 and devoted his time to study and writing. In 1853 he completed his *Essai sur les fables de La Fontaine* (essay on the fables of La Fontaine), written as the thesis for his doctorate at the Sorbonne. He immediately began an essay on Livy, which, entered in competition, won for him an award from the French Academy in 1855. Early in 1854, however, Taine had suffered a breakdown in health because of his arduous program of writing.

After a period of enforced rest he resumed his literary activities, contributing articles on various subjects to periodicals and entering literary society. One series of articles, published as *Les Philosophes classiques du XIX siècle en France* (the classic philosophers of the nineteenth century in France), first suggested Taine's theory of the application of scientific methods to psychological and metaphysical research. The book attracted considerable interest and helped to spread the author's critical fame. A revised version of his doctoral essay on La Fontaine was published in 1861.

In 1864 Taine received two appointments, both of which gave him security and left him free to study and write. He became examiner at Saint-Cyr and professor of aesthetics and art history at L'École des Beaux Arts. In the same year he published a study of John Stuart Mill, *English Positivism*. In the meantime his famous *History of English Literature* had appeared, a work illustrating how determinism could be applied to the study of literature by utilizing the elements of race, milieu, and moment. From 1864 to 1870 Taine fulfilled his tasks at Saint-Cyr and lectured at L'École des Beaux Arts. A general study of the philosophy of art appeared in 1865, followed by volumes on various phases of art and the philosophy of art. He married the daughter of an architect in 1868.

The Franco-Prussian War ended that happy period in Taine's life and turned his thinking to new paths. Anxious to ascertain the cause of France's weakness and political instability, and feeling that they were traceable to the French Revolution of 1789, Taine began what was to be his greatest work, his study of the origins of contemporary France. He worked at it constantly, even giving up his professorship in 1884 to avail himself of more time; even so, he left it unfinished when he died in Paris in 1893. The methods that Taine used in this work were the same quasi-scientific and deterministic methods he had already used successfully in his studies of literature and art. The book marked Taine as one of the great intellectual leaders of the nineteenth century, the leader of a generation in France that sought in art, literature, and history truth that could be regarded as "objective" and "scientific."

Bernadette Lynn Bosky

Bibliography

Eustis, Alvin Allen. *Hippolyte Taine and the Classical Genius*. Berkeley: University of California Press, 1951. Focuses on Taine's assessment of classical society and its artists, noting the importance the critic places on social conditions and on the production of high-quality art.

Goetz, Thomas H. *Taine and the Fine Arts*. Madrid: Playor, 1973. Extensive analysis of Taine's writings on the fine arts, focusing particularly on those about sculpture and painting.

Gullace, Giovanni. *Taine and Brunetiere on Criticism*. Lawrence, Kans.: Coronado Press, 1982. Excellent analysis of Taine's ideas about art in *Philosophy of Art*.

Kahn, Sholom Jacob. *Science and Aesthetic Judgement: A Study in Taine's Critical Method*. New York: Columbia University Press, 1953. Extended scholarly examination of Taine's writings on art, exploring ways he is able to balance the need for objective analysis with the more elusive art of judgment, especially value judgment.

Lombardo, Patrizia. "Hippolyte Taine Between Art and Science." *Yale French Studies* 77 (1990). A worthwhile article.

Weinstein, Leo. *Hippolyte Taine*. New York: Twayne, 1972. General study of the writer. Discusses Taine's analysis of the nature of art and the conditions necessary for its production. Examines his judgments on the art of Europe, his notion of the ideal, and the emphasis he places on personal and national "character" in creating great art.

Ted Tally

American playwright and screenwriter

Born: Winston-Salem, North Carolina; April 9, 1952

DRAMA: *Terra Nova*, pr. 1977; *Hooters*, pr., pb. 1978; *Coming Attractions*, pr. 1980; *Silver Linings*, pr. 1981; *Little Footsteps*, pr., pb. 1986.
SCREENPLAYS: *White Palace*, 1990 (adaptation of Glenn Savan's novel); *The Silence of the Lambs*, 1991 (adaptation of Thomas Harris's novel); *The Juror*, 1996 (adaptation of George D. Green's novel); *Before and After*, 1996 (adaptation of Rosellen Brown's novel); *All the Pretty Horses*, 2000 (adaptation of Cormac McCarthy's novel); *Red Dragon*, 2002 (adaptation of Harris's novel).
TELEPLAY: *The Father Clements Story*, 1987 (with Arthur Heineman).

Ted Tally is an important and influential screenwriter who began his career as a playwright for the New York stage. His plays continue to be performed in regional theaters. Tally grew up in Greensboro, North Carolina, as the bookish son of two teachers. He received his undergraduate degree from Yale University in 1974 and then studied playwriting at the Yale School of Drama, alongside the notable future playwrights Christopher Durang and Wendy Wasserstein.

Tally's first New York productions grew out of plays he developed as a student at Yale. The first of these was *Terra Nova*, based on diaries and other documents relating the story of English sea captain Robert Scott and his fatal expedition to the South Pole. This play, Tally's master's thesis, was first produced at the Yale School of Drama in 1977 and later the same year, after revisions, at the Yale Repertory Theatre in a production starring Lindsay Crouse and Michael Gross. Although *Terra Nova* was not produced in New York until 1984, its success at Yale generated interest in New York for subsequent plays, including *Hooters*, *Coming Attractions*, *Silver Linings*, and *Little Footsteps*. These plays are comedies, in contrast to *Terra Nova*, which is a serious and moving portrait of obsession and dedication, ending in the deaths of the principal characters. Such serious and dark themes did not return to Tally's work until the publication of his screenplays, especially the Academy Award-winning *The Silence of the Lambs*. *Hooters*, for example, is an extended anecdote about two college-age boys trying to pick up slightly older women at the beach. *Little Footsteps* treats similar characters at the point in life where they are married and expecting a child.

During the 1980's Tally wrote primarily for the stage, with productions that received mixed reviews and the occasional award (including an Obie Award for the 1984 production of *Terra Nova*). Tally began to experiment with writing for television and film, recognizing that such writing could bring financial security. At the request of British director Lindsay Anderson, Tally began to work on an epic screenplay set in India during the time of British occupation. This screenplay, called "Empire," was completed but never produced. Subsequently, Tally continued to write screenplays and adaptations of his own plays. He was paid for these works commissioned by studios, yet he was frustrated because none of them became films. His first produced screenplay was a television film called *The Father Clements Story*, based on the true story of a priest who adopted a child.

Tally's first screenplay to be filmed was *White Palace*, an offbeat love story starring Susan Sarandon and James Spader. Tally's early plays all include romantic or erotic relationships (including *Terra Nova*, which weaves in the story of Scott's marriage), and he has said that he cannot imagine writing a script that excludes women characters. *White Palace*, like *All the Pretty Horses* a decade later, shows Tally's skill in writing about powerful romantic attachments, a counterpoint to his macabre work in *The Silence of the Lambs* and *Red Dragon*.

Before and After can be seen as transitional for Tally in terms of subject matter. In this project, he adapted the work of an accomplished novelist, Rosellen Brown, whose work focuses on moral dilemmas. In this novel, the ethical crisis stems from a murder apparently committed by a teenage boy and from the responses to this act by his parents. The father (played by Liam Neeson) wants to protect his son, whereas the mother (Meryl Streep) argues that the truth must be revealed. The story, then, is focused on relationships, in keeping with Tally's earlier work, but moves toward looking at darker human motives, as he does in his next projects. Unfortunately, negative critical reaction to *Before and After* made Tally question the worth of writing for a medium where critics can so quickly dismiss one's serious efforts (this problem would return after *All the Pretty Horses*).

Both *The Silence of the Lambs* and *Red Dragon* are adapted from novels by Thomas Harris about a cannibalistic serial killer Dr. Hannibal Lecter. By chance, Tally read the manuscript of *The Silence of the Lambs* shortly before its hardcover publication and was able to express his interest and be hired as screenwriter. The sensationalistic aspects of the plot are balanced by thoughtful treatment of the central character, young Federal Bureau of Investigation agent Clarice Starling (played by Jodie Foster). The film brought financial security and acclaim to Tally, who won an Academy Award for his screenplay. He chose not to work on the sequel, *Hannibal* (Foster and *The Silence of the Lambs* director Jonathan Demme also opted out), but Tally later took on the project of *Red Dragon*, an earlier Harris novel also featuring Hannibal Lecter.

As Tally's screenwriting career developed, he showed little inclination to return to playwriting. He decided in the late 1980's to concentrate on one form of writing and found his niche in adapting novels to film. His early success with *Terra Nova*, a historical play based on extant documents, proved a template for his later satisfaction in using an established plot as the basis for his scripts, allowing him to concentrate on the practical aspects of structuring a story. Unlike some playwrights who turn to screenwriting for its financial rewards with the intention of using the money to fuel further work for the stage, Tally has preferred the challenge of adapting novels for the screen.

Diane M. Ross

Bibliography

Bliss, Michael, and Christina Banks. *What Goes Around Comes Around: The Films of Jonathan Demme*. Carbondale: Southern Illinois University Press, 1996. The book devotes a chapter to *The Silence of the Lambs*, the work that revolutionized Tally's career.

Engel, Joel. "Ted Tally." In *Screenwriters on Screenwriting*. New York: Hyperion, 1995. This chapter is devoted to an interview with Tally on the craft of screenwriting.

Tally, Ted. "A Conversation with Ted Tally." Interview by Michael Winship. *Writer's Guild of America East Newsletter*, December 6, 2002. This article provides a detailed interview with Tally about his career and the influences on his work, including discussion of the difference between writing plays and screenplays.

Amy Tan

American novelist

Born: Oakland, California; February 19, 1952
Identity: Chinese American

LONG FICTION: *The Joy Luck Club*, 1989; *The Kitchen God's Wife*, 1991; *The Hundred Secret Senses*, 1995; *The Bonesetter's Daughter*, 2001.
NONFICTION: "The Language of Discretion," 1990 (in *The State of the Language*, Christopher Ricks and Leonard Michaels, editors).
CHILDREN'S/YOUNG ADULT LITERATURE: *The Moon Lady*, 1992; *The Chinese Siamese Cat*, 1994.

Amy Ruth Tan was born February 19, 1952, in Oakland, California, to John Tan, a minister and electrical engineer, and Daisy Chan (formerly Tu Ching), a vocational nurse. (Her mother was also a member of a club like the one depicted in Tan's first novel, *The Joy Luck Club*). Her parents had moved to the United States from China three years before she was born. When Tan was fifteen, her father and one of her brothers died; her mother took her and her younger brother to Switzerland, where Tan finished high school. Later the family returned to the United States, and Tan attended and graduated from San Jose State University. She married tax attorney Lou DeMattei.

In spite of her considerable literary success, Amy Tan's writing career was unplanned. After holding various jobs, including work as a consultant to programs for disabled children, reporter, managing editor, associate publisher for *Emergency Medicine Reports*, freelance writer, and technical writer, Tan sought counseling to learn to curb her workaholic tendencies. When her therapist fell asleep three times during their counseling sessions, however, Tan instead began taking jazz piano lessons and writing fiction as a form of therapy and a way to cut her working hours. She eventually joined the Squaw Valley Community, a fiction writers' workshop. A short story she wrote, which was published in *Seventeen*, gained the attention of a literary agent, who suggested that she submit a proposal for a novel based on her mother's friends and family. Tan's hobby developed into a lucrative career when that novel, *The Joy Luck Club*, was published in 1989. (A film version, for which Tan collaborated on the screenplay, was released in 1993.) Both this first novel, her second novel, *The Kitchen God's Wife*, and fourth novel, *The Bonesetter's Daughter*, were enormous popular and critical successes.

Chronicling the lives of Chinese American women and their Chinese immigrant mothers, These three novels explore the conflicting and confusing emotions associated with female individuation. Like the characters she writes about in *The Joy Luck Club*, *The Kitchen God's Wife*, and *The Bonesetter's Daughter*, Tan admits that she once experienced ambivalent feelings about her Chinese background. However, Tan has said that through writing *The Joy Luck Club* she was able to discover "how very Chinese" she is and how much has stayed with her that she had tried to deny.

Amy Tan comes from a rich tradition of Asian American women writers. Like her predecessor Maxine Hong Kingston, for example, Tan concerns herself with the controversial issue of female individuation and suggests plausible methods for how women can come to a clear understanding of self. Also, like Kingston, Tan uses Chinese myth as a means of explaining and highlighting the problems with self-awareness that many Chinese women experience regardless of whether they are immigrants or native-born Americans of Chinese ancestry.

The singularity of Tan's vision lies in her intense focus on the mother-daughter relationship and her insistence that female individuation occurs ultimately as a result of bringing that particular parent-child relationship into proper order. According to Tan, successful individuation for women involves unification with the mother rather than separation from her. Thus, June May in *The Joy*

Luck Club, Pearl in *The Kitchen God's Wife*, and Ruth Young in *The Bonesetter's Daughter* must mend their broken relationships with their mothers in order to become strong women in their own right. June May's trip to China to fulfill her deceased mother's dream of returning home and finding her other two daughters is an important undertaking. The trip frees her from guilt over the past failures in her relationship with her mother. Likewise, June May comes to understand that the tension that characterized her relationship with her mother resulted more from their similarities than from their differences. This realization, in turn, encourages her to celebrate rather than denounce the likenesses between her mother and herself. She can now be confident and be comfortable with the woman she has become.

In *The Kitchen God's Wife*, Tan highlights the issue of female individuation by narrowing her consideration of the mother-daughter relationship to focus exclusively on Winnie Louie and her daughter Pearl. In so doing she calls particular attention to the relationship between the freed female voice and successful female individuation. Because Winnie finds the freedom to tell her story openly and honestly, she is finally freed from the demons that have haunted her for a lifetime. Pearl, in turn, is freed by her mother's openness and finds the strength to share courageously her own secret. By breaking the silence between them and revealing her secret to her daughter, Winnie makes it possible for Pearl to connect emotionally with her and become a complete person.

In *The Bonesetter's Daughter*, Tan's exploration of the mother-daughter relationship becomes more personal. One character develops Alzheimer's disease, as did Tan's own mother. Tan's works reflect both a traditional and unique perspective on the issue of female individuation and bridge the gap between generations of Asian American women writers. She honestly portrays Asian American women's lives and in so doing gives voice to the joys, fears, defeats, and triumphs of all women.

Cheryl Abrams Collier

Bibliography

Benanni, Ben, ed. *Paintbrush: A Journal of Poetry and Translation* 22 (Autumn, 1995). A special issue of the journal focusing on Tan and on *The Joy Luck Club* in particular. Includes articles on mothers and daughters, memory and forgetting.

Bloom, Harold, ed. *Amy Tan*. Philadelphia: Chelsea House, 2000. Bloom also provides an introduction to the installment in the Modern Critical Views series. Pulls together the comments of contemporary critics.

Cheung, King-Kok. *An Interethnic Companion to Asian American Literature*. Cambridge, England: Cambridge University Press, 1997. An essay collection with a critical overview of Asian American literary studies. Most interesting to readers of Tan's novels are essays by Sau-ling Cynthia Wong, Shirley Geok-lin Lim, Jinqi Ling, and Donald Geollnicht.

Cooperman, Jeannette Batz. *The Broom Closet: Secret Meanings of Domesticity in Postfeminist Novels by Louise Erdrich, Mary Gordan, Toni Morrison, Marge Piercy, Jane Smiley, and Amy Tan*. New York: Peter Lang, 1999. A study of the role of traditionally feminine concerns, such as marriage and family, in the works of these postfeminist writers.

Ho, Wendy. *In Her Mother's House: The Politics of Asian American Mother-Daughter Writing*. Walnut Creek, Calif.: AltaMira Press, 1999. Includes two chapters dedicated specifically to Tan, "Losing Your Innocence But Not Your Hope: Amy Tan's Joy Luck Mothers and Coca-Cola Daughters," and "The Heart Never Travels: The Incorporation of Fathers in the Mother-Daughter Stories of Maxine Hong Kingston, Amy Tan, and Fae Myenne Ng."

Huh, Joonok. *Interconnected Mothers and Daughters in Amy Tan's "The Joy Luck Club."* Tucson, Ariz.: Southwest Institute for Research on Women, 1992. Examines the mother and adult child relationship in Tan's novel. Includes a bibliography.

Huntley, E. D. *Amy Tan: A Critical Companion*. Westport, Conn.: Greenwood Press, 1998. Writing for general readers and students, Huntley introduces and discusses Tan's novels in the context of Asian American fiction. A feature of the book is the incorporation of several critical approaches to the novels. Analyzes major themes such as the crone figure, food, clothing, language, biculturalism, and mothers and daughters. Includes useful bibliography.

Lim, Elaine. *Asian American Literature: An Introduction to the Writings and Their Social Context*. Philadelphia: Temple University Press, 1982. The first critical guide to Asian American literature, Lim's book is an essential introduction to the historical and literary contexts of Tan's work.

Tan, Amy. "Amy Tan." Interview by Barbara Somogyi and David Stanton. *Poets and Writers* 19, no. 5 (September 1, 1991): 24-32. One of the best interviews with Tan. Tan speaks about her childhood and her early career as a business writer, her decision to write fiction, her success with *The Joy Luck Club*, and some of its autobiographical elements.

Jun'ichirō Tanizaki

Japanese novelist

Born: Tokyo, Japan; July 24, 1886
Died: Yugawara, Japan; July 30, 1965

LONG FICTION: *Itansha no kanashimi*, 1917; *Chijin no ai*, 1924-1925 (serial), 1925 (book; *Naomi*, 1985); *Kōjin*, 1926; *Tade kuu mushi*, 1928-1929 (serial), 1936 (book; *Some Prefer Nettles*, 1955); *Manji*, 1928-1930; *Bushūkō hiwa*, 1931-1932 (serial), 1935 (book; *The Secret History of the Lord of Musashi*, 1982); *Sasameyuki*, 1943-1948 (serial), 1949 (book; *The Makioka Sisters*, 1957); *Shōshō Shigemoto no haha*, 1950 (*The Mother of Captain Shigemoto*, 1956); *Kagi*, 1956 (*The Key*, 1960); *Fūten rōjin nikki*, 1961-1962 (serial), 1962 (novella; *Diary of a Mad Old Man*, 1965).

SHORT FICTION: "Kirin," 1910; "Shisei," 1910 ("The Tattooer," 1963); "Shōnen," 1910; "Hōkan," 1911; "Akuma," 1912; "Kyōfu," 1913 ("Terror," 1963); "Otsuya goroshi," 1913; "Haha o kouru ki," 1919 ("Longing for Mother," 1980); "Watakushi," 1921 ("The Thief," 1963); "Aoi Hano," 1922 ("Aguri," 1963); "Mōmoku monogatari," 1931 ("A Blind Man's Tale," 1963); "Ashikari," 1932 (English translation, 1936); "Shunkinshō," 1933 ("A Portrait of Shunkin," 1936); *Hyofu*, 1950; "Yume no ukihashi," 1959 ("The Bridge of Dreams," 1963); *Yume no ukihashi*, 1960; *Kokumin no bungaku*, 1964; *Tanizaki Jun'ichirō shu*, 1970; *Seven Japanese Tales*, 1981; *The Gourmet Club: A Sextet*, 2001 (Anthony H. Chambers and Paul McCarthy, translators).

DRAMA: *Aisureba koso*, pb. 1921; *Okumi to Gohei*, pb. 1922; *Shirogitsune no yu*, pb. 1923 (*The White Fox*, 1930); *Mumyō to Aizen*, pb. 1924; *Shinzei*, pb. 1949.

NONFICTION: *Bunsho no dukohon*, 1934; "In'ei raisan," 1934 ("In Praise of Shadows," 1955); *Kyō no yume, Ōsaka no yume*, 1950; *Yōshō-jidai*, 1957 (*Childhood Years: A Memoir*, 1988).

TRANSLATION: *Genji monogatari*, 1936-1941, 1951-1954 (of Murasaki Shikibu's medieval *Genji monogatari*).

MISCELLANEOUS: *Tanizaki Jun'ichirō zenshu*, 1930 (12 volumes); *Tanizaki Jun'ichirō zenshu*, 1966-1970 (28 volumes).

Jun'ichirō Tanizaki (tahn-ee-zahk-ee) explored Japanese traditionalism and the male infatuation with dominant women in a wide-ranging body of work embracing novels, novellas, short stories, plays, and essays. He was the son of the struggling owner of a printing establishment and spent his childhood growing up in the Nihonbashi section of Tokyo. His mother was quite attractive, and the young Tanizaki, as later autobiographical statements attest, was enthralled by her beauty. He was a handsome youth, often bullied by his classmates. In primary school, his precociousness was recognized by a teacher who guided him in exploring the Japanese and Chinese classics, giving him an early appreciation of traditions and literary aesthetics. At the First Municipal High School in Tokyo, he was an outstanding student and went on to study in the Japanese literature department at Tokyo Imperial University, where he joined the student literary magazine *Shinshichō* (new thought tides). Because he could not pay his university fees, he did not finish his degree studies, choosing instead to pursue writing as a career.

His first substantial works were two plays published in 1910, but it was "The Tattooer," an erotic short story describing the coming to life of a spider etched on the back of a drugged courtesan and the enraptured entrapment of the tattooer in the transformed beauty of his "victim," that launched his literary career. In 1911 this Poe-like creation and other works won for Tanizaki the praise of Nagai Kafū, a writer-critic whom Tanizaki admired and who characterized Tanizaki as a fellow struggler against the prevailing naturalist school of writing and its emphasis on describing reactions to real-life situations. Many of his early works—"Shōnen" (children), "Akuma" (demon), and "Kyōfu" (terror)—reflecting *fin de siècle* influences of Charles Baudelaire, Oscar Wilde, and Edgar Allan Poe and his personal infatuation with the hedonistic macabre, are characterized by "diabolism" (*akumashugi*), his preoccupation with the perverse and deviant.

Tanizaki was married for the first time in 1915; the marriage, which ended in divorce in 1930, was complicated by a liaison between his wife and his friend the writer Haruo Sato and by Tanizaki's fascination for his sister-in-law Seiko. The writer's involved personal life received autobiographical treatment in *Itansha no kanashimi* (sorrows of a heretic), about a gifted writer and the sadistic carnal attentions of his prostitute lover, and "Longing for Mother," published a year after his mother died, concerning the narrator's dream quest for his departed mother. These and other stories, serialized in magazines and newspapers, developed Tanizaki's fixation on women characters representative of the idealized mother or the domineering sexual siren ministering to the lustful desires of emotionally repressed men. Other important writings from this period include an autobiographical novel, a two-act play set in Edo, and a rare political novel, perhaps inspired by the Russian Revolution. Tanizaki also wrote plays in the early 1920's, exploring the theme of guilt and happiness involving two men competing for the love of one woman, and dallied with filmmaking. Important short stories from this period include "The Thief" and "Aguri."

On September 1, 1923, the great Kantō earthquake devastated the Tokyo-Yokohama region, prompting Tanizaki to move to the Osaka region. This move interrupted the writing of *Naomi*, a long work (reminiscent of *Pygmalion*) about the effort to change a Japanese bar girl into a sophisticated woman capable of mingling in refined circles with foreigners. For some years, Tanizaki had been intrigued by the West, considering Europe to be a more vibrant civilization than the Orient. Though his early stories explored dissolute Japanese themes shrouded in the native past, he had, nevertheless, an admiration for things Western, as seen in *Naomi*.

He continued a flirtation with a Western lifestyle while residing near the port city of Kobe with its large foreign enclave, but gradually he discovered in the more traditional ways of the Kansai region (especially as characterized by the softspoken women of the area) an appreciation for vestiges of a fading past which rekindled childhood memories of what was no longer available in a Tokyo being rebuilt into a modern city. This interest in the customs, language, and style of the Osaka-Kyoto-Nara region became manifest in his writings, particularly the serialized novels *Manji* and *Some Prefer Nettles*. The former explored the intertwined relationship of two men and two women who relate to shared events from their different perspectives. Tanizaki had the dialogue translated into the Kansai dialect to give the story a sense of location. *Some Prefer Nettles* went beyond the contemporary localism of *Manji* to mark a complete return to the author's nativist roots. Kaname, the main character, in the midst of a failing marriage complicated by a Eurasian prostitute who merely satisfies him and a wife, Misako, who is leaving him for her lover, becomes captivated by the harmonious traditional relationship between his father-in-law and his young mistress, Ohisa. In exploring what is lacking in his own "modern" relationships and discovering what his in-law has in his, Kaname comes to an appreciation of old Japan.

Tanizaki married a young Kansai woman in 1931, but he soon became infatuated with Matsuko Morita (who became his third and last wife), the wife of a wealthy merchant, who inspired him to write "A Blind Man's Tale" and *The Secret History of the Lord of Musashi*. Other important works from this time are "Ashikari" and "A Portrait of Shunkin." These writings reflected what Tanizaki described in his 1934 essay "In Praise of Shadows" as a preference for the traditional aesthetic over glaring modernism.

The Makioka Sisters, a novel chronicling the history of a declining Osaka family in the prewar years, was banned by the wartime military authorities for its acceptance of Westernisms. When the book was fully published in the late 1940's, it won several awards and reestablished Tanizaki's reputation. Tanizaki returned to Heian Japan for inspiration in *The Mother of Captain Shigemoto* to reconstruct fictitiously the perverse romance of a famous courtier and her lover. The story of an aged professor's sexual dalliances related in his and his wife's diaries in *The Key*, published in the *Chūō Kōron* journal, was a huge success. "The Bridge of Dreams" once again delved into the theme of mother fixation. *Diary of a Mad Old Man*, a humorous account of love in old age, was his last major work.

Analyses of Tanizaki's literary career usually focus on the transitions in his life and the resulting effects on his writings. The decadent fascination with fetishes, sadism, excreta, and other perversities found in his early fiction are attributed to personal sexual ambivalances stemming from his childhood maternal fixation and adult marriage problems, expressed in a writing style liberated by exposure to Western writers. With his move to the Kansai region and ensuing disenchantment with occidental modernity, Tanizaki is said to have turned to the Japanese past as a new source of exoticism. During this middle period, he eschewed current events, returning to the classical and medieval ages for inspiration. With the completion of *The Makioka Sisters*, he turned to the recent but disappearing past while accepting the modernity of the times. His postwar writings were freed from an obsession with the past, and his lifelong exploration of sensual idealism was resuscitated in his final works.

The shifts from occidentalism to orientalism or from diabolism to classicism that many see in Tanizaki's oeuvre are debatable. What transcends these speculations is the indisputable quality of literary craftsmanship shown in Tanizaki's mastery of language and sensory detail (smells, tastes, sounds, colors) employed in an exploration of the hedonistically decadent. Weak men sexually enraptured by demoniac femmes fatales and haunting mother figures provide the motifs for delving into tradition and history. In 1927 the novelist Ryūnosuke Akutagawa criticized Tanizaki for his fixation on the fanciful and depraved at the cost of artistic value. Tanizaki rejected this critique, defending the "architectural beauty" of his writings. Indeed, despite the infatuation with prurient elements, his fiction captures an elemental Japaneseness expressed in an aesthetic of sensuality indelibly stamped with the author's personality.

William M. Zanella

Bibliography

Chambers, Anthony Hood. *The Secret Window: Ideal Worlds in Tanizaki's Fiction*. Cambridge, Mass.: Harvard University Press, 1994. Chapters on "ideal worlds," *The Secret History of the Lord of Musashi*, "A Portrait of Shunkin," *The Makioka Sisters*, *The Mother of Captain Shigemoto*, and "The Bridge of Dreams." Includes notes and bibliography.

Gessel, Van C. *Three Modern Novelists: Soseki, Tanizaki, Kawabata*. New York: Kodansha International, 1993. Concentrates on Tanizaki's handling of the theme of modernism. With detailed notes but no bibliography.

Golley, Gregory L. "Tanizaki Junichiro: The Art of Subversion and the Subversion of Art." *The Journal of Japanese Studies* 21 (Summer, 1995): 365-404. Examines the "return to Japan" inaugurated by Tanizaki's *Some Prefer Nettles*.

Ito, Ken K. *Visions of Desire: Tanizaki's Fictional Worlds*. Stanford, Calif.: Stanford University Press, 1991. Chapters on Tanizaki's handling of the "Orient" and the "West," on his treatment of the past, "The Vision of the Blind," "Fair Dreams of Hanshin," "Writing as Power," and "A Mad Old Man's World." Includes notes, bibliography, and a section on names and sources.

Lippit, Noriko Miuta. *Reality and Fiction in Modern Japanese Literature*. White Plains, N.Y.: M. E. Sharpe, 1980. Sections on Tanizaki deal with his aesthetic preference for fantasy and complex structure, with a comparison to Edgar Allan Poe. Includes notes.

Peterson, Gwenn Boardman. *The Moon in the Water: Understanding Tanizaki, Kawabata, and Mishima*. Honolulu: University of Hawaii Press, 1979. The section on Tanizaki includes discussions of "Fifty Years of Meiji Man," "Reality and Illusion:

Dream and Shadow," "The Ambiguities of Love and Marriage," "Chronicles of Modern Japan," and works available in English as well as a partial chronology.

Rubin, Jay. *Injurious to Public Morals: Writers and the Meiji State*. Seattle: University of Washington Press, 1984. The author tackles censorship in Japan and analyzes the relationship between writers and the government. The sections on Tanizaki, an apolitical period writer, suggest ways censorship affected his early career. Contains interesting discussions of the bans on his short stories. Includes chronology, notes, bibliography, and an index.

Suzuki, Tomi. *Narrating the Self: Fictions of Japanese Modernity*. Stanford, Calif.: Stanford University Press, 1996. See especially the epilogue, "Tanizaki's Speaking Subject and the Creation of Tradition." Includes notes and bibliography.

Thornbury, Barbara E. "Kagura, Chaban, and the Awaji Puppet Theatre: A Literary View of Japan's Performing Arts." *Theatre Survey* 35 (May, 1994): 55-64. Discusses the traditional performing works of Tanizaki Jun'ichirō and Uno Chiyo; claims that for both authors the traditional performing arts were a connection between the present and past, an important element in Japan's cultural identity—and one that could be lost.

Booth Tarkington

American novelist

Born: Indianapolis, Indiana; July 29, 1869
Died: Indianapolis, Indiana; May 19, 1946

LONG FICTION: *The Gentleman from Indiana*, 1899; *Monsieur Beaucaire*, 1900; *The Conquest of Canaan*, 1905; *His Own People*, 1907; *The Flirt*, 1913; *Penrod*, 1914; *The Turmoil*, 1915; *Penrod and Sam*, 1916; *Seventeen*, 1916; *The Magnificent Ambersons*, 1918; *Ramsey Milholland*, 1919; *Alice Adams*, 1921; *Gentle Julia*, 1922; *The Midlander*, 1923; *Growth*, 1923 (includes *The Turmoil*, *The Magnificent Ambersons*, and *The Midlander*, the last here renamed *National Avenue*); *Penrod Jashber*, 1929; *Young Mrs. Greeley*, 1929; *Presenting Lily Mars*, 1933; *Little Orvie*, 1934; *The Heritage of Hatcher Ide*, 1941; *The Fighting Littles*, 1941; *Kate Fennigate*, 1943; *Image of Josephine*, 1945.

SHORT FICTION: *In the Arena*, 1905; *The Fascinating Stranger, and Other Stories*, 1923.

DRAMA: *The Guardian*, pb. 1907 (with Harry Leon Wilson); *Mister Antonio*, pr. 1916; *The Gibson Upright*, pb. 1919 (with Wilson); *Clarence*, pr. 1919.

NONFICTION: *The World Does Move*, 1928 (reminiscence).

Newton Booth Tarkington was born in Indianapolis, Indiana, on July 29, 1869. He attended Phillips Exeter Academy and Purdue University and graduated from Princeton University. Primarily interested in art, he had hoped to make drawing his career, but financial necessity turned him to writing. He was a prolific writer, with successful ventures in the short story and the drama, but it is chiefly as a novelist that he is remembered. After an inauspicious beginning he gradually achieved popularity among readers and considerable acclaim from critics. His first popular success in fiction was *Monsieur Beaucaire*, a romantic novella that helped call attention to his first novel, *The Gentleman from Indiana*, which had appeared a year before, in 1899. Today Tarkington is perhaps most widely known for his stories of youth and teenagers: *Penrod, Penrod and Sam, Penrod Jashber*, and *Seventeen*. These are "American boy" stories, comic but human and appealing. The Penrod books, extremely popular and financially rewarding for Tarkington, were among the first contemporary novels to be adapted to film. His most critically acclaimed novel, *Alice Adams*, appeared in 1921 and won the Pulitzer Prize in fiction in 1922. *The Magnificent Ambersons* had earlier won the same prize. In 1933 Tarkington was awarded the Gold Medal of the National Institute of Arts and Letters. Tarkington was twice married, to Laurel Louisa Fletcher in 1902 and to Susannah Robinson in 1912.

Tarkington suffered difficulties with his eyesight for years and became totally blind in 1930, but his sight was partially restored by a series of operations. For the last thirty-five years of his life he divided his time between his family home in Indianapolis and the summer resort in Kennebunkport, Maine, that he called "the house that Penrod built."

Richard A. Hill

Bibliography

Fennimore, Keith J. *Booth Tarkington*. New York: Twayne, 1974. A volume in Twayne's United States Authors series, this book is an excellent introduction to Tarkington's life and works.

LeGates, Charlotte. "The Family in Booth Tarkington's Growth Trilogy." *Midamerica: The Yearbook of the Society for the Study of Midwestern Literature* 6 (1979): 88-99. The family occupies the center of Tarkington's world, and LeGates's discussion of it is exemplary.

Mayberry, Susanah. *My Amiable Uncle: Recollections About Booth Tarkington*. West Lafayette, Ind.: Purdue University Press, 1983. An important contribution to the biography of Tarkington.

Noverr, Douglass A. "Change, Growth, and the Human Dilemma in Booth Tarkington's *The Magnificent Ambersons*." *Society for the Study of Midwestern Literature Newsletter* 11 (1981): 14-32. This article treats primarily one novel, but it has value for anyone seeking to understand the major themes of Tarkington's work.

Woodress, James. *Booth Tarkington, Gentleman from Indiana*. Philadelphia: Lippincott, 1955. An important biography of Tarkington, this volume offers some analysis of the novels. Considered the standard biography by many critics.

Andrey Tarkovsky

Russian director and screenwriter

Born: Moscow, Soviet Union (now in Russia); April 4, 1932
Died: Paris, France; December 29, 1986

SCREENPLAYS: *Katok i skripka*, 1960 (with Andrey Mikhalkov-Konchalovsky; *The Steamroller and the Violin*, 1981); *Ivanovo detstvo*, 1962 (with Mikhail Papava and Vladimir Bogomolov; based on Bogomolov's novella *Ivan*; *My Name Is Ivan*, 1963, also known as *Ivan's Childhood*); *Andrei Rublev*, 1966 (with Mikhalkov-Konchalovsky; English translation, 1968 [censored version], 1983 [original version]); *Solaris*, 1972 (with Friedrich Gorenstein; based on Stanisław Lem's novel); *Zerkalo*, 1974 (with Aleksandr Misharin; *The Mirror*, 1983); *Ctankep*, 1979 (*Stalker*, 1982); *Nostalghia*, 1983 (with Tonino Guerra; *Nostalgia*, 1984); *Offret*, 1986 (*The Sacrifice*, 1986).

NONFICTION: *Die Versiegelte Zeit*, 1986 (*Sculpting in Time: Reflections on the Cinema*, 1986); *Time Within Time: The Diaries, 1970-1986*, 1991.

Between 1962 and 1986, Andrey Arsenyevich Tarkovsky (tahr-KAWF-skee) directed some of the best films of the twentieth century. Ingmar Bergman called him "the most important director of our time." Born in Moscow and raised in Tuchkovo, Tarkovsky was always torn between his Russian roots and his international role as an artist. Soviet authorities restricted the release and promotion of his films in Russia and abroad. When he defected to the West in July, 1984, it was with profound ambivalence: Like the character in his 1983 film *Nostalgia*, he suffered from a powerful sense of disorientation, homesickness, and loss. He died two years later in Paris, from cancer, at the age of fifty-six.

Tarkovsky's films show an unrelenting concern for the human spirit in an age of rapid technological advances. Humankind, he believed, must turn inward and renew its concern with spirituality or else run the risk of self-annihilation. His final film, *The Sacrifice*, is a testament to this idea: A man takes drastic personal action—he burns down his house and refuses to speak—as a nuclear war looms imminent. Tarkovsky certainly did not see the materialistic, consumer-oriented West as the answer to the world's spiritual woes. His films explore the boundaries of personal freedom versus an ideal moral order; this duality serves as the fundamental conflict of his protagonists. They want unlimited freedom, but they strive to realize moral perfection.

Tarkovsky spent his early childhood in Tuchkovo, a rural farming village. His father, a soldier in World War II, came home intermittently. His mother stayed home at the family farm and took care of the children. Tarkovsky idealized his parents. His father, Arseniy, was a poet and translator; his mother, Maria Ivanovna, was an actress. Andrey knew that he also would work in the arts but did not know exactly how.

After leaving the Institute of Oriental Languages in 1954, Tarkovsky spent a year as a geological prospector in Siberia. His work involved solitary walks for hundreds of miles over vast, desolate landscapes. This experience undoubtedly shows in his films; they are often set in extreme, remote locales, the severity of which puts his characters to constant tests of faith.

Tarkovsky graduated from the All-Union State Cinematography Institute in 1960. His first major film, *Ivan's Childhood*, won the Golden Lion prize at the Venice Film Festival in 1962. The film tells the story of a Russian boy's daring reconnaissance efforts during World War II. Tarkovsky saw *Ivan's Childhood* as a turning point; its success gave him confidence in his abilities as a director and visual poet—he created ingenious filmic images. Falling snow, for example, is later echoed by falling bits of paper, shredded documents, as the Russians enter Berlin.

In *Andrei Rublev*, Tarkovsky depicted the great Russian icon painter in the turbulent Middle Ages. Growing up in a monastery, Rublev painted with talent, but it was only after he saw the horrors of the outside world (Tartars on horseback killing people with abandon, pagans holding fertility rites) did he learn to paint with passion. The film illustrates Tarkovsky's belief that personal convictions must be validated by actual experience to have true value.

The 1972 film *Solaris* takes place on a space station above a planet whose seas produce hallucinations in the minds of their observers. The protagonist, Kelvin, is confronted with a replication of his wife, who had killed herself on Earth. His conscience brings her back and allows him to try to right his past behavior. Tarkovsky's visual poetry achieves a dazzling beauty in this film. He compares flowing algae to Kelvin's wife's hair to tassles on her shawl. *Solaris* is also a sort of meditation on immortality—how people live on after they die.

The Mirror is Tarkovsky's most autobiographical film. For its setting, he returned to his childhood home and rebuilt the house in which he had once lived, to re-create the past. He even rented a neighboring field and planted buckwheat, the crop that grew there when he was young. His mother's character is central to *The Mirror*; the same actress, Margarita Terekhova, plays both his wife and mother.

With *Stalker* in 1979, Tarkovsky returned to science fiction. A "zone" is established when a meteorite destroys a village. The zone is a treacherous forbidden place navigated by "stalkers" who serve as guides. On this occasion, a stalker escorts a scientist and a writer to seek the special room in the village where one's most longed-for desires can be obtained.

Tarkovsky's last two films were made outside Russia. *Nostalgia*, filmed in Italy and cowritten with his friend Tonino Guerra, depicts the struggles of a Russian poet as he researches the life of a Russian émigré musician. The poet is distraught with longing for his native land and family. He is torn between the past and present, between love for his wife and feelings for his beautiful Italian translator. *The Sacrifice*, filmed in Sweden with the help of Ingmar Bergman's production team, is set at a house by a seacoast as a nuclear war becomes inevitable. The film questions what individuals can do to avert such a catastrophe and wonders if love expressed through sacrifice is an appropriate response.

Alan Ziskin

Bibliography

"Back to the Future, Soviet Style." *Premiere* 3, no. 10 (June, 1990): 38. A favorable review of the video release of Tarkovsky's 1972 film *Solaris*.

LeFanu, Mark. *The Cinema of Andrei Tarkovsky*. London: BFI, 1987. Provides excellent criticism of each film and makes insightful observations about Tarkovsky's work as a whole.

Liehm, Mira, and Antonin Liehm. *The Most Important Art: Eastern European Film After 1945*. Berkeley: University of California Press, 1977. Survey of postwar film production in Eastern Europe; includes several indexes and a bibliography.

Tarkovsky, Andrey. *Time Within Time: The Diaries*. New York: Verso, 1993. Includes interviews with the filmmaker.

Turovskaya, Maya. *Tarkovsky: Cinema as Poetry*. Boston: Faber & Faber, 1989. Includes an introduction by Ian Christie as well as an index and a bibliography.

Torquato Tasso

Italian poet and playwright

Born: Sorrento, Kingdom of Naples (now in Italy); March 11, 1544
Died: Rome (now in Italy); April 25, 1595

POETRY: *Rinaldo*, 1562 (English translation, 1792); *Gerusalemme liberata*, 1581 (*Jerusalem Delivered*, 1600); *Rime*, 1581, 1591, 1593 (*From the Italian of Tasso's Sonnets*, 1867); *Gerusalemme conquistata*, 1593 (*Jerusalem Conquered*, 1907); *Le sette giornate del mondo creato*, 1607.

DRAMA: *Aminta*, pr. 1573 (verse play; English translation, 1591); *Il re Torrismondo*, pb. 1587 (verse play).

NONFICTION: *Allegoria del poema*, 1581; *Dialoghi*, 1581; *Apologia*, 1586; *Discorsi dell'arte poetica*, 1587; *Lettere*, 1587, 1588, 1616-1617; *Discorsi del poema eroico*, 1594 (*Discourses on the Heroic Poem*, 1973).

Torquato Tasso (TAHS-soh) was the son of Bernardo Tasso, a famous Italian poet exiled from Naples during his son's childhood. Tasso spent his early years in Naples with his mother, who sent him to school with the Jesuits. When he was ten, he joined his father at Pesaro, where he and the heir to the duke of Urbino were tutored together. In 1557 his father sent him to study law at the University of Padua. Finding the law uninteresting, he turned before long to the study of philosophy and poetry. A few of his poems appeared as early as 1561, but real fame came with the publication of *Rinaldo*, a romantic epic published while the eighteen-year-old author was still a student at Padua.

After a short period of study at the University of Bologna, Tasso returned to Padua, and by 1565 he had found a wealthy patron in Cardinal Luigi d'Este, a member of the noble house of Ferrara that Tasso was to celebrate in his *Jerusalem Delivered* (the later title of an epic poem that he had begun at Bologna). The next five years of his life were happy and busy ones, except for the death of his father in 1569. A year later Tasso traveled with the cardinal to Paris, where he met a number of French writers of the period. A short time later a difference of opinion on religious matters caused him to exchange the cardinal's patronage for that of Duke Alfonso d'Este of Ferrara. *Aminta*, Tasso's charming pastoral drama, added to his literary fame after its initial presentation at Ferrara in 1573.

Jerusalem Delivered, Tasso's masterpiece, was completed the following year and was read publicly to the duke of Ferrara and the court in 1575. Having chosen Vergil as his model, Tasso followed the Roman poet's strict adherence to unity, style, and form but with the addition of a Christianity so ardent that he went repeatedly to the Inquisition to confess his fears that he and the work might be unintentionally heterodox. The subject matter of the poem is the First Crusade, the theme dealing with the efforts of the forces of evil, personified by the beautiful sorceress Armida, to keep the crusaders under Godfrey of Bouillon from capturing the Holy City. Although classic in form, the poem is closer to medieval romance in its use of allegory and in the romantic interest supplied by love affairs between Christian knights and pagan heroines. Following the reading of *Jerusalem Delivered*, Tasso became ill, probably of malaria, and suffered delusions that attempts were being made on his life. When he asked for permission to leave the court, the duke was patient but firm in his refusal; perhaps he feared that Tasso, if angered or allowed to leave Ferrara, might dedicate his poem to the Medici family of Florence. Probably Tasso became temporarily insane about this time, for in 1577 he was placed under the medical care of the Franciscans at Ferrara.

In July of that year he escaped, disguised as a peasant, and went to Sorrento to take refuge with his sister Cornelia. His condition improved, and he was in Ferrara again in 1578. After a year spent wandering about Italy, he returned to Ferrara and openly accused Duke Alfonso of trying to poison him. He was then confined to an insane asylum for seven years. Although denied liberty of movement, he was permitted to receive visitors and was given spacious apartments in which to live. In 1580, an inaccurate partial version of *Jerusalem Delivered* was printed in Venice under the title *Goffredo*. A year later the complete work was published at Ferrara under its present title, *Jerusalem Delivered*. Publication was by order of the duke after Tasso's manuscript had been seized along with his other effects. When the work appeared, he received nothing for the poem which made him famous throughout Europe.

Through the effects of friendly Vincenzio Gonzaga, prince of Mantua, Tasso was released in 1586 and allowed to go to Mantua to live under the protection of the prince. There he wrote *Il re Torrismondo* before he became a wanderer again. From 1587 to 1594 he traveled aimlessly about Europe, a victim of physical illness, mental weakness, and poverty. *Jerusalem Conquered*, a sequel to *Jerusalem Delivered* (but a much inferior work), was published in 1593. In 1594 arrangements were made to crown him poet laureate at the court of Pope Clement VIII and to grant him a suitable pension. Honors and money came too late. Before the ceremony could be performed, Tasso retired to the monastery of St. Onofrio, near Rome, and announced that he was entering the monastery to die, as he did less than a month later, on April 25, 1595—the very day scheduled for his crowning. The laurel wreath was laid on his coffin.

James S. Whitlark

Bibliography

Boulting, William. *Tasso and His Times*. New York: Haskell House, 1968. A biography of Tasso that places him in context, identifying the influences on his work.

Looney, Dennis. *Compromising the Classics: Romance Epic Narrative in the Italian Renaissance*. Detroit: Wayne State University Press, 1996. Looney examines Italian Romance epic narratives, including those of Tasso, Matteo Maria Boiardo, and Lodovico Ariosto. Includes a bibliography and an index.

Niccoli, Gabriel Adriano. *Cupid, Satyr, and the Golden Age: Pastoral Dramatic Scenes of the Late Renaissance*. New York: Peter Lang, 1989. Niccoli examines the works of a number of pastoral dramatists from the late Renaissance, including Tasso's *Aminta*. Bibliography and index included.

Reynolds, Henry. *Tasso's "Aminita" and Other Poems*. Salzburg, Austria: Instit für Anglistik und Amerikanistik, Universität Salzburg, 1991. A modern publication of seventeenth century writer Reynolds's analysis of Tasso's famous work. Includes a bibliography and an index.

Allen Tate

American poet and biographer

Born: Winchester, Kentucky; November 19, 1899
Died: Nashville, Tennessee; February 9, 1979

POETRY: *The Golden Mean, and Other Poems*, 1923 (with Ridley Wills); *Mr. Pope, and Other Poems*, 1928; *Poems, 1928-1931*, 1932; *The Mediterranean, and Other Poems*, 1936; *Selected Poems*, 1937; *The Winter Sea*, 1944; *Poems, 1920-1945*, 1947; *Poems, 1922-1947*, 1948; *Poems*, 1960; *The Swimmers, and Other Selected Poems*, 1971; *Collected Poems, 1919-1976*, 1977.

LONG FICTION: *The Fathers*, 1938.

NONFICTION: *Stonewall Jackson: The Good Soldier*, 1928; *Jefferson Davis: His Rise and Fall*, 1929; *Reactionary Essays on Poetry and Ideas*, 1936; *Reason in Madness, Critical Essays*, 1941; *On the Limits of Poetry: Selected Essays, 1928-1948*, 1948; *The Hovering Fly, and Other Essays*, 1949; *The Forlorn Demon: Didactic and Critical Essays*, 1953; *The Man of Letters in the Modern World: Selected Essays, 1928-1955*, 1955; *Collected Essays*, 1959; *Essays of Four Decades*, 1968; *The Poetry Reviews of Allen Tate, 1924-1944*, 1983.

John Orley Allen Tate was born in Winchester, Kentucky, on November 19, 1899, the third son of Eleanor Varnell and John Orley Tate. His early education was somewhat sporadic, but in 1918 he entered Vanderbilt University, where he began to dedicate himself to literature in the company of such writers as John Crowe Ransom, Donald Davidson, and Robert Penn Warren, with whom he was active in the Fugitive and Agrarian movements. In 1924 Tate married Caroline Gordon. In 1959 he married Isabella Gardner, and, in 1966, Helen Heinz.

Best known as a poet, Tate is also the author of biographies of Stonewall Jackson and Jefferson Davis as well as of *The Fathers*, a complex, brilliant novel set against the background of the Civil War. His many critical essays have constituted a shaping force in modern literature. In addition, he served as consultant in poetry to the Library of Congress (1943-1944), edited *The Sewanee Review* (1944-1945), and taught at several universities, including Princeton, the University of North Carolina at Greensboro, and the University of Minnesota.

Tate's earlier poetry, best represented by the famous "Ode to the Confederate Dead," is classical in attitude as well as in execution. The ode is a profound meditation which transcends its nominal subject to treat the theme of the self's struggles in a faithless era. Another major poem, "The Mediterranean," parallels Tate's interest in his own past with Aeneas's search for a home after the fall of Troy. In later poetry, Tate softened the austerity of his classicism in poems which seek to integrate physical and imaginative vision; these efforts culminate in "The Maimed Man," "The Swimmers," and "The Buried Lake."

As a critic, Tate has been identified with the New Critics, who argued for the autonomous nature of the literary work, the reading of which should not be influenced by knowledge external to the work itself. It should be noted, however, that his approach to literature did not employ the "scientific" method of such New Critics as I. A. Richards. In an almost Socratic fashion, Tate sought to unravel in detail the terms on which a literary work presents itself to a reader. Allen Tate's essays and poems, each shedding light on the other, stand as major achievements in American literature.

Jonathan S. Cullick

Bibliography

Bishop, Ferman. *Allen Tate*. New York: Twayne, 1967. Though composed while Tate was still writing, Bishop's book offers a good survey of his life and work up to that point; Tate's final years did not change much. Includes chronology, detailed notes and references, and select bibliography.

Brooks, Cleanth, and Allen Tate. *Cleanth Brooks and Allen Tate: Collected Letters, 1933-1976*. Edited by Alphonse Vinh. Columbia: University of Missouri Press, 1998. A selection of letters that constitute a feisty and enjoyable account of the history of two leading participants in the literary critical wars during an era when the way to read and to teach poetry in the English language was being profoundly recast.

Dupree, Robert S. *Allen Tate and the Augustinian Imagination: A Study of the Poetry*. Baton Rouge: Louisiana State University Press, 1983. Dupree has accomplished here a thorough traversal of Tate's poetry, but he does confine his attention to the poetry. His approach is methodical and comprehensive, disclosing ingenious insights. Includes an index, a bibliography, and notes.

Hammer, Langdon. *Hart Crane and Allen Tate*. Princeton, N.J.: Princeton University Press, 1993. Three chapters are devoted to Tate, the focus of the study being on the two poets' relationship within the framing context of literary modernism. Includes bibliography, index.

Huff, Peter A. *Allen Tate and the Catholic Revival: Trace of the Fugitive Gods*. New York: Paulist Press, 1996. Examines Tate in the context of the Catholic Revival following the "lost generation" post-World War I years. Tate incorporated the revival's Christian humanism into his critique of secular industrial society.

Squires, Radcliffe. *Allen Tate: A Literary Biography*. New York: Bobbs-Merrill, 1971. Written before Tate's death, this book is primarily a writing biography—that is, it considers the life of the writer with reference to his writings. Benefits from the personal acquaintance of Squires with Tate. Contains much anecdotal material, bibliography, indexes, and notes.

_______, ed. *Allen Tate and His Work: Critical Evaluations*. Minneapolis: University of Minnesota Press, 1972. Squires here assembles essays on all phases of Tate's writing, editing, teaching, and life. Contains a bibliography.

Stewart, John Lincoln. *The Burden of Time: The Fugitives and the Agrarians*. Princeton, N.J.: Princeton University Press, 1965. This study focuses more on the intellectual movements associated with Tate than on Tate himself. Because, however, these movements formed a large part of his life, they are revealing. Includes substantial comments on both poetry and criticism, and the coverage is thorough and deep. Includes footnotes and a bibliography.

Underwood, Thomas A. *Allen Tate: Orphan of the South*. Princeton, N.J.: Princeton University Press, 2000. A biographical study of Tate and his part in the Agrarian and Fugitive movements. Includes bibliographical references and index.

James Tate

American poet

Born: Kansas City, Missouri; December 8, 1943

POETRY: *The Lost Pilot*, 1967; *The Oblivion Ha-Ha*, 1970; *Hints to Pilgrims*, 1971, 1982; *Absences: New Poems*, 1972; *Viper Jazz*, 1976; *Riven Doggeries*, 1979; *Constant Defender*, 1983; *Reckoner*, 1986; *Distance from Loved Ones*, 1990; *Selected Poems*, 1991; *Worshipful Company of Fletchers*, 1994; *Shroud of the Gnome*, 1997; *Police Story*, 1999; *Memoir of the Hawk*, 2001.
LONG FICTION: *Lucky Darryl*, 1977 (with Bill Knott).
SHORT FICTION: *Hottentot's Ossuary*, 1974; *Dreams of a Robot Dancing Bee: Forty-four Stories*, 2002.
NONFICTION: *The Route as Briefed*, 1999.
EDITED TEXT: *The Best American Poetry, 1997*, 1997.

James Vincent Tate grew up in the Midwest and was educated at the University of Missouri at Columbia and at Kansas State College, where he received his B.A. He began writing poems seriously during these years and, on the basis of their quality, he was admitted to the University of Iowa's Creative Writing program, one of the best of its kind. By the time he received his M.F.A. degree in 1967, he had begun a teaching career of his own and achieved some small acclaim as a poet. From 1966 to 1967, he subsidized his studies as a graduate instructor and saw a few of his poems collected in a small monograph printed in limited edition, *Cages*, as well as anthologized in *Poets of the Heartland*. Shortly thereafter he won the Yale Younger Poets Series competition, which led to the publication of his first full-fledged book of poems, *The Lost Pilot*. It was an auspicious debut. Tate, the series' youngest winner, was hailed as one of the most promising voices of his generation.

He spent the 1967 to 1968 academic year at the University of California at Berkeley as a visiting lecturer, after which he returned to the East Coast and for two years taught at Columbia University. After spending 1970 to 1971 in Boston as poet-in-residence at Emerson College, he began teaching at the University of Massachusetts at Amherst. By this time Tate had to his credit nearly a dozen monograph-length works published in limited editions by fine arts presses; a second book, *The Oblivion Ha-Ha*, issued by a major publisher (Little, Brown); a third book, *Absences*, nearing publication; and a lengthy list of publications in an array of magazines and literary journals, including *The New Yorker*, *The Nation*, and the *Paris Review*.

Tate went on to win the Pulitzer Prize in 1991 for his *Selected Poems*, a volume providing striking evidence of his productivity. His other work notwithstanding, *The Lost Pilot* may be his most beloved work, and the one where his most immediate roots as poet are to be found. In this work can be heard echoes of such Midwestern poets as John Knoepfle, Father Raymond Roseliep, or David Madden.

If his roots are in evidence, however, so are concerns that proved to be central to Tate's later works. At the time of Tate's birth, his father was a pilot serving overseas in the Army Air Corps; he was killed in 1944 before seeing his child. In "The Lost Pilot," which is dedicated to his father, Tate ponders with childlike wonder the ties he feels toward a man he never knew; in his imagination and soul his father is alive to a degree he probably never would have been had he survived. "The Book of Lies" begins with the lines "I'd like to have a word/ with you. Could we be alone/ for a minute? I have been lying/ until now . . . ." In these poems and elsewhere in the volume can be seen the need to bridge the gulf between the speaker of the poem and a world beyond, a search for a language and a voice that can somehow make sense of personal experience and articulate it in ways that make sense publicly.

Though the style of Tate's next books is different, the same kind of concern can be seen in such poems as "Shadowboxing," in which through a metaphor supplied by the title Tate examines the tension that binds lovers together at the same time it keeps them apart: "Come here, let me touch you, you say./ He comes closer. Come close, you say. Then. *Whack!* And/ you start again, moving around and around . . ."

In his work, Tate addresses how and why people are better defined by the absences in their lives than by that which they can inventory; throughout there is a search for a language with which to codify and organize the experiences that make human beings most human. The best of Tate's later work builds upon what was accomplished earlier. Here, too, the loneliness of the human condition remains his central concern. The title poem of *The Lost Pilot*, for example, is recalled in the title poem of *Distance from Loved Ones*, which ponders the intimacies shared by parent and child at the same time that it explores how those roles keep the two apart.

In *Worshipful Company of Fletchers*, which won the National Book Award, Tate's mood and style become a little darker. Here, Tate has moved his strategies from previous books into a single thrust of reasoning aimed at the disenchanted world of adulthood and its mundane circumstances. He is the confirmed orphan living without benefit of a father's counsel or affection. In this and succeeding books, the poems report events from a slightly skewed perspective.

Stylistically, an increasing concern with the form of the poems can be discerned. Most notable is Tate's attempt to distill a poetic conceit into the simplest of forms while at the same time the line-by-line appearance of the poem is prosaic. It is as if Tate has become mistrustful of poetic form over the years, or perhaps more aware of the limitations of poetry as a means of connecting human beings.

Jay Boyer

Bibliography

Levis, Larry. "Eden and My Generation." In *Conversant Essays: Contemporary Poets on Poetry*, edited by James McCorkle. Detroit: Wayne State University Press, 1990. A broad-ranging survey of the lines and forces of contemporary poetry, in which James Tate is located, and of its major theme in the loss of Eden.

McDaniel, Craig. "James Tate's Secret Co-Pilot." *New England Review* 23, no. 2 (Spring, 2002): 55-74. Examines Tate's development as a poet in relationship to Fyodor Dostoevski's prose and how it influenced "The Lost Pilot."

Rosen, R. D. "James Tate and Sidney Goldfarb and the Inexhaustible Nature of the Murmur." In *American Poetry Since 1960: Some Critical Perspectives*, edited by Robert B. Shaw. Cheshire, England: Carcanet Press, 1973. Argues that both Tate and Goldfarb belong to a generation that uses poetry to escape from the postwar age; their writing, notes Rosen, is that of moral outlaws.

Tate, James. *The Route as Briefed*. Ann Arbor: University of Michigan Press, 1999. Collects Tate's interviews, essays, and occasional writings together, where he comments on his composing method, or fields questions from various interviewers about the peculiar nature of his lyric arguments, his influences, and the like.

Upton, Lee. *The Muse of Abandonment: Origin, Identity, Mastery in Five American Poets*. London: Associated University Presses, 1998. A critical study of the works of five twentieth century American poets, including Tate, and their points of view on alienation, power, and identity. Includes bibliographical references and index.

Edward Taylor

American poet

Born: Near Sketchley, Leicestershire, England; c. 1645
Died: Westfield, Massachusetts; June 24, 1729

POETRY: *The Poetical Works of Edward Taylor*, 1939 (Thomas H. Johnson, editor); *The Poems of Edward Taylor*, 1960 (Donald E. Stanford, editor); *A Transcript of Edward Taylor's Metrical History of Christianity*, 1962 (Stanford, editor); *Edward Taylor's Minor Poetry*, 1981 (volume 3 of *The Unpublished Writings of Edward Taylor*, 1981; Thomas M. Davis and Virginia L. Davis, editors).

NONFICTION: *Christographia*, 1962 (Norman S. Grabo, editor); *Diary*, 1964 (F. Murphy, editor); *Edward Taylor's Treatise Concerning the Lord's Supper*, 1966 (Grabo, editor).

MISCELLANEOUS: *The Unpublished Writings of Edward Taylor*, 1981 (3 volumes; Thomas M. Davis and Virginia L. Davis, editors).

The manuscripts that contained some three hundred poems by New England mystic Edward Taylor had lain untouched for more than two centuries before they were resurrected by Thomas H. Johnson in 1937. Johnson edited a selection of the poems and in 1939 published them, along with a biographical sketch and a critical introduction, in *The Poetical Works of Edward Taylor*. Taylor, who wrote in a style imitative of the seventeenth century Metaphysical poets, demonstrated a fairly high degree of poetical competency, especially in the long, semidramatic "God's Determinations," which has been called "perhaps the finest single poetic achievement in America before the nineteenth century."

As for the author of the poems, little is known about him before his arrival in Boston in 1668. He was born in or near Sketchley, Leicestershire, probably in the year 1645. He may have attended a Nonconformist school and come to America because he could not take the oath of conformity then demanded of all English clergymen. He may have attended the University of Cambridge or one of the dissenting academies before he left for New England. It is certain, however, that he early began training for the ministry, as he had been brought to the colonies by the Act of Uniformity of Charles II. Passed in 1662, this law required all schoolmasters and ministers to take an oath of allegiance to the Anglican Church, an action he was prevented from taking by his Puritan religious orthodoxy.

Following his arrival in Massachusetts, his activities were well documented. First, he was admitted to Harvard College as a sophomore in 1668 and was given the post of college butler; he graduated in 1671. Next, he went to the settlement of Westfield as minister and remained there for the rest of his life, marrying twice, having fourteen children, acting as a physician, and in general caring for the physical as well as the spiritual well-being of his flock.

All this time he was writing his poetry. He courted his first wife, Elizabeth Fitch of Norwich, Connecticut, through letters and verse and married her in 1674. She gave birth to his first eight children and died fifteen years later. Taylor's grief was recorded in one of his most moving poems, "A Funerall Poem upon the Death of My Ever Endeared and Tender Wife." At the age of about fifty, in 1692, he remarried, to Ruth Wyllys of Hartford, with whom he had six children and who survived him by six months. He received his M.A. degree from Harvard in 1720. The responsibility he bore in meeting his congregation's medical as well as spiritual needs is reflected in his "Preparatory Meditations." The manuscript of his poems was inherited by his grandson, Ezra Stiles, who respected his ancestor's injunction that "his heirs should never publish it." The poems were deposited in the library of Yale College during Stiles's presidency, and they remained there until their discovery in 1937.

Bibliography

Gatta, John. *Gracious Laughter: The Meditative Wit of Edward Taylor.* Columbia: University of Missouri Press, 1989. Gatta, an insightful expositor of Taylor's poetry, opened up a new avenue of inquiry into Taylor's acknowledged supremacy as a colonial poet, positing his wit as the bridge between his theology and his poetics. Includes comprehensive bibliography.

Grabo, Norman. *Edward Taylor.* Rev. ed. Boston: Twayne, 1988. Biocritical introduction to Taylor's life and work is an excellent source of explication of Taylor's aesthetic and theological influences.

Hammond, Jeffrey A. *Edward Taylor: Fifty Years of Scholarship and Criticism.* Columbia, S.C.: Camden House, 1993. Five chapters examine Taylor scholarship in chronological order, from its beginnings to the later decades of the twentieth century. Includes bibliography and index.

Keller, Karl. *The Example of Edward Taylor.* Amherst: University of Massachusetts Press, 1975. A groundbreaking biocritical work of Taylor's poetry. Keller argues convincingly that Taylor must be viewed as a Christian humanist and calls for—and achieves—a reevaluation of Taylor as colonial America's foremost poet and aesthetician.

Miller, David G. *The Word Made Flesh Made Word: The Failure and Redemption of Metaphor in Edward Taylor's "Christographia."* Selinsgrove, Pa.: Susquehanna University Press, 1995. Provides a reading of Taylor's *Christographia* sermon material and a study of the use of metaphorical language in the sermons.

Rowe, Karen E. *Saint and Sinner: Edward Taylor's Typology and the Poetics of Meditation.* Cambridge, England: Cambridge University Press, 1986. Rowe notes the relationship between Puritan typology—its use of Old Testament narratives as a guide to the meaning of the mundane devotional life of colonial believers—and its role in Taylor's craftsmanship as a poet. Includes appendices that examine the relationship between individual Taylor poems and their sources in sermons.

Schuldiner, Michael, ed. *The Tayloring Shop: Essays on the Poetry of Edward Taylor.* Newark: University of Delaware Press, 1997. This collection of critical essays on Taylor's poems provides readers with insights into several traditions of the past that informed Taylor's poetry, from the Puritan concept of nature to Puritan casuistry. Includes bibliographical references and index.

Elizabeth Taylor

English novelist

Born: Reading, Berkshire, England; July 3, 1912
Died: Penn, Buckinghamshire, England; November 19, 1975

LONG FICTION: *At Mrs. Lippincote's*, 1945; *Palladian*, 1946; *A View of the Harbour*, 1947; *A Wreath of Roses*, 1949; *A Game of Hide and Seek*, 1951; *The Sleeping Beauty*, 1953; *Angel*, 1957; *In a Summer Season*, 1961; *The Soul of Kindness*, 1964; *The Wedding Group*, 1968; *Mrs. Palfrey at the Claremont*, 1971; *Blaming*, 1976.

SHORT FICTION: *Hester Lilly, and Twelve Short Stories*, 1954 (pb. in England as *Hester Lilly, and Other Stories*, 1954); *The Blush, and Other Stories*, 1958; *A Dedicated Man, and Other Stories*, 1965; *The Devastating Boys, and Other Stories*, 1972.

CHILDREN'S/YOUNG ADULT LITERATURE: *Mossy Trotter*, 1967.

Elizabeth Taylor was born to Oliver Coles, an insurance inspector, and Elsie Fewtrell Coles, whom Taylor credited with nurturing her imagination and creating an interest in literature. As a child, Elizabeth Coles spent a lot of time in the Reading public library. She attended the Abbey School in Reading. In 1930, at the age of eighteen, she became a governess and a few years later a librarian at High Wycombe. In 1936 she married John William Kendell Taylor, a manufacturer, with whom she had a son, Renny, and a daughter, Joanna.

Elizabeth Taylor began to write in the years following her marriage. Several short stories were published in *Time and Tide*, *Harper's Bazaar*, *Harper's Magazine*, and *Adelphi*. During World War II she lived at Scarborough while her husband was in the Royal Air Force. She drew upon this experience for her first published novel, *At Mrs. Lippincote's*, a comedy of manners that portrays life in wartime England.

After the war she and her family settled in the country village of Penn, Buckinghamshire, which Taylor considered a congenial atmosphere for a novelist. There she wrote a total of twelve novels, four short story collections, and a children's book. *A View of the Harbour* is a satire of the gothic novel. Taylor's lighthearted treatment of the genre is reminiscent of Jane Austen's *Northanger Abbey* (1818). *A View of the Harbour*, which depicts life in an English seaside village, was praised by reviewers for its economy of expression, scenic accuracy, and objective characterizations.

One of Taylor's interests was painting, and in 1949 she presented, in *A Wreath of Roses*, a main character who lives for her art but whose career and idyllic village life are threatened by violence in the form of a strangler—a situation symbolic of the precarious position of civilization in a competitive, materialistic, violent world.

Critics tended to praise Taylor, often comparing her to Austen, Virginia Woolf, Elizabeth Bowen, and Barbara Pym, but she never became widely popular. Bowen and Ivy Compton-Burnett, respected novelists who shared the problem of reaching an audience, wrote to Taylor to offer their appreciation of *A Game of Hide and Seek* in 1951. Bowen compared it to Austen's *Persuasion* (1818) and Emily Brontë's *Wuthering Heights* (1847). Taylor's 1953 novel *The Sleeping Beauty* was another critical success. One aspect that was cited—the comic sense conveyed through the conversation of minor characters—was a technique associated with the work of Compton-Burnett, a writer much admired by Taylor. Her critical study of Compton-Burnett's novels was published by *Vogue*.

In 1954, *Hester Lilly, and Twelve Short Stories* was published, the first of four books of short stories. Taylor's work in this genre produced further critical acclaim. She was called one of the greatest living short-story writers by a critic who, ironically, was not appreciative of her novels. Many of the stories originally appeared in *The New Yorker*. Her association with the magazine helped to increase her popularity, and it also indicated to some critics that she was more than a chronicler of domestic tranquillity. More recent promoters of her fiction include the famous novelists Angus Wilson, Kingsley Amis, Elizabeth Jane Howard, and Anne Tyler.

The 1957 novel *Angel* is considered by many to be the high point of Taylor's output. In 1984 the Book Marketing Council selected it as one of the "Best Novels of Our Time." The work tells the story of Angelica Deverell, a popular author of romantic novels, who is not gifted enough to realize how bad her writing is. Taylor's ability to make this "purveyor of twaddle" into a sympathetic character is an indication of her artistry.

In a Summer Season deals with a middle-aged woman who, to the disapproval of friends, neighbors, and relatives, marries a much younger man. The results are both funny and tragic and are revealed with great skill and elegance, something that can be said about most of Taylor's works. Her subsequent books—*The Soul of Kindness*; *A Dedicated Man, and Other Stories*, *The Wedding Group*, *Mrs. Palfrey at the Claremont*, *The Devastating Boys, and Other Stories*, and the posthumously published *Blaming*—appeared to much critical acclaim but were appreciated by only a small readership. This situation changed, however, in the 1980's, when many of her books were reissued and won a new and much larger audience for Taylor.

Noel Schraufnagel

Bibliography

Baldwin, Dean. "The English Short Story in the Fifties." In *The English Short Story, 1945-1980*, edited by Dennis Vannata. New York: Twayne, 1985. Argues that "shaming nature," which is what Tory does at the beginning of Taylor's story "A Red-Letter Day," is a good description of the theme, for she is unable to connect with her son; she is the prototype of the modern parent—alienated, awkward, divorced—unable to say where she has failed.

Gillette, Jane Brown. "'Oh, What a Something Web We Weave': The Novels of Elizabeth Taylor." *Twentieth Century Literature* 35 (Spring, 1989): 94-112. Discusses Taylor's fiction in three stages: the early period, in which she is critical of the distortion of the imagination; the middle period, in which she moderates her criticism; and the later years, when she celebrates the creative imagination.

Grove, Robin. "From the Island: Elizabeth Taylor's Novels." *Studies in the Literary Imagination* 9 (1978): 79-95. Discusses the critical neglect of Taylor's work. Argues that her books claim that watching the mind's ironies and reflections on itself is a natural and nourishing activity. Discusses the comic nature of her work.

Hicks, Granville. "Amour on the Thames." *Saturday Review* 44 (January 21, 1961): 62. Hicks compares Taylor to Jane Austen. Brief comments about her work generally, with more extended comments on *In a Summer Season*.

Kingham, Joanna. Introduction to *A Dedicated Man, and Other Stories*, by Elizabeth Taylor. London: Virago Press, 1993. An article based on an interview with Taylor in 1971, in which she talks about when and why she started to write, her writing habits, her reactions to feminism, and the things that give her pleasure. Taylor's daughter talks about her childhood and her relationship with her mother.

Leclercq, Florence. *Elizabeth Taylor*. Boston: Twayne, 1985. In this general introduction to Taylor's work, Leclercq says that what makes Taylor's stories so fascinating is her "crystallization of one particular 'moment of being'." Argues that her craft is more clearly defined in her stories than in her novels.

Taylor, Elizabeth. "England." *Kenyon Review*, 1969, 469-473. In her contribution to this symposium on the short story, Taylor says some stories are nearer to poetry than the novel; others are like paintings, full of suggestion and atmosphere; the unity of the short story gives an impression of perfection, of being lifted into another world, instead of sinking into it, as one does with the novel.

Mildred D. Taylor

American novelist

Born: Jackson, Mississippi; September 13, 1943
Identity: African American

CHILDREN'S/YOUNG ADULT LITERATURE: *Song of the Trees*, 1975; *Roll of Thunder, Hear My Cry*, 1976; *Let the Circle Be Unbroken*, 1981; *The Friendship*, 1987; *The Gold Cadillac*, 1987; *The Road to Memphis*, 1990; *Mississippi Bridge*, 1990; *The Well: David's Story*, 1995; *The Land*, 2001.

Mildred Delois Taylor has distinguished and endeared herself to thousands of readers, young and old, through her unique depiction of the American black experience, both painful and joyful, both traumatic and heroic. She was born in the segregated South to parents who did not want to raise their children under racism. When Taylor was still an infant, the family moved from Jackson, Mississippi, to Toledo, Ohio, where her father found employment in a factory. In the course of the family's frequent journeys south to visit relatives, Taylor became sensitive to the different manifestations of racial prejudice in the North and South. The family had to drive through the night when motels did not accept them, and they had to avoid the main roads for fear of being pulled over and harassed by police. (The story of such humiliation and fear would eventually be told in her novella *The Gold Cadillac*.) Taylor also learned a great deal about the South through the family stories that riveted her attention and that would provide both the inspiration and much of the content for her Logan stories.

Racism was not confined to the South, however. On a family trip to California when she was nine, Taylor discovered that for them second-class citizenship stretched from coast to coast: There were motels and restaurants all along the way that did not welcome blacks. She learned more about America when she and her family moved into a solid middle-class neighborhood and watched their white neighbors raise the For Sale signs in their front yards. The desire to tell the truth of her people's experience grew inside the young student, especially when she noted again and again that her school texts consistently rendered a distorted version of black history in America. However, the stories she wrote during her high school and college years were not yet publishable, and her aspirations to become a writer were put on hold when, after graduating from the University of Toledo in 1965, Taylor joined the Peace Corps and taught English and history for two very happy years in Ethiopia. In September, 1968, she enrolled in the School of Journalism at the University of Colorado. There she also became a leader in the Black Student Alliance, which helped bring about black studies and black education programs on many campuses.

Eventually Taylor settled in Los Angeles, where she began to pursue the art of writing seriously. It was there too that she married a man from Central America in 1972. Although the marriage would fail, her writing did not. In October, 1973, she entered a writing contest sponsored by the Council on Interracial Books for Children. A few months later she learned that she had won; the signing of her first book contract followed, and in the spring of 1975 *Song of the Trees* introduced the Logan family to the reading public. This novella, based on family history, presents a unified black family whose dignity and pride as landowners make them stand tall against the white racists who tried to steal their trees. The work was cited as an Outstanding Book of the Year by *The New York Times*. Taylor's dream had come true: She had become an author.

The Logan books that followed continued to reflect the writer's immersion in the family story-well, filled during those many visits to the South when young Mildred had eagerly soaked up from her father and her uncles the oral history of black families and characters whose courage and self-respect defied the racism that tried to reduce them to insignificance. Those stories about parents, grandparents, great-grandparents, aunts, uncles, cousins, neighbors, and friends were sometimes humorous, often tragic, but they were important, for they taught her her own history and compelled her to write about it. *Roll of Thunder, Hear My Cry* featured young Cassie Logan as its spunky narrator, through whom the reader experiences black family life in rural Mississippi during the Depression. The Logans struggle to keep their land, their lives, and their dignity when bigotry and injustice threaten to take it all away. The book's powerful narrative creates a deeply sympathetic portrayal through richly detailed characters and dramatic action, spiced with many moments of mischief and humor. The novel won the Newbery Medal and many other awards. It was all the encouragement Taylor needed.

The five Logan novels that followed succeed admirably in maintaining this high quality of rendering racial discrimination and humiliation through vibrant prose, compelling characters, and provocative themes. Again and again the malignant and frequently terrifying presence of white contempt and hate inflicts its evil on blacks, both children and adults. Taylor's Civil War and Reconstruction era prequel to *Roll of Thunder, Hear My Cry*, 2001's *The Land*, won Coretta Scott King Book Award, Scott O'Dell Historical Fiction Award, and PEN Center West Literary Award for children's literature.

Taylor avoids indulging in the stereotyping that she had discovered in the textbooks of her youth: The whites in her fiction can be vicious, like Charlie Simms; they can also be noble, like Jeremy Simms. Although the blacks are often shaken and bent by the power and meanness of white neighbors, they are not broken. Through fierce pride, loving family bonds, and a strong spirit of community, the Logans and others cope and survive. Taylor's novels engender anger in the reader but ultimately not so much bitterness as hope—hope in the power of family, moral goodness, dignity, and self-respect to defeat the evils of racism.

Henry J. Baron

Bibliography

Bosmajian, Hamida. "Mildred Taylor's Story of Cassie Logan: A Search for Law and Justice in a Racist Society." *Children's Literature* 24 (1996): 141-160. A perceptive essay that explores the treatment of racism and justice in Taylor's works, especially in relation to Cassie Logan. A solid examination of themes common to Taylor's writings.

Crowe, Chris. *Presenting Mildred D. Taylor.* New York: Twayne, 1999. This introduction to Taylor and her work provides biographical information; cultural context, especially of the Civil Rights movement, for her novels; critical analysis; and a bibliography.

Harper, Mary Turner. "Merger and Metamorphosis in the Fiction of Mildred D. Taylor." *Children's Literature Association Quarterly* 13 (Summer, 1988): 75-80. Examines the first four books as culturally conscious fiction.

Osa, Osayimwense. "Africanism in African American Children's Literature: Mildred Taylor's *Song of the Trees* and *The Friendship* and Eleanora Tate's *The Secret of Gumbo Grave*." *Obsidian* 3 (Spring, 2001): 89-99. Discusses the way the two writers, in drawing upon their childhoods for their fiction, also demonstrate the continuities of African themes in African American literature.

Scales, Pat. "Mildred D. Taylor: Keeper of Stories." *Language Arts* 80 (January, 2003): 240-244. A short profile of Taylor and her novels.

Smith, Karen. "A Chronicle of Family Honor: Balancing Rage and Triumph in the Novels of Mildred D. Taylor." In *African American Voices in Young Adult Literature: Tradition, Transition, Transformation*, edited by Karen P. Smith. Metuchen, N.J.: Scarecrow Press, 1994. Smith explores the treatment of the African American family in Mississippi during the Depression.

Taxel, Joel. "Reclaiming the Voice of Resistance: The Fiction of Mildred Taylor." In *The Politics of the Textbook*, edited by Michael W. Apple and Linda K. Christian-Smith. New York: Routledge, 1991. Demonstrates Taylor's power and the forthrightness of her treatment of African American history and heritage, particularly in her first two novels.

Peter Taylor

American short-story writer

Born: Trenton, Tennessee; January 8, 1917
Died: Charlottesville, Virginia; November 2, 1994

SHORT FICTION: *A Long Fourth, and Other Stories*, 1948; *The Widows of Thornton*, 1954; *Happy Families Are All Alike*, 1959; *Miss Leonora When Last Seen, and Fifteen Other Stories*, 1963; *The Collected Stories of Peter Taylor*, 1968; *In the Miro District, and Other Stories*, 1977; *The Old Forest, and Other Stories*, 1985; *The Oracle at Stoneleigh Court*, 1993.
LONG FICTION: *A Woman of Means*, 1950; *A Summons to Memphis*, 1986; *In the Tennessee Country*, 1994.
DRAMA: *Tennessee Day in Saint Louis: A Comedy*, pr. 1956; *A Stand in the Mountains*, pb. 1965; *Presences: Seven Dramatic Pieces*, pb. 1973.
NONFICTION: *Conversations with Peter Taylor*, 1987 (Hubert H. McAlexander, editor).
EDITED TEXT: *Randall Jarrell, 1914-1965*, 1967 (with Robert Lowell and Robert Penn Warren).

Though he published several plays and novels, Peter Hillsman Taylor is best known as one of America's finest short-story writers. From the 1930's to the 1990's his prizewinning narratives have continued to be regarded as major achievements in a golden age of short fiction writing. During an era of great social change, Taylor's publication record was amazingly steady.

The settings of his fiction and his focus on upper-middle-class Southern culture have roots in Taylor's own Tennessee background. Born in the rural Tennessee, Taylor at the age of seven moved with his family to Nashville, two years later to St. Louis, and then in 1932 to Memphis. After graduation from high school and a brief trip abroad, he enrolled at Southwestern at Memphis and became acquainted with Allen Tate, who was his freshman English instructor. In the next few years, in the course of transferring to Vanderbilt University and then to Kenyon College, Taylor met the significant critic-teachers and nascent poets who would prove to be not only major literary influences but also lifelong friends—Tate, John Crowe Ransom, Randall Jarrell, and Robert Lowell. The formalist strain in these associations, as well as Taylor's southern consciousness, was enhanced by his brief encounters as a graduate student at Louisiana State University with Robert Penn Warren and Cleanth Brooks.

Taylor was one of the American writers of the post-World War II period who was nurtured by academia and the critical support it gave to a generation of creative artists. In turn, many of the writers, like Taylor, reciprocated by becoming teachers in creative writing programs at various universities. Throughout his writing career, Taylor taught at universities as varied as the Women's College of the University of North Carolina at Greensboro, the University of Chicago, Ohio State University, the University of Virginia,

Harvard University, and Memphis State University. As well as affording him an economic base, these involvements with higher education provided Taylor with consistent contact with American youth during a period of cultural turmoil.

Yet there is little evidence in his work that he was influenced by the radicalism manifested in the 1960's and 1970's. His fiction instead seems to reflect the steadiness of his personal life. While friends such as Tate, Lowell, and Jarrell underwent the anguish of divorce, had mental breakdowns, or committed suicide, Taylor's life progressed along more conventional lines. He remained married to Eleanor Lilly Ross, whom he had wed in 1943, and together they reared their two children, restored old houses, and pursued their respective writing careers. Eleanor Ross Taylor has published several volumes of poetry. After retiring from academic life, Taylor continued to write. He died of pneumonia, at his home in Charlottesville, at the age of seventy-seven and within weeks of the publication of his last work, *In the Tennessee Country*.

The family and its different generations and extended branches form the central matter of Taylor's fiction and serve to structure his elaborate intertwining of social, psychological, and historical materials. Typically, the stories are tightly crafted, reflecting the influence of Taylor's early teachers and his poet friends. At times Taylor worked from poetry to prose in composing his stories, and several of his later narratives have been published in verse form. Throughout his career, Taylor's stories evidenced his formalist roots; they are invariably carefully articulated character dramas, modulated by his own delicate taste, demonstrating a controlled and complex set of implications. In one of his earliest and most successful pieces, "A Spinster's Tale," the narrator's sense of being the only woman in the family is amplified and irritated by the idea of the town drunk, Mr. Speed, as the symbolic embodiment of what she believes is an uninhibited and untrustworthy masculine world surrounding her. In her ultimate encounter with this pathetic drunk at the story's conclusion, she not only discovers that she has the emotional strength to summon the police but also begins to sense, with some fear, the cruelty that has been inextricably mixed in her newfound strength.

More typical of Taylor's domestic analysis is "Guests," a story examining the visit of country cousins, the Kincaids, to their city relatives, the Harpers. On the surface, the narrative presents a social comedy in which Henrietta Harper's insistent social hospitality is adamantly resisted by a defensively proud Annie Kincaid, much to the discomfort of Johnny Kincaid, whose shifting dispositions seem so often the social prizes over which the women struggle. The hidden pathos of the growing personal distance created by different social histories is suggested in the speculations of the narrator, Edmund Harper, about his cousin Johnny: "Here is such a person as I might have been, and I am such a one as he might have been." While Taylor's characters do not often seem uniquely striking, the sense of the self weighing its enhanced or diminished social power creates a vividly convincing picture of the domestic history of an era.

"The Old Forest," a story set in the 1930's, sketches, through the puzzled desperation of narrator Nat Ramsey, the very different feminine possibilities of his working-class date, Lee Ann Deehart, and his upper-middle-class fiancé, Caroline Braxley. In the search for the mysteriously vanished Lee Ann the characters seem to gain insights that result in their being established more firmly in their respective social roles.

At its finest, Taylor's fiction is an acute mixture of psychological insight tempered by acceptance and, at times, forgiveness, with an intense sense of history. As they interact, his characters often endeavor to experience other social possibilities, only to see at last in what they are not the labyrinthine cultural depths of their own social being. The calm, retrospective narration of his 1986 Pulitzer Prize-winning novel *A Summons to Memphis* and of his last novel, *In the Tennessee Country*, continues this interplay of psychological and social consciousness. While Phillip Carver reveals in *A Summons to Memphis* the complex workings of family and of upper-class Tennessee society, his memories show him hovering, most of all, above his own sense of self.

Walter Shear
Rebecca Godwin Smith

Bibliography

Graham, Catherine Clark. *Southern Accents: The Fiction of Peter Taylor*. New York: P. Lang, 1994. An insightful study. Includes bibliographical references.

Griffith, Albert J. *Peter Taylor*. Rev. ed. Boston: Twayne, 1990. An excellent introductory study.

Kramer, Victor A., Patricia A. Bailey, Carol G. Dana, and Carl H. Griffin. *Andrew Lytle, Walker Percy, Peter Taylor: A Reference Guide*. Boston: G. K. Hall, 1983. One of the later and most complete bibliographies of Taylor's work and the reviews and criticism.

McAlexander, Hubert H. *Critical Essays on Peter Taylor*. New York: G. K. Hall, 1993. A solid collection of critical and interpretive essays on Taylor's writing.

________. *Peter Taylor: A Writer's Life*. Baton Rouge: Louisiana State University Press, 2001. A biography written with the close cooperation of its subject. In fact, McAlexander, who edited *Conversations with Peter Taylor* and a collection of essays on the writer, was hand-picked by Taylor, and his portrait is admiring.

Robinson, Clayton. "Peter Taylor." In *Literature of Tennessee*, edited by Ray Will-Banks. Rome, Ga.: Mercer University Press, 1984. This article relates Taylor's fiction to his early years and explains his mother's influence on his techniques and subject matter.

Robison, James C. *Peter Taylor: A Study of the Short Fiction*. Boston: Twayne, 1987. This volume is not only an extended study of Taylor's writings but also contains two interviews with the author as well as essays by a number of critics. Robison's comments are occasionally wide of the mark, but he is an earnest and generally intelligent reader of Taylor's work. Essential reading.

Stephens, C. Ralph, and Lynda B. Salamon, eds. *The Craft of Peter Taylor*. Tuscaloosa: The University of Alabama Press, 1995. A collection of essays on Taylor's work, including discussions of his poetics, his focus on place, his relationship to the Agrarians, his treatment of absence, his role in American pastoralism, and such stories as "The Other Times," "The Old Forest," and "The Hand of Emmagene."

Taylor, Peter. "Interview with Peter Taylor." Interview by J. H. E. Paine. *Journal of the Short Story in English* 9 (Fall, 1987): 14-35. The most extended interview with Taylor, dealing with his techniques and influences.

Wright, Stuart T. *Peter Taylor: A Descriptive Bibliography, 1934-1987.* Charlottesville: University Press of Virginia, 1988. Published for the Bibliographical Society of the University of Virginia. Remains indispensable.

Sheila Ortiz Taylor

American novelist

Born: Los Angeles, California; September 25, 1939
Identity: Mexican American, gay or bisexual

LONG FICTION: *Faultline*, 1982; *Spring Forward/Fall Back*, 1985; *Southbound*, 1990; *Coachella*, 1998.
POETRY: *Slow Dancing at Miss Polly's*, 1989.
NONFICTION: *Emily Dickinson: A Bibliography, 1850-1966*, 1968; *Imaginary Parents*, 1996.

Sheila Ortiz Taylor is often considered the first Chicana lesbian novelist. Her first and most acclaimed novel, *Faultline*, was republished in 1995 because of increased awareness of its importance not only in lesbian and Chicano literature but as a significant work of fiction. The novel has been published in British, German, Greek, Italian, and Spanish translations, and in 1995 film rights were bought by Joseph May Productions. The novel also won several awards, although it was often neglected by critics and mainstream reviewers.

Ortiz Taylor grew up in a Mexican American family in Southern California, an experience she records in *Imaginary Parents*. The book, a mixture of fact and fiction, is true to the spirit of her childhood in the 1940's and 1950's. Her older sister's color prints accompany the text and represent a different version of the shared past. In her preface Ortiz Taylor writes that the book could be called autobiography, memoir, poetry, nonfiction, creative nonfiction, fiction, or codex (a manuscript book); she herself calls it an *ofrenda*, an offering of small objects with big meanings set out in order. The book reimagines the past and recreates the parents and extended family who have since died; it also provides an insightful Chicana perspective into what she calls the strange Southern California culture of the war years.

It was during the post-World War II years of the early 1950's that Ortiz Taylor, then twelve or thirteen years old, realized that she wanted to write. She attended California State University at Northridge and graduated magna cum laude. She earned her M.A. from the University of California, Los Angeles, in 1964, and her Ph.D. in English from the same university in 1973 with a dissertation on "Form and Function in the Picaresque Novel."

Taylor's own novels often follow the episodic traditions of the picaresque, although they transform the rogue hero into an adventurous lesbian protagonist who challenges boundaries and resists stereotyped categorization. In *Faultline* the main character, Arden Benbow, who was an English major in college, is the mother of six when she falls in love with another woman. Together they create a loving homelife, which includes an African American gay male drag queen as a baby-sitter, an assortment of pets (as many as three hundred rabbits), and various friends and neighbors who are attracted by Arden's energy and enthusiasm. Although he himself is involved with another woman and does not want to be bothered with the children, Arden's former husband files a custody suit on the grounds that Arden's lesbianism makes her an unfit mother. Arden refuses to pretend to be someone she is not, and her life-affirming spirit triumphs. The book ends with a legally nonbinding double wedding between Arden and her lover Alice and between two of their gay male friends.

A similar sense of hopefulness and triumph in the face of opposition, which some reviewers have referred to as utopian, pervades *Spring Forward/Fall Back*, and the same spirit informs Taylor's poetry and other writings. Taylor has a keen eye for detail and is clear about oppression and stagnated prejudicial attitudes. Her writings also show survival techniques in a hostile culture, among them the invocation of humor, love, and goodwill toward others. Her protagonists refuse to be beaten down, and they enjoy and respect life.

Taylor's professional career has been in teaching English at several universities, most notably at Florida State University, where she began teaching literature in the early 1970's. Her courses include many on women writers, and she has served as Director of Women's Studies. She has given many public readings nationally and internationally, and in 1991 she was awarded a Fulbright Fellowship to teach at the University of Erlangen-Nürnberg.

Taylor's work shows a continuing fascination with the novel form and its many variations. She sees herself as an author who creates convincing forgeries that are intended to illuminate life. Her works show her challenging herself by shifting subject matter, style, and approach. She never repeats simple patterns or formulas from previous works. This approach to writing is also reflected in her central characters, who meet challenges with creativity and vitality and accept risk as a part of the lived life.

Many readers have found Taylor's texts to be engaging. Her work is therefore not restricted to special audiences. Like the literal lesson of the geological faultlines where earthquakes appear, Taylor's works illustrate that chance and change are inevitable, that for individuals and societies it is important to avoid rigidity, and that challenges must be met actively with love, humor, and imagination.

Lois Marchino

Bibliography

Bruce-Novoa, Juan. *RetroSpace: Collected Essays on Chicano Literature*. Houston: Arte Publico Press, 1990. Asserts that Taylor's writings show that there is no monolithic Chicano culture or literature and cites *Faultline* as the best novel written by a Chicana.

_______. "Sheila Ortiz Taylor's *Faultline:* A Third Woman Utopia." *Confluencia: Revista Hispánica de Cultura y Literatura* 6 (Spring, 1991). A lengthy discussion about the novel.

Christian, Karen. "Will the 'Real Chicano' Please Stand Up? The Challenge of John Rechy and Sheila Ortiz Taylor to Chicano Essentialism." *Americas Review* 20 (Summer, 1992). An excellent extended treatment of the importance of gay and lesbian writing in Chicano literature, with special attention to the style and content of *Faultline*.

Zimmerman, Bonnie. *Safe Sea of Women*. Boston: Beacon Press, 1990. Taylor is one of several writers discussed in this study of lesbian fiction in the late twentieth century.

Esaias Tegnér

Swedish poet

Born: Kyrkerud, Sweden; November 13, 1782
Died: Östrabo, Sweden; November 2, 1846

POETRY: *Svea*, 1811 (English translation, 1840); *Nattvardsbarnen*, 1820 (*The Children of the Lord's Supper*, 1841); *Axel*, 1822 (English translation, 1838); *Frithiofs saga*, 1825 (*Frithiof's Saga*, 1833).
NONFICTION: *Esaias Tegnérs brev*, 1953-1976 (11 volumes; Nils Palmborg, editor).

Esaias Tegnér (tehng-NAYR), born in the Värmland district of Sweden in 1782, was the son of Esaias Lucasson, a clergyman who changed his name to Tegnerus, after the town of Tegnaby in Småland. The poet subsequently changed his name to Tegnér. Left fatherless in childhood, the boy received some tutoring through the assistance of the crown bailiff and later, with the aid of his brother's employer, was able to enter the University of Lund. After receiving his degree in philosophy in 1802 Tegnér remained at the university as lecturer and professor of Greek for twenty-two years. During this period he gradually became recognized as Sweden's leading national poet. After some early failures, he achieved overnight fame in 1808 with his "War Song of the Militia of Scania." Three years later his patriotic poem *Svea* won him the grand prize of the Swedish Academy.

Together with Arvid Afzelius and Erik Geijer, Tegnér developed the Gothic League, which opposed modernist European trends in Swedish literature, and in 1819 he was appointed a life member of the academy. Drawing principally on Icelandic sagas and Norse folk tales, Tegnér made his great contributions to Swedish literature in *The Children of the Lord's Supper*, which was made famous by Henry Wadsworth Longfellow's 1841 translation; *Frithiof's Saga*, now translated into almost every European language; and his long narrative poem *Axel*.

In 1824 Tegnér was named to the bishopric of Växjö, but his health broke under the burden of diocesan and parliamentary duties, and for a time he became mentally ill. He recovered sufficiently, however, to fulfill the duties of his church office from 1841 until his death at Östrabo in 1846. Two epic poems, *Gerda* and *Kronbruden*, remained unfinished when he died.

Irene Struthers

Bibliography

Bellquist, John Eric. "Tegnér's First Romantic Poem." *Scandinavica* 31, no. 1 (May, 1992).

Boyesen, Hjalmar Hjorth. "Esaias Tegnér." In *Essays on Scandinavian Literature*. Reprint. New York: Charles Scribner's Sons, 1911.

Brandes, Georg Morris Cohen, and Rasmus Bjorn Anderson. *Creative Spirits of the Nineteenth Century*. New York: Thomas Y. Crowell, 1923.

Hilen, Andrew R. *Longfellow and Scandinavia: A Study of the Poet's Relationship*. New Haven, Conn.: Yale University Press, 1947.

Longfellow, Henry Wadsworth. "Tegnér's *Frithiofs Saga*." *The North American Review* 45, no. 96 (July, 1837): 149-185.

"Tegnér." *The Saturday Review* 60, no. 1557 (August 29, 1885): 280-282.

Werin, Algot Gustaf. *Tegnér*. 2 vols. Stockholm: Dictum, 1974-1976.

Pierre Teilhard de Chardin

French theologian and paleontologist

Born: Sarcenat, France; May 1, 1881
Died: New York, New York; April 10, 1955
Identity: Catholic

NONFICTION: *Early Man in China*, 1941; *Le Phénomène humain*, 1955 (*The Phenomenon of Man*, 1955); *L'Apparition de l'homme*, 1956 (*The Appearance of Man*, 1965); *Lettres de voyage (1923-1939)*, 1956 (partial translation as *Letters from a Traveler*, 1962); *Le Milieu divin*, 1957 (*The Divine Milieu*, 1960); *Nouvelles Lettres de voyage (1939-1955)*, 1957 (partial translation as *Letters from a Traveler*, 1962); *La Vision du passé*, 1957 (*The Vision of the Past*, 1966); *L'Avenir de l'homme*, 1959 (*The Future of Man*, 1965); *Génèse d'une pensée: Lettres 1914-1919*, 1961 (*The Making of a Mind: Letters from a Soldier-Priest, 1914-1919*, 1965); *Hymne de l'univers*, 1961 (*Hymn of the Universe*, 1961); *L'Énergie humaine*, 1962 (*Human Energy*, 1969); *L'Activation de l'énergie*, 1963 (*Activation of Energy*, 1970); *Lettres d'Égypte, 1905-1908*, 1963 (*Letters from Egypt, 1905-1908*, 1965); *La Place de l'homme dans la nature*, 1963 (*Man's Place in Nature*, 1966); *Science et Christ*, 1965 (*Science and Christ*, 1968); *Écrits du temps de la guerre (1916-1919)*, 1965 (*Writings in Time of War*, 1968); *Lettres à Léontine Zanta*, 1965 (*Letters to Leontine Zanta*, 1969); *Lettres d'Hastings et de Paris, 1908-1914*, 1966 (pb. in 2 volumes: *Letters from Paris, 1912-1914*, 1967; *Letters from Hastings, 1908-1912*, 1968); *Accomplir l'homme, lettres inédites, 1926-1952*, 1968 (*Letters to Two Friends, 1926-1952*, 1968); *Comment je crois*, 1969 (*How I Believe*, 1969); *Christianity and Evolution*, 1971; *Toward the Future*, 1975; *On Love and Happiness*, 1984; *Letters of Teilhard de Chardin and Lucile Swan*, 1993.
MISCELLANEOUS: *Oeuvres de Pierre Teilhard de Chardin*, 1955-1976 (13 volumes); *Pierre Teilhard de Chardin: Writings*, 1999.

In his work as geologist, paleontologist, and Jesuit priest, Marie-Joseph-Pierre Teilhard de Chardin (tay-yahr duh shahr-dan) combined his scientific beliefs and Christian convictions in an idealistic, evolutionary vision of the universe. He was born in 1881 in Sarcenat, a small town in south central France. The fourth child of a large family, Teilhard absorbed from his father, a farmer, an interest in geology, and from his mother, a devout Roman Catholic, a deep belief in the truths of Christianity. In 1892 he entered a Jesuit boarding school near Lyons. By the time he was sixteen, he knew he had a vocation to the religious life, and on March 20, 1899, he entered the Jesuit novitiate in Aix-en-Provence.

Teilhard was a model novice, and after a two-year initiation into the Jesuit way of life, he took his vows of poverty, chastity, and obedience in Laval, where he continued his training. However, anticlerical legislation forced Teilhard and other Jesuits to leave France for the Channel island of Jersey, where he studied Scholastic philosophy. In 1905 Teilhard began teaching physics and chemistry in the Jesuit College of the Holy Family in Cairo, where he also had the chance to do geological and paleontological research.

From 1908 to 1912 Teilhard studied theology at Hastings in southern England. He began discovering connections between his scientific and religious beliefs. Evolution was the bridge between these two visions of the world, and for Teilhard they complemented rather than contradicted each other. In Teilhard's vision, Jesus Christ represents the crucial point in the universe's evolution, as matter and spirit are so deeply intertwined in his person that he embodies the world's true fulfillment. By 1911, when he was ordained a priest, Teilhard was a fervent evolutionist.

In 1912, after completing his theological training, Teilhard went to Paris to study under Marcellin Boule, an expert on Neanderthals, at the Institute of Human Paleontology. On a trip to England in 1913, he became involved in what later became known as the "Piltdown hoax." Though evolutionary theorist Stephen Jay Gould later claimed that Teilhard was the deceiver behind the hoax, most scholars believe that the Jesuit paleontologist was as deceived as others by these artificially aged animal and human bones.

Teilhard's final year of Jesuit training, at Canterbury in England, was interrupted by the outbreak of World War I. He served as a stretcher-bearer in various regiments and in many campaigns. His bravery and self-sacrifice merited numerous decorations. After his demobilization in March of 1919, he returned to his scientific career. His studies in geology, botany, and zoology culminated in 1922 when he received a doctorate from the Sorbonne. His doctoral thesis dealt with the fossil mammals of the Eocene period, some forty million years ago, when mammalian species rapidly multiplied and diversified.

From 1922 to 1926 Teilhard was an assistant professor of geology at the Institut Catholique in Paris. He lectured that before Charles Darwin, theologians had encountered few problems when they taught that one man (Adam) had corrupted humanity by his original sin and that another man (Jesus Christ) saved everyone by his sacrifice on the cross but that modern scientists have shown that the universe is not centered on the earth and that terrestrial life is not centered on humankind. Teilhard believed that the reality of evolution necessitated a revision of the dogma of original sin.

In 1923 Teilhard left France to do scientific research in China. During the next ten years, interspersed with periodic trips back to France, he worked in Tientsin with Émile Licent, a Jesuit paleontologist, and went on paleontological expeditions to the Ordos and Gobi Deserts in Mongolia. He enjoyed oscillating between Paris and China. In the East he was helping to reconstruct ancient life-forms, including early human beings, while in France his vision of Christ as the moving spirit of evolution was influencing a small but growing group of disciples. His most important work during this time was probably his dating of the bones of Sinanthropus, commonly known as Peking Man, and his discovery, with Henri Breuil, that Peking Man had been a toolmaker. This was also the period when he wrote *The Divine Milieu*, a systematization of his personal way to God, although it was not published until after his death.

Despite his inability to publish his insights on evolution and religion, he remained loyal to the Jesuit Order and to the Roman Catholic Church. Nevertheless, he spread his ideas through his extensive travels; in the 1930's he made several trips to the United States, where he made friends with scientists at the Museum of Natural History in New York. His life and work in China became increasingly dangerous because of the Japanese invasion. When the war against Japan was confined to China, Teilhard was able to travel to France and the United States, but when World War II began, he was unable to leave Peking. The Japanese occupation of northern China seriously hindered his geological and paleontological work.

Largely isolated from the outside world, Teilhard began to compose what became his most important work, *The Phenomenon of Man*. He hoped to bridge the gap between non-Christians and Christians over the question of the future of humankind. For Julian Huxley, who later became Teilhard's friend, the core idea of *The Phenomenon of Man* was that humankind, the end product of billions of years of the universe's development, now carries the promise of evolution, which it can realize by enhancing human knowledge and love. Teilhard completed *The Phenomenon of Man* in 1940 and sent it to Rome in 1941 to be approved by religious censors. He did not learn until 1944 that permission had been refused.

After the war Teilhard visited Paris and Rome in an unsuccessful attempt to get permission to publish his philosophical and theological writings. Unable to get a chair he sought at the Collège de France, Teilhard made the Wenner-Grenn Foundation of Anthropological Research in New York City the base of his activities during the last years of his life. He privately circulated his books and essays, and they exerted considerable influence.

During the summer of 1954, he made his last visit to France. He lectured on the origins of humankind and visited his birthplace before he returned to New York. A short time before his death, he composed a spiritual testament that revealed how he united his love for God and his faith in an evolving world. At a dinner at the French consulate in New York on March 15, 1954, he declared to relatives and friends that he would like to die on the day commemorating the resurrection of Christ, and on Easter Sunday, April 10, 1955, after saying a private mass and attending a public High Mass at Saint Patrick's Cathedral, he died among friends. He was seventy-four years old.

Although many of Teilhard's scientific works were published during his lifetime, the works he most wanted disseminated—his poetically theological attempts to unify traditional Christianity and modern science—were denied publication by church officials. Despite his dissatisfaction with these decisions, Teilhard remained loyal to the Catholic church and the Society of Jesus. After his death, his private writings made their way into print, resulting in widespread discussion of his ideas. Many scientists saw Teilhard's speculations as idealistically romantic, whereas orthodox Catholics thought that his views underestimated sin and grace and overestimated evolution's power to enlighten Christian theology. Nevertheless, Teilhard's writings expressed the longings of many for a mystical vision of the universe—permeated with God's love and becoming progressively better.

Robert J. Paradowski

Bibliography

Cowell, Siôn. *The Teilhard Lexicon: Understanding the Language, Terminology, and Vision of the Writings of Pierre Teilhard de Chardin, the First English-Language Dictionary of His Writings*. Portland, Oreg.: Sussex Academic Press, 2001. An excellent companion to the writings of Teilhard. Includes bibliography.

Cuénot, Claude. *Teilhard de Chardin: A Biographical Study*. London: Burns & Oakes, 1965. Remains the standard life.

King, Thomas M. *Teilhard de Chardin*. Wilmington, Del.: M. Glazier, 1988. Finds a place for Teilhard in the lineage of Christian mystics.

King, Ursula. *Towards a New Mysticism: Teilhard de Chardin and Eastern Religions*. New York: Seabury Press, 1980. Examines Teilhard's surprisingly negative estimation of Buddhism, Hinduism, Taoism, and Confucianism.

Roberts, Noel. *From Piltdown Man to Point Omega: The Evolutionary Theory of Teilhard de Chardin*. New York: Peter Lang, 2000. Covers a vast array of topics related to Teilhard and his vision, including biological evolution, fossils, Charles Darwin, Christian doctrine, Creationism, and much more.

Alfred, Lord Tennyson

English poet

Born: Somersby, Lincolnshire, England; August 6, 1809
Died: Near Haslemere, Surrey, England; October 6, 1892

POETRY: *Poems by Two Brothers*, 1827 (with Charles Tennyson and Frederick Tennyson); *Poems, Chiefly Lyrical*, 1830; *Poems*, 1832 (imprinted 1833); *Poems*, 1842; *The Princess*, 1847; *In Memoriam*, 1850; *Maud, and Other Poems*, 1855; *Idylls of the King*, 1859-1885; *Enoch Arden, and Other Poems*, 1864; *The Holy Grail, and Other Poems*, 1869 (imprinted 1870); *Gareth and Lynette*, 1872; *The Lover's Tale*, 1879; *Ballads and Other Poems*, 1880; *Tiresias, and Other Poems*, 1885; *Locksley Hall Sixty Years After, Etc.*, 1886; *Demeter, and Other Poems*, 1889; *The Death of Œnone, and Other Poems*, 1892.

DRAMA: *Queen Mary*, pb. 1875; *Harold*, pb. 1876; *Becket*, wr. 1879, pb. 1884; *The Falcon*, pr. 1879 (one act); *The Cup*, pr. 1881; *The Foresters*, wr. 1881, pr., pb. 1892; *The Promise of May*, pr. 1882; *The Devil and the Lady*, pb. 1930 (unfinished).

NONFICTION: *The Letters of Alfred Lord Tennyson: Volume 1, 1821-1850*, 1981 (Cecil Y. Lang and Edgar F. Shannon, editors); *The Letters of Alfred Lord Tennyson: Volume 2, 1851-1870*, 1987 (Lang and Shannon, editors); *The Letters of Alfred Lord Tennyson: Volume 3, 1871-1892*, 1990 (Lang and Shannon, editors).

MISCELLANEOUS: *The Works of Tennyson*, 1907-1908 (9 volumes; Hallam, Lord Tennyson, editor).

Alfred Tennyson (TEHN-uh-suhn), the fourth son of the Rev. G. C. Tennyson, rector of the parish at Somersby in Lincolnshire, was born in 1809. His literary output began at the age of six, with blank verse scribbled on a slate, and culminated some seventy-five years later with the much-quoted "Crossing the Bar." In between came poetry that is sometimes magnificent, often vapid and mawkish, but always characteristic of an age alternately self-confident and self-conscious, the age of Victoria.

Somersby was a quiet village with fewer than a hundred inhabitants. Tennyson's father was talented (a dabbler in poetry, painting, architecture, and music), and his mother, whose maiden name was Elizabeth Fytche, was noted for her gentleness and sweet disposition. In this setting Tennyson's talent developed early. While he was attending Louth Grammar School he broke into print with *Poems by Two Brothers*, a collection which actually contained the works of three members of a talented family—Alfred, Frederick, and Charles. This juvenile volume shows the influence of George Gordon, Lord Byron, whom Alfred admired so greatly that when he heard of his death he took a lonely, sad walk and carved into the sandstone, "Byron is dead."

In 1828 Tennyson went to Trinity College, Cambridge. There he took an interest in politics and became a member of the Apostles, a club of young literary men. Among these friends was Arthur Henry Hallam, whose later death at the age of twenty-three so affected Tennyson that he published nothing for ten years. Hallam is elegized in *In Memoriam*, a loose collection of philosophical lyrics that seems to be groping for, but never quite reaching, the handhold of faith. At Cambridge Tennyson won the chancellor's medal for his poem "Timbuctoo," and it was there he brought out in 1830 his first important volume, *Poems, Chiefly Lyrical*. Although some of the reviews of this book were unkind, perhaps justifiably so, and although the influence of another Romantic poet, John Keats, is very evident, the volume marked the beginning of a career almost unmatched in popularity for a poet during his lifetime.

Two years later came another volume, which included "The Lady of Shalott" and "The Lotus Eaters," two poems in the smooth, melancholy tone of Tennyson at his best. Then came Hallam's death and the ten years of silence. Hallam was Tennyson's close friend and the fiancé of his sister Emily; when Tennyson heard the news of his unexpected death in Vienna, he was shocked and shaken. Later he began working on *In Memoriam*, a labor that lasted for seventeen years. Not until 1842 did Tennyson publish again, bringing out two volumes, one of which contained "Morte d'Arthur," the beginning of a series on the Arthurian legends which became *Idylls of the King*. Also in 1842 appeared "Locksley Hall," one of Tennyson's most popular poems.

Tennyson's most auspicious year was 1850. After unwise speculation had left him penniless and two bouts with nervous prostration had damaged his health, his affairs took a threefold upsurge: He married Emily Sellwood, he published *In Memoriam*, and he was appointed poet laureate to succeed William Wordsworth. Outstanding among his "official" poems as laureate is his "Ode on the Death of the Duke of Wellington," a stiff but moving tribute. The laureateship became the first step toward elevation to the peerage, an honor bestowed on him by an admiring Queen Victoria. Tennyson had twice refused this honor (tendered to him first through William Gladstone and then through Benjamin Disraeli), but he accepted it in 1883, becoming baron of Aldworth and Farrington. Even before he became a peer, Tennyson's popularity had been great (ten thousand copies of the first series of *Idylls of the King*, published in 1859, were sold within a few weeks), but now this tall, gaunt man, the idealized figure of a poet, became almost a living legend. After his death there was a reaction against his sentimentality and "Victorianism," but poems like "The Lotus Eaters," "Tithonus," and "Ulysses" still ring strong and true.

Tennyson's life was quiet and unhurried. Most of it he spent at his home, Farringford, on the Isle of Wight and, after 1867, at Blackdown in Surrey, where he lived in a house which he named Aldworth. In this later period he tried his hand at poetic dramas: *Queen Mary*, *Harold*, and *Becket*. Only the last became a success on the stage. In 1889, *Demeter, and Other Poems* came out, twenty thousand copies of which were sold within a week. On his eightieth birthday, Tennyson received tributes from all over the world. Though the end of his life was not far away, he still had the strength to write a romantic play, *The Foresters*, a drama on the Robin Hood theme, which was produced at Daly's Theatre in New York in 1892. Tennyson died at eighty-three at his home, Aldworth House, and was buried in the Poets' Corner of Westminster Abbey.

George F. Horneker

Bibliography

Hood, James W. *Divining Desire: Tennyson and the Poetics of Transcendence*. Aldershot, Vt.: Ashgate, 2000. Hood examines religious transcendence in the works of Tennyson. Includes bibliography and index.

Howe, Elisabeth A. *The Dramatic Monoglogue*. New York: Twayne, 1996. This study of dramatic monologues looks at the works of Tennyson, Robert Browning, T. S. Eliot, and Ezra Pound. Includes bibliography and index.

Levi, Peter. *Tennyson*. London: Macmillan, 1994. This biography studies the life and work of Tennyson.

Ormond, Leonée. *Alfred Tennyson: A Literary Life*. New York: St. Martin's Press, 1993. A biographical study that examines Tennyson's life as a poet and writer. Includes bibliography and index.

Potter, Lois, ed. *Playing Robin Hood: The Legend as Performance in Five Centuries*. Newark: University of Delaware Press, 1998. This study of the legend of Robin Hood examines how the story has been presented in literature, including in Tennyson's *The Foresters*. Includes bibliography and index.

Smith, Elton Edward. *Tennyson's "Epic Drama."* Lanham, Md.: University Press of America, 1997. Smith examines the dramatic works of Tennyson. Includes bibliography and index.

Thorn, Michael. *Tennyson*. New York: St. Martin's Press, 1993. A biography of Tennyson that covers his life and works. Includes bibliography and index.

Tucker, Herbert F., ed. *Critical Essays on Alfred, Lord Tennyson*. New York: Maxwell Macmillan International, 1993. A collection of essays on Tennyson. Includes index and bibliography.

Terence

Roman playwright

Born: Carthage (now in Tunisia); c. 190 B.C.E.
Died: En route from Greece; 159 B.C.E.

DRAMA: *Andria*, 166 B.C.E. (English translation, 1598); *Hecyra*, 165 B.C.E. (*The Mother-in-Law*, 1598); *Heautontimorumenos*, 163 B.C.E. (*The Self-Tormentor*, 1598); *Eunuchus*, 161 B.C.E. (*The Eunuch*, 1598); *Phormio*, 161 B.C.E. (English translation, 1598); *Adelphoe*, 160 B.C.E. (*The Brothers*, 1598).

Publius Terentius Afer, known as Terence (TEHR-uhnts), was probably born in the North African city of Carthage in 190 or 185 B.C.E. The sole source of knowledge about his life is the fourth century grammarian and commentator Donatus, who, in his commentary on Terence's plays, preserves a biographical extract from Suetonius's lost *De viris illustribus*. Terence was brought to Rome in childhood as a slave but was given the education of a gentleman by his master, the senator M. Terentius Lucanus. After having been given his freedom, the young man took the name of his former master and added the cognomen Afer (African).

His intellectual brilliance and personal charm won Terence a place among the aristocratic literary coterie in Rome, a group of young men intent on Hellenizing Roman society and bringing Greek literature and its refinements to the Romans. His personal attractiveness, which secured him the patronage of Caecilius, the poet, and the backing of the literary and aristocratic party, stood Terence in good stead when he was accused of plagiarism and of receiving "help" from his noble friends. Although the elegance and purity of his style and language—surprising in one so young, and a foreigner—indicate that the accusation may have had some basis in truth, he was successful in repelling the charges and continued to be lionized by Roman society.

Around 160 B.C.E. Terence spent some time in Greece, probably studying Greek life and institutions for future use in his writing. Tradition has it that he was lost at sea in 159 B.C.E., as he was returning to Rome bearing a translation of the plays of Menander.

Six plays of Terence have survived: *Andria*, *The Mother-in-Law*, *The Self-Tormentor*, *The Eunuch*, *Phormio*, and *The Brothers*, all produced between 166 and 160 B.C.E. Like the works of Plautus, they are modeled on Greek comedies, primarily those of Menander, but they also show the influence of Diphilus and Apollodorus. Terence seems to have taken greater liberties with the plots and characterizations of the Greek originals than did Plautus, and he often combined scenes from several different plays. Nevertheless, he remained truer to the spirit and style of his sources. Unlike Plautus, his language is consistently temperate and refined, and he avoids the incongruity of introducing Roman allusions or traditions into his plays. Terence seems to have been less concerned with the applause of the masses than with achieving a fusion of the purity of cultivated Latin with the smoothness of Attic Greek, and he strove to introduce Greek culture and sophistication to a Rome that must have appeared to him vulgar, if not barbaric.

Terence's plays are characterized by complex but careful plot construction and by a sense of the probability of the incidents he portrays. Consistency and moderation in speech and characterization, quite different from the extravagance of Plautus's writing, mark his work. All six comedies deal with the love entanglements of young men, usually involving two love relationships, one with a wellborn young woman and one with a courtesan, and complicated by the presence of a parent (or parents). Although the characterization in the early plays follows closely the stock types of Greek comedy, Terence's later plays show considerable development toward a subtle and sympathetic understanding of human psychology.

Thomas J. Sienkewicz

Bibliography

Forehand, Walter. *Terence*. Boston: Twayne, 1985. A basic biography of Terence, with literary criticism of his works. Includes some general discussion of Latin drama. Contains bibliography and index.

Goldberg, Sander M. *Understanding Terence*. Princeton, N.J.: Princeton University Press, 1986. Goldberg provides a brief biography of Terence, along with analysis of his works and of Latin drama in general.

Snowden, Frank M., Jr. *Blacks in Antiquity: Ethiopians in the Greco-Roman Experience*. Cambridge, Mass.: Belknap Press of Harvard University Press, 1970. The author examines the role of blacks in the Greek and Roman worlds.

Sutton, Dana Ferrin. *Ancient Comedy: The War of the Generations*. New York: Maxwell Macmillan International, 1993. This study of ancient comedy looks at Terence, Menander, and Plautus. Includes bibliography and index.

Studs Terkel

American journalist and historian

Born: New York, New York; May 16, 1912

NONFICTION: *Giants of Jazz*, 1957, revised 1975; *Division Street: America*, 1967; *Hard Times: An Oral History of the Great Depression*, 1970; *Working: People Talk About What They Do All Day and How They Feel About What They Do*, 1974; *Talking to Myself: A Memoir of My Times*, 1977; *American Dreams: Lost and Found*, 1980; *"The Good War": An Oral History of World War Two*, 1984; *Chicago*, 1986; *The Great Divide: Second Thoughts on the American Dream*, 1988; *Race: How Blacks and Whites Think and Feel About the American Obsession*, 1992; *Coming of Age: The Story of Our Century by Those Who Have Lived It*, 1995; *My American Century*, 1997; *The Spectator: Talk About Movies and Plays with the People Who Make Them*, 1999; *Will the Circle Be Unbroken? Reflections on Death, Rebirth, and Hunger for a Faith*, 2001.

DRAMA: *Amazing Grace*, pr. 1967.

Louis "Studs" Terkel (TUR-kuhl) was a broadcast journalist and author of several books. His father, tailor Samuel Terkel, and mother, seamstress Anna (Finkel) Terkel, emigrated from Bialystok, Poland, to the Bronx, where Louis, the youngest of three boys, was born and grew up with people from a wide variety of ethnic backgrounds.

When Terkel was nine, his family moved to Chicago, where his parents ran a rooming house. He enjoyed observing and conversing with the renters there, and he credited his career as an interviewer in part to his interaction with those guests. Terkel acquired his nickname from his fascination with novelist James T. Farrell's character Studs Lonigan in *Young Lonigan* (1932). "Naturally I identified with (Lonigan) because we had nothing in common," he said. He spoke constantly of Lonigan to his friends, who consequently dubbed him Studs.

In 1939 Terkel married Ida Goldberg, a social worker of Ukrainian descent who was raised in Wisconsin. The two met through a theater group and discovered their common interest in progressive politics and similarities in other areas of their lives. They had one son, Paul.

After receiving a bachelor's degree in philosophy from the University of Chicago in 1932 and a J.D. from its law school two years later, Terkel realized his career was not going to be as glamorous as that of his lawyer-hero, Clarence Darrow, so Terkel began seeking work elsewhere: in the civil service; as an actor in Chicago; in the radio division of the Works Progress Administration (WPA) Writers Project; and, because a perforated eardrum prevented him from serving in combat when he was called up for military duty, as an entertainer for the military.

In the 1940's he began working with radio, doing radio commentary and later hosting *Studs Terkel's Wax Museum*. In 1950 he began his own television show, *Studs' Place*, featuring himself as the manager of a small café, three actors as café workers, and different people as guests each week. The program's dialogue was spontaneous and informal, and the show helped define the genre of Chicago-style television.

Then in 1953, Terkel's liberal political views caused him to be viewed with suspicion by Senator Joseph McCarthy and the House Committee on Un-American Activities, and he was subsequently blacklisted. The television station dropped *Studs' Place*, and no one else would employ him. Then Chicago radio station WFMT offered him work as a disc jockey, later giving him his own show, *The Studs Terkel Program*.

His radio broadcasts included interviews with people from all walks of life, from the local community activist to the internationally known orchestra conductor. Terkel liked to do programs with unusual twists, such as discussing the opening of an art show by playing pieces of music which people said reminded them of that artist's work.

Terkel saw himself primarily as a radio interviewer. In 1957 he wrote a book on jazz musicians, thirteen giants of a musical genre he loved. Several years later his publisher and an actress friend saw a book of interviews—anthropologist Jan Myrdal's *Report from a Chinese Village* (1965)—and encouraged Terkel to write a similar book about an American city. He finally accepted the challenge, interviewed a cross-section of Chicago residents, and produced *Division Street: America*.

He described his books as memory books, not history books. In them he used his skills as interviewer to encourage the subjects to speak, and as editor, to allow them to speak for themselves. Aside from a prologue to the book and brief descriptions of each interviewee, the text of many of his books consists solely of interviews edited to read as monologues.

His books featured the opinions of those others had overlooked: the common man who went about his business, not necessarily making headline news but having an interesting story nonetheless. Terkel commented that he wrote *Working* to "do something in the present that would have been terrific if other people had done it for their own times in the past," that is, to have interviewed the workers building the pyramids—the ones who gave the sweat while the pharaohs got the glory.

His 2001 book on life and death, *Will the Circle Be Unbroken?*, helped him cope with the 1999 death of his wife of sixty years. He found comfort in talking with the subjects of his book. With this work, as with many of his others, he left his personal views out. However, he described himself as "an agnostic, which is what someone once told me is a cowardly atheist."

Terkel encouraged his interviewees to talk to him by putting them at ease and showing genuine interest in what they had to say. He avoided discussing the very private aspects of their lives, stating that as he did not like people invading his personal space, he tried not to invade theirs.

In 1998, he became Distinguished Scholar-in-Residence at the Chicago Historical Society, and in 2002 he founded the Studs and Ida Terkel Author Fund "to support promising authors in a range of fields who share [his] fascination with everyday life in America."

Terkel carved out his niche in the broadcasting world by "celebrating the uncelebrated people of the world . . . giving voice to the voices of those we never hear." He preserved for posterity a slice of Americana often overlooked—the opinions, hopes, and dreams of the ordinary person.

Elena C. Hines

Bibliography

Baker, James T. *Studs Terkel*. New York: Twayne, 1992. Baker gives a comprehensive overview of Terkel's life and career. The book is written in an engaging style and includes a bibliography.

Parker, Tony. *Studs Terkel: A Life in Words*. New York: Henry Holt, 1996. Parker presents condensed interviews with Terkel and with Terkel's family members, friends, and coworkers. Offers intriguing insights into Terkel as a person.

Stern, Richard G. "Studs Terkel." *The Antioch Review* 53 (Fall, 1995): 454-464. Stern makes some prefatory comments about Terkel in his post-radio WFMT days and then prints text of one of Terkel's interviews of him. The interview showcases the background research Terkel does for interviews and also how he deflects questions that probe into his own life.

Megan Terry
(Megan Duffy)

American playwright

Born: Seattle, Washington; July 22, 1932

DRAMA: *Ex-Miss Copper Queen on a Set of Pills*, pr. 1963; *Calm Down Mother*, pr. 1965; *Keep Tightly Closed in a Cool Dry Place*, pr. 1965; *Comings and Goings*, pr. 1966; *The Gloaming, Oh My Darling*, pr. 1966; *Viet Rock: A Folk War Movie*, pr., pb. 1966 (music by Marianne de Pury); *The Magic Realists*, pr. 1966; *The People vs. Ranchman*, pr. 1967; *Massachusetts Trust*, pr. 1968; *Megan Terry's Home: Or, Future Soap*, pr. 1968 (televised), pr. 1974 (staged); *The Tommy Allen Show*, pr. 1969; *Approaching Simone*, pr. 1970; *Three One-Act Plays*, pb. 1970; *Couplings and Groupings*, pb. 1973; *Nightwalk*, pr. 1973 (with Sam Shepard and Jean-Claude van Itallie); *Babes in the Bighouse*, pr., pb. 1974; *Fifteen Million Fifteen-Year-Olds*, pr. 1974; *Hothouse*, pr., pb. 1974; *The Pioneer*, pr. 1974; *Pro Game*, pr. 1974; *100,001 Horror Stories of the Plains*, pr. 1976 (with Judith Katz, James Larson, and others); *Brazil Fado*, pr., pb. 1977; *Sleazing Toward Athens*, pr. 1977, revised pr., pb. 1986; *Willa-Willie-Bill's Dope Garden*, pb. 1977; *American King's English for Queens*, pr., pb. 1978; *Attempted Rescue on Avenue B: A Beat Fifties Comic Opera*, pr., pb. 1979; *Goona Goona*, pr. 1979; *Mollie Bailey's Traveling Circus: Featuring Scenes from the Life of Mother Jones*, pr. 1981; *Kegger*, pr. 1982; *Family Talk*, pr., pb. 1986; *Sea of Forms*, pr. 1986 (with Jo Ann Schmidman); *Dinner's in the Blender*, pr., pb. 1987; *Walking Through Walls*, pr., pb. 1987 (with Schmidman); *Amtrak*, pr. 1988; *Headlights*, pr., pb. 1988; *Retro*, pr. 1988; *Body Leaks*, pr. 1990 (with Schmidman and Sora Kimberlain); *Do You See What I'm Saying?*, pr., pb. 1990; *Belches on Couches*, pr. 1992 (with Schmidman and Kimberlain); *India Plays*, pr. 1992; *Sound Fields: Are We Hear*, pr. 1992 (with Schmidman and Kimberlain); *Star Path Moon Stop*, pr. 1995; *Plays*, pb. 2000; *No Kissing in the Hall*, pr. 2002.

TELEPLAYS: *The Dirt Boat*, 1955; *One More Little Drinkie*, 1969.

RADIO PLAYS: *Sanibel and Captiva*, 1968; *American Wedding Ritual Monitored/Transmitted by the Planet Jupiter*, 1972.

EDITED TEXT: *Right Brain Vacation Photos: New Plays and Production Photographs, 1972-1992*, 1992 (with Jo Ann Schmidman and Sora Kimberlain).

Megan Terry, the daughter of Joseph Duffy, Jr., and Marguerite Cecelia (née Henry) Duffy, was born Marguerite (Megan) Duffy; she changed her last name to Terry in homage to her Welsh heritage. Speaking of her great-grandmother, who with her seven children crossed the country in a covered wagon, Terry once said "I come from a pioneer culture, so I'm kind of different from people raised in the East. Women worked side by side with the men. I was taught to build houses. . . . My grandfather was a great engineer who built bridges and railroads. I grew up using tools. I think that's important." Terry has spoken of the women in her life who were particularly influential: her mother, grandmothers, aunts, great-aunts, and cousins, whom she has described as "fantastic women. I love to be with them. I go home several times a year just so I can hang out with them! They're all beautiful, bright, witty, full of the devil. Terrific singers."

Terry attended the Banff School of Fine Arts at the University of Alberta, Edmonton, where she was trained in theater design. In 1956 she earned her B.A. in drama from the University of Seattle, Washington. As a teenager she was trained in other aspects of the theater when she participated in the Seattle Repertory Playhouse. Here she watched actors do improvisations in workshops and acting classes. She also learned that some actors can be effective storytellers, which inspired her to begin writing.

During 1954-1956 Terry taught drama at the Cornish School of Allied Arts, where she reorganized the Cornish Players, a group that toured the northwest United States for two years. She also conducted workshops at various colleges and universities, and she worked as a sculptor, painter, and theater designer. When she moved to New York in 1956 Terry became a founding member of the Open Theatre (with Joseph Chaikin), the New York Theatre Strategy, and the Women's Theatre Council. She revolutionized the American theater by creating the first rock musical and antiwar play, *Viet Rock*, which was given its premiere at La Mama Experimental Theatre Club in New York and was chosen to inaugurate the first season of the Yale Repertory Theatre under the artistic directorship of Robert Brustein. In 1974 she joined Jo Ann Schmidman to become playwright-in-residence and literary manager of the Omaha Magic Theater, the oldest and most productive feminist theater troupe in the United States.

In 1970 Terry's play *Approaching Simone*, which is based on the life of the French philosopher and mystic Simone Weil, was awarded an Obie for best new play. In 1977 Terry was awarded the Silver Medal for Distinguished Contribution and Service in American Theater by the American Theater Association. Together with Schmidman and the Omaha Magic Theater Company, Terry has produced plays that offer alternatives to realism. In 1983 she was awarded the Dramatists Guild Annual Award in recognition of her sustained work as a writer of conscience and controversy. The governor of Nebraska named her artist of the year in 1992. In 1994 she was voted a lifetime member of the College Fellows of the American Theater.

Terry's work has consistently addressed social problems. In *Sleazing Toward Athens* she focuses on the excessively materialistic orientation of college students. In *Kegger* she confronts adolescent alcohol abuse. *Attempted Rescue on Avenue B* explores women coming to terms with nonprocreative forms of power, and the fears and possibilities that accompany such confrontations. *Goona Goona* takes domestic violence and child abuse as its subjects in a slapstick Punch-and-Judy format, and *Babes in the Bighouse*, the first full-length play Terry developed after joining the Omaha Magic Theater, is set in a women's prison and explores connections between incarceration and sexual stereotyping. *Do You See What I'm Saying?* explores the lives of seven homeless women in their struggle to help each other survive on the streets. *Sound Fields: Are We Hear* is a full-length musical that examines the relationships between human beings and the earth, as well as their ethical responsibilities toward the earth.

Terry's theater pieces combine sculpture, music, dance, video, chanting, and visual arts. She and members of the Omaha Magic Theater have built a subscription community in the small Midwestern city of Omaha, and they regularly tour and conduct workshops and seminars in arts communities and academic institutions elsewhere. In the course of these activities Terry has attained an international reputation as a leading figure in American feminist theater.

Lynda Hart

Bibliography

Bell-Metereau, Rebecca, and Anne Fletcher. "Megan Terry." In *Critical Survey of Drama*, edited by Carl Rollyson. 2d rev. ed. Pasadena, Calif.: Salem Press, 2003. A thorough overview of Terry's life and playwriting career, with analyses of most of her important dramatic works.

Betsko, Kathleen, and Rachel Koenig, eds. *Interviews with Contemporary Women Playwrights*. New York: Beech Tree, 1987. Includes a full-length interview with Terry on her writing and life.

Diamond, Elin. "(Theoretically) Approaching Megan Terry: Issues of Gender and Identity." *Art and Cinema* 1 (Fall, 1987). Terry is the main focus of discussion.

Keyssar, Helene. "Making Magic Public: Megan Terry's Traveling Family Circus." In *Making a Spectacle: Feminist Essays on Contemporary Women's Theatre*, edited by Lynda Hart. Ann Arbor: University of Michigan Press, 1989. Terry is the main focus of discussion.

_______. "Megan Terry: Mother of American Feminist Theatre." In *Feminist Theatre*. New York: Grove Press, 1985. Details Terry's contributions to the development of a collaborative feminist theater in the United States. In addition to providing thorough bibliographic information and notes, this essay offers a valuable overview and analysis of Terry's vital impact on American drama.

Klein, Kathleen Gregory. "Language and Meaning in Megan Terry's 'Musicals.'" *Modern Drama* 27 (December, 1984): 574-583. Focusing on the plays *American King's English for Queens*, *Babes in the Bighouse*, *Brazil Fado*, and *The Tommy Allen Show*, Klein details how Terry's work elucidates the relationship of language to gender. This insightful article draws connections between Terry's work and the traditions of B-movie musicals, television, and popular culture, with an emphasis on the language of Terry's musicals.

Leavitt, Dinah L. "Megan Terry." In *Women in American Theatre*, edited by Helen Krich Chinoy and Linda Walsh Jenkins. New York: Crown, 1981. A brief overview of Terry's works and life.

Natalle, Elizabeth. *Feminist Theatre: A Study in Persuasion*. Metuchen, N.J.: Scarecrow Press, 1985. This survey of feminist theater features a ten-page bibliography, an index, and nine pages of analysis of Terry's role in the development of feminist theater. The discussion focuses primarily on *American King's English for Queens* and *Babes in the Bighouse*, placing them in the context of feminist concerns.

Savran, David, ed. *In Their Own Words: Contemporary American Playwrights*. New York: Theater Communications Group, 1988. Includes a full-length interview with Terry.

William Makepeace Thackeray

English novelist

Born: Calcutta, India; July 18, 1811
Died: London, England; December 24, 1863
Pseudonyms: Ikey Solomons, Jr., M. A. Titmarsh, George Savage Fitz-Boodle

LONG FICTION: *Catherine: A Story*, 1839-1840 (as Ikey Solomons, Jr.); *The History of Samuel Titmarsh and the Great Hoggarty Diamond*, 1841 (later as *The Great Hoggarty Diamond*, 1848); *The Luck of Barry Lyndon: A Romance of the Last Century*, 1844 (commonly known as *Barry Lyndon*); *Vanity Fair: A Novel Without a Hero*, 1847-1848; *The History of Pendennis: His Fortunes and Misfortunes, His Friends and His Greatest Enemy*, 1848-1850; *Rebecca and Rowena: A Romance upon Romance*, 1850 (as M. A. Titmarsh); *The History of Henry Esmond, Esquire, a Colonel in the Service of Her Majesty Q. Anne*, 1852 (3 volumes); *The Newcomes: Memoirs of a Most Respectable Family*, 1853-1855; *The Virginians: A Tale of the Last Century*, 1857-1859; *Lovel the Widower*, 1860; *The Adventures of Philip on His Way Through the World, Shewing Who Robbed Him, Who Helped Him, and Who Passed Him By*, 1861-1862; *Denis Duval*, 1864.

SHORT FICTION: *The Yellowplush Papers*, 1837-1838; *Some Passages in the Life of Major Gahagan*, 1838-1839; *Stubb's Calendar: Or, The Fatal Boots*, 1839; *Barber Cox and the Cutting of His Comb*, 1840; *The Bedford-Row Conspiracy*, 1840; *Comic Tales and Sketches*, 1841 (2 volumes); *"The Confessions of George Fitz-Boodle," and "Some Passages in the Life of Major Gahagan,"* 1841-1842; *Men's Wives*, 1843 (as George Savage Fitz-Boodle); *A Legend of the Rhine*, 1845 (as M. A. Titmarsh); *Jeames's Diary: Or, Sudden Wealth*, 1846; *The Snobs of England, by One of Themselves*, 1846-1847 (later as *The Book of Snobs*, 1848, 1852); *Mrs. Perkin's Ball*, 1847 (as Titmarsh); *"Our Street,"* 1848 (as Titmarsh); *A Little Dinner at Timmins's*, 1848; *Doctor Birch and His Young Friends*, 1849 (as Titmarsh); *The Kickleburys on the Rhine*, 1850 (as Titmarsh); *A Shabby Genteel Story, and Other Tales*, 1852; *The Rose and the Ring: Or, The History of Prince Giglio and Prince Bulbo*, 1855 (as Titmarsh); *Memoirs of Mr. Charles J. Yellowplush [with] The Diary of C. Jeames De La Pluche, Esqr.*, 1856.

POETRY: *The Chronicle of the Drum*, 1841.

NONFICTION: *The Paris Sketch Book*, 1840 (2 volumes; as M. A. Titmarsh); *The Irish Sketch Book*, 1843 (2 volumes; as Titmarsh); *Notes of a Journey from Cornhill to Grand Cairo, by Way of Lisbon, Athens, Constantinople, and Jerusalem, Performed in the Steamers of the Penninsular and Oriental Company*, 1846 (as Titmarsh); *The English Humourists of the Eighteenth Century*, 1853; *Sketches and Travels in London*, 1856; *The Four Georges: Sketches of Manners, Morals, Court and Town Life*, 1860.

William Makepeace Thackeray (THAK-uh-ree) was born in Calcutta, India (where his father was in the service of the East India Company), in 1811, and died in London in 1863. At least until 1859, when George Eliot's *Adam Bede* (1859) appeared, he was Charles Dickens's only possible rival as the leading Victorian novelist.

Thackeray's father, Richmond Thackeray, died in 1815; his mother thereafter married Captain Henry Carmichael-Smyth, the original of Thackeray's fictional Colonel Newcome. In 1822 the boy was sent to the Charterhouse School, where he experienced real cruelty. A school bully flattened his nose beyond repair, rendering him physically grotesque. For the rest of his life Thackeray was acutely self-conscious about his appearance. He was an indifferent student at Cambridge University, leaving without taking a degree. Lacking a definite aim or goal in life, he spent time in Weimar, where he had a private audience with Johann Wolfgang von Goethe. For a while he lived a bohemian life as an art student in Paris; he then read for the law at the Middle Temple, but he disliked it so heartily that he never practiced. After losing most of his considerable inheritance through a combination of folly and ill luck, Thackeray thought he would make his living as an artist. He sought to illustrate Dickens's *The Posthumous Papers of the Pickwick*

Club (1836-1837), but Dickens turned him down. Fortunately for posterity Thackeray turned to literature, but he always loved art and he later illustrated many of his own writings.

Thackeray began his career by burlesquing popular contemporary novelists whose work he considered mawkish, absurd, or morally vicious for *Fraser's Magazine*; the most important outcome of these labors was his *Catherine*, in which he attacked the vogue of the crime story. A more important enterprise, *Barry Lyndon*, was an eighteenth century rogue story, influenced by Thackeray's admiration for Henry Fielding's *Jonathan Wild* (1743). The writer did not really catch the public fancy until he published *Vanity Fair* in 1847-1848. From then on, though his sales always ran far behind those of Dickens, his reputation and fortune were secure.

In the 1850's he made two lecture tours of the United States, where he was welcomed by the best society. On his first tour he dined at the White House and met such literary luminaries as Henry Wadsworth Longfellow, William Cullen Bryant, and Washington Irving. His literary career concluded with his appointment as the first editor of the *Cornhill Magazine* in 1859. His domestic happiness was clouded by the death of his second infant daughter and the mental illness of his wife, Isabella Shaw, whom he married in 1836, and who outlived him by many years. In his relations with his daughters he showed all the tenderness of which his kindly, but in some ways weak, nature was capable.

Thackeray was at once a cynic and a sentimentalist. The judgments he makes of his characters are often conventional, but he portrays them with a powerful realism that was no doubt shocking to many readers of his day. Many of his most successful characters are, in one way or another, rogues. "The Art of Novels," he declared, "is to represent Nature; to convey as strongly as possible the sentiment of reality." The heightening and idealism proper to "a tragedy or a poem or a lofty drama" he ruled out. Not by this alone was he differentiated from Dickens but also by his upper-class point of view, his lack of Dickens's enthusiasm, vitality, and inexhaustible sympathy, and his more bookish, elegant style. Thackeray's world, in its main aspects, comprises Mayfair and bohemia.

Though the two great writers did not fail to appreciate each other, Dickens was inclined to resent his rival's somewhat superior and aristocratic air toward "the art that he held in trust." He also envied the success of *Vanity Fair*. The strained relations of the two novelists suffered a total breach from an imbroglio involving a fellow member of the Garrick Club which was repaired only days before Thackeray's unexpected death. The loss of his rival brought Dickens genuine grief.

Vanity Fair is generally regarded as Thackeray's magnum opus. It is a stunning panorama of a corrupt upper- and middle-class society against the background of the Waterloo crisis. Its heroine, Becky Sharp, is, along with Daniel Defoe's Moll Flanders, the most celebrated woman rogue in English fiction. Another masterpiece is *The History of Henry Esmond, Esquire*, a novel in the form of a memoir, presenting various intrigues in an eighteenth century London that in some ways was more congenial to Thackeray's mind and spirit than was his own time. The novel's cool, autumnal elegance and perfect distinction of style make it one of the world's great novels. It has, too, in Beatrix Esmond, one of the most subtly and completely portrayed of all heroines of fiction. *The History of Pendennis* is an attempt to use for fiction the materials of Thackeray's own life in the manner and spirit of Fielding's *Tom Jones* (1749). *The Newcomes*, a family novel covering three generations, is a *Vanity Fair* with a broader scope. *The Virginians* depicts Henry Esmond's grandsons in the American Revolution and in London. *Denis Duval*, a brilliant adventure story which marks a turning to romance, Thackeray unfortunately did not live to finish.

Thackeray's achievement, like that of his master Fielding, is central in the development of the English novel. Though he lacked Dickens's imaginative fecundity, he was a masterful stylist and had an unerring sense of social and psychological realism. After well more than a century, Thackeray's reputation as one of the great English novelists is secure.

Robert G. Blake

Bibliography

Bloom, Harold, ed. *William Makepeace Thackeray*. New York: Chelsea House, 1987. A collection of essays on various aspects of Thackeray's fiction, including such issues and concepts as humor, realism, characterization, point of view, and irony.

_______. *William Makepeace Thackeray's "Vanity Fair."* New York: Chelsea House, 1987. In addition to Bloom's original introductory essay, the volume reprints seven critical essays on the novel. Subjects range from Dorothy Van Ghent's evaluation of Becky Sharp to H. M. Daleski's consideration of the form of Thackeray's most important work.

Clarke, Michael M. *Thackeray and Women*. De Kalb: Northern Illinois University Press, 1995. Examines Thackeray's treatment of women characters. Includes bibliographical references and an index.

Dodds, John Wendell. *Thackeray: A Critical Portrait*. New York: Oxford University Press, 1941. This scholarly study of Thackeray's genius and the art of his fiction includes an assessment of his short satirical sketches and stories. An important book in Thackeray criticism. Includes an index.

Fletcher, Robert P. "'The Foolishest of Existing Mortals': Thackeray, 'Gurlyle,' and the Character(s) of Fiction." *Clio* 24 (Winter, 1995): 113-125. Discusses Thomas Carlyle's and Thackeray's different conceptions of history and fiction. Claims that a contrast between their opinions on novels and knowledge uncovers the anxiety in Carlyle's preference for history over fiction.

Harden, Edgar F. *Thackeray the Writer: From Journalism to "Vanity Fair."* New York: St. Martin's Press, 1998. A thorough study of Thackeray's literary career.

_______. *"Vanity Fair": A Novel Without a Hero*. New York: Twayne, 1995. A clear, understandable review of the seminal novel. Excellent for any student of *Vanity Fair*.

Mudge, Isadore Gilbert, and M. Earl Sears. *A Thackeray Dictionary: The Characters and Short Stories Alphabetically Arranged*. 1910. Reprint. New York: Humanities Press, 1962. An essential reference. "Chronological List of Novels and Stories" includes the titles under which many of Thackeray's short sketches and stories were published and republished. "Synopses" provides invaluable annotations on the contents of all of Thackeray's works. "Dictionary" is an alphabetical reference for his characters.

Shillingsburg, Peter. *William Makepeace Thackeray: A Literary Life*. New York: Palgrave, 2001. An excellent introduction to the life of the great novelist. Thorough and scholarly but accessible.

Taylor, D. J. *Thackeray: The Life of a Literary Man*. New York: Carroll and Graf, 2001. A lengthy biography that argues for Thackeray's preeminence among nineteenth century English novelists. Sheds much light on his work.

Theocritus

Greek poet

Born: Syracuse, Sicily (now in Italy); c. 308 B.C.E.
Died: Syracuse, Sicily (now in Italy); c. 260 B.C.E.

POETRY: *Idylls*, c. 270 B.C.E. (English translation, 1684).

Theocritus (thee-AHK-ruht-uhs), a lyric and semidramatic poet, is regarded as the father of pastoral poetry. Little factual biographical information exists. Much of what has sometimes passed for fact about him has been inferred from his writings, and in some cases doubt has been cast on works attributed to him. It would appear reasonable to assume, however, that he was born about 308 B.C.E. in Syracuse, Sicily (though claims have also been made for Cos), and that he studied as a youth and young man under the Greek master Philetas, in Cos. Becoming certain of his craft as a poet, Theocritus appealed to Hiero the Second, ruler of Syracuse, for Hiero's support as a patron (probably in 275 B.C.E.) but was refused. Shortly thereafter, a similar plea to Ptolemy Philadelphus brought success, and Theocritus took up residence in Alexandria sometime between 275 and 270 B.C.E. How long he stayed there and where he went afterward is a question on which there is only conjecture. Probably he went to Cos, perhaps back to Syracuse, where he probably died about 260 B.C.E.

Much of Theocritus's poetry illustrates the love the ancient Greeks had for their homeland. Apparently the poet, far away from Greece in Alexandria, wrote much of his poetry in the pastoral convention to express the love he had for Greece. Theocritus was a skilled literary craftsman, and his style is vivid and graceful. His work shows a love of nature and a sophisticated ability with drama, satire, and characterization. His most famous poems, the bucolics, are pastoral poems on mythical subjects. The epics, a later work, includes poems to Hiero and Ptolemy and to their respective spouses. There is also a series of epigrams of doubtful authenticity and equally doubtful date. The poems of Theocritus are often referred to as idylls, a word bestowed upon them by ancient authors. Credit is usually given to Theocritus for being the inventor of pastoral poetry, and he probably was, although modern scholarship, by showing how Theocritus borrowed ideas and fragments from earlier authors, has somewhat diminished the reputation he once enjoyed. Theocritus inspired later Greek poets, including Moschus of Syracuse. His most successful follower, however, was the Roman poet Vergil, who, in his *Eclogues* (43-37 B.C.E.), introduced pastoral conventions into Latin poetry. Theocritus also influenced later poets such as Edmund Spenser.

Jonathan L. Thorndike

Bibliography

Burton, Joan B. *Theocritus's Urban Mimes: Mobility, Gender, and Patronage*. Berkeley: University of California Press, 1995. Burton presents sophisticated readings of Theocritus's urban mimes. Unlike Theocritus's bucolic poems, his urban mimes represent women in more central and powerful roles.

Haber, Judith. *Pastoral and the Poetics of Self-Contradiction*. New York: Cambridge University Press, 1994. A review of the origins and development of the pastoral tradition, with an especially acute focus on the criticism and interpretations of Theocritus over the centuries.

Halperin, David. *Before Pastoral: Theocritus and Ancient Tradition of Bucolic Poetry*. New Haven: Yale University Press, 1983. A reexamination of Theocritus's place as the originator of the pastoral poetry. Halperin credits him with more originality and greater influence than do previous critics.

Hubbard, Thomas. *Pipes of Pan*. Ann Arbor: University of Michigan Press, 1998. A review of the pastoral tradition from ancient Greece to the European Renaissance, with special attention paid to Theocritus as originator and prime exponent.

Hunter, Richard. "Commentary." In *Theocritus: "Idylls," a Selection*. New York: Cambridge University Press, 1999. Provides an excellent selection of Theocritus's verse and good background to his themes, including city and town life, pastoral poetry, and art of the ancient Mediterranean region.

________. *Theocritus and the Archaeology of Greek Poetry*. New York: Cambridge University Press, 1996. An interesting study of the historical and literary context of the Greek archaic age from which Theocritus's poems emerged. Focuses more on the hymns, mimes, and erotic poems of Theocritus than on his pastorals.

Walker, Steven F. *Theocritus*. Boston: Twayne, 1980. A study providing a solid introduction and background to the author, his world, and his works.

Zimmerman, Clayton. *The Pastoral Narcissus: A Study of the First Idyll of Theocritus*. Lanham, Md.: Rowman and Littlefield, 1994. Links Theocritus's poem on Narcissus to the visual arts in the Hellenistic period.

Paul Theroux

American novelist and travel writer

Born: Medford, Massachusetts; April 10, 1941

LONG FICTION: *Waldo*, 1967; *Fong and the Indians*, 1968; *Murder in Mount Holly*, 1969; *Girls at Play*, 1969; *Jungle Lovers*, 1971; *Saint Jack*, 1973; *The Black House*, 1974; *The Family Arsenal*, 1976; *Picture Palace*, 1978; *The Mosquito Coast*, 1981; *Half Moon Street: Two Short Novels*, 1984; *O-Zone*, 1986; *My Secret History*, 1989; *Chicago Loop*, 1990; *Millroy the Magician*, 1994; *My Other Life*, 1996; *On the Edge of the Great Rift: Three Novels of Africa*, 1996 (includes *Fong and the Indians*, *Girl at Play*, and *Jungle Lovers*); *Kowloon Tong*, 1997; *The Collected Short Novels*, 1999; *Hotel Honolulu*, 2001.

SHORT FICTION: *Sinning with Annie, and Other Stories*, 1972; *The Consul's File*, 1977; *World's End*, 1980; *The London Embassy*, 1982; *The Collected Stories*, 1997.

DRAMA: *The Autumn Dog*, pr. 1981.

SCREENPLAY: *Saint Jack*, 1979 (with Peter Bogdanovich and Howard Sackler).

NONFICTION: *V. S. Naipaul: An Introduction to His Work*, 1972; *The Great Railway Bazaar: By Train Through Asia*, 1975; *The Old Patagonian Express: By Train Through the Americas*, 1979; *The Kingdom by the Sea: A Journey Around Great Britain*, 1983; *Sailing Through China*, 1983; *The Imperial Way*, 1985 (with Steve McCurry); *Sunrise with Seamonsters: Travels and Discoveries, 1964-1984*, 1985; *Patagonia Revisited*, 1985 (with Bruce Chatwin); *Riding the Iron Rooster: By Train Through China*, 1988; *To the Ends of the Earth: The Selected Travels of Paul Theroux*, 1990; *The Happy Isles of Oceania: Paddling the Pacific*, 1992; *Travelling the World: The Illustrated Travels of Paul Theroux*, 1992; *The Pillars of Hercules: A Grand Tour of the Mediterranean*, 1995; *Sir Vidia's Shadow: A Friendship Across Five Continents*, 2000; *Fresh-Air Fiend: Travel Writings, 1985-2000*, 2000; *Nurse Wolf and Dr. Sacks*, 2001; *Dark Star Safari: Overland from Cairo to Cape Town*, 2002.

CHILDREN'S/YOUNG ADULT LITERATURE: *A Christmas Card*, 1978; *London Snow: A Christmas Story*, 1979.

Paul Edward Theroux (thuh-REW) is the primary delineator in fiction of Americans in exile and is the best-known American travel writer of his time. He is the son of Albert Eugene, who was a shoe-leather salesman, and Anne Dittami Theroux, a teacher. Among his six siblings is novelist Alexander Theroux. Young Theroux sought privacy from his large family by reading and decided to become a writer when he was fourteen.

After high school, he attended the University of Maine for one year and graduated from the University of Massachusetts in 1963. He then briefly went to graduate school at Syracuse University before joining the Peace Corps. He taught English at Soche Hill College in Limbe, Malawi, until October, 1965, when he was arrested and deported for spying and aiding revolutionaries attempting to overthrow the country's dictator. Theroux had volunteered to be a messenger for the dictator's leading opponent, not realizing that the man was plotting an assassination. Expelled from the Peace Corps, he lectured at Makerere University in Kampala, Uganda, until 1968. His first novel, *Waldo*, was published in 1967, the year he married Anne Castle, a fellow teacher; they have two sons. Theroux taught Jacobean drama at the University of Singapore from 1968 until 1971, when he decided to write full-time. He lived for many years in England, his wife's native country. Following their divorce, he returned to the United States and settled in East Sandwich, Massachusetts.

Theroux's fiction reflects his experiences: Most of it deals with exiles, usually Americans, in Africa, Asia, Latin America, and England. *Fong and the Indians* presents a Chinese Catholic living in Kenya and subjected to the prejudice of Africans, Americans, and the British. *Jungle Lovers* chronicles two Americans trying to improve the lives of the citizens of Malawi and discovering strong resistance to change. Since Theroux's fiction is ironic and skeptical, the Americans' motives are ambiguous. The hero of *Saint Jack*, perhaps Theroux's best novel, is a middle-aged American hustler and pimp in Singapore. *The Black House*, a subtle horror tale, concerns an English anthropologist who returns to England after years in Uganda to find himself so alienated that he has an affair with a beautiful woman created by his imagination.

In 1975 Theroux's career entered a new phase with the publication of *The Great Railway Bazaar.* Always in love with trains and travel, he took a four-month trip through Asia and turned his impressions into a surprise best-seller. Such travel writing had not been popular since the 1930's, but Theroux's book, a distinctive blend of colorful details, decadence, wit, and anger, almost singlehandedly created a new readership, paving the way for his books about Latin America, England, and China, as well as similar works by writers such as Bruce Chatwin and Jonathan Raban. Before his first travel book, Theroux's novels were generally well received by reviewers and ignored by readers. Afterward, such novels as *The Family Arsenal* and *The Mosquito Coast* became best-sellers.

Theroux writes realistic fiction, almost comedies of manners, earning for him comparisons with Anthony Trollope, Henry James, W. Somerset Maugham, and Evelyn Waugh. On another level, his works are darkly ironic, violent explorations of the nature of evil similar to the fiction of Joseph Conrad, Graham Greene, and V. S. Naipaul. Although most of his protagonists are Americans, his view of the world is said by many commentators to be Anglicized: It is concerned with the decline of the international influence of the writers from his adopted country. Also, his writings about England, as with the short-story collection *The London Embassy* and the travel book *The Kingdom by the Sea*, emphasize the economic and social decay of Great Britain.

Theroux's infatuation with the expatriate experience is also in the English tradition, an approach to fiction that, like his travel writing, allows him to contrast cultures. His characters often find themselves at the mercy of social, political, and natural forces over which they have no control. They fail all the more when they fool themselves into thinking that they have complete control over their circumstances. In *Doctor Slaughter*, one of two short novels in *Half Moon Street*, an American scholar in London enjoys exerting power over men as a high-class prostitute only to be devastated when she realizes that she has become merely a pawn in international politics. The protagonist of *The Mosquito Coast* uproots his family from Massachusetts because he despises what America has become, but once in the Honduran jungle, he tries to turn it into another version of what he has fled, leading to madness and death. The protagonist of *Saint Jack*, a corrupt version of the title character in Joseph Conrad's *Lord Jim* (1900), considers himself a tainted saint, unselfishly devoted to his clients. Still, he is the least self-deluded of Theroux's characters, recognizing the individual's responsibility not to make the world any worse than it need be. Theroux seems torn between a cynicism about human nature and an almost Dickensian belief in the possibilities of individual goodness beneath society's decadent, violent surface.

Several of Theroux's novels, such as *My Secret History* and *My Other Life*, are partly autobiographical, but also partly imaginings of what the writer's life might have been if certain things had been different. Others, such as *Hotel Honolulu*, are based in Theroux's experience as a traveler and a writer (the protagonist of the former novel is a blocked writer) but wander further afield. In all cases, however, Theroux is acknowledged as a writer who has amassed an unrivaled knowledge of the world and its inhabitants which he puts to good purpose in all of his writing.

Michael Adams

Bibliography

Beecroft, Simon. "*Sir Vidia's Shadow:* V. S. Naipaul, the Writer, and *The Enigma of Arrival.*" *Journal of Commonwealth Literature* 35, no. 1 (2000): 71-85. Presents a structural analysis of Theroux's book on the breakdown of his long friendship with Naipaul, comparing it with Naipaul's own book *The Enigma of Arrival.*

Bell, Robert F. "Metamorphoses and Missing Halves: Allusions in Paul Theroux's *Picture Palace.*" *Critique: Studies in Modern Fiction* 22, no. 3 (1981): 17-30. Discusses concepts of the interchangeability of identities, the double image, and the gap existing between art and life.

Coale, Samuel. *Paul Theroux.* Boston: Twayne, 1987. Part of Twayne's United States Authors series, this book provides a comprehensive look at Theroux's work as well as providing a chronology of events in the author's life. Includes references for each chapter and a bibliography of both primary and secondary sources and an index.

Glaser, E. "The Self-Reflexive Traveler: Paul Theroux on the Art of Travel and Travel Writing." *Centennial Review* 33 (Summer, 1989): 193-206. This article provides more insight into what motivates Theroux's writing and traveling. This in-depth profile and interview of Theroux is invaluable in the light of the scarcity of book-length works about him; includes some references.

Kerr, Douglas. "A Passage to *Kowloon Tong:* Paul Theroux and Hong Kong, 1997." *Journal of Commonwealth Literature* 34, no. 2 (1999): 75-84. Discusses Theroux's representation in his novel of the transfer of power over Hong Kong from Britain to China, and the response to the novel in Hong Kong and China.

O'Connor, Teresa F. "Jean Rhys, Paul Theroux, and the Imperial Road." *Twentieth Century Literature* 38 (Winter, 1992): 404-414. Considers the possible influence of Rhys's unpublished manuscript "Imperial Road" on Theroux's work.

Dylan Thomas

Welsh poet

Born: Swansea, Wales; October 27, 1914
Died: New York, New York; November 9, 1953

POETRY: *Eighteen Poems*, 1934; *Twenty-five Poems*, 1936; *The Map of Love*, 1939; *New Poems*, 1943; *Deaths and Entrances*, 1946; *Twenty-six Poems*, 1950; *In Country Sleep*, 1952; *Collected Poems, 1934-1952*, 1952; *The Poems of Dylan Thomas*, 1971 (Daniel Jones, editor).
LONG FICTION: *The Death of the King's Canary*, 1976 (with John Davenport).
SHORT FICTION: *Portrait of the Artist as a Young Dog*, 1940; *Selected Writings of Dylan Thomas*, 1946; *A Child's Christmas in Wales*, 1954; *Adventures in the Skin Trade, and Other Stories*, 1955; *A Prospect of the Sea, and Other Stories*, 1955; *Early Prose Writings*, 1971; *The Followers*, 1976; *The Collected Stories*, 1984.
DRAMA: *Under Milk Wood: A Play for Voices*, pr. 1953 (public reading), pr. 1954 (radio play), pb. 1954, pr. 1956 (staged; musical settings by Daniel Jones).
SCREENPLAYS: *Three Weird Sisters*, 1948 (with Louise Birt and David Evans); *No Room at the Inn*, 1948 (with Ivan Foxwell); *The Doctor and the Devils*, 1953; *The Beach at Falesá*, 1963; *Twenty Years A'Growing*, 1964; *Rebecca's Daughters*, 1965; *Me and My Bike*, 1965.
RADIO PLAYS: *Quite Early One Morning*, 1944; *The Londoner*, 1946; *Return Journey*, 1947; *Quite Early One Morning*, 1954 (22 radio plays).
NONFICTION: *Letters to Vernon Watkins*, 1957 (Vernon Watkins, editor); *Selected Letters of Dylan Thomas*, 1966 (Constantine FitzGibbon, editor); *Poet in the Making: The Notebooks of Dylan Thomas*, 1968 (Ralph Maud, editor); *Twelve More Letters by Dylan Thomas*, 1969 (FitzGibbon, editor).
MISCELLANEOUS: *"The Doctor and the Devils," and Other Scripts*, 1966 (two screenplays and one radio play).

Dylan Marlais Thomas, born in Swansea, Wales, in 1914, is widely considered to be the greatest British poet of his generation. In addition to poetry, he wrote a famous radio play (*Under Milk Wood*), an autobiography, and highly imaginative short stories as well as screenplays and essays. He gained celebrity in Great Britain for British Broadcasting Corporation (BBC) radio broadcasts of his and other poets' works and received international acclaim for his public readings in the United States, where he died on November 9, 1953, of alcohol abuse and related causes.

Though Thomas's total poetic output is modest, he was not so much a slow writer as a careful one, altering some of his poems more than two hundred times. He insisted that his work be read at its face value, preferably aloud. (Thomas once said that he wanted to be *read*, not *read into*.) His lyrical gifts are often linked to his Welsh background, along with the influence of particular poets, notably Gerard Manley Hopkins. Much of the criticism of the obscurity of his work has been irrelevant, because readers are supposed to allow the words to work on them, which they do in spite of the many private and esoteric references. Still, Thomas's painstakingly crafted poetry was the product of a highly dialectical intellect and holds up to close rational analysis.

Thomas was a complex figure, a man of effusive good will who suffered agonies of guilt. While he tortuously worked through to a celebration of Christian belief in God and nature, his personal life revealed a man who wished to believe, to find faith, but could not without great difficulty. Extremely sensitive, he projected his own guilt onto the world at large—its hypocrisy and greed, its general inhumanity. Two symptoms of this paradox were his telling the truth beyond the edge of tact and his profligate wastefulness of money, though he was miserable when the first resulted in hurt feelings and the second in poverty.

Many of Thomas's poems reflect his love of the Welsh countryside. The setting of one of his most famous poems, "Fern Hill," is his aunt and uncle's farm, which he visited as a child. Much of what he had to say in these poems is concerned with that Edenic country world—its harmony with the rhythm of the earth in its emphasis on birth, marriage, death, rebirth, and a simple faith in God—or with the lost world of childhood innocence.

Thomas was educated in the Swansea grammar school, in which his strict, agnostic father was an English master. His juvenile poetry and prose were published frequently in the grammar school literary magazine. When his first volume, *Eighteen Poems*, appeared, it was received enthusiastically by critics such as Edith Sitwell, though not by the general public, some of whom wrote virulent abuses to the *Sunday Times*. His poetry of this period was concerned almost entirely with personal problems and was made perhaps deliberately obscure by private imagery and a highly personalized rhetorical style.

Until World War II Thomas lived in London much of the time. Short but broad, of huge energy, he had experiences that were in many ways those of any proud rural innocent; always scornful of hypocrisy and the unnatural, he found much to reject in the city. At the same time, his great warmth and talent made him many friends among its literary leaders. His way of adapting to this life was to mock convention with droll acts. During the war he served as an antiaircraft gunner; the sight of the war's courage and suffering induced his second creative phase, one which revealed poignant feelings for others. When he began reading poetry over the BBC, he developed a following among the general public. With the publication of *Deaths and Entrances* in 1946, which contains some of his most celebrated poems, Thomas's literary reputation grew considerably.

With the printing of *Collected Poems* in 1952 he became a major public figure on the basis of the book's enthusiastic reception by reviewers and critics. His later poetry had begun to reveal the change in his attitude from one of doubt and fear to faith and hope, with love of God gained through love of humankind and the world of nature. It also was more accessible. It was at this time, however, that he became unbearably dissatisfied with life. Part of this feeling may have been due to his growing fear of alienation from his Irish-born wife, Caitlin, and their three children; part of it may have been the effect of his fear of losing his powers. In addition, he was miserable as a public figure. He was anxious before strangers. Although he was deeply appreciated by the audiences he read to, most of these people were interested in the poet of public fame, not in the private man. For a man with a huge capacity and need to love and be loved, this experience may have been devastating. Whatever the causes, Thomas produced mostly fiction and verse plays the last few years of his life. Of these, the unfinished *Adventures in the Skin Trade* deals with his urban experiences, *Under Milk Wood* with his village reminiscences. Both these works, along with his unfinished series of poems titled "In Country Heaven" (of which *In Country Sleep*, published in 1952, was a part), are celebrations of "the love of Man and in praise of God, and I'd be a damn' fool if they weren't."

James J. Balakier

Bibliography

Ackerman, John. *Dylan Thomas: His Life and Work*. New York: St. Martin's Press, 1996. A biography describing the life and writings of Thomas.

_______. *Welsh Dylan: Dylan Thomas's Life, Writing, and His Wales*. 2d ed. Bridgend, Wales: Seren, 1998. This biography of Dylan looks at his homeland, Wales, and shows how the area influenced his writings.

Davies, James A. *A Reference Companion to Dylan Thomas*. Westport, Conn.: Greenwood Press, 1998. A handbook that provides quick and easy reference to facts about the poet and his life. Includes bibliography and index.

Ferris, Paul. *Dylan Thomas: The Biography*. Rev. ed. Washington, D.C.: Counterpoint, 2000. This volume presents an account of the playwright's upbringing in Wales, his education, his move to London and marriage, his travels during the postwar years, and his writing. Includes bibliography and index.

Hardy, Barbara Nathan. *Dylan Thomas: An Original Language*. Athens: University of Georgia Press, 2000. Hardy looks at Thomas's use of language in his writings, including his use of Welsh-derived terms. Includes bibliography and index.

Jones, R. F. G. *Time Passes: Dylan Thomas's Journey to "Under Milk Wood."* Sydney: Woodworm Press, 1994. An account of the literary development of Thomas, including analysis of *Under Milk Wood*. Includes bibliography and index.

Korg, Jacob. *Dylan Thomas*. Rev. ed. New York: Twayne, 1992. A basic biography of Thomas that covers his life and works. Includes bibliography and index.

Sinclair, Andrew. *Dylan the Bard: A Life of Dylan Thomas*. New York: Thomas Dunne Books, 2000. Sinclair provides the story of Thomas's life as a poet and writer. Includes bibliography and index.

Joyce Carol Thomas

American novelist, poet, and playwright

Born: Ponca City, Oklahoma; May 25, 1938
Identity: African American

LONG FICTION: *Marked by Fire*, 1982; *Bright Shadow*, 1983; *Water Girl*, 1986; *The Golden Pasture*, 1986; *When the Nightingale Sings*, 1992; *House of Light*, 2001.

DRAMA: *A Song in the Sky*, pr. 1976; *Look! What a Wonder!*, pr. 1976; *Magnolia*, pr. 1977; *Ambrosia*, pr. 1978; *Gospel Roots*, pr. 1981; *I Have Heard of a Land*, pr. 1989; *When the Nightingale Sings*, pr. 1991 (adaptation of her novel).

POETRY: *Bittersweet*, 1973; *Crystal Breezes*, 1974; *Blessing*, 1975; *Black Child*, 1981; *Inside the Rainbow*, 1982.

EDITED TEXT: *A Gathering of Flowers: Stories About Being Young in America*, 1990.

CHILDREN'S/YOUNG ADULT LITERATURE: *Brown Honey in Broomwheat Tea*, 1993; *Gingerbread Days*, 1995; *Cherish Me*, 1998.

Joyce Carol Thomas, novelist, poet, and playwright, was born May 25, 1938, in Ponca City, Oklahoma, the fifth child in a family of nine children. Her father was a bricklayer, and her mother was a hairstylist. As a child, Thomas picked cotton with her family. This involved living temporarily with other families. Thomas especially enjoyed staying with the ten children of the Lightsey family. There, her fascination with stories began—both listening to the tales of others and telling her own. When she was ten, her family migrated to Tracy, California, to pick tomatoes. There she worked with many Mexican families and became interested in their language, which she described as "singing."

As a young mother, Thomas worked days as a telephone operator and attended night school, graduating from San Jose State University in 1964 with a B.A. in Spanish. She then taught high school French and Spanish classes in Palo Alto, California, while attending Stanford University and earning her M.A. in 1967. She divorced her first husband, Gettis Withers, in 1968 and married Roy Thomas. Her daughter and three sons all respected their mother's busy schedule, allowing her time and space for her writing.

From 1969 to 1982, Thomas taught drama and English at Contra Costa College in San Pablo, at St. Mary's College in Moraga, and at San José State University. In 1983, she served as visiting professor at Purdue University in Indiana and taught from 1989 to 1995 at the University of Tennessee. She also lectured at several other American universities as well as conducting poetry seminars in Nigeria and Haiti.

From 1973 to 1978, Thomas began to publish poems and plays. Her poetry appeared in numerous periodicals, such as the *American Poetry Review*, *Black Scholar*, and the *Yardbird Reader*, and in the anthology *Calafía: The California Poetry* (1979). Her first collection of poems, *Bittersweet*, was quickly followed by *Crystal Breezes* and *Blessing*. In 1982, she published *Inside the Rainbow*, which gathered most of these poems and added some new ones. In her poetry, Thomas deals with general human realities, but she also captures her own experiences in poems such as "Double Rock Baptist Church" and with references to "fat back" frying and "scrubbing chitlin grease." Her poetry is known for its honest rendering of human experience as well as for its celebration of the African American cultural heritage.

The fifteen poems of *Black Child* were written after the tragic murders of several children in Atlanta. Her preface advised that the living recommit their lives to the young. In addition to her poems for adults, Thomas has addressed young readers in *Brown Honey in Broomwheat Tea*, *Gingerbread Days*, and *Cherish Me*, as well as other poem collections designed for preschool children. Thomas continued to celebrate the importance of children and their families in a community context.

Poetry was Thomas's first writing form, and even when she became known for plays and then for fiction, poetry was never far away. She insisted, "Poetry wakes me up at midnight." This love of language and ear for speech also flowered in her first drama, *A Song in the Sky*, which she produced in 1976. Six more plays quickly followed, some of which she produced herself.

In 1982 her career took a new path: She published her first novel, *Marked by Fire*, sometimes labeled as a novel for young adults. Children are often featured in Thomas's work, and this novel focuses on the young Abyssinia Jackson, who, as Thomas had done, works in the cotton fields outside of Ponca City, Oklahoma. Thomas here draws upon her sensitivity to language, folk stories, and small-town ritual. The novel was named Outstanding Book of the Year by *The New York Times* and also Best Book for Young Adults by the American Library Association. It then won the 1983 American Book Award for children's fiction in paperback. *Marked by Fire* and its sequel, *Bright Shadow*, became required reading in several high schools and universities. The sequel explores Abyssinia's young womanhood and shows Thomas's ability to create vivid, memorable images and strong African American characters. *Water Girl* focuses on her move to California, and the life of Abyssinia's lover, Carl Lee, is told in *The Golden Pasture*.

In 1990, Thomas edited *A Gathering of Flowers*, expanding her scope, for this collection includes various other American ethnic groups. Thomas's writing has often been compared to that of Toni Morrison, Maya Angelou, and Alice Walker. Certainly her poetry and fiction have made a significant contribution to American letters.

Marie J. K. Brenner

Bibliography

Henderson, Katherine Usher. "Joyce Carol Thomas." In *Inter/View: Talks with America's Writing Women*, edited by Mickey Pearlman and Katherine Usher Henderson. Lexington: University Press of Kentucky, 1990. Highlights Thomas's attitude toward the pleasures and freedoms of outside space and her ability to exalt African American culture with no lingering bitterness.

"Joyce Carol Thomas." In *Contemporary Literary Criticism*, edited by Daniel G. Marowski. Vol. 35. Detroit: Gale, 1985. Provides an early compilation of materials on Thomas's fiction, including portions of the reviews of her first two novels.

Toombs, Charles P. "Joyce Carol Thomas." In *Afro-American Fiction Writers After 1955*, edited by Thadious M. Davis and Trudier Harris. Vol. 33 in *Dictionary of Literary Biography*. Detroit: Gale, 1984. Provides a concise overview of Thomas's life, including samples of her poetry and first two Abyssinia novels.

Yalom, Marilyn, ed. *Women Writers of the West Coast: Speaking of Their Lives and Careers*. Santa Barbara, Calif.: Capra Press, 1983. Discusses Thomas's real-life western settings as well as the centrality of women characters in her fiction.

Lewis Thomas

American essayist and science writer

Born: Flushing, New York; November 25, 1913
Died: New York, New York; December 3, 1993

NONFICTION: *The Lives of a Cell: Notes of a Biology Watcher*, 1974; *The Medusa and the Snail: More Notes of a Biology Watcher*, 1979; *Late Night Thoughts on Listening to Mahler's Ninth Symphony*, 1983; *The Youngest Science*, 1983 (memoir); *Et Cetera, Et Cetera: Notes of a Word-Watcher*, 1990; *The Fragile Species*, 1992.
POETRY: *Could I Ask You Something? Notes of a Medicine Watcher*, 1984.

Lewis Thomas was one of the most important American essayists and science writers of the late twentieth century. He was the son of Dr. Joseph Thomas, a successful general practitioner who later became a surgeon, and Grace (Peck) Thomas, a nurse. Dr. Thomas often took his son Lewis along with him while he made house calls. In his memoir, *The Youngest Science*, Thomas describes growing up in a medical family at a time when a general practitioner was still expected to make house calls but, beyond accurate diagnosis, could do little to cure ordinary diseases. This therapeutic nihilism had gradually changed by World War II, with the discovery of penicillin, sulfadiazine, and other new miracle drugs. In his essays, Thomas traces the transformation of modern medicine into a clinical science through discoveries in immunology and biochemistry.

Thomas was a precocious student who skipped several grades, graduated from the McBurney School in Manhattan at the age of fifteen, majored in biology at Princeton University, and then entered Harvard Medical School in 1933. After completing his clinical training in neurology, pathology, and immunology, he married Beryl Dawson, in 1941 (they later had three daughters). He then served with the U.S. Navy as a virologist in the Pacific and afterward embarked on a brilliant career in biomedical research and administration. He served as dean of the New York University and the Yale University schools of medicine, and as chancellor of the Sloan-Kettering Cancer Institute in New York. For most of his career, Thomas was a medical researcher and administrator at the Rockefeller Institute, The Johns Hopkins University, Tulane University, the University of Minnesota, New York University and Bellevue Hospital, and Yale University. He became a successful essayist in his fifties almost by accident.

Though Thomas wrote some poetry as an undergraduate, and later published more than two hundred articles for professional journals, he only started writing essays for *The New England Journal of Medicine* in 1971. His monthly column there, "Notes of a Biology Watcher," proved so successful that Viking Press published his first essay collection, *The Lives of a Cell*, in 1974. Much to Thomas's surprise, it became a best-seller and won for him a National Book Award in 1975. Thomas continued writing for *The New England Journal of Medicine* until 1978, collecting additional essays for a second collection, *The Medusa and the Snail*. He appeared as a regular columnist for *Discover* magazine, publishing a third essay volume, *Late Night Thoughts on Listening to Mahler's Ninth Symphony*, the same year as his memoir, *The Youngest Science*. Thomas indulged his passion for language in his next essay collection, *Et Cetera, Et Cetera: Notes of a Word-Watcher*. In the introduction Thomas admits, "My sole qualification for writing these essays on (mostly) Indo-European roots is that I've been enchanted and obsessed by them for over twenty years. . . ." In *The Fragile Species*, Thomas's last essay collection, he continues to share his eclectic concerns, ranging from the development of his profession to AIDS, aging, and his cat Jeoffry.

In his essays, Thomas employs an informal discursive style—brief, factual, witty, and optimistic. His mastery of the short essay form resulted from the editorial constraints on his monthly columns. One of Thomas's recurrent themes throughout his essays is the importance of symbiosis, the tendency of organisms to link together to create mutually beneficial relationships. Partnerships are essential in nature, where everything is interdependent. Organicism is the root metaphor in Thomas's writing, beginning with *The Lives of a Cell*. He imagines that Earth's biosphere is an integrated whole, with the human community functioning as a kind of global nervous system. In *The Medusa and the Snail*, he argues that symbiosis and altruism are the driving forces behind this global cooperation, evident everywhere, from the ecology of the cell to the behavior of social insects to a multitude of host-parasite partnerships throughout nature. Nothing exists absolutely alone. The ultimate symbiont is planet Earth, seen by Thomas as a gigantic living cell, surrounded by a self-regulating atmosphere. In his third essay volume, *Late Night Thoughts on Listening to Mahler's Ninth Symphony*, Thomas tempers his optimistic sense of the promise of science with an increased awareness of the risks of unrestrained militarism and the threat of nuclear war.

Thomas's memoir, *The Youngest Science*, is divided between personal reminiscence and medical history, with the early chapters describing Thomas's childhood and education and the later chapters recounting his medical career. In his discussion of the development of modern medicine, Thomas is preoccupied with the trade-offs between high-quality bedside care and high technology in the practice of medicine. The Whitney Museum has published a limited edition of Thomas's poetry, *Could I Ask You Something?*, with illustrations by Alfonso Ossorio.

Et Cetera, Et Cetera further explores topics developed in earlier essays such as the human capacity for error and children's remarkable capacity for learning language; it also documents what happens when Thomas lets himself loose in a room full of dictionaries.

The Fragile Species is a collection and adaptation of various addresses and lectures given by Thomas from 1984 to 1990. It was the last collection he published prior to his death in 1993.

Perhaps Thomas's most important accomplishment was his ability to reach a broad public audience, touching upon a wide range of scientific and general topics and using the concise, familiar essay form to articulate his unique personal vision. His literary success was and is an inspiration to other physicians and medical scientists to maintain the tradition of medical humanism in an age of overspecialization. He died of Waldenstrom's disease a week after his eightieth birthday.

Andrew J. Angyal
Beverly J. Matiko

Bibliography

Angyal, Andrew J. *Lewis Thomas*. Boston: Twayne, 1989. The first full-length study of Thomas's life and work.

Bearn, Alexander G. Obituary. *Nature* 367 (January 6, 1994): 23. Thomas's role in the medical community and as an eloquent spokesperson for it are discussed.

Bernstein, Jeremy. "Profiles: Biology Watcher." In *Experiencing Science: Profiles in Discovery*. New York: Basic Books, 1978. An accurate introduction to Thomas's career.

Flannery, Maura C. "Notes on a Biology Watcher." *The American Biology Teacher* 56, no. 6 (September, 1994): 374. A tribute that focuses on Thomas's impact on biology teachers.

Nemerov, Howard. "Lewis Thomas, Montaigne, and Human Happiness." In *New and Selected Essays*. Carbondale: Southern Illinois University Press, 1985. An insightful essay by a talented writer.

Rosenblatt, Roger. "Lewis Thomas." *The New York Times Magazine*, November 21, 1993, 650. Reports on his interviews with the terminally ill Thomas in an essay published just two weeks before Thomas's death.

Thomas à Kempis
(Thomas Hammerken)

German ecclesiastic and essayist

Born: Kempen, the Rhineland (now in Germany); 1379
Died: Monastery of St. Agnietenberg, near Zwolle, Bishopric of Utrecht (now in the Netherlands); August 8, 1471

NONFICTION: *Imitatio Christi*, c. 1427 (*The Imitation of Christ*, c. 1460-1530).

Thomas à Kempis (TAHM-uhs uh KEHM-puhs), born Thomas Hammerken (or Hemerken), probably in 1379, was the son of a peasant whose wife was the keeper of an old-fashioned dame school for small children. At the age of twelve, Thomas was sent to the chapter school at Deventer, where among his teachers was Florens Radewijns (Florentius Radewyn). Known at Deventer as Thomas from Kempen, the scholar gradually assumed the name by which posterity knows him. When it became apparent to Thomas and his teachers that he was suited for a monk's life, he went in 1399 to the monastery of St. Agnietenberg, near Zwolle, where the prior was his brother John. Thomas entered the Augustinian order in 1406 and was ordained a priest in 1413 or 1414.

The remainder of his long life was spent in that monastery, except for a brief period of exile from 1429 to 1432, during the Utrecht schism. Thomas copied a great deal of material, earning money for his monastery by his labors. He also wrote original material, for which dates of composition are too vague to have any value. Included in his works are biographies of Gerhard Groot, Florentius Radewyn, and the Flemish St. Louise. He also wrote many tracts and a chronicle of the monastery of St. Agnietenberg.

The most important of the writings with which his name is associated is *The Imitation of Christ*. This work, which states the aims of a true Christian and describes the means to achieve these aims, is an extremely well known and influential religious work. Although Thomas à Kempis's authorship has been disputed, the arguments advanced against his authorship have only seemed to strengthen the belief that the work is really from his pen. Thomas was made subprior of St. Agnietenberg in 1425. He died there on August 8, 1471.

Allen H. Redmon

Bibliography

Creasy, William C. Introduction to *The Imitation of Christ*, by Thomas à Kempis. Macon, Ga.: Mercer University Press, 1989.

Easwaran, Eknath. *Seeing with the Eyes of Love: Reflections on a Classic of Christian Mysticism*. Tomales, Calif.: Nilgiri Press, 1991.

Hyma, Albert. *The Brethren of the Common Life*. Grand Rapids, Mich.: Wm. B. Eerdmans, 1950.

_______. *The Christian Renaissance: A History of "Devotio Moderno."* 1924. Reprint. Hamden, Conn.: Archon, 1965.

Post, R. R. *The Modern Devotion: Confrontation with Reformation and Humanism*. Leiden, the Netherlands: E. J. Brill, 1968.

Thomas Aquinas

Italian theologian

Born: Roccasecca, north of Naples, Kingdom of Sicily (now in Italy); 1224 or 1225
Died: Fossanova, Latium, Papal States (now in Italy); March 7, 1274
Identity: Catholic

NONFICTION: *Scriptum super "Libros sententiarum,"* 1252-1256 (English translation, 1923); *Summa contra gentiles*, c. 1258-1264 (English translation, 1923); *Summa theologiae*, c. 1265-1273 (*Summa Theologica*, 1911-1921).

Thomas Aquinas (TAHM-uhs uh-KWI-nuhs) is generally agreed to be the towering figure in medieval theology, and to him goes the principal credit for applying the philosophical doctrines of Aristotle to Christianity. The joining of these seemingly divergent streams of thought in the philosophical movement known as Scholasticism has had tremendous influence on subsequent theological and philosophical thinking.

Thomas was well prepared by his background for the work that was to engage far and away the major portion of his efforts. Born at Roccasecca, near Aquino, Italy, in 1224 or 1225, the son of Count Landolfo of Aquino, he was raised in an atmosphere of ease. Having studied at the Abbey of Monte Cassino, he went from there, in 1239, to Naples to study the liberal arts. He then entered the Order of St. Dominic (c. 1243), abandoning his life of privilege to become a "begging friar."

Thomas was fortunate to be able to study under Albert the Great (Albertus Magnus) in Paris from 1245 to 1248. While with Albert in Cologne, after his studies in Paris, he was ordained to the priesthood. Shortly thereafter he received advanced degrees in theology. He spent the rest of his life teaching and writing his great treatises—such as his commentary on the *Sentences* of Peter Lombard (c. 1100-c. 1160)—in Rome, Paris, and Naples.

Of his works, the two most important are his *Summa contra gentiles*, which defends Christianity in the area of natural theology, and *Summa Theologica*, a work whose three divisions are related to God, Man, and Christ and in which Thomas attempted to summarize all human knowledge. This monumental treatise was left unfinished when he died of a sudden illness on March 7, 1274, at Fossanova, Italy, while traveling to the General Council of Lyons. St. Thomas Aquinas, canonized in 1323, remains a central thinker in Christian theology because of his synthesization of past knowledge and his application of the principles of scholastic reasoning to religion.

Craig Payne

Bibliography

Davies, Brian. *Aquinas*. New York: Continuum, 2002.
Inglis, John. *On Aquinas*. Belmont, Calif.: Wadsworth/Thompson Learning, 2002.
Milbank, John. *Truth in Aquinas*. New York: Routledge, 2001.
Nichols, Aidan. *Discovering Aquinas: An Introduction to His Life, Work, and Influence*. London: Darton Longman & Todd, 2002.
Oguejiofor, J. Obi. *The Philosophical Significance of Immortality in Thomas Aquinas*. Lanham, Md.: University Press of America, 2001.
Pope, Stephen, ed. *The Ethics of Aquinas*. Washington, D.C.: Georgetown University Press, 2002.
Shanley, Brian J. *The Thomast Tradition*. Boston: Kluwer, 2002.
Wippel, John F. *The Metaphysical Thought of Thomas Aquinas: From Finite Being to Uncreated Being*. Washington, D.C.: Catholic University of America Press, 2000.

Daniel Pierce Thompson

American novelist

Born: Charlestown, Massachusetts; October 1, 1795
Died: Montpelier, Vermont; June 6, 1868

LONG FICTION: *The Adventures of Timothy Peacock, Esq.*, 1835; *The Green Mountain Boys*, 1839; *Locke Amsden: Or, The Schoolmaster*, 1847; *The Rangers*, 1851.

Born of an old American family that reached Massachusetts early in the seventeenth century, and with an ancestor supposed to have been killed at the Battle of Lexington, Daniel Pierce Thompson had reason to be interested in history. Shortly after his birth, at Charlestown, Massachusetts, his family moved to Berlin, Vermont, a frontier settlement with neither school nor library. The chance discovery of a volume of poetry inspired him to get an education. After studying by himself and at a preparatory school, he entered Middlebury College with advanced standing, financing his studies by the sale of his sheep and by poems and articles he contributed to magazines.

After graduation, Thompson tutored the son of a rich southern planter and met Thomas Jefferson, who turned the young man's thoughts toward the law. After some study, Thompson returned to Vermont and was admitted to the bar. He codified the laws of Vermont in 1834. His first work of fiction was the anti-Masonic *Adventures of Timothy Peacock, Esq.*, whom he called a "Masonic Quixote." Association with survivors of the revolutionary period inspired his novel *The Green Mountain Boys*, first printed on a small newspaper press. Immediately successful, the novel went through fifty editions in twenty years. Its sequel was *The Rangers*, published in 1851. Thompson also edited the antislavery publication *Green Mountain Freeman* (1849-1856).

Thompson was an old-fashioned Yankee with a keen sense of humor. A contemporary portrait shows him with thin features, a jutting chin, a long nose, and a tangled mop of hair. He died at Montpelier, Vermont, in 1868.

Bibliography

Brooks, Van Wyck. *The Flowering of New England*. 1936. Reprint. Boston: Houghton Mifflin, 1981.

Flitcroft, J. E. *The Novelist of Vermont: A Biographical and Critical Study of Daniel Pierce Thompson*. Cambridge, Mass.: Harvard University Press, 1929.

Knoles, Lucia Z. "Daniel Pierce Thompson." In *Nineteenth-Century American Fiction Writers*, edited by Kent P. Ljungquist. Vol. 202 in *Dictionary of Literary Biography*. Detroit: Gale Group, 1999.

D'Arcy Wentworth Thompson

Scottish scientist and classicist

Born: Edinburgh, Scotland; May 2, 1860
Died: St. Andrews, Scotland; June 21, 1948

NONFICTION: *A Glossary of Greek Birds*, 1895, new edition 1936; *On Aristotle as a Biologist*, 1911; *On Growth and Form*, 1917, new edition 1942; *Science and the Classics*, 1940; *A Glossary of Greek Fishes*, 1947.
TRANSLATIONS: *The Fertilisation of Flowers*, 1893 (of Hermann Müller's *Die Befruchtung der Blumen durch Insekten*); *Historia Animalium*, 1910 (of Aristotle).
MISCELLANEOUS: *A Bibliography of Protozoa, Sponges, Coelenterata, and Worms for the Years 1861-1883*, 1885.

Although he made important contributions to biology and classical literature, Sir D'Arcy Wentworth Thompson is best known for using mathematics and physics to study the structure, function, and development of living things. His father was a classical scholar and educator, and his mother was the daughter of a veterinary surgeon. D'Arcy's mother died giving birth to him, and he consequently formed an intensely strong bond with his father, who profoundly influenced his son's character and career. The elder Thompson, a passionate humanist with advanced views on education, was fluent in Latin and Greek, which he taught to his young son, who learned to read, write, and speak these classical languages with astonishing ease. After attending Edinburgh Academy, the young Thompson entered the University of Edinburgh as a medical student in 1877.

In 1880 Thompson won a scholarship at Trinity College, Cambridge University, where he studied zoology under Francis M. Balfour and physiology under Michael Foster. In 1883, he achieved first-class honors in his exams for his B.A. degree, and during the following year he taught physiology under Foster's direction. He began his sixty-four-year association with University College, Dundee, in 1884, when he was appointed professor of biology. (When this college was incorporated into the University of St. Andrews in 1917, he assumed the chair of natural history at the united college.) In Dundee, he compiled a bibliography of world literature on protozoa, sponges, coelenterates, and worms, which was published in 1885, and he translated Hermann Müller's monumental treatise *Die Befruchtung der Blumen durch Insekten* in 1893 under the title *The Fertilisation of Flowers*. To aid his teaching, Thompson built a museum of zoology at Dundee. He also combined his expertise in science with his immense classical learning to publish *A Glossary of Greek Birds* in 1895. As a member of the British-American commission on the fur-seal fisheries in the Bering Sea, he traveled to the Pribilof Islands in 1896 and 1897, during which time he learned much about marine phenomena that he would later publish in reports and scientific papers on oceanography.

After returning to Scotland and his teaching duties, he married Maureen Drury in 1901, a union that would eventually result in three daughters. Thompson, an entertaining conversationalist, was an attractive man, said to have "the build of a Viking" and "the pride of bearing that comes from good looks known to be possessed." Nevertheless, he was more the scholar than a social creature, and his wife provided him with the "peace, quiet, and freedom" that he valued. He eventually published more than three hundred papers in a wide variety of fields. His publications in the classics led to his becoming president of an important classical association. His mathematical papers appeared in the journals of the Royal Society and other scientific organizations. His oceanographic studies and interest in the conservation of fisheries and fur seals in northern Europe led to his becoming a founding member of the International Council for the Exploration of the Sea. He served on this council from 1902 to 1947, and for many years he was chairman of its Statistical Committee and editor of the *Bulletin statistique*.

In his 1911 presidential address to a section of a British scientific association, Thompson spoke on the "greater problems of biology," in which he discussed what he called "the exploration of the borderline of morphology and physics." His 1908 paper in the journal *Nature* on the shapes of eggs and the causes that determine them had already shown how his thinking about biological structure was evolving. He was taking a new approach in which he stressed the mathematical aspects of organic form. These studies, which he continued to develop during World War I, culminated in a book, first published in 1917, that P. B. Medawar has called "beyond comparison the finest work of literature in all the annals of science that have been recorded in the English tongue." Thompson wrote *On Growth and Form* to show how "[c]ell and tissue, shell and bone, leaf and flower" are simply combinations of bits of matter that have been moved and shaped by forces acting according to the laws of physics. Like Thompson, the ancient Greeks saw the problems of the structures of living things as essentially mathematical. For example, in his chapter "On the Comparison of Related Forms," Thompson demonstrated how related organic forms can be mapped using René Descartes's method of coordinates. Traditionally, biologists had described the shapes of living things in their own technical terms; Thompson wanted to define these forms in the precise language of mathematics.

Though the five hundred copies of *On Growth and Form* that were initially published took many years to sell, the book became an object of veneration for those who appreciated Thompson's departures from traditional biological methods. The book is now seen as a seminal scientific investigation that deeply influenced developments in such diverse fields as developmental biology, marine biology, and paleontology. Many critics praised the book as a great literary accomplishment, with its lucid style and wealth of quotations from ancient and modern writers. Other critics saw the book's importance as freeing scientists from the fashions of the day to reveal how biology could be approached in a fresh and imaginative new way.

After the book was published, Thompson continued to write papers on morphology in the years between the two world wars. He started to revise *On Growth and Form* in 1922, but the work was interrupted by sundry professional duties. His many scientific papers dealt with a mind-boggling variety of topics, from the internal ear of the sunfish and the arrangement of feathers on a hummingbird to directions on how to catch a cuttlefish. He also wrote a large number of classical essays, book reviews, and obituaries. In the 1930's he served as president of various organizations, including the Royal Society of London, and in 1936 he was invited to deliver the Lowell Lectures in Boston. Both Cambridge and Oxford gave him honorary degrees, and in 1937 he was knighted.

During World War II Thompson completed his revision of *On Growth and Form*. Science had developed rapidly between the times of the first and second editions, and he was aware of the new ideas in biology in genetics and evolution and the new ideas in physics in quantum mechanics. Thompson only alluded to these new ideas in the second edition, which stressed, as its ancestor had, the formative power of physical forces on living things. He continued to see evolutionary changes in terms of physical forces acting upon individual organisms in their lifetimes rather than in terms of modifications made on successive generations of organisms over long periods, the view of traditional Darwinists. In his 1942 edition Thompson, a theoretician rather than an experimenter, largely ignored experiments that had been done that threw new light on several of the findings in his 1917 edition. He also neglected the work of many chemists who had shown how the structures and functions of chemical substances can help explain how biological structures originate and act. Despite these and other criticisms, *On Growth and Form* continued to be highly regarded by many scholars.

Thompson's last book marked a return to his earliest interests. In his *Glossary of Greek Fishes*, published in 1947, he gathered information about all the fishes mentioned in ancient Greek literature and used his immense zoological knowledge to illuminate these references. In his eighties he was asked about his feelings on death. He responded that the natural world had not yet become tedious to him but that he was prepared to acknowledge that his "long and happy holidays" on Earth had been "just enough" for him to do what he could, and he was content with his "full share of modest happiness." He died in 1948, having recently returned from a trip to India, where he spoke to a large audience on the skeletal structure of birds. At the end, as throughout his life, he continued to integrate his loves of language and nature, seeing things that others had seen but thinking and expressing thoughts that no one else ever had.

Robert J. Paradowski

Bibliography

Bonner, John Tyler. "D'Arcy Thompson." *Scientific American*, August, 1952. A good place to start for those unfamiliar with Thompson.

_______. Introduction to his abridged edition of *On Growth and Form*, by D'Arcy Wentworth Thompson. Cambridge, England: Cambridge University Press, 1961. A critical analysis of Thompson's work in the light of modern scientific discoveries.

Clark, W. Le Gros, and P. B. Medawar, eds. *Essays on Growth and Form*. Oxford, England: Clarendon Press, 1945. This detailed discussion of Thompson's work contains helpful analyses.

Dobell, Clifford. *Obituary Notices of the Fellows of the Royal Society*, no. 18 (1949). Contains a good brief biography of Thompson.

Newman, James R. *The World of Mathematics*. Vol 2. London: G. Allen and Unwin, 1960. This classic anthology has an enthusiastic appraisal of Thompson's life and achievements.

Thompson, Ruth D'Arcy. *D'Arcy Wentworth Thompson, the Scholar Naturalist, 1860-1948*. New York: Oxford University Press, 1958. Ruth's biography of her father remains essential reading for those interested in the man and his work. The book also has a valuable postscript by P. B. Medawar.

Francis Thompson

English poet, biographer, and critic

Born: Preston, Lancashire, England; December 18, 1859
Died: London, England; November 13, 1907

POETRY: *Poems*, 1893 (includes "The Hound of Heaven"); *Sister Songs*, 1895; *New Poems*, 1897.
NONFICTION: *Health and Holiness: A Study of the Relations Between Brother Ass the Body and His Rider the Soul*, 1905; *Shelley*, 1909; *Saint Ignatius Loyola*, 1909; *The Life and Labours of Saint John Baptist de la Salle*, 1923; *Francis Thompson, Literary Criticisms: Newly Discovered and Collected*, 1948 (T. L. Connolly, editor); *The Letters of Francis Thompson*, 1969 (John Walsh, editor).
MISCELLANEOUS: *The Works of Francis Thompson*, 1913 (3 volumes; Wilfred Meynell, editor).

Francis Thompson, the son of a homeopathist, was brought up in the Roman Catholic faith and educated at Ushaw College in preparation for becoming a priest. At the age of seventeen, in accordance with his father's desire, he began to study medicine at Owens College, Manchester. A frail and timid young man, he found medical study repugnant. After six years he gave up the attempt to become a physician and went to London, where he became addicted to opium and sank into the direst poverty. For a time he earned his living selling matches and newspapers. In the spring of 1888 he sent two poems to Wilfred Meynell, the editor of *Merrie England*, who accepted them for publication. With Meynell and his wife, Alice, as his patrons and supporters, the poet tried to break the opium habit.

Thompson's first volume of poetry, simply titled *Poems*, contained "The Hound of Heaven," a poem that despite its strict Catholic dogma became immediately popular. The poem recounts God's pursuit of the speaker, who is ultimately saved from despair. In addition to Catholic mysticism, which informs particularly his early works, Thompson was tremendously influenced by the English Metaphysical poets of the seventeenth century. Thompson produced few works, and he probably never lived up to his potential. He was never able to break his addiction to opium. He died of tuberculosis on November 13, 1907, and was buried under his own epitaph: "Look for me in the nurseries of Heaven."

Katherine Hanley

Bibliography

Halladay, Jean R. *Eight Late Victorian Poets Shaping the Artistic Sensibility of an Age: Alice Meynell, John Davidson, Francis Thompson, Mary Coleridge, Katherine Tynan, Arthur Symons, Ernest Dowson, Lionel Johnson*. Lewiston, N.Y.: Edwin Mellen Press, 1993.

Parekh, Pushpa Naidu. *Response to Failure: Poetry of Gerard Manley Hopkins, Francis Thompson, Lionel Johnson, and Dylan Thomas*. New York: P. Lang, 1998.

Waldron, Robert G. *The Hound of Heaven at My Heels: The Lost Diary of Francis Thompson*. San Francisco: Ignatius Press, 1999.

Hunter S. Thompson

American journalist

Born: Louisville, Kentucky; July 18, 1937

NONFICTION: *Hell's Angels: A Strange and Terrible Saga*, 1967; *Fear and Loathing in Las Vegas: A Savage Journey to the Heart of the American Dream*, 1972 (also known as *Fear and Loathing in Las Vegas, and Other American Stories*); *Fear and Loathing: On the Campaign Trail '72*, 1973; *The Great Shark Hunt: Strange Tales from a Strange Time*, 1979; *The Curse of Lono*, 1983 (with Ralph Steadman); *Generation of Swine: Tales of Shame and Degradation in the '80's*, 1988; *Songs of the Doomed: More Notes on the Death of the American Dream*, 1990; *Better than Sex: Confessions of a Political Junkie*, 1994; *The Proud Highway: Saga of a Desperate Southern Gentleman, 1955-1967*, 1997 (Douglas Brinkley, editor); *Fear and Loathing in America: The Brutal Odyssey of an Outlaw Journalist, 1968-1976*, 2000 (Brinkley, editor); *The Kingdom of Fear: Loathsome Secrets of a Star-Crossed Child in the Final Days of the American Century*, 2003.
SHORT FICTION: *Screw-jack*, 2000.
LONG FICTION: *The Rum Diary*, 1998.

Hunter Stockton Thompson—"gonzo" journalist, legendary wild man, and would-be local politician—was born in Louisville in 1937 to Jack R. and Virginia Thompson; his father was an insurance agent. Thompson stood out as an intelligent, charismatic individual and a troublemaker in high school. He was a member of the Athenaeum, the school's prestigious literary society, but he also began to have run-ins with the law and was arrested more than once. He finally served thirty days in jail while his friends were graduating from high school.

Thompson joined the Air Force in 1955 and was stationed at Eglin Air Proving Ground in Florida, where he began writing entertaining sports articles for the base newspaper. He soon chafed under the restrictions of military life, however, and he managed to get his separation papers in 1957. Thompson moved to New York, where he worked as a copyboy for Time-Life, read F. Scott Fitzgerald, Ernest Hemingway, and William Faulkner, wrote fiction, and met Sandy Dawn Conklin, the woman he would marry in 1963. He soon went west to Big Sur, California. Then, in 1962, he moved to Brazil and wrote pieces for the *National Observer*, truly beginning his life as a journalist.

Returning to the United States, he moved to San Francisco in 1964, after having bought property (Owl Farm) in Woody Creek, Colorado, near Aspen. His and Sandy's son, Juan Fitzgerald Thompson, was born in March of 1964. In California Thompson received an offer to write a magazine piece about the notorious motorcycle gang Hell's Angels; the article spawned book offers, eventually coming to fruition as *Hell's Angels*. Thompson, an inveterate motorcyclist, spent considerable time riding and partying with the Angels. The book was well received.

The frenetic style for which Thompson became famous, "gonzo journalism," was born in a piece written for *Scanlon's Monthly*, "The Kentucky Derby Is Decadent and Depraved," published in the fall of 1970. Thompson had found himself unable to complete the article and, with the deadline upon him, gave pages of handwritten notes to the magazine, which published them essentially as they were—disjointed and frantic, with the "journalist's" descriptions of his own actions and feelings more important than the event he was supposed to have been covering. Gonzo journalism is Thompson's form of participatory journalism, and his style projects an on-the-edge immediacy.

Also in 1970, Thompson began a five-year stint as the "national affairs editor" at Jann Wenner's *Rolling Stone*, then a newspaper-style weekly. Many of his signature pieces were first published in the magazine through the years. *Fear and Loathing in Las Vegas* appeared serially in *Rolling Stone* beginning in 1971.

Fear and Loathing in Las Vegas is a work like no other, a conflation of real events and exaggerated paranoid fantasies, and a description of alcohol and recreational drug use of preposterous proportions. Mexican American activist and attorney Oscar Zeta Acosta accompanied Thompson on his trip to Las Vegas, which in reality was an attempt to get away from Los Angeles to finish a story they were working on for *Rolling Stone*. Acosta is referred to as Thompson's "Samoan attorney" and as Dr. Gonzo in the book, and Thompson adopts the persona of sportswriter "Raoul Duke"; the use of thinly fictionalized personas is one of Thompson's characteristic techniques in his writing and life (he often calls himself Dr. Thompson, for example, although he has no college degree of any sort).

A review in *The New York Times* called the book "a kind of mad, corrosive prose poetry" and placed Thompson among writers such as Norman Mailer and Tom Wolfe. Both loved and reviled, the book has sufficiently stood the test of time to be reissued in 1996 as part of the Modern Library series. Thompson, as the *Rolling Stone* editors saw immediately, wrote in his own voice, "inventing his own vocabulary," coining such evocative phrases as "fear and loathing," "bad craziness," and "greed-heads": "When the going gets weird," he wrote, "the weird turn pro."

Thompson has been captivated by politics all his adult life. At the national level, he developed a particular fascination with Richard M. Nixon, viewing him as all that is "dark and venal" in the American psyche; Nixon inspired Thompson to new heights of invective, so much so that Thompson dedicated *The Great Shark Hunt* to Nixon, who, he said, "never let me down." Thompson covered George McGovern's 1972 presidential campaign, first in the primaries, then against incumbent Nixon; the account was published as *Fear and Loathing: On the Campaign Trail '72*. At the local level, in 1970 Thompson had run for sheriff of Pitkin County, Colorado—he was by then living at his farm in Woody Creek—on the Freak Power ticket, losing the election narrowly. In the ensuing years, Thompson has remained one of the area's more controversial but influential political figures. When, in 1995, he sided with opponents of a proposed airport expansion, the measure went down to defeat.

As the 1970's progressed, Thompson went overseas to cover stories—or at least to write about his own experiences and perceptions of events—including, in 1974, a world heavyweight boxing championship in Zaire and, in 1975, the fall of Saigon. By the late 1970's his marriage to Sandy was in trouble, and the two went through a difficult divorce that dragged on for nearly two years.

In the 1980's and early 1990's Thompson wrote articles and went on college lecture tours, but he spent most of his time at home in Colorado. Collections of his writings appeared in 1988 and 1990. In 1990, he was forced to go to court on drug possession charges resulting from a police search that occurred after a woman accused him of harassing her at his home. Thompson was acquitted; he maintained that the trial was politically motivated—a "lifestyle bust."

The descriptions and effects of Thompson's intake of alcohol and, particularly, a variety of other drugs, form a significant and unique part of his writing. Eventually the drug use began to take its toll. *The Curse of Lono*, for example, is a rehashing of the style of earlier works without their brilliance. People who have known Thompson have spoken of his "great dark side," of his heavy alcohol and drug use, and of the depression and pain that must underlie his anger, recurrent desires for revenge, and fascination with violence. Nevertheless, as the creator of a unique form of New Journalism he has left a mark on American writing—and on popular culture as well, having been portrayed by Bill Murray in the 1980 film *Where the Buffalo Roam* and Johnny Depp in director Terry

Gilliam's 1998 film of *Fear and Loathing in Las Vegas*, as well as being caricatured as "Uncle Duke" in Garry Trudeau's *Doonesbury* comic strip beginning in 1974.

McCrea Adams

Bibliography

Carroll, E. Jean. *Hunter: The Strange and Savage Life of Hunter S. Thompson*. New York: Dutton, 1993. Full-length biography. Includes the essay "Young Doctor Thompson," which appeared in *Esquire* (February, 1993).

Crouse, Timothy. *The Boys on the Bus*. 1973. Reprint. New York: Random House, 2003. Thompson is featured in Crouse's depiction of the press corps on the 1972 campaign, offering an alternative account to Thompson's *Fear and Loathing: On the Campaign Trail, '72*.

Draper, Robert. *Rolling Stone Magazine: The Uncensored History*. New York: Doubleday, 1990. Mentions Thompson's contributions to the magazine.

McKeen, William. *Hunter S. Thompson*. Boston: Twayne, 1991. Offers biographical information and analyses of Thompson's major works through the early 1990's.

Perry, Paul. *Fear and Loathing: The Strange and Terrible Saga of Hunter S. Thompson*. New York: Thunder's Mouth Press, 1992. An unauthorized biography by an editor who has worked with Thompson.

Whitmer, Peter O. *When the Going Gets Weird: The Strange Life and Twisted Times of Hunter S. Thompson*. New York: Hyperion, 1993. Full-length biography by a clinical psychologist that attempts to demythologize Thompson's raucous life and reputation.

James Thomson

Scottish poet and playwright

Born: Ednam, Roxburgh, Scotland; September 7, 1700
Died: Richmond, Yorkshire, England; August 27, 1748

POETRY: *Winter*, 1726; *Summer*, 1727; *Spring*, 1728; *Autumn*, 1730; *The Seasons*, 1730, revised 1744 (includes 4 previous titles); *A Hymn*, 1730; *Liberty*, 1735-1736; *The Castle of Indolence: An Allegorical Poem*, 1748.

DRAMA: *The Tragedy of Sophonisba*, pb. 1730; *Agamemnon*, pr., pb. 1738; *Edward and Eleonora*, pb. 1739; *Alfred*, pr., pb. 1740 (with David Mallet); *Tancred and Sigismunda*, pr., pb. 1745; *Coriolanus*, pr., pb. 1749.

James Thomson was for more than a century considered a major British poet. His masterpiece, *The Seasons*, was among the best-selling poems between 1730 and 1850, and it was often ranked with John Milton's *Paradise Lost* (1667) as the representative British work.

Although a contemporary of Alexander Pope, who made the heroic couplet standard in the age, Thomson wrote most of his work in blank verse. He further departs from the Augustan tradition in his use of nature. His evocative descriptions of nature, expressed in simple language, free of the self-conscious artificiality of his contemporaries, foreshadowed the Romantic movement.

Thomson's affinity with nature can be traced to his early days in the small Scottish village of Ednam. Educated at Edinburgh University, he traveled to London in 1725 and passed through a series of patrons, pensions, and tutorial positions—a frequent pattern among writers in eighteenth century London. The phenomenal success of the individual poems of *The Seasons* (originally published separately) helped make him financially independent, and his works in translation were popular in France, Spain, and Germany. In 1736 he moved to Kew Gardens, then a rural district outside London, where he spent the remainder of his life.

The Seasons is a reflective landscape poem in blank verse that describes nature and the turn of the year with great variety and fullness. The four books, each devoted to a season, reveal the classical influence of Vergil's *Georgics* (c. 37-29 B.C.E.) in their rural patriotism as well as the modern scientific influence of Isaac Newton's *Opticks* (1704) in the play of light and color in their bucolic imagery. The poem's passages on beauty, truth, and goodness elevate it beyond the merely picturesque, for they expound a philosophy of the natural, social, political, and moral realms of humankind. Its moral tone and rural subject make *The Seasons* a perfect merger of two great English literary traditions, the Augustan and the Romantic.

The Castle of Indolence, an imitation of Edmund Spenser's *The Faerie Queene* (1590-1596), recounts the enticement of weary pilgrims into the castle of Wizard Indolence and the subsequent destruction of the wizard and the castle by the Knight of Arms and Industry. The lush music of the poem's style is more memorable than its allegorical exhortation to cultivate the virtues of Industry.

Thomson was also a popular playwright, and his heroic tragedies with patriotic themes were performed regularly at Drury Lane by David Garrick and James Quin. It is of some historical interest that *Alfred*, a masque written in collaboration with David Mallet, contains the famous patriotic song "Rule, Britannia." Thomson's major importance, however, rests upon his early mastery of poetic forms—blank verse and the Spenserian stanza—and subjects which were atypical of an age dominated by reason and the heroic couplet.

H. George Hahn

Bibliography

Balakier, Ann Sewart. *The Spatial Infinite at Greenwich in Works by Christopher Wren, James Thornhill, and James Thomson: The Newton Connection*. Lewiston, N.Y.: Edwin Mellen Press, 1995.

Irlaum, Shaun. *Elations: The Poetics of Enthusiasm in Eighteenth-Century Britain*. Stanford, Calif.: Stanford University Press, 1999.

Sambrook, James. *James Thomson, 1700-1748: A Life*. New York: Oxford University Press, 1991.

Terry, Richard, ed. *James Thomson: Essays for the Tercentenary*. Liverpool, England: Liverpool University Press, 2002.

Henry David Thoreau

American nature writer and poet

Born: Concord, Massachusetts; July 12, 1817
Died: Concord, Massachusetts; May 6, 1862

NONFICTION: *A Week on the Concord and Merrimack Rivers*, 1849; *Walden: Or, Life in the Woods*, 1854; *Excursions*, 1863; *The Maine Woods*, 1864; *Cape Cod*, 1865; *Letters to Various Persons*, 1865 (Ralph Waldo Emerson, editor); *A Yankee in Canada, with Anti-Slavery and Reform Papers*, 1866; *Early Spring in Massachusetts*, 1881; *Summer*, 1884; *Winter*, 1888; *Autumn*, 1892; *Familiar Letters of Henry David Thoreau*, 1894 (F. B. Sanborn, editor).
POETRY: *Poems of Nature*, 1895; *Collected Poems of Henry Thoreau*, 1943 (first critical edition); *Journal*, 1981-1997 (5 volumes).
MISCELLANEOUS: *The Writings of Henry David Thoreau*, 1906; *Collected Essays and Poems*, 2001.

Henry David Thoreau (thuh-ROH), defier of labels, was born before his time. If written thirty or forty years later, *Walden* might have surged to success on the tide of nature interest which benefited such writers as John Burroughs and John Muir. As it was, Thoreau was largely ignored by his own generation, which dismissed him as an impractical reformer. It was only later that he was recognized as one of the most original thinkers and one of the best prose writers of his time.

Along with Ralph Waldo Emerson and Nathaniel Hawthorne, Thoreau is often referred to as a member of the "Concord Group"; of this trio, however, Thoreau alone could claim the town as his birthplace. The second son of John and Cynthia (Dunbar) Thoreau, he grew up in Concord village, attending the local school—apparently an excellent one—in preparation for Harvard, which he entered at the age of sixteen. Despite financial difficulties during the next four years, he graduated in 1837, well versed in languages and skilled in writing. Already a nonconformist, during his Harvard days he disregarded honors, neglected unappealing studies, and deplored the necessity of spending five dollars for a diploma.

Unlike his literary contemporaries, Thoreau never prepared for a profession. After graduation from college he taught school in Concord for a time, together with his brother John, with whom he made a trip on the Concord and Merrimack Rivers in 1839. John, to whom Thoreau was devoted, died of tetanus in 1842. John was ill with tuberculosis at the time, a disease which took their father and, finally, Thoreau himself.

It was about 1840 that Thoreau decided to become a writer. The decision made no change in his simple manner of life. Intermittently he worked at lead pencil making (his father's business), did surveying, or made gardens. It was in the capacity of gardener that he became a member of Emerson's household in 1841, though his services came to include helping Emerson to edit the Transcendentalist journal *The Dial*. Despite critic James Russell Lowell's contention that Thoreau was the imitator of his employer, it seems equally likely that Emerson's interest in nature and nature lore was gained, at least in part, from Thoreau.

The independence and fearlessness of Thoreau's nature led him to speak out actively against whatever he found reason to regard as wrong. He strongly championed John Brown and the Abolitionists, for example, at a time when such a stand was highly unpopular. In 1845, following the example of Bronson Alcott, he went to jail rather than pay poll tax to a government that, as Thoreau saw it, countenanced war and slavery. He provided a living embodiment of Emerson's doctrines of self-reliance and nonconformity, but it is notable that he did so without forfeiting the love and respect of those who knew him best.

Perhaps the most important activity of Thoreau's life began in 1845, when he retired to a little hut at Walden Pond near Concord. There he lived for more than two years, cultivating a small plot of ground and attempting to prove that people need not go beyond their own resources for sustenance and enjoyment. The literary result of this experiment was *Walden*, his best-known work. Published in 1854, this book provided the first and best example of that literary product especially identified with the United States, the "nature book."

Aside from *Walden*, the only other of Thoreau's books published during his lifetime was *A Week on the Concord and Merrimack Rivers*, of which the public took little notice, only two hundred or so copies being sold. It was not until after his death that the bulk of Thoreau's writing was published, although some articles and addresses had made their appearances in contemporary periodicals, chiefly in *The Dial* and *Putnam's Magazine*. Since his death, his complete journal has been published and hailed as a masterpiece; even though his total writing output is slim in comparison with that of some of his fellow New Englanders, it is sufficient to give him belated recognition as one of the truly original and vigorous writers of the century.

The nineteenth century neglect of Thoreau, which continued for a decade or two after his death, was partly the result of the inaccurate estimates of his worth made by such respected critics as Lowell. The nature school, arising at the end of the nineteenth century, played a part in his literary revival; nevertheless, Thoreau's essential value as a writer depends only partly on his subject matter. Clarity of expression, shrewdness, and occasional humor combine to form an individual prose style of compelling charm. His integrity shines through his work, and his positive views on nature and government constitute a continuing challenge to a civilization bowed down by frustrations and complexities.

Richard Tuerk

Bibliography

Cain, William E. *A Historical Guide to Henry David Thoreau*. New York: Oxford University Press, 2000. Historical and biographical context and treatment of Thoreau.

Hahn, Stephen. *On Thoreau*. Belmont, Calif.: Wadsworth, 2000. A concise study intended to assist a beginning student in understanding Thoreau's philosophy and thinking. Includes bibliographical references.

Harding, Walter. *The Days of Henry Thoreau*. New York: Alfred A. Knopf, 1965. This fine scholarly biography remains useful. Harding places the poetry insightfully in the pattern of Thoreau's life. Includes illustrations, a bibliographical note, and an index.

Harding, Walter, and Michael Meyer. *The New Thoreau Handbook*. New York: New York University Press, 1980. This standard basic reference on Thoreau is generally the first source to be consulted for help. Contains a considerable amount of factual information about the writings and the writer, arranged for easy access. Includes chronologies, indexes, and cross-references.

Howarth, William. *The Book of Concord: Thoreau's Life as a Writer.* New York: Viking Press, 1982. Howarth presents a writer's biography, paying particular attention to the relationship between the life and the writings and showing exactly how the work evolved. Includes a list of sources, an index, notes, and a number of drawings.

Myerson, Joel, ed. *The Cambridge Companion to Henry David Thoreau*. New York: Cambridge University Press, 1995. A guide to the works and to the biographical, historical, and literary contexts. Includes a chronology and further readings.

Richardson, Robert D. *Henry Thoreau: A Life of the Mind*. Berkeley: University of California Press, 1986. This study focuses primarily on the development of Thoreau's leading themes and the formulation of his working philosophy. Richardson offers clear accounts of some of the writer's complex theories. Provides notes, a bibliography, and an index.

Salt, Henry S. *Life of Henry David Thoreau*. Reprint. Hamden, Conn.: Archon Books, 1968. Written by a former master of Eton who wrote the first biography of Thoreau, in 1890, this is the 1908 (third) version, valuable for the insight it offers into both a late nineteenth century figure and some of his contemporaries, including anecdotes and facts gathered from Samuel Arthur Jones, F. B. Sanborn, Ernest W. Vickers, Raymond Adams, Fred Hosmer, and Mohandas K. Gandhi.

Schneider, Richard J., ed. *Thoreau's Sense of Place: Essays in American Environmental Writing*. Iowa City: University of Iowa Press, 2000. A collection of essays which address a central question in Thoreau studies: How immersed in a sense of place was Thoreau really, and how has this sense of place affected the tradition of nature writing in the United States?

Tauber, Alfred I. *Henry David Thoreau and the Moral Agency of Knowing*. Berkeley: University of California Press, 2001. Tauber shows how Thoreau's metaphysics of self-knowing informed all that this multifaceted writer, thinker, and scientist did. A clear presentation of the man in the context of social and intellectual history.

Waggoner, Hyatt H. *American Poets: From the Puritans to the Present*. New York: Houghton Mifflin, 1968. This volume is a comprehensive and detailed history of American poetry. Waggoner gives Thoreau appropriate space and a sympathetic treatment. An appendix, detailed notes, an extensive bibliography, and a good index supplement the volume.

Thucydides

Greek historian

Born: Probably Athens, Greece; c. 459 B.C.E.
Died: Place unknown; c. 402 B.C.E.

NONFICTION: *Historia tou Peloponnesiacou polemou*, 431-404 B.C.E. (*History of the Peloponnesian War*, 1550).

Thucydides (thyew-SIHD-uh-deez) was the son of Olorus, an Athenian citizen. The date of his birth is uncertain; it has been put as early as 471 B.C.E. and as late as 455 B.C.E. He may have spent part of his youth in Thrace, where his family owned gold-mining rights. He says that he began his history of the Peloponnesian War at the moment when the war broke out, so he was presumably living at Athens in 431. He was certainly there the following year during the plague, of which he fell ill.

In 424 he was appointed, jointly with Eucles, to defend the coastal region bordering on Thrace and was entrusted with a naval squadron. His failure to prevent the capture of Amphipolis when it was invaded by the Spartans provoked the Athenians to send him into exile. He passed his twenty years of banishment in visiting the cities of the enemy and the principal battlefields of the war and in collecting from veterans of the war the historical materials needed for his work. He returned to Athens about 403. He did not live to complete his great work—the *History of the Peloponnesian War* ends in 411, seven years before the peace was finally made. His death is supposed to have occurred at the hands of an assassin about 402 B.C.E. Thucydides is classified as the first scientific historian. Compared with Herodotus, his predecessor, whom Thucydides criticized for his failure to verify facts and stories before using them, he went to extremes to guarantee the accuracy of his own work.

Thucydides' *History* is both highly objective and highly dramatic. In the numerous orations which he reports or constructs, he shows his precise understanding of ideological issues. His narratives are marvelously vivid; among the most memorable are his accounts of the plague in Athens and of the Syracusan campaign, which ended with the imprisonment of the expeditionary force in the rock quarries and which had a direct effect on the defeat of Athens by Sparta.

Glenn L. Swygart

Bibliography

Conner, W. Robert. *Thucydides*. 2d ed. Princeton, N.J.: Princeton University Press, 1985.

Debner, Paula. *Speaking the Same Language: Speech and Audience in Thucydides' Spartan Debates*. Ann Arbor: University of Michigan Press, 2001.

Gomme, Arnold W. *A Historical Commentary on Thucydides*. 5 vols. Oxford, England: Clarendon Press, 1945-1981.

Gustafson, Lowell S., ed. *Thucydides' Theory of International Relations: A Lasting Possession*. Baton Rouge: Louisiana State University Press, 2000.

Hornblower, Simon. *Thucydides*. 2d ed. London: Duckworth, 1987.

Luginbill, Robert D. *Thuycidides on War and National Character*. Boulder, Colo.: Westview Press, 1999.

Price, Jonathan J. *Thucydides and Internal War*. New York: Cambridge University Press, 2001.

James Thurber

American short-story writer

Born: Columbus, Ohio; December 8, 1894
Died: New York, New York; November 2, 1961

SHORT FICTION: *Is Sex Necessary?*, 1929 (with E. B. White); *The Owl in the Attic, and Other Perplexities*, 1931; *The Seal in the Bedroom, and Other Predicaments*, 1932; *My Life and Hard Times*, 1933; *The Middle-Aged Man on the Flying Trapeze*, 1935; *Let Your Mind Alone!, and Other More or Less Inspirational Pieces*, 1937; *The Last Flower: A Parable in Pictures*, 1939; *Fables for Our Time and Famous Poems Illustrated*, 1940; *My World—and Welcome to It!*, 1942; *The Great Quillow*, 1944; *The White Deer*, 1945; *The Thurber Carnival*, 1945; *The Beast in Me, and Other Animals: A New Collection of Pieces and Drawings About Human Beings and Less Alarming Creatures*, 1948; *The Thirteen Clocks*, 1950; *Thurber Country: A New Collection of Pieces About Males and Females, Mainly of Our Own Species*, 1953; *Further Fables for Our Time*, 1956; *The Wonderful O*, 1957; *Alarms and Diversions*, 1957; *Lanterns and Lances*, 1961; *Credos and Curios*, 1962.

DRAMA: *The Male Animal*, pr., pb. 1940 (with Elliott Nugent); *Many Moons*, pb. 1943; *A Thurber Carnival*, pr. 1960 (revue).
NONFICTION: *The Thurber Album*, 1952; *The Years with Ross*, 1959; *Selected Letters of James Thurber*, 1982.

Generally considered the greatest American humorist since Mark Twain, James Grover Thurber was born on December 8, 1894, in Columbus, Ohio, the setting for many of his comic reminiscences. His father was active in local politics; his mother had a histrionic gift of comic impersonation that gave his mind "a sense of confusion that . . . never left it." When Thurber was six, his older brother accidentally shot him with an arrow in the left eye, which was replaced with a glass one. In Columbus, Thurber attended the public schools and Ohio State University, where he wrote for the campus paper and for the student monthly, of which he became editor in chief.

In June, 1918, Thurber left Ohio State University without taking a degree. He had tried to enlist in the armed forces but was rejected because of his eyesight. Instead, he became a code clerk for the State Department, first in Washington, D.C., then at the American embassy in Paris. In the summer of 1920, Thurber returned to Columbus, where for the next four years he was a reporter and columnist for the Columbus *Dispatch*. In 1922 Thurber married Althea Adams of Columbus. Two years later, he resigned from the *Dispatch* to try his hand at freelance writing. In 1925 he went with his wife to France to write a novel, which never materialized. Instead, he became a reporter for the Paris, and later the Riviera, edition of the *Chicago Tribune*. After a year in France, the Thurbers returned to the United States, and Thurber began work as a reporter for the New York *Evening Post*.

In February, 1927, Thurber finally began his real career when he met E. B. White, the celebrated writer for *The New Yorker*, and *The New Yorker* editor Harold Ross, who hired him. Thurber contributed to "The Talk of the Town" column and submitted his own comic stories and essays. In 1929 he and White collaborated on what was for both a first book, *Is Sex Necessary?*, which spoofed books on sex therapy. Here Thurber found one of his recurring themes, "the melancholy of sex," which he would develop into a full-scale mock war between men and women. *Is Sex Necessary?* also introduced Thurber as a cartoonist and illustrator. White found that he had been filling wastebaskets with penciled drawings, which White rescued, inked in, and persuaded the publishers to include as illustrations. All Thurber's subsequent books except four fairy-tale and fantasy books were illustrated by the author, and his cartoons and drawings soon became a hallmark of *The New Yorker.*

In 1931 Thurber published his first book alone, *The Owl in the Attic, and Other Perplexities*. The first section, a series of eight stories about Mr. and Mrs. Monroe, deals with the sort of matrimonial relationship that was to become a major subject of his later work. The domination of the American male by the American female and the innocence of animals figure in *The Seal in the Bedroom, and Other Predicaments*, Thurber's first book of cartoons and drawings. A self-taught draftsman, Thurber developed a unique and instantly recognizable style that renders people and objects in linear outline, flowing gracefully but without shading or cross-hatching. In 1933 Thurber published *My Life and Hard Times*, a comic autobiography that many readers consider his most amusing work. In it, Thurber carries to burlesque extremes some of the episodes of his boyhood and college days. It is a prime example of his definition of his humor as "emotional chaos told about calmly and quietly in retrospect."

Thurber's men and his own personae in his writings often suffer from hesitation, neuroses, hypochondria, apprehension, and fragmentation of character. The real Thurber bore little resemblance to these characters; friends and interviewers noted that far from being shy and trapped, Thurber was confident and assured. The antihero features in *The Middle-Aged Man on the Flying Trapeze*, one of Thurber's best collections of stories and essays, published in 1935. In their subdued way, Thurber's protagonists are often frustrated romantics, like Walter Mitty. Thurber objected to any attempts to regiment the freewheeling imagination, and *Let Your Mind Alone!* includes a number of pieces satirizing inspirational and self-help books, which Thurber believed were trying to discipline readers into a pedestrian conformity to a dull norm.

Despite the birth of his daughter Rosemary in 1931, Thurber's marriage had been troubled for a long time, and in 1935 he was divorced. Several stories written around this time—"One Is a Wanderer" and "The Evening's at Seven"—are serious, poignant studies of loneliness. That same year, however, Thurber married Helen Wismer, a magazine editor, and this marriage endured for the rest of his life. As for the battle of the sexes, Thurber said that it was a gimmick, that he admired vibrant and intelligent women. His is a mock misogyny: He truly believed that women could manage things better than men.

During the late 1930's and early 1940's, the war years, Thurber produced several successful books, both serious and humorous, that pointedly denounced or mocked human behavior: *The Last Flower*, a poignant book-length cartoon denouncing war; *The Male Animal*, a play written in collaboration with college friend Elliott Nugent (later a successful actor and director), which continued the battle-of-the-sexes theme and championed academic freedom while it attacked right-wing witch-hunting on the campus of a midwestern university; *Men, Women, and Dogs*, his second book of cartoons; and *My World—and Welcome to It!*, which contains his best-known short story, "The Secret Life of Walter Mitty," featuring a protagonist who triumphs over a nagging wife by retreating into a fantasy world in which he is the superhero he wishes to be.

While Thurber was having all these artistic successes, the sight in his remaining eye began to deteriorate, and despite a series of operations, he gradually became blind. After 1951, he had to give up drawing altogether; his later books are illustrated by earlier drawings, sometimes reversed or rearranged. Fortunately for his writing, he could memorize several entire versions of a story or essay before dictating it. During his operations, Thurber wrote a few stories reflecting frustration and rage—"The Cane in the Corridor" and "The Whip-poor-will," for example. Thurber's reaction was usually more positive, and he soon turned to writing fairy tales that entertain with a gentle and humane moral. The first two of these,

Many Moons and *The Great Quillow*, were written for children; the third and best tale, *The White Deer*, is for adults as well.

In 1945 Thurber had his biggest success, with *The Thurber Carnival*, an anthology of his best work up to that time. One obstacle to recognition of Thurber as a serious and significant artist was the fact that his work was in miniature short stories, essays, cartoons, and drawings—but *The Thurber Carnival* provided an overview that allowed a more appreciative focus on his entire body of work. By 1948, Thurber was receiving the recognition he deserved. In 1949 Columbia University gave him the Laughing Lions Award for humor, and over the next four years he received honorary doctorates from Kenyon College, Williams College, and Yale University.

The Thurber Album appeared in 1952—a departure from Thurber's usual humor, being a series of well-researched biographical sketches of family members, friends, and Ohio State University professors who offered positive role models for American values. In 1956 *Further Fables for Our Time* satirized intellectual and political intolerance, rumor, and vicious innuendo, winning the American Library Association's Liberty and Justice Award. In 1957 another book-length fantasy, *The Wonderful O*, told the story of a pirate whose mother tries to ban the letter *o* on an island, only to have the islanders rebel and reaffirm the *o* in "love," "valor," and "freedom." Thurber visited England in 1958 and was the first American since Mark Twain to be "called to the table" for *Punch*'s Wednesday luncheon. In 1959 he published *The Years with Ross*, a book-length sketch of his time with the founder of *The New Yorker*. He won a Tony Award for adapting some of his short pieces into a revue, *A Thurber Carnival*, which was produced successfully in New York in 1960. In September, Thurber joined the cast, playing himself for eighty-eight performances in a sketch titled "File and Forget." The next year, 1961, he revisited Europe and published another collection, *Lanterns and Lances*. On October 4, Thurber was stricken with a blood clot in the brain, underwent emergency surgery, and rallied—but he died of pneumonia on November 4. He is buried in Columbus, Ohio.

Though Thurber is now firmly established as the major American humorist of the twentieth century, admired by writers such as T. S. Eliot, Dylan Thomas, and Edmund Wilson, his work, like that of all great humorists, has an underlying seriousness in its satire on war, failed communication between the sexes, political intolerance and extremism, thought control, and linguistic degeneration; it offers an astute commentary on human nature, addressing the predicaments and perplexities of modern times.

Robert E. Morsberger

Bibliography

Grauer, Neil A. *Remember Laughter: A Life of James Thurber*. Lincoln: University of Nebraska Press, 1994. A biography that examines the context of Thurber's work. Provides an interesting discussion of the background to the writing of "The Secret Life of Walter Mitty" and its reception when first published in *The New Yorker*.

Kaufman, Anthony. "'Things Close In': Dissolution and Misanthropy in 'The Secret Life of Walter Mitty.'" *Studies in American Fiction* 22 (Spring, 1994): 93-104. Discusses dissolution and misanthropy in the story; argues that Mitty's withdrawal is symptomatic not of mild-mannered exasperation with a trivial world but of anger; concludes that Mitty is the misanthrope demystified and made middle-class—the suburban man who, unable to imagine or afford the drama of a retreat into the wilderness, retreats inward.

Kenney, Catherine McGehee. *Thurber's Anatomy of Confusion*. Hamden, Conn.: Archon Books, 1984. A survey of Thurber's creative world, including discussions of his most characteristic works. Discusses *Fables for Our Time* and such stories as "The Greatest Man in the World" and "The Secret Life of Walter Mitty."

Kinney, Harrison. *James Thurber: His Life and Times*. New York: Henry Holt, 1995. A biography that focuses largely on Thurber's relationship to the development of *The New Yorker* magazine. Discusses how Thurber made use of overheard conversation, wordplay, and literary allusions in his stories.

Long, Robert Emmet. *James Thurber*. New York: Continuum, 1988. This biographical and critical study divides Thurber's works into drawings, fiction, autobiography, fables, fairy tales, and occasional pieces, giving each a chapter. Includes a bibliography.

Wallace Thurman

American novelist

Born: Salt Lake City, Utah; August 16, 1902
Died: New York, New York; December 22, 1934
Identity: African American

LONG FICTION: *The Blacker the Berry*, 1929; *Infants of the Spring*, 1932.
DRAMA: *Harlem*, pr. 1929 (with William Jourdan Rapp).

Wallace Henry Thurman may have seen the death of the Harlem Renaissance after *Infants of the Spring*, but while it was alive his imagination and critical attention helped to keep it healthy. Thurman was born on August 16, 1902, in Salt Lake City, Utah, to Beulah and Oscar Thurman. His parents soon separated, and he was raised by his maternal grandmother, Emma Jackson, to whom he dedicated his first novel, *The Blacker the Berry.* Thurman enrolled briefly at the University of Utah, then moved to California and started a premedical curriculum at the University of Southern California. He did not finish his studies because he became involved in the type of work that was to absorb his energies for the rest of Thurman's brief life: He began to write a column for a black Los Angeles newspaper, and he edited a magazine. The magazine lasted six months, the longest any of Thurman's independent editorial projects would last.

Thurman arrived in Harlem in 1925 and worked for meals as a jack-of-all-trades on a small magazine whose editor knew the staff of the black-radical magazine *The Messenger*; Thurman was later hired as managing editor of *The Messenger.* Editorial and administrative work suited Thurman, and he continued in it throughout the renaissance; he was, in fact, one of the few younger renaissance figures who had a steady, predictable source of income.

By the time he began work on *The Messenger,* he had been around Harlem enough to know all the major figures of the renaissance. His most important acquaintance was the poet, novelist, and playwright Langston Hughes, who roomed across the hall from him in the boardinghouse that served as the model for "Niggerati Manor" in *Infants of the Spring*. Hughes brought to Thurman in 1927 a request to serve as editor of a new magazine for publishing experimental and unconventional literature by younger black writers. Black magazines which published art and literature (the National Association for the Advancement of Colored People's *The Crisis* and the Urban League's *Opportunity*, for example) were not primarily literary magazines, and the idea of Hughes and his friends was that a strictly literary magazine with solely artistic criteria was necessary. The new magazine, *Fire!!*, was visually stunning (designed by African American artist Aaron Douglas) and editorially adventurous, a tribute to Thurman's abilities. Unfortunately the magazine was too adventurous for most of the readers who bought that first issue (more than one short story, for example, contained sexually unorthodox characters), and the final blow for the project was that the remaining copies of the first issue were destroyed by a fire in the apartment where they were stored. With no inventory and no income, the group could not continue publication. Thurman took it upon himself to repay the debt for the paper, printing, and binding of this high quality publication; repayment took about four years.

The next year Thurman founded a general interest magazine, which he called *Harlem*. Again the magazine was well designed and edited; moreover it was not so controversial as *Fire!!*, but it, too, failed after one issue. Thurman did not have time to mourn the failure because he was busy writing and working on the editorial staff of Macauley Publishing Company, the company that published *The Blacker the Berry* in 1929. This novel, which details the effects of color prejudice and self-hatred among African Americans, received mixed reviews. Thurman was more successful in February, 1929, with a production of the play *Harlem*, written with William Jourdan Rapp and based on one of the controversial short stories in the defunct *Fire!!* The play ran at the Apollo Theatre in New York City for ninety-three performances, had successful road company tours, and was revived on Broadway in October of 1929.

Thurman briefly tried his hand at writing "social problem" screenplays for an independent filmmaker in Hollywood, then went back to Harlem, where he wrote his most important work, *Infants of the Spring*, also published by his employer, Macauley. The title is taken from a passage in William Shakespeare's *Hamlet* which summarizes Thurman's view of the Harlem Renaissance; he believed that it had been killed before it had flowered. He also believed that the "canker" was internal: The Harlem Renaissance, in his opinion, died of too much self-consciousness and self-indulgence. This harsh evaluation was not fully accepted in 1932 when the novel was published, nor has it been since, but the novel has been recognized as a skillfully satirical *roman à clef.* The novel, which follows the lives of black writers and artists living in a rooming house called Niggerati Manor, includes deftly drawn (and quartered) characters such as Tony Crews (Langston Hughes) and Sweetie Mae Carr (Zora Neale Hurston).

Thurman contracted tuberculosis in the early 1930's and died of it in New York City on December 22, 1934. In his autobiography, *The Big Sea* (1940), Hughes affectionately and critically limns Thurman as a man whose critical bent caused him to see flaws in everything, including his own writing. According to Hughes, Thurman wanted to be a great literary figure and believed that he was "merely" a journalist. With *Infants of the Spring*, Thurman's literary ambitions and his journalistic talent work together; the result is a satirical novel that is still read with enjoyment, long after both the satirist and the objects of his satire have passed from the scene. Posterity seems to have judged Thurman more kindly than he judged himself.

Isaac Johnson

Bibliography

Gaither, Renoir W. "The Moment of Revision: A Reappraisal of Wallace Thurman's Aesthetics in *The Blacker the Berry* and *Infants of the Spring*." *CLA Journal* 37, no. 1 (1993). A reevaluation that is worth reading.

Hughes, Langston. *The Big Sea*. 1940. Reprint. Columbia: University of Missouri Press, 2002. Hughes presents in his autobiography a fascinating character sketch of Thurman.

Notten-Krepel, Eleonore van. *Wallace Thurman's Harlem Renaissance*. Leiden, the Netherlands: Author, 1994. A full-length study.

Walden, Daniel. "The Canker Galls . . . Or, The Short Promising Life of Wallace Thurman." In *The Harlem Renaissance Reexamined*, edited by Victor A. Kramer and Robert A. Russ. Rev. and expanded ed. Troy, N.Y.: Whitston, 1997. A close look at Thurman's life.

Louise A. Tilly

American historian, feminist, and sociologist

Born: Orange, New Jersey; December 13, 1930

NONFICTION: *The Rebellious Century, 1830-1930*, 1975 (with Charles Tilly and Richard Tilly); *Women, Work, and Family*, 1978, 2d edition 1987 (with Joan W. Scott); *Computer Chips and Paper Clips: Technology and Women's Employment*, 1986 (with Heidi Hartmann and Robert Kraut); *Politics and Class in Milan, 1881-1901*, 1992; *Individual and Gender Inequality*, 1993.

EDITED TEXTS: *Class Conflict and Collective Action*, 1981 (with Charles Tilly); *Feminist Re-Visions: What Has Been and Might Be*, 1983 (with Vivian Patraka); *Women, Politics, and Change*, 1990 (with Patricia Gurin); *The European Experience of Declining Fertility, 1850-1970: The Quiet Revolution*, 1992 (with John Gillis and David Levine); *European Integration in Social and Historical Perspective: 1850 to the Present*, 1997.

TRANSLATION: *Mémé Santerre: A French Woman of the People*, 1985 (of Serge Grafteau).

Louise Audino Tilly has been a pioneer in using sociological and statistical methods in the historical study of women, labor, and family life in modern Europe. She was the daughter of Hector (an engineer) and Piera (an artist) Audino. After graduating with a B.A. with high honors in history from Rutgers University in 1952, she married sociologist Charles Tilly in 1953. Two years later, she graduated with an M.A. from Boston University and in 1974 was awarded a Ph.D. from the University of Toronto. She is the mother of four children: Christopher, Kathryn, Laura, and Sarah.

Tilly has had an active and successful academic career. In 1971, she began her teaching career at the Flint campus of the University of Michigan, and since then she has taught at several major universities, including the University of Michigan in Ann Arbor and Princeton University. In 1984, she became a professor of history and sociology at the New School for Social Research in New York, where she also served as chair of the Committee on Historical Studies. She has evaluated grant proposals for numerous foundations, including the National Endowment for the Humanities. In 1993, she was elected president of the American Historical Association, one of the most prestigious achievements within the historical profession.

Her writings have dealt with various aspects of social history, conditions of workers, and changing gender roles. In methods, she has emphasized quantitative data, sociological concepts, and comparisons among various places in the world. Her works have examined the lives of average persons rather than leaders and the wealthy elite; they have focused on the small-scale effects of large-scale social change within particular historical settings. Like many social historians, she has attempted to orient her work to themes relevant to current issues and possible social reforms.

Tilly has authored or coauthored at least eleven books and has published scores of scholarly articles in journals of history and sociology. Her first book, *The Rebellious Century*, written with Charles and Richard Tilly, was a comparative analysis of violent upheavals in France, Italy, and Germany, from the revolution of 1830 until the eve of Adolf Hitler's accession to power. The highly influential work *Women, Work, and Family*, written with Joan Scott, is a comparative study of working-class women's lives in Europe. It explores the impact of the Industrial Revolution on women's employment opportunities and family relations. Using sophisticated statistical techniques, Scott and Tilly demonstrated that women generally worked because of the financial needs of their families and that, in the workplace, they were under male authority with increasing frequency.

Tilly's book *Politics and Class in Milan, 1881-1901* explores the relationship between the working class and the rise of the socialist movement in the city of Milan. Tilly also translated and edited *Mémé Santerre: A French Woman of the People*, which gives a firsthand account of a poor woman who was born in 1891. Because the family of Mémé Santerre migrated seasonally between work in the hand-weaving of linen and commercial agriculture, Tilly believes that the book provides an exceptionally rich description of work early in the twentieth century.

Tilly has not written her books and articles for a large audience; she has written them mostly for professional historians and social scientists. Early in the twenty-first century, she was busy working on an ambitious project concerning the ways in which modernization, socioeconomic classes, and the development of welfare states have shaped gender relations and family structures throughout the world.

Thomas Tandy Lewis

Bibliography

Scanlon, Jennifer, and Shaaron Cosner. *American Women Historians, 1700's-1900's: A Biographical Dictionary.* Westport, Conn.: Greenwood Press, 1996. An excellent summary of the lives, careers, and writings of a large number of female historians, including Tilly.

Zinsser, Judith P. *History and Feminism: A Glass Half Full.* New York: Twayne, 1993. An interesting and informative account of feminist historiography since the 1970's, with an emphasis on individual writers.

Tirso de Molina
(Gabriel Téllez)

Spanish playwright

Born: Madrid, Spain; 1580(?)
Died: Almazán, Spain; February, 1648

DRAMA: *El vergonzoso en palacio*, wr. 1611(?), pb. 1624 (*The Bashful Man at Court*, 1991); *Marta la piadosa*, wr. 1615, pb. 1636; *Don Gil de las calzas verdes*, wr. 1615, pb. 1635 (*Don Gil of the Green Breeches*, 1991); *El condendado por desconfiado*, wr. 1615(?), pb. 1634 (*The Saint and the Sinner*, 1952; also known as *Damned for Despair*, 1986); *La venganza de Tamar*, wr. 1621, pb. 1634 (*Tamar's Revenge*, 1988; also known as *The Rape of Tamar*, 1999); *El burlador de Sevilla*, wr. 1625(?), pb. 1630 (*The Trickster of Seville*, 1923); *La prudencia en la mujer*, wr. 1627-1633, pb. 1634 (*Prudence in Woman*, 1964).

NONFICTION: *Los cigarrales de Toledo*, 1624; *Deleytar aprovechando*, 1635; *Historia general de la orden de Nuestra Señora de las Mercedes*, 1639.

Tirso de Molina (TEER-soh day moh-LEE-nah), Lope de Vega Carpio, and Pedro Calderón de la Barca are the triad of the great Golden Age dramatists of Spain. Tirso's birth, around 1580, places him chronologically between the two other masters; in style and content, however, he belongs more to Lope's dramatic cycle, and Tirso's *Los cigarrales de Toledo* (the orchards of Toledo) contains a defense of Lopean theater.

Little is known of Tirso's early life, although there is much speculation that he was born Gabriel Téllez of aristocratic, though illegitimate, birth. He studied at the University of Alcalá de Henares and entered the Mercedarian Order of Friars in 1600 or 1601. He was living in Toledo in 1613 when he met Lope de Vega, and his play *Don Gil of the Green Breeches* was performed in that city in 1615. Tirso had started writing for the theater several years before, and *The Bashful Man at Court* is probably the first play he wrote. (Because of the uncertainty surrounding the first performance of many Golden Age plays, the date given is generally that of the first appearance in print.)

In 1616 he was sent by his order to Hispaniola. On his return two years later, he increasingly immersed himself in his writing and in the exciting life of Madrid, the capital of the Spanish empire. His friendship with Lope opened many doors, and more of his plays were performed; soon he was basking in the applause of both public and critics. The authorities, however, were not won over. In 1626, he was banished to the backwater of Trujillo. The reason given was that a priest should not contribute to the "corruption" of others nor be seen in the "lewd" company of actors. No one knows the real motive behind this punishment, but it is widely believed that those in power had little or no toleration for Tirso's thinly veiled criticism of the nobility and government of his day.

A good churchman as well as a good dramatist, Tirso then devoted himself to the affairs of the Mercedarians. He was named the order's historian in 1632 and edited a history of the order, but he never stopped writing plays. Some four hundred *comedias* are attributed to him; eighty are extant, although a few are of doubtful authorship.

In 1630 Tirso published his greatest work, which saw the first appearance of one of the archetypal figures of world literature, Don Juan of *The Trickster of Seville*. Don Juan is a rebel who knowingly breaks every social and moral law; fittingly, he is damned for his actions. Other writers, notably José de Zorrilla, have changed the psychological and social focus of the seventeenth century play, but it is Tirso's Don Juan, mocking and satirical, whose characterization has lent itself to so many interpretations.

One of the great debates of Tirso's time centered on the importance of faith, grace, predestination, and free will in attaining salvation. Don Juan had been condemned for overconfidence, for relying too much on the mercy of God; in *The Saint and the Sinner*, however, Tirso presents the flip side of the coin. In this work, the religious man Paulo loses his salvation because he has lost confidence in God's mercy and, in his denial of free will, gives way to despair and his own spiteful pride. Questions of free will and predestination are always relevant, but Tirso's genius lies in his ability to put a human face on these abstract concepts. Paulo and Don Juan are characters of flesh and blood whose human frailties are very real.

Tirso has also been renowned for his portrayal of strong women characters, and some critics have insinuated that their psychological realism stems from Tirso's knowledge of their secrets in the confessional. In 1633 *Prudence in Woman* introduced María de Molina to the stage; many consider her to be the most heroic female representation in Spanish theater. *Prudence in Woman* concerns a mother, acting as regent, who valiantly defends her son's right to the throne while beset on all sides by ruthless nobles. The plot parallels the historical situation in Spain after the death of Phillip III in 1621. More than any other Golden Age playwright, Tirso consistently—and more or less openly—attacked corruption, political intrigue, and folly.

Tirso paid the price for this audacity. He never returned to Madrid, and although many of his plays were published during his lifetime, the number of performances diminished. In 1648 he died in virtual oblivion in Almazán, Soria, his work forgotten until its reappraisal at the beginning of the nineteenth century.

Charlene E. Suscavage

Bibliography

Albrecht, Jane. *Irony and Theatricality in Tirso de Molina*. Ottawa, Canada: Dovehouse Editions, 1994. This study of Tirso de Molina also examines the Spanish theater of his time. Includes bibliography and index.

Halkhoree, P. R. K. *Social and Literary Satire in the Comedies of Tirso de Molina*. Ottawa, Canada: Dovehouse Editions, 1989. This study examines the use of social satire in the comedies of Tirso de Molina. Includes bibliography.

Hesse, Everett Wesley. *Tirso's Art in "La venganza de Tamar": Tragedy of Sex and Violence*. York, S.C.: Spanish Literature Publishing, 1991. Provides a critical analysis of Tirso de Molina's *Tamar's Revenge*. Includes bibliography.

Hughes, Ann Nickerson. *Religious Imagery in the Theater of Tirso de Molina*. Macon, Ga.: Mercer, 1984. Hughes presents a study of Tirso de Molina's plays in respect to his handling of religious imagery. Includes bibliography.

Levin, Leslie. *Metaphors of Conversion in Seventeenth Century Spanish Drama*. Rochester, N.Y.: Tamesis, 1999. This study of seventeenth century Spanish theater focuses on Tirso de Molina and Pedro Calderón de la Barca and the topic of conversion. Includes bibliography.

Sola-Solé, Josep M., and Geroge E. Gingras, eds. *Tirso's Don Juan: The Metamorphosis of a Theme*. Washington, D.C.: Catholic University of America Press, 1988. This collection of papers from a symposium on Tirso de Molina held in Washington, D.C., in November, 1985, discusses the dramatist's depiction of the Don Juan character in *The Trickster of Seville*. Includes bibliography.

Wilson, Margaret. *Tirso de Molina*. Boston: Twayne, 1977. A basic biography of Tirso de Molina that covers his life and works. Includes bibliography and index.

Alexis de Tocqueville

Political theorist

Born: Paris, France; July 29, 1805
Died: Cannes, France; April 16, 1859

NONFICTION: *De la démocratie en Amérique*, 1835, 1840 (*Democracy in America*, 1835, 1840); *L'Ancien Régime et la révolution*, 1856 (*The Old Régime and the Revolution*, 1856); *Memoirs, Letters, and Remains of Alexis de Tocqueville*, 1861 (2 volumes); *Souvenirs de Alexis de Tocqueville*, 1893 (*The Recollections of Alexis de Tocqueville*, 1896, 1949); *Writings on Empire and Slavery*, 2001 (Jennifer Pitts, editor).

Alexis de Tocqueville (tawk-veel) was born in Paris in 1805. As a child he displayed great powers of intelligence, and he was fortunate enough to be allowed to develop them through study and travel. His journey to the United States resulted in his first book, a study of the penal system of both the Old and New Worlds. This book, which appeared in 1832, was based on a long and hard exploration of a year's duration, during which he familiarized himself with the nature of American culture. Another book, one which was to make him famous, was also a consequence of this journey. *Democracy in America* immediately raised Tocqueville to the status of a great European author.

Democracy in America was the answer of an empiricist to political theories derived largely from speculation. It was based on close study of institutions rather than on a theory of human nature, and it covered in great detail the economics, legal structure, and social structure of the United States. It covered, too, the dangers of democracy: the probability of increased centralization of power, the encroachment of oligarchy on popular rights. In the years after the publication of this great work Tocqueville took an active part in government and became a fascinated observer of the violent political changes of the 1830's and 1840's. During this period of his life, Tocqueville was building a factual and philosophical foundation for his last historical masterpiece.

The preoccupation of Tocqueville during these years was decidedly not with ideas or theories but with what he called the realities of authority, morality, and religion. He was opposed to revolutionary activities that would, in the name of reform, destroy these positive values. His fear was of too much freedom, of the destruction of the European community by private interests. He wrote of the dangers from two directions: from a plutocracy that would become more and more selfish, considering the working classes as of no more value than the machines they operated, and from the despotism of the working classes themselves.

In his books, letters, and personal life he consistently stated that institutions that worked badly were preferable to those that did not work at all. He foretold the new despotism of the twentieth century, and he characterized it as the product of a time that had abandoned its past. The ties of caste, class, corporation, and family were essential to his view of orderly government, and he discerned that these ties were rapidly becoming weaker even in his own lifetime. What would replace them was private interest, whether of the mob, the middle classes, or a ruling clique. The one way to stop this danger, he believed, was through freedom. Political freedom, he stated in his last work, was the one agent that could unite the varying interests of the modern state.

After the revolution of 1848 in France, Tocqueville was elected to the new legislature. In 1851 this position led to a brief imprisonment for opposing the *coup d'etat* of Louis Napoleon. In 1854, Tocqueville traveled to Germany to study the origins of feudalism. This study was part of his research into the background of the French Revolution that began in 1789. The result of this research was *The Old Régime and the Revolution.* Tocqueville's thesis, never before articulated, was that the revolution was accomplished in the minds of men long before the events of 1789.

Bathed in the laurels of this masterpiece, Tocqueville visited England for the last time in 1857. Back in Paris the following spring, while working on a second volume on the French Revolution, this one on the actual events, he suddenly became very ill. His health failed to improve, and he and his wife moved to the warmer climate of Cannes, where he died on April 16, 1859. The second volume on the French Revolution was left to posterity only in the form of notes, which were later organized by the editors of his complete works.

Glenn L. Swygart

Bibliography

Commager, Henry Steele. *Commager on Tocqueville.* Columbia: University of Missouri Press, 1993. Analysis of Tocqueville's writings. Includes an index.

Ledeen, Michael Arthur. *Tocqueville on American Character: Why Tocqueville's Brilliant Exploration of the American Spirit Is as Vital and Important Today as It Was Nearly Two Hundred Years Ago.* New York: St. Martin's Press, 2000. Evaluates Tocqueville's American travels and their impact on him and his writings.

Mansfield, Harvey C., Delba Winthrop, and Philippe Raynaud. *Tyranny and Liberty: Big Government and the Individual in Tocqueville's Science of Politics.* London: Institute of United States Studies, University of London, 1999. Covers Tocqueville's ideas on liberty, wealth, and equality as well as government.

Welch, Cheryl B. *De Tocqueville.* New York: Oxford University Press, 2001. Biography puts Tocqueville in the revolutionary context of his time.

J. R. R. Tolkien

English novelist and philologist

Born: Bloemfontein, South Africa; January 3, 1892
Died: Bournemouth, Hampshire, England; September 2, 1973

LONG FICTION: *The Hobbit*, 1937; *The Lord of the Rings*, 1955 (includes *The Fellowship of the Ring*, 1954; *The Two Towers*, 1954; *The Return of the King*, 1955); *The Silmarillion*, 1977; *The Book of Lost Tales I*, 1983; *The Book of Lost Tales II*, 1984; *The Lays of Beleriand*, 1985; *The Shaping of Middle-Earth*, 1986; *The Lost Road, and Other Writings*, 1987; *The Return of the Shadow: The History of "The Lord of the Rings," Part One*, 1988; *The Treason of Isengard: The History of "The Lord of the Rings," Part Two*, 1989; *The War of the Ring: The History of "The Lord of the Rings," Part Three*, 1990; *Sauron Defeated, the End of the Third Age: The History of "The Lord of the Rings," Part Four*, 1992; *Morgoth's Ring*, 1993; *The War of the Jewels*, 1994; *The Peoples of Middle-Earth*, 1996 (previous 12 novels collectively known as The History of Middle-Earth).

SHORT FICTION: *Tree and Leaf*, 1964, revised 1988; *Unfinished Tales of Numenor and Middle-Earth*, 1980 (Christopher Tolkien, editor); *The Book of Lost Tales*, 1983-1984.

DRAMA: *The Homecoming of Beorhtnoth Beorhthelm's Son*, pb. 1953.

POETRY: *Songs for the Philologists*, 1936 (with E. V. Gordon et al.); *The Adventures of Tom Bombadil*, 1962; *The Road Goes Ever On: A Song Cycle*, 1967; *The Lays of Beleriand*, 1985.

NONFICTION: *A Middle English Vocabulary*, 1922; *The Letters from J. R. R. Tolkien*, 1981 (Humphrey Carpenter, editor); *The Monsters and the Critics, and Other Essays*, 1983.

EDITED TEXTS: *Sir Gawain and the Green Knight*, 1925 (with E. V. Gordon); *Ancrene Wisse: The English Text of the Ancrene Riwle*, 1962.

TRANSLATIONS: *"Sir Gawain and the Green Knight," "Pearl," and "Sir Orfeo,"* 1975; *The Old English Exodus*, 1981; *Finn and Hengest: The Fragment and the Episode*, 1982.

MISCELLANEOUS: *The Tolkien Reader*, 1966.

CHILDREN'S/YOUNG ADULT LITERATURE: *Farmer Giles of Ham*, 1949; *Smith of Wootton Major*, 1967; *The Father Christmas Letters*, 1976; *Roverandom*, 1998.

John Ronald Reuel Tolkien (TAHL-keen) was born in Bloemfontein, South Africa, one of two sons of Arthur Reuel and Mabel Suffield Tolkien. When he was four years old, his father died, and his mother returned to England, to a town near Birmingham. The verdant English countryside to which he was moved made an immediate impression on the boy; it was to become the locale for his now-famous fantasy world. Tolkien's first teacher was his mother, and from her he acquired a love of languages and fantasy. Following her death in 1904 he and his brother were raised by Father Francis Xavier Morgan, a Roman Catholic priest. Tolkien received his secondary education at King Edward VI School in Birmingham and then attended Exeter College, Oxford, where he received his bachelor's degree in 1915. He then joined the Lancashire Fusiliers and served on the Western Front until the end of World War I. In 1916 he married Edith Mary Bratt; together they would have a daughter and three sons.

After the war, Tolkien returned to the University of Oxford and earned his master's degree in 1919. His love of language led him to work for two years as an assistant on the *Oxford English Dictionary*. Between 1920 and 1925 he taught English at the University of Leeds. In 1925 he returned to Oxford as a professor of Anglo-Saxon at Pembroke College, soon becoming the Rawlinson and Bosworth Professor of Anglo-Saxon. He was elected a fellow of Pembroke College in 1926 and was Merton Professor of English Language and Literature from 1945 until his retirement in 1959. During these years he continued his work in Anglo-Saxon and medieval literature and lore, publishing monographs and articles on works such as *Beowulf* and Geoffrey Chaucer's *The Canterbury Tales*.

When he was forty-five years old, *The Hobbit*, a novel for children, was published. It became an immediate success. Ostensibly based upon stories which he had created for the amusement of his children, *The Hobbit*, a heroic tale of dragons, giants, and heroes, appealed to both children and adults. Far more profound was *The Lord of the Rings*, which occupied him for fifteen years. This three-part work, which described the fantastic secondary world of Middle-Earth, with its own languages, history, customs, people, and geography, became enormously popular. Tolkien fan clubs and fan magazines emerged and flourished. During these years Tolkien received numerous awards and honors, ranging from children's book awards to honorary doctorates.

Although he officially retired from his professorship in 1959 Tolkien continued to write about Middle-Earth. At his death in 1973 he left behind many notes and partially completed manuscripts. Some of these were collated by his son, Christopher Tolkien, and published in 1977 as *The Silmarillion*, the story of the creation of Middle-Earth. *The Book of Lost Tales*, a collection of Tolkien's stories, was edited and published by his son in 1983 and 1984. Other posthumous works have followed.

Tolkien made his fictional world come alive. Because his fantasy world was firmly rooted in the medieval tradition, Tolkien's professional specialty, and because he was a perfectionist regarding detail, his descriptions of Middle-Earth are consistent and absorbing. Within this world, heroic adventures could and did take place. That too was part of the medieval epic literary tradition. Tolkien used many of the traditional characteristics of the epic in his works: heroes, quests, visits to the underworld, and noble deaths in battle. His variation on the theme was his unheroic hero. Middle-Earth had to be saved by ordinary and even humble heroes. Moreover, the effort had to be commensurate with the result; good could not triumph without hardship and suffering.

While Tolkien stated that his works were neither allegorical nor topical, his stories have strong relevance for the modern world. His experiences in the trenches of World War I, as well as the totalitarianism of the pre- and post-World War II era, affected him deeply and often surface in his work. Tolkien was concerned with the problem of power—whether it be political, spiritual, or personal. All of his characters are forced to choose whether to accept or to reject power. Tolkien was also concerned with the theme of good versus evil. Although he has been criticized as simplistic, his attitude was not only medieval but also modern. He created a world in which dignity is alive and good can triumph over evil.

Tolkien's significance lies in his ability to write literature which appeals to all ages. At the simplest level, his stories appeal to children. At a higher level, the heroic tales are delightful fiction. At a still higher level, the work enters the realm of ethical philosophy. Tolkien's fantasy world provides a place where moral values exist and quests can still be achieved.

William S. Brockington, Jr.

Bibliography

Carpenter, Humphrey. *Tolkien: A Biography*. London: Allen and Unwin, 1977. Written with access to Tolkien's unpublished letters and diaries, this mostly chronological narrative traces the development of the world of Middle-Earth from Tolkien's philological work. An extensive section of black-and-white photographs, a detailed bibliography, a family genealogy, and an index add to the value of this standard biography.

Clark, George, and Daniel Timmons, eds. *J. R. R. Tolkien and His Literary Resonances: Views of Middle Earth*. Westport, Conn.: Greenwood Press, 2000. A collection of fourteen essays devoted to Tolkien's Middle-Earth works, including an examination of Tolkien's images of evil.

Crabbe, Katharyn W. *J. R. R. Tolkien*. Rev. ed. New York: Continuum, 1988. A study of Tolkien's writings unified by a vision of "the quest." After a brief biographical chapter, Crabbe considers Tolkien's use of languages to delineate character in his major works.

Curry, Patrick. *Defending Middle-Earth: Tolkien, Myth, and Modernity*. London: HarperCollins, 1997. Curry examines the relevance of Tolkien's mythological creation, especially in terms of its depiction of struggle of community, nature, and spirit against state. There are chapters on politics, ecology, and spirituality.

Reynolds, Patricia, and Glen GoodKnight, eds. *Proceedings of the J. R. R. Tolkien Centenary Conference, 1992*. Altadena, Calif.: Mythopoeic Press, 1995. As the title suggests, this is a collection of papers given at the Tolkien conference held at Keble College, Oxford, in 1992 and represents a significant collection of views on Tolkien.

Shippey, T. A. *J. R. R. Tolkien: Author of the Century*. Boston: Houghton Mifflin, 2001. A critical review of Tolkien's work that takes to task critics inclined to relegate the founder of modern fantasy to the ranks of his inferior literary descendants.

Ernst Toller

German playwright

Born: Samotschin, Germany (now Szamocin, Poland); December 1, 1893
Died: New York, New York; May 22, 1939
Identity: Jewish

DRAMA: *Die Wandlung*, pr., pb. 1919 (*Transfiguration*, 1935); *Masse-Mensch*, pr. 1920 (*Masses and Man*, 1924); *Die Maschinenstürmer*, pr., pb. 1922 (*The Machine-Wreckers*, 1923); *Hinkemann*, pr., pb. 1923 (English translation, 1926); *Der entfesselte Wotan*, pb. 1923; *Die Rache des verhöhnten Liebhabers*, pr. 1923 (*The Scorned Lover's Revenge*, 1936); *Hoppla, wir leben!*, pr., pb. 1927 (*Hoppla! Such Is Life!*, 1928); *Feuer aus den Kesseln*, pr., pb. 1930 (*Draw the Fires!*, 1935); *Wunder in Amerika*, pr., pb. 1931 (with Hermann Kesten; *Miracle in America*, 1934); *Die blinde Göttin*, pr. 1932 (*The Blind Goddess*, 1934); *Seven Plays*, pb. 1935; *Blind Man's Buff*, pr. 1936 (with Denis Johnston, based in part on Toller's play *Die blinde Göttin*) *Nie wieder Friede!*, wr. 1936, pb. 1978 (*No More Peace!*, 1936); *Pastor Hall*, wr. 1938-1939, pb. 1946 (English translation, 1939).

POETRY: *Gedichte der Gefangenen*, 1921; *Das Schwalbenbuch*, 1924 (*The Swallow-Book*, 1924); *Vormorgen*, 1924.

NONFICTION: *Justiz: Erlebnisse*, 1927; *Quer durch: Reisebilder und Reden*, 1930 (*Which World—Which Way? Travel Pictures from America and Russia*, 1931); *Eine Jugend in Deutschland*, 1933 (*I Was a German*, 1934); *Briefe aus dem Gefängnis*, 1935 (*Letters from Prison*, 1936).

Ernst Toller (TAWL-ur) was one of the most popular playwrights in Germany and abroad in the 1920's, with translations in twenty-seven languages, although his fame quickly faded during the 1930's. Toller's creativity showed both in his activism and in his writings.

Toller's first play, for example, was the antiwar drama *Transfiguration*, which made him famous. While its rhetoric may today seem stale and sermonizing, the play proved a public success. Also, as early as 1917, Toller very effectively used excerpts from it, both in public readings and in leaflets, to encourage people to become politically active. As Toller evolved toward skeptical realism, his work continued to be inseparable from his life, which provided him with three major themes: the outsider, pacifism, and the socialist revolution with its paradoxes.

Born into the Jewish minority of the German-speaking population of a Polish part of Prussia, Toller witnessed, on one hand, the anti-Semitism of the Germans, and on the other, German feelings of superiority toward the Poles. His youth was otherwise uneventful, but the conflict of establishing his individuality led Toller away from Judaism. He later had his name removed from the register of his hometown's Jewish community.

World War I was the first major influence on Toller that converted him to pacifism. When the war started in 1914, he was swept up in the patriotism and volunteered for duty. Posted, upon his own request, to a machine-gun unit, Toller began to see all soldiers, even the enemy, as his brothers. After a nervous breakdown in May, 1916, he never returned to active duty and began his activism to win people over to his newly found nonviolent ideals, which would lead to the second major influence on Toller: the Munich revolution.

After leaving the front, Toller attended university and slowly turned to revolutionary socialism, but his ethical ideas were strongly influenced by Gustav Landauer, a contemporary who defined his brand of socialism in terms of pacifism and anti-Marxism. As a student in Heidelberg, Toller began to agitate against the ongoing war, barely evaded arrest, and left for Berlin in January, 1918. There he met the antiwar politician Kurt Eisner at a January, 1918, meeting of the Independent Social Democratic Party. Toller followed him to Munich and helped to organize a workers' strike in support of a peace without annexations. The strike collapsed on February 4, and Toller was arrested for attempted treason but was released.

The failed January strike was the precursor to Toller's involvement in the revolution in Bavaria, which lasted only six months. It began under Eisner's leadership as an unbloody coup on November 8, 1918. After Eisner's assassination on February 21, 1919, confusion ensued, and eventually Bavaria was declared a Soviet republic on April 7. Toller served as president for six days and later as field commander of the Red Army for ten days. He resigned when it became clear that he, the pacifist, refused to follow orders to have prisoners executed and that the Communist leadership would not follow his urging to negotiate with the advancing troops. These events created the legend of Toller as the writer-revolutionary.

On May 3, 1919, the revolution ended in bloodshed, but Toller was able to hide until June 4, 1919. He was sentenced to five years in prison. During these years he finished *Transfiguration* and wrote four other plays. Toller still considered himself a socialist but stayed away from party politics. He also wrote other works in prison; his last book of poetry, *The Swallow-Book*, was inspired by the swallows that nested in his cell.

Toller served his full sentence, refusing to be pardoned just on account of his literary fame. When he was released in 1924, Germany had shifted toward the political right. At the same time, Toller was at the height of his fame during the remaining 1920's and used his energy for both literary endeavors and political activism. While from 1924 to 1933 his residence was in Berlin, he traveled through the United States and much of Europe, including the Soviet Union. He supported human rights and was also an early campaigner against Nazism; modifying his pacifism, he believed that Western democracy had to resist Nazi barbarism.

Many works of this period were written in collaboration with others. Toller also explored other media. *Draw the Fires!*, considered his finest play, had first been planned as a film. In 1933 the Nazis seized power, and later that year Toller traveled to Switzerland for radio broadcasts; he never returned to Germany, because his life was in danger. His books were among those publicly burned.

Also in 1933, Toller published his autobiography, as part of his ongoing political activities that then included the cause of political refugees. He eventually settled in London in February, 1934. With much of his work published in English translation and amid wide publicity, Toller was again a celebrity. In 1935 he married Christiane Grautoff, a young actress whom he had met in 1932. The years the couple lived in London were among Toller's happiest times. However, his belief that the Nazis ought to be opposed militarily, as espoused in his play *No More Peace!*, met little interest in the England of the appeasement era.

From October, 1936, to February, 1937, Toller visited the United States, again on a lecture tour, and returned later in 1937 to work in Hollywood for Metro-Goldwyn-Mayer. None of his scripts, however, had a chance of being filmed, and in February, 1938, he left, disappointed and depressed, for New York, while his wife stayed in Hollywood. His work became more difficult because he was not comfortable writing in English, so he had to rely on a translator. His last play, *Pastor Hall*, loosely based on Martin Niemöller's resistance to Nazism, was performed posthumously.

Toller's last political ambition, providing humanitarian food aid to Republican Spain, was about ready to be realized when it was rendered obsolete by the defeat of Republican Spain by Francisco Franco's fascists. Deeply disappointed, faced with declining popularity, and isolated in part because of his separation from his wife, Toller committed suicide in his room at the Mayflower Hotel in New York on May 22, 1939.

Ingo R. Stoehr

Bibliography

Dove, Richard. *He Was a German: A Biography of Ernst Toller.* London: Libris, 1990. Detailed and evenhanded account of Toller's life, including a discussion of his works and the main intellectual influences on him.

Jordan, James. "One of Our War Poets Is Missing: The Case of Ernst Toller." *Oxford German Studies* 25 (1996): 24-25. Shows how Toller developed the theme of war into antiwar poetry of the highest quality.

Lamb, Stephen. "Intellectuals and the Challenge of Power: The Case of the Munich 'Räterepublik.'" In *The Weimar Dilemma: Intellectuals in the Weimar Republic*, edited by Anthony Phelan. Manchester, England: Manchester University Press, 1985. Discusses Toller's youthful activism in the light of revolutionary reality as well as different versions of ethical socialism espoused by Kurt Eisner and Gustav Landauer.

Pittock, Malcolm. *Ernst Toller.* Boston: Twayne, 1979. Focuses on the interpretation of Toller's literary work. Contains a chronology and brief survey of Toller's life.

Melvin B. Tolson

American poet

Born: Moberly, Missouri; February 6, 1898
Died: Dallas, Texas; August 29, 1966
Identity: African American

POETRY: *A Gallery of Harlem Portraits*, wr. 1932, pb. 1979; *Rendezvous with America*, 1944; *Libretto for the Republic of Liberia*, 1953; *Harlem Gallery: Book I, The Curator,* 1965; *"Harlem Gallery," and Other Poems of Melvin B. Tolson*, 1999.
DRAMA: *A Fire in the Flint*, pr. 1952 (adaptation of Walter White's novel).
NONFICTION: *Caviar and Cabbage: Selected Columns by Melvin B. Tolson from the "Washington Tribune," 1937-1944*, 1982; *The Harlem Group of Negro Writers*, 2001.

Melvin Beaunorus Tolson was a paradox; he was both a populist and an academic, a folk poet and a modernist. He was heavily influenced by the poets of the Harlem Renaissance, but he filtered its influence through a conscious adoption and adaptation of modernist techniques. The resulting poetry has become a Rorschach test for generations of literary critics.

Tolson grew up in small towns in Missouri and Iowa, the son of a "circuit riding" Methodist minister. He graduated from high school in Kansas City, Missouri, and in 1918 entered Fisk University in Nashville. After his first year at Fisk, he transferred to Lincoln University (another traditionally black college) near Philadelphia. In 1922, while still attending Lincoln, he married Ruth Southall. They had four children by 1928.

Tolson graduated from Lincoln in 1923. The next year he accepted an appointment as instructor in English and speech at Wiley College in Marshall, Texas. He would spend the rest of his life as a full-time teacher at small black colleges: first at Wiley, then, from 1947 to his retirement in 1965, at Langston University in Langston, Oklahoma, with an appointment in English and drama. By all accounts he was a gifted and well-respected teacher and administrator. He coached the Wiley College debating team to national prominence. Between 1937 and 1944 he wrote an opinion column for the *Washington Tribune*. He produced, directed, and wrote plays, and he directed theater companies in both Marshall and Langston. Tolson also ran for mayor of Langston and was elected to several terms. He had a full, engaged life in the black community. At the same time, as an artist, he lived in isolation. He was never part of an artists' community, and his writing time had to be stolen from his full-time work as a teacher and administrator.

That artistic isolation was relieved briefly in the 1931-1932 academic year, when he lived in New York City in order to attend Columbia University. As part of his work toward a master's degree in English, he interviewed writers of the Harlem Renaissance. That brief contact inspired his first major work, *A Gallery of Harlem Portraits*. Various poems from that poem sequence, or "book," were published during the 1930's, but the entire work was never published during his lifetime. Harlem, however, became his Mecca and his muse. His first major published poem, "Dark Symphony," was an affirmation of black pride and progress, in the declamatory, populist manner of some of Langston Hughes's work. The poem consists of six sections, each with a musical tempo or performance notation. "Black Symphony" received first prize in a 1939 contest sponsored by the American Negro Exposition. The judges of that contest were Harlem Renaissance writers Hughes, Arna Bontemps, and Frank Marshall Davis. "Dark Symphony" was published in *The Atlantic Monthly* in 1941 and became Tolson's best-known poem. His next book of poetry, *Rendezvous with America*, published in 1944, included "Dark Symphony."

Tolson was to publish just two more books of poetry before his death in 1966: *Libretto for the Republic of Liberia* and *Harlem Gallery: Book I, The Curator*. President William S. V. Tubman named Tolson poet laureate of Liberia in 1947 and commissioned a poem celebrating Liberia's upcoming centennial. The poem Tolson wrote was *Libretto for the Republic of Liberia*, a twenty-nine-page work (followed by sixteen pages of notes) organized into eight sections, each named for one of the notes in the musical scale. *Harlem Gallery* consists of 155 pages organized into twenty-four cantos, one for each letter of the Greek alphabet.

In *Libretto for the Republic of Liberia* and in *Harlem Gallery*, Tolson used the techniques of allusion and startling juxtaposition associated with Ezra Pound and T. S. Eliot. *Libretto for the Republic of Liberia* and *Harlem Gallery* were, consequently, less direct and more difficult than *Rendezvous with America*. Tolson's serious (though not solemn) use of modernist techniques made him unusual among black poets. Allen Tate, a modernist poet and member of a group of southern writers called the Fugitives, wrote an introduction to *Libretto for the Republic of Liberia* praising Tolson for being a modernist and praising the poem as an important work of art. Tate also suggested that no other black poets were working along lines fruitful for creating important work. Some critics have disagreed vigorously with Tate's general assessment of black poetry, and some have disagreed with his specific assessment of Melvin Tolson. Some have believed that Tolson erred in trying to please white critics (he solicited Tate's introduction), while others have said that he was not pleasing white critics but choosing the most useful working methods for his talents. Scholars agree, however, that in all of Tolson's work he is a satirist, a master of black English as well as academic English, and an irrepressible humorist.

Isaac Johnson

Bibliography

Berube, Michael. "Masks, Margins, and African American Modernism: Melvin Tolson's Harlem Gallery." *PMLA* 105, no. 1 (January, 1990): 57-69. A major reconsideration (and defense) of Tolson's ideas, strategies, and tactics.

Farnsworth, Robert M. *Melvin B. Tolson, 1898-1966: Plain Talk and Poetic Prophecy*. Columbia: University of Missouri Press, 1984. A complete biography.

Flasch, Joy. *Melvin B. Tolson*. New York: Twayne, 1972. This is the first extended consideration of Tolson's life and works, produced by the company that published his last two books of poetry.

Nelson, Raymond. "Harlem Gallery: An Advertisement and User's Manual." *The Virginia Quarterly Review* 75, no. 3 (Summer, 1999): 528-543. A thoughtful, urbane, jargon-free introduction to *Harlem Gallery* and to the rest of Tolson's work.

Nielsen, Aldon L. "Melvin B. Tolson and the Deterritorialization of Modernism." *African American Review* 26, no. 2 (Summer, 1992): 241-255. A brilliant analysis of the uses Tolson makes of modernism.

Tolson, Melvin B., Jr. "The Poetry of Melvin B. Tolson (1898-1966)." *World Literature Today* 64, no. 3 (Summer, 1990): 395-400. Tolson's son, professor of French at the University of Oklahoma, provides personal insight into his father's ideas and methods.

Tatyana Tolstaya

Russian novelist and short-story writer

Born: Leningrad, Soviet Union (now St. Petersburg, Russia); May 3, 1951

LONG FICTION: *Kys*, 2001 (*The Slynx*, 2003).

SHORT FICTION: *Na zolotom kryl'tse sideli*, 1987 (*On the Golden Porch*, 1989); *Sleepwalker in a Fog*, 1992.

NONFICTION: "Intelligentsia and Intellectuals," 1989; "In a Land of Conquered Men," 1989; "Apples as Citrus Fruit," 1990; "President Potemkin," 1991; *Pushkin's Children: Writings on Russia and Russians*, 2003.

During the late 1980's Tatyana Tolstaya (tohl-STI-yah) came to be considered one of the greatest talents in Russian literature. She and her six siblings, all of whom grew up with unusual privileges for the time, were grandchildren of the historical novelist Aleksei Nikolaevich Tolstoy, himself a relative of Leo Tolstoy. Tolstaya's other grandfather was Mikhail Lozinskii, a minor poet and well-known translator.

Tolstaya came of age during the period in the Soviet Union that came to be referred to as "the stagnation," years during the Brezhnev era that show remarkably little original prose literature. Many of the more interesting writers, among them Aleksandr Solzhenitsyn, Andrei Sinyavsky, and Vasily Aksyonov had already left the country. Others, including Yuri Trifonov and Lidia Chukovskaya, who never left the Soviet Union, were also out of the picture, due to either death or the lack of publishing opportunities. The impoverished monumentalism of the official genre of Socialist Realism had reached its nadir.

After Leonid Brezhnev's death in 1982 a liberalizing atmosphere began that eventually culminated with the rise of Mikhail Gorbachev in 1987 and the period called glasnost, a reference to the opening of the closed, controlled society created by Soviet socialism. It is not coincidental that Tatyana Tolstaya began writing at about this time. In 1983 came the publication of her first story, "Kleem i nozhnitsami" (with glue and scissors), which set the stage for such later stories as "On the Golden Porch."

The period of openness brought with it the so-called new thinking, which undoubtedly played a significant role in the success of Tolstaya's next story, "Peters." This complex psychological work focuses on the childhood of a boy made to conform to a despotic older generation, personified in his grandmother, who does not allow him to grow in a natural fashion but attempts to create a robotlike compendium of "good manners." The origin of the final letter *s* in the name derives from the nineteenth century custom of reducing the word for "sir" to this sound, which was added, in deference, by a person of the lower classes in speaking to someone from the nobility. With a twist of irony, Tolstaya presents the act of preparing for life as the life-draining force of the twentieth century Soviet era. In this the work is reminiscent of Boris Pasternak's *Doctor Zhivago* (1957), where, however, the principals are all unmasked, playing their natural parts; in "Peters" the force is masked, the role of the intimate exchanged for the baton of the despot.

Tolstaya's prose does not show the linear quality typical of Soviet writing. The deeply textured language, in which thought and action sometimes become meshed, would probably not have been accepted for publication in Russia at an earlier time. Tolstaya has been absolutely uncompromising in her writing, never allowing any changes to her texts whatsoever.

Tolstaya has achieved considerable success among English-language readers, especially in the United States. The translation of thirteen of her stories in *On the Golden Porch*, met with enthusiastic critical attention in *The New York Times* and elsewhere. Her second collection, *Sleepwalker in a Fog* met with similar success, making Tolstaya a very well-known literary figure in the United States.

"New-thinking" Russia was actually not as open as its name would seem to imply. Tolstaya was subjected to considerable pressure from editors and censors to conform to the "taste" of the political structure, even to the extent of being denied a place in the Writers' Union for a year on the basis of her ideological failures. Her straightforward, uncompromising style resists control from the power structures, and she persists in her artistic denunciation of Soviet society. In some of her stories she uses words with politically negative associations, like "dorevolutsionnyi" (prerevolutionary), which she transforms into something positive, a nostalgic longing for the loss of continuity with the Old Russia. Tolstaya's eventual path cannot be predicted, but her estimable early contribution to literature promises much for the future.

Christine D. Tomei

Bibliography

Chapple, Richard L. "Tatyana Tolstaya's Russian Family Portrait Gallery." *Midwest Quarterly* 32 (Winter, 1991): 156-166. A profile of the writer and her work.

Goscilo, Helena. *The Explosive World of Tatyana N. Tolstaya's Fiction*. Armonk, N.Y.: M. E. Sharpe, 1996. This is a critical review of Tolstaya's oeuvre, covering her whole career to the date of publication.

_______. "Monsters Monomaniacal, Marital, and Medical: Tat'iana Tolstaya's Regenerative Use of Gender Stereotypes." In *Sexuality and the Body in Russian Culture*, edited by Jane Costlow et al. Stanford, Calif.: Stanford University Press, 1993. This chapter discusses Tolstaya's symbolism and sound sources in her prose.

_______. "Tatyana Tolstaia's 'Dome of Many-Colored Glass': The World Refracted Through Multiple Perspectives." *Slavic Review* 47 (Summer, 1988): 280-290. A detailed scholarly analysis of Tolstaya's stories. Includes explanatory and reference footnotes, several of them in Russian and untranslated.

See, Carolyn. "In the Russian Tradition." *Los Angeles Times Book Review*, January 19, 1992, 3. A review of *Sleepwalker in a Fog*; suggests that the point in the stories is their timelessness; calls them elegant, overwritten mystical tales that are everything that communism was not.

Wisniewska, Sophia T. "Tat'iana Tolstaia." In *Russian Women Writers*, edited by Christine D. Tomei. New York: Garland, 1999. This is a critical biography of Tolstaya and her contribution to Russian literature.

Zalygin, Sergei, ed. *The New Soviet Fiction: Sixteen Short Stories*. New York: Abbeville Press, 1989. This 318-page anthology contains one story by Tolstaya, one of only three women represented. Zalygin's critical introduction analyzes the state of fiction in the Soviet Union during *perestroika* and *glasnost*.

Leo Tolstoy

Russian novelist

Born: Yasnaya Polyana, Russia; September 9, 1828
Died: Astapovo, Russia; November 20, 1910

LONG FICTION: *Detstvo*, 1852 (*Childhood*, 1862); *Otrochestvo*, 1854 (*Boyhood*, 1886); *Yunost'*, 1857 (*Youth*, 1886); *Semeynoye schast'ye*, 1859 (*Family Happiness*, 1888); *Kazaki*, 1863 (*The Cossacks*, 1872); *Voyna i mir*, 1865-1869 (*War and Peace*, 1886); *Anna Karenina*, 1875-1877 (English translation, 1886); *Smert' Ivana Il'icha*, 1886 (*The Death of Ivan Ilyich*, 1887); *Kreytserova sonata*, 1889 (*The Kreutzer Sonata*, 1890); *Voskreseniye*, 1899 (*Resurrection*, 1899); *Khadzi-Murat*, wr. 1904, pb. 1911 (*Hadji Murad*, 1911).

SHORT FICTION: *Sevastopolskiye rasskazy*, 1855-1856 (*Sebastopol*, 1887); *The Kreutzer Sonata, the Devil, and Other Tales*, 1940; *Notes of a Madman, and Other Stories*, 1943; *Tolstoy Tales*, 1947.

DRAMA: *Vlast tmy*, pb. 1887 (*The Power of Darkness*, 1888); *Plody prosveshcheniya*, pr. 1889 (*The Fruits of Enlightenment*, 1891); *Zhivoy trup*, pr., pb. 1911 (*The Live Corpse*, 1919); *I svet vo tme svetit*, pb. 1911 (*The Light Shines in Darkness*, 1923); *The Dramatic Works*, pb. 1923.

NONFICTION: *Ispoved'*, 1884 (*A Confession*, 1885); *V chom moya vera*, 1884 (*What I Believe*, 1885); *O zhizni*, 1888 (*Life*, 1888); *Kritika dogmaticheskogo bogosloviya*, 1891 (*A Critique of Dogmatic Theology*, 1904); *Soedinenie i perevod chetyrekh evangeliy*, 1892-1894 (*The Four Gospels Harmonized and Translated*, 1895-1896); *Tsarstvo Bozhie vnutri vas*, 1893 (*The Kingdom of God Is Within You*, 1894); *Chto takoye iskusstvo?*, 1898 (*What Is Art?*, 1898); *Tak chto zhe nam delat?*, 1902 (*What to Do?*, 1887); *O Shekspire i o drame*, 1906 (*Shakespeare and the Drama*, 1906); *The Diaries of Leo Tolstoy, 1847-1852*, 1917; *The Journal of Leo Tolstoy, 1895-1899*, 1917; *Tolstoi's Love Letters*, 1923; *The Private Diary of Leo Tolstoy, 1853-1857*, 1927; *"What Is Art?," and Essays on Art*, 1929; *L. N. Tolstoy o literature: Stati, pisma, dnevniki*, 1955; *Lev Tolstoy ob iskusstve i literature*, 1958; *Leo Tolstoy: Last Diaries*, 1960.

CHILDREN'S/YOUNG ADULT LITERATURE: *Azbuka*, 1872; *Novaya azbuka*, 1875 (*Stories for My Children*, 1988); *Russkie knigi dlya chteniya*, 1875; *Classic Tales and Fables for Children*, 2002 (includes selections from *Azbuka* and *Novaya azbuka*).

MISCELLANEOUS: *The Complete Works of Count Tolstoy*, 1904-1905 (24 volumes); *Tolstoy Centenary Edition*, 1928-1937 (21 volumes); *Polnoye sobraniye sochinenii*, 1928-1958 (90 volumes).

Among the world's greatest novelists, Leo Nikolayevich Tolstoy (TAWL-stoy) also wrote an important body of nonfiction advocating pacifism and social justice. The fourth son of Princess Marya Nikolayevna Volkonsky and Nikolay Ilyich Tolstoy, a retired lieutenant colonel and gentleman farmer, Tolstoy was born on the family estate of Yasnaya Polyana, Tula Province, Russia, on September 9 (August 28 according to the Russian Julian calendar), 1828. His mother died two years later in giving birth to her fifth child; her death may explain why Tolstoy, who fathered thirteen children, developed a terror of childbirth and in his novels portrayed it as a harrowing experience. Although he could not have remembered much about his mother, he drew on accounts of her to create Princess Marya in *War and Peace*. His father, who died when Leo was nine years old, served as the model for Nikolay Rostov in that work, and many of Tolstoy's other relatives and acquaintances provided him with characters for his fiction, as he himself was the model for Levin in *Anna Karenina*.

Tolstoy's youth was carefree and dissipated. In 1846 he enrolled in Kazan University to prepare for a diplomatic career but left after a year of studying Oriental languages. He would later become adept at Greek (which he claimed he taught himself in three months), Hebrew, German, French, and English, all of them represented in his fourteen-thousand-volume library. Despite a rigorous program of self-improvement that he established for himself after leaving the university, he spent the next four years as a typical Russian aristocrat (Tolstoy was a count), traveling between his country estate and the cities of St. Petersburg and Moscow. Though he eventually abandoned this social milieu, his experiences in high society allowed him to paint vivid portraits of its members.

Bored, in 1851 he joined the army and served in the Caucasus and in the Crimean War. He would reject this life, too, but he learned at first hand what war was like. In *War and Peace*, he presents the Battle of Austerlitz not as a grand panorama of clashing armies and heroic encounters but rather from the limited perspective of a soldier engaged in the action. As an officer, he would also have met characters like Count Vronsky and his circle, so well depicted in *Anna Karenina*. More immediately, he used his observations to create a series of sketches that appeared as *Sebastopol*; many of these stories contrast the quiet bravery of common soldiers with the vainglorious posturing of their officers.

Resigning his commission in 1856, Tolstoy turned his attention to improving the lot of the peasants who lived on his land, setting up a school, publishing textbooks, and traveling to Western Europe to observe teaching methods. In 1862 he married the eighteen-year-old Sofia Andreyevna Bers, sixteen years his junior. The next decade and a half, in which he created his two monumental novels, *War and Peace* and *Anna Karenina*, would be the happiest and most productive of his life. In his later years, he became increasingly concerned with religion, pacifism, and social issues, writing a large number of tracts attacking the established church, war, and injustice. Like his character Levin, he worked alongside the peasants. He also made his own shoes, became a vegetarian, and refused to allow others to serve him. He wrote his novel *Resurrection* to raise money for the Dukhobars, a group of pacifists seeking to emigrate to Canada. Like much of his writing in this period, the novel attacks the Russian Orthodox church, which excommunicated him in 1901. Several times he attempted to abandon the trappings of aristocracy. In November, 1910, he made the last of these efforts, dying in a railway station in Astapovo on his way to his beloved Caucasus.

Tolstoy not only produced two of the world's greatest novels but also revolutionized the genre. In 1851 he tried in "A History of Yesterday" to re-create a typical day in his life. Rejecting the Romantic fiction popular at the time, he sought to describe life in all of its contradictions and complexity while at the same time depicting the psychological motivations of his characters as they revealed themselves through subtle gestures and simple expressions. From this literary experimentation came works of epic proportions and epic stature. *War and Peace* contains more than 550 characters, at least 50 of them significant; *Anna Karenina* treats 143, and again some 50 play important roles in the work. Both are social histories, the one of the period 1805 to 1814, the other of the 1860's, and while Tolstoy focuses on the aristocratic world he knew so intimately, he shows a keen understanding of the common people as well. In his work, Tolstoy combines psychological probing with the novel of manners on a grand scale. Although he writes in the third person as an omniscient author, he allows his characters to reveal themselves.

Tolstoy's preeminence as a writer of fiction is unquestioned. John Galsworthy and E. M. Forster are only two of the many who have called *War and Peace* the greatest novel ever written, and another critic has commented that if God wrote a novel, it would be *Anna Karenina*. More problematic is Tolstoy's position as a reformer. Yet even here he has been influential. In his own day, he was regarded as the conscience of the nation as he pleaded for the lives of revolutionaries condemned to death, and Mahatma Gandhi found his works deeply inspirational. Though Tolstoy often adopted extreme positions, he has come to be recognized as a serious thinker, even if his religious and social tracts pale before the brilliance of his novelistic achievement.

Joseph Rosenblum

Bibliography

Bayley, John. *Leo Tolstoy.* Plymouth, England: Northcote House, 1997. Criticism and interpretation of Tolstoy's work.

Bloom, Harold, ed. *Leo Tolstoy.* New York: Chelsea House, 1986. A collection of critical essays. The views expressed give a good sampling of the wide range of opinions about Tolstoy prevalent among Western critics. Many of these critics assign a prominent place in literary history to Tolstoy, comparing him to, among others, Homer and Johann Wolfgang von Goethe. Includes bibliography.

Orwin, Donna Tussig. *Tolstoy's Art and Thought, 1847-1880.* Princeton, N.J.: Princeton University Press, 1993. Divided into three parts, which coincide with the first three decades of Tolstoy's literary career, Orwin's study attempts to trace the origins and growth of the Russian master's ideas. After focusing on Tolstoy's initial creative vision, Orwin goes on to analyze, in depth, his principal works.

Rowe, William W. *Leo Tolstoy.* Boston: Twayne, 1986. Concise introduction to Tolstoy's life and work, with special emphasis on the major novels and later didactic writings. Discusses, briefly, most of Tolstoy's major concerns. Excellent treatment of individual characters in the major novels. Includes bibliography.

Seifrid, Thomas. "Gazing on Life's Page: Perspectival Vision in Tolstoy." *PMLA* 113 (May, 1998): 436-448. Suggests that the typical visual situation in Tolstoy's fiction is perspectival; argues that Tolstoy's impulse can be linked with the material nature of books and that this linkage has implications for Russian culture as well as for the relationship between the verbal and the visual in general.

Steiner, George. *Tolstoy or Dostoevsky: An Essay in the Old Criticism.* 2d ed. New Haven, Conn.: Yale University Press, 1996. This welcome reappearance of a classic study of the epic versus the dramatic, first published in 1959, carries only a new preface. In it, however, Steiner makes a compelling case for the reprinting, in the age of deconstructionism, of this wide-ranging study not just of individual texts but of contrasting worldviews.

Tolstaia, Sophia Andreevna. *The Diaries of Sophia Tolstoy.* Translated by Cathy Porter, edited by O. A. Golinenko et al. New York: Random House, 1985. This massive personal record of Tolstoy's wife, detailing their life together, spans the years 1862-1910. Sophia Tolstoy kept an almost daily account of her husband's opinions, doubts, and plans concerning his literary activity and social ventures as well as of his relationship with other writers and thinkers. Her notes give a fascinating and intimate view of the Tolstoy family and of the extent to which it served as background for many of the literary episodes. Illustrated.

Tolstoy, Alexandra. *Tolstoy: A Life of My Father.* 1953. Reprint. New York: Octagon Books, 1973. Many of Tolstoy's offspring, relations, and peers wrote about him. This is a good place to begin for those who wish to understand why Tolstoy inspired such reverence in those around him.

Wilson, A. N. *Tolstoy.* New York: W. W. Norton, 1988. A long but immensely readable biography, breezy, insightful, and opinionated, by a highly regarded British novelist. Illustrated; includes a useful chronology of Tolstoy's life and times as well as notes, bibliography, and index.

Giuseppe Tomasi di Lampedusa

Italian novelist and essayist

Born: Palermo, Sicily, Italy; December 23, 1896
Died: Rome, Italy; July 25, 1957

LONG FICTION: *Il gattopardo*, 1958 (*The Leopard*, 1960).
SHORT FICTION: *Racconti*, 1961 (partial translation as *Two Stories and a Memory*, 1962).
NONFICTION: "Lezioni su Stendhal," 1959 (in *Paragone* IX, April).
MISCELLANEOUS: *The Siren, and Selected Writings*, 1995.

Giuseppe Tomasi di Lampedusa (toh-MAH-see dee lahm-pay-DEW-zah) was born into an aristocratic Sicilian family in 1896. He traveled widely and spent some years in London and Paris, but he lived most of his life in a decaying family palace in Palermo.

At his father's behest, Lampedusa studied law and prepared to enter the diplomatic corps, but his university career was interrupted when he was called up for duty in the Italian army in 1915. He was captured and served time in an Austro-Hungarian prison camp, from which he eventually escaped. In 1932 he married the Latvian psychoanalyst Alexandra Wolff-Stormersee and in 1956 adopted a son, Gioacchino Lanza, who would carry on his title.

Lampedusa wrote a number of essays that demonstrate a profound knowledge of French and English literature, but he published very little during his lifetime; among his papers were found essays on Stendhal, Prosper Mérimée, and Gustave Flaubert. He first appeared on the literary scene in 1954 at a literary congress with his cousin, the Sicilian poet Luigi Piccolo. Years earlier he had expressed the intention of writing a novel based on the life of his great-grandfather, who had been an astronomer and mathematician. In this book he wanted to set the biography of his grandfather among the historical events that had affected his family and the Sicilian people while expressing his own emotions and ideas with regard to himself, his family, and history.

On his return from the congress, at the age of sixty and feeling death to be near, Lampedusa began writing his novel. Finishing it in 1956, he submitted the manuscript to publishers who were, unfortunately, bound to find his view of history pessimistic and reactionary. One letter of rejection from a prominent Italian novelist employed as a publisher's reader reached Lampedusa as he lay dying of lung cancer.

Another novelist, Giorgio Bassani, received the manuscript of *The Leopard* from a friend. Amazed that such a book should be written by an unknown writer, Bassani perceived its value immediately and telephoned Palermo to speak to Lampedusa, only to learn that he had died. *The Leopard* was published the following year, to international acclaim.

Grove Koger

Bibliography

Cowart, David. "The Turning Point." In *History and the Contemporary Novel*. Carbondale: Southern Illinois University Press, 1989. A scholarly treatment.
Gilmour, David. *The Last Leopard: A Life of Giuseppe di Lampedusa*. New York: Pantheon Books, 1991. A complete biography.
Pacifici, Sergio. "Giuseppe Tomasi di Lampedusa: The View from Within." In *The Modern Italian Novel: From Pea to Moravia*. Carbondale: Southern Illinois University Press, 1979. *The Leopard* is analyzed in the wider context of Italian literature.

Charles Tomlinson

English poet

Born: Stoke-on-Trent, Staffordshire, England; January 8, 1927

POETRY: *Relations and Contraries*, 1951; *The Necklace*, 1955, rev. ed. 1966; *Seeing Is Believing*, 1958, 1960; *A Peopled Landscape*, 1963; *American Scenes, and Other Poems*, 1966; *The Way of a World*, 1969; *Renga: A Chain of Poems*, 1971 (with Octavio Paz, Jacques Roubaud, and Edoardo Sanguineti); *Written on Water*, 1972; *The Way In, and Other Poems*, 1974; *The Shaft*, 1978; *Selected Poems, 1951-1974*, 1978; *The Flood*, 1981; *Airborn = Hijos del Aire*, 1981 (with Octavio Paz); *Notes from New York, and Other Poems*, 1984; *Collected Poems*, 1985, expanded 1987; *The Return*, 1987; *Annunciations*, 1989; *The Door in the Wall*, 1992; *Jubilation*, 1995; *Selected Poems, 1955-1997*, 1997; *The Vineyard Above the Sea*, 1999.
TRANSLATIONS: *Versions from Fyodor Tyutchev, 1803-1873*, 1960 (with Henry Gifford); *Castilian Ilexes: Versions from Antonio Machado, 1875-1939*, 1963 (with Gifford); *Ten Versions from "Trilce" by César Vallejo*, 1970 (with Gifford); *Translations*, 1983; *Selected Poems*, 1993 (of Attilio Bertolucci).

NONFICTION: *The Poem as Initiation*, 1967; *Some Americans: A Personal Record*, 1981; *Isaac Rosenberg of Bristol*, 1982; *Poetry and Metamorphosis*, 1983; *The Sense of the Past: Three Twentieth Century British Poets*, 1983; *The Letters of William Carlos Williams and Charles Tomlinson*, 1992; *William Carlos Williams and Charles Tomlinson: A Transatlantic Connection*, 1998; *American Essays: Making It New*, 2001.

EDITED TEXTS: *Marianne Moore: A Collection of Critical Essays*, 1969; *William Carlos Williams: A Critical Anthology*, 1972; *Selected Poems*, 1976, revised 1985 (of William Carlos Williams); *Selected Poems*, 1979 (poems of Octavio Paz); *The Oxford Book of Verse in English Translation*, 1980; *Poems of George Oppen, 1908-1984*, 1990; *Eros English'd: Classical Erotic Poetry in Translation from Golding to Hardy*, 1992.

MISCELLANEOUS: *Words and Images*, 1972; *In Black and White: The Graphics of Charles Tomlinson*, 1976; *Eden: Graphics and Poetry*, 1985.

Alfred Charles Tomlinson is a contemplative poet in the tradition of William Wordsworth and Wallace Stevens. Mindful of the transience and interdependence of all natural things, he focuses on the concrete, sensible world and its relationship to human knowledge. His poems typically begin with meticulous observation of the changing surfaces of the natural world, but Tomlinson always moves beyond mere observation toward meditation, exploring the ways we discover meaning in the act of perception. In "Aesthetic," one of his earliest poems, he asserts that "Reality is to be sought, not in concrete,/ But in space made articulate."

Tomlinson was educated at Queens College, Cambridge, where he received a B.A. in 1948, and London University, where he received an M.A. in 1955. In 1956 he joined the faculty of the University of Bristol, where he taught until his retirement in 1982; he has also, over the years, traveled widely and held several visiting professorships, including one in the southwestern United States. A painter as well as a poet, he has had many one-man shows, and he has continued to receive many literary awards. He married Brenda Raybould in 1948, becoming the father of two daughters. They made their permanent home in Gloucestershire, England.

Rejecting the insularity of much contemporary English poetry, Tomlinson has found poetic inspiration in the work of various American and European poets. He has translated the work of several modern poets and has collaborated with a number of his contemporaries, including the Mexican poet Octavio Paz. Tomlinson's favorite subjects are rocks, mountains, water, light, and the moon and sun; as he paints his subjects, he captures gradations of coloration as well as volume, shape, and texture. While recording such changeable appearances, he addresses the predicament of locating meaning in a world of flux. For Tomlinson, the discovery of meaning requires a recognition of the world's otherness. By acknowledging a world beyond the self, we move, he writes in "Antecedents," out of the "shut cell" of our solitude toward an "earned relation/ With all that is other." This "relation," grounded in accurate perception, leads to a sense of equilibrium between the world and the self. The "basic theme" of his work, he says in *Some Americans*, is "that one does not need to go beyond sense experience to some mythic union, that the 'I' can be responsible only in relationship and not by dissolving itself away into ecstasy or the Oversoul."

Seeing Is Believing, like *A Peopled Landscape*, expresses Tomlinson's deep respect for English history, but once again, the poet focuses on the ethical implications of the act of perception. The mind, the imagination, and the eye work in unison to perceive the world and to discern meaning, as his title *Seeing Is Believing* suggests. Indeed, to translate seeing into meaning entails moral responsibility; one must always respect the separateness, the individuality, indeed, the autonomy, of the perceived object. "I leave you," he writes of a tree he has just described, "to your own meaning, yourself alone." Elsewhere, he speaks of Paul Cézanne, who knew how to paint his mountains "unposed," to accept the object as it always "is."

Tomlinson's later poetry continues to broaden the ethical and political implications of his art. In *The Way of a World* and *Written on Water*, he is increasingly willing to "fix a meaning" on the world. Some of his finest poems from these and subsequent books consider various historical figures, examining the consequences of human egotism in the world. One of his most memorable political poems, "Assassin," explores the all-consuming ego of Trotsky's murderer, who imagines altering the course of history with an act of violence. In *The Shaft* Tomlinson further develops his political interests in several poems about the French Revolution. His more recent work continues to explore historical and contemporary themes while maintaining a focus on the nature and limits of perception as a basis for shaping the self and living ethically in the world.

Stylistically, Tomlinson's verse is characterized by impressive range and variety. He can write spare, lucid descriptions notable for their precision, a mode of expression learned partly from the American poets William Carlos Williams and Marianne Moore. Tomlinson has also mastered a graceful, meditative style with roots in the poetry of Wordsworth, a style rich and suggestive but remarkably free of showy verbal effects. Given his subject, it is understandable that the "I" is restrained. Effects of language, rhythm, image, and sound reinforce the relativistic nature of observed experience and knowledge—that all experience depends upon the interdependence of mind and object, and of object and the universal flux.

Lois Gordon
Michael Hennessy

Bibliography

Clark, Timothy. *Charles Tomlinson*. Plymouth, England: Northcote House, 1999. Clark gives a brief but wide-ranging introduction to Tomlinson's career, covering not only his poetry but also his work as a translator, as a graphic artist, and as a collaborator in writing experimental, multilingual poetic sequences. Features a detailed biographical outline, examples of Tomlinson's graphics, a bibliography, notes, and index.

John, Brian. *The World as Event: The Poetry of Charles Tomlinson.* Montreal: McGill-Queen's University Press, 1989. John says that Tomlinson's poetry creates a language of the senses, enlarges definitions, and pursues understanding of experience. Includes a photograph, notes, a bibliography, and an index.

King, P. R. "Seeing and Believing: The Poetry of Charles Tomlinson." In *Nine Contemporary Poets: A Critical Introduction.* New York: Methuen, 1979. A substantial study, this essay presents Tomlinson's poetry as an independent endeavor in which the poet uses his painter's eye to search for a right relationship between people and places, time and history, to find delight in the act of seeing as the self adjusts to reality. Notes, a bibliography, and an index.

Kirkham, Michael. *Passionate Intellect: The Poetry of Charles Tomlinson.* Liverpool: Liverpool University Press, 1999. This book provides a detailed critical reading of Tomlinson's poetry from the 1950's through the 1980's. Kirkham presents Tomlinson's work in an "unfolding sequence," focusing on the poet's "unified vision of the natural-human world." Includes a bibliography, notes, and an index.

O'Gorman, Kathleen, ed. *Charles Tomlinson: Man and Artist.* Columbia: University of Missouri Press, 1988. Eleven essays, two interviews, a poem, a chronology, and a foreword by Donald Davie cover Tomlinson's career. Six essays present different perspectives on his poetry, and two provide overviews of his development. Three essays study interrelationships of his painting and poetry. Illustrations, bibliography, and index.

Swigg, Richard. *Charles Tomlinson and the Objective Tradition.* Lewisburg, Pa.: Bucknell University Press, 1994. Swigg explores Tomlinson's place in an Anglo-American poetic tradition of "objectivity" that values the world's otherness, its existence apart from the ego of the poet. Focuses on the ways in which various writers within this tradition have influenced Tomlinson. A bibliography, notes, and index are included.

Weatherhead, A. Kingsley. "Charles Tomlinson." In *The British Dissonance: Essays on Ten Contemporary Poets.* Columbia: University of Missouri Press, 1983. Explores the question raised by Tomlinson about whether form is in objective reality or imposed by subjective perception. Presents Tomlinson as a poet who bridges many of the divisions separating contemporary poets and their themes. Includes notes, a bibliography, and an index.

H. M. Tomlinson

English novelist and travel writer

Born: Wanstead, Essex, England; June 21, 1873
Died: London, England; February 5, 1958

LONG FICTION: *Gallions Reach*, 1927; *All Our Yesterdays*, 1930; *The Snows of Helicon*, 1933; *Mars His Idiot*, 1935; *All Hands!*, 1937 (also known as *Pipe All Hands!*); *The Day Before*, 1939; *Morning Light*, 1946; *The Trumpet Shall Sound*, 1957.

NONFICTION: *The Sea and the Jungle*, 1912 (travel); *Old Junk*, 1918; *London River*, 1921; *Waiting for Daylight*, 1922; *Tidemarks*, 1923 (travel); *Gifts of Fortune*, 1926; *Under the Red Ensign*, 1926 (also known as *The Foreshore of England*); *Thomas Hardy*, 1929; *Between the Lines*, 1930; *Norman Douglas*, 1931; *Out of Soundings*, 1931; *Below London Bridge*, 1934 (travel); *South to Cadiz*, 1934 (travel); *The Wind Is Rising*, 1941; *The Turn of the Tide*, 1946; *The Face of the Earth*, 1950; *Malay Waters*, 1950; *The Haunted Forest*, 1951; *A Mingled Yarn*, 1953.

Henry Major Tomlinson was born in 1873 in Wanstead, Essex, but spent his youth around the London docks. At the age of twelve he was employed as a shipping clerk. Hating the drudgery of the work, he nevertheless loved the ships with which his labors brought him in contact. Even while working, he found time to read extensively, some of his favorite authors being Walt Whitman, Herman Melville, Ralph Waldo Emerson, and Henry David Thoreau. He married Florence Hammond in 1898.

Tomlinson started writing early in his life and began submitting his work to editors in hopes of escaping the shipping office, but he was thirty-one before he was able to leave his job as a clerk. He became a member of the editorial staff of the London *Morning Leader* in 1904 and remained in this position until 1909, when he embarked on a long trip across the Atlantic and up the Amazon River on a tramp steamer. This voyage and his experiences on it are the source for *The Sea and the Jungle*, his best-known travel book. Tomlinson joined the staff of the London *Daily News* in 1912, serving as a war correspondent in France and Belgium from 1914 to 1917. In 1917 he became literary editor of *The Nation and thenaeum*, a post he left six years later to pursue writing full-time.

With the publication of *Gallions Reach* in 1927, Tomlinson achieved success as a novelist, and subsequently he devoted much of his attention to fiction. This first novel, a romance set in the Far East, won the Femina-Vie Heureuse Prize and caused Tomlinson to be associated, as an author, with Joseph Conrad. Perhaps the primary resemblance between them is their devotion to the sea, although Tomlinson also shared Conrad's conviction that the human state of mind, the thought process, is more important than action as such.

Tomlinson went on to write seven more novels, many of them autobiographical. His essays—collected in such volumes as *Old Junk*, *London River*, and *Waiting for Daylight*—earned him a popular following and are distinguished by a style of impressive imagery, verbal beauty, and poetic introspection. They range in subject matter from his beloved London to the drawbacks of technological progress. Better still are such travel books as *The Sea and the Jungle* and *Tidemarks*, the former of which is regarded as a classic of its kind. Tomlinson died in London in 1958.

Grove Koger

Bibliography

Connell, Evan S. Preface to *The Sea and the Jungle*, by H. M. Tomlinson. Marlboro, Vt.: Marlboro Books, 1989.

Crawford, Fred D. *H. M. Tomlinson*. Boston: Twayne, 1981.

Hopkins, Kenneth. Introduction to *H. M. Tomlinson: A Selection from His Writings*. London: Hutchinson, 1953.

Krasner, James. "The Geometric Jungle: Imperialistic Vision in the Writings of Alfred Russel Wallace, H. M. Tomlinson, and Joseph Conrad." In *The Entangled Eye: Visual Perception and the Representation of Nature in Post-Darwinian Narrative*. New York: Oxford University Press, 1992.

John Kennedy Toole

American novelist

Born: New Orleans, Louisiana; 1937
Died: Biloxi, Mississippi; March 26, 1969

LONG FICTION: *A Confederacy of Dunces*, 1980; *The Neon Bible*, 1989.

John Kennedy Toole will perhaps always be touted more for his potential than for his accomplishments, for his first published novel, *A Confederacy of Dunces*, was not printed until eleven years after his death. Born in 1937 in New Orleans, Louisiana, Toole was the son of John Toole, a car salesman, and Thelma Ducoing Toole, a teacher. The author, who had written his first novel at the age of sixteen, received a B.A. from Tulane University in 1958 and an M.A. in English from Columbia University the following year. After teaching at the University of Southwestern Louisiana, Toole served in the army, writing *A Confederacy of Dunces* while stationed in Puerto Rico from 1962 to 1963. Later Toole returned to New Orleans, where he worked toward a Ph.D. at Tulane University and taught at Saint Mary's Dominican College. In late 1968, he left New Orleans to travel and a few months later committed suicide in his car in Biloxi, Mississippi. He was thirty-one years old.

The Neon Bible, which Toole wrote at the age of sixteen, was finally cleared for publication in 1989, following legal battles among the author's heirs. The novel is set in a small southern town in the 1940's and focuses on young David, who must deal with eccentric family members and the rigid, unforgiving religious fanaticism of the small-town community. David's crisis occurs when his father departs to fight in the war, his favorite aunt leaves town, and the preacher takes his mother away.

The publication of *A Confederacy of Dunces* has a unique history. Between 1963 and 1966, Toole negotiated with the publishing house Simon and Schuster, which, after commanding numerous revisions, finally rejected the work in 1966. Toole apparently gave up hope of the novel's ever being published. After Toole's death, however, his mother sent the worn, nearly illegible carbon copy to eight more publishers during the next seven years. In 1976 she began repeated efforts to persuade novelist Walker Percy, teaching at Loyola University in New Orleans, to read her son's novel. In the novel's foreword, Percy describes his unsuccessful attempts to dodge Thelma Toole as well as his eventual determination to see the novel through to its publication by Louisiana State University Press in 1980. Despite the many rejections by publishers, *A Confederacy of Dunces* was a surprising critical success, selling forty-five thousand hardcover copies in five printings and later appearing on *The New York Times* paperback best-seller list for more than a month. The novel was awarded the 1980 Pulitzer Prize in fiction and was honored with a nomination for the prestigious Faulkner Award in 1981.

A Confederacy of Dunces is about thirty-year-old Ignatius J. Reilly, obese, educated, and lazy, who sponges off his garish, alcoholic mother in the colorful city of New Orleans. Ignatius, whose name recalls Saint Ignatius Loyola, the founder of the Jesuit Order, is a proponent of medieval philosophy and values. He reads the work of the Roman Christian philosopher Boethius, who advocates passive acceptance of life's events. Ignatius records his thoughts and observations in Big Chief Tablets, which are strewn around his dank monk's-cell of a room. He practices celibacy and upholds the ideals of theology and geometry and of taste and decency. Meanwhile, he escapes into the worlds of television and film while verbalizing his disgust at the vulgarity of such forms of entertainment; he consumes massive quantities of junk food and

Dr. Nut soda despite a pyloric valve that causes intestinal distress when he is emotionally upset.

Ignatius's search for employment, at his mother's insistence, generates several subplots. At first he tries to work at the Levy Pants Company, a dying business in which almost no one, not even the owner, takes an interest. Ignatius decorates the office with hand-painted signs, rids the business of its problem of a backlog of files by discarding them, and incites unenthusiastic factory workers to riot in legitimate protest of squalid working conditions. He also befriends Miss Trixie, a senile octogenarian who shows up for work in her nightgown, mumbles incessantly about a Christmas turkey she was promised but never received, and begs to be allowed to retire. Ignatius's next job as a hot dog salesman for Paradise Vendors is even less profitable, for he eats more hot dogs than he sells and often slips away to the movies.

In frequent correspondence with Myrna Minkoff, a New York political reformer whom he met in college and with whom he shares a love-hate relationship, Ignatius rebuffs her suggestions that all of his problems are sexual and organizes a group of French Quarter homosexuals in a plan to reform the world. Other subplots involve Ignatius's mother, who declares independence from her son and becomes socially active, and the female proprietor of a strip joint, The Night of Joy, who peddles pornography and exploits her employees.

A Confederacy of Dunces has received much critical praise for the ingenuity of its characters and for the intricacy of its plot but mostly for its unique humor and the vividness of its language and local color. Some critics have been made uneasy by the overreliance on coincidence in the novel, but perhaps more disturbing to some has been the difficulty in categorizing the work. Ignatius J. Reilly is so repulsive, and his treatment of his mother is so insensitive and cruel, that it is misleading to label him a comic hero. The title of the novel is from Jonathan Swift's writing: "When a true genius appears in the world, you may know him by this sign, that the dunces are all in confederacy against him." The novel is also in the mold of a Swiftian satire. Toole's hero is roguish, but the reader finds that this unpleasant character casts aspersions that likely echo the reader's own sentiments against the crassness, the materialism, and the decadence of society. Unlike the protagonist in traditional satires, however, Ignatius embraces many of the very hypocrisies, obscenities, and insensitivities against which he rails.

Lou Thompson

Bibliography

McNeil, David. "*A Confederacy of Dunces* as Reverse Satire: The American Subgenre." *Mississippi Quarterly* 38 (1984/1985). Particularly insightful article, which emphasizes the novel's place in the literary tradition of reverse satire, in which the protagonist hypocritically exemplifies the very ideals he criticizes.

Nelson, William. "The Cosmic Grotesque in Recent Fiction." *Thalia* 5 (1982/1983). Examines *A Confederacy of Dunces*' grotesque elements which nullify expectations of convention and resolution.

Nevils, René Pol, and Deborah George Hardy. *Ignatius Rising: The Life of John Kennedy Toole*. Baton Rouge: Louisiana State University Press, 2001. A biography of the troubled writer and his southern gothic family.

Rudnicki, Robert Walter. "Toole's Proboscis: Some Effluvial Concerns in *The Neon Bible*." *Mississippi Quarterly* 47, no. 2 (1994). Compares Toole's two novels.

Jean Toomer

American poet

Born: Washington, D.C.; December 26, 1894
Died: Doylestown, Pennsylvania; March 30, 1967
Identity: African American

POETRY: "Banking Coal," in *Crisis*, 1922; *Cane*, 1923 (prose and poetry); "Blue Meridian," in *New American Caravan*, 1936; *The Wayward and the Seeking*, 1980 (prose and poetry; Darwin T. Turner, editor); *The Collected Poems of Jean Toomer*, 1988.
DRAMA: "Balo," in Alain Locke's *Plays of Negro Life*, pb. 1927.
NONFICTION: "Winter on Earth," in *The Second American Caravan*, 1929; "Race Problems and Modern Society," 1929; *Essentials: Definitions and Aphorisms*, 1931; "The Flavor of Man," 1949.

Jean Toomer published only a single work of lasting literary importance, *Cane*, but that one volume has earned for him a distinguished place in American literary history. He was born Nathan Eugene Toomer in Washington, D.C., on December 26, 1894. His father, Nathan Toomer, abandoned his wife, Nina Pinchback, before their son was born. Raised in his maternal grandparents' home, Toomer was influenced by his grandfather, Pinckney Benton Stewart Pinchback, a proud and once-powerful man who had served as lieutenant governor of post-Civil War Louisiana during Reconstruction. Through much of his adolescence, the young man was known as Eugene Pinchback, and it was only when he began to pursue a literary career that he adopted his father's surname and changed Eugene to Jean.

Light-skinned and racially mixed, P. B. S. Pinchback had made his political career as a black; however, during Toomer's childhood the family lived in an exclusive white neighborhood on Washington's Bacon Street. Racial identity was an issue that Toomer considered carefully, and by the time he went to college, he had rejected identification with either race; instead, he embraced the label "American."

When Toomer was a teenager, the family moved to a black neighborhood, where he finished high school at the segregated M Street High School. After graduation, he attended a series of colleges: the University of Wisconsin, Massachusetts College of Agriculture, the American College of Physical Training, the University of Chicago, and the City College of New York. He never stayed at any school long enough to earn a degree, and he switched his academic interests several times.

Toomer's early interest in literature was inspired by his Uncle Bismark, who spent hours in bed surrounded by an eclectic array of books. It was not, however, until Toomer was studying at the City College of New York and had begun to meet literary figures such as E. A. Robinson, Waldo Frank, and Van Wyck Brooks that he thought seriously of writing as a career. Disappointed by his first efforts, Toomer returned to Washington and accepted an invitation to manage a school in Sparta, Georgia, for a few months. In Georgia, Toomer shared the life of the poor blacks who were served by the school, and he was moved by this introduction to rural black life. Encouraged by Frank after his return to New York in 1922, Toomer turned his experience in Georgia into *Cane*. The manuscript, which was finished by the spring of 1923, showed the influence of contemporary prose experimentation, combining prose and poetry in a three-part structure that begins in the rural South, moves to the urban North, and then returns to the South. In *Cane*, Toomer attempted to bridge the gap between the rural black heritage and the New Negro of the 1920's, creating a complex intermingling of black and white, rural and urban, primitive and civilized. *Cane* did not sell well, but it was a striking critical success, particularly among the other young black intellectuals who were forming the basis of the Harlem Renaissance.

Much of the critical reaction angered Toomer because it focused on his role as a black writer, a racial limitation that Toomer rejected. In reaction, he cut himself off from the literary crowd that had fostered his career. Although he published a few stories during the 1920's and a long narrative poem in 1936, he was unable to find a publisher for his other literary work. In the summer of 1924, Toomer traveled to George Ivanovitch Gurdjieff's Institute for Harmonious Development of Man in Fontainebleau, France. From that time until his marriage to Margery Latimer in 1932 Toomer worked as a teacher of the Gurdjieff philosophy, first in Harlem and then in Chicago. In 1934 after the death of his first wife in childbirth, he married Marjorie Content, and they settled in Doylestown, Pennsylvania. In 1940 he joined the Society of Friends, for whom he wrote several pamphlets. After 1950, he was generally incapacitated by illness, and he died in 1967 in Doylestown. Interest in Toomer was revived after *Cane* was reprinted in 1967. The general recognition that *Cane* is one of the outstanding achievements of the Harlem Renaissance guarantees Toomer a continuing place in American literary history.

Carl Brucker

Bibliography

Benson, Joseph, and Mabel Mayle Dillard. *Jean Toomer.* Boston: Twayne, 1980. The first book-length study of Toomer, this volume is an excellent introduction to Toomer's life, work, and place in American literature. After a biographical chapter, the book examines Toomer's novel *Cane* and representative later works. Includes a bibliography.

Byrd, Rudolph P. "Jean Toomer and the Writers of the Harlem Renaissance: Was He There with Them?" In *The Harlem Renaissance: Revaluations*, edited by Amritjit Singh, William S. Shiver, and Stanley Brodwin. New York: Garland, 1989. In this article, Byrd argues that Toomer should not be considered part of the Harlem Renaissance because he was not in Harlem for many of the Renaissance's most important years, he did not associate himself with other Harlem writers, and he refused to be labeled as a "Negro" writer.

Fabre, Geneviève, and Michel Feith, eds. *Jean Toomer and the Harlem Renaissance*. New Brunswick, N.J.: Rutgers University Press, 2001. A collection of essays by European and American scholars highlighting Toomer's bold experimentations as well as his often ambiguous responses to the questions of his time.

Hajek, Friederike. "The Change of Literary Authority in the Harlem Renaissance: Jean Toomer's *Cane*." In *The Black Columbiad: Defining Moments in African American Literature and Culture*, edited by Werner Sollos and Maria Diedrich. Cambridge, Mass.: Harvard University Press, 1994. Argues that one of the main unifying elements in *Cane* is the concept of changing authority, which occurs in three phrases corresponding to the three sections of the text.

Kerman, Cynthia. *The Lives of Jean Toomer: A Hunger for Wholeness*. Baton Rouge: Louisiana State University Press, 1988. This book gives an account of the various stages of Jean Toomer's life and his attempts to find spiritual guidance and revelation throughout his lifetime. An interesting account of a fascinating life.

O'Daniel, Therman B., ed. *Jean Toomer: A Critical Evaluation*. Washington, D.C.: Howard University Press, 1988. This large volume contains forty-six essays and an extensive bibliography. The essays are arranged thematically, and cover Toomer's life; his work as novelist, short-story writer, poet, and playwright; his friendships with other writers; religious and male-female themes; and various interpretations of *Cane*. An excellent and accessible collection.

Scruggs, Charles, and Lee VanDemarr. *Jean Toomer and the Terrors of American History*. Philadelphia: University of Pennsylvania Press, 1998. Scruggs and VanDemarr examine sources such as Toomer's early writings on politics and race, his extensive correspondence with Waldo Frank, and unpublished portions of his autobiographies to illustrate the ways in which the cultural wars of the 1920's influenced Toomer's *Cane* and his later attempt to escape from the racial definitions of American society.

Wagner-Martin, Linda. "Toomer's *Cane* as Narrative Sequence." In *Modern American Short Story Sequences*, edited by J. Gerald Kennedy. Cambridge, England: Cambridge University Press, 1995. Discusses *Cane* as a modernist tour de force of mixed genre. Examines "Blood-Burning Moon" as Toomer's ideal fiction construct that provides insight into the structural and thematic radicalism of the collection.

Susan Allen Toth

American memoirist

Born: Ames, Iowa; June 24, 1940

NONFICTION: *Blooming: A Small-Town Girlhood*, 1981 (autobiography); *Ivy Days: Making My Way Out East*, 1984 (autobiography); *How to Prepare for Your High-School Reunion, and Other Midlife Musings*, 1988; *A House of One's Own: An Architect's Guide to Designing the House of Your Dreams*, 1991 (with James Stageberg); *My Love Affair with England*, 1992; *England as You Like It: An Independent Traveler's Companion*, 1995; *England for All Seasons*, 1997; *Victoria: The Heart of England*, 1999.

EDITED TEXT: *Reading Rooms*, 1991 (with John Coughlan).

Susan Allen Toth is an important Midwestern chronicler of the life of the common person. Her writing shows how a relatively mundane life may seem intriguing if it is told with sensitivity and sympathy for humanity. Born in Ames, Iowa, where she also grew up, she had a quiet and happy childhood with her mother, Hazel Erickson Allen Lipa, an English teacher at Iowa State University, and her sister, Karen, one year older than Toth. Her father, Edward Douglas Allen, a promising economist at Iowa State, died when she was seven years old; her mother did not remarry until Toth's college years.

Toth's childhood and adolescence are recorded in detail in her first book, *Blooming: A Small-Town Girlhood*, which is a thematic collection of reminiscences from her grade-school years to her arrival at Smith College. The book depicts incidents and people, apprehensions and successes, that shape the person she would become in adulthood. *Blooming* also describes Toth's early propensity for omnivorous reading, her immersion in the Protestant work ethic (from baby-sitting to detasseling corn), and the social and psychological importance of cultivating many girlfriends and boyfriends.

Blooming's eleven chapters explore Toth's early interests and experiences: the town swimming pools and her family's summer lake retreat, her friends and classes and parties, holiday celebrations, and preparations for and departure to college. *Ivy Days: Making My Way out East*, a memoir of Toth's four years at Smith College and her first two years of graduate school at the University of California at Berkeley, has seven chapters that tell of Toth's alliance with and adjustments to all sorts of other women, her fledgling attempts at social drinking and smoking, her embarrassments and boredom on uninteresting or threatening dates, her apprehensions and successes in college classes, and her enchantment with campus scenery and with East Coast families of her friends.

Ivy Days is not only more mature chronologically than her first book but also tighter in its prose and more symbolic in its language. Apples packed in a bag for lunch on the train home from college symbolize freedom and health, a quilt made by her aunt signifies solace and love in her claustrophobic dormitory room in Lawrence House, and six-foot-long college scarves curled on other girls' shoulders broadcast popularity and romantic involvement. *Ivy Days* is a book at once universal and particular in its topics of uprooting, moving, becoming homesick, and reaching out to others.

Ivy Days is also about charting direction for life. Toth embarks on a history major after considering art history and economics, but two months later she finds governmental abstractions and legislative acts uninteresting when compared with the writing of Henry David Thoreau and Thomas Carlyle, which delights her. Her experiences as an English major are not all positive, however: A devastating comment from a creative writing instructor causes her to give up writing short stories for the next eighteen years.

After one summer working in Boston for the *Harvard Business Review* and another going to summer school in London, Toth graduated from college, not with the summa cum laude for which she had striven (illness having caused her to do poorly on the final examination) but with magna cum laude distinction and with her mother and stepfather in attendance at the ceremony. The last dozen pages of the book cover her Berkeley years and her meeting and falling in love with Louis E. Toth, whom she married in 1963. They had one child, Jennifer Lee. Since 1969 Toth has been on the writing faculty at Macalester College in St. Paul, Minnesota.

Toth's third book, *How to Prepare for Your High-School Reunion, and Other Midlife Musings*, chronicles her feelings and concerns at the stage of mid-life, following her divorce in 1974 and her remarriage to architect James Stageberg in 1985. Here she presents emotions and insights about single parenting, adult dating, adjustments in a happy second marriage, college teaching, tranquillity in nature, and fascination with material things. In one essay, childhood reminiscence about an inappropriate gift purchased for her mother concerns, more important, parental love. In other essays she recommends five steps of preparation for attending a class reunion, offers suggestions and encouragement to would-be writers, shows how she combats an emotional crisis, and shares fears of violence and crime in an urban neighborhood. In three of the final essays Toth hypothesizes about her maternal grandmother's life and the lessons Toth learned from her without ever meeting her.

In addition to coming-of-age domestic prose, Toth has written two entertaining, conversational, autobiographical travel guides: *My Love Affair with England* and *England as You Like It: An Independent Traveler's Companion*. A third book on England, *England for All Seasons*, was published in 1997. Toth's guides encourage leisurely travel and well-planned exploration of small areas and highlight destinations that are her personal favorites. All three books are informative and readable.

Toth is also adept at composing book-length essays on other topics. She coedited (with John Coughlan) *Reading Rooms: America's Foremost Writers Celebrate Our Public Libraries* and coauthored (with her architect-husband) *A House of One's Own: An Architect's Guide to Designing the House of Your Dreams*. In addition, her stories, reviews, and essays have appeared in *Family Portraits: Remembrances by Twenty Distinguished Writers* (1989) and in such publications as *North American Review*, *Cleveland Plain Dealer*, *The New York Times*, *Harper's*, *Woman's Day*, and *Vogue*.

Toth has said that she has been influenced by E. B. White's varied sentence structure, his use of the surprising image, and his zest for life amid fear and self-doubt. She is an avid admirer of Henry David Thoreau, for his spare and strong style and his moral philosophy. From Sarah Orne Jewett she learned to write about small things and the quiet, domestic life. In her personal revelations Toth is unpretentious, self-deprecating, and unembarrassed. Her books concern humanity in general, and she uses commonplace subjects, such as picking raspberries or buying knee socks, to illustrate truths about life. Her style is modest and matter-of-fact, and her prose reveals universal life experiences of growth and exploration. Critics have noted that her work is well-received in part because her vivid memories spark similar reminiscences in her readers.

Jill B. Gidmark

Bibliography

Bartley, Robert. "Remembrance of Growing Up in America's Heartland." *The Wall Street Journal*, June 11, 1981, p. 26. A review of *Blooming*.

Knickerbocker, Laura. "Bookshelf: Not So Bright College Years at Smith." *The Wall Street Journal*, August 20, 1984. A lukewarm review of *Ivy Days*.

Lochner, Frances C., ed. *Contemporary Authors*. Vol. 105. Detroit: Gale Research, 1982. Offers a brief biography of Toth, a useful listing of her publications, and a short comment from the author on her goals in writing.

Skarda, Patricia L. "Susan Allen Toth." In *Dictionary of Literary Biography Yearbook 1985*, edited by Jean W. Ross. Detroit: Gale, 1986. A reference entry on Toth.

Albion Winegar Tourgée

American novelist

Born: Williamsfield, Ohio; May 2, 1838
Died: Bordeaux, France; May 21, 1905
Pseudonym: Henry Churton

LONG FICTION: *Toinette*, 1874 (as Henry Churton; better known as *A Royal Gentleman*, 1881); *A Fool's Errand*, 1879; *Bricks Without Straw*, 1880; *Hot Plowshares*, 1883; *Murvale Eastman, Christian Socialist*, 1890.
NONFICTION: *The Code of Civil Procedure of North Carolina*, 1868; *A Digest of Cited Cases*, 1878; *The Invisible Empire*, 1880.

Albion W. Tourgée (toor-ZHAY), a Union soldier in the Civil War, wrote to justify the Radical Republican idea of Reconstruction. Other minor American writers used Reconstruction themes, but unlike Tourgée they were native southerners, they did not experience Reconstruction directly, and they were not involved in its politics. Tourgée was thus unique.

Tourgée grew up in Ohio and graduated from Rochester College in 1862. His war career lasted less than two years, and in 1865 he moved to North Carolina. As a carpetbag lawyer he wanted to help establish racial equality and generally to improve and enlighten the South. He later realized how radical and naïve these ideas were. Disillusioned, he fictionalized his experiences under the title *A Fool's Errand*.

The book is the best of his more than twenty novels. It is largely autobiographical—the central figure of the fool is an idealistic Michigan lawyer who moves to the South and finds himself *persona non grata* as he tries to help African Americans obtain their rights. A certain amount of suspense and violent action helps rescue the book from Tourgée's heavy burden of moralizing. Particularly memorable are the vivid accounts of Ku Klux Klan threats and atrocities. Comfort Servosse, the fool, finally realizes that the South cannot change instantly. He admires the courage and courtesy of southern aristocrats but hates their stubbornness and prejudice. His sad concluding moral is curiously prescient, calling for federal action to help educate blacks and hoping that strong black leadership will arise. Tourgée departs from accurate self-portrayal in that he idealizes the fool beyond credibility. He himself was frequently intemperate and slanderous, a contrast to the dignified character of Servosse.

Most of Tourgée's other novels are thought of as pieces of third-rate sentimentalism—bad imitations of his idol, James Fenimore Cooper. Stereotyped characters and wholly implausible situations abound. When, as in *A Fool's Errand*, he confined himself to the times and situations he knew, he managed to rise to second-rate status. Other novels in this category are *Bricks Without Straw*, dealing with the rise of an African American protagonist, and *A Royal Gentleman*, with a miscegenation theme, showing how one southern gentleman could not give up his belief in the inferiority of blacks. Tourgée's earliest books were his best. In addition to his writing, he served variously as superior court judge, codifier of state law, newspaper columnist, magazine editor, and consul to Bordeaux.

Bibliography

Dibble, Roy F. *Albion W. Tourgée*. 1921. Reprint. Port Washington, N.Y.: Kennikat Press, 1968.

Gross, Theodore L. *Albion W. Tourgée*. New York: Twayne, 1963.

Olsen, Otto H. *Carpetbagger's Crusade: The Life of Albion Winegar Tourgée*. Baltimore: The Johns Hopkins University Press, 1965.

Stiller, Richard. *The White Minority: Pioneers for Racial Equality*. New York: Harcourt Brace Jovanovich, 1977.

Cyril Tourneur

English playwright

Born: Place unknown; c. 1575
Died: Kinsale, Ireland; February 28, 1626

DRAMA: *The Revenger's Tragedy*, pr. 1606-1607 (authorship uncertain); *The Atheist's Tragedy: Or, The Honest Man's Revenge*, pr. c. 1607; *The Plays of Cyril Tourneur*, pb. 1978.
POETRY: *The Transformed Metamorphosis*, 1600.
MISCELLANEOUS: *The Works of Cyril Tourneur*, 1929, 1963 (Allardyce Nicoll, editor).

Cyril Tourneur (TUR-nur), about whom little is known, was perhaps the son of Captain Richard Turnor, a follower of Sir Thomas Cecil. The young Tourneur, probably born about 1575, was a follower of the Cecils also, and he served the Vere family and the earl of Essex at different times during his career. Much of that career was spent in military or diplomatic service. He probably served with the English forces in the Netherlands in the early years of the seventeenth century.

A verse satire, *The Transformed Metamorphosis*, was published in 1600, and *The Revenger's Tragedy*, which has traditionally been ascribed to Tourneur, was published in 1607. Tourneur's literary reputation rests chiefly on this play, although it was not ascribed to him until 1656, some fifty years after its performance, and its authorship has been contested. Indeed, a majority of contemporary critics now attributes the play to Thomas Middleton. Considerable arguments have been made both for and against Tourneur's authorship of this work, based on various approaches to analyzing the play; the truth will probably never be known for certain. Another surviving play, *The Atheist's Tragedy*, was published in 1611 and is certainly Tourneur's work. The Stationers' Register contains an entry in 1612 of *The Nobleman*, a tragicomedy by Cyril Tourneur, but this play and *The Arraignment of London*, for which he wrote one of the acts for Henslowe's company, have both been lost. Four other literary works are often ascribed, again with considerable uncertainty, to Tourneur: *A Grief on the Death of Prince Henry* (1913), a pamphlet titled *Laugh and Lie Down* (1605), the elegy "On the Death of a Child but One Year Old," and the poem "Of Lady Anne Cecil . . . ."

Tourneur was a government courier in 1613 and a campaign soldier again in 1614. Imprisoned by the Privy Council in 1617, he was released on Sir Edward Cecil's bond. In 1625 he accompanied Sir Edward on a naval expedition against Spain. As lord marshall of the fleet, Sir Edward appointed Tourneur secretary to the Council of War and secretary to the Marshall's Court, but the first appointment was not approved. The expedition failed; Sir Edward's flagship, the *Royal Anna*, was badly damaged, with many of the crew killed or wounded, among them Tourneur. The ship reached port in Kinsale, Ireland, where Tourneur was put ashore. He died there of his wounds on February 28, 1626.

Unlike many of the Elizabethan and Jacobean dramatists, Tourneur seems to have devoted most of his life to his active military career and relatively little of it to writing for the stage. T. M.

Parrott considers him "a poet expressing himself in dramatic form rather than a professional playwright." The morbid splendor of the two surviving plays traditionally attributed to Tourneur has attracted much critical interest.

William Ryland Drennan

Bibliography

Camoin, François A. *The Revenge Convention in Tourneur, Webster, and Middleton.* Salzburg: Institut für Englische Sprache und Literatur, Universität Salzburg, 1972. Stresses the complexity of moral views among Jacobean playwrights, which led to the questioning nature of their works. Emphasizes the different techniques of Elizabethan and Jacobean playwrights writing revenge plays.

Jacobson, Daniel J. *The Language of "The Revenger's Tragedy."* Salzburg: Institut für Englische Sprache and Literatur, Universität Salzburg, 1974. Jacobson investigates such aspects of Tourneur's language as antithesis, irony, and paradox.

Murray, Peter. *A Study of Cyril Tourneur.* Philadelphia: University of Pennsylvania Press, 1964. This full-length study of Tourneur provides a definitive discussion of the authorship question for *The Revenger's Tragedy.* Tourneur's two plays are analyzed in detail for their art and thought. Murray also gives considerable attention to *The Transformed Metamorphosis* but little or no attention to other minor works.

Schuman, Samuel. *Cyril Tourneur.* Boston: Twayne, 1977. A basic biography covering the life and providing critical analysis of the works of Tourneur. Includes an index.

White, Martin. *Middleton and Tourneur.* New York: St. Martin's Press, 1992. White compares and contrasts the works of Thomas Middleton and Tourneur. Includes a bibliography and an index.

Michel Tournier

French novelist and short-story writer

Born: Paris, France; December 19, 1924

LONG FICTION: *Vendredi: Ou, Les Limbes du Pacifique*, 1967, revised 1978 (*Friday: Or, The Other Island*, 1969); *Le Roi des Aulnes*, 1970 (*The Ogre*, 1972; also known as *The Erl-King*); *Les Météores*, 1975 (*Gemini*, 1981); *Gaspard, Melchior, et Balthazar*, 1980 (*The Four Wise Men*, 1982); *Gilles et Jeanne*, 1983 (*Gilles and Jeanne*, 1987); *La Goutte d'or*, 1985 (*The Golden Droplet*, 1987); *Eléazar: Ou, La Source et le buisson*, 1996 (*Eleazar, Exodus to the West*, 2002).

SHORT FICTION: *Le Coq de Bruyère*, 1978 (*The Fetishist, and Other Stories*, 1983); *Le Médianoche amoureux: Contes et nouvelles*, 1989 (*The Midnight Love Feast*, 1991).

NONFICTION: *Canada: Journal de voyage*, 1977 (travel journal); *Le Vent Paraclet*, 1977 (essays; *The Wind Spirit*, 1988); *Le Vol du vampire: Notes de lecture*, 1981 (criticism); *Le Vagabond immobile*, 1984 (with Jean-Max Troubeau); *Le Tabor et le Sinai: Essais sur l'art contemporain*, 1988; *Le Miroir des idées: Traite*, 1994 (*The Mirror of Ideas*, 1998); *Le Pied de la lettre: Trois cents mots propres*, 1994; *Célébrations: Essais*, 1999; *Journal extime*, 2002.

CHILDREN'S/YOUNG ADULT LITERATURE: *Vendredi: Ou, La Vie Sauvage*, 1971 (*Friday and Robinson: Life on the Esperanza Island*, 1972); *Les Rois mages*, 1983 (adaptation of his novel *The Four Wise Men*).

TRANSLATION: *Les Archives secrètes de la Wilhelmstrasse*, 1950-1953 (4 volumes; of the secret archives of the German Ministry of Foreign Affairs).

Michel Édouard Tournier (tewr-nyay) is one of the most widely read, most honored, and certainly most controversial and thought-provoking of contemporary European writers. He was born in Paris on December 19, 1924, the son of Alphonse and Marie-Madeleine (Fournier) Tournier, who had met while studying German at the Sorbonne. Alphonse's educational career was curtailed by World War I; after being wounded, he abandoned professional ambitions and founded an international bureau which dealt with musicians' copyrights. Tournier's favorite toy was the phonograph; from childhood on, he enjoyed music but even more the power of the spoken word. Marie-Madeleine's legacy was equally formative. While she gave up her teaching plans for child-rearing, she never lost her love for Germany, which she passed on to her children. Tournier's maternal great-uncle, Gustave Fournier, had taught German in Dijon, and tales about Gustave and Edouard, Tournier's grandfather, during the Prussian occupation of the 1870's form the basis of some of Tournier's autobiographical vignettes in *The Wind Spirit.* His own childhood was laced with train excursions to the Black Forest; these happy occasions took place within the growing shadow of Nazism. Tournier was not a diligent student nor was he a prodigious reader. Yet he was attracted to writers such as Hans Christian Andersen, whose works combine fantasy with reality. Tournier has said that he wishes his own works to be comprehensible to any twelve-year-old child. His stories in *The Fetishist, and Other Stories*, his rewriting of Daniel Defoe's *Robinson Crusoe* (1719) in *Friday*, and the novel *The Four Wise Men* reflect his early reading.

When he was four years old, Tournier underwent a routine tonsillectomy. To the nervous and hypersensitive young boy, the operation was a nightmare, an invasion. It gave Tournier a sense of alienation and a mistrust of other people. This feeling of solitude and separation was furthered by his experiences during World War II. Too young for active service, Tournier first saw the war from a perspective of youthful exuberance. At the beginning of the Occupation, his family lived in the Parisian suburbs, but their home was soon commandeered by German officers, and the Tourniers were socially categorized by their *germanistik* sympathies. The family moved to an apartment in Neuilly while Tournier stayed at a summer cottage in Villers-sur-Mer and, later on, in the village of Lusigny. In spring, 1944, by chance he was away from Lusigny when his foster family was deported to Buchenwald for having helped the Maquis. Tournier's love of German culture made Nazi excesses even more intolerable to him, but he admits that he, like the majority of the French, never considered joining the Resistance. From 1942 to 1945, Tournier studied philosophy at the Sorbonne under Gaston Bachelard and Jean-Paul Sartre. He also was influenced by fellow student Gilles Deleuze. In 1946 Tournier went to the university in Tübingen for a proposed three-week study of German philosophers; he stayed there for four years. In July, 1949, however, Tournier suffered the setback which ended his academic career: He failed his Sorbonne doctoral exam. It was a bitter blow, yet it may also be seen as the beginning of his literary vocation.

From 1949 to 1958, Tournier worked in radio and television production, first for a French station, and then as an announcer for Europe No. 1. He lived in a Parisian hotel with other painters and writers. He also worked as a translator of contemporary German texts, most notably those of Erich Maria Remarque, into French, and he took courses from Claude Lévi-Strauss. In 1958, Tournier became head of translation services for Editions Plon, where he worked until 1968. From 1960 to 1965, he also hosted a television series, *La Chambre bleue* (the darkroom), which dealt with photography. Tournier has been called France's foremost "amateur" photographer, and the motif of image versus reality undergirds his writings. In 1967, Tournier, who already enjoyed considerable success in intellectual pursuits, published *Friday*, his flipside version of Defoe's *Robinson Crusoe*. A study of human isolation and sensuality, it enjoyed immediate critical success, winning the Grand Prix de Roman of the French Academy. The novel was a popular success as well; in fact, Tournier's novels generally top the French best-seller lists for weeks, even months.

The 1970's were a time of artistic development for Tournier. In 1970 *The Ogre* won the Prix Goncourt. Set against a background of World War II, its portrayal of Fascism, pederasty, and alienation is both repulsive and compelling. Tournier's personal background has led critics to speculate extensively on the novel's verisimilitude and *roman à clef* qualities. Tournier was elected to the Académie Goncourt in 1972, and throughout the early 1970's he traveled extensively; among the places he visited were Japan, Iceland, Canada, and Northern Africa. These trips were reflected in his own favorite work, *Gemini*, a study of twinship and solitude, sublimation and desire. Unfriendly critics have denounced *Gemini* as morally reprehensible, but more favorable readers applaud its candid and intellectual approach to questions of sexual identity and power. During the 1970's, Tournier also devoted time to writing children's stories and to his hobby of photography. In 1975 Tournier was honored as a Chevalier de la Légion d'Honneur.

Tournier has frequently remarked upon the importance of rites of passage as are reflected in his novels of the 1980's such as *The Four Wise Men*, a recasting of the Nativity story, and *Gilles and Jeanne*, the account of Bluebeard Gille de Rais's perverted veneration of Joan of Arc. During this decade, Tournier also developed more fully the motifs of duality, of ethnic and psychological separation. He reveled in challenging mythical and historical "truths." *The Golden Droplet*, which was made into a film in 1988, aroused much critical debate with its denunciation of dominant political ideology, popular culture, and racism via the adventures of its neo-Candide Berber protagonist, Idriss. In *The Midnight Love Feast* Tournier played again with framework tales (*The Arabian Nights* and *The Decameron*), blending and contrasting Western and non-Western traditions.

In the 1990's, Tournier continued to distill his major theme of duality. *Le Miroir des idées* (the mirror of ideas) contains philosophical essays, dedicated to Gaston Bachelard, which explore polarities. Photography has resurfaced, preeminent and paradoxical, in his study of the works of the controversial Czech photographer Jan Saudek, *Le Pied de la lettre* (treat as equal). Michel Tournier himself has lived for more than thirty years in a former rectory in the valley of the Chevreuse.

Katherine C. Kurk

Bibliography

Anderson, Christopher. *Michel Tournier's Children: Myth, Intertext, Initation*. New York: P. Lang, 1998. Focuses on Tournier's writing for and about children, especially his use of myth and patterns of rites of passage in his narratives.

Cloonan, William. *Michel Tournier*. Boston: Twayne, 1985. Biographical information and overviews of the critical response to major works.

Davis, Colin. *Michel Tournier: Philosophy and Fiction*. New York: Oxford University Press, 1988. Davis provides a reliable, comprehensive study.

Edwards, Rachel. *Myth and the Fiction of Michel Tournier and Patrick Granville*. Lewiston, N.Y.: E. Mellen Press, 1999. A comparative study.

Gascoigne, David. *Michel Tournier*. Washington, D.C.: Berg, 1996. A solid introduction to Tournier's life and works.

Petit, Susan. *Michel Tournier's Metaphysical Fictions*. Philadelphia: J. Benjamins, 1991. A reliable, comprehensive study.

Arnold Toynbee

English historian

Born: London, England; April 14, 1889
Died: York, Yorkshire, England; October 22, 1975

NONFICTION: *Nationality and the War*, 1915; *The New Europe*, 1915; *The Western Question in Greece and Turkey*, 1922; *Greek Historical Thought from Homer to the Age of Heraclitus*, 1924; *Greek Civilisation and Character*, 1924; *The World After the Peace Conference*, 1925; *Turkey*, 1926 (with K. P. Kirkwood); *A Journey to China*, 1931; *A Study of History*, 1934-1961 (12 volumes); *Christianity and Civilization*, 1940; *Civilization on Trial*, 1948; *The Prospects of Western Civilization*, 1949; *The World and the West*, 1953; *An Historian's Approach to Religion*, 1956; *Christianity Among the Religions of the World*, 1957; *East to West: A Journey Round the World*, 1958; *Hellenism: The History of a Civilization*, 1959; *Between Oxus and Jumma*, 1961; *The Present-Day Experiment in Western Civilization*, 1962; *Between Niger and Nile*, 1965; *Hannibal's Legacy: The Hannibalic War's Effects on Roman Life*, 1965 (2 volumes); *Cities on the Move*, 1970; *Surviving the Future*, 1971.

Among philosophers of history, Arnold Joseph Toynbee is unique in having made a profound appeal to scholars and general readers alike. His most impressive work is his twelve-volume *A Study of History*, which received immediate acclaim from historians and philosophers of history and afforded exciting reading to thousands who read the work through abridgements.

Toynbee, born in London on April 14, 1889, was educated at Winchester and then at Balliol College, Oxford. His academic record enabled him to be a scholar at both schools. From 1912 to 1915 he was a fellow and tutor at Balliol. Later in his life, when his scholarly activities had given him distinguished status among commentators on history, he was awarded various honorary degrees from Oxford, Birmingham, Columbia, Cambridge, and Princeton Universities.

During World War I Toynbee worked at various governmental jobs, including a period with the British Foreign Office in 1918 as a member of the staff in the political intelligence department. He was a member of the Middle Eastern Section of the British Delegation to the Peace Conference in Paris in 1919.

Having engaged in the practical application of his knowledge of Middle Eastern affairs, Toynbee returned to academic life in his position as Koraes Professor of Byzantine and Modern Greek Language, Literature, and History at London University from 1919 to 1924. Recognition of his increasing expertise in his fields brought him the distinction of becoming director of studies at the Royal Institute of International Affairs and research professor of international history at the University of London. He held these posts on a Sir Daniel Stevenson Foundation grant from 1925 until his retirement in 1955.

In the meantime Toynbee had initiated what developed into an impressive series of publications. In addition to writing such books as *The New Europe*, *The Western Question in Greece and Turkey*, and *Greek Historical Thought from Homer to the Age of Heraclitus*, Toynbee, as both editor and writer, dealt with contemporary international history in a series of yearbooks with the general title *Survey of International Affairs* (1920-1946).

During World War II Toynbee was a director of foreign research and press services at the Royal Institute of International Affairs, and from 1943 to 1946 he was director of the research department of the British Foreign Office. He was once again a member of the British delegation at the Peace Conference in 1946. Starting in 1934 he was an editor of *British Commonwealth Relations*. Toynbee's monumental work in *A Study of History* had its beginnings in 1922; engaged in other tasks, he worked on the project intermittently until its completion in 1954, a period of study and writing at the Institute for Advanced Study in Princeton, New Jersey, having enabled him to complete the final volumes. A frequent visitor to the United States, he made his permanent home in London.

The distinctive feature of Toynbee's study of history is his claim that civilizations, not nations, are the determining factors in history, and that the life of a civilization is the story of its challenges and responses to environmental conditions. He provoked considerable critical attack with his contention that history shows the influence of God on historical events.

Toynbee's last years were spent traveling and speaking throughout the world, including many trips to the United States, as well as in continued writing. He also spent much time defending his historical theories, primarily by defining and clarifying terms that he frequently used in his writing. He was continually in demand as a speaker and, although his health was failing, he always tried to comply. Toynbee and his wife finally retired to York, in northern England, where he died on October 22, 1975.

Glenn L. Swygart

Bibliography

McNeill, William. *Arnold J. Toynbee: A Life*. New York: Oxford University Press, 1989. Written at the request of Toynbee's son, this is the authoritative biography.

Perry, Marvin. *Arnold Toynbee and the Western Tradition*. New York: P. Lang, 1996. Places Toynbee's work in the context of his time.

Thompson, Kenneth W. *Toynbee's Philosophy of World History and Politics*. Baton Rouge: Louisiana State University Press, 1985. Relies on extracts from Toynbee's writings.

Toynbee, Arnold. *Arnold Toynbee: A Selection from His Works*, edited by E. W. F. Tomlin. New York: Oxford University Press,

1978. Defines and clarifies key phrases used repeatedly by Toynbee.

_______. "The Way to Coexistence." *UNESCO Courier*, February, 1994. A concise article.

Urban, G. R. *Toynbee on Toynbee*. New York: Oxford University Press, 1974. Urban presents the published result of radio discussions with Toynbee.

Thomas Traherne

English poet

Born: Herefordshire, England; c. 1637
Died: Teddington, London, England; October, 1674

POETRY: *A Serious and Patheticall Contemplation of the Mercies of God*, 1699 (better known as *Thanksgivings*); *The Poetical Works of Thomas Traherne*, 1903; *Traherne's Poems of Felicity*, 1910.

NONFICTION: *Roman Forgeries*, 1673; *Christian Ethicks*, 1675; *Meditations on the Six Days of the Creation*, 1717; *Centuries of Meditations*, 1908.

The seventeenth century meditative religious poet Thomas Traherne (truh-HURN) did not acquire literary fame until the late nineteenth century, for the poems and the prose reflections, *Centuries of Meditations*, on which his reputation rests, were lost for more than two hundred years after his death, reappearing finally at a London bookseller's in 1897. Consequently, little is known about the poet's quiet life. Most of the extant information was recorded by Anthony à Wood, a seventeenth century man of letters, in his *Athenae Oxonienses* (1691-1692), a collection of brief biographical sketches of all the Oxford graduates he considered noteworthy.

Traherne was the son of a shoemaker who had come from a once-prominent Welsh family. His Celtic heritage links Traherne with Henry Vaughan, another seventeenth century religious poet whose works reveal a mystical concept of the relationship between humans and nature as well as a soul seeking to return to its original state of innocence when it was one with God.

Both Thomas and his elder brother, Philip, were provided with financial support for a good education, apparently by another Philip Traherne, a wealthy innkeeper of their village, who was probably a relative. Thomas entered Brasenose College, Oxford, in 1652. He was granted the degree of bachelor of arts in 1656 and received his master of arts in 1661, after his ordination to the priesthood in the Church of England in December, 1657. He remained a staunch, if somewhat unorthodox, Anglican throughout his life.

Traherne accepted the position of rector of the parish of Credenhill, near Hereford, soon after his ordination, but, according to the custom of the time, he evidently spent at least part of the years of his tenure there in Oxford, studying for the degree of bachelor of divinity, which was granted in 1669, and doing research in the Bodleian Library for his scholarly treatise, *Roman Forgeries*.

It was probably during the time at Credenhill that Traherne wrote many of his meditations glorifying the innocence and wonder of childhood and lamenting the corruption that wealth and the desire for it brings. His best poems and meditations dramatize his conception of Felicity, the "Highest Bliss," which he experienced naturally as a child, subsequently lost, and then regained in adulthood. Traherne's imagery for expressing his Felicity reflects an excitement for the new open spatial model of the universe that replaced the closed Ptolemaic system. As he wrote in one of his meditations:

> Were nothing made but a Naked Soul, it would See nothing out of it Self. For Infinite Space would be seen within it. And being all sight it would feel it self as it were running parallel with it. And that truly in an Endless manner, because it could not be conscious of any Limits: nor feel it self present in one Center more than another. This is an infinite sweet mystery: to them that have Taste[d] it.

By 1669 Traherne had joined the staff of Sir Orlando Bridgeman, Lord Keeper of the Great Seal under Charles II, as chaplain. When Bridgeman retired to Teddington, a London suburb not far from Hampton Court, in 1672, Traherne accompanied him and remained in service there until his death, at the age of thirty-seven, in 1674.

The sophisticated, witty court near which Traherne spent the last few years of his life was a world completely foreign to his temperament. His intensely introspective meditations on innocence, childhood, and the beauties of nature reveal him as the true contemporary not of urbane Restoration classicists such as Edmund Waller and John Dryden but of poets such as Henry Vaughan, George Herbert, William Blake, and William Wordsworth, fellow seekers after a pure and uncorrupted spiritual state of Felicity.

James J. Balakier

Bibliography

Day, Malcolm M. *Thomas Traherne*. Boston: Twayne, 1982. Day's study of Traherne's meditations and poems focuses on his use of abstraction, paradox, and repetition to evoke in his readers a sight of eternity unlike the childlike vision earlier critics described in his work. Day provides a biographical chapter, thoughtful analyses of Traherne's work, a chronology, and an annotated select bibliography.

De Neef, A. Leigh. *Traherne in Dialogue: Heidegger, Lacan, and Derrida*. Durham, N.C.: Duke University Press, 1988. De Neef's study investigates the applicability to Traherne's work of three popular theories, with their themes of being, psychic identity, desire, and "the discursive economy of supplementarity."

Hawkes, David. "Thomas Traherne: A Critique of Political Economy." *The Huntington Library Quarterly* 62, nos. 3/4 (2001): 369-388. An examination of one isolated and idiosyncratic attempt by Traherne to question the most basic assumptions of political economy after the Restoration in England.

Lane, Belden C. "Traherne and the Awakening of Want." *Anglican Theological Review* 81, no. 4 (Fall, 1999): 651-664. Lane examines Traherne's argument that want is the very essence of God's being.

Stewart, Stanley. *The Expanded Voice: The Art of Thomas Traherne*. San Marino, Calif.: Huntington Library, 1970. Although the bulk of his book is devoted to Traherne's prose, Stewart devotes two chapters to the poetry, which is discussed in the context of a literary tradition. Contains two extensive readings of Traherne's poems, "The Preparative" and the lesser known "Shadows in the Water."

Georg Trakl

Austrian poet

Born: Salzburg, Austro-Hungarian Empire (now in Austria); February 3, 1887
Died: Kraków, Galicia, Austro-Hungarian Empire (now in Poland); November 3, 1914

POETRY: *Gedichte*, 1913; *Sebastian im Traum*, 1914; *Die Dichtungen*, 1918; *Aus goldenem Kelch*, 1939; *Decline: Twelve Poems*, 1952; *Twenty Poems of Georg Trakl*, 1961; *Selected Poems*, 1968; *Poems*, 1973; *Georg Trakl: A Profile*, 1983.
DRAMA: *Fata Morgana*, pr. 1906 (lost); *Totentag*, pr. 1906 (lost).
MISCELLANEOUS: *Gesammelte Werke*, 1949-1951 (3 volumes); *Dichtungen und Briefe*, 1969 (poetry and letters).

Even though Georg Trakl (TRAHK-uhl), in his shockingly short lifetime, produced only a slender number of poems, many critics consider these among the greatest to have been produced in the twentieth century, ranking with the work of Rainer Maria Rilke, Federico García Lorca, William Butler Yeats, T. S. Eliot, Osip Mandelstam, and Anna Akhmatova. In 1917 Rilke declared that "Trakl's poetry is to me an object of sublime existence . . . [which has] mapped out a new dimension of the spirit." Trakl's life was filled with almost incessant suffering caused by depression, incest, and addiction to drugs. He was born into a prosperous Protestant family in Salzburg's overwhelmingly Catholic society. His mother was a taciturn woman who suffered from depression, became addicted to opium, and often retired to her room for days on end. The father also held himself aloof from his seven sons and single daughter. Georg formed a close attachment to his sister, Grete, and he focused in many of his poems on the erotic attraction between a brother and a sister. Most Trakl scholars accept the likelihood of an incestuous intimacy between Georg and his sister. Grete Trakl, who suffered from emotional disturbances similar to those of her brother, shot herself three years after his death.

Trakl was an indifferent student at school, but, having been taught French by an Alsatian governess, he read the Symbolist poets Charles Baudelaire, Paul Verlaine, and Arthur Rimbaud as well as the German poets Friedrich Hölderlin, Eduard Mörike, and Stefan George, and the Austrian Hugo von Hofmannsthal. His thought was also strongly influenced by Søren Kierkegaard, Friedrich Nietzsche, and particularly Fyodor Dostoevski. In early adolescence he was introduced to narcotics by a pharmacist's son, and toward the end of his school years he grew moody and unsociable, began to talk of suicide, drank heavily, carried a bottle of chloroform around with him, and dipped his cigarettes in an opium solution.

In 1905, after it had become evident that Trakl would not be able to finish his secondary schooling, he began a three-year apprenticeship in a Salzburg pharmacy. In 1908 he went to Vienna for a two-year program at the university to obtain his pharmaceutical degree. Trakl's life there remained lonely, and he moved frequently from one furnished room to another. He did produce some poems, but critics consider them unremarkable.

In 1910, immediately upon his having obtained his degree, Trakl was conscripted into the Austrian army for a one-year term during which he served in the medical corps. Upon his return to civilian life he began to work in a Salzburg pharmacy, but, emotionally oppressed and unable to keep his job, he reenlisted in the army. In April, 1912, he was sent to work in the pharmacy of a military hospital in Innsbruck, where he stayed for half a year. This time was a turning point in Trakl's life. He was befriended by Ludwig von Ficker, the editor of the biweekly journal *Der Brenner*, who became his patron, intellectual guide, and surrogate parent for the remaining two and a half years of Trakl's life. Every issue of *Der Brenner*, from late 1912 until Trakl's death, published at least one of his poems. Almost all the work on which Trakl's reputation as a major poet is founded was composed after he had joined the literary circle presided over by Ficker.

From December, 1912, through January, 1913, Trakl wrote "Helian," his first major as well as his longest poem. This difficult work, which has been subjected to varying interpretations, moves toward death and then toward rebirth, contrasting images of decay, dissolution, and demonism with pastoral landscapes and an idyllic past. Critics have stressed two other areas of meaning in "Helian": its prophecy of the decline of Occidental civilization and its use of Christian imagery without commitment to a specifically Christian range of meanings. Like his French Symbolist forerunners, Trakl concentrates on the suggestive power of images and lines rather than on the exposition of a sequence of ideas or events. The work represents a significantly new development in German poetry. By 1913 Trakl had become irreversibly addicted to drugs. In December he nearly died of an overdose of veronal. In July, 1914, he received a considerable sum of money anonymously from the philosopher Ludwig Wittgenstein, who was dispossessing himself of his material inheritance. Wittgenstein wrote to Ficker about Trakl's poetry: "I don't understand it; but its *tone* delights me. It is the *tone* of genius." In August, 1914, Trakl left Innsbruck for Galicia, as a lieutenant attached to Austria's medical corps. A few weeks later, after having either threatened or attempted suicide, he was diagnosed as schizophrenic. His treatment consisted of being locked up in a cell. There Trakl, at the age of twenty-seven, died of an overdose of cocaine.

Perhaps no other twentieth century poet has been open to more contradictory interpretations than Trakl. The perspectives of critics have ranged from arch-Christian to expressionist, ethical, and psychoanalytic. Most critics tend to agree, however, that Trakl laments the difficulty of living in an age of cultural decline and spiritual corruption and that, at least in some of his poems, he affirms an existential Christian faith akin to that of Kierkegaard and a compassion akin to that of Dostoevski.

Gerhard Brand

Bibliography

Graziano, Frank, ed. *Georg Trakl: A Profile*. Durango, Colo.: Logbridge-Rhodes, 1983. This biographical study of Trakl's work concentrates on the poet's family relations, drug addiction, poverty, and depression as well as the influence of World War I.

Sharp, Francis Michael. *The Poet's Madness: A Reading of Georg Trakl*. Ithaca, N.Y.: Cornell University Press, 1981. Critical interpretation of selected poems by Trakl. Includes the texts of poems in English and German.

Williams, Eric. *The Mirror and the Word: Modernism, Literary Theory, and Georg Trakl*. Lincoln: University of Nebraska Press, 1993. A critical study of Trakl's works that focuses on his contributions to modernism in Austria. Includes bibliographical references and index.

_______, ed. *The Dark Flutes of Fall: Critical Essays on Georg Trakl*. Columbia, S.C.: Camden House, 1991. A collection of essays on the works of Trakl. Includes bibliographical references and index.

Tomas Tranströmer

Swedish poet

Born: Stockholm, Sweden; April 15, 1931

POETRY: *17 dikter*, 1954; *Hemligheter på vägen*, 1958; *Den halvfärdiga himlen*, 1962; *Klanger och spår*, 1966; *Mörkerseende*, 1970 (*Night Vision*, 1971); *Twenty Poems of Tomas Tranströmer*, 1970; *Windows and Stones: Selected Poems*, 1972 (May Swenson, translator); *Elegy: Some October Notes*, 1973; *Citoyens*, 1974; *Selected Poetry of Paavo Haavikko and Tomas Tranströmer*, 1974; *Östersjöar*, 1974 (*Baltics*, 1975); *Friends You Drank Some Darkness: Three Swedish Poets*, 1975 (with Harry Martinson and Gunnar Ekelöf); *Sanningsbarriären*, 1978 (*Truth Barriers: Poems by Tomas Tranströmer*, 1980); *Dikter, 1954-1978*, 1979; *How the Late Autumn Night Novel Begins*, 1980; *Det vilda torget*, 1983 (*The Wild Marketplace*, 1985); *Tomas Tranströmer: Selected Poems, 1954-1986*, 1987; *The Blue House = Det blå huset*, 1987; *Collected Poems*, 1987; *Sorgegondolen*, 1996 (*Sorrow Gondola*, 1997); *New Collected Poems*, 1997; *Samlade dikter, 1954-1996*, 2001.

TRANSLATION: *Tolkningar*, 1999 (of many poets including James Wright, Robert Bly, and Sandor Weores).

NONFICTION: *Air Mail: Brev, 1964-1990*, 2001 (with Robert Bly).

MISCELLANEOUS: *För levende och döda*, 1989 (*For the Living and the Dead: New Poems and a Memoir*, 1996).

Tomas Gösta Tranströmer (TRAHNS-trur-mur) is widely regarded as Sweden's best poet since World War II. He was born to Gösta and Helmy Tranströmer, who divorced when Tomas was only three, leaving him with a strong sense of the absence of a father figure. Tranströmer graduated from the University of Stockholm in 1956, married Monica Blach in 1958, and has raised two daughters. He has maintained a dual career as a psychologist and poet. Tranströmer worked at the Psychological Institute in Stockholm from 1957 to 1959, later worked in a boys' reformatory in Roxtuna from 1960 to 1965, and subsequently worked as a special consultant and counselor for delinquent boys and people with disabilities in Vaesteraas.

Tranströmer's career as a poet began when he was only sixteen and was quickly established by his first collection, *17 Dikter*, published in 1954 when the poet was only twenty-three. This early work immediately identified Tranströmer as one who loves landscapes and specializes in joining images rarely associated with one another. He and others have called his work surrealistic, introducing the unreal or supernatural in the midst of the seemingly familiar.

Tranströmer's second work, *Hemligheter på vägen*, was inspired by the poet's travels in the Balkans, Italy, and Turkey and by his experiences with the paintings of Vincent van Gogh and Francisco Goya. With his third volume, *Den halvfärdiga himlen*, Tranströmer further developed the tensions in his poetry between the positive and the malevolent sides of life. Some of his best poems from this volume are those treating music, such as "Allegro," "C Major," and "Nocturne." His fourth volume, *Klanger och spår*, continues to develop themes involving travel and music but utilizes looser poetic forms, sometimes shifting to a prose form. His next volume, *Night Vision*, confirmed his reputation among English-language readers as a significant contemporary poet. Since that time his work has come to be translated into thirty different languages, and he has been translated into English more than any other living Swedish poet.

Aside from several collections consisting primarily of previously published works, Tranströmer's next major work was *Baltics*, translated skillfully by Samuel Charters, treating the life of his grandfather and other family members on an island off the east coast of Sweden. This lyrical narrative of life on the island demonstrates well the author's ability to control and interweave images throughout a sequence of poems, making this book one of his finest poetic achievements to date.

His eighth major work, *Truth Barriers*, translated by Robert Bly, one of Tranströmer's best translators, demonstrates well the range of his styles and use of images. In this work one finds the familiar references to places and music and art, but convictions are still refreshingly personal and new. For example, "Schubertiana" describes the reality that music creates, which is greater than the bustling business of New York City or any other place. As Bly did in *Friends, You Drank Some Darkness: Three Swedish Poets* (1975), which includes a fine selection of Tranströmer's poetry, he included the original Swedish version of the poems for reference.

Identifying the specific qualities of Tranströmer's poetry that make it viable in Swedish as well as many other languages is not easy. His finely crafted style, his use of surprising images, and his love of nature, family, and art all play a prominent role. The lyrical qualities of his work sometimes remind one of Dylan Thomas or Gerard Manley Hopkins. Tranströmer's love of music and his skill in playing the piano are evident in both the content and the style of his poetry. Furthermore, his religious sensibilities, while not entirely predictable or orthodox, are prominent and genuine, giving depth to his work. Finally, his work as a psychologist has caused him to look deeply into the nature of life.

Tranströmer has noted, "My poems are meeting places. Their intent is to make a sudden connection between aspects of reality that conventional languages and outlooks ordinarily keep apart." He adds (in a letter to Hungarian poets), "What looks at first like a confrontation turns out to be connection." The gaps between his images are well placed and neatly used. Tomas Tranströmer's career as a poet has been punctuated by important prizes such as the Petrarca Prize in 1981, the Bonniers Poetry Prize in 1983, the Grand Prize of the Nordic Council in 1989, the Neustadt International Prize for Literature in 1990, the Nordic Prize of the Swedish Academy in 1991, and the Horst Bienik Prize of the Bayerische Akademie des Schönen Kunste in 1992 for his career achievements. His work is steadily gaining maturity and much-deserved recognition.

Daven M. Kari

Bibliography

Bankier, Joanna. "Breaking the Spell: Subversion in the Poetry of Tomas Tranströmer." *World Literature Today* 64, no. 4 (Autumn, 1990): 591. A discussion of several of Tranströmer's poems that describe how socialization imposes a role and turns life into a set of ritualized performances that minimize stylized movement.

Bly, Robert. "Tomas Tranströmer and 'The Memory.'" *World Literature Today* 64, no. 4 (Autumn, 1990): 570-573. A useful biocritical overview.

Fulton, Robin. Introduction to *New Collected Poems*, by Tomas Tranströmer. Newcastle upon Tyne, England: Bloodaxe Books, 1997. An excellent brief biographical and analytical overview.

Ivask, Ivar. "The Universality of Openness: The Understated Example of Tomas Tranströmer." *World Literature Today* 64, no. 4 (Autumn, 1990): 549. A profile of Tranströmer and the international recognition he has found through his poetry.

Kaplinski, Jaan. "Presentation to the Jury." *World Literature Today* 64, no. 4 (Autumn, 1990): 552. Kaplinski describes Tranströmer as one of the most outstanding poets of the present age and as a fitting recipient of the Neustadt International Prize for Literature. A listing of his works is offered.

Rossel, Sven H. Review of *Tolkningar*, by Tomas Tranströmer. *World Literature Today* 74, no. 1 (Winter, 2000): 253. Rossel's review includes biographical information on Tranströmer's career and work.

Sjoberg, Leif. "The Architecture of a Poetic Victory: Tomas Tranströmer's Rise to International Pre-eminence." *Scandinavian Review* 78, no. 2 (Autumn, 1990): 87. Tranströmer has enjoyed sensational publicity and critical acclaim. Reasons for this unusual success are outlined. Two of Tranströmer's poems are included.

Soderberg, Lasse. "The Swedishness of Tomas Tranströmer." *World Literature Today* 64, no. 4 (Autumn, 1990): 573. The poetry of Tranströmer is examined, and ways in which his poetry can be described as being specifically Swedish are discussed.

B. Traven
(Berick Traven Torsvan)

Novelist and short-story writer

Born: Chicago, Illinois(?); March 5, 1890(?)
Died: Mexico City, Mexico; March 26, 1969
Pseudonym: Ret Marut

LONG FICTION: *Das Totenschiff*, 1926 (*The Death Ship*, 1934); *Der Wobbly*, 1926 (*The Cotton-Pickers*, 1956); *Der Schatz der Sierra Madre*, 1927 (*The Treasure of the Sierra Madre*, 1934); *Die Brücke im Dschungel*, 1929 (*The Bridge in the Jungle*, 1938); *Die weisse Rose*, 1929 (*The White Rose*, 1965); *Der Karren*, 1931 (*The Carreta*, 1936); *Der Marsch ins Reich der Caoba*, 1933 (*March to Caobaland*, 1960); *Sonnen-Sschöpfung*, 1936 (*The Creation of the Sun and the Moon*, 1968); *Die Rebellion der Gehenkten*, 1936 (*The Rebellion of the Hanged*, 1952); *Die Troza*, 1936 (*Trozas*, 1994); *Ein General kommt aus dem Dschungel*, 1940 (*General from the Jungle*, 1954); *Macario*, 1950 (English translation, 1966).

SHORT FICTION: *Der Busch*, 1928; *The Night Visitor, and Other Stories*, 1966; *The Kidnapped Saint, and Other Stories*, 1975; *To the Honorable Miss S. . . . , and Other Stories*, 1981 (as Ret Marut).

NONFICTION: *Land des Frühlings*, 1928 (travel); *Regierung*, 1931 (*Government*, 1935).

Almost every statement about B. Traven (TRAHV-uhn), the most famous international literary mystery of the twentieth century, must end with a question mark. In a comment on his life and work, Traven said, "Of an artist or writer, one should never ask an autobiography, because he is bound to lie. . . . If a writer, who he is and what he is, cannot be recognized by his work, either his books are worthless, or he himself is." His readers should look for him, he said, along and between the lines of his works.

From the beginning, he would not allow his life and personality to be exploited for publicity. In 1963 he refused a literary prize from Germany. His agents in Mexico City protected him from most of the numerous letters addressed to him, many from editors all over the world.

Although many scholars and writers have attempted to solve the mystery of B. Traven, few facts are known about his life; almost every bit of "information" about Traven's background is currently challenged by at least one reputable source. Traven's birthplace and date are not known for certain. Most scholars, however, agree that one of Traven's earliest identities was as Ret Marut, a German actor and political activist who shunned the public spotlight. After leaving Europe, Marut appeared in Mexico around 1923 or 1924. Shortly after that, from Mexico, Traven offered his earliest books to publishers in Germany. In 1925 *The Cotton-Pickers* appeared in serial form in a German newspaper.

While he was living in Mexico, Traven adopted at least two other identities, T. Torsvan and Hal Croves, supposedly B. Traven's agent. Croves worked with John Huston on the filming of Traven's novel *The Treasure of the Sierra Madre*. Throughout his lifetime, Traven is reported to have used at least twenty-seven different aliases. Many researchers are convinced that Traven is more than one person, as his writing shows such linguistic diversity. Apparently, Traven wrote and spoke German, French, Spanish, and English fluently; he also spoke two of the unwritten Indian languages of southeastern Mexico.

Interest in Traven's life and writings increased dramatically after his death. By 1994 all his novels had been translated into English. His sixteen novels are concerned with the common man, laboring on ships and in the jungles of Mexico. His characters speak the slang of the early twentieth century with an immigrant accent. There is much description of landscapes and seascapes, and he has a special interest in depicting strong, courageous women, children, and the personalities of certain animals. The hard-core center of most of his realistic fiction is work. Among his books are sociological studies, documentaries, Mexican travel books (illustrated with his own photographs), and Mexican folktales. His outlook was that of the self-educated worker—sardonic and ironic; it was expressed, even in crawling misery, with wit and ribald humor. His novels depict people with a great appetite for life struggling to survive, always within the immediate vicinity of death.

One third of Traven's novels were written in the first person. Whether told in the third person or in the first, his novels aggressively state his radical revolutionary sentiments. He is alienated not only from Western civilization in general but also from any formal creed or ideology in particular. In *The Death Ship*, Gerald Gales, who reappears in several of the novels, speaks of national and international bureaucracy as the irreconcilable enemy of individual freedom. Though one may be tempted, because of Traven's radical thinking and adventurous life, to associate him with Jack London, he is more a philosophical revolutionary in the tradition of Henry David Thoreau, whose love of privacy he shared. Much of his work resembles American proletarian fiction, although most of it was written several years before novels in that genre began to appear. Moreover, because of the attitude toward life that he and his characters demonstrate in action and speech, Traven may be regarded as one of the finest of the "tough-guy" novelists.

Mary Mahony

Bibliography

Baumann, Michael. *B. Traven: An Introduction*. Albuquerque: University of New Mexico Press, 1976. Excellent introduction to Traven.

Chankin, Donald. *Anonymity and Death: The Fiction of B. Traven*. University Park: Pennsylvania State University Press, 1975. Provides insightful psychoanalytical analyses of character and theme.

Mezo, Richard. *A Study of B. Traven's Fiction: The Journey to Solipaz*. San Francisco: Mellen Research University Press, 1993. This literary analysis of Traven's writing is extremely helpful.

Raskin, Jonah. *My Search for B. Traven*. New York: Methuen, 1980. Raskin's recounting of his search into Traven's mysterious past attempts to trace Traven through his manuscripts.

Schurer, Ernst, and Philip Jenkins, eds. *B. Traven: Life and Work*. University Park: Pennsylvania State University Press, 1987. Excellent introduction to Traven. Collects many of the best essays about his life and writing.

Stone, Judy. *The Mystery of B. Traven*. Los Altos, Calif.: Kaufmann, 1977. Stone's recounting of her search into Traven's past includes excerpts from her interviews with Traven.

Wyatt, Will. *The Secret of Sierra Madre: The Man Who Was B. Traven*. San Diego, Calif.: Harcourt Brace Jovanovich, 1985. Wyatt's presents information gathered for his BBC documentary in the book.

Sophie Treadwell

American playwright and journalist

Born: Stockton, California; October 3, 1885
Died: Tucson, Arizona; February 20, 1970

DRAMA: *An Unwritten Chapter*, pr. 1915 (adaptation of her serial "How I Got My Husband and How I Lost Him"); *Claws*, pr. 1918; *Gringo*, pr. 1922; *O, Nightingale*, pr. 1925; *Machinal*, pr. 1928; *Ladies Leave*, pr. 1929; *For Saxophone*, wr. 1934; *Plumes in the Dust*, pr. 1936; *Hope for a Harvest*, pr. 1941; *Highway*, pr. 1944; *Woman with Lilies*, wr. 1948-1967, pr. 1967 (as *Now He Doesn't Want to Play*).
LONG FICTION: *One Fierce Hour and Sweet*, 1959.
TELEPLAYS: *Hope for a Harvest*, 1953 (adaptation of her play); *Highway*, 1954 (adaptation of her play).

Sophie Anita Treadwell was born in 1885 to Alfred B. and Nettie Fairchild Treadwell. When Sophie was five, her father moved to San Francisco. During her childhood, she and her mother sometimes lived with her father, sometimes not. She attended the University of California at Berkeley from 1902 to 1906. There she was involved in theater and, despite struggles with poverty and illness, graduated with a bachelor of letters degree with an emphasis in French.

Following her graduation, Treadwell moved to Los Angeles, where she performed in vaudeville. In 1908 her friend Constance Skinner, who had been a drama critic, arranged for Treadwell to type the memoirs of actress Helena Modjeska. It was Modjeska who encouraged Treadwell's ambitions to be a dramatist. Also in 1908, Treadwell began her career as a journalist at the *San Francisco Bulletin*.

In 1910 she married noted journalist and sports reporter William O. McGeehan. After her marriage, she retained her maiden name and continued her active participation in the movement for women's suffrage. She wrote frequently on women's issues, and one of her serials, "How I Got My Husband and How I Lost Him," was adapted for the stage and produced under the title *An Unwritten Chapter* in San Francisco in 1915.

Treadwell was an accredited war correspondent during World War I, one of the first American women to serve in such a capacity. She spent four months in France in 1915, writing for the *San Francisco Bulletin* and *Harper's Weekly*. During the war, she also continued to write plays, including *Claws*, produced in a 1918 showcase.

During the 1920's Treadwell used information from her investigations as a reporter in creating dramas. For example, she covered the aftermath of the Mexican Revolution in the early 1920's, obtaining an exclusive interview with Pancho Villa for the *New York Tribune*. This provided her with the background for *Gringo*, her first Broadway production (1922), which featured a character based on Villa.

In 1927 Treadwell attended the murder trial of Ruth Snyder, a sensational event that was headline news for much of the year. Snyder was convicted of conspiring with her lover Judd Gray to murder her husband. Both died in the electric chair; Snyder was the first woman so executed in New York. The trial provided the inspiration for Treadwell's most successful play, *Machinal*, produced on Broadway in 1928. The play was produced in London (under the title *The Life Machine*) in 1931. In 1933 Treadwell visited Moscow for the Russian production of *Machinal*. Revived Off-Broadway in 1960, it remains her best-known work.

Travel was also important to Treadwell. She and McGeehan took two long trips through Europe and Africa. After McGeehan's death in 1933 and that of her mother in 1934, Treadwell traveled to Egypt and the Far East. During this period she continued to write plays; *For Saxophone* was copyrighted in 1934, and *Plumes in the Dust* was produced on Broadway in 1936.

Like *Machinal*, *For Saxophone* is an experiment in expressionism. Although it has never been produced or published, the play has generated a surprising amount of critical comment. Considered Treadwell's most innovative work, it extends the expressionistic techniques used in *Machinal* to include music. Although other American playwrights, including Eugene O'Neill and Elmer Rice, were experimenting with expressionism in the 1920's, Treadwell tried to expand the form as a way to focus on women as subjects in drama. That she could not get *For Saxophone* produced was a huge disappointment.

In 1949 Treadwell adopted a German baby, William, and divided her time during the next few years among Europe, Mexico, Connecticut, and California. From 1956 to 1965, she lived mostly in Spain, writing novels and seeking cures for a variety of illnesses. In 1965 she moved to Tucson, Arizona, where she remained for the rest of her life. The University of Arizona produced *Woman with Lilies* under the title *Now He Doesn't Want to Play* in 1967. When Treadwell died in 1970, she left her estate to the Tucson diocese of the Roman Catholic Church; royalties for her work are used to support local orphanages.

Work of feminist scholars intent on restoring women playwrights to the theatrical canon has given Sophie Treadwell a place in the history of American theater. Continued revivals of *Machinal* and its positive critical reception have assured that place.

Elsie Galbreath Haley

Bibliography

Bywaters, Barbara L. "Marriage, Madness, and Murder in Sophie Treadwell's *Machinal*." In *Modern American Drama and the Female Canon*, edited by June Schlueter. Rutherford, N.J.: Fairleigh Dickinson University Press, 1990. A critical analysis of *Machinal* from a feminist perspective.

Dickey, Jerry. *Sophie Treadwell: Research and Production Sourcebook*. Westport, Conn.: Greenwood Press, 1997. A comprehensive research resource, including a production history of each of the twelve Treadwell plays that had been produced by 1995.

Heck-Rabi, Louise. "Sophie Treadwell: Agent for Change." In *Women in American Theatre*, edited by Helen Krich Chinoy and Linda Walsh Jenkins. New York: Theatre Communications Group, 1987.

Rose Tremain

English novelist and short-story writer

Born: London, England; August 2, 1943

LONG FICTION: *Sadler's Birthday*, 1976; *Letter to Sister Benedicta*, 1979; *The Cupboard*, 1981; *The Swimming Pool Season*, 1985; *Restoration*, 1989; *Sacred Country*, 1992; *The Way I Found Her*, 1997; *Music and Silence*, 1999.

SHORT FICTION: *The Colonel's Daughter, and Other Stories*, 1984; *The Garden of the Villa Mollini, and Other Stories*, 1987; *Evangelista's Fan, and Other Stories*, 1994; *Collected Short Stories*, 1996.

CHILDREN'S/YOUNG ADULT LITERATURE: *Journey to the Volcano*, 1988.

Rose Tremain, born Rose Thomson, began writing at the age of ten, when her father's sudden abandonment of his family motivated her to express her feelings through the written word. It was only after being encouraged by the novelist Angus Wilson in a university course that she began seriously to consider becoming an author, however; Wilson was very important to, and supportive of, her subsequent development. She studied at the Sorbonne in Paris and the University of East Anglia before becoming a teacher of English, French, and history at the junior high school level in Great Britain. After working as a subeditor and researcher for the BPC Publishing Group, she became a full-time writer in the mid-1970's and published her first novel, *Sadler's Birthday*, in 1976.

Although young authors are often advised to write what they know, Tremain took quite a different tack in creating a body of work that ranges widely over historical periods and human types. The protagonist of her first novel, for example, is a seventy-six-year-old man who is about to have another birthday, but Jack Sadler is not entirely sure exactly when this will occur. Alone and in failing health, he nonetheless carries on with the determination to make sense out of the past events that periodically pop up in his consciousness, and the result is an intriguing story that belies its commonplace materials. *Letter to Sister Benedicta*, in which a fiftyish housewife copes with her husband's debilitating stroke, and *The Cupboard*, whose protagonist is an eighty-seven-year-old writer explaining the reasons for her suicide, also demonstrate a remarkable ability to write sympathetically about the kinds of older subjects who are too often scorned by authors anxious to appear youthful and contemporary.

Tremain's literary status was significantly enhanced by her selection as one of *Granta*'s Best of Young British Novelists in 1983. This special issue of the magazine has achieved cult status among students of contemporary British literature for its perspicacity in selecting writers who usually go on to fulfill their early promise: Martin Amis, Pat Barker, Julian Barnes, Ian McEwen, and Salman Rushdie are among the most prominent in what was a brilliant piece of literary forecasting by editor Bill Buford. Tremain's inclusion in this select company was a deserved acknowledgment of what she had already published as well as an accurate, and very influential, prediction of her subsequent accomplishments.

Restoration, which won the *Sunday Express* Book of the Year Award in 1989 and was also short-listed for Great Britain's most prestigious literary honor, the Booker Prize, is one of her most accomplished novels. Set in the years following the restoration of King Charles II to the English throne in the late seventeenth century, the narrative relates the volatile adventures of physician Robert Merivel, whose vicissitudes begin when he agrees to marry one of the king's mistresses in exchange for an estate and a title. Although he understands that the marriage is not supposed to be consummated, Merivel nonetheless falls in love with his wife and is banished from court. Following further tribulations in a rural insane asylum and an affair with a deeply disturbed woman, he is eventually restored to his former social position after experiences that have taught him much about society's demands on the sensitive individual.

In 1991, Tremain's status as a widely respected writer enabled her to make further acknowledgment of her appreciation of Angus Wilson's early support of her work. Penguin Books, Wilson's publisher, was planning to let all of his titles go out of print without making any provision for transferring them to another firm. Tremain and several other writers raised such a public fuss about this matter that a new company, House of Stratus, was funded by arts-supporting agencies to keep Wilson's books available.

Tremain's 1999 novel *Music and Silence* is set in seventeenth century Denmark, and like *Restoration*, it features an emotionally fragile commoner who becomes entangled in the affairs of a king and his court. Peter Claire is a talented lute player who becomes romantically involved with the favorite servant of the king's nymphomaniac wife, and the atmosphere of murky plots and ambiguous motives is beautifully rendered. The novel is much more than a page-turner, however, as Tremain also explores the complex relationships between great art and the demands of everyday human existence.

Twice married and twice divorced, with a daughter from her first marriage, Tremain was at the beginning of the twenty-first century living with the acclaimed biographer Richard Holmes in Norfolk and London. She has frequently taught creative writing at the university level and has also written for television, radio, and film. She has been active in PEN's campaign to free imprisoned writers, and her literary honors include the James Tait Black Memorial Prize in 1993 and France's Prix Fémina du Roman Étranger in 1994 (both for *Sacred Country*) and the Whitbread Novel Award in 1999 (for *Music and Silence*).

Paul Stuewe

Bibliography

Biswell, Andrew. "A Boy and His Fictions Try to Forget Real Life." Review of *The Way I Found Her*, by Rose Tremain. *The Boston Globe*, July 26, 1998, p. F3. An extensive review that focuses on Tremain's clever construction of her novel.

Buford, Bill, ed. "The Best of Young British Novelists 1." *Granta* 7 (March, 1983). Although the biographical information provided for Tremain is minimal, the inclusion of her short story "I Married a White Russian" in this special issue of the prestigious magazine set the British literary community's stamp of approval upon her work.

Fendler, Susanne, and Ruth Wittlinger. "Rose Tremain's *Restoration* and Thatcherism." *Culture and Communication* 3 (Winter, 2000): 29-50. A convincing argument for the influence of contemporary politics on Tremain's novel of seventeenth century court intrigues.

George Macaulay Trevelyan

English historian

Born: Welcombe, near Stratford-on-Avon, England; February 16, 1876
Died: Cambridge, England; July 21, 1962

NONFICTION: *England in the Age of Wycliffe*, 1899, revised 1904; *England Under the Stuarts*, 1904, revised 1925; *Garibaldi's Defence of the Roman Republic*, 1907; *Garibaldi and the Thousand*, 1909; *Garibaldi and the Making of Italy*, 1911; *History of England*, 1926, revised 1937, corrected 1952; *England Under Queen Anne*, 1930-1934 (3 volumes); *The English Revolution, 1688-89*, 1938; *English Social History*, 1942; *An Autobiography, and Other Essays*, 1949; *A Layman's Love of Letters*, 1954 (lectures).

Historian George Macaulay Trevelyan (trih-VEHL-yuhn) was the third son of Sir George Otto Trevelyan, who was himself a historian and author as well as the editor of *The Life and Letters of Lord Macaulay* (1876) by his uncle Thomas Babington Macaulay. The younger Trevelyan was born at Stratford-on-Avon, England, on February 16, 1876. His brief autobiography relates some of the chief events of his life. From the beginning his imagination was stirred by history, and his political bias was Liberal, following in the tradition of his father and his great-uncle. It is significant that throughout his life he read poetry with pleasure. He speaks of "the poetry of history"—the idea that other persons once walked on the same ground on which the present generation walks.

Trevelyan was educated at Harrow and at Trinity College, Cambridge, and though he took up an academic career—writing, lecturing, and producing his first book, *England in the Age of Wycliffe*—he soon came to believe that he had to leave the college to write independent of scholastic criticism, able as he was to finance such a break. He contracted to write *England Under the Stuarts* as one book in a multivolume history by various authors. He married, and he soon began a three-volume study of Giuseppe Garibaldi. Other books followed, most notably his survey, *History of England*.

With these achievements behind him, he returned to academic life, accepting the Regius Professorship of Modern History at Cambridge University. He was awarded the Order of Merit in 1930. Later he became Master of Trinity College. Meanwhile, other books appeared; especially noteworthy are the short work *The English Revolution, 1688-89* and the large study *England Under Queen Anne*. Finally, there was one more great achievement, *English Social History*, which surveyed six centuries.

The turbulent and disquieting world events of Trevelyan's lifetime caused him increasingly to view those events in a historical context, but they did not transform him into a bitter pessimist. Instead, he continued his calling to explain the lessons of those events to his and future generations. Trevelyan's last years were spent in disabled retirement, a lonely widower after fifty-two years of happy marriage, content to meditate on his life and on the conditions in the world. As friends came often to visit and to read to him, he waited patiently for death, which came at age eighty-six in his home at Cambridge.

Glenn L. Swygart

Bibliography

Cannadine, David. *G. M. Trevelyan*. New York: W. W. Norton, 1992. A long-awaited biography. Includes index and bibliography.

"Lyrical Historian." *The New York Review of Books*, July 15, 1993. Suggests that Trevelyan's works as a historian are outdated and no longer relevant.

Moorman, Mary Trevelyan. *George Macaulay Trevelyan: A Memoir.* North Pomfret, Vt.: Hamilton, 1980. Written by Trevelyan's daughter. Includes index and bibliography.

"The True Voice of Clio." *Times Literary Supplement*, May 2, 1980. Predicts that time will elevate Trevelyan's standing among twentieth century historians.

William Trevor
(William Trevor Cox)

Irish short-story writer, novelist, and playwright

Born: Mitchelstown, County Cork, Ireland; May 24, 1928

SHORT FICTION: *The Day We Got Drunk on Cake, and Other Stories*, 1967; *The Ballroom of Romance, and Other Stories*, 1972; *The Last Lunch of the Season*, 1973; *Angels at the Ritz, and Other Stories*, 1975; *Lovers of Their Time, and Other Stories*, 1978; *Beyond the Pale, and Other Stories*, 1981; *The Stories of William Trevor*, 1983; *The News from Ireland, and Other Stories*, 1986; *Family Sins, and Other Stories*, 1990; *Collected Stories*, 1992; *Ireland: Selected Stories*, 1995; *Outside Ireland: Selected Stories*, 1995; *Marrying Damian*, 1995 (limited edition); *After Rain*, 1996; *The Hill Bachelors*, 2000.

LONG FICTION: *A Standard of Behaviour*, 1958; *The Old Boys*, 1964; *The Boarding-House*, 1965; *The Love Department*, 1966; *Mrs. Eckdorf in O'Neil's Hotel*, 1969; *Miss Gomez and the Brethren*, 1971; *Elizabeth Alone*, 1973; *The Children of Dynmouth*, 1976; *Other People's Worlds*, 1980; *Fools of Fortune*, 1983; *Nights at the Alexandra*, 1987; *The Silence in the Garden*, 1988; *Two Lives*, 1991; *Juliet's Story*, 1991; *Felicia's Journey*, 1994; *Death in Summer*, 1998; *The Story of Lucy Gault*, 2002.

DRAMA: *The Elephant's Foot*, pr. 1965; *The Girl*, pr. 1967 (televised), pr., pb. 1968 (staged); *A Night Mrs. da Tanka*, pr. 1968 (televised), pr., pb. 1972 (staged); *Going Home*, pr. 1970 (radio play), pr., pb. 1972 (staged); *The Old Boys*, pr., pb. 1971 (adaptation of his novel); *A Perfect Relationship*, pr. 1973; *The Fifty-seventh Saturday*, pr. 1973; *Marriages*, pr., pb. 1973; *Scenes from an Album*, pr. 1975 (radio play), pr., pb. 1981 (staged).

RADIO PLAYS: *Beyond the Pale*, 1980; *Autumn Sunshine*, 1982.

NONFICTION: *A Writer's Ireland: Landscape in Literature*, 1984; *Excursions in the Real World*, 1993.

EDITED TEXT: *The Oxford Book of Irish Short Stories*, 1989.

William Trevor's fertile imagination can scarcely be summed up in two adjectives, but if one were so limited, then "gothic" and "elegiac" would do very well. Though not an experimentalist, he has developed a flexible narrative form that conveys a wide variety of attitudes, shifts of tone, speaking voices, and descriptive passages that, while not pretending to rival the accomplishments of his master, James Joyce, have succeeded in establishing Trevor as a leading fiction writer on both sides of the Atlantic. Born William

Trevor Cox in a small town in County Cork, Ireland, Trevor was educated in a haphazard way until he entered St. Columba's College in Dublin in 1942. In 1950 he earned his baccalaureate from Trinity College and for the next decade or so eked out a living teaching school while working as a sculptor. Although one of his sculptures won a prize in 1952, he gave up sculpting a few years afterward in favor of writing. Meanwhile, he had left Ireland for England, where he eventually made his home in Devonshire after teaching in Rugby and Taunton and then working in advertising in London.

Moving to England was motivated strictly by economics, as work was hard to find in Ireland after graduation from Trinity College. Nevertheless, Trevor evidently found the English social and intellectual climate congenial, which explains his continued residence. More important, he found there a singular advantage to his writing, the advantage one enjoys as an acute observer of a culture different from one's own. Hence, his early stories and novels treat English subjects and involve English men and women; only later did he begin to focus upon his native Ireland. Perhaps the advantage of living away from his homeland for an extended period gave him the perspective he felt he needed. In any event, while books such as *The Old Boys* and *The Children of Dynmouth* deal impressively with English themes and English characters, short stories such as "Attracta" in *Lovers of Their Time, and Other Stories* and the title story in *The News from Ireland, and Other Stories* reveal Trevor's sure handling of Irish subjects, in both historical and contemporary settings.

The gothic aspect of Trevor's imagination shows itself in the assemblage of misfits, oddballs, and eccentrics that populate almost all of his fiction. Studdy and Nurse Clock in *The Boarding-House* also demonstrate its sinister side. Bitter rivals and indeed enemies, they link up in an unholy alliance to become the sole beneficiaries of an unusual bequest, but they are ultimately thwarted by their own greed and a failure to grasp the warped intelligence of those they are trying to cheat. Young Timothy Gedge, by contrast, seems to understand only too well the weaknesses of his victims, as he tries to insinuate himself into their lives. If like Studdy he is a confidence man, his youth and his loneliness combine to make him finally a creature more pathetic than wicked, though Trevor does not underestimate the potential—and real—evil of which Gedge is capable.

The presence of evil in the world and the inability of many human beings to communicate effectively with one another explain the sadness, or the elegiac quality, that colors so much of Trevor's work. *Nights at the Alexandra* develops this quality to an extraordinary degree. The keynote sounds with the opening short paragraph: "I am a fifty-eight-year-old provincial. I have no children. I have never married." This statement is the unintended legacy that Alexandra Messinger, an Englishwoman married to a German, leaves young Harry. She and her husband have fled from Nazi Germany and are living in a small Irish town during the "Emergency" (as the Irish called World War II). Told from the vantage point of many years later, *Nights at the Alexandra* recounts the story of a youngster who, badly misunderstood by his parents and siblings, becomes a loner. Much taken by the beautiful, mysterious but kindly woman many years her husband's junior, Harry defies parental orders not to visit with the strangers and ultimately elects to work in Herr Messinger's newly erected cinema instead of his father's lumberyard. Built despite wartime shortages and named for Frau Messinger, the cinema is her husband's gift to her and to the town. When it finally opens, however, Frau Messinger has died and her husband leaves the town and Cloverhill, the home where Harry visited them, forever. The illness is never named or explained, but it doubtless derives in part from an early heartbreak Frau Messinger experienced, the inability to give her husband a child, her deep sense of gratitude to him for his love and devotion, and in general the profound isolation she finds in these alien surroundings. "We can live without anything but love, Harry," she says at one point. "Always remember that." Yet though she has love, she dies, and dying, she takes with her any chance Harry may have to love, though he lives on.

Trevor has written plays for stage and television, many of them adapted from his own stories or novels. He believes short stories lend themselves better to films than novels do, but he has adapted both for radio and television, including "Beyond the Pale," "Voices from the Past," "The Love of a Good Woman," "Matilda's England," *Elizabeth Alone*, and "The Ballroom of Romance."

Widely regarded as one of the finest storytellers and craftsmen writing in English, Trevor has been the recipient of numerous awards. Among these are the Royal Society of Literature Award, the Allied Irish Banks' Prize for Literature, and the Whitbread Prize for Fiction. His novel *The Story of Lucy Gault* was shortlisted for the Booker Prize in 2002. He is also a member of the Irish Academy of Letters and has been named an honorary Commander, Order of the British Empire.

Jay L. Halio

Bibliography

Bonaccorso, Richard. "William Trevor's Martyrs for Truth." *Studies in Short Fiction* 34 (Winter, 1997): 113-118. Discusses two types of Trevor characters: those who try to evade the truth and those who gravitate, often in spite of themselves, toward it.

Fitzgerald-Hoyt, Mary. "The Influence of Italy in the Writings of William Trevor and Julia O'Faolain." *Notes on Modern Irish Literature* 2 (1990): 61-67. Compares the two writers' use of Italian settings.

Haughey, Jim. "Joyce and Trevor's Dubliners: The Legacy of Colonialism." *Studies in Short Fiction* 32 (Summer, 1995): 355-365. Compares how James Joyce's "Two Gallants" and Trevor's "Two More Gallants" explore the complexities of Irish identity; argues that Trevor's story provides an updated commentary on the legacy of Ireland's colonial experience. Both stories reveal how Irish men, conditioned by colonization, are partly responsible for their sense of cultural alienation and inferiority.

MacKenna, Dolores. *William Trevor: The Writer and His Work*. Dublin: New Island, 1999. Offers some interesting biographical details; includes a bibliography and an index.

Morrison, Kristin. *William Trevor*. New York: Twayne, 1993. A useful study of Trevor's fiction, including a chronology of significant events in the author's life, a selected bibliography of his works, and a list of secondary works.

Paulson, Suzanne Morrow. *William Trevor: A Study of the Short Fiction*. New York: Twayne, 1993. This introduction to Trevor's stories examines four common themes from Freudianism to feminism: psychological shock, failed child/parent relationships, patriarchal repressiveness, and materialism in the modern world. Also contains an interview with Trevor and a number of short reviews of his stories.

Schirmer, Gregory A. *William Trevor: A Study of His Fiction*. New York: Routledge, 1990. A general discussion, organized chronologically.

Yuri Trifonov

Russian novelist and short-story writer

Born: Moscow, Soviet Union (now in Russia); August 28, 1925
Died: Moscow, Soviet Union (now in Russia); March 28, 1981

LONG FICTION: *Studenty*, 1950 (*Students*, 1953); *Utoleniye zhazhdy*, 1963 (*Thirst Acquenched*, 1964); *Otblesk kostra*, 1965; *Obmen*, 1969 (novella; *The Exchange*, 1978); *Predvaritel'nye itogi*, 1970 (novella; *Taking Stock*, 1978); *Dolgoe proshchaniye*, 1971 (novella; *The Long Goodbye*, 1978); *Neterpenie*, 1973 (*The Impatient Ones*, 1978); *Drugaya zhizn'*, 1975 (*Another Life*, 1983); *Dom na naberezhnoy*, 1976 (*The House on the Embankment*, 1983); *Starik*, 1978 (*The Old Man*, 1984); *Vremya i mesto*, 1981; *Ischeznoveniye*, 1987 (*Disappearance*, 1991).

SHORT FICTION: *Pod solntsem*, 1959; *V kontse sezona*, 1961; *Fakely na Flaminio*, 1965; *Igry v sumerkakh*, 1970; *Oprokinutyy dom*, 1981; *The Exchange, and Other Stories*, 1991.

NONFICTION: *Kak slovo nashe otzovetsiya . . .*, 1985.

MISCELLANEOUS: *Sobranie sochinenii*, 1985-1987 (4 volumes).

Yuri Valentinovich Trifonov (tri-FAWN-awf) was one of the Soviet Union's leading prose writers of the 1960's and 1970's. He was born in Moscow on August 28, 1925, the son of Valentin Trifonov, a longtime revolutionary activist. The elder Trifonov, who had joined the Bolshevik Party in 1904, had suffered imprisonment and exile under the czarist regime. By the time of the Russian Revolution of 1917, Valentin Trifonov was a member of the revolutionary council in Petrograd, and during the civil war of 1918-1921, he helped to organize units of the Red Army. His prominent position allowed him to obtain an apartment in "the house on the embankment," a large gray structure in Moscow for high government officials and, later, the setting for Trifonov's novel of that name. In 1937, during the purges ordered by Joseph Stalin, Trifonov's father was arrested, and the following year he was executed. An important influence on Trifonov's career was the effort to come to terms both with the revolutionary activities of his father and with his father's disappearance while Trifonov was still very young.

In 1938 Trifonov's mother was also arrested; until her release in 1946, he and his sister were raised by his grandmother. At the beginning of World War II, he was briefly evacuated to Central Asia, but then he returned to Moscow, where he worked at an airplane factory. In 1944 Trifonov, who had written both poetry and prose throughout his youth, entered the Gorky Literary Institute—Russia's leading writers' school. There he concentrated on prose, publishing his first stories, which were based on travels to Armenia and to the Kuban region, in 1947. He graduated from the institute in 1949; his thesis was the novel *Students*, which deals with academic life during the postwar years. The book was awarded a Stalin Prize and brought Trifonov early renown.

There was then a thirteen-year hiatus until the appearance of his next novel, *Thirst Acquenched*, which deals with the construction of an irrigation canal in Turkmenistan. His travels to the area resulted as well in the volume of stories *Pod solntsem* (under the sun). During the 1960's Trifonov also wrote numerous stories and sketches on sports, which formed the basis for several collections.

The first signs of Trifonov's later interests can be found in the factually based narrative *Otblesk kostra* (the fire's gleam), an account of Valentin Trifonov's role in the revolution and its aftermath. Although inspired by actual documents and memoirs, the book is less a conventional biography than an attempt on the part of the narrator to understand several key moments in his father's life. Even when Trifonov is simply describing actual events, he allows himself to manipulate the material to create an artistically more satisfying work; hence, while he resisted the efforts to assign this story of his father to any one genre, many critics persist in calling it a novel. Trifonov's interest in the biography of revolutionaries can also be seen in *The Impatient Ones*, a portrayal of Andrey Zhelyabov, who, as a member of the People's Will Party, conspired to assassinate Alexander II in 1881.

Trifonov gained renewed fame not so much through his historically based writings as through a series of stories and novellas from the late 1960's and early 1970's, in which he depicted a spiritual malaise within the urban middle and upper classes that had grown up in the shadow of Stalinism. Particularly important in this regard is his "Moscow cycle," which originally consisted of the novellas *The Exchange*, *Taking Stock*, and *The Long Goodbye*, but which most would extend to include the majority of his subsequent novels as well. While the three novellas are not overtly political, they offer an implicit critique of Soviet society by showing an entire generation of people who no longer believe, or are even interested, in revolutionary ideals. Their lives are totally occupied with efforts to achieve success, but they have discovered that neither acclaim from their peers nor material possessions provides satisfaction. In his later novels Trifonov combined his portrayals of contemporary society with investigations into the events that formed his characters. By the end of the 1970's, Trifonov was attaining new heights with each work; thus his sudden death at age fifty-five, from a heart attack following a routine kidney operation, came as a great shock to all who follow Russian literature.

Trifonov's writing did not so much broaden as deepen. During the final decade of his life, he again and again returned to situations that he had treated earlier, exploring similar situations from different angles and trying to gain a deeper understanding of his characters, of the eras that he had lived through, and ultimately of both his father and of himself. Trifonov served as a spokesman for his generation. During the time that Leonid Brezhnev governed the Soviet Union, when most writers were too timid to examine the Stalinist legacy, Trifonov pushed back the limits of what was permissible within Soviet literature. In addition to treating once-forbidden topics, his works are notable most of all for their honesty: His villains are usually deserving of some sympathy, and his protagonists elicit more pity than praise. Those whose outlook was formed during the Revolution find themselves ill-equipped for life afterward, while their descendants, those of Trifonov's age, have compromised all too often. Perhaps his most lasting achievement, then, was to chronicle the moral void sensed by many of his contemporaries, who no longer believed in the exemplars of the past and could find no heroes in the present.

Barry P. Scherr

Bibliography

Austin, Paul M. "From Helsingfors to Helsinki: Jurij Trifonov's Search for His Past." *Scando-Slavica* 32 (1986).

Gillespie, David C. *Iurii Trifonov: Unity Through Time*. New York: Cambridge University Press, 1992. A critical study of Trifonov's work.

Kolesnikoff, Nina. *Yury Trifonov: A Critical Study*. New York: Cambridge University Press, 1991. Traces the evolution of Trifonov's work, from Socialist Realism through the Moscow novellas and *Disappearance*.

McLaughlin, Sigrid. "Antipov's *Nikiforov Syndrome:* The Embedded Novel in Trifonov's *Time and Place*." *Slavic and East European Journal* 32 (1988). A particularly informative article.

Pankin, B. "A Circle or a Spiral? On Iurii Trifonov's Novels." *Soviet Studies in Literature* 14, no. 4 (1978). Offers detailed comments on the three Moscow novellas, as well as on *Another Life* and *The House on the Embankment*.

Paton, S. "The Hero of His Time." *Slavonic and East European Review* 64 (1986). A general study of Trifonov's mature period.

Schneidman, N. N. "The New Dimensions of Time and Place in Iurii Trifonov's Prose of the 1980's." *Canadian Slavonic Papers* 27 (1985). An overall introduction to Trifonov's late work.

Woll, Josephine. "Trifonov's *Starik:* The Truth of the Past." *Russian Literature Triquarterly* 19 (1986). A study of an individual work.

Lionel Trilling

American critic

Born: New York, New York; July 4, 1905
Died: New York, New York; November 5, 1975

NONFICTION: *Matthew Arnold*, 1939; *E. M. Forster*, 1943; *The Liberal Imagination: Essays on Literature and Society*, 1950; *Freud and the Crisis of Our Culture*, 1955; *The Opposing Self*, 1955 (criticism); *A Gathering of Fugitives*, 1956 (criticism); *Beyond Culture: Essays on Learning and Literature*, 1965; *Sincerity and Authenticity*, 1972 (criticism); *Mind in the Modern World*, 1973; *Prefaces to "The Experience of Literature,"* 1979; *The Last Decade, Essays and Reviews, 1965-1975*, 1979; *Speaking of Literature and Society*, 1980 (Diana Trilling, editor); *The Moral Obligation to Be Intelligent: Selected Essays*, 2000 (Leon Wieseltier, editor).

LONG FICTION: *The Middle of the Journey*, 1947.

SHORT FICTION: *Of This Time, of That Place, and Other Stories*, 1979.

EDITED TEXTS: *The Portable Matthew Arnold*, 1949; *The Selected Letters of John Keats*, 1951; *The Experience of Literature: A Reader with Commentaries*, 1967; *The Life and World of Sigmund Freud*, 1970; *Literary Criticism: An Introductory Reader*, 1970; *The Oxford Anthology of English Literature*, 1973 (with others).

Lionel Trilling grew up in a Jewish neighborhood in New York City. Except for some of his youthful writing, he shunned specifically Jewish themes and identified his work with the great traditions of literature in Europe and the United States. His initial plan was to become a novelist, but he enrolled in Columbia University and became an astute student and critic, eventually obtaining his Ph.D. In fact, Trilling's dissertation, on Matthew Arnold, became a highly acclaimed book. Like Arnold, Trilling became not only a literary critic but also a critic of culture. Along with Edmund Wilson, Trilling has come to be regarded as perhaps the pivotal critic of his generation, defining the dominant character of American literature and assessing the literature itself in profoundly moral and historical terms.

Trilling's elegant, sober style helped to shape the literary tastes of a generation. In an enormously influential collection of essays, *The Liberal Imagination*, for example, he praises Henry James for his style, point of view, sensitivity, and complexity while deploring Theodore Dreiser's well-meaning but clumsy and vapid rhetoric. Trilling maintains that in novels such as *The Princess Casamassima* (1886) James exhibited a political sensitivity and shrewdness that was every bit as valuable as Dreiser's—more so, because the literary value of James's work was so much greater. The point of such evaluations for Trilling's generation was that they rectified the rather provincial bias of earlier critics who were wary of James's European biases and too eager to elevate new American writers such as Dreiser to canonical status.

Trilling was particularly interested in the relationship between works of art and culture. As a result, he drew on a number of different academic disciplines, such as history, philosophy, and psychology. He was especially curious as to how Sigmund Freud's ideas about the mind might be applied to the study of literary works. While he had enormous respect for works of art, he thought that they were open to analysis using the vocabulary of the modern social sciences.

In *The Liberal Imagination*, Trilling articulates his stance as a critic heavily involved in determining the character of the age while assessing its roots in the past. In *Beyond Culture*, he extends his range by looking closely at the quality of American education. He is troubled by the way modern literature has been absorbed into the college curriculum, even though the producers of that literature had been against the institutionalization of knowledge. What will be the fate of the great modern works of literature in a setting that is itself conventionalized? Trilling seeks, in other words, to remind his readers (many of whom are academics) of the subversive value of literature which questions, rather than supports, the status quo. Implicit in Trilling's argument is the notion that revolutionary ideas of modern literature should not be allowed to be domesticated. Somehow teachers have to give students a feel for the iconoclasm of art.

In "Some Notes for an Autobiographical Lecture," Trilling explains how he first became engaged with Matthew Arnold and then how the example of Arnold turned Trilling toward the writing of an intellectual biography that was to have a profound impact on all of his criticism. In the beginning, Arnold represented the poet as the passive vehicle through which the stresses and strains of his culture get expressed. In the end, the poet became a rebel defiant of culture, someone who wanted to change it. That is also the kind of critic Trilling became: Never sure that literature, the teaching of literature, or the writing of literary criticism were self-justifying activities, he actively took on the point of view of society and argued for and against it. In an autobiographical lecture, Trilling calls his stance "novelistic," by which he seems to mean that all of his assumptions have to be tested against experience and that ideas are not sacrosanct—they have no permanent truth—but must be constantly reevaluated in a changing environment. While many critics might echo Trilling's sentiments, very few have embedded this novelistic imagination in their prose. Trilling's work, read in its entirety, confirms that his views of literature and society continued to develop in response to the changing times.

Carl Rollyson

Bibliography

Heilbrun, Carolyn G. *When Men Were the Only Models We Had: My Teachers Barzun, Fadiman, and Trilling*. Philadelphia: University of Pennsylvania Press, 2002. Memoir by a former student of Trilling.

Krupnick, Mark. *Lionel Trilling and the Fate of Cultural Criticism*. Evanston, Ill.: Northwestern University Press, 1986. Primarily concerned with Trilling's influence and his merit as a literary critic.

Leitch, Thomas M. *Lionel Trilling: An Annotated Bibliography*. New York: Garland, 1993. A valuable research tool.

O'Hara, Daniel T. *Lionel Trilling: The Work of Liberation*. Madison: University of Wisconsin Press, 1988. Examines the broad range of Trilling's work.

Shoben, Edward J., Jr. *Lionel Trilling: Mind and Character*. New York: F. Ungar, 1981. A general study of Trilling's complete works. It provides biographical information as well as a study of Trilling's influential novel *The Middle of the Journey*.

Tanner, Stephen L. *Lionel Trilling*. Boston: Twayne, 1988. A succinct critical overview.

Trilling, Diana. *The Beginning of the Journey: The Marriage of Diana and Lionel Trilling*. New York: Harcourt Brace, 1993. A biographical and autobiographical memoir.

Anthony Trollope

English novelist

Born: London, England; April 24, 1815
Died: London, England; December 6, 1882

LONG FICTION: *The Macdermots of Ballycloran*, 1847; *The Kellys and the O'Kellys*, 1848; *The Warden*, 1855; *Barchester Towers*, 1857; *The Three Clerks*, 1858; *Doctor Thorne*, 1858; *The Bertrams*, 1859; *Castle Richmond*, 1860; *Framley Parsonage*, 1860-1861; *Orley Farm*, 1861-1862; *The Small House at Allington*, 1862-1864; *Rachel Ray*, 1863; *Can You Forgive Her?*, 1864-1865; *Miss Mackenzie*, 1865; *The Belton Estate*, 1865-1866; *The Claverings*, 1866-1867; *The Last Chronicle of Barset*, 1867; *Phineas Finn, the Irish Member*, 1867-1869; *He Knew He Was Right*, 1868-1869; *The Vicar of Bulhampton*, 1869-1870; *The Eustace Diamonds*, 1871-1873; *Phineas Redux*, 1873-1874; *The Way We Live Now*, 1874-1875; *The Prime Minister*, 1875-1876; *The American Senator*, 1876-1877; *Is He Popenjoy?*, 1877-1878; *John Caldigate*, 1878-1879; *The Duke's Children*, 1879-1880; *Dr. Wortle's School*, 1880; *Ayala's Angel*, 1881; *The Fixed Period*, 1881-1882; *The Landleaguers*, 1882-1883; *Mr. Scarborough's Family*, 1882-1883.

SHORT FICTION: *Tales of All Countries*, 1861, 1863; *Lotta Schmidt, and Other Stories*, 1867; *An Editor's Tales*, 1870; *Why Frau Frohmann Raised Her Prices, and Other Stories*, 1882.

NONFICTION: *The West Indies*, 1859; *North America*, 1862; *Clergymen of the Church of England*, 1865-1866; *Travelling Sketches*, 1865-1866; *The Commentaries of Caesar*, 1870 (translation); *Australia and New Zealand*, 1873; *South Africa*, 1878; *Thackeray*, 1879; *Lord Palmerston*, 1882; *Autobiography*, 1883; *The Letters of Anthony Trollope*, 1951 (Bradford A. Booth, editor).

The father of Anthony Trollope (TRAHL-uhp), Thomas Anthony Trollope, was an eccentric barrister who lost his wealth in wild speculations; his mother, Frances Trollope, kept the family together by fleeing to Belgium to escape creditors and by writing a total of 114 volumes, mostly novels. Her best-known work today is *Domestic Manners of the Americans* (1832), a caustic and grossly exaggerated account of the United States she observed on a trip to Cincinnati in 1823 in an unsuccessful attempt to set up a great bazaar. As his older brother, Thomas Adolphus, was also a writer, Anthony was following a well-established family tradition.

According to his posthumous *Autobiography*, Trollope was born in London on April 24, 1815; he grew into an ungainly, oafish, and unpopular boy who spent miserable and friendless years at Harrow and Winchester, where he learned nothing. When he was nineteen, he sought work in London, first as a clerk and then as a civil servant with the post office. He hated his work and his lonely life in the city, and seven years later he accepted with relief an appointment as traveling postal inspector in Ireland (1841-1859). Later his duties carried him on brief trips to all the continents of the world. In Ireland Trollope's pleasant experiences with genial country people and an exhilarating landscape helped him develop into a more confident and optimistic person.

He married Rose Haseltine and at the age of thirty began to write, his first novels being inspired by the ruins of an Irish mansion. His early works were failures, but he persevered under difficult conditions until *The Warden* found a responsive audience in 1855. This "scene from clerical life," its setting the Episcopal establishment of Barchester, presents a detailed account of the day-to-day events of provincial life in Victorian England. Its sequel, *Barchester Towers*, with its incorrigible comic character, Bertie, was so successful that it was followed by four other novels on the same theme, the whole group constituting the perennially popular "Chronicles of Barsetshire." During this same period, Trollope also wrote other novels, the best of which are *The Three Clerks*, an autobiographical account of the English civil service, and *Orley Farm*, a work which combines a plot involving a forged will with genre pictures of family life in the country.

In 1867, now confident of his powers, Trollope resigned from the post office and became interested in politics. He stood as Liberal candidate for Parliament in 1868 but was defeated. Nevertheless, he cut an impressive figure, chatting in the London literary clubs and riding to the hounds in southern England. All these interests are faithfully embodied in a series sometimes called the parliamentary novels, among them *Phineas Finn, the Irish Member*; *Phineas Redux*; *The Prime Minister*; and *The Duke's Children*. Trollope could not compete with Benjamin Disraeli in this field (just as he was unable to compete with Charles Dickens in depicting city life among the lower and middle classes), and despite their appealing portraits of political life and character, his parliamentary series was not widely read. Trollope continued to turn out novel after novel—mild satires, histories, romances, travelogues, novels of manners, and even, in *The Fixed Period*, a futuristic work about life in 1980. A curiously interesting work is the story of an erring woman, *Can You Forgive Her?*—a novel as close as he ever came to modern realism.

Despite the fact that he wrote some sixty novels in all, it cannot be said of Trollope that he made the world his stage. He surveys generally a rather narrow scene, usually rural and provincial, peopled by mild villains and tame heroes. No powerful philosophical or social conviction charges his writing, and no keen analysis of human psychology opens the inner beings of his characters. "A novel," he said, "should give a picture of common life enlivened by humor and sweetened by pathos." In this endeavor Trollope succeeded so completely that Henry James said of him, "His great, his inestimable merit was a complete appreciation of the usual." Trollope died on December 6, 1882, as the result of a stroke suffered one month earlier.

Trollope's posthumously published *Autobiography* disappointed his admirers and dampened his reputation, for he candidly confessed that he wrote 250 words per hour, completing eight to sixteen pages a day. He is said to have earned some seventy thousand pounds from his writings. Despite the fact that he was not an inspired writer, he amused an entire generation with pleasant tales, the best of which have considerable value as sociological insights into a more tranquil age forever past.

Bibliography

Felber, Lynette. *Gender and Genre in Novels Without End: The British Roman-Fleuve.* Gainesville: University Press of Florida, 1995. Discusses Trollope's Palliser novels, Dorothy Richardson's *Pilgrimage* (1938, 1967), and Anthony Powell's *A Dance to the Music of Time* (1955-1975). An excellent study.

Hall, N. John. *Trollope: A Biography.* Oxford, England: Clarendon Press, 1991. Draws heavily on the great Victorian's own words and pays particular attention to Trollope's travel writing and his final decade.

_______, ed. *The Trollope Critics.* Basingstoke, Hampshire, England: Macmillan, 1981. A good critical anthology for introductory purposes. Includes twenty Trollope critics and covers a wide range of topics. Contains bibliography.

Halperin, John. *Trollope and Politics.* New York: Macmillan, 1977. This study focuses on each of the six Palliser novels and includes several more general chapters. Contains a select bibliography and indexes.

Mullen, Richard, and James Munson. *The Penguin Companion to Trollope.* New York: Penguin, 1996. A thorough guide to Trollope's life and works. With index and bibliography.

Pollard, Arthur. *Anthony Trollope.* Boston: Routledge and Kegan Paul, 1978. Pollard seeks to put all of Trollope's novels and a variety of miscellaneous works within the context of his life and time. Stresses Trollope's evocation of his age and his guiding moral purpose. Includes an index.

Terry, R. C., ed. *Trollope: Interviews and Recollections.* New York: St. Martin's Press, 1987. This invaluable collection is a useful adjunct to the numerous biographies of Trollope. Terry collects forty-six memories of Trollope by a host of individuals who knew him at various points in his life. Includes critical evaluations of Trollope's work.

Wright, Andrew. *Anthony Trollope: Dream and Art.* Basingstoke, Hampshire, England: Macmillan, 1983. This brief study of fifteen of Trollope's novels sees them as contemporary fictions, transfiguring life in a certain way. Contains a bibliography and an index.

John Townsend Trowbridge

American novelist

Born: Ogden Township, New York; September 18, 1827
Died: Arlington, Massachusetts; February 12, 1916

LONG FICTION: *Neighbor Jackwood*, 1856; *Cudjo's Cave*, 1863.
SHORT FICTION: *Coupon Bonds, and Other Stories*, 1871.
POETRY: *The Vagabonds, and Other Poems*, 1869.

John Townsend Trowbridge (TROH-brihj) considered his forty-odd novels as little more than hack work. He believed his only serious and great literary efforts were the series of volumes of didactic narrative poetry which later generations have forgotten, as they have almost forgotten his novels. Trowbridge was born on a farm in Ogden Township, New York, on September 18, 1827, and spent his childhood there. As he grew up, bad eyesight caused him difficulty in school. Because of his handicap, he was largely self-taught; nevertheless, he acquired a great deal of learning, including a knowledge of French, Latin, and Greek. After completing a year at the academy in Lockport, New York, Trowbridge traveled to the Midwest. He taught school in Illinois in 1845, then moved back to Lockport to teach school there for a year. In 1847 he went to New York City and began to make a reputation for himself as a writer, contributing his work principally to *Dollar Magazine*.

During the period from 1849 to 1860, Trowbridge edited periodicals and wrote for *The Atlantic Monthly*, the *Youth's Companion*, and *Our Young Folks*. His interest in writing for boys and his success in pleasing their tastes won for him the editorship of *Our Young Folks*, a position he held from 1860 to 1873. He made his own a type of adventure fiction that was popular with adolescent boys and of interest to some adults; *Cudjo's Cave* is an excellent example of the type.

In 1860 Trowbridge married Cornelia Warren, who died four years later, leaving two children. The following year Trowbridge moved his family to Arlington, Massachusetts, near Boston. His second marriage was to Sarah Newton, of Arlington, in 1873. Among Trowbridge's friends were such diverse literary personalities as Oliver Wendell Holmes, Henry Wadsworth Longfellow, and Walt Whitman. He died at Arlington on February 12, 1916.

Bibliography

Sloane, David E. E. "John Townsend Trowbridge." In *Nineteenth-Century American Fiction Writers*, edited by Kent P. Ljungquist. Vol. 202 in *Dictionary of Literary Biography*. Detroit: Gale Research, 1999.

Trowbridge, John Townsend. *My Own Story: With Recollection of Noted Persons*. Boston: Houghton Mifflin, 1903.

Wilson, Edmund. "Northerners in the South: Frederick L. Olmsted, John T. Trowbridge." In *Patriotic Gore: Studies in the Literature of the American Civil War*. New York: W. W. Norton, 1994.

Dalton Trumbo

American novelist and screenwriter

Born: Montrose, Colorado; December 9, 1905
Died: Los Angeles, California; September 10, 1976
Pseudonyms: Millard Kaufman, Ian McLellan Hunter, Ben Perry, Robert Rich, Sally Stubblefield, Sam Jackson

LONG FICTION: *Eclipse*, 1935; *Washington Jitters*, 1936; *Johnny Got His Gun*, 1939; *The Remarkable Andrew*, 1940.

DRAMA: *The Biggest Thief in Town*, pr. 1949 (also known as *Aching Rivers* and *The Emerald Staircase*).

SCREENPLAYS: *Road Gang*, 1936 (with Tom Reed); *Love Begins at Twenty*, 1936 (with Abem Finkel and Harold Buckley); *Devil's Playground*, 1937 (with Liam O'Flaherty and Jerome Chodorov); *Fugitives for a Night*, 1938; *A Man to Remember*, 1938; *The Flying Irishman*, 1939 (with Ernest Pagano); *Five Came Back*, 1939 (with Jerry Cady and Nathanael West); *Career*, 1939; *Curtain Call*, 1940; *A Bill of Divorcement*, 1940; *We Who Are Young*, 1940; *Kitty Foyle*, 1940; *The Remarkable Andrew*, 1942 (adaptation of his novel); *A Guy Named Joe*, 1943; *Tender Comrade*, 1943; *Thirty Seconds over Tokyo*, 1944; *Our Vines Have Tender Grapes*, 1945; *Gun Crazy*, 1949 (as Millard Kaufman); *Roman Holiday*, 1953 (as Ian McLellan Hunter); *Carnival Story*, 1954 (uncredited, with Hans Jacoby and Kurt Neumann); *The Boss*, 1956 (as Ben Perry); *The Brave One*, 1956 (as Robert Rich); *The Girl with the Green Eyes*, 1957 (as Sally Stubblefield); *Spartacus*, 1960 (as Sam Jackson); *Exodus*, 1960; *Town Without Pity*, 1961 (uncredited, with Sylvia Rinehart and Georg Hurdalek); *The Last Sunset*, 1961; *Lonely Are the Brave*, 1962; *The Sandpiper*, 1965 (with Michael Wilson); *Hawaii*, 1966 (with Daniel Taradash); *The Fixer*, 1968; *Johnny Got His Gun*, 1971 (adaptation of his novel); *The Horsemen*, 1971; *F.T.A.*, 1972 (with others); *Executive Action*, 1973; *Papillon*, 1973.

NONFICTION: *The Time of the Toad*, 1972; *Additional Dialogue: Letters of Dalton Trumbo, 1942-1962*, 1970.

Born in Montrose, Colorado, in 1905, James Dalton Trumbo was the son of Orus Trumbo and Maud Tillery Trumbo, parents with limited financial resources who nevertheless were ambitious for their son. The family moved from Montrose to Grand Junction, Colorado, the site of most of Trumbo's fiction, where they lived until 1924. When he was in the fourth grade, his mother became a Christian Scientist, and the whole family attended her church. According to Trumbo, Christian Science was responsible for his lack of fear. From his father, an unsuccessful businessman, he acquired the inability to lie, a characteristic that later would lead to his imprisonment. In his youth Trumbo had a variety of jobs, but the most influential one was as a cub reporter for the *Grand Junction Sentinel*, an afternoon daily owned and edited by Walter Walker, who befriended him. In addition to being a good writer, Trumbo was also an excellent speaker who won prizes for debating and oratory in high school. Although his family was poor, he attended the University of Colorado in Boulder, but when his father lost his job in Grand Junction, Trumbo had to leave school. During his one year in college he wrote for the *Silver and Gold*, the school newspaper; helped edit the college yearbook; was invited to write for the *Colorado Dodo*, the campus humor magazine; and was invited to join Sigma Delta Chi, the national honorary society for journalism.

In 1925 Trumbo joined his family in Los Angeles, where he worked for eight years at the Davis Perfection Bakery, which also provided him with pro-labor material that he later used in his novels. After his father's death, Trumbo became the family breadwinner and supplemented his salary with bootlegging, which became the source for a story he wrote for *Vanity Fair* in 1932. He began to take writing courses at the University of Southern California and wrote several unpublished novels that concerned the bakery and Grand Junction. Soon he was working for *The Film Spectator* (later *The Hollywood Spectator*), which led to a position in the story department at Warner Bros. Studio, where in 1934 Trumbo became a junior writer specializing in scripts for "B" films. A year later he published his first novel, *Eclipse*, in England. A thinly veiled account of life in Grand Junction, it chronicled the rise and fall of a small-town capitalist and angered many people in Grand Junction.

Although *Washington Jitters*, his second novel, appeared in 1936, his writing was primarily for film. He worked for Columbia Studios, Metro-Goldwyn-Mayer, and RKO in the next two years, and he married Cleo March in 1938. He began work on *Johnny Got His Gun*, his most critically acclaimed novel, in 1937; when it was serialized in *The Daily Worker*, a Communist newspaper, he was criticized for his leftist views. The novel won the American Booksellers Award in 1940, the same year he published *The Remarkable Andrew* and was nominated for an Oscar for his script for *Kitty*

Foyle. In the 1940's he was the best-paid screenwriter in Hollywood (three thousand dollars per week or seventy-five thousand dollars per picture), but the Communist scare resulted in his being blacklisted.

One of the Unfriendly Nineteen called to appear before the House Committee on Un-American Activities in 1947, Trumbo, who had joined the Communist Party in 1943, was cited for contempt of court when he refused to cooperate with the committee. In 1948 he was sentenced to a year in jail and, after appeals failed, served his time in a federal penitentiary in Ashland, Kentucky, 1950-1951. From the time he was subpoenaed until 1961, he was a victim of the Waldorf Agreement, which denied suspected communists work in the entertainment industry. Trumbo continued to work writing stories and scripts but had to use other people's names. During this period he wrote many scripts, usually at reduced pay because studio executives exploited him and other blacklisted writers. Using the name Robert Rich, he won an Academy Award for his script of *The Brave One* but did not receive the Oscar for it with his own name on it until 1975. Because the studios frequently used several writers, some of them blacklisted, on a project, it is difficult to know how many scripts Trumbo actually wrote. When Otto Preminger announced that he was hiring Trumbo to script his film *Exodus*, the blacklist was over for Trumbo, who actually wrote few screenplays after 1960.

Trumbo's literary and cinematic reputation rests mainly on *Johnny Got His Gun*, which he adapted to film and directed, besides raising money to produce it. Based on many of Trumbo's experiences (Joe Bonham, the protagonist, is Trumbo's alter ego), the film won the 1971 Prix special du Jury at Cannes, and Trumbo won the International Critics Award. He was also the recipient of the 1970 Laurel Prize given by the Writers Guild, an organization Trumbo remained loyal to despite studio efforts to break it up. He died in Los Angeles in 1976.

Thomas L. Erskine

Bibliography

Cook, Bruce. *Dalton Trumbo*. New York: Charles Scribner's Sons, 1977. Though he covers Trumbo's fiction, Cook's emphasis is on Trumbo's screenplays, and when he does discuss the novels, he tends to stress their filmic qualities. Conversations with many of Trumbo's associates and friends are sprinkled throughout the book, providing the political and intellectual context.

French, Warren. *The Social Novel at the End of an Era*. Carbondale: Southern Illinois University Press, 1966. French faults Trumbo's fiction for its obtrusive political harangues, which reduce the novels to tracts, and believes that *Johnny Got His Gun* is a revolutionary story rather than a cautionary tale.

Kriegel, Leonard. "Dalton Trumbo's *Johnny Got His Gun*." In *Proletarian Writers of the Thirties*, edited by David Madden. Carbondale: Southern Illinois University Press, 1968. Kriegel discusses the Communist myth involving *Johnny Got His Gun* and finds the second part of the novel propagandistic.

Norden, Martin E. "*Johnny Got His Gun:* The Evolution of an Antiwar Statement." In *Hollywood's World War I Motion Picture Images*, edited by Peter Rollins. Bowling Green, Ohio: Bowling Green State University Popular Press, 1997. Concerns the political context in which the novel was written.

Marina Tsvetayeva

Russian poet

Born: Moscow, Russia; October 9, 1892
Died: Yelabuga, Tatar Autonomous Soviet Republic, Soviet Union (now in Russia); August 31, 1941

POETRY: *Vecherny albom*, 1910; *Volshebny fonar*, 1912, 1979; *Iz dvukh knig*, 1913; *Versty I*, 1922; *Stikhi k Bloku*, 1922, 1978; *Razluka*, 1922; *Psikheya*, 1923; *Remeslo*, 1923; *Posle Rossii*, 1928 (*After Russia*, 1992); *Lebediny stan*, 1957 (*The Demesne of the Swans*, 1980); *Selected Poems of Marina Tsvetayeva*, 1971; *Poem of the End: Selected Narrative and Lyrical Poetry*, 1998.

DRAMA: *Konets Kazanovy*, pb. 1922; *Fortuna*, pb. 1923; *Metel*, pb. 1923; *Priklyuchenie*, pb. 1923; *Tezey*, pb. 1927 (also known as *Ariadna*); *Fedra*, pb. 1928.

NONFICTION: *Proza*, 1953; *Izbrannaia Proza v Dvukh Tomakh: 1917-1937*, 1979; *A Captive Spirit: Selected Prose*, 1980; *Art in the Light of Conscience: Eight Essays on Poetry*, 1992.

MISCELLANEOUS: *Izbrannye proizvedeniya*, 1965 (selected works).

Marina Tsvetayeva (tsvih-TAH-yuh-vuh) benefited greatly from having educated, artistic parents. Her mother, Maria, a talented pianist, and her father, Ivan, a respected art history professor at the University of Moscow and the founding director of Russia's first fine arts museum, gave her a love of music and literature and an appreciation of tradition, heritage, and art. Governesses and boarding schools in Switzerland and Germany taught her poise, independence, and European languages and strengthened her determination to follow the career she had begun at age six, when she wrote her first poems. Her mother died from tuberculosis in 1906. Upon completing high school in 1909, Tsvetayeva traveled alone to Paris, where she cultivated a provocative personal style and delved into French poetry at the Sorbonne. Her privately published first book of lyric poems, *Vecherny albom* (evening album), won the immediate attention of such major poets as Nikolai Gumilyov, Valery Bryusov, and Max Voloshin. Voloshin became her close friend and mentor, introduced her to literary circles, and encouraged her efforts.

In 1912, Tsvetayeva married Sergei Efron, a military cadet from an old-line Jewish publishing family, who helped her privately publish two other collections, *Volshebny fonar* (the magic lantern) and *Iz dvukh knig* (from two books). These highly original, very personal lyrical poems—precise, sharp, fast-paced, yet deeply passionate—received high critical praise and marked her as a promising poet, confident in her creative abilities. Her daughter Ariadna (Alya), born in 1912, became the star of her poetry at that time. Tsvetayeva became close friends with Aleksandr Blok, Vladimir Mayakovsky, and Boris Pasternak, all respected poets, and corresponded with Marcel Proust and Rainer Maria Rilke about art and poetry. The lyrical diary *Versty I* (mileposts I) records a love affair (one of many in her life) with another poet, Osip Mandelstam.

While Efron fought as an officer with the White Army during the revolutionary events of 1917 and the Russian Civil War, Tsvetayeva was stranded in Bolshevik Moscow, alone, with two small daughters. Her political sympathies, forcefully expressed in *The Demesne of the Swans*, a tribute to the czar and the Whites, gained her no well-wishers. The clear-sighted, futuristic poems of this period predicted dangers others optimistically dismissed, and her diaries and prose sketches suggest Tsvetayeva felt something antispiritual and antipersonal—and therefore deeply hostile—in communism.

Impractical, impoverished, and self-absorbed, Tsvetayeva put both daughters in an orphanage so they would have food during the bitter winter of 1919-1920. When Alya became seriously ill, Tsvetayeva nursed her at home; in the meantime, however, Irina died of malnutrition. In the spring of 1922, on the verge of literary acceptance in Russia, Tsvetayeva followed Efron to Berlin, then Prague. There, she wrote prolifically until 1925, when, following the birth of a son, Georgy, the family moved to Paris.

Paris was home for Tsvetayeva for the next fourteen years. She published widely, using her small literary income to support the family. Financial necessity, however, forced her to turn from poetry to prose (literary portraits, memoirs, autobiographical reminiscences, and essays on art) to earn enough to survive, for Efron's Soviet sympathies and active politics as a secret Soviet agent had alienated Tsvetayeva from the Parisian-Russian literary cliques. Alya, converted to communism by her father, followed him to the Soviet Union in 1937; Georgy agitated to join them. Fearful of war, disturbed at émigré hostility, and eager to join her family, Tsvetayeva revised her manuscripts, collected her poetry, appended explanatory notes, and deposited these valuable possessions in various safe places as her legacy to the world in case her fears proved true.

On June 12, 1939, with the world on the brink of World War II, she left Le Havre for Russia. After a brief respite, she entered a personal nightmare beyond her worst imagining: Her daughter and sister were sent to a gulag, Efron was executed as an enemy of the people, and she was shunned by all but a few brave friends. Upon being evacuated to Yelabuga in the Tatar Autonomous Republic to escape a German offensive, unable to bear her son's hostility and her own loneliness, Tsvetayeva hanged herself on August 31, 1941. She was buried, unmourned, in an anonymous pauper's grave.

Her creations are amazingly varied: ten collections of short poems, sixteen long poems, eight verse dramas, autobiography, historical-lyrical prose, essays, literary portraits, correspondence about art with famous writers and personalities, and personal diaries recording her poetic vision. Her subjects include antique mythology, Russian folk myth, European medieval legends, German romanticism, legendary historical personalities, fairy tales, and gypsy songs. Her techniques mix old orthography, tongue twisters, proverbs, bright metaphors, shifting intonations and rhythms, contrast, oxymoron, and numerous innovations. The publication of works previously unavailable in Russia has brought a deeper understanding of her contribution. Her poetry is praised for its terse diction, experimental syntax and rhythm, verbless constructions, and effective mingling of biblical idiom, classical and Russian mythology, folk stories and folk language, archaisms, and the motifs Russians have always loved: the motherland, sacrifice, art, and love.

Paulina L. Bazin
Gina Macdonald

Bibliography

Brodsky, Joseph. "A Poet and Prose." In *Less than One: Selected Essays*. New York: Farrar, Straus and Giroux, 1986. Brodsky discusses Tsvetayeva's prose as an extension of her poetry, employing poetic devices, such as assonance and enjambment, and following an organic rather than linear structure.

Cixous, Hélène. *Readings: The Poetics of Blanchot, Joyce, Kafka, Kleist, Lispector, and Tsvetayeva*. Translated by Verena Andermatt Conley. Minneapolis: University of Minnesota Press, 1991. A comparative analysis of a variety of innovative writers by a noted French feminist thinker, geared toward a scholarly audience.

Feiler, Lilly. *Marina Tsvetayeva: The Double Beat of Heaven and Hell*. Chapel Hill, N.C.: Duke University Press, 1994. This psychological biography draws on both classical and postmodernist psychoanalytic theory—Sigmund Freud's notion of pre-Oedipal narcissism and Julia Kristeva's concept of depression as "the hidden face of Narcissus"—to explain the contradictory impulses evident throughout Tsvetayeva's work.

Makin, Michael. *Marina Tsvetaeva: Poetics of Appropriation*. Oxford, England: Clarendon Press, 1993. Eschewing biographical interpretation, Makin stresses Tsvetayeva's reliance on literary antecedents. The text is well documented, contains a comprehensive source list, and provides original translations of the poetry discussed.

Schweitzer, Viktoria. *Tsvetaeva*. Translated by Robert Chandler and H. T. Willetts. New York: Farrar, Straus and Giroux, 1992. This biography portrays Tsvetayeva as alienated from the world since early childhood by her poetic sensibilities. The author argues that a compulsive "need to be needed" kept Tsvetaeva grounded in events of the real world. Includes bibliography, chronology, index, and biographical notes.

Barbara W. Tuchman

American historian

Born: New York, New York; January 30, 1912
Died: Greenwich, Connecticut; February 6, 1989

NONFICTION: *The Lost British Policy: Britain and Spain Since 1700*, 1938; *Bible and Sword: England and Palestine from the Bronze Age to Balfour*, 1956; *The Zimmermann Telegram*, 1958; *The Guns of August*, 1962; *The Proud Tower: A Portrait of the World Before the War, 1890-1914*, 1966; *Stilwell and the American Experience in China, 1911-1945*, 1971; *A Distant Mirror: The Calamitous Fourteenth Century*, 1978; *Practicing History: Selected Essays*, 1981; *The March of Folly: From Troy to Vietnam*, 1984; *The First Salute: A View of the American Revolution*, 1988.

Best known as a skillful popularizer of history, Barbara Wertheim Tuchman (TUHK-muhn) was a member of a distinguished family. Her maternal grandfather, Henry Morgenthau, Sr., was ambassador to Turkey and later Mexico under President Woodrow Wilson. Her uncle, Henry Morgenthau, Jr., served as secretary of the Treasury under Franklin Delano Roosevelt. Her father, Maurice Wertheim, was an international banker, philanthropist, art collector, and sportsman.

In the 1920's Tuchman spent many summers traveling with her parents in Europe. In 1929 she entered Radcliffe College. Following graduation, she accompanied her grandfather, Henry Morgenthau, Sr., to the World Economic Conference in London. Tuchman began working for the Institute of Pacific Relations in 1933. In 1935 she was sent by the institute to work in Tokyo and returned later in the same year to the United States, where she began working for *The Nation*. Tuchman traveled to Spain for *The Nation* in 1937 as a correspondent covering the Spanish Civil War. In 1940 she married Lester R. Tuchman, a physician. During World War II she worked as an editor for the Office of War Information preparing material on the Far East for broadcast in Europe.

As a homemaker and mother of three girls, Tuchman put her career on hold for many years. Joking with a journalist, she referred to herself as a "Park Avenue matron." She mentioned that it was difficult to find the time and place to write, a problem that she later solved by working in a cabin without a telephone at her country home at Cos Cob in southern Connecticut. Tuchman often said that she was glad she was unencumbered by the Ph.D. She believed that if she had continued in academic work her talents for narrative history would have been "stifled." Despite the lack of a graduate degree, Tuchman served as president of the Society of American Historians from 1970 to 1973.

Tuchman's first three best-sellers focus on the World War I era. The first, *The Zimmermann Telegram*, is a detailed account of the American discovery of the German telegram that offered Mexico the return of territories it lost to the United States if it would enter World War I on the side of Germany. Tuchman's next book, *The Guns of August*, concentrates on the opening encounters of World War I and suggests that they foreshadowed the long, drawn-out, and bloody war that followed; a film adaptation of the book was made in 1964. Tuchman followed *The Guns of August* with *The Proud Tower*, a portrait of society in Western Europe and America prior to World War I. Aristocrats, anarchists, and artists are depicted in Tuchman's evocative exploration of a world that has disappeared.

In *Stilwell and the American Experience in China, 1911-1945* Tuchman presents a biography of the American general in charge of advising the Chinese government before and during World War II. Tuchman's use of Stilwell's diaries reveals that "Vinegar Joe" Stilwell had both to fight the inertia of Chiang Kai-shek and to keep the Nationalists and Communists fighting the Japanese instead of each other.

Tuchman's *A Distant Mirror: The Calamitous Fourteenth Century* shows the effects of the Hundred Years' War and the bubonic plague on Western Europe. The narrative also traces the life of Enguerrand de Coucy VII, subject of the king of France and allied by marriage to the English king. Tuchman presents a grim picture of peasant and bourgeois uprisings, rapacious armies, and an aristocracy no longer able to lead.

Many of Tuchman's books discuss poor governmental decisions brought about by "groupthink." In Tuchman's view, leaders and even whole societies proceed in dangerous directions despite what seem like obvious warning signs. This theme is particularly evident in *The March of Folly*, which discusses four episodes of societal folly: the Trojans' mistake in bringing the wooden horse into the city, the Renaissance popes' corruption and lack of understanding of the need for reform, the English aristocracy's misrule of the American colonies, and the American government's failure in Vietnam. Tuchman's last book, *The First Salute*, traces events of the American Revolution, a subject partially developed in earlier studies.

For her work Tuchman received plaudits, and many of her books were best-sellers. Critics praised her lively narrative style and her ability to depict character. She was scorned, however, by some professional writers, who found her command of language unsure. In addition, some professional historians found her narrative histories old-fashioned and her interpretations biased. Despite this criticism, Tuchman received the Pulitzer Prize in 1963 for *The Guns of August* and in 1972 for *Stilwell and the American Experience in China*.

In the last year of her life Tuchman had planned to write a murder mystery, but she was unable to achieve this goal. At the time of her death *The First Salute* was on *The New York Times* best-seller list. Tuchman died from complications following a stroke.

Charles S. Pierce, Jr.

Bibliography

Bowman, Kathleen. *New Women in Social Sciences.* Mankato, Minn.: Creative Education Press, 1976. Especially useful on Tuchman's early works.

Coles, H. L. Review of *Stilwell and the American Experience in China*, by Barbara W. Tuchman. *Journal of American History* 58 (December, 1971). The work in question is called "a model biography."

Davis, C. D. Review of *The Proud Tower*, by Barbara W. Tuchman. *Journal of American History* 53 (September, 1966). Tuchman is faulted for loose organization.

Fromkin, David, and James Chace. "What Are the Lessons of Vietnam?" *Foreign Affairs* 63, no. 4 (1985). States that Tuchman felt American leaders during the Vietnam War "saw the futility of the U.S. effort but did not revise strategy."

Pace, Eric. "Barbara Tuchman Dead at 77: A Pulitzer-Winning Historian." *The New York Times*, February 7, 1989. Gives a sympathetic evaluation of the author and her work.

See, Carolyn. "Barbara Tuchman." *Kenyon Review* 12 (Winter, 1990). Presents a feminist approach to Tuchman's life and work.

Trask, David. "Popular History and Public History: Tuchman's *The March of Folly*." *Public History* 7, no. 4 (1985). Discusses Tuchman's methodology.

Frederick Goddard Tuckerman

American poet

Born: Boston, Massachusetts; February 4, 1821
Died: Greenfield, Massachusetts; May 9, 1873

POETRY: *Poems*, 1860, 1863; *The Sonnets of Frederick Goddard Tuckerman*, 1931 (Witter Bynner, editor); *The Complete Poems of Frederick Goddard Tuckerman*, 1965 (N. Scott Momaday, editor).

Frederick Goddard Tuckerman was born to one of Boston's wealthiest merchant families. Tuckerman's father made a fortune in dry goods and real estate; his mother, Sophia May Tuckerman, came from a fervently abolitionist family. Frederick, their third son, was named for a cousin whose accidental drowning in Lake Zurich had been memorialized by William Wordsworth. During Tuckerman's childhood his family joined the Episcopalian church, which remained a lifelong influence upon him.

Tuckerman was educated at Bishop Hopkins's school in Burlington, Vermont, and at Boston Latin. He entered Harvard University in 1837, immediately after Ralph Waldo Emerson's "American Scholar" address, and his Greek tutor was the mystic Calvinist poet Jones Very. Tuckerman spent only one year at college before an eye ailment forced him to withdraw; after one year of recuperation he entered Harvard's Law School, received his LL.B. in 1842, and after passing the bar examination began work in a law office. However, Tuckerman much preferred his studies in literature, botany, and astronomy to the practice of law, and he spent much time on long walking tours through western Massachusetts and the White Mountains of New Hampshire with his brother Edward, a botanist.

On June 17, 1847, Tuckerman married Hannah Jones and settled in Greenfield, in the Berkshire Mountains of western Massachusetts. With the death of his father he had inherited enough to allow him to abandon law. Tuckerman was fascinated with Greenfield's rich colonial history. He devoted himself to literary and scientific studies and wrote short, reflective lyric poems, mostly meditations on love and nature as well as longer narratives. In such works as "The Question" he adapted old forms and conventions to new American themes.

Frederick and Hannah (whom he called "Anna") had a son, Edward, in 1850, who was followed by their daughter, Anna, in 1853. In 1851 Tuckerman accompanied his mother on a three-month trip to England. He and Anna made the grand European tour in 1854 to 1855; the zenith of this trip was a three-day visit with Alfred, Lord Tennyson, at Farringford.

On May 7, 1857, Anna gave birth to a son, Frederick; five days later she died of puerperal fever. Tuckerman began writing sonnets inspired by his struggles with her death and his attempts to make sense of his loss. *Poems*, privately printed in 1860, contains his early lyrics and narratives, as well as two masterful, irregular sonnet sequences, which provide a complex and powerful testament to the nineteenth century battle between Romanticism and more conventional religious experience. Tuckerman wrote of his attraction to Transcendentalism: He longed to "follow those that go before the throng,/ Reasoning from stone to star, and easily/ Exampling this existence." However, like Herman Melville, Emily Dickinson, and Nathaniel Hawthorne, he also realized the dangers of Emersonian idealism. Tuckerman's irregular elegiac sonnets portray an imperfect and incomplete natural world that must be jettisoned, not embraced:

> No more thy meaning seek, thine anguish plead,
> But leaving straining thought and stammering word,
> Across the barren azure pass to God:
> Shooting the void in silence like a bird,
> A bird that shuts his wings for better speed.

Hawthorne and Emerson warned Tuckerman that his work would not be successful commercially. Critics, resistant to experimental prosody, rebuked Tuckerman for not knowing how to write a "correct" sonnet. Although an English edition of *Poems* was published in 1863 and followed by two American reprints, the work made little impression on his contemporaries. Tuckerman gradually withdrew from society, and his children were raised by his brother Edward. The Civil War brought the death of his close friend Colonel George D. Wells, but even more painful was the sudden death of his son Edward at Harvard University in 1871. Although Tuckerman continued to write in these later years, he did not pursue publication. Three shorter sonnet cycles and a long ode titled "The Cricket" were among his papers at his death in 1873.

In 1909 Walter Prichard Eaton came across a copy of *Poems*; impressed by the book, he brought Tuckerman to the attention of the literary world. Witter Bynner discovered the three unpublished sonnet cycles and edited *The Sonnets of Frederick Goddard Tuckerman* in 1931. N. Scott Momaday edited *The Complete Poems of Frederick Goddard Tuckerman* in 1965. Since then Tuckerman's work has been frequently anthologized, providing an instructive outsider's commentary on Transcendentalism.

Catherine Wilcoxson Parrish

Bibliography

Donoghue, Denis. *Connoisseurs of Chaos: Ideas of Order in Modern American Poetry.* 2d ed. New York: Columbia University Press, 1984. This wide-ranging study devotes a chapter to recurrent oppositional themes in Tuckerman's poetry: public and private, human and natural, physical and metaphysical, and truth and ambiguity. Also offers brief comparisons of Tuckerman to other modern poets such as Emily Dickinson, T. S. Eliot, William Empson, Wallace Stevens, and Walt Whitman.

England, Eugene. *Beyond Romanticism: Tuckerman's Life and Poetry.* Albany: State University of New York Press, 1991. A combined biography and critical study. Examines how Tuckerman was molded by, and yet reacted against, Romanticism. Includes extensive readings of individual poems, an index, and a bibliography.

_______. "Tuckerman and Tennyson: 'Two Friends . . . on Either Side of the Atlantic.'" *New England Quarterly* 57 (June, 1984): 225-239. Essay explores how Tuckerman's poetry was strongly influenced by his friendship with Alfred, Lord Tennyson. The first half examines letters between the two men; the second half demonstrates how, through his close study of the English poet, Tuckerman moved beyond him as a model and established his own unique poetic identity.

Golden, Samuel. *Frederick Goddard Tuckerman.* New York: Twayne, 1966. Provides basic information about Tuckerman's life and several readings of his poems. Some of Golden's biographical reconstructions, however, are based too fully on Tuckerman's sonnets and not fully enough on other kinds of historical materials.

Hudgins, Andrew. "'A Monument of Labor Lost': The Sonnets of Frederick Goddard Tuckerman." *Chicago Review* 37, no. 1 (Winter, 1990): 64-79. A critical study of Tuckerman's sonnets.

Seed, David. "Alone with God and Nature: The Poetry of Jones Very and Frederick Goddard Tuckerman." In *Nineteenth Century American Poetry*, edited by A. Robert Lee. Totowa, N.J.: Barnes and Noble, 1985. A comparative study of the poetry of Tuckerman and Jones Very.

Frank Tuohy

English short-story writer and novelist

Born: Uckfield, Sussex, England; May 2, 1925
Died: Shepton Mallet, Somerset, England; April 11, 1999

SHORT FICTION: *The Admiral and the Nuns, with Other Stories*, 1962; *Fingers in the Door, and Other Stories*, 1970; *Live Bait, and Other Stories*, 1978; *The Collected Stories*, 1984.
LONG FICTION: *The Animal Game*, 1957; *The Warm Nights of January*, 1960; *The Ice Saints*, 1964.
NONFICTION: *Portugal*, 1970; *Yeats*, 1976.

The writing of John Francis Tuohy (TEW-ee) is distinguished by two qualities: the excellence of his craft and the pessimism of his outlook. He was born May 2, 1925, in Uckfield, England, the son of Patrick Gerald Tuohy, Irish, and Dorothy Annandale Tuohy, Scottish. He was educated in Stowe School, King's College, Cambridge. During World War II he was ineligible for military service because of a defective heart valve, later corrected by surgery. He graduated from the University of Cambridge in 1946, then embarked on a career teaching English language and literature in foreign countries, including Finland, Brazil, Poland, Japan, and the United States. He has also written reviews and articles for newspapers and journals. His wide travels and his interest in journalism not only provided him with the settings for his novels and many of his stories, which center on the lives of expatriates and their interaction with one another and with foreign nationals, but also were influential in his seeing himself as an observer of the world, not as a writer expressing his inner self. The chief subject of his fiction became the contrast and conflict of manners and cultures.

Tuohy's novel *The Ice Saints*, set in Poland, tells the story of a Polish professor, his wife, and their son, who inherits a fortune from his mother's English relatives. Rose Nicholson, the boy's aunt, goes to Poland in the guise of a tourist, visits her sister's family, and tries to persuade the boy, Tadeusz, to return to England, where he can enjoy his fortune. During her visit, Rose has an affair with a Polish government agent, who reveals the family's secret to the government, spoiling any hope they may have had to get Tadeusz out of the country. Without descending to propaganda, *The Ice Saints* paints a grim picture of life behind the Iron Curtain. Tuohy's vision of the Polish is of a people condemned to secrecy and duplicity. On the other hand, his English heroine is condemned by her own lack of discretion. The net effect is one of hopelessness, alleviated only by Tuohy's dry humor.

Tuohy's short stories can be categorized handily with respect to their settings: English tales and foreign tales. His collections mix both kinds. The stories set in England tend to focus on comedy of manners, in the tradition of E. M. Forster and Angus Wilson. The stories set abroad tend to be more dramatic, if more cynical. *The Admiral and the Nuns, with Other Stories* features pieces set in Brazil and Poland, as well as in England. The title story features the character of the daughter of a British admiral educated in English convent schools, married to a Polish pioneer living in the Brazilian jungle. Another story in this collection tells the tale of an aged Polish nobleman reduced to working as a courier in a cocaine smuggling operation. *Fingers in the Door, and Other Stories* features exclusively English settings, and some critics have disparaged it for lack of conflict and contrast. In *Live Bait, and Other Stories*, Tuohy adds Japan and America to his stable of settings, both for the same purpose of showing the discomfort created for the characters by the confrontation of cultures.

Although not favored by academic critics, Tuohy's writing received high praise from reviewers and fellow writers. His first short-story collection, *The Admiral and the Nuns, with Other Stories*, received the Katherine Mansfield-Menton prize, and *Live Bait, and Other Stories* won the William Heinemann Memorial Award. His third novel, *The Ice Saints*, generally considered his best, received both the James Tait Black Memorial Prize and the Geoffrey Faber Memorial Prize. In England he was elected a Fellow of the Royal Society of Literature in 1965. In 1972, The American Institute of Arts and Letters bestowed on him the E. M. Forster Award. In 1994, he received the $20,000 Bennett Award from *The Hudson Review*.

Besides his novels and stories, Tuohy also wrote a travelogue, *Portugal*, and a biography of the Irish poet William Butler Yeats. This latter work, called simply *Yeats*, was praised for its concise, straightforward treatment of the poet's life and works. The book is notable for its intelligent use of photographs and illustrations.

James T. Jones

Bibliography

Flower, Dean. "Frank Tuohy and the Poetics of Depression." *The Hudson Review* 49 (Spring, 1996): 87-96. Suggests that such collections as *Fingers in the Door, and Other Stories* and *The Admiral and the Nuns, with Other Stories* may be out of print because most readers probably found them too depressing; concludes that what makes all of Tuohy's works worth reading is their anguished and inconsolable tone.

King, Francis. "Obituary: Frank Tuohy." *The Independent*, April 15, 1999, p. 6. A biographical sketch of Tuohy's life and literary career, commenting on his early fiction, his resemblance to W. Somerset Maugham in his attitude toward sex, and his receiving the Katherine Mansfield-Menton Prize for his first volume of short stories.

Prescott, Peter S. "The Whiplash Effect." Review of *The Collected Stories*, by Frank Tuohy. *Newsweek*, February 4, 1985, 78. Prescott argues that Tuohy's stories are "extremely pessimistic" but powerful in their portrayal of human pain.

Snow, C. P. "Snapshot Album." Review of *Fingers in the Door, and Other Stories*, by Frank Tuohy. *Financial Times* (London), May 14, 1970. Snow remarks that Tuohy's "great gifts" are concentration, "intensive exactness," and a language that is "as firm and limpid as English can be."

Wilson, Jason. "Foreigners Abroad: Frank Tuohy's Three Novels." *London Magazine*, July, 1992. Jason Wilson, although writing mostly about Tuohy's long fiction, which he praises as still perceptive about "Britons abroad" even though thirty years out of print, finds his novels "episodic, linked short stories."

Ivan Turgenev

Russian novelist

Born: Orel, Russia; November 9, 1818
Died: Bougival, France; September 3, 1883

LONG FICTION: *Rudin*, 1856 (*Dimitri Roudine*, 1873; better known as *Rudin*, 1947); *Asya*, 1858 (English translation, 1877); *Dvoryanskoye gnezdo*, 1859 (*Liza*, 1869; also known as *A Nobleman's Nest*, 1903; better known as *A House of Gentlefolk*, 1894); *Nakanune*, 1860 (*On the Eve*, 1871); *Pervaya lyubov*, 1860 (*First Love*, 1884); *Ottsy i deti*, 1862 (*Fathers and Sons*, 1867); *Dym*, 1867 (*Smoke*, 1868); *Veshniye vody*, 1872 (*Spring Floods*, 1874; better known as *The Torrents of Spring*, 1897); *Nov*, 1877 (*Virgin Soil*, 1877); *The Novels of Ivan Turgenev*, 1894-1899 (15 volumes).

SHORT FICTION: *Zapiski okhotnika*, 1852 (*Russian Life in the Interior*, 1855; better known as *A Sportsman's Sketches*, 1932); *Povesti i rasskazy*, 1856.

DRAMA: *Neostorozhnost*, pb. 1843 (*Carelessness*, 1924); *Bezdenezhe*, pb. 1846 (*A Poor Gentleman*, 1924); *Kholostyak*, pr. 1849 (*The Bachelor*, 1924); *Zavtrak u predvoditelya*, pr. 1849 (*An Amicable Settlement*, 1929); *Nakhlebnik*, wr. 1849, pb. 1857 (*The Family Change*, 1924); *Razgovor na bolshoy doroge*, pr. 1850 (*A Conversation on the Highway*, 1924); *Mesyats v derevne*, wr. 1850, pb. 1855 (*A Month in the Country*, 1924); *Provintsialka*, pr. 1851 (*A Provincial Lady*, 1934); *Gde tonko, tam i rvyotsya*, wr. 1851, pr. 1912 (*Where It Is Thin, There It Breaks*, 1924); *Vecher v Sorrente*, wr. 1852, pr. 1884 (*An Evening in Sorrento*, 1924); *The Plays of Ivan Turgenev*, pb. 1924 (2 volumes); *Three Plays*, pb. 1934.

POETRY: *Parasha*, 1843; *Senilia*, 1882, 1930 (better known as *Stikhotvoreniya v proze*; *Poems in Prose*, 1883, 1945).

NONFICTION: "Gamlet i Don Kikhot," 1860 ("Hamlet and Don Quixote," 1930); *Literaturnya i zhiteyskiya vospominaniya*, 1880 (*Literary Reminiscences and Autobiographical Fragments*, 1958); *Letters*, 1983 (David Lowe, editor); *Turgenev's Letters*, 1983 (A. V. Knowles, editor).

MISCELLANEOUS: *The Works of Iván Turgenieff*, 1903-1904 (6 volumes).

Ivan Sergeyevich Turgenev (tewr-GYAYN-yuhf), the first of the great Russian novelists to be read widely in Europe, was born in Orel, Russia, in 1818. He was the second of three sons born to his unhappily married parents: harsh and tyrannical Varvara Petrovna Lutovinov, who had inherited large estates at twenty-six after an unhappy childhood, and cold, handsome, philandering Sergey Nikolayeyvich Turgenev, an impecunious young cavalry officer who had married this woman six years his senior for her money. The child, who was to be known as the most European of the great Russian masters, first saw Europe at the age of four with his family and its entourage.

Turgenev spent his earliest years in the elegance of the family mansion on the Spasskoye estate. When the family moved to their Moscow house in 1827, Turgenev began to prepare for the entrance examinations to Moscow University. By the time he entered, in 1834, he had fallen under the influence of Georg Wilhelm Friedrich Hegel and Friedrich Schiller. In the same year, however, Colonel Turgenev transferred his son to St. Petersburg University. Then, with his wife away in Italy, the aloof colonel died.

Turgenev had written since childhood, and at St. Petersburg he continued his attempts, seeing two of his poems published a year after his graduation in 1837. In 1838 he went to Berlin to study intensively for a career as a teacher of literature, returning to St. Petersburg in 1841 to prepare for his M.A. examinations. Under the impact of an unhappy love affair, however, he failed to take his degree. The poem *Parasha*, published in 1843, signaled Turgenev's escape from romanticism and was praised by critics for its sensitive simplicity.

When he resigned from the civil service job he had taken in 1842, his mother sharply reduced his allowance, and from that time on their relationship steadily became more acrimonious. He met Madame Pauline Viardot, the magnetic opera singer to whom he was to be devoted for the rest of his life, alternately her enchanted and despairing admirer. He published a realistic sketch in *The Contemporary Review* and then others in a similar vein. In February, 1847, he left Russia with Viardot and her husband, despite his mother's frantic efforts to prevent him from doing so. He left the Viardots at Berlin, and in Paris, Brussels, and Lyons he continued to work on what were to be *A Sportsman's Sketches*. Taking up residence at Courtavenel, the Viardots' summer home, in the summer of 1848, he stayed into 1849. By the summer of 1850, when he returned home because of his mother's deteriorating health, he had also composed many poems and more than half a dozen plays. For the most part these were comedies conspicuous for their dialogue. Although some were successfully staged, Turgenev was always extremely critical of them.

His mother's death in November, 1850, made him a rich man. In March, 1852, however, he found himself under arrest: A laudatory article on Nikolai Gogol shortly after Gogol's death, combined with the suspicion created by his sketches as they appeared, caused Turgenev's arrest by the czar's political police. He was confined in jail for a month and then placed under house arrest at Spasskoye for a year and a half. *A Sportsman's Sketches*, collected in book form in August, 1852, was an immediate and resounding success. The realistic treatment of Russian life, particularly the plight of the peasants, was so influential that it helped bring about the emancipation of the serfs nine years later. Regaining his freedom, Turgenev worked on his first novel during 1855. Published in *The Contemporary Review* in January and February of 1856, *Rudin* was the story of a utopian who had eloquence, honesty, faith, and enthusiasm but was not strong enough to achieve real love or political usefulness.

Turgenev dropped his literary work for a time in 1856 to return to Pauline Viardot in France, but her departure with another man left him desolate, and illness completed his misery. His return to Russia in 1858 was the beginning of three years of fruitful work. In January *The Contemporary Review* published *A House of Gentlefolk*, into which Turgenev had put many of his emotions arising from his relationships with Viardot and with his own family. This melancholy novel of infidelity, worldliness, and wasted lives was a resounding success. Now the most celebrated of Russian writers, he immediately set to work, this time in Vichy, on a novel based on a manuscript given him by a young soldier rightly convinced that he would not survive the Crimean War to complete it. It became *On the Eve*, appearing in *The Russian Herald* in January and February, 1860. On one level a depiction of a love affair, on another level it was a foreshadowing of the Russia to come, when in the 1860's so many of the nation's youth were to band together against czarist autocracy.

Acrimonious political controversies, quarrels with Ivan Goncharov and Leo Tolstoy, and estrangement from Viardot saddened Turgenev, but he completed *Fathers and Sons*, which was published in March, 1862, in *The Russian Monthly*. This classic novel presented the age-old conflict between generations, but it was also localized in provincial Russia and set in a critical period. In Bazaroff (often spelled Bazarov), Turgenev created one of the first of the nihilists, those who wanted to sweep away the old and apply the tenets and methods of science to politics and other human affairs. The novel incensed both young and old, extremists and reactionaries. Turgenev, surprised and hurt, was attacked from all sides.

Except for brief visits home, the years between 1863 and 1871 were spent in Baden-Baden, some of them with the Viardot family. In March, 1867, he published another novel, *Smoke*, in *The Russian Herald*. This love story, with its portrayal of aristocrats and young revolutionaries, like *Fathers and Sons*, pleased no one. Sympathizing with neither side, castigating political persons and follies, he became a target for criticism from all quarters. During these years he continued his prolific output of short stories. The best of them, such as "A Lear of the Steppes" and "First Love," bore the same hallmarks of his art, as did his novels: the psychological insight, the melancholy realism, the delicate nuances, the subtle creation of mood, and the sensitive pastel landscapes. After spending parts of 1870 and 1871 in England and Scotland, he published the short, nonpolitical novel *The Torrents of Spring* in 1872, in *The European Herald*. It was a great success and was very soon reprinted. In 1874 Turgenev moved into a suite of rooms in the house of the Viardots, where Henry James visited him in 1875.

Turgenev spent six years planning and writing his last novel, *Virgin Soil*, published in *The European Herald* in 1877. This novel, presenting to the reader a wide variety of the types who were to become revolutionaries, portrayed an aristocratic class that did not perceive itself to be in the process of dissolution. It also predicted with a high degree of accuracy the course that future events were to take in the writer's unhappy country. Although the novel was a best-seller in France, England, and the United States, it was a failure in Russia, and Turgenev resolved to renounce fiction. In 1878 he began composing his *Poems in Prose*, reflections upon politics, philosophy, and his own intimate concerns. Though he was still a pessimistic agnostic, some of these works showed a lightening and a heartening at examples of courage and defiance of death.

Turgenev's brief return to Russia in 1879 was a triumph in which honors and acclaim greeted him, and he was hailed as a pioneer and master. The academic honors conferred on him in Russia were soon matched by great universities in France and England. By 1882, however, when he had returned to the Viardot household, his health had begun to decline rapidly. Although he was told that he was suffering from angina pectoris, it was actually cancer of the spinal cord that confined him to his bed. By September he had virtually abandoned hope, but he lived on through a year of torment, dying in 1883. His funeral in St. Petersburg, attended by delegations from 180 different organizations, was an occasion of national mourning, an acknowledgment of the passing of a master of Russian literature.

Vasa D. Mihailovich

Bibliography

Allen, Elizabeth Cheresh. *Beyond Realism: Turgenev's Poetics of Secular Salvation*. Stanford, Calif.: Stanford University Press, 1992. Argues that readers should not turn to Turgenev merely for transparent narratives of nineteenth century Russian life; attempts to expose the unique imaginative vision and literary patterns in Turgenev's work. Discusses Turgenev's development of narrative techniques in *A Sportsman's Sketches*, analyzing several of the major stories, such as "Bezhin Meadow" and "The Singers."

Brouwer, Sander. *Character in the Short Prose of Ivan Sergeevic Turgenev*. Atlanta: Rodopi, 1996. An excellent look at Turgenev's characters in the short fiction.

Costlow, Jane T. *Worlds Within Worlds: The Novels of Ivan Turgenev*. Princeton, N.J.: Princeton University Press, 1990. A useful discussion of Turgenev's long fiction. Includes bibliographical references and an index.

Gregg, Richard. "Turgenev and Hawthorne: The Life-Giving Satyr and the Fallen Faun." *Slavic and East European Journal* 41 (Summer, 1997): 258-270. Discusses Nathaniel Hawthorne's influence on Turgenev and comments on the common motif that their "mysterious" stories shared (the uncanny spell, curse, or blight). Claims that Turgenev's explicit admiration for those works of Hawthorne in which that motif is to be found attests to a bond of sympathy between the two writers.

Knowles, A. V. *Ivan Turgenev*. Boston: Twayne, 1988. An excellent introductory study, with a biographical sketch, chapters on the start of Turgenev's literary career, and the establishment of his reputation and his first three novels. Subsequent chapters on his later novels, letters, final years, and his place in literature. Includes chronology, notes, and an annotated bibliography.

Seeley, Frank Friedeberg. *Turgenev: A Reading of His Fiction*. New York: Cambridge University Press, 1991. Seeley prefaces his study of Turgenev's fiction with an outline of Turgenev's life and a survey of his poetry and plays. This volume incorporates later findings and challenges some established views, especially the traditional notion of the "simplicity" of Turgenev's works. Seeley stresses the psychological treatment that Turgenev allotted to his characters.

Sheidley, William E. "'Born in Imitation of Someone Else': Reading Turgenev's 'Hamlet of the Shchigrovsky District' as a Version of Hamlet." *Studies in Short Fiction* 27 (Summer, 1990): 391-398. Discusses the character Vasily Vasilyevych as the most emphatic and the most pathetic of the Hamlet types in *A Sportsman's Sketches*. Contends that in a striking flash of metafictional irony, Vasily recognizes himself as the walking embodiment of the Hamlet stereotype. Sheidley points out the different implications of the Hamlet character in Elizabethan tragedy and nineteenth century character sketch.

Troyat, Henri. *Turgenev*. New York: Dutton, 1988. A sound narrative biography by a seasoned biographer. Troyat examines closely the contradictions of Turgenev's character and how they relate to his work. A perfect introductory book, written in an accessible but nevertheless learned style. Provides notes, bibliography, illustrations, and detailed index.

Valentino, Russell Scott. *Vicissitudes of Genre in the Russian Novel: Turgenev's "Fathers and Sons," Chernyshevsky's "What Is to Be Done?," Dostoevsky's "Demons," Gorky's "Mother."* New York: Peter Lang, 2001. This study compares Turgenev's use of characterization and gender with that of other Russian novelists.

Waddington, Patrick, ed. *Ivan Turgenev and Britain*. Providence, R.I.: Berg, 1995. Essays on Turgenev's reputation in England and in the United States, including reviews by distinguished critics such as Frank Harris, Virginia Woolf, and Edmund Gosse. Waddington provides a comprehensive introduction, explaining the historical context in which these reviews appeared. With extensive notes and bibliography.

Woodward, James B. *Turgenev's "Fathers and Sons."* London: Bristol Classical Press, 1996. Part of the Critical Studies in Russian Literature series, this is an excellent study of the novel. Provides bibliographical references and an index.

Frederick Jackson Turner

American historian

Born: Portage, Wisconsin; November 14, 1861
Died: Pasadena, California; March 14, 1932

NONFICTION: *The Significance of the Frontier in American History*, 1894; *The Frontier in American History*, 1920; *The Significance of Sections in American History*, 1932.

Frederick Jackson Turner was born, and received his earliest education, in Portage, Wisconsin. Located along the Wisconsin River at the edge of the 1861 frontier, and named for the portage route for many years used by local American Indians, Portage was an ideal place for the training of a future frontier historian. His father was a journalist, a political figure, and something of a local historian. As a young man, Turner attended the University of Wisconsin, where Professor William Francis Allen had an influence on him. He received his A.B. degree from the University of Wisconsin in 1884. After a few years of interest in journalism and elocution, Turner returned to historical studies, taking an M.A. at Wisconsin in 1888. He began working on manuscripts at the Wisconsin State Historical Society, and from that work came his doctoral dissertation, "The Character and Influence of the Indian Trade in Wisconsin," accepted at The Johns Hopkins University for his Ph.D. in 1890. Among the history professors at Johns Hopkins who influenced Turner were Herbert Baxter Adams, whose scholarship Turner admired but whose frontier theories Turner rejected, and a future U.S. president, Woodrow Wilson, whose ideas influenced the development of Turner's frontier thesis.

Turner was a member of the history staff at his alma mater, Wisconsin, from 1889 to 1910, although he had opportunities during that time to move to posts at other universities. He became a significant figure in the study of American history through a paper presented in 1893 to the American Historical Society when it met at the World's Fair in Chicago. In this famous paper he suggested that the frontier was the factor that made American history unique and that the closing of the frontier in 1890 marked a distinct change in the course of American history and culture.

Turner's work as a historian led to his receiving a number of honorary degrees: an LL.D. from the University of Illinois, 1908; a Litt.D. from Harvard University, 1909; a Ph.D. from Royal Frederick University, Christiania, Norway, 1911; and a Litt.D. from the University of Wisconsin, 1921.

In 1909 to 1910 Turner became president of the American Historical Association. In 1910 he left Wisconsin to accept a professorship at Harvard, where he taught and worked on his research until his retirement in 1924. His essays, including "The Significance of the Frontier," were published in the volume titled *The Frontier in American History* in 1920. Another group of essays appeared as *The Significance of Sections in American History* in 1932. For the latter volume the author was awarded a Pulitzer Prize shortly after his death. Following his retirement from Harvard, Turner lived for a time in Wisconsin but later moved to California and became a research associate at the Huntington Library, having his residence in Pasadena, where he died in 1932 when a blood clot stopped his heart.

Like many historians Turner much preferred research to the laborious task of writing, and the product of his pen is remarkably limited. However, what he did write has remained a source of knowledge, intrigue, admiration, and controversy. His basic thesis that the advancing frontier was the determining factor in the development of American democracy, and that the ending of the frontier would create yet unseen problems in the United States, has been challenged and even ridiculed but never disproved.

Glenn L. Swygart

Bibliography

Billington, Ray Allen. *Frederick Jackson Turner: Historian, Scholar, Teacher.* New York: Oxford University Press, 1973. A complete biography of Turner. Includes bibliography.

Bogue, Allan G. *Frederick Jackson Turner: Strange Roads Going Down*. Norman: University of Oklahoma Press, 1998. Biography includes index and bibliographical references.

Faragher, John Mack. Commentary in *Rereading Frederick Jackson Turner.* New Haven, Conn.: Yale University Press, 1998. Commentary on the published essays of Turner.

_______. "The Frontier Trail: Rethinking Turner and Reimagining the American West." *American Historical Review* 98 (February, 1993). Centennial evaluation of Turner's frontier thesis, which declares it no longer relevant and says that it should be replaced by a more regional view.

Jacobs, Wilbur R. *The Historical World of Frederick Jackson Turner.* New Haven, Conn.: Yale University Press, 1968. Insight into Turner's life, based largely on his correspondence.

Limerick, Patricia Nelson. "Turnerians All: The Dream of a Helpful History in an Intelligible World." *American Historical Review* 100 (June, 1995). Centennial evaluation of Turner's frontier thesis, which comments on Turner's desire to reshape frontier scholarship.

McClay, Wilfred M. "A Tent on the Porch." *American Heritage* 44 (July/August, 1993). Evaluation of Turner's frontier thesis declares that Turner is still relevant.

Mattson, Vernon, and William Marion. *Frederick Jackson Turner: A Reference Guide.* Boston: G. K. Hall, 1985. Essential guide to Turner research.

Scott Turow

American novelist

Born: Chicago, Illinois; April 12, 1949

LONG FICTION: *Presumed Innocent*, 1987; *The Burden of Proof*, 1990; *Pleading Guilty*, 1993; *The Laws of Our Fathers*, 1996; *Personal Injuries*, 1999; *Reversible Errors*, 2002.
NONFICTION: *One L*, 1977.
EDITED TEXT: *Guilty as Charged: The Penguin Book of New American Crime Writing*, 1996.

Scott Turow (tuh-ROH) is a successful Chicago attorney who has written best-selling fictional and nonfictional portrayals of the lives of lawyers and law students which both entertain and grapple with important moral and ethical issues confronting the legal system. Turow received his bachelor's degree from Amherst College in 1970 and his M.A. in 1974 from Stanford University.

When he entered Harvard University Law School in the fall of 1975, he wrote down his reflections and experiences on the pressures and stresses to which he and his fellow students were subjected at this highly competitive and prestigious law school. His book analyzing these experiences was published in 1977 as *One L* and was immediately popular with both current and prospective law students, as well as with lawyers and the public. In many ways Harvard Law School has long served as a model for legal education in the United States, and the portrayal of the experience there from a student perspective helped encourage much critical examination. While this first book was nonfiction, it was told as a story and was highly entertaining—a precursor to the author's later success as a popular novelist.

Following Turow's graduation from Harvard Law School in 1978, he returned to Chicago, where he was admitted to the Illinois Bar and worked as a criminal prosecutor, serving as an assistant U.S. attorney from 1978 to 1986. Turow's tenure at the U.S. attorney's office in Chicago had included the time frame in which a widely publicized federal government "sting" operation entitled Operation Greylord had resulted in the indictment and successful prosecution of many local judges for taking bribes, fixing cases, and other corrupt acts. It was during his term in that job that he began in his spare time (including on the train during his commute downtown to his job) to write on yellow legal pads, recording a gritty, realistic portrayal of the workings of a county prosecutor's office. The resulting legal thriller, *Presumed Innocent*, was published in 1987 and became a best-seller. It is told in the first person by a male prosecutor who is ultimately charged with, prosecuted for, and then acquitted of the murder of a female colleague with whom he previously had an extramarital affair. In addition to the portrayal of the courtroom drama, the novel focuses on issues such as how local politics and individual ambition may influence the operation of the criminal justice system, as well as issues of prosecutorial and judicial corruption. The novel was later the basis for a popular film starring Harrison Ford in the protagonist's role.

From the U.S. attorney's office Turow moved to a position as a private attorney at a large Chicago firm, Sonnenschein, Carlin, Nath, and Rosenthal, becoming a partner there in 1986. He subsequently published *The Burden of Proof* in 1990, a novel in which the first-person narrator and protagonist is a private criminal defense lawyer (the same attorney who defended the accused prosecutor in *Presumed Innocent*) who is confronted with the initially inexplicable suicide of his wife. Conflicting duties and loyalties of this lawyer then arise out of the local U.S. attorney's investigation into the financial affairs of a major client of his who is also his brother-in-law. This novel was later made into a television miniseries. Turow's third novel, *Pleading Guilty*, focuses on a large private law firm's internal investigation of the suspected embezzlement of lawsuit settlement funds by one of its partners. The novel weaves a complex tale involving the past career of the narrator (the lawyer assigned by the firm to investigate the missing funds) as a police officer who exposed his own partner's corruption, the hidden personal life of the suspected embezzler (who engaged in a homosexual love affair with a sports referee and then became involved in a gambling scheme involving the games at which his lover was officiating), and the involvement of an officer of the law firm's largest client in an offshore banking attempt to hide the stolen funds.

The Laws of Our Fathers revisits the character Sonia Klonsky from *The Burden of Proof*; now a Superior Court judge, she is presiding over the murder trial of a young black man accused of arranging the death of his mother, a ghetto activist. *Personal Injuries* entails an elaborate FBI sting operation that uses a corrupt lawyer who has been bribing judges to entrap an even more corrupt judge who is believed to be next in line to become chief justice of Kindle County. *Reversible Errors* contrasts the reactions of two couples when the innocence of a convicted murderer comes to light: one pair are former lovers, the prosecuting attorney and police officer who conspired to convict the man, the other are his court-appointed defense attorney and the now-disgraced judge who heard the case.

Turow's first six novels take place in a fictional Kindle County in Illinois—which is smaller than Cook County, Illinois, but still a large metropolis. Because some characters, geographic locales, and background reappear, readers of Turow's novels have the feeling of returning to familiar terrain. Taken together, the novels present a full-bodied and complex portrayal of life in the urban legal community. The popularity of the books among the general public, but even more so among the legal community, is due in no small measure to their portrayals of lawyers as multifaceted, real persons with complex personal lives and dilemmas that are not always amenable to easy solution.

Bernard J. Farber

Bibliography

Bennett, Julie K. "The Trials of a Novelist." *North Shore* 10, no. 9 (September, 1987). Examines Turow's life and work.

Diggs, Terry K. "Through a Glass Darkly." *American Bar Association Journal* 82 (October, 1996). Compares the realities of the legal life with its representation in the novels of Turow and John Grisham.

Doyle, James M. "'It's the Third World down There!' The Colonialist Vocation and American Criminal Justice." *Harvard Civil Rights-Civil Liberties Law Review* 27 (Winter, 1992). The work of Turow is compared with earlier portrayals of criminal justice in the works of Rudyard Kipling and Joseph Conrad.

Gray, Paul. "Burden of Success: As a High-Powered Lawyer and Novelist, Scott Turow Has Become the Bard of the Litigious Age." *Time*, June 11, 1990. Discusses aspects of Turow's legal fiction.

Lundy, Derek. *Scott Turow: Meeting the Enemy.* Toronto: ECW Press, 1995. An admiring examination of Turow's background and his work. Discusses Turow's personal views on life, authorship, fame, and the law, and provides analyses of Turow's early short stories and first three novels.

Watson, Jay. "Making Do in the Courtroom: Notes on Some Convergences Between Forensic Practice and Bricolage." *Studies in Law, Politics, and Society Annual* 14 (1994). The judicial process portrayed in *Presumed Innocent* is compared to real life.

Amos Tutuola

Nigerian novelist and short-story writer

Born: Abeokuta, Nigeria; 1920
Died: Ibadan, Nigeria; June 8, 1997

LONG FICTION: *The Wild Hunter in the Bush of Ghosts*, wr. c. 1948, pb. 1983; *The Palm-Wine Drinkard*, 1952; *My Life in the Bush of Ghosts*, 1954; *Simbi and the Satyr of the Dark Jungle*, 1955; *The Brave African Huntress*, 1958; *Feather Woman of the Jungle*, 1962; *Ajaiyi and His Inherited Poverty*, 1967; *The Witch-Herbalist of the Remote Town*, 1981; *Pauper, Brawler, and Slanderer*, 1987.

SHORT FICTION: "The Elephant Woman," 1956; "Ajayi and the Witchdoctor," 1959; "The Duckling Brothers and Their Disobedient Sister," 1961; "Akanke and the Jealous Pawnbroker," 1974; "The Pupils of the Eyes," 1974; "The Strange Fellows Palm-Wine Tapster," 1984; "Tort and the Dancing Market Woman," 1984; *Yoruba Folktales*, 1986; *The Witch Doctor and Other Stories*, 1990.

NONFICTION: *Tutuola at the University: The Italian Voice of a Yoruba Ancestor*, 2001 (lectures; Alessandro Di Maio, editor).

The reputation of Amos Tutuola (tew-tew-OH-lah) has been the subject of much controversy. Unlike the majority of African writers, who are not only university educated (and therefore well versed in and influenced by the formal structures of Western literature) but also often employ their second language with as much skill as a native speaker, Tutuola had none of this academic preparation. He began school at the age of twelve, was trained as a blacksmith, and, finding no opportunity for plying his trade, became a government messenger in Lagos. It could hardly be imagined that he might become a recognized author as a result of his daily habit of scribbling down stories on scraps of paper to abate his boredom while awaiting errand jobs as a messenger. Yet, perhaps by sheer accident of discovery and with some luck, Tutuola, an apprentice craftsman with no formal education beyond six years in missionary primary schools, is given the distinction of having written the first major modern African novel in English. Tutuola's rise to international fame is marked by the publication of *The Palm-Wine Drinkard* in 1952.

The history of his achievement is extraordinary. Attracted by an advertisement from the United Society for Christian Literature, Tutuola worked feverishly on a draft of *The Palm-Wine Drinkard*. Clearly, the novel was unsuitable for this group. Yet it was provocative, and an intelligent reader saw its potential; it was sent to publishers Faber and Faber in London, whose editors agreed to publish it. The result established Tutuola's career at the cost of much debate, which generally separated British and African critics. While Tutuola was heralded abroad as a naïve native genius (partly as a result of Dylan Thomas's enthusiastic review in the *Observer* in 1952), African critics at home viewed the untutored bard as a literary burglar with little or no imagination. The basic argument was whether Tutuola's natural style was brilliantly innovative or embarrassingly incompetent. Dylan Thomas called the novel "a thronged, grisly, and bewitching story," and he admired its unusual style. Educated Africans protested that Faber's determination to publish the work without the usual editorial corrections indicated a patronizing colonial attitude that showed a preference for a childish quality in an African writer.

This debate, so impassioned for more than three decades, cooled with Tutuola's subsequent publications. He came to be seen as a novice writer who did not meet conventional expectations but opened up a rare world, simultaneously original and naïve. The title of his first novel is indicative of the issues raised: Is "drinkard" an accidental error, or is the usage calculatingly ingenious in its subtle modification of the expected term "drunkard"? Regardless of such questions, Tutuola's book has achieved a fame he has not been able to equal since. After nine printings in the United States, it was translated into languages as different as Finnish, Japanese, and Serbian. It was developed into an opera and dramatized as a play repeatedly performed by the University of Ibadan's Travelling Theatre, both in English and in a version using Yoruba, Tutuola's native language.

The story tells of a "drinkard" whose phenomenal liquor supplies are cut off when his tapster, responsible for extracting his daily ration of palm wine, falls from a tree to his death. Driven by deprivation, the drinkard determines to follow him down to "the land of the Deads" and effect his release so that he may again serve his thirsty needs. This situation establishes that archetypal pattern, familiar in all continents, of the visitor venturing into the shades to rescue one whom death had stolen. The actual incidents are wildly imaginative, with the traveler experiencing punishments and excitements before returning with a healing and reconciling benefice to all in his village.

Tutuola continued to write novels in a similar vein. The pattern was the telling of Yoruba myth but in a manner that allowed him to incorporate a mixture of modern experience, Greek legend, Nordic monsters, and pure imagination into a unique narrative form. There are magic, bizarre transformations, and ghosts. One of the ghosts in *My Life in the Bush of Ghosts* has multiple television sets in her fingertips. The plots of all Tutuola's books are remarkable and outrageous. The stories remain compelling and the language ingenious, though there is some sense of repetition when the novels are read in succession; the astounding originality of the first book is reduced to the expected through familiarity.

There is some evidence that in his later novels Tutuola exhibits greater facility and calculation in the way he handles structure and dialogue. Yet his was a natural, instinctive talent for the most part; if he had learned any more sophisticated contrivances, they probably would have undermined the ingenuity of this remarkable storyteller. Tutuola's many honors include being named a Noble Patron of Arts by the Pan African Writers Association in 1992.

John F. Povey
Pamela J. Olubunmi Smith

Bibliography

Achebe, Chinua. "Work and Play in Tutuola: *The Palm-Wine Drinkard*." *Okike* 14 (1978): 25-33. A perceptive article by one of Tutuola's fellow countrymen and one of Africa's greatest novelists.

Afolayan, A. "Language and Sources of Amos Tutuola." In *Perspectives on African Literature*, edited by Christopher Heywood. New York: African Publishing Corporation, 1971. This essay assesses the writer's contribution to Yoruba literature from a Yoruba perspective.

Armstrong, Robert G. "Amos Tutuola and Kola Ogunmola: A Comparison of Two Versions of *The Palm-Wine Drinkard*." *Callaloo* 3 (1980): 165-174. A useful source study and comparison.

Bruchac, Amos. "Amos Tutuola." In *Critical Survey of Long Fiction*, edited by Carl Rollyson. 2d rev. ed. Pasadena, Calif.: Salem Press, 2000. A thorough overview of Tutuola's life and career, emphasizing his novels.

Collins, Harold R. *Amos Tutuola*. Boston: Twayne, 1969. A standard introductory study, with chronology, notes, and bibliography.

Irele, Abiola. "Tradition and the Yoruba Writer: Daniel O. Fagunwa, Amos Tutuola, and Wole Soyinka." In *The African Experience in Literature and Ideology*. London: Heineman, 1981. Irele's chapter should be compared to Afolayan's essay in *Perspectives on African Literature* (above).

Langford, Michele, ed. *Contours of the Fantastic in Two West African Novels*. New York: Greenwood Press, 1990. Contains Joyce Watford's essay, "Techniques of the Fantastic in Two West African Novels."

Lindfors, Bernth, ed. *Critical Perspectives on Amos Tutuola*. Washington, D.C.: Three Continents Press, 1975. An excellent source of discussions providing critical insights into Tutuola's individual novels.

Onyeberechi, Sydney E. "Myth, Magic, and Appetite in Amos Tutuola's *The Palm-Wine Drinkard*." *MAWA Review* 4 (1989): 22-26. Often cited as one of the best studies of Tutuola's masterpiece.

Owomoyela, Oyekan. *Amos Tutuola Revisited*. New York: Twayne, 1999. An excellent introduction to Tutuola's life and works. Good for the beginning student.

Palmer, Eustace. "Twenty-five Years of Amos Tutuola." *International Fiction Review* 5 (1978): 15-24. A good overview of the novelist's career and his reputation.

Quayson, Ato. "Treasures of an Opulent Fancy: Amos Tutuola and the Folktale Narrative." In *Strategic Transformation in Nigerian Writing*. Bloomington: Indiana University Press, 1997. A sound treatment of an important element in the writer's fiction.

Mark Twain

(Samuel Langhorne Clemens)

American novelist, travel writer, short-story writer, essayist, and memoirist

Born: Florida, Missouri; November 30, 1835
Died: Redding, Connecticut; April 21, 1910

LONG FICTION: *The Gilded Age*, 1873 (with Charles Dudley Warner); *The Adventures of Tom Sawyer*, 1876; *The Prince and the Pauper*, 1881; *Adventures of Huckleberry Finn*, 1884; *A Connecticut Yankee in King Arthur's Court*, 1889; *The American Claimant*, 1892; *Tom Sawyer Abroad*, 1894; *The Tragedy of Pudd'nhead Wilson*, 1894; *Personal Recollections of Joan of Arc*, 1896; *Tom Sawyer, Detective*, 1896; *A Double-Barrelled Detective Story*, 1902; *Extracts from Adam's Diary*, 1904; *Eve's Diary*, 1906; *A Horse's Tale*, 1906; *Extract from Captain Stormfield's Visit to Heaven*, 1909; *Report from Paradise*,1952 (Dixon Wecter, editor); *Mark Twain's Mysterious Stranger Manuscripts*, 1969 (William M. Gibson, editor).

SHORT FICTION: *The Celebrated Jumping Frog of Calaveras County, and Other Sketches*, 1867; *Mark Twain's (Burlesque) Autobiography and First Romance*, 1871; *Mark Twain's Sketches: New and Old*, 1875; *Punch, Brothers, Punch! and Other Sketches*, 1878; *The Stolen White Elephant, and Other Stories*, 1882; *Merry Tales*, 1892; *The £1,000,000 Bank-Note, and Other New Stories*, 1893; *The Man That Corrupted Hadleyburg, and Other Stories and Essays*, 1900; *King Leopold's Soliloquy: A Defense of His Congo Rule*, 1905; *The $30,000 Bequest, and Other Stories*, 1906; *The Curious Republic of Gondour, and Other Whimsical Sketches*, 1919; *Letters from the Earth*, 1962; *Mark Twain's Satires and Burlesques*, 1967 (Franklin R. Rogers, editor); *Mark Twain's Which Was the Dream? and Other Symbolic Writings of the Later Years*, 1967 (John S. Tuckey, editor); *Mark Twain's Hannibal, Huck and Tom*, 1969 (Walter Blair, editor); *Mark Twain's Fables of Man*, 1972 (Tuckey, editor); *Life as I Find It*, 1977 (Charles Neider, editor); *Early Tales and Sketches*, 1979-1981 (2 volumes; Edgar M. Branch and Robert H. Hirst, editors); *A Murder, a Mystery, and a Marriage*, 2001 (Roy Blount, Jr., editor).

DRAMA: *Colonel Sellers*, pr., pb. 1874 (adaptation of his novel *The Gilded Age*); *Ah Sin*, pr. 1877 (with Bret Harte).

NONFICTION: *The Innocents Abroad*, 1869; *Roughing It*, 1872; *A Tramp Abroad*, 1880; *Life on the Mississippi*, 1883; *Following the Equator*, 1897; *How to Tell a Story, and Other Essays*, 1897; *My Début as a Literary Person*, 1903; *What Is Man?*, 1906; *Christian Science*, 1907; *Is Shakespeare Dead?*, 1909; *Mark Twain's Speeches*, 1910 (Albert Bigelow Paine, editor); *Europe and Elsewhere*, 1923 (Paine, editor); *Mark Twain's Autobiography*, 1924 (2 volumes; Paine, editor); *Mark Twain's Notebook*, 1935 (Paine, editor); *Letters from the Sandwich Islands, Written for the Sacramento Union*, 1937 (G. Ezra Dane, editor); *Mark Twain in Eruption*, 1940 (Bernard DeVoto, editor); *Mark Twain's Travels with Mr. Brown*, 1937 (Franklin Walker and Dane, editors); *The Love Letters of Mark Twain*, 1949 (Dixon Wecter, editor); *Mark Twain to Mrs. Fairbanks*, 1949 (Wecter, editor); *Mark Twain of the Enterprise: Newspaper Articles, and Other Documents, 1862-1864*, 1957 (Henry Nash Smith and Frederick Anderson, editors); *Traveling with the Innocents Abroad: Mark Twain's Original Reports from Europe and the Holy Land*, 1958 (Daniel Morley McKeithan, editor); *Mark Twain-Howells Letters: The Correspondence of Samuel L. Clemens and William D. Howells, 1872-1910*, 1960 (Smith and William M. Gibson, editors); *The Autobiography of Mark Twain*, 1961 (Charles Neider, editor); *Mark Twain's Letters to His Publishers, 1867-1894*, 1967 (Hamlin Hill, editor); *Clemens of the Call: Mark Twain in San Francisco*, 1969 (Edgar M. Branch, editor); *Mark Twain's Correspondence with Henry Huttleston Rogers, 1893-1909*, 1969 (Lewis Leary, editor); *Mark Twain's Notebooks and Journals*, 1975-1979 (3 volumes; Anderson et al., editors); *Mark Twain Speaking*, 1976 (speeches; Paul Fatout, editor); *Mark Twain Speaks for Himself*, 1978 (journalism; Fatout, editor); *Mark Twain's Letters*, 1988-2002 (6 volumes; Branch et al., editors); *Mark Twain's Own Autobiography: The Chapters from the "North American Review,"* 1990 (Michael J. Kiskis, editor); *Mark Twain's Aquarium: The Samuel Clemens Angelfish Correspondence, 1905-1910*, 1991 (John Cooley, editor).

MISCELLANEOUS: *The Portable Mark Twain*, 1946 (Bernard DeVoto, editor); *Collected Tales, Sketches, Speeches, and Essays, 1853-1891*, 1992 (Louis J. Budd, editor); *Collected Tales, Sketches, Speeches, and Essays, 1891-1910*, 1992 (Budd, editor).

Mark Twain is both the greatest humorist American literature has produced and one of its most important novelists. Born Samuel Langhorne Clemens, the son of John Marshall and Jane Lampton Clemens, in the small town of Florida, Missouri, he spent his boyhood in nearby Hannibal on the banks of the Mississippi River, a setting that would figure prominently in many of his best works. His father died before he turned twelve, and he quit school and went to work as a printer's apprentice a few years later. While working on his older brother's newspaper, he began writing humorous sketches. In 1852, he published his first piece in the East, "The Dandy Frightening the Squatter," which appeared in a Boston magazine. A year later, he left Hannibal and found work as a printer in several eastern cities before deciding, at the age of twenty-one, to set out for South America. While traveling down the Mississippi River by steamboat, however, he altered his plans and persuaded a steamboat pilot to teach him his trade.

Twain's career as a pilot was cut short by the Civil War, and after a two-week stint in a Missouri militia unit, he went with his brother to Nevada. There, he made unsuccessful forays into silver mining and adopted the pseudonym "Mark Twain"—a nautical phrase meaning two fathoms deep—while working for a Virginia City newspaper. After relocating to San Francisco, he wrote the story that would win him national recognition, "The Celebrated Jumping Frog of Calaveras County" (early titles vary). The story shows Twain already a master of the deadpan, Western-flavored tall tale, and its use of dialect introduces the idiomatic style that would help earn him a place among the giants of American literature.

As a reporter for the *Sacramento Union*, Twain traveled to Hawaii in 1866 and sent home humorous travel sketches in the form of letters. In 1867, he embarked for Europe and the Holy Land as a newspaper travel correspondent, and his revised and expanded sketches were published in his first major book in 1869, *The Innocents Abroad*. That book's immense popularity soon made its author a familiar figure on the lecture circuit. In 1870, Twain married Olivia Langdon, with whom he had four children, only one of whom outlived him. The couple eventually resettled in Hartford, Connecticut, where they remained for twenty years. *Roughing It*, Twain's comical recollections of his time in the West, was published in 1872 and was followed the next year by *The Gilded Age*, a social and political satire that he cowrote with his friend Charles Dudley Warner.

In 1876, Twain published what would become one of his best-loved novels, *The Adventures of Tom Sawyer*. Drawing on his memories of his childhood in Hannibal, Twain created a rollicking portrait of an American boyhood characterized by high spirits, a thirst for adventure, and an irrepressible talent for mischief. The book became a classic and has never been out of print.

In 1884, Twain completed a novel he had begun eight years earlier. Generally acknowledged as his greatest work, *Adventures of Huckleberry Finn* is a scathing social satire disguised as a young boy's adventure. During the course of Huck's trip downriver with the runaway slave Jim, he encounters the hypocrisy, greed, and cruelty of "civilized" society and notes, in the book's famous final passage, "I reckon I got to light out for the Territory ahead of the rest, because Aunt Sally she's going to adopt me and sivilize me, and I can't stand it. I been there before." Criticized as crude and vulgar by some at the time of its publication, *Adventures of Huckleberry Finn* has since entered the ranks of the most important and influential American novels; it was praised by Ernest Hemingway as the beginning of modern American fiction.

Although Twain's final years were marred by business failures and personal sorrow (the deaths of his wife and two daughters), Twain found himself a celebrated and beloved public figure, recognized throughout the world and a legend in his own time. His last years were devoted to philosophical works, often dark and bitter in tone, and to his autobiography, a portion of which was edited and published after his death by his official biographer, Albert Bigelow Paine. When Twain died of heart disease in 1910, he left an immense body of unpublished writings in various stages of completion.

Mark Twain's reputation as a writer has grown in the years since his death as the richness of his legacy has come to be appreciated by subsequent generations of readers and critics. He is often credited with giving American literature its first uniquely American voice, and the color and vibrancy of his work stand in stark contrast to the elegant language and seriousness of tone that mark other nineteenth century novels. Yet Twain's command of language was one of his chief strengths, and his genius lay in his ability to make even the roughest of dialects serve his purposes as eloquently as the most refined and educated of accents. Twain brought the energy and truth-stretching humor of the West to his work and used it to entertain society with an account of its own foibles and vices.

Janet Lorenz

Bibliography

Camfield, Gregg. *The Oxford Companion to Mark Twain*. New York: Oxford University Press, 2003. Collection of original essays, including several by other scholars, on diverse aspects of Twain's life and writing, with encyclopedia reference features.

Emerson, Everett. *Mark Twain: A Literary Life*. Philadelphia: University of Pennsylvania Press, 2000. A complete revision of Emerson's *The Authentic Mark Twain* (1984), this masterful study traces the development of Twain's writing against the events in his life and provides illuminating discussions of many individual works.

Fishkin, Shelley Fisher. *Lighting Out for the Territory: Reflections on Mark Twain and American Culture*. New York: Oxford University Press, 1996. A broad survey of Mark Twain's influence on modern culture, including the many writers who have acknowledged their indebtedness to him; discusses Twain's use of Hannibal, Missouri, in his writings; charts his transformation from a southern racist to a committed antiracist.

Kaplan, Justin. *Mr. Clemens and Mark Twain*. New York: Simon & Schuster, 1966. Pulitzer Prize-winning biography that remains the best general work on Twain's life after 1861.

LeMaster, J. R., and James D. Wilson, eds. *The Mark Twain Encyclopedia*. New York: Garland, 1993. Comprehensive reference work broadly similar in organization to Rasmussen's *Mark Twain A to Z*, differing in devoting most of its space to literary analysis.

Leonard, James. S., ed. *Making Mark Twain Work in the Classroom.* Durham, N.C.: Duke University Press, 1999. Collection of essays by leading Twain scholars designed for students and teachers. Special attention is given to *A Connecticut Yankee in King Arthur's Court, Joan of Arc, Innocents Abroad*, and *Adventures of Huckleberry Finn*.

Messent, Peter B. *Mark Twain.* New York: St. Martin's Press, 1997. A standard introduction to Twain's life and works by a leading British scholar of American literature. Provides bibliographical references and an index.

________. *The Short Works of Mark Twain: A Critical Study.* Philadelphia: University of Pennsylvania Press, 2001. Detailed exploration of Twain's shorter works that takes the innovative approach of examining how Twain planned the individual collections in which they were first published in book form.

Paine, Albert Bigelow. *Mark Twain: A Biography.* 3 vols. 1912. Reprint. Philadelphia: Chelsea House, 1997. Often reprinted, this immense study by Twain's authorized biographer and editor remains the fullest study of Twain's life and benefits from Paine's close personal acquaintance with Twain and his access to sources that no longer exist.

Rasmussen, R. Kent. *Mark Twain A to Z.* New York: Facts on File, 1995. The most comprehensive single-volume reference tool on Twain. Virtually every character, theme, place, and biographical fact can be researched in this volume. Contains the most complete chronology ever compiled.

Sloane, David E. E. *Student Companion to Mark Twain.* New York: Greenwood Press, 2001. Essays on aspects of Twain's life, with special chapters on individual books.

Wilson, James D. *A Reader's Guide to the Short Stories of Mark Twain.* Boston: G. K. Hall, 1987. Detailed summaries and analyses of sixty-five stories, including several that appear within Twain's travel books.

Anne Tyler

American novelist

Born: Minneapolis, Minnesota; October 25, 1941

LONG FICTION: *If Morning Ever Comes*, 1964; *The Tin Can Tree*, 1965; *A Slipping-Down Life*, 1970; *The Clock Winder*, 1972; *Celestial Navigation*, 1974; *Searching for Caleb*, 1976; *Earthly Possessions*, 1977; *Morgan's Passing*, 1980; *Dinner at the Homesick Restaurant*, 1982; *The Accidental Tourist*, 1985; *Breathing Lessons*, 1988; *Saint Maybe*, 1991; *Ladder of Years*, 1995; *A Patchwork Planet*, 1998; *Back When We Were Grownups*, 2001.

SHORT FICTION: "The Common Courtesies," 1968; "Who Would Want a Little Boy?," 1968; "With All Flags Flying," 1971; "The Bride in the Boatyard," 1972; "The Base-Metal Egg," 1973; "Spending," 1973; "Half-Truths and Semi-Miracles," 1974; "The Geologist's Maid," 1975; "A Knack for Languages," 1975; "Some Sign That I Ever Made You Happy," 1975; "Your Place Is Empty," 1976; "Average Waves in Unprotected Waters," 1977; "Foot-Footing On," 1977; "Holding Things Together," 1977; "Uncle Ahmad," 1977; "Under the Bosom Tree," 1977; "Linguistics," 1978; "Laps," 1981; "The Country Cook," 1982; "Teenage Wasteland," 1983; "Rerun," 1988; "A Woman Like a Fieldstone House," 1989; "People Who Don't Know the Answers," 1991.

CHILDREN'S/YOUNG ADULT LITERATURE: *Tumble Tower*, 1993 (illustrations by Mitra Modarressi).

Although Anne Tyler's books have always been popular with general readers, acclaim from critics came more slowly. With *Dinner at the Homesick Restaurant*, however, Tyler's position in American literature was firmly established. In addition to her many short stories and novels, Tyler is much in demand as a book reviewer. She has achieved her greatest success and recognition as a witty yet serious and compassionate observer of human nature, with a polished style, a strong sense of irony, and an uncanny ability to create memorable characters and to reproduce their speech as if she had actually heard it.

Tyler is the only daughter of Lloyd Parry and Phyllis (Mahon) Tyler; there were also four boys in the family, a circumstance that appears in reverse in Tyler's first novel, *If Morning Ever Comes*, in which the main character is an only son with six sisters. Tyler denies that her novels are autobiographical. Although she was reared in North Carolina, she does not consider herself a southern writer, despite the repeated statement to that effect on the jackets of most of her books. Nor does she consider herself a feminist writer; she is more interested in people than in movements.

Tyler graduated from Duke University in 1961, having begun college at the age of sixteen. A course on the short story taught by the writer Reynolds Price had a great impact on her, though not on her style. After doing graduate study in Russian at Columbia University, she married Taghi Modarressi, a psychiatrist, in 1963, and the couple had two daughters, Tezh and Mitra.

A longtime resident of Baltimore, Maryland, Tyler has set most of her novels in various parts of that city. She has used other locations only briefly and secondarily, including small towns in North Carolina and Pennsylvania and such cities as New York, New Orleans, and Paris. She once said that what she was doing in her novels was populating a town—not with people she knew, but with people about whom she had written. Such comments are rare, however, as Tyler shuns publicity, does not give readings, and almost never grants interviews.

Winner of the National Book Critics Circle Award in 1986, *The Accidental Tourist* was filmed in 1987; the film also won awards, though the reviews were mixed. Critics responded to Tyler's next book, *Breathing Lessons*, in much the same way; while the book remained on best-seller lists for several months, won the Pulitzer Prize in fiction in 1989, and was filmed in 1994, some critics found it sentimental, slapstick, and banal, while others were unreserved in their enthusiastic praise.

All Tyler's novels draw on a family or a familylike community as a context in which to observe how the characters play out their lives and their relations with one another. The author's viewpoint varies over a wide range of possibilities: a young boy in *If Morning Ever Comes*; a teenage girl in *A Slipping-Down Life*; a wife in *Earthly Possessions*; an elderly, dying mother in *Dinner at the Homesick Restaurant*, in which parts of the story are also told by each of the woman's three children; and a young uncle, turned single parent, who shares the narrative with two nieces and a nephew in *Saint Maybe*. In *The Ladder of Years* a woman runs away from her family while on a beach vacation and reinvents herself in the image she feels more truly represents herself, while the protagonist of *Back When We Were Grownups* starts the novel with the realization that she had grown up to become "the wrong person" and attempts to discover whether it is still possible to become the right one. These examples show how Tyler varies her narrative voice, which is always sure and credible.

Tyler's characters are often eccentric and quirky, but they are just as often, in the same book, pitiable in their idiosyncrasies, misunderstandings, and failures. Tyler's world is a comic one where ordinary people make mistakes yet learn to cope with life's problems, take personal risks, and find alternative ways to survive. Contemporary society constantly challenges Tyler's characters with its changing traditions and sex-roles, its urban decline, and its clutter. Her protagonists find they cannot cling to the past but must move forward, make adult choices, learn to satisfy their own needs while reaching out to others, deal with modern complexity, and tolerate human difference. The more inclusive and complicated their worlds become, Tyler suggests, the more vital and fulfilled they will be.

Natalie Harper
Susan S. Kissel

Bibliography

Bail, Paul. *Anne Tyler: A Critical Companion*. Westport, Conn.: Greenwood Press, 1998. Contains a biography, literary influences on Anne Tyler, and individual chapters that discuss twelve of Tyler's novels in terms of plot, characters, themes, literary devices, historical settings, and narrative points of view as they apply to individual novels. Extensive bibliography.

Croft, Robert W. *Anne Tyler: A Bio-Bibliography*. Westport, Conn.: Greenwood Press, 1995. Includes a biography which includes four chapters, each followed by endnotes and an extensive bibliography, divided into primary and secondary sources, with a list of Anne Tyler's papers at Duke University.

_______. *An Anne Tyler Companion*. Westport, Conn.: Greenwood Press, 1998. A critical study of Tyler's fiction. Includes a bibliography and an index.

Evans, Elizabeth. *Anne Tyler*. New York: Twayne, 1993. Contains biography and an overview of Tyler's works. Includes a useful bibliography of primary and secondary sources.

Jansen, Henry. *Laughter Among the Ruins: Postmodern Comic Approaches to Suffering*. New York: P. Lang, 2001. Tyler is discussed along with Iris Murdoch, John Irving, and Cees Nooteboom in this study of postmodern literary comedy.

Kissel, Susan S. *Moving On: The Heroines of Shirley Ann Grau, Anne Tyler, and Gail Godwin*. Bowling Green, Ohio: Bowling Green State University Popular Press, 1996. Topics include Tyler's heroines and her identity as a southern writer. Includes a bibliography and an index.

Petry, Alice Hall. "Bright Books of Life: The Black Norm in Anne Tyler's Novels." *The Southern Quarterly* 31, no. 1 (Fall, 1992): 7-13. A study of Tyler's favorable portrayals of African Americans as wise and knowing characters.

Quiello, Rose. *Breakdowns and Breakthoughts: The Figure of the Hysteric in Contemporary Novels by Women*. New York: P. Lang, 1996. Discusses the work of Margaret Drabble, Kate O'Brien, and Anne Tyler. Includes a bibliography and an index.

Robertson, Mary F. "Anne Tyler: Medusa Points and Contact Points." In *Contemporary American Women Writers: Narrative Strategies*, edited by Catherine Rainwater and William J. Scheick. Lexington: University Press of Kentucky, 1985. A discussion of the narrative form of Tyler's novels, focusing on her disruption of the conventional expectations of family novels.

Salwak, Dale, ed. *Anne Tyler as Novelist*. Iowa City: University of Iowa Press, 1994. A collection of essays addressing Tyler's development, attainments, and literary reputation.

Stephens, C. Ralph, ed. *The Fiction of Anne Tyler*. Jackson: University Press of Mississippi, 1990. A collection of essays selected from papers given in 1989 at the Anne Tyler Symposium in Baltimore and representing a range of interests and approaches.

Voelker, Joseph C. *Art and the Accidental in Anne Tyler*. Columbia: University of Missouri Press, 1989. The first book-length study of Anne Tyler's fiction, this volume focuses on the development of Tyler's aesthetics and her treatment of character, particularly her view of selfhood as mystery and of experience as accidental.

Tristan Tzara
(Sami Rosenstock)

Romanian-born French poet and essayist

Born: Moineşti, Romania; April 4, 1896
Died: Paris, France; December 24, 1963

POETRY: *La Première Aventure céleste de Monsieur Antipyrine*, 1916; *La Deuxième Aventure céleste de Monsieur Antipyrine*, wr. 1917, pb. 1938; *Vingt-cinq poèmes*, 1918; *De nos oiseaux*, 1923; *Mouchoir de nuages*, 1925; *Indicateur des chemins de coeur*, 1928; *L'Arbre des voyageurs*, 1930; *L'Homme approximatif*, 1931 (*Approximate Man, and Other Writings*, 1973); *Où boivent les loups*, 1932; *L'Antitête*, 1933; *Primele Poème*, 1934 (English translation, 1976); *Grains et issues*, 1935; *Midis gagnés*, 1939; *Terre sur terre*, 1946; *Entre-temps*, 1946; *Le Signe de vie*, 1946; *Le Fruit permis*, wr. 1946, pb. 1956; *Phases*, 1949; *Sans coup férir*, 1949; *Parler seul*, 1950; *De mémoire d'homme*, 1950; *La Première main*, 1952; *La Face intérieure*, 1953; *À haute flamme*, 1955; *La Bonne heure*, 1955; *Miennes*, 1955; *Le Temps naissant*, 1955; *Parler seul*, 1955; *Frère bois*, 1957; *La Rose et le chien*, 1958.

LONG FICTION: *Faites vos jeux*, 1923.

DRAMA: *Mouchoir de nuages*, pb. 1924 (*Handkerchief of Clouds*, 1972); *Le Coeur à gaz*, wr. 1921, pb. 1946 (*The Gas Heart*, 1964); *La Fuite*, pb. 1947.

NONFICTION: *Sept manifestes Dada*, wr. 1917-1918, pb. 1924 (*Seven Dada Manifestoes*, 1977); *Le Surréalisme et l'après-guerre*, 1947; *L'Art Océanien*, 1951; *Picasso et la poésie*, 1953; *L'Égypte face à face*, 1954; *Lampisteries*, 1963 (English translation, 1977).

MISCELLANEOUS: *Œuvres completes*, 1975-1991 (6 volumes).

As a young man, Tristan Tzara (tsah-rah), known as Sami Rosenstock until he changed his name in 1915, studied math and philosophy at the University of Bucharest. He wrote poetry in Romanian during this time, but his literary career did not begin in earnest until after he moved to Switzerland during World War I, where he helped to create Dada, one of the twentieth century's most revolutionary and influential, albeit short-lived, artistic movements.

It must be said that "art" and "movement" are words that apply to Dada only in an ironic sense, because its members rejected everything that the word "art" had signified in European culture up to that point and were equally opposed to the idea of an organized, goal-oriented collective enterprise such as the word "movement" implies. Dada began in 1916 in Zurich, a city that hosted many Europeans who were seeking refuge from the violence and hopelessness of the war. The movement consisted of a small circle of young, primarily German-speaking artists and poets, who staged a series of events at a café called the Cabaret Voltaire. These events are now considered the precursors of more recent avant-garde experiments such as the theatrical, improvisational "happenings" of the 1960's and the "performance art" of the 1980's.

In part because much of his early work was performed in public, Tzara is considered to have made important contributions to the theater as well as to poetry. Tzara established himself as a creative force and theorist of Dada, and his first major published work, *La Première aventure céleste de Monsieur Antipyrine* (the first heavenly adventure of Mr. Antipyrine), is an illustration of some of the characteristics associated with the movement: provocation, iconoclasm, disregard for artistic convention, and spontaneity and openness toward new or previously unrecognized sources of inspiration. He pioneered the technique of "automatic writing," or writing with as little conscious intellectual control as possible, borrowed material from African folk songs, and made use of pure sound unrelated to conventional meaning. He published his first "Dada Manifesto" in 1918, a radical and uncompromising statement that contributed to his reputation as leader of the movement, even though he was only one of several people who were particularly influential during the Zurich phase of Dada.

After the war ended in 1918, Dada evolved in two separate directions: toward Berlin, where an artistic avant-garde thrived until its suppression by the Nazis in the 1930's, and toward Paris, where Tzara and a growing number of followers continued to perform and publish Dadaist "art" until the early 1920's. As the French Dada group disbanded, several of its members and much of its subversive energy became part of the Surrealist movement, formed under the strict leadership of French writer André Breton. Unlike Dada, the radical spirit of which some say it betrayed, Surrealism set explicit goals for its practitioners, such as the use of the psychological concept of the unconscious as a source for art and the liberation of society from middle-class taboos. Although Breton received some of the inspiration for Surrealism from Dada, he feuded with Tzara, who for several years remained aloof from the movement.

Tzara married artist Greta Knutson in 1925, and the couple had a son, Christophe, in 1927. In 1929 he began to publish in Surrealist journals, in spite of the tension with Breton. Some of Tzara's most highly regarded works date from his Surrealist period, including *Approximate Man*, *Où boivent les loups* (where the wolves drink), *L'Antitête* (the antihead), and *Grains et issues* (seeds and bran). While continuing in the Dadaist spirit, these poems differ from his earlier ones by virtue of a greater reliance on imagery and theme. Tzara is the only major French poet to have played such an important role in both the Dada and Surrealist groups.

Tzara broke with the Surrealists in 1935, mainly for political reasons. While Surrealists had always claimed political and social revolution as part of their program, Tzara became disillusioned with their inability or unwillingness to implement those goals. Attracted to Communism, he went to Spain to show support for the Republicans fighting the Fascists in the Civil War (1936-1939) and joined the French Communist Party when he became a French citizen in 1947. After the German occupation of France in 1940, Tzara was persecuted because of his Jewish origins and political activity. He went underground and joined the propaganda arm of the French Resistance. His newfound commitment to freedom and social justice proved to be an important influence on his poetry. Compared to the more radical experimentalism and dominance of sound over meaning characteristic of his early works, his poetry from the late 1930's onward displays a greater lyrical dimension, at times idealistic in tone. He left the Communist Party in 1956 after the Soviet invasion of Hungary but nevertheless remained strongly committed to social reform and to a politically inspired concept of poetry as part of the concrete, daily lives of all members of humanity. In his final years he also devoted himself to writing literary and art criticism and to recording the history of Dada and its influence.

M. Martin Guiney

Bibliography

Cardinal, Roger. "Adventuring into Language." *The Times Literary Supplement*, October 13, 1978, 1156. A review of the first few volumes of Tzara's complete works, which had just been published in France. Provides a short but useful introduction to several of the major issues in his poetry.

Caws, Mary Ann. Introduction to *Approximate Man, and Other Writings*, by Tristan Tzara. Translated by Caws. Detroit: Wayne State University Press, 1973. This book is an excellent selection of English translations of Tzara's poetry, and the introduction provides a helpful guide to each phase of his work.

_______, ed. *Surrealist Painters and Poets: An Anthology*. Cambridge, Mass.: MIT Press, 2001. Contains translations of several prose pieces by Tzara as well as works by many of his contemporaries, providing an overview of the context in which he operated. Includes many illustrations.

Marcus, Greil. *Lipstick Traces: A Secret History of the Twentieth Century*. Cambridge, Mass.: Harvard University Press, 1989. A highly original and accessible study of nihilistic movements in art, music, and literature, from Dada to punk rock. Tzara is only one of many figures discussed here, but this book deserves mention because of its broad historical scope and excellent analysis of the relationship between popular culture and the avant-garde.

Peterson, Elmer. *Tristan Tzara: Dada and Surrational Theorist*. New Brunswick, N.J.: Rutgers University Press, 1971. A primary critical work on Tzara in English. Includes many illustrations.

Nicholas Udall

English playwright and translator

Born: Southampton, Hampshire, England; December, 1505(?)
Died: London, England; December, 1556

DRAMA: *Ralph Roister Doister*, pr. c. 1552.
NONFICTION: *Compendiosa totius anatomie delineatio*, 1552.
TRANSLATIONS: *Floures for Latine Spekynge*, 1534 (of Terence); *Apopthegmes*, 1542 (of Erasmus); *The Paraphrase of Erasmus upon the New Testament*, 1549 (of Erasmus); *A Discourse or Tractise of Petur Martyr*, 1550 (of Peter Martyr's *Tractatie de Sacramente*).

Born about 1505, Nicholas Udall (YEW-dahl) was educated at Winchester and Corpus Christi College, Oxford, where he served as lecturer from 1526 to 1528. At the age of twenty-seven or twenty-eight, he assisted in the preparation of verses for Anne Boleyn's coronation. From 1533 to 1547 he was vicar of Braintree, Essex, and from 1534 to 1541 he was headmaster of Eton. In 1534 he published a significant collection, *Floures for Latine Spekynge*, and in 1538 he was paid for "playing before my Lord." His career at Eton ended in disgrace, however, for he was accused of theft and other misconduct and dismissed.

For the next fourteen years, Udall was writer, tutor, and churchman under patronage of members of the royal household. His principles as churchman were flexible enough to permit his serving Edward VI as a Protestant and Mary Tudor as a Catholic. Before the latter he performed or produced various dialogues and interludes. The date of his only surviving play, *Ralph Roister Doister*, is uncertain, but it was probably 1552, for evidence suggests it was first performed at Windsor Castle in September, 1552. The printed epilogue praises "our most noble Queen," but this might have been an addition for a later performance before Elizabeth I.

Udall was a prominent scholar of his day. In 1549 he published *The Paraphrase of Erasmus upon the New Testament*, a translation of the Dutch humanist's Latin commentaries on the New Testament on which he had collaborated with Princess Mary Tudor. By royal order, Udall's *Paraphrase* became the prescribed biblical commentary for all clergy, and along with the English Bible and the *Book of Common Prayer*, it appeared in every church pulpit in England. In 1555 Udall was appointed headmaster of Westminster School; he died the next year. His most important work, *Ralph Roister Doister*, bears the marks of his many talents as a humanist, a classical scholar, and a teacher.

Frank Day

Bibliography

Boas, Frederick F. *An Introduction to Tudor Drama*. 1933. Reprint. New York: AMS Press, 1978. Contains basic facts about Udall and his works, including his relationship with Queen Mary and a lawsuit against him in the early 1500's. Offers a comment on the classical influences on Udall, the "most representative" English playwright in the three decades between John Heywood and the major Inns of Court dramas of the 1560's.

Cartwright, Kent. *Theatre and Humanism: English Drama in the Sixteenth Century*. New York: Cambridge University Press, 1999. Cartwright examines the influence of Humanism on English drama in the 1500's. Udall followed Humanism and received instruction in it. Includes bibliography and index.

Edgerton, William. *Nicholas Udall*. New York: Twayne, 1965. The biographical sections are enlarged by references to major historical events. *Respublica* is dismissed as probably not by Udall. The longest chapter is devoted to *Ralph Roister Doister*, with emphasis on the dating problem and on the presence of Latin influence in the comedy. Includes annotated bibliography.

Walker, Greg. *The Politics of Performance in Early Renaissance Drama*. New York: Cambridge University Press, 1998. Walker examines the theater of Great Britain, focusing on the writers Udall, David Lindsay, John Heywood, and Thomas Norton. Includes bibliography and index.

Alfred Uhry

American playwright and screenwriter

Born: Atlanta, Georgia; December 3, 1936

DRAMA: *Here's Where I Belong*, pr. 1968 (lyrics; book by Alex Gordon, music by Robert Waldman; adaptation of John Steinbeck's novel *East of Eden*); *The Robber Bridegroom*, pr. 1975 (lyrics and libretto; music by Waldman; adaptation of Eudora Welty's novella); *Chapeau*, pr. 1977; *Swing*, pr. 1980 (lyrics; book by Conn Fleming, music by Waldman); *Little Johnny Jones*, pr. 1982 (adaptation of George M. Cohan's musical); *America's Sweetheart*, pr. 1985 (lyrics and libretto; music by Robert Waldman; adaptation of John Kobler's book *Capone: The Life and World of Al Capone*); *Driving Miss Daisy*, pr. 1987; *The Last Night of Ballyhoo*, pr. 1996; *Parade*, pr. 1998.

SCREENPLAYS: *Mystic Pizza*, 1988 (with others); *Driving Miss Daisy*, 1989 (adaptation of his play); *Rich in Love*, 1993 (adaptation of Josephine Humphreys' novel).

Pulitzer Prize-winning dramatist Alfred Uhry (YEWR-ee) was born on December 3, 1936, in Atlanta to Ralph K. and Alene Fox Uhry. His father was a furniture designer and artist; his mother was a social worker. Uhry earned a B.A. degree from Brown University in 1958. During his undergraduate years, he wrote the book and lyrics for annual student musical presentations. On June 13, 1959, Uhry married Joanna Kellogg, a schoolteacher. They had four daughters: Emily, Elizabeth, Kate, and Nell.

When Uhry first went to New York, he worked for composer Frank Loesser as a lyricist. Then he joined the faculty of Calhoun High School, a private school in New York City, where he taught English and drama until 1980. For the next several years, until 1984, Uhry was affiliated with the Goodspeed Opera House, working on comedy scripts for television. In 1985 he resumed teaching for three years at New York University in New York City, as instructor of lyric writing. A key experience in Uhry's life was the opportunity to work with the composer Robert Waldman for a number of years.

During the 1960's and 1970's, Uhry worked mainly as a lyricist and librettist. In 1968 he wrote the lyrics for *Here's Where I Belong*, a musical adapted from John Steinbeck's novel *East of Eden*. It closed after one performance. Uhry's work as lyricist and librettist for a two-act musical based on Eudora Welty's novella *The Robber Bridegroom* in 1975 fared much better. It was produced on Broadway, and it earned him a nomination for the Drama Desk Award in 1975 and the Tony Award, the American Theatre Wing Award, and the League of American Theatres Award in 1976. A surprise hit, this musical ran on Broadway for almost 150 performances during the 1976-1977 season. Uhry had several such successes throughout the 1970's and early 1980's, with *Chapeau*, a musical; *Swing*, which was performed at the John F. Kennedy Center for the Performing Arts in 1980; *Little Johnny Jones*; and *America's Sweetheart*, based on John Kobler's book about Al Capone.

After realizing that he had spent years doing what he did not really want to do, Uhry decided that the time was right to write a play. For him, researching a subject was unnecessary; he would draw from family experiences. He knew a family legend about his grandmother, who continued to drive long past the time she could do so safely. The family finally forced her to accept the services of a chauffeur. With the Off-Broadway production of his first full-length play, *Driving Miss Daisy*, Uhry got his big break. In the play, the twenty-five-year relationship between the elderly grandmother and the black chauffeur provided Uhry a chance to reveal some of the changes in attitudes and relationships that took place during that era of civil rights struggles between the 1950's and the 1970's. With great subtlety, Uhry addresses a number of issues of the era, including race and ethnicity, the rich and the poor, the Jew and the Gentile, and conflicts between the old and the young.

Driving Miss Daisy earned Uhry the 1988 Pulitzer Prize in drama as well as the Outer Critics Circle award. The play enjoyed 664 performances, making it the longest-running play in the history of the Alliance Theatre Company, and there were 1,195 Off-Broadway performances of the play. The following year *Driving Miss Daisy* was awarded the Los Angeles Drama Critics Circle Award. In 1990 Uhry received the Academy Award (Oscar) for the best screenplay adaptation.

Uhry continued to produce screenplays throughout the 1980's. In 1988 he collaborated with Amy Jones and Perry and Randy Howze on completing the script for the 1988 film *Mystic Pizza*, which centers on three young women employees in a pizza parlor, each with some emotional crisis involving love relationships. Uhry's contributions were chiefly in the areas of plot resolution and in introducing humor in appropriate places in the play. The following year he worked with Bruce Beresford, a film director with whom he had collaborated earlier, on adapting Josephine Humphreys' novel *Rich in Love*, about a South Carolina family whose youngest daughter comes of age during a family crisis precipitated by the mother abandoning the family.

Uhry continued to write screenplays while pondering what he could do to follow the highly successful *Driving Miss Daisy*. To his surprise, the answer came when the Cultural Olympiad in his hometown commissioned him to write a play for the Olympic Arts Festival which ran concurrently with the 1996 Olympic Games in Atlanta. As with *Driving Miss Daisy*, Uhry turned to past family events as a source of inspiration for *The Last Night of Ballyhoo*. The play is set in an antebellum house in a German-Jewish neighborhood in Atlanta, much like his uncle's house. Characters based on his relatives are concerned with The Ballyhoo, a country-club gala hosted around the holiday season by the most elite of southern Jewish society during the years between World War I and World War II. *The Last Night of Ballyhoo* won Uhry a Tony nomination as well as a spot on the shortlist for the Pulitzer Prize.

Victoria Price

Bibliography

Berney, K. A., ed. *Contemporary American Dramatists*. Detroit: St. James Press, 1994. Provides biographic data and contains a bibliography of Uhry's work, with commentary on his awards.

Matuz, Roger, ed. *Contemporary Southern Writers*. Detroit: St. James Press, 1999. Provides helpful critical comments on Uhry's work and identifies as central the themes of aging and social expectations. Focuses almost exclusively on *Driving Miss Daisy* after touching on biographical notes and a bibliography of Uhry's work.

Riggs, Thomas, ed. *Contemporary Dramatists*. 6th ed. Detroit: St. James Press, 1999. Following basic biographical information and lists of publications and critical studies of some of Uhry's works, the article focuses on his career development and the evolution of *Driving Miss Daisy* in particular.

Laurel Thatcher Ulrich

American historian

Born: Sugar City, Idaho; July 11, 1938

NONFICTION: *A Beginner's Boston*, 1970 (with others); *Good Wives: Image and Reality in the Lives of Women in Northern New England, 1650-1750*, 1982; *A Midwife's Tale: The Life of Martha Ballard, Based on Her Diary, 1785-1812*, 1990; *The Significance of Trivia*, 1992; *The Age of Homespun: Objects and Stories in the Creation of an American Myth*, 2001.

MISCELLANEOUS: *All God's Critters Got a Place in the Choir*, 1995 (with Emma Lou Thayne).

Laurel Thatcher Ulrich compares her career as a scholar and writer to a patchwork quilt. Her success has not resulted from any kind of deliberate plan, and she was forced to work with the materials that were at hand, but her life shows a definite pattern. She was born Laurel Thatcher in Sugar City, Idaho, a predominantly Mormon town; her family, the Thatchers, figured prominently in the community and had been among the original group of Mormon pioneers to settle the area. In her essay "Family Scriptures," in *Dialogue* 20 (1987), she describes her Grandfather Thatcher as a "book of remembrance," a source of stories and information about her family and her community. For her, his stories constituted "family scriptures," in that they were sacred to her and to her family. She writes, "Scriptures clarify by sifting out eternal principles from the grainy confusion of ordinary life." Her later work as a historian shows this same concern for the patterns that emerge from the "trivia" of ordinary life.

Laurel Ulrich attended the University of Utah, where she studied English and excelled in debate, winning the western regional championship. She also met and married Gael Dennis Ulrich. As she and her husband pursued their academic careers, hers was interrupted by the birth of five children. She writes in her essay "Patchwork," from *All God's Critters Got a Place in the Choir*, that her career developed in a rather roundabout manner. In the 1970's she found herself a "faculty wife" at the University of New Hampshire with an M.A. in English. She entered the Ph.D. program at New Hampshire in history and progressed from graduate student to part-time instructor to tenured professor. In 1995 she became James Duncan Phillips Professor of Early American History and director of the Charles Warren Center of Studies in American History at Harvard University. Her multiple roles as mother, wife, scholar, and dedicated Mormon made her progress slow, but her multiple roles also prepared her to enter into fields of scholarship that few others had previously considered or valued.

Ulrich's work shows a concern for the importance of commonplace experience. Her first published work was *A Beginner's Boston*, a book that claims to be the first guidebook to Boston. Although many writers contributed to the book, the preface acknowledges Laurel Ulrich as the "driving force" behind the project. The book itself is not as extraordinary as the manner in which it was written. *A Beginner's Boston* began as a fund-raiser for the Relief Society of the Cambridge Ward, an "educational and charitable organization for Mormon women" for the local congregation of the Church of Jesus Christ of Latter-day Saints (Mormons). The book resulted from the volunteer labor of a number of women and represents the kind of collaborative work by women that Ulrich examines among New England women during the colonial period in her two historical works, *Good Wives* and *A Midwife's Tale*.

In *Good Wives* Ulrich contests common scholarly views on the lives of colonial women. She reconstructs the patterns of women's lives from court records, probate inventories, diaries, and other documents to show that women during the period 1650 to 1750 participated in many more social roles than scholars had previously thought: housewife, deputy husband, consort, mother, mistress, neighbor, Christian, and heroine. To describe these roles, Ulrich uses three archetypal women from the Old Testament: Bathsheba, Eve, and Jael. Bathsheba represents the economic role of women, Eve represents sex and reproduction, and Jael relates to "the intersection between religion and aggression."

Ulrich is probably best known for *A Midwife's Tale*. This work is based on the diary of Martha Moore Ballard, a colonial midwife and mother of nine from Hallowell, Maine. The diary covers twenty-seven years of Ballard's career. Although previous historians had known of the diary, they dismissed it as "trivial" because it appeared to be a mere chronicle of the everyday tasks performed by colonial women. With her belief that nothing in the lives of women is trivial, Ulrich turned her attention to the diary and discovered the patterns reflected in the ordinary chores of women. She indicates how the activities recorded in Martha Ballard's diary reveal important economic, social, and medical practices of the time.

Although Laurel Ulrich decided early in her career as a historian not to study Mormon history, she turned her remarkable critical skills to her own experience. For more than twenty years, Ulrich contributed essays to *Exponent II*, a Boston-based quarterly newspaper inspired by the nineteenth century Mormon women's magazine *Woman's Exponent* (1872-1914). Many of these essays are collected in *All God's Critters Got a Place in the Choir*, written with the Mormon poet-essayist Emma Lou Thayne. As in her historical work, Ulrich examines the patterns that emerge in the everyday activities of Mormon women, in her own life and the lives of those around her. In "Seeing Without Seeing" she describes her memories of seeing Helen Keller at Salt Lake City's Tabernacle. In "Improve the Shining Moments" she takes her inspiration from a popular Mormon hymn and talks about the importance of learning from the commonplace and ordinary. She describes her own experience learning to "read" cloth and realizing the tremendous number of patterns that can be constructed from "white" cloth. In "Ode to Autumn" Ulrich discusses her dual role as mother and scholar, and in "Border Crossings" she describes her often uncomfortable position as a "Mormon feminist." (She had originally entitled this essay "Confessions of an OxyMormon.") In *The Age of Homespun*, Ulrich used a set of seventeenth to nineteenth century handmade household objects as starting points for discussions of the realities of everyday life for the makers and owners of those objects. Laurel Thatcher Ulrich has won numerous awards and fellowships for her work, including the Pulitzer Prize and Bancroft Prize for history.

Gary Layne Hatch

Bibliography

Donath, J. R. Review of *The Age of Homespun*, by Laurel Thatcher Ulrich. In *Magill's Literary Annual 2002*. Pasadena, Calif.: Salem Press, 2002. Notes that the book "is not a work of revisionist history" and that "Ulrich offers readers a chance to reexamine and reconnect with the experiences and values of people who produced, used, and saved some wonderfully meaningful objects."

Dunn, Mary Maples, Patricia Cline Cohen, Marla R Miller, and Laurel Thatcher Ulrich. "Dialogue: Paradigm Shift Books—*A Midwife's Tale* by Laurel Thatcher Ulrich." *Journal of Women's History* 14, no. 3 (Autumn, 2002): 133-161. A discussion of the impact of *A Midwife's Tale* by a panel that includes Ulrich herself.

Taylor, Alan. "Threads of History." *The New Republic* 226, nos. 8/9 (March 4, 2002): 38-41. In this extensive review of *The Age of Homespun*, Taylor also examines Ulrich's career as a historian.

Ulrich, Laurel Thatcher. "Document: Martha's Diary and Mine." *Journal of Women's History* 4 (Fall, 1992): 157-160. Ulrich's acceptance speech for the Bancroft Prize offers insights on how she was able to interpret and squeeze the most historical meaning out of Ballard's diary.

_______. "A Pail of Cream." *The Journal of American History* 89, no. 1 (June, 2002): 43-47. Ulrich describes how feminism and history helped her examine her rural childhood.

Miguel de Unamuno y Jugo

Spanish novelist, playwright, poet, and philosopher

Born: Bilbao, Spain; September 29, 1864
Died: Salamanca, Spain; December 31, 1936

LONG FICTION: *Paz en la guerra*, 1897 (*Peace in War*, 1983); *Amor y pedagogía*, 1902; *Niebla*, 1914 (*Mist: A Tragicomic Novel*, 1928); *Abel Sánchez: Una historia de pasión*, 1917 (*Abel Sánchez*, 1947); *Tres novelas ejemplares y un prólogo*, 1920 (*Three Exemplary Novels and a Prologue*, 1930); *La tía Tula*, 1921 (*Tía Tula*, 1976); *San Manuel Bueno, mártir*, 1931 (*Saint Manuel Bueno, Martyr*, 1956); *Dos novelas cortas*, 1961 (James Russell Stamm and Herbert Eugene Isar, editors).

SHORT FICTION: *El espejo de la muerte*, 1913; *Soledad y otros cuentos*, 1937; *Abel Sánchez, and Other Stories*, 1956.

DRAMA: *La esfinge*, wr. 1898, pr. 1909; *La venda*, wr. 1899, pb. 1913; *La difunta*, pr. 1910; *El pasado que vuelve*, wr. 1910, pr. 1923; *Fedra*, wr. 1910, pr. 1918 (*Phaedra*, 1959); *La princesa doña Lambra*, pb. 1913; *Soledad*, wr. 1921, pr. 1953; *Raquel encadenada*, wr. 1921, pr. 1926; *El otro*, wr. 1926, pr., pb. 1932 (*The Other*, 1947); *Sombras de sueño*, pb. 1930; *El hermano Juan: O, El mundo es teatro*, wr. 1927, pb. 1934; *Teatro completo*, pb. 1959, 1973.

POETRY: *Poesías*, 1907; *Rosario de sonetos líricos*, 1911; *El Cristo de Velázquez*, 1920 (*The Christ of Velázquez*, 1951); *Rimas de dentro*, 1923; *Teresa*, 1924; *Romancero del destierro*, 1928; *Poems*, 1952; *Cancionero: Diario poético*, 1953 (partial translation as *The Last Poems of Miguel de Unamuno*, 1974.

NONFICTION: *De la enseñanza superior en España*, 1899; *Nicodemo el fariseo*, 1899; *Tres ensayos*, 1900; *En torno al casticismo*, 1902; *De mi país*, 1903; *Vida de Don Quijote y Sancho, según Miguel de Cervantes Saavedra, explicada y comentada por Miguel de Unamuno*,

1905 (*The Life of Don Quixote and Sancho According to Miguel de Cervantes Saavedra Expounded with Comment by Miguel de Unamuno*, 1927); *Recuerdos de niñez y de mocedad*, 1908; *Mi religión y otros ensayos breves*, 1910; *Soliloquios y conversaciones*, 1911 (*Essays and Soliloquies*, 1925); *Contra esto y aquello*, 1912; *Del sentimiento trágico de la vida en los hombres y en los pueblos*, 1913 (*The Tragic Sense of Life in Men and Peoples*, 1921); *L'Agonie du Christianisme*, 1925 (in French; in Spanish as *La agonía del Cristianismo*, 1931; *The Agony of Christianity*, 1928, 1960); *Cómo se hace una novela*, 1927 (*How to Make a Novel*, 1976); *La ciudad de Henoc*, 1941; *Cuenca ibérica*, 1943; *Paisajes del alma*, 1944; *La enormidad de España*, 1945; *Visiones y commentarios*, 1949.
MISCELLANEOUS: *Obras completas*, 1959-1964 (16 volumes).

Miguel de Unamuno y Jugo (ew-nah-MEW-noh ee HEW-goh) is one of the most significant and controversial figures in the history of modern thought. He was known primarily as an essayist at the beginning of his career, but later criticism has focused on his renovation of the novel and on his poetry. Although he has become inseparably associated with the area of Castile, especially Salamanca, Unamuno was a Basque, born in Bilbao on September 29, 1864. His father, a baker, who died when Unamuno was only six years old, had settled in that city upon his return from Mexico, where he had hoped to win fame and fortune. In his first novel, *Peace in War*, Unamuno admittedly describes himself in his portrayal of the young orphan, Pachico, some of whose most vivid memories were of the 1874 Carlist siege and bombardment of Bilbao.

A philologist by training, Unamuno in 1891 accepted the post of professor of Greek and Romance philology at the University of Salamanca. Except for his years in exile, Unamuno would never leave the university, which he considered one of the two safe and stable components of his life. The other was his marriage to Concepción (Concha) Lizárraga, which lasted for forty-three years; the couple had nine children.

Unamuno was one of the leaders of the famous literary group known as the "generation of '98." Using Spain's defeat in the Spanish-American War as a rallying point, writers such as Antonio Machado, Pío Baroja, José Martinez Ruiz, and Unamuno tried to analyze the reasons underlying Spain's decline and provide a philosophical framework for its regeneration in the twentieth century. In *En torno al casticismo* (on authenticity) Unamuno first developed his theory of "intrahistory," the cultural, unchanging base of a people, its authentic identity as compared with the trivial facts and figures of recorded "history."

Spain as a theme dominates Unamuno's early essays and poetry, but in 1904, the prolonged illness and death of his son Raimundo provoked a spiritual crisis that was to influence profoundly all Unamuno's life and later work. Long branded as a political troublemaker, Unamuno now became known as a religious heretic as his inner doubts and fears became the obsession of his public writings. *The Tragic Sense of Life in Men and Peoples*, praised as one of the masterworks of twentieth century thought, is Unamuno's manifesto of a philosophy of struggle in a world where humankind's longing for meaning and faith clashes with cold rationality and science. This preoccupation with the metaphysical dilemmas of the twentieth century has led to Unamuno's inclusion as a precursor of existentialism.

In his search for an effective vehicle in which to describe the essence of humankind, Unamuno turned to the narrative and the stage. Novels such as *Abel Sánchez* and *Mist*, which in its famous confrontation scene between character and creator anticipated Luigi Pirandello's play *Sei personaggi in cerca d'autore* (pr., pb. 1921; *Six Characters in Search of an Author*, 1922), not only solidified Unamuno's place in vanguard literary circles but also earned for him a steadily growing reading public. Therefore, his deportation from Spain in 1924, motivated by his strident criticism of the dictatorship of Miguel Primo de Rivero, caused an immediate outcry in the international literary and diplomatic community. His return in 1930, after more than five years in exile, was a personal triumph. He was reappointed rector of Salamanca and elected as deputy to the Cortes, the Spanish parliament. In 1934 he was named lifetime rector of the University of Salamanca but suffered the double blow of the death of his wife and one of his children. Critical of the indecisiveness of the Republic, at first he had supported General Francisco Franco, but he soon became one of the general's most outspoken critics. Dismissed from his post, Unamuno died, during virtual house arrest by the angered Franco, on December 31, 1936.

Unamuno's plays consist of philosophy set into dialogue. A reading of them is better than their performance. His best-known drama, *The Other*, with identical twins as protagonists, reveals his complete rejection of any final answer even in a work of fiction. One brother kills the other and, driven to suicide by remorse, takes to the grave the secret of his own identity and that of his victim. Unamuno believed that humankind was adrift in a sea of contradictions and that in order to arrive at the vital core, it was necessary to strip away all the layers of pseudocivilization and intellectualism. The constant conflicts between death and immortality, reason and faith, science and life, and reality and illusion torment Unamuno's man of flesh and blood (*carne y hueso*). Such dualities can never be resolved, and Unamuno's work, therefore, is a study in unanswered questions and contradiction. Labeled a heretic, he yet could write one of the finest religious poems in the Spanish language, *The Christ of Velázquez*, a series of meditations on aspects of the famous painting of the crucified Christ. Frustrated at his country's apparent inertia and subjugation to the past, in 1898 Unamuno exclaimed that Don Quixote must die so that Spain, rid of madness, could be set free to face the future, but, almost immediately, he completely reversed his opinion and eulogized the knight as the authentic living symbol of Spain's past, present, and future. In *Saint Manuel Bueno, Martyr*, the philosopher who scorned unquestioning acceptance presents a hero-priest who, himself unable to believe, strives to preserve the innocent faith of his people.

Unamuno's place as one of the dominant thinkers of twentieth century literature and philosophy has never seriously been challenged, though there has been harsh criticism of the quality of his fiction and his poetry and of the relevance of his philosophic writings. Intense and relentless, Unamuno himself was never objective, and the same can be said of much of the early evaluation of his work. Critics, many of them supporters of Unamuno's contemporary José Ortega y Gasset, charged that Unamuno was devoted only to a cult of his own personality and that what had the appearance of learned commentary was, in reality, anarchic indulgence. Criticism also was divided along lines of political affiliation. Called a "bad son of Spain" by those who resented his constant attacks, after his death he became a symbol of resistance to the Franco dictatorship. Detractors also derided the harshness and lack of musicality of his verse and ridiculed its drumming cadence, devoid of any pretense of polish.

However, Unamuno believed that he would be remembered primarily as a poet, and late twentieth century criticism has indeed affirmed the value of his verse. His sonnets, above all, have come to be regarded as examples of the finest in all Hispanic poetry. A growing awareness of Unamuno's role in the development of existentialism has encouraged a revival of interest in his novels and essays, and his reputation has been enhanced by the number of major writers, such as James Baldwin and Jorge Luis Borges, who have confessed their debt to him. It must be admitted, however, that alongside the positive reevaluation, there still exists vehement criticism. This debate would have pleased Unamuno, who wrote to provoke and incite and who abhorred indifference.

Charlene E. Suscavage

Bibliography

Ch'oe, Chae-Sok. *Greene and Unamuno: Two Pilgrims to La Mancha*. New York: Peter Lang, 1990. This comparison of the Christian fiction of Unamuno and Graham Greene sheds light on the religious themes employed by Unamuno in his dramatic works. Includes bibliography and index.

Ellis, Robert Richmond. *The Tragic Pursuit of Being: Unamuno and Sartre*. Tuscaloosa: University of Alabama Press, 1988. This work compares and contrasts the existentialism revealed in the works of Unamuno and Jean-Paul Sartre. Includes bibliography and index.

Hansen, Keith W. *Tragic Lucidity: Discourse of Recuperation in Unamuno and Camus*. New York: Peter Lang, 1993. A comparison of the political and social views of Unamuno and Albert Camus, as evidenced in their literary works. Includes bibliography.

Nozick, Martin. *Miguel de Unamuno*. New York: Twayne, 1971. A basic biography of Unamuno that covers his life and works. Includes bibliography.

Round, Nicholas G., ed. *Re-reading Unamuno*. Glasgow, Scotland: University of Glasgow Department of Hispanic Studies, 1989. This collection of papers from a conference on Unamuno provides literary criticism of his works. Includes bibliographies.

Sinclair, Alison. *Uncovering the Mind: Unamuno, the Unknown, and the Vicissitudes of Self*. New York: Manchester University Press, 2002. An examination of the fictional works of Unamuno in respect to his portrayal of the self. Includes bibliography and index.

Wyers, Frances. *Miguel de Unamuno, the Contrary Self*. London: Tamesis, 1976. A look at the image of self in the literary works of Unamuno. Includes bibliography.

Sigrid Undset

Norwegian novelist

Born: Kalundborg, Denmark; May 20, 1882
Died: Lillehammer, Norway; June 10, 1949

LONG FICTION: *Fru Marta Oulie*, 1907; *Fortaellingen om Viga-Ljot og Vigdis*, 1909 (*Gunnar's Daughter*, 1936); *Jenny*, 1911 (English translation, 1921); *Varen*, 1914; *Kransen*, 1920 (*The Bridal Wreath*, 1923); *Husfrue*, 1921 (*The Mistress of Husaby*, 1925); *Korset*, 1922 (*The Cross*, 1927; previous 3 novels collectively known as *Kristin Lavransdatter*, 1929); *Olav Audunssøn i Hestviken* and *Olav Audunssøn og hans børn*, 1925-1927 (*The Master of Hestviken*, 1928-1930, 1934; includes *The Axe*, 1928, *The Snake Pit*, 1929, *In the Wilderness*, 1929, and *The Son Avenger*, 1930); *Gymnadenia*, 1929 (*The Wild Orchid*, 1931); *Den brændende busk*, 1930 (*The Burning Bush*, 1932); *Ida Elisabeth*, 1932 (*Ida Elizabeth*, 1933); *Den trofaste husfru*, 1933 (*The Faithful Wife*, 1937); *Madame Dorthea*, 1939 (English translation, 1940); *Sigurd og hans tapre venner*, 1955 (pb. in German as *Die Saga von Vilmund Vidutan und seiner Gefährten*, 1931; *Sigurd and His Brave Companions*, 1943).

SHORT FICTION: *Den lykkelige alder*, 1909; *Fattige skjæbner*, 1912; *Splinten av troldspeilet*, 1917 (includes "Fru Hjelde" [*Images in a Mirror*, 1938]); *De kloge jomfruer*, 1918; *Four Stories*, 1969.

DRAMA: *I graalysningen*, wr. 1908 (one act).

POETRY: *Ungdom*, 1910.

NONFICTION: *Et kvindesynspunkt*, 1919; *Kimer i klokker*, 1924; *Katolsk propaganda*, 1927; *Etapper I and II*, 1929, 1933 (*Stages on the Road*, 1934); *Begegnungen und Trennungen: Essays über Christentum und Germanentum*, 1931; *Elleve år*, 1934 (*The Longest Years*, 1935); *De søkte de gamle stier*, 1936; *Norske helgener*, 1937 (*Saga of Saints*, 1934); *Selvportretter og landskapsbilleder*, 1938 (*Men, Women, and Places*, 1939); *Tillbake til fremitiden*, 1942 (*Return to the Future*, 1942); *Lykkelige dager*, 1947 (*Happy Times in Norway*, 1942); *Caterina av Siena*, 1951 (*Catherine of Siena*, 1954); *Artikler og taler fra krigstiden*, 1953; *Sigrid Undset on Saints and Sinners*, 1993 (Deal W. Hudson, editor).

MISCELLANEOUS: *The Unknown Sigrid Undset: Jenny, and Other Works*, 2001 (novel, short fiction, and letters).

Sigrid Undset (UHN-seht) was the daughter of Ingvald Martin Undset, a distinguished Norwegian archaeologist, and Anna Charlotte Gyth from the Danish town of Kalundborg. As a child, Sigrid lived with her mother's family while her father conducted research in Mediterranean countries. When he became a lecturer at the University of Norway, the family moved to Christiania (now Oslo), where two additional daughters were born. Undset was deeply influenced by her father's work and applied his scientific rigor to an exploration of medieval culture in Norway. She was educated at a private academy under the direction of the considerate Fru Ragna Nielsen, who permitted Sigrid and her sisters to remain at the school after their father died and financial resources were limited. Despite the expectations of her mother and instructors, Undset had little interest in a university education; she preferred a career as a painter. She enrolled in a business school, however, in order to help support her family.

For ten years, Undset held a clerical position, which, although monotonous, gave her considerable insight into working-class women and their family and social relationships, material that she began to use for short stories and her first novel. During these years as an office worker, her study of Scandinavian folklore became more intense, and she wrote a novel based on Norse legends. However, it was not until the publication of *Jenny* in 1911 that Undset received widespread recognition as a compelling novelist. The success of this novel allowed her to commit herself to a writer's career.

In 1912 she married A. C. Svarstad, a Norwegian painter with three children from a previous marriage. Undset and Svarstad had three children together, but after ten years together they agreed to a separation as Undset became more and more imbued with Roman Catholicism. She was convinced that the only true visionaries of history were the Christian saints. Because her husband had married her while divorced, Undset's marriage was annulled by the Roman Catholic Church, which she joined as a convert from Lutheranism in 1924.

During the following decade, Undset's greatest books were published. *The Bridal Wreath*, *The Mistress of Husaby*, and *The Cross* became the famous trilogy *Kristin Lavransdatter*, issued as a single volume in 1929. This signature work is often considered a timeless masterpiece, and it has been translated into several languages. In 1928 Undset received the Nobel Prize in Literature. The Swedish Academy recognized her intimate knowledge of medieval laws, culture, and history, majestically portrayed as a powerful continuity of life; they also noted her ability to weigh the civilizations of the past against those of the present, especially with regard to human fortitude and spirituality. Undset's other magnum opus is *The Master of Hestviken*, a tetralogy set in the Middle Ages. This collection comprises *The Axe*, *The Snake Pit*, *In the Wilderness*, and *The Son Avenger.*

Undset remained a prolific writer throughout the 1930's; numerous short stories, essays, memoirs, historical studies, and contemporary novels were published with regularity until the outbreak of World War II. Chief among these are *Saga of Saints* and *Men, Women, and Places*. Much of her later writing reinforces her deep and abiding attachment to Roman Catholicism. Because she was a strong advocate of religious and racial tolerance, the German Nazi propaganda criticized her ideas. Nevertheless, she remained in Norway and volunteered as a government censor until her oldest son was killed during the defense of Norway during the German invasion. She escaped through Sweden with her younger son (her daughter had died a few years before) and made her way to the United States, where she lived through the war years, giving occasional lectures.

Upon her return to Norway, King Haakon VII bestowed upon her the Grand Cross of the Order of Saint Olav, making her the first woman commoner to receive such an honor. In her final years, Undset lived quietly at Lillehammer in a house dating back to Viking times until she died after suffering a paralytic stroke. She collected old lace and other Norse antiques and spent much of her time contemplating those aspects of Norwegian history that amplify the preoccupations and revelations of womanhood.

Robert J. Frail

Bibliography

Bayerschmidt, Carl F. *Sigrid Undset*. New York: Twayne, 1970. An introductory study, with chapters on Undset's life, early works, social novels, middle age, and later novels. Includes notes and bibliography.

Beyer, Harald. *A History of Norwegian Literature*. Edited and translated by Einar Haugen. New York: New York University Press, 1956. Includes an essay on Undset's place in the history of Norwegian realism.

Brunsdale, Mitzi. *Sigrid Undset: Chronicler of Norway*. New York: Berg, 1988. Provides a useful introduction to Norwegian culture and literature, a short biography of Undset, analysis of her early novels and later masterpieces, and a final chapter assessing her achievement. With chronology, notes, and a bibliographical essay.

Hudson, Deal W., ed. *Sigrid Undset on Saints and Sinners—New Translations and Studies: Papers Presented at a Conference Sponsored by the Wethersfield Institute, New York City, April 24, 1993*. San Francisco: Ignatius Press, 1993. Contains essays titled "A Life of Sigrid Undset," "Sigrid Undset: Holiness and Culture," and "In the Blood: The Transmission of Sin in *The Master of Hestviken*."

Lytle, Andrew. *Kristin: A Reading*. Columbia: University of Missouri Press, 1992. Lytle's reading aims to recover an appreciation for what he deems a neglected twentieth century classic.

Lytle, a novelist and critic, provides an especially sensitive, indeed a model, reading of a complex literary work.

Solbakken, Elisabeth. *Redefining Integrity: The Portrayal of Women in the Contemporary Novels of Sigrid Undset*. New York: Peter Lang, 1992. Examines Undset's feminism and treatment of woman characters in the long fiction.

Undset, Sigrid. *The Unknown Sigrid Undset: Jenny, and Other Works*. Translated by Tiina Nunnally, edited by Tim Page. South Royalton, Vt.: Steerforth Press, 2001. A translation of the long-out-of-print *Jenny* and two other short stories, plus some letters by Undset. Includes a valuable introduction.

Giuseppe Ungaretti

Italian poet

Born: Alexandria, Egypt; February 8, 1888
Died: Milan, Italy; June 1, 1970

POETRY: *Il porto sepolto*, 1916; *Allegria di naufragi*, 1919; *La Guerre*, 1919; *L'allegria*, 1931, 1942 (includes revisions of *Il porto sepolto* and *Allegria di naufragi*); *Sentimento del tempo*, 1933; *Il dolore*, 1947; *La terra promessa*, 1950; *Gridasti, soffoco . . .* , 1951; *Un grido e paesaggi*, 1952; *Life of a Man*, 1958; *Il taccuino del vecchio*, 1960; *Morte delle stagioni*, 1967; *Dialogo*, 1968; *Giuseppe Ungaretti: Selected Poems*, 1969; *Vita d'un uomo: Tutte le poesie*, 1969; *Selected Poems of Giuseppe Ungaretti*, 1975; *The Buried Harbour: Selected Poems of Giuseppe Ungaretti*, 1990 (Kevin Hart, translator and editor); *The Major Selection of the Poetry of Giuseppe Ungaretti*, 1997.

TRANSLATIONS: *Traduzioni*, 1936 (various poems and authors); *Venti-due sonetti de Shakespeare: Scelti e tradotti da Giuseppe Ungaretti*, 1944; *Vita d'un uomo: Quaranta sonetti di Shakespeare tradotti*, 1946; *L'Après-midi et le monologue d'un faune di Mallarmé*, 1947; *Vita d'un uomo: Da Góngora e da Mallarmé*, 1948; *Vita d'un uomo: "Fedra" di Jean Racine*, 1950; *Finestra del caos*, 1961 (of Murilo Mendes); *Vita d'un uomo: "Visioni" di William Blake*, 1965.

NONFICTION: *Il povero nella città*, 1949; *Il deserto e dopo*, 1961; *Innocence et memoire*, 1969; *Lettere a un fenomenologo*, 1972; *Vita d'un uomo: Saggi e interventi*, 1974.

Giuseppe Ungaretti (ewng-gah-REHT-tee) was born in Alexandria, Egypt, and spent his first twenty-four years there. In 1912 he moved to Paris, where, while attending the Sorbonne, he met many gifted artists, including the poets Paul Valéry and Guillaume Apollinaire and the painters Pablo Picasso and Georges Braque. Ungaretti joined the Italian army when World War I broke out, and during the war he continued to write and to develop his skill as a poet. Like many writers of his generation, Ungaretti was strongly influenced by various aspects of modernism, with its rejection of many traditional views of the nature and function of art.

According to the modernist perspective, advances in physical science had proved traditional views of religion, ethics, and the human psyche to be superstitious nonsense, and, consequently, such views were regarded as reactionary and irrelevant. One seemingly insoluble implication of this new worldview was that it left the individual isolated in a universe whose only reality was that of physics and chemistry, and, despite the many conveniences afforded by new technology, few found great comfort in that version of reality. The destruction wrought in Europe by new technology and old politics during World War I certainly forced writers and other artists to recognize that the new era had brought its own horrors. Like the American novelist Ernest Hemingway, Ungaretti saw the war as a manifestation of the social and psychological fragmentation of the modern world. Confronted by a chaotic universe, Ungaretti sought to create an artistic harmony in his poetry, even when the poetry itself spoke of chaos.

At the time of Ungaretti's arrival in Paris in 1912, the city had long been a center of artistic experimentation, especially in poetry. From the work of Gérard de Nerval through that of Charles Baudelaire and Arthur Rimbaud to the work of such Symbolist poets as Stéphane Mallarmé, nineteenth century Paris had produced a remarkable variety of brilliant experiments in poetic form and content. Ungaretti's friends Apollinaire and Valéry were interested in developing a poetry appropriate to contemporary civilization, and Ungaretti's early poetry reveals his own determination to break with tradition. He avoided rhyme and punctuation, and his poems were often obscure. Although Ungaretti eventually adopted a somewhat more traditional poetic form, critics continued to accuse him of excessive obscurity.

In 1936 the literary critic Francesco Flora called Ungaretti's poetry "hermetic," implying that any meaning contained in the poems was completely sealed within the poems and consequently remained inaccessible to the reader. As a consequence, Ungaretti came to be designated as a proponent of "Hermeticism," and the poets Salvatore Quasimodo and Eugenio Montale, both influenced by Ungaretti, were regarded as his fellow Hermeticists. It is possible that some of the obscurity of Hermeticist poetry resulted from the threat of retribution from Fascist censors during this time, but it is clear that for Ungaretti the very difficulty of producing poetic art inevitably entailed a corresponding aesthetic demand upon the reader.

In 1936 Ungaretti moved to Brazil, where he spent six years as a university professor. The poetry he produced after arriving in São Paulo displays a greater clarity than much of the earlier work, possibly because personal grief overwhelmed him during this period. Devastated by the death of his young son, Ungaretti tried to express his emotions in his art. In 1942 he returned to Italy, where he taught at the University of Rome until 1957. During this phase of his academic career he continued to publish collections of poetry, along with various translations from French, English (including Shakespeare), and Spanish literature.

Ungaretti died in 1970. His career resembles those of several of his contemporaries in some respects, particularly in the modernist themes and techniques that preoccupied his generation, but he is also a unique figure. An Italian born and raised in Egypt, educated among the gifted avant-garde artists of Paris, Ungaretti lived a life in which he moved from rejection of the arbitrariness of convention to an understanding that poetic form is itself essential. Like the Irish poet William Butler Yeats, Ungaretti continually sought to ground himself in a larger reality, and, as did Yeats, he found in his artistic maturity a calm authority and dignity of expression. Wherever he lived, this poet remained attuned to the highest possibilities of his art. Having lived on three continents and through two world wars, and having spent thirty years of his long life outside the circles of European culture, Giuseppe Ungaretti survived the merely clever and consequently short-lived fashions of modernism to establish himself as a major figure among the European poets of the twentieth century.

Robert W. Haynes

Bibliography

Godorecci, Maurizio. "The Poetics of the Word in Ungaretti." *Romance Languages Annual* 9 (1997): 197-201. A critical analysis of selected poems by Ungaretti.

Jones, Frederic J. *Giuseppe Ungaretti: Poet and Critic*. Edinburgh: Edinburgh University Press, 1977. An assessment of Ungaretti's life and career. Includes bibliographic references.

Moevs, Christian. "Ungaretti: A Reading of 'Alla noia.'" *Forum Italicum* 25, no. 2 (Fall, 1991): 211-227. A critical study of one of Ungaretti's poems.

O'Connor, Desmond. "The Poetry of a Patriot: Ungaretti and the First World War." *Journal of the Australasian Universities Language and Literature Association* 56 (November, 1981): 201-218. An analysis of Ungaretti's poetic treatment of World War I.

Samson-Talleur, Linda. "Ungaretti, Leopardi, and the Shipwreck of the Soul." *Chimeres* 16, no. 1 (Autumn, 1982): 5-19. A comparative study of the works of two poets.

John Updike

American novelist, short-story writer, and poet

Born: Shillington, Pennsylvania; March 18, 1932

LONG FICTION: *The Poorhouse Fair*, 1959; *Rabbit, Run*, 1960; *The Centaur*, 1963; *Of the Farm*, 1965; *Couples*, 1968; *Bech: A Book*, 1970; *Rabbit Redux*, 1971; *A Month of Sundays*, 1975; *Marry Me: A Romance*, 1976; *The Coup*, 1978; *Rabbit Is Rich*, 1981; *The Witches of Eastwick*, 1984; *Roger's Version*, 1986; *S.*, 1988; *Rabbit at Rest*, 1990; *Memories of the Ford Administration*, 1992; *Brazil*, 1994; *In the Beauty of the Lilies*, 1996; *Toward the End of Time*, 1997; *Bech at Bay: A Quasi-Novel*, 1998; *Gertrude and Claudius*, 2000.

SHORT FICTION: *The Same Door*, 1959; *Pigeon Feathers, and Other Stories*, 1962; *Olinger Stories: A Selection*, 1964; *The Music School*, 1966; *Museums and Women, and Other Stories*, 1972; *Problems, and Other Stories*, 1979; *Three Illuminations in the Life of an American Author*, 1979; *Too Far to Go: The Maples Stories*, 1979; *The Chaste Planet*, 1980; *Bech Is Back*, 1982; *The Beloved*, 1982; *Trust Me*, 1987; *Brother Grasshopper*, 1990 (limited edition); *The Afterlife, and Other Stories*, 1994; *Licks of Love: Short Stories and a Sequel, "Rabbit Remembered,"* 2000; *The Complete Henry Bech: Twenty Stories*, 2001.

DRAMA: *Three Texts from Early Ipswich: A Pageant*, pb. 1968; *Buchanan Dying*, pb. 1974.

POETRY: *The Carpentered Hen, and Other Tame Creatures*, 1958; *Telephone Poles, and Other Poems*, 1963; *Dog's Death*, 1965; *Verse*, 1965; *The Angels*, 1968; *Bath After Sailing*, 1968; *Midpoint, and Other Poems*, 1969; *Seventy Poems*, 1972; *Six Poems*, 1973; *Cunts (Upon Receiving the Swingers Life Club Membership Solicitation)*, 1974; *Query*, 1974; *Tossing and Turning*, 1977; *Sixteen Sonnets*, 1979; *Five Poems*, 1980; *Jester's Dozen*, 1984; *Facing Nature*, 1985; *Mites, and Other Poems in Miniature*, 1990; *A Beautiful Alphabet of Friendly Objects*, 1995; *Americana, and Other Poems*, 2001.

NONFICTION: *Assorted Prose*, 1965; *Picked-Up Pieces*, 1975; *Hugging the Shore: Essays and Criticism*, 1983; *Just Looking: Essays on Art*, 1989; *Self-Consciousness: Memoirs*, 1989; *Odd Jobs: Essays and Criticism*, 1991; *Golf Dreams: Writings on Golf*, 1996; *More Matter: Essays and Criticism*, 1999.

EDITED TEXT: *The Best American Short Stories of the Century*, 2000.

John Hoyer Updike is widely acclaimed as one of the most accomplished stylists and prolific writers of his generation; his fiction represents a penetrating chronicle of the changing morals and manners of American society. He was born in Shillington, Pennsylvania, on March 18, 1932, the only child of Wesley and Linda Grace Hoyer Updike. His father was a mathematics teacher at the high school and supported the family in lean times, first in the old parental home in Shillington, and later on a farm in Plowville, ten miles outside Shillington. A number of short stories, such as "Flight," and the novels *The Centaur* and *Of the Farm* draw upon this experience. After attending schools in Shillington, Updike went to Harvard University in 1950 on a full scholarship, majoring in English. He was editor of the Harvard *Lampoon* and graduated in 1954 with highest honors. In 1953 he married Radcliffe student Mary Pennington, the daughter of a Unitarian minister; they were to have four children.

In 1954 Updike sold the first of many stories to *The New Yorker.* After a year in Oxford, England, where Updike studied at the Ruskin School of Drawing and Fine Art, he returned to the United States to a job as a staff writer with *The New Yorker,* for which he wrote the "Talk of the Town" column. In April of 1957, fearing the city scene would inhibit his writing. Updike and his family left New York for Ipswich, Massachusetts. He continued to sell stories to *The New Yorker* while working on longer fiction. His first book was a collection of verse, *The Carpentered Hen, and Other Tame Creatures*, published in 1958. The next year he published his first novel, *The Poorhouse Fair,* set in a retirement home. The novel received favorable reviews and won the Rosenthal Award. His first collection of short stories, *The Same Door,* also appeared in 1959. During this time Updike was active in Ipswich community life and attended the Congregational church—a setting depicted in a number of works. In 1974 the Updikes were divorced. In 1977 Updike remarried to Martha Bernhard.

During this same period—the late 1950's and early 1960's—Updike faced a crisis of faith prompted by his consciousness of death's inevitability. The works of such writers as Søren Kierkegaard and, especially, Karl Barth, the Swiss neoorthodox theologian, helped Updike come to grips with this fear and to find a basis for faith. Many of Updike's works explore theological and religious issues. In a real sense, Updike has become a kind of late twentieth century Nathaniel Hawthorne; his works, like Hawthorne's, are saturated with religious and theological concerns. In fact, three of his novels, *A Month of Sundays*, *Roger's Version*, and *S.*, form an updated version of Hawthorne's *The Scarlet Letter* (1850).

Updike's work published during the 1960's established him as one of America's important serious writers. In 1960 he published *Rabbit, Run*, the first in a series of novels about a middle-class man and his family set in a small city in Pennsylvania. He returned to this character at intervals of a decade with *Rabbit Redux*, *Rabbit Is Rich* (which won the Pulitzer Prize in fiction in 1981), *Rabbit at Rest*, and the novella *Rabbit Remembered*. Each of these novels deals seriously with a man interacting with his changing culture, adapting but not fully capitulating to it, seeking always for something certain, if not transcendent. In 1962 Updike's second story collection, *Pigeon Feathers, and Other Stories*, appeared, and in 1963, another collection of verse, *Telephone Poles, and Other Poems*, was published. His novel *The Centaur,* also published in 1963, earned for Updike the National Book Award and election to the National Institute of Arts and Letters, making Updike the youngest writer ever to be so elected. In 1966 the collection of stories *The Music School* appeared.

In 1964-1965 Updike traveled to Eastern Europe as part of a cultural exchange program. A number of works reflect that experience, in particular his collection *Bech*. In 1973 Updike traveled, under State Department auspices, to Africa; his novel *The Coup* reflects that journey. With three collections of essays and reviews—*Assorted Prose*, *Picked-Up Pieces*, and *Hugging the Shore*—Updike has shown himself to be an excellent literary critic and cultural commentator as well as a gifted writer of fiction.

Updike's mature fiction has been concerned with the fate of eros in the upper-middle-class suburbs of the eastern United States. His fiction provides a vivid chronicle of the sexual mores and strained and broken marriages of contemporary America. Most of his protagonists are enmeshed in the compromises of modern life, in the horizontal, while yet yearning for the transcendent, the recovery of the vertical dimension. For many of his characters, sexual ecstasy, even with its attendant disappointments, replaces the passions of faith. In such works as *Couples*—a best-seller that received favorable treatment in *Time* and *Life* magazines and garnered Updike a large sum for the film rights—the Rabbit books, *Marry Me*, and the story collections *Museums and Women* and *Problems, and Other Stories*, Updike focuses on marriage and its discontents, especially the various stages of marital disintegration. If innocence, real or imagined, is irrecoverable in Updike's fiction, if his characters often seem engulfed by moral squalor, they yet possess a lively and admirable energy, a spiritual striving, and a vital resistance to entropy that points to something quite other than defeat. Inseparable from the energy of his characters' striving is the astonishing variety and richness of Updike's narratives, reflecting a conviction that the vocation of writing, as with Henry James, constitutes a necessary assault upon the precincts of death. Thus, in both thematic seriousness and narrative range, Updike has produced a body of writings of the highest order.

John G. Parks

Bibliography

Boswell, Marshall. *John Updike's Rabbit Tetralogy: Mastered Irony in Motion*. Columbia: University of Missouri Press, 2001. A study of Harry Angstrom's literary journey through life.

Broer, Lawrence R., ed. *Rabbit Tales: Poetry and Politics in John Updike's Rabbit Novels*. Tuscaloosa: University of Alabama Press, 1998. Twelve essays that demonstrate that Updike's Rabbit novels are a carefully crafted fabric of changing hues and textures, of social realism and something of grandeur. Includes bibliographical references and index.

Detweiler, Robert. *John Updike*. Rev. ed. Boston: Twayne, 1984. An excellent introductory survey of Updike's work through 1983. Contains a chronology, a biographical sketch, analysis of the fiction and its sources, a select bibliography, and an index.

Greiner, Donald J. *The Other John Updike: Poems, Short Stories, Prose, Play.* Athens: Ohio University Press, 1981. While devoting a considerable amount of space to other critics, Greiner, who has written three books about Updike, here traces Updike's artistic development in his writing that both parallels and extends the themes of the novels.

Luscher, Robert M. *John Updike: A Study of the Short Fiction.* New York: Twayne, 1993. An introduction to Updike's short fiction, dealing with his lyrical technique, his experimentation with narrative structure, his use of the short-story cycle convention, and the relationship between his short fiction and his novels. Includes Updike's comments on his short fiction and previously published critical essays representing a variety of critical approaches.

Miller, D. Quentin. *John Updike and the Cold War: Drawing the Iron Curtain.* Columbia: University of Missouri Press, 2001. Studies the influence of Cold War society and politics in forming Updike's worldview.

O'Connell, Mary. *Updike and the Patriarchal Dilemma: Masculinity in the Rabbit Novels.* Carbondale: Southern Illinois University Press, 1996. Examines the themes of men, masculinity, and patriarchy in Updike's Rabbit series. Includes an index and bibliography.

Pritchard, William H. *Updike: America's Man of Letters.* South Royalton, Vt.: Steerforth Press, 2000. A biography of the novelist, whom Pritchard sees as the heir to such American storytellers as William Dean Howells and Henry James, alone in a sea of metafiction.

Schiff, James A. *John Updike Revisited.* New York: Twayne, 1998. Schiff offers a critical reexamination of most of Updike's works up to 1998. Includes bibliographical references and index.

_______. *Updike's Version: Rewriting "The Scarlet Letter."* Columbia: University of Missouri Press, 1992. Schiff explores the influence of Hawthorne's novel on Updike's oeuvre. Contains an index and bibliography.

Tallent, Elizabeth. *Married Men and Magic Tricks: John Updike's Erotic Heroes.* Berkeley, Calif.: Creative Arts, 1982. Offers, in Judie Newman's words, "a ground-breaking exploration of the erotic dimensions of selected works." A long-needed analysis that includes a feminist perspective missing from much previous Updike criticism.

Trachtenberg, Stanley, ed. *New Essays on "Rabbit, Run."* Cambridge, England: Cambridge University Press, 1993. Essays in this collection address Updike's notable novel and such themes as middle-class men in literature. With bibliographical references.

Leon Uris

American novelist

Born: Baltimore, Maryland; August 3, 1924
Died: Shelter Island, New York; June 21, 2003
Identity: Jewish

LONG FICTION: *Battle Cry*, 1953; *The Angry Hills*, 1955; *Exodus*, 1958; *Mila 18*, 1960; *Armageddon*, 1964; *Topaz*, 1967; *QB VII*, 1970; *Trinity*, 1976; *The Haj*, 1984; *Mitla Pass*, 1988; *Redemption*, 1995; *A God in Ruins*, 1999.

SCREENPLAYS: *Battle Cry*, 1955 (adaptation of his novel); *Gunfight at the OK Corral*, 1957.

NONFICTION: *Exodus Revisited*, 1959 (photographs by Dimitrios Harissiadis; also known as *In the Steps of Exodus*); *Ireland, a Terrible Beauty: The Story of Ireland Today*, 1975 (photographs by Jill Uris); *Jerusalem: Song of Songs*, 1981 (photographs by Jill Uris).

Leon Marcus Uris (YEWR-ihs) endures as one of the most popular—and controversial—American novelists. Born on August 3, 1924, in Baltimore, the son of Wolf William and Anna Blumberg Uris, he was educated in the Baltimore and Philadelphia city schools before enlisting in the United States Marine Corps in 1942. He served with the Marines in the Pacific and in Northern California and was honorably discharged in 1946. In 1945, while stationed near San Francisco, he met and married Marine Sergeant Betty Katherine Beck, with whom he had three children: Karen, Mark, and Michael. To support his family while struggling to publish, he worked as a home delivery manager for the *San Francisco Call-Bulletin*. When he finally sold an article on football to *Esquire* in 1950, he decided to work on a novel about World War II because "the real Marine story had not been told." That novel was *Battle Cry*, and its astonishing success in 1953 established him as a full-time writer. This realistic account of World War II introduced the formula that Uris would follow throughout his canon: rather stereotyped characters whose personal drama is played out against a background of international crisis.

The triumph of *Battle Cry*, made into a successful film in 1955 with a script by the novelist, was not to be repeated with Uris's second novel, *The Angry Hills*. Published in 1955, it is a less ambitious and less appealing story of Greek resistance fighters during the Nazi Occupation. The novel repeated the Uris approach, however, being loosely based on the diary of an uncle who had fought in Greece as a volunteer in the Palestinian brigade. In the late 1950's

Uris's fortunes soared once again. In addition to writing the screenplay for the successful Western *Gunfight at the OK Corral*, he published *Exodus*, a novel which not only stands as the author's greatest literary accomplishment but also entered mass culture as the definitive popular work on the birth of modern Israel. This success, coupled with the equivalent popularity of the film, which starred Paul Newman, established Uris as the unofficial historian of modern Judaism. It is because of his treatment of Jews and Arabs that he has engendered much controversy.

In *Exodus Revisited*, a work of photojournalism published with Dimitrios Harissiadis, a picture of Hasidic children is contrasted to a full-length photograph of a "modern" young woman: "A very few Jews cling to the ways of the ghetto. But Israel pins her hopes on her tough and wonderful sabras." It is this obvious polarization that has bothered even Jewish critics. Throughout his works, Uris is uncompromising in his treatment of Arabs as primitive and misled in politics.

After four more novels, a second marriage, and a six-year hiatus (during which he researched the background of modern Ireland), Uris produced his second greatest work. *Trinity* is a sprawling novel which dramatizes the background of modern Ireland from the potato famine to the Easter Rebellion of 1916. Very much like *Exodus* in theme, characterization, and structure, the novel was both a critical and a popular success. To do research for the novel, he and his third wife, Jill Peabody Uris, a professional photographer whom he had married in 1970, spent nearly a year traveling throughout Ireland. This expedition resulted in another photographic essay, *Ireland, a Terrible Beauty*, which actually appeared a year before the novel, in 1975. In 1995, Uris published *Redemption*, a novel set in Ireland during World War I that treats some of the same families that appeared in *Trinity*.

It was not until 1984 that the Uris name again appeared on the best-seller lists, but when it did, it accompanied the most controversial work of his controversial career: *The Haj*. In what appeared to many critics and readers as a classic example of chutzpah, this champion of Zionism chose to write the modern history of the Palestinians from an Arab point of view. Perhaps because the novel seems to conclude that the Jews are the Arabs' "bridge out of darkness," the novel was generally savaged by the critics.

In *Mitla Pass*, published in 1988, Uris turned again to the familiar subjects of Zionism and Israeli-Arab conflict, this time the 1956 struggle over the Suez Canal. Although the structure of the story follows the traditional Uris formula of individuals caught up in conflicts of global significance, there is a different emphasis. The book seems much more personal, more of an "author's life" than the other novels.

Redemption returned to Irish history, carrying on the story of two of the families from *Trinity*, the Larkins and the Hobbeses, into World War I and its aftermath, contrasting the conflicts in Ireland with the battlefields of continental Europe and Turkey. *A God in Ruins* takes place in 2008, featuring a Catholic presidential candidate who was, unbeknownst to himself, born a Jew. Uris uses the plot as an opportunity to explore questions of religion and politics in the United States, but the novel was generally felt to be a weak effort, overwhelmed by excessive flashbacks. Uris died in 2003.

It is perhaps surprising that Uris did not do more in the area of motion pictures, considering his early success and the cinematic quality of his narratives. The majority of his novels have been filmed, but when Uris worked on the screenplays, his strong personality clashed with those of the filmmakers. As Sharon Downey and Richard Kallan observed, Leon Uris was "a reader's writer and a critic's nightmare." Yet when his material meshed with his abilities, he became a dramatic chronicler of the events that shaped the modern world.

Daniel J. Fuller
Richard Tuerk

Bibliography

Cain, Kathleen Shine. *Leon Uris: A Critical Companion*. Westport, Conn.: Greenwood Press, 1998. Explores the plots, themes, and characters of Uris's work.

Downey, Sharon D., and Richard A. Kallan. "Semi-Aesthetic Detachment: The Fusing of Fictional and External Worlds in the Situational Literature of Leon Uris." *Communication Monographs*, September, 1982. Shows how Uris uses history in his first eight novels.

Furman, Andrew. "A New 'Other' Emerges in American Jewish Literature: Philip Roth's Israel Fiction." *Contemporary Literature* 36 (Winter, 1995). Discusses *Exodus* in the context of Philip Roth's fiction set in Israel, such as *The Counterlife* (1986) and *Operation Shylock* (1993).

Gonshak, Henry. "'Rambowitz' Versus 'Schlemiel' in Leon Uris's *Exodus*." *Journal of American Culture* 22 (Spring, 1999). Compares the ways in which Uris depicts Jewish people in his novel.

Manganaro, Elise Salem. "Voicing the Arab: Multivocality and Ideology in Leon Uris' *The Haj*." *MELUS* 15, no. 4 (Winter, 1988). Treats Uris's Arab characters as "ugly" misrepresentations.

Weissbrod, Rachel. "*Exodus* as Zionist Melodrama." *Israel Studies* 4 (Spring, 1999). An in-depth analysis of *Exodus*.

Luis Miguel Valdez

American playwright and political activist

Born: Delano, California; June 26, 1940
Identity: Mexican American

DRAMA: *The Theft*, pr. 1961; *The Shrunken Head of Pancho Villa*, pr. 1965; *Las dos caras del patroncito*, pr. 1965; *La quinta temporada*, pr. 1966; *Los vendidos*, pr. 1967; *Dark Root of a Scream*, pr. 1967; *La conquista de México*, pr. 1968 (puppet play); *No saco nada de la escuela*, pr. 1969; *The Militants*, pr. 1969; *Vietnam campesino*, pr. 1970; *Helguistas*, pr. 1970; *Bernabé*, pr. 1970; *Soldado razo*, pr., pb. 1971; *Actos*, pb. 1971 (includes *Las dos caras del patroncito*, *La quinta temporada*, *Los vendidos*, *La conquista de México*, *No saco nada de la escuela*, *The Militants*, *Vietnam campesino*, *Huelguistas*, and *Soldado razo*); *Las pastorelas*, pr. 1971 (adaptation of a sixteenth century Mexican shepherd's play); *La Virgen del Tepeyac*, pr. 1971 (adaptation of *Las cuatro apariciones de la Virgen de Guadalupe*); *Los endrogados*, pr. 1972; *Los olivos pits*, pr. 1972; *La gran carpa de los rasquachis*, pr. 1973; *Mundo*, pr. 1973; *El baille de los gigantes*, pr. 1973; *El fin del mundo*, pr. 1975; *Zoot Suit*, pr. 1978; *Bandido!*, pr. 1981, revised pr. 1994; *Corridos*, pr. 1983; *"I Don't Have to Show You No Stinking Badges!,"* pr., pb. 1986; *Luis Valdez—Early Works: Actos, Bernabé, and Pensamiento Serpentino*, pb. 1990; *Zoot Suit, and Other Plays*, pb. 1992; *Mummified Deer*, pr. 2000.

SCREENPLAYS: *Zoot Suit*, 1982 (adaptation of his play); *La Bamba*, 1987.

TELEPLAYS: *Fort Figueroa*, 1988; *La Pastorela*, 1991.

EDITED TEXT: *Aztlan: An Anthology of Mexican American Literature*, 1972 (with Stan Steiner).

MISCELLANEOUS: *Pensamiento Serpentino: A Chicano Approach to the Theatre of Reality*, 1973.

Luis Miguel Valdez (VAL-dehz), political activist, playwright, director, essayist, and founder of El Teatro Campesino, is the most prominent figure in modern Chicano theater. Born on June 26, 1940, to migrant farmworker parents, he was second in a family of ten brothers and sisters. In spite of working in the fields from the age of six, Valdez completed high school and received a scholarship to San Jose State College, where he developed his early interest in theater. *The Shrunken Head of Pancho Villa* was written while Valdez was a student there. After receiving a bachelor's degree in English and drama in 1964, he joined the San Francisco Mime Troupe, whose work was based on *commedia dell'arte* and the theater of Bertolt Brecht. These experiences heavily influenced Valdez's work, especially in terms of style and production.

A 1965 meeting with César Chávez, who was organizing migrant farmworkers in Delano, California, led to the formation of El Teatro Campesino, the cultural and propagandistic arm of the United Farm Workers (UFW) union. Valdez created short improvisational pieces, called *actos*, for the troupe. All the *actos* are characterized by the use of masks, stereotyped characters, farcical exaggeration, and improvisation. *Las dos caras del patroncito* (the two faces of the boss) and *La quinta temporada* (the fifth season) are *actos* from this early period that highlight the plight of the farmworkers and the benefits of unionization. Valdez left the union in 1967, bringing El Teatro Campesino with him to establish El Centro Campesino Cultural. He wanted to broaden the concerns of the troupe by fostering Chicanos' pride in their cultural heritage and by depicting their problems in the Anglo culture. *Los vendidos* (the sellouts), for example, satirizes Chicanos who attempt to assimilate into a white, racist society, and *La conquista de Mexico* (the conquest of Mexico) links the fall of the Aztecs with the internal dissension of Chicano activists. In 1968 El Teatro Campesino moved toward producing full-length plays, starting with Valdez's *The Shrunken Head of Pancho Villa*. Expressionistic in style, the play explores the conflict between two brothers—an assimilationist and a *pachuco*, a swaggering street kid—and the impact this extremism has on the tenuous fabric of a Chicano family. Recognition followed, with an Obie Award in New York in 1969 for "creating a workers' theater to demonstrate the politics of survival" and an invitation to perform at the Theatre des Nations festival in Nancy, France. Later in 1969, Valdez and the troupe moved to Fresno, California, where they founded an annual Chicano theater festival, and Valdez began teaching at Fresno State College.

In 1971 Valdez moved his company permanently to the small town of San Juan Bautista in California. There, Teatro Campesino underwent a fundamental transformation, as the group began increasingly to emphasize the spiritual side of their work, as derived from prevalent Christian as well as newfound Aztec and Mayan roots. This shift from an agitational focus to a search for spiritual solutions was met with anger by formerly admiring audiences in Mexico City at the Quinto Festival de los Teatros Chicanos in 1974. The company continued to flourish, however, touring campuses and communities yearly and giving financial support and advice to other theater troupes.

Fame came with *Zoot Suit*, the first Chicano play to reach Broadway. Although its run was relatively brief, owing to negative criticism, the play was very popular on the West Coast and was made into a film in 1981, with Valdez both the director and the writer of the screenplay. During the 1980's, Valdez and El Teatro Campesino continued to tour at home and abroad, presenting works by Valdez and collectively scripted pieces that interpret the Chicano experience. The 1986 comedy *"I Don't Have to Show You No Stinking Badges!"* is about the political and existential implications of acting, both in theater and in society. In 1987 Valdez wrote the screenplay for the successful film *La Bamba*, the story of Ritchie Valens, a young Chicano pop singer who died in an airplane crash in the late 1950's. This work reached a large audience.

After a gap in playwriting of almost fifteen years, Valdez wrote *Mummified Deer.* This play reaffirms his status as the "father of Chicano drama" and continues his exploration of his heritage through the juxtaposition of ritual and realism. The play takes its inspiration from a newspaper article concerning the discovery of a sixty-year-old fetus in the body of an eighty-four-year old woman. According to scholar Jorge Huerta, the mummified fetus serves as a metaphor for "the Chicanos' Indio heritage, seen through the lens of his own Yaqui blood." The play's major dramatic action operates in the historical/fictional past.

Valdez's contributions to contemporary Chicano theater are extensive. Writing individually and with others, he has redefined the cultural forms of the barrio: the *acto*, a short comic piece intended to move the audience to political action; the *mito* (myth), which characteristically takes the form of an allegory based on Indian ritual, in an attempt to integrate political activism and religious ritual; and the *corrido*, a reinvention of the musical based on Mexican American folk ballads. He has placed the Chicano experience onstage in all of its political and cultural complexity, creating what no other American playwright has, a genuine workers' theater that has made serious drama popular, political drama entertaining, and ethnic drama universal.

Lori Hall Burghardt

Bibliography

Broyles-Gonzales, Yolanda. *El Teatro Campesino: Theater in the Chicano Movement*. Austin: University of Texas Press, 1994. Study drawing on previously unexamined materials, such as production notes and interviews with former ensemble members, to demystify the roles Valdez and El Teatro Campesino played in the development of a Chicano theater aesthetic.

Elam, Harry J., Jr. *Taking It to the Streets: The Social Protest Theatre of Luis Valdez and Amiri Baraka*. Ann Arbor: University of Michigan Press, 2001. Explores the political, cultural, and performative similarities between El Teatro Campesino and Baraka's Black Revolutionary Theater. An intriguing examination of the political theater of these two marginalized groups, Chicanos and African Americans, and their shared aesthetic.

Huerta, Jorge A. *Chicano Theatre: Themes and Forms*. Ypsilanti, Mich.: Bilingual Press, 1982. Well-written and -illustrated study that begins with Valdez's experiences in Delano in 1965. It contains an excellent immediate description with dialogue of these first energies and is written in the present tense for immediacy and energy. Provides some discussion of the beginnings of the San Francisco mime troupe and strong description of the *actos* and their literary history in Europe.

_______. "Labor Theatre, Street Theatre, and Community Theatre in the Barrio, 1965-1983." In *Hispanic Theatre in the United States*, edited by Nicolas Kanellos. Houston: Arte Publico Press, 1984. Placed at the end of a longer study of Hispanic theater, this essay takes on more importance by indicating Valdez's contribution in a continuum of history. Good on contemporaries of El Teatro Campesino; strong bibliography.

Kanellos, Nicolas. *Mexican American Theater: Legacy and Reality*. Pittsburgh: Latin American Literary Review Press, 1987. Begins with an examination of Valdez's transformation from director of El Teatro Campesino to the urban commercial playwright of *Zoot Suit* in 1978. Cites Valdez's contribution to the "discernible period of proliferation and flourishing in Chicano theatres" from 1965 to 1976, then moves on to examine other offshoots of the impulse.

Morales, Ed. "Shadowing Valdez." *American Theatre* 9 (November, 1992): 14-19. Excellent essay on Valdez, his followers, his film plans, his shelved Frida Kahlo project, and later productions in and around Los Angeles, with production stills. Includes an essay entitled "Statement on Artistic Freedom" by Valdez, in which he defends his nontraditional casting.

Pottlitzer, Joanne. *Hispanic Theater in the United States and Puerto Rico: A Report to the Ford Foundation*. New York: Ford Foundation, 1988. This volume provides a brief history to 1965 and discusses the Hispanic theater during the upheaval of the Vietnam War. Also examines the theater's activities and budget and pays homage to the inspiration of El Teatro Campesino and Valdez. Supplemented by an appendix and survey data.

Valdez, Luis Miguel. "*Zoot Suit* and the Pachuco Phenomenon: An Interview with Luis Valdez." Interview by Roberta Orona-Cordova. In *Mexican American Theatre: Then and Now*, edited by Nicolas Kanellos. Houston: Arte Publico Press, 1983. The opening of the film version of *Zoot Suit* prompted this interview, in which Valdez reveals much about his motives for working, his view of Chicano literature and art, and his solutions to "the entrenched attitude" that will not allow Chicano participation in these industries.

Luisa Valenzuela

Argentine novelist and short-story writer

Born: Buenos Aires, Argentina; November 26, 1938

LONG FICTION: *Hay que sonreír*, 1966 (*Clara*, 1976); *El gato eficaz*, 1972; *Como en la guerra*, 1977 (*He Who Searches*, 1979); *Libro que no muerde*, 1980; *Cola de lagartija*, 1983 (*The Lizard's Tail*, 1983); *Novela Negra con Argentinos*, 1990 (*Black Novel with Argentines*, 1992); *Realidad nacional desde la cama*, 1990 (*Bedside Manners*, 1995); *La travesía*, 2001.
SHORT FICTION: *Los heréticos*, 1967 (*The Heretics: Thirteen Short Stories*, 1976); *Aquí pasan cosas raras*, 1975 (*Strange Things Happen Here: Twenty-six Short Stories and a Novel*, 1979); *Cambio de armas*, 1982 (*Other Weapons*, 1985); *Donde viven las águilas*, 1983 (*Up Among the Eagles*, 1988); *Open Door: Stories*, 1988; *Simetrías*, 1993 (*Symmetries*, 1998); *Cuentos completos, y uno más*, 1998.
NONFICTION: *Peligrosas palabras*, 2001 (essays).

Luisa Valenzuela (vah-lehn-ZWAY-lah), Argentine novelist, short-story writer, journalist, and scriptwriter, is one of Argentina's most significant authors to emerge since the boom in Latin American literature during the 1960's. As the daughter of Luisa Mercedes Levinson, a prominent Argentine writer, Valenzuela was initiated at an early age into the world of the written word. Her father, Pablo Francisco Valenzuela, was a doctor. She was reared in Belgrano and received her early education from a German governess and an English tutor. In 1945, she attended Belgrano Girls' School and then an English high school. She began writing for the magazine *Quince Abriles* in 1953 and completed her studies at the National Preparatory School Vicente López in 1955. Subsequently she graduated with a bachelor of arts degree from the University of Buenos Aires. She wrote for the Buenos Aires magazines *Atlántida*, *El Hogar*, and *Esto Es* and worked with Jorge Luis Borges in the National Library of Argentina. She also wrote for the Belgrano Radio and was a tour guide in 1957. It was during this time that her first short stories were published, in the magazine *Ficción*.

In 1958, when she was twenty years old, Valenzuela left Buenos Aires to become the Paris correspondent for the Argentine daily newspaper *El Mundo*. There she wrote programs for Radio Télévision Française and participated in the intellectual life of the then-famous *Tel Quel* group of literary theorists and structuralists. She married French merchant marine Theodore Marjak, resided in Normandy, and gave birth to a daughter, Anna-Lisa, in 1958. Three years later she returned to Buenos Aires and joined Argentina's foremost newspaper, *La Nación*, where she became assistant editor. After she was divorced from her husband in 1965, she went to the University of Iowa's Writers' Workshop on a Fulbright grant in 1969. In 1972, she received a scholarship to study pop culture and literature in New York. She then became an avid traveler, living in Spain, Mexico, New York, and Buenos Aires; participating in conferences; continuing her journalism; and cultivating her fiction.

Her first novel, *Clara*, presents the story of a naïve country girl turned prostitute in Buenos Aires; the girl's picaresque adventures in a male world alternate between the humorous and the sinister. As the novel progresses, the antiheroine's forthrightness slowly changes into a pathos under the constant attack of the city's anonymity, alienation, and male brutality. Valenzuela won the Instituto Nacional de Cinematografía Award in 1973 for the script "Hay que sonreír," based on her first novel. Her New York-Greenwich Village experience resulted in *El gato eficaz* (the efficient cat), an experimental novel sustained largely by the innovative use of language and an imaginative plot. In 1975, she returned to Buenos Aires and joined the staff of the journal *Crisis*. After participating in more workshops and conferences, she left Buenos Aires and settled in New York in 1978, where she conducted creative writing workshops and taught Latin American literature at Columbia University, as well as at other universities in the United States.

Although she has lived much of her life outside Argentina, Valenzuela, like other Argentine women writers, could not escape her involvement with an Argentine society torn by violence, class struggle, dictatorship, and dehumanization. Thus, much of her fiction, though written and published outside her native country, where it was banned, treats such themes as violence, political repression, and cultural repression, especially as they relate to women. Yet, as critics point out, her work continually undermines social and political myths while (unlike that of so many political writers) refusing to replace old mythic structures with new but equally arbitrary and authoritative ones.

Genevieve Slomski

Bibliography

Bach, Caleb. "Metaphors and Magic Unmask the Soul." *Americas* 47 (January/February, 1995): 22-28. Notes that Valenzuela is distressed by the cultural banality common the world over. Says that her prose involves the reader by posing questions rather than suggesting simplistic solutions; claims her books are not for the lazy reader.

Hoeppner, Edward H. "The Hand That Mirrors Us: Luisa Valenzuela's Re-Writing of Lacan's Theory of Identity." *Latin American Literary Review* 20 (January-June, 1992): 9-17. Provides a thoughtful study of Valenzuela's works in the light of psychoanalytic theory.

Logan, Joy. "Southern Discomfort in Argentina: Postmodernism, Feminism, and Luisa Valenzuela's *Simetrías*." *Latin American Literary Review* 24 (July-December, 1996): 5-17. Argues that in the fairy-tale section of *Symmetries*, Valenzuela's critique of Western patriarchal practices is most clear. Claims that the collection is a textual performance of the interplay between postmodernism and feminism.

McNab, Pamela J. "Sexual Silence and Equine Imagery in Valenzuela and Cortazar." *Bulletin of Hispanic Studies* 76 (April, 1999): 263-279. Compares the way in which both Valenzuela and Julio Cortazar use horse imagery to fill the gap between language and silence in their short stories.

Magnarelli, Sharon. "Simetrías: 'Mirror, Mirror, on the Wall. . . .'" *World Literature Today* 69 (Autumn, 1995): 717-726. Argues that the collection *Symmetries* is organized around motifs of language and power. Analyzes "Tango," "Transfigurations," and the title story "Symmetries" in terms of the motif of parallel situations and responses.

Marting, Diane. "Gender and Metaphoricity in Luisa Valenzuela's 'I'm Your Horse in the Night.'" *World Literature Today* 69 (Fall, 1995): 702-708. A survey and critique of previous interpretations of the story, accompanied by a close reading in which Marting argues that the story criticizes the man for his retrograde treatment of the woman who loves him.

Tomlinson, Emily. "Rewriting Fictions of Power: The Texts of Luisa Valenzuela and Marta Traba." *Modern Language Review* 93 (July, 1998): 695-709. Discusses the feminist exploration of themes of power in the writings of the two authors.

Juan Valera

Spanish novelist

Born: Cabra, Spain; October 18, 1824
Died: Madrid, Spain; April 18, 1905

LONG FICTION: *Mariquita y Antonio*, 1861; *Pepita Jiménez*, 1874 (*Pepita Ximenez*, 1886); *Las ilusiones del doctor Faustino*, 1875; *El comendador Mendoza*, 1877 (*Commander Mendoza*, 1893); *Pasarse de listo*, 1878 (*Don Braulio*, 1892); *Doña Luz*, 1879 (English translation, 1891); *Juanita la larga*, 1896; *Genio y figura*, 1897; *Morsamor*, 1899.

SHORT FICTION: *Cuentos y diálogos*, 1882; *Algo de todo*, 1883; *Cuentos, diálogos y fantasías*, 1887; *Cuentos y chascarrillos andaluces*, 1898 (with Narciso Campillo, Conde de las Navas, and Doctor Thebussem); *De varios colores*, 1898.

DRAMA: *Tentativas dramáticas*, pb. 1879; *Teatro*, pb. 1908.

POETRY: *Ensayos poéticas*, 1844; *Poesías*, 1858; *Canciones, romances y poemas*, 1885.

NONFICTION: *De la naturaleza y carácter de la novela*, 1860; *Estudios críticos sobre literatura, política, y costumbres de nuestros días*, 1864; *Crítica literaria*, 1864-1871; *Disertaciones y juicios literarios*, 1878; *Nuevos estudios críticos*, 1883; *Apuntes sobre el nuevo arte de escribir novelas*, 1887; *Carta al señor don Juan Valera*, 1888; *Cartas americanas*, 1889; *Nuevas cartas americanas*, 1890; *Las mujeres y las academias*, 1891; *Ventura de la Vega: Estudio biográfico crítico*, 1891; *Ecos argentinos*, 1901.

EDITED TEXTS: *Florilegio de cuentos, leyendas y tradiciones vulgares*, 1860; *Florilegio de poesías castellanas del siglo XIX*, 1902-1904.

TRANSLATION: *Poesía y arte en los árabes en España y Sicilia*, 1867, 1868, 1871 (of Adolf F. Schack's *Poesie und Kunst der Araber in Spanien und Sicilien*).

MISCELLANEOUS: *Obras completas*, 1905-1935 (53 volumes); *Obras completas*, 1947-1958 (3 volumes).

Juan Valera (vah-LAY-rah), in full Juan Valera y Alcalá Galiano, was born October 18, 1824, in Cabra, a hill town some thirty-five miles southeast of Córdoba, Spain. His parents were distinguished if not affluent, his mother of the Spanish nobility, his father a naval officer. His maternal uncle was the famous orator and politician Antonio Alcalá Galiano. Valera attended a good secondary school in Málaga from 1837 to 1840, studied law in Granada's Colegio del Sacro Monte and in Madrid, and—back in Granada—graduated in 1844. Though an avid reader of literary classics, he was not a diligent student. It might be noted that many a nineteenth century Spanish undergraduate law major never intended a career in jurisprudence. Such degrees were closer to what would be considered today as the bachelor of arts. Valera, however, despite predictable excursions into the field of literature (a few poems in magazines and a volume of verses whose publication was subsidized by his father as a graduation present), actually attempted to practice law in Madrid.

Valera's family connections gave him entrée into high society. It was a pleasant but unremunerative existence; he soon had to think of correcting his course. Diplomacy appeared a more likely choice, and, after a slow start, it proved a good one. He obtained an unofficial post in Naples, working for his friend the great Romantic author the Duque de Rivas, at the time Spanish ambassador, from 1847 to 1849. Valera was sent to Lisbon in 1850 and to Rio de Janeiro in 1851. There followed a post in Dresden (1855) and a visit to Russia (1856).

Returning to Spain, Valera ran for the office of deputy (similar to the position of congressman) in 1858, an office he held during two not very outstanding terms. In 1865, he received his first really important diplomatic appointment as minister in Frankfurt. In 1868, Isabel II lost her throne; Valera became undersecretary of state for most of one year. He even helped choose Amadeo of Savoy as the new king of Spain in 1870 and was made director of public instruction for a very short time. The king soon abdicated, leaving Valera out of political favor. For seven years, Valera devoted himself to writing.

During previous lulls in his public career, he had already managed to produce a volume of poetry in 1858, helped found two satiric literary magazines in the two succeeding years, and was editor in chief for the middle-of-the-road *El contemporáneo* (where his first, unfinished novel, *Mariquita y Antonio*, appeared in 1861). Although he had only one book to his credit, the 1858 volume of poetry (an earlier one in 1844 had sold so poorly that he had had it withdrawn from the market), he was elected in 1861 into the Spanish Academy, whose standards, it must be admitted, were somewhat less strict than those of its sister institution in France. His first collection of essays appeared in 1864: *Estudios críticos sobre literatura, política, y costumbres de nuestros días* (critical studies on contemporary literature, politics, and customs). In 1867, by then in his early forties, he married Dolores Delavat, a daughter of a career diplomat, whom he had first known in Rio de Janeiro in 1851. She was half his age, stubborn, and extravagant; he was usually strapped for funds, given to sarcasm, and notably fond of affairs of the heart (an early addiction still catered to long after his marriage). It was not an especially happy union, although they never separated, and the last few years proved somewhat calmer.

From 1881 to 1883, needing funds to support a growing family along with his extravagant wife, Valera accepted a post as minister in Lisbon, where the accusation of certain financial and political improprieties almost led to a duel. He resigned the position, supposing that his career was ruined. On the contrary, the next year, he was appointed minister to the United States in Washington, D.C. His wife stayed in Spain with the children. Washington, like almost all of his appointments, seemed a mixed blessing. He was forever impugning the climate, the manners, the dress, or the tastes of the places—European or American—where he served his country. American men he termed dull moneygrubbers, though, as always, he enjoyed the women. One of them, Katherine Lee Bayard, the twenty-eight-year-old daughter of the secretary of state, loved him deeply enough to commit suicide in 1886, on hearing that he was to return to Spain. Despite her death and that of his eldest son from typhoid, he seems to have enjoyed his transatlantic stay. Besides his usual active social life, he found time to read generously from American literature, even translating a few poems by James Russell Lowell and John Greenleaf Whittier with an eye to adding fifty or so more to make up a whole book, a project that died aborning.

Valera's last two diplomatic posts were as minister in Brussels, from 1886 to 1887, and, after a six-year lapse, in Vienna, from 1893 to 1895. There ended his diplomatic career, rendered untenable by questionable health and increasing blindness. Returning to Madrid, he resumed his pursuit of literature. Even in government harness, he had produced *Cartas americanas* and *Nuevas cartas americanas* (new American letters), discussing Latin American writers such as the Nicaraguan *Modernismo* poet Rubén Darío. Full-time commitment allowed for three more novels—*Juanita la larga* (shrewd Juanita), usually considered his best after *Pepita Ximenez*; *Genio y figura* (the title a shortened version of "genio y figura hasta la sepultura," an expression signifying "what's bred in the bone will be with you until you die"); and his historical novel, *Morsamor*—as well as short stories, essays, polemics, and an extensively annotated five-volume anthology of nineteenth century Spanish poetry. Valera died peacefully on April 18, 1905, in the very act of composing a discourse to be delivered before his beloved Spanish Academy.

The author-cum-diplomat was a proud man, at times even haughty, and a chronic complainer, occasionally belligerent. He was often guilty of provincialism, not above denigrating foreign writers who dared pass judgment on things Spanish. He could be superficial and flighty, traits he exhibited all of his adult years. That he used some dozen publishers during his writing career is somewhat unusual, though the large body of his oeuvre may to some extent justify what seems to indicate a difficult personality. He was quite outspoken, a characteristic not always found among professional diplomats. Yet, despite his thorniness, he was normally kind to writers of his own generation in Spain (even too kind, some critics have objected), and he encouraged young writers and scholars. The public tends to expect social and moral perfection in its famous men. Valera might fail his critics, but he remains basically a man to honor and respect.

Armand E. Singer

Bibliography

Bianchini, Andreina. "*Pepita Jiménez*: Ideology and Realism." *Hispanofila* 33, no. 2 (January, 1990): 33-51. An examination of the novel's relationship to ideology and idealism. Discusses the three-part structure of the work.

DeCoster, Cyrus Cole. *Juan Valera*. New York: Twayne, 1974. An informative biography. Contains an overview of Valera's life and literary career and analyzes his literary characters and themes.

Ford, J. D. M. *Main Currents of Spanish Literature*. 1919. Reprint. New York: Biblio and Tannen, 1968. In these critical lectures delivered at the Lowell Institute in Boston, Valera's novels are considered high points of Spanish American literature. Text includes a bibliographical note.

Lott, Robert E. *Language and Psychology in "Pepita Jimenez."* Urbana: University of Illinois Press, 1970. A well-regarded study of the language and psychology found in *Pepita Jiménez*. The first part is an analysis of language, style, and rhetorical devices. The second section is a psychological examination of characters.

Taylor, Teresia Langford. *The Representation of Women in the Novels of Juan Valera: A Feminist Critique*. New York: P. Lang, 1997. This study focuses on the underlying patriarchal ideology in Valera's texts. Includes bibliographical references and an index.

Trimble, Robert. *Chaos Burning on My Brow: Don Juan Valera in His Novels*. San Bernardino, Calif.: Borgo Press, 1995. A critical study. Includes an index and a bibliography.

Turner, Harriet S. "Nescit Labi Virtus: Authorial Self-Critique in *Pepita Jiménez*." *Kentucky Romance Quarterly* 35, no. 3 (August, 1988): 347-357. Examines the omniscient narrator, the writer, the use of irony, and the relationship to virtue.

Paul Valéry

French poet and playwright

Born: Sète, France; October 30, 1871
Died: Paris, France; July 20, 1945

POETRY: *La Jeune Parque*, 1917 (*The Youngest of the Fates*, 1947; also known as *The Young Fate*); *Album de vers anciens*, 1920 (*Album of Early Verse*, 1971); *Charmes: Ou, Poèmes*, 1922 (*Charms*, 1971).
SHORT FICTION: "La Soirée avec Monsieur Teste," 1896 ("An Evening with Monsieur Teste," 1925).
DRAMA: *Amphion*, pr., pb. 1931 (musical drama; English translation, 1960); *Sémiramis*, pr., pb. 1934 (musical drama; English translation, 1960); *Cantate du Narcisse*, pr. 1939 (musical drama; *The Narcissus Cantata*, 1960); *Mon Faust*, pb. 1946 (*My Faust*, 1960).
NONFICTION: *Introduction à la méthode de Léonard de Vinci*, 1896 (serial), 1919 (book; *Introduction to the Method of Leonardo da Vinci*, 1929); *Eupalinos: Ou, L'Architecte*, 1921 (dialogue; *Eupalinos: Or, The Architect*, 1932); *Variété*, 1924-1944 (5 volumes); *L'âme et la danse*, 1925 (dialogue; *Dance and the Soul*, 1951); *Analecta*, 1926 (*Analects*, 1970); *Regards sur le monde actuel*, 1931 (*Reflections on the World Today*, 1948); *Degas, danse, dessin*, 1938 (*Degas, Dance, Drawing*, 1960); *Les Cahiers*, 1957-1961.
MISCELLANEOUS: *Selected Writings*, 1950; *The Collected Works of Paul Valéry*, 1956-1975 (15 volumes).

Paul Valéry (va-lay-ree) was the son of an Italian mother and a Corsican father. He first attended school in his hometown of Sète, France, then spent 1884 through 1888 at the *lycée* of Montpellier. His career there was undistinguished. Judging himself too untalented in mathematics to attend the Naval Academy, Valéry turned his interest to the arts, especially poetry. Among the chief literary influences on him at this time were Victor Hugo, Théophile Gautier, and Charles Baudelaire; by 1889 Valéry had written a number of poems.

He served in the military from 1889 to 1890, during which time he developed an interest in Symbolist poetry. His reading of Joris-Karl Huysmans's 1884 novel *Against the Grain* directed Valéry to the poetry of Paul Verlaine and, particularly, Stéphane Mallarmé. In 1890 he met Pierre Louÿs, who put him in touch with Mallarmé, José-Maria de Hérédia, and André Gide. Louÿs also began publishing Valéry's poetry in his literary journal, *La Conque*. In the meantime Valéry devoted himself to the study of law, again at Montpellier.

In 1892, caught up in a personal crisis, Valéry went to spend his vacation in Genoa, Italy, with his aunt. In the course of an October night of anxiety and insomnia, he became obsessed with the idea that the emotional and aesthetic life distorted and crippled intellectual clarity and activity. He decided to reject writing and the artistic life to devote himself to what he valued most: self-knowledge and the consideration of the intellect and the life of thought.

In 1894 Valéry went to Paris to seek government service. He became a member of Mallarmé's "Tuesday Circle" of Symbolist writers. In 1895 he entered the Ministry of War. The next year he published *Introduction to the Method of Leonardo da Vinci* and "An Evening with Monsieur Teste." Valéry left the Ministry of War in 1900 to become private secretary for his friend, Edouard Lebey, an influential businessman. He held this position for twenty-two years, until Lebey's death. Valéry was also married in 1900. His position with Lebey took little time, and he spent many hours each day during these two decades noting his observations of his mental and intellectual activity: He watched the self in thought, in dream, and in time, and he examined the relation of thought and language. His metaphor for himself during these years was that of a man caught in the labyrinth of his own thought, attempting vainly to find the thread that would guide him out. This writing resulted in more than 250 notebooks.

In 1912, twenty years after he had given up poetry, Valéry was asked by Gide and another friend to publish an edition of his early poems; *Album of Early Verse* finally appeared in 1920. This project resulted in a single new poem, *The Young Fate*. The success of this poem led Valéry to write and publish more poetry, most notably his famous "Cemetery by the Sea" (1920). *Charms*, a collected volume of his poetry written after *The Young Fate*, was published in 1922, and Valéry's reputation grew rapidly.

Although first identified with the Symbolists because of his association with people such as Mallarmé and Verlaine, Valéry's later work took him on an introspective course of his own. His writing is delicately balanced and lyrical, yet often obscure. His philosophical probing led to the formulation of aesthetic and poetic theories that had a major influence on later writers.

With the death of Lebey in 1922, Valéry devoted himself completely to the life of a writer. He was lionized by the reading public, and his essays and prefaces were in great demand. The French Academy elected him to the chair of Anatole France in 1925. He received many other honors in the 1920's and 1930's, the period when he wrote most of his celebrated dialogues, and in 1937 he took the chair of poetry at the Collège de France. Continuing to teach during World War II and the Occupation, Valéry did much to encourage the Resistance. He died just after the liberation, and he was buried in the cemetery beside the sea in Sète.

Sandra C. McClain

Bibliography

Anderson, Kirsteen. *Paul Valéry and the Voice of Desire*. Oxford, England: Legenda, 2000. An exploration of the power of voice as image and theme throughout Valéry's writing. Anderson highlights the tension between a dominant "masculine" imaginary and the repressed "feminine" dimension which underpins Valéry's work.

Gifford, Paul, and Brian Stimpson, eds. *Reading Paul Valéry: Universe in Mind.* New York: Cambridge University Press, 1998. A collection of essays by internationally recognized scholars offering a comprehensive account of Valéry's work. Perspectives are offered on the immense range of Valéry's experimental and fragmentary writings.

Kluback, William. *Paul Valéry: Illusions of Civilization.* New York: Peter Lang, 1996. A discussion of the meaning of civilization, in particular, Western civilization, as it was investigated in the philosophical works of Valéry. Studies the infrastructure of Valéry's philosophy as it embraced the questions of civilization, history, evil, love, and mortality.

_______. *Paul Valéry: The Realms of the "Analecta."* New York: Peter Lang, 1998. A study of a particular aspect of Valéry's philosophical work, the *Analects*. This is the realm of the imagination, of the image and metaphor. Readers are presented with epigrams that are designed to confuse and challenge their thinking.

Putnam, Walter C. *Paul Valéry Revisited.* New York: Twayne, 1995. An introductory biography and critical study of selected works by Valéry. Includes bibliographical references and index.

César Vallejo

Peruvian poet

Born: Santiago de Chuco, Peru; March 16, 1892
Died: Paris, France; April 15, 1938
Identity: American Indian (Chimu)

POETRY: *Los heraldos negros*, 1918 (*The Black Heralds*, 1990); *Trilce*, 1922 (English translation, 1973); *Poemas en prosa*, 1939 (*Prose Poems*, 1978); *Poemas humanos*, 1939 (*Human Poems*, 1968); *España, aparta de mí este cáliz*, 1939 (*Spain, Take This Cup from Me*, 1974); *Obra poética completa*, 1968; *Poesía completa*, 1978; *César Vallejo: The Complete Posthumous Poetry*, 1978; *Selected Poems*, 1981.

LONG FICTION: *Fábula salvaje*, 1923 (novella); *El tungsteno*, 1931 (*Tungsten*, 1988).

SHORT FICTION: *Escalas melografiadas*, 1923; *Hacia el reino de los Sciris*, 1967; *Paco Yunque*, 1969.

DRAMA: *La piedra cansada*, pb. 1979; *Colacho hermanos: O, Presidentes de América*, pb. 1979; *Lock-Out*, pb. 1979; *Entre las dos orillas corre el río*, pb. 1979; *Teatro completo*, pb. 1979.

NONFICTION: *Rusia en 1931: Reflexiones al pie del Kremlin*, 1931, 1965; *El romanticismo en la poesía castellana*, 1954; *Rusia ante el segundo plan quinquenal*, 1965; *El arte y la revolución*, 1973; *Contra el secreto profesional*, 1973.

César Vallejo (vah-YAY-hoh) vies with the Chilean poet Pablo Neruda for recognition as the best Spanish American poet of the twentieth century, yet the semantic difficulty of his poetry has often meant that he is not as well known outside the Spanish-speaking world as he deserves to be. Author of a novel, a novella, four dramas, a collection of short stories, a collection of essays on Marxism and literary theory, two books on Soviet Russia, and more than two hundred newspaper articles, Vallejo is mainly remembered for his poetry.

Born the eleventh child to a family of mixed Spanish and Indian origins, Vallejo as a child witnessed at first hand hunger, poverty, and the injustices done to Indians. His first book of poems, *The Black Heralds*, showed him still to be under the influence of *modernismo*—which favored allusions to Greco-Roman mythology—but also hinted at the emergence of a radically new personal poetic voice. The major theme of this collection was anguish at the injustice and futility of life, a feeling that was deepened by the death of his older brother, Miguel. Some poems in *The Black Heralds* openly question God's role in the universe, some demonstrate the stirrings of an Amerindian consciousness, and others hint at the growth of social concern for the plight of the Indians.

In 1920, Vallejo's involvement in political matters concerning the Indian population led to his imprisonment for nearly three months. This experience heightened his feeling of loss at the death of his mother and contributed to a state of depression that was to torment him for the rest of his life. *Trilce* was conceived during his imprisonment; in this work, Vallejo used startling and innovative techniques—such as neologisms, colloquialisms, and typographical innovation—to express his anguish at the disparity that he felt existed between human aspirations and the limitations of human existence.

In 1923, Vallejo left Peru for Europe; he was never to return to his homeland. While in Paris, he was unable to find stable employment; he barely made a living from translations, language tutoring, and political writing. His experience of poverty was accompanied by a growing interest in Marxism. In the late 1920's, Vallejo became a frequent visitor to the bookstore of *L'Humanité*, the Communist newspaper. He read Marxist and Leninist theory, and as a result, his work reflected this shift toward the political sphere. He also traveled twice to the Soviet Union during these years to see Communism at work firsthand. Vallejo was expelled from France in 1930 for his political activities (he had to go to Spain), and he joined the Communist Party in 1931.

While he published no new poetic works during the 1930's, he continued to write poetry based on his experience of life in Europe. About half of these poems, which were published posthumously under the title *Human Poems*, focus on the collective experience of humankind. A number of the poems express enthusiasm for the collective ethos of communism, some express dismay at the exploitation and pain experienced by the proletariat, and others express disillusionment with politics and politicians.

In July, 1936, the Spanish Civil War broke out, and Vallejo was irresistibly drawn to this international political struggle. He traveled to Spain on two separate occasions and wrote some emotional poems about the conflict, subsequently collected in *Spain, Take This Cup from Me*. Some of the best poems of this collection focus on a Republican war hero. "Masa" (Mass), for example, perhaps Vallejo's most famous poem, focuses on a moment on the battlefield when a dead Republican militiaman is miraculously brought back to life through the collective love of humankind.

Vallejo died on Good Friday in 1938, muttering that he wanted to go to Spain, on the very day that Francisco Franco's troops split the Republican forces in two by reaching the Mediterranean Sea, thereby sealing the fate of the Republicans. Vallejo thus did not live to see the demise of the Republican forces he supported. A number of poems were discovered among his posthumous papers by his widow, Georgette de Vallejo, who the following year published them under the title *Human Poems*. They had been written from the late 1920's to the mid-1930's and had been typed up over a period of about six months preceding Vallejo's death.

Stephen M. Hart

Bibliography

Britton, R. K. "Love, Alienation, and the Absurd: Three Principal Themes in César Vallejo's *Trilce*." *Modern Language Review* 87 (July, 1992). Demonstrates how Vallejo's poetry expresses the anguished conviction that humankind is simply a form of animal life subject to the laws of a random, absurd universe.

Buelow, Christiane von. "Vallejo's 'Venus de Milo' and the Ruins of Language." *PMLA* 104 (January, 1989). Provides a close analysis that convincingly shows how Vallejo's poetry dismembers the very structure of language itself.

Franco, Jean. *César Vallejo: The Dialectics of Poetry and Silence*. New York: Cambridge University Press, 1976. A good introduction to Vallejo's work.

Hart, Stephen, ed. *César Vallejo: Selected Poems*. London: Bristol Classical Press, 2000. Hart's introduction and notes on Vallejo include excerpts of poetry in Spanish. (The text is in English.) Also includes a bibliography and glossary.

Higgins, James. *The Poet in Peru: Alienation and the Quest for a Super-Reality*. Liverpool, England: Cairns, 1982. Contains a good overview of the main themes of Vallejo's poetry.

Vallejo, César. *César Vallejo: The Complete Posthumous Poetry*. Translated by Clayton Eshleman and José Rubia Barcia. Berkeley: University of California Press, 1978. Offers translations of the later poems and contains a helpful introduction to Vallejo's work.

Vālmīki

Indian poet

Born: Ayodhya(?), India; fl. c. 500 B.C.E.
Died: India; date unknown

POETRY: *Rāmāyana*, c. 500 B.C.E. (*The Ramayana*, 1870-1874).

Vālmīki (vahl-MEE-kee) is one of those ancient authors who tantalize scholars because so little is known or can be known about them. According to Hindu tradition, Vālmīki lived in 867,000 B.C.E.; Westernized scholars have offered their own guesses ranging from about 700 B.C.E. to approximately 500 C.E. Vālmīki may be a legend that people long ago created to account for a great work of literature. The traditional story is that Vālmīki was a highway robber. Priests told him to ask his family, whom he supported through his thefts, whether they would be willing to share in hell the torments he would reap for his sins. His relatives declined. Distraught, he again consulted the priests, who told him to repeat the holy syllables "ma" and "rā." Immobile, he complied while an anthill (*valmīka*) slowly arose around him (the source of his name). A thousand years later, the priests returned. Only then did Vālmīki realize that he had been chanting the name Rāma. Thereafter, to Vālmīki came Nārada, the messenger of the gods, who recited to the now-holy man the virtues and adventures of Rāma, the ideal hero and an incarnation of Vishnu. When he had heard the tale, Vālmīki mourned that he had no poetic power to pass on the tale to other men, until one day he saw a hunter kill a heron. Moved by his pity for the bird and his anger at the man, Vālmīki began to express himself in Sanskrit poetry. While he was reciting *slokas*, the god Brahmā appeared and ordered Vālmīki to use his newfound poetic power to sing of Rāma, his love for Sītā, and Rāma's victory over the demons. The story of Rāma is famous and has been retold many times, regardless of whoever may have composed it first. Later renditions of the *Ramayana* include Kshmendra's *Ramayana-Kathasara-Manjari*, Bhoja's *Ramayana-Champu*, and Tulsīdās's

Ram-Charit-Manas. While Vālmīki may or may not have ever lived, the poem attributed to him still holds meaning for its readers. Untold millions of people in India and beyond have found inspiration and pleasure in the *Ramayana*.

James S. Whitlark

Bibliography

Kam, Garrett. *Ramayana in the Arts of Asia*. Singapore: Select Books, 2000.

Nagar, Shanti Lal. *Genesis and Evolution of the Rama Katha in Indian Art, Thought, Literature, and Culture: From the Earliest Period to the Modern Times*. Delhi: B. R., 1999.

Pandurangarava, Ai. *Valmiki*. New Delhi: Sahitya Akademi, 1994.

_______. *Women in Valmiki*. Hyderabad, India: Andhra Mahila Sabha, 1978.

Pati, Madhusudana. *The Ramayana of Valmiki: A Reading*. Bhubaneswar, India: Orissa Sahitya Akademi, 1999.

Richman, Paula, ed. *Questioning Ramayanas: A South Asian Tradition*. Berkeley: University of California Press, 2001.

Vanamail, Devi. *Sri Rama Lila: The Story of the Lord's Incarnation as Sri Rama, Narrated by Sage Valmiki in the Ramayana*. New Delhi: Aryan Books International, 2000.

Vartaka, Padmakara Vishnu. *The Scientific Dating of the Ramayana and the Vedas*. Pune, India: Veda Vidnyana Mandala, 1999.

Sir John Vanbrugh

English playwright and architect

Born: London, England; January 24, 1664 (baptized)
Died: London, England; March 26, 1726

DRAMA: *The Relapse: Or, Virtue in Danger*, pr., pb. 1696; *Aesop, Part I*, pr. 1696; *Part II*, pr., pb. 1697 (adaptation of Edmé Boursault's play *Les Fables d'Ésope*); *The Provok'd Wife*, pr., pb. 1697; *The Country House*, pr. 1698 (adaptation of Florent-Carton Dancourt's play *La Maison de campagne*); *The Pilgrim*, pr., pb. 1700 (adaptation of John Fletcher's play *The Pilgrim*); *The False Friend*, pr., pb. 1702 (adaptation of Alain-René Lesage's play *Le Traître puni*); *Squire Trelooby*, pr., pb. 1704 (with William Congreve and William Walsh; adaptation of Molière's play *Monsieur de Pourceaugnac*); *The Confederacy*, pr., pb. 1705 (adaptation of Dancourt's play *Les Bourgeoises à la mode*); *The Mistake*, pr. 1705 (adaptation of Molière's play *Le Dépit amoureux*); *The Cuckold in Conceit*, pr. 1707 (adaptation of Molière's play *Sganarelle: Ou, Le Cocu imaginaire*); *A Journey to London*, pb. 1728 (unfinished; also known as *The Provok'd Husband*, pr., pb. 1728, with revisions by Colley Cibber).

NONFICTION: *A Short Vindication of "The Relapse" and "The Provok'd Wife,"* 1698.

MISCELLANEOUS: *The Complete Works of Sir John Vanbrugh*, 1927-1928 (4 volumes; Bonamy Dobrée and Geoffrey Webb, editors).

John Vanbrugh (VAHN-bruh) excelled in two art forms: playwriting and architecture. His father was a London merchant, his mother a daughter of Sir Dudley Carleton. Little is known of the events of Vanbrugh's early life before he became associated with the theater, except that he reportedly studied architecture in France from 1683 to 1685. He was commissioned as an officer in the British army in 1686 and served for several years. While in France in 1690 he was imprisoned for several months in the Bastille as a suspected English spy. His first play to be published, *The Relapse*, was an original work produced in 1696. *The Provok'd Wife*, another original play, was presented in 1697 but had probably been written about 1691. Other plays which he wrote or cowrote were adaptations from earlier English or continental dramatists.

The Relapse was a sequel to Colley Cibber's *Love's Last Shift* (1696). Like other dramatists of the 1690's, Vanbrugh depended on comedy of manners, sex, and lively action to carry along his plays. Social problems are introduced into the plays at times, but usually just for the purpose of making some cynical humor out of them. Notable in *The Relapse* is the sudden conversion of a debauched and faithless husband to marital constancy; such a reformation at the end of an immoral play was the dramatist's reply to charges hurled at the stage at the time that it was presenting immorality. Vanbrugh's plays, popular during his lifetime, were published in a collected edition in 1730, just four years after his death. On the side of notoriety rather than fame, Vanbrugh was one of the dramatists attacked for immorality by Jeremy Collier in his *Short View of the Immorality and Profaneness of the English Stage* (1698). Vanbrugh's published replies to Collier's attacks reveal a sophisticated understanding of comic theory.

As an architect, Vanbrugh designed Castle Howard, the Haymarket Theater, Blenheim Palace, and (with Nicholas Hawksmoor) the Clarendon Building at Oxford. Vanbrugh was knighted in 1723. He was married in 1719 to Henrietta Yarborough; they had several children, of whom a boy and a girl survived. Vanbrugh's personality and well-constructed, good-humored plays continue to hold interest for many readers and playgoers in modern times.

Paul Varner

Bibliography

Berkowitz, Gerald M. *Sir John Vanbrugh and the End of Restoration Comedy.* Amsterdam: Rodopi, 1981. Examines the works of Vanbrugh in the context of the transition from Restoration comedy to new forms of comedy. Includes bibliography and index.

Bull, Jon. *Vanbrugh and Farquhar.* New York: St. Martin's Press, 1998. Analyzes the work of Vanbrugh and George Farquhar in the context of English drama in the seventeenth and eighteenth centuries. Includes bibliography and index.

Downes, Kerry. *Sir John Vanbrugh: A Biography.* New York: St. Martin's Press, 1987. Examines the life and works of this dramatist and architect. Includes bibliography and index.

McCormick, Frank. *Sir John Vanbrugh: The Playwright as Architect.* University Park: Pennsylvania State University Press, 1991. McCormick provides both critical analysis of Vanbrugh's works and discussion of his role as architect. Includes bibliography and index.

Ridgway, Christopher, and Robert Williams. *Sir John Vanbrugh and Landscape Architecture in Baroque England, 1690-1730.* Stroud, England: Sutton in association with the National Trust, 2000. Although this work focuses on Vanbrugh as an architect, it provides valuable insights into his life and the times in which he lived. Includes bibliography and index.

Mark Van Doren

American poet

Born: Hope, Illinois; June 13, 1894
Died: Torrington, Connecticut; December 10, 1972

POETRY: *Spring Thunder, and Other Poems*, 1924; *7 P.M., and Other Poems*, 1926; *Now the Sky, and Other Poems*, 1928; *Jonathan Gentry*, 1931; *A Winter Diary, and Other Poems*, 1935; *The Last Look, and Other Poems*, 1937; *Collected Poems, 1922-1938*, 1939; *The Mayfield Deer*, 1941; *Our Lady Peace, and Other War Poems*, 1942; *The Seven Sleepers, and Other Poems*, 1944; *The Country Year*, 1946; *The Careless Clock: Poems About Children in the Family*, 1947; *New Poems*, 1948; *Humanity Unlimited: Twelve Sonnets*, 1950; *In That Far Land*, 1951; *Mortal Summer*, 1953; *Spring, and Other Poems*, 1953; *Selected Poems*, 1954; *Morning Worship, and Other Poems*, 1960; *Collected and New Poems, 1924-1963*, 1963; *The Narrative Poems*, 1964; *That Shining Place: New Poems*, 1969; *Good Morning: Last Poems*, 1973.

LONG FICTION: *The Transients*, 1935; *Windless Cabins*, 1940; *Tilda*, 1943; *Home with Hazel*, 1957.

SHORT FICTION: *Nobody Say a Word, and Other Stories*, 1953; *Collected Stories*, 1962-1968.

DRAMA: *The Last Days of Lincoln*, pb. 1959; *Three Plays*, pb. 1966 (includes *Never, Never Ask His Name*, pr. 1965).

NONFICTION: *Henry David Thoreau*, 1916 (master's thesis); *The Poetry of John Dryden*, 1920 (dissertation); *Shakespeare*, 1939; *Private Reader*, 1942; *Liberal Education*, 1942; *Noble Voice*, 1946; *Nathaniel Hawthorne*, 1949; *The Autobiography of Mark Van Doren*, 1958; *The Happy Critic, and Other Essays*, 1961; *The Essays of Mark Van Doren*, 1980.

CHILDREN'S/YOUNG ADULT LITERATURE: *Dick and Tom: Tales of Two Ponies*, 1931; *Dick and Tom in Focus*, 1932; *The Transparent Tree*, 1940.

EDITED TEXTS: *An Anthology of World Poetry*, 1928; *The Oxford Book of American Prose*, 1932; *Walt Whitman*, 1945; *The Portable Emerson*, 1946.

Mark Albert Van Doren (van DOHR-uhn) was a distinguished American poet, critic, fiction writer, editor, and educator. He was born in Hope, Illinois, the son of Dr. Charles Lucius Van Doren (a medical doctor) and Dora Ann Butz. Mark Van Doren remained on his parents' farm until he was six years old. Subsequently he, his parents, and his four brothers relocated to Urbana, Illinois.

Following the path of his older brother Carl, Mark Van Doren studied at the University of Illinois at Urbana. After he completed his bachelor's degree in 1914, he enrolled in the master's English program. Van Doren took a course in nineteenth century prose writers under the tutelage of Professor Stuart Sherman, who introduced Van Doren to Henry David Thoreau's writings. Van Doren chose the writings of Thoreau as the subject for his master's thesis. In 1915 he was awarded his master's degree.

Van Doren continued his studies at Columbia University in New York, where his brother Carl had studied previously and had become an English literature professor. Carl was very influential in Van Doren's academic career. Carl suggested Van Doren's dissertation topic: John Dryden's poetry. Van Doren received his Ph.D. in 1920.

During the fall of 1920, Van Doren became an English professor at Columbia. During his tenure, he taught several future literary critics, such as Lionel Trilling, Maxwell Geismar, and John Gassner, as well as publishers Donald Dike and Robert Giroux and novelist Jack Kerouac. Demonstrating his passion for teaching, Van Doren remained at Columbia until he retired in 1959. He came out of retirement in 1963 to accept a position at Harvard University as a visiting professor. He continued to write until his death in 1972.

During the 1920's, Van Doren was literary editor as well as film critic of the liberal weekly *The Nation*. While serving as literary editor from 1924 to 1928, Van Doren published the works of such poets as Hart Crane, Robert Graves, and Allen Tate. Also, several other members of the Van Doren family, including brother Carl, Irita (Carl's first wife), and writer and editor Dorothy Graffe (Mark's future wife), held different positions on *The Nation*. In 1922, Mark and Dorothy were married. They became the parents of two sons, Charles and John. Dorothy wrote a biography of Van Doren called *The Professor and I* in 1959.

Van Doren established himself as a significant poet when he published *Spring Thunder, and Other Poems*, consisting of early pastoral lyrics. Some of his other typical works of poetry include *Jonathan Gentry*, a narrative poem; *A Winter Diary, and Other Poems*, his frontier legend; *Our Lady Peace*, war poems; *The Seven Sleepers, and Other Poems*, war poems; *The Country Year*, poems on rural life; and *Good Morning: Last Poems*, expressions of peaceful acceptance in anticipation of death. Although Van Doren covered a variety of topics in his poetry, some of his common themes concern family, friends, nature, death, American legends, animals, and World War II.

Van Doren began his career as a critic when he published *Henry David Thoreau* in 1916. Other critical works include *The Poetry of John Dryden*, *Shakespeare*, and *Nathaniel Hawthorne*. Van Doren's major critical writings can be found in *Private Reader* and *The Happy Critic, and Other Essays*.

Included in Van Doren's fiction are four novels: *The Transients*, *Windless Cabins*, *Tilda*, and *Home with Hazel*. Some of his best short stories can be found in *Nobody Say a Word, and Other Stories*. Also to his credit are three books of children's fiction: *Dick and Tom*, *Dick and Tom in Focus*, and *The Transparent Tree*.

Van Doren's voluminous works earned for him many awards and commendations. In 1940 Van Doren won a Pulitzer Prize for *Collected Poems*. He received Columbia University's Alexander Hamilton Medal in 1959, earned the Hale Award in 1960, won the Huntington Hartford Creative Award in 1962, and received the Emerson Thoreau Award in 1963. Additionally, he was the recipient of numerous honorary degrees. Famous poets Robert Frost, T. S. Eliot, and Allen Tate commended Van Doren for his craftsmanship.

Mark Van Doren wrote more than one thousand poems, but only a few critics have given serious consideration to his poetry. Some have suggested that it is unnecessary to analyze or interpret his work because it is not difficult to understand. In fact, many critics have used the term "lucidity" when referring to his poetry.

Nila M. Bowden

Bibliography

Bradbury, Eric, et al., eds. *The Penguin Companion to American Literature*. New York: McGraw-Hill, 1971. This source gives a few biographical details and lists many of Van Doren's major works.

Curley, Maurice Kramer, et al., eds. *Modern American Literature*. Vol. 3. New York: Frederick Ungar, 1969. This source provides critical commentary on Van Doren's works. Several different critics and sources are represented.

Hart, James D., ed. *The Oxford Companion to American Literature*. New York: Oxford University Press, 1995. This source gives a listing of Van Doren's major works.

Perkins, George, et al., eds. *Benét's Reader's Encyclopedia of American Literature*. New York: HarperCollins, 1991. Includes a biography with emphasis on Van Doren's major works.

Rood, Karen L., ed. *American Literary Almanac from 1608 to the Present*. New York: Bruccoli Clark Layman, 1988. This source includes details about Mark Van Doren as well as discussions about other literary figures with whom he associated.

Mona Van Duyn

American poet

Born: Waterloo, Iowa; May 9, 1921

POETRY: *Valentines to the Wide World*, 1959; *A Time of Bees*, 1964; *To See, to Take*, 1970; *Bedtime Stories*, 1972; *Merciful Disguises*, 1973; *Letters from a Father, and Other Poems*, 1982; *Near Changes*, 1990; *If It Be Not I: Collected Poems, 1959-1982*, 1993; *Firefall: Poems*, 1993; *Selected Poems*, 2002.

Mona Jane Van Duyn (van DIN), the first woman to be named poet laureate in the United States, was born in Waterloo, Iowa, in 1921. Neither of her parents was particularly literary, and her father used to urge her to stop reading (an activity Van Duyn learned to enjoy early in her life) and go outdoors to play. Van Duyn developed an early love of poetry despite its unsympathetic treatment by her parents and even by her teachers, who often used memorizing assignments as punishment for unruly students.

After her high school graduation, Van Duyn's father tried to discourage her from going to college. She managed to leave home for Iowa State Teachers' College (now the University of Northern Iowa) only after a long, intense campaign and only because she had won a scholarship. In college, Van Duyn's writing finally received serious attention from one of her teachers; one of her English professors helped to direct her reading and urged her to begin trying to publish her work. She received her B.A. in 1942 and an M.A. from the University of Iowa in 1943, the same year that she married Jarvis Thurston, an English professor. During the next twenty-five years, Van Duyn held a variety of teaching posts at the University of Iowa, the University of Louisville, and Washington University. During the same period, she and her husband founded and edited *Perspective*, a literary journal.

Van Duyn's first two books, *Valentines to the Wide World* and *A Time of Bees*, and the positive critical attention they received, led her to decide that teaching occupied too much of her energies. She ended her career as a full-time teacher in 1967, although she continued to conduct workshops and poetry readings.

After the publication of her second book, Van Duyn began to receive prizes and awards for her work. In 1966 she was one of the first five American poets to win a grant from the National Endowment for the Arts, and in 1970 she won the prestigious Bollingen Prize for poetry. During this period, she also served as poetry consultant for the Olin Library Modern Literature Collection of Washington University (the university at which her own papers are housed). In 1971 *To See, to Take* won the National Book Award, and in 1972, the year of *Bedtime Stories*, Van Duyn received a Guggenheim Fellowship.

The volume *Near Changes* won the 1991 Pulitzer Prize in poetry, and in 1992 Van Duyn became the first woman appointed as poet laureate consultant in poetry by the Library of Congress. After the laureate appointment, she noted that she hoped to use her position to nurture younger poets by inviting them to read in the Library of Congress's reading series.

Van Duyn has said of her work style that she writes only when she has ideas and does not try to maintain a daily writing schedule. When she is ready to compose, she proceeds by patient revision—composing a few lines, typing them out, and then revising them before she goes on to the next few lines. Van Duyn has drawn on all parts of her world for inspiration; her poems sometimes refer to her family life (she has protested the label "domestic," noting that many men also write about their home lives without receiving such a label), but they also come from history, literature, the subject of poetry itself, and even newspaper items. Still, her most vivid work seems to center on household settings and to involve characters who seem like family members (Van Duyn is reserved about discussing her private life so no conclusions can necessarily be drawn about it from her poems). They become the means by which Van Duyn addresses the themes that dominate her work—love and the difficulties of experiencing love in a flawed world.

Van Duyn is a formalist who uses and adapts traditional forms such as sonnets (which she sometimes pares into "minimalist" sonnets) as well as other stanza forms. She also relies on rhyme (often slant rhyme), sometimes for witty effects. The range of Van Duyn's subjects—from the detective story, to an aunt's letters (which combine apocalyptic religious vision with family chitchat), to the death of an elderly parent in a nursing home, to references to Plato and Alexander Pope—gives her work room to address her central idea, that the poem is the vehicle that can lead readers to understand the world and their relationships to the other people in it.

Ann D. Garbett

Bibliography

Augustine, Jane, and William T. Hamilton. "Mona Van Duyn." In *Critical Survey of Poetry*, edited by Philip K. Jason. 2d rev. ed. Pasadena, Calif.: Salem Press, 2003. A good introductory essay to Van Duyn's life and writings through *Firefall.*

Burns, Michael, ed. *Discovery and Reminiscence: Essays on the Poetry of Mona Van Duyn*. Fayetteville: University of Arkansas Press, 1998. Contains tributes by fellow poets, critical and interpretative essays, biographical notes, and "Matters of Poetry," the revised text of Van Duyn's 1993 lecture at the Library of Congress.

Hall, Judith. "Strangers May Run: The Nation's First Woman Poet Laureate." *The Antioch Review* 52, no. 1 (Winter, 1994): 141. Hall examines Van Duyn's work in an effort to discover why she was the first woman to be appointed poet laureate of the United States.

Prunty, Wyatt. *"Fallen from the Symboled World": Precedents for the New Formalism*. New York: Oxford University Press, 1990. In this work on American poetry in the twentieth century, Prunty discusses Van Duyn in the chapter "Pattern of Similitude."

Jean-Claude van Itallie

American playwright

Born: Brussels, Belgium; May 25, 1936

DRAMA: *War*, pr. 1963; *Almost Like Being*, pr. 1964; *The Hunter and the Bird*, pr. 1964; *I'm Really Here*, pr. 1964; *America Hurrah*, pr. 1966 (trilogy; includes *The Interview*, *TV*, and *Motel*); *Where Is De Queen?*, pr. 1966; *War, and Four Other Plays*, pb. 1967; *The Serpent: A Ceremony*, pr. 1968; *The King of the United States*, pr. 1972, revised pb. 1973 (as *Mystery Play*); *A Fable*, pr. 1975; *Bag Lady*, pr. 1979; *Naropa*, pb. 1980; *The Tibetan Book of the Dead: Or, How Not to Do It Again*, pr. 1983; *Early Warnings*, pr. 1983 (includes *Bag Lady*, *Sunset Freeway*, and *Final Orders*); *Pride*, pr. 1985 (in *Faustus in Hell*); *Paradise Ghetto*, pr. 1987; *The Traveller*, pr. 1987; *Ancient Boys*, pr. 1989; *Struck Dumb*, pr. 1989; *The Odyssey*, pr. 1991 (musical); *America Hurrah, and Other Plays*, pb. 2001.

DRAMA TRANSLATIONS: *The Seagull*, pr. 1973 (of Anton Chekhov); *Cherry Orchard*, pr. 1977 (of Chekhov); *Medea*, pr. 1979 (of Euripides); *Three Sisters*, pr. 1979 (of Chekhov); *Uncle Vanya*, pb. 1980 (of Chekhov); *The Balcony*, pr. 1985 (of Jean Genet); *The Master and Margarita*, pr. 1993 (of Mikhail Bulgakov); *Chekhov: The Major Plays*, pb. 1995.
SCREENPLAY: *Three Lives for Mississippi*, 1971.
TELEPLAYS: *Hobbies: Or, Things Are All Right with the Forbushers*, 1967; *Take a Deep Breath*, 1969; *Picasso: A Painter's Diary*, 1980.
NONFICTION: *The Playwright's Workbook*, 1997.

Jean-Claude van Itallie (van IHT-ahl-lee) was born in Brussels, Belgium, May 25, 1936, son of investment banker Hugo Ferdinand and Marthe Mathilde Caroline (Levy) van Itallie. The family emigrated to the United States in 1940. He grew up comfortably in Great Neck, New York, but came to view the suburbs as a horrible place to live. Because his grandfather piqued his interest in history, he went on to major in the history and literature of Russia, France, and England at Harvard, graduating in 1958. He set up an apartment in New York City and a country home in Charlemont, Massachusetts. Van Itallie has routinely taken residencies at theaters and universities, working on production of his plays and teaching playwriting. These include the Yale School of Drama, New York University, the Naropa Institute and the University of Colorado in Boulder, and Kent State University, Ohio, where he has donated his papers. A private man, van Itallie maintains inner harmony through practicing yoga and Buddhism.

In 1959 van Itallie began graduate school at New York University and studied acting at the Neighborhood Playhouse. He took his first job in 1960 as editor of the *Transatlantic Review.* Next, he wrote teleplays for the religious television program *Look Up and Live*, simultaneously writing experimental one-act plays for the budding Off-Off-Broadway theater. He became playwright-in-residence at the newly formed Open Theatre and established a lasting professional relationship with director Joseph Chaikin. They worked together with the actors to develop new performance techniques, striving for ways to establish emotional contacts with the audience by combining the experimental with the classical, metaphorically depicted in their first production, *War.* Van Itallie presented three one-act plays, *The Interview*, *TV*, and *Motel*, in the 1966 social-political satire *America Hurrah.* The production attracted both critical and popular attention and established the experimental Off-Off-Broadway theater as a viable artistic force. Chaikin began to work with his troupe on improvisations about the Creation and Fall, while van Itallie gave their work structure and words, resulting in *The Serpent: A Ceremony*, which established both their international reputations.

Until this time, van Itallie had focused more on gesture and movement than on dialogue to create his plays. However, in the 1970's he changed his focus to language, translating four of Anton Chekhov's plays. He worked with Chaikin on the 1973 production of his adaptation of *The Seagull* as well as on his original play, *A Fable*, an adult picaresque journey, in 1975. Having embraced Buddhism, van Itallie wrote two plays about the healing effect of acknowledging the split between the body and the mind, *Naropa* and *The Tibetan Book of the Dead: Or, How Not to Do It Again*, a production which combined the improvisation and movement from the Open Theatre and the language of the classics.

Van Itallie returned to the one-act play form in 1979 with the acclaimed *Bag Lady*, a metaphor for reducing one's life to essentials. In the 1980's he wrote *Paradise Ghetto*, which told of the Nazi detention camp at Theresienstadt. In his tale of this Nazi showcase for the International Red Cross, van Itallie superimposed the personalities of Open Theatre actors onto the prisoners, developing contrasting cabaret sketches with poignant characters that left the audience feeling the triumph of the human experience.

In May, 1984, Joseph Chaikin suffered a stroke and van Itallie spent much of his time nursing him back to health. In January, 1985, van Itallie and Chaikin began working to create a play that takes its characters from reality to a dream state and back to reality. He also wrote *Struck Dumb*, a performance piece for Chaikin to use while he was recovering.

Van Itallie's *Ancient Boys* is his addition to the body of literature responding to the AIDS epidemic. He has also continued to translate and to adapt the classics with his musical version of *The Odyssey.* Van Itallie attempts to create clear theatrical metaphors that communicate to the entire being: the head, the heart, the gut, and the groin, synthesizing a truth that causes the audience to say, "Ah, yes!"

Gerald S. Argetsinger

Bibliography

"Ages of the Avant-Garde." *Performing Arts Journal* 16 (January, 1994). A detailed account of van Itallie's writing.

Bryer, Jackson R., ed. *The Playwright's Art: Creating the Magic of Theater.* New York: Thunder's Mouth Press, 1997. Considers van Itallie's aesthetic.

Cohn, Ruby. *New American Dramatists, 1960-1990.* 2d ed. New York: St. Martin's Press, 1991. Joseph Chaikin's theatrical relationship with van Itallie is explored.

Lahr, John. *Up Against the Fourth Wall.* New York: Grove Press, 1970. Important early assessment of van Itallie's work.

Plunka, Gene. *Jean-Claude van Itallie and the Off-Broadway Theater.* Newark: University of Delaware Press, 1999. Assesses van Itallie's role in the history of Off-Broadway theater. Includes an extensive bibliography.

Serif 8 (Winter, 1972). Jean-Claude van Itallie special issue. Important early assessment of van Itallie's work.

Carl Van Vechten

American novelist and critic

Born: Cedar Rapids, Iowa; June 17, 1880
Died: New York, New York; December 21, 1964
Identity: Gay or bisexual

LONG FICTION: *Peter Whiffle: His Life and Works*, 1922; *The Blind Bow-Boy*, 1923; *The Tattooed Countess*, 1924; *Firecrackers*, 1925; *Nigger Heaven*, 1926; *Spider Boy*, 1928; *Parties*, 1930.

NONFICTION: *Music After the Great War*, 1915; *Music and Bad Manners*, 1916; *Interpreters and Interpretations*, 1917; *The Merry-Go-Round*, 1918; *The Music of Spain*, 1918; *In the Garret*, 1920; *Interpreters*, 1920; *The Tiger in the House*, 1920; *Red*, 1925; *Excavations*, 1926; *Sacred and Profane Memories*, 1932; *Fragments from an Unwritten Autobiography*, 1955; *Keep A-inchin' Along: Selected Writings of Carl Van Vechten About Black Art and Letters*, 1979 (Bruce Kellner, editor); *The Letters of Gertrude Stein and Carl Van Vechten, 1913-1946*, 1986 (Edward Burns, editor); *Letters of Carl Van Vechten*, 1987 (Kellner, editor); *Remember Me to Harlem: The Letters of Langston Hughes and Carl Van Vechten, 1925-1964*, 2001 (Emily Bernard, editor).

Carl Van Vechten (van VEHK-tuhn) moved deftly through three careers: He began as a music, dance, and drama critic, producing several volumes of wide-ranging, urbane essays; then he devoted himself to fiction, writing seven well-received novels in a decade that saw the first publications of Ernest Hemingway, F. Scott Fitzgerald, and John Dos Passos; finally, he became a noted photographer, specializing in portraits of writers and artists.

Van Vechten's father was a banker turned insurance company executive; his mother was a college graduate, suffragist, and political and social activist. Born when his parents were in their forties, Van Vechten had two siblings much older than he and so spent his childhood surrounded by four adults. Predictably, this atmosphere nurtured a precocious child. By the time he was an adolescent, Van Vechten had thoroughly immersed himself in whatever cultural offerings could be found in Cedar Rapids—opera, theater, and concerts that stopped in the city on tour—and began to apply his own talents to amateur theatrical productions and family piano recitals. Physically he was an awkward youth—too tall too early, with large buck teeth—and his omnivorous appetite for culture made him feel socially awkward among his peers. Longing to escape from the complacent bourgeois existence of Cedar Rapids, he enrolled at the University of Chicago and, in 1899, took his first steps east, a direction that would eventually lead to New York and then to Paris.

At college, Van Vechten studied with Robert Morss Lovett and William Vaughn Moody. He also began writing passionately and composing music. After graduating in 1903, he took a job on the *Chicago American*; he was assigned to write short news pieces and collect photographs to illustrate news stories. He soon decided, however, that, for his purposes, Chicago was little better than Cedar Rapids. In 1906, he left for New York.

Van Vechten's first writing assignment there was an opera review for Theodore Dreiser, then editor of *Broadway Magazine*. Soon Van Vechten joined the staff of *The New York Times* as assistant to the music critic. From 1908 to 1909, he served as Paris correspondent for the *Times*, a post which brought him into close contact with leading European dancers, sculptors, artists, and writers. When he returned to New York in the spring of 1909, he resumed his job as music critic, but he longed to return to Europe. He would return to Paris in 1914. Van Vechten was open about his homosexuality but married twice. In 1912 he divorced Anna Elizabeth Snyder, a childhood friend he had married five years before. Shortly after the divorce, he met the Russian-Jewish actress Fania Marinoff, whom he would soon marry. In 1913, he met Mabel Dodge, the irrepressible center of her own vibrant salon. In 1914, at the second performance of Igor Stravinsky's *Le Sacre du Printemps* in Paris, he met Gertrude Stein, at whose rue de Fleurus home he would soon encounter the leading figures of Parisian cultural life.

From 1915 to 1932 Van Vechten wrote an astonishing number of books—first several volumes of essays on music and the arts, then seven novels. He preferred the experimental and the daring, particularly the works of young artists being performed, written, and conducted in the United States and on the Continent. The enthusiasm with which he greeted such works helped earn their acceptance by his readers. He predicted the enduring greatness of Stravinsky at a time when some wondered if what they were hearing was, indeed, music. He approached his task as critic with "curiosity and energy," he said, and his tastes, idiosyncratic as they were, reflected his certainty in empathizing with the aims of modern artists.

In 1928 his brother died, leaving Van Vechten a substantial bequest that allowed him financial independence. This event coincided with, and perhaps made possible, his new career, that of photographer. He had his first show in 1934 and became a portrait photographer of such writers and artists as Stein, Truman Capote, George Gershwin, Leontyne Price, and William Faulkner.

Van Vechten was the founder of several libraries and archives, including the James Weldon Johnson Memorial Collection (black art and literature) at Yale, the George Gershwin Memorial Collection (music) at Fisk University, the Rose McClendon Memorial Collection (photographs of famous blacks) at Howard University, and the Florine Stettheimer Memorial Collection (fine arts) at Fisk.

The spirit of the jazz age, the roaring twenties, and the "lost generation" is well depicted in the saucy and irreverent novels of Van Vechten. In all his diverse endeavors, Van Vechten was witty, cosmopolitan, and above all, unconventional. He publicized the work of such writers as Faulkner, Ronald Firbank, and especially Stein, who remained his close friend until her death and who assigned him as her literary executor. He was among the first critics to recognize the exciting cultural renaissance flourishing in Harlem and devoted much effort to helping establish the careers of Countée Cullen, Langston Hughes, James Weldon Johnson, Bessie Smith, Ethel Waters, and other African American artists. He saw himself as a popularizer and supporter of avant-garde artists, and, with a clear eye and self-assurance, he brought to the attention of the American public exotic figures ranging from Vaslav Nijinsky and Erik Satie to Mary Garden and Stravinsky.

Van Vechten, more than many of his contemporaries, lived the literary life with seemingly boundless enthusiasm. His verve animates all of his writing, including the essays he frequently contributed to such trend-setting journals as *Trend*, *The Smart Set*, and *Vanity Fair*, and this effervescent spirit informs his novels as well. His wide interests, diverse friendships, and tireless pursuit of the new, the brilliant, and the innovative make Van Vechten a fascinating guide to cultural life in the United States in the first decades of the twentieth century.

Linda Simon

Bibliography

Coleman, Leon. *Carl Van Vechten and the Harlem Renaissance*. New York: Garland, 1998. Essentially a biography on Van Vechten, emphasizing his interest and influence in the arts. Contains much valuable background information on Van Vechten and his relationships with fellow writers, artists, and dancers during the 1920's.

Lueders, Edward. *Carl Van Vechten*. New York: Twayne, 1965. A critical study on Van Vechten containing a brief biography, a discussion of his novels and other works, an afterword, a chronology, and a bibliography. A knowledgeable, sympathetic study by Leuders, who defends Van Vechten's work from critics' attacks on its superficiality and pointlessness.

_______. *Carl Van Vechten and the Twenties*. Albuquerque: University of New Mexico Press, 1955. Discusses Van Vechten's novels and volumes on music and art in the context of the hectic high life of the 1920's. Lueders, a friend of Van Vechten and critic of his work, has written an interesting study of this author and the decade during which he produced his novels.

Van Vechten, Carl. *Letters of Carl Van Vechten*. Edited by Bruce Kellner. New Haven, Conn.: Yale University Press, 1987. An intimate portrait of Van Vechten, as seen through his letters to friends, fellow authors, publishers, artists, biographers, and family members. The letters have been selected from private collections and private and public institutions.

Van Vechten, Carl, and Langston Hughes. *Remember Me to Harlem: The Letters of Langston Hughes and Carl Van Vechten, 1925-1964*. Edited by Emily Bernard. New York: Alfred A. Knopf, 2001. Provides an inside view of the Harlem Renaissance as well as insight into Van Vechten's relationships with fellow authors and musicians.

Mario Vargas Llosa

Peruvian novelist

Born: Arequipa, Peru; March 28, 1936

LONG FICTION: *La ciudad y los perros*, 1962 (*The Time of the Hero*, 1966); *La casa verde*, 1965 (*The Green House*, 1968); *Los cachorros*, 1967 (novella; *The Cubs*, 1979); *Conversación en la catedral*, 1969 (*Conversation in the Cathedral*, 1975); *Pantaleón y las visitadoras*, 1973 (*Captain Pantoja and the Special Service*, 1978); *La tía Julia y el escribidor*, 1977 (*Aunt Julia and the Scriptwriter*, 1982); *La guerra del fin del mundo*, 1981 (*The War of the End of the World*, 1984); *La historia de Alejandro Mayta*, 1984 (*The Real Life of Alejandro Mayta*, 1986); *¿Quién mató a Palomino Molero?*, 1987 (*Who Killed Palomino Molero?*, 1987); *El hablador*, 1987 (*The Storyteller*, 1989); *Elogio de la madrastra*, 1988 (*In Praise of the Stepmother*, 1990); *Lituma en los Andes*, 1993 (*Death in the Andes*, 1996); *Los cuadernos de don Rigoberto*, 1997 (*The Notebooks of Don Rigoberto*, 1998); *Fiesta del Chivo*, 2000 (*The Feast of the Goat*, 2001).

SHORT FICTION: *Los jefes*, 1959 (*The Cubs, and Other Stories*, 1979).

DRAMA: *La señorita de Tacna*, pb. 1981 (*The Young Lady from Tacna*, 1990); *Kathie y el hipopótamo*, pb. 1983 (*Kathie and the Hippopotamus*, 1990); *La Chunga*, pb. 1987 (English translation, 1990); *Three Plays*, pb. 1990; *El loco de los balcones*, pb. 1993.

NONFICTION: *La novela en América Latina: Dialogo*, 1968; *Literatura en la revolución y revolución en literatura*, 1970 (with Julio Cortázar and Oscar Collazos); *La historia secreta de una novela*, 1971; *Gabriel García Márquez: Historia de un deicidio*, 1971; *El combate imaginario*, 1972; *García Márquez y la problemática de la novela*, 1973; *La novela y el problema de la expresión literaria en Peru*, 1974; *La orgía perpetua: Flaubert y "Madame Bovary,"* 1975 (*The Perpetual Orgy: Flaubert and "Madame Bovary,"* 1986); *José María Arguedas: Entre sapos y halcones*, 1978; *La utopia arcaica*, 1978; *Entre Sartre y Camus*, 1981; *Contra viento y marea, 1964-1988*, 1983-1990 (3 volumes); *A Writer's Reality*, 1991 (Myron I. Lichtblau, editor); *Fiction: The Power of Lies*, 1993; *Pez en el agua*, 1993 (*A Fish in the Water: A Memoir*, 1994); *Making Waves*, 1996; *Cartas a un joven novelista*, 1997 (*Letters to a Young Novelist*, 2002); *Claudio Bravo: Paintings and Drawings*, 1997 (with Paul Bowles); *El lenguaje de la pasión*, 2001 (*The Language of Passion*, 2003); *La verdad de las mentiras*, 2002.

Peru's leading contemporary novelist, Jorge Mario Pedro Vargas Llosa (VAHR-gahs YOH-sah), is regarded as one of the creators (along with such writers as Julio Cortázar, Gabriel García Márquez, and Carlos Fuentes) of the new Latin American novel. Born in the town of Arequipa in southern Peru, Mario Vargas Llosa was the son of Ernesto Vargas Maldonado and Dora Llosa Ureta. His parents were divorced before he was born, and he was taken by his mother to live at Cochabama, Bolivia, with her parents, who spoiled him. When he was nine, he and his mother left for Piura, in northwestern Peru; however, a year later, his parents remarried, and they moved the family to Lima.

The pampered and sensitive boy found himself no longer the center of attention. At the Catholic school he attended in Lima, he was younger than most of his classmates and was consequently ridiculed. At home, his artistic activities had to be kept from his father, who (like many Peruvians) regarded writing as no work for a man. For Vargas Llosa, literature became an escape and, as he later described it, a way of justifying his existence. Intending to "make a man of him," Vargas Llosa's father sent his son to a military academy in Lima, the Leoncio Prado. The machismo and brutality he encountered there proved highly traumatic for the young man.

This experience ended in 1952, when Vargas Llosa returned to Piura for his final year of secondary school. In Piura he worked part-time on the newspaper *La Industria* and wrote a play called "La huida" (the escape). Returning to Lima, Vargas Llosa studied for his degree in literature at the University of San Marcos, while being employed as a journalist with Radio Panamericana and the newspaper *La Crónica*. In 1955 he married Julia Urquidi, a Bolivian; the marriage ended in divorce. In 1965 he married his first cousin Patricia Llosa, with whom he had two sons and a daughter.

Vargas Llosa made a brief visit to Paris in 1958 and won a prize in a short-story competition sponsored by *La Revue française*. The winning story, "El desafío" (the challenge), was published in his first book of short stories. The book won for Vargas Llosa the Premio Leopoldo Alas award in Spain, where it was published in 1959. That same year the author traveled to the University of Madrid on a scholarship but decided to move on to Paris without completing his doctoral dissertation. He lived there for seven years, working as a Berlitz teacher, as a journalist, and with URTF, the French radio and television network.

In Paris, Vargas Llosa met other Latin American and French writers and intellectuals but worked and wrote in relative isolation until the publication of his first novel, *The Time of the Hero*, which caused a sensation throughout the Spanish-speaking world. Highly experimental in style, the novel portrays an educational institution that deliberately corrupts innocence and perverts idealism in its students (indicting both the Leoncio Prado and the Peruvian military regime that it represents). The Peruvian military authorities burned a thousand copies of the book on the grounds of the Leoncio Prado and dismissed the work as the product of a demented Communist mind. In Spain, however, it received the Premio de la Crítica Española, and it has been translated into more than a dozen languages.

The Green House appeared three years later. The title refers both to a Piura brothel and to the rain forest. The social messages—the complicity between army and church, the horrors of human exploitation—coexist with the intense inner conflicts of the characters. Some critics disparaged the novel's characters as one-dimensional, failing to understand that for Vargas Llosa a novel is primarily a chronicle of action, not an inner revelation of the forces that motivate action. The book was awarded numerous prizes in Spain and Peru.

In 1966 Vargas Llosa left Paris for London, accepting an appointment as visiting lecturer in Latin American literature at the University of London; he also traveled and lectured throughout Great Britain and Europe. He then spent a semester as writer-in-residence at the University of Washington in Seattle.

After the publication of his third novel, *Conversation in the Cathedral*, a monumental two-volume indictment of Peruvian life under the corrupt dictatorship of Manuel Udria (he ruled from 1948 to 1956), Vargas Llosa lectured briefly at the University of Puerto Rico. The doctoral dissertation he had begun in 1959, a study of the fiction of his close friend Gabriel García Márquez, was finally published in 1971. Two years later a fourth novel appeared: *Captain Pantoja and the Special Service*. While it once again attacked the unholy alliance of church, army, and brothel, it was written in a new farcical style. This comic vein continues in the author's next novel, *Aunt Julia and the Scriptwriter*, a satirical account of the discovery of a Bolivian genius in his genre: radio melodramas.

Besides being a writer of fiction, Vargas Llosa has published much literary criticism. For him, writing literary criticism is a creative act, not unlike that of writing a novel or a short story, in which the critic indulges in the same arbitrariness and fantasy as the author.

Finally, Vargas Llosa has taken an active role in Peruvian politics, running for president in 1990. As a spokesman for democratic centrism, he has been harshly criticized by his erstwhile colleagues on the left. Not only in speeches and journalistic pieces but also in novels such as *The Real Life of Alejandro Mayta* and *The Feast of the Goat*, Vargas Llosa has cast a skeptical eye on revolutionary ideology and its real-world outcomes. Political controversy, however, has not diminished his reputation as one of the leading writers in Latin America.

Genevieve Slomski

Bibliography

Booker, M. Keith. *Vargas Llosa Among the Postmodernists*. Gainesville: University Presses of Florida, 1994. One of the most comprehensive treatments of Vargas Llosa's work. Includes chapters such as "The Reader as Voyeur" and "Literature and Modification."

Castro-Klaren, Sara. *Understanding Mario Vargas Llosa*. Columbia: University of South Carolina Press, 1990. Offers an insightful analysis of Vargas Llosa's major works of fiction and views the works in their political and cultural context.

Cevallos, Francisco Javier. "García Márquez, Vargas Llosa, and Literary Criticism: Looking Back Prematurely." *Latin American Research Review* 26, no. 1 (1991): 266-275. An interesting article about Vargas Llosa and his peer Gabriel García Márquez.

Farnsworth, Elizabeth. "The Temptation of Mario." *Mother Jones* 14, no. 1 (January, 1989): 22-28. A smartly written popular biography of Vargas Llosa, set in the middle of his presidential campaign.

Gerdes, Dick. *Mario Vargas Llosa*. Boston: Twayne, 1985. A varied and useful collection of critical essays by Gerdes; includes a chronology of events and a bibliography.

Guillermoprieto, Alma. *Looking for History: Dispatches from Latin America*. New York: Pantheon, 2001. Discusses Vargas Llosa's political career.

Kerr, R. A. *Mario Vargas Llosa: Critical Essays on Characterization*. Potomac, Md.: Scripta Humanistica, 1990. Offers a varied and in-depth study of characterization in Vargas Llosa's major works.

Kristal, Efra'n. *Temptation of the Word: The Novels of Mario Vargas Llosa*. Nashville: Vanderbilt University Press, 1999. Kristal examines the overarching reasons for Vargas Llosa's political passions and divides Vargas Llosa's writing career into sections corresponding to results of his ideas on capitalism and the decline of the Cuban Revolution.

Lutes, Todd Oakley. *Shipwreck and Deliverance: Politics, Culture and Modernity in the Works of Octavio Paz, Gabriel García Márquez and Mario Vargas Llosa*. Lanham, Md.: University Press of America, 2003. A comparative study of three of the most important Latin American writers of the twentieth century.

Moses, Michael Valdez. *The Novel and the Globalization of Culture*. New York: Oxford University Press, 1995. Discusses the cultural context of Vargas Llosa's major works of fiction.

Williams, Raymond L. *Mario Vargas Llosa*. New York: Ungar, 1986. Provides a detailed overview of the author's life and work.

Henry Vaughan

Welsh poet

Born: Newton-on-Usk, Wales; April 17, 1622
Died: Llansantfffraed, Wales; April 23, 1695

POETRY: *Poems*, 1646; *Silex Scintillans*, parts 1 and 2, 1650, 1655; *Olor Iscanus*, 1651; *Thalia Rediviva*, 1678; *The Secular Poems of Henry Vaughan*, 1958 (E. L. Marilla, editor); *The Complete Poetry of Henry Vaughan*, 1964 (French Fogle, editor).

MEDICAL TRANSLATIONS: *Hermetical Physick*, 1655 (of Heinrich Nolle); *The Chymists Key to Open and to Shut*, 1657 (of Nolle).

NONFICTION: *The Mount of Olives: Or, Solitary Devotions*, 1652.

MISCELLANEOUS: *The Works of Henry Vaughan*, 1914, 1957 (L. C. Martin, editor).

A number of seventeenth century poets won new popularity in the mid-twentieth century in the wake of a revived interest in the Metaphysical poetry of John Donne. Among them is Henry Vaughan (vawn), whose works reflect the influence of the religious lyrics of Donne and his disciple George Herbert.

Vaughan came from a middle-class Welsh family. He was born in 1622 in Newton-on-Usk, Brecknockshire, and, with his twin brother Thomas, received his early education from Matthew Herbert, a clergyman who lived in a nearby village. The two young men probably entered Jesus College, Oxford, together in 1638; the records of Thomas's matriculation, but not of Henry's, are still extant.

Thomas Vaughan remained in Oxford to receive his degree and was later ordained a priest in the Church of England, but Henry went on to London in 1640 to study law. There is little factual evidence of his activities at that time, but he probably took advantage of the opportunity to become familiar with contemporary literature. His first volume of poetry reveals his knowledge of the works of many of the Cavalier poets of the court of Charles I.

Vaughan seems to have abandoned his legal studies about 1642 with the outbreak of the Civil Wars, and he served in King Charles's army. He was also employed as clerk to Sir Marmaduke Lloyd, chief justice of the Brecon Circuit, Vaughan's home district.

Vaughan's first book of poems was published in 1646. The verses included in it, polished love lyrics addressed to his lady, Amoret, are full of classical allusions and Platonic sentiments in the Caroline tradition of Thomas Carew, John Suckling, and Thomas Randolph. Vaughan wrote other such poems, but they were not published until later decades, partly because of unpopular political references; the Puritans controlled South Wales after 1646. A second, perhaps stronger, reason was Vaughan's increasing preoccupation with religion. His growing seriousness was apparently intensified by the death of his younger brother William in 1648. His religious thought was also influenced by that of Thomas, who had turned his attention from orthodox Anglicanism to neo-Platonism, mysticism, and the occult sciences. Henry's poetry reflects a neo-Platonic concept of childhood as a state during which people gradually grow away from the union with God that preceded their birth. Humankind's constant yearning for the renewal of this perfect unity of the human and the divine is the subject of many of his lyrics.

Vaughan settled in his father's home, the village of Newton-on-Usk, in 1646 and married Catherine Wise of Warwickshire soon afterward. At some time in the next decade he began practicing medicine. No evidence has been discovered to indicate when or where he received his medical training. The self-trained physician was a common feature in rural areas like his. His wife died in 1653, leaving her husband with four young children. Two years later he married his wife's sister, Elizabeth, with whom he had four more children.

Vaughan's prose and poetic works appeared with regularity during the years from 1650 to 1655. The best of his poems appeared in *Silex Scintillans*, published in two parts, in 1650 and 1655, and in *Olor Iscanus*, in 1651. *Silex Scintillans* (the flashing flint) is a two-part sequence of religious verse in the manner of Herbert, whom Vaughan calls his master. Whereas Herbert wrote from a priest's position in *The Temple* (1633), however, Vaughan wrote as a pious individual who prays often and meditates over the Bible. The two parts are organized around poems of conversion, repentance, forgiveness, death, and judgment. *Olor Iscanus* (the swan of Usk) continues the secular themes of Vaughan's poems from 1646 but emphasizes the rural life of retirement rather than the urban life of arts and politics. Vaughan places himself as the poet of the Usk River, which flowed through his native countryside. Vaughan disowned these secular lyrics when he published the second part of *Silex Scintillans*, and his first modern editors tended to pass over them, but readers have come increasingly to recognize that the sacred and secular poems reflect a single poetic sensibility.

Vaughn's devotional essays, the *Mount of Olives*, came out in 1652, followed by translations of several religious and medical treatises. He published almost nothing for almost twenty years after this burst of creative activity. His final volume, *Thalia Rediviva*, a collection of his own later poems and of several by his brother, Thomas, who had died in 1666, appeared in 1678. Vaughan lived to a venerable age for his century, dying at the age of seventy-three in Llansantffraed.

Thomas Willard

Bibliography

Calhoun, Thomas O. *Henry Vaughan: The Achievement of "Silex Scintillans."* Newark: University of Delaware Press, 1981. Calhoun claims that *Silex Scintillans* is in the tradition of lyric sequences that originated with Petrarch's *Le Rime*. After outlining that tradition, Calhoun examines the revisions in *Silex Scintillans* in terms of biographical details, historical events, and stylistic concerns.

Davies, Stevie. *Henry Vaughan*. Chester Springs, Pa.: Dufour Editions, 1995. A concise historical narrative of the life and works of Henry Vaughan. Includes an index and a bibliography.

Friedenreich, Kenneth. *Henry Vaughan*. Boston: Twayne, 1978. Friedenreich discusses three characteristics of Vaughan's style—the Welsh language, the Bible, and Hermetic philosophy—and illustrates their impact on Vaughan's work. *Olor Iscanus, Silex Scintillans*, and the major prose receive most of the attention. Includes lengthy analyses of individual poems, a chronology, and a select annotated bibliography.

Rudrum, Alan, ed. *Essential Articles for the Study of Henry Vaughan*. Hamden, Conn.: Archon Books, 1987. Rudrum has reprinted twenty-one articles, only two of which are excerpts from books on Vaughan. Major Vaughan scholars analyze individual poems such as "The Night" and "Regeneration" and discuss Vaughan's subjects such as nature, infancy, Hermeticism, and mysticism.

Young, R. V. *Doctrine and Devotion in Seventeenth-Century Poetry: Studies in Donne, Herbert, Crashaw, and Vaughan*. Rochester, N.Y.: D. S. Brewer, 2000. Young provides a critical interpretation of English early modern and Christian poetry. Includes bibliographical references and index.

Ivan Vazov

Bulgarian novelist, poet, and playwright

Born: Sopot, Bulgaria; June 27, 1850
Died: Sofia, Bulgaria; September 22, 1921

LONG FICTION: *Pod igoto*, 1889-1890 (serial), 1893 (book; *Under the Yoke*, 1894); *Nova zemya*, 1896; *Kazalarskata tsaritsa*, 1903; *Svetoslav terter*, 1907.

SHORT FICTION: *Selected Stories*, 1967.

DRAMA: *Sluzhbogontsi*, pb. 1903; *Borislav*, pb. 1909; *Ivaylo*, pb. 1911.

POETRY: *Izbavlenie*, 1878; *Gusla*, 1881; *Epopeya na zabravenite*, 1881-1884; *Polya i gori*, 1884; *Pod nasheto nebe*, 1900; *Pesni za makedoniya*, 1916; *Ne shte zagine*, 1920; *Selected Poems*, 1976.

NONFICTION: *Velika Rilska pustina*, 1904 (*The Great Rila Wilderness*, 1969).

Ivan Minchov Vazov (VA-zof), for thirty years the outstanding writer in Bulgaria, was that country's first great writer in the various creative genres of the novel, poetry, and drama. During his most influential years, from 1890 to 1920, his name was used to characterize these years as "the Vazov period."

Vazov received his elementary education in his native town of Sopot and at Plovdiv. The son of a conservative, well-to-do merchant, he enjoyed a comfortable childhood. He left Bulgaria when he was nineteen, and his first creative work, poems on patriotic and revolutionary themes, were published in Bucharest in the 1870's.

During this time he made a business trip to Romania and met the revolutionary writers Lyuben Stoychev Karavelov and Khristo Botev. Inspired by them and by the prerevolutionary poet Petko Rachev Slaveykov, he decided to give up his studies and devote his work to the revolutionary cause.

After the liberation of Bulgaria from Turkish rule in 1878, he returned to his country and served as judge of the circuit court in Berkovitsa. From 1886 to 1889 he was a political exile in Odessa, having opposed Stefan Nikolov Stambolov's Bulgarian government. When he returned to Sofia he settled down to a life of prolific writing, achieving his most notable success in 1893 with the novel *Under the Yoke*, a story of the beginnings of the Bulgarian revolt against the Turks.

All his novels, plays, and poems were praised for expressing sympathy for the common people. On October 2, 1920, he was honored by a national jubilee celebrating his completion of fifty years of creative work. He died of a heart attack in Sofia on September 22, 1921.

Vasa D. Mihailovich

Bibliography

Manning, Clarence Augustus. *The History of Modern Bulgarian Literature*. New York: Bookman Associates, 1960.

Moser, Charles A. *A History of Bulgarian Literature, 1865-1944*. The Hague, the Netherlands: Mouton, 1972.

Protokhristova, Kleo. "Ivan Vazov." In *Modern Slavic Literature*, compiled by Vasa D. Mihailovich. 2 vols. New York: Frederick Ungar, 1972-1976.

_______, ed. *South Slavic Writers Before World War II*. Vol. 147 in *Dictionary of Literary Biography*. New York: Gale Research, 1995.

Thorstein Veblen

American economist

Born: Manitowoc County, Wisconsin; July 30, 1857
Died: Palo Alto, California; August 3, 1929

NONFICTION: *The Theory of the Leisure Class*, 1899; *The Theory of Business Enterprise*, 1904; *The Blond Race and the Aryan Culture*, 1913; *The Instinct of Workmanship and the State of the Industrial Arts*, 1914; *Imperial Germany and the Industrial Revolution*, 1915; *An Inquiry into the Nature of Peace and the Terms of Its Perpetuation*, 1917; *The Higher Learning in America: A Memorandum on the Conduct of Universities by Business Men*, 1918; *The Place of Science in Modern Civilisation, and Other Essays*, 1919; *The Engineers and the Price System*, 1921; *Absentee Ownership and Business Enterprise in Recent Times: The Case of America*, 1923; *Elimination of the Unfit*, 1950; *Essays, Reviews, and Reports*, 1973.

Thorstein Bunde Veblen (VEHB-luhn) was born to Norwegian immigrant parents on a farm in Wisconsin when that state was still largely on the frontier. In 1865 the family moved to a 290-acre farm in Minnesota in a Norwegian community where Old World ways and speech were dominant. When Veblen was seventeen, his father, eager for his children to be educated, enrolled his son at Carleton College in Northfield, Minnesota.

After graduation Veblen went to Madison, Wisconsin, where he taught for a year (1880-1881) at Monona Academy. Afterward, he enrolled at The Johns Hopkins University. Failing to receive a fellowship there, he left before the first term's end for Yale University, where he took a Ph.D. in philosophy in 1884. That same year two of his writings appeared: an essay on the philosophy of Immanuel Kant in the *Journal of Speculative Philosophy* and an essay on the surplus federal revenue of 1837. The latter won the John Addison Porter Prize.

Unable to find a job despite his publications and his doctorate, Veblen returned to the farm in Minnesota, where he led an unhappy life. After marrying Ellen May Rolfe, whom he had known in college, he moved with her to a farm in Iowa. In 1891 he obtained a fellowship at Cornell University, continuing to write for academic journals. Through a friend he received a teaching fellowship at the new University of Chicago in 1892, where he remained until 1906. During this period he also served as editor of the *Journal of Political Economy* from 1896 to 1905, and his two best-known works—*The Theory of the Leisure Class* and *The Theory of Business Enterprise*—were published, making him famous outside academic circles.

Because of marital problems Veblen moved west, where he taught at Stanford University for slightly more than two years, leaving because of a love affair in 1909. Returning to the Midwest to teach at the University of Missouri in 1911, he married a second time. He held his academic position at Missouri for seven years, continuing to write his controversial books. After a brief period as an editor of the *Dial* he became a faculty member at the New School for Social Research in 1919. Over the years his thought and writings became more bitter and increasingly revolutionary. When his second wife died in 1926, he returned to his mountain cabin near Palo Alto, California, living with his stepdaughter until his death from heart disease just after his seventy-second birthday.

Veblen's was a stormy life. He was the subject of one of H. L. Mencken's most derisive essays in the first series of his *Prejudices*, published in 1919. Mencken ridiculed Veblen's tortured style and what he considered the essential hollowness of the ideas, concluding that Veblen was merely a "geyser of pish-posh." Nevertheless, Veblen's writings had a considerable influence on social and economic thought among those who opposed his theories as well as among those who admired them.

Victoria Gaydosik

Bibliography

Dowd, Douglas Fitzgerald. *Thorstein Veblen*. Rev. ed. New Brunswick, N.J.: Transaction, 2000. Depicts Veblen as a penetrating thinker, one who cast a fresh eye on the contemporary American passion for making money.

Jorgenson, Elizabeth. *Thorstein Veblen: Victorian Firebrand*. Armonk, N.Y.: M. E. Sharpe, 1999. Biography sets to correct previous popular impression of Veblen as a notorious womanizer, examining his enlightened views on women's equality in society.

Louca, Francisco, and Mark Perlman. *Is Economics an Evolutionary Science? The Legacy of Thorstein Veblen*. Northampton, Mass.: E. Elgar, 2000. Collection of essays makes clear both the strengths and weaknesses of Veblen's theories, which regarded economic laws as evolutionary, not absolute.

Spindler, Michael. *Veblen and Modern America: Revolutionary Iconoclast*. Sterling, Va.: Pluto, 2002. Study sets Veblen's work in its social and intellectual context, spelling out its main concepts and reestablishing the extent of its influence. Portrays Veblen as a seminal analyst and critic of American culture.

"Thorstein Veblen in Contemporary Perspective." *Social Science Quarterly* 60, no. 3 (December, 1979). A special issue devoted to an overview of scholarship on Veblen.

Tilman, Rick. *The Intellectual Legacy of Thorstein Veblen*. Westport, Conn.: Greenwood Press, 1996. Provides historical context, describing the changes in the American society and economy to which Veblen's writings respond.

Lope de Vega Carpio

Spanish playwright

Born: Madrid, Spain; November 25, 1562
Died: Madrid, Spain; August 27, 1635

DRAMA: *Los comendadores de Córdoba*, wr. 1596-1598, pb. 1609; *El nuevo mundo descubierto por Cristóbal Colón*, wr. 1596-1603, pb. 1614 (*The Discovery of the New World by Christopher Columbus*, 1950); *El mayordomo de la duquesa de Amalfi*, wr. 1599-1606, pb. 1618 (*The Majordomo of the Duchess of Amalfi*, 1951); *El anzuelo de Fenisa*, wr. 1602-1608, pb. 1617; *La corona merecida*, wr. 1603, pb. 1620; *La noche toledana*, wr. 1605, pb. 1612; *Los melindres de Belisa*, wr. 1606-1608, pb. 1617; *El acero de Madrid*, wr. 1606-1612, pb. 1618 (*Madrid Steel*, 1935); *Castelvines y Monteses*, wr. 1606-1612, pb. 1647 (English translation, 1869); *La niña de plata*, wr. 1607-1612, pb. 1617; *Peribáñez y el comendador de Ocaña*, wr. 1609-1612, pb. 1614 (*Peribáñez*, 1936); *La buena guarda*, wr. 1610, pb. 1621; *Las flores de don Juan, y rico y pobre trocados*, wr. 1610-1615, pb. 1619; *El villano en su rincón*, wr. 1611, pb. 1617 (*The King and the Farmer*, 1940); *Fuenteovejuna*, wr. 1611-1618, pb. 1619 (*The Sheep-Well*, 1936); *Lo cierto por lo dudoso*, wr. 1612-1624, pb. 1625 (*A Certainty for a Doubt*, 1936); *El perro del hortelano*, wr. 1613-1615, pb. 1618 (*The Gardener's Dog*, 1903); *El caballero de Olmedo*, wr. 1615-1626, pb. 1641 (*The Knight from Olmedo*, 1961); *La dama boba*, pb. 1617 (*The Lady Nit-Wit*, 1958); *Amar sin saber a quién*, wr. 1620-1622, pb. 1630; *El mejor alcalde, el rey*, wr. 1620-1623, pb. 1635 (*The King, the Greatest Alcalde*, 1918); *Los Tellos de Meneses I*, wr. 1620-1628, pb. 1635; *El premio del bien hablar*, wr. 1624-1625, pb. 1636; *La moza de cántaro*, wr. 1625-1626, pb. 1646?; *El guante de doña Blanca*, wr. 1627-1635, pb. 1637; *El castigo sin venganza*, pb. 1635 (based on Matteo Bandello's novella; *Justice Without Revenge*, 1936); *Four Plays*, pb. 1936; *Las bizarrías de Belisa*, pb. 1637; *Five Plays*, pb. 1961.

LONG FICTION: *La Arcadia*, 1598; *El peregrino en su patria*, 1604 (*The Pilgrim: Or, The Stranger in His Own Country*, 1621); *Los pastores de Belén*, 1612; *Novelas a Marcia Leonarda*, 1621; *La Dorotea*, 1632.

POETRY: *La Dragontea*, 1598; *El Isidro*, 1599; *La hermosura de Angélica*, 1602; *Rimas*, 1602; *El arte nuevo de hacer comedias en este tiempo*, 1609 (*The New Art of Writing Plays*, 1914); *Jerusalén conquistada*, 1609; *Rimas sacras*, 1614; *La Circe*, 1621; *La filomena*, 1621; *Triunfos divinos*, 1625; *La corona trágica*, 1627; *Laurel de Apolo*, 1630; *Amarilis*, 1633; *La gatomaquia*, 1634 (*Gatomachia*, 1843); *Rimas humanas y divinas del licenciado Tomé de Burguillos*, 1634; *Filis*, 1635; *La Vega del Parnaso*, 1637.

NONFICTION: *Égloga a Claudio*, 1637.

The architect of the Golden Age of the theater in Spain was Lope Félix de Vega Carpio (VAY-gah KAHR-pyoh), often just Lope de Vega, who could justly boast that when he started writing plays only two companies of actors were performing, whereas at the end of his career forty companies employing at least a thousand people were providing the Spanish capital with plays. Scholarship sets his total dramatic output at about eight hundred plays. At least 507 of these are unquestionably his, and many of the others are in his handwriting. The total body of his work is more than any other dramatist can claim, and though many plays were written in less than one day, none is wholly insignificant, none untouched by his genius. Publishers sent shorthand experts to the theater to copy his plays and pirate them. In the provinces managers advertised their offerings as by Lope de Vega to be sure of an audience. So great was his popularity that anything excellent, from food to jewels, was referred to as "of Lope."

This *monstruo de la naturaleza* (prodigy of nature), as Miguel de Cervantes called him, was the son of a worker in gold. An ecclesiastical patron entered him in the University of Alcalá de Henares, and in 1580 he was a student at Salamanca, but a love affair with the wife of an actor kept him from taking orders as he had planned. This was the first of many love affairs, all of which he transmuted into important literary works. Friends had only to suggest a form of literature he had not attempted to have him compose for them a good example of it. The theater was his great love. Able to write a play in verse almost faster than a scribe could copy it, he seized on anything as a plot idea. The medical fad of taking iron for the blood inspired *Madrid Steel*. A proverb was the seed of *The Gardener's Dog*.

In his rhymed *The New Art of Writing Plays* Lope de Vega laid down the rules under which he wrote: "In the first act, state your case; in the second, your events, so that not till the middle of the third does anybody begin to suspect what is going to come of it all. . . . Do not permit the solution till you come to the last scene." As a result his dramas are full of suspense. Action, not philosophy, was what his audiences wanted, and he confessed that the audience dictated his plots, chose his characters, and wrote his plays. Though he knew the rules of the classical theater, he admitted that, with a half dozen exceptions, he broke them to please the people and to be true to life. Prose and poetry, he hoped, would gain him fame, and he made no secret of the fact that he wrote plays for money.

Although his genius touched all types of drama, his popularity rested chiefly on the type called *comedias de capa y espada*, or cape-and-sword plays, which were full of intrigue and complications and included masked nobles and women disguised as men. The plots commanded the characters, and stock impulses motivated the action (love easily transferred, jealousy easily aroused, honor easily offended). An entertaining and involved plot kept the spectators guessing until matrimony at the final curtain washed away all stains on family honor. The outcome of these plays is not always logical. In his treatise on playwriting, Lope de Vega declared: "At times, that which is contrary to logic for that very reason is pleasing."

He was also successful in religious plays with saints as heroes, in comedies of manners with lower-class characters, and in heroic plays with historical or legendary characters, such as *The Sheep-Well* and *The King, the Greatest Alcalde*. In addition he composed several hundred *autos sacramentales*, short plays for the Corpus Christi season and other Church holy days.

Lope de Vega was also fertile in nondramatic works. The epic poem *La hermosura de Angélica* (the beauty of Angelica) runs to eleven thousand lines, and he penned ten thousand lines in poetic tribute to Madrid's patron Saint Isidor. The epic *Jerusalén conquistada* (Jerusalem conquered) is twice that long. In 1598 he composed *La Dragontea*, an epic in ten cantos about the misdeeds of Francis Drake, and wrote two thousand lines about the loves and adventures of a cat in his mock epic *Gatomachia*. Fifteen hundred sonnets resulted from his poetic musing. In prose he wrote *La Arcadia*, a pastoral novel. His favorite novel, *La Dorotea*, was inspired by his first love; frequently revised, it was finally published in 1632.

In his personal life, however, Lope de Vega's reputation was less admirable. His sexual escapades and resulting legal difficulties were the talk of all Spain. As a boy he showed precocity, composing poetry when he was only five and writing a play at the age of twelve. He ran away from school with a companion and toured Spain until a pawnbroker grew suspicious at the wealth they displayed and turned them over to the police.

At the university he perfected himself chiefly in fencing, singing, and dancing. Once his studies were over, he surrendered to his love for the theater and by the age of fifteen was seeing his plays professionally performed. His love for adventure led him in 1583 to join a naval expedition to the Azores; he returned to an intensive life of writing. Five years later he was banished from Madrid on penalty of death for a criminal libel against the family of his mistress, Elena Osorio, the daughter of a theatrical manager for whom he provided plays. From exile in Valencia he wooed Isabel de Urbina and returned boldly to the capital to elope with her. Nineteen days after their marriage he left her to join the Armada; he used his leisure from military duties to write an epic poem.

Rough seas and the death of his brother made war unattractive, and following Isabel's death he spent the next forty years in a succession of love intrigues and scandals. His two favorite children were illegitimate. Friend and associate of the nobility, serving the duke of Alba, the marques of Malpica, and the count of Lemos, he reached the depths as panderer for the dissipated duke of Sessa.

However, he had his moments of repentance. In 1609 he became a *familiar* of the Inquisition. He joined three religious confraternities in two years. When his second wife, Juana, and their son Carlos died almost simultaneously, Lope de Vega entered holy orders. In 1614, however, when he was ordained priest in Toledo, he was at the same time providing mistresses for Sessa and carrying on a love affair of his own. In 1614 he met Marta de Nevares, the great love of his life, whom he immortalized as Amaryllis in his poetry and whom he cared for tenderly during her illness, blindness, and descent into madness.

Lope de Vega was a strange compound of sensuality, pettiness, conceit, servility, and genius. Over time the last quality has outweighed all the rest, and it was that quality that all Madrid recognized on Tuesday, August 28, 1635, when he was accorded funeral honors such as have seldom been equaled for a person of letters.

When his grave, San Estéban, was remodeled in the eighteenth century, no distinguishing mark was put on his coffin, so that the whereabouts of Lope de Vega's present grave are uncertain. He left his monument in the creation of Spanish theater, however.

He established the play of three acts, set down rules of versification for the expression of various emotions and situations, and brought to the stage a richness of poetic inspiration unequaled in Spanish literature. He reflected the life, customs, and ideas of the sixteenth and seventeenth centuries with naturalness and poetic freedom. Inferior to Tirso de Molina in handling comedy, incapable of the poetic heights of Pedro Calderón de la Barca, less careful than Pedro Antonio de Alarcón in character portrayal and analysis, Lope de Vega Carpio nevertheless surpassed all his contemporaries in skill at blending poetry and life, which he painted in vivid colors, although he did not interpret it deeply. He gave freedom and importance to women and dignity to the lower classes and produced an enormous number of masterpieces at the time when variety was necessary to encourage a theatergoing public and bring to greatness the theater of the Golden Age in Spain.

Charlene E. Suscavage

Bibliography

Fox, Diane. *Refiguring the Hero: From Peasant to Noble in Lope de Vega and Calderón.* University Park: Pennsylvania State University Press, 1991. Fox examines the image of the hero and class status in the works of Lope de Vega and Pedro Calderón de la Barca. Includes bibliography and index.

McKendrick, Melveena. *Playing the King: Lope de Vega and the Limits of Conformity.* Rochester, N.Y.: Tamesis, 2000. An examination of Lope de Vega's portrayal of the monarchy in his works. Includes bibliography and index.

Morrison, Robert R. *Lope de Vega and the Comedia de Santos.* New York: Peter Lang, 2000. This study examines the religious drama of Lope de Vega. Includes bibliography and index.

Ostlund, DeLys. *The Re-creation of History in the Fernando and Isabel Plays of Lope de Vega.* New York: Peter Lang, 1997. Ostlund examines the historical aspects of the dramas of Lope de Vega. Includes bibliography and index.

Smith, Marlene K. *The Beautiful Woman in the Theater of Lope de Vega: Ideology and Mythology of Female Beauty in Seventeenth Century Spain.* New York: Peter Lang, 1998. A discussion of the feminine beauty as portrayed in the works of Lope de Vega. Includes bibliography and index.

Wright, Elizabeth R. *Pilgrimage to Patronage: Lope de Vega and the Court of Philip III, 1598-1621.* Lewisburg, Pa.: Bucknell University Press, 2001. This study focuses on the patronage system and the interactions between politics and the life and work of Lope de Vega. Includes bibliography and index.

Giovanni Verga

Italian novelist

Born: Catania, Kingdom of the Two Sicilies (now in Sicily, Italy); September 2, 1840
Died: Catania, Sicily, Italy; January 27, 1922

LONG FICTION: *Amore e patria*, 1857; *I carbonari della montagna*, 1861-1862; *Sulle lagune*, 1863 (serial), 1975 (book); *Una peccatrice*, 1866 (*A Mortal Sin*, 1995); *Storia di una capinera*, 1871 (*Sparrow: The Story of a Songbird*, 1994); *Eva*, 1873; *Eros*, 1874; *Tigre reale*, 1875; *I malavoglia*, 1881 (partial translation as *The House by the Medlar Tree*, 1890, 1953; complete translation, 1964); *Il marito di Elena*, 1882; *Mastro-don Gesualdo*, 1889 (English translation, 1893, 1923).

SHORT FICTION: *Primavera ed altri racconti*, 1876; *Vita dei campi*, 1880 (*Under the Shadow of Etna*, 1896); *Novelle rusticane*, 1883 (*Little Novels of Sicily*, 1925); *Per le vie*, 1883; *Vagabondaggio*, 1887; *I ricordi del capitano D'Arce*, 1891; *Don Candeloro e C'.*, 1894; *Dal tuo al mio*, 1905 (adaptation of his play); *Cavalleria Rusticana, and Other Stories*, 1926; *The She-Wolf, and Other Stories*, 1958.

DRAMA: *Rose caduche*, wr. 1873-1875, pb. 1928; *Cavalleria rusticana*, pr., pb. 1884 (adaptation of his short story; *Cavalleria Rusticana: Nine Scenes from the Life of the People*, 1893); *In portineria*, pb. 1884 (adaptation of his short story "Il canario del N. 15"); *La lupa*, pr., pb. 1896 (adaptation of his short story); *La caccia al lupo*, pr. 1901 (adaptation of his short story; *The Wolf Hunt*, 1921); *La caccia alla volpe*, pr. 1901; *Dal tuo al mio*, pr. 1903; *Teatro*, pb. 1912.

NONFICTION: *Lettere al suo traduttore*, 1954; *Lettere a Dina*, 1962, 1971; *Lettere a Luigi Capuana*, 1975.

Widely considered the greatest Italian novelist after Alessandro Manzoni, Giovanni Verga (VAYR-gah) was born in Catania, Sicily, in 1840, of a family supposed to have come from Aragon in the thirteenth century. The Vergas were a family of patriots. The grandfather was an underground fighter for independence and a deputy to the first Sicilian parliament in 1812. During Giovanni's boyhood, his mother encouraged him to read. Although he gave her credit for his decision at the age of fifteen to become a novelist, biographers point out that his teacher Pietro Abato wrote poems and novels and assigned classwork that caused the young student to write a six-hundred-page novel about George Washington and the American Revolution. Fortunately, Verga knew more about the subjects of his later fiction.

Instead of entering the university in 1860, he persuaded his father to let him use the money to publish another manuscript he had completed in four volumes—*I carbonari della montagna*, concerning the adventures of his grandfather. During the next fifteen years Verga lived in Florence and Milan. In these cities, under the influence of the French writers, he wrote passable novels of middle-class life, among them the sentimental *Sparrow: The Story of a Songbird*. In Milan he described adultery in high society in *Eva* and *Tigre reale*.

From this distance Verga could look back on his childhood home and draw upon his impressions of Sicilian life. He scorned being classified. When some found in him the masked pity and underlying pessimism of a Thomas Hardy and others called him a supporter of Verism, with its anti-Romanticist reaction, he retorted that "works of art may be born of any -ism. The main thing is for it to be born."

The years from 1878 to 1880, after he returned to Milan following the death of his favorite sister in Sicily, marked the turning point in his career. His renewed interest in the Sicilian peasants and fishermen as subjects of art was shown in the collection of short stories that contained "Cavalleria Rusticana," a tale of primitive passion and violence that he was to dramatize in 1884 and then use as the libretto for an opera. His greatest fame came from *The House by the Medlar Tree*, a novel dealing with Sicilian fishermen defeated in their struggle for existence, with their town as the real protagonist. Verga's hometown, under the disguise of Trezza, also figured in his last great novel, *Mastro-don Gesualdo*, which tells of the downfall of a proud, ambitious peasant.

The foreword to *The House by the Medlar Tree* had announced Verga's intent to write a Sicilian *comedie humaine* that would show "the slow, inevitable flow of the rivers of social life." Writing was hard for him, though, and during the last twenty years of his life spent in his native town in southern Sicily he wrote and published little. He died at Catania on January 27, 1922.

The style of Verga's writing, mentioned by all critics, grew from his admiration for a moving story by a sea captain that he read when young and which appealed to him in spite of its colloquial and illiterate style. Although an aristocrat, Verga tried to make his own writing echo the speech of simple peasants. For most readers the wealth of detail and the keen observation of the life and customs of the lower class give his novels of southern Italy their greatest appeal. D. H. Lawrence was moved to translate *Mastro-don Gesualdo* and two volumes of short stories in order to give pleasure to readers ignorant of Italian.

Bibliography

Adams, Robert Martin. "The Godfather's Grandfather." *The New York Review of Books* 31 (December 20, 1984): 46-49. A discussion of Verga's works, including *The She-Wolf, and Other Stories*; notes that his reputation stems from the sparse, realistic stories of Sicilian peasants that he wrote in the 1880's; claims that Verga's haunting studies of the destructive power of sex and money retain much of their impact.

Cecchetti, Giovanni. *Giovanni Verga*. Boston: Twayne, 1978. A solid introductory study with chapters on Verga's formative years and his maturity, with separate chapters on *The House by the Medlar Tree* and *Mastro-don Gesualdo*. Includes chronology, notes, and an annotated bibliography.

_______. Introduction to *The She-Wolf, and Other Stories*, by Giovanni Verga. Berkeley: University of California Press, 1958. This volume contains the best of Verga's short fiction available in translation. Divided in two parts, with selections of stories from Verga's early and late period. Cechetti emphasizes that this translation was made "as literal as possible" in order to "render the spirit as well as the letter of the original."

Hemmings, F. W. J., ed. *The Age of Realism*. Baltimore: Penguin Books, 1974. Contains an essay, "Giovanni Verga: From 'Verismo' to Realism." A short but perceptive discussion of Verga's career, situating him in the context of European realism.

Lane, Eric. Introduction to *Short Sicilian Novels*, by Giovanni Verga, translated by D. H. Lawrence. London: Daedalus Books, 1984. Lane's introduction provides the reader with an accurate historical overview and with perspicacious critical observations. The three-page chronology proves to be useful and informative and one of the best compiled on Verga.

Lucente, Gregory. "The Ideology of Form in Verga's 'La lupa': Realism, Myth, and the Passion of Control." *Modern Language Notes* 95 (1980): 105-138. Lucente argues that the interaction of realistic and mythic structures in "The She-Wolf" determines its logic; contends that within the social world of the story, the basic opposition of passion and control (irrational/rational, nature/culture, libido/superego) is pushed to a transcendent realm in terms of pure expression and absolute repression.

Patruno, Nicholas. *Language in Giovanni Verga's Early Novels*. Chapel Hill: University of North Carolina Press, 1977. An excellent study that examines, analyzes, and determines the linguistic norm of the early works of Giovanni Verga, namely *Una peccatrice, Eva, Tigre reale*, and *Eros*. This work comprises a historical introduction and an explanation of phonology and lexicon used by Verga in his early novels.

Vergil
(Publius Vergilius Maro)

Roman poet

Born: Andes, near Mantua, Cisalpine Gaul (now in Italy); October 15, 70 B.C.E.
Died: Brundisium (now Brindisi, Italy); September 21, 19 B.C.E.

POETRY: *Eclogues*, 43-37 B.C.E. (also known as *Bucolics*; English translation, 1575); *Georgics*, c. 37-29 B.C.E. (English translation, 1589); *Aeneid*, c. 29-19 B.C.E. (English translation, 1553).

Publius Vergilius Maro, known as Vergil (VUR-juhl), author of one of the most familiar epics in all literature, was born in the village of Andes, in what is today northern Italy, on October 15, 70 B.C.E., only a few decades before the end of the Golden Age of the Roman Republic. It is claimed that his father was a potter who, through hard work and an advantageous marriage, had become a landowner prosperous enough to give his son a superior education. The youth studied under eminent teachers at Cremona and Milan and under the Greek poet and grammarian Parthenius at Naples. At the age of twenty-three Vergil went to Rome to study not only poetry and philosophy but also mathematics and physics under Siro the Epicurean, whose philosophy affected Vergil and his writings throughout his life.

Although he was a shy, rustic, and slow-spoken youth, his personal charm and the literary ability evident in his early poems won Vergil the friendship of some of the most cultivated and powerful men in Rome, among them Octavian, Maecenas, Pollio, Horace, and Cornelius Gallus. His popularity was such that in 41 B.C.E., when his farm was threatened with seizure, along with surrounding territories to be divided among the victorious soldiers of the triumvirs returning from the battle of Philippi, his friends were able to intercede at Rome to have it saved. Despite his popularity in the capital, however, Vergil spent much time in retirement on his beloved farm, studying Greek and Roman history and literature.

With the encouragement of his friend Asinius Pollio, Vergil continued work on the *Eclogues*, which were begun around 43 (some scholars say 45) and finally completed about 37 B.C.E. These idyllic pastoral poems were based on the *Idylls* of the third century B.C.E. Sicilian poet Theocritus. The setting, structure, and language of the *Eclogues* are highly imitative, but their greater complexity and artificiality reflect a wider range of observation and the background of a more highly developed civilization. They are also original in their extensive use of allegory and their many laudatory references to the author's friends.

After the publication of the *Eclogues*, Vergil took up residence at a country estate near Naples, where he spent most of the rest of his life. It was there that he wrote the *Georgics*, a didactic poem in four books on the subject of husbandry. Written at the request of Maecenas, who wished to revive an interest in the old Roman virtues of industry and a fondness for rustic life, the poems are considered to be the most technically polished and elaborate of all Vergil's work. Unlike the rather dry, strictly didactic *Works and Days* (c. 700 B.C.E.) of the Greek poet Hesiod, on which they were based, the *Georgics* were obviously never intended to teach the specific techniques of successful agriculture to anyone who did not know them already. What they aimed to do, and did most successfully, was to interest the reader in the lost art of agriculture by making it attractive and interesting to him. This the author did by means of graceful language, imaginative imagery, concrete illustrations, and digressions on various subjects which added much to the charm, if not to the unity, of the work.

Vergil was forty-one years old before he embarked on his lifelong ambition, the composition of a Homeric epic which would commemorate the glory of Rome and his friend the Emperor Augustus and would win back the Roman people, unsettled and corrupted by long civil strife, to their primitive religion and ancient virtues. Ancient legend has Vergil working on the *Aeneid* for eleven years, but seven seems more accurately to fit the evidence. While traveling in Greece, Vergil fell ill to a fever and returned homeward as far as Brundisium before dying on September 21, 19 B.C.E. Final revisions were not yet completed, but Augustus ordered—against Vergil's stated wishes—that the work be preserved.

Vergil chose as his topic the voyage of the Trojan hero Aeneas to Italy after the fall of Troy, because Aeneas was the only character in the Homeric tale whom poets had connected with the legendary founding of Rome. Although Vergil borrowed heavily not only from Homer but also from Apollonius, Greek tragedy, and the Latin epic poet Ennius, the total conception and expression were all his own. The skillful handling of the hexameters, the imagery, and the characterizations of the central figures were all original, as was the interweaving of numerous old tales and legends into one comprehensive whole. In the character of Queen Dido, particularly, one finds a "modern" treatment of romantic love and its effects on the human character largely foreign to Greek classical literature. The *Aeneid* is a literary rather than a "true" epic in that it is the result of conscious artistic effort rather than of natural, gradual evolution. However, there is nothing artificial in Vergil's deeply rooted patriotic sentiment nor in his unquestioning belief in the divine origin and destiny of the Roman state. His *Aeneid* remains today one of the most stirring productions of a great civilization.

Alan Cottrell

Bibliography

Bernard, John D., ed. *Vergil at 2000: Commemorative Essays on the Poet and His Influence*. New York: AMS Press, 1986. Fifteen essays by noted scholars, concerning most aspects of Vergilian scholarship, including the author's life and style and his historical background and influence.

Comparetti, Domenico. *Vergil in the Middle Ages*. Translated by E. F. M. Benecke. 1895. Reprint. Princeton, N.J.: Princeton University Press, 1997. A masterpiece of intellectual history, this work covers the poet's reception and identity from antiquity to late medieval times (through Dante). Comparetti looks not only at Vergil's critical reception but also at the popular Christian folklore surrounding him and at his impact upon Italian and European self-identity.

Hardie, Philip R. *Virgil*. Oxford, England: Oxford University Press, 1998. Offers interpretation and criticism of the *Aeneid* and the *Georgics*.

Jenkyns, Richard. *Virgil's Experience, Nature, and History: Times, Names, and Places*. New York: Clarendon Press, 1998. This large-scale work examines Vergil's ideas of nature and historical experience as compared with similar ideas throughout the ancient Western world. Jenkyns also discusses the influence of Vergil's works on later thought, particularly regarding views of nature, the landscape, and the environment.

Levi, Peter. *Virgil: His Life and Times*. New York: St. Martin's Press, 1999. A thorough introduction to Vergil for the beginning student.

Martindale, Charles, ed. *The Cambridge Companion to Virgil*. New York: Cambridge University Press, 1997. This collection of twenty-one essays (including the editor's introduction) is divided into four sections covering the translation and reception of Vergil's works, his poetic career, historical contexts, and the content of his thought. A helpful dateline is included as well as some illustrations and numerous bibliographies.

Otis, Brooks. *Virgil: A Study in Civilized Poetry*. Norman: University of Oklahoma Press, 1995. This classic work argues for Vergil as a sophisticated poet who presented mythic, well-known material in a new and meaningful style to his urban readers. Covers the *Aeneid*, the *Bucolics*, and the *Georgics*. A useful survey of Vergilian scholarship is included as a foreword in the 1995 edition.

Perkell, Christine, ed. *Reading Vergil's "Aeneid": An Interpretive Guide*. Norman: University of Oklahoma Press, 1999. Contains several essays covering various aspects of the work on a book-by-book basis. The editor also provides an introduction discussing the work's historical background and themes. Several essays on such topics as influences and characters conclude this fine study.

Verbart, Andre. "Milton on Vergil: Dido and Aeneas in *Paradise Lost*." *English Studies* 78 (March, 1997): 111-126. Discusses the relationship between Vergil and John Milton's Adam and Eve. Notes that in Milton's epic, Adam's first words to Eve echo Aeneas's last words to Dido; notes four other parallels that had never been noted and comments on how Vergil's work affected the structure of Milton's epic.

Paul Verlaine

French poet

Born: Metz, France; March 30, 1844
Died: Paris, France; January 8, 1896
Identity: Gay or bisexual

POETRY: *Poèmes saturniens*, 1866; *Fêtes galantes*, 1869 (*Gallant Parties*, 1912); *La Bonne Chanson*, 1870; *Romances sans paroles*, 1874 (*Romances Without Words*, 1921); *Sagesse*, 1881; *Jadis et naguère*, 1884; *Amour*, 1888; *Parallèlement*, 1889, 1894; *Femmes*, 1891 (English translation, 1977); *Bonheur*, 1891; *Chansons pour elle*, 1891; *Liturgies intimes*, 1892; *Odes en son honneur*, 1893; *Élégies*, 1893; *Dans les limbes*, 1894; *Épigrammes*, 1894; *Chair, dernière poésies*, 1896; *Invectives*, 1896; *Hombres*, 1903 (English translation, 1977); *Selected Poems*, 1948; *Femmes/Hombres*, 1977 (includes English translation of *Femmes* and *Hombres*).

SHORT FICTION: *Louise Leclercq*, 1886; *Histoires comme ça*, 1903.

DRAMA: *Les Uns et les autres*, pr. 1884; *Madame Aubin*, pr. 1886.

NONFICTION: *Poètes maudits*, 1884; *Mes hôpitaux*, 1891; *Quinze Jours en Hollande*, 1892; *Mes prisons*, 1893; *Confessions*, 1895 (*Confessions of a Poet*, 1950); *Les Mémoires d'un veuf*, 1896; *Charles Baudelaire*, 1903; *Critiques et conférences*, 1903; *Souvenirs et promenades*, 1903; *Voyage en France par un français*, 1903.

Paul Marie Verlaine (vur-lehn) was the son of a former captain of engineers of Napoleon's army. He was educated in Paris and then secured a minor position with an insurance company, a job that provided a small salary while leaving him time for creative work. In 1870 he married Mathilde Mauté. In the following year he formed the friendship with Arthur Rimbaud that was to affect his life so profoundly. His close relationship with Rimbaud, with whom he was infatuated, would prove extremely important to the development of Verlaine's mature poetry. With Rimbaud, a much younger man, Verlaine wandered through England, France, and

Belgium. He had long been drinking heavily, and the journey ended disastrously when he tried to shoot Rimbaud in an altercation over Verlaine's wife. This act cost Verlaine two years in prison at Mons, during which time he converted to Catholicism; Rimbaud went to North Africa to begin a dissolute life of drugs and gunrunning, eventually contracting syphilis. After his relationship with Verlaine, he never wrote again. When Verlaine returned to France in 1875, his wife divorced him. He then went to England again to earn his living as a teacher of French.

Verlaine had begun his poetic career in the Parnassian school, led by Leconte de Lisle, whose members aimed at a severity in poetry. Soon he slipped away from them into the eighteenth century fantasies of *Fêtes galantes*. This phase was not Verlaine's important work. His greatest significance, beginning with *Romances Without Words*, lies in his contribution to the Symbolist movement.

The poets included in this general movement were at first known as the "decadents," a term that Verlaine was willing to accept. The name "Symbolists" was suggested by Jean Moréas, and the school derived primarily from Charles Baudelaire's poem "Correspondences," in which nature is described as a "forest of symbols." Symbolism was a reaction against the austere impersonality of the Parnassians and can perhaps best be described by quoting Stéphane Mallarmé's comment: "To name an object is to suppress three-fourths of the enjoyment of the poem. . . . to suggest it, there is the dream." Thus Symbolist poetry consists largely of vague suggestions and half-hints, by which the poet tries to express "the secret affinities of things with his soul." Verlaine said in his poem "The Art of Poetry," "no color, only the nuance" and "Take eloquence and wring its neck"—a protest against the sonorous declamations of poetry such as Victor Hugo's. Symbolist practice led inevitably to poetry that became more and more "private" as each poet developed a personal set of symbols, the ultimate, perhaps, being Rimbaud's insistence that for him each vowel had a different color. Poetry, then, finally came to resemble music; its purpose was the evocation of a mood, and the subject was unimportant. Behind the Symbolists clearly stood the figure of Edgar Allan Poe, whom Baudelaire had introduced to France in the 1860's. In France the Symbolist movement led to Mallarmé and finally to Paul Valéry; in England it influenced the young William Butler Yeats and Gerard Manley Hopkins. The Symbolists' concept of developing a private language has had a profound influence on modern poetry.

Although Verlaine regained sufficient respectability to be invited to lecture in England in 1894, his later years were marked by poverty, drunkenness, and debauchery. He alternated between cafés and hospitals until his death in 1896.

John Jacob

Bibliography

Blackmore, A. M., and E. H. Blackmore, eds. *Six French Poets of the Nineteenth Century: Lamartine, Hugo, Baudelaire, Verlaine, Rimbaud, Mallarmé*. New York: Oxford University Press, 2000. This anthology of poetry is preceded by an introduction, notes on text and translations, a select bibliography, and a chronology.

Ivry, Benjamin. *Arthur Rimbaud*. Bath, Somerset, England: Absolute Press, 1998. A biography of Rimbaud which details his two-year affair with Verlaine. Ivry delves deeply into the relationship, and especially its sexual aspects including possible dalliances with other men, misogynistic outbursts, and graphically sexual poems.

Lehmann, John. *Three Literary Friendships: Byron and Shelley, Rimbaud and Verlaine, Robert Frost and Edward Thomas*. New York: Henry Holt, 1984. An examination of the way these friendships influenced each poet's work. J. R. Combs, commenting for *Choice* magazine, notes, "[Lehmann] argues convincingly that after Verlaine and Rimbaud became friends and lovers, they became more productive literarily."

Lepelletier, Edmond Adolphe de Bouhelier. *Paul Verlaine: His Life, His Work*. Translated by E. M. Lang. New York: AMS Press, 1970. The only English translation of the hefty 1909 biography.

Nicolson, Harold George. *Paul Verlaine*. 1921. Reprint. New York: AMS Press, 1997. This venerable biography remains useful.

Robb, Graham. "Rimbaud, Verlaine, and Their Season in Hell." *New England Review* 21, no. 4 (Fall, 2000): 7-20. An excerpt from *Rimbaud*, a biography of nineteenth century poet Arthur Rimbaud by Graham Robb, is presented. The selection features an altercation Rimbaud experienced with his friend and lover, poet Paul Verlaine, in which violence broke out after Rimbaud announced his intention to leave Verlaine and return to his wife and children.

Sorrell, Martin. Introduction to *Selected Poems*, by Paul Verlaine. New York: Oxford University Press, 1999. Sorrell's introduction is useful for beginning students in this bilingual edition of 170 newly translated poems by Verlaine.

Jules Verne

French novelist

Born: Nantes, France; February 8, 1828
Died: Amiens, France; March 24, 1905

LONG FICTION: *Cinq Semaines en ballon*, 1863 (*Five Weeks in a Balloon*, 1876); *Voyage au centre de la terre*, 1864 (*A Journey to the Centre of the Earth*, 1872); *Voyages et aventures du capitaine Hatteras*, 1864-1866 (2 volumes; includes *Les Anglais au pôle nord*, 1864 [*English at the North Pole*, 1874], and *Le Désert de glace*, 1866 [*Field of Ice*, 1876]; also known as *Adventures of Captain Hatteras*, 1875); *De la terre à la lune*, 1865 (*From the Earth to the Moon*, 1873); *Les Enfants du capitaine Grant*, 1867-1868 (3 volumes; *Voyage Round the World*, 1876-1877; also known as *Captain Grant's Children*, includes *The Mysterious Document*, *Among the Cannibals*, and *On the Track*); *Vingt mille lieues sous les mers*, 1869-1870 (*Twenty Thousand Leagues Under the Sea*, 1873); *Autour de la lune*, 1870 (*From the Earth to the Moon . . . and a Trip Around It*, 1873); *Une Ville flottante*, 1871 (*A Floating City*, 1876); *Aventures de trois russes et de trois anglais*, 1872 (*Meridiana: The Adventures of Three Englishmen and Three Russians in South Africa*, 1873); *Le Tour du monde en quatre-vingts jours*, 1873 (*Around the World in Eighty Days*, 1873); *Docteur Ox*, 1874, 1876 (in *Dr. Ox's Experiment and Master Zacharius*, 1876); *L'Île mystérieuse*, 1874-1875 (3 volumes; includes *Les Naufrages de l'air*, *L'Abandonné*, and *Le Secret de l'île*; *The Mysterious Island*, 1875); *Le Chancellor*, 1875 (*Survivors of the Chancellor*, 1875); *Michel Strogoff*, 1876 (*Michael Strogoff*, 1876-1877); *Hector Servadac*, 1877 (English translation, 1878); *Les Cinq Cents Millions de la Bégum*, 1878 (*The Begum's Fortune*, 1880); *La Maison à vapeur*, 1880 (*The Steam House*, 1881; includes *The Demon of Cawnpore* and *Tigers and Traitors*); *La Jangada*, 1881 (2 volumes; *The Giant Raft*, 1881; includes *Down the Amazon* and *The Cryptogram*); *Mathias Sandorf*, 1885 (English translation, 1886); *Robur le conquerant*, 1886 (*The Clipper of the Clouds*, 1887); *Sans dessus dessous*, 1889 (*The Purchase of the North Pole*, 1891); *Le Château ds Carpathes*, 1892 (*The Castle of the Carpathians*, 1893); *L'Île à hélice*, 1895 (*Floating Island*, 1896; also known as *Propeller Island*, 1965); *Face au drapeau*, 1896 (*For the Flag*, 1897); *Le Sphinx des glaces*, 1897 (*An Antarctic Mystery*, 1898; also known as *The Mystery of Arthur Gordon Pym*); *Le Superbe Orénoque*, 1898 (*The Mighty Orinoco*, 2002); *Le Village aérien*, 1901 (*The Village in the Treetops*, 1964); *Maître du monde*, 1904 (*Master of the World*, 1914); *La Chasse au météore*, 1908 (*The Chase of the Golden Meteor*, 1909); *Les Naufrages du "Jonathan,"* 1909 (*The Survivors of the "Jonathan,"* 1962); *Le Secret de Wilhelm Storitz*, 1910 (*The Secret of Wilhelm Storitz*, 1965); *L'Étonnante Aventure de la mission Barsac*, 1920 (2 volumes; *Into the Niger Bend*, 1919; *The City in the Sahara*, 1965); *Paris au XXᵉ siècle*, 1994 (*Paris in the Twentieth Century*, 1996).

SHORT FICTION: *Maître Zacharius: Ou, L'Horloger qui a perdu son âme*, 1854; *Docteur Ox*, 1874, 1976; *Dr. Ox's Experiment and Master Zacharius*, 1876; *Hier et demain*, 1910 (*Yesterday and Tomorrow*, 1965).

DRAMA: *Les Pailles rompues*, pr. 1850; *Colin Maillard*, pb. 1853 (libretto); *Les Compagnons de la Marjolaine*, pr. 1855 (libretto).

NONFICTION: *Géographie illustrée de la France et de ses colonies*, 1867-1868 (with Théophile Lavellée); *Histoire des grandes voyages et grand voyageurs*, 1870-1873 (3 volumes; with Gabriel Marcel; *Celebrated Travels and Travellers*, 1879-1881).

Born in 1828, Jules Verne, who was to become one of the best-known science-fiction writers of all time, had a quiet childhood in Nantes. He attended the local *lycée* before going to Paris, intending to study law. However, through the influence of writers such as Victor Hugo and Alexandre Dumas, he discovered that he preferred literary work. He wrote operas, collaborated with the younger Dumas on some plays, and tried travel writing. His first success came with the publication of *Five Weeks in a Balloon*. The popularity of this novel encouraged Verne to continue writing near-future scientific adventure, often involving journeys into known and unknown realms. These "voyages extraordinaires" included *A Journey to the Centre of the Earth*, *From the Earth to the Moon*, and *Twenty Thousand Leagues Under the Sea*.

Adopting literary techniques similar to the mid-century French realists, Verne included carefully prepared scientific and geographical data to provide plausible backgrounds for his novels. The subject matter and lively action of Verne's tales soon gained for him an immense following in France and abroad. His novels coincided with the popular interest in science and technology beginning to sweep people's imaginations during the second half of the nineteenth century. Their popularity is attested by the great number of translations and foreign editions. Each novel described a scientific or technological development and its consequences, many of which have proved startlingly accurate and have inspired writers and scientists. By combining the physical sciences with the elements of fiction, he helped to create a form of literature later called science fiction.

The most famous of Verne's novels, *Twenty Thousand Leagues Under the Sea*, a pioneer work, introduced an advanced submarine to literature decades before the world's navies could build and use such a vessel. In this case, as in others, he anticipated future technology; his *Nautilus*, propelled by electricity, functions on principles similar to those of modern undersea craft.

Although Verne's novels achieved wide and enduring fame, they did not receive careful critical attention until the last third of the twentieth century. Scholars began to consider his novels against the background of their literary, scientific, and social context and to analyze his artistic techniques.

In his own time, Verne was honored by the French government, acclaimed by the French intellectuals, and beloved by readers the world over, having popularized science more effectively than any previous writer. Subsequently, his renown and literary standing have grown in France and throughout the world.

Timothy C. Miller

Bibliography

Butcher, William. *Verne's Journey to the Centre of the Self: Space and Time in the Voyages Extraordinaires*. London: Macmillan, 1990. A comprehensive study of Verne's science fiction, with detailed notes and a comprehensive bibliography.

Costello, Peter. *Jules Verne: Inventor of Science Fiction*. New York: Scribner's, 1978. A readable biography that puts the fiction in historical context. Includes a bibliography.

Jules-Verne, Jean. *Jules Verne*. New York: Taplinger, 1976. Written by Verne's grandson, this readable and entertaining biography draws on material in the family archives and explores Verne's methods and the experiences that led to his stories and novels. Also a good portrait of the times in which Verne lived and wrote. Includes detailed bibliography and index.

Lottmann, Herbert. *Jules Verne: An Exploratory Biography*. New York: St. Martin's Press, 1996. A graceful study by a veteran biographer of many French subjects. The detailed notes reflect extensive new research.

Lynch, Lawrence. *Jules Verne*. New York: Twayne, 1992. A reliable introductory study with chapters on Verne's early life, his early fiction, his period of masterpieces, and his final fictions. Includes an appendix listing film adaptations of Verne, detailed notes, a chronology, and an annotated bibliography.

Martin, Andrew. *The Mask of the Prophet: The Extraordinary Fictions of Jules Verne*. Oxford, England: Clarendon Press, 1990. Attempts to recapture Verne for modern readers, focusing on his fictions of subversion and law and disorder, and on the prophetic nature of fiction itself.

Gore Vidal

American novelist, playwright, and critic

Born: West Point, New York; October 3, 1925
Pseudonym: Edgar Box

LONG FICTION: *Williwaw*, 1946; *In a Yellow Wood*, 1947; *The City and the Pillar*, 1948, revised 1965; *The Season of Comfort*, 1949; *A Search for the King: A Twelfth Century Legend*, 1950; *Dark Green, Bright Red*, 1950; *The Judgment of Paris*, 1952, revised 1965; *Death in the Fifth Position*, 1952 (as Edgar Box); *Death Before Bedtime*, 1953 (as Box); *Death Likes It Hot*, 1954 (as Box); *Messiah*, 1954, revised 1965; *Julian*, 1964; *Washington, D.C.*, 1967; *Myra Breckinridge*, 1968; *Two Sisters: A Memoir in the Form of a Novel*, 1970; *Burr*, 1973; *Myron*, 1974; *1876*, 1976; *Kalki*, 1978; *Creation*, 1981; *Duluth*, 1983; *Lincoln*, 1984; *Empire*, 1987; *Hollywood: A Novel of America in the 1920's*, 1990; *Live from Golgotha*, 1992; *The Smithsonian Institution*, 1998; *The Golden Age*, 2000.

SHORT FICTION: *A Thirsty Evil: Seven Short Stories*, 1956.

DRAMA: *Visit to a Small Planet: A Comedy Akin to a Vaudeville*, pr. 1957; *The Best Man: A Play About Politics*, pr. 1960; *Romulus: A New Comedy*, pr., pb. 1962; *An Evening with Richard Nixon*, pr. 1972.

SCREENPLAYS: *The Catered Affair*, 1956; *Suddenly Last Summer*, 1959 (with Tennessee Williams); *The Best Man*, 1964 (adaptation of his play); *Last of the Mobile Hot-Shots*, 1969; *Caligula*, 1977.

TELEPLAYS: *Visit to a Small Planet, and Other Television Plays*, 1956; *Dress Gray*, 1986.

NONFICTION: *Rocking the Boat*, 1962; *Reflections upon a Sinking Ship*, 1969; *Homage to Daniel Shays: Collected Essays, 1952-1972*, 1972; *Matters of Fact and of Fiction: Essays, 1973-1976*, 1977; *The Second American Revolution and Other Essays, 1976-1982*, 1982; *At Home: Essays, 1982-1988*, 1988; *The Decline and Fall of the American Empire*, 1992; *Screening History*, 1992; *United States: Essays, 1952-1992*, 1993; *Palimpsest: A Memoir*, 1995; *Virgin Islands, A Dependency of United States: Essays, 1992-1997*, 1997; *Gore Vidal, Sexually Speaking: Collected Sex Writings*, 1999; *The Last Empire: Essays, 1992-2000*, 2000; *Dreaming War: Blood for Oil and the Cheney-Bush Junta*, 2002; *Perpetual War for Perpetual Peace: How We Got to Be So Hated*, 2002.

MISCELLANEOUS: *The Essential Gore Vidal*, 1999 (Fred Kaplan, editor).

Regarded as one of the most promising novelists to emerge in the period after World War II, Gore Vidal (vee-DAHL) not only created an important body of fiction but also became an influential man of letters, rivaling his contemporary John Updike in the scope and consistency of his work. Born Eugene Luther Vidal to a politically prominent family—he adopted his name "Gore" in honor of his grandfather, Oklahoma senator Thomas P. Gore, and is a distant cousin of former vice president Al Gore—Vidal grew up in Washington, D.C., and has written novels and essays that have the authoritative character of one steeped in politics, but he first came to prominence with the war novel *Williwaw*. His reputation took a sharp downturn with the publication of his third novel, *The City and the Pillar*, largely because of its then shockingly sympathetic portrayal of a homosexual protagonist. Several novels on both contemporary and historical themes followed, but Vidal found himself unable to make enough money as a writer or to attract the critical praise that would ensure his career as a novelist. Consequently he turned to writing for films and television, becoming one of the four or five best television writers before adapting his teleplay *Visit to a Small Planet* for a successful run on the Broadway stage. He wrote a number of plays for stage, screen, and television.

Having achieved some degree of fame and financial security, Vidal returned to the novel in 1964, publishing *Julian*, a brilliant historical novel that re-creates the life of a fourth century Roman emperor who renounced Christianity. He subsequently created a dazzling series of historical novels and contemporary satires. Vidal's fictional magnum opus is a six-volume series of novels that presents American history in the same acerbic terms as his essays. The first of the books to be written is the last chronologically, the contemporary novel *Washington, D.C.* The second novel, *Burr*, for example, sides with one of history's losers, creating sympathy for a political leader who had none of the pomposity or hypocrisy of Alexander Hamilton, George Washington, or Thomas Jefferson. If Vidal has an American hero, it is Abraham Lincoln, who is the subject of what is perhaps Vidal's greatest novel. Lincoln is presented as a political genius who broke certain constitutional restraints to save the Union. *Lincoln*, when viewed in the context of Vidal's other historical novels, suggests that the president's very greatness may have contributed to the follies and abuses of power Vidal chronicles so entertainingly in *1876*. Vidal concludes the series with *Empire*, set at the turn of the century, and *Hollywood*, set in the 1920's. The series traces and reflects the history of the United States through the lives of Aaron Burr and his fictitious descendants.

Vidal's lucid prose stands in marked contrast to the baroque experimentalism of Norman Mailer and other celebrated contemporaries. In fact, in his essays Vidal attacked much of contemporary American fiction, finding it esoteric and obscure, a literature produced for discussion in the American classroom, not a body of writing that will survive for a general audience. Vidal's models have been writers such as Edith Wharton, clear-eyed social critics and novelists of manners. Throughout his career Vidal used fiction to question the received truths of the political establishment and of what he called the heterosexual dictatorship. Having discussed homosexuality in *The City and the Pillar*, Vidal raised the stakes by centering *Myra Breckinridge* and its sequel *Myron* on a transsexual. In *Messiah* and *Kalki* he uses a quasi-science-fictional approach to examine human beings' fascination with death; *Kalki* features a character who wipes out most of humanity. Vidal offended almost everyone with *Live from Golgotha*, a farcical stew of Christianity, computers, and time travel, narrated by St. Paul's male lover. Under the pseudonym Edgar Box, Vidal also tried his hand at mystery and detective fiction with novels such as *Death in the Fifth Position*, *Death Before Bedtime*, and *Death Likes It Hot*.

For many literary critics, Vidal the essayist predominates over Vidal the novelist. In some of his fiction, characterization seems weak, and he often seems more interested in the points he has to make than in the people he has created. There are, however, major exceptions to this judgment. *Burr*, in which the historical figure's voice blends perfectly with Vidal's, is a triumph—as is *Lincoln*, in which Vidal restrains his sarcasm in favor of a sober yet lively narrative that reveals Lincoln's political intelligence in all of its magnificence.

Carl Rollyson
Arthur D. Hlavaty

Bibliography

Baker, Susan, and Curtis S. Gibson. *Gore Vidal: A Critical Companion*. Westport, Conn.: Greenwood Press, 1997. A helpful book of criticism and interpretation of Vidal's work. Includes bibliographical references and index.

Dick, Bernard F. *The Apostate Angel: A Critical Study of Gore Vidal*. New York: Random House, 1974. An entertaining and perceptive study, based on interviews with Vidal and on use of his papers at the University of Wisconsin at Madison. Dick focuses on Vidal's work rather than on his biography. The book contains footnotes and a bibliography.

Harris, Stephen. *The Fiction of Gore Vidal and E. L. Doctorow: Writing the Historical Self*. New York: P. Lang, 2002. Discusses Vidal's strong identification with history as reflected in his writing.

Kaplan, Fred. *Gore Vidal: A Biography*. New York: Doubleday, 1999. A comprehensive biography of the novelist, playwright, scriptwriter, essayist, and political activist who helped shape American letters during the second half of the twentieth century.

Kiernan, Robert F. *Gore Vidal*. New York: Frederick Ungar, 1982. This study of Vidal's major writings tries to assess his place in American literature and gives astute descriptions of the Vidalian style and manner. The book, which uses Vidal's manuscript collection, contains a brief note and bibliography section.

Parini, Jay, ed. *Gore Vidal: Writer Against the Grain*. New York: Columbia University Press, 1992. Vidal's distaste for much of the academic study of contemporary fiction has been mirrored in a lack of academic study of his work. Jay Parini sought to redress the balance by compiling this work, which deals with both Vidal's fiction and nonfiction.

Alfred de Vigny

French poet

Born: Loches, France; March 27, 1797
Died: Paris, France; September 17, 1863

POETRY: *Poèmes*, 1822; *Eloa*, 1824; *Poèmes antiques et modernes*, 1826, 1829, 1837; *Les Destinées*, 1864.
LONG FICTION: *Cinq-Mars*, 1826 (*Cinq-Mars: Or, A Conspiracy Under Louis XIII*, 1847); *L'Alméh*, 1831; *Stello*, 1832; *Daphné*, 1912.
SHORT FICTION: *Servitude et grandeurs militaires*, 1835 (*The Military Necessity*, 1919).
DRAMA: *Le More de Venise*, pr. 1829 (translation of William Shakespeare's *Othello*); *La Maréchale d'Ancre*, pr. 1831; *Quitte pour la peur*, pr. 1833 (one act); *Chatterton*, pr., pb. 1835.
NONFICTION: *Le Journal d'un poète*, 1867.

In French literature Alfred Victor, Comte de Vigny (veen-yee), is important as a great pioneer of the Romantic movement in the nineteenth century, but to speakers of English he is best known as the author of *Cinq-Mars*, a historical romance. Vigny, following a long family tradition, began his career as an officer in the French army in 1814, at the age of seventeen. He retired from military life in 1827, after thirteen years of peacetime service. Before retiring he had already begun to write, and a volume of his verse, *Poèmes*, had been published in 1822. This volume was followed by a series of narrative poems, including *Eloa* in 1824.

Vigny's early poetry, collected in 1837, was, according to his own preface to that edition, philosophic thought clothed in the form of poetic art. Alfred de Musset, Victor Hugo, and Alphonse de Lamartine, all later important French Romantic poets, were influenced by Vigny's work. In his later poetry he tried to analyze human problems and present them through biblical symbols.

In addition to his poetry and his very popular novel *Cinq-Mars*, Vigny translated works of William Shakespeare into French, wrote studies of the poet in modern society in *Stello*, wrote plays (including one about the English poet Thomas Chatterton), and published a volume of sketches and essays on military life.

In private life Vigny was unfortunate. He was married to an Englishwoman, Lydia Bunbury, in 1825, but she shortly afterward became permanently disabled. From 1831 to 1838 Vigny was the lover of Marie Dorval, a celebrated actress, but the affair ended unhappily. He was barely elected to the French Academy in 1845. Twice he ran unsuccessfully for the French Assembly, in 1848 and 1849. Vigny died of cancer September 17, 1863.

Pierre L. Horn

Bibliography

Bowman, Frank Paul. "The Poetic Practices of Vigny's *Poèmes philosophiques*." *Modern Language Review* 60 (1965): 359-368. Vigny was famous for his use of Stoic philosophy in his poems. This essay examines Vigny's skill in persuading his readers to admire his characters, who maintain their dignity in the face of true suffering.

Doolittle, James. *Alfred de Vigny*. New York: Twayne, 1967. This short book is a good introduction in English to Vigny's lyric poetry and to his more famous historical novels, including *Cinq-Mars* and *The Military Necessity*. Includes bibliography.

McGoldrick, Malcolm. "The Setting in Vigny's 'La Mort du loup.'" *The Language Quarterly* 29, nos. 1/2 (Winter/Spring, 1991): 104-114. In one of Vigny's best-known poems, the speaker is a hunter who kills a wolf but finally comes to admire the dying wolf's courageous efforts to protect his family. Shows how the setting in a forest isolates the hunter from others and makes him reflect on the consequences of his actions.

McLeman-Carnie, Janette. "Monologue: A Dramatic Strategy in Alfred de Vigny's Rhetoric." *Nineteenth-Century French Studies* 23, nos. 3/4 (Spring/Summer, 1988): 253-265. Some of Vigny's most famous poems are dramatic monologues in which the speaker conveys his understanding of what he sees before him. Vigny was also a dramatist, and this essay examines his skill in making his readers identify with the internal struggles of his speakers.

Shwimer, Elaine K. *The Novels of Alfred de Vigny: A Study of Their Form and Composition*. New York: Garland, 1991. Critical study includes bibliographic references.

Wren, Keith. *Vigny's "Les Destinées."* London: Grant & Cutler, 1985. A thoughtful study of Vigny's posthumously published book of poetry. This short book describes the artistry and philosophical depth of this work.

José Antonio Villarreal

American novelist

Born: Los Angeles, California; July 30, 1924
Identity: Mexican American

LONG FICTION: *Pocho*, 1959; *The Fifth Horseman*, 1974; *Clemente Chacón*, 1984.
SHORT FICTION: "The Last Minstrel in California" and "The Laughter of My Father" (in *Iguana Dreams*, 1992).

The parents of José Antonio Villarreal (VEE-yah-ree-AHL) were born in Mexico and moved to the United States in 1921. His father fought for Pancho Villa during the Mexican Revolution. Villarreal's family served as migrant workers in the fields of California before settling in Santa Clara in 1930. As a child he read such works as classical mythology, Mark Twain's *Tom Sawyer* (1876) and *Huckleberry Finn* (1884), Jonathan Swift's *Gulliver's Travels* (1726), and Henry Fielding's *Tom Jones* (1749). He has cited James Otis's *Toby Tyler, Or, Ten Weeks with a Circus* (1881) as his favorite childhood book.

Villarreal received a B.A. in English from the University of California at Berkeley. He has taught at various universities, including the University of Colorado, the University of Texas at El Paso, the University of Texas-Pan American, the University of Santa Clara, and the Universidad Nacional Autónoma de México.

Villarreal has the distinction of having written what is considered to be the first Chicano novel, *Pocho*, published in 1959, before the Civil Rights movement began in earnest. Villarreal maintains his individuality within the Chicano movement; he acknowledges his cultural debt not only to the Chicano culture but to the mainstream cultures of the United States and Mexico as well. He considers Chicano literature to be a part of American literature and compares Chicano writers to the regional writers of the southern or western United States. He acknowledges Mexican literature as an influence on his writing but feels that, except for the difference of language, the literatures of Mexico and the United States are very similar.

Villarreal considers the best Chicano literature to be that which informs the rest of American society about the condition of Hispanics living in the United States. He does not hesitate to criticize radical propagandistic writings by Chicanos which, in his opinion, alienate the general public and are read only by Chicanos, who are already familiar with their predicament. Villarreal has gone as far as to say that Chicano literature has come to be considered a separate and distinct body of literature largely because of the promotional efforts of academics who must justify their jobs and graduate programs.

Villarreal's first novel, *Pocho*, suggests that the Mexican Revolution was the beginning of the proliferation of Hispanic communities in the American Southwest. Subsequently, many other Chicano novelists have also referred to the revolution as the point of departure for Chicano culture. The novel's title is a derogatory term for an Americanized Chicano. The father of the protagonist, Richard Rubio, had participated in the Mexican Revolution and then crossed into the United States. As he matures, Richard rejects his parents' Mexican Catholic values in order to assimilate into American society. As he witnesses a demonstration by farm and cannery workers, Richard's perspective is detached—he seems to have forgotten that his own birth was in a melon field in California's Imperial Valley. Villarreal modeled *Pocho* after James Joyce's *A Portrait of the Artist as a Young Man* (1916).

In his second novel, *The Fifth Horseman*, Villarreal took his assimilationist philosophy one step further by attempting to write a novel that could be considered part of the Mexican literary tradition, even though the novel is written in English. As in *Pocho*, the Mexican Revolution provides the historical setting. Several scenes appear to be strongly influenced by Mexican novels about the revolution.

The Fifth Horseman also recalls the many American novels about the Mexican Revolution that were written in the 1920's and 1930's, long before the Chicano rights movement; moreover, the novel's title is even reminiscent of *The Four Horsemen of the Apocalypse* (1916), the novel about World War I by the Spaniard Vicente Blasco Ibáñez. By thus acknowledging his American, Mexican, and Spanish heritage, Villarreal asserts his belief that the best literature is universal.

In his third novel, *Clemente Chacón*, Villarreal depicts the plight of Chicanos in the 1960's and 1970's. The narrative has certain surreal qualities, which are perhaps the author's way of suggesting that Chicanos had become totally divorced from their history by the second half of the twentieth history. For example, in the novel's epilogue, a senator from Texas named Porfirio Díaz talks to the U.S. president about the problem of illegal Mexican aliens.

Douglas Edward LaPrade

Bibliography

Alarcón, Daniel Cooper. *The Aztec Palimpsest: Mexico in the Modern Imagination*. Tucson: University of Arizona Press, 1997. Discusses images of Mexico in *Pocho*.

Bruce-Novoa, Juan. *Chicano Authors: Inquiry by Interview*. Austin: University of Texas Press, 1980. Includes an interview with Villarreal that is an excellent source of information about the author's childhood and education; the interview also offers valuable insights into Villarreal's attitudes toward Chicano literature and literature in general.

Leal, Luis. "*The Fifth Horseman* and Its Literary Antecedents." Introduction to *The Fifth Horseman*. Garden City, N.Y.: Doubleday, 1974. This essay makes many references to Mexican and American novels about the Mexican Revolution that serve as sources or background for *The Fifth Horseman*.

Saldívar, Ramón. *Chicano Narrative*. Madison: University of Wisconsin Press, 1990. Includes a subchapter entitled "*Pocho* and the Dialectics of History," which explains how the protagonist must ignore history in order to assimilate in the United States.

Victor Villaseñor

American novelist, short-story writer, biographer, and screenwriter

Born: Carlsbad, California; May 11, 1940
Identity: Mexican American

LONG FICTION: *Macho!*, 1973.
SHORT FICTION: *Walking Stars: Stories of Magic and Power*, 1994.
SCREENPLAY: *The Ballad of Gregorio Cortez*, 1982.
NONFICTION: *Jury: The People vs. Juan Corona*, 1977; *Rain of Gold*, 1991; *Wild Steps of Heaven*, 1996; *Thirteen Senses: A Memoir*, 2001.

Victor Edmundo Villaseñor (VEE-yah-sehn-YOHR) is one of the significant chroniclers of the Mexican American experience; his novel *Macho!* was, along with Richard Vásquez's 1970 novel *Chicano*, one of the first Chicano novels issued by a mainstream publisher. Villaseñor was born to Mexican immigrant parents in Carlsbad, California. His parents, Lupe Gomez and Juan Salvador Villaseñor, who had immigrated with their families when young, were middle class, and Victor and his four siblings were brought up on their ranch in Oceanside. Villaseñor struggled with school from his very first day, being dyslexic and having spoken Spanish rather than English at home. He dropped out of high school, feeling that he would "go crazy" if he did not, and went to work on his parents' ranch. He briefly attended college at the University of San Diego, where he discovered that reading books could be something other than drudgery, but left college after flunking most of his courses. He became a boxer for a brief period, then went to Mexico, where he suddenly became aware of Mexican art, literature, and history. He began to be proud of his heritage, rather than confused and ashamed, meeting Mexican doctors and lawyers—"heroes," he says—for the first time. He read extensively.

Returning to California at his parents' insistence, Villaseñor worked in construction beginning in 1965 and painstakingly taught himself how to write. James Joyce's *A Portrait of the Artist as a Young Man* (1916) was particularly inspirational. He wrote extensively, producing many novels and short stories. They were steadily rejected until Bantam Books decided to take a chance and publish *Macho!* in 1973. The novel's protagonist is a young man named Roberto García, and the novel covers roughly a year in his life, first in his home village in Mexico, then in California, then in Mexico again. Somewhat unwillingly, Roberto journeys northward with a group of *norteños* from his village to earn money working in the fields of California. Roberto's personification of—and finally, inability to fully accept—the traditional social code of machismo; his conflicts with others, notably fellow *norteño* Pedro; and the larger labor struggle between migrant workers and landowners in California provide the central action of the book. *Macho!* received favorable reviews. The year of its initial publication Villaseñor married Barbara Bloch, the daughter of his editor; they have two sons, David and Joe. Villaseñor built a house on his parents' property, and as his sons grew older he enjoyed horseback riding with them.

Villaseñor's second major published work was nonfiction. *Jury: The People vs. Juan Corona* details the trial of a serial killer. Villaseñor had read about the case after *Macho!* had been accepted for publication, and it captured his interest—Corona had been arrested for murdering twenty-five derelicts. Villaseñor extensively interviewed the members of the jury that convicted Corona and thoroughly examined the complex and controversial trial. (The jury had deliberated for eight grueling days before reaching a verdict.) After the book's publication, he received some criticism for his interpretations of the events.

Villaseñor subsequently wrote the screenplay for *The Ballad of Gregorio Cortez*, based partly on writer Américo Paredes's account of the adventures of Cortez, a real-life figure, eluding the Texas Rangers around 1900. Villaseñor tells the story using multiple points of view, effectively relating the story of a man driven by circumstances into the life of a bandit while showing the prejudices and racism of the times. Written for television, the film won an award from the National Endowment for the Humanities; it was also released to theaters.

Rain of Gold, published in 1991 after more than ten years of research and writing, is the multigenerational story of Villaseñor's family. It begins in the days before the turbulence of the Mexican Revolution and continues through life after migration to the United States in the early twentieth century, and it is told with some dramatic fictionalization. It was dubbed the "Chicano *Roots*" by those who compared it with Alex Haley's story of his African American family's history. *Rain of Gold* tells readers much about Mexican history and about anti-Hispanic prejudice in the American Southwest. The book was almost published two years earlier by G. P. Putnam's, but Villaseñor became unhappy with the company at the last minute for insisting that the book be called "Rio Grande" ("a John Wayne movie," he scoffed) and wanting to cut its length and call it fiction in order to boost sales. The company agreed to let him buy back his book, for which Villaseñor remortgaged his home. Published in its original form and with the original title (a translation of La Lluvia de Oro, his mother's birthplace in Mexico) by Arte Público, it was well received and was widely considered Villaseñor's masterwork.

Wild Steps of Heaven recounts the history of Villaseñor's father's family in the highlands of Jalisco, Mexico, before the events covered in *Rain of Gold*; Villaseñor considered it part two of a "Rain of Gold" trilogy, and he planned to follow it with the story of his mother's family. He draws on stories told by his father and members of his extended family, relating them in a folkloric style that sometimes verges on Magical Realism. *Walking Stars: Stories of Magic and Power*, published two years before *Wild Steps of Heaven*, consists of stories for young readers that attempt both to entertain and to inspire; each of the stories, most based on events in the early lives of his parents, concludes with notes in which the author discusses the stories' meanings, emphasizing the spiritual magic that people's lives embody.

McCrea Adams

Bibliography

Barbato, Joseph. "Latino Writers in the American Market." *Publishers Weekly*, February 1, 1991, pp. 17-21. Discusses the publishing of *Rain of Gold* and includes an interview with Villaseñor.

Guilbault, Rose Del Castillo. "Americanization Is Tough on 'Macho.'" In *American Voices: Multicultural Literacy and Critical Thinking*, edited by Dolores Laguardia and Hans P. Guth. Mountain View, Calif.: Mayfield, 1992. Focuses on the concept of macho, central to Villaseñor's first book; also has an interview with Villaseñor.

Kelsey, Verlene. "Mining for a Usable Past: Acts of Recovery, Resistence, and Continuity in Victor Villaseñor's *Rain of Gold*." *Bilingual Review* 18 (January-April, 1993): 79-85. Extensive review and close reading of Villaseñor's book.

Tatum, Charles M. *Chicano Literature*. Boston: Twayne, 1982. Includes a discussion of Villaseñor.

François Villon
(François de Montcorbier)

French poet

Born: Paris, France; 1431
Died: Unknown; 1463(?)

POETRY: *Le Lais*, wr. 1456, pb. 1489 (*The Legacy*, 1878; also known as *Le Petit Testament*, *The Little Testament*); *Le Grand Testament*, wr. 1461, pb. 1489 (*The Great Testament*, 1878); *Ballades en jargon*, 1489 (*Poems in Slang*, 1878); *Les Œuvres de Françoys Villon*, 1533 (Clément Marot, editor); *The Poems of Master François Villon*, 1878; *Ballads Done into English from the French of François Villon*, 1904; *The Testaments of François Villon*, 1924; *The Complete Works of François Villon*, 1928; *The Poems of François Villon*, 1954, 1977, 1982 (includes *The Legacy*, *The Great Testament*, and some shorter poems; Galway Kinnell, translator).

Nothing is known of the background and youth of François Villon (vee-yohn) except that he was born in Paris in 1431, of poor parents. His father died early; his mother was still living in 1461. His name was actually François de Montcorbier, but he took the name of his patron (and probable relative) Guillaume de Villon, a priest and professor of canon law in Paris. He was also known in court records as François des Loges. The patron sent young Villon to the University of Paris, at that time one of the greatest in Europe, where he received the degree of bachelor of arts in 1449 and that of master of arts in 1452.

Shortly after finishing his education Villon began a long series of embroilments with the law, incidents that scholars have recreated from documents in the Paris archives. On June 5, 1455, he was involved in a street brawl with one Jehan le Mardi and a priest named Phillippe Chermoye, as a result of which Chermoye died of his wounds. Villon was banished and fled the city, but the sentence was remitted on the basis of self-defense. Back in Paris the next year, he was so badly beaten in another brawl that he planned to go to Angers. Before leaving, however, around Christmas of 1456, he and some disreputable friends robbed the chapel of the College of Navarre. The robbery was discovered in the spring; one of the gang turned king's evidence, and Villon was again banished from Paris. For four years he wandered about France. In 1457 he was a visitor at the court of Charles, duc d'Orléans, himself one of the great French medieval poets, and he was also sheltered by Jean II of Bourbon. He was unable to keep out of trouble; in 1460 he was sentenced to death in Orléans and was freed only as a result of the general amnesty proclaimed on the state entry of the duke's infant daughter. The summer of 1461 found him in prison at Meung; again he owed his release to the royal house, for in honor of Louis XI, who was passing through the city, all prisoners were pardoned.

The autumn of 1462 found him back in Paris and again involved in a complicated web of trouble in which the old robbery figured. He was thrown into the Châtelet prison, tortured, and sentenced to be hanged. When he agreed to pay restitution the Parlement de Paris commuted his sentence to ten years of banishment from the city. His movements can be traced in Paris during one further year. After that, like the troubadours of his time, he may have lived until his death in a monastery. Rabelais stated that he found refuge in London, but there is no evidence for this claim.

Villon's poetry, which is highly personal, lends itself to biographical interpretation. His *Testaments* are long, rambling poems in eight-line stanzas interspersed with *ballades* and *lais*. By using the form of a "testament" ironically, he was able to include many people with whom he had dealings, bequeathing to each some appropriate memento, paying off old scores, and expressing gratitude. The value of the poems to later readers lies in the unrivaled picture of France at the close of the Middle Ages. It is possible to visualize the swarming city of Paris, the church where his mother went to pray, the taverns, the brothel where he lived with Fat Margot—for Villon had seen all aspects of contemporary life, from the court of Charles d'Orléans to the prison of Le Châtelet. He was the first great poet of the city, the first to make art from the harsh physical realities and from his unsentimental vision of medieval urban life.

There is also the revelation of his fascinating personality, that of a man who could jest about the gallows he had, more than once, narrowly escaped and the next moment write the *ballade* of his mother praying. Though Villon made the conventional gesture of blaming his ill-luck on Fortune, he clearly knew that his troubles were of his own making, that he was hopelessly enmeshed in vice, that the gibbet was perilously close. The only consolation he could draw was from the favorite theme of the fifteenth century, death—"the Dance of Death," Death the Leveller—which comes to high and low alike. Ignored during the neoclassic seventeenth century, Villon's poetry was revived by the Romanticists as part of the renewed interest in medieval literature. It appealed particularly to writers who enjoyed glimpses of the turbulent century that had produced such contrasts as Jeanne d'Arc and François Villon.

John Jacob

Bibliography

Anacker, Robert. *François Villon*. New York: Twayne, 1968. As Anacker's bibliography indicates, this was the first book-length study of Villon's poetry in English since 1928. Writing for the general reader, Anacker limits the scholarly apparatus to a dozen notes and references but gives an overview of Villon's world before analyzing *The Legacy/The Guest Testament* and miscellaneous poems, ending with an assessment of Villon's poetic achievement.

Brereton, Geoffrey. "François Villon." In *An Introduction to the French Poets: Villon to the Present Day*. 2d ed. London: Methuen, 1973. Brereton balances his commentary between Villon the poet and Villon's poetry, giving a general assessment of Villon's poetic technique and personality as it is reflected in the poetry.

Burl, Aubrey. *Danse Macabre: François Villon, Poetry, and Murder in Medieval France*. Stroud, Gloucestershire, England: Sutton, 2000. Biography studies Villon within the context of fifteenth century Paris, seeking out the truth behind the poet's crimes as well as the surpassing depth and beauty of his poetry.

Daniel, Robert R. *The Poetry of Villon and Baudelaire: Two Worlds, One Human Condition*. New York: Peter Lang, 1997. Daniel traces many themes that Villon shared with Charles-Pierre Baudelaire, such as mortality and the *danse macabre*, or dance of death. The result is an illumination of the poetry of a modern and a medieval poet that highlights Villon's medieval and modern characteristics.

Fox, John. *The Poetry of Villon*. New York: Thomas Nelson and Sons, 1962. Focuses on Villon's poetry rather than his personality. Fox's study takes a commonsensical approach to the text by allowing for multiple interpretations of it and looks closely in separate chapters at the sound and rhythm in Villon's poetry, at the word order and phrasing, and at theme, image, and symbol.

Freeman, Michael. *François Villon in His Works: The Villain's Tale*. Atlanta: Rodopi, 2000. Arguing that no analysis of Villon is complete without taking into account the Paris in which he lived, this book describes that rough place and also tells how Villon consciously fashioned his own image.

Simpson, Louis, trans. Preface to *François Villon's "The Legacy" and "The Testament."* Ashland, Oreg.: Story Line, 2000. Simpson's preface provides a useful introduction to Villon's life and times, and the notes provide commentary on Villon's language and clarify the many obscure allusions that enrich Villon's poetry.

Taylor, Jane H. M. *The Poetry of François Villon: Text and Context*. New York: Cambridge University Press, 2001. Study highlights the flair and originality of Villon's poetry, showing how it appealed to his contemporary readers.

Helena María Viramontes

American novelist and short-story writer

Born: East Los Angeles, California; February 26, 1954
Identity: Mexican American

LONG FICTION: *Under the Feet of Jesus*, 1995; *Their Dogs Came with Them*, 2000.
SHORT FICTION: *The Moths, and Other Stories*, 1985; "Miss Clairol," 1987; "Tears on My Pillow," 1992; "The Jumping Bean," 1993.
NONFICTION: "Nopalitos: The Making of Fiction," 1989; "Why I Write," 1995.
EDITED TEXTS: *Chicana Creativity and Criticism: Charting New Frontiers in American Literature*, 1987, revised 1996 (with María Herrera-Sobek); *Chicana (W)rites: On Word and Film*, 1995 (with Herrera-Sobek).

Helena María Viramontes (VEE-rah-MON-tays) made a name for herself as a fiction writer, educator, and active participant in Latino literary and artistic groups. One of the founders of Southern California Latino Writers and Filmmakers, Viramontes also lectured in New Delhi, India, and participated in a women's writing discussion group in the People's Republic of China. Her work was included in several major anthologies, including *The Oxford Book of Women's Writing in the United States* (1995).

The major themes of Viramontes's fiction, the oppression of women and the problems faced by working-class Chicanos, can be traced to her childhood experiences. Viramontes's parents, Mary Louise and Serafin Viramontes, met as migrant workers and settled in East Los Angeles, where Viramontes was raised with six sisters and three brothers. In "Nopalitos," she depicts her mother as a kind, energetic woman who often took in friends and relatives who needed a place to stay. Viramontes describes her father, a construction worker, as a man who worked hard but responded to the stresses of his job and family responsibilities with drinking and angry outbursts.

Viramontes started writing while attending Immaculate Heart College, from which she received a B.A. in English in 1975. In 1977 her story "Requiem for the Poor" received first prize in a competition sponsored by the California State University in Los Angeles's *Statement* magazine; in 1978 she received the same prize for "The Broken Web." In 1979 she entered the creative writing program at the University of California at Irvine (UCI), where her story "Birthday" won first prize for fiction in the University's Chicano Literary Contest.

After leaving the UCI creative writing program in 1981 Viramontes continued to write and to take a leading role in local literary and artistic organizations. Two short stories, "Snapshots" and "Growing," were published in *Cuentos: Stories by Latinas* (1983); in 1984 "The Broken Web" appeared in the anthology *Woman of Her Word*. These and other stories first published in magazines such as *XhismeArte* and *Maize* were gathered in Viramontes's first book, *The Moths, and Other Stories*.

The stories in *The Moths, and Other Stories* focus on women, usually Latinas, struggling against traditional social and cultural roles. Oppressive fathers, misguided husbands, and priests who are blind to women's real needs and problems contribute to the pain experienced by Viramontes's female protagonists. However, the rebellious adolescent girls in "Growing" and "The Moths" find that their mothers collaborate in the loss of freedom and in the social limitations placed upon *mujeres*, or women. In "The Long Reconciliation" Amanda, a married Mexican woman, chooses to abort a child rather than allow it to starve, but the price she must pay is her husband's rejection and abandonment. The concerns of older women are also depicted in "Snapshots" and "Neighbors." In "The Cariboo Cafe" Viramontes extends her representation of women to include the plight of Central American mothers whose children have been "disappeared." In addition to sharing common themes, the stories in *The Moths* are linked by Viramontes's skillful handling of multiple narrators and stream of consciousness.

In 1987 Viramontes, along with María Herrera-Sobek, organized a conference at UCI on Mexican American women writers. Viramontes's short story "Miss Clairol" was included in the conference proceedings, *Chicana Creativity and Criticism*, which she also coedited. Viramontes's growing reputation was enhanced in 1989 by a National Endowment for the Arts grant, an invitation to attend a storytelling workshop with Nobel Prize laureate Gabriel García Márquez at the Sundance Institute, and the publication of her autobiographical essay "Nopalitos" in *Breaking Boundaries: Latina Writing and Critical Readings*. In 1991 she was awarded a residency at the Millay Colony for the Arts.

Viramontes returned to the University of California writing program in 1992, the same year in which "Tears on My Pillow" appeared in *New Chicana/Chicano Writing*. In 1993 Viramontes received her M.F.A., completed the manuscript that was published as *Under the Feet of Jesus* in 1995, and published another story, "The Jumping Bean," in the anthology *Pieces of the Heart*. Viramontes began to teach creative writing at Cornell University in the fall of 1993.

Viramontes's novel *Under the Feet of Jesus* combines realism with lyrical passages to depict the harsh circumstances faced by a family of migrant farmworkers. Abandoned by her husband, Petra, the mother, lives with Perfecto, a man thirty-seven years her senior, who is torn between his obligations to Petra and her family and his desire to return to his home in Mexico. Perfecto's gentleness and concern for Petra contrast sharply with the kind of male characters that dominate *The Moths*. The novel focuses upon thirteen-year-old Estrella, whose life has been one of impermanence and loss. Though drained by exhaustion and poverty, Estrella finds the strength to fight the injustice of her life when her first love, Alejo, falls ill after being exposed to pesticides. After the family has spent all the money they have on a useless medical examination for Alejo, Estrella threatens a nurse with a crowbar, recovers the family's money, and enables Alejo to receive treatment at a hospital. The novel ends with Estrella perched on the roof of a barn she had longed to climb, an image that conveys her determination, heroism, and triumph.

Maura Ives

Bibliography

Carbonell, Ana Maria. "From Llarona to Gritona: Coatlicue in Feminist Tales by Viramontes and Cisneros." *MELUS* 24 (Summer, 1999): 53-74. Analyzes the representations of the Mexican goddess Coatlicue and the folkloric figure of the wailing ghost La Llarona in the works of Mexican American women writers Viramontes and Sandra Cisneros.

Green, Carol Hurd, and Mary Grimley Mason. *American Women Writers*. New York: Continuum, 1994. Includes a brief biographical sketch as well as an analysis of the short stories in *Moths*.

Moore, Deborah Owen. "La Llarona Dines at the Cariboo Cafe: Structure and Legend in the Works of Helena María Viramontes." *Studies in Short Fiction* 35 (Summer, 1998): 277-286. Contrasts the distant and close-up narrative perspectives in Viramontes's work.

Richards, Judith. Review of *Chicana Creativity and Criticism:*

Charting New Frontiers in American Literature, by Helena María Viramontes. *College Literature* 25 (Spring, 1998): 182. Points to the emergence of urban working-class women as protagonists, the frequent use of child and adolescent narrators, and autobiographical formats that focus on unresolved issues as characteristics of Chicana literature.

Swyt, Wendy. "Hungry Women: Borderlands Mythos in Two Stories by Helena María Viramontes." *MELUS* 23 (Summer, 1998): 189-201. Discusses the short stories "The Broken Web" and "Cariboo Cafe."

Yarbo-Bejarano, Yvonne. Introduction to *The Moths, and Other Stories*, by Helena María Viramontes. Houston, Tex.: Arte Público Press, 1995. Discusses Viramontes's portrayal of women characters who struggle against the restrictions placed on them by the Chicano culture, the church, and the men in these women's lives.

Elio Vittorini

Italian novelist

Born: Syracuse, Sicily, Italy; July 23, 1908
Died: Milan, Italy; February 12, 1966

LONG FICTION: *Il garofano rosso*, wr. 1933, pb. 1948 (*The Red Carnation*, 1952); *Erica e i suoi fratelli*, wr. 1936, pb. 1954 (*Erica*, 1960); *Conversazione in Sicilia*, 1937 (serial), 1941 (*In Sicily*, 1948; also known as *Conversation in Sicily*); *Uomini e no*, 1945 (*Men and Not Men*, 1985); *Il sempione strizza l'occhio al frejus*, 1947 (novella; *The Twilight of the Elephant*, 1951; also known as *Tune for an Elephant*, 1955); *Le donne di Messina*, 1949, 1964 (*Women of Messina*, 1973); *La garibaldina*, 1950 (novella; *La Garibaldina*, 1960); *The Dark and the Light*, 1960 (includes *La Garibaldina* and *Erica*); *Le città del mondo*, 1969 (unfinished); *Le opera narrative*, 1974; *The Twilight of the Elephant, and Other Novels*, 1974.

SHORT FICTION: *Piccola borghesia*, 1931; *Nome e lagrime e altri racconti*, 1972 (collected fragments).

NONFICTION: *Diario in pubblico*, 1957, 1970; *Le due tensioni*, 1967; *Gli anni del politecnico: Lettere, 1945-1951*, 1977 (3 volumes).

EDITED TEXTS: *Teatro spagnolo*, 1941; *Americana*, 1943, 1968.

MISCELLANEOUS: *Nei morlacchi: Viaggio in Sardegna*, 1936 (prose poem and travelogue; reissued in part as *Sardegna come un'infanzia*, 1952); *A Vittorini Omnibus*, 1960; *Opere*, 1974 (10 volumes).

Elio Vittorini (vee-toh-REE-nee) is remembered chiefly as one of Sicily's great twentieth century authors, although only two of his major works deal with that island: *In Sicily* and *La Garibaldina*. Vittorini was born on July 23, 1908, in Syracuse, Sicily, the son of a railway stationmaster. He had little formal education, which contributed to his problems as a writer. In the 1930's he worked as a newspaper editor and translator—he had taught himself English and translated a number of American authors, including Ernest Hemingway and John Steinbeck. When the Spanish Civil War began in 1936 and Germany and Italy began supporting the Franco forces, Vittorini rejected Italian Fascism and began working against it. His book *In Sicily*, serialized in 1937, is an anti-Fascist novel. Its anti-Fascism is couched in such ambiguous terms and situations, however, that at first the Fascist censors permitted it to be published. Later, after numerous complaints from government officials, the book was banned.

Vittorini joined the Communist Party of Italy, then underground, and worked with the Resistance. His novel *Men and Not Men* is the story of the Milan underground's fight in the winter of 1944, when Italy was occupied by German forces. Its style clearly borrows from the plain and repetitive style of Hemingway and other American authors. Despite its stylistic failings, it signifies Vittorini's search for a poetic fiction. After the war, Vittorini continued working as an editor. His postwar works, such as *The Twilight of the Elephant* and *La Garibaldina*, were shorter than standard novels. His last long novel was *Women of Messina*, published in 1949. Of these works, only *La Garibaldina* has come close to achieving the fame of *In Sicily*.

In his last years, Vittorini was influential chiefly for his editorial work for the publishers Einaudi, Bompiani, and Mondadori, where he continued to promote the translation of foreign authors and to edit an influential series of texts. He also issued several minor nonfiction works, which added little to his reputation; his creative period was over. He did not write much in his last years, although his importance in Italian literature was ensured by the continuing popularity of *In Sicily* as well as *La Garibaldina*. In the United States and other English-speaking countries, both novels were translated and praised. The American edition of *In Sicily* boasts an introduction, full of praise, by Hemingway, while the British version had that honor done by Stephen Spender. Vittorini died in Milan on February 12, 1966.

Philip Brantingham

Bibliography

Bonsaver, Guido. *Elio Vittorini: The Writer and the Written*. Leeds, England: Northern Universities Press, 2002. Studies

Vittorini's work from an Italian perspective. Includes passages in Italian with English translations.

Heiney, Donald. *Three Italian Novelists: Moravia, Pavese, Vittorini*. Ann Arbor: University of Michigan Press, 1968. A clear and insightful study of Vittorini as an "operatic" novelist.

Jeannet, Angela, and L. K. Barnett, eds. *New World Journeys: Contemporary Italian Writers and the Experience of America*. Westport, Conn.: Greenwood Press, 1977. Includes index and bibliography.

Pacifici, Sergio. *The Modern Italian Novel: From Pea to Moravia*. Carbondale: Southern Illinois University Press, 1979. A view of Vittorini's place in contemporary Italian literature.

Potter, Joy Hambuechen. *Elio Vittorini*. Boston: Twayne, 1979. In the Twayne World Authors series. A full-length study.

Gerald Vizenor

American novelist and short-story writer

Born: Minneapolis, Minnesota; October 22, 1934
Identity: American Indian (Ojibwa)

LONG FICTION: *Darkness in Saint Louis Bearheart*, 1978, revised 1990 (as *Bearheart: The Heirship Chronicles*); *Griever: An American Monkey King in China*, 1987; *The Trickster of Liberty: Tribal Heirs to a Wild Baronage*, 1988; *The Heirs of Columbus*, 1991; *Dead Voices: Natural Agonies in the New World*, 1992; *Hotline Healers: An Almost Browne Novel*, 1997; *Chancers*, 2000.

SHORT FICTION: *Anishinabe Adisokan: Stories of the Ojibwa*, 1974; *Wordarrows: Indians and Whites in the New Fur Trade*, 1978; *Earthdivers: Tribal Narratives on Mixed Descent*, 1981; *Landfill Meditation: Crossblood Stories*, 1991.

SCREENPLAY: *Harold of Orange*, 1984.

POETRY: *Matsushima: Pine Islands*, 1984 (originally pb. as four separate volumes of haiku during the 1960's).

NONFICTION: *Thomas James White Hawk*, 1968; *The Everlasting Sky: New Voices from the People Named the Chippewa*, 1972; *Tribal Scenes and Ceremonies*, 1976; *Crossbloods: Bone Courts, Bingo, and Other Reports*, 1990; *Interior Landscapes: Autobiographical Myths and Metaphors*, 1990; *Manifest Manners: Postindian Warriors of Survivance*, 1994; *Fugitive Poses: Native American Indian Scenes of Absence and Presence*, 1998; *Postindian Conversations*, 1999.

EDITED TEXTS: *Summer in the Spring: Ojibwe Lyric Poems and Tribal Stories*, 1981 (revised as *Summer in the Spring: Anishinaabe Lyric Poems and Stories*, 1993); *Native American Perspectives on Literature and History*, 1992 (with Alan R. Velie); *Narrative Chance: Postmodern Discourse on Native American Indian Literatures*, 1993; *Native American Literature: A Brief Introduction and Anthology*, 1995.

MISCELLANEOUS: *The People Named the Chippewa: Narrative Histories*, 1984; *Shadow Distance: A Gerald Vizenor Reader*, 1994.

Gerald Vizenor is often recognized as the most innovative writer of Native American fiction ever to put pen to paper. Born to Clement William Vizenor and LaVerne Lydia Peterson Vizenor, he was raised in Minneapolis from the age of two primarily by his father's family (originally from the White Earth Reservation), following the unsolved murder of his father. After weathering a less than ideal childhood, tempered by Anishinabe trickster tales, Vizenor joined the National Guard at fifteen and the Army at eighteen.

Stationed in Japan for several important formative years, he returned to civilian life in 1955 and began college at New York University. He transferred to the University of Minnesota the next year, where he earned a B.A. in 1960. In 1959 he married Judith Horns, with whom he had a son, Robert Vizenor; in 1969, they were divorced. He married Laura Hall in 1981. During the early 1960's Vizenor first began to write about the problems faced by city-dwelling Native Americans. His inside perspective as a social worker, his community activism and journalism, and his report on the trial of Thomas James White Hawk eventually led him to work as a *Minneapolis Tribune* reporter. He moved north temporarily to direct the Indian Studies Program at Bemidji State University in 1971-1972 and studied at Harvard University in 1973 before returning to the *Tribune* as a staff and editorial writer.

In the late 1970's and early 1980's, Vizenor taught at both Berkeley and the University of Minnesota, and then at Tianjin University, China. In 1984 he returned to Berkeley, leaving for the University of California at Santa Cruz in 1987 and serving as provost of Kresge College in 1989-1990. He then held the David Burr Chair of Letters at the University of Oklahoma before returning again to Berkeley, in 1992, as professor of Native American literature. He continued as editor of the American Indian Literature and Critical Studies series (which he founded) for the University of Oklahoma Press.

First published as a poet in 1960 and renowned for his haiku, Vizenor is probably best known for his novels, perhaps better described as colorful tapestries of strangely talented characters and trickster figures. Additionally, through his large body of nonfiction, Vizenor has contributed immeasurably to modern American ethnic studies, notably in his unceasing efforts to define in dynamic—as opposed to static—terms what it means to be Native American. Appropriately, he has coined the term "crossblood" to signify people of mixed Native American and immigrant ancestry. As Native American and post-immigrant American identities continue to evolve, that concept becomes increasingly relevant.

Although incensed by the many abuses Native Americans have endured, Vizenor has nonetheless never embraced either violence or victim status. Indeed, his own accounts from the early 1970's, published initially as reportage in the *Minneapolis Tribune* and later in works such as *Interior Landscapes*, reveal the often comic ineptitude of many self-styled revolutionary radicals: Most are described as city-bred opportunists with little real understanding of the ideals, language, and culture of the various rural tribal peoples they have attempted, often inaccurately, to represent. In startlingly fresh style, Vizenor resolves conflicts with humor, skewering radical wannabes, mainstream media materialists, and nabobs of new-age philosophizing left and right, often directing his sharpest gibes—as he does in *Manifest Manners*—at all who continue to invent and perpetuate the publicly accepted mythic and romanticized images of Native Americans. His novel *Chancers* embodies most of these characteristics, taking on the topic of the repatriation of Native American bones from museums in a tale that involves tricksters, human sacrifice (of professors by graduate students), resurrected spirits, and more.

Although his work is often challenging to read, his appeal should prove enduring, for his writing illuminates the perils and passions not only of Native Americans but also of all people. His ironic humor, artistically subtle wordplay, unusual plot twists that blur boundaries between the real and the imaginary, and odd characters living in a frustratingly capricious world have won for him an enthusiastic following among readers of postmodern American literature. Throughout his writing, but especially in his fiction, Gerald Vizenor reveals himself as the pre-eminent literary trickster of modern American authors.

William Matta

Bibliography

Barry, Nora Baker. "Postmodern Bears in the Texts of Gerald Vizenor." *MELUS* 27 (Fall, 2002): 93-112. Countering the trend to discuss Vizenor's work by focusing on his trickster figures, Barry turns attention to his use of the mythologically important figure of the bear in his work.

Blaeser, Kimberly. *Gerald Vizenor: Writing in the Oral Tradition.* Norman: University of Oklahoma Press, 1996. Blaeser emphasizes Vizenor's own awareness of ironic contrasts between his eclecticism and his sense of continuity with the tribal past.

Haseltine, Patricia. "The Voices of Gerald Vizenor: Survival Through Transformation." *American Indian Quarterly* 9, no. 1 (Winter, 1985): 31. In discussing Vizenor's multiplicity, Haseltine suggests that one strata of it arises from dream vision experience.

Isernhagen, Hartwig. *Momaday, Vizenor, Armstrong: Conversations on American Indian Writing*. American Indian Literature and Critical Studies series 32. Norman: University of Oklahoma Press, 1999. Although Vizenor has given many interviews, this work brings him into the context of N. Scott Momaday's works, which have been a major influence on Vizenor's.

Lee, A. Robert, ed. *Loosening the Streams: Interpretations of Gerald Vizenor.* Bowling Green, Ohio: Bowling Green State University Popular Press, 2000. A collection of essays on a wide range of topics; includes a bibliography.

Monsma, Bradley John. "'Active Readers . . . Obverse Tricksters': Trickster-Texts and Cross-Cultural Reading." *Modern Language Studies* 26 (Fall, 1996): 83-98. Monsma investigates to what extent Vizenor's use of the trickster theme expects both the readers and the author to be tricksters.

Owens, Louis, ed. *Studies in American Indian Literatures: The Journal of the Association for the Study of American Indian Literatures* 9 (Spring, 1997). This special issue devoted to Vizenor contains articles on his contrasts between tribal and legal identity; the way Samuel Beckett, John Bunyan, and he use the past in comparable ways; his employment of Buddhist and wasteland imagery; and his changing poetic vision.

Eric Voegelin

German philosopher and historian

Born: Cologne, Germany; January 3, 1901
Died: Palo Alto, California; January 19, 1985

NONFICTION: *Der autoritäre Staat: Ein Versuch über das ōsterreichische Staatsproblem*, 1936 (*The Authoritarian State: An Essay on the Problem of the Austrian State*, 1999); *The New Science of Politics*, 1952; *Order and History*, 1956-1987 (includes *Israel and Revelation*, 1956; *The World of the Polis*, 1957; *Plato and Aristotle*, 1957; *The Ecumenic Age*, 1974; and *In Search of Order*, 1987); *Wissenschaft, Politik, und Gnosis*, 1959 (*Science, Politics, and Gnosticism: Two Essays*, 1968); *Anamnesis: Zur Theorie, Geschiche und Politik*, 1966 (*Anamnesis*, 1978); *From Enlightenment to Revolution*, 1975; *Faith and Political Philosophy: The Correspondence Between Leo Strauss and Eric Voegelin, 1934-1964*, 1993; *Collected Works of Eric Voegelin*, 1995- (34 volumes projected).

Eric Hermann Wilhelm Voegelin (VURG-uh-lihn) is one of the most important political philosophers and historians of the twentieth century. He was born to Otto Stefan Voegelin, a civil engineer, and Elisabeth Ruchl Voegelin. In 1910 his family moved to Vienna, Austria, where Voegelin entered a *Realgymnasium* that had a strong emphasis on ancient and modern languages and the sciences. He completed his Ph.D. in 1922 at the University of Vienna in the political science program of the law faculty. From 1923 to 1924 he was an assistant in the law faculty at the university. In 1924 he received a Laura Spellman Rockefeller Fellowship, which allowed him to study in the United States and France for three years. In 1929 he was appointed as a *Privatdozent* and then, in 1936, as an associate professor of law at the University of Vienna. In 1932 he married Lissy Onken. In 1938 he was dismissed from his faculty position, largely because of his criticisms of the Nazi ideology on race. That same year he fled to the United States. From 1938 to 1939 he held short-term appointments at Harvard University and Bennington College, and in 1939 he became an assistant professor in the political science department of the University of Alabama at Tuscaloosa. Three years later he joined the political science department of Louisiana State University, where he was made Boyd Professor of Government in 1952. In 1958 he accepted an invitation from the University of Munich to hold its first chair in political science. In 1969 he returned to the United States as Henry Salvatori Distinguished Scholar at the Hoover Institution in Stanford, California. He spent the remainder of his career at Stanford.

Of the five books Voegelin published in German before leaving Austria, two dealt critically with the idea of racial superiority and one examined the nature and character of the authoritarian state. The fourth introduced the concept of political religions, that is, social and political orders that purport to save humankind from economic, social, and political disorder, and the fifth examined American political and social theory. Voegelin's reputation, however, rests primarily on the work published after his forced emigration. In 1952 he published *The New Science of Politics*, a criticism of positivistic social science which also introduced his concept of modern Gnosticism, the pervasive belief in the soteriological power of knowledge. In 1956 he published the first volume of his magnum opus, *Order and History*. This volume, *Israel and Revelation*, examined the concept of political order and disorder in the Ancient Near East. The second and third volumes, *The World of the Polis* and *Plato and Aristotle*, examined the experiential and theoretical developments in Greece that led to the creation of philosophy and political science as the cornerstone of the Western understanding of political order and disorder. Three more volumes were scheduled to appear in 1958 and 1959: the first, to be titled *Empire and Christianity*, was to cover the rise of multicivilizational empires through the end of the Middle Ages; the other two, "The Protestant Centuries" and "The Crisis of Western Civilization," were to cover the twentieth century. Only the next planned volume, *The Ecumenic Age*, appeared, but not until twenty years later, in 1974, and a fifth volume, *In Search of Order*, was published posthumously, in 1987.

Three other important books appeared in the interval: *Anamnesis* contains a critical analysis of positivist science and a theoretical discussion of what a science of politics must encompass; *Science, Politics, and Gnosticism* develops the concept of later Gnosticism more fully; and *From Enlightenment to Revolution* provides a critical analysis of the eighteenth and nineteenth century efforts to establish a new science of society and history. When the fourth volume of *Order and History* did appear, Voegelin explained that civilizational data and theoretical changes had delayed the project. *The Ecumenic Age* examines the period of ecumenic empires, and *In Search of Order* contains a series of essays on modern political philosophers, including Georg Wilhelm Friedrich Hegel.

Voegelin's primary concern, reflected in all his works, was the attempt to understand the origins of the political disorders that convulsed the first half of the twentieth century. He was convinced that the prevailing positivistic, "value-free" approach could not address the crisis. His alternative was to develop a historical analysis of political order and disorder as a way of setting the current crisis in context. Voegelin's approach gained for him a wide audience in the United States and Europe, although his criticisms of positivism drew sharp responses from advocates. Overall, however, his work was highly praised by leading scholars in philosophy and political science, and it has been compared to the work of Arnold Toynbee, Ernst Cassirer, and Pitirim Sorokin.

Stephen A. McKnight

Bibliography

Cooper, Barry. *Eric Voegelin and the Foundations of Modern Political Science*. Columbia: University of Missouri Press, 1999. Examines developments in the philosophy of history and political science.

_______. *The Political Theory of Eric Voegelin*, Lewiston, N.Y.: E. Mellen Press, 1986. Contains a good discussion of historiogenesis.

Hughes, Glenn. *Mystery and Myth in the Philosophy of Eric Voegelin*. Columbia: University of Missouri Press, 1993. Critical study.

McKnight, Stephen A., ed. *Eric Voegelin's Search for Order in History: Expanded Edition*. Baton Rouge: Louisiana State University Press, 1987. Provides an interdisciplinary analysis of *The New Science of Politics* and *Order in History*.

Ranieri, John J. *Eric Voegelin and the Good Society*. Columbia: University of Missouri Press, 1995. Critical study.

Sandoz, Ellis. *The Voegelinian Revolution: A Biographical Introduction*. New Brunswick, N.J.: Transaction, 2000. Sandoz provides an intellectual biography.

Paula Vogel

American playwright

Born: Washington, D.C.; November 16, 1951
Identity: Gay or bisexual

DRAMA: *Meg*, pr., pb. 1977; *Apple Brown Betty*, pr. 1979; *Desdemona: A Play About a Handkerchief*, pr. 1979; *The Last Pat Epstein Show Before the Reruns*, pr. 1979; *The Oldest Profession*, pr. 1981; *Bertha in Blue*, pr. 1981; *And Baby Makes Seven*, pr. 1986; *The Baltimore Waltz*, pr., pb. 1992; *Hot 'n' Throbbing*, pr. 1993; *The Baltimore Waltz, and Other Plays*, pb. 1996; *How I Learned to Drive*, pr., pb. 1997; *The Mineola Twins*, pr. 1997; *The Mammary Plays*, pb. 1998.

Paula Anne Vogel was born to a working-class family in Washington, D.C. After her parents' divorce, she was raised by her mother. Vogel's family life, education, and early career were not free of problems, but the challenges and failures she faced taught her lessons and helped her build the resilience necessary for life as a writer. She first became interested in drama in high school and began working as a stage manager for school productions. She began college at Bryn Mawr but lost her scholarship and finished her undergraduate education at Catholic University in Washington, where she earned her B.A. in 1974. She hoped to attend graduate school at the Yale School of Drama, but her application was rejected. She entered a Ph.D. program at Cornell University but left in 1977, not having completed her dissertation. By then her playwriting career had begun to experience some success.

Vogel's first theatrical success came with *Meg*, a three-act play examining the life and martyrdom of the Catholic saint Sir Thomas More, as seen from the perspective of his daughter Margaret. The play won the 1977 American College Theater Festival award for best new play and was produced at the Kennedy Center for the Performing Arts in Washington, D.C. Vogel's interest in exploring traditionally male stories from the vantage point of women characters can also be seen in *Desdemona*, in which the story of William Shakespeare's *Othello* (pr. 1604) is retold from the point of view of Othello's wife. Vogel turns the innocent young woman of Shakespeare's play into a wicked, deceitful character embodying Othello's worst nightmares.

A major breaktrough in Vogel's career came in 1992 with *The Baltimore Waltz*, a play inspired by the time she spent helping her brother Carl in his final battle with acquired immunodeficiency syndrome (AIDS). The play is a tribute to her brother and an indictment of the medical establishment and of society's treatment of terminally ill patients. Despite its dark subject matter, *The Baltimore Waltz* has a surreal story line and a comic touch. The play won the prestigious Obie Award for best Off-Broadway play.

If *The Baltimore Waltz* secured her place in the canon of American theater, it was *How I Learned to Drive* that brought Vogel to the attention of an international audience. The play takes an unusual approach to the difficult subject of child abuse by portraying the abuser as a complex, sometimes even likable, figure, rather than a one-dimensional villain. The play earned for Vogel many of the top honors for New York theater in 1997, among them the Obie in playwriting, the Lucille Lortel Award for best play, and The New York Drama Critics Circle Best Play Award. In 1998 it was awarded the Pulitzer Prize in drama.

In addition to her original works, Vogel's contribution to American theater has included teaching young playwrights and nurturing new talent. She served on the faculty of theater arts at Cornell from 1978 to 1982 and in Brown University's M.F.A. program in playwriting beginning in 1985. She has also served as a consultant and taught playwriting workshops at a long and varied list of institutions, including the Perseverance Theatre in Juneau, Alaska; the Saratoga International Theatre Institute; McGill University in Montreal, Quebec; St. Elizabeths Hospital in Washington, D.C.; and even a maximum security women's prison.

By the time she wrote *The Baltimore Waltz*, Vogel had publicly acknowledged her lesbian sexual orientation and had begun to discuss the ways in which it influenced her writing. Though she made clear in interviews that she did not intend to write "lesbian plays" or to speak for the entire gay community, her works do often deal with some of the more complex and less frequently acknowledged aspects of human sexuality and family life, from pedophilia and incest in *How I Learned to Drive* to the lives of older prostitutes in *The Oldest Profession* to lesbian adoption and parenting in *And Baby Makes Seven*.

It is not only in her choice of subjects, though, that Vogel pushes artistic boundaries. Her work also shows experimentation with theatrical form and narrative voice, and it is this that most attracts critical attention to her work. In addition to the numerous prizes she has garnered for individual plays, some of her more prestigious awards include a Guggenheim Fellowship, several National Endowment for the Arts Fellowships, a McKnight Fellowship, the Pew Charitable Trust Senior Residency Award, and a residency at the Rockefeller Foundation's Bellagio Center. The success of Vogel's writing has allowed her to continue expanding her artistic reach and to begin working in new forms, including musical theater, film adaptations of her plays, and long fiction.

Janet E. Gardner

Bibliography

Bigsby, C. W. E. "Paula Vogel." In *Contemporary American Playwrights*. Cambridge, England: Cambridge University Press, 1999. Vogel is one of ten playwrights whose careers are overviewed in this volume.

Friedman, Sharon. "Revisioning the Woman's Part: Paula Vogel's

Desdemona." *New Theatre Quarterly* 15 (May, 1999): 131-141. Examines the complex gender issues in Vogel's Shakespeare-inspired play and the ways in which Vogel pushes the boundaries of feminist theater.

Nourveh, Andrea J. "Flashing Back: Dramatizing the Trauma of Incest and Child Sexual Abuse." *Theatre Symposium: A Journal of the Southern Theatre Conference* 7 (1999): 49-63. Considers Vogel's treatment of adolescent sexual abuse in *How I Learned to Drive* and compares it to that of American playwright Marsha Norman.

Richardson, Brian. "Voice and Narration in Postmodern Drama." *New Literary History: A Journal of Theory and Interpretation* 32 (Summer, 2001): 681-694. Compares Vogel's experimentation with narrative voice in *Hot 'n' Throbbing* with that of Irish playwright Samuel Beckett in his later works.

Vogel, Paula. "Driving Ms. Vogel." Interview by David Savran. *American Theatre* 15 (October, 1998): 16 ff. Interview topics include the success of *How I Learned to Drive*, Vogel's early work in the theater, and incidents in her life that have inspired her writing.

_______. "Paula Vogel: No Need for Gravity." Interview by Stephanie Coen. *American Theatre* 10 (April, 1993): 26-28. An interview in which Vogel discusses, among other things, the political content of her plays, her views on teaching playwriting, and the economic climate of the American theater.

Cynthia Voigt

American novelist and short-story writer

Born: Boston, Massachusetts; February 25, 1942

CHILDREN'S/YOUNG ADULT LITERATURE: *Homecoming*, 1981; *Dicey's Song*, 1982; *Tell Me if the Lovers Are Losers*, 1982; *A Solitary Blue*, 1983; *The Callender Papers*, 1983; *Building Blocks*, 1984; *The Runner*, 1985; *Jackaroo*, 1985; *Izzy, Willy-Nilly*, 1986; *Come a Stranger*, 1986; *Stories About Rosie*, 1986; *Sons from Afar*, 1987; *Tree by Leaf*, 1988; *Seventeen Against the Dealer*, 1989; *On Fortune's Wheel*, 1990; *The Vandemark Mummy*, 1991; *David and Jonathan*, 1992; *Orfe*, 1992; *The Wings of a Falcon*, 1993; *When She Hollers*, 1994; *The Bad Girls*, 1997; *Bad, Badder, Baddest*, 1997; *Elske*, 1999; *It's Not Easy Being Bad*, 2000; *Bad Girls in Love*, 2002.

LONG FICTION: *Glass Mountain*, 1991.

EDITED TEXT: *Shore Writer's Sampler II: Stories and Poems*, 1988 (with David Bergman).

Cynthia Irving Voigt (voyt) has produced dozens of young adult novels. *Dicey's Song* merited the Newbery Medal in 1983 and the American Library Association (ALA) Best Children's Book citation. *A Solitary Blue* was named a Newbery Honor Book in 1984 and the ALA Best Young Adult Book. Although many of her other novels have received awards and favorable reviews, Voigt says the real pleasure of being an author comes during the writing itself. She continues to write prolifically from her home in Deer Isle, Maine.

Frederick C. and Elise (Keeney) Irving provided a stable home in rural Connecticut for their daughter Cynthia, her two sisters, and twin brothers. She attended Dana Hill boarding school in Massachusetts, where she developed self-reliance. During her youth, Voigt read books that stimulated her mind and imagination and influenced her to become a writer. She graduated from Smith College in 1963 and began working for an advertising agency in New York City.

In 1964 she married and moved to Santa Fe, New Mexico, where she attended college long enough to earn a teaching certificate. Previously, she had vowed never to teach, but she discovered that she loved her young students and the classroom setting. In 1965 she moved to the East Coast and taught at Glen Burnie, Maryland, and then at The Key School in Annapolis. In 1971, her daughter, Jessica, was born. That same year, she divorced her husband. In 1974 she married Walter Voigt, a teacher of classical languages at The Key School. In 1977 her son, Peter (Duffle), was born. A reduced teaching schedule allowed her to begin writing *Tell Me if the Lovers Are Losers* and *The Callender Papers*. These novels received recognition after her award-winning successes with *Homecoming*, *Dicey's Song*, and *A Solitary Blue*.

Voigt's Tillerman series includes *Homecoming*, *Dicey's Song*, *A Solitary Blue*, *The Runner*, *Come a Stranger*, *Sons from Afar*, and *Seventeen Against the Dealer*. Some of the issues confronting her well-drawn characters include child abandonment, alienation from adults, poverty, racism, and physical and emotional changes that occur during adolescence. Voigt's inspiration for the series came after she saw a group of children waiting in a car parked in front of a supermarket. She wondered to herself what would happen if nobody ever came back for those kids. Her fictional answer to that question began with *Homecoming*, as Dicey Tillerman and her abandoned siblings, James, Maybeth, and Sammy, begin an arduous journey from New England to their grandmother's home in Maryland.

A Solitary Blue, *Sons from Afar*, and *Seventeen Against the Dealer* are sequels to *Homecoming* and *Dicey's Song*. The Tillerman family and their friends continue to struggle with emotional handicaps that threaten future maturity and happiness. *The Runner* and *Come a Stranger* are prequels. The story of the children's uncle, "Bullet" Tillerman, in *The Runner* gives insight into Gram's stubborn, eccentric personality when her needy grandchildren arrive in *Homecoming*. Mina Smith's previous experience with racism and rejection in *Come a Stranger* explains why she befriends Dicey.

Voigt's preference for writing a series allows her to develop characters beyond the pages of one book. Her historical adventure novels *Jackeroo*, *On Fortune's Wheel*, *The Wings of a Falcon*, and *Elske* have a medieval, Viking-like setting and courageous protagonists with generational family ties. In the course of the series, a masked woman bandit robs the rich to help her destitute community, pirates kidnap youths and sell them into slavery, heroic youths escape and return home, and a clever girl restores the rightful queen to the throne.

Voigt's series Bad Girls involves preteens Margalo and Mikey as they scheme to achieve popularity in middle school. Each girl has a unique personality. Always clever and mischievous, they combine talents to confront authorities in the classroom, peers on the playground, and parents getting a divorce. Adolescent crushes, social cliques, athletic competition, and fashion consciousness contribute to their humorous situations.

Family relationships undergird most of Voigt's other fiction. Her well-developed characters strive for resolution of realistic teenage conflicts and situations involving self-discovery, physical disabilities, the rock music business, drugs, ethnic prejudices, homosexuality, and incest.

Martha E. Rhynes

Bibliography

"Cynthia Voigt." In *Children's Literature Review*, edited by Alan Hedbled and Thomas McMahon. Vol. 48. Detroit: Gale, 1998. Article includes major works, biography, analysis of major works, interviews, and commentaries.

"Profile of Cynthia Voigt." In *Fifth Book of Junior Authors and Illustrators*, edited by Sally Holmes Holtze. New York: H. W. Wilson, 1983. Voigt tells of her childhood ambition to become a writer, authors who influenced her, her education, marriage, and family. Includes a bibliography.

Reid, Suzanne Elizabeth. *Presenting Cynthia Voigt*. New York: Twayne, 1995. This biography contains photographs, a chronology of Voigt's life and publishing history, and six chapters on adolescent-related themes in the novels. Includes notes and references, a selected bibliography, and an index.

Vladimir Voinovich

Russian novelist

Born: Stalinabad, Tadzhik, Soviet Union (now Dushanbe, Tajikistan); September 26, 1932

LONG FICTION: *Zhizn' i neobychainye priklyucheniya soldata Ivana Chonkina*, 1975 (*The Life and Extraordinary Adventures of Private Ivan Chonkin*, 1977); *Ivan'kiada, ili rasskaz o vselenii pisatelya Voynovicha v novuyu kvartiru*, 1976 (satire; *The Ivankiad: Or, The Tale of the Writer Voinovich's Installation in His New Apartment*, 1977); *Pretendent na prestol: Novye priklyucheniya soldata Ivana Chonkina*, 1979 (*Pretender to the Throne: The Further Adventures of Private Ivan Chonkin*, 1981); *Moscorep*, 1986 (*Moscow 2042*, 1987); *Shapka*, 1988 (*The Fur Hat*, 1989); *Khochu byt' chestnym: Povesti*, 1989 (collected novellas); *Monumentalnaia propaganda*, 2000 (*Monumental Propaganda*, 2003).

NONFICTION: *Antisovetskiy Sovetskiy Soyuz*, 1985 (*The Anti-Soviet Soviet Union*, 1986); *Delo No. 34840: Sovershenno nesekretno*, 1994 (autobiography); *Zamysel: Kniga*, 1995, expanded 1999; *Portret na fone mifa*, 2002.

MISCELLANEOUS: *Putem vzaimnoy perepiski*, 1979 (letters and short fiction; *In Plain Russian: Stories*, 1979); *Maloe sobranie sochinenii: v 5 tomakh*, 1993.

Vladimir Nikolaevich Voinovich (voy-NOH-vihch) is an outstanding Soviet satirist of the post-Stalin era. He joined the dissidents in the 1960's and himself emigrated to Munich in December, 1980, continuing his writing career abroad. According to his own account in "A Few Words About Myself" in *The Anti-Soviet Soviet Union*, he was born in Dushanbe (then Stalinabad), Tajikistan, on September 26, 1932. His father, of Serbian origin, was a journalist; his mother, who was Jewish, was a mathematics teacher. His distant ancestors served in the Russian navy, and nearer forebears were writers and scholars with a Serbian focus. His father was arrested during the Stalinist purges in the late 1930's but was released, fleeing with his son to live with relatives in the Ukraine in time to participate in World War II.

Postwar conditions in Ukraine did not allow his parents to support Vladimir, though he began school there and established the habit of reading with the same enthusiasm as his parents. The practice was fortunate, since further schooling was sporadic. At age eleven, he began to support himself, working at miscellaneous jobs—on collective farms, on the railroad, in factories, even a short time in radio. He spent about two years at the Moscow Pedagogical

Institute from 1957 to 1959. He served in the army for four years and began writing poetry and songs there, achieving quick recognition. One of the songs, "Fourteen Minutes to Go," about Soviet cosmonauts, became enormously popular; Premier Nikita Khrushchev himself sang it to greet Soviet astronauts as they returned from space. In 1960, Voinovich wrote his first story, "We Live Here," published in *Novy mir* in 1961. The story was well received by critics looking for new literature, but it was attacked by party-line critics for the "alien poetic of depicting life as it is." A campaign of attacking the writer's work began in earnest in 1963. Voinovich's support of Yuli Daniel and Andrei Sinyavsky in 1968 placed him with the dissidents as literary policy hardened and publication abroad was punishable.

It became clear to him that he would be unable to publish his first novel, *The Life and Extraordinary Adventures of Private Ivan Chonkin*, in the Soviet Union; the book is a hilarious satire about a loyal, good-hearted, but ordinary soldier who is sent to a corrupt and lazy collective farm on orders from a Stalinist army official, who promptly forgets him. In 1973, Voinovich sent part of the book abroad for publication, a practice sure to be censured; that year, he also signed a letter in support of Aleksandr Solzhenitsyn and wrote letters attacking literary practices of the time. Dismissal from the Writers' Union followed, making it impossible for him to earn his living as a writer. Unlike others of the so-called Third Wave of emigrating Russian writers, however, Voinovich stayed in the Soviet Union for another seven years "under constant KGB pressure, in an atmosphere of incessant threats, blackmail, and provocation." He continued to write and to send his work and comments abroad, and much of his work circulated in *samizdat* (illegal copies passed from hand to hand) in his own country.

In 1980 he addressed a satirical letter to the newspaper *Izvestiya* on the government's treatment of the dissident physicist Andrei Sakharov; he was subsequently allowed to emigrate, and he settled in Munich. Six months later, he was stripped of his Soviet citizenship by Premier Leonid Brezhnev. The first of the works he sent abroad before his exile were translated in 1977. The completed version of *The Life and Extraordinary Adventures of Private Ivan Chonkin* appeared in that year, a work that convinced Western readers that such a phenomenon as a riotously comical novel could emerge from the Soviet Union. The work made his reputation abroad, and *The Ivankiad* followed close on its heels. This autobiographical account of his mock-epic efforts to convince the Soviet bureaucracy of his right to a larger apartment (his wife was going to have a baby) exposed the dynamics of petty corruption in housing and literature, areas of continuing Soviet problems.

In Plain Russian followed in 1979, a collection of his open letters to various powers, together with short fiction published both in the Soviet Union and abroad but never available in a single volume. The year 1979 also brought *Pretender to the Throne*, a bitter work about the further adventures of Private Chonkin. In exile, Voinovich continued to publish. A collection of sketches about life in the Soviet Union, permeated with a fine sense of its ironies, came out in translation in 1986. The paradoxical title was *The Anti-Soviet Soviet Union*, the thesis being that the government of the country was the worst enemy of itself and its people. The sketches recalled works by Soviet satirists of the 1920's, but Voinovich's work aimed to supply information about the lives of the Soviet people, news of whose everyday life was simply unavailable to Westerners. Scarcity and shoddiness of consumer goods, interference by secret police, and censorship and prescription in literary life were some of the topics that came under Voinovich's knife. Voinovich noted at the end of this work that changes began under Premier Mikhail Gorbachev. The novel *Moscow 2042* involves a flight from late twentieth century Munich by an expatriate Soviet writer to a Moscow of the future. This dystopian work increased the range of Voinovich's satire: The West as well as the Soviet Union came under his gaze.

Voinovich's novels and short works focus on ordinary life, as seen through the eyes of human types recognizable everywhere. The general decency, kindliness, and susceptibility to fear and guilt of his characters as they encounter the cruelties and absurdities of life in a dogma-dominated society sustain his view that he is not a political writer, but simply a writer, his political fate to the contrary. His works examine the gap between power-mad rulers and ordinary people who want only to live ordinary lives and experience usual human pleasures; in his fiction, this gap is the source not of tragedy (though at times tragic loss looms) but of a comedy that manages to land telling blows meant to prompt change.

After his exile—his Russian citizenship was restored to him in 1990—Voinovich also published articles in the Western periodical press. He established himself as the outstanding satirist of his generation, moving because of his exile finally to a subject matter beyond the confines of his own country. Some critics have found his attitude toward women sexist, but the books have attained wide readership because of their pace and boisterous and savagely critical humor. Underlying the Gogolian satire, however, is the assertion of human claims and unregenerate orneriness in the face of the outrages of totalitarianism.

Martha Manheim
Vasa D. Mihailovich

Bibliography

Dalton-Brown, Sally. "Signposting the Way to the City of Night: Recent Russian Dystopian Fiction." *Modern Language Review* 90 (January, 1995): 103. *Moscow 2042* is one of several novels discussed in a study of dystopian themes in post-*glasnost* fiction.

Kasack, Wolfgang. "Vladimir Voinovich and His Undesirable Satires." In *Fiction and Drama in Eastern and Southeastern Europe: Evolution and Experiment in the Postwar Period*, edited by Henrik Birnbaum and Thomas Eekman. Columbus, Ohio: Slavica, 1980. Worthy of attention.

Khan, Halimur. "Folklore and Fairytale Elements in Vladimir Voinovich's Novel *The Life and Extraordinary Adventures of Private Ivan Chonkin*." *Slavic and East European Journal* 40 (Fall, 1996): 494-518. Discusses the relationship between folktale and satire in Voinovich's novel.

Matich, Olga, and Michael Heim, eds. *The Third Wave: Russian Literature in Emigration*. Ann Arbor, Mich.: Ardis, 1984. Contains discussion of issues by Soviet émigré dissidents, including Voinovich, as well as bio-bibliographical data.

Novikov, Tatyana. "The Poetics of Confrontation: Carnival in V. Voinovich's *Moscow 2042*." *Canadian Slavonic Papers* 42 (December, 2000): 491-505. Analyzes Voinovich's dystopian novel using Mikhail Bakhtin's theory of the carnivalesque,

Porter, R. C. *Four Contemporary Russian Writers*. New York: Berg, 1989. Voinovich's work is profiled, along with that of Valentin Rasputin, Chingiz Aitmatov, and Georgii Vladimov. Good coverage of Voinovich's work up to the point of the fall of the Soviet Union.

Rancour-Laferriere, Daniel. "From Incompetence to Satire: Voinovich's Image of Stalin as Castrated Leader of the Soviet Union in 1941." *Slavic Review* 50 (Spring, 1991): 36. Voinovich's *The Life and Extraordinary Adventures of Private Ivan Chonkin* is analyzed.

William T. Vollmann

American novelist

Born: Santa Monica, California; July 28, 1959

LONG FICTION: *You Bright and Risen Angels: A Cartoon*, 1987; *The Ice-Shirt*, 1990; *Whores for Gloria*, 1991; *Fathers and Crows*, 1992; *Butterfly Stories*, 1993; *The Rifles*, 1994; *The Atlas*, 1996; *The Royal Family*, 2000; *Argall*, 2001.

SHORT FICTION: *The Rainbow Stories*, 1989; "The Saviors," 1999.

NONFICTION: *An Afghanistan Picture Show: Or, How I Saved the World*, 1992; *Open All Night*, 1995 (photography by Ken Miller); "Across the Divide," 2000.

William T. Vollmann, who burst onto the crowded late twentieth century literary scene and showed that there was still something new to say, spent the first five years of his life in Santa Monica, California. Beginning in 1964, his family made a series of moves: first to Hanover, New Hampshire, where his father taught business at Dartmouth College, then to Rhode Island, and finally to Indiana, where Vollmann attended high school. At age nine, while living in New Hampshire, Vollmann experienced a tragedy that informed his subsequent life: His six-year-old sister drowned in a pond after he had been told to watch her. Vollmann blamed himself and his daydreaming for her death, mockingly dubbing himself William the Blind when he began to write the novels of his epic Seven Dreams series; two tragic women protagonists of this work are named Born Swimming and Born Underwater. His painful early lessons about the need to try to save others, to expiate one's guilt, and to be unflinchingly observant, all echo throughout his writing.

Vollmann was accepted into the college program of Deep Springs (located in Death Valley, as he sardonically observed), which emphasized service to others and self-reliance; he completed the program with a senior year at Cornell University, from which he graduated with honors. He followed this with graduate studies in comparative literature at the University of California at Berkeley. In 1982, still burning with a desire to save others and influenced by T. E. Lawrence and Ernest Hemingway, Vollmann went to Afghanistan to fight for the mujahideen. He described this well-intentioned but quixotic foray with rich irony, years later, in his travel memoir, *An Afghanistan Picture Show: Or, How I Saved the World*. In 2000, he returned to Afghanistan, both literally and in print, with a lengthy and vivid piece of reportage about the then-ruling Taliban, "Across the Divide," published in *The New Yorker* on May 15, 2000.

Vollmann worked as a computer programmer in the mid-1980's. His experience in California's Silicon Valley resulted in his first published novel, *You Bright and Risen Angels*, for which he received a Whiting Writers' Award in 1988. The plot is a satirical allegory of the conflict between democracy and authoritarianism, in which democracy triumphant turns into the next oppressive regime. The characters are witty caricatures, playing their roles in a vast, complex computer game realized in the form of a novel. A major subplot involves the history of electricity.

In his next major work, *The Rainbow Stories*, a collection of stories that form an episodic novel, the author creates portraits of damaged sociopaths from the urban underclass, whom comfortable citizens regard as subhuman. While retaining some cartoon-like elements in describing them, Vollmann presented their unsettling humanity for the specific purpose of winning them sympathy, as he later acknowledged.

With *The Ice-Shirt*, the first volume of the Seven Dreams series, Vollmann becomes a time traveler, combining a grim subplot about the sordid side of North American life with a brilliant reinvention of Norse sagas about the Viking discovery of the New World, layered with Norse and Inuit mythology. He traveled extensively, doing onsite research in Norway and in the areas where Vikings and American Indians met (and according to Vollmann, clashed violently) around the year 1000 C.E. In this and subsequent volumes deeply probing the roots of American culture, Vollmann's stylistic techniques grow ever more resourceful.

As the volumes of Seven Dreams are completed, the unifying theme of the ruination of North America, through technology, human self-destructiveness, and the mutual blindness of cultures, comes into focus: *Fathers and Crows* (volume 2), about the conquest, conversion, and loss of French Canada; *Argall* (volume 3), about Samuel Argall, an Indian killer and slaver in the days of Pocahontas and John Smith; and *The Rifles* (volume 6), about the doomed nineteenth century expedition of Sir John Franklin to locate the Northwest Passage. It is a parade of follies and self-delusions, a heartbreaking and bloody human comedy, at which the gods must laugh. Vollmann is aware that his panoramic conception of plot, combined with ironic meditations upon history, suggests the work of Leo Tolstoy, while the thousand-year range of his epic (the years 1000 through 2000 C.E.) echoes the *Metamorphoses* of Ovid (c. 8 C.E.).

Vollmann goes back and forth between the epic and the intimate, seeking to explain the most perplexing and perverse human phenomena on both the large and the small scales. He suggests that the need to love, twisted by an inability to love, results in the need to inflict pain, as exhibited by the schoolyard bully (*Butterfly Stories*); Ignatius Loyola, founder of the Jesuit Order (*Fathers and Crows*); and Adolf Eichmann, Holocaust criminal (from an analysis of him and modern skinheads in *The Rainbow Stories*), all of whom create countless martyrs.

With *The Royal Family*, Vollmann returned to the subject of the sex industry, which, as critics wearily pointed out, he had already explored in *Whores for Gloria*, *Butterfly Stories*, and *The Atlas*. The second half of *The Royal Family* is the less original and appears to owe much to the fantasy world of the Marquis de Sade. However, the first half contains realistic portraits which expand the scope of Vollman's character delineations. Most interesting is the portrait of Henry Tyler, at first glance a stock character based upon the hard-boiled private investigator of popular detective novels. The pursuit of an elusive mystery woman, a stock situation of detective stories, is masterfully handled from the start and generates the suspense expected from a popular page-turner. Tyler's brother John is unhappily married to Irene, the love of Henry Tyler's life—another stock situation. Vollmann exquisitely delineates the myriad annoyances and misunderstandings that turn wedded bliss into marital hell. All of this reaffirms that a convincing description of ordinary people is, in fact, a much bolder enterprise than the pyrotechnics of Vollmann's precocious, experimental novels. Before one can congratulate Vollmann on breaking new ground once again, the luminous "ordinary" woman, Irene, ends her life, the mystery woman is found, and Henry Tyler, losing his previous personality, surrenders his entire being to sadomasochistic addictions of abasement and self-abasement, described in repetitive detail.

Vollman's cultural background is one of world literature and a generous share of science, religion, and philosophy. He is acutely aware of the interconnectedness of all human cultures and phenomena. A provocative novelist and a voraciously curious observer and adventurer, he helped bring the twentieth century to conclusion with a bang and continues to promise new revelations.

D. Gosselin Nakeeb

Bibliography

Bell, Madison Smartt. "William T. Vollmann." *The New York Times Magazine*, February 6, 1994, 18-21. Lively analysis of Vollmann as a creator of metafiction and his dangerous onsite research about street people, the experience of being tortured, and living alone at the North Pole.

Ulin, David L. "Northern Exposure." *The Nation* 258, no. 11 (March 21, 1994): 384-387. An article by a reviewer who has become acquainted in depth with Vollmann's work. Offers restrained appreciation of *The Rifles*.

Vollmann, William T. "Across the Divide." *The New Yorker* 76, no. 11 (May 14, 2000): 58-73. Vollmann, at the top of his form, revisits Afghanistan, combining vivid reportage and keen analysis with flashbacks to his visit in 1982.

_______. "Interview with William T. Vollmann." Interview by Larry McCaffery. *The Review of Contemporary Fiction* 13, no. 2 (Summer, 1993): 9-24. A rich and detailed interview that produced a virtual autobiography of the author, who describes his personal history, philosophical views, and the writers who most influenced him.

"William T. Vollman." In *World Authors: 1990-1995*, edited by Clifford Thompson. New York: H. W. Wilson, 1999. Helpful biographical background.

Voltaire

(François-Marie Arouet)

French novelist and playwright

Born: Paris, France; November 21, 1694
Died: Paris, France; May 30, 1778

LONG FICTION: *Zadig: Ou, La Destinée, histoire orientale*, 1748 (originally as *Memnon: Histoire orientale*, 1747; *Zadig: Or, The Book of Fate*, 1749); *Le Micromégas*, 1752 (*Micromegas*, 1753); *Histoire des voyages de Scarmentado*, 1756 (*The History of the Voyages of Scarmentado*, 1757; also known as *History of Scarmentado's Travels*, 1961); *Candide: Ou, L'Optimisme*, 1759 (*Candide: Or, All for the Best*, 1759; also known as *Candide: Or, The Optimist*, 1762, and *Candide: Or, Optimism*, 1947); *L'Ingénu*, 1767 (*The Pupil of Nature*, 1771; also known as *Ingenuous*, 1961); *L'Homme aux quarante écus*, 1768 (*The Man of Forty Crowns*, 1768); *La Princesse de Babylone*, 1768 (*The Princess of Babylon*, 1769).

SHORT FICTION: *Le Monde comme il va*, 1748 (revised as *Babouc: Ou, Le Monde comme il va*, 1749; *Babouc: Or, The World as It Goes*, 1754; also known as *The World as It Is: Or, Babouc's Vision*, 1929); *Memnon: Ou, La Sagesse humaine*, 1749 (*Memnon: Or, Human Wisdom*, 1961); *La Lettre d'un Turc*, 1750; *Le Blanc et le noir*, 1764 (*The Two Genies*, 1895); *Jeannot et Colin*, 1764 (*Jeannot and Colin*, 1929); *L'Histoire de Jenni*, 1775; *Les Oreilles du Comte de Chesterfield*, 1775 (*The Ears of Lord Chesterfield and Parson Goodman*, 1826).

DRAMA: *Œdipe*, pr. 1718 (*Oedipus*, 1761); *Artémire*, pr. 1720; *Mariamne*, pr. 1724 (English translation, 1761); *L'Indiscret*, pr., pb. 1725 (verse play); *Brutus*, pr. 1730 (English translation, 1761); *Ériphyle*, pr. 1732; *Zaïre*, pr. 1732 (English translation, 1736); *La Mort de César*, pr. 1733; *Adélaïade du Guesclin*, pr. 1734; *L'Échange*, pr. 1734; *Alzire*, pr., pb. 1736 (English translation, 1763); *L'Enfant prodigue*, pr. 1736 (verse play; prose translation as *The Prodigal*, 1750?); *La Prude: Ou, La Grandeuse de Cassette*, wr. 1740, pr., pb. 1747 (verse play; adaptation of William Wycherley's play *The Plain Dealer*); *Zulime*, pr. 1740; *Mahomet*, pr., pb. 1742 (*Mahomet the Prophet*, 1744); *Mérope*, pr. 1743 (English translation, 1744, 1749); *La Princesse de Navarre*, pr., pb. 1745 (verse play; music by Jean-Philippe Rameau); *Sémiramis*, pr. 1748 (*Semiramis*, 1760); *Nanine*, pr., pb. 1749 (English translation, 1927); *Oreste*, pr., pb. 1750; *Rome sauvée*, pr., pb. 1752; *L'Orphelin de la Chine*, pr., pb. 1755 (*The Orphan of China*, 1756); *Socrate*, pb. 1759 (*Socrates*, 1760); *L'Écossaise*, pr., pb. 1760 (*The Highland Girl*, 1760); *Tancrède*, pr. 1760; *Don Pèdre*, wr. 1761, pb. 1775; *Olympie*, pb. 1763; *Le Triumvirat*, pr. 1764; *Les Scythes*, pr., pb. 1767; *Les Guèbres: Ou, La Tolérance*, pb. 1769; *Sophonisbe*, pb. 1770 (revision of Jean Mairet's play); *Les Pélopides: Ou, Atrée et Thyeste*, pb. 1772; *Les Lois de Minos*, pb. 1773; *Irène*, pr. 1778; *Agathocle*, pr. 1779.

NONFICTION: *An Essay upon the Civil Wars of France . . . and Also upon the Epick Poetry of the European Nations from Homer Down to Milton*, 1727; *Histoire de Charles XII*, 1731 (*The History of Charles XII*, 1732); *Le Temple du goût*, 1733 (*The Temple of Taste*, 1734); *Letters Concerning the English Nation*, 1733; *Lettres philosophiques*, 1734 (originally published in English as *Letters Concerning the English Nation*, 1733; also known as *Philosophical Letters*, 1961); *Discours de métaphysique*, 1736; *Éléments de la philosophie de Newton*, 1738 (*The Elements of Sir Isaac Newton's Philosophy*, 1738); *Vie de Molière*, 1739; *Le Siècle de Louis XIV*, 1751 (*The Age of Louis XIV*, 1752); *Essai sur les mœurs et l'esprit des nations*, 1756, 1763 (*The General History and State of Europe*, 1754-1757, 1759); *Traité sur la tolérance*, 1763 (*A Treatise on Religious Toleration*, 1764); *Dictionnaire philosophique portatif*, 1764, enlarged 1769 (as *La Raison par alphabet*, also known as *Dictionnaire philosophique*; *A Philosophical Dictionary for the Pocket*, 1765; also known as *Philosophical Dictionary*, 1945, enlarged 1962); *Commentaires sur le théâtre de Pierre Corneille*, 1764; *Avis au public sur les parracides imputés aux calas et aux Sirven*, 1775; *Correspondence*, 1953-1965 (102 volumes).

MISCELLANEOUS: *The Works of M. de Voltaire*, 1761-1765 (35 volumes), 1761-1781 (38 volumes); *Candide, and Other Writings*, 1945; *The Portable Voltaire*, 1949; *Candide, Zadig, and Selected Stories*, 1961; *The Complete Works of Voltaire*, 1968-1977 (135 volumes; in French).

The man who, under the name of Voltaire (vohl-tayr), was to be remembered as the foremost spokesman of the Age of Enlightenment, was born François-Marie Arouet in Paris on November 21, 1694. The son of a prosperous lawyer who numbered among his friends members of the nobility and the literary aristocracy, young François-Marie grew up in an atmosphere of wit and culture. At the age of eleven, already known in Paris as an unusually clever rhymer of verses, he was invited to the salon of the celebrated Ninon de l'Enclos, thus gaining early entrée into a dazzling world of free morals and free thought. Although from a Jansenist family, François-Marie received his formal education at the Jesuit Collège Louis-le-Grand, where he acquired a solid classical background, familiarity with poetry and drama, and a number of noble and influential friends who were to serve him well throughout his lifetime.

While still in his school days, he became a member of the cultivated, freethinking, epicurean, and rather debauched "Society of the Temple." Resisting his father's efforts to make him a lawyer, he insisted that he would be a poet. Soon his biting verses mocking those in high places had earned for him several brief exiles from Paris and, in 1717, an eleven-month sojourn in the Bastille. He emerged from prison with a finished draft of *Oedipus*, the first of the more than fifty plays he was to write during his lifetime. Some of these plays were failures, others were spectacular successes on the contemporary stage, but none has survived the test of time. Although they are interesting in their frequently exotic settings, their use of characters from French history, and their introduction of some of the elements of the less formal English drama upon the rigorously defined classical stage of France, it is for their historic interest rather than their literary or dramatic merit that they are read today.

A few years later, following another brief term in prison, a three-year exile in England brought François-Marie, who by this time had changed his name to Arouet de Voltaire, into the society of such men as Alexander Pope, Jonathan Swift, and John Gay and into contact with the ideas of Francis Bacon, John Locke, and Isaac Newton. As a result of this sojourn, much of the intellectual activity of Voltaire's most productive period was devoted to synthesizing the two streams of rationalistic, freethinking ideas, French and English. Voltaire returned to France with his deism and skepticism strengthened and with a strong desire to cultivate liberal thought in his homeland. One of his first weapons in this cause was the *Philosophical Letters*, which, in characteristically brief, epigrammatic sentences, described the political liberty, religious tolerance, and commercial enterprise of the British, contrasting them with conditions in France. When this volume was published, its implied criticism of French law, religion, and institutions incurred royal wrath, which forced Voltaire to flee Paris and take up residence with various wealthy sponsors in the provinces.

At the home of one of these sponsors, Voltaire met the Marquise du Châtelet, the brilliant and learned woman who was to be his mistress and intellectual companion for fifteen years. The years he spent with her at Cirey were fruitful ones of intellectual development and consolidation. During that time he was appointed royal historiographer, was elected to the French Academy, wrote numerous plays, worked on several volumes of historical criticism—including the rationalistic, freethinking *General History and State of Europe* (also known as *Essay on Manners*), which was not published until 1754, and published the tale *Zadig* in 1747. After the Marquise du Châtelet's death in 1749, Voltaire spent three years at the court of his great admirer and patron, Frederick the Great of Prussia, years which had been intended for the creation in reality of the Platonic ideal of a philosopher-king but which were marked by increasingly bitter quarrels and disillusionment. Upon his return to France, Voltaire, grown rich from writings, pensions, and shrewd business ventures, purchased and settled on a great estate at Ferney, conveniently close to the Swiss border. It was during his life there that his *A Treatise on Religious Toleration* was written and the first volume of the *Philosophical Dictionary*, a work which epitomized Voltaire's rationalism and his universal interests, was published. At Ferney he wrote articles for Denis Diderot's *Encyclopédie* and dedicated himself to the extirpation of "L'Infâme," the intolerance and superstition which he believed to be the inevitable accompaniment of organized religion. In the midst of numerous sustained interests and activities, he spent three days writing *Candide*, the work for which he is best remembered.

In *Candide: Or, The Optimist*, the fantastically improbable travels, adventures, and misfortunes of the young Candide, his fiancé Cunegonde, and his tutor Pangloss are recounted in a terse, dry, understated style. Voltaire, never an unqualified optimist, and progressively disillusioned by his mistress's death, the failure of his schemes for Frederick the Great, the gratuitous horror and suffering of the great Lisbon earthquake of 1755, and his acquaintance with the universal folly and wickedness of humankind derived from his wide reading, makes his exaggerated adventure tale an ironic attack on the optimistic philosophy of Gottfried Wilhelm Leibniz and Pope, who contended that this was "the best of all possible worlds." By endowing his characters initially with a good fortune and every prospect for happiness, and then leading them through every conceivable misfortune into resigned old age, Voltaire makes the point that only by taking life as it comes and avoiding theoretical speculation about its meaning can one ward off despair. Richly spiced with a wit and humor which are as fresh today as when they were created, *Candide* is nevertheless the thoughtful and embittered product of a mind more concerned with communicating an idea than with skillful characterization or pure entertainment.

Early in 1778 Voltaire entered Paris in triumph to oversee the production of his latest play, *Irène*. There, in his hour of greatest glory, he died on May 30. The man whose clear, direct style made him the greatest spokesman for the anticlerical and rationalistic ideas of the Enlightenment, had died "in a state of sin," and his body had to be smuggled out of Paris at night to prevent its ignominious burial in a common ditch.

Bibliography

Besterman, Theodore. *Voltaire*. 3d ed. Chicago: University of Chicago Press, 1976. This biography by a Voltaire scholar provides coverage of the writer's life and works. Includes bibliography and index.

Bird, Stephen. *Reinventing Voltaire: The Politics of Commemoration in Nineteenth Century France*. Oxford, England: Voltaire Foundation, 2000. An examination of the critical response to Voltaire, particularly in the nineteenth century. Includes bibliography and indexes.

Carlson, Marvin A. *Voltaire and the Theatre of the Eighteenth Century*. Westport, Conn.: Greenwood Press, 1998. An examination of the French theater in the eighteenth century and Voltaire's role. Includes bibliography and index.

Gray, John. *Voltaire*. New York: Routledge, 1999. A biography of Voltaire that covers his life and works, while concentrating on his philosophy. Includes bibliography.

Knapp, Bettina Liebowitz. *Voltaire Revisited*. New York: Twayne, 2000. A basic biography of Voltaire that describes his life and works. Includes bibliography and index.

Mason, Haydn, ed. *Studies for the Tercentenary of Voltaire's Birth, 1694-1994*. Oxford, England: Voltaire Foundation, 1994. Contains essays on Voltaire's works and life, including one on the French theater in the 1690's. Includes bibliography.

Kurt Vonnegut

American novelist, short-story writer, and essayist

Born: Indianapolis, Indiana; November 11, 1922

LONG FICTION: *Player Piano*, 1952; *The Sirens of Titan*, 1959; *Mother Night*, 1961; *Cat's Cradle*, 1963; *God Bless You, Mr. Rosewater: Or, Pearls Before Swine*, 1965; *Slaughterhouse-Five: Or, The Children's Crusade, a Duty-Dance with Death*, 1969; *Breakfast of Champions: Or, Goodbye Blue Monday*, 1973; *Slapstick: Or, Lonesome No More!*, 1976; *Jailbird*, 1979; *Deadeye Dick*, 1982; *Galápagos*, 1985; *Bluebeard*, 1987; *Hocus Pocus*, 1990; *Timequake*, 1997; *God Bless You, Dr. Kevorkian*, 1999 (novella) .

SHORT FICTION: *Canary in a Cat House*, 1961; *Welcome to the Monkey House*, 1968; *Bagombo Snuff Box: Uncollected Short Fiction*, 1999.

DRAMA: *Penelope*, pr. 1960, revised pr., pb. 1970 (as *Happy Birthday, Wanda June*).

TELEPLAY: *Between Time and Timbuktu: Or, Prometheus-5, a Space Fantasy*, 1972.

NONFICTION: *Wampeters, Foma, and Granfalloons (Opinions)*, 1974; *Palm Sunday: An Autobiographical Collage*, 1981; *Fates Worse than Death: An Autobiographical Collage of the 1980's*, 1991; *Like Shaking Hands with God: A Conversation About Writing*, 1999 (with Lee Stringer).

CHILDREN'S/YOUNG ADULT LITERATURE: *Sun Moon Star*, 1980 (with Ivan Chermayeff).

Few comic fiction writers since Mark Twain have achieved the combination of popularity and critical acclaim attained by social satirist Kurt Vonnegut (VON-uh-guht) or had similarly long and productive careers. Born in Indianapolis, Indiana, on November 11, 1922, to Kurt Vonnegut, Sr., and the former Edith Lieber, Vonnegut was the youngest of three gifted children. His brother, Bernard, has made noteworthy contributions to the science of meteorology, and his sister, Alice, who died of cancer at age forty-one, showed talent as a sculptor. Vonnegut's father and paternal grandfather were architects, while the Liebers owned a prosperous local brewery. Unfortunately, anti-German prejudice inspired by World War I plus financial setbacks resulting from Prohibition and the Great Depression reduced the family's fortunes. Kurt, Jr., went to Shortridge High School in Indianapolis, where he wrote for its *Daily Echo* newspaper.

A student in biochemistry at Cornell University from 1940 to 1942, Vonnegut wrote for the *Cornell Sun*, decrying American involvement in World War II. Nevertheless, he enlisted in the U.S. Army early in 1943. The war years brought Vonnegut the double trauma of his mother's suicide and his own capture by German troops during the Battle of the Bulge. His experiences as a war prisoner in Dresden during that city's destruction by incendiary bombs in February of 1945 provide much of the material for *Slaughterhouse-Five*, his most acclaimed novel.

Soon after his repatriation, Vonnegut married Jane Marie Cox and became a student in anthropology at the University of Chicago, working part-time as a police reporter. After the university's rejection of his master's thesis, Vonnegut, in 1947, accepted a job as a writer of public-relations copy for the General Electric Company in Schenectady, New York. This experience inspired him with a hatred of corporate insensitivity and an awareness of the destructive social impact of science and technology, themes of importance in *Player Piano*, his first novel, published in 1952, and much of the rest of his writing. Technology was already the villain in his first accepted short story, "Report on the Barnhouse Effect," which appeared in the February, 1950, issue of *Collier's*.

By 1951, having moved from Schenectady to Cape Cod, Vonnegut had begun writing full time, relying mainly on the sale of short stories for his livelihood. When the short-story market weakened in the late 1950's, his desire to publish further novels became an urgent need. His second novel, *The Sirens of Titan*, appeared in 1959, attracting little immediate critical attention despite its eventual high reputation among Vonnegut's works. The book narrates the wanderings of a reluctant space traveler, Malachi Constant, whose life, like the lives of many of Vonnegut's characters, is determined not by will but by cosmic accident; Constant achieves some measure of fulfillment only when he discovers his capacity to love.

The declared theme of Vonnegut's third novel, *Mother Night*, is that "We are what we pretend to be, so we must be careful about what we pretend to be." The novel's central character, Howard W. Campbell, Jr., plays his double role as spy and collaborator so well that he loses himself in his own and the world's duplicity.

Two more novels of the 1960's, *Cat's Cradle* and *God Bless You, Mr. Rosewater*, augmented Vonnegut's reputation among an increasingly devoted cult readership and anticipated themes which would receive definitive treatment in *Slaughterhouse-Five*, the book for which Vonnegut is best known. In *Slaughterhouse-Five*, the loving, unstable innocent is Billy Pilgrim, who evangelizes his consoling religious message despite having witnessed the technological marvel of incendiary warfare at Dresden and despite knowing (because he has become "unstuck in time") precisely how technology will end the universe. The culmination of years of struggle to cope creatively with the horrors Vonnegut had experienced in World War II, *Slaughterhouse-Five* brought its author international acclaim.

The catharsis of completing his "Dresden novel" and the success of the film adaptation of *Slaughterhouse-Five* led Vonnegut to consider abandoning the novel form. He experimented with new devices in the next novels that many readers found perplexing. *Breakfast of Champions* includes the first publication of Vonnegut's simple line drawings in a book that attempts to dispel its author's personal despondency while lamenting the collapse of a national culture. Readers either celebrated it or found it trivial, and it enjoyed at once Vonnegut's best initial sales and worst reviews. *Slapstick* and *Jailbird* were both found pessimistic and enervated by reviewers, but they show continuing growth in Vonnegut's versatility within the novel's form, his unrelenting assiduity as a social commentator, and the increasingly subtle weaving of autobiography into his fiction. In *Deadeye Dick*, his tenth novel and the first after his sixtieth birthday, the autobiographical allusions abound, despite the warning, "This is fiction, not history, so should not be used as a reference book." Again experimental, *Deadeye Dick* is metafictional (its setting being the world of *Breakfast of Champions*) and punctuated by recipes and "playlets"

Three years in the writing, *Galápagos* is a brilliant novel that questions the perception of evolution as continuing upward progress. Here those who survive a million years into the future do so through intellectual devolution. *Bluebeard* reflects Vonnegut's long-held interest in the visual arts. In these later books, Vonnegut's male protagonists are increasingly debilitated, physically and emotionally, and are led to health by the stronger women. The narrator of *Hocus Pocus* is another battered survivor who looks back over his life as a collection of "if only" fragments. The tone of these three novels is far more positive than that of the previous group, however, and they have been well received. Nearly forty years after *Player Piano*, *Hocus Pocus* showed Vonnegut returning to the same setting and many similar themes, such as the human search for purpose, the perils of uncontrolled technology, and the costs of short-sighted military, scientific, and political ambitions. However, the novelist continued to grow in authority, in originality, and in the assurance of the authorial voice over the course of an unusually long career.

In 1997 Vonnegut published what he proclaimed would be his last book, *Timequake*. This loosely structured novel placed his favorite character, the long-suffering Kilgore Trout, and Vonnegut himself in a future time warp in which everyone on Earth is forced to relive a ten-year period. A work of metafiction is laced with personal reminiscences about Vonnegut's real life and relatives. *God Bless You, Dr. Kevorkian*, which appeared two years later, recounts an imaginary "near-death" experience at the hands of the controversial practitioner of assisted-suicide and contains interviews with thirty famous dead people, ranging from William Shakespeare to Adolf Hitler. *Bagombo Snuff Box*, which also appeared in 1999, comprises previously uncollected magazine stories from the early 1950's. This book is most interesting for the revealing introductions and afterword that Vonnegut wrote for it.

Robert H. O'Connor
Peter J. Reed

Bibliography

Allen, William Rodney. *Understanding Kurt Vonnegut*. Columbia: University of South Carolina Press, 1991. Allen's study, part of the Understanding Contemporary American Literature series, places Vonnegut, and especially *Slaughterhouse-Five*, in the literary canon. Contains an annotated bibliography and an index.

Boon, Kevin A., ed. *At Millennium's End: New Essays on the Work of Kurt Vonnegut*. Albany: State University of New York Press, 2001. A collection of eleven essays examining the novelist's moral vision.

Broer, Lawrence R. *Sanity Plea: Schizophrenia in the Novels of Kurt Vonnegut*. Ann Arbor: University of Michigan Press, 1989. Comprehensive work covering Vonnegut's major fiction from the perspective of his admitted struggles with depression.

Klinkowitz, Jerome. *"Slaughterhouse-Five": Reforming the Novel and the World*. Boston: Twayne, 1990. Study of *Slaughterhouse-Five* that debunks earlier, fatalistic interpretations of the novel, relating the postmodern form of the novel to the real-world condition from which it arises.

_______. *Vonnegut in Fact: The Public Spokesmanship of Personal Fiction*. Columbia: University of South Carolina Press, 1998. Discussion of Vonnegut as a redeemer of the novelistic form, tracing his integration of autobiography and fiction within his body of work.

Klinkowitz, Jerome, Julie Huffman-Klinkowitz, and Asa B. Pieratt, Jr. *Kurt Vonnegut, Jr.: A Comprehensive Bibliography*. Hamden, Conn.: Archon Books, 1987. An authoritative bibliography of works by and about Vonnegut. Lists Vonnegut's works in all their editions, including the short stories in their original places of publication, dramatic and cinematic adaptations, interviews, reviews, secondary sources, and dissertations.

Klinkowitz, Jerome, Julie Huffman-Klinkowitz, Asa B. Pieratt, Jr., and David L. Lawler, eds. *Vonnegut in America: An Introduction to the Life and Work of Kurt Vonnegut*. New York: Delacorte Press, 1977. A collection of essays ranging from biography and an "album" of family photographs to Vonnegut as satirist, science-fiction writer, and short-story writer. Discusses his reputation in the Soviet Union and Europe.

Klinkowitz, Jerome, and John Somer, eds. *The Vonnegut Statement*. New York: Delacorte Press, 1973. Collection of essays examining the nature and sources of Vonnegut's reputation, from his college writing years through his writing of *Slaughterhouse-Five*. Includes an interview and a bibliography.

Leeds, Marc. *The Vonnegut Encyclopedia: An Authorized Compendium*. Westport, Conn.: Greenwood Press, 1995. A concordance and encyclopedia identifying Vonnegut's most frequently recurring images and all his characters; indispensable for serious students of Vonnegut.

Merrill, Robert, ed. *Critical Essays on Kurt Vonnegut*. Boston: G. K. Hall, 1990. A comprehensive collection of essays on Vonnegut's works and career, which includes reviews, previously published essays, and articles commissioned for this work. The extensive introduction traces in detail Vonnegut's career and critical reception from the beginnings to 1990.

Mustazza, Leonard, ed. *The Critical Response to Kurt Vonnegut*. Westport, Conn.: Greenwood Press, 1994. Presents a brief history of the critical response to Vonnegut and critical reviews.

Rasmussen, R. Kent. Review of *Timequake*, by Kurt Vonnegut. In *Magill's Literary Annual 1998*, edited by John D. Wilson. Pasadena, Calif.: Salem Press, 1998. Review of *Timequake* that places the novel within the context of Vonnegut's life and related fiction.

Reed, Peter J. *The Short Fiction of Kurt Vonnegut*. Westport, Conn.: Greenwood Press, 1997. A critical study of the author's short fiction. Includes a bibliography and an index.

Reed, Peter J., and Marc Leeds, eds. *The Vonnegut Chronicles: Interviews and Essays*. Westport, Conn.: Greenwood Press, 1996. Vonnegut discusses, among other topics, postmodernism and experimental fiction. Includes a bibliography and an index.

Vonnegut, Kurt, Jr. Interview by Wendy Smith. *Publishers Weekly* 228 (October 25, 1985): 68-69. Vonnegut discusses his writing career, censorship, and his work; notes that Vonnegut is an ardent foe of book censorship and has strong words for those who seek to limit the free speech of others.

Mihály Vörösmarty

Hungarian poet and playwright

Born: Kápolnásnyék, Hungary; December 1, 1800
Died: Pest, Hungary; November 19, 1855

POETRY: *Zalán futása*, 1825; *Minden munkái*, 1864 (12 volumes); *Összes munkái*, 1884-1885 (8 volumes); *Összes mûvei*, 1960-1979 (18 volumes).

DRAMA: *Csongor és Tünde*, pr. 1830; *A kincskeresök*, pr. 1833; *Vérnász*, pb. 1833; *A fátyol titkai*, pr. 1834; *Árpád ébredése*, pr. 1837; *Marót Ban*, pb. 1838.

DRAMA TRANSLATIONS: *Julius Caesar*, pr. 1848 (of William Shakespeare's play); *Lear király*, pr. 1856 (of Shakespeare's play *King Lear*).

Widely considered Hungary's greatest nationalist writer, Mihály Vörösmarty (vuh-ruh-SHMAHR-tee) wrote during Hungary's social reforms era of 1825-1849. In contrast to the sixteenth and seventeenth centuries, the eighteenth century saw Hungary's Magyar language become almost obsolete with the upsurge of German and Latin in the arts, particularly in literature. By the early nineteenth century, however, a movement toward Hungarian patriotism had begun, and by the time Vörösmarty came of age, he was writing during a period of patriotic and linguistic nationalism and literary rejuvenation. Some writers of this period, including Vörösmarty, are credited with enriching the Magyar language by inventing new words and usages.

Born into a Catholic family that remained impoverished despite ties to nobility, Vörösmarty was schooled by Cistercian monks at Szekesfejervar and later by the Piarist clergy at Pest. When his father died in 1811, the family's poverty increased. By age fifteen, and for many years thereafter, Vörösmarty earned money for his law studies by hiring himself out as a private tutor. Writing poetry in addition to his studies, he lived an often penurious existence and supplemented his income by writing reviews and other pieces for newspapers. Eventually, he left his law studies and devoted himself to his literary efforts. His first widely successful published work was *Zalán futása* (the flight of Zalán), an epic poem detailing Hungary's conquest by Árpád during the ninth century. This heroic epic helped mark a literary shift from classical to the more romantic in Hungary and revived the genre of the epic poem, neglected in Hungary since the seventeenth century. The poem's publication also served to solidify Vörösmarty's acceptance among the established writers of the day, such as Sandor Kisfaludy and his brother Karoly Kisfaludy, and Ferenc Kolcsey, author of Hungary's national anthem, "Himnusz." Its impressive artistic quality notwithstanding, *Zalán futása* owes a portion of its success to the nation's increased patriotism of the time. Vörösmarty's tribute to Hungary's glorious past was just what the Hungarian people wanted, and he endeavored to give them more.

In addition to his deep stirrings of patriotism, Vörösmarty also found himself tormented by his unrequited love for Etelka Perczel, a young lady of social status considerably higher than his own. Born of his nearly all-consuming passion for her were several sentimental shorter poems, among them "Fair Helen," a lighter narrative poem describing the inevitably tragic love between King Matthias and the lovely Ilonka. Readers, warmly receptive to the poem's sentimentality after years of the more classical literature, loved it. In 1828, adding to his meager income and increasing fame, Vörösmarty was appointed editor of a popular magazine, *Tudományos Gyûjtemény*. Two years later, he was inducted, as the inaugural member, into the newly established Hungarian Academy. Eventually, he succeeded Karoly Kisfaludy as the academy's director, earning an annual wage of five hundred forints. To acknowledge the historical and literary importance of Sandor and Karoly Kisfaludy's work, Vörösmarty helped found the Kisfaludy Society. He also established in 1837 the most highly respected critical periodical in Hungary, *Figyelmezo*.

Despite his roles as editor, director, and champion of literature, Vörösmarty persevered in his own writing. Some of his best-known work was produced during this time: "Szozat" ("The Call"), a patriotic appeal, became Hungary's second national anthem soon after its publication in 1837. Broadening his literary reach, he also began writing dramas and between 1823 and 1831 composed four plays. Critics appear equally divided between designating *Csongor és Tünde* and *Vérnász* his best drama. *Csongor és Tünde* is a rather fanciful fairy-tale play, full of symbolism and suggestive of William Shakespeare's *A Midsummer Night's Dream* (c. 1595-1596). *Vérnász* won a prestigious Hungarian Academy award.

Vörösmarty married relatively late in life (1843). His new bride, Laura Csajághy, is credited with having inspired a series of beautifully romantic lyric poems. With these contemplative pieces, Vörösmarty established a new genre, at which he excelled. Perhaps his best known of these love poems is "A merengõhöz" (1843, to a daydreamer). In 1848, Vörösmarty and a small number of other writers undertook the project of translating several of William Shakespeare's plays into the Magyar language. Vörösmarty completed *Julius Caesar* (c. 1599-1600) and *King Lear* (c. 1605-1606) himself.

Having thus far lived a life of fierce patriotism, Vörösmarty was horrified by events of 1848-1849 and all the War of Independence entailed. Fully embracing the cause, he became a member of the Parliament, but during the Austrian oppression that followed the war, he was forced into exile. He and his three children lived a life of misery until he received amnesty for his nationalistic wartime activities. During his final years, Vörösmarty was able to produce several fine poems, but they showed a darkened perspective, a pessimism regarding what he considered Hungary's catastrophe. "Vén cigány" (1854; the old gypsy) suggests Hungary's apocalyptic destruction, though a glint of hope emerges at poem's end.

Vörösmarty died in 1855, ironically in the same house that Karoly Kisfaludy had died in twenty-five years earlier. November 21, the date of his funeral, was named a national day of mourning, and a national fund was established for the support of his children.

Cherie Castillo

Bibliography

De George, Iby. *Mihály Vörösmarty: A Historical Study of the Poet's Life in Relation to Hungarian Theatre and Drama*. New York: City College of New York, 1982. Introduces critical interpretation of some of Vörösmarty's work, including his dramas. Includes bibliographical references.

Jones, David Mervyn. *Five Hungarian Writers*. Oxford, England: Clarendon Press, 1966. Jones looks extensively at five prominent writers, including Vörösmarty, and their works' significance both within and outside Hungarian literature.

Mark, Thomas R. "The First Hungarian Translation of Shakespeare's Complete Works." *Shakespeare Quarterly* 16, no. 1 (Winter, 1965): 105-115. To fill what they saw as a void in Hungarian literature, Hungarian writers, including Vörösmarty, began translating William Shakespeare's plays into the Hungarian language. Mark discusses a variety of results, such as the thirteen plays somewhat unsuccessfully translated by an eighteen-year-old girl, and Vörösmarty's eloquent translation of *Julius Caesar* and *King Lear.*

Lev Vygotsky

Russian psychologist

Born: Orsha, Belorussia (now in Belarus); November 17, 1896
Died: Moscow, Soviet Union (now in Russia); June 11, 1934

NONFICTION: *Myshlenie i rech: Psikhologicheskie issledovaniya*, 1934 (*Thought and Language*, 1962); *Umstvennoe razvitie detei v protsesse obucheniya*, 1935; *Izbrannye psikhologicheskie issledovaniya*, 1956; *Razvitie vysshykh psikhicheskikh funktsii*, 1960; *Psikhologiya iskusstvo*, 1965, 1968 (*The Psychology of Art*, 1971); *Mind in Society: The Development of Higher Psychological Processes*, 1978; *Sobranie sochinenii*, 1982-1984 (*The Collected Works of L. S. Vygotsky*, 1987-1999 [6 volumes]); *The Vygotsky Reader*, 1994.

Lev Semenovich Vygotsky (vi-GOT-skee) pioneered work in psychology which belatedly influenced the study of art, literature, linguistics, and education as well as psychology. What little is known of his life comes from the accounts of his colleagues. He was born in 1896 in White Russia, the son of a small-town banker. He was educated by private tutors and later in the Jewish *Gymnasium*, where he developed an interest in Jewish history and culture. He attended medical school in Moscow in deference to his parents' practical concerns, but he later switched to the study of law, to be nearer humanistic subjects. While pursuing his studies at Moscow University, Vygotsky also attended Shanyavskii People's University, an unofficial institution established in reaction to government repression at the state universities. Following his graduation from Moscow University, Vygotsky returned to the provinces to teach literature and psychology. He attracted the notice of professional psychologists at a convention in 1924, at which he delivered a brilliantly original paper. His wife, Roza, accompanied him to Moscow in 1924, when he joined the staff of the Institute of Psychology there.

In the ten years following his appointment to the Psychological Institute, Vygotsky was extraordinarily productive. He founded a new institute for the study of children with physical handicaps and learning disabilities. While maintaining a heavy schedule as a researcher and lecturer, he produced a great number of articles and book-length studies. At the time of his death, of tuberculosis, in 1934, much of this work had not yet been published. As a result of the caprices of Stalinism, Vygotsky's approach to psychology fell out of favor, and it was not until the 1950's that his work began to appear again in the Soviet Union. Between the 1950's and the 1980's, many of his works were published for the first time, along with reissues of previously published material.

Vygotsky reacted against the work of such contemporaries as Ivan Pavlov, who, he believed, placed too much emphasis on reactions as the primary component of human behavior. In the early 1920's Vygotsky developed his concept of "mediation," which distinguishes humans from other animals in their ability to connect stimuli and responses by means of various kinds of links, such as language. These means of mediation then become themselves stimuli of more complex responses, or "inner language," as Vygotsky called it. Vygotsky also assumed that language and thought developed independently, both in the individual and in the history of the human species. This presupposition led him to postulate that intelligence is a function of the ability to connect signs with concepts. On the basis of this presupposition, he developed the Vygotsky blocks, a test for schizophrenia which was the only one of Vygotsky's concepts widely known before the 1960's, when his works were first translated into English.

Vygotsky's first book, *The Psychology of Art*, unpublished even in Russian until 1965, was a revision of his doctoral thesis at the Moscow Institute of Psychology. This work, which reveals a broad interest in literature and philosophy, exhibits two important qualities of Vygotsky's thought: first, his notion that human psychology is a very complex phenomenon; and second, that psychology is a means to study culture, rather than an end in itself. In other works of the 1920's Vygotsky addressed the divisions and schools of psychology in his day and outlined his own method, compatible with Marxism but not rigidly subject to it.

In the early 1930's Vygotsky collected seven essays and fitted them together to compose his most important and influential work, *Thought and Language*. In this book Vygotsky again surveys various approaches to the subject, focusing primarily on that of his contemporary Jean Piaget. He argues that speech and thought have different roots and that the two are joined only at a given stage in the development of the individual, after which they exert a mutual influence on future development. The child, he showed, exhibits both speech without meaning and intellectual activity without words. It is the joining and subsequent interaction of the systems of language and thought that mark the maturation of the child. His natural interest in the learning process led Vygotsky to study children in educational settings. There he observed that two forms of conceptual learning can be distinguished: one formal and systematic, the other spontaneous and loosely organized. This division led, in turn, to his theory of "inner speech," whereby the social function of communication in language is internalized as a set of psychological relations.

Vygotsky and his slightly younger colleague Alexander Luria undertook pioneering studies in cross-cultural psychology, comparing the reasoning processes of uneducated rural people with those of people who had varying levels of formal education. Luria, who went on to enjoy a long career and attained worldwide recognition as a neuropsychologist, always credited Vygotsky's influence and played a part in the revival of his work. Vygotsky's researches also led him into the field of psychopathology; one of his papers on mental illness, "Thought in Schizophrenia," was published in English in 1934.

Vygotsky left his mark not only on Soviet psychology—in his resistance to crudely dogmatic Marxist ideology and insistence on a pluralistic methodology, and in his influence on the work of his students—but also on the fields of art, literature, and linguistics. The belated translation of his works into English has brought increasing recognition of Vygotsky's immense contribution to twentieth century thought.

James T. Jones

Bibliography

Kozulin, Alex. "Vygotsky in Context." Introduction to *Thought and Language*, by L. S. Vygotskii. Cambridge, Mass.: MIT Press, 1986. A long introductory essay in this revised and expanded edition. Particularly valuable.

Luria, A. R. *The Making of Mind: A Personal Account of Soviet Psychology*, edited by Michael Cole and Sheila Cole. Cambridge, Mass.: Harvard University Press, 1979. Includes a tribute to Vygotsky and a recollection of Luria's work with him.

McCrone, John. "Champion of the Transformed Mind." *New Scientist* 144 (October 7, 1994). A journal article on Vygotsky's work.

Wertsch, James V. *Vygotsky and the Social Formation of Mind*. Cambridge, Mass.: Harvard University Press, 1985. A thorough study of Vygotsky in English. Includes an extensive bibliography.

Jane Wagner

American screenwriter, director, and producer

Born: Morristown, Tennessee; February 2, 1935

DRAMA: *Appearing Nitely*, pr. 1977 (with Lily Tomlin); *The Search for Signs of Intelligent Life in the Universe*, pr. 1985.
SCREENPLAYS: *Moment by Moment*, 1978; *The Incredible Shrinking Woman*, 1981; *The Search for Signs of Intelligent Life in the Universe*, 1991 (adaptation of her play).
TELEPLAYS: *J. T.*, 1969 (adaptation of her book); *Lily*, 1973 (with Lily Tomlin, Richard Pryor, and others); *Earthwatch*, 1975 (education special); *Lily Tomlin*, 1975 (with Tomlin and others); *People*, 1975; *Lily: Sold Out*, 1981 (with others); *Lily for President?*, 1982 (with Tomlin and others); *Edith Ann: A Few Pieces of the Puzzle*, 1994; *Edith Ann: Homeless Go Home*, 1995; *Culture Wars*, 1995 (documentary; with Tina DiFeliciantonio); *Edith Ann's Christmas: Just Say Noel*, 1996.
CHILDREN'S/YOUNG ADULT LITERATURE: *J. T.*, 1969; *Edith Ann: My Life So Far*, 1996.

A native of Tennessee, Jane Wagner toured as a leading actress with the famed Barter Theater during her early and mid-teens. At the age of seventeen, she moved to New York City to pursue her interests in art studies. She studied painting and sculpture at the School of Visual Arts and established herself as a textile designer for various firms, including Kimberly-Clark and Fieldcrest. Her best known textile creation is the "Teach Me, Read Me" collection of bedsheets for children, which have become part of the permanent collection at the Brooklyn Museum of Art.

Wagner's first credited writings were the teleplay and associated book *J. T.*, an inner-city drama. The play won her a Peabody Award (1969), while the book won the Georgia Children's Book Award (1972). *J. T.* also led to her affiliation with actress Lily Tomlin, who was attracted by Wagner's humor and insightful writing. Wagner wrote scripts for Tomlin's appearances in the television series *Rowan and Martin's Laugh-In* during the early 1970's. In 1976, she wrote the screenplay *The Incredible Shrinking Woman*, which was performed by Tomlin. Wagner also wrote two Tony Award-winning Broadway shows for Tomlin, *Appearing Nitely* and *The Search for Signs of Intelligent Life in the Universe*. Between 1973 and 1982, Wagner wrote seven television specials for Tomlin. Wagner was awarded Emmys for *Lily*, *Lily Tomlin*, *Lily: Sold Out*, and *Lily for President?* She also received a Writer's Guild Award for *Lily*.

The Search for Signs of Intelligent Life in the Universe established Wagner as a unique writer in the literary world. For this work, she was honored with special citations from the New York Drama Critics Circle and the New York Drama Desk. It was the first play to appear on *The New York Times* best-seller list in twenty years, remaining there for many weeks. The film version of the play was released in 1991 and received wide acclaim. Wagner wrote the screenplay and the title song, "We Are the Ones." The play was revived in 1996 and played for twenty-six weeks in the Booth Theater on Broadway. During 2001 and 2002, it played before sold-out audiences in Los Angeles, San Francisco, and London.

In the mid-1990's, Wagner turned her talents to writing three animated teleplays about a precocious five-year-old girl: *Edith Ann: A Few Pieces of the Puzzle*, *Edith Ann: Homeless Go Home*, and *Edith Ann's Christmas: Just Say Noel*. All three specials received rave reviews and excellent ratings. She received her second Peabody Award for *Edith Ann's Christmas: Just Say Noel*. In 1996, she released her book *Edith Ann: My Life So Far*.

Wagner is not only a talented writer but also an accomplished director and producer of films as well as a writer of song lyrics. She scripted and directed the film *Moment by Moment* that starred Tomlin and John Travolta. In 1988, Wagner and Tina DiFeliciantonio founded the filmmaking company known as Naked Eye Productions. The films they produced include *Tom's Flesh*, a Sundance Film Festival winner for short filmmaking; *Girls Like Us*, a Sundance Film Festival Grand Jury Prize winner; *Two or Three Things, but Nothing for Sure*, which received a National Emmy Award nomination; and *Walk This Way*, a first place winner in the Chicago International Children's Film Festival.

Wagner has lectured at numerous universities and served on many panels and juries, including those of the Sundance Film Festival and the Emmy Awards. In 1998, the Lily Tomlin and Jane Wagner Cultural Arts Center was opened in Los Angeles. The center presents live theater performances, art exhibits, and other events for the benefit of the community. Among other things, the earned revenues are used to provide services for people suffering from acquired immunodeficiency syndrome (AIDS) and for helping young playwrights, artists, and performers start their careers.

Alvin K. Benson

Bibliography

Gavin, Christy. *American Women Playwrights, 1964-1989: A Research Guide and Annotated Bibliography.* New York: Garland, 1993. Documents the work and critical analysis of women playwrights since the early 1960's. Contains an excellent bibliography and annotated list of works related to individual playwrights, including Jane Wagner.

Murphy, Brenda, ed. *The Cambridge Companion to American Women Playwrights*. Cambridge, England: Cambridge University Press, 1999. Addresses the cultural, historical, critical, and ideological aspects of women playwrights, including Jane Wagner, and their work throughout the history of American theater.

John Wain

English novelist, biographer, literary critic, and short-story writer

Born: Stoke-on-Trent, Staffordshire, England; March 14, 1925
Died: Oxford, England; May 24, 1994

LONG FICTION: *Hurry on Down*, 1953 (pb. in U.S. as *Born in Captivity*); *Living in the Present*, 1955; *The Contenders*, 1958; *A Travelling Woman*, 1959; *Strike the Father Dead*, 1962; *The Young Visitors*, 1965; *The Smaller Sky*, 1967; *A Winter in the Hills*, 1970; *The Pardoner's Tale*, 1978; *Young Shoulders*, 1982 (pb. in U.S. as *The Free Zone Starts Here*); *Where the Rivers Meet*, 1988; *Comedies*, 1990; *Hungry Generations*, 1994.

SHORT FICTION: *Nuncle, and Other Stories*, 1960; *Death of the Hind Legs, and Other Stories*, 1966; *The Life Guard*, 1971; *King Caliban, and Other Stories*, 1978.

DRAMA: *Harry in the Night: An Optimistic Comedy*, pr. 1975; *Johnson Is Leaving: A Monodrama*, pb. 1994.

TELEPLAY: *Young Shoulders*, 1984 (with Robert Smith).

RADIO PLAYS: *You Wouldn't Remember*, 1978; *A Winter in the Hills*, 1981; *Frank*, 1982.

POETRY: *Mixed Feelings*, 1951; *A Word Carved on a Sill*, 1956; *A Song About Major Eatherly*, 1961; *Weep Before God: Poems*, 1961; *Wildtrack: A Poem*, 1965; *Letters to Five Artists*, 1969; *The Shape of Feng*, 1972; *Feng: A Poem*, 1975; *Poems for the Zodiac*, 1980; *Thinking About Mr. Person*, 1980; *Poems, 1949-1979*, 1981; *Twofold*, 1981; *Open Country*, 1987.

NONFICTION: *Preliminary Essays*, 1957; *Gerard Manley Hopkins: An Idiom of Desperation*, 1959; *Sprightly Running: Part of an Autobiography*, 1962; *Essays on Literature and Ideas*, 1963; *The Living World of Shakespeare: A Playgoer's Guide*, 1964; *Arnold Bennett*, 1967; *A House for the Truth: Critical Essays*, 1972; *Samuel Johnson*, 1974; *Professing Poetry*, 1977; *Samuel Johnson, 1709-1784*, 1984 (with Kai Kin Yung); *Dear Shadows: Portraits from Memory*, 1986.

CHILDREN'S/YOUNG ADULT LITERATURE: *Lizzie's Floating Shop*, 1981.

EDITED TEXTS: *Contemporary Reviews of Romantic Poetry*, 1953; *Interpretations: Essays on Twelve English Poems*, 1955; *International Literary Annual*, 1959, 1960; *Fanny Burney's Diary*, 1960; *Anthology of Modern Poetry*, 1963; *Selected Shorter Poems of Thomas Hardy*, 1966; *Selected Shorter Stories of Thomas Hardy*, 1966; *Thomas Hardy's "The Dynasts,"* 1966; *Shakespeare: "Macbeth," a Casebook*, 1968, revised 1994; *Shakespeare: "Othello," a Casebook*, 1971; *Johnson as Critic*, 1973; *The New Wessex Selection of Thomas Hardy's Poetry*, 1978 (with Eirian James).

John Barrington Wain was a British man of letters of major importance, most famous for his early novel *Hurry on Down* and for his prize-winning biography of Samuel Johnson. He was born in Stoke-on-Trent, Staffordshire, England, on March 14, 1925, the son of Arnold A. Wain and Anne Wain. A man of humble background, Arnold Wain had become a dentist, the first professional person in his family. Generous and compassionate, he served as a preacher in the Church army, a city councillor, and a magistrate, and he became a model for his son, who paid tribute to his father in *Dear Shadows*.

After attending school at Newcastle-under-Lyme, Wain, who had been rejected by the army for poor eyesight, went to Oxford and entered St. John's College. At Oxford University, he met Charles Williams and was tutored by C. S. Lewis. He also came to know Richard Burton and with him participated in Shakespeare productions under the direction of the dynamic, unconventional don Nevill Coghill. Nevill inspired his students to love Shakespeare and, by acting on his convictions in the face of criticism from his peers, became another role model for Wain. In 1946 Wain received his B.A.; from 1946 to 1949, when he received his M.A., he was Fereday Fellow at Oxford. Meanwhile, in 1947, he married Marianne Urmston and became a lecturer in English at the University of Reading, where he remained until 1955. He resigned this position to become a freelance writer. The next year, his marriage was dissolved.

With the publication of a book of poetry in 1951, *Mixed Feelings*, Wain's meteoric rise in reputation began. It was followed by another volume of poetry, which despite its conventionality was praised for voicing the anguish of humankind in the twentieth century. In 1953 he published the picaresque novel *Hurry on Down*, the story of an aimless university graduate who wanders through British society seeking a niche where he can feel at home. Despite Wain's protests, this book brought him the label of "angry young man" (applied to those postwar writers who were attacking the English class structure). Critics predicted a bright future for Wain; many of them assumed that he would be the primary writer of his generation. During the decade, he produced three more novels and a critical work on Gerard Manley Hopkins. In 1953, he was chosen to edit a British Broadcasting Corporation (BBC) program featuring new writers. That same year, he edited two books of essays and a two-volume literary annual.

In 1960, Wain married Eirian James, with whom he eventually had three sons. His new happiness was reflected in what is probably his best book written during this period, *Sprightly Running*, which surveys the first thirty-five years of his life honestly and often joyfully. In the 1960's, Wain's energy was evidenced by a steady outpouring of work, including seven editions of works by writers as diverse as Alexander Pope, Fanny Burney, Thomas Hardy, and William Shakespeare and two books of criticism. As the decade proceeded, he published four volumes of poetry, which steadily became more experimental in form than his earlier works, as well as more concerned with social and political matters. He also brought out two collections of short stories and wrote three novels, which like the poetry were more serious and more pessimistic than his previously published fiction. Yet reviewers continued to be lukewarm about both his poetry and his fiction.

Despite the attractiveness of *Sprightly Running*, it was not until the 1970's that Wain attained the eminence which had been predicted for him. Although along with favorable comments, critics continued to voice disappointment in his poetry and his fiction, which seemed to stop just short of brilliance, Wain was acknowledged as a distinguished man of letters. In 1973 he was honored with the place of professor of poetry at Oxford. Then came a work which fulfilled Wain's early promise. Interestingly, it was a work of criticism, his perceptive biography of Samuel Johnson, which was universally admired and earned for Wain the James Tait Black Memorial Prize. It was followed by a novel, *The Pardoner's Tale*, which was admired by most critics, some of whom called it his best fictional work, and then by another well-reviewed novel, *Young Shoulders*, in 1982. In 1981 a work in another genre, *Lizzie's Floating Shop*, had been published; it won for Wain the Whitbread Award for children's literature. Readers also were delighted with another autobiographical volume, *Dear Shadows*, which, like its predecessor *Sprightly Running*, was not presumptuous but honest, warm, and frequently insightful.

Wain's beloved wife Eirian died in 1987; he then married Patricia Dunn the following year. Despite ill health and diminished vision, Wain labored on at his, ultimately, final project, the three novels that constitute the Oxford Trilogy: *Where the Rivers Meet*, *Comedies*, and *Hungry Generations*. This epic work covers three decades in the life of Peter Leonard, from his undergraduate years at Oxford in the mid-1920's, through World War II, to the ending in 1956. The novels include a multitude of characters who all speak their minds about politics, world news, and the progress of society. In 1994, the year the last volume of the trilogy was published, Wain died of a stroke at the John Radcliffe Hospital in Oxford.

Throughout the acclaimed Johnson biography, Wain had emphasized the need for courage in a tragic world, for reason in an irrational world, and for tradition in a world which is changing, not necessarily for the better. These Johnsonian themes are also Wain's themes. In *Dear Shadows*, Wain writes about eight people, four famous and four unknown, who were important in his life. In them, he saw the qualities he admires: his father's courage and sense of duty, the Stratford landlady's commonsensical look at hasty passion, and Nevill Coghill's determined revival of the Shakespearean tradition in twentieth century Oxford. Although none of Wain's imaginative works has quite fulfilled the expectations of the critics who so praised his first novel, the fact that year after year he brought out works in various genres which are always respectable and often very good suggests that his place in literary history is secure. He did not limit himself to one area but influenced his age through works of many kinds, not least of which is his scholarly biography of one of the greatest men of letters in English literature, Dr. Samuel Johnson.

Rosemary M. Canfield Reisman

Bibliography

Amis, Kingsley. *Kingsley Amis: Memoirs*. New York: Summit Books, 1991. Gives a vivid glimpse of in-fighting among aspiring writers. Amis hints wryly that Wain envied the bestsellerdom of *Lucky Jim* that placed his own first novel, *Hurry on Down*, into the shade.

Bayley, John. "Obituary: John Wain." *The Independent*, May 25, 1994, p. 14. In this biographical sketch of Wain's life and literary career, Bayley compares him with Kingsley Amis and praises his biography of Samuel Johnson.

Burgess, Anthony. *The Novel Now: A Guide to Contemporary Fiction*. New York: W. W. Norton, 1967. Expanded from an earlier study, Burgess's work groups Wain with other class-conscious British fiction writers.

Gerard, David E. *John Wain: A Bibliography*. Westport, Conn.: Meckler, 1987. Contains a comprehensive annotated bibliography of Wain's work. Lists materials of critical and biographical interest, including radio, television, and sound recordings. Also includes other critical and biographical references and reviews of works by Wain.

Gindin, James. "The Moral Center of John Wain's Fiction." In *Postwar British Fiction: New Accents and Attitudes*. Berkeley: University of California Press, 1962. Gindin contends that Wain creates characters who always exhibit dignity and moral commitment. Considers Wain's first four novels and his stories in the volume *Nuncle, and Other Stories*. In an introductory essay, Gindin evaluates Wain in the context of other authors from the 1950's.

Hatziolou, Elizabeth. *John Wain: A Man of Letters*. London: Pisces

Press, 1997. The first extensive biography to come out after Wain's death. Includes an index.

Heptonstall, Geoffrey. "Remembering John Wain." *Contemporary Review* 266 (March, 1995): 144-146. A brief discussion of Wain's central themes of faithlessness and the assumption that there are no assumptions; discusses Wain's rejection of realism and his intention to speak imaginatively. An excellent overview.

Pickering, Jean. "The English Short Story in the Sixties." In *The English Short Story, 1945-1960*, edited by Dennis Vannatta. Boston: Twayne, 1985. A comprehensive study of Wain as a writer of short fiction.

Rabinovitz, Rubin. "The Novelists of the 1950's: A General Survey." In *The Reaction Against Experiment in the English Novel, 1950-1960*. New York: Columbia University Press, 1967. Rabinovitz places Wain in the context of novelists who embraced traditional values rather than those who experimented with unconventional ideas or forms, aligning Wain's novels with those of Arnold Bennett and eighteenth century picaresque novelists.

Salwak, Dale. *Interviews with Britain's Angry Young Men*. San Bernardino, Calif.: Borgo Press, 1984. This useful resource characterizes Wain as an "eighteenth century man." Engages Wain in a discussion of the role of criticism in the author's life, his goals as a writer, his response to the phenomenon of the Angry Young Men, and the sources and themes in several of his novels.

_______. *John Wain*. Boston: Twayne, 1981. After a chapter introducing Wain's life and art, the text contains four chapters on his novels. "Other Fiction, Other Prose" covers Wain's stories, poems, and biographical works. A selected bibliography completes the text.

Salwak, Dale, and Rosemary M. Canfield Reisman. "John Wain." In *Critical Survey of Long Fiction*, edited by Carl Rollyson. 2d rev. ed. Pasadena, Calif.: Salem Press, 2000. A good general introduction to Wain's novels. Includes a brief biography.

Taylor, D. J. *After the War: The Novel and English Society Since 1945*. London: Chatto and Windus, 1993. An attempt to define the nature of postwar writing. Wain is grouped with William Cooper and Kingsley Amis as being antimodernist, or opposed to the psychological emphasis and stylistic complexity of James Joyce and Virginia Woolf, and antiromantic.

Diane Wakoski

American poet

Born: Whittier, California; August 3, 1937

POETRY: *Coins and Coffins*, 1962; *Discrepancies and Apparitions*, 1966; *The George Washington Poems*, 1967; *Inside the Blood Factory*, 1968; *The Moon Has a Complicated Geography*, 1969; *The Magellanic Clouds*, 1970; *The Motorcycle Betrayal Poems*, 1971; *Smudging*, 1972; *Dancing on the Grave of a Son of a Bitch*, 1973; *Looking for the King of Spain*, 1974; *Virtuoso Literature for Two and Four Hands*, 1975; *Waiting for the King of Spain*, 1976; *The Man Who Shook Hands*, 1978; *Cap of Darkness*, 1980; *The Magician's Feastletters*, 1982; *The Collected Greed, Parts 1-13*, 1984 (part 1 pb. in 1968); *The Rings of Saturn*, 1986; *Emerald Ice: Selected Poems, 1962-1987*, 1988; *Medea the Sorceress*, 1991; *Jason the Sailor*, 1993; *The Emerald City of Las Vegas*, 1995; *Argonaut Rose*, 1998; *The Butcher's Apron: New and Selected Poems, Including "Greed: Part 14,"* 2000.

NONFICTION: *Creating a Personal Mythology*, 1975; *Toward a New Poetry*, 1980.

Diane Wakoski has become well known for the "personal mythology" she has woven by imaginatively reworking her own history into mythic poem-stories. Born in the small California town of Whittier, Wakoski endured a childhood marked by poverty, separation from her father, and feelings of disassociation from her family and community. When she was fifteen months old, her father joined the Navy, and from then on she saw him only on his brief visits home, while his marriage to her mother came apart. Wakoski's feelings of abandonment from this early experience played a large role in her later life and influenced her writing. She began writing poems when she was seven years old. Later, attending Fullerton High School, she was encouraged in her writing by her teachers. She also belonged to a poetry club that met after school, and she haunted the school library.

Wakoski attended the University of California at Berkeley, where her teachers included poets Thomas Parkinson, Thom Gunn, and Josephine Miles. Writers who strongly influenced her at this stage of her career included Wallace Stevens, Federico García Lorca, and Gertrude Stein. After earning a bachelor's degree in English in 1960, she moved to New York City with composer La Monte Young; there she worked in a bookstore, acquired a temporary teaching credential, and taught in a junior high school. Throughout this time she wrote prolifically. Her first book, *Coins and Coffins*, which contains a number of dramatic narrative poems, was published in 1962. In 1965 she married a photographer, S. Shepard Sherbell; they were later divorced, and she married Michael Watterland in 1973.

Although Wakoski has been given the label "confessional poet," she has several times stated her dislike for the term, which to her implies that using one's personal experience in writing is wrong, that the experiences described are neurotic, and that imagination plays no role in transforming such experience into poetry with larger implications. She began creating her own personal mythology when she was still in college, after falling in love with Greek tragedy and with the long story poems of California writer Robinson Jeffers.

She makes reference in some poems to having borne two children out of wedlock, and in a long autobiographical essay published in 1984 she describes giving this son and daughter up for adoption. However, many other characters who appear in Wakoski's poems (including "the King of Spain," "the Blue Moon Cowboy," "George Washington," and others) are either fictitious or are very loosely based on people the poet has known. Even the "Dianes" who turn up from work to work are often just aspects of the writer's self, creatures who change personality from poem to poem.

Much of Wakoski's work has been sparked by the failure of various relationships with men, and her most commercially successful book, *The Motorcycle Betrayal Poems*, came as the result of her breakup with motorcycle racer Tony Weinberger. The book is dedicated "to all those men who betrayed me at one time or another, in hopes they will fall off their motorcycles and break their necks."

Wakoski was for a number of years an itinerant poet, giving as many as eighty readings a year and teaching occasional writing workshops. In the early 1970's she held posts at colleges and universities throughout the United States and won National Endowment for the Arts and Guggenheim fellowships while continuing to write voluminously. In 1975 she began an affiliation with Michigan State University in East Lansing, where she eventually became a permanent faculty member in the English department. In 1983 she married photographer Robert Turney, her third husband. Throughout her career she has won a large following of readers, but she received little critical honor until 1989, when she was awarded the Poetry Society of America's William Carlos Williams Award for *Emerald Ice*.

Much of Wakoski's work draws heavily on place. California, her early home, recurs throughout her poems, as does Las Vegas, where she has often been a visiting writer. Las Vegas plays a large role in her thirteen-part poem *Greed*, which was published in small segments beginning in 1968 and gathered under one cover in 1984. A fourteenth part was published in *The Butcher's Apron* in 2000.

The author of more than forty books of poetry, Wakoski has long been one of the most prolific of contemporary American poets. Her work revolves around a quest for beauty and for love, sex, and romance. She seldom writes in established poetic forms but rather lets each poem find its own form organically. Wakoski's poems are often extraordinarily beautiful in their juxtaposition of everyday objects and philosophical ideas.

Penelope Moffet

Bibliography

Brown, David M. "Wakoski's 'The Fear of Fat Children.'" *The Explicator* 48, no. 4 (Summer, 1990): 292-294. Brown observes how the poem's common diction and grotesque imagery work to create a successful postmodern confessional in which the speaker expresses not only guilt but also the urge for self-reformation.

Gannon, Catherine, and Clayton Lein. "Diane Wakoski and the Language of Self." *San Jose Studies* 5 (Spring, 1979): 84-98. Focusing on *The Motorcycle Betrayal Poems*, Gannon and Lein discuss the betrayal motif in terms of the speaker's struggle for identity. The poems' speaker uses the moon image to consider possible alternative images for herself, and in the last poem of the book she achieves a "richer comprehension of her being."

Hughes, Gertrude Reif. "Readers Digest." *Women's Review of Books* 18, no. 7 (April, 2001): 14-16. Treats *The Butcher's Apron* along with collected works volumes by Carolyn Kizer and Kathleen Raine. Gives high praise to "Greed, Part 14," which is granted the status of a major long poem that redeems much else in the collection.

Lauter, Estella. *Women as Mythmakers: Poetry and Visual Art by Twentieth-Century Women*. Bloomington: Indiana University Press, 1984. Lauter devotes one chapter to Wakoski's handling of moon imagery in several of the poet's books. There is also a related discussion of Isis and Diana as aspects of the speaker's personality.

Martin, Taffy Wynne. "Diane Wakoski's Personal Mythology: Dionysian Music, Created Presence." *Boundary 2: A Journal of Postmodern Literature* 10 (Fall, 1982): 155-172. According to Martin, Wakoski's sense of absence and lost love prompts desire, which in turn animates the poetry, giving it life. Martin also discusses Wakoski's mythmaking, her use of digression as a structural device, and her use of musical repetition.

Newton, Robert. *Diane Wakoski: A Descriptive Bibliography*. Jefferson, N.C.: McFarland, 1987. Newton unravels Wakoski's career in print through its first quarter century.

Ostriker, Alicia Luskin. *Stealing the Language: The Emergence of Women's Poetry in America*. Boston: Beacon Press, 1986. An outstanding history of women's poetry, Ostriker's book includes extended readings of some of Wakoski's works, especially *The George Washington Poems*. For the most part, Ostriker focuses on the divided self (the all-nothing and the strong-weak) in Wakoski's poetry and discusses the ways in which the poet's masks and disguises become flesh. There is an extensive bibliography concerning women's poetry.

Wakoski, Diane. Interview by Taffy Wynne Martin. *Dalhousie Review* 61 (Autumn, 1981): 476-496. Martin elicits detailed answers from Wakoski about a wide range of topics: part 10 of *Greed*, her relationships with her parents, the literary influences on her poetry, and her responses to many new American poets. Of particular interest is Wakoski's discussion of how memory functions as narrative and how it can structure a poem.

_______. *Toward a New Poetry*. Ann Arbor: University of Michigan Press, 1980. The book includes not only Wakoski's criticism, much of which is commentary to her own poetry, but also five revealing interviews, only two of which had previously been published in major journals. In the introduction, Wakoski lists her "best" poems, the ones she believes illustrate her personal mythology, her use of image and digression, and the kind of music she thinks is important to contemporary poetry.

Derek Walcott

West Indian poet and playwright

Born: Castries, St. Lucia, West Indies; January 23, 1930
Identity: African descent

POETRY: *Twenty-five Poems*, 1948; *Poems*, 1951; *In a Green Night: Poems, 1948-1960*, 1962; *Selected Poems*, 1964; *The Castaway, and Other Poems*, 1965; *The Gulf, and Other Poems*, 1969; *Another Life*, 1973; *Sea Grapes*, 1976; *The Star-Apple Kingdom*, 1979; *The Fortunate Traveller*, 1981; *Midsummer*, 1984; *Collected Poems, 1948-1984*, 1986; *The Arkansas Testament*, 1987; *Omeros*, 1990; *Poems, 1965-1980*, 1992; *The Bounty*, 1997; *Tiepolo's Hound*, 2000.

DRAMA: *Henri Christophe: A Chronicle*, pr., pb. 1950; *The Sea of Dauphin*, pr., pb. 1954; *The Wine of the Country*, pr. 1956; *Ione*, pr. 1957; *Ti-Jean and His Brothers*, pr. 1957, revised pr. 1958 (music by Andre Tanker); *Drums and Colours*, pr. 1958; *Malcochon: Or, Six in the Rain*, pr. 1959; *Dream on Monkey Mountain*, pr. 1967; *Dream on Monkey Mountain, and Other Plays*, pb. 1970; *In a Fine Castle*, pr. 1970; *The Joker of Seville*, pr. 1974 (adaptation of Tirso de Molina's *El burlador de Sevilla*; music by Galt MacDermot); *The Charlatan*, pr. 1974; *O Babylon!*, pr. 1976; *Remembrance*, pr. 1977; *"The Joker of Seville" and "O Babylon!": Two Plays*, pb. 1978; *Pantomime*, pr. 1978; *Marie LaVeau*, pr. 1979; *"Remembrance" and "Pantomime,"* pb. 1980; *Beef, No Chicken*, pr. 1981; *The Last Carnival*, pr. 1982; *The Isle Is Full of Noises*, pr. 1982; *A Branch of the Blue Nile*, pr. 1983; *To Die for Grenada*, pr. 1986; *Three Plays*, pb. 1986; *Ghost Dance*, pr. 1989; *Viva Detroit*, pr. 1990; *Steel*, pr. 1991 (music by MacDermot); *The Odyssey*, pr. 1992, pb. 1993; *Walker*, pr. 1992, revised pb. 2002; *The Capeman: A Musical*, pr. 1997, pb. 1998 (music by Paul Simon); *The Haitian Trilogy*, pb. 2001.

NONFICTION: "Meanings: From a Conversation with Derek Walcott," 1970 (in *Performing Arts*); *The Antilles: Fragments of Epic Memory*, 1993 (Nobel lecture); *Homage to Robert Frost*, 1996 (with Joseph Brodsky and Seamus Heaney); *What the Twilight Says: Essays*, 1998.

Derek Alton Walcott is one of the most highly regarded poets writing in English, let alone from the English-speaking Caribbean. His prodigious talent and energy were recognized early in Castries, St. Lucia, and his mother, Alix Walcott, encouraged him, his older sister, and his twin brother, Roderick Walcott (also an accomplished playwright), in their art. Their father, Warwick Walcott, wrote and painted watercolors as an avocation; he died at age thirty-five when the twin brothers were one year old. Derek Walcott has won numerous awards and fellowships for his writing, among them the Welsh Arts Council International Writers Prize (1980), the John D. and Catherine MacArthur Foundation Prize (1981), the *Los Angeles Times* Book Award (1986) for his *Collected Poems, 1948-1984*, the Queen's Gold Medal for Literature (1989), the St. Lucia Cross (1993), and the Nobel Prize in Literature (1992). He is a Fellow of the Royal Society of Literature (1966) and an honorary member of the American Academy and Institute of Arts and Letters (1979).

Walcott attended St. Mary's College in Castries and the University of the West Indies in Jamaica, earning a B.A. in English, French, and Latin in 1953. With his mother's financial help, he published his first volume of poems in 1948. His first play, *Henri Christophe*, was produced in 1950 by the student drama society at Jamaica. He taught Latin and other subjects in Grenada, St. Lucia, and Trinidad until 1959, when he founded the Little Carib Theatre Workshop (later known as the Trinidad Theatre Workshop). He worked with the company until 1976, writing many of his most important plays for actors he had trained. Among the plays premiered there were *Ti-Jean and His Brothers*, *Dream on Monkey Mountain* (which won an Obie Award in 1971), *The Joker of Seville*, and *O Babylon!* In that same period, he finished six volumes of poetry, including *Another Life*, the book-length autobiographical poem that, like William Wordsworth's *The Prelude* (1850), chronicles the growth of the poet's imagination.

In the late 1970's, Walcott taught at Yale, Columbia, Harvard, and New York universities before accepting a full-time post at Boston University in 1981; after 1985 this became a visiting professorship. Dividing his time between teaching in the United States and living in St. Lucia and Trinidad permitted the division within his African and European heritage (which he defined in "A Far Cry from Africa" and other early poems) to be elaborated in terms of the metropolitan state and the developing islands. The placing of his poetry in both halves of the New World reveals an ambitious effort to bring into creative tension the conflicts of his divided life as a part-black and part-white man of the postcolonial world of the Americas. That effort is mounted in a literary context. Thus his poetry draws upon the tradition within which he locates his work, that of Andrew Marvell, John Milton, Henry Vaughan, Thomas Traherne, John Donne, W. H. Auden, Dylan Thomas, William Butler Yeats, and many others, including Robert Lowell and especially Homer, whose works underlie Walcott's best-known work *Omeros*—as well as in a historical context of a postslavery, postcolonial society.

The racial and political ironies of Walcott's West Indian situation are also the subject of his plays from the late 1970's, *Remembrance* and *Pantomime*. In the latter, a white Englishman and a black calypsonian from Trinidad exchange places in rehearsing a music-hall version of Robinson Crusoe, in which Crusoe is black and Friday is white. They play out their oppositions to reach a relationship that is nearly brotherhood, though Crusoe has to ask Friday for a raise.

Walcott has both been criticized for writing a self-indulgent, highly wrought poetic line and praised for a line that is Elizabethan in grandeur and richness. Some critics have accused him of betraying the very people his poetry should speak to and for: the indigent, Creole-speaking West Indian who likely cannot read the poetry that Walcott writes. Such critics favor Jamaican "dub" and reggae-based poetry, but they misconstrue the importance of the Trinidadian calypso in Walcott's work, and indeed in the East Caribbean. Walcott the lyric poet and narrative poet is also a dramatic poet, and his plays and poems elucidate each other. A thorough assessment of Walcott's work cannot be made without integrating the poet and playwright with the painter who swore on his eighteenth birthday to put his island into paint and words and who has been admirably successful at the task for decades. His ability to paint these images so lyrically in words was recognized by his being awarded the Nobel Prize in Literature in 1992. He was the first black man to win the award, and the prize brought attention to West Indian writers in general. Walcott's best work may be those poems, such as *Another Life*, that, whatever the foregrounded subject, take as their realm the villages of St. Lucia—Anse La Raye, Dennery, Choiseul, Gros Islet, Vieuxfort, Soufriere, and the city of Castries—and the spectacular forests, mountains, and seas of the Caribbean.

Robert Bensen

Bibliography

Bloom, Harold, ed. *Derek Walcott*. New York: Chelsea House, 2003. A collection of essays intended to provide an overview of the critical reception of Walcott's work.

Bobb, June D. *Beating a Restless Drum: The Poetics of Kamau Brathwaite and Derek Walcott*. Trenton, N.J.: African World Press, 1998. Examines the influence of colonization and slavery on the Caribbean's most important anglophone poets, linking them to a specifically Caribbean tradition rooted in African mythologies and other influences. Bibliography, index.

Burnett, Paula. *Derek Walcott: Politics and Poetics*. Gainesville: University Press of Florida, 2001. Sees the drama and poetry together designed to create a legacy for modern Caribbean society, incorporating myth, identity, and aesthetics. Notes, bibliography, index.

Davis, Gregson, ed. *The Poetics of Derek Walcott*. Durham, N.C.: Duke University Press, 1997. A collection of critical essays on the poetry. The cornerstone essay is one in which Walcott reflects on poetics, illuminating his masterpiece *Omeros*. Other contributors focus on central thematic concerns as well as modes of expression.

Hamner, Robert D. *Derek Walcott*. New York: Twayne, 1993. Hamner conducts a thorough exploration of Walcott's plays, poems, and critical articles, ending with *The Star-Apple Kingdom*. The text is supplemented by a selected bibliography of both primary and secondary sources and an index.

King, Bruce. *Derek Walcott: A Caribbean Life*. New York: Oxford University Press, 2000. The first literary biography, with reference to letters, diaries, uncollected and unpublished writings, and interviews in the Caribbean, North America, and Europe.

Thieme, John. *Derek Walcott*. New York: St. Martin's Press, 1999. An introductory biography and critical interpretation of selected works. Includes bibliographical references and index.

Alice Walker

American novelist, short-story writer, poet, and essayist

Born: Eatonton, Georgia; February 9, 1944
Identity: African American

LONG FICTION: *The Third Life of Grange Copeland*, 1970; *Meridian*, 1976; *The Color Purple*, 1982; *The Temple of My Familiar*, 1989; *Possessing the Secret of Joy*, 1992; *By the Light of My Father's Smile*, 1998.

SHORT FICTION: *In Love and Trouble: Stories of Black Women*, 1973; *You Can't Keep a Good Woman Down*, 1981; *The Complete Stories*, 1994; *Alice Walker Banned*, 1996 (stories and commentary).

POETRY: *Once: Poems*, 1968; *Five Poems*, 1972; *Revolutionary Petunias, and Other Poems*, 1973; *Goodnight, Willie Lee, I'll See You in the Morning: Poems*, 1979; *Horses Make a Landscape Look More Beautiful*, 1984; *Her Blue Body Everything We Know: Earthling Poems, 1965-1990 Complete*, 1991; *Absolute Trust in the Goodness of the Earth: New Poems*, 2003.

NONFICTION: *In Search of Our Mothers' Gardens: Womanist Prose*, 1983; *Living by the Word: Selected Writings, 1973-1987*, 1988; *Warrior Marks: Female Genital Mutilation and the Sexual Blinding of Women*, 1993 (with Pratibha Parmor); *The Same River Twice: Honoring the Difficult*, 1996; *Anything We Love Can Be Saved: A Writer's Activism*, 1997; *The Way Forward Is with a Broken Heart*, 2000; *Sent by Earth: A Message from the Grandmother Spirit After the Attacks on the World Trade Center and Pentagon*, 2001.

CHILDREN'S/YOUNG ADULT LITERATURE: *Langston Hughes: American Poet*, 1974; *To Hell with Dying*, 1988; *Finding the Green Stone*, 1991.

EDITED TEXT: *I Love Myself When I Am Laughing . . . and Then Again When I Am Looking Mean and Impressive: A Zora Neale Hurston Reader*, 1979.

Alice Malsenior Walker identifies herself as a "womanist"—that is, by her definition, as a black feminist who seriously concerns herself with the double oppression of racism and sexism. These two themes dominate Walker's poetry, fiction, and prose. Born in 1944 to Georgia sharecroppers, Minnie Lue and Willie Lee (memorialized in *Goodnight, Willie Lee, I'll See You in the Morning*), Walker grew up in the small town of Eatonton. Her childhood was scarred, literally and figuratively, by a BB gun wound to her eye when she was eight years old. Although the scar and loss of sight were partially repaired by an operation when she was fourteen, Walker acknowledges the part played by this accident in her becoming a writer. It forced her to withdraw from social contacts, but it allowed her to retreat into a world of daydreams ("not of fairytales—but of falling on swords, of putting guns to my heart or head, and of slashing my wrists with a razor") and a world of reading and writing.

A scholarship for handicapped students sent Walker to Spelman College (a setting used in *Meridian*) in 1961; after two years, she transferred to Sarah Lawrence College, from which she graduated in 1965. Here another painful personal experience precipitated her first volume of poetry, *Once*. Returning to college in the fall of 1964 from a summer in Africa, Walker faced the realization that she was pregnant, without money, and without support. She seriously considered suicide before securing an abortion. After graduation, Walker was awarded fellowships to both the Bread Loaf Writers' Conference and the MacDowell Colony, where she began writing her first novel, *The Third Life of Grange Copeland*, in 1967, the year she published her first short story, "To Hell with Dying." In that same year, Walker married Melvyn R. Leventhal, a civil rights lawyer whom she had met through her active involvement in the movement. They had one child, Rebecca Grant, before their divorce in 1976.

Walker has acknowledged the influence of Emily Dickinson, William Carlos Williams, E. E. Cummings, and Matsuo Bashō on her poetry, which she sees as having much in common with improvisational jazz. Her lines are of irregular length; the poems are frequently short. Walker's poetry is marked by an informal tone and a straightforward, unafraid, realistic approach to her subject matter. Her most effective subject is her own childhood. The clean, fresh, unadorned style of Walker's poetry also marks her volumes of short fiction. In *You Can't Keep a Good Woman Down*, Walker experiments with nonfiction fiction as she weaves a historical perspective into the fictional fabric. In "Coming Apart," for example, the narrator forces her black husband to see how pornography, black and white, continues the exploitation begun in slavery by introducing him to inserted passages from black writers Audre Lorde, Luisah Teish, and Tracy A. Gardner.

Walker's novels similarly illustrate consistency of theme—oppression—with variety of structure. Her first novel, *The Third Life of Grange Copeland*, is a chronologically ordered, realistic novel following its black sharecropper protagonist through three generations in pursuit of integrity and dignity. Her second novel, *Meridian*, opens in Chicokemo, Mississippi, where ascetic Meridian Hill is working among the poor; the arrival of a friend and lover from her days as an activist in the Civil Rights movement throws the novel into a series of flashbacks.

The Color Purple is an epistolary novel in which Celie, the young protagonist, overcome by physical and emotional abuse initiated by her father and continued by her husband, writes to God and to her sister, Nettie, exposing her painful life. It was this novel, adapted to the screen in 1985 under the direction of Steven Spielberg, which brought fame to Alice Walker. Although the film, a box-office success, was accused by many reviewers of having trivialized the novel, Walker herself was happy with the production, on which she was a consultant, because it brought a story of black women, told in authentic black speech, into the marketplace. The Washington Square paperback edition of *The Color Purple* sold more than a million copies.

In her fourth novel, *The Temple of My Familiar*, Walker sustains a similar account of black women, but this time she also takes on the enormous challenge of rewriting the spiritual history of the universe. Despite the presence of Miss Celie and Miss Shug, two beloved characters from *The Color Purple*, the novel earned little critical praise or favorable media attention. *Possessing the Secret of Joy* relates the story of an African woman who endures terrible physical and emotional suffering in order to demonstrate her loyalty to the people of her tribe. Because of the polemical nature of the story, this novel also did not garner the same commendatory reception that the earlier novels received.

Walker's years of civil rights involvement grew out of a conviction that black writers must also be actively engaged in black issues: "It is unfair to the people we expect to reach to give them a beautiful poem if they are unable to read it." Her own activist stance is seen clearly in her *In Search of Our Mothers' Gardens*, as well as in her untiring efforts to reestablish the reputation of the neglected black writer Zora Neale Hurston (by editing a collection of her short stories, *I Love Myself When I Am Laughing . . . and Then Again When I Am Looking Mean and Impressive*) and to make the black poet Langston Hughes more available to children (*Langston Hughes: American Poet*).

In the 1990's and early 2000's, Walker focused more on her activism and nonfiction work as a means to convey her views. In March, 2003, she was arrested outside the White House, in Washington, D.C., along with Maxine Hong Kingston, while protesting the war with Iraq.

The crazy ("not patchwork") quilt is an essential metaphor in Walker's work: It is the central symbol in her powerful short story "Everyday Use"; it is also the vehicle in *The Color Purple* which allows Sofia, while quilting with Celie, to give her the courage to be. Walker has said that the enigmatic structure of her novel *Meridian* imitates the design of a quilt. In all the works of Alice Walker one finds a commitment to the preservation of the black heritage—the traditions, the culture, the family; to the necessity for putting an end to violence and injustice; to the relationship between individual dignity and community dignity; and to an insistence that women applaud their godliness.

Catharine F. Seigel
Traci S. Smrcka

Bibliography

Bloom, Harold, ed. *Alice Walker*. New York: Chelsea House, 1989. A book-length compilation of the best criticism on Walker. Authors Diane F. Dadoff and Deborah E. McDowell explore the resonant Zora Neale Hurston/Alice Walker relationship. Naturally radical feminism is addressed in this study, and Bloom discusses the mother/daughter motif in Walker's works.

Bloxham, Laura J. "Alice [Malsenior] Walker." In *Contemporary Fiction Writers of the South*, edited by Joseph M. Flora and Robert Bain. Westport, Conn.: Greenwood Press, 1993. A general introduction to Walker's "womanist" themes of oppression of black women and change through affirmation of self. Provides a brief summary and critique of previous criticism of Walker's work.

Butler-Evans, Elliott. *Race, Gender, and Desire: Narrative Strategies in the Fiction of Toni Cade Bambara, Toni Morrison, and Alice Walker.* Philadelphia: Temple University Press, 1989. Focuses on the connections between gender, race, and desire, and their relationship to the narrative strategies in the fiction of these three contemporary writers. Includes somewhat lengthy endnotes and a bibliography.

Dieke, Ikenna, ed. *Critical Essays on Alice Walker.* New York: Greenwood Press, 1999. Especially well suited for use in college literature classrooms, this collection gives particular attention to Walker's poetry and her developing ecofeminism.

Gates, Henry Louis, Jr., and K. A. Appiah, eds. *Alice Walker: Critical Perspectives Past and Present.* New York: Amistad, 1993. Contains reviews of Walker's first five novels and critical analyses of several of her works of short and long fiction. Also includes two interviews with Walker, a chronology of her works, and an extensive bibliography of essays and texts.

Gentry, Tony. *Alice Walker.* New York: Chelsea House, 1993. This biography is geared toward the high school student. The text is simple to read but thorough in providing biographical information about Walker and discussing her writing. A chronology and brief bibliography are also included.

Lauret, Maria. *Alice Walker.* New York: St. Martin's Press, 2000. Provocative discussions of Walker's ideas on politics, race, feminism, and literary theory. Of special interest is the exploration of Walker's literary debt to Zora Neale Hurston, Virginia Woolf, and even Bessie Smith.

Wade-Gayles, Gloria. "Black, Southern, Womanist: The Genius of Alice Walker." In *Southern Women Writers: The New Generation*, edited by Tonette Bond Inge. Tuscaloosa: University of Alabama Press, 1990. An excellent, thorough introduction to the life and literary career of Walker. Placing emphasis on Walker's voice as a black, southern woman. Argues that Walker's commitment is to the spiritual wholeness of her people. Supplemented by a bibliography of Walker's works, endnotes, and a useful secondary bibliography.

Walker, Rebecca. *Black, White, and Jewish: Autobiography of a Shifting Self.* New York: Riverhead, 2001. A self-indulgent but nevertheless insightful memoir by Alice Walker's daughter. Rebecca Walker, who describes herself as "a movement child," grew up torn between two families, two races, and two traditions, always in the shadow of an increasingly famous and absorbed mother.

Winchell, Donna Haisty. *Alice Walker.* New York: Twayne, 1992. Provides a comprehensive analysis of Walker's short and long fiction. A brief biography and chronology precede the main text of the book. Each chapter refers to specific ideas and themes within Walker's works and focuses on how Walker's own experiences define her characters and themes. Following the narrative is a useful annotated bibliography.

Joseph A. Walker

American playwright, actor, and educator

Born: Washington, D.C.; February 24, 1935
Identity: African American

DRAMA: *The Believers*, pr. 1968 (with Josephine Jackson); *The Harangues*, pr. 1969, revised pb. 1971 (as *Tribal Harangue Two*); *Ododo*, pr. 1970; *Yin Yang*, pr. 1972; *The River Niger*, pr. 1972; *Antigone Africanus*, pr. 1975; *The Lion Is a Soul Brother*, pr. 1976; *District Line*, pr. 1984.

SCREENPLAY: *The River Niger*, 1976 (adaptation of his play).

NONFICTION: "Broadway Vitality," 1973; "The Hiss," 1980; "Themes of the Black Struggle," 1982.

Joseph A. Walker was born to working-class parents, Joseph and Florine Walker. He earned a B.A. from Howard University in philosophy in 1956 and minored in drama. Walker spent much of his time in college working on productions with the university's Howard Players. In 1955 he played the character Luke in James Baldwin's premier production of *The Amen Corner* at Howard University. After graduating, he served in the U.S. Air Force, becoming a first lieutenant before his honorable discharge in 1960. He earned his M.F.A. in drama from Catholic University in 1963 and was later awarded the Ph.D. from New York University. He divorced Barbara Brown in 1965, and in 1970 he married Dorothy Dinroe.

Walker's teaching career began in junior high and high schools in Washington, D.C., and he subsequently taught at the City College of New York and at Howard University. He later became a professor in the theater division of the Fine Arts Department at Rutgers University. In his early years, he performed with the Negro Ensemble Company (NEC), which produced several of his plays, and from 1970 to 1971 he was playwright in residence at Yale University. Walker performed in numerous stage productions during the late 1960's and early 1970's, including *The Believers*. He also performed in films, such as *April Fools* (1969) and *Bananas* (1971).

In 1970 Walker and his wife, Dinroe-Walker, founded a musical-dance repertory company called Demi-Gods. Walker's *Ododo* (the truth), a revolutionary, African American historical review, and *Yin Yang*, an African American view of the conflict between good and evil (featuring black women as God and Satan), were moderate successes. Walker's emerging artistry climaxed, however, with the highly successful play *The River Niger.*

Walker is best known for *The River Niger,* which received many awards, including a Tony Award for best play, several Obie Awards, the Elizabeth Hull-Kate Warriner Award from the Drama Guild, the Audelco Award, the John Gassner Award from the Outer Critics Circle, and a Drama Desk Award for most promising playwright. He also received a Guggenheim Fellowship in 1973 and a Rockefeller Foundation grant in 1979. *The River Niger* was a beacon of the Black Arts movement of the 1970's because it was unquestionably semiautobiographical theater examining the realities of a struggling black family and the African American symbolic vision of the African heritage. The play also treats universal philosophical themes, such as parents' relationships with and responsibilities to their grown children, protest and self-actualization, and the function of poetry and art in the lives of working-class families.

Barbara and Carlton Mollette in *Black Theatre: Premise and Presentation* (1992) refer to Walker in their chapter "Afrocentric Heroes" because *The River Niger* embodies traditional African-centered values that prioritize the success of the family and the prosperity of the race. In an African-centered analysis, Walker's other plays, such as *Ododo*, *Yin Yang*, and *Believers* (which addresses the oppression and self-defense strategies of African American men), are culturally significant. Some critics regarded the direct racial and revolutionary context of these plays as threatening, whereby the subtle, or sophisticated, racial context of *The River Niger* found a wider audience. *The River Niger* was adapted into a film production in 1976. Walker wrote the screenplay for the film, which starred Cicely Tyson and James Earl Jones.

Christel N. Temple

Bibliography

Barthelemy, Anthony. "Mother, Sister, Wife: A Dramatic Perspective." *Southern Review* 21, no. 3 (Summer, 1985): 770-789. Barthelemy compares and analyzes the dysfunctions of man-woman relationships in three of Walker's plays. He presents Walker's repetitive use of stereotypical women's roles in defining the positions and roles forced on black women by both their families and society in general.

Clurman, Harold. "Theater: *The River Niger.*" *The Nation* 215, no. 21 (December 25, 1972): 668. Although Clurman praises Walker's technique in *The River Niger,* he finds fault with Walker's use of symbolism in *Ododo*. He suggests that Walker is not sure which historical truths about black-white relationships he wants to tell, so he tries to make the play tell them all. This lack of focus, Clurman states, distorts and creates internal contradiction within both plays.

Kauffmann, Stanley. "Theater: *The River Niger.*" *The New Republic* 169, no. 12 (September 29, 1973): 22. Kauffmann criticizes many of Walker's techniques in *The River Niger,* in particular his lack of subtlety with character motivations and dialogue, but appreciates both the real affection his characters show for one another and the recognition with which black audiences have responded to the play.

Lee, Dorothy. "Three Black Plays: Alienation and Paths to Recovery." *Modern Drama* 19, no. 4 (December, 1975): 397-404. Lee argues that the alienation theme, when addressed in the context of African American concerns, is also a metaphor for the human condition. Describes Walker as seeking definitions of a sense of community or its telling absence, both uniquely black and universally relevant.

Meyers, Julia M. "Joseph A. Walker." In *Critical Survey of Drama*, edited by Carl Rollyson. 2d rev. ed. Pasadena, Calif.: Salem Press, 2003. A thorough overview of Walker's life and career as a playwright, including both a biographical sketch and analyses of several of his plays.

Margaret Walker

American poet, novelist, and essayist

Born: Birmingham, Alabama; July 7, 1915
Died: Chicago, Illinois; November 30, 1998
Identity: African American

LONG FICTION: *Jubilee*, 1966.

POETRY: *For My People*, 1942; *The Ballad of the Free*, 1966; *Prophets for a New Day*, 1970; *October Journey*, 1973; *For Farish Street Green*, 1986; *This Is My Century: New and Collected Poems*, 1989.

NONFICTION: *How I Wrote "Jubilee,"* 1972; *A Poetic Equation: Conversations Between Nikki Giovanni and Margaret Walker*, 1974; *Richard Wright: Daemonic Genius*, 1987; *How I Wrote "Jubilee," and Other Essays on Life and Literature*, 1990; *God Touched My Life: The Inspiring Autobiography of the Nun Who Brought Song, Celebration, and Soul to the World*, 1992; *On Being Female, Black, and Free: Essays by Margaret Walker, 1932-1992*, 1997 (Maryemma Graham, editor); *Conversations with Margaret Walker*, 2002 (Graham, editor).

MISCELLANEOUS: *Margaret Walker's "For My People": A Tribute*, 1992.

Margaret Walker, poet, novelist, essayist, orator, and critic, is known for her humanistic approach to issues of race and for the totality of her historical perspective. She began publishing poetry in the 1930's in magazines such as *Poetry*, *Opportunity*, and *Crisis*, but is perhaps best known for her novel *Jubilee*.

Margaret Abigail Walker was born July 7, 1915, in Birmingham, Alabama. Her father, Sigismund Walker, had emigrated from Buff Bay, Jamaica, to study for the ministry and received a degree in 1913 from Gramman Theological Seminary in Atlanta, Georgia. A Methodist minister, Sigismund bequeathed to his daughter a love of literature and an acute knowledge of the Bible. Likewise, Walker's mother, Marian Dozier Walker, a music teacher, played ragtime music for Margaret and read a variety of poetry to her. Both of Walker's parents encouraged her to pursue the highest academic goals possible.

Margaret Walker completed high school at age fourteen in New Orleans, where the family had moved when she was seven, and she enrolled at New Orleans University (now Dillard University). At the encouragement of Langston Hughes, Walker left the South after her sophomore year and eventually finished her bachelor's degree at Northwestern University in 1935. She also published her first poem that year in *Crisis*. Upon graduating from Northwestern, Walker began working full time for the Works Progress Administration (WPA) Writers' Project. On her assignment as a junior writer, Walker came into contact with such writers as James Phelan, Katherine Dunbar, Frank Yerby, Fenton Johnson, and Richard Wright.

Her friendship with Wright was perhaps the most important and rewarding aspect of Walker's time at the WPA. Their relationship was mutually supportive as Walker and Wright worked diligently to publish for the first time in national journals and books. Wright helped Walker improve the structure of her poetry, while Walker helped him revise some of his works. Wright encouraged Walker's decision to delay work on her Civil War novel, which eventually became *Jubilee*, and Walker helped Wright research *Native Son* (1940). Walker's relationship with Wright came to an abrupt end in June, 1939, when Wright accused her of spreading rumors about him and refused to speak to her again.

In the same year, Walker moved to Iowa City, Iowa, and enrolled in the University of Iowa Writers' Workshop. Under the mentorship of instructor Paul Engle, she completed an M.A. in 1940, using as her master's thesis a collection of poems which were published two years later by Yale University Press as *For My People*. With the publication of this volume, which won for Walker the Yale University Young Poets Award, Walker became the first African American woman to win a prestigious national literary competition. The collection was also the first book of poetry published by an African American woman since Georgia Douglas Johnson's *The Heart of a Woman, and Other Poems* in 1918. Throughout *For My People*, Walker calls for action against racism, demands change, and warns that the failure to do so would eventually lead to violence.

After teaching at Livingstone College in North Carolina (1941) and West Virginia State College (1942), Margaret Walker married Firnist James Alexander on June 13, 1943. She gave birth to her first child in 1944 and, a year later, returned to teach at Livingstone College. She also resumed research on *Jubilee*. In 1949 Walker began her long teaching career at Jackson State College (now Jackson State University) in Jackson, Mississippi, which ended when she retired from teaching in 1979. After tracing her grandmother's family's path from Greenville, Alabama, to Dawson, Georgia, in the early 1950's, Walker located her grandmother's younger sister, who gave her a picture of Walker's great-grandmother, the family Bible, and the chest that her great-grandmother had brought from the plantation. These discoveries proved important in Walker's shaping of *Jubilee*—she eventually used the image of her great-grandmother to help create the novel's protagonist, Vyry; similarly, the chest is used as an important symbol in the novel.

In 1962, Walker returned to the University of Iowa Writers' Workshop to begin work on a Ph.D. in English. Using *Jubilee* as her dissertation, she completed all the requirements for the degree in 1965 and published the novel in 1966. Noted for its realistic representation of the daily existence and folklore of slaves, *Jubilee* chronicles the life of Vyry Ware Brown through her childhood and young adulthood as a slave and as an adult during the Civil War and Reconstruction. Walker unites the oral tradition passed on to her by her maternal grandmother—Vyry's story is essentially a fictionalized account of Walker's great-grandmother's life—with historical facts about slavery to create in *Jubilee* a novel that embodies history while encompassing Walker's humanistic vision. As with her poetry, *Jubilee* demonstrates Walker's belief that African Americans have risen above their victimization to become forceful and complex agents of change and shapers of history.

The poetry and essays that Walker published after *Jubilee* are as important as the novel. Her collection *Prophets for a New Day*, for example, offers a moving record of the triumphs and sorrows of the Civil Rights movement. Likewise, *A Poetic Equation* and *How I Wrote "Jubilee," and Other Essays on Life and Literature* present crucial statements of Walker's artistic vision. Margaret Walker's celebration of African American life, culture, and history has made her an indelible figure in American literature. She died from breast cancer in 1998 at the age of eighty-three.

Cheryl Abrams Collier

Bibliography

Berke, Nancy. *Women Poets on the Left: Lola Ridge, Genevieve Taggard, Margaret Walker.* Gainesville: University Press of Florida, 2001. Discusses political poetry in the United States and places these three poets in that context. Includes bibliographical references and index.

Carmichael, Jacqueline Miller. *Trumpeting a Fiery Sound: History and Folklore in Margaret Walker's "Jubilee."* Athens: University of Georgia Press, 1998. Places *Jubilee* in historical and critical context of American, African American, and women's literature. Includes bibliographical references and index.

Collier, Eugenia. "Fields Watered with Blood: Myth and Ritual in the Poetry of Margaret Walker." In *Black Women Writers (1950-1980): A Critical Evaluation*, edited by Mari Evans. Garden City, N.Y.: Anchor Press/Doubleday, 1984. Presents important insights into Walker's poetry.

Graham, Maryemma, ed. *Fields Watered with Blood: Critical Essays on Margaret Walker.* Athens: University of Georgia Press, 2001. A solid collection of critical and interpretive essays. Includes bibliographical references and index.

Gwin, Minrose. *Black and White Women of the Old South: The Peculiar Sisterhood in American Literature.* Knoxville: University of Tennessee Press, 1985. Offers an important discussion of Walker and her work.

Pettis, Joyce. "Margaret Walker: Black Woman Writer of the South." In *Southern Women Writers: The New Generation*, edited by Tonette Bond Inge. Tuscaloosa: University of Alabama Press, 1990. Offers an important discussion of Walker and her work.

Walker, Margaret. "The Fusion of Ideas: An Interview with Margaret Walker Alexander." Interview by Maryemma Graham. *African American Review* 27 (Summer, 1993). Useful and insightful interview.

Walker, Melissa. *Down from the Mountaintop: Black Women's Novels in the Wake of the Civil Rights Movement, 1966-1989.* New Haven, Conn.: Yale University Press, 1991. Offers an important treatment of *Jubilee.*

David Foster Wallace

American novelist, short-story writer, and essayist

Born: Ithaca, New York; February 21, 1962

LONG FICTION: *The Broom of the System*, 1987; *Infinite Jest*, 1996.
SHORT FICTION: *Girl with Curious Hair*, 1989; *Brief Interviews with Hideous Men: Stories*, 1999.
NONFICTION: *Signifying Rappers: Rap and Race in the Urban Present*, 1990 (with Mark Costello); *A Supposedly Fun Thing I'll Never Do Again: Essays and Arguments*, 1997; *Up, Simba! Seven Days on the Trail of an Anticandidate*, 2000.

David Foster Wallace grew up in Urbana, Illinois, the son of a philosophy professor and community college English teacher. He was a talented, competitive tennis player whose gifts for the game included oversweating in order to keep well ventilated and the ability to ascertain the differential complications between the angles of the court and the unpredictable midwestern winds that often seized balls while in play. Wallace majored in philosophy at Amherst College. His professors believed he would become an important philosopher, but after taking time off to drive a school bus, he completed his senior thesis as a creative piece, which would soon be picked up as a rough draft of his first novel, *The Broom of the System.* From there, he headed west for Arizona State University's creative writing program.

The Broom of the System earned for Wallace a Whiting Writer's Award and gained the twenty-five-year-old some cult and critical notoriety. The novel's story line is built on phone messages, literary magazine submissions, and psychotherapy sessions. Readers come to realize that the central character's search for her missing grandmother is actually a pursuit of her own identity. Wallace uses stylized wordplay to represent the notion that something's value is nothing more or less than its function, a concept fostered by the philosopher Ludwig Wittgenstein's idea that language is a means by which reality is constructed. His postmodernist plot fragmentation, need to express philosophical ideas through fiction, and old-fashioned concern for character development are reflective of Wallace's wide range of early influences, which include Donald Barthelme and Tobias Wolff. They are also staple concepts that persist throughout Wallace's work.

His second book, *Girl with Curious Hair,* is a short-story collection assimilating American history, pop culture, and its icons with central characters that embody certain ideologies. A slacker takes an internship with Lyndon Johnson in "Lyndon," while "Little Expressionless Animals" deals with the plans of the producers of *Jeopardy!*, the television game show, to eject a long-running champion because of her sexual orientation. This focus on pop culture is carried over into Wallace's nonfiction with *Signifying Rappers*, a book cowritten with Mark Costello, wherein two white males use an obscure language to discuss the violence, misogyny, and arrogance often associated with hip-hop. Throughout his early years as a writer, Wallace was praised for the inventiveness and energy displayed in his writing, sometimes referred to as a genius restoring opulence to fiction after the dominance of minimalism.

Though Wallace compared a writer's fame to that of a local meteorologist, the early attention scathed him. Just as his writing reflects brilliance mixed with humility, Wallace was unsure whether to believe those who dubbed him genius or the lurking internal whisper sometimes calling him fake. Driven by self-doubt and confusion as to what it means to be a famous writer, Wallace went through a three-year period of using drugs and alcohol during the late 1980's and early 1990's, while living in Boston and Syracuse. Eventually, he checked into a psychiatric ward and was put on suicide watch. While details remain vague, friends have said Wallace sought the help of recovery programs. In the end, he came to realize he lacked the stomach for heavy drinking and the nervous system necessary for constant drug use. In 1990 he took a teaching position at Illinois State University and took up residence in a sparsely decorated home, with no television set, located amid cornfields.

Personal experience seems to have played a heavy role in Wallace's 1,079-page novel, the highly publicized *Infinite Jest.* Wallace said that he wanted to write something sad. The book parallels a substance abuse program with an elite tennis academy and revolves around the search for a film titled "Infinite Jest," to which viewers become addicted. Central characters are a tennis star, an addict from a rehabilitation center, and a group of wheelchair-bound Quebecois separatists; all want to use the film as a weapon. The novel's massive length and its 304 footnotes are reflective of Wallace's need not to spare a detail, a trait that seems to arise from both his meticulousness and his effulgence. While acknowledging the difficulty he posed for readers, he imagined the book's audience akin to himself: educated people in their twenties and thirties who read persistently in the hope of eventual payoff.

This affinity for details and footnotes carried over into his essay writing. Contracted to write various essays for *Harper's* and other magazines, Wallace attempted to capture and interpret his time. He allowed his own life, his attitude, and his ideas to spill through. The result was a body of essays in which he is the central character, experiencing and commenting upon everything, from luxury cruises to cracked midwestern tennis courts. For a while, his phone rang constantly, bringing offers to write what he described as assignments for which his instructions basically involved standing in a certain location, turning 360 degrees, and describing what he saw. He published the essays, unabridged, in 1997's *A Supposedly Fun Thing I'll Never Do Again.* That same year, he was awarded the MacArthur Foundation Fellowship, otherwise known as the "genius grant."

Upon his return to fiction, Wallace was interested in writing about sex and relationships. In 1999 he published *Brief Interviews with Hideous Men*, a collection of short stories and imagined interviews. While some readers continued to applaud his ability to invent ways of storytelling, others wondered where to find the emotion of the story. Still, many found the writing to be within Wallace's normal range of hilarious, unsettling, and almost unbearable edginess.

His originality has placed him somewhere between the camps of Thomas Pynchon and Thomas Wolfe; meaning is often found within the cracks of his narratives. Wallace's truest self seems to come out in his essays. The brilliance and competitiveness displayed early in his life shine through with the originality of his work, making him a force in American literature.

Jason Skipper

Bibliography

Olsen, Lance. "Termite Art, or Wallace's Wittgenstein." *The Review of Contemporary Fiction* 13, no. 2 (Summer, 1993). Demonstrates the ways in which philosopher Ludwig Wittgenstein greatly influenced Wallace's writing: Both use cynicism as a means to an end, rather than as an end in itself.

Rother, James. "Reading and Riding the Post-scientific Wave: The Shorter Fiction of David Foster Wallace." *The Review of Contemporary Fiction* 13, no. 2 (Summer, 1993). Seeks to demonstrate how Wallace's work differs from popular postmodern literature. Rother argues that the writer's "craftiness" is just part of his pursuit for higher meaning.

Wallace, David Foster. "An Interview with David Foster Wallace." Interview by Larry McCaffrey. *The Review of Contemporary Fiction* 13, no. 2 (Summer, 1993). In an extensive and cerebral interview, Wallace demonstrates the outspokenness and intelligence for which his work is often lauded.

Lewis Wallace

American novelist

Born: Brookville, Indiana; April 10, 1827
Died: Crawfordsville, Indiana; February 15, 1905

LONG FICTION: *The Fair God: Or, The Last of the 'Tzins—A Tale of the Conquest of Mexico*, 1873; *Ben Hur: A Tale of the Christ*, 1880; *The Prince of India*, 1893.

Although General Lewis (Lew) Wallace spent his professional life (as a soldier and a politician) as a realist, in his novels he chose to move opposite the prevailing realistic literary movement and return to the romantic concept of fiction. This stand proved popular with the reading public, and his romanticized *Ben Hur: A Tale of the Christ*, published in 1880, became a best-seller.

Wallace, born in Brookville, Indiana, on April 10, 1827, studied for the bar and practiced law until the outbreak of the Mexican War, in which he served. Wallace was elected Indiana state senator in 1856, serving until the beginning of the Civil War. He rose to the rank of major-general during the Civil War (participating in the Battle of Shiloh and the 1864 defense of Washington, D.C.), served as president of court in the Andersonville prison trials, and served as a member of the court that tried the Lincoln conspirators.

Wallace retired from the army in 1865 and later acted as governor of the New Mexico Territory from 1878 to 1881 (during which time he wrote *Ben Hur*) and represented the United States as minister to Turkey (1881-1885). After his retirement from public life he wrote biographies, a tragedy in blank verse, and *The Prince of India*. His first novel, *The Fair God: Or, The Last of the 'Tzins—A Tale of the Conquest of Mexico*, published in 1873, is often considered his best. *Ben Hur* is a dramatization of the story of Jesus, sentimentalized in action and language but vivid and memorable in its authentic detail. *The Prince of India*, published in 1893, was based upon his experiences as United States minister to Turkey and presents the legendary character of the Wandering Jew. Wallace died in Crawfordsville, Indiana, on February 15, 1905.

Tom Frazier

Bibliography

McGee, Irving. *"Ben Hur" Wallace: The Life of General Lew Wallace*. Berkeley: University of California Press, 1947.

Morsberger, Robert E., and Katherine M. Morsberger. *Lew Wallace, Militant Romantic*. New York: McGraw-Hill, 1980.

Vinson, James, ed. *Great Writers of the English Language: Novelists and Prose Writers*. New York: St. Martin's Press, 1979. Places Wallace and his career in perspective.

Wallace, Lewis. *Smoke, Sound, and Fury: The Civil War Memoirs of Major-General Lew Wallace, U.S. Volunteers*, edited by Jim Leeke. San Francisco: Strawberry Hill Press, 1998.

Edward Lewis Wallant

American novelist

Born: New Haven, Connecticut; October 19, 1926
Died: Norwalk, Connecticut; December 5, 1962
Identity: Jewish

LONG FICTION: *The Human Season*, 1960; *The Pawnbroker*, 1961; *The Tenants of Moonbloom*, 1963; *The Children at the Gate*, 1964.

Edward Lewis Wallant was born October 19, 1926, in New Haven, Connecticut. The son of Sol and Ann (Mendel) Wallant, he received his elementary and secondary education in public schools and briefly attended the University of Connecticut before joining the U.S. Navy as a gunner's mate aboard the USS *Glennon* in 1944. After World War II ended he attended Pratt Institute (1947-1950) and later the New School for Social Research (1954-1955). Beginning in 1950 Wallant worked as a graphic artist for several advertising agencies. In 1957 he became art director at the McCann Erikson agency, and he held this position at the time of his death. His first novel, *The Human Season*, was published in 1960, and it received the Jewish National Book Award. It was followed in 1961 by *The Pawnbroker*. Both works received high critical acclaim. Wallant received a Guggenheim Fellowship in 1962. On December 5, 1962, he died suddenly of an aneurysm; his untimely death cut short a career of unusual promise. He left behind two additional novels, which were published posthumously: *The Tenants of Moonbloom* and *The Children at the Gate*.

In spite of the recognition he gained, Wallant's writing did not fit into the styles that were then fashionable. His profound sense of humor, although it depended to some extent upon absurdities, was not based upon existentialism, and although he was Jewish and was particularly concerned with Jewish themes, he was not generally described as a "Jewish writer"—in part because he regularly superimposed Christian symbolism on his Jewish characters and settings. His striking and sometimes grotesque characterizations, and his caustic wit and sly humor, are peculiarly his own. His fictional world, though full of problems and ridiculous situations, is not the conventionalized blind universe of irrationality, hopelessness, and despair. Wallant admired the human spirit and believed in its infinite possibilities.

William V. Davis

Bibliography

Ayo, Nicholas. "The Secular Heart: The Achievement of Edward Lewis Wallant." *Critique: Studies in Modern Fiction* 12 (1970): 86-94. Compares Wallant to Fyodor Dostoevski to convey the former's grim realism and emphasis of changes of heart, looking expressly at the religious element in Wallant's characters.

Galloway, David. *Edward Lewis Wallant*. Boston: Twayne, 1979. A full-length treatment of Wallant. Includes a chronology, notes, and an annotated bibliography.

Gurko, Leo. "Edward Lewis Wallant as Urban Novelist." *Twentieth Century Literature* 20 (October, 1974): 252-261. Examines Wallant's metaphoric use of the city, which is ugly, perverted, dangerous, and cruel. Gurko claims, however, that in its sprawling vitality, the city also contains "seeds of its own reconstruction."

Lewis, Robert W. "The Hung-Up Heroes of Edward Lewis Wallant." *Renascence* 24 (1972): 70-84. This substantial discussion examines all of Wallant's novels, especially *The Pawnbroker*, paying particular attention to his sensitive, intellectual characters and his themes of suffering and rebirth. Also looks at his use of myth.

Schulz, M. F. "Wallant and Friedman: The Glory and Agony of Love." *Critique: Studies in Modern Fiction* 10 (1968): 31-47. Compares Wallant and Bruce Jay Friedman, particularly in their use of humor and the theme of love. Finds Wallant's characters examples of growth in sensibility and his novels affirmations of order and rebirth.

Stanford, Raney. "The Novels of Edward Wallant." *Colorado Quarterly* 17 (1969): 393-405. Examines some of Wallant's characters and themes, concentrating especially on *The Tenants of Moonbloom* and *The Pawnbroker.* Wallant's characters tend to undergo rebellion that leads to their rebirth.

Edmund Waller

English poet

Born: Coleshill, Hertfordshire, England; March 3, 1606
Died: Hall Barn, Beaconsfield, Buckinghamshire, England; October 21, 1687

POETRY: *Poems*, 1645, 1664, 1686, 1690, 1693; "A Panegyrick to My Lord Protector," 1655; "A Poem on St. James' Park as Lately Improved by His Majesty," 1661; "Instructions to a Painter," 1666; *Divine Poems*, 1685; *The Second Part of Mr. Waller's Poems*, 1690.
DRAMA: *Pompey the Great*, pb. 1664 (translation of Pierre Corneille); *The Maid's Tragedy*, pb. 1690 (adaptation of Francis Beaumont and John Fletcher).
NONFICTION: *The Workes of Edmund Waller in This Parliament*, 1645; *Debates of the House of Commons from the Year 1667 to the Year 1694*, 1763 (10 volumes; with others).
MISCELLANEOUS: *The Works of Edmund Waller, Esq., in Verse and Prose*, 1729 (Elijah Fenton, editor).

Edmund Waller was an innovative seventeenth century English poet. As a youth, he had several years of private instruction, as did most of the literary figures of his time. Thereafter he was sent to Eton and to Cambridge. Waller was married in 1631, after having served for several years as a member of Parliament. A son and a daughter were born before his wife's death in 1634. After she died Waller retired to Beaconfield, where he lived the life of a wealthy country gentleman. He wrote at this time some of the poems that were to make him famous, especially those love poems to a married woman he called Sacharissa (who was indifferent to his verse).

In Parliament once again, Waller distinguished himself as a speaker. He became known as a moderate, and was therefore out of place, as his surroundings were becoming increasingly revolutionary. After attempting to conciliate the king and the House of Commons, Waller tried to arrange to liberate the former. As a result he was placed under arrest and then banished to France. He spent the next six years in France and Italy; during this time, he married his second wife, and his poems were published in England, purportedly without his permission. In 1651 Waller received a pardon from Parliament, and in 1652 he returned to England. He soon reached accommodation with Oliver Cromwell's regime; in 1655 he published his famous "A Panegyrick to My Lord Protector," and was appointed a commissioner of trade. When the monarchy was later restored he managed to dispel a reputation for ingratiating himself with Cromwell, and he became popular with Cromwell's enemies. He was among the first to welcome the newly arrived Charles II, with a poem titled "Upon His Majesty's Happy Return." He continued his service in Parliament and distinguished himself in the cause of religious toleration for Catholics and Protestant dissenters. At court he was a literary model for the younger men who admired his poetry.

Soon after Waller's second wife died in 1677, he retired to the woods and gardens of his home at Hall Barn. In these last years he apparently underwent a religious conversion; rejecting his earlier works, he returned to meditations on spiritual themes. He died at Hall Barn on October 21, 1687, surrounded by his children and grandchildren, at the age of eighty-one.

Waller's work consisted of short lyrical poems, for the most part on love. He was an important innovator, giving to the couplet the form, smoothness, and precision that later poets were to admire and imitate. He can be thought of as one of the best of the seventeenth century poetic craftsmen. His poems are not read much today, yet Waller's technical work had great influence; he endowed the poets of the eighteenth century with the couplet, which became their favorite mode of verse. He endowed them, too, with a diction and an attitude toward poetry that dominated literary life for a considerable time after his death. Classicism in English poetry is attributable not only to the Roman verse that serves as its models but also to men like Waller and Sir John Denham, who tried to replace the poetry of the early seventeenth century. Under their influence poetry became less intellectual and more lyrical. In essence, Waller brought back harmonics to English verse and laid the groundwork for poets as distinguished as John Dryden and Alexander Pope.

Bibliography

Chernaik, Warren L. *The Poetry of Limitation: A Study of Edmund Waller.* New Haven, Conn.: Yale University Press, 1968. Vividly depicts the political, cultural, and literary context in which Waller wrote his Cavalier lyric poetry, formal occasional poems, and heroic satire, but there are few extended analyses of his works. Contains a chapter accounting for the rise and fall of Waller's literary reputation.

Gilbert, Jack G. *Edmund Waller.* Boston: Twayne, 1979. Gilbert explores the complex relationship between Waller's political career and poetry, devotes separate chapters (with extended analyses of some poems) to the lyric and the political poems, and concludes by defining Waller's view of art and fixing his position in English literature. Includes a chronology and an annotated select bibliography.

Hillyer, Richard. "Edmund Waller's Sacred Poems." *Studies in English Literature, 1500-1900* 39, no. 1 (Winter, 1999): 155-169. At age 79, Waller published *Divine Poems*, the fruits of his late rebirth that crowned the final collected edition of his works printed during his lifetime. Waller's sacred poems are discussed.

Kaminski, Thomas. "Edmund Waller, English Precieux." *Philological Quarterly* 79, no. 1 (Winter, 2000): 19-43. Kaminski places Waller in a seventeenth-century context that should enable the reader to grasp both what was new in his poetry and why it should have been praised so highly during his life and for nearly a century after his death.

Miner, Earl. *The Cavalier Mode from Jonson to Cotton*. Princeton, N.J.: Princeton University Press, 1971. Miner uses Waller to demonstrate past Ben Jonson Cavalier motifs and provides lengthy analyses of "At Penshurst" and "A Poem on St. James' Park as Lately Improved by His Majesty," two topographical poems that express the social order that characterizes Cavalier poetry.

Piper, William Bowman. *The Heroic Couplet*. Cleveland: Case Western Reserve University, 1969. Provides an overall assessment of Waller's use of the heroic couplet, from the early imperfections to the mature style reflected in "A Poem on St. James' Park."

Richmond, H. M. "The Fate of Edmund Waller." In *Seventeenth-Century English Poetry: Modern Essays in Criticism*, edited by William R. Keast. Rev. ed. London: Oxford University Press, 1971. Richmond attributes Waller's decline in popularity and in literary merit to his faults as a person (his feigned madness, bribery, and informing to save his life), rather than to his poetic talents and the lack of the thought/feeling tension associated with the metaphysical poets.

Horace Walpole

English novelist, essayist, and historian

Born: London, England; September 24, 1717
Died: London, England; March 2, 1797

LONG FICTION: *The Castle of Otranto*, 1765.
SHORT FICTION: *Hieroglyphic Tales*, 1785.
DRAMA: *The Mysterious Mother*, pb. 1768.
NONFICTION: *Aedes Walpolianae*, 1747; *A Catalogue of the Royal and Noble Authors of England*, 1758; *Anecdotes of Painting in England*, 1762-1771; *Historic Doubts on the Life and Reign of Richard III*, 1768; *Description of the Villa of Horace Walpole*, 1774; *Essay on Modern Gardening*, 1785; *The Works of Horatio Walpole, Earl of Orford*, 1798-1825 (9 volumes; also pb. 1999 in 5 volumes); *Reminiscences*, 1805; *Memoirs of the Last Ten Years of the Reign of George II*, 1822; *Memoirs of the Reign of George III*, 1845; *Letters*, 1857-1859 (9 volumes; Peter Cunningham, editor); *Journal of the Reign of George III from 1771 to 1783*, 1859; *Letters*, 1903-1905 (16 volumes; Mrs. Paget Toynbee, editor); *The Yale Edition of Horace Walpole's Correspondence*, 1937-1983 (49 volumes; W. S. Lewis, editor).

A brilliant essayist, historian, and letter-writer and a notable novelist, dramatist, and amateur antiquary, Horace (christened Horatio) Walpole (WAWL-pohl) was born in London on September 24, 1717. He was the third son and youngest child of Catherine Shorter and Sir Robert Walpole, the great eighteenth century British prime minister. Walpole was raised at Houghton Hall, a miniature palace that had an art collection rivaling the best in Italy and a semi-naturalistic garden that provided Walpole with a frame of mind through which he later looked on life. The grand scale of the building seems to have convinced Master Walpole that he belonged to the nobility.

At the age of ten Walpole was sent to Eton, where he formed friendships with boys like Thomas Ashton, Henry Conway, Thomas Gray, and Richard West and belonged to the Quadruple Alliance, a literary group whose members included Gray and West. This involvement stimulated Walpole's love of literature. After graduating from Eton, Walpole went to Cambridge. In March of 1739 he left Cambridge without earning a degree and invited Gray to be his companion on a Grand Tour of the Continent, which lasted about two and a half years. The Grand Tour has been regarded as one of the major events of Walpole's life. It gave him the friendship of the famous American Horace Mann, whom Walpole met in Florence and with whom he corresponded extensively for the next fifty years of his life, although he never saw him again; his correspondence with Mann was the largest of his many correspondences. The tour also furnished Walpole with the friendship of John Chute, who later helped him design his toy castle Strawberry Hill. Furthermore, it provided Walpole with a perspective with which to create the Italian settings for *The Castle of Otranto* and *The Mysterious Mother.*

Following his return to England, Walpole became a member of Parliament, serving from 1741 to 1768. In 1748 he purchased a cottage in Twickenham, which for the remainder of his life he spent remodeling into a pseudo-Gothic castle. Strawberry Hill became famous as Walpole's home, as the center of his enthusiasm for Gothic architecture, as the home of Strawberry Hill Press, and as a kind of park-museum-showplace. By his work on Strawberry Hill, Walpole—an eighteenth century celebrity who knew everybody and went everywhere—was to make a name for himself as a gardener and an architect. His tragic drama, *The Mysterious Mother,* a punishment dream, was published by Strawberry Hill Press, but his famous gothic novel *The Castle of Otranto* was not.

The supernatural elements of *The Castle of Otranto* were designed to provide terror for Walpole's readers; they do so no longer. In *The Castle of Otranto* Walpole delineates the customs of the Middle Ages, a period he regards as rife with superstition. In doing so, he conveys anti-Catholic feelings. Notably, the novel contains a strict unity of action, for everything therein occurs over a period of three days and two nights at the castle and its surroundings. The genesis for the novel was a dream about a gigantic hand in armor on a staircase. This dream can be associated with life at Strawberry Hill. What Walpole discloses in *The Castle of Otranto* is his infantile desire for a sensual relationship with his mother. Incest and patricide are the novel's themes. In the resolution of the dream, Theodore, a young peasant with a strawberry birthmark, marries the virtuous princess Isabella and is transformed into a noble prince.

The Castle of Otranto was inspired by Walpole's rage over the problems of his cousin, Henry Conway, who was dismissed in 1764 from his regiment of dragoons' command for voting in Parliament against General Warrants. For Walpole, Conway was a mother substitute. Walpole's mother had died in 1737, when he was twenty. The relationship between Walpole and Conway has been called a homosexual one, a kind of Oedipal attraction. Walpole came to Conway's defense with a pamphlet called *A Counter Address to the Public on the Late Dismission of a General Officer.* He tried to show that Conway did not merit banishment for his conduct in Parliament and claimed that the total ruin of Conway was not proper. Without question, Walpole's anger and frustration over the Conway affair in 1764 affected the writing of *The Castle of Otranto* in that year. *The Castle of Otranto* is a wish-fulfillment fantasy.

Other facets of Walpole's life are also important. His memoirs, covering the last half of the eighteenth century, were written in a conscious effort to be the historian of his times. Few men have planned their engagement with posterity so carefully. Walpole was determined to achieve a lasting reputation independent of his father. A vast amount of information on the culture and affairs of England and the Continent is contained in Walpole's letters. They are a source of extensive historical knowledge and have been compared in value to a thousand of the documentary films of the twentieth century.

Walpole became the fourth earl of Orford in 1791. He never married. Mme du Deffand, the famous blind sixty-nine-year-old French debauchée of wit, was in love with him; his relationship with her represented a gratification of hidden impulses. She personified his protective mother, whom he overvalued as a child. Mary Berry, a twenty-one-year-old neighbor, seems to have been in love with him as well. He called her one of his "twin wives." Walpole's most famous aphorism is this: "Life is a comedy to those who think, a tragedy to those who feel." He died in London on March 2, 1797, at the age of seventy-nine and was buried in the vault beneath the Lilliputian church on the grounds of the Houghton Hall estate.

James Norman O'Neill

Bibliography

Brownell, Morris. *The Prime Minister of Taste: A Portrait of Horace Walpole.* New Haven, Conn.: Yale University Press, 2001. A biography focusing on Walpole's career as a collector and patron of the arts.

Fothergill, Brian. *The Strawberry Hill Set: Horace Walpole and His Circle.* Boston: Faber and Faber, 1983. An intellectual biography and sociological study of Walpole in the context of his time.

Jacobs, Edward H. *Accidental Migrations: An Archeology of Gothic Discourse.* Lewisberg, Pa.: Bucknell University Press, 2000. Evaluates Walpole's contribution to the development of the gothic genre.

Kallich, Martin. *Horace Walpole.* Boston: Twayne, 1971. A solid bio-critical study of Walpole. It contains a useful chronology and chapters on Walpole's life, his political career, and his role as a social butterfly in eighteenth century England, as well as analyses of *The Castle of Otranto, The Mysterious Mother,* and *Hieroglyphic Tales.*

Ketton-Cremer, R. W. *Horace Walpole: A Biography.* 3d ed. Ithaca, N.Y.: Cornell University Press, 1964. The standard biography of Walpole.

Mowl, Timothy. *Horace Walpole: The Great Outsider.* London: Murray, 1996. An intellectual biography emphasizing Walpole as a legislator, writer, collector, and homosexual.

Sabor, Peter, ed. *Horace Walpole: The Collected Critical Heritage, Eighteenth Century.* New York: Routledge, 1996. A substantial collection of critical essays on Walpole's works.

Van Luchene, Stephen Robert. "The Castle of Otranto." In *Essays in Gothic Fiction from Horace Walpole to Mary Shelley.* New York: Arno Press, 1980. Considers *The Castle of Otranto*'s influence on gothic fiction to be threefold: It ushered in stock characters, established set narrative techniques, and conveyed an idealized view of the Middle Ages.

Sir Hugh Walpole

English novelist

Born: Auckland, New Zealand; March 13, 1884
Died: Keswick, Cumberland, England; June 1, 1941

LONG FICTION: *The Wooden Horse*, 1909; *Maradick at Forty*, 1910; *Mr. Perrin and Mr. Traill*, 1911 (also known as *The Gods and Mr. Perrin*); *The Prelude to Adventure*, 1912; *Fortitude*, 1913; *The Duchess of Wrexe*, 1914; *The Golden Scarecrow*, 1915; *The Dark Forest*, 1916; *The Green Mirror*, 1917; *Jeremy*, 1919; *The Secret City*, 1919; *The Captives*, 1920; *The Young Enchanted*, 1921; *The Cathedral*, 1922; *Jeremy and Hamlet*, 1923; *The Old Ladies*, 1924; *Portrait of a Man with Red Hair*, 1925; *Harmer John*, 1926; *Jeremy at Crale*, 1927; *Wintersmoon*, 1928; *Hans Frost*, 1929; *Rogue Herries*, 1930; *Above the Dark Circus*, 1931 (also known as *Above the Dark Tumult*); *Judith Paris*, 1931; *The Fortress*, 1932; *Vanessa*, 1933; *Captain Nicholas*, 1934; *The Inquisitor*, 1935; *A Prayer for My Son*, 1936; *John Cornelius*, 1937; *The Joyful Delaneys*, 1938; *The Sea Tower*, 1939; *The Bright Pavilions*, 1940; *The Blindman's House*, 1941; *The Killer and the Slain*, 1942; *Katherine Christian*, 1943.
SHORT FICTION: *The Thirteen Travellers*, 1921; *The Silver Thorn*, 1928; *All Souls' Night*, 1933; *Head in Green Bronze*, 1938.
NONFICTION: *Joseph Conrad*, 1916; *The English Novel*, 1925; *Anthony Trollope*, 1928; *A Letter to a Modern Novelist*, 1932; *The Apple Trees*, 1932.

Hugh Seymour Walpole (WAWL-pohl) was born in Auckland, New Zealand, March 13, 1884, the son of an English minister serving as incumbent of St. Mary's Pro-Cathedral in Auckland. As a boy, Walpole was sent to school in Cornwall, England. His family returned to England and lived in Durham, a cathedral city; Walpole's father served as bishop of Edinburgh from 1910 until his death in 1929.

Hugh Walpole was educated at King's College, Canterbury, and Emanuel College, Cambridge. He began writing novels while still an undergraduate, but without success in his early ventures. His first successful novel was *Fortitude*, published in 1913, and his popularity as a writer of fiction on both sides of the Atlantic began with that work.

During World War I Walpole worked in Russia with the Red Cross, and two novels grew out of his experiences there: *The Dark Forest* and *The Secret City*, awarded the James Tait Black Memorial Prize. Most of Walpole's books have a romantic tinge, and many of them enjoyed large sales. His most successful novels are parts of a tetralogy covering two hundred years of English social history: *Rogue Herries*, *Judith Paris*, *The Fortress*, and *Vanessa*.

At the time of King George VI's coronation, Walpole was knighted and proudly bore his title. Prolific in his novel writing, Walpole also wrote short stories, critical studies, and plays; wrote scenarios for films in both Hollywood and Britain; and enjoyed great success on numerous lecture tours to the United States and in Britain. W. Somerset Maugham caricatured him as the character Alroy Kear in *Cakes and Ale*. Walpole died at Brackenburn, his home in the Lake District, on June 1, 1941.

Victoria Gaydosik

Bibliography

Coveney, Peter. *Poor Monkey: The Child in Literature*. Rev. ed. Harmondsworth, England: Penguin, 1967.

Dane, Clemence. *Tradition and Hugh Walpole*. 1929. Reprint. Port Washington, N.Y.: Kennikat Press, 1972.

Hart-Davis, Rupert. *Hugh Walpole*. New York: Macmillan, 1952.

Steele, Elizabeth. "A Change of Villains: Hugh Walpole, Henry James, and Arnold Bennett." *Colby Library Quarterly* 17 (September, 1981).

_______. *Hugh Walpole*. New York: Twayne, 1972.

Steen, Marguerite. *Hugh Walpole: A Study*. London: Ivor Nicholson and Watson, 1933.

Swinnerton, Frank. *Figures in the Foreground*. 1964. Reprint. Freeport, N.Y.: Books for Libraries Press, 1970.

Martin Walser

German playwright and novelist

Born: Wasserburg, Germany; March 24, 1927

DRAMA: *Der Abstecher*, pr., pb. 1961 (*The Detour*, 1963); *Eiche und Angora*, pr., pb. 1962 (*The Rabbit Race*, 1963); *Überlebensgross Herr Krott: Requiem für einen Unsterblichen*, pr. 1963; *Der schwarze Schwan*, pr., pb. 1964; *Die Zimmerschlacht*, pr., pb. 1967 (*Home Front*, 1971); *Wir werden schon noch handeln*, pr. 1968 as *Der schwarze Flügel*, pb. 1968; *Ein Kinderspiel*, pb. 1970, pr. 1972; *Aus dem Wortschatz unserer Kämpfe*, pb. 1971; *Ein reizender Abend*, pr. 1971; *Das Sauspiel: Szenen aus dem 16. Jahrhundert*, pr., pb. 1975; *In*

Goethes Hand: Szenen aus dem 19. Jahrhundert, pr., pb. 1982; *Die Ohrfeige*, pr. 1984; *Ein fliehendes Pferd*, pr., pb. 1985 (adaptation of his novel); *Das Sofa*, pb. 1992; *Kaschmir in Parching*, pb. 1995.

LONG FICTION: *Ehen in Philippsburg*, 1957 (*The Gadarene Club*, 1960; also known as *Marriage in Philippsburg*); *Halbzeit*, 1960; *Das Einhorn*, 1966 (*The Unicorn*, 1971); *Die Gallistl'sche Krankheit*, 1972; *Der Sturz*, 1973; *Jenseits der Liebe*, 1976 (*Beyond All Love*, 1982); *Ein fliehendes Pferd*, 1978 (*Runaway Horse*, 1980); *Seelenarbeit*, 1979 (*The Inner Man*, 1984); *Das Schwanenhaus*, 1980 (*The Swan Villa*, 1982); *Brief an Lord Liszt*, 1982 (*Letter to Lord Liszt*, 1985); *Brandung*, 1985 (*Breakers*, 1987); *Dorle und Wolf*, 1987 (*No Man's Land*, 1989); *Jagd*, 1988; *Die Verteidigung der Kindheit*, 1991; *Ohne Einander*, 1993; *Finks Kreig*, 1996; *Ein springender Brunnen*, 1998; *Der Lebenslauf der Liebe*, 2001; *Tod eines Kritikers*, 2002.

SHORT FICTION: *Ein Flugzeug über dem Haus und andere Geschichten*, 1955; *Liebegeschichten*, 1964; *Selected Stories*, 1982; *Gesammelte Geschichten*, 1983; *Messmers Gedanken*, 1985; *Fingerübungen eines Mörders: 12 Geschichten*, 1994.

NONFICTION: *Beschreibung einer Form: Versuch über Franz Kafka*, 1961; *Erfahrungen und Leseerfahrungen*, 1965; *Heimatkunde*, 1968; *Wie und wovon handelt Literatur*, 1973; *Wer ist ein Schriftsteller?*, 1979; *Selbstbewusstsein und Ironie*, 1981; *Liebeserklärungen*, 1983; *Variationen eines Würgegriffs: Bericht über Trinidad und Tobago*, 1985 (travel); *Heilige Brocken*, 1986; *Über Deutschland reden*, 1988; *Vormittag eines Schriftstellers*, 1994; *Ansichten, Einsichten: Aufsätze zur Zeitgeschichte*, 1997; *Deutsche Sorgen*, 1997; *Erfahrungen beim Verfassen einer Sonntagsrede: Friedenspreis des Deutschen Buchhandels 1998*, 1998; *Ich vertraue—Querfeldein*, 2000.

MISCELLANEOUS: *Werke in zwölf Bänden*, 1997 (12 volumes).

Martin Walser (VAHL-sur) is certainly to be ranked among the most prominent West German writers since 1945. Born in the picturesque Bodensee area of southern Germany, Walser was the child of innkeepers. He attended a local school during the Nazi era and graduated from secondary school in 1946. He went to several German universities and completed his studies in 1951 with a dissertation on Franz Kafka. While still a student, he worked for a number of years with a southern German radio and television station, and he married in 1950. Walser won the prestigious prize of the "Gruppe 47" organization of German writers in 1955 and has since been an independent and prolific author. He has taught as a guest professor at a number of universities in the United States and in England, and he has been the recipient of numerous prizes for literature.

Walser's initial efforts at writing were deeply influenced by his early reading of Kafka's works, in which he identified with the profound and pervasive sense of isolation, and much of his writing during the 1950's represents an attempt to come to terms with the literary and psychological influence of the Prague writer. Gradually Walser began to realize the crucial role played by social and economic factors in determining the individual's sense of self and the quality of interaction with others. Although Walser's works still touch upon existential themes such as aging, love and sexuality, and death, these "socialist" themes came to predominate in his writings as of the 1960's.

Walser's first novel, *The Gadarene Club*, suggests his efforts at emancipation from the influence of Kafka and his adoption of a critical stance toward German society. Written in a complex series of internal monologues, the novel focuses on several characters and their lives in the upper-middle-class social circles of a fictitious southern German city of Philippsburg. Walser levels a sharp and ironic critique of the shallow and egocentric social, sexual, and political machinations of his characters in a societal system that promotes the psychological estrangement of its members. The novels *Halbzeit* (halftime), *The Unicorn*, and *Der Sturz* (the fall) form a loose trilogy of texts that examine the character Anselm Kristlein and continue Walser's critical probing of the falsity and self-deception of middle-class German society from the economic boom period after the war until the beginning of the 1970's. Texts such as *Die Gallistl'sche Krankheit* (the Gallistl illness), the story of Josef Gallistl's rejection of his upper-middle-class life and his adoption of socialist values, continue these themes. Other works, among them *Runaway Horse* and *Breakers*, examine love and marriage, sexuality and aging, and issues of male identity in modern industrial society.

In his plays, too, Walser provides an often ironic portrait of character types—from capitalists in *Überlebensgross Herr Krott* (larger-than-life Mr. Krott) and former Nazi doctors in *Der schwarze Schwan* (the black swan) to authoritarian bourgeois families in *Ein Kinderspiel* (a child's game)—of modern German society and they evidence, to a degree, the influence of Bertolt Brecht's satiric-didactic dramatic techniques and Friedrich Dürrenmatt's grotesque parodies. The play *Die Ohrfeige* (the slap) depicts the situation of the unemployed, their anger and helplessness as well as their fundamental lack of comprehension of the industrial system that determines their lives.

Walser's writings, much like those of Heinrich Böll, present a critical vision of German society in the postwar period and as such they spring from a deeply humanistic and utopian sense of a kind of social organization that could be. His critique of modern capitalist societies and the kinds of personality distortion such societal structures produce in the individual suggest a romantic longing for a feeling of authentic community in which mutual cooperation (and not ruthless competition), self-respect, and love of others (and not neurotic self-doubt and veiled aggression) regulate human interaction. As a critic of modern social consciousness, Walser gives the reader a sadly accurate but nevertheless optimistic view of his contemporary situation.

Thomas F. Barry

Bibliography

Oswald, Franz. *The Political Psychology of the White-Collar Worker in Martin Walser's Novels*. New York: P. Lang, 1998. Discusses the differing critical and reader receptions of Walser's fiction between 1957 and 1978 in West Germany, East Germany, and the United States.

Pilipp, Frank. *The Novels of Martin Walser: A Critical Introduction*. New York: Camden House, 1991. A comprehensive study of Walser's output in all genres between 1976 and 1988.

_______, ed. *New Critical Perspectives on Martin Walser.* Columbia, S.C.: Camden House, 1994. An examination of contemporary critiques of Walser's works. Bibliography and index.

Schlunk, Jürgen E., and Armand E. Singer, eds. *Martin Walser: International Perspectives*. New York: Peter Lang, 1987. A collection of papers presented at the International Martin Walser Symposium at the West Virginia University in April, 1985. Bibliographies.

Taberner, Stuart. *Distorted Reflections: The Public and Private Uses of the Author.* Atlanta: Rodopi, 1998. A study of the way in which political engagement serves as a subtext in the novels of Uwe Johnson, Günter Grass, and Walser.

Waine, Anthony Edward. *Martin Walser: The Development as Dramatist, 1950-1970.* Bonn: Bouvier, 1978. Waine traces Walser's development as a playwright until 1970. Bibliography and index.

Robert Walser

Swiss short-story writer

Born: Biel, Switzerland; April 15, 1878
Died: Herisau, Switzerland; December 25, 1956

SHORT FICTION: *Fritz Kochers Aufsätze*, 1904; *Aufsätze*, 1913; *Geschichten*, 1914; *Kleine Dichtungen*, 1914; *Der Spaziergang*, 1917 (*The Walk, and Other Stories*, 1957); *Prosastücke*, 1917; *Kleine Prosa*, 1917; *Poetenleben*, 1918; *Seeland*, 1919; *Die Rose*, 1925; *Selected Stories*, 1982 (foreword by Susan Sontag); *Aus dem Bleistiftgebiet: Mikrogramme aus den Jahren 1924-1925*, 1985; *Masquerade, and Other Stories*, 1990.

LONG FICTION: *Geschwister Tanner,* 1907; *Der Gehülfe*, 1908; *Jakob von Gunten*, 1909 (English translation, 1969); *Der "Räuber"-Roman*, 1972 (*The Robber,* 2000).

DRAMA: *Aschenbrödel*, pr. 1901 (fairy-tale play; *Cinderella*, 1985); *Schneewittchen*, pr. 1901 (fairy-tale play; *Snowwhite*, 1985); *Die Knaben*, pr. 1902 (sketch); *Komödie: Theatralisches*, pb. 1919.

POETRY: *Gedichte*, 1909; *Unbekannte Gedichte*, 1958.

MISCELLANEOUS: *Eine Ohrfeige und Sonstiges*, 1925 (*A Slap in the Face Et Cetera*, 1985); *Das Gesamtwerk*, 1966-1975 (13 volumes); *Robert Walser Rediscovered: Stories, Fairy-Tale Plays and Critical Responses*, 1985.

The prominent German publisher Siegfried Unseld called Robert Walser (VAHL-sur) "the greatest unknown author in the German language in [the twentieth] century." This prolific, dedicated, but very independent writer of short prose, novels, playlets, and poems gained considerable recognition early in his career, most notably from Franz Kafka and Christian Morgenstern, Hugo von Hofmannsthal and Hermann Hesse. As time went on, however, his unconventional works failed to appeal to a broader audience. Virtually forgotten for several decades, he was rediscovered in the 1960's and is viewed not only as a leading Swiss author of the twentieth century but also as one of the first modernist writers of self-conscious fiction.

Robert Otto Walser was the second-youngest of eight children. His father, Adolf Walser, was a congenial man who tried his hand, unsuccessfully, at a number of business ventures. His mother, Elisa Marti Walser, and two of his brothers suffered from mental instability. Robert was closest to his sister Lisa, a schoolteacher, and his successful brother Karl, who illustrated several of his books. At the age of fourteen, Walser left school and learned the banking trade. For some time he toyed with the idea of becoming an actor but eventually turned to literature instead.

In 1896 Walser moved to Zurich, where he remained until 1905, constantly changing residences and clerical jobs, which was to become a pattern in his life. It was there that his first works, six poems, were published in the Swiss newspaper *Der Bund*, which in turn led to an invitation to publish additional poems, prose pieces, and playlets in the new literary journal *Die Insel* in Munich. Walser's breakthrough came in 1904, when the publishing house Insel in Leipzig published his first book, *Fritz Kochers Aufsätze* (Fritz Kocher's essays), supposedly the compositions of a gifted young schoolboy. This early work contains many of the themes, motifs, and narrative techniques that became Walser's trademark. Although the slim volume with its amusing drawings by his brother Karl received high critical praise, it sold so poorly that the publisher reneged on his commitment to a second book of poems and dramas. This was the first of a number of similar occasions where one of Walser's works was received with initial enthusiasm but then failed to sell, which invariably led to the publishers' dropping Walser from their lists. In the spring of 1905, still convinced that his first book could be a commercial success, Walser joined his brother Karl in cosmopolitan Berlin to embark on a career as a freelance writer. Soon after, however, he enrolled in a school for domestic servants, an experience he later fictionalized in his novel *Jakob von Gunten*, and worked in a castle in Upper Silesia as a footman. For most of his life he was obsessed with the role of the servant.

It was during his Berlin years, 1905 to 1913, that Walser produced most of his novels in quick succession, notably *Geschwister Tanner* (the Tanner siblings), *Der Gehülfe* (the assistant), and *Jakob von Gunten*. These largely autobiographical novels had scant plots and shifting viewpoints, and all feature closely related central characters in lowly positions who engage in contradictory self-analysis. They are vaguely based on Walser's Zurich years and on his experiences as the secretary of a Swiss inventor and as a student in the school for servants in Berlin. Although Walser had vowed that he would sooner join the army than become "a supplier to magazines," he continued to produce large numbers of short texts, many of which found their way into periodicals and newspapers throughout German-speaking Europe. During the later Berlin years, however, when his novels did not elicit the desired critical response and he found it more and more difficult to place his shorter prose pieces, his productivity began to suffer, and he grew increasingly despondent.

In 1913, disappointed, nearly destitute, and convinced that he had failed as a novelist, Walser returned to his native Biel, where he spent the next seven years (1913-1921). For much of the time he lived quietly in a spare attic room in the Hotel Blaues Kreuz (a temperance hostel) on what he described as "the periphery of bourgeois existence," always in financial straits and always struggling to find a publisher for his works. Several volumes of more traditional, almost neo-Romantic short prose appeared during the Biel period, much of it inspired during long walks in the environs of Biel: *Kleine Prosa* (short prose), for which he received a prize, *Prosastücke* (prose pieces), *Poetenleben* (poets' lives), and *Seeland* (lakeland). It was in Biel that Walser devised a new and rather peculiar method of writing, his "pencil system." He filled many large sheets of paper with increasingly small, seemingly illegible texts that were long thought to be written in a form of private shorthand. These "microgrammes" turned out to be first drafts of prose pieces, playlets, and poems, many of which he wrote in Bern from 1924 to 1931. The novel *Der "Räuber"-Roman* (the "robber" novel), a witty novel about an artist in search of material, is now regarded as the most enduring narrative work in what have become known as Walser's microscripts.

In 1921 Walser moved to Bern, where, once again, he changed residences more than a dozen times. He was extremely productive but found few outlets for his works. Several manuscripts were rejected by publishers, and the last work that Walser was able to publish himself, *Die Rose* (the rose), a collection of demanding short texts, was poorly received. As the pieces he sent out to journals became more radical, they were rejected with increasing frequency. By the late 1920's Walser was living the life of a recluse. At times he drank heavily and suffered from severe bouts of anxiety. When he began hallucinating and hearing voices, he was committed to the mental hospital Waldau near Bern and diagnosed a schizophrenic, a diagnosis that is no longer believed to have been accurate. In Waldau, Walser continued to write sporadically, but after his involuntary transfer to a public institution in Herisau in 1933 he ceased writing altogether.

Until he died of a heart attack on Christmas Day in 1956 at the age of seventy-eight, he performed simple manual work and took long solitary walks in the hills of eastern Switzerland. From 1936 until his death he was visited several times a year by the Swiss critic and journalist Carl Seelig, who ultimately became Walser's legal guardian and literary executor. Seelig recorded their conversations and published them in 1957 as *Wanderungen mit Robert Walser* (walks with Robert Walser), now regarded as a significant contribution to Walser scholarship. Walser, like several other unorthodox German-Swiss writers of his generation, gained wider public recognition after his death than he had in life. Many of his works were published posthumously. The rediscovery of Walser began, very slowly, in the late 1950's, thanks to the efforts of Seelig. Interest in this author grew dramatically in the late 1970's, around the centenary of his birth, when a new edition of his collected works and several translations reached a broader, more diversified audience. Critical interest in Walser reached new heights in 1985 when the first volumes of his microscripts appeared.

Judith Ricker-Abderhalden

Bibliography

Avery, George. *Inquiry and Testament: A Study of the Novels and Short Prose of Robert Walser.* Philadelphia: University of Pennsylvania Press, 1968. This introduction to Walser is aimed at both the general reader and the student of German literature. Deals with themes, style, and structure of his fiction in the context of European literary developments of the early twentieth century.

Cardinal, Agnes. *The Figure of Paradox in the Work of Robert Walser.* Stuttgart, Germany: H.-D. Heinz, 1982. Cardinal's examination of Walser's technique is informative and interesting. Includes a bibliography.

Gass, William H. "Robert Walser." In *Finding a Form.* New York: Alfred A. Knopf, 1996. Gass argues that Walser's narrators frequently split their point of view between surface reality and a picture-postcard world. The result, Gass contends, is a complex prose style that reveals Walser to be a postmodernist long before the fashion.

Hamburger, Michael. "Explorers: Musil, Robert Walser, Kafka." In *A Proliferation of Prophets: Essays on German Writers from Nietzsche to Brecht.* Manchester, England: Carcanet Press, 1983. Views "freedom and ambivalence" as hallmarks of Walser's art, claiming that he combines the freedom of the essay and the poem with the art of prose fiction.

Harman, Mark. "Stream of Consciousness and the Boundaries of Self-Conscious Fiction: The Works of Robert Walser." *Comparative Criticism* 6 (1984): 119-134. Views the fairy tales, short prose, and novels of Walser as parts of an "autobiographical construct." Despite their confessional aspects, Walser's works are products of craftsmanship and reflection.

_______, ed. *Robert Walser Rediscovered: Stories, Fairy-Tale Plays, and Critical Responses.* Hanover, N.H.: University Press of New England, 1985. Along with translations, some previously published, are commentaries by major critics, contemporary and modern. Includes chronology, notes, bibliography, and an index of Walser's works.

Hinson, Hal. "Brothers of Invention." *The Washington Post*, April 18, 1996, p. G1. In this interview, Stephen and Timothy Quay discuss their film adaptation of Walser's novella "Jakob von Gunten." They talk about what drew them to Walser's work and how they tried to adapt his theme and style to film.

Sontag, Susan. Foreword to *Selected Stories*, by Robert Walser. Translated by Christopher Middleton et al. Manchester, England: Carcanet New Press, 1982. Views Walser as a "miniaturist" in short prose and comments on the "refusal of power" and compassionate despair of his work. See also Christopher Middleton's "Postscript."

Izaak Walton

English biographer

Born: Stafford, Staffordshire, England; August 9, 1593
Died: Winchester, Hampshire, England; December 15, 1683

NONFICTION: *The Life and Death of Dr. Donne*, 1640; *The Life of Sir Henry Wotton*, 1651; *The Compleat Angler: Or, The Contemplative Man's Recreation*, 1653; *The Life of Mr. Richard Hooker*, 1665; *The Life of Mr. George Herbert*, 1670.

Izaak Walton, often called the first professional English biographer, was born near Stafford in 1593. In his youth he was apprenticed to an ironmonger in London. Becoming a freeman in the company in 1618, he prospered as a dealer in ironware until his retirement during the English civil war. Although he was a Royalist in his sympathies and although his interests were literary, he never became involved in the political or literary contentions of the times. In retirement he devoted himself to his favorite pastime, fishing, and developed the charming yet authoritative discourse in *The Compleat Angler.* Largely self-educated, Walton began his literary career in his late forties when he was commissioned by Sir Henry Wotton to collect material for a projected life of John Donne. Walton, who called himself "the poorest, the meanest, of all [Donne's] friends," had been a member of Donne's parish of St. Dunstan's. When Wotton died before writing the biography, Walton undertook the task. The result, published as an introduction to the 1640 edition of Donne's *Sermons*, has become an integral part of the great editions of Donne's poetry and prose. Walton followed this biography with a life of Wotton in 1651. He subsequently wrote biographies of such worthies as Bishop Sanderson, Richard Hooker, and George Herbert.

Walton presented all his material from a Christian point of view, including *The Compleat Angler.* More than a study of a man's recreational pursuits, this book also champions the Christian virtues of peace, friendship, and goodness as opposed to the money-getting scramble of the city. One of Walton's aims, to show how one may find peace of mind, typified a pervading seventeenth century desire to seek relief from the world's woes in nature and the works of God. The effortless clarity of the style and the freshness of the anecdotes make the work especially attractive, just as the personality of Walton himself facilitated the many friendships that allowed him to gather material for his less well-known biographies. The bucolic appeal of *The Compleat Angler* is universal; the more than three hundred editions printed since 1653 testify to its enduring popularity.

Victoria Gaydosik

Bibliography

Loges, Max. "The Origins of Angling." *Aethlon: The Journal of Sport Literature* 10 (Spring, 1993).

Marshall, Gerald. "Time in Walton's *Lives*." *Studies in English Literature, 1500-1900* 32 (Summer, 1992).

Martin, Jessica. *Walton's Lives: Conformist Commemorations and the Rise of Biography.* New York: Oxford University Press, 2001.

Radcliffe, David Hill. "'Study to Be Quiet': Genre and Politics in Izaak Walton's *Compleat Angler*." *English Literary Renaissance* 22 (Winter, 1992).

Smith, Nigel. "Oliver Cromwell's Angler." *The Seventeenth Century* 8 (Spring, 1993).

Stanwood, P. G. *Izaak Walton.* New York: Twayne, 1998.

Wendorf, Richard. "'Visible Rhetorick': Izaak Walton and Iconic Biography." *Modern Philology* 82 (February, 1985).

Joseph Wambaugh

American novelist

Born: East Pittsburgh, Pennsylvania; January 22, 1937

LONG FICTION: *The New Centurions*, 1970; *The Blue Knight*, 1972; *The Choirboys*, 1975; *The Black Marble*, 1978; *The Glitter Dome*, 1981; *The Delta Star*, 1983; *The Secrets of Harry Bright*, 1985; *The Golden Orange*, 1990; *Fugitive Nights*, 1992; *Finnegan's Week*, 1993; *Floaters*, 1996.

SCREENPLAYS: *The Onion Field*, 1979 (adaptation of his book); *The Black Marble*, 1980 (adaptation of his novel).

TELEPLAY: *Echoes in the Darkness*, 1987 (adaptation of his book).

NONFICTION: *The Onion Field*, 1973; *Lines and Shadows*, 1983; *Echoes in the Darkness*, 1987; *The Blooding*, 1989; *Fire Lover: A True Story*, 2002.

Joseph Wambaugh (WAHM-baw), in full Joseph Aloysius Wambaugh, Jr., was born into what he described as a family of "steelworkers, bar owners, and champion drinkers." His father and mother, Anne Malloy Wambaugh, moved from Pennsylvania to California with their only child in 1951.

Three years later, Wambaugh joined the United States Marine Corps, serving until 1957. In the middle of his tour, he married Dee Allsup. They settled in Ontario, California, where Wambaugh worked in the Kaiser steel mill and attended college part-time. In 1958, he received an associate of arts degree in English literature from Chaffey College in Alta Loma, California. Two years later he was awarded his bachelor of arts from California State University, Los Angeles.

The year 1960 was a remarkable one in Wambaugh's life. In addition to receiving his B.A., he entered into the career that would eventually have a huge impact on crime fiction and the true crime genre: He joined the Los Angeles Police Department (LAPD), wearing badge number 178.

Wambaugh told one interviewer that he loved his job as a cop, in part because he found that in a single night, he "sometimes learned things that a man could not expect to learn in a month or a year." He continued his studies in night school, receiving his master's degree in 1968. The Watts riot of 1965 may have been the major catalyst for Wambaugh's writing about the rough streets of Los Angeles from the viewpoint of young policemen. His first efforts were short stories, all of which were rejected for publication. Finally, an *Atlantic Monthly* editor advised Wambaugh to try a novel. The result was *The New Centurions*.

While reviewers noted some typical first-novel faults, such as one-dimensional characterizations and clumsy exposition, they also praised the book for being exciting and readable. The first of Wambaugh's novels, it became a best-seller. In a 1996 interview, Wambaugh said, "I was the first person, I think, to write a book about cops that was not a police procedural." His insightful and complex characterizations of cops transformed a kind of pulp fiction into a more literary form of writing.

In 1973 Wambaugh published *The Onion Field*, a book frequently compared to Truman Capote's *In Cold Blood* (1965). *The Onion Field* recounts the events surrounding the real-life kidnapping and murder of a police officer in an onion field outside Bakersfield, California. As in his first two books, Wambaugh lures the reader into the psyche of his cop characters. *The Onion Field* proved to be one his most popular works.

By this time, Wambaugh had risen to the rank of detective sergeant in the LAPD, working the burglary detail in the Hollenbeck Division. However, his increasing celebrity began to interfere with his police duties. He finally retired from the department on March 8, 1974, after fourteen years on the force.

Wambaugh began to work in television and film at about this time. Between 1973 to 1977, he served as creative consultant on two television series, NBC's *Police Story*, and CBS's *The Blue Knight*. In 1977, the film version of *The Choirboys* was released, without Wambaugh's blessing. He wrote the initial screenplay, but when the studio revised the script and completely changed the ending, Wambaugh sued to have his name expunged from the credits. He won the suit. Other lawsuits and litigation surrounded Wambaugh's nonfiction. He was sued for defamation of character by the cop protagonist of *Lines and Shadows*. One of the alleged villains of *Echoes in the Darkness* brought a suit against the author for violating his civil rights. An investigation into whether Wambaugh had access to privileged information was launched in England after the publication of *The Blooding*. Wambaugh spent hundreds of thousands of dollars fighting these cases and vowed never to write nonfiction again. Then, after the 1996 publication of *Floaters*, he announced that he was retiring altogether.

His retirement lasted six years, ending with the publication of another nonfiction book. In 2002, intrigued by the case of a California serial arsonist, Wambaugh wrote *Fire Lover*. It was his first book to center on a fire department rather than a police department. As he did with all of his true crime books, Wambaugh performed extensive research and careful interviews, enlisting the assistance of investigators who actually worked the case. In more than three decades of writing, Wambaugh received awards from the Mystery Writers of America and the International Association of Crime Writers. He is credited with influencing crime writers in the print, film, and television industries.

Janet M. Ball

Bibliography

Dunn, Adam. "Burning Down the House." *Book* 22 (May/June, 2002): 19. Background of Wambaugh's first book after a six-year hiatus.

Hitt, Jack. "Did the Writer Do It?" *GQ* 68, no. 7 (July, 1998): 172. Detailed yet highly readable explanation of a lawsuit against Wambaugh stemming from his writing of *Echoes in the Darkness*.

Jeffrey, David K. "Joseph Wambaugh: Overview." In *St. James Guide to Crime and Mystery Writers*, edited by Jay P. Pederson. 4th ed. Detroit: St. James Press, 1996. This article leans heavily toward literary criticism, with intermittent biographical information.

Schunk, Thomas C., and William Hoffman. "Joseph Wambaugh." In *Critical Survey of Long Fiction*, edited by Carl Rollyson. 2d rev. ed. Pasadena, Calif.: Salem Press, 2000. A thorough overview of Wambaugh's life and career, emphasizing his novels.

Van Dover, J. Kenneth. *Centurions, Knights, and Other Cops: The Police Novels of Joseph Wambaugh*. San Bernardino, Calif.: Brownstone Books, 1995. A critical study of Wambaugh's first fourteen books. Includes an excellent chronology of his life.

Wambaugh, Joseph. "Ship to Shore with Joseph Wambaugh: Still a Bit Paranoid Among the Palms." Interview by Andy Meisler. *The New York Times*, June 13, 1996, p. C1. An interview with Wambaugh on his boat, *Bookworm*, near the San Diego harbor. The article explores some of Wambaugh's views and gives a brief description of his career.

Wang Wei

Chinese poet

Born: District of Qi, Taiyuan, Shanxi Province, China; 701
Died: Changan (now Xian), China; 761

POETRY: Major poems, including "Written While Crossing the Yellow River to Qing-he," "To the Frontier," "For Vice-Magistrate Zhang," and "The Deer Enclosure," can be found in *The Poetry of Wang Wei: New Translations and Commentary*, 1980 (Pauline Yu, translator); and in *Laughing Lost in the Mountains: Poems of Wang Wei*, 1991 (Willis Barnstone, Tony Barnstone, and Xu Haixin, translators).

The Tang Dynasty (618-907) in China was a golden age of poetry in Chinese civilization, in which more than fifty thousand poems were composed by twenty-three hundred poets. In part this was because of the policies of a woman named Wu Zhao, originally the young concubine of the Emperor Tai Zong and later, beginning in 690, the only woman in Chinese history to rule as sovereign in her own right. As a way of enlarging the social base of the governing classes, and of eroding in the process the power of the traditional aristocracy that had opposed her rise to power, Wu Zhao reformed the examination system through which scholars became officials. She made it more open to all, and she also made the composition of poetry a major part of the system.

The outpouring of poetry that resulted reached its pinnacle during the period extending from 713 to 765, which scholars have designated the High Tang. Wang Wei (wahng way), along with Du Fu (or Tu Fu) and Li Bo (or Li Po), is one of the three major poets of this period and the Chinese poet most frequently translated into English. Whereas Du Fu embodies the Confucian virtues of compassion and service, and Li Bo the romantic, spontaneous individualism of Daoist spirituality, Wang Wei is best known for his meditative, Buddhist-inspired nature poetry.

In reality Wang displays quite a wide range of accomplishment, and not a small part of his identity as a poet involves his ability to encompass opposites. In essence he might most accurately be considered a recluse-official: an official who serves conscientiously and whose career grows steadily throughout his life but one who writes an exquisitely understated contemplative poetry of retreat from the world.

From the beginning Wang Wei encompasses both extremes of the political spectrum that emerged during his lifetime. On one hand, he is related to powerful old aristocratic families on both sides of his family. On the other, as an immensely gifted and talented scholar he was able to move through the system of official examinations as one of the new, self-made literati of his time.

Wang Wei was something of a child prodigy. He began composing poetry at the age of nine and left home for the capital of Changan at the age of fifteen. There he proved himself not only an accomplished poet but a painter and musician as well. At one point he wrote that painting was his truest and deepest calling. Certainly he casts a painterly eye on the objects and landscapes he portrays in his poetry. Su Dongpo, the well-known Song Dynasty poet, wrote of Wang Wei's work: "In his poetry there is painting, and in his painting poetry."

As a young man in the capital, Wang joined the entourage of Li Fan, the younger brother of the Emperor Xuanzong and the period's foremost patron of the arts, and proved himself a quick success in the glittering and complex society of the Tang court. In 721 he passed the most difficult and most prestigious of the official examinations, the *jinshi*, or "presented scholar," examination, which typically only 1 or 2 percent of candidates passed annually. He was then appointed to a position with the bureau of music, and his poetry at the time tended toward the complex, celebratory style of the court.

After a short period in office, Wang was involved in political trouble, perhaps the result of his close association with an imperial prince at a time when the emperor was trying to curb the influence of the princes, and in 723 Wang was sent to assume a minor position in Shandong Province at Zhizhou. He probably served in this position for about four years, during which time he mastered the style of the rich body of exile poetry, with its variations on the theme of loneliness and its complex treatment of duty and service. Many years later, in 738, during a mission to the northwest, he would master the style of frontier poetry, which typically evoked vast, impersonal landscapes and the clash of warfare.

Before his return to the capital in 734, Wang undertook an extensive tour of the eastern provinces, during which he became interested in several kinds of religious experience: in local shamanistic cults, popular Daoism, and meditative Buddhism, studying with a Chan (or Zen) Buddhist master. All these religious interests came to be reflected in the poetry of this period. However, Wang's quality of austere simplicity and the nonjudgmental acceptance of a mind perfectly at one with the objects of nature that it beholds probably derived from his experiences with Chan Buddhist meditation; these are the characteristics that mark his subsequent, and most admired, poems.

During the tumultuous rebellion of An Lu-shan in 755, the emperor fled from the capital, and Wang Wei was captured by rebel forces and forced to serve in their regime. He was then charged with collaboration when the monarchy was restored in 757. Finally he was exonerated, largely on the basis of the eloquence with which he lamented the downfall of the emperor in two poems written during the rebellion. Despite, or perhaps because of, these episodes in his career, he continued to write meditative, reclusive poems. In 759, two years before his death—as he continued to write exquisite poems expressing renunciation of and retreat from the world of officialdom—he was promoted to the highest post he had yet attained, assistant secretary of state.

Bruce M. Wilson

Bibliography

Barnstone, Tony, Willis Barnstone, and Xu Haixin, trans. *Laughing Lost in the Mountains: Poems of Wang Wei*. Hanover, N.H.: University Press of New England, 1991. Excellent translation of 171 poems. The critical introduction, "The Ecstasy of Stillness," by the Barnstones provides insights into these poems.

Robinson, G. W., trans. *Poems of Wang Wei*. Harmondsworth, Middlesex, England: Penguin, 1973. With a lucid introduction about the poet's life and poetic achievements.

Wagner, Marsha L. *Wang Wei*. Boston: Twayne, 1981. An excellent study of Wang Wei's poems and his career, with elaborate notes and a useful bibliography. Covers his accomplishments as a nature poet, court poet, Zen Buddhist poet, and painter.

Walmsley, Lewis Calvin, and Dorothy Brush Walmsley. *Wang Wei: The Painter-Poet*. Rutland, Vt.: Tuttle, 1968. An examination of Wang Wei's poems in the context of the art of Chinese traditional painting. With helpful illustrations.

Weinberger, Eliot. *Nineteen Ways of Looking at Wang Wei*. Mount Kisco, N.Y.: Moyer Bell, 1987. This little book offers insights into the art of translating Chinese poems. With commentary by both Weinberger and Octavio Paz.

Young, David, trans. *Five T'ang Poets: Wang Wei, Li Po, Tu Fu, Li Ho, Li Shang-yin*. Oberlin, Ohio: Oberlin College Press, 1990. Provides an opportunity for appreciating Wang Wei along with contemporary poets during the Tang Dynasty.

Yu, Pauline. *The Poetry of Wang Wei: New Translations and Commentary*. Bloomington: Indiana University Press, 1980. Excellent translations of 150 poems with insightful commentary. Also includes the Chinese texts of the poems.

Mary Augusta Ward

English novelist

Born: Tasmania, Australia; June 11, 1851
Died: London, England; March 24, 1920

LONG FICTION: *Milly and Olly*, 1881; *Miss Bretherton*, 1884; *Robert Elsmere*, 1888; *The History of David Grieve*, 1892; *Marcella*, 1894; *The Story of Bessie Costrell*, 1895; *Sir George Thessady*, 1896; *Eleanor*, 1900; *Lady Rose's Daughter*, 1903; *Fenwick's Career*, 1906; *The Testing of Diana Mallory*, 1908; *Daphne: Or, Marriage à la Mode*, 1909; *Canadian Born*, 1910 (pb. in U.S. as *Lady Merton*); *The Case of Richard Meynell*, 1911; *The Mating of Lydia*, 1913; *The Coryston Family*, 1913; *Delia Blanchflower*, 1914.
NONFICTION: *Unbelief and Sin*, 1881; *England's Efforts: Letters to an American Friend*, 1916.
TRANSLATION: *Amiel's Journal: The Journal Intime of Henri Frederic Amiel*, 1885.

Mary Augusta Ward, née Mary Augusta Arnold and also known as Mrs. Humphry Ward, was a best-selling novelist in the late nineteenth and early twentieth centuries. The first of eight children born to Thomas Arnold and Julia Sorrell, she was the granddaughter of Thomas Arnold, headmaster of Rugby, and niece of Matthew Arnold, the famous poet and critic. When the family returned to England from Tasmania in 1854, following her father's conversion to Roman Catholicism, she was sent to Fox How, the Arnold family home in Westmoreland, to be raised by her grandmother and Aunt Francis Arnold, while her father served at the Catholic University in Dublin. During this period she attended the Rock Terrace School for Young Ladies and came under the influence of the Evangelical Vicar of Shiffnal.

Thomas Arnold returned to the Church of England in 1865 and was rewarded with a lectureship at Oxford University, where Mary joined him in 1867. She served as researcher in the Bodleian Library for her father as well as for Mark Pattison, the rector of Lincoln, who had her read Spanish church records from the fifth and sixth centuries. Her first publication, "A Westmoreland Story," appeared in *The Churchman's Companion* in July, 1870, and was followed by a pamphlet, *A Morning in the Bodleian*, in 1871. Edward Freeman asked her to write a volume on Spain for the historical series he was editing, a project she did not feel ready to take on. Much in demand in the social life of Oxford, she met Thomas Humphry Ward, to whom she was married on April 6, 1872. For the next several years she wrote articles for *Macmillan's Magazine*, the *Saturday Review*, and the *Oxford Spectator* to supplement her husband's meager salary as a tutor.

In 1874, the year her first child, Dorothy, was born, Ward served as secretary of the Committee for Lectures for Women at Oxford, work which led to the founding of the first women's residence hall at Oxford. In 1879 she accepted the invitation of Henry Ware to write entries on early Spanish saints and ecclesiastics for the *Dictionary of Christian Biography*. In the following two years she contributed 209 articles. The year 1880 saw the publication of *Ward's Poets*. In that same year Humphry Ward accepted a position on the *Times*, where he eventually became art critic. In the next year Mary published *Unbelief and Sin*, a response to John Wordsworth's Bampton Lecture, which accused those who held unorthodox religious views of committing a heinous sin. The family settled in Russell Square, Bloomsbury, where Mary wrote articles for the *Times* and, from February, 1883, to June, 1885, produced a monthly article for *Macmillan's*. She continued her editing of *Ward's Poets* and published her translation of *Amiel's Journal: The Journal Intime of Henri Frederic Amiel*.

Ward's best-known novel, *Robert Elsmere*, was begun in 1884. She submitted the first few chapters to Macmillan, who rejected it, but found a publisher in Smith, Elder, and Company and received an advance of two hundred pounds. The hero of the novel, rejecting the tenets of traditional Christianity, founds his own new version of the faith, the New Brotherhood, and finds an enthusiastic following. The work appealed to the Victorian reading public, quickly became a best-seller, and was rapidly translated into most European languages. On the success of this novel, Ward was able to sell her next book, *The History of David Grieve*, a novel about a "new" Christianity, for seven thousand pounds. With their newfound prosperity, the Wards built a country house, Lower Grayswood, in Surrey, but they soon bought Stocks, near Tring, for a traditional house with a history was more to Mary's taste for heritage.

The Story of Bessie Costrell, one of Ward's most compact novels, is a powerful story of a peasant woman succumbing to the temptation to steal and eventually drowning herself. *Sir George Thessady* traces the development of a social conscience in an aristocratic member of Parliament. Ward had her own social conscience: In 1897 she established the Passmore Edwards Settlement in Bloomsbury, London (now called Mary Ward House) to serve the young people of the area by providing a comfortable setting for them to attend lectures on philosophical and cultural topics.

In 1908 Ward traveled to the United States and Canada. This trip resulted in two novels. She wrote *Daphne: Or, Marriage à la Mode* as an attack on American divorce laws, which she saw as a threat to the Anglican church, for to her the church was the foundation of all that was worthwhile in civilization. *Canadian Born* (published in the United States as *Lady Merton*) is a celebration of Canadian culture. President Theodore Roosevelt, who had received her at the White House, asked her to help make the United States aware of England's effort in World War I. The result was *England's Efforts: Letters to an American Friend*. During the conflict she became one of the first women war correspondents.

As the women's suffrage movement came into full bloom, Ward registered her opposition, for she believed that women should work behind the scenes and that to demonstrate was unseemly. She portrayed the kind of activist woman she detested in *The Coryston Family* and *Delia Blanchflower*. Late in 1919 she fell ill. In early 1920, as her health declined, she received two outstanding honors, an honorary doctorate from the University of Edinburgh and appointment as one of the first seven women magistrates of England. She died on March 24.

Early critics saw Mary Augusta Ward as the successor of George Eliot. However, as the world became progressively liberal, she became more conservative. Although she was a skillful and talented novelist, her audience moved away from her and turned to other writers. She is, nevertheless, worth reading for her vivid characterizations and for her portrayal of the mood of an age.

J. Don Vann

Bibliography

Jones, Enid Huws. *Mrs. Humphry Ward*. New York: St. Martin's Press, 1973. This book's publication advanced the knowledge of the novelist because the author had access to materials not previously available.

Peterson, William S. *Victorian Heretic: Mrs. Humphry Ward's "Robert Elsmere."* Leicester, England: Leicester University Press, 1976. Connects that novel with the novelist's religious conflicts.

Smith, Esther Marian Greenwell. *Mrs. Humphry Ward*. Boston: Twayne, 1980. A convenient handbook.

Sutherland, John. *Mrs. Humphry Ward: Eminent Victorian, Pre-eminent Edwardian*. New York: Oxford University Press, 1990. A detailed biography that analyzes Ward's private life within the context of her times.

Charles Dudley Warner

American essayist, editor, and novelist

Born: Plainfield, Massachusetts; September 12, 1829
Died: Hartford, Connecticut; October 20, 1900

NONFICTION: *My Summer in a Garden*, 1870; *Saunterings*, 1872; *Backlog Studies*, 1873; *Baddock, and That Sort of Thing*, 1874; *My Winter on the Nile, Among the Mummies and Moslems*, 1876, revised 1881; *In the Levant*, 1876; *Being a Boy*, 1877; *In the Wilderness*, 1878; *Captain John Smith, Sometime Governor of Virginia, and Admiral of New England: A Study of His Life and Writings*, 1881; *Washington Irving*, 1881; *A Roundabout Journey*, 1883; *Papers on Penology*, 1886 (with others); *Their Pilgrimage*, 1886; *A-hunting the Deer, and Other Essays*, 1888; *On Horseback: A Tour in Virginia, North Carolina, and Tennessee, with Notes on Travel in Mexico and California*, 1888; *Studies in the South and West, with Comments on Canada*, 1889; *As We Were Saying*, 1891; *Our Italy, Southern California*, 1891; *The Work of Washington Irving*, 1893; *As We Go*, 1894; *The Relation of Literature to Life*, 1897; *The People for Whom Shakespeare Wrote*, 1897; *Fashion in Literature: And Other Literary and Social Essays and Addresses*, 1902.

LONG FICTION: *The Gilded Age: A Tale of Today*, 1873 (with Mark Twain); *A Little Journey in the World*, 1889, revised 1899; *The Golden House*, 1894; *That Fortune*, 1899.

EDITED TEXTS: *The Book of Eloquence: A Collection of Extracts in Prose and Verse, from the Most Eloquent Authors and Poets*, 1866; *A Library of the World's Best Literature*, 1896-1897 (30 volumes); *Biographical Dictionary and Synopsis of Books Ancient and Modern*, 1902 (2 volumes).

MISCELLANEOUS: *The Complete Writings of Charles Dudley Warner*, 1904 (15 volumes).

Charles Dudley Warner typifies conservative American authors between 1865 and the advent of literary naturalism—popular because they were genial, witty, and somewhat shallow.

Warner's parents were farmers. When Charles was five, his father died, leaving two hundred acres and admonishing Charles to attend college. In 1837, his mother took him to a guardian in Claremont, Massachusetts, and four years later to her brother in Cazenovia, New York.

In 1847 Warner attended the Oneida Conference Seminary in Cazenovia and a year later entered Hamilton College in Clinton, New York. His puritanical upbringing discouraged frivolity; his college years were therefore marked by scrupulous, protracted reading. He published a few articles in the *Knickerbocker Magazine*. During graduation ceremonies in 1851, he presented an eloquent address. After tedious work in printing and publishing establishments, Warner compiled *The Book of Eloquence*, featuring passages from British and American authors whose works he revered, and printed it privately in 1853 and commercially in 1866.

Warner improved chronically poor health by working from 1853 to 1854 as a railway surveyor in Missouri. He returned to New York State in 1855, living with an uncle in Binghamton, working in real-estate conveyancing, and reading law there and soon after in Philadelphia. In 1856 he married Susan Lee, a seminary classmate; the couple never had children. Warner earned his law degree at the University of Pennsylvania and passed the bar examination in 1858. A two-year stint of law practice in Chicago (1858-1860) was unprofitable, partly owing to the Panic of 1857, and convinced him that he should try writing, research, and editing.

Joseph Hawley, whom Warner had known at Hamilton, invited him to move to Hartford, Connecticut, to become his associate editor at the *Hartford Press*. When the Civil War began, Hawley joined the Union army, leaving Warner (whose nearsightedness kept him from military duty) as editor in chief. He displayed such editorial skills that soon after General Hawley returned to civilian life and entered politics, Warner consolidated the *Hartford Press* with the *Hartford Courant*, of which he became part owner. In 1868 he took his wife for a leisurely year in England and on the Continent, during which time he dispatched travel essays to his *Courant*.

Back in Hartford, Warner bought a house and three acres outside the city, later named the place Nook Farm, and began welcoming numerous persons of grace, wit, and literary accomplishments—including William Dean Howells, novelist, editor, and critic; Mark Twain, world-famous humorist; antiquarian J. Hammond Trumbull; Joseph Hopkins Twichell, ex-Union Army chaplain; Harriet Beecher Stowe, author of *Uncle Tom's Cabin* (1852), and her siblings, Henry Ward Beecher, clergyman and author (phenomenally popular until disgraced for alleged adultery in 1874), and suffragist Isabella Beecher Hooker.

Warner's literary career began with *My Summer in a Garden*, a collection of philosophical *Hartford Courant* columns on garden work and joys. It was guaranteed success when the Reverend Beecher recommended it to his own Boston publisher and provided a pleasant introduction. Warner's career advanced with *Saunterings*, his collection of *Courant* essays sent from abroad. Its popularity encouraged him to publish eight more travel books, reflecting his comfortable sojourns, brief or extended, in Africa, California, Canada, France, Egypt, Mexico, Spain, and elsewhere and voicing his conservative lament that cultural values were eroding.

Backlog Studies was his first book of critical essays on society and literature. A burning backlog, symbol of conservative influence here, radiates heat slowly, consistently, and influentially. Of several such books that followed, the only exciting ones propose improvements in public education, open-ended prison sentences for reform-minded inmates, and American and international copyright reforms.

Warner's solid biography of Washington Irving inaugurated his influential American Men of Letters series. His huge *A Library of the World's Best Literature* was popular in its day and netted him thousands of dollars. His superficial *Biographical Dictionary and Synopsis of Books Ancient and Modern*, however, is now embarrassing; for example, Dante rates only six lines.

Almost solely through his association with Mark Twain in coauthoring *The Gilded Age* is Warner remembered today. In it, however, his chapters mainly feature melodramatic plotting and effete Victorian morality, whereas Twain's chapters satirizing political corruption and greedy land speculators inspired historians to call the last decades of America's nineteenth century the Gilded Age. The three novels Warner wrote without Twain's help also dramatize the disastrous consequences of ruthless moneygrubbing. Warner is a near-perfect example of late nineteenth century cultural critics: largely self-educated, genteel, sincere, and persuasive, espousing conservative ideals destined to be shattered by events they rarely saw looming on the horizon.

Robert L. Gale

Bibliography

Andrews, Kenneth. *Nook Farm: Mark Twain's Hartford Circle.* Cambridge, Mass.: Harvard University Press, 1950. Indispensable study of Warner's Hartford associates.

Fields, Annie. *Charles Dudley Warner.* New York: McClure, Phillips, 1904. Laudatory, old-fashioned biography.

Van Egmond, Peter. "Charles Dudley Warner." In *American Literary Critics and Scholars, 1850-1880*, edited by John W. Rathbun and Monica M. Grecu. Vol. 64 in *Dictionary of Literary Biography.* Detroit: Gale, 1988. Discussion of Warner as enlightened conservative critic.

Marina Warner

English critic, novelist, and journalist

Born: London, England; November 9, 1946

NONFICTION: *The Dragon Empress: Life and Times of Tz'u-hsi 1835-1908*, 1972; *Alone of All Her Sex: The Myth and Cult of the Virgin Mary*, 1976; *Joan of Arc: The Image of Female Heroism*, 1981; *Monuments and Maidens: The Allegory of Female Form*, 1985; *Managing Monsters: Six Myths of Our Times*, 1994; *From the Beast to the Blonde: On Fairy Tales and Their Tellers*, 1994; *No Go the Bogeyman: Scaring, Lulling, and Making Mock*, 1998; *Fantastic Metamorphoses, Other Worlds: Ways of Telling the Self*, 2002.

LONG FICTION: *In a Dark Wood*, 1977; *The Skating Party*, 1982; *The Lost Father*, 1988; *Indigo: Or, Mapping the Waters*, 1992; *The Leto Bundle*, 2000.

SHORT FICTION: *The Mermaids in the Basement: Stories*, 1993; *Murderers I Have Known, and Other Stories*, 2002.

CHILDREN'S/YOUNG ADULT LITERATURE: *The Crack in the Teacup*, 1979; *The Impossible Day*, 1981; *The Impossible Night*, 1981; *The Impossible Bath*, 1982; *The Impossible Rocket*, 1982; *The Wobbly Tooth*, 1984.

EDITED TEXT: *Wonder Tales: Six Stories of Enchantment*, 1994.

Marina Sarah Warner's literary career has been prolific, encompassing a number of topics and genres. In addition to her principal works of nonfiction and fiction, she has been a journalist and has written some children's literature and screenplays for television. However, two main themes emerge as concerns of her major works: feminism and myth. Indeed, many of her writings demonstrate the links between these two ideas.

Many of Warner's interests stem from her family and education. She was born in London. Her father, Esmund, was a bookseller and her mother, Emilia Terzuli, was a teacher. Marina Warner was raised as a Roman Catholic and was educated in convent schools in England, Egypt, and Belgium. She received her degree at Oxford (Lady Margaret Hall) in French and Italian. Her literary talents were evident in her work as editor of *Isis*, the university magazine at Oxford, and in her early career as a journalist, for which she received the *Daily Telegraph* Young Writer of the Year award in 1970. By the early 1970's she had begun to write full-time. Her first book was a biography of Tz'u-hsi, the empress dowager of China in the late nineteenth century. This work showed Warner's promise as a historical writer in its ability to convey the intrigue of the Chinese court and in her portrayal of Tz'u-hsi as a strong, forceful woman.

In 1976 the book for which Marina Warner is best known was published. *Alone of All Her Sex: The Myth and Cult of the Virgin Mary* examines the various manifestations through the centuries of the myth and cult of the Virgin Mary. Her interest in this subject is rooted in her education in Catholic convent schools, where the Virgin was upheld as an exemplar of ideal womanhood. After leaving the Catholic Church, Warner wanted to examine why this myth of female virginity was so powerful. Her book utilizes an impressive amount of evidence drawn from religious studies, anthropology, history, and art history to advance her thesis that the cult of the Virgin was degrading to women. This book shows how Warner investigates the mythological content of an idea to expose its misogynistic core. Warner's next work of nonfiction, *Joan of Arc: The Image of Female Heroism*, delved into the mythology surrounding another woman, Joan of Arc. Rather than approach the subject as a biography, Warner looked into the context that made Joan credible to her contemporaries and then considered how this historical figure evolved into a symbol of female heroism in subsequent centuries.

Around this time Marina Warner also began to write fiction. Her first novel, *In a Dark Wood*, concerns two brothers, one a Jesuit who is writing a historical biography, the other a magazine publisher. This novel thus draws on several facets of Warner's life, her Catholic religious background and her writing career as a historian and journalist. Her second novel is *The Skating Party*. While the main characters come from the contemporary world of academia, the novel reworks a classical Greek story found in Homer's *Iliad* that tells how, at his mother's instigation, her son seduces the young woman who is his father's lover. The critical consensus was that these early novels demonstrated less literary polish than her more convincing writings on historical topics.

Warner's next major book, *Monuments and Maidens: The Allegory of Female Form*, returned to nonfiction treatment of a subject that combines feminism and symbolism. This book looks at monumental, usually allegorical, depictions of females in Western art and shows how modern female leaders often consciously or unconsciously adopt some of the visual symbolism portrayed in these depictions. Like her earlier writing, Warner's historical study of visual and literary imagery about certain aspects of women's persona illuminates contemporary attitudes toward women's place in society.

Two works of fiction followed. *The Lost Father* is Warner's most ambitious novel. The density of its historical, allegorical, mythological, and psychological components reveals the attributes that Warner brings to her works as a cultural historian. The story utilizes autobiographical material about Warner's maternal family in southern Italy. It reflects the ambivalent place of women in this Italian culture, where a strong matriarchy preserves the almost heroic mythological status of the father figure. *Indigo: Or, Mapping the Waters* also traces a family history from a Caribbean island to modern London. It is rich in literary references, especially to William Shakespeare's *Tempest*, and is richly textured with mythic tales and psychological insights.

Three works published during 1993 to 1994 focus on the function of myth. Two nonfiction studies, *From the Beast to the Blonde: On Fairy Tales and Their Tellers* and *Managing Monsters: Six Myths of Our Times*, are complementary. The first investigates the mythic origins of fairy tales, while the second looks at the way myths function in contemporary life. Together, they demonstrate Warner's thesis that the continuities of myth reinforce gender stereotypes. *No Go the Bogeyman* started out as an attempt to consider male figures in folklore and folktale as Warner had previously assessed female figures, but ended up as a study of the grotesque in folk and popular culture, a theme continued in *Fantastic Metamorphoses, Other Worlds*, which addresses shape-shifting. *Mermaids in the Basement* is a collection of short stories in which Warner refashions archetypal plots, especially from the Bible, in contemporary settings. Because their main characters are women, the stories continue Warner's exploration of the inherent nature of women's experience. Warner's interest in myth also informs her novel *The Leto Bundle*, which shifts between past and present and between mortal and goddess, drawing on the myth of Leto, the mother of Artemis and Apollo. As Constance Markey observed in a review of *The Lost Father*, all of Warner's works reveal her to be an author with "the heart of a poet and the mind of a scholar."

Karen Gould

Bibliography

Coakley, Sarah. "Mariology and 'Romantic Feminism': A Critique." In *Women's Voices: Essays in Contemporary Feminist Theology*, edited by Teresa Elwes. London: Marshall Pickering, 1992. This essay categorizes several contemporary discussions of Mariology according to type of feminism. Warner's book is discussed as an example of deconstructionist Mariology.

Colby, Vineta, ed. *World Authors, 1975-1980*. New York: Wilson, 1985. Includes a biographical overview.

Corn, Alfred. "Old Wives, Fairy Godmothers." *The Nation* 261 (November 20, 1995): 612-615. An extensive review of *From the Beast to the Blonde*.

Luhrmann, Tanya. "Things That Go Bump." *New York Times Book Review* 148 (March 14, 1999): 14-15. Review of *No Go the Bogeyman* written by a folklorist.

Weil, Judith. "*The White Devil* and Old Wives' Tales." *Modern Language Review* 94 (April, 1999): 328-340. Uses Warner's theories about mythology and folklore to analyze John Webster's Jacobean drama.

Rex Warner

English novelist

Born: Birmingham, Warwickshire, England; March 9, 1905
Died: Wallingford, Oxfordshire, England; June 24, 1986

LONG FICTION: *The Wild Goose Chase: An Allegory*, 1937; *The Professor: A Forecast*, 1938; *The Aerodrome: A Love Story*, 1941; *Why Was I Killed? A Dramatic Dialogue*, 1944; *Men of Stones: A Melodrama*, 1949; *Escapade: A Tale of Average*, 1953; *The Young Caesar*, 1958; *Imperial Caesar*, 1960; *Pericles the Athenian*, 1963; *The Converts: A Novel of Early Christianity*, 1967; *The Stories of the Greeks*, 1967 (includes *Men and Gods*, *Greeks and Trojans*, and *The Vengeance of the Gods*).

POETRY: *Poems*, 1937 (revised as *Poems and Contradictions*, 1945).

NONFICTION: *The English Public Schools*, 1945; *The Cult of Power*, 1946; *John Milton*, 1949; *E. M. Forster*, 1950; *Men and Gods*, 1950; *Views of Attica and Its Surroundings*, 1950; *Ashes to Ashes: A Post-mortem on the 1950-51 Tests*, 1951 (with Lyle Blair); *Eternal Greece*, 1951 (with Martin Hurliman); *Greeks and Trojans*, 1951; *The Vengeance of the Gods*, 1954; *Athens*, 1956; *The Greek Philosophers*, 1958; *Men of Athens: The Story of Fifth Century Athens*, 1972.

CHILDREN'S/YOUNG ADULT LITERATURE: *The Kite*, 1936; *Look at Birds*, 1962; *Athens at War*, 1970.

TRANSLATIONS: *The "Medea" of Euripides*, 1944; *The "Prometheus Bound" of Aeschylus*, 1947; *The Persian Expedition*, 1949 (Xenophon); *The "Hippolytus" of Euripides*, 1950; *The "Helen" of Euripides*, 1951; *History of the Peloponnesian War*, 1954 (Thucydides); *The Fall of the Roman Republic: Six Lives*, 1958 (Plutarch); *War Commentaries of Caesar*, 1960; *Poems*, 1960 (George Seferis); *The Oresteia*, 1961 (Aeschylus); *The Confessions of St. Augustine*, 1963; *History of My Times*, 1966 (Xenophon); *On the Greek Style: Selected Essays on Poetry and Hellenism*, 1966 (Seferis); *Moral Essays*, 1971 (Plutarch).

EDITED TEXT: *Look up at the Skies!*, 1972 (poems and prose of Gerard Manley Hopkins).

MISCELLANEOUS: *Personal Impressions: Talks on Writers and Writing*, 1986 (British Broadcasting Corporation scripts).

Rex Warner was described by the distinguished British author and literary critic V. S. Pritchett as "the only outstanding novelist of ideas whom the decade of ideas produced." Warner was preeminently a novelist of ideas, a translator from Greek and Latin of great distinction, and a classicist of uncommon breadth and style. Reginald Ernest Warner was born in 1905. Educated at St. George's School in Harpenden, he there showed his prowess at cricket and rugby football as well as in debating contemporary issues and in writing poetry, all the while excelling in classical studies. He was awarded a scholarship to Wadham College, Oxford, and was tutored by the renowned classicist Sir Maurice Bowra. While he obtained a first-class pass in classical moderations, he had to take a leave of absence and did not distinguish himself in his final examinations; as a result, he had to dismiss the possibility of a university appointment in the classics.

While at Oxford, however, Warner became close friends with Cecil Day Lewis, Stephen Spender, and W. H. Auden, who encouraged his writing of poetry and included his work in journals and anthologies. It was there, too, that his interest in politics (the Great Strike of 1926) and philosophy developed. An immediate result was his essay on education in *The Mind in Chains: Socialism and the Cultural Revolution* (1937), edited by Day Lewis. Another was his pamphlet *We're Not Going to Do Nothing* (published under Day Lewis's name in 1937), a reply to Aldous Huxley's open question, What are the British going to do about the growing imminence of war in Europe? Huxley advocated nonviolent resistance to war, violence being morally wrong. Warner advocated a world alliance of socialist states under the leadership of the labor movement in Great Britain, guided by the principle of production for use rather than for profit. This belief lasted throughout his lifetime and informed his fictions, though it became more generalized in the later novels; in all of them, however, there is seen the same tension between individual freedom and public authority.

The "classical" novels (loosely described as historical fiction) complement the early ones (usually considered allegorical novels) by showing that humankind has always been concerned with the problems of power, responsibility, and motivation: The past is used to illustrate (and provide parallels to) the contemporary condition. Always the model is the Greek democratic ideal; always Rex Warner is a novelist of political relevance. He is also socially responsible; he was the child of a dissenting clergyman and a teacher, and so he is always concerned with the moral choices available and is motivated by concern for the public good. (It is not insignificant that he edited selections from Gerard Manley Hopkins and John Bunyan.) The final speech of George, one of the principal characters in *The Wild Goose Chase*, seems to sum up the values that are extolled in all of Warner's work, whether in poems, essays, or fictions: "We attach great value—to comradeship, and to profane love, to hard work, honesty, the sight of the sun, reverence to those who have helped us." Warner was intensely loyal to his Oxford (and, later, American) friends; he never lost faith in the possibility of international peace and national tranquillity if the public good was advanced before private profit. He loved nature, and he had an ineradicable (though perhaps inchoate) sense of religion. His commitment to literature as the index of high culture was absolute. For his dedication to the classics, he was awarded the Order of the Phoenix by the king of the Hellenes.

Some of Warner's special interests, other than Greece and Rome, were Egypt, English village life, Charles Dickens (whom he praised for his "extraordinary fecundity of creation"), Fyodor Dostoevski (whom he thought to be the Russian equivalent of Dickens), and the modern fascination with the cult of power—the worship of violence, lawlessness, and the setting-up of the individual against the community and even the universe. The cult of power, he wrote, takes the hero out of tragedy and begins by denying the reality of the religious background—God, necessity, law, social conscience. As he admired Dickens and Dostoevski, he deprecated others—including D. H. Lawrence and Adolf Hitler—as "moral anarchists" committed to blood, sex, virility, and violence. In many ways, the 1946 nonfiction work *The Cult of Power* is the key to understanding Warner's political and social thought; like all of his writing, it is remarkable for its clear, inimitable Attic style.

Warner was director of the British Institute in Athens from 1945 until 1947; he then taught in the Berlin Technical Institute. Later, he taught for a year at Bowdoin College and, from 1963 until his retirement in 1974, at the University of Connecticut. He was awarded the degree of doctor of letters, *honoris causa*, by Rider University in 1968.

Alan L. McLeod

Bibliography

McLeod, A. L. *Rex Warner, Writer: An Introductory Essay*. Sydney: Wentworth Press, 1960. Devoted to Warner's writing, has chapters on his poetry, fiction, belles lettres, and classical studies. Includes bibliography.

_______, ed. *A Garland for Rex Warner.* Mysore, India: Literary Half-Yearly Press, 1985. Has essays by scholars from throughout the world on Warner's juvenilia, novels, and "fictional biographies."

Reeve, N. H. *The Novels of Rex Warner: An Introduction.* New York: St. Martin's Press, 1989. A critical overview.

Tabachnick, Stephen Ely. *Fiercer than Tigers: The Life and Works of Rex Warner.* East Lansing: Michigan State University Press, 2002. Deeply researched biography of Warner.

Sylvia Townsend Warner

English short-story writer

Born: Harrow, Middlesex, England; December 6, 1893
Died: Maiden Newton, Dorset, England; May 1, 1978

SHORT FICTION: *"Some World Far from Ours," and "Stay Corydon, Thou Swain,"* 1929; *Elinor Barley*, 1930; *Moral Ending, and Other Stories*, 1931; *The Salutation*, 1932; *More Joy in Heaven, and Other Stories*, 1935; *Twenty-four Short Stories*, 1939 (with Graham Greene and James Laver); *The Cat's Cradle Book*, 1940; *A Garland of Straw, and Other Stories*, 1943; *The Museum of Cheats*, 1947; *Winter in the Air, and Other Stories*, 1955; *A Spirit Rises*, 1962; *A Stranger with a Bag, and Other Stories*, 1966 (pb. in U.S. as *Swans on an Autumn River: Stories*, 1966); *The Innocent and the Guilty: Stories*, 1971; *Kingdoms of Elfin*, 1977; *Scenes of Childhood*, 1981; *One Thing Leading to Another, and Other Stories*, 1984; *Selected Stories of Sylvia Townsend Warner*, 1988; *The Music at Long Verney: Twenty Stories*, 2001 (Michael Steinman, editor).

LONG FICTION: *Lolly Willowes: Or, The Loving Huntsman*, 1926; *Mr. Fortune's Maggot*, 1927; *The True Heart*, 1929; *Summer Will Show*, 1936; *After the Death of Don Juan*, 1938; *The Corner That Held Them*, 1948; *The Flint Anchor*, 1954.

POETRY: *The Espalier*, 1925; *Time Importuned*, 1928; *Opus 7*, 1931; *Whether a Dove or a Seagull: Poems*, 1933; *Boxwood*, 1957; *Azrael, and Other Poems*, 1978; *Twelve Poems*, 1980; *Collected Poems*, 1982.

NONFICTION: *Jane Austen*, 1951; *T. H. White: A Biography*, 1967; *Letters*, 1982; *The Diaries of Sylvia Townsend Warner*, 1994 (Claire Harman, editor); *I'll Stand by You: Selected Letters of Sylvia Townsend Warner and Valentine Ackland*, 1998 (Susanna Pinney, editor) *The Element of Lavishness: Letters of Sylvia Townsend Warner and William Maxwell, 1938-1978*, 2001 (Michael Steinman, editor).

Sylvia Townsend Warner, though published often, has received sparse critical attention assessing her importance as a writer of short fiction, novels, poems, biographies, and translations. She was born in Harrow on the Hill, Middlesex, England, on December 6, 1893. Her father, George Townsend Warner, was a Harrow School housemaster, but Sylvia did not receive a formal education. Her mother, Eleanor (Hudleston) Warner, taught her to read, her father taught her history, and a governess tutored her in general subjects. By the age of ten, Sylvia was reading extensively in her father's library. She favored books on the occult, a subject that would later influence much of her writings. After her father died in 1916 she took a job in a munitions factory during World War I. She then moved to London to study music and was a member of the editorial committee that compiled the ten volumes of *Tudor Church Music* (1922-1929), which took ten years to complete.

Warner's first book of poetry, *The Espalier*, was published in 1925. Her first novel, *Lolly Willowes*, was printed in 1926 and was selected by the newly established Book-of-the-Month Club. Warner's second novel, *Mr. Fortune's Maggot*, published in 1927, was chosen by the Literary Guild. Despite this early popularity of her novels, Warner received little critical acclaim for them; she became best known for her short stories. From 1936 to 1978, *The New Yorker* published 144 of her stories. After her second book of poetry, *Time Importuned*, was published in 1928, Warner's first collection of short fiction came out in *"Some World Far from Ours," and "Stay, Corydon, Thou Swain,"* in 1929. Her prose style was often praised for its conciseness, precise wording, fast-moving action, and ironic tone. In 1930 Warner and her partner Valentine Ackland moved to the country, where Warner wrote and Ackland opened an antique shop. Always active, Warner studied the black arts, elves, and mysticism. She also became an accomplished cook. She used much of this knowledge in her writings. In 1935 Warner became active in the Communist Party. In 1936 she and Ackland sailed to Barcelona, Spain, to volunteer their services to the Red Cross. (Warner and Ackland would live together until Ackland's death in 1969.) Also in 1936, Warner's novel *Summer Will Show* was published. It is considered by some critics to be her best work.

In 1939 Warner published *Twenty-four Short Stories* (including stories by Warner, Graham Greene, and James Laver), which was followed by another short-story collection, *The Cat's Cradle Book*, in 1940. Then her *A Garland of Straw, and Other Stories* saw print in 1943. These stories show her continued interest in Spanish life, first seen in her novel *After the Death of Don Juan*. Some of these stories depict the effects on individuals of the Spanish Civil War and appear more angry than playful. More short-story collections and novels followed over the next eight years. Her last novel, *The Flint Anchor*, appeared in 1954. After this publication, another book of short stories, *Winter in the Air, and Other Stories*, went on sale in 1955, and a collection of poems, *Boxwood*, was published in 1957. In 1962 Warner's stories were collected in *A Spirit Rises*. Her prolific output continued, and her writings were still popular even when she was in her eighties. A short-story collection, *Kingdoms of Elfin*, and a collection of poems, *Azrael, and Other Poems*, were published shortly before her death.

Del Corey

Bibliography

Ackland, Valentine. *For Sylvia: An Honest Account*. New York: W. W. Norton, 1985. A brief but poignant autobiography by Warner's lover, detailing the years with Warner and the painful separation caused by Ackland's struggle with alcoholism. Bea Howe's lengthy foreword discusses her firsthand understanding of the influence of Ackland on Warner's personal and professional life.

Brothers, Barbara. "Through the 'Pantry Window': Sylvia Townsend Warner and the Spanish Civil War." In *Rewriting the Good Fight: Critical Essays on the Literature of the Spanish Civil War*, edited by Frieda S. Brown et al. East Lansing: Michigan State University Press, 1989. Places Warner in the context of her contemporaries regarding the period of the Spanish Civil War. Includes bibliography.

Dinnage, Rosemary. "An Affair to Remember." *The New York Times*, March 7, 1999. A review of *I'll Stand by You: Selected Letters of Sylvia Townsend Warner and Valentine Ackland*; comments on Warner's offbeat short stories from *The New Yorker*, claiming the short story was well suited to her whimsy. Discusses her relationship with Valentine Ackland.

Harmon, Claire. *Sylvia Townsend Warner: A Biography*. London: Chatto & Windus, 1989. An even and thorough biography with illustrations, a bibliography, and an index. Deals openly and prominently with the relationship between Valentine Ackland and Warner. Gives a biographical and historical context of Warner's work but includes little critical detail.

Loeb, Marion C. "British to the Core." *St. Petersburg Times*, August 6, 1989, p. 7D. A review of *Selected Stories of Sylvia Townsend Warner*; notes that her stories deal with the world of civil servants, vicars' wives, and pensioners; comments on her graceful, lyrical style.

Maxwell, William, ed. Introduction to *Letters,* by Sylvia Townsend Warner. New York: Viking, 1982. The novelist and editor for *The New Yorker* and Warner's longtime personal friend shows great admiration for Warner's work. Maxwell notes her historical astuteness, her "ironic detachment," and her graceful formalism of language. Also considers the letters in the light of their being a writer's "left-over energy" and written without the inhibition of editorial or critical judgment. Includes a brief biographical sketch.

Perenyi, Eleanor. "The Good Witch of the West." *The New York Review of Books* 32 (July 18, 1985): 27-30. Argues that Warner's writing reputation has suffered from the inability of critics to categorize her writings, which include dozens of short stories and seven novels. Notes that the publication of her letters has sparked new interest and that their talk of dreams and visitations suggests that Warner harbored "more than a touch of the witch."

Strachan, W. J. "Sylvia Townsend Warner: A Memoir." *London Magazine* 19, no. 8 (November, 1979): 41-50. An overview of Warner's fiction, with a close look at the elements of fantasy and realism. *Kingdoms of Elfin* and *Lolly Willowes*, for example, seem incongruent given Warner's activity during World War I, but such realistic works as *The Flint Anchor* demonstrate her earthy, pragmatic quality.

Tomalin, Claire. "Burning Happiness." *The New York Times*, February 18, 1996. A review of *The Diaries of Sylvia Townsend Warner*; discusses the nature of her feminism and her communism. Notes the depth of her grief for Valentine Ackland after Ackland's death.

Updike, John. "Jake and Olly Opt Out." *The New Yorker* 55 (August 20, 1979): 97-102. In this comparative review of Kingsley Amis's *Jake's Thing* (1978) and Warner's *Lolly Willowes*, Updike looks at the role of nature in Warner's work and discerns a subtle strain of feminism. He argues that, unlike Amis and other former poets-turned-novelists, Warner's poetic style retains elements of "magic and music" and that her talent merits a much greater recognition than she has received.

Robert Penn Warren

American poet and novelist

Born: Guthrie, Kentucky; April 24, 1905
Died: West Wardsboro, near Stratton, Vermont; September 15, 1989

POETRY: *Thirty-six Poems*, 1935; *Eleven Poems on the Same Theme*, 1942; *Selected Poems, 1923-1943*, 1944; *Brother to Dragons: A Tale in Verse and Voices*, 1953; *Promises: Poems, 1954-1956*, 1957; *You, Emperors, and Others: Poems, 1957-1960*, 1960; *Selected Poems: New and Old, 1923-1966*, 1966; *Incarnations: Poems, 1966-1968*, 1968; *Audubon: A Vision*, 1969; *Or Else—Poem/Poems, 1968-1974*, 1974;

Selected Poems, 1923-1975, 1976; *Now and Then: Poems, 1976-1978*, 1978; *Being Here: Poetry, 1977-1980*, 1980; *Rumor Verified: Poems, 1979-1980*, 1981; *Chief Joseph of the Nez Percé*, 1983; *New and Selected Poems, 1923-1985*, 1985; *The Collected Poems of Robert Penn Warren*, 1998 (John Burt, editor).

LONG FICTION: *Night Rider*, 1939; *At Heaven's Gate*, 1943; *All the King's Men*, 1946; *World Enough and Time: A Romantic Novel*, 1950; *Band of Angels*, 1955; *The Cave*, 1959; *Wilderness: A Tale of the Civil War*, 1961; *Flood: A Romance of Our Time*, 1964; *Meet Me in Green Glen*, 1971; *A Place to Come To*, 1977.

SHORT FICTION: *Blackberry Winter*, 1946; *The Circus in the Attic, and Other Stories*, 1947.

NONFICTION: *John Brown: The Making of a Martyr*, 1929; *Modern Rhetoric*, 1949 (with Cleanth Brooks); *Segregation: The Inner Conflict in the South*, 1956; *Selected Essays*, 1958; *The Legacy of the Civil War: Meditations on the Centennial*, 1961; *Who Speaks for the Negro?*, 1965; *Democracy and Poetry*, 1975; *Portrait of a Father*, 1988; *New and Selected Essays*, 1989; *Cleanth Brooks and Robert Penn Warren: A Literary Correspondence*, 1998 (James A. Grimshaw, Jr., editor); *Selected Letters of Robert Penn Warren*, 2000-2001 (2 volumes; William Bedford Clark, editor).

DRAMA: *Proud Flesh*, pr. 1947; *All the King's Men*, pr. 1958 (adaptation of his novel).

EDITED TEXTS: *An Approach to Literature*, 1936 (with Cleanth Brooks and John Thibault Purser); *Understanding Poetry: An Anthology for College Students*, 1938 (with Brooks); *Understanding Fiction*, 1943 (with Brooks); *Faulkner: A Collection of Critical Essays*, 1966; *Randall Jarrell, 1914-1965*, 1967 (with Robert Lowell and Peter Taylor); *American Literature: The Makers and the Making*, 1973 (with R. W. B. Lewis).

Robert Penn Warren is the only American writer to have won the Pulitzer Prize in both fiction and poetry. Indeed, he won the award three times: for *All the King's Men*, a novel inspired by the legend of Huey Long, the southern populist politician; for *Promises*, a midlife resurgence of poetic power; and again for *Now and Then*, a demonstration of undiminished poetic skill published in the eighth decade of his life. As a college professor who wrote textbooks, Warren contributed significantly to changes in the teaching of literature in the United States. Warren also wrote excellent literary criticism as well as social and historical commentary.

Warren was born in Guthrie, a tiny community in southwestern Kentucky. As a young man, Warren's father had aspired to become a poet and a lawyer, but he became a small-town banker instead. With three children of his own and a family of young half brothers and sisters inherited when his father died, he had no time to develop his taste for poetry. Robert Penn Warren said he felt as if he had stolen his father's life, since he realized the literary ambitions of which his father had only dreamed.

Warren's relationship with his father had a profound effect on his fiction, which often concerns a young man with ambivalent feelings for a real or surrogate father. However, his early poetry, as well as his much later biographical narrative of Jefferson Davis, reflected the influence of his beloved maternal grandfather, Gabriel Thomas Penn, a onetime Confederate cavalryman who had lived on a tobacco farm and had been an ardent reader of poetry and military history. On his grandfather's farm in the summertime, the young Robert was steeped in stories of the Civil War and the local tobacco wars, both of which would find their way into his fiction. His first novel, *Night Rider*, dramatized the Kentucky tobacco war between growers and the monopolistic tyranny of the tobacco company. By the time Warren wrote *Wilderness*, he had a much less romantic view of that conflict than he had had as a child, when he believed that the Civil War was the great American epic.

Warren's talent for writing was discovered and fostered in his college years at Vanderbilt University by the poet John Crowe Ransom, who was teaching English there. Ransom encouraged him to write poetry, and Donald Davidson, who was teaching English literature, let Warren write imitations of *Beowulf* and Geoffrey Chaucer instead of the usual term papers. In 1924 Warren became the youngest member of a local literary society who called themselves the Fugitives and included Ransom, Davidson, and Allen Tate, who roomed with Warren.

After graduation from Vanderbilt, Warren earned a master's degree at the University of California at Berkeley in 1927. The next year, he was doing postgraduate work at Yale University, and the following year he attended Oxford University as a Rhodes scholar. In 1929 he published his first book, the biography *John Brown: The Making of a Martyr*, written with a distinctly southern perception of that fanatic abolitionist.

At Louisiana State University (LSU), where Warren taught from 1934 to 1936, he absorbed the legends and the spectacle of Huey Long, who provided the germ of the character Willie Stark in *All the King's Men*. This novel displays themes that appear throughout the Warren canon: the quest for identity and personal responsibility, the relation of son to father, the conflict between idealism and practical circumstances, the use of the past and the problems inherent in the writing of history. In 1947 *All the King's Men* won for Warren his first Pulitzer Prize, and two years later the novel was made into an Academy Award-winning film.

At LSU Warren also made the acquaintance of Cleanth Brooks, which resulted in one of the most fruitful partnerships in American letters. They cooperated at first to create and edit an excellent literary magazine, *The Southern Review*, but went on to produce literature textbooks such as *Understanding Poetry*, *Understanding Fiction*, and *Modern Rhetoric*, which did more than anything else to propagate the methods of the New Criticism.

In 1930, Warren married Emma Brescia, whom he divorced in 1951, shortly after accepting a position at Yale University. In 1952, he married the writer Eleanor Clark. They had two children: Rosanna and Gabriel. Warren left Yale in 1956 but returned to the faculty from 1961 to 1973 and as professor emeritus from 1973 to 1989. He continued his distinguished career as a teacher, poet, novelist, critic, editor, and lecturer virtually to the end of his long life.

In February, 1986, the Librarian of Congress named him the first official poet laureate of the United States. Warren died at his summer home in West Wardsboro on September 15, 1989.

Katherine Snipes
Jonathan S. Cullick

Bibliography

Blotner, Joseph. *Robert Penn Warren: A Biography*. New York: Random House, 1997. Blotner's was the first biography published following Warren's death in 1989. Blotner began his work while Warren was still alive and had the good fortune to have the cooperation not only of his subject but also of the larger Warren family. Blotner's book is straightforward and chronological; it makes a good beginning.

Bohner, Charles. *Robert Penn Warren*. Rev. ed. Boston: Twayne, 1981. An excellent all-purpose introduction, divided into thematic sections with subdivisions. Provides a chronology, notes, and an index. Also includes a bibliography in which secondary sources receive brief summaries regarding their merit and suitability.

Burt, John. *Robert Penn Warren and American Idealism*. New Haven, Conn.: Yale University Press, 1988. Burt describes his work as traversing "regions" of Warren's work: the elegies, the narrative poems, and three major novels—*Night Rider, All the King's Men*, and *World Enough and Time*. What unifies these works, Burt maintains, is Warren's ambivalence about experience, an ambivalence endemic to American idealism.

Clark, William Bedford, ed. *Critical Essays on Robert Penn Warren*. Boston: G. K. Hall, 1981. The selection covers both the poetry and prose and includes twenty contemporary reviews, an interview, and eight in-depth articles. Among the authors are Malcolm Cowley, John Crowe Ransom, and Harold Bloom.

Grimshaw, James A. *Understanding Robert Penn Warren*. Columbia: University of South Carolina Press, 2001. An introduction to the novels, poems, and plays. Includes an introductory biography, bibliographical references, and an index.

Justus, James H. *The Achievement of Robert Penn Warren*. Baton Rouge: Louisiana State University Press, 1981. A cogent study of Warren's work from the premise that the latter largely derives from the cultural circumstances of time and place in his career. The book is divided into four sections dealing, respectively, with Warren's themes, poetry, nonfiction prose, and novels.

Madden, David, ed. *The Legacy of Robert Penn Warren*. Baton Rouge: Louisiana State University Press, 2000. A collection of critical and biographical essays on Warren's life and work. Includes bibliographical references and an index.

Ruppersburg, Hugh. *Robert Penn Warren and the American Imagination*. Athens: University of Georgia Press, 1990. Ruppersburg considers the Warren opus an attempt to define a national identity. Subscribing to Warren's notion that he was not a historical writer, Ruppersburg places Warren in a contemporary context, emphasizing such modern American concerns as civil rights and nuclear warfare.

Szczesiul, Anthony. *Racial Politics and Robert Penn Warren's Poetry*. Gainesville: University Press of Florida, 2002. Addresses Warren's poetry in terms of his political views, especially those relating to race and civil rights. Includes bibliographical references and index.

Watkins, Floyd C., John T. Hiers, and Mary Louise Weaks, eds. *Talking with Robert Penn Warren*. Athens: University of Georgia Press, 1990. A collection of twenty-four interviews, extending from 1953 to 1985, in which Warren talks about his work with characteristic honesty, openness, folksiness, and wit from the joint perspective of writer, interpreter, and critic. The group of interviewers includes Ralph Ellison, Marshall Walker, Bill Moyers, Edwin Harold Newman, Floyd C. Watkins, and Eleanor Clark.

Booker T. Washington

American philosopher and memoirist

Born: Near Hale's Ford, Virginia; April 5, 1856
Died: Tuskegee, Alabama; November 14, 1915
Identity: African American

NONFICTION: *The Future of the American Negro*, 1899; *The Story of My Life and Work*, 1900; *Up from Slavery*, 1901; *Working with the Hands*, 1904; *The Story of the Negro*, 1909; *My Larger Education*, 1911.

Recognized during the early years of the twentieth century as the principal, though controversial, spokesman for African Americans, Booker Taliaferro Washington also won fame for his well-known rags to riches autobiography, *Up from Slavery*. He was born a slave of a white father and a black mother on a Virginia plantation, and the Civil War occurred early in his life. At age nine, moving with his mother and stepfather to West Virginia, where his stepfather went to work in the salt mines, Washington developed a hunger for education. Mrs. Lewis Ruffner, the wife of the mine's owner, encouraged and helped him enter the Hampton Institute of Virginia, an industrial school for African Americans and American Indians.

Washington graduated from Hampton in 1875, but his early career as a teacher ended abruptly when he was appointed in 1881 to organize and head the Tuskegee Normal School and Industrial Institute in Alabama. He spent the bulk of the rest of his life building Tuskegee through his philosophy of the dignity of hard work and thrift. He envisioned that African Americans would succeed in the postwar South through practical education and economic development. A master administrator and communicator, Washington attracted financial support, and within twenty years Tuskegee could boast a faculty of 125 and a student body that numbered more than a thousand.

Washington became a famous and controversial figure in 1895, when he delivered a much-reported speech at the Atlanta Exposition, sometimes referred to as the "Atlanta compromise" address. In his speech he extolled the value of African Americans and whites working together in the common cause of economically building the South. Perhaps the most famous quotation from the speech suggests that "we can be as separate as the fingers yet one as the hand in all things essential to mutual progress." The speech, like all his writing, is full of anecdote and employs a visionary oratorical style; it brought his audience to its feet.

While many lauded him as a black Moses, some African Americans, most notably W. E. B. Du Bois, believed that he demanded too little and gave too much in his program of accommodating whites and their view of their own superiority. Washington believed that African Americans should forgo political activism and concentrate on becoming useful, financially independent citizens. Du Bois, on the other hand, found such a "gospel of work and money" a limiting vision and a betrayal of African Americans. Though Washington played the accommodationist in public, however, the posthumous publication of his papers reveals that behind the scenes he was politically active, secretly financing court challenges of jury bans on blacks, segregationalist transportation laws, and peonage. H. G. Wells insightfully saw in Washington's public accommodationism a "strategic cunning" covering his genuine indignation at racial injustice, a position Washington increasingly gave voice to in his later years.

Washington's newfound fame led to the opportunity to have his ideas read by a prepared and interested public. His first book, *The Future of the American Negro*, is a collection of essays and speeches in which he develops his philosophy concerning race problems, their origins, and how to move positively into the future. He argues for the centrality of industrial education in the progress of African Americans in the South and in the movement toward racial harmony. He views higher education as impractical to the needs of most blacks, scorning the image of a youth studying French grammar in a one-room cabin. Publicly, he promoted the idea that African Americans should earn their civil rights through education and self-reliance.

The fame initiated by his speech in Atlanta enabled him to succeed Frederick Douglass as the most visible spokesman for African Americans and led to his publication of an autobiography. His first attempt, with a ghost writer, was called *The Story of My Life and Work*; it was brief, poorly written, and padded with speeches. With Max Bennett Thrasher he tried again, this time doing much more of the writing himself, practicing a plain eloquence that has made *Up from Slavery*, the story of his rise from plantation to power, an inspiration to millions. A minor classic that is often compared with Benjamin Franklin's autobiography, it describes a black American dream that goes literally from the rags of slavery to the riches of Tuskegee's considerable assets. Like Washington himself, however, the book is controversial. Though called the last slave narrative published in the United States, which tells a story with some similarities to Douglass's autobiographies, it has also been called a tool with which Washington solicited political and financial support for the "Tuskegee machine." Two subsequent autobiographies, *Working with the Hands* and *My Larger Education*, are sequels to *Up from Slavery* focusing on his work at Tuskegee and his fund-raising and diplomatic activities. Like the second half of Franklin's autobiography, they lack the energy and drama of the quest for success, merely filling in the picture of Washington's public role.

Raised in the age of Horatio Alger and laissez-faire, during a period in which the Supreme Court was upholding segregation laws and disfranchisement, Washington, perhaps inevitably, believed that tact over political activism was the best path to progress for African Americans. He was a complex man whose life story continues to generate controversy, inspiring both resentment and respect.

Dennis R. Perry

Bibliography

Baker, Houston A. *Turning South Again: Re-thinking Modernism/Re-reading Booker T.* Durham, N.C.: Duke University Press, 2001. Analysis of Washington's philosophy and writings.

Harlan, Louis R. *Booker T. Washington: The Making of a Black Leader.* New York: Oxford University Press, 1972. Harshly critical of Washington as the white leaders' candidate for black leadership.

McElroy, Frederick L. "Booker T. Washington as Literary Trickster." *Southern Folklore* 49, no. 2 (1992). Analyzes how Washington revises Frederick Douglass's rhetoric.

Mansfield, Stephen. *Then Darkness Fled: The Liberating Wisdom of Booker T. Washington*. Nashville: Cumberland House, 1999. A sympathetic analysis and biography.

Munslow, Alan. *Discourse and Culture*. New York: Routledge, 1992. The issues dividing W. E. B. Du Bois and Washington are clearly and evenhandedly explained.

Verney, Kevern. *The Art of the Possible: Booker T. Washington and Black Leadership in the United States, 1881-1925.* New York: Routledge, 2001. Presents all sides of the debate begun by W. E. B. Du Bois.

Jakob Wassermann

German novelist

Born: Fürth, Bavaria (now in Germany); March 10, 1873
Died: Alt-Aussee, Austria; January 1, 1934
Identity: Jewish

LONG FICTION: *Die Juden von Zirndorf*, 1897 (*The Jews of Zirndorf*, 1918; also known as *Dark Pilgrimage*, 1933); *Die Geschichte der jungen Renate Fuchs*, 1900; *Alexander in Babylon*, 1905 (English translation, 1949); *Caspar Hauser: Oder, Die Trägheit des Herzens*, 1908 (*Caspar Hauser*, 1928); *Das Gänsemännchen*, 1915 (*The Goose Man*, 1922); *Christian Wahnschaffe*, 1919 (*The World's Illusion*, 1920); *Oberlins drei Stufen und Sturreganz*, 1922 (*Oberlin's Three Stages*, 1925); *Ulrike Woytich*, 1923 (*Gold*, 1924); *Faber: Oder, Die verlorenen Jahre*, 1924 (*Faber: Or, The Lost Years*, 1925; with *Der unbekannte Gast*, below, the previous 3 titles make up the series *Der Wendekreis*); *Laudin und die Seinen*, 1925 (*Wedlock*, 1926); *Der Aufruhr um den Junker Ernst*, 1926 (*The Triumph of Youth*, 1927); *Der Fall Maurizius*, 1928 (*The Maurizius Case*, 1929); *Etzel Andergast*, 1931 (*Doctor Kerkhoven*, 1932); *Joseph Kerkhovens dritte Existenz*, 1934 (*Kerkhoven's Third Existence*, 1934); *Olivia*, 1937.

SHORT FICTION: *Der unbekannte Gast*, 1920 (volume 1 of series *Der Wendekreis*); *World's Ends: Five Stories*, 1927 (translates all but the title story of *Der unbekannte Gast*).

DRAMA: *Die ungleichen Schalen*, pb. 1912.

NONFICTION: *Deutsche Charaktere und Begebenheiten*, 1915-1924 (biography; 2 volumes); *Mein Weg als Deutscher und Jude*, 1921 (autobiography; *My Life as German and Jew*, 1933); *Lebensdienst*, 1928 (autobiography); *Christoph Columbus: Der Don Quichote des Ozeans*, 1929 (*Christopher Columbus: Don Quixote of the Seas*, 1930); *Hofmannsthal der Freund*, 1930; *Bula Matari, Das Leben Stanleys*, 1932 (*Bula Matari: Stanley, Conqueror of a Continent*, 1933); *Selbstbetrachtungen*, 1933 (autobiography); *Briefe an seine Braut und Gattin Julie, 1900-1929*, 1940 (first published as *The Letters of Jakob Wassermann to Frau Julie Wassermann*, 1935).

Perhaps no writer of modern times, with the possible exception of Francis Thompson, has suffered greater indignities than Jakob Wassermann (VAHS-sehr-mahn) in the struggle to vindicate himself as an artist. He was born of Jewish parentage to his merchant father, a man with a narrow, conservative outlook who allowed his second wife, the boy's unsympathetic stepmother, to regulate the life of the household. In his childhood Wassermann's literary talents were ruthlessly curbed on the principle that if he should become a writer he would be poor and therefore worthless. In 1889 he was sent to Vienna, where his uncle was the proprietor of a factory; unable to bear the routine of business, Wassermann made a temporary escape to Munich with the plan of studying to enter the university. Lacking money, he returned home and was sent to Vienna again, this time to learn the export trade. Less than a year later, he left his new job. Conscripted into the army for the required year of military duty, he became the butt of anti-Semitic pranks and insults from comrades.

After completing his year of service he held a government job in Nuremberg until, inheriting a small sum of money, he ventured to Munich again and remained as long as his resources allowed. He briefly found employment in Freiburg but then, destitute again, he roamed as a beggar in the Black Forest before working his way with odd jobs to Zurich and then once more to Munich. A turn in his fortunes occurred, just in time to avert the collapse of his health, when in 1895 he became engaged as secretary to the writer Ernst von Wolzogen. Shortly thereafter, he was hired as an editorial assistant by the manager of the satirical Munich periodical *Simplicissimus*, which was then in its first year of publication. Some of his poems and tales appeared in that journal in 1896, and one story gained him a prize of three hundred marks. Between 1897 and 1900 his novels *Dark Pilgrimage* and *Die Geschichte der jungen Renate Fuchs* (the story of young Renate Fuchs) were published to positive reviews, inaugurating the succession of major novels that established his literary reputation. In 1898 he returned to Austria, to live there the rest of his life, and in 1901 he married Julie Speyer. After separating from her in 1919 and obtaining a divorce several years later, he married Marta Karlweis. On New Year's Day, 1934, he died at Alt-Aussee, where he had resided for ten years.

Wassermann was strongly admired by Arthur Schnitzler, Hugo von Hofmannsthal, and Thomas Mann. His work is impressive for the scope of its themes. He was especially interested in the problems of ethical conduct and was devoted to the ideals of democratic liberalism.

Bibliography

Blankenagel, J. C. "Jakob Wassermann's Views on America." *German Quarterly* 27 (1954). A study in English.

Garrin, Stephen H. *The Concept of Justice in Jakob Wassermann's Trilogy*. Las Vegas: P. Lang, 1979. A critical study.

Regensteiner, Henry. "The Obsessive Personality in Jakob Wassermann's Novel *Der Fall Maurizius*." *Literature and Psychology* 14 (1964). A worthwhile article on *The Maurizius Case*.

Wassermann, Jakob. *My Life as German and Jew*. Translated by S. N. Brainin. New York: Coward-McCann, 1933. A primary source for biographical material.

Wendy Wasserstein

American playwright

Born: Brooklyn, New York; October 18, 1950
Identity: Jewish

DRAMA: *Any Woman Can't*, pr. 1973; *Happy Birthday, Montpelier Pizz-zazz*, pr. 1974; *When Dinah Shore Ruled the Earth*, pr. 1975 (with Christopher Durang); *Uncommon Women and Others*, pr. 1975 (one act), pr. 1977 (two acts); *Isn't It Romantic*, pr. 1981, revised pr. 1983; *Tender Offer*, pr. 1983 (one act); *The Man in a Case*, pr., pb. 1986 (one act; adaptation of Anton Chekhov's short story); *Miami*, pr. 1986 (musical); *The Heidi Chronicles*, pr., pb. 1988; *The Heidi Chronicles, and Other Plays*, pb. 1990; *The Sisters Rosensweig*, pr. 1992; *An American Daughter*, pr. 1997; *Waiting for Philip Glass*, pr., pb. 1998 (inspired by William Shakespeare's Sonnet 94); *The Festival of Regrets*, pr. 1999 (libretto); *Old Money*, pr. 2000; *Seven One-Act Plays*, pb. 2000.

NONFICTION: *Bachelor Girls*, 1990; *Shiksa Goddess: Or, How I Spent My Forties*, 2001.

CHILDREN'S/YOUNG ADULT LITERATURE: *Pamela's First Musical*, 1996.

SCREENPLAY: *The Object of My Affection*, 1998 (adaptation of Stephen McCauley's novel).

TELEPLAYS: *The Sorrows of Gin*, 1979 (from the story by John Cheever); *"Drive," She Said*, 1984; *The Heidi Chronicles*, 1995 (adaptation of her play); *An American Daughter*, 2000 (adaptation of her play).

Wendy Wasserstein (WAHS-ur-steen) was the youngest of the five children of Morris W. Wasserstein, a textile manufacturer, and Lola Scheifer Wasserstein, an amateur dancer. When she was thirteen her family moved to the East Side of Manhattan. There she attended the Calhoun School, where she wrote the school's musical revue for the mother/daughter luncheons. At Mount Holyoke College she studied to be a congressional intern. Her interest in theater was sparked by a summer playwriting course at Smith College and by her experiences at Amherst College, where she spent her junior year. Wasserstein earned her B.A. in history from Mount Holyoke, and thereafter her M.A. in creative writing from City University of New York. In 1973 her play "Any Woman Can't," a satire about a woman whose failure as a tap dancer leads her to marry an egotistical sexist, was produced Off-Broadway at Playwrights Horizons.

In 1973 Wasserstein entered the Yale Drama School, and one year later her play *Happy Birthday, Montpelier Pizz-zazz*, a cartoonish caricature of college life focusing on the male domination of women, was first produced. She collaborated with Christopher Durang on *When Dinah Shore Ruled the Earth*, a parody of beauty contests, which was produced at the Yale Cabaret Theater. These early plays about the suppression of women display an absurdist humor that depends on comic caricatures and a broad use of irony.

In her one-act thesis production at Yale, *Uncommon Women and Others*, her style moved closer to realism. She subsequently expanded the play into a full-length comedy that was eventually produced Off-Broadway by the Phoenix Theater on November 21, 1977. The drama opens on a reunion between five women and then flashes back six years to their senior year in college. The play abounds in contrasts, among them that between the women's present condition and their past expectations. After sipping sherry and folding their napkins at Mrs. Plumm's gatherings the women leave and discuss masturbation and the possibilities of male menstruation. Contrasts are also reflected in the women's inner turmoil. At times all of them are self-assured, but Wasserstein also shows one woman wishing she were more like the others. In *Uncommon Women and Others* Wasserstein brings to the drama a community of women who can share their emotions, express their insecurities, and play out their fantasies together as they face an uncertain future. Featuring Meryl Streep and Swoosie Kurtz, the play appeared on Public Broadcasting System (PBS) television in 1978, and critics began to hail Wasserstein as a promising new playwright.

After adapting John Cheever's short story "The Sorrows of Gin" for a television production on PBS, Wasserstein's next play, *Isn't It Romantic*, opened Off-Broadway in 1981. Many critics faulted the play for being loosely constructed and full of unnecessary jokes; after seven revisions, the work was reopened at Playwrights Horizons on December 15, 1983, and this time it won critical acclaim as well as achieving box-office success, running to 733 performances.

In 1983 Wasserstein's one-act play *Tender Offer*, which concerns a father who misses his daughter's dance recital, was produced by the Ensemble Studio Theatre. In 1986 her one-act adaptation of Anton Chekhov's short story "The Man in a Case" was produced by the Acting Company. She rocketed back into national prominence on December 11, 1988 with *The Heidi Chronicles*, the play that established her as a noted playwright as well as a popular success. Moving in time from 1965 to 1989, a middle-aged art professor relives the hope and disillusionment of the women's movement. *The Heidi Chronicles* is a dreamlike play filled with songs of a bygone era, recurring images, and relived moments, as the past is shown always encroaching into the present. Heidi is always aware not only of her personal history but also of the history of her generation caught in the sweep of social change, ever on the path of self-discovery. *The Heidi Chronicles* won a number of awards, including those of the New York Drama Critics Circle, the Outer Critics Circle, and the Drama Desk. The play also led to Wasserstein's becoming the third woman in a decade to win the Pulitzer Prize in drama and the first woman to win a Tony Award for an original drama.

Wasserstein's *The Sisters Rosensweig*, which opened at Lincoln Center on October 22, 1992, focuses on three Jewish-American sisters who examine their lives and explore their future options during a birthday weekend in London. Although the play is set against the backdrop of social and political upheaval, the larger social world is kept at a distance as the characters struggle with their identity, examine their life choices, and try to seize a moment of happiness. Both a critical and box office success, the play moved to Broadway's Ethel Barrymore Theatre and was nominated for a Tony Award.

Spanning more than twenty-five years of social change, Wasserstein's plays depict a generation reflecting on its lost ideals and examining new possibilities. Her plays focus on character rather than plot, and they are thought-provoking without being preachy, comedic without sacrificing sentiment, and theatrical without losing believability. Even though her output has not been extensive, with two critically acclaimed Broadway hits and a series of prestigious awards, Wasserstein has established herself as a significant American playwright.

Paul Rosefeldt

Bibliography

Ciociola, Gail. *Wendy Wasserstein: Dramatizing Women, Their Choices, and Their Boundaries*. Jefferson, N.C.: McFarland, 1998. Suggests that Wasserstein has not received sufficient critical attention because of her commercial success and takes Wasserstein's career as a starting point for a discussion of debates over the nature and scope of feminist aesthetics.

Frank, Glenda. "The Struggle to Affirm: The Image of Jewish-Americans on Stage." In *Staging Difference: Cultural Pluralism in American Theatre and Drama*, edited by Marc Maufort. New York: P. Lang, 1995. Discusses Wasserstein's Jewish American identity.

Hoban, Phoebe. "The Family Wasserstein." *New York*, January 4, 1993. Covers the influence of Wasserstein's family on her work.

Keyssar, Helene. "Drama and the Dialogic Imagination: *The Heidi Chronicles* and *Fefu and Her Friends*." In *Feminist Theater and Theory*, edited by Keyssar. New York: St. Martin's Press, 1997. Discusses Wasserstein's play along with a play by Maria Irena Fornes as "ostensibly" feminist works.

Rose, Phyllis Jane. "Dear Heidi—An Open Letter to Dr. Holland." *American Theater* 6 (October, 1989): 26. Written in letter form, this essay is a provocative, in-depth feminist critique of the images of women as presented in *The Heidi Chronicles*.

Rosen, Carol. "An Unconventional Life." *Theater Week*, November 8, 1992. Discusses *The Heidi Chronicles* and other works but concentrates on *The Sisters Rosensweig*.

Whitfield, Stephen. "Wendy Wasserstein and the Crisis of (Jewish) Identity." In *Daughters of Valor: Contemporary Jewish American Women Writers*, edited by Jay Halio and Ben Siegel, Newark: University of Delaware Press, 1997. Discusses the ways in which Jewish concerns are addressed in Wasserstein's writing.

Hugo Wast
(Gustavo Adolfo Martínez Zuviría)

Argentine novelist

Born: Córdoba, Argentina; October 23, 1883
Died: Buenos Aires, Argentina; March 28, 1962

LONG FICTION: *Alegre*, 1905; *Flor de durazno*, 1911 (*Peach Blossom*, 1929); *Casa de los cuevos*, 1916 (*The House of the Ravens*, 1924); *Valle negro*, 1918 (*Black Valley*, 1928); *La corbata celeste*, 1920; *Pata de zorra*, 1924; *Desierto de piedra*, 1925 (*Stone Desert*, 1928); *Myriam la conspiradora*, 1926; *Lucía Miranda*, 1929.
NONFICTION: *Año X*, 1960 (history).

Gustavo Adolfo Martínez Zuviría, known in literature as Hugo Wast (vahst), was born in Córdoba, Argentina, in 1883. While still a university student he wrote his first novel, *Alegre*, published in 1905. Then he went on to become a doctor of laws, in 1907, and joined the University of Santa Fe as professor of economics and sociology. Politics also attracted him, and he served several terms in the Argentine Congress. He was the longtime director of Argentina's National Library; later he served as minister of education.

After two juvenile attempts at novel writing, he published a serious novel about unmarried love, *Peach Blossom*, in 1911. Afraid that the critics of Buenos Aires would scorn any work of a provincial author, he signed it with an anagram of his first name, from which he made "Hugo Wast." The novel proved a success. During the next forty years, Wast published thirty-three books, many of them through a company that he organized. His books have appeared with Spanish and Chilean imprints in nearly three hundred editions, and nearly a million and a half copies have been sold. In addition, some seventy translations have appeared in eleven different languages.

Wast's best-selling novel, *The House of the Ravens*, won for him a prize from El Ateneo in 1915. For *Black Valley* he won the gold medal of the Spanish Academy, which later made him a corresponding member and enlarged its dictionary by the inclusion of words from his writing. *Stone Desert* was awarded the Grand National Prize of Argentine Literature for the year of its appearance.

Wast's novels can be divided into several groups. One series, for example, covers the history of his country from the earliest days of exploration and conquest, as told in *Lucía Miranda*, through the struggle for independence shown in *Myriam la conspiradora* (Myriam the conspirator), the period of the dictatorship dramatized in *La corbata celeste* (the blue necktie), and into the future in later novels.

Wast's training in economics and sociology is apparent in his problem novels set in rural regions and in his fictional treatment of urban problems in others. He had young readers in mind for several novels, especially the amusing 1924 work *Pata de zorra*, named for a fortune teller who tries to help a university student pass his examination in Roman law. It is for the number of readers whom Wast's writings have attracted, rather than for any particular influence he has exerted on his contemporaries, that he merits a place in Argentine literature.

Bibliography

Hespelt, E. H. "Hugo Wast, Argentine Novelist." *Hispania* 7 (1924).

Magaldi, Juan Bautista. *En torno a Hugo Wast*. Buenos Aires: Ediciones del Peregrino, 1995.

Moreno, Juan Carlos. *Genio y figura de Hugo Wast*. Buenos Aires: Editorial Universitaria de Buenos Aires, 1969.

Sedgwick, Ruth. "Hugo Wast, Argentina's Most Popular Novelist." *Hispanic American Historical Review* 9 (1929).

Frank Waters

American novelist

Born: Colorado Springs, Colorado; July 25, 1902
Died: Taos, New Mexico; June 3, 1995
Identity: American Indian (Cheyenne)

LONG FICTION: *Fever Pitch*, 1930 (also known as *The Lizard Woman*); *The Wild Earth's Nobility*, 1935; *Below Grass Roots*, 1937; *The Dust Within the Rock*, 1940; *People of the Valley*, 1941; *River Lady*, 1942 (with Houston Branch); *The Man Who Killed the Deer*, 1942; *The Yogi of Cockroach Court*, 1947; *Diamond Head*, 1948 (with Branch); *The Woman at Otowi Crossing*, 1966; *Pike's Peak: A Family Saga*, 1971 (completely rewritten, one-volume novel based on *The Wild Earth's Nobility*, *Below Grass Roots*, and *The Dust Within the Rock*); *Flight from Fiesta*, 1986.

NONFICTION: *Midas of the Rockies: The Story of Stratton and Cripple Creek*, 1937; *The Colorado*, 1946; *Masked Gods: Navaho and Pueblo Ceremonialism*, 1950; *The Earp Brothers of Tombstone: The Story of Mrs. Virgil Earp*, 1960; *Book of the Hopi*, 1963; *Leon Gaspard*, 1964, revised 1981; *Pumpkin Seed Point: Being Within the Hopi*, 1969; *To Possess the Land: A Biography of Arthur Rockford Manby*, 1973; *Mexico Mystique: The Coming Sixth World of Consciousness*, 1975; *Mountain Dialogues*, 1981; *Brave Are My People: Indian Heroes Not Forgotten*, 1993; *Of Time and Change: A Memoir*, 1998; *Pure Waters: Frank Waters and the Quest for the Cosmic*, 2002 (Barbara Waters, editor).

MISCELLANEOUS: *A Frank Waters Reader: A Southwestern Life in Writing*, 2000 (Thomas J. Lyon, editor).

First nominated for the Nobel Prize in Literature in 1985, Frank Waters holds a place in American literature as a significant western writer. His mother was from a prominent mining family, and his father was part Cheyenne. Waters early became conscious of this duality in his parentage, especially after experiencing a mystical moment at his family's gold mine on Pikes Peak. This transcendental glimpse of the underlying unity of the earth became a pivotal experience in his life and work, reinforcing his need to reconcile dualities and leading him to a lifelong study of Eastern philosophy; traditional Native American beliefs, myths, and rituals; and Jungian psychoanalysis. He studied engineering for three years at Colorado College before dropping out in 1924 to work, first in the oil fields of Wyoming and later as an engineer in California. Throughout his career, he expressed both the mystical and the rational sides of his experience in novels of poetic, intuitive insight and in essays, biographies, and anthropological studies of Native American cultures.

Two of Waters's initial attempts to give fictional form to his ideas, *The Yogi of Cockroach Court* (begun in 1927 but not published until 1947) and *Fever Pitch*, reflect his early problem of blending idea and form while exploring such themes as the yogic doctrines of Buddhism, the mystical experiences of wholeness and enlightenment, and the dynamic relationship of people to their environment. Driven by his own desire for reconciliation, Waters wrote an epic autobiographical trilogy that realistically tells the pioneer story of gold mining in the Rocky Mountains from 1870 to 1920: *The Wild Earth's Nobility*, *Below Grass Roots*, and *The Dust Within the Rock*. The first volume is based on his grandfather Dozier (renamed Rogier), who experiences moments of expanded consciousness and becomes obsessed to the point of madness by his effort to extract both gold and the hidden principle of existence from his Pikes Peak mine. The second book reflects Waters's emotionally divisive childhood, as Rogier's grandson, March Cable, is caught between his white mother and part-Native American father, who fight for emotional dominance over their son. In the third book, March comes to terms with his own duality, achieving a symbolic synthesis of the Anglo (granite) and Native American (adobe) elements within his psyche. Waters later published a more focused, one-volume redaction of the trilogy under the title *Pike's Peak*.

After moving to Taos, New Mexico, in 1940 to study Pueblo culture, Waters wrote *People of the Valley*, the ethnic history of New Mexico as objectified in the pastoral life of Maria, a Hispano-Indian. The novel is a convincing inside view of the central character, who attains the wisdom of a seer and total harmony with her environment. Maria's life as a wild, natural, free product of the land dramatizes the evolution of human consciousness. This work was followed by *The Man Who Killed the Deer*, Waters's own favorite and an outstanding novel about the Native American. Artfully blending idea and form, Waters authentically portrays the Native American vision as he narrates the dilemmas of Martiniano, the protagonist. Changed by his "white" schooling and estranged from both cultures, Martiniano becomes physically and spiritually wounded when he violates the laws of each culture by killing a deer out of season and neglecting the prerequisite killing ceremony. Gradually he returns to the regenerative tribal rituals, finding healing and wholeness through the transforming power of the Cosmic Mother.

In trying to resolve the dualities of his background, Waters never quite settled his personal life. He was married four times: to Lois Moseley (1944-1946), to Jane Somervell (1947-1955), to Rose Marie Woodell (1961-1965), and to Barbara A. Hayes (married 1979). He had no children.

The Woman at Otowi Crossing, based on the real-life story of Edith Warner, is one of Waters's most admired novels. The protagonist, Helen Chalmers, opens a tearoom on the Rio Grande during World War II, adjacent to the Atomic City of Los Alamos and across the river from San Ildefonso Pueblo. An ordinary white woman, Chalmers unexpectedly has a transcendental experience of the timeless, which drives her toward self-fulfillment. Her "knowing" is deepened by her participation in the Pueblo Kiva rituals, where she experiences the essential unifying force of creation. A friend of both the Native Americans and the atomic scientists, she becomes a bridge between two value systems at that point where the ancient and modern worlds touch. Although the novel is more explicitly didactic than Waters's earlier Native American novels, he convincingly portrays metaphysical themes in a compelling, realistic narrative, enmeshed in the ordinary and commonplace. In *Flight from Fiesta* Waters imaginatively dramatizes the purging of the old, atavistic hate between Native American and white through the enigmatic relationship between Elsie, a ten-year-old girl in rebellion against her materialistic parents, and Inocencio, an old Pueblo whose pottery she destroys in a tantrum. Set in Santa Fe during an annual fiesta in the 1950's, the novel portrays the adventures of the two characters who, mysteriously drawn to each other, flee from the fiesta, traveling through far-flung western towns, mountains, deserts, and Pueblo dwellings. Their reconciliation clearly has allegorical implications, but Waters makes the abstractions palatable by rendering them through sharp, vivid images and evocative landscapes that authenticate the narrative.

In his novels and in such nonfiction works as *Masked Gods*, *Book of the Hopi*, *Mexico Mystique*, and *Mountain Dialogues*, Waters's primary concern is the relationship of people to the land, the white and Native American races' conflicting relationship to the earth, and the evolution of human consciousness. Believing that humankind is one at the deepest level of consciousness, Waters speculates that, in the dialectical process of history, various cultures are, in their unique ways, traveling toward the realization of a great conscious unity. Waters's most important achievement is his artful, lifelike portrayal of these themes in his novels, of ideas that are thoroughly grounded in the actual circumstances of their southwestern regional settings. Waters died June 3, 1995, having been nominated several times for the Nobel Prize in Literature.

Clifford D. Edwards

Bibliography

Adams, Charles L., ed. *Studies in Frank Waters*. Las Vegas: Frank Waters Society, 1978-1990. Contains a number of excellent critical essays.

Blackburn, Alexander. *A Sunrise Brighter Still: The Visionary Novels of Frank Waters*. Athens: Ohio University Press, 1991. Chapters on each of Waters's novels, with an introduction that surveys the writer's purposes and his career and a conclusion arguing that Waters is a major American writer. Includes detailed notes and extensive bibliography.

Deloria, Vine, Jr., ed. *Frank Waters: Man and Mystic*. Athens: Ohio University Press, 1993. Memoirs of Waters and commentaries on his novels, emphasizing his prophetic style and sense of the sacred. Also provides criticism and interpretation of Waters's work, looking specifically at Waters's place in the history of mysticism in literature and Western literature.

Lyon, Thomas J. *Frank Waters*. New York: Twayne, 1973. Analyzes Waters's themes and artistic style. After sketching Waters's life, Lyon examines his nonfiction, showing him to be a writer of ideas with a sacred theory of the earth and Hopi mythic values. Lyon also discusses his minor works, the children's biography of Robert Gilruth, his book reviews, and his essays on writing. Contains a chronology, notes and references, a selected annotated bibliography, and an index.

Waters, Barbara. *Celebrating the Coyote: A Memoir.* Denver: Divina, 1999. A memoir by Waters's last wife. She discusses her life with him and her grief at losing him.

James D. Watson

American biologist and memoirist

Born: Chicago, Illinois; April 6, 1928

NONFICTION: *Molecular Biology of the Gene*, 1965, 4th revised edition 1987 (with others); *The Double Helix: A Personal Account of the Discovery of the Structure of DNA*, 1968 (memoir); *The DNA Story: A Documentary History of Gene Cloning*, 1981 (with John Tooze); *Molecular Biology of the Cell*, 1983 (with others); *Recombinant DNA: A Short Course*, 1983 (with Tooze and David Kurtz); *A Passion for DNA: Genes, Genomes, and Society*, 2000; *Genes, Girls, and Gamow*, 2001 (also known as *Genes, Girls, and Gamow: After the Double Helix*, 2002).

James Dewey Watson played a pivotal role in the discovery of the structure of the deoxyribonucleic acid (DNA) molecule. His parents were James Dewey Watson, a businessman, and Jean (Mitchell) Watson, a couple whose English and Scotch-Irish roots in the Midwest went back for several generations. They provided their son and their daughter Elizabeth with a comfortable childhood and an excellent education, beginning with nursery school at the University of Chicago. James was a child prodigy who developed the habit of reading widely, a practice that stood him in good stead when he was an ebullient member of the *Quiz Kids* radio show. He attended the Horace Mann Elementary School for eight years and the South Shore High School for two years. Aside from birdwatching, which he found a pleasant way to learn about ornithology, he had no special interest in science until he read Sinclair Lewis's *Arrowsmith* (1925), the story of a medical doctor's experiences with the joys and frustrations of research. This novel stimulated him to dream that he would make great scientific discoveries.

In the summer of 1943, when he was only fifteen years old, he received a tuition scholarship to the University of Chicago's four-year experimental college. As an undergraduate, he was principally interested in birds and avoided taking any advanced chemistry and physics courses, although he did outstanding work in the courses of his program, obtaining A's even from professors who rarely gave them. In 1947 he received a bachelor of science degree in zoology and a bachelor of philosophy degree. With a fellowship for graduate study in zoology at Indiana University, he went to Bloomington, where he came under the influence of two Nobel Prize-winning scientists, the geneticist Hermann J. Muller and the microbiologist Salvador E. Luria. Watson's thesis, under the direction of Luria, was a study of the effect of high-energy X rays on the multiplication of bacteria-destroying viruses (bacteriophages). After receiving his Ph.D. in 1950, Watson, who had come to share Luria's passion to understand the chemistry of viruses, was awarded a Merck Postdoctoral Fellowship by the National Research Council to continue his work in Copenhagen at the laboratories of the biochemist Herman Kalckar and the microbiologist Ole Maaløe. In the spring of 1951 Watson traveled with Kalckar to a symposium at Naples, where he met Maurice Wilkins, who was studying DNA crystals with X rays. This meeting stimulated Watson to change the direction of his research from bacteriophages to the structural chemistry of proteins and nucleic acids. Fortunately, Luria was able to arrange for Watson to work with John Kendrew, a molecular biologist at the Cavendish Laboratory of the University of Cambridge.

Watson arrived at Cambridge in the fall of 1951 and began to assist Kendrew with his X-ray studies of the protein myoglobin. Since the myoglobin molecule released the secrets of its structure only grudgingly, Watson grew bored with the hard work and modest results, and when he met Francis Crick, a British physicist who was working desultorily on a doctoral thesis involving the X-ray diffraction of proteins, he discovered that they shared an enthusiasm about the gene and the way it replicated. Watson and Crick decided to collaborate. It seemed to both of them that the gene's secrets could be attacked only when its structure was known, which meant deciphering the structure of DNA. With a fellowship from the National Foundation for Infantile Paralysis, Watson began his most productive period. The inspiration for the work of Watson and Crick was Linus Pauling, the American chemist who had deciphered the structures of numerous molecules, from the mineral molybdenite to the fibrous and globular proteins. Originally, Crick believed that solving DNA's structure was the job of Maurice Wilkins and Rosalind Franklin at King's College, London, but as time went on, Watson and Crick became impatient with the slow progress of the X-ray diffraction studies of the King's College group. The failure of Crick's colleagues at the Cavendish Laboratory to discover the structure of proteins before Pauling made a deep impression on Crick and Watson. Pauling had solved the structure by using his deep knowledge of structural chemistry to impose constraints on the molecular models he constructed. Watson and Crick believed that they could solve DNA's structure in the same way, and they raced to reach the solution before Pauling. Their experiments, with the help of findings by Franklin at King's College, resulted in their discovery of the double helix as the mechanism for the duplication of the DNA molecule. Watson and Crick described the double helix in their now-famous paper published in *Nature* on April 25, 1953.

Watson left the Cavendish Laboratory in the fall of 1953 to become a senior research fellow in biology at the California Institute of Technology. Watson had become interested in ribonucleic acid (RNA), and in Pasadena he was able to work with Alexander Rich, a medical doctor who had collaborated with Pauling, in X-ray diffraction studies of RNA. In 1955 Watson returned to the Cavendish Laboratory to work again with Crick. During their year together, they published several papers on the general principles of viral structure. In 1956 Watson joined the biology department at Harvard University, where he quickly passed through the academic ranks, becoming full professor in 1961, and where he established a research laboratory in which many future leaders in molecular biology were trained. Watson's major interest in the late 1950's and early 1960's was the role of RNA in protein synthesis, and one of the important conclusions that he and his coworkers helped to establish was that protein synthesis requires the ordered interaction of three types of RNA. In 1962 Watson shared the Nobel Prize in Physiology or Medicine with Crick and Wilkins for his part in the discovery of the three-dimensional structure of DNA. With the prestige bestowed by the Nobel Prize, he became an effective spokesperson for molecular biology. In 1965 he published a textbook, *Molecular Biology of the Gene*, which, through its successive editions, became the vade mecum for molecular biologists from college freshmen to practicing scientists.

The year 1968 marked several important events in Watson's life. On March 28, he married Elizabeth Lewis, with whom he would have two sons. Later in the year, he left Harvard to assume the directorship of the Cold Spring Harbor Laboratory on the North Shore of Long Island. According to some of his subordinates, he ran the laboratory as a benevolent despot, but he had a perceptive eye for important research problems and talented workers. In 1968 he also published *The Double Helix*, a controversial account of how the structure of DNA was discovered. Some scientists, including Crick and Wilkins, objected to Watson's unfavorable portrayal of them. Several reviewers thought that *The Double Helix* distorted the work of scientists into a race for prizes. But the book had its defenders, who praised Watson's honesty for depicting the confused motives and competitive personalities that comprise science as it is actually practiced. These reviewers believed that Watson's book was a much-needed amendment to the traditional picture of science as objective and impersonal.

During his early tenure at Cold Spring Harbor Laboratory, Watson initiated a large-scale study of how viruses can make cells cancerous, and in the process he established the laboratory as a key site for studying the molecular biology of animal cells. In the 1970's Watson was awarded the prestigious John J. Carty Gold Medal of the National Academy of Sciences and the Presidential Medal of Freedom. In 1975 he was one of the founders and participants of the Asilomar Conference on the possible dangers of recombinant DNA research. He had a jaundiced view of what was accomplished, noting that the participants pretended to act responsibly but were actually irresponsible in approving recommendations that did not adversely affect anyone's work. In 1988 Watson became involved in a project that had the potential to rival the size and scope of the Apollo moon-landing program: to map completely the genetic instructions for making a human being. Despite criticism, the National Institutes of Health began funding the Human Genome Project, and Watson became its director. He expressed great enthusiasm for the project's goals, though the project's success would involve troubling ethical questions. Watson saw a mapped human genome as having the potential to do much good, for example, in helping to understand and eventually eliminate many genetic diseases; however, he was driven to resign his directorship in 1992 after a federal probe into his financial interests in biotechnology companies. The next year, he was named chairman of the International Science Foundation.

Watson is most likely to be remembered among the wider public for *The Double Helix* because it frankly described for the first time the human circumstances behind a great scientific discovery. This memoir, which has been translated into many foreign languages and made into a major film, helped to shape a generation's view of science. Many scientists who were idealistic about their research regretted this influence. On the other hand, there is little doubt that Watson, who as a young man dreamed of scientific glory, achieved his dream.

Robert J. Paradowski
Trey Strecker

Bibliography

Edelson, Edward. *Francis Crick and James Watson and the Building Blocks of Life*. New York: Oxford University Press, 1998. A balanced presentation of the process of discovering the structure of DNA. Includes many sidebars and other aids to help the general reader understand the basics of molecular biology.

McElheny, Victor K. *Watson and DNA: Making a Scientific Revolution*. Cambridge, Mass.: Perseus, 2003. An unauthorized biography, focusing on Watson's scientific career and his influence in shaping twentieth century scientific thought.

The New York Times, February 25, 2003, pp. F1-F4. Five articles assess the importance of Watson and Crick's work, fifty years after their ground-breaking discovery of the structure of DNA. Includes a profile of the two, an analysis of their *Nature* paper, discussion of the repercussions of their work, including the Human Genome Project, and much else.

Strathern, Paul. *The Big Idea: Crick, Watson, and DNA*. New York: Anchor Books, 1999. Details the working partnership between Watson and Crick.

Evelyn Waugh

English novelist

Born: London, England; October 28, 1903
Died: Combe Florey, near Taunton, Somerset, England; April 10, 1966

LONG FICTION: *Decline and Fall*, 1928; *Vile Bodies*, 1930; *Black Mischief*, 1932; *A Handful of Dust*, 1934; *Scoop*, 1938; *Put Out More Flags*, 1942; *Brideshead Revisited*, 1945, 1959; *Scott-King's Modern Europe*, 1947; *The Loved One*, 1948; *Helena*, 1950; *Men at Arms*, 1952; *Love Among the Ruins: A Romance of the Near Future*, 1953; *Officers and Gentlemen*, 1955; *The Ordeal of Gilbert Pinfold*, 1957; *The End of the Battle*, 1961 (also known as *Unconditional Surrender*); *Basil Seal Rides Again: Or, The Rake's Regress*, 1963; *Sword of Honour*, 1965 (includes *Men at Arms*, *Officers and Gentlemen*, and *The End of the Battle*).

SHORT FICTION: *Mr. Loveday's Little Outing*, 1936; *Tactical Exercise*, 1954; *Charles Ryder's Schooldays, and Other Stories*, 1982; *The Complete Stories of Evelyn Waugh*, 1999.

NONFICTION: *Rossetti: His Life and Works*, 1928; *Labels*, 1930; *Remote People*, 1931; *Ninety-two Days*, 1934; *Edmund Campion: Jesuit and Martyr*, 1935; *Waugh in Abyssinia*, 1936; *Robbery Under the Law*, 1939; *The Holy Places*, 1952; *The Life of the Right Reverend Ronald Knox*, 1959; *Tourist in Africa*, 1960; *A Little Learning*, 1964; *The Diaries of Evelyn Waugh*, 1976 (Christopher Sykes, editor); *The Letters of Evelyn Waugh*, 1980 (Mark Amory, editor).

From the 1940's until his death in 1966, Evelyn Arthur St. John Waugh (waw) served as *bête noire* for left-wing critics on both sides of the Atlantic, a role he seemed to enjoy. He was born in London on October 28, 1903, the second son of Arthur Waugh, author and managing director of the publishing firm of Chapman and Hall, and Catherine Charlotte Raban. Evelyn's father and brother, Alec, had attended Sherborne School, but Alec had been expelled and shortly thereafter published *The Loom of Youth* (1917), a sensational exposé of public school life. Sherborne was thus out of the question for Evelyn, so he attended Lancing College before going up to Oxford University.

In 1925 Waugh left Hertford College, Oxford, with a modest third-class degree in history. As a young man whose father and elder brother were firmly established as professional writers and editors, he might have been thought a natural candidate for a literary career himself. Instead, he tried several fields first—including art, to which he was strongly attracted—before turning to letters. He served brief tenures as a schoolmaster at two obscure public schools. The experience was a profoundly unhappy one, which led to Waugh's attempted suicide by drowning, yet it also furnished the material for his first novel. In the autumn of 1927, Waugh met Evelyn Gardner. The two were soon married, and Waugh's literary career was launched with two books: *Rossetti*, a commercial failure published in 1928, and *Decline and Fall*, a critical and commercial success appearing the same year. *Decline and Fall* is a madcap satire in the style of Voltaire's *Candide* (1759), with an ironic depiction of Oxford, spurious and neurotic schoolmasters, and the penal system (which Waugh likens to an English public school).

In 1930 his *Vile Bodies* satirized the Bright Young People, the English equivalent of flappers in the United States. This novel, like his first, was wildly funny, and he had found his audience. In contrast, his personal life was in ruins—just as he achieved literary success, his wife of fewer than two years deserted him for another man. That he peppered his novels with faithless young wives for the rest of his career testifies to the depth of his bitterness. In 1929 he had begun traveling in the Mediterranean with his wife. After his divorce, he traveled incessantly for three years—in Abyssinia, Africa, and South America. The results of this compulsive peregrination were the travel books *Labels, Remote People*, and *Ninety-two Days* as well as considerable raw material for future novels.

Waugh's third novel, *Black Mischief*, appeared in 1932. It is certainly a satire of British colonialism, concluding with a scene in which the strains of a Gilbert and Sullivan composition go wafting out over the wacky African kingdom of Azania. A number of critics, though, purport to find the book racist and are extremely hostile to it. *Black Mischief* introduces Basil Seal, a lovable—and sometimes not so lovable—young rogue, who reappears in subsequent novels. Two years later, Waugh published his most pessimistic novel, *A Handful of Dust*. Its protagonist, Tony Last, like Paul Pennyfeather of *Decline and Fall* and Adam Fenwick-Symes of *Vile Bodies*, is an innocent wandering through a world of ravenous beasts. Tony's fate, unlike that of his predecessors, is tragic, while the novel's comedy is dark and its irony heavy. In 1935 Waugh was awarded the Hawthornden Prize for *Edmund Campion*, his study of Oxford's Jesuit martyr in the reign of Elizabeth I.

In 1937, after a long and anxious wait for a dispensation from Rome, Waugh was finally free to marry Laura Herbert. Two years earlier, he had covered the Abyssinian war as a newspaper correspondent. The result was *Waugh in Abyssinia*, a book whose punning title he did not choose. His last novel of the 1930's, *Scoop*, recounts the hilarious adventures of unscrupulous journalists as they cover an absurd war in the primitive African nation of Ishmaelia.

At the outbreak of World War II, Waugh secured an army commission, only after encountering considerable difficulty as a result of his age. In 1942 *Put Out More Flags* was published. *Brideshead Revisited*, written while its author was on leave from active service, was published in May, 1945. The novel was easily Waugh's most popular. It also, for the first time, tied Waugh inextricably to the flaws of his first-person narrator. Charles Ryder is perceived as smug, snobbish, superficially attracted to the aristocracy, and contemptuous of the common man. Finally, *Brideshead Revisited* was the first novel in which Waugh placed the practice of Catholicism at the very heart of the narrative. It sold widely, especially in the United States, but most critics attacked its structure, its sentiments, or both.

Waugh published several novellas during the postwar period. *Scott-King's Modern Europe* reflects Waugh's dismay at the postwar Europe that Great Britain had helped to fashion. *The Loved One*, which is on the surface a spoof of the American funeral industry, is, beyond that, a Juvenalian attack upon Anglo-American materialism in general. *Love Among the Ruins* is the bitter portrait of an arid and soulless Great Britain of the future. *Helena* is the only historical novel in the Waugh canon. *Helena*, fiction based upon scanty historical data, is the story of the mother of Constantine the Great, the first Christian emperor. She was canonized for her legendary discovery of the true cross. In the years following his return to civilian life, Waugh settled his family in the country, first at Piers Court, Stinchcombe, in Gloucestershire, later at Combe Florey in Somerset.

Four novels mark the final phase of Waugh's career. *The Ordeal of Gilbert Pinfold* is an autobiographical novel based upon a psychotic episode Waugh had recently experienced. His war trilogy, *Men at Arms*, *Officers and Gentlemen*, and *Unconditional Surrender*, roughly parallels the author's military service: the sometimes awkward training period of an aging subaltern, combat in the disastrous campaign on Crete, and service as liaison to partisans in Yugoslavia. Waugh's American publisher changed the title of the third novel to *The End of the Battle*, doubtless due to his awareness that the surrender cited was as much Great Britain's surrender to expediency as the Axis Powers' surrender to the Allies. The trilogy was subsequently revised slightly and published in one volume under the title *Sword of Honour*. Waugh's last work of fiction was *Basil Seal Rides Again*, a very slight novella treating Basil in middle age.

On Easter Sunday, April 10, 1966, shortly after returning home from Mass, Waugh fell dead from a massive heart attack. Even those critics who do not share his love for the past and his revulsion for the present have judged him one of the finest novelists and probably the foremost satirist of the twentieth century.

Patrick Adcock

Bibliography

Carens, James F., ed. *Critical Essays on Evelyn Waugh*. Boston: G. K. Hall, 1987. Contains twenty-six essays divided into three sections: general essays, essays on specific novels, and essays on Waugh's life and works. In his lengthy introduction, Carens provides a chronological overview of Waugh's literary work and a discussion of Waugh criticism. Includes index and bibliography.

Cook, William J., Jr. *Masks, Modes, and Morals: The Art of Evelyn Waugh*. Rutherford, N.J.: Fairleigh Dickinson University Press, 1971. Considers Waugh's novels squarely in the ironic mode, tracing Waugh's development from satiric denunciation to comic realism to romantic optimism to ironic realism. Cook provides lengthy analyses of the novels, which he suggests move from fantasy to reality and from satire to resignation. Includes index and bibliography.

Crabbe, Katharyn. *Evelyn Waugh*. New York: Continuum, 1988. Crabbe's book is most helpful: She provides a chronology of Waugh's life, a short biography, and five chapters of detailed criticism on Waugh's major novels. A concluding chapter on style is followed by a bibliography and an index.

Davis, Robert Murray. *Evelyn Waugh: Writer*. Norman, Okla.: Pilgrim Books, 1981. Drawing from previously unavailable manuscript materials, Davis examines Waugh's fiction in terms of his artistic technique, his extensive revisions, and his reworking of his novels. After an opening chapter on Waugh's biography of Dante Gabriel Rossetti, Davis focuses exclusively on the novels, *Brideshead Revisited* and *Sword of Honour* in particular. Includes index.

Hastings, Selina. *Evelyn Waugh: A Biography*. Boston: Houghton Mifflin, 1994. Hastings notes that hers is not an academic biography such as Stannard has written but a lively attempt to recapture Waugh's personality as it seemed to him and to his friends.

Lane, Calvin W. *Evelyn Waugh*. Boston: Twayne, 1981. Indispensable for Waugh scholars, Lane's relatively short volume contains a detailed chronology, a biography stressing the factors influencing his literary career, and lengthy treatments of Waugh's novels. Includes a bibliography and four interviews with Waugh.

Stannard, Martin. *Evelyn Waugh*. New York: W. W. Norton, 1987. A scholarly, well-documented account of Waugh's early literary career, Stannard's biography provides valuable publication details about the novels and uses Waugh's diaries and letters. Also contains many photographs and illustrations, a genealogical chart of Waugh's ancestry, a selected bibliography, and an excellent index.

_______. *Evelyn Waugh: No Abiding City, 1939-1966*. London: Dent, 1992. The second volume of a meticulous, scholarly biography. Includes notes, bibliography, illustrations, and two indexes: a general index and one of Waugh's work.

Mary Webb

English novelist

Born: Leighton-Under-the-Wrekin, Shropshire, England; March 25, 1881
Died: St. Leonards, Sussex, England; October 8, 1927

LONG FICTION: *The Golden Arrow*, 1916; *Gone to Earth*, 1917; *The House in Dormer Forest*, 1920; *Seven for a Secret*, 1922; *Precious Bane*, 1924; *Armour Wherein He Trusted*, 1929.
POETRY: *Fifty-one Poems*, 1946.
MISCELLANEOUS: *The Spring of Joy: A Little Book of Healing*, 1917 (poems and essays); *Poems and "The Spring of Joy,"* 1928; *Collected Works*, 1928-1929; *The Essential Mary Webb*, 1949.

Mary Gladys Meredith Webb was the daughter of an English-Welsh schoolmaster portrayed as a charming, sympathetic man in his daughter's first novel, *The Golden Arrow.* Webb was educated largely at home, although she spent two years at a private school in Southport, England. She began to write when she was a child, trying her hand at stories and poetry. In 1912 she married Henry Bertram Law Webb, also a schoolmaster. She suffered constant ill health and developed Graves' disease. Webb's five novels appeared from 1916 to 1924, with almost no recognition at the time of their publication from either readers or critics. Her only award was the Femina-Vie Heureuse Prize for 1924-1925, which she received for *Precious Bane*. An unfinished novel, *Armour Wherein He Trusted*, was published posthumously. When Webb died she was practically unknown, but in 1928 Prime Minister Stanley Baldwin praised her novels at a Royal Literary Fund dinner. After that recognition, her fame began to grow; her five novels were reprinted shortly thereafter, with introductions by Baldwin, G. K. Chesterton, and others.

Webb is evocative of many earlier writers, especially George Eliot and Elizabeth Gaskell. Her novels tend to concentrate on inner meanings that sometimes cause her books to stray away from the reality of most contemporary fiction. Webb's frequent didacticism, too, is contrary to the tastes of many modern readers. In *The Golden Arrow* are two pairs of lovers, one pair exemplary and the other foolish. The contrasts are always obvious, and the author frequently invades the narrative with intrusive commentary and moralizing. In *The House in Dormer Forest* there is a contrast again, this time between one family that is close to nature and another that is grasping and materialistic. Once more Webb is obvious in preferring the former to the latter and asking the reader to do the same. In this novel, as in her others, there are stock characters, such as the plain, despised woman of hidden sweetness who is saved from wasting a life by the timely arrival of a husband who is the epitome of masculinity and who has high, idealistic values. Other novels are *Gone to Earth*, *Seven for a Secret*, and *Precious Bane*, the latter being Webb's best-known novel. Her unfinished novel, *Armour Wherein He Trusted*, took the author out of the setting she had habitually used—contemporary Shropshire—into medieval times, for the work was to be a historical romance set against the background of the First Crusade. Also published was *The Spring of Joy*, a volume of essays and poetry written during her adult years. This collection has a preface by Walter de la Mare, in which he points out that her poetry and prose both contain certain poetic elements and that her prose rhythms derive from such specific seventeenth century authors as Sir Thomas Browne, author of *Religio Medici* (c. 1635) and *Urn Burial* (1658). Her *Gone to Earth* was filmed in 1948, and a popular television drama series of *Precious Bane* was produced in 1989. Although the popularity of her novels waned as a result of Stella Gibbons's spoof *Cold Comfort Farm* (1932), since then it has revived considerably.

David Barratt

Bibliography

Barale, Michele. *Daughters and Lovers: The Life and Writing of Mary Webb.* Middletown, Conn.: Wesleyan University Press, 1986. Good critical study.

Cavaliero, Glen. *The Rural Tradition in the English Novel, 1900-1939.* New York: Macmillan, 1977. Cavaliero makes some interesting observations regarding Webb as a provincial novelist.

Coles, Gladys. *Mary Webb.* Chester Springs, Pa.: Dufour Editions, 1990. Good biography; includes bibliography.

Dickens, Gordon. *Mary Webb: A Narrative Bibliography of Her Life and Works.* Shrewsbury, England: Shropshire Libraries, 1981. This thirty-three-page pamphlet makes an excellent starting place.

Paterson, John, and Evangeline Paterson. "Reality and Symbol in the Work of Mary Webb." In *Humanistic Geography and Literature*, edited by Douglas Pocock. Totowa, N.J.: Barnes & Noble Books, 1981. An interesting chapter.

Wrenn, Dorothy. *Goodbye to Morning: A Biographical Study of Mary Webb.* Shrewsbury, England: Wilding & Son, 1964. Well-researched biography.

Walter Prescott Webb

American historian

Born: Piney Woods, Panola County, Texas; April 3, 1888
Died: Austin, Texas; March 8, 1963

NONFICTION: *Growth of a Nation: The United States of America*, 1928 (history; with E. C. Barker and W. E. Dodd); *The Story of Our Nation: The United States of America*, 1929 (history; with Barker and Dodd); *The Great Plains*, 1931 (history); *Our Nation Grows Up*, 1933 (history; with Barker and Dodd); *The Texas Rangers*, 1935 (history); *The Building of Our Nation*, 1937 (history; with Barker and Henry Steele Commager); *Divided We Stand: Crisis of a Frontierless Democracy*, 1937; *The Great Frontier*, 1952 (history); *More Water for Texas*, 1954; *An Honest Preface, and Other Essays*, 1959; *Flat Top: A Story of Modern Ranching*, 1960.
EDITED TEXT: *The Handbook of Texas*, 1950.

Walter Prescott Webb grew up in an impoverished area of western Texas, and he had little schooling until 1905, when his family, having had a good crop, moved from their farm to the town of Kent, Texas. In 1906, after a year of school in Kent, the future historian was granted a certificate to teach in rural schools. After a year of teaching he returned for a higher certificate from the normal school, continuing as a public school teacher. He graduated from the University of Texas in 1915, with an A.B. degree, taking his M.A. in 1920 and his Ph.D. in 1932 from the same university. He also did graduate work at the Universities of Wisconsin and Chicago. He had become an instructor at the University of Texas in 1918; he spent his career there, rising to the rank of professor by 1933.

He also had special appointments: He became a consulting historian for the National Park Service in 1937, and he was granted a Guggenheim Fellowship in 1938; he was Harkness lecturer at the University of London in 1938 and Harmsworth Professor of American History at Oxford University in 1942-1943. His fellow historians elected him president of the American Historical Association in 1958, the same year in which he received the award of the American Council of Learned Societies. He was also honored as a writer: His *The Great Plains* earned for him the Lonbat Prize from Columbia University. He received an honorary M.A. from Oxford in 1942, and a D.Litt. from Southern Methodist University in 1951.

As a writer Webb wanted to make westerners see what lay all about them. His historical theses were not altogether popular, sometimes offending southerners, sometimes fellow historians, sometimes chambers of commerce, sometimes corporations. He believed that his greatest work, done during the late 1950's, was establishing a theory of European history (including the western hemisphere). Based upon the expansion of Europeans into America, Webb posited that the prosperity of all European civilization from 1500 to 1950 resulted from the American frontier. Webb's death came just before he turned seventy-five, the result of an automobile crash.

Bibliography

Barzun, Jackie, et al. *Essays on Walter Prescott Webb and the Teaching of History*. College Station: Texas A&M University Press, 1985.

Furman, Necah Stewart. *Walter Prescott Webb: His Life and Impact*. Albuquerque: University of New Mexico Press, 1976.

Jacobs, Wilbur R. *Turner, Bolton, and Webb: Three Historians of the American Frontier.* Seattle: University of Washington Press, 1979.

Kingston, Mike. *Walter Prescott Webb in Stephens County*. Austin, Tex.: Eakin Press, 1985.

Owens, William A. *Three Friends: Roy Bedichek, J. Frank Dobie, Walter Prescott Webb*. Garden City, N.Y.: Doubleday, 1969.

Reinhartz, Dennis, and Stephen E. Maizlish, eds. *Essays on Walter Prescott Webb and the Teaching of History*. College Station: Texas A&M University Press, 1985.

Rundell, Walter. *Walter Prescott Webb*. Austin, Tex.: Steck-Vaughn, 1971.

Shannon, Fred A. *An Appraisal of Walter Prescott Webb's "The Great Plains": A Study in Institutions and Environment*. 1939. Reprint. Westport, Conn.: Greenwood Press, 1979.

Max Weber

German sociologist

Born: Erfurt, Prussia (now in Germany); April 21, 1864
Died: Munich, Germany; June 14, 1920

NONFICTION: *Gesammelte Aufsätze zur Religionssoziologie*, 1920-1921 (3 volumes: volume 1, *Die protestantische Ethik und der Geist des Kapitalismus* [first pb. 1904-1905; *The Protestant Ethic and the Spirit of Capitalism*, 1930]; *Die protestantischen Sekten und der Geist des Kapitalismus* [*The Protestant Sects and the Spirit of Capitalism*, 1946]; *Die Wirtschaftsethik der Weltreligionen* [first pb. 1915; *The Social Psychology of the World Religions*, 1946, and *The Religion of China: Confusianism and Taoism*, 1951], 1920; volume 2, *Hinduismus und Buddhismus*, 1921 [*The Religion of India: The Sociology of Hinduism and Buddhism*, 1958]; volume 3, *Das antike Judentum*, 1921 [*Ancient Judaism*, 1952]); *Die rationalen und soziologischen Grundlagen der Musik*, 1921 (*The Rational and Social Foundations of Music*, 1958); *Die Stadt*, 1922 (*The City*, 1958); *Wirtschaft und Gesellschaft*, 1922 (translations include *The Theory of Social and Economic Organization*, 1947; *Max Weber on Law in Economy and Society*, 1954; *The Sociology of Religion*, 1963; and *Economy and Society: An Outline of Interpretive Sociology*, 1968); *Wirtschaftsgeschichte*, 1923 (*General Economic History*, 1927); *From Max Weber: Essays in Sociology*, 1946; *Max Weber on the Methodology of the Social Sciences*, 1949; *Sociological Writings*, 1994.

Max Weber (VAY-bur) was one of the founding fathers of modern social science. He was born in 1864 to a solidly established middle-class Prussian family. His father was a successful lawyer and parliamentarian, his mother a woman of culture and piety. Weber spent most of his first twenty-nine years in his parents' household, first in Erfurt, then in Berlin, where it became a meeting place for prominent politicians and celebrated scholars. In 1882 Weber began his studies in law at the University of Heidelberg, continuing at the universities of Berlin and Göttingen. He became a lecturer in law at the University of Berlin, where he was an enormously productive scholar. From 1894 to 1897, Weber taught economics at the universities of Freiburg and Heidelberg.

In 1893, at age twenty-nine, Weber married and moved out of his parents' home. In 1897 his father died, only a few weeks after he and Max had quarreled violently. Believing that he had contributed to his father's death, Weber suffered a nervous breakdown. Chronically overburdened by his work and now suffering from exhaustion, remorse, and depression, Weber was forced to suspend his academic work over the next four years. From 1901 on, Weber began to recover and gradually resumed his scholarly work. He accepted a position as an associate editor of the *Archiv für Sozialwissenschaft und Sozialpolitik* (archives for social science and social welfare), which he helped build into the leading social science journal in Germany. Later in the decade, he cofounded, with Ferdinand Tönnies and Georg Simmel, the German Sociological Society.

It was in *Archiv für Sozialwissenschaft und Sozialpolitik* in 1904 that Weber published probably the best known of all of his works, *The Protestant Ethic and the Spirit of Capitalism*, which traced the development of capitalism in the West to the contributions of Calvinism. Seeking to steer between a vulgar Marxian economic determinism and an equally one-sided idealistic determinism, he offered the monograph as a modest illustration of "how ideas become effective forces in history." His subsequent analyses of the religions of China, India, and ancient Judaism extended the argument by examining the absence of full-blown capitalism where religious and cultural norms were not supportive.

In 1919 Weber accepted a chair at the University of Munich, where he delivered two classic lectures, "Science as a Vocation" and "Politics as a Vocation." These lectures highlight the tensions in Weber's own life between scientific neutrality and political commitment. The years from 1918 to 1920 were a time of especially intense political activity for Weber: He helped found the German Democratic Party, served as adviser to the German delegation to the Versailles peace conference, helped draft the new Weimar Constitution, and unsuccessfully sought nomination to the newly constituted assembly. Throughout the war and postwar years, Weber labored on his never-to-be-completed magnum opus, *Economy and Society* (the incomplete three volumes were published posthumously). In June, 1920, Weber died of pneumonia; his last words were "The Truth is the Truth."

The unifying theme throughout Weber's diverse works is his preoccupation with the concept of "rationalization," the progressive shift from a world organized and legitimated on the bases of tradition, charisma, and sentiment, to one organized and legitimated on the basis of reason, logic, and efficiency. For Weber, this "disenchantment of the world," rooted in ancient Judaism, the Enlightenment, and accelerated in later times by industrialization and urbanization, has found its highest expressions in the economic system of capitalism and the organizational system of bureaucracy. Weber's analysis of bureaucracy still dominates theory and research on the subject.

His contributions to the methodology of the social sciences have also been highly influential. He acknowledged that, in order to establish causality, both natural and human sciences must demonstrate an association among factors. He argued that, whereas in the natural world interactions mean nothing to the insentient objects and organisms involved, human interaction is based on intention, motivation, and shared symbols. Hence, no scientific explanation of human interaction is adequate without reference to this level of meaning, a methodological procedure and imperative he called *Verstehen* (understanding).

Originally trained as a student of law, Weber's interests and scholarship ranged across jurisprudence, political science, economics, sociology, comparative religions, and the histories of several nations and civilizations, both ancient and modern. Although he is chiefly regarded as a sociologist, his influence on all these fields has been decisive and enduring.

Robert B. Pettit

Bibliography

Albrow, Martin. *Max Weber's Construction of Social Theory.* New York: St. Martin's Press, 1990. Excellent extended introduction to most of the elements of Weber's social theory, including his personal, historical, and intellectual background. Carefully organizes and clarifies the many complicated thematic strands of Weber's work.

Brubaker, Rogers. *The Limits of Rationality: An Essay on the Social and Moral Thought of Max Weber.* London: George Allen and Unwin, 1984. Careful and persuasive presentation of Weber's profoundly influential concept of "rationalization" in its various forms. Presents Weber as an ethicist and analyst of modernity and its crises.

Collins, Randall. *Max Weber: A Skeleton Key.* Beverly Hills, Calif.: Sage Publications, 1986. Superb brief introduction to Weber's life and thought as well as to some of the critical issues in Weber scholarship. Excellent starting point for further study.

Diggins, John Patrick. *Max Weber: Politics and the Spirit of Tragedy.* New York: Basic Books, 1996. A passionately and clearly written account of Weber's life as well as of his ethical and political perspective. Uses Weber's lifelong interest in the United States as a vehicle to explore his relevance to late twentieth century American thought and history.

Lehmann, Hartmut, and Guenther Roth, eds. *Weber's Protestant Ethic: Origins, Evidence, Contexts.* Cambridge, England: Cambridge University Press, 1995. Excellent collection of scholarly essays covering a wide range of late twentieth century assessments of Weber's famous Protestant ethic thesis.

Morrison, Ken. *Marx, Durkheim, Weber: Formations of Modern Social Thought.* Thousand Oaks, Calif.: Sage Publications, 1995. Provides an accessible and careful survey of Weber's key works in sociology and methodology. Includes a helpful glossary of Weberian terminology.

Ritzer, George. *The McDonaldization of Society.* Rev. ed. Thousand Oaks, Calif.: Pine Forge Press, 1996. A stimulating, troubling, and highly readable application of the Weberian concept of rationalization in an analysis of the "iron cages" of late twentieth century life.

Weber, Marianne. *Max Weber: A Biography.* Translated by Harry Zohn. New York: Wiley, 1975. An account of Weber's life and times, amounting to an intellectual portrait of Weber and post-World War I Germany by an intimate participant.

John Webster

English playwright

Born: London, England; c. 1577-1580
Died: London, England; before 1634

DRAMA: *Westward Ho!*, pr. 1604 (with Thomas Dekker); *Northward Ho!*, pr. 1605 (with Dekker); *The White Devil*, pr. c. 1609-1612; *The Duchess of Malfi*, pr. 1614; *The Devil's Law-Case*, pr. c. 1619-1622; *Monuments of Honour*, pr., pb. 1624; *A Cure for a Cuckold*, pr. c. 1624-1625 (with William Rowley); *Appius and Virginia*, pr. 1634 (?; with Thomas Heywood).

John Webster is known for being the author of *The White Devil* and *The Duchess of Malfi*. Few other facts about his life are known with any certainty. The scant amount of biographical information about this remarkable writer is an indication of the slight esteem Renaissance England granted to its great drama. It also points out how exceptional is the relatively large amount of information surviving about William Shakespeare.

Because Webster stated in the epistle to his *Monuments of Honour* that he was "born free" of the Guild of Merchant Tailors (or Merchant Taylors' Company), it is a reasonable assumption that the John Webster who appears in the guild records in 1571 and 1576 was his father. A John "Wobster" was a member of an Anglo-German acting company in 1596, and a John Webster was admitted to the Middle Temple in 1598. Possibly these references are to the dramatist. Thomas Heywood referred to the dramatist as being dead in 1635; the actual year of his death is unknown, however, and he may have died as much as ten years earlier.

The early part of Webster's dramatic career was spent as a collaborator in Philip Henslowe's prolific stable of playwrights; his chief collaborators were John Marston and Thomas Dekker. The first year any record of his theatrical activity exists is 1602. Webster is thought to have married a woman named Sara Peniall in March of 1605. Between 1610 and 1615 he reached his prime with the two celebrated tragedies that make his reputation. *The White Devil* and *The Duchess of Malfi* have a number of similarities. Both portray a world of macabre evil in which good characters are tormented by the ambitious, lustful, and vengeful. Both are set in sixteenth century Italy and involve murderous plotters. In both, church and state are corrupt. In these dark masterpieces Webster reveals himself as a powerful poet and an excellent man of the theater. Nothing in the plays he wrote either before or after these masterpieces indicates a comparable power.

Victoria Gaydosik

Bibliography

Aughterson, Kate. *Webster: The Tragedies.* New York: Palgrave, 2001. An analysis of the tragic works of Webster. Includes bibliography and index.

Cervo, Nathan A. "Webster's *The White Devil.*" *The Explicator* 57, no. 2 (Winter, 1999): 73-75. Cervo examines Webster's *The White Devil*, focusing on Brachiano's reference to Saint Anthony's fire.

Goldberg, Dena. *Between Worlds: A Study of the Plays of John Webster.* Waterloo, Ontario, Canada: Wilfrid Laurier University Press, 1987. Webster, born into the Elizabethan world, spoke frequently of its institutions and laws. That world was crumbling during the early years of Webster's maturity. According to Goldberg, the second world is that of revolutionary fervor in the 1640's; Webster, dead before 1640, is a prerevolutionary. He is an iconoclast, but he sees potential for a new order.

Oakes, Elizabeth. "The Duchess of Malfi as a Tragedy of Identity." *Studies in Philology* 96, no. 1 (Winter, 1999): 51-67. This essay examines the Duchess of Malfi's behavior as a widow, placing it within the context of the society in which she lived.

Ranald, Margaret Loftus. *John Webster.* Boston: Twayne, 1989. This brief, general, and quite readable overview of Webster's life and work contains basic information about dating, sources, and texts. Critical sections are distinguished by the absence of esoteric argument. Includes lengthy annotated bibliography.

Waage, Frederick O. *"The White Devil" Discover'd: Backgrounds and Foregrounds in Webster's Tragedy.* New York: Peter Lang, 1984. Extremely close readings of the play (the foreground) follow the action carefully. Knowledge of historical events and contemporary publications (the background) contribute to interpretation.

Wymer, Rowland. *Webster and Ford.* New York: St. Martin's Press, 1995. Wymer compares and contrasts the works of English dramatists John Ford and Webster. Includes bibliography and index.

Frank Wedekind

German playwright

Born: Hanover, Kingdom of Hanover (now in Germany); July 24, 1864
Died: Munich, Germany; March 9, 1918

DRAMA: *Der Schnellmaler*, pb. 1889; *Frühlings Erwachen*, pb. 1891 (*Spring's Awakening*, 1960); *Der Erdgeist*, pb. 1895 (*Earth Spirit*, 1914); *Der Kammersänger*, pr., pb. 1899 (*The Tenor*, 1946); *Die junge Welt*, pb. 1900; *Der Marquis von Keith*, pr., pb. 1901 (*The Marquis of Keith*, 1955); *Die Büchse der Pandora*, pr., pb. 1904 (*Pandora's Box*, 1918); *Hidalla: Oder, Karl Hetmann der Zwergriese*, pb. 1904; *Tod und Teufel*, pb. 1905 (revision of his play *Totentanz*; *Death and Devil*, 1952); *Musik*, pr., pb. 1908; *Die Zensur*, pb. 1908; *Oaha*, pb. 1908; *König Nicolo: Oder, So ist das Leben*, pb. 1911 (*Such Is Life*, 1929); *Schloss Wetterstein*, pb. 1912 (*Wetterstein Castle*, 1952); *Franziska*, pr., pb. 1912, revised pr. 1914 (verse play; English translation, 1998); *Simson*, pr., pb. 1914; *Bismarck*, pb. 1916; *Herakles*, pb. 1917, pr. 1919; *Die Kaiserin von Neufundland*, pb. 1924 (ballet scenario); *Five Tragedies of Sex*, pb. 1952; *The Lulu Plays*, pb. 1967.

LONG FICTION: *Mine-Haha: Oder, Über die körperliche Erziehung der jungen Mädchen*, 1903.

SHORT FICTION: *Feuerwerk*, 1906.

POETRY: *Die vier Jahreszeiten*, 1905; *Lautenlieder*, 1920; *Ich habe meine Tante geschlachtet*, 1967.

NONFICTION: *Schauspielkunst*, 1910.

MISCELLANEOUS: *Die Fürstin Russalka*, 1897; *Prosa, Dramen, Verse*, 1960-1964 (2 volumes).

Benjamin Franklin Wedekind (VAY-duh-kihnt), one of the most controversial of *fin de siècle* German writers, was the son of a world-traveling doctor who, at sixty-four, had married an actress less than half his age. Born in Hanover, Kingdom of Hanover, on July 24, 1864, Wedekind graduated from Lenzburg in Switzerland in 1883. Later he worked as a journalist and as traveling secretary for Herzog's Circus. While he was with the circus he became convinced that humans are essentially animals who are healthiest when they live entirely by their instincts, uncorrupted by bourgeois education.

After a brief period as secretary to a Parisian art dealer, Wedekind went to Munich and wrote his first play, *Der Schnellmaler* (the world of youth), the story of a girls' boarding school. It was followed by *Spring's Awakening*, which presents an adolescent youth tormented by sexual drives and ruthlessly curbed by the iron discipline of society—an attempt on Wedekind's part to out-

Nietzsche Friedrich Nietzsche. He also attacked Henrik Ibsen and the realists of the preceding generation for being too genteel and middle-class. As writer, actor, and director of the Munich Theater, he believed that the stage needed "beasts of prey," and he proceeded to supply them.

Lulu, the heroine of *Earth Spirit* and *Pandora's Box*, is a Dionysiac character who becomes sex incarnate and is finally cut down by Jack the Ripper. The hero of *The Marquis of Keith* conceives of love as a sexual orgy, drives his wife to suicide, tries to build a bawdy house with stolen money but fails, and is abandoned by his mistress. These plays are not simply acted; they are mimed, danced, and screamed, as if Wedekind had Caliban within every character. Toward the end of his career, however, Wedekind reformed, thanked the judges who had condemned *Pandora's Box*, and expressed a reverence for the church.

Wedekind's plays bridge the naturalistic realism of Ibsen and August Strindberg to German expressionism. His characters tend to be caricatures depicting specific ideas and personality types. The confrontations between social outcasts and society, with actors speaking at one another instead of conversing, directly influenced Bertold Brecht's development of epic theater. Wedekind's plays were often banned by German censors and were later among those condemned by Adolf Hitler. The postwar German theater revived Wedekind's plays as curiosities of emotional and imaginative excess; later, the sexual revolution of the late twentieth century resulted in productions based on their sexual politics.

Gerald S. Argetsinger

Bibliography

Boa, Elizabeth. *The Sexual Circus: Wedekind's Theatre of Subversion*. New York: B. Blackwell, 1987. An analysis of Wedekind's works that focuses on his portrayal of sexuality. Bibliography and index.

Chick, Edson. *Dances of Death: Wedekind, Brecht, Dürrenmatt, and the Satiric Tradition*. Columbia, S.C.: Camden House, 1984. Chick examines the use of satire by the German dramatists Wedekind, Bertolt Brecht, and Friedrich Dürrenmatt. Bibliography and index.

Izenberg, Gerald N. *Modernism and Masculinity: Mann, Wedekind, Kandinsky Through World War I*. Chicago: University of Chicago Press, 2000. Izenberg looks at modernism and masculinity in the pre-World War I works of Wedekind, Thomas Mann, and Wassilly Kandinsky. Bibliography and index.

Jones, Robert A., and Leroy R. Shaw, comps. *Frank Wedekind: A Bibliographic Handbook*. 2 vols. New Providence, R.I.: K. G. Saur, 1996. A bilingual bibliography on the playwright. Includes indexes.

Lewis, Ward B. *The Ironic Dissident: Frank Wedekind in the View of His Critics*. Columbia, S.C.: Camden House, 1997. Lewis analyses Wedekind's dramatic works, focusing on the comments of critics over the years. Bibliography and index.

Skrine, Peter N. *Hauptmann, Wedekind, and Schnitzler*. New York: St. Martin's Press, 1989. Skrine provides criticism and interpretation of the modern German dramatists Wedekind, Gerhart Hauptmann, and Arthur Schnitzler. Bibliography and index.

Jerome Weidman

American novelist, short-story writer, and playwright

Born: New York, New York; April 4, 1913
Died: New York, New York; October 6, 1998
Identity: Jewish

LONG FICTION: *I Can Get It for You Wholesale*, 1937; *What's in It for Me?*, 1938; *I'll Never Go There Anymore*, 1941; *The Lights Around the Shore*, 1943; *Too Early to Tell*, 1946; *The Price Is Right*, 1949; *The Hand of the Hunter*, 1951; *Give Me Your Love*, 1952; *The Third Angel*, 1953; *Your Daughter Iris*, 1955; *The Enemy Camp*, 1958; *Before You Go*, 1960; *The Sound of Bow Bells*, 1962; *Word of Mouth*, 1964; *Other People's Money*, 1967; *The Center of the Action*, 1969; *Fourth Street East: A Novel of How It Was*, 1970; *Last Respects*, 1972; *Tiffany Street*, 1974; *The Temple*, 1975; *A Family Fortune*; 1978; *Counselors-at-Law*, 1980.

SHORT FICTION: *The Horse That Could Whistle "Dixie," and Other Stories*, 1939; *The Captain's Tiger*, 1947; *A Dime a Throw*, 1957; *My Father Sits in the Dark, and Other Selected Stories*, 1961; *Where the Sun Never Sets, and Other Stories*, 1964; *The Death of Dickie Draper, and Nine Other Stories*, 1965.

DRAMA: *Fiorello!*, pr. 1959 (libretto with George Abbott; music and lyrics by Sheldon Harnick and Jerry Bock); *Tenderloin*, pr. 1960 (libretto with Abbott; music and lyrics by Harnick and Bock); *I Can Get It for You Wholesale*, pr. 1962 (libretto, music by Harold Rome; adaptation of his novel); *Cool Off!*, pr. 1964 (libretto; music by Howard Blackman); *Pousse-Café*, pr. 1966 (libretto; music by Duke Ellington); *Ivory Tower*, pr. 1968 (with James Yaffe); *The Mother Lover*, pr. 1969; *Asterisk! A Comedy of Terrors*, pr., pb. 1969.

SCREENPLAYS: *The Damned Don't Cry*, 1950 (with Harold Medford); *The Eddie Cantor Story*, 1953 (with Ted Sherdeman and Sidney Skolsky); *Slander*, 1957.

TELEPLAY: *The Reporter*, 1964 (series).

NONFICTION: *Letter of Credit*, 1940 (travel); *Back Talk*, 1963 (essays); *Praying for Rain*, 1986 (memoir).
EDITED TEXTS: *A Somerset Maugham Sampler*, 1943; *Traveler's Cheque*, 1954; *The First College Bowl Question Book*, 1961 (with others).

Of Jewish background, Jerome Weidman (WID-muhn) was the son of Joseph and Annie (Falkovitz) Weidman. His father was an Austrian immigrant; his mother was from Hungary. Because his parents knew hardly any English, Weidman did not speak that language fluently until he was five years old. He married Elizabeth Ann Payne, a writer, in 1943. Among their children are Jeffrey and John Whitney.

Weidman attended City College (now City College of the City University of New York) from 1931 to 1933, Washington Square College from 1933 to 1934, and New York University Law School from 1934 to 1937. His military and wartime service included work in the U.S. Office of War Information from 1942 to 1945. Before becoming a full-time writer, he worked at various jobs such as soda jerk, newsboy, stenographer, mail clerk, and accountant. He was a member of the Authors Guild and the Dramatists Guild of the Authors League of America, of which he was president from 1969 to 1974, and the Writers Guild of America, East.

When Weidman graduated from high school, the Great Depression was at its height. He read for entertainment and held a job in the New York City garment district for a weekly salary of eleven dollars. His writing career was spurred by ten dollars he received when a magazine accepted a short story he wrote and submitted. His first novel, *I Can Get It for You Wholesale*, was written as a result of a contest he entered; he wrote a chapter each night. The novel portrays its Jewish protagonist as ruthless and traces his path from upstart to ambitious manufacturer who is unable to find happiness in life. Although the novel did not win the contest, it was eventually published, and critical response was very positive. The book was successful enough that Weidman followed up with a sequel, *What's in It for Me?* The sequel continues to depict the protagonist as a man unable to love, a despicable human being, lacking any sensibilities.

With the success of his first novel, Weidman quit law school at age twenty-four to become a full-time writer. He was compared by critics to writers such as Ernest Hemingway and William Faulkner. Weidman was ultimately prolific. During his literary career, he produced a vast body of works, including novels, short stories, dramas, screenplays, and even a television series. He proved himself a disciplined and skilled storyteller and observer of modern life and Jewish immigrant culture in the United States. In many of his works, ambitious characters are successful at first but are defeated in the end because they sacrifice their morality and integrity to gain financial rewards. Some of his characters fail to differentiate between ephemeral material happiness and real human sensibilities. All these concerns reflect Weidman's personal experience of the Depression years and the lack of material wealth around him during his youth. Weidman portrayed these dislocations in human greed and desire with meticulous accuracy.

Along with his ethnic roots and childhood experiences, Weidman's travels in North America, the Mediterranean region, and England inspired him and provided material for his works, which have been translated into many languages. Interestingly, his parents read his books in Hebrew because of their lack of English comprehension. Weidman earned a number of prestigious awards such as the Pulitzer Prize in drama, the New York Drama Critics Circle Award, and the Tony Award in 1960 for the musical play *Fiorello!*, which ran for 795 nights on Broadway. A musical version of *I Can Get It for You Wholesale* ran for 300 nights and was later made into a feature-length film in 1951.

Not all critics were kind to Weidman's works, and the author took the negative reviews seriously. He was, in fact, somewhat hurt and surprised by them, because he thought he worked hard as a storyteller and had something serious to contribute to the literary world and to his readers. His response was to continue writing.

As a first-generation Jewish American writer, Weidman never discounted his roots and humble background, always finding ways to work autobiographical details into his books. His reminiscences include those of seeking cultural identity, the generation gap, stereotypes in the Gentile world, and getting away from the urban ghetto. His stories reflect this unique American immigrant experience with a Yiddish flare and a cadenced English dialogue. As a writer, he also had a special talent for drawing material from Eastern European tales and legends, especially in his short stories. He also was a keen observer of mundane details, turning them from banalities to insightful and interesting facets of everyday life in his stories. Though his literary fame wavered from time to time during his fifty-year career, Weidman retained his audience with a prolific body of works because he was good at storytelling. His works are still read widely and continue to be studied seriously.

H. N. Nguyen

Bibliography

Blicksilver, Edith. "Jerome Weidman." In *Twentieth-Century American-Jewish Fiction Writers*, edited by Daniel Walden. Vol. 28 in *Dictionary of Literary Biography*. Detroit: Gale, 1984. Entry on Weidman's life and prolific body of works.

Sarafin, Steven R., ed. "Jerome Weidman." In *Encyclopedia of American Literature*. New York: Continuum, 1999. Overview of Weidman's writing career.

Weidman, Jerome. "Interview with Jerome Weidman." Interview by John Barkman. *Saturday Review* 45 (July 28, 1962): 38-39. Weidman discusses his literary career and his intent as a writer.

Simone Weil

French philosopher and critic

Born: Paris, France; February 3, 1909
Died: Ashford, Kent, England; August 24, 1943

NONFICTION: *La Pesanteur et la grâce*, 1947 (*Gravity and Grace*, 1952); *L'Enracinement*, 1949 (social criticism; *The Need for Roots*, 1952); *Attente de Dieu*, 1950 (*Waiting for God*, 1951); *La Connaissance surnaturelle*, 1950; *Intuitions pré-chrétiennes*, 1951; *Lettre à un religieux*, 1951 (*Letter to a Priest*, 1953); *La Condition ouvrière*, 1951 (social criticism); *Cahiers*, 1951-1956 (3 volumes; *The Notebooks of Simone Weil*, 1956); *La Source grecque*, 1953; *Oppression et liberté*, 1953 (*Oppression and Liberty*, 1958); *Intimations of Christianity Among the Ancient Greeks*, 1957 (includes selections from *Intuitions pré-chrétiennes* and *La Source grecque*); *Leçons de philosophie de Simone Weil*, 1959 (*Lectures on Philosophy*, 1978); *Écrits historiques et politiques*, 1960; *Pensées sans ordre concernant l'amour de Dieu*, 1962; *Selected Essays: 1934-1943*, 1962; *Seventy Letters*, 1965; *On Science, Necessity, and the Love of God*, 1968; *First and Last Notebooks*, 1970; *Gateway to God*, 1974; *Simone Weil: An Anthology*, 1986.
DRAMA: *Venise sauvée*, pb. 1955.
POETRY: *Poèmes*, 1968.
MISCELLANEOUS: *Écrits de Londres et dernières lettres*, 1957; *The Simone Weil Reader*, 1977; *Formative Writings, 1929-1941*, 1987; *Œuvres*, 1999.

The writings of Simone Adolphine Weil (vay) had significant influence on religious and political thought in the second half of the twentieth century. Weil was the second child of Jewish agnostics Bernard and Selma Weil. She expressed social concerns at an early age—when only five years old, she steadfastly refused to eat sugar as long as French soldiers could not get it. The strain of humility that runs through Weil's adult writings also began early; the achievements of her brother André, a prodigy who went on to enjoy a distinguished career as a mathematician, eroded her self-confidence. In this, as in so much else, Weil was a mixture of opposites, and her writings also reveal a strong consciousness of her intellectual powers and a morally judgmental tone bordering on arrogance. At the age of twelve Weil endured the first of the migraine headaches that tortured her throughout her life and from which she may have distilled some of her intense compassion for human suffering.

Weil was awarded her *baccalauréat* with distinction at the age of fifteen. After studies with the famed French philosopher Emile-Auguste Chartier (known by his pen name, Alain), she passed first in the extremely competitive entrance examination of the École Normale Supérieure. A brilliant and precocious student, she became deeply involved in social and political causes. Following her graduation in 1931, Weil began teaching philosophy at a girls' *lycée*. School boards shuffled her from one school to another, nervous at her picketing and her writing for leftist journals. By 1932 she was publishing in the *Révolution Prolétarienne* such articles as "Reflections on the Causes of Liberty and Social Oppression." In her notebooks of this period Weil reflected on the social alienation caused by workers' increasing enslavement to industrial society.

To get experience of workers' lives at first hand, Weil left teaching in 1934 to work at a Renault auto factory. *The Need for Roots* presents her conclusions about the obligations of the state to the individual. Weil's antifascist convictions led her in 1936 to join a unit training for the Spanish Civil War. Her pacifism kept her from battle but not from injury: While working as a cook, she badly burned herself with oil and was forced to return after only two months. Weil's writing through the 1930's addressed the problems of economic depression, fanatical politics, and war. Her chief preoccupation became increasingly evident: how to reduce human suffering and to find meaning amid that suffering.

During leisure enforced by deteriorating health, Weil began reading the English metaphysical poets. George Herbert's "Love" (III) inspired the first of her mystical revelations. The religious concerns that came to dominate her thought provide the thematic pulse of *Waiting for God*, a posthumously published collection of meditations and reflections. Here Weil criticizes the oversimplifying rationalism of Christian doctrine, insisting that God cannot be discovered through the senses or intellect.

On May 17, 1942, Weil and her family escaped Nazi-occupied France and fled to the United States, but the complacency there struck her as insensitive to the suffering of her embattled compatriots. In November she went to England, where she wrote *The Need for Roots*, a response to the request of the Free French in London to report on possibilities for the regeneration of France. *The Need for Roots* is a passionate intellectual plea for the West to recover its spiritual heritage as the first step to solving political problems. Weil discusses the spiritual significance of physical labor, delineates the needs of the soul, and outlines the social principles upon which a truly Christian nation might be built. In the famous preface to the English translation of this book, also published posthumously, T. S. Eliot calls Weil "a woman of genius, of a kind of genius akin to that of the saints." The war notebooks include writing Weil did in the United States and England in 1942 and 1943, the last pages penned a few days before her death. Weil died at the age of thirty-four of pulmonary tuberculosis and starvation as a consequence of her refusal to eat more than what she assumed people in occupied France were rationed.

Critics have pointed to contradictions in Weil's thought. Intensely religious, she rejected her Jewish background and refused baptism in the Christianity she adopted. She is both Marxist and mystical; in her writing, seventeenth century religious fervor accompanies twentieth century intellectualism. It is the very inclusiveness of that paradoxical perspective that has drawn countless readers to her work. Weil has a reputation as a creative thinker, intensely realistic in her awareness of suffering and passionately idealistic in her hopes to lessen that suffering.

Steven C. Walker
Brandie Siegfried

Bibliography

Coles, Robert. *Simone Weil: A Modern Pilgrimage*. 1987. Reprint. Woodstock, Vt.: Skylight Paths, 2001. Insightful and accessible study of Weil, an introductory survey of her life and work. This edition contains a new foreword by the author.

Courtine-Denamy, Sylvie. *Three Women in Dark Times: Edith Stein, Hannah Arendt, Simone Weil, or "Amor Fati, Amor Mundi."* Translated by G. M. Goshgarian. Ithaca, N.Y.: Cornell University Press, 2000. A study of these three Jewish women philosophers against the background of wartime Europe.

Gray, Francine du Plessix. *Simone Weil*. New York: Viking, 2000. Well-written introduction for general readers.

Hellman, John. *Simone Weil: An Introduction to Her Thought*. Philadelphia: Fortress Press, 1984. Offers helpful commentary on Weil in relation to her contemporaries.

McLane-Iles, Betty. *Uprooting and Integration in the Writings of Simone Weil*. New York: P. Lang, 1987. Gives special consideration to Weil's contributions to science.

Petrement, Simone. *Simone Weil: A Life*. New York: Schocken Books, 1988. An excellent source of biographical information. Petrement was a close friend of Weil, and her substantial, well-documented book provides a comprehensive account of Weil's life.

Winch, Peter. *Simone Weil: "The Just Balance."* New York: Cambridge University Press, 1989. A sophisticated study that focuses on the uneasy mix of religion and philosophy in Weil's thought.

Peter Weiss

German-born Swedish playwright

Born: Nowawes, near Berlin, Germany; November 8, 1916
Died: Stockholm, Sweden; May 10, 1982

DRAMA: *Der Turrm*, pr. 1949 (radio play), pb. 1963, pr. 1967 (staged; *The Tower*, 1966); *Die Versicherung*, wr. 1952, pr. 1966; *Nacht mit Gästen*, pr., pb. 1963 (*Night with Guests*, 1969); *Die Verfolgung und Ermordung Jean Paul Marats, dargestellt durch die Schauspielgruppe des Hospizes zu Charenton unter der Anleitung des Herrn de Sade*, pr., pb. 1964 (*The Persecution and Assassination of Jean-Paul Marat as Performed by the Inmates of the Asylum of Charenton Under the Direction of the Marquis de Sade*, 1965, better known as *Marat/Sade*); *Die Ermittlung*, pr., pb. 1965 (*The Investigation*, 1966); *Gesang vom lusitanischen Popanz*, pr., pb. 1967 (*Song of the Lusitanian Bogey*, 1970); *Diskurs über die Vorgeschichte und den Verlauf des lang andauernden Befreiungskrieges in Viet Nam als Beispiel für die Notwendigkeit des bewaffneten Kampfes der Unterdrückten gegen ihre Unterdrücker sowie über die Versuche der Vereinigten Staaten von Amerika die Grundlagen der Revolution zu vernichten*, pb. 1967 (better known as *Viet Nam Diskurs*; *Discourse of the Progress of the Prolonged War of Liberation in Viet Nam and the Events Leading Up to It as Illustration of the Necessity for Armed Resistance Against Oppression and on the Attempts of the United States of America to Destroy the Foundations of Revolution*, 1970, better known as *Vietnam Discourse*); *Wie dem Herrn Mockingpott das Leiden ausgetrieben wird*, pr., pb. 1968 (*How Mister Mockingpott Was Cured of His Suffering*, 1971); *Dramen in zwei Bänden*, pb. 1968 (2 volumes); *Trotski im Exil*, pr., pb. 1970 (*Trotsky in Exile*, 1972); *Hölderlin*, pr., pb. 1971; *Der Prozess*, pr., pb. 1975 (adaptation of Franz Kafka's novel); *Der neue Prozess*, pr. 1982 (revised adaptation of Kafka's novel; *The New Trial*, 2001).

LONG FICTION: *Der Schatten des Körpers des Kutschers*, 1960 (*The Shadow of the Coachman's Body*, 1969); *Abschied von den Eltern*, 1961 (*The Leavetaking*, 1966); *Fluchtpunkt*, 1962 (*Vanishing Point*, 1966); *Das Gespräch der drei Gehenden*, 1963 (*The Conversation of the Three Wayfarers*, 1970); *Die Ästhetik des Widerstands*, 1975-1981 (3 volumes).

NONFICTION: *Arbeitspunkte eines Autors in der geteilten Welt*, 1965; *Notizen zum kulturellen Leben der Demokratischen Republik Vietnam*, 1968 (*Notes on the Cultural Life of the Democratic Republic of Vietnam*, 1970); *Rapporte*, 1968-1971 (2 volumes); *Notizbücher, 1971-1980*, 1981; *Notizbücher, 1960-1971*, 1982.

Peter Ulrich Weiss (vis) is considered one of the most prominent playwrights and novelists of the German postwar era. Born in a suburb of Berlin to a Jewish family on November 8, 1916, he originally wanted to be a painter. When the Nazis came to power in the 1930's, Weiss's family emigrated to England, and he then studied for several years at the art academy in Prague. He then finally moved to Sweden in 1939, where he spent the remainder of his life, becoming a Swedish citizen in 1945. Weiss began writing in 1946 at the age of thirty, and his first poetic efforts were written in Swedish. He was also involved at this time in making experimental films and documentaries. In 1952 Weiss began living with the Swedish artist Gunilla Palmstierna, who did the stage design for many of his later plays. A politically committed individual, he traveled to North Vietnam in 1968 to observe at firsthand the effects of the war there. Throughout the course of his career, Weiss was the recipient of numerous literary prizes and honors. He died May 10, 1982, in Stockholm.

Weiss's first writings were highly experimental, surreal narratives. *The Shadow of the Coachman's Body* presents a first-person narrator who records his highly associative, almost hallucinatory impressions over a six-day period. Weiss's early interest in film is apparent in this text in which objects, events, and characters are recorded in a neutral fashion as they occur. *The Conversation of the Three Wayfarers* shares the same disjointed, surreal perspective as the author's first novel. It records the three narrators' conversations, which consist of fantasies, vaguely remembered events, and meandering observations on life. These texts suggest Weiss's attempt to come to terms with the discrepancies between the objective complexity of reality and his subjective perception of it. *The Leavetaking* and *Vanishing Point* are autobiographical novels in which Weiss seeks, here in a more personal way, to assess the nature of his reality. They deal with existential themes of personal alienation, the difficulty of authentic communication, and the individual's search for an identity separate from family and friends. These works represent Weiss's growing realization of the close interrelationship between self and society.

The dialectical play *Marat/Sade* brought Weiss international acclaim. It is a work about the history of ideas and political realities of revolution and social change. Its fictional premise is that of a play about the assassination of the progressive French revolutionary Jean-Paul Marat that is being staged and directed by the infamous sexual libertine Marquis de Sade within the Charenton mental asylum. This play-within-a-play becomes a dialogue between Marat and Sade on the nature of humankind, society, and the possibility of progress. Marat represents the optimistic Enlightenment position of the perfectibility of man, that the goals of the revolution—liberty, social equality, and brotherhood—can be realized. Sade presents a darker, more pessimistic picture in which perverse sexuality and repressed desire produce a society of irrational violence and destruction. Weiss's dramatic writing is strongly influenced by the practice of the Brechtian stage; that is, he uses songs and cabaret-style techniques to present his message. The dramatic oratorio *The Investigation* deals with the horror of the Nazi concentration camps and addresses in broad terms the issue of modern political oppression. The political plays *Song of the Lusitanian Bogey* and *Vietnam Discourse* present strongly propagandistic condemnations of the history of capitalist colonization and exploitation in developing nations such as Angola and Vietnam. Weiss used, as he does in many of his works, extensive documentary sources in writing these plays.

The plays *Trotsky in Exile* and *Hölderlin* deal with the situation of the politically committed but alienated intellectual. In the former play, the socialist exile, who was at odds with the other early theoreticians of Marxism, reflects upon what he sees as the misguided course of the Russian revolution and speaks for the ideals of true socialism and the creative freedom of the visionary writer-intellectual. Weiss sees his own situation as a committed socialist author as being analogous in certain respects to that of Trotsky. In the latter play, based on the tragic life of the eighteenth century German poet Friedrich Hölderlin, Weiss again explores the fate of the socialist intellectual artist whose inspired visions of a just and equitable society place him both at the forefront of the revolutionary thought of his era and at odds with the less progressive spirit of the times. The play *Der Prozess* is an adaptation of the 1925 novel by Franz Kafka, which was translated into English as *The Trial* (1937). Weiss did the original stage adaptation in 1975 and revised it as *Der neue Prozess* (*The New Trial*) in 1982. Kafka's novel deals with existential and psychological themes of the estranged personality which Weiss then transformed into a socialist critique of alienation in a capitalist society.

Weiss's last major work was the extended novel *Die Ästhetik des Widerstands* (the aesthetics of resistance). It is a mixture of fictional, autobiographical, and documentary materials in which the author speculates in the guise of the narrator about what his life might have been like had he been born into the lower classes. He discusses the socialist commitment that has been so significant in his life. Weiss's final literary work returns, in certain respects, to the autobiographical concerns of his first writings and summarizes the social concerns that had dominated his creative work throughout his career.

Thomas F. Barry

Bibliography

Cohen, Robert. *Understanding Peter Weiss*. Columbia: University of South Carolina Press, 1993. Cohen presents the life and analyzes the work of Weiss. Includes bibliography and index.

Ellis, Roger. *Peter Weiss in Exile: A Critical Study of His Works*. Ann Arbor: University of Michigan Research Press, 1987. Ellis examines the political and social views of Weiss and how they manifested themselves in his work. Includes bibliography and index.

Herman, Jost, and Marc Silverman, eds. *Rethinking Peter Weiss*. New York: Peter Lang, 2000. The essays in this work are revised versions of lectures presented in November, 1998, at the University of Wisconsin. Includes bibliography.

Vance, Kathleen A. *The Theme of Alienation in the Prose of Peter Weiss*. Las Vegas: Peter Lang, 1981. Vance provides a critical analysis of Weiss's works, focusing on the theme of alienation. Includes bibliography.

Denton Welch

English novelist, short-story writer, and memoirist

Born: Shanghai, China; March 29, 1915
Died: Crouch, Kent, England; December 30, 1948
Identity: Gay or bisexual

LONG FICTION: *Maiden Voyage*, 1943; *In Youth Is Pleasure*, 1944; *A Voice Through a Cloud*, 1950 (unfinished).
SHORT FICTION: *Brave and Cruel*, 1948; *A Last Sheaf*, 1951; *The Stories of Denton Welch*, 1985.
POETRY: *Dumb Instrument: Poems and Fragments*, 1976.
NONFICTION: *I Left My Grandfather's House*, 1958; *The Journals of Denton Welch*, 1984.

To Dame Edith Sitwell, one of his earliest admirers, Maurice Denton Welch was "a born writer." To Maurice Cranston, he was "a born solipsist," to C. E. M. Joad, he was a latter-day decadent, and to Julian Symons, the harshest of his critics, he was "a pathetic rather than a tragic figure" whose writings betray the author's "complete narcissistic self-absorption" and "the poverty of his subjects." Welch saw himself as a monk dedicated to a single task, devoted to an art forged in his own image—an art that is not so much narcissistic as self-exploring, perhaps even self-creating. The intense and often sensuous subjectivity of his writing, especially of the later works, is its most distinguishing feature. Situated at the very center of his writing and his world, his "I" exists as the author's attempt to reconstitute the self—both physical and psychological—that had been largely destroyed as a result of a near-fatal accident in 1935. His "I" exists less as a participant in the events described than as a spectator, as a presiding, recording consciousness. What distinguishes Welch's subjectivity from mere narcissism and his gaze from mere voyeurism is the manner in which he manages to transform them to narrative advantage. His preoccupation with his own subjective self constitutes his attempt to fill the emptiness he felt within. As he wrote in his journal, "Now I am alone here in the afternoon, with freezing mist outside, and nothing in me." Although his self-absorption may be traced to more or less specific physiological and psychological causes, the results extend well beyond the merely pathological to the forging of a decidedly new form of narrative art that is all the more surprising given just how derivative and unexceptional his poems and paintings are.

Welch was born on March 29, 1915, in Shanghai, China. Never close to his father, a well-to-do businessman, he was devoted to his American-born mother, from whose death in 1927 he never entirely recovered. In 1935, Welch sustained injuries in a bicycle crash; it would eventually cause his death thirteen years later. Trained as an artist, Welch soon turned to writing and in 1940 published an article about a visit to painter Walter Sickert in Cyril Connolly's *Horizon*. In 1942, he began keeping a journal of considerable literary merit as well as biographical interest. His first novel appeared the following year. *Maiden Voyage* is, as are all Welch's novels and many of his stories, autobiographical in subject and episodic in form. "After I had run away from school," the novel begins, "no one knew what to do with me." The narrator-protagonist hardly knows what to do with himself. He leaves Repton, then leaves England for China, then leaves his father's house to explore that strange land, and then returns to England, where he enrolls in art school. Written in a simple style suggestive of the narrator-protagonist's own youthfulness, *Maiden Voyage* proves a surprisingly mature work, one in which (as poet W. H. Auden has noted) "scientific objectivity" and "subjective terror" are strangely combined. Welch's second novel, *In Youth Is Pleasure*, was less well received. Only half as long as *Maiden Voyage*, its action and cast of characters more condensed, *In Youth Is Pleasure* focuses more narrowly and relentlessly on the sexual—or, rather, the homosexual—aspect of the search for self-knowledge by the protagonist, Orville Pym, in a largely hostile, at times even terrifying, world surrounding the hotel where Pym goes between school terms with his father and two brothers. A number of reviewers found it difficult to sympathize with a character so narcissistic and "desperately miserable" as Pym. However, the more important reason the novel fails is the use of a third-person narrator, which, as critic Maurice Cranston has pointed out, "demanded an interest in the external world which Denton Welch could not sustain."

Welch did not live to complete his third—and many contend, his best—novel, *A Voice Through a Cloud*. In part, the reason was physical: Pain began to make it difficult for him to write for more than a few minutes at a time. Also, Welch turned to the writing of short stories that would bring him the income he sorely needed following the death of his father. Many of these stories of failed sexual encounters Welch collected in *Brave and Cruel*, while others appear in *A Last Sheaf*, compiled by Eric Oliver, Welch's companion during his final years. Even in its unfinished state, *A Voice Through a Cloud* is a remarkable work. Narrated by "Maurice," the novel deals with Welch's accident and recovery, but in a way that is, as John Updike pointed out, as much metaphorical as it is autobiographical. The novel proclaims the human being's "terrible fragility" and the author's painstaking effort "to reconstitute human experience particle by particle." Here the metaphorical maiden voyage from illness to recovery ends with yet another beginning as Maurice, well if not quite whole, goes to live on his own, no longer needing the help of Dr. Frawley, on whom he had come to depend both as patient and as son. Maurice is, as his journals show Welch was, free but unfulfilled, at least until he came to terms with his feelings for Oliver, at long last entering into precisely the kind of relationship that he, like so many of his narrators and characters, had previously only observed.

What Welch depicted in his writing—his novels and stories as well as his journals—is not a world such as one finds in the realistic fiction written by the majority of other English writers during the 1940's. It is instead a sensibility marked by the intensity of his perception, and marked, too, by its power to evoke rather than merely narrate or (despite the brilliance of Welch's startling imagery) describe. Freely mixing candor with guilt, subjective desire with clinical detachment, he broke free of the upper-middle-class prejudices and perspective for which his work has at times been attacked to forge in his writing what he could not in his life: a new form, one which (as critic Ruby Cohn has noted) prefigures the slightly later New Novel in France and the works of the Angry Young Men in England. If his scale was small—smaller in fact than that of Jane Austen, a writer he greatly admired—the intensity of his vision and the scrupulous honesty with which he portrayed his limited world were inversely great.

Robert A. Morace

Bibliography

Crain, Caleb. "It's Pretty, but Is It Broken?" *The New York Times*, June 20, 1999. Discusses Welch as the "champion of preciousness," fascinated with picnics and antiques. Comments on the relationship of Welch's homosexuality and physical disability to his writing.

De-la-Noy, Michael. *Denton Welch: The Making of a Writer.* New York: Viking, 1984. This standard biography uses much material never before published. The biographer uses many of Welch's letters, letters to Welch from his friends, and materials from personal recollections of those who knew him.

Gooch, Brad. "Gossip, Lies, and Wishes." *The Nation* 240 (June 8, 1985): 711-713. Gooch praises Welch for his ability to make even the smallest objects into mementos by the precision of his writing. Though Welch seems haunted by death and time, he is never morbid and can, at times, be flippant about tombs and graveyards.

Hollinghurst, Alan. "Diminished Pictures." *The Times Literary Supplement*, no. 4264 (December 21, 1984): 1479-1480. Hollinghurst finds Welch's aestheticism anything but precious. It helped him focus his attention on art objects during times of great physical and mental pain. He wrote to save himself and to enrich his life.

Phillips, Robert. *Denton Welch*. New York: Twayne, 1974. The only book-length critical treatment of all of Welch's work. Phillips's interpretations are thorough, though he tends to find Freudian and Jungian patterns most helpful. He points out some of the affinities that Welch shared with D. H. Lawrence and James Joyce.

Skenazy, Paul. "The Sense and Sensuality of Denton Welch." *The Washington Post Book World*, April 6, 1986, p. 1. A review of *The Stories of Denton Welch* that comments on Welch's focus on the texture of social rituals rather than narrative structure and plot tension; asserts one reads Welch not for character revelation but to experience his sensibility. Notes that nearly all the stories concern a confused outsider seeking security and love.

Updike, John. "A Short Life." In *Picked-Up Pieces*. New York: Alfred A. Knopf, 1975. Updike calls Welch an authentic existential writer insofar as his agony enabled him to create a world particle by particle. He sees Welch's autobiographical account of his terrible accident as "a proclamation of our terrible fragility."

James Welch

American novelist and poet

Born: Browning, Montana; November 18, 1940
Died: Missoula, Montana; August 4, 2003
Identity: American Indian (Gros Ventre and Blackfoot)

LONG FICTION: *Winter in the Blood*, 1974; *The Death of Jim Loney*, 1979; *Fools Crow*, 1986; *The Indian Lawyer*, 1990; *The Heartsong of Charging Elk*, 2000 (also known as *Heartsong*).
POETRY: *Riding the Earthboy Forty*, 1971, revised 1975.
NONFICTION: *Killing Custer: The Battle of Little Bighorn and the Fate of the Plains Indians*, 1994 (with Paul Stekler).

James Welch, whose various writings present the American Indians of his native Montana, was born to a mother of the Gros Ventre tribe and a father of the Blackfoot tribe. He attended reservation schools but graduated from a high school in Minneapolis. From the University of Montana in Missoula he received a B.A. degree in 1965 and a master's degree in 1967. He settled with his wife in Missoula, Montana. He died there of a heart attack in 2003, at the age of sixty-two.

The title of his collection of fifty-four poems, *Riding the Earthboy Forty*, refers to a family named Earthboy who had a ranch of forty acres. The poem that lends its name to the volume describes a first-person narrator responding romantically to Earthboy, who "farmed the sky with words." Earthboy is buried on his former farm, however, and his spirit declares that "dirt is where the dreams must end," suggesting tension between the needs of living and aspirations of spirit.

After drafting his first novel, *Winter in the Blood*, Welch showed the manuscript to an editor friend, Bill Kitteridge, who offered extensive criticism. Welch thereupon reworked the story, doing much of the work during a stay in Greece. In this work the unnamed first-person narrator wastes his time in town and at his mother's farm until he discovers his roots, especially his grandfather, Yellow Calf, who saved his ostracized grandmother, who was from a different tribe, from starvation. This knowledge, accompanied by a sense of the ghostly presence of his ancestors, freshens the narrator's interest in his life and in his potential wife. The story suggests that realization of their roots and of their heroic ancestors can save American Indians.

The Death of Jim Loney received ambivalent responses, in part because the story depicts the despair that assaults a man whom others love. Welch's hero is a man as lonely as his name, who ends by seeking to be shot by the reservation policeman. Aspects of this character come from the author's life, but Welch denies that the novel is essentially autobiographical.

Fools Crow was more warmly received and garnered a number of awards. Set between 1867 and 1870, this major work treats the Montana Blackfeet from the perspective of a young man coming of age who longs for recognition and respect within his village. After a raid to steal horses, White Man's Dog has his name changed to suggest his cleverness in having fooled the Crow enemy. Yet he feels remorse for having stabbed to death a Crow youth during the raid. The people in this novel accept dreams and visions as important directives from the gods and their spirit ancestors. The white settlers take the Blackfeet land and bring smallpox, but when Fools Crow's people fight back, the U.S. Cavalry responds with the massacre of a village on the Marias River in the winter of 1870. In Fools Crow's vision his people endure even though they are subject to white people.

The Indian Lawyer depicts Sylvester Yellow Calf, who has starred in high school basketball, graduated from Stanford Law School, and risen to partnership in a law firm in Montana's capital. The omniscient narrator presents the thinking of many characters who attempt to influence Yellow Calf. In this novel the writing lacks the poetry and imaginative reach of *Fools Crow*, but Welch presents an American Indian who succeeds in the larger society.

The Heartsong of Charging Elk depicts the dilemmas facing Native Americans as the frontier closed. The protagonist is an Oglala Sioux who has joined Buffalo Bill's Wild West Show; laid up with broken ribs and influenza in Marseilles, France, he panics that the show has abandoned him and rushes out of the hospital in a delirium to find what is now the only family he has. Charging Elk wanders through Marseilles, prey to memories and ghosts, as he tries to find his way home both literally and metaphorically.

In the nonfiction *Killing Custer* Welch returns to the nineteenth century, narrating the events leading to and following from the Battle of the Little Bighorn on June 25, 1876.

Many of Welch's fictional characters live in northern Montana and claim Browning as home. Even the successful lawyer returns here when he needs advice and encouragement. Descriptions of the lovely summers and brutal winters of Welch's birthplace give realistic depth to his stories, and his characters delight at the sight of an eagle or a mountain lion and in the landscape. Welch's Blackfeet must address the challenge of living in a white-dominated society. Within his locale and Indian roots, Welch created characters who differ widely in outlook and situation, but all his characters search for direction and value in life.

Emmett H. Carroll

Bibliography

Beidler, Peter G., ed. *American Indian Quarterly* 4 (May, 1978). A symposium on *Winter in the Blood* for a special edition of *American Indian Quarterly*; three papers deal with the central character's alienation, three others discuss the novel's tone.

Gish, Robert F. "Word Medicine: Storytelling and Magic Realism in James Welch's *Fools Crow*." *American Indian Quarterly* 14, no. 4 (Fall, 1990). Compares the novel to a Homeric poetic epic.

McFarland, Ronald E. "'The End' in James Welch's Novels." *American Indian Quarterly* 17, no. 3 (1993). Looks for the themes in the novels' endings.

_______. *Understanding James Welch*. Columbia: University of South Carolina Press, 2000. An introduction to the writer and his work. Includes a thorough bibliography.

_______, ed. *James Welch*. Lewiston, Idaho: Confluence Press, 1986. A collection of critical articles on Welch's first four books. Of special interest is a 1984 interview in which Welch suggests that his family background inspired aspects of his stories. The collection also includes a chronology of his life and writings.

Nelson, Robert M. *Place and Vision: The Function of Landscape in Native American Literature*. New York: P. Lang, 1993. Discusses the philosophy of place that emerges from Welch's depictions of landscape.

Schort, Blanca. *Storied Voices in Native American Texts: Harry Robinson, Thomas King, James Welch, and Leslie Marmon Silko*. New York: Routledge, 2003. Analyzes the oral narrative traditions underlying Welch's, and others', work.

Velie, Alan R. "Blackfeet Surrealism: The Poetry of James Welch." In *Four American Indian Literary Masters*. Norman: University of Oklahoma Press, 1982. A critical study of Welch's single volume of poetry.

Fay Weldon

English novelist, short-story writer, and playwright

Born: Alvechurch, Worcestershire, England; September 22, 1931

LONG FICTION: *The Fat Woman's Joke*, 1967 (also known as . . . *And the Wife Ran Away*, 1968); *Down Among the Women*, 1971; *Female Friends*, 1974; *Remember Me*, 1976; *Words of Advice*, 1977 (also known as *Little Sisters*, 1978); *Praxis*, 1978; *Puffball*, 1980; *The President's Child*, 1982; *The Life and Loves of a She-Devil*, 1983; *The Shrapnel Academy*, 1986; *The Rules of Life*, 1987; *The Heart of the Country*, 1987; *The Hearts and Lives of Men*, 1987; *Leader of the Band*, 1988; *The Cloning of Joanna May*, 1989; *Darcy's Utopia*, 1990; *Growing Rich*, 1992; *Life Force*, 1992; *Affliction*, 1993 (also known as *Trouble*); *Splitting*, 1995; *Worst Fears*, 1996; *Big Women*, 1997 (also known as *Big Girls Don't Cry*); *Rhode Island Blues*, 2000; *The Bulgari Connection*, 2001.

SHORT FICTION: *Watching Me, Watching You*, 1981; *Polaris, and Other Stories*, 1985; *Moon over Minneapolis: Or, Why She Couldn't Stay*, 1991; *Angel, All Innocence, and Other Stories*, 1995; *Wicked Women: A Collection of Short Stories*, 1995; *A Hard Time to Be a Father*, 1998.

DRAMA: *Permanence*, pr. 1969; *Time Hurries On*, pb. 1972; *Words of Advice*, pr., pb. 1974; *Friends*, pr. 1975; *Moving House*, pr. 1976; *Mr. Director*, pr. 1978; *Action Replay*, pr. 1979 (also known as *Love Among the Women*); *After the Prize*, pr. 1981 (also known as *Wordworm*); *I Love My Love*, pr. 1981; *Tess of the D'Urbervilles*, pr. 1992 (adaptation of Thomas Hardy's novel); *The Four Alice Bakers*, pr. 1999; *The Reading Group*, pb. 1999.

TELEPLAYS: *Wife in a Blonde Wig*, 1966; *The Fat Woman's Tale*, 1966; *What About Me*, 1967; *Dr. De Waldon's Therapy*, 1967; *Goodnight Mrs. Dill*, 1967; *The Forty-fifth Unmarried Mother*, 1967; *Fall of the Goat*, 1967; *Ruined Houses*, 1968; *Venus Rising*, 1968; *The Three Wives of Felix Hull*, 1968; *Hippy Hippy Who Cares*, 1968; *£13083*, 1968; *The Loophole*, 1969; *Smokescreen*, 1969; *Poor Mother*, 1970; *Office Party*, 1970; *On Trial*, 1971 (in *Upstairs, Downstairs* series); *Hands*, 1972; *The Lament of an Unmarried Father*, 1972; *A Nice Rest*, 1972; *Old Man's Hat*, 1972; *A Splinter of Ice*, 1972; *Comfortable Words*, 1973; *Desirous of Change*, 1973; *In Memoriam*, 1974; *Poor Baby*, 1975; *The Terrible Tale of Timothy Bagshott*, 1975; *Aunt Tatty*, 1975 (adaptation of Elizabeth Bowen's story); *Act of Rape*, 1977; *Married Love*, 1977 (in *Six Women* series); *Pride and Prejudice*, 1980 (adaptation of Jane Austen's novel); *Honey Ann*, 1980; *Watching Me, Watching You*, 1980 (in *Leap in the Dark* series); *Life for Christine*, 1980; *Little Miss Perkins*, 1982; *Loving Women*, 1983; *Redundant! Or, The Wife's Revenge*, 1983.

RADIO PLAYS: *Spider*, 1972; *Housebreaker*, 1973; *Mr. Fox and Mr. First*, 1974; *The Doctor's Wife*, 1975; *Polaris*, 1978; *Weekend*, 1979 (in *Just Before Midnight* series); *All the Bells of Paradise*, 1979; *I Love My Love*, 1981.

NONFICTION: *Letters to Alice on First Reading Jane Austen*, 1984; *Rebecca West*, 1985; *Sacred Cows: A Portrait of Britain, Post-Rushdie, Pre-Utopia*, 1989; *Godless in Eden*, 1999; *Auto da Fay*, 2002.

CHILDREN'S/YOUNG ADULT LITERATURE: *Wolf the Mechanical Dog*, 1988; *Party Puddle*, 1989; *Nobody Likes Me*, 1997.

EDITED TEXT: *New Stories Four: An Arts Council Anthology*, 1979 (with Elaine Feinstein); *Godless in Eden: A Book of Essays*, 1999.

Fay Weldon is a major contemporary writer on women's issues, noted for short fiction and novels as well as for plays for stage, radio, and television. She was born Franklin Birkinshaw on September 22, 1931, in Alvechurch, Worcestershire, England, to Frank Thornton Birkinshaw, a doctor, and Margaret Jepson Birkinshaw, a writer of romantic novels. Her maternal grandfather and an uncle were also writers. Weldon was reared in New Zealand. When she was five, her parents were divorced; she spent the rest of her childhood in an all-female household, consisting of her mother, her grandmother, and her sister, and then was educated at a girls' school. After returning to England, Weldon attended Hampstead Girls' High School, London. In 1949 she went to St. Andrews University in Fife, Scotland, and received her master's degree in economics and psychology in 1954. In the 1950's Weldon worked as a report writer for the British Foreign Office, spent some time as a market researcher for the London *Daily Mirror*, and then became an advertising copywriter. After a brief, disastrous marriage in 1958, in 1960 she married Ronald (Ron) Weldon, an antique dealer, painter, and jazz musician; their marriage lasted until 1994. Weldon subsequently married poet Nick Fox.

Although Weldon had worked on novels in the 1950's, her career as a successful writer should be dated from the year 1966, when three of her plays were produced on British television. Her first novel, *The Fat Woman's Joke*, which was published a year later, grew out of the teleplay *The Fat Woman's Tale*. Witty, satirical, and conversational, it set the pattern for her later works, which have consistently dealt with women's problems as seen through women's eyes. In 1969 Weldon's first play was produced in London; it was followed by six others during the next decade. Meanwhile, she continued to write novels, short stories, and numerous teleplays, including an award-winning episode of the popular series *Upstairs, Downstairs*. In the 1970's she also wrote a number of radio plays; in 1973, she won the Writers' Guild Award for one of them, *Spider*, and in 1978, she won the Giles Cooper Award for *Polaris*. In every genre she was praised for skillful plot development, witty and realistic dialogue, and an accurate delineation of the plight of all women, single or married, who are victims of their biological drives and of the men who dominate society. Although her themes remain the same, critics are impressed by Weldon's seemingly endless powers of invention. In the early work *Remember*

Me, for example, a dead divorced wife comes back to haunt her ex-husband; in *Puffball*, a pregnant woman, alone in Somerset, is beset by a witch; and in what is perhaps Weldon's most famous later novel, *The Life and Loves of a She-Devil*; an abandoned wife takes an elaborate revenge on her husband and on the wealthy romance writer who stole him from her.

In addition to her own fiction and plays, Weldon has written acclaimed scripts based on the works of other writers, including *Aunt Tatty*, based on a short story by Elizabeth Bowen, and the five-part dramatization of Jane Austen's 1813 novel *Pride and Prejudice*, that was shown in England and in the United States in 1980. Her interest in Austen led to the publication of an unusual book, *Letters to Alice on First Reading Jane Austen*, which is cast as a series of letters from the novelist to a fictional niece. In addition to analyses of Austen's novels and details about her life, the book includes Weldon's comments on the art of fiction and on her own work. In 1985 Weldon's book *Rebecca West* was structured similarly. In this case Weldon supposes herself to be writing fictitious letters to another writer, Rebecca West, after the birth in 1914 of West's son by H. G. Wells. In keeping with her feminist posture, she praises West's determined unconventionality but also reminds her that a satisfying life does not depend on Wells or on any other man.

Weldon's novels and stories tend to be rational rather than vituperative, witty rather than shrill. Both men and women are targets of her satire, men because they so often insist on bolstering their own insecurities by bullying the women who love them or who are involved with them, and women because they conspire in their own subjugation, assuming that thus they will keep the men they so desperately need in order to maintain their own identities. Extreme feminists criticize Weldon because her men are not monsters; most of them are weak. Like Bobbo in *The Life and Loves of a She-Devil*, they collapse as soon as women cease to adore them. Such critics also complain that Weldon's women are often as foolish as the men. Other critics disagree, pointing out that her incisive social commentary may lay the groundwork for a new maturity and respect in relationships between men and women, based on a new balance in the lives of women such as Weldon herself.

In 2001, Weldon received a great deal of criticism for her novel *The Bulgari Connection* when it was revealed that she had accepted an undisclosed but large sum of money from the Italian jewelers Bulgari for "product placement" within the work—essentially, for using her novel as a form of advertising for the company. The practice has been increasingly used, and increasingly deplored, in film, and Weldon's complicity in bringing it into the world of print was felt by many to be a triumph of crass commercialism over art. The novel itself received mixed reviews, with many feeling that it was classic Weldon satire, while others felt the novelist was merely marking time and repeating a formula.

Rosemary M. Canfield Reisman
David Barratt

Bibliography

Barreca, Regina, ed. *Fay Weldon's Wicked Fictions*. Hanover, N.H.: University Press of New England, 1994. This important volume contains thirteen essays by various writers, in addition to five by Weldon. The editor's introduction provides a useful overview of Weldon criticism. Indexed.

Cane, Aleta F. "Demythifying Motherhood in Three Novels by Fay Weldon." In *Family Matters in the British and American Novel*, edited by Andrea O'Reilly Herrera, Elizabeth Mahn Nollen, and Sheila Reitzel Foor. Bowling Green, Ohio: Bowling Green State University Popular Press, 1997. Cane points out that in *Puffball, The Life and Loves of a She-Devil*, and *Life Force*, dysfunctional mothers produce daughters who are also dysfunctional mothers. Obviously, it is argued, Weldon agrees with the feminist position about mothering, that it cannot be improved until women cease to be marginalized.

Dowling, Finuala. *Fay Weldon's Fiction*. Rutherford, N.J.: Fairleigh Dickinson University Press, 1998. An examination of the themes and techniques in Weldon's fiction, with emphasis on the novels but relevance to the short fiction as well.

Faulks, Lana. *Fay Weldon*. Boston: Twayne, 1998. An introduction to Weldon's life and work. Focusing on the novels, Faulks sees Weldon's work as "feminist comedy" contrasting with feminist writing that depicts women as oppressed. Also examines Weldon's experiments with narrative techniques.

Salzmann-Brunner, Brigitte. *Amanuenses to the Present: Protagonists in the Fiction of Penelope Mortimer, Margaret Drabble, and Fay Weldon*. New York: Peter Lang, 1988. Examines the women in these authors' works, with opportunities for some comparisons and contrasts.

H. G. Wells

English novelist and scholar

Born: Bromley, Kent, England; September 21, 1866
Died: London, England; August 13, 1946

LONG FICTION: *The Time Machine: An Invention*, 1895; *The Wonderful Visit*, 1895; *The Island of Dr. Moreau*, 1896; *The Wheels of Chance: A Holiday Adventure*, 1896; *The Invisible Man: A Grotesque Romance*, 1897; *The War of the Worlds*, 1898; *When the Sleeper Wakes: A Story of the Years to Come*, 1899; *Love and Mr. Lewisham*, 1900; *The First Men in the Moon*, 1901; *The Sea Lady*, 1902; *The Food of the*

Gods, and How It Came to Earth, 1904; *Kipps: The Story of a Simple Soul*, 1905; *In the Days of the Comet*, 1906; *The War in the Air, and Particularly How Mr. Bert Smallways Fared While It Lasted*, 1908; *Tono-Bungay*, 1908; *Ann Veronica: A Modern Love Story*, 1909; *The History of Mr. Polly*, 1910; *The New Machiavelli*, 1910; *Marriage*, 1912; *The Passionate Friends*, 1913; *The Wife of Sir Isaac Harman*, 1914; *The World Set Free: A Story of Mankind*, 1914; *Bealby: A Holiday*, 1915; *The Research Magnificent*, 1915; *Mr. Britling Sees It Through*, 1916; *The Soul of a Bishop: A Novel—with Just a Little Love in It—About Conscience and Religion and the Real Troubles of Life*, 1917; *Joan and Peter: The Story of an Education*, 1918; *The Undying Fire: A Contemporary Novel*, 1919; *The Secret Places of the Heart*, 1922; *Men Like Gods*, 1923; *The Dream*, 1924; *Christina Alberta's Father*, 1925; *The World of William Clissold: A Novel at a New Age*, 1926 (3 volumes); *Meanwhile: The Picture of a Lady*, 1927; *Mr. Blettsworthy on Rampole Island*, 1928; *The King Who Was a King: The Book of a Film*, 1929; *The Autocracy of Mr. Parham: His Remarkable Adventure in This Changing World*, 1930; *The Buplington of Blup*, 1933; *The Shape of Things to Come: The Ultimate Resolution*, 1933; *The Croquet Player*, 1936; *Byrnhild*, 1937; *The Camford Visitation*, 1937; *Star Begotten: A Biological Fantasia*, 1937; *Apropos of Dolores*, 1938; *The Brothers*, 1938; *The Holy Terror*, 1939; *Babes in the Darkling Wood*, 1940; *All Aboard for Ararat*, 1940; *You Can't Be Too Careful: A Sample of Life, 1901-1951*, 1941.

SHORT FICTION: *The Stolen Bacillus and Other Incidents*, 1895; *The Plattner Story, and Others*, 1897; *Thirty Strange Stories*, 1897; *Tales of Space and Time*, 1899; *The Vacant Country*, 1899; *Twelve Stories and a Dream*, 1903; *The Country of the Blind, and Other Stories*, 1911; *A Door in the Wall, and Other Stories*, 1911; *The Short Stories of H. G. Wells*, 1927 (also pb. as *The Complete Stories of H. G. Wells*, 1966); *The Favorite Short Stories of H. G. Wells*, 1937 (also pb. as *The Famous Short Stories of H. G. Wells*, 1938).

NONFICTION: *Text-Book of Biology*, 1893 (2 volumes); *Honours Physiography*, 1893 (with Sir Richard A. Gregory); *Certain Personal Matters*, 1897; *A Text-Book of Zoology*, 1898 (with A. M. Davis); *Anticipations of the Reaction of Mechanical and Scientific Progress upon Human Life and Thought*, 1902 (also known as *Anticipations*); *The Discovery of the Future*, 1902; *Mankind in the Making*, 1903; *A Modern Utopia*, 1905; *Socialism and the Family*, 1906; *The Future in America: A Search After Realities*, 1906; *This Misery of Boots*, 1907; *New Worlds for Old*, 1908; *First and Last Things: A Confession of Faith and Rule of Life*, 1908; *The Great State: Essays in Construction*, 1912 (also known as *Socialism and the Great State*); *The War That Will End War*, 1914; *An Englishman Looks at the World: Being a Series of Unrestrained Remarks upon Contemporary Matters*, 1914 (also known as *Social Forces in England and America*); *God, the Invisible King*, 1917; *The Outline of History: Being a Plain History of Life and Mankind*, 1920; *Russia in the Shadows*, 1920; *The Salvaging of Civilization*, 1921; *A Short History of the World*, 1922; *Socialism and the Scientific Motive*, 1923; *The Open Conspiracy: Blue Prints for a World Revolution*, 1928; *Imperialism and the Open Conspiracy*, 1929; *The Science of Life: A Summary of Contemporary Knowledge About Life and Its Possibilities*, 1929-1930 (with Julian S. Huxley and G. P. Wells); *The Way to World Peace*, 1930; *What Are We to Do with Our Lives?*, 1931 (revised edition of *The Open Conspiracy*); *The Work, Wealth, and Happiness of Mankind*, 1931 (2 volumes); *After Democracy: Addresses and Papers on the Present World Situation*, 1932; *Evolution: Fact and Theory*, 1932 (with Huxley and G. P. Wells); *Experiment in Autobiography: Discoveries and Conclusions of a Very Ordinary Brain Since 1866*, 1934 (2 volumes); *The New America: The New World*, 1935; *The Anatomy of Frustration: A Modern Synthesis*, 1936; *World Brain*, 1938; *The Fate of Homo Sapiens: An Unemotional Statement of the Things That Are Happening to Him Now and of the Immediate Possibilities Confronting Him*, 1939; *The New World Order: Whether It Is Obtainable, How It Can Be Attained, and What Sort of World a World at Peace Will Have to Be*, 1940; *The Common Sense of War and Peace: World Revolution or War Unending?*, 1940; *The Conquest of Time*, 1942; *Phoenix: A Summary of the Inescapable Conditions of World Reorganization*, 1942; *Science and the World Mind*, 1942; *Crux Ansata: An Indictment of the Roman Catholic Church*, 1943; *'42 to '44: A Contemporary Memoir upon Human Behaviour During the Crisis of the World Revolution*, 1944; *Mind at the End of Its Tether*, 1945.

CHILDREN'S/YOUNG ADULT LITERATURE: *The Adventures of Tommy*, 1929.

Herbert George Wells, whose parents ran a china shop, was one of England's most prolific and best-known writers. Although he had to work for a living early in life, he was determined to get an education and rise in the world. After a period as a draper's apprentice and a chemist's assistant, he attended Midhurst Middleschool, where he was a teacher and a student. In 1884 he won a scholarship at the Royal College of Science, studying under the biologist and advocate of Charles Darwin's theory of evolution, Thomas Henry Huxley, an experience that made a lasting impression on him. Two years later he founded the *Science Schools Journal*, combining his interests in teaching and science writing. In 1890 he earned a bachelor of science degree from London University. He began tutoring until tuberculosis forced him to give up teaching. While convalescing, he began to write essays and stories, and in 1891 he published an essay in the *Fortnightly Review*, marking the beginning of his long and active career. In the same year, Wells married Isabel Mary Wells, a cousin. In 1893 he completed *Text-Book of Biology*. During this period, he taught in a correspondence school and did various kinds of writing. In 1895 he divorced his wife, after a two-year separation, and married Amy Catherine "Jane" Robbins, a former student, with whom he had two sons.

In 1895 Wells published *The Stolen Bacillus and Other Incidents*, a collection of short stories; later that year, he published *The Time Machine*, the first of his "scientific romances," his term for what became science fiction. An immediate success, this novel was frequently compared to the work of Jules Verne, but Wells protested that he wrote for political ends, while he thought Verne did not. Wells continued his scientific speculations in such books as *The Wonderful Visit*, *The Island of Dr. Moreau*, *The Invisible Man*, and *The War of the Worlds*. Like many of his works, these novels combined biological and historical projection with Darwinian theory. They also included social satire as well as warnings about the potentials of science, and they earned him the reputation of a visionary. The power and excitement inherent in his fiction were amply demonstrated in 1938, when a radio adaptation of *The War of the Worlds* created a few hours of panic throughout the United States, with many listeners believing that an invasion from space was occurring.

In *The Wheels of Chance*, Wells wrote the first of his novels dealing with the attempts of the lower middle class to rise in the world; this series includes *Kipps*, *Love and Mr. Lewisham*, and *The History of Mr. Polly*. Like Charles Dickens, Wells described the lives of ordinary people with generosity and sympathy. Around the turn of the twentieth century, he developed friendships with such writers as Joseph Conrad, Arnold Bennett, Henry James, George Bernard Shaw, and Stephen Crane.

From about 1905 to the period of World War I, Wells wrote realistic novels, what he called "social fables," using social as well as political ideas. He created some highly individualized characters. Examples of his work from this period include *Ann Veronica*, *Mr. Britling Sees It Through*, and *This Misery of Boots*. *New Worlds for Old* was an explanation of Wells's own version of socialism. For a time, he belonged to the Fabian Society, a socialist group, but his political utopia came to be more like Plato's republic than a socialist or communist state. He later renounced socialism as tyranny.

In *Tono-Bungay*, Wells began a group of novels based on contemporary historical themes and Darwinian theory, including *The New Machiavelli*, *The Passionate Friends*, and *The Research Magnificent*. After World War I, Wells achieved international fame with *The Outline of History*, a chronological survey of civilization. This book sold more than two million copies. Wells followed it with *A Short History of the World*. These books, along with his many books of scientific and social speculation, made Wells one of the most influential writers of his time.

In his writings and other activities after World War I, Wells made a bid for political recognition. To this period belongs *Russia in the Shadows*. In 1922 Wells the man entered politics as a candidate for Parliament on the Labour Party ticket. Defeated, he made a second unsuccessful attempt in 1923. After the death of his second wife in 1927, he lived mostly in London.

From 1929 to 1930, Wells published *The Science of Life*, a learned and monumental work written in collaboration with his son George and Julian Huxley, the son of Thomas. During the 1930's, Wells showed much interest in the New Deal experiments in the United States; his writing during the decade reflected current economic and political problems. Three years before his death, Wells completed a thesis on personality and was awarded the doctor of science degree from London University. He lived to see the end of World War II, having predicted, and then lamented, the use of the atomic bomb.

H. G. Wells is perhaps best known for his scientific romances, which helped to prepare the way for the genre of science fiction. His literary achievements, however, were vast and diverse. Through his eagerness to instruct and to entertain his readers, he produced many kinds of works on politics, history, society, and science. He was an undaunted, independent, iconoclastic, and sometimes impatient idealist. He thought that it was his duty to alert readers to future implications of scientific progress and that he could reconcile his hope for a better world with Darwinian ideas. His works reflect the struggles of his personal life and the intellectual and moral dilemmas of his times.

Timothy C. Miller

Bibliography

Batchelor, John. *H. G. Wells*. Cambridge, England: Cambridge University Press, 1985. An important examination of Wells's work. Includes an index and a bibliography.

Costa, Richard Hauer. *H. G. Wells*. Rev. ed. Boston: Twayne, 1985. A sympathetic survey of Wells's career and influence, with an emphasis on the major novels in the context of literary traditions before and after Wells. Includes a chronology, a review of contemporary trends in Wells criticism, notes, an annotated bibliography, and an index.

Hammond, J. R. *An H. G. Wells Chronology*. New York: St. Martin's Press, 1999. A guide to Wells's life and work. Includes bibliographical references and an index.

_______. *An H. G. Wells Companion*. New York: Barnes & Noble Books, 1979. Part 1 describes Wells's background and his literary reputation. Part 2 is an alphabetical listing and annotation of every title Wells published. Part 3 provides succinct discussions of his short stories; part 4 contains a brief discussion of book-length romances, and part 5 addresses individual novels. Part 6 is a key to characters and locations. Includes an appendix on film versions of Wells's fiction and a bibliography. An indispensable tool for the Wells scholar.

_______. *A Preface to H. G. Wells*. New York: Longman, 2001. A sound and concise introduction to Wells, with biographical information and critical analysis.

Haynes, Roslynn D. *H. G. Wells: Discoverer of the Future*. London: Macmillan, 1980. This is a thorough study of the influence of science on Wells's fiction and sociological tracts. It shows how science helped Wells to achieve an analytical perspective on the problems of his time, from art to philosophy. Includes bibliography and index.

Huntington, John, ed. *Critical Essays on H. G. Wells*. Boston: G. K. Hall, 1991. Essays on his major writings, including *Tono-Bungay* and *The History of Mr. Polly* as well as discussions of his science fiction and his treatment of social change, utopia, and women. Includes an introduction but no bibliography.

Smith, David C. *H. G. Wells: Desperately Mortal—A Biography*. New Haven, Conn.: Yale University Press, 1986. A scholarly biography of Wells, covering every aspect of his life and art. Includes very detailed notes and bibliography.

Irvine Welsh

Scottish novelist and short-story writer

Born: Edinburgh, Scotland; 1958

LONG FICTION: *Trainspotting*, 1993; *Marabou Stork Nightmares*, 1995; *Filth*, 1998; *Glue*, 2001; *Porno*, 2002.
SHORT FICTION: *The Acid House*, 1994; *Ecstasy: Three Tales of Chemical Romance*, 1996.
DRAMA: *Headstate*, pr. 1994; *You'll Have Had Your Hole*, pr., pb. 1998; *Blackpool*, pr. 2002 (musical; with Harry Gibson).
SCREENPLAY: *The Acid House*, 1999 (adaptation of his short stories).
MISCELLANEOUS: *The Irvine Welsh Omnibus*, 1997.

Even in an age accustomed to hyping first novels as instant classics, the commercial and critical success of Irvine Welsh has been remarkable. Indeed, Welsh was not only one of the most successful writers of the 1990's but also among the most influential. Welsh did not singlehandedly bring about the Scottish literary renaissance; Alasdair Gray, James Kelman, Iain Banks, and Janice Galloway had already laid the groundwork. However, Welsh focused the world's attention on Scotland, demonstrating how multiform the nation and its literature are and making the publication of Scottish fiction outside Scotland more viable than it had been for decades. Equally important, Welsh ushered in a new kind of fiction directed at the kind of young readers who did not take their cues from the literary reviews and British broadsheets. In doing so, he helped bring about another change, in the way such books are packaged and marketed. What makes Welsh successful and the extent of his influence so remarkable is that it derives from a book he did not actually set out to write. Once it was written, he never thought it would be published, and, once it was published, he never thought it would be read, least of all by the kind of reader for which it was intended.

That reader is the kind of character that populates *Trainspotting* and Welsh's other writing: disaffected, young, mainly male no-hopers, drunk or drugged, under- or unemployed, from Edinburgh (or rather from Leith, the docklands area where Welsh was born, or one of the postwar housing estates, such as Muirhouse, where he grew up). Welsh's Edinburgh is not the city of tourism, with its Castle and Edinburgh Festival. It is the city with an underbelly of acquired immunodeficiency syndrome (AIDS), heroin, and casual violence.

Welsh's fiction may not be overtly political, but it is nonetheless as connected to Scotland's political and socioeconomic situation as it is to particular streets, neighborhoods, and pubs. It grows out of the national mood of angry impotence following the failure of the 1979 referendum that would have given Scotland a greater—but still very limited—measure of independence after nearly three hundred years of union with England and more than a decade of the corrosive effects of Margaret Thatcher's policies on the Scottish economy and Scottish working-class values. Having left Edinburgh in 1978 for the London punk scene, Welsh stayed on to reap some of the benefits from the mid-1980's real estate boom. Back in Edinburgh by the decade's end, he became acutely aware of, and outraged by, the effects of AIDS and heroin on his class and generation.

Trainspotting is largely the story of five down-and-outers: friends, or rather associates, realistically rendered yet allegorical in a way, each representing a certain kind of response to their collective condition. With its loose plot and structure, the novel creates a momentum that depends more on cumulative effect, fast pace, and montage than on conventional causality and continuity. It is *Trainspotting*'s raw energy and demoniac urgency, its bleak vision and black humor, and the authenticity with which a nonjudgmental Welsh creates a coherent world rather than a conventional story that gives the novel its immense power.

Praised by mainstream reviewers, *Trainspotting* also appealed to young readers, especially those active in the club scene, many of whom read the novel only after reading Welsh's second book, *The Acid House*. These twenty-one stories and novella demonstrate an impressive range and versatility on Welsh's part, from conventional realism to punk send-ups involving inversions of various kinds. There is less use of dialect here than in *Trainspotting* but similar interest in the socially disaffected and disenfranchised. Welsh's second novel, *Marabou Stork Nightmares*, is his most ambitious work, an intricately layered narrative, or interweaving of narratives, in which Roy Strang seeks to come to terms with and to escape his past (especially a violent gang rape).

Since its publication, Welsh's reputation, if not his place on British best-seller lists, has suffered considerably. *Ecstasy: Three Tales of Chemical Romance* was hastily written and then rushed into print to coincide with the release of Danny Boyle's well-received film version of *Trainspotting* (1996). Although vastly different in style, the three novellas of *The Acid House* (one a revenge comedy, the second a revenge tragedy, and the third quite literally a chemical romance) all center on drugs, including the purported benefits of ecstasy and the irresponsibility of pharmaceutical companies that produce legal but harmful drugs such as thalidomide.

Filth, Welsh's version of the "tartan noir" detective fiction of Ian Rankin, betrays the sentimental streak that Welsh had previously avoided altogether (*Trainspotting*) or used sparingly and more effectively (*Marabou Stork Nightmares*). The sentimentality here is all the more glaring because it caps a novel that seemed to many reviewers written mainly to shock its audience. (Many felt the same way about Welsh's modern version of a Jacobean revenge play staged that same year, the aptly if obscenely titled, *You'll Have Had Your Hole*.) *Glue*, published three years later, is everything *Filth* is not: expansive, even generous. Like Glaswegian Alan

Spence's *The Magic Flute* (1990), it follows its four main characters over several generations and offers fleeting, teasing glimpses of the central characters of *Trainspotting*. Distinctive as his work his, Welsh has proven a surprisingly versatile writer, working in a variety of forms, including stage musical, and an adaptable one; two of his books have been adapted for the screen, four for the stage.

Robert A. Morace

Bibliography

Craig, Cairns. *The Modern Scottish Novel: Narrative and the National Imagination*. Edinburgh: Edinburgh University Press, 1999. Situates Welsh, specifically *Trainspotting*, in the context of Scottish fiction and Scottish national identity, particularly the dialectic of the fearful and the fearless.

Crawford, Robert. *Devolving English Literature*. 2d ed. Edinburgh: Edinburgh University Press, 2000. Discussion of *Trainspotting* plays an important role in the afterword to the second edition of Crawford's seminal study of the Scottishness of English literature.

Morace, Robert A. *Irvine Welsh's "Trainspotting."* New York: Continuum, 2001. Includes biography, bibliography, and extended analysis of *Trainspotting:* the novel, its reception, and stage and screen adaptations.

Redhead, Steve. *Repetitive Beat Generation*. Edinburgh: Rebel, 2000. Contains one of the best and longest interviews with Welsh. The introduction establishes the cultural context of his fiction. Also includes interviews with related literary figures, including John King and fellow Scots Duncan McLean, Gordon Legge, Alan Warner, and Kevin Williamson.

Eudora Welty

American short-story writer and novelist

Born: Jackson, Mississippi; April 13, 1909
Died: Jackson, Mississippi; July 23, 2001

LONG FICTION: *The Robber Bridegroom*, 1942; *Delta Wedding*, 1946; *The Ponder Heart*, 1954; *Losing Battles*, 1970; *The Optimist's Daughter*, 1972.

SHORT FICTION: *A Curtain of Green, and Other Stories*, 1941; *The Wide Net, and Other Stories*, 1943; *The Golden Apples*, 1949; *Short Stories*, 1950; *Selected Stories of Eudora Welty*, 1954; *The Bride of the Innisfallen, and Other Stories*, 1955; *The Collected Stories of Eudora Welty*, 1980; *Moon Lake, and Other Stories*, 1980; *Retreat*, 1981.

NONFICTION: *Music from Spain*, 1948; *The Reading and Writing of Short Stories*, 1949; *Place in Fiction*, 1957; *Three Papers on Fiction*, 1962; *One Time, One Place: Mississippi in the Depression, a Snapshot Album*, 1971; *A Pageant of Birds*, 1974; *The Eye of the Story: Selected Essays and Reviews*, 1978; *Ida M'Toy*, 1979; *Miracles of Perception: The Art of Willa Cather*, 1980 (with Alfred Knopf and Yehudi Menuhin); *Conversations with Eudora Welty*, 1984 (Peggy Whitman Prenshaw, editor); *One Writer's Beginnings*, 1984; *Eudora Welty: Photographs*, 1989; *A Writer's Eye: Collected Book Reviews*, 1994 (Pearl Amelia McHaney, editor); *More Conversations with Eudora Welty*, 1996 (Prenshaw, editor); *Country Churchyards*, 2000; *On William Hollingsworth, Jr.*, 2002; *On Writing*, 2002 (includes essays originally published in *The Eye of the Story*); *Some Notes on River Country*, 2003.

CHILDREN'S/YOUNG ADULT LITERATURE: *The Shoe Bird*, 1964.

MISCELLANEOUS: *Stories, Essays, and Memoir*, 1998.

Eudora Alice Welty is one of the greatest writers of Southern fiction. She was born in Jackson, Mississippi, on April 13, 1909, the daughter of Mary Chestina Andrews Welty, a teacher originally from West Virginia, and Christian Webb Welty, originally from Ohio. Soon after marrying, the young couple moved to Jackson, Mississippi, where Welty's father eventually became president of a life insurance company. After she left Jackson High School, Welty attended Mississippi State College for Women for two years and then transferred to the University of Wisconsin, where she received her bachelor of arts degree in 1929. By this time, Welty had decided to become an author, but her father considered writing a risky career and persuaded her to study at the Columbia University Graduate School of Business in New York. After studying advertising for a year, Welty returned home to Jackson at the beginning of the Depression. In 1931 her beloved father died.

At this time, Welty began to write regularly, while working at various jobs, several with newspapers, one with a radio station. The most important position for her literary career was one as a publicity agent for the Works Progress Administration, which sent her all over Mississippi, taking photographs and interviewing people, developing a sense of her native Mississippi, the setting for most of her fiction, and collecting ideas for her stories. In 1936 she had a one-person show of her photographs in New York City; that same year, her first story, "Death of a Traveling Salesman," appeared in a small magazine called *Manuscript*. Soon her work was being accepted by *The Southern Review*, then edited by Robert Penn Warren and Cleanth Brooks, and by other publications of national circulation. In 1941 "A Worn Path" and "Why I Live at the P.O." were published in *The Atlantic Monthly*, and "A Worn Path" won second prize in the O. Henry Memorial Contest; that year, too, her first collection of short stories, *A Curtain of Green*, appeared, with an introduction by Katherine Anne Porter. With her literary reputation established, Welty was now able to devote full time to her writing.

From that time on, Welty's short stories were published regularly, both in magazines and in collected editions, and just as regularly won prizes. Welty herself received Guggenheim Fellowships in 1942 and in 1949; the second enabled her to travel in France, Italy, and England. Her 1942 novella, *The Robber Bridegroom*, containing history, legend, and fairy tale, received praise from fellow southerner William Faulkner. In 1946 Welty's first full novel, *Delta Wedding*, appeared. Other novels followed, winning critical acclaim, such as the William Dean Howells Medal of the American Academy in 1955 for *The Ponder Heart*, which was dramatized and ran successfully on Broadway in 1956. During the years that followed, Welty lectured at various colleges and universities, becoming more widely known; however, it was not until the publication in 1970 of *Losing Battles* that Welty attained national fame. The book which followed in 1972, *The Optimist's Daughter*, based on the long illness and death of Welty's mother, won the Pulitzer Prize.

In addition to Welty's fame as a fiction writer, works such as *The Eye of the Story* established her importance as a critic. For the understanding of her own work and of the process of fiction in general, valuable critical comments are found in the memoir *One Writer's Beginnings*. In this book, Welty explains how her childhood observation prepared her for the kind of writing she was to do. For example, she says, she noticed that one friend of her mother, whose stories delighted her, always structured her stories in scenes. From the monologues of that same lady, she learned that economical speech does not reveal so much about a character as the rambling, digressive talk that is so typical of the South and which Welty reproduces perfectly. These lessons from her childhood are evident in one of Welty's most popular short stories, "Petrified Man." Essentially, the story is one long scene in a beauty shop. Through her own vivid descriptions and through the revealing, gossipy talk of the three characters, Welty not only produces an image of life at a point in time and space but also illustrates her theme: that women can dominate men to the point of turning men into freaks.

Writing from within a society that takes family ties and obligations seriously, Welty frequently chooses a time of crisis or ceremony for a story or a novel, when family and community are brought together and all of their intricate relationships can be revealed. In "The Wide Net," the disappearance of a young wife, who has left a suicide note, is the excuse for a group of men to come together in order to drag the river for her body. It is ironic that in this seemingly tragic situation, the men find themselves having a good time, and even the young husband briefly forgets the reason for the activity. Typically, both he and his wife (who has not actually killed herself) have learned something by the end of the story: he, that however worrisome she is, he cannot be happy without her, and she, that by cultivating her irrationality, she can enchant and control him. Similar revelations come to the young characters involved in ritual events, such as the marriage in *Delta Wedding*, the courtroom trial in *The Ponder Heart*, the family reunion in *Losing Battles*, and the funerals in "The Wanderers" and in *The Optimist's Daughter*. These characters learn that change is part of life, that joy and sorrow are intertwined, and that only through mutual respect and forgiveness can the family and the community survive.

In the 1960's, Welty was attacked by liberal critics for her failure to crusade for civil rights. Her answer can be found in the essay "Must the Novelist Crusade?" in *The Eye of the Story*, where she insists that propagandistic writing would destroy the imaginative writer, whose mission is to explore the underlying meaning of human life. By awakening her readers to the dignity of the humblest human being, to the importance of tolerance, and to the good that can be exerted by a family or a community, Welty established her lasting place in literature and may well have accomplished more for humanity than some of her more confrontational contemporaries.

Rosemary M. Canfield Reisman
Suzan Harrison

Bibliography

Devlin, Albert J. *Eudora Welty's Chronicle: A Story of Mississippi Life*. Jackson: University Press of Mississippi, 1983. Devlin analyzes certain works, such as *Delta Wedding*, in great detail. He offers insightful criticism and suggests that Welty's writing contains a historical structure, spanning from the territorial era to modern times.

Georgia Review 53 (Spring, 1999). A special issue on Welty celebrating her ninetieth birthday, with articles by a number of writers, including Doris Betts, as well as a number of critics and admirers of Welty.

Manning, Carol S. *With Ears Opening Like Morning Glories: Eudora Welty and the Love of Storytelling*. Westport, Conn.: Greenwood Press, 1985. An advanced book offering a critical interpretation of Welty's writing. Manning believes that the root of Welty's creativity is the Southern love of storytelling. Offers a select bibliography.

Marrs, Suzanne. *One Writer's Imagination: The Fiction of Eudora Welty*. Baton Rouge: Louisiana State University Press, 2002. A combination of critical analysis and memoir, written by a longtime friend of Welty who is also a scholar and the archivist of Welty's papers. Discusses the effects of both close personal relationships and social and political events on Welty's imagination and writing.

Mississippi Quarterly 50 (Fall, 1997). A special issue on Welty, with essays comparing Welty to William Faulkner, Edgar Allan Poe, and Nathaniel Hawthorne, and discussions of the women in Welty's stories, her political thought, and her treatment of race and history.

Mortimer, Gail L. *Daughter of the Swan: Love and Knowledge in Eudora Welty's Fiction*. Athens: University of Georgia Press, 1994. Concentrates primarily on the short stories and discusses one novel, *The Optimist's Daughter*, in detail.

Pierpont, Claudia Roth. *Passionate Minds: Women Rewriting the World*. New York: Alfred A. Knopf, 2000. Evocative interpretive essays on the life paths and works of twelve women, including Welty, connecting the circumstances of their lives with the shapes, styles, subjects, and situations of their art.

Vande Kieft, Ruth M. *Eudora Welty*. Rev. ed. Boston: Twayne, 1987. Vande Kieft offers an excellent critical analysis of Welty's major works, an overview of Welty's career, and an annotated secondary bibliography. A well-written, useful study for all students.

Waldron, Ann. *Eudora: A Writer's Life*. New York: Doubleday, 1998. The first complete but unauthorized biography of Welty. Offers a balanced study of her life as well as sensitive and sensible analyses of her short stories and novels.

Westling, Louise Hutchings. *Sacred Groves and Ravaged Gardens: The Fiction of Eudora Welty, Carson McCullers, and Flannery O'Connor.* Athens: University of Georgia Press, 1985. Westling examines the lives and works of Welty and the other authors in terms of their common concerns as women, such as their relationships with men and with their mothers. Offers a provocative and original viewpoint.

Weston, Ruth D. *Gothic Traditions and Narrative Techniques in the Fiction of Eudora Welty*. Baton Rouge: Louisiana State University Press, 1994. Discusses Welty's use of the gothic tradition in her fiction; provides original readings of a number of Welty's short stories.

Franz Werfel

Czech novelist and playwright

Born: Prague, Bohemia, Austro-Hungarian Empire (now in Czech Republic); September 10, 1890
Died: Beverly Hills, California; August 26, 1945
Identity: Jewish

LONG FICTION: *Nicht der Mörder, der Ermordete ist schuldig: Eine Novelle*, 1920 (*Not the Murderer*, 1937); *Verdi: Roman der Oper*, 1924 (*Verdi: A Novel of the Opera*, 1925); *Der Tod des Kleinbürgers*, 1927 (novella; *The Man Who Conquered Death*, 1927; also known as *The Death of a Poor Man*, 1927); *Der Abituriententag: Die Geschichte einer Jugendschuld*, 1928 (*Class Reunion*, 1929); *Barbara: Oder, Die Frömmigkeit*, 1929 (*The Pure in Heart*, 1931; also known as *The Hidden Child*, 1931); *Die Geschwister von Neapel*, 1931 (*The Pascarella Family*, 1932); *Kleine Verhältnisse*, 1931 (novella; *Poor People*, 1937); *Die vierzig Tage des Musa Dagh*, 1933 (*The Forty Days of Musa Dagh*, 1934); *Höret die Stimme*, 1937 (*Hearken unto the Voice*, 1938); *Twilight of a World*, 1937 (novellas); *Cella: Oder, Die Überwinder*, wr. 1937-1938, pb. 1954 (*Cella: Or, The Survivors*, 1989); *Der veruntreute Himmel: Die Geschichte einer Magd*, 1939 (*Embezzled Heaven*, 1940); *Das Lied von Bernadette*, 1941 (*The Song of Bernadette*, 1942); *Stern der Ungeborenen: Ein Reiseroman*, 1946 (*Star of the Unborn*, 1946).

SHORT FICTION: *Geheimnis eines Menschen*, 1927 (*Saverio's Secret*, 1937); *Erzählungen aus zwei Welten*, 1948-1952 (part of *Gesammelte Werke*).

DRAMA: *Der Besuch aus dem Elysium*, pb. 1912; *Die Versuchung*, pb. 1913; *Die Troerinnen des Euripedes*, pb. 1915 (a free adaptation of Euripides' *The Trojan Women*); *Die Mittagsgöttin*, pb. 1919; *Spiegelmensch*, pb. 1920; *Bocksgesang*, pb. 1921 (*Goat Song*, 1926); *Schweiger*, pb. 1922 (English translation, 1926); *Juárez und Maximilian*, pb. 1924 (*Juárez and Maximilian*, 1926); *Paulus unter den Juden*, pr., pb. 1926 (*Paul Among the Jews*, 1928); *Das Reich Gottes in Böhmen*, pr., pb. 1930 (*The Kingdom of God in Bohemia*, 1931); *Der Weg der Verheissung*, pb. 1935 (*The Eternal Road*, 1936); *In einer Nacht*, pr., pb. 1937; *Jacobowsky und der Oberst*, pr. 1944 (*Jacobowsky and the Colonel*, 1944).

POETRY: *Der Weltfreund*, 1911; *Wir sind*, 1913; *Einander*, 1915; *Der Gerichtstag*, 1919; *Poems*, 1945 (Edith Abercrombie Snow, translator).

NONFICTION: *Die christliche Sendung: Ein offener Brief an Kurt Hiller*, 1917.

MISCELLANEOUS: *Gesammelte Werke*, 1948-1975 (16 volumes).

Franz Werfel (VEHR-fuhl) was born into a Jewish family of Prague on September 10, 1890. His father, the owner of a glove factory, was intensely interested in art and music, but he saw in his son only a future partner and an heir to the business; consequently, he opposed the boy's early inclinations toward literature. Young Werfel was educated at the local *Gymnasium* and spent two years, 1909 to 1910, at the University of Prague. Having had the pleasure of seeing some of his work in print, Werfel had little interest in an academic career, preferring to spend his time writing and discussing literature with friends, who included such recognized writers as Gustav Meyrink, Max Brod, and Otokar Březina.

After leaving the university in 1910, Werfel went to Hamburg, Germany. There he took a job in a business firm but continued to write. Following a year of compulsory military service, from 1911 to 1912, he settled for a time in Leipzig, where he became a publisher's reader. With the beginning of World War I, he took a pacifist stand, publishing pacifist poems such as "Der Krieg," "Wortmacher des Krieges," and "Der Ulan," all of which appeared in

Einander. Despite his attitude toward the war, Werfel was called into the service as an officer in an artillery regiment and served during 1916 to 1917. In 1916 his adaptation of Euripides' *The Trojan Women* had a successful season on the Berlin stage and in other cities. By the time he was thirty, Werfel had made for himself a reputation in both poetry and drama; in addition, he already had written and published a short novel, *Not the Murderer.*

During the early 1920's Werfel's work was primarily in drama. *Spiegelmensch* opened simultaneously on stages in Dusseldorf, Leipzig, and Stuttgart. Werfel's first play to appear on the American stage was *Goat Song*, produced in New York in 1926. One of his most popular plays was *Juárez and Maximilian*, which after a successful run in Europe was translated into English and produced in New York before being made into a motion picture. Three religious plays were written somewhat later in Werfel's career: *Paul Among the Jews*, *The Kingdom of God in Bohemia*, and *The Eternal Road*. The last-named, a presentation of early Jewish history, was translated into English and produced in New York in 1936.

From 1925 on, Werfel was interested primarily in fiction, and a series of stories and short novels preceded his more important novels. In the United States his popularity came with the publication of *The Forty Days of Musa Dagh*, a novel based on the Armenian resistance to the Turks. *Hearken unto the Voice* showed the author's continued interest in the Jews and their history. *Embezzled Heaven*, also popular in the United States, illustrates how Werfel's religiosity caused him to become highly sympathetic to Roman Catholicism.

After World War I Werfel lived in Vienna. At the time of the *Anschluss* he fled to Paris, only to become a fugitive once again when the Germans invaded France. Eventually he reached the United States and safety. While escaping from the Germans, he had found a temporary refuge at Lourdes. While there, he vowed to write a book about the young woman who had seen a vision of the Virgin Mary at that shrine. *The Song of Bernadette* fulfilled that vow. A play, *Jacobowski and the Colonel*, was successfully produced in New York in 1944, and a collection of his verse, *Poems*, translated by Edith A. Snow, was published in 1945. Werfel and his wife, Anna, who was the widow of the composer Gustav Mahler, moved to Hollywood, where Werfel continued to write despite failing health. His last novel, *Star of the Unborn*, was completed only days before he succumbed to a heart attack on August 26, 1945.

Betsy P. Harfst

Bibliography

Everett, Susanne. *The Bride of the Wind: The Life and Times of Alma Mahler-Werfel*. New York: Viking, 1992. This biography of Werfel's wife describes their life together and depicts twentieth century Austria. Includes bibliography and index.

Heizer, Donna K. *Jewish-German Identity in the Orientalist Literature of Else Lasker-Schüler, Friedrich Wolf, and Franz Werfel.* Columbia, S.C.: Camden House, 1996. Heizer compares and contrasts the works of Werfel, Else Lasker-Schüler, and Friedrich Wolf, paying particular attention to the issue of Jewish-German identity. Includes bibliography and index.

Huber, Lothar, ed. *Franz Werfel: An Austrian Writer Reassessed.* New York: St. Martin's Press, 1989. A collection of papers presented at an international symposium on Werfel, discussing his life and works. Includes bibliography.

Jungk, Peter Stephan. *Franz Werfel: A Life in Prague, Vienna, and Hollywood*. New York: Grove Weidenfeld, 1990. A biography of Werfel that covers his life and works. Includes bibliography and indexes.

Michaels, Jennifer E. *Franz Werfel and the Critics*. Columbia, S.C.: Camden House, 1994. An examination of the critical reaction to Werfel's literary works. Includes bibliography and index.

Wegener, Hans. *Understanding Franz Werfel*. Columbia: University of South Carolina Press, 1993. A critical analysis and interpretation of the works of Werfel. Includes bibliography and index.

Glenway Wescott

American novelist and critic

Born: Kewaskum, Wisconsin; April 11, 1901
Died: Rosemont, New Jersey; February 22, 1987

LONG FICTION: *The Apple of the Eye*, 1924; *The Grandmothers: A Family Portrait*, 1927; *The Pilgrim Hawk: A Love Story*, 1940; *Apartment in Athens*, 1945.

SHORT FICTION: *. . . Like a Lover*, 1926; *Good-bye, Wisconsin*, 1928; *The Babe's Bed*, 1930; *Twelve Fables of Aesop*, 1954.

POETRY: *The Bitterns: A Book of Twelve Poems*, 1920; *Natives of Rock: XX Poems, 1921-1922*, 1925.

NONFICTION: *Elizabeth Madox Roberts: A Personal Note*, 1930; *Fear and Trembling*, 1932; *A Calendar of Saints for Unbelievers*, 1932; *Images of Truth: Remembrances and Criticism*, 1962; *The Best of All Possible Worlds: Journals, Letters, and Remembrances, 1914-1937*, 1975; *Continual Lessons: The Journals of Glenway Wescott, 1937-1955*, 1990.

EDITED TEXTS: *The Maugham Reader*, 1950; *Short Novels of Colette*, 1951.

Glenway Wescott, born in Kewaskum, Wisconsin, on April 11, 1901, was a midwesterner by birth and education. He attended public schools in various Wisconsin towns and spent two years (1917-1919) at the University of Chicago. His family had hoped he would enter the ministry, while he entertained some hope of becoming a professional musician. After World War I he spent a year in Germany, then returned to live for a short time in New Mexico. His first book was a volume of poetry, *The Bitterns*, published in 1920; this was followed by a second book of verse, *Natives of Rock*, in 1925. His first novel, *The Apple of the Eye*, was completed during a period of several months that Wescott spent in New York City. Set in rural Wisconsin, the novel relates the conflicts and forces involved in a boy's search for an understanding of the world and sex, a series of problems similar to those probed by many contemporary novelists, who seemed to be fascinated by the problems of the adolescent in the modern world. After the publication of his novel Wescott went again to Europe, and during the next eight years he was one of a large colony of American writers who lived abroad in the 1920's.

While in Europe he wrote *The Grandmothers*, which has received more acclaim from readers and critics than any of his other novels. It earned for Wescott the Harper Prize Novel Award for the year of publication. The novel, a saga of pioneer life in early Wisconsin, unfolds as it appears to Alwyn Tower, a young man who is very much like the author and who comes across an old family photograph album. His curiosity, awakened by the album, leads him to piece together the story of his family and relate the story as he finds it. This novel, like most of Wescott's fiction, interprets humanity through the desires and motives of typical human beings. The novel is illustrative, too, of the flowing, cadenced prose which is one of Wescott's strong points as a writer. The prose approaches the cadences of folk literature, and it was particularly well chosen for a novel about American pioneer life. Other works which appeared during the author's years of expatriation were *Good-bye Wisconsin*, a volume of short stories; *The Babe's Bed*, a long short story; *Fear and Trembling*, a volume of essays; and *A Calendar of Saints for Unbelievers*. The most interesting of these works is *The Babe's Bed*, a meditation in which a young man dreams about the possible future of a baby nephew.

Returning to the United States in 1934, Wescott settled on a farm in Hunterdon County, New Jersey. *The Pilgrim Hawk*, published in 1940, is a novel which indicated that the author had managed to weather successfully a period of inactivity such as is sometimes fatal to a writer's reputation. Ineligible for military service during World War II, Wescott sought to aid his country in other ways. An attempt to write a novel which would help Americans understand what had produced Nazism proved unsuccessful, however. An encounter with a Greek underground leader led Wescott to write another novel, *Apartment in Athens*, which describes the effect of the German occupation on one family in Athens, Greece, during World War II. The book was chosen by a national book club for its list and achieved a wide body of readers.

Early in the 1950's Wescott turned to critical writing. He edited *The Maugham Reader* and *Short Novels of Colette*. From this point in his career Wescott became more of a public man of letters than an active writer. He wrote and delivered speeches, was active in the arts community, serving on boards and committees, gave talks and readings, appeared on television and radio, and participated in symposia and conferences. In 1962 he published a collection of literary essays, *Images of Truth*, which established him as an influential critic. He died in 1987 on his family's farm in rural New Jersey, where he had lived for many years.

Bibliography

Baker, Jennifer Jordan. "'In a Thicket': Glenway Wescott's Pastoral Vision." *Studies in Short Fiction* 31 (Spring, 1994): 95-187. Explores the paradox of the Midwest as isolating and repressive as well as simple and idyllic in one of Wescott's best-known stories, "In a Thicket." Shows how Wescott treats this tension with narrative conventions and the narrative perspective of traditional pastoral.

Benfey, Christopher. "Bright Young Things." *The New York Times*, March 21, 1999, sec. 7, p. 9. A review of *When We Were There: The Travel Albums of George Platt Lynes, Monroe Wheeler, and Glenway Wescott*; comments on Wescott's fussy style but claims that his novella *The Pilgrim Hawk* is a brilliant work that can stand comparison with those of William Faulkner or D. H. Lawrence. Asserts that the central image of the novella comes from Wescott's relationship with George Platt Lynes.

Calisher, Hortense. "A Heart Laid Bare." *The Washington Post*, January 13, 1991, p. X5. In this review of Wescott's journals, *Continual Lessons*, Calisher provides a brief biographical sketch of Wescott; claims that he was not a true original as a novelist, but rather he was a reporter of a nonfictive kind. Contends that the image of Wescott from the journals is that of a writer not quite in the closet and not quite out of it.

Johnson, Ira. *Glenway Wescott: The Paradox of Voice*. Port Washington, N.Y.: Kennikat Press, 1971. A full-length, valuable study of Wescott, with extensive critical commentary on his major works. Includes bibliography and plot summaries of his novels.

Kahn, Sy Myron. *Glenway Wescott: A Critical and Biographical Study*. Ann Arbor, Mich.: University Microfilms, 1957. Much of the biographical information that is included in Kahn's dissertation cannot be found anywhere else. By showing how Wescott's experiences influenced each of his major works, Kahn has made an indispensable contribution to Wescott scholarship.

Rosco, Jerry. "An American Treasure: Glenway Wescott's *The Pilgrim Hawk*." *The Literary Review* 15 (Winter, 1988): 133-142. Rosco's analysis of Wescott's famous novella is taken from information provided by Wescott himself during his last interview.

Rueckert, William H. *Glenway Wescott*. New York: Twayne, 1965. A useful introduction to the works of Wescott, chronicling his development as a writer. Largely a sympathetic study of Wescott but points out that his ideas on the novel are limiting and that this has affected his work. Includes bibliography.

Wescott, Glenway. *Continual Lessons: The Journals of Glenway Wescott, 1937-1955*. Edited by Robert Phelps and Jerry Rosco. New York: Farrar, Straus and Giroux, 1990. Wescott's diaries provide a glimpse of his life.

Arnold Wesker

English playwright

Born: London, England; May 24, 1932

DRAMA: *Chicken Soup with Barley*, pr. 1958; *The Kitchen*, pr. 1959, revised pr., pb. 1961; *Roots*, pr., pb. 1959; *I'm Talking About Jerusalem*, pr., pb. 1960; *The Wesker Trilogy*, pb. 1960 (includes *Chicken Soup with Barley*, *Roots*, and *I'm Talking About Jerusalem*); *Chips with Everything*, pr., pb. 1962; *The Nottingham Captain: A Moral for Narrator, Voices and Orchestra*, pr. 1962 (libretto; music by Wilfred Josephs and David Lee); *The Four Seasons*, pr. 1965; *Their Very Own and Golden City*, pr. 1965; *The Friends*, pr., pb. 1970; *The Old Ones*, pr. 1972; *The Wedding Feast*, pr. 1974 (adaptation of Fyodor Dostoevski's story); *The Journalists*, pb. 1975; *Love Letters on Blue Paper*, pr. 1976 (televised), pr. 1977 (staged; adaptation of his short story); *The Merchant*, pr. 1976, revised pb. 1985 (based on William Shakespeare's play *The Merchant of Venice*); *The Plays of Arnold Wesker*, pb. 1976, 1977 (2 volumes); *Caritas*, pr., pb. 1981; *Four Portraits of Mothers*, pr. 1982; *Annie Wobbler*, pr. 1983 (staged version of the radio play *Annie, Anna, Annabella*); *The Sullied Hand*, pr. 1984; *Yardsale*, pr. 1984 (radio play), pr. 1987 (staged); *One More Ride on the Merry-Go-Round*, pr. 1985; *Whatever Happened to Betty Lemon*, pr. 1986; *Badenheim 1939*, pr. 1987 (adaptation of Aharon Appelfeld's novel); *Beorhtel's Hill*, pr. 1989; *Little Old Lady*, pr. 1989 (for children); *One-Woman Plays*, pb. 1989; *The Mistress*, pb. 1989; *Shoeshine*, pr. 1989 (for children); *When God Wanted a Son*, pr. 1989; *The Kitchen, and Other Plays*, pb. 1990; *Lady Othello, and Other Plays*, pb. 1990; *Shylock, and Other Plays*, pb. 1990; *Three Women Talking*, pr. 1992; *Blood Libel*, pb. 1994; *Wild Spring, and Other Plays*, pb. 1994; *Break, My Heart*, pr. 1997; *Denial*, pr. 2000.

SHORT FICTION: *Love Letters on Blue Paper*, 1974; *Said the Old Man to the Young Man: Three Stories*, 1978; *Love Letters on Blue Paper, and Other Stories*, 1980; *The King's Daughters: Twelve Erotic Stories*, 1998.

SCREENPLAY: *The Kitchen*, 1961.

TELEPLAY: *Menace*, 1963.

RADIO PLAYS: *Annie, Anna, Annabella*, 1983; *Bluey*, 1985.

NONFICTION: *Fears of Fragmentation*, 1970; *Journey into Journalism*, 1977; *The Journalists: A Triptych*, 1979; *Distinctions*, 1985; *As Much as I Dare*, 1994 (autobiography); *The Birth of Shylock and the Death of Zero Mostel*, 1997.

CHILDREN'S/YOUNG ADULT LITERATURE: *Fatlips: A Story for Young People*, 1978.

MISCELLANEOUS: *Six Sundays in January*, 1971 (stories and plays).

Arnold Wesker, one of the many English dramatists of the stage revolution that began with John Osborne's *Look Back in Anger* in 1956, made his reputation with a trio of plays about the working classes called *The Wesker Trilogy*, composed of *Chicken Soup with Barley*, *Roots*, and *I'm Talking About Jerusalem*. More to the point, his name became associated with the term "kitchen-sink drama," owing to the realistic depiction of life in his play *The Kitchen*, concerning the routine of daily life in a restaurant kitchen. This same realism exists in his play about military life, *Chips with Everything*, which joins those works previously mentioned as the fifth of Wesker's best-known plays. All are highly detailed, humorous, and compassionate studies of life among the poor. All are drawn from his own personal and family life and are based on his strong convictions about the necessity for social change.

Born in East London (Stepney) to Joseph, a tailor, and Leah Perlmutter Wesker, of Russian-Hungarian-Jewish extraction, Wesker held assorted jobs as carpenter, plumber, bookshop assistant, farmworker, and pastry cook. He spent two years in the Royal Air Force and enrolled in a course at the London School of Film Technique, entering *The Kitchen* in *The Observer* play competition in 1956, the year the stage revolution began. Although the play was rejected by theater managers at the time, like so many of his contemporaries whose plays were staged in provincial theaters and who maintained an association with a particular theater, Wesker found his home in the Belgrade Theatre, Coventry. As a moralist and social activist, he worked hard in Centre 42, an organization with the purpose of bettering life for the working classes, especially in regard to the importance of art in their lives. As a result of his political activism, he spent some time in prison for his part in a protest staged by the Campaign for Nuclear Disarmament. *The Kitchen* has its roots in Wesker's own experiences and in those of his mother, who supplemented the family income with restaurant kitchen jobs. The structure of the play takes on the order in which workers arrive at a restaurant in the course of a day, the rhythms of life in the kitchen increasing to a frenzied pitch with the lunch and dinner rushes.

Like *The Kitchen*, Wesker's trilogy is drawn from his own experience, this time from his own family and community life in London's East End. In all three plays, characters of the same family continue from one generation to the next. The first of the three plays to be staged, *Chicken Soup with Barley*, begins in the 1930's in the context of the fascistic anticommunist marches that took place in the Jewish East End. Despite the domestic quarrels of the family of Harry and Sarah Kahn, larger issues and events unify them and their idealistic son and daughter, Ronnie and Ada. World War II, the Russian invasion of Hungary, Harry's paralyzing stroke, Sarah's desperate attempt to keep the family together—all these events affect the moral and political idealism of Ronnie. In the second play of the trilogy, *Roots*, the scene is Norfolk, where Beatie Bryant and her family are awaiting the arrival of her fiancé, Ronnie, who upsets the expectations of the family by his decision not to marry Beatie. She, in turn, has experienced her own self-discovery, in contrast with the narrow-mindedness of her family and neighbors. *I'm Talking About Jerusalem* continues the Kahn family chronicles, this time in Norfolk, where Ronnie is helping Ada and her husband Dave move into a new home. More disillusionment sets in as all three, along with an old friend who is visiting them, confront a variety of personal failures. Dave is involved in petty thievery; Ronnie talks about his failed relationship with Beatie; Harry is confined to a mental institution; and a voice on the radio announces the Conservative victory of 1959. The four friends in their current situation present a vivid contrast with their optimistic idealism in *Chicken Soup with Barley*, a play in which their vision of a humane society based on brotherhood had been so strong. Despite the anguish in all of them, their idealism, although diminished, remains in the form of their recognition of the small gains that have been realized.

Originally written as a novel, *Chips with Everything* is based on Wesker's experience in the Royal Air Force. Written in Brechtian style, the play is drawn from Wesker's own letters. Pip Thompson, the main character, although middle-class, is an idealist who insists on forgoing his middle-class prerogatives for a commissioned rank. His sympathies for the military underclass and his opposition to authority, on the other hand, are challenged by officers and by his own personal revulsion to the vulgarity of the very class he champions. *Chips with Everything* was hailed by New Critics such as Kenneth Tynan and rejected as proselytizing propaganda by critics who opposed Wesker's left-wing view of the outdated English class system. Between the two extremes are those critics who see Wesker's plays as compassionate, humane, and moral.

Wesker's later plays are clearly distinguished from his early plays by the focus on personal relationships, bordering at times on the sentimental or fanciful. *The Friends*, for example, is concerned with a group of friends who react to the central character, Esther, who is dying of leukemia. All of Esther's friends are in the interior decorating industry, and their aesthetic community is the integrating principle of the drama. A Chekhovian situation prevails as the idea of death is the catalyst that drives various characters into revealing their inner selves. The vision here is highly personalized, and the sharp focus of the early plays seems diffused. Lyrical in tone and poetic in imagery, the style of the later plays contrasts sharply with the realism and social criticism of the early dramas. Yet the strong affirmation of family, community, and social idealism remains the thematic hallmark throughout Wesker's plays. Wesker has received several honors. In 1985 he was made a Fellow of the Royal Society for Literature, and in 1989 he was made an honorary Litt.D. of the University of East Anglia.

Susan Rusinko
David Barratt

Bibliography

Alter, Iska. "'Barbaric Laws, Barbaric Bonds': Arnold Wesker's *The Merchant*." *Modern Drama* 31 (December, 1988): 536-547. Traces some of the intertextual ambiguities, especially concerning the insistent use of the law by Shylock. Wesker's historical research is noted to shift the play from Romance to political realism.

Brown, John Russell. *Theatre Language: A Study of Arden, Osborne, Pinter, and Wesker.* London: Allen Lane, 1972. Brown analyzes the language of *Roots*, *The Kitchen*, and *Chips with Everything*, dealing particularly with the way Wesker maintains theatricality by substituting talk for action in his drama.

Dornan, Reade W. *Arnold Wekser Revisited.* Boston: Twayne, 1994. An overview of the critical reception of Wekser's major works, biographical chapters, and a useful bibliography of primary and secondary sources.

_______, ed. *Arnold Wesker.* New York: Garland, 1998. One of the Casebook series, it consists of eighteen essays on various aspects of Wesker's plays by an international array of critics.

Hayman, Ronald. *Arnold Wesker.* 3d ed. London: Heinemann, 1979. This volume in the Contemporary Playwrights series includes chapters on specific plays, two interviews with Wesker, and a clearly written, informative introduction to the earlier Wesker. Bibliography, biographical outline, and photographs.

Leeming, Glenda. "Articulacy and Awareness: The Modulation of Familiar Themes in Wesker's Plays of the Seventies." In *Contemporary English Drama*, edited by C. W. E. Bigsby. New York: Holmes and Meier, 1981. Leeming reviews the development of Wesker's drama from *The Old Ones* through *The Merchant.* She sees particularly an interiorization of a number of themes. The protagonists' awareness of their own suffering is located as the axis for the development.

_______. *Wesker the Playwright.* New York: Methuen, 1983. This volume is probably the fullest account of Wesker's work written up to the date of its publication. Contains a chapter on each of his plays, an appendix, a select bibliography, an index, and photographs.

_______, ed. *Wesker on File.* New York: Methuen, 1985. This invaluable small collection consists both of reviewers' and Wesker's own comments on his plays as well as on his work in general. Chronology and select bibliographies.

Wilcher, Robert. *Understanding Arnold Wesker.* Columbia: University of South Carolina Press, 1991. An analysis of the plays and stories. Originally a series of lectures by the Senior Lecturer at the University of Birmingham, England.

Cornel West

American philosopher

Born: Tulsa, Oklahoma; June 2, 1953
Identity: African American

NONFICTION: *Prophesy Deliverance! An Afro-American Revolutionary Christianity*, 1982; *Prophetic Fragments*, 1988; *The American Evasion of Philosophy: A Genealogy of Pragmatism*, 1989; *Breaking Bread: Insurgent Black Intellectual Life*, 1991 (with Bell Hooks); *The Ethical Dimensions of Marxist Thought*, 1991; *Beyond Eurocentrism and Multiculturalism*, 1993 (2 volumes); *Keeping Faith: Philosophy and Race in America*, 1993; *Race Matters*, 1993; *Jews and Blacks: Let the Healing Begin*, 1995 (with Michael Lerner; revised as *Jews and Blacks: A Dialogue on Race, Religion, and Culture in America*, 1996); *The Future of the Race*, 1996 (with Henry Louis Gates, Jr.); *Restoring Hope: Conversations on the Future of Black America*, 1997 (Kelvin Shawn Sealey, editor); *The Future of American Progressivism: An Initiative for Political and Economic Reform*, 1998 (with Roberto Mangabeira Unger); *The War Against Parents: What We Can Do for America's Beleaguered Moms and Dads*, 1998 (with Sylvia Ann Hewlett); *The Cornel West Reader*, 1999; *The African-American Century: How Black Americans Have Shaped Our Country*, 2000 (with Gates); *Cornel West: A Critical Reader*, 2001 (George Yancy, editor).

EDITED TEXTS: *Theology in America: Detroit II Conference Papers*, 1982 (with Caridad Guidote and Margaret Coakley); *Post-Analytic Philosophy*, 1985 (with John Rajchman); *Out There: Marginalization and Contemporary Cultures*, 1991; *White Screens, Black Images: Hollywood from the Dark Side*, 1994 (with James Snead and Colin MacCabe); *Encyclopedia of African-American Culture and History*, 1996 (with Jack Salzman and David Lionel Smith); *Struggles in the Promised Land: Towards a History of Black-Jewish Relations in the United States*, 1997 (with Jack Salzman); *The Courage to Hope: From Black Suffering to Human Redemption*, 1999 (with Quinton Hosford Dixie); *Taking Parenting Public: The Case for a New Social Movement*, 2002 (with Sylvia Ann Hewlett and Nancy Rankin).

Cornel Ronald West, the son of civilian Air Force administrator Clifton L. West, Jr., and his wife, Irene Bias West, a schoolteacher, had, before his fortieth birthday, established himself firmly among the leading public intellectuals in the United States. Both in his writing and in public appearances that are marked by his riveting charisma, West provokes thought, reaction, and controversy.

Born in Tulsa, Oklahoma, West was graduated from Harvard University magna cum laude in 1973. Princeton University awarded him the master's degree in 1975 and the Ph.D. in 1980. He began his teaching career as an assistant professor of philosophy at Union Theological Seminary in New York City, with which he was affiliated from 1977 to 1983 and again in 1988. Between 1984 and 1987 West taught at the Yale University Divinity School. He was professor of religion and director of African American studies at Princeton University from 1989 to 1994, then professor of religion and African American studies at Harvard from 1994. In 2002 he returned to Princeton as the Class of 1943 University Professor of Religion as part of a highly publicized exodus from the Harvard African American studies department precipitated by differences between the faculty and the university's president.

West is noted for the development of a form of pragmatism he has labeled "prophetic pragmatism." Much affected by his association at Princeton with Richard Rorty, perhaps the most significant living pragmatic philosopher in the United States, West, in *The American Evasion of Philosophy: A Genealogy of Pragmatism*, has taken Rorty's approach further than Rorty was able or willing to do. Realizing that Rorty, generally praised for his antifoundationalism, his rejection of human cruelty, and his support of pluralism, is conservative in his calculatedly ethnocentric views, West cautions obliquely that Rorty's views and his new pragmatism are not without pitfalls. West's work, deeply rooted in both Christianity and Marxism, out of which grows his vigorous moral philosophy, establishes a new kind of morality, much of it based upon traditional ideas that have endured for centuries. In *Race Matters*, for example, West calls for people of different ethnicities to arrive at a meeting of the minds and to bring about change through coalescing their ideas rather than through polar opposition.

His earlier *Prophesy Deliverance! An Afro-American Revolutionary Christianity* and *Prophetic Fragments* both created a new context within which to view black liberation theology. In these works and in *Race Matters*, West postulates theories regarding the redistribution of wealth for the common good, a Marxist notion that has made West highly controversial. The titles of the individual essays in *Race Matters* suggest the scope of West's interests: "Nihilism in Black America," "The Pitfalls of Racial Reasoning," "The Crisis of Black Leadership," "Demystifying the New Black Conservatism," "Beyond Affirmative Action: Equality and Identity," "On Black-Jewish Relations," "Black Sexuality: The Taboo Subject," and "Malcolm X and Black Rage." Not only do the titles of these essays illustrate West's range, but they suggest as well the direction of his future work. The essays in *Race Matters* are marked by keen, clear-cut reasoning. West is ever the skillful logician capable of applying the fundamental processes of pure reason to current problems relating to race. If one has any quibble with this tactic, which serves West extremely well, it might be that the underlying foundation of much of his logic is deductive rather than inductive. Reasoning from such a base often results in a dogmatic absolutism rather than in a liberating relativism.

In his collaboration with Michael Lerner, *Jews and Blacks: Let the Healing Begin*, West examines the tensions between blacks and Jews. The authors postulate building accords that will eradicate such tensions. In the 1996 revised edition of this book, newly titled *Jews and Blacks: A Dialogue on Race, Religion, and Culture in America*, the authors introduce a valuable new perspective into their original work.

West's writing consistently addresses with impressive intellectual vigor matters relating to racism, sexism, socialism, Eurocentrism, and multiculturalism. His collaboration with Bell Hooks (who deliberately uses all lowercase letters in the spelling of her name), *Breaking Bread: Insurgent Black Intellectual Life*, deals with these topics and comments cogently on black culture in America today. West and Hooks not only raise questions rooted in philosophy, sociology, economics, and theology, but also address matters of fashion and the arts within the black community. In this book they demonstrate their genuine compassion for the downtrodden and reveal their concern for improving the lots of such people.

Keeping Faith: Philosophy and Race in America examines the intellectual life of African Americans in the United States. It focuses on politics and government as they affect the lives of blacks and seems at times prophetic, given the aftermath of the 1992 Rodney King police brutality trial and the outcome of the 1995 O. J. Simpson trial.

R. Baird Shuman

Bibliography

Cowan, Rosemary. *Cornel West: The Politics of Redemption*. Malden, Mass.: Blackwell, 2002. An introduction to West's works and philosophy, especially as they relate to contemporary politics and sociology.

Johnson, Clarence Shole. *Cornel West and Philosophy*. New York: Routledge, 2002. A comprehensive examination of West's philosophy from his conceptions of pragmatism, existentialism, Marxism, and Prophetic Christianity to his writings on black-Jewish relations, affirmative action, and the role of black intellectuals.

West, Cornel. "Cornel West." Interview by John Nichols. *The Progressive* 61 (January, 1997: 26-29. In this extended interview, Nichols broaches questions about radical democracy, about the future of which West is pessimistic. West calls on political progressives to respect the religious concerns of African Americans.

Wood, Mark David. *Cornel West and the Politics of Prophetic Pragmatism*. Urbana: University of Illinois Press, 2000. Evaluates and critiques the political consequences of West's pragmatic philosophy.

Yancy, George, ed. *Cornel West: A Critical Reader*. Cambridge, Mass.: Blackwell, 2001. A collection of eighteen essays on the philosopher and academician. West is considered an important intellectual figure in African American studies and in the world of critical thinking.

Jessamyn West

American short-story writer and novelist

Born: North Vernon, Indiana; July 18, 1902
Died: Napa, California; February 23, 1984

SHORT FICTION: *The Friendly Persuasion*, 1945; *Cress Delahanty*, 1953; *Love, Death, and the Ladies' Drill Team*, 1955; *Except for Me and Thee: A Companion to the Friendly Persuasion*, 1969; *Crimson Ramblers of the World, Farewell*, 1970; *The Story of a Story, and Three Stories*, 1982; *Collected Stories of Jessamyn West*, 1986.

LONG FICTION: *The Witch Diggers*, 1951; *Little Men*, 1954 (pb. in *Star: Short Novels*, Frederik Pohl, editor); *South of the Angels*, 1960; *A Matter of Time*, 1966; *Leafy Rivers*, 1967; *The Massacre at Fall Creek*, 1975; *The Life I Really Lived*, 1979; *The State of Stony Lonesome*, 1984.

DRAMA: *A Mirror for the Sky*, pb. 1948 (libretto).

SCREENPLAY: *Friendly Persuasion*, 1956.

POETRY: *The Secret Look: Poems*, 1974.

NONFICTION: *To See the Dream*, 1957; *Love Is Not What You Think*, 1959; *Hide and Seek: A Continuing Journey*, 1973 (autobiography); *The Woman Said Yes: Encounters with Life and Death, Memoirs*, 1976; *Double Discovery: A Journey*, 1980.

EDITED TEXT: *The Quaker Reader*, 1962.

Jessamyn West is noted for her perceptive short stories and novels, particularly for those which deal with nineteenth century Quakers establishing homes on the midwestern frontier and for those which re-create the Southern California frontier of her childhood in the early twentieth century. Born in North Vernon, Indiana, on July 18, 1902, the first child of Eldo Roy and Grace Anna Milhous West, Mary Jessamyn West moved to rural Orange County, California, with her parents when she was six years old. (U.S. president Richard Milhous Nixon was her first cousin.) There, spending much of her time outdoors, she learned to love nature. She also developed a passion for reading and a fierce sense of personal responsibility that was certainly influenced by her being the oldest of three children.

After she graduated from Fullerton High School in 1919 she continued her education, receiving a bachelor of arts degree in English from Whittier College in 1923. That year she married Harry Maxwell McPherson, a teacher, who also had a Quaker background. After working for five years as a teacher and as a secretary in Hemet, California, in 1929 she resigned to work on a doctorate in English literature at the University of California at Berkeley. It was there that she developed her enthusiasm for Henry David Thoreau, whose influence can be seen in her work. When her work was almost concluded, she was diagnosed with advanced tuberculosis. After some time in a sanatorium, West was sent home, and during this period of enforced inactivity she began to write.

By the time West published her first short story, she was thirty-six years old. It is not surprising that seven years later, when her first book appeared, *The Friendly Persuasion*, it was the work of a mature writer. West gathered her material during her illness, when her mother, who was nursing her, reminisced about her childhood in Indiana. The book was above all the story of a happy marriage, based on mutual respect and faith in God. The arguments between the fun-loving, strong-willed Jess Birdwell and his equally strong-willed, strict wife, Eliza Cope Birdwell, a Quaker minister, were always resolved through prayer and love. Critics praised West for her appealing characters, for her original and precise style, and above all for her convincing depiction of the gentle Quaker way of life. Coming at the end of World War II, such stories brought their readers much-needed reassurance.

After an unsuccessful poetic opera based on the life of John James Audubon and a novel set on an Indiana poor farm, West returned to the form which had made her famous, the series of related sketches. *Cress Delahanty* was West's first essay into her other source of material: life in rural Orange County, California, in the period of her own youth. The adolescent heroine was praised, as the Birdwells had been, and again critics noted West's skill in pointing out the human truths that are evident in slight occurrences.

In the years which followed, West wrote primarily fiction, in the forms of short stories, as those collected in *Love, Death, and the Ladies' Drill Team*, and novels, such as *South of the Angels*. Only in *Except for Me and Thee* did she return to the form of related sketches. She also did some screen writing, including the script for *Friendly Persuasion* (pb. 1955, released in 1956), which won the Palme d'Or at the Cannes Film Festival and received six Academy Award nominations. Her book *To See the Dream* tells of her experiences during the making of the film. In the later years of her life, West wrote several important autobiographical books. Early in the 1970's, she retreated for three months to a trailer by the Colorado River, where she wrote the meditative, reminiscent *Hide and Seek*. Unlike that work, *The Woman Said Yes*, published in 1976, raised a storm of controversy because in it she admitted not only to having considered suicide when she was in ill health but also to having aided her cancer-stricken sister to kill herself, a situation that she had treated fictionally in *A Matter of Time*. In 1983 West completed her last work, the novel *The State of Stony Lonesome*. She died of a stroke in Napa, California, on February 23, 1984.

The predominant theme of West's work is the tension between the needs of the individual and the demands of love. In *The Friendly Persuasion* and in *Except for Me and Thee*, for example, the ebullient Irish Quaker Jess Birdwell must frequently decide whether to take an action that appears harmless to him yet offends the sensibilities of his loving but firm Quaker minister wife, Eliza. In keeping with her Quaker background, West stresses the importance of the individual conscience. When a character follows the demands of his conscience, he can triumph over pain. Each person must test his or her deeds and words by their motivation. If these deeds and words proceed from hatred, they will destroy him or her; if they proceed from love, they will enable him or her to triumph over heartbreak. It was perhaps this test that West used when she responded to her sister's desire for death. In this situation, she made her own decision and acted as her conscience moved her.

West was always beloved by the reading public and praised by critics. Since her death, though, the academic world seems to have rediscovered her, finding that her work is much more complex than a quick reading may suggest. Although her characters may be ordinary, their feelings and their motivations are complicated; although her plots may not at first glance appear dramatic, they involve the most serious decisions of the human spirit. Even West's language, rich in metaphor and humor, lyrically descriptive and highly symbolic, deserves further study. No longer considered a local-color writer, West is now viewed as a historian of the human condition.

Rosemary M. Canfield Reisman

Bibliography

Barron, James. "Jessamyn West, Author of Stories About Quakers in Indiana, Dies." *The New York Times*, February 24, 1984, p. B16. In this obituary of West, Barron briefly traces her personal and literary life and comments on her focus on Quakers.

Betts, Doris. "Skillful Styles from Two Storytellers." *Los Angeles Times*, February 26, 1987. A review of *Collected Stories of Jessamyn West*; comments on her narrators as observers, her characters as eccentrics, and her animals as lovable.

Farmer, Ann Dahlstrom. *Jessamyn West: A Descriptive and Annotated Bibliography*. Lanham, Md.: Scarecrow Press, 1998. A helpful tool for students of West. Includes an index.

Prescott, P. S. "The Massacre at Fall Creek." *Newsweek*, April 14, 1975, 86. According to Prescott, the ingredients in a "good old-fashioned novel" combine suspense, violence, and villainy with sentiment. *The Massacre at Fall Creek* is a concrete example of this genre. Jessamyn West's expertise, according to Prescott, extends not only to the "good old-fashioned novel" but also to other literary forms as well.

Shivers, Alfred S. *Jessamyn West*. Rev. ed. New York: Twayne, 1992. This biography of West probes the religious influences of her Quaker beliefs on her literary endeavors, thus providing an essential clue to her character and personality. Shivers incorporates his literary criticism of her works.

Yalom, Marilyn, and Margo B. Davis, eds. *Women Writers of the West Coast: Speaking of Their Lives and Careers*. Santa Barbara, Calif.: Capra Press, 1983. Discusses the role of religion—in this case, Quakerism—in West's life and work.

Nathanael West

(Nathan Weinstein)

American novelist and screenwriter

Born: New York, New York; October 17, 1903
Died: El Centro, California; December 22, 1940

LONG FICTION: *The Dream Life of Balso Snell*, 1931; *Miss Lonelyhearts*, 1933; *A Cool Million: The Dismantling of Lemuel Pitkin*, 1934; *The Day of the Locust*, 1939.

SCREENPLAYS: *Follow Your Heart*, 1936 (with Lester Cole and Samuel Ornitz); *The President's Mystery*, 1936 (with Cole); *Ticket to Paradise*, 1936 (with Jack Natteford); *It Could Happen to You*, 1937 (with Ornitz); *Born to Be Wild*, 1938; *I Stole a Million*, 1939; *Five Came Back*, 1939 (with Jerry Cady and Dalton Trumbo); *Men Against the Sky*, 1940.

MISCELLANEOUS: *Novels and Other Writings*, 1997 (includes long fiction, letters, and unpublished writings).

Nathanael West's literary life has an irony that almost parodies his own novels. An original and very serious craftsman, he achieved in his short life little fame, except among a discerning few, and no popular success. Paperback editions of his novels have sold hundreds of thousands of copies in numerous editions, and West's 1939 satire of Hollywood, *The Day of the Locust*, was made into a widely acclaimed motion picture in 1975.

West was born Nathan Weinstein in New York City on October 17, 1903. He attended DeWitt Clinton High School but performed so poorly that he had to doctor his transcript to matriculate at Tufts University in 1921. There West's grades plummeted so rapidly (he did not attend classes) that school administrators asked for his withdrawal after only one term. By another ruse he was admitted to Brown University with the high grades and cumulative credits of a different Nathan Weinstein, but even then West performed so poorly that he barely received his baccalaureate degree in 1924. At Brown he was nicknamed "Pep" for the opposite characteristics the word suggests. Literary friends included I. J. Kapstein, Quentin Reynolds, and S. J. Perelman, who later married his sister Laura. He wrote few pieces for undergraduate publications. In Paris during 1925-1926 he came under Surrealist influences and began work on his first novel, *The Dream Life of Balso Snell*, a fantasy on his hero's wanderings inside the Trojan horse, where he meets a naked man in a derby writing about Saint Puce (a flea who lived in Christ's armpit) and a twelve-year-old boy wooing his schoolmistress with Russian journals. This work was ignored following its publication in 1931.

Back in New York, West managed one of his father's hotels, which he populated with largely freeloading writers and friends. He also began using his pen name—because, as he once claimed, "Horace Greeley said, 'Go West young man!' so I did." A widening circle of literary friendships brought work as editor of *Contact* with William Carlos Williams in 1932 and as associate on *Americana* with George Grosz in 1933. *Contact* and a third little magazine, *Contempo*, contained early drafts of *Miss Lonelyhearts*, the story of an advice-to-the-lovelorn columnist who is destroyed when he takes too seriously the problems and miseries of his correspondents. This minor classic was issued in 1933 by a publisher who shortly afterward went bankrupt. By the time copies and plates were rescued from the unpaid printer by another publishing house, demand for the book had ceased.

West's third and weakest novel, *A Cool Million*, is a broad satire on the Horatio Alger myth, in which Lemuel Pitkin loses his teeth, eye, scalp, money, and eventually his life after being victimized by capitalists, communists, and neo-fascists. It was quickly remaindered.

Unsuccessful as an editor and writer, West moved to California in 1935 and took up residence in a seedy Hollywood apartment, where he was surrounded by movie stuntmen and bit players. In time he was able to pick up regular script work on a string of B-movies with titles such as *I Stole a Million* and *Bachelor Girl*. It was dreary work but provided West with crucial material for his most mature work, *The Day of the Locust*, published in 1939. In 1940 he married Eileen McKenney, of *My Sister Eileen* fame. Seven months later, on December 22, they were killed together in an auto crash at El Centro, California.

Although *The Day of the Locust* has Hollywood as its locale and minor actors and hangers-on from the periphery of the studios as its characters, the novel is no more about motion pictures than *Miss Lonelyhearts* is about newspapers. Fantastic and exaggerated in theme and treatment, West's two chief novels convey, more clearly than most twentieth century fiction, a sense of horror and revulsion at the universe in which humankind lives and the world people make for themselves.

Steven C. Weisenburger

Bibliography

Bloom, Harold, ed. *Nathanael West*. New York: Chelsea House, 1986. This useful collection includes essays on all of West's work in a representative selection. S. E. Hyman's essay is a valuable introduction to West. Contains bibliography.

_______. *Nathanael West's "Miss Lonelyhearts."* New York: Chelsea House, 1987. This valuable collection offers nine essays from a variety of viewpoints on *Miss Lonelyhearts*. Includes a chronology and a bibliography.

Martin, Jay, ed. *Nathanael West: A Collection of Critical Essays*. Englewood Cliffs, N.J.: Prentice-Hall, 1971. This collection contains some brief critical commentaries by West himself as well as analyses by others. Martin's introductory essay is a useful summary. Some of the others presuppose a fairly sophisticated reader. Includes bibliography.

Siegel, Ben, ed. *Critical Essays on Nathanael West*. New York: G. K. Hall, 1994. Divided into two sections—reviews and essays. In addition to the comprehensive introduction surveying West's life and career, the essay section provides studies of individual novels and of West's work as a whole. Includes notes and index but no bibliography.

Veitch, Jonathan. *American Superrealism: Nathanael West and the Politics of Representation in the 1930's*. Madison: University of Wisconsin Press, 1997. Contains separate chapters on each novel as well as an introduction discussing the "crisis of representation in the 1930's." Includes detailed notes but no bibliography.

Widmer, Kingsley. *Nathanael West*. Boston: Twayne, 1982. Widmer's general introduction concentrates on "West as the prophet of modern masquerading, role-playing, and its significance" while offering useful analyses of West's work. Lengthy notes and an annotated bibliography are provided.

Wisker, Alistair. *The Writing of Nathanael West*. New York: St. Martin's Press, 1990. Chapters on each novel and a series of appendices on various aspects of West's work, including his handling of violence, his unpublished fiction, and revisions of his work. Includes notes and bibliography.

Paul West

English-born American novelist

Born: Eckington, Derbyshire, England; February 23, 1930

LONG FICTION: *A Quality of Mercy*, 1961; *Tenement of Clay*, 1965; *Alley Jaggers*, 1966; *I'm Expecting to Live Quite Soon*, 1970; *Caliban's Filibuster*, 1971; *Bela Lugosi's White Christmas*, 1972; *Colonel Mint*, 1972; *Gala*, 1976; *The Very Rich Hours of Count von Stauffenberg*, 1980; *Rat Man of Paris*, 1986; *The Place in Flowers Where Pollen Rests*, 1988; *Lord Byron's Doctor*, 1989; *The Women of Whitechapel and Jack the Ripper*, 1991; *Love's Mansion*, 1992; *The Tent of Orange Mist*, 1995; *Sporting with Amaryllis*, 1996; *Terrestrials*, 1997; *Life with Swan*, 1999; *The Dry Danube: A Hitler Forgery*, 2000; *O.K.: The Corral, the Earps, and Doc Holliday*, 2000; *A Fifth of November*, 2001; *Cheops: A Cupboard for the Sun*, 2002.

SHORT FICTION: *The Universe and Other Fictions*, 1988.

POETRY: *Poems*, 1952; *The Spellbound Horses*, 1960; *The Snow Leopard*, 1964.

NONFICTION: *The Growth of the Novel*, 1959; *Byron and the Spoiler's Art*, 1960, 2d edition 1992; *I, Said the Sparrow*, 1963; *The Modern Novel*, 1963; *Robert Penn Warren*, 1964; *The Wine of Absurdity: Essays in Literature and Consolation*, 1966; *Words for a Deaf Daughter*, 1969; *Out of My Depths: A Swimmer in the Universe*, 1983; *Sheer Fiction*, 1987-1994 (3 volumes); *Portable People*, 1990 (drawings by Joe Servello); *My Mother's Music*, 1995; *A Stroke of Genius: Illness and Self-Discovery*, 1995; *The Secret Lives of Words*, 2000; *Master Class: Scenes from a Fiction Workshop*, 2001; *Oxford Days: An Inclination*, 2002.

EDITED TEXT: *Byron: Twentieth Century Views*, 1963.

Paul Noden West is one of America's most imaginative and innovative contemporary writers and finest literary stylists. He was born in Eckington, England, on February 23, 1930, the son of Alfred and Mildred (Noden) West. From his earliest days, West was surrounded by book lovers—parents, grandparents, and relatives—who viewed the written word as sacred and who considered nearly any book a worthy addition to an ever-growing canon of literary experiences, experiences they considered as valid as those of everyday life for authenticating the self and one's existence in the world. West quickly assimilated this reverence for the word and literary text as experience and applied it to his studies at Oxford and Columbia universities. Between the childhood encouragement to sample literature from around the world and the Oxford mentoring that exhorted him to experience literature, learning, and activities outside the traditional academic setting, it is not surprising that West developed an eclectic, comparative taste in literature and in the versatility and variety of his literary craft.

Even a cursory examination of West's works reveals their thematic variety and stylistic richness as well as the originality of his imagination. His themes include psychic abuse, failed relationships, societal indifference, and spiritual inadequacy, but a positive side exists in his writing as well. Self-discovery and survival are strong forces in his works. The dialectical tensions between the forces of genocide and the keepers of peace reinforce the paradoxical nature of existence in an indifferent, imperfect, yet potentially rich universe. This thematic richness and variety is the product of West's interconnected beliefs about the human condition. Throughout his works, West juxtaposes a picture of a universe in flux, filled with a plurality of experience, to one of an arbitrary and imperfect world, self-absorbed and heedless of its members. West reveals that the tension and confrontation between these paradoxical sides of an absurd world produce both the darker sides of human behavior and being and the potentiality in life. Consequently, his works suggest the need to perceive the universe and life more inclusively and recognize the productive capacity of the imagination to construct meaning and even a measure of happiness in an absurd world.

West's particular significance in contemporary literature rests strongly with his stylistic genius; he ranks with James Joyce, Vladimir Nabokov, Marcel Proust, and Virginia Woolf in his ability to craft simultaneously lyrical and dense, elegant and economical tours de force. He captures the exciting, arbitrary nature of words for reflecting a universe in flux. West's career has moved in a steady arc from the realism of the *Alley Jaggers* trilogy through the experimentalism of *Caliban's Filibuster* and *Gala* to a sustained production of historical fiction. In these later novels he has imaginatively explored Count von Stauffenberg, the putative assassin of Adolf Hitler, a Parisian street person, Jack the Ripper, his own parents' adolescence and courtship, and Chinese women conscripted by the Japanese to act as prostitutes. West has given historical fiction a depth and stylistic exuberance unmatched by most practitioners of the form. In all these novels, there is also a sustained examination of the creative possibilities of an artistic sensibility, with character after character practicing some personal, highly individual art.

West's fiction demands fluidity of the novel as an organic, dynamic genre and of the reader as collaborator in the creative process of constituting the text as aesthetic object. It is for these contributions to contemporary literature that West's peers awarded him the prestigious American Academy and Institute of Arts and Letters Literature Award in 1985, and the Lannan Prize for Fiction and France's Grand Prix Halpérine-Kaminsky in 1993.

Joseph F. Pestino
David W. Madden

Bibliography

McGuire, Thomas G. "The Face(s) of War in Paul West's Fiction." *War, Literature, and the Arts* 10 (Spring/Summer, 1998): 169-186. Traces the persistence of West's rumination on warfare and conflict. Three principal novels—*The Very Rich Hours of Count von Stauffenberg*, *The Place in Flowers Where Pollen Rests*, and *Rat Man of Paris*—form the basis of the argument. The journal also contains an interview with West and three of the author's short fictions.

Madden, David W. "Indoctrination to Pariahdom: Liminality in the Fiction of Paul West." *Critique* 40 (Fall, 1998): 49-70. Examines five of West's novels to explain the confusions and violence found so frequently there. The essay argues that each novel presents characters suspended in a liminal state from which they have difficulties extracting themselves.

_______. *Understanding Paul West*. Columbia: University of South Carolina Press, 1993. A book-length study on West that provides an overview of his work through *The Women of Whitechapel*. Intended as an introductory study to West's life and fiction, it traces the development of the themes of identity, artistic creation, and imagination's freedom.

_______, ed. *The Review of Contemporary Fiction* 11 (Spring, 1991). A special half-issue devoted to West. Contains thirteen essays, an interview, and a primary bibliography of West's work up to *The Women of Whitechapel*, examining his novels from a variety of perspectives. The collection also features three short fictions from West.

Pope, Dan. "A Different Kind of Post-Modernism." *The Gettysburg Review* 3 (Autumn, 1990); 658-669. Looks at West's short-story collection *The Universe and Other Fictions* in the company of Rick DeMarinis's *The Coming Triumph of the Free World* (1988) and T. Coraghessan Boyle's *If the River Was Whiskey* (1989). A fine sustained consideration of West's short fiction.

Saltzman, Arthur M. "Beholding Paul West and *The Women of Whitechapel*." *Twentieth Century Literature* 40 (Summer, 1994): 256-271. Examines West's fourteenth novel in terms of the author's wit and inventive verbal energy and the uneasy balance between ontology and linguistic inventiveness.

Rebecca West
(Cicily Isabel Fairfield)

English novelist

Born: London, England; December 21, 1892
Died: London, England; March 15, 1983

LONG FICTION: *The Return of the Soldier*, 1918; *The Judge*, 1922; *Harriet Hume: A London Fantasy*, 1929; *War Nurse: The True Story of a Woman Who Lived, Loved, and Suffered on the Western Front*, 1930; *The Harsh Voice*, 1935; *The Thinking Reed*, 1936; *The Fountain Overflows*, 1956; *The Birds Fall Down*, 1966; *This Real Night*, 1984; *Cousin Rosamund*, 1985; *Sunflower*, 1986.

NONFICTION: *Henry James*, 1916; *The Strange Necessity: Essays and Reviews*, 1928; *Ending in Earnest: A Literary Log*, 1931; *St. Augustine*, 1933 (biography); *Black Lamb and Grey Falcon*, 1941 (travel); *The Meaning of Treason*, 1947 (history; revised as *The New Meaning of Treason*, 1964); *A Train of Powder*, 1955 (history); *The Court and the Castle*, 1957 (literary criticism); *The Young Rebecca: Writings of Rebecca West*, 1982 (journalism); *Family Memories*, 1987.

MISCELLANEOUS: *Rebecca West: A Celebration*, 1977.

Rebecca West is best known for her contribution to nonfiction writing, in which she showed a remarkable facility for blending the genres of history, travel, biography, and literary criticism. Ranking just below such masterpieces as *Black Lamb and Grey Falcon* and *The Meaning of Treason* are her works *The Fountain Overflows* and *The Birds Fall Down*. It does her a disservice to separate her fiction and nonfiction, for all of her mature writing is informed by a strongly novelistic sensibility.

West was born Cicily Isabel Fairfield. Her father, Charles Fairfield, was of Anglo-Irish descent and made something of a reputation for himself as a staunch defender of individualism in debates with George Bernard Shaw and Herbert Spencer, two of the most important and influential thinkers in Victorian England. When her father died in 1902, however, West found herself in straitened circumstances, one of four daughters whom her mother had somehow to support. She never forgot the feeling of shabbiness in her early years, and by the age of nineteen, determined to make her mark as an actress, she changed her name to Rebecca West after a character in Henrik Ibsen's play *Rosmersholm* (pb. 1886; English translation, 1889). When West was advised that she had minimal talent as an actress, she took up her pen as a militant feminist journalist. She dared to attack even the most advanced thinkers of her time, including H. G. Wells, who eventually became her lover. She had a son with him, but they later parted in bitterness, with West feeling keenly the special burdens placed on women in male-dominated, double-standard societies.

In addition to her feminist journalism (collected in *The Young Rebecca*), West produced searing criticism of Augustine, a highly sexed man and yet a saint, cushioned in life by his devoted mother and also a worldly man capable of abandoning a mistress of long-standing once he dedicated himself to the Church. In her acclaimed *Black Lamb and Grey Falcon*, a travel account and historical study of the Balkans on the eve of World War II, various woman characters are given dominant roles, and West herself speaks in her own voice about her youthful impressions of Eastern Europe. Her husband, Henry Maxwell Andrews, accompanied her on this trip, and through his incisive contributions to the dialogue and his quietly supportive presence, it is clear that West found a male companion entirely comfortable with her formidable intelligence and restless quest to understand her time in history.

Many critics, misled by the many different genres in which she wrote, have doubted that there is a major theme or thread in West's work. In fact, in her fiction and nonfiction West's concerns have been the same: war, treason, marriage—the institutions and events that bind society together or rend it apart. In her early novel *The Return of the Soldier*, two women (a wife and cousin) are perplexed by the return of their soldier, who in his shell-shocked state does not remember them but longs for a woman he loved many years earlier. The gap that suddenly opens up in his life and in theirs—between the loving husband and relative and his amnesiac alter ego, the young, impulsive lover of another woman from a lower social class—is evocative of West's effort to capture both the personal and the historical dimensions of experience in the war-torn world of the twentieth century.

Whether writing about the Nuremberg Trials in *The Meaning of Treason* or about petty criminals in *A Train of Powder*, West conveys an extraordinary sense of the range of human society. She understands both the historical forces that inform individual actions and the peculiarities of individual behavior that her father so cherished. Some of her novels, it is thought, are overwhelmed by her intellectuality, but on balance she must be considered as one of the greatest imaginative minds of the twentieth century.

Carl Rollyson

Bibliography

Deakin, Motley F. *Rebecca West*. Boston: Twayne, 1980. Clear examination of major genres and themes in West's writing. Provides detailed commentary on theme, character, style, and setting in West's novels.

Glendinning, Victoria. *Rebecca West: A Life*. New York: Alfred A. Knopf, 1986. Detailed account of West's life, focusing particularly on the early years. Provides insight into West's development as a writer.

Orel, Harold. *The Literary Achievement of Rebecca West*. London: Macmillan, 1986. Analyses West's life and her critical stance. Compares and contrasts characters, style, idiom, and recurring themes in her novels.

Rollyson, Carl E. *The Literary Legacy of Rebecca West*. San Francisco: International Scholars, 1998. A thorough book of criticism and interpretation of West. Includes bibliographical references and an index.

_______. *Rebecca West: A Life*. New York: Scribner, 1996. Detailed biography discussing West's importance to twentieth century literature, tracing the development of her long career and illustrating the connections between her fiction and nonfiction.

Scott, Bonnie Kime. *Refiguring Modernism*. 2 vols. Bloomington: Indiana University Press, 1995. The first volume of this set discusses women of 1928, and the second volume offers postmodern feminist readings of Virginia Woolf, Djuna Barnes, and West.

Edward Noyes Westcott

American novelist and short-story writer

Born: Syracuse, New York; September 27, 1846
Died: Syracuse, New York; March 31, 1898

LONG FICTION: *David Harum: A Story of American Life*, 1898.
SHORT FICTION: *The Teller*, 1901.

Edward Noyes Westcott is something of an anomaly in the history of American literature, being a banker turned author. The son of a dentist, he attended the public schools in Syracuse until he was sixteen and then left school to take a job as a junior clerk in a local bank. At the age of twenty he left Syracuse to work for an insurance company in New York City. He returned to Syracuse, however, to become a teller and cashier in banks in that city. In 1874 he married Jane Dows of Buffalo, New York, and the couple had three children, two sons and a daughter.

Eager to get ahead in life and to provide for his children's education, Westcott formed the company of Westcott and Abbott, a banking and brokerage house, in 1880. For several years the firm was successful, but the bankruptcy of an allied company caused its failure in the late 1880's, at which time Westcott took a job with the Syracuse water commission.

Having to retire because of tuberculosis in 1895, Westcott went to the Adirondack Mountains to recuperate. While there he began to write for his own amusement. In 1895 he went to Naples, still searching for good health. While there he wrote *David Harum*, his famous novel about a shrewd but good-hearted Yankee with a penchant for horse trading. The novel, rejected by six publishing houses before it was finally accepted, appeared in 1898, just a few months after Westcott's death. Its success was immediate, with six printings within three months. The novel was immensely popular in the early twentieth century. Within two years more than 400,000 copies were sold, and the eventual sales exceeded one million copies. In 1901 *The Teller*, a group of stories, with some letters by Westcott, was published.

The popularity of *David Harum* continued with stage and film adaptations. The novel, among the first of a type that portrays the Yankee character as hard on the outside but gentle and kind within, is competently written, but its literary value is slight, and scholars, unlike the public, have passed it by with but little attention.

Bibliography

Case, Richard G. "The Westcott and *David Harum*." *Courier* 10 (Winter, 1973): 3-14.

Glassie, Henry. "The Use of Folklore in *David Harum*." *New York Folklore Quarterly* 23 (September, 1967): 163-185.

Hitchcock, Helen Sargent. "David Harum Philosophizes Again." *New York Times Magazine* 17 (July, 1938): 10, 16.

Kurtz, Jeffrey B. "Edward Noyes Westcott." In *Nineteenth-Century American Fiction Writers*, edited by Kent P. Ljungquist. Vol. 202 in *Dictionary of Literary Biography*. Detroit: Gale Group, 1999.

Vance, Arthur Turner. *The Real David Harum: The Wise Ways and Droll Sayings of One "Dave" Hannum, of Homer, N.Y., the Original of the Hero of Mr. Westcott's Popular Book*. New York: Baker and Taylor, 1900.

Edith Wharton

American novelist

Born: New York, New York; January 24, 1862
Died: St.-Brice-sous-Forêt, France; August 11, 1937

LONG FICTION: *The Touchstone*, 1900; *The Valley of Decision*, 1902; *Sanctuary*, 1903; *The House of Mirth*, 1905; *Madame de Treymes*, 1907; *The Fruit of the Tree*, 1907; *Ethan Frome*, 1911; *The Reef*, 1912; *The Custom of the Country*, 1913; *Summer*, 1917; *The Marne*, 1918; *The Age of Innocence*, 1920; *The Glimpses of the Moon*, 1922; *A Son at the Front*, 1923; *Old New York*, 1924 (4 volumes; includes *False Dawn*, *The Old Maid*, *The Spark*, and *New Year's Day*); *The Mother's Recompense*, 1925; *Twilight Sleep*, 1927; *The Children*, 1928; *Hudson River Bracketed*, 1929; *The Gods Arrive*, 1932; *The Buccaneers*, 1938.
SHORT FICTION: *The Greater Inclination*, 1899; *Crucial Instances*, 1901; *The Descent of Man*, 1904; *The Hermit and the Wild Woman*, 1908; *Tales of Men and Ghosts*, 1910; *Xingu, and Other Stories*, 1916; *Here and Beyond*, 1926; *Certain People*, 1930; *Human Nature*, 1933; *The World Over*, 1936; *Ghosts*, 1937; *The Collected Short Stories of Edith Wharton*, 1968; *Collected Stories, 1891-1910*, 2001 (Maureen Howard, editor); *Collected Stories, 1911-1937*, 2001 (Howard, editor).
POETRY: *Verses*, 1878; *Artemis to Actæon*, 1909; *Twelve Poems*, 1926.

NONFICTION: *The Decoration of Houses*, 1897 (with Ogden Codman, Jr.); *Italian Villas and Their Gardens*, 1904; *Italian Backgrounds*, 1905; *A Motor-Flight Through France*, 1908; *Fighting France from Dunkerque to Belfort*, 1915; *French Ways and Their Meaning*, 1919; *In Morocco*, 1920; *The Writing of Fiction*, 1925; *A Backward Glance*, 1934; *The Letters of Edith Wharton*, 1988; *The Uncollected Critical Writings*, 1997 (Frederick Wegener, editor); *Yrs. Ever Affly: The Correspondence of Edith Wharton and Louis Bromfield*, 2000 (Daniel Bratton, editor).

Edith Newbold Jones Wharton (HWAWRT-uhn) is one of the masters of American realistic fiction. She was born in New York City on January 24, 1862, into a family that held a high place in New York society. Throughout her life, Wharton valued the refined manners and charms of fashionable society, but she was also deeply conscious of its superficiality and pettiness. By the time she was a teenager, private tutoring and extensive travel in Europe had made her fluent in German, French, and Italian as well as English. Wharton's writings frequently reveal her wide range of intellectual interests, which encompassed history, art, sociology, and science as well as literature. Her artistic and intellectual interests were not shared by Edward Wharton, the man she married on April 29, 1885. The couple spent much of each year in Europe, but they also lived in New York City and Newport, Rhode Island, and eventually in Lenox, Massachusetts. The unsatisfying nature of her married life, both physically and intellectually, may explain why issues of marriage and divorce dominate many of her best novels and short stories.

After a nervous breakdown, Wharton turned to the writing of fiction in the mid-1890's, partly as a form of therapy. In 1878, a collection of her verse had been privately printed. Although Wharton tried her hand at poetry at other times, she was rarely more than a competent crafter of conventional verse. Her collaboration with the architect Ogden Codman, Jr., in the writing of *The Decoration of Houses* reflected her interest in architectural form and interior design, an interest that also shapes her fiction, which frequently uses the description of rooms and houses as an index to a character's moral and social standing. Wharton published nonfiction at various points throughout her career, producing a number of impressive essays and reviews as well as several vivid books of travel. Her literary reputation, however, rests almost entirely on her fiction.

Wharton's early short stories and first novella, *The Touchstone*, won the admiration of many critics, although some thought that she was imitating Henry James too closely, and others complained of a lack of human warmth in her treatment of issues and characters. Her first long novel, *The Valley of Decision*, was an unsuccessful attempt to explore the social turmoil of Italian civilization at the dawn of the Napoleonic era. In 1905 Wharton won both popular and critical acclaim for *The House of Mirth*, which charts the moral development and social decline of Lily Bart. In 1907 Wharton moved to France, where, except for tours abroad and brief visits to the United States, she spent the rest of her life. The sharp contrast between French and American values is the subject of her novella *Madame de Treymes*. Less successful was her attempt to deal with social issues, most notably labor unrest and euthanasia, in *The Fruit of the Tree*. A passionate affair with Morton Fullerton hastened the collapse of Wharton's marriage, which finally ended in divorce in 1913. Wharton's literary reputation was enhanced by her continued triumphs in the short-story form, where her achievements ranged from powerful ghost stories to ironic masterpieces of social comedy.

The publication of *Ethan Frome* in 1911 showed decisively that Wharton's subjects were not limited to fashionable New York. In this novella, which some rank as her best work, Wharton provided a powerfully tragic vision of a wasted life set within a New England rural landscape that is both emotionally stark and symbolically fascinating. Wharton engaged in other experiments with the novel form. *The Reef* is a densely textured psychological novel that is similar in some ways to the later novels of James. Her next novel, *The Custom of the Country*, is a satire that focuses on the pretensions of a pretty but vulgar young woman who destroys others in her rise to social prominence and wealth. The outbreak of World War I in 1914 led Wharton to charity work on behalf of the refugees who were crowding into her beloved Paris and to literary work, both fiction and nonfiction, in support of the Allied cause. Her two World War I novels, *The Marne* and *A Son at the Front*, are not highly regarded, but this period also saw the publication of *Summer*, a powerful novel about the seduction and betrayal of a New England girl, which can be seen as a passionate counterpart to the coldly delineated tragedy of *Ethan Frome*.

After the war, Wharton returned to the subject of New York society, attempting to capture its social history during the last three decades of the nineteenth century in *The Age of Innocence*, which won for her the Pulitzer Prize. The novel tells of Newland Archer, a dilettante whose infatuation with the vibrant Ellen Olenska threatens his engagement to the bland but virtuous May Welland. The four novellas that make up *Old New York* all deal with individuals in conflict with social values; the two that focus on women, *The Old Maid* and *New Year's Day*, are quite effective.

Wharton spent her final years at her two homes in France. A few critics have been interested in her portrayal of the literary artist Vance Weston in *Hudson River Bracketed* and *The Gods Arrive*, but the other novels written in the 1920's and 1930's have been generally dismissed. This period, however, also saw the composition of some of Wharton's finest short stories, her memoir *A Backward Glance*, and an attempt to define her literary principles in *The Writing of Fiction*. At the time of her death in 1937, there was some sentiment that Wharton may have been overrated, but the literary artistry of *The House of Mirth*, *Ethan Frome*, and *The Age of Innocence* continued to attract critics and readers. The publication of R. W. B. Lewis's biography in 1975 and the advent of feminist criticism aroused new interest in Wharton's life and works. She is now widely recognized as one of the two or three most important women writers of fiction in the literary history of the United States and praised as an artist who endowed the novel of manners with a remarkable blend of social analysis and psychological depth.

Alfred Bendixen

Bibliography

Ammons, Elizabeth. *Edith Wharton's Argument with America*. Athens: University of Georgia Press, 1980. Ammons proposes that Wharton's "argument with America" concerns the freedom of women, an argument in which she had a key role during three decades of significant upheaval and change. Examines the evolution of Wharton's point of view in her novels and discusses the effect of World War I on Wharton. Contains a notes section.

Banta, Martha. "The Ghostly Gothic of Wharton's Everyday World." *American Literary Realism: 1870-1910* 27 (Fall, 1994): 1-10. An analysis of Wharton's ghost story "Afterward" and her novella *Ethan Frome* as illustrative of the nineteenth century craving for a circumscribed experience of the bizarre.

Beer, Janet. *Kate Chopin, Edith Wharton, and Charlotte Perkins Gilman: Studies in Short Fiction*. London: Macmillan, 1997. Beer devotes two chapters of Wharton's short fiction, focusing primarily on the novellas in one chapter and the regional stories about New England in the other.

Bell, Millicent, ed. *The Cambridge Companion to Edith Wharton*. Cambridge, England: Cambridge University Press, 1995. Essays on the works as well as on Wharton's handling of manners and race. Bell gives a critical history of Wharton's fiction in her introduction. Includes a chronology of Wharton's life and publications and a bibliography.

Bendixen, Alfred, and Annette Zilversmit, eds. *Edith Wharton: New Critical Essays*. New York: Garland, 1992. Studies of *The House of Mirth*, *The Fruit of the Tree*, *Summer*, *The Age of Innocence*, *Hudson River Bracketed*, and *The Gods Arrive* as well as on Wharton's treatment of female sexuality, modernism, language, and gothic borrowings.

Benstock, Shari. *No Gifts from Chance: A Biography of Edith Wharton*. New York: Charles Scribner's Sons, 1994. Although Benstock applies a feminist perspective to Wharton's life, she does not claim that Wharton was a feminist. Using primary materials not previously available, she provides a detailed account on Wharton's early life.

Dwight, Eleanor. *Edith Wharton: An Extraordinary Life*. New York: Abrams, 1994. A lively, succinct biography. Illustrated. Includes detailed notes, chronology, and bibliography.

Fracasso, Evelyn E. *Edith Wharton's Prisoner of Consciousness: A Study of Theme and Technique in the Tales*. Westport, Conn.: Greenwood Press, 1994. Analyzes stories from three periods of Wharton's career. Focuses on her technique in treating the theme of imprisonment. Deals with people trapped by love and marriage, imprisoned by the dictates of society, victimized by the demands of art and morality, and paralyzed by fear of the supernatural.

Gimbel, Wendy. *Edith Wharton: Orphancy and Survival*. New York: Praeger, 1984. Drawing upon psychoanalytic theories and feminist perspectives, Gimbel analyzes the four works that she sees as key to understanding Wharton: *The House of Mirth*, *Ethan Frome*, *Summer*, and *The Age of Innocence*. The analyses of these works, with their deeply psychological overtones, are well worth reading.

Lewis, R. W. B. *Edith Wharton: A Biography*. 2 vols. New York: Harper and Row, 1975. An extensive study on Wharton, whom Lewis calls "the most renowned writer of fiction in America." Notes that Wharton thoughtfully left extensive records, made available through the Beinecke Library at Yale, on which this biography is based. Essential reading for serious scholars of Wharton or for those interested in her life and how it shaped her writing.

Lindberg, Gary H. *Edith Wharton and the Novel of Manners*. Charlottesville: University Press of Virginia, 1975. Presents Wharton's style with a keen understanding of the ritualism of the social scenes in her work. Strong analytical criticism with a good grasp of Wharton's use of irony.

McDowell, Margaret B. *Edith Wharton*. Boston: Twayne, 1975. A perceptive biography and analysis of Wharton's body of writings. Chapter 6 discusses her most important short fiction.

Nettels, Elsa. *Language and Gender in American Fiction: Howells, James, Wharton, and Cather*. Charlottesville: University Press of Virginia, 1997. Nettels examines American writers struggling with the problems of patriarchy.

Phillis Wheatley

African-born American poet

Born: West Coast of Africa (possibly the Senegal-Gambia region); 1753(?)
Died: Boston, Massachusetts; December 5, 1784
Identity: African American

POETRY: *Poems on Various Subjects, Religious and Moral*, 1773; *The Poems of Phillis Wheatley*, 1966, 1989 (Julian D. Mason, Jr., editor).

MISCELLANEOUS: *Memoir and Poems of Phillis Wheatley: A Native African and a Slave*, 1833; *The Collected Works of Phillis Wheatley*, 1988 (John Shields, editor).

Although other African Americans published individual poems before her, Phillis Wheatley is often regarded as the first African American poet. In 1773 she became the first black American to publish a book of poetry: *Poems on Various Subjects, Religious and Moral*.

Wheatley was born on the west coast of Africa, probably in 1753. At age seven or eight, she was kidnapped from her parents' home, sold to slave traders, and brought to America. John Wheatley, a prosperous tailor, and his wife, Susannah, purchased the slave girl at a Boston slave market in 1761 and gave her the name Phillis. She became Mrs. Wheatley's personal maid.

The Wheatleys were strict Methodists who attempted to turn their slaves into literate and cultured Christians. Within eighteen months of her purchase, Phillis Wheatley had learned to speak, read, and write in English and had begun to study Latin as well. At an early age, she was exposed to the Bible, the classical Greek and Roman works, and contemporary British poets. While still in her teens, with her masters' encouragement, Wheatley began to write poems.

At age fourteen, Wheatley published her first poem in a Newport, Rhode Island, newspaper. The elegy "On the Death of Mr. George Whitefield" appeared in 1770 and brought the young poet some recognition. The poem was included in *Poems on Various Subjects*, first published in London in 1773. That volume of thirty-eight poems brought Wheatley widespread attention. She became known as the "sable muse" and was cited in England and America as an example of the impressive intellectual potential of African slaves.

The volume comprises religious poems, elegies, and historical poems, written, for the most part, in the neoclassical style of eighteenth century British and colonial writers. Most of the poems consist of series of rhyming couplets reminiscent of those of Alexander Pope, the British poet whom Wheatley greatly admired.

The elegies are generally considered the finest poems in *Poems on Various Subjects*, the best ones rivaling those of an earlier colonial poet, Anne Bradstreet. Their subjects include ministers, physicians, dignitaries, and family friends. Like Bradstreet, Wheatley often accepts death with the hope of an everlasting afterlife. In "To a Lady and Her Children, On the Death of Her Son and Their Brother," for example, Wheatley urges the family members of a deceased child to cease their mourning and look forward to the day when they can join their loved one on heaven's shores.

Wheatley visited England as her collection was published and met various dignitaries, including Benjamin Franklin. When she returned to America, her mistress, Mrs. Wheatley, died, and Phillis was set free by Mr. Wheatley. She became an ardent supporter of the colonial cause during the American Revolution, and she met General George Washington in 1775 when he was headquartered in Boston. Wheatley honored Washington with a poem titled "To His Excellency General Washington."

Wheatley continued to publish poetry in newspapers and pamphlets; she tried to publish another volume of poems in 1779 but was unable to attract a publisher. After *Poems on Various Subjects*, Wheatley produced more than fifty other poems, some of which have been lost. Many of her letters, however, did survive and were later published.

Only a handful of Wheatley's poems deal with the issue of slavery, and those poems often make contradictory statements about the institution. In "On Being Brought From Africa to America," for example, Wheatley states, "'Twas mercy brought me from my *Pagan* land,/ Taught my benighted soul to understand/ That there's a God, that there's a *Saviour* too." Nonetheless, she ends the poem, "Remember, *Christians*, *Negroes*, black as *Cain*,/ May be refin'd, and join th' angelic train." In "To the University of Cambridge, in New England," she states that the "Father of mercy" brought her "in safety from those dark abodes" of Africa; yet her tribute to the earl of Dartmouth condemns slavery as "the iron chain" that enslaves the land. Moreover, in poems such as "To S. M., A Young African Painter," Wheatley shows a pride in her race rarely seen in eighteenth century writing. In her poems, Wheatley never uttered powerful condemnations of slavery. In her private letters, however, Wheatley was sometimes harsh on the slave system.

Wheatley married John Peters, a freed slave, in 1778. The couple had three children, all of whom died in infancy. Wheatley continued to write poems, and she tried to run a small private school. Through most of their marriage, however, Wheatley and her husband lived in poverty, and he was eventually briefly imprisoned for failing to pay debts. In December, 1784, Wheatley, thirty-one years old, in ill health and poor spirits, died. Her third child died a few days later.

Although Thomas Jefferson once denigrated the poems of Phillis Wheatley as "below the dignity of criticism," her poetry was generally well received during her lifetime. Through the 1830's, Wheatley's poems were enthusiastically reprinted by abolitionists who used her work as evidence that African slaves had an intellectual capacity equal to that of white people, a position not widely accepted before the Civil War. Ironically, proponents of slavery also used her work to demonstrate the benefits of slavery, claiming that only as a slave in the United States could a black African experience achievements such as those of Wheatley.

James Tackach

Bibliography

Barker-Benfield, G. J., and Catherine Clinton, comps. *Portraits of American Women: From Settlement to the Present*. New York: St. Martin's Press, 1991. A collection of essays that locate the histories of women and men together by period. Includes portraits of Phillis Wheatley and others designed to appeal to a wide range of readers. Includes bibliographical references.

Bassard, Katherine Clay. *Spiritual Interrogations: Culture, Gender, and Community in Early African American Women's Writing*. Princeton, N.J.: Princeton University Press, 1999. A historical analysis that includes a discussion of the works of Wheatley. Includes bibliographical references and index.

Jones, Jacqueline. "Anglo-American Racism and Phillis Wheatley's 'Sable Veil,' 'Length'ned Chain,' and 'Knitted Heart.'" In *Women in the Age of the American Revolution*, edited by Ronald Hoffman and Peter J. Albert. Charlottesville: University Press of Virginia, 1989. This sometimes difficult study includes fascinating biographical information and offers a close reading of dozens of poems. Jones delineates the importance of *Poems on*

Various Subjects, Religious and Moral as an early commentary on slavery and on American female thought.

Richmond, Merle. *Phillis Wheatley*. New York: Chelsea House, 1988. Written for young adults, this biography is lively and informative. The dozens of illustrations include a portrait of Wheatley and a sample of her handwriting. Contains suggestions for further reading, a chronology, and an index.

Rinaldi, Ann. *Hang a Thousand Trees with Ribbons: The Story of Phillis Wheatley*. New York: Harcourt, 1996. This fictionalized biography is aimed at younger readers and is written in the style Wheatley might have used to write her own autobiography. In addition to relating the events of her life, starting with her abduction from Senegal, she discusses writing and its significance. Rinaldi appends a note explaining issues of fact and fiction in her work.

Robinson, William H. *Phillis Wheatley: A Bio-Bibliography*. Boston: G. K. Hall, 1981. After a brief biography and review of the critical reception, this volume presents an annotated list of representative writings about Wheatley from 1761 to 1979. Includes reprinted appendices commenting on two of the poems and an extensive index.

_______. *Phillis Wheatley and Her Writings*. New York: Garland, 1984. A fine introduction to Wheatley, by an eminent Wheatley scholar. Presents a brief biography, the text of all the poems and surviving letters (several in facsimile) with an analysis, nine appendices providing background information, bibliography, and index.

_______, ed. *Critical Essays on Phillis Wheatley*. Boston: G. K. Hall, 1982. This collection of sixty-five essays contains early comments and reviews, including several by Wheatley herself, important reprinted essays from 1834 to 1975, and five critical evaluations original to this book. An editor's introduction provides a biographical and critical overview. Includes chronology and index.

E. B. White

American novelist, poet, and scholar

Born: Mount Vernon, New York; July 11, 1899
Died: North Brooklin, Maine; October 1, 1985

SHORT FICTION: *Is Sex Necessary? Or, Why You Feel the Way You Do*, 1929 (with James Thurber); *The Second Tree from the Corner*, 1954.

POETRY: *The Lady Is Cold*, 1929; *The Fox of Peapack, and Other Poems*, 1938; .

NONFICTION: *Every Day Is Saturday*, 1934; *Farewell to Model T*, 1936; *Quo Vadimus? Or, The Case for the Bicycle*, 1939; *One Man's Meat*, 1942; *World Government and Peace: Selected Notes and Comment, 1943-1945*, 1945; *The Wild Flag*, 1946; *Here Is New York*, 1949; *The Elements of Style*, 1959, 2d edition 1972, 3d edition 1979, 4th edition 1999 (with William Strunk, Jr.); *The Points of My Compass*, 1962; *The Egg Is All*, 1971; *Letters of E. B. White*, 1976; *Essays of E. B. White*, 1977; *Writings from "The New Yorker," 1925-1976*, 1990.

CHILDREN'S/YOUNG ADULT LITERATURE: *Stuart Little*, 1945; *Charlotte's Web*, 1952; *Trumpet of the Swan*, 1970.

EDITED TEXTS: *Ho-Hum: Newsbreaks from "The New Yorker,"* 1931; *Another Ho-Hum*, 1932; *A Subtreasury of American Humor*, 1941 (with Katherine Sergeant White); *Onward and Upward in the Garden*, 1979 (by Katherine Sergeant White).

MISCELLANEOUS: *An E. B. White Reader*, 1966 (William W. Watt and Robert W. Bradford, editors); *Poems and Sketches of E. B. White*, 1981 .

Elwyn Brooks White was a multifaceted writer. Although he has more than twenty volumes to his credit, his recognition is primarily for four types of literature: a style manual, fiction, poetry, and children's literature.

White was born in Mount Vernon, New York, on July 11, 1899. His father manufactured pianos with a New York business. E. B. lived the pleasant suburban life. After serving in the Army as a private in 1918, White entered Cornell University in Ithaca, New York. He wrote for *The Cornell Daily Star*. One of White's professors was William Strunk, Jr. Strunk used his book *The Elements of Style* in the course. This book—with its grammar glossary, advice on pronoun uses, punctuation rules, and (later) suggestions for avoiding sexism—would prove significant to White.

After White graduated in 1921, he traveled and worked many jobs, including reporter for the United Press, the American Legion News Service, and the *Seattle Times*. He returned to New York in 1924 and worked as an advertising copywriter, a production assistant, and finally at the newly formed *The New Yorker*.

The first literary editor of *The New Yorker* was Katherine Sergeant Angell. In 1929 White and Angell married; they had three children. Their friends included Dorothy Parker, a short story writer, poet, theater critic, and screenwriter; Robert Benchley, a drama critic, actor, and humorist; Stephen Leacock, a modern language instructor, humorist, and chair of the Economics and Political Science Department at McGill University; and James Thurber, a cartoonist, children's writer, and humorist. White worked with Thurber to produce *Is Sex Necessary?*, a spoof of the sex manuals of the day.

White worked with *The New Yorker* for eleven years. In addition to his editorial essays, he also wrote of the complexities of modern life, the failures of technology, war, the joys of both rural and urban life, and nature. His *Ho-Hum* and *Another Ho-Hum* were collections of essays. In *The Wild Flag*, White assembled some articles that had previously appeared in his *New Yorker* columns "Talk of the Town." These essays reflected his support of the United Nations and internationalism; all the essays were informed and clear.

White's poetry appeared in two volumes: *The Lady Is Cold* and *The Fox of Peapack, and Other Poems*. Critics noted the wit and exquisite form of the poems. In 1935 the Macmillan Company commissioned White to edit Strunk's *The Elements of Style*. In addition to this first edit, White later revised the manual for the 1959, 1972, and 1979 editions. *The Elements of Style* became the standard English-language style guide.

In 1938 the Whites moved to North Brooklin, Maine. The animals and the rural peace furnished story ideas and helped allay White's bouts of depression. E. B. White teamed up with his wife to edit *A Subtreasury of American Humor*, published in 1941. He also wrote a monthly column titled "One Man's Meat" for *Harper's* from 1938 to 1943. His compilation of these columns formed *One Man's Meat*. Two years later he expanded the collection; *One Man's Meat* remained in print for fifty-five years. White found time to contribute poetry and other writings to *Harper's*.

One night when White was traveling by rail, he dreamed about a mouse named Stuart Little. The next morning he wrote down fragments of the dream. Over a period of twelve years, he continued to add to the tale. Though he intended the story for his six-year-old niece, she was grown before he finished *Stuart Little*, now a children's literature classic.

Charlotte's Web was White's second children's book. *Publishers Weekly* reported in 2001 that *Charlotte's Web* was the all-time best-selling paperback children's book. Its setting reflected White's rural life. The story line came from his concern with the death of animals. A spider that wove intricate webs and a pig became the main characters. *Charlotte's Web* won the Newbery Honor Medal (1953), the Lewis Carroll Shelf Award (1958), the George G. Stone Center for Children's Books Recognition of Merit Award (1970), and the New England Round Table of Children's Libraries Award (1973). In 1970 White accepted the Laura Ingalls Wilder Award—a major children's literature prize—for *Stuart Little* and *Charlotte's Web*.

White's third children's book was *The Trumpet of the Swan*. A reversal-of-fortune story, it tells how Louis, a mute swan, compensates by playing the trumpet. Louis gives hope to challenged readers and encourages acceptance of others. *The Trumpet of the Swan* won the Sue Hefley Award from the Louisiana Association of School Librarians (1974) and the Young Hoosier Award from the Indiana School Librarians Association (1975).

In 1971 White earned the National Medal for Literature. In 1973 children voted *The Trumpet of the Swan* as their favorite book in both Oklahoma (Sequoyah Award) and Kansas (the William Allen White Award at Emporia State University). In 1978 he received a Pulitzer Prize special citation for his writings as a whole. The International Board on Books for Young People honored this third children's book as an internationally important literature example. White received the National Institute of Arts and Letters' Gold Medal for Essays and Criticism; in 1973 the members of the National Institute elected him to the American Academy of Arts and Letters, a society of fifty members. He received honorary degrees from seven colleges and universities. E. B. White died of Alzheimer's disease on October 1, 1985, in North Brooklin, Maine.

Anita Price Davis

Bibliography

Elledge, Scott. *E. B. White: A Biography*. New York: W. W. Norton, 1984. The first full-length biography on White.

Roback, Diane, and Jason Britton, eds. "All-Time Bestselling Children's Books." *Publishers Weekly*, December 17, 2001, 1-25. Among paperback books as of 2001, *Charlotte's Web* ranked number 1; *Stuart Little*, 53; and *Trumpet of the Swan*, 83.

Sampson, Edward C. *E. B. White*. New York: Twayne, 1974. An early study from Twayne's United States Authors series.

"White, Elwyn Brooks." In *Something About the Author*. Vol. 100. Detroit: Gale, 1999. White states that he always wrote for himself, not an audience.

Patrick White

Australian novelist and playwright

Born: London, England; May 28, 1912
Died: Sydney, Australia; September 30, 1990
Identity: Gay or bisexual

LONG FICTION: *Happy Valley*, 1939; *The Living and the Dead*, 1941; *The Aunt's Story*, 1948; *The Tree of Man*, 1955; *Voss*, 1957; *Riders in the Chariot*, 1961; *The Solid Mandala*, 1966; *The Vivisector*, 1970; *The Eye of the Storm*, 1973; *A Fringe of Leaves*, 1976; *The Twyborn Affair*, 1979; *Memoirs of Many in One*, 1986.

SHORT FICTION: *The Burnt Ones*, 1964; *The Cockatoos: Shorter Novels and Stories*, 1974; *Three Uneasy Pieces*, 1987.

DRAMA: *Return to Abyssinia*, pr. 1947; *The Ham Funeral*, wr. 1947, pr. 1961; *The Season at Sarsaparilla*, pr. 1962; *A Cheery Soul*, pr. 1963; *Night on Bald Mountain*, pr. 1963; *Four Plays*, pb. 1965, revised pb. 1985-1994 (as *Plays*; 2 volumes); *Big Toys*, pr. 1977; *Signal Driver*, pr. 1982; *Netherwood*, pr., pb. 1983; *Shepherd on the Rocks*, pr. 1987.

SCREENPLAY: *The Night of the Prowler*, 1976.
POETRY: *The Ploughman, and Other Poems*, 1935.
NONFICTION: *Flaws in the Glass: A Self-Portrait*, 1981; *Patrick White Speaks*, 1989; *Patrick White: Letters*, 1996 (David Marr, editor).

Patrick Victor Martindale White was not only a major Australian novelist but also one of the outstanding English-language writers of the twentieth century. A second-generation Australian, he was born in London in 1912 while his parents were on a visit there. Both his parents belonged to landholding families in the Hunter Valley of New South Wales. After his early education in Australia, he was sent to England for four years at Cheltenham, a preparatory school. He returned to Australia to train for life as a grazier but persuaded his family to let him return to England, where he took a degree in modern languages at Cambridge University. He would later stay in England, beginning his literary career. His first novel, *Happy Valley*, was published in England in 1939. *The Living and the Dead* was hurriedly completed as White shuttled between America and England awaiting service in World War II; it is, accordingly, the least satisfactory of his novels. *The Aunt's Story*, begun in England but completed en route to Australia after the war, represents a major advance and is one of his two best novels. (*The Eye of the Storm*, written twenty-five years later, is the other.)

After settling in Australia, White entered his major creative period. Believing that Australia lacked a spiritual dimension, he tried to provide that in his next two novels, writing about the two great Australian movements, the pioneer settlement of the land in *The Tree of Man* and the exploration of the continent in *Voss*. Though perhaps not his best novel, *Voss* is often and validly considered the "great Australian novel"; in 1986, it was made into an opera, with the libretto written by David Malouf. *The Tree of Man* brought world attention to White, and his reputation continued to rise with *Voss* and *Riders in the Chariot*, his most ambitious novel, embracing Judaism as well as Christianity, Europe as well as Australia, and aboriginal as well as Caucasian aspects of Australian life.

The Solid Mandala marks the beginning of White's decline, which continued with the publication of *The Vivisector.* His achievement was such, however, that he was already a strong contender for the Nobel Prize in Literature when *The Vivisector* appeared. The Nobel Prize committee looked with disfavor upon the negative portrait of an artist in *The Vivisector* (the artist dissects his subjects for his own purposes), and it may be this disfavor that spurred White on to a recovery of his powers in *The Eye of the Storm*. That novel secured for him the Nobel Prize in 1973, the first time that the award was given to an English-language writer outside the United Kingdom or the United States. Yet the Nobel Prize seemed to have constrained White, for the novels that followed *The Eye of the Storm* are rather slight or unattractive. *A Fringe of Leaves* tells a good story well but is one of White's less important works, while *The Twyborn Affair* and *Memoirs of Many in One* are decidedly strange and unprepossessing. White later announced that he had finished writing.

White also wrote short stories but showed no special talent for short fiction. His short stories lack the spiritual dimension of his novels and reveal his less pleasant side. They show at times a derisive enjoyment of the characters' distress and an interest in disturbed states of mind. White also wrote a number of plays. His early plays might have had more significance had they been performed when they were written—*The Ham Funeral* is an early and interesting example of what was later called the Theater of the Absurd—but the delay lessened their impact and discouraged White's theatrical career. Late in his life, with his reputation established, he again turned to the theater, but the late plays tend to be marred by moralizing.

It is as a novelist and especially as one of the great stylists of the English language that White will be remembered. He wrote at least four major novels (*The Aunt's Story*, *The Tree of Man*, *Voss*, and *The Eye of the Storm*) and one flawed masterpiece (*Riders in the Chariot*), an achievement few novelists in English can equal. White's novels were concerned very early with establishing an arbitrary and unclear distinction between the living and the dead (the title of his second novel) or the elect and the nonelect. Mostly his elect are social outsiders with some special gift of perception or creativity—visionaries of a kind. Here White's homosexuality came into play; he regarded homosexuality as a gift for the artist. As expressed in the works, it becomes an examination of artistic insight as well as the doubleness of human beings in the form of androgyny. Among the ranks of his outsiders are Theodora Goodman, Stan Parker, Laura Trevelyan, the four riders in the chariot, Arthur Brown, Hurtle Duffield, and Elizabeth Hunter. A corollary of this theme is his series of Christ figures, of whom Voss is the first and Arthur Brown the last. After *The Solid Mandala*, White's elect figures are stripped of their association with Christ and accorded merely human status, with some unpleasant characteristics, such as those of Hurtle Duffield and Elizabeth Hunter.

One becomes aware in a number of White's novels of an ongoing battle between the protagonist and his or her mother or a mother figure. That is most obviously the case in *The Aunt's Story*, *Voss*, *The Eye of the Storm*, and *The Twyborn Affair. The Eye of the Storm* contains the greatest elevation of the mother in Elizabeth Hunter (a thinly disguised version of White's own mother) and the greatest self-abasement of her offspring; however, White's growing self-disgust had already manifested itself in *The Solid Mandala*. This self-disgust is developed at greater length in the portrait of the artist in *The Vivisector* and resumed in the two novels *The Twyborn Affair* and *Memoirs of Many in One*. There is no mellowing or maturing in the late White, only disintegration. His best work was done in the years 1948 to 1960; after that date, only *The Eye of the Storm* shows a resurgence of his massive talents. After a long illness, White died at his home in Sydney on September 30, 1990.

John B. Beston
L. L. Lee

Bibliography

Bliss, Carolyn. *Patrick White's Fiction: The Paradox of Fortunate Failure*. New York: St. Martin's Press, 1986. This study offers an excellent introduction to White's overall thematic concerns.

Argues that all White's writing stems from a paradox—that is, the failures so often experienced by the characters can in fact lead to their successful redemption.

Collier, Gordon. *The Rocks and Sticks of Words: Style, Discourse, and Narrative Structure in the Fiction of Patrick White.* Amsterdam: Rodopi, 1992. Deconstructs White's themes and techniques in his fiction.

During, Simon. *Patrick White.* New York: Oxford University Press, 1996. Explores the life and works of White.

Edgecombe, Rodney Stenning. *Vision and Style in Patrick White: A Study of Five Novels.* Tuscaloosa: University of Alabama Press, 1989. Addresses five novels, including *The Eye of the Storm*, considered by Edgecombe to be White's greatest. Links the books by exploring the metaphysical thoughts they share and examines White's distinctive style. This style affirms his novels' thematic emphasis on alienation, isolation, and the subsequent search for a vision to free the individual from spiritual imprisonment.

Marr, David. *Patrick White: A Life.* New York: Knopf, 1992. Written with White's cooperation. The biographer had complete freedom. Even though a dying White found the biography painful reading, he did not ask the author to change a word. A monumental accomplishment, with detailed notes, bibliography, and helpful appendices.

Morley, Patricia. *The Mystery of Unity: Theme and Technique in the Novels of Patrick White.* Montreal: McGill-Queen's University Press, 1972. Shows how White's fiction makes use of the international tradition along with the archetypes of Western literature. Morley argues that, through his intertextuality, White gives a unified view of a world beset by pain and suffering, but one that will offer salvation for those who seek it.

Weigel, John A. *Patrick White.* Boston: Twayne, 1983. Introduces White and his work by tracing his life and discussing each of his novels, as well as his plays. Although introductory and general, the book serves well the beginning reader of White's fiction. Includes a secondary bibliography and a chronology.

Williams, Mark. *Patrick White.* New York: St. Martin's Press, 1993. Includes many chapters that explore White's fiction titles in depth as well as discussions centered on the themes and contexts of his works. Bibliography and index.

Wolfe, Peter. *Laden Choirs: The Fiction of Patrick White.* Lexington: University Press of Kentucky, 1983. While not taking any particular thematic stand, this book offers a substantial analysis of each of White's novels. Focuses in part on White's style, demonstrating how it affects narrative tension, philosophical structure, and the development of character.

_______, ed. *Critical Essays on Patrick White.* Boston: G. K. Hall, 1990. A wide-ranging collection edited by one of White's most astute critics. Includes a section of autobiographical essays by White and a helpful bibliography.

T. H. White

English novelist

Born: Bombay, India; May 29, 1906
Died: Piraeus, Greece; January 17, 1964
Pseudonym: James Aston
Identity: Gay or bisexual

LONG FICTION: *Darkness at Pemberley*, 1932; *Farewell Victoria*, 1933; *The Sword in the Stone*, 1938; *The Witch in the Wood*, 1939; *The Ill-Made Knight*, 1940; *Mistress Masham's Repose*, 1946; *The Elephant and the Kangaroo*, 1947; *The Master: An Adventure Story*, 1957; *The Candle in the Wind*, 1958; *The Once and Future King*, 1958 (a tetralogy including *The Sword in the Stone*, *The Witch in the Wood*, *The Ill-Made Knight*, and *The Candle in the Wind*); *The Book of Merlyn: The Unpublished Conclusion to "The Once and Future King,"* 1977.

NONFICTION: *England Have My Bones*, 1936 (autobiography); *The Age of Scandal: An Excursion Through a Minor Period*, 1950 (anecdotes); *The Goshawk*, 1951; *The Scandalmonger*, 1952 (anecdotes); *The Godstone and the Blackymor*, 1959 (autobiography); *America at Last*, 1965 (autobiography).

TRANSLATION: *The Book of Beasts*, 1954 (of medieval bestiary).

Although Terence Hanbury White was born in India, he spent most of his adult life in the British Isles. His parents' bitter divorce colored his childhood and contributed to lifelong emotional problems. Educated at Cheltenham College and Queen's College, Cambridge, he taught school at Stowe Ridings, Buckinghamshire. There he began his writing career in 1930, at first publishing novels under the pseudonym James Aston. A suppressed homosexual (for which he blamed his mother), White began psychotherapy in 1935 and tried unsuccessfully to have a "normal" love life. In 1937 he resigned his teaching job to devote himself full-time to writing. His first major success was *The Sword in the Stone*, published in 1938. From 1938 to 1945 White, a pacifist, lived in Ireland. He returned to England after World War II to live on the tiny island of Aldernay in the English Channel.

White's greatest success was his retelling of Sir Thomas Malory's *Le Morte d'Arthur* (1485), which gave him financial security in 1960 after it became the basis for Lerner and Loewe's musical *Camelot*. The four novels—*The Sword in the Stone*, *The Witch in the Wood*, *The Ill-Made Knight*, and *The Candle in the Wind*—with some revisions were collected under the title *The Once and Future King* in 1958. *The Book of Merlyn*, the original conclusion of White's Arthuriad, was written during World War II and sent to White's London publisher in 1941. Because of its pacifist theme, however, the book was rejected and only published posthumously in 1977.

In these retellings of the legends of King Arthur, White shows a vast knowledge of the Middle Ages and a keen appreciation of medieval culture. More important, he is able to make the sometimes shadowy figures of the legends vital and real, often interpreting his characters with the aid of modern psychology. In the portrayal of Morgause in *The Witch in the Wood* White presents a thinly disguised and bitter picture of his own mother, but the character of King Arthur is sympathetically depicted. The king becomes an almost tragic figure as he struggles, in the face of mounting opposition, to build an ideal kingdom founded on law and justice instead of on naked force.

White, known to his friends as Tim, was a lonely, often tortured but brilliant and charming man. He would combat depression sometimes with heavy drinking but more often by enthusiasm for what he called his "crazes": he learned to fly a plane, to fish for salmon, to train hawks, to speak Gaelic, and later in life to sign the deaf alphabet and to read braille. Interested in helping individuals who were blind or deaf, he invited them for summer holidays at his home in Aldernay. On Aldernay he also formed a hopeless and unrevealed love for a twelve-year-old boy he called "Zed," which tormented his final years. While on a Mediterranean cruise following a lecture tour of the United States (described in the posthumous *America at Last*), White was found dead in his cabin in the port of Piraeus, Greece, apparently of heart failure. He was buried in the Protestant cemetery in Athens.

White's nonfiction best exemplifies the wide range of his knowledge and interest. *The Age of Scandal* and *The Scandalmonger*, for example, are anthologies of gossipy and scandalous anecdotes about men and women of eighteenth century England. *The Goshawk* is an account of his attempt to train a hawk after the manner of a medieval falconer; *The Book of Beasts* is a translation of a medieval bestiary (a collection of legends about actual and legendary animals); and *England Have My Bones*, *The Godstone and the Blackymor*, and *America at Last* are autobiographical accounts of White's life in England, Ireland, and the United States.

Jay Ruud

Bibliography

Brewer, Elisabeth. *T. H. White's "The Once and Future King."* Cambridge, England: D. S. Brewer, 1993. Examines White's work and other Arthurian romances, historical fiction, and fantastic fiction. Includes bibliography and index.

Crane, John K. *T. H. White*. New York: Twayne, 1974. A competent overview of White's work. For the beginning student.

Irwin, Robert. "T. H. White." In *The St. James Guide to Fantasy Writers*, edited by David Pringle. Detroit: St. James Press, 1996. A good summary account of White's fantasies.

Kellman, Martin. *T. H. White and the Matter of Britain*. Lewiston, N.Y.: E. Mellen Press, 1988. Kellman studies the Arthurian legend in detail.

Manlove, C. N. *The Impulse of Fantasy Literature*. Kent, Ohio: Kent State University Press, 1983. The chapter on White carefully relates his work to the book's other subjects and the tradition of British fantasy.

Warner, Sylvia Townsend. *T. H. White: A Biography*. London: Cape/Chatto & Windus, 1967. A sensitive biography, whose central conclusions are summarized in Warner's introduction to *The Book of Merlyn*.

Colson Whitehead

American novelist and journalist

Born: New York, New York; 1969
Identity: African American

LONG FICTION: *The Intuitionist*, 1999; *John Henry Days*, 2001.

Colson Whitehead has been hailed as one of the United States' most talented and innovative young writers. As a child growing up in New York City, he decided that he wanted to be a novelist after reading Stephen King's novels. Whitehead matriculated at Harvard University; after he was not accepted into Harvard's creative writing seminars, he studied English and comparative literature. Upon receiving a B.A. in 1991, he became an editorial assistant at *The Village Voice*; he wrote music, television, and book reviews and eventually became the newspaper's television editor. While working at *The Village Voice*, he met and married Natasha Stovall, a photographer and writer. Whitehead's essays have appeared in other publications, such as *The New York Times*, *Vibe*, *Spin*, and *Newsday*.

Although Whitehead worked in San Francisco, where he wrote about Internet events, and taught in the University of Houston's creative writing program during the spring semester for several years, he is a self-described lifelong New Yorker. He and his wife made their home in Brooklyn. On September 11, 2001, Whitehead and Stovall stood on a hill in Brooklyn's Fort Greene Park and looked out on lower Manhattan. They watched the World Trade Center's two towers burn and collapse after the terrorist attacks of that morning. One of Whitehead's most eloquent and memorable essays, "Lost and Found," (*The New York Times*, November 11, 2001), pays tribute to the Twin Towers, New York City, and memories.

Whitehead continues to write essays, yet he is best known for his fiction. In his first novel, *The Intuitionist*, he pits an urban department of elevator inspectors' two contentious groups against each other: the Intuitionists and the Empiricists. The novel's protagonist, Lila Mae Watson, is the first African American woman in the department. She is known as the most competent inspector until an elevator, inspected by her, freefalls. Elated Empiricists blame the accident on Watson, an Intuitionist. Determined to find out what happened, Watson investigates in a work that critics have described as a racial allegory, comic fantasy, and mystery.

The Intuitionist, a finalist for the PEN/Hemingway Award for First Fiction in 1999, won the Quality Paperback Book Club's New Voices Award, 1999, and the Whiting Writers' Award, 2000. *The Intuitionist* was published when Whitehead was twenty-nine; consequently, critics proclaimed that he was one of the most talented of the younger generation of writers. His debut novel garnered comparisons with novels by Don DeLillo, Ralph Ellison, Joseph Heller, Toni Morrison, and Thomas Pynchon. Excerpts from Whitehead's novels began appearing in such anthologies as *Step into a World: A Global Anthology of the New Black Literature* (2000), edited by Kevin Powell, and *Giant Steps: The New Generation of African American Writers* (2000), edited by Kevin Young.

The Intuitionist and Whitehead's second novel, *John Henry Days*, focus on racial as well as gender issues. Whitehead became aware of John Henry, the legendary railroad figure, when he was an elementary school student. When Whitehead's teacher showed his class a cartoon about Henry, Whitehead was intrigued. Although he had read Marvel comics, John Henry represented a phenomenon Whitehead had never seen before—an African American superhero. Years later, Whitehead decided to write about Henry; however, he postponed beginning the novel until he felt capable of presenting the nineteenth century folk hero differently from the image depicted in the various versions of the ballad of John Henry. Thus in his novel, Whitehead emphasizes Henry's humanity rather than portraying him as a mythical figure. Henry, an Industrial Age figure, is contrasted with J. Sutter, a young, African American freelance journalist who represents the Digital Age and is sent to Talcott, West Virginia, to write about a three-day festival held in Henry's honor.

The critical acclaim bestowed upon Whitehead's second novel surpassed the favorable commentary conferred upon *The Intuitionist*. *John Henry Days* won the New York Public Library Young Lions' Fiction Award, 2002, and was a finalist for the National Book Critics Circle Award and the Pulitzer Prize. It was selected as the 2001 *New York Times* Editor's Choice and was cited as the "Best Book of the Year" by reviewers at the *Los Angeles Times*, *The San Francisco Chronicle*, *The Washington Post*, and Salon.com. Established writers such as Ishmael Reed and John Updike acknowledged Whitehead's talents as a novelist. *The Intuitionist* and *John Henry Days* also merited the attention of the John D. and Catherine T. MacArthur Foundation; Whitehead was one of twenty-four 2002 MacArthur Fellows awarded $500,000 grants.

Whitehead has received more favorable critical recognition in three years than many of his peers receive after decades of writing.

Linda M. Carter

Bibliography

Franzen, Jonathan. "Freeloading Man." *The New York Times Book Review*, May 13, 2001, 8. Novelist Franzen reviews *John Henry Days*, focusing on Whitehead's theme of men's problems in contemporary society.

Hill, Logan. "Whitehead Revisited." *New York Magazine* 34 (May 7, 2001): 38. Provides updates on Whitehead's career weeks prior to the release of *John Henry Days*.

Krist, Gary. "The Ascent of Man." *The New York Times Book Review*, February 7, 1999, 9. Review of *The Intuitionist* that predicts a successful career as a novelist for Whitehead.

Mari, Christopher. "Colson Whitehead." In *Current Biography Yearbook* 2001, edited by Clifford Thompson. New York: H. W. Wilson, 2001. Emphasis on Whitehead's two novels; few details about his personal life.

Porter, Evette. "Writing Home." *Black Issues in Higher Education* 4 (May/June, 2002): 36. Contains concise biographical information.

Reed, Ishmael. "Rage Against the Machine." *The Washington Post Book World*, May 20, 1991, 5. Review of *John Henry Days* which commends Whitehead for daring to go beyond literary conventions.

Updike, John. "Tote That Ephemera." *The New Yorker* 77 (May 7, 2001): 87-89. A review of *John Henry Days* that acknowledges Whitehead's talents as a gifted writer.

Whitehead, Colson. "Tunnel Vision." Interview by Daniel Zalewski. *The New York Times Book Review*, May 13, 2001, 8. An interview with Whitehead, who discusses his inspiration for *The Intuitionist* and *John Henry Days* as well as how he constructed his second novel.

John Whiting

English playwright

Born: Salisbury, Wiltshire, England; November 15, 1917
Died: Duddleswell, Sussex, England; June 16, 1963

DRAMA: *Paul Southman*, pr. 1946 (radio play), pr. 1965 (staged); *A Penny for a Song*, pr. 1951, revised pr. 1962; *Saint's Day*, pr. 1951; *Marching Song*, pr., pb. 1954; *The Gates of Summer*, pr. 1956; *The Devils*, pr., pb. 1961 (adaptation of Aldous Huxley's book *The Devils of Loudun*); *No Why*, pb. 1961; *Conditions of Agreement*, pr. 1965; *The Nomads*, pr. 1965; *The Collected Plays of John Whiting*, pb. 1969 (2 volumes); *No More A-Roving*, pb. 1975, pr. 1979 (radio play), pr. 1987 (staged); *Plays: One*, pb. 1999; *Plays: Two*, pb. 2001.
SCREENPLAYS: *The Ship That Died of Shame*, 1955 (with Michael Relph and Basil Dearden); *The Good Companions*, 1957 (with T. J. Morrison and J. L. Hodgson); *The Captain's Table*, 1959 (with Bryan Forbes and Nicholas Phipps); *Young Cassidy*, 1965.
TELEPLAY: *A Walk in the Desert*, 1960.
RADIO PLAYS: *Eye Witness*, 1949; *The Stairway*, 1949; *Love's Old Sweet Song*, 1950; *No More A-Roving*, 1975.
MISCELLANEOUS: *The Art of the Dramatist, and Other Pieces*, 1969 (short fiction, criticism, lectures; Ronald Hayman, editor).

John Robert Whiting, while virtually unknown to general audiences, is recognized by serious critics as a major force in twentieth century drama. He was born in Salisbury, England, on November 15, 1917, the son of a retired army officer turned lawyer. An indifferent student who later claimed that he had never passed an examination, Whiting left his upper-middle-class schooling at age seventeen to train as an actor at the Royal Academy of Dramatic Art. With the outbreak of World War II, he enlisted in the Royal Artillery. After marrying actress Jackie Mawson in 1940, he returned to acting at the end of the war, joining John Gielgud's company in 1951.

In spite of this lengthy association with the theater, Whiting exhibited no interest in writing plays until a casual conversation with a friend in 1946 inspired him to make the attempt. During the following five years he wrote four plays—half of his entire canon of stage drama—as well as four radio plays for the British Broadcasting Corporation (BBC). His first stage play was *A Penny for a Song*, a comedy set during the Napoleonic Wars. Directed by Peter Brook, it was performed in March, 1951. A vivid, theatrical play, it traces the rise and fall of Sir Timothy Humpage as he attempts to preserve happiness and a sense of purpose—illusions for Whiting—at the expense of self-deception. "We find reality unbearable. . . . And so we escape, childlike, into the illusion," one of the characters says. In September of 1951, Whiting's second stage play, *Saint's Day*, was performed at the Arts Theatre Club. It closed after three weeks amid hostile popular criticism and audience rejection, a pattern which was to continue during most of Whiting's life. With a central theme of self-destruction, the play sets forth in bleak terms the tragedy of the elderly poet Paul Southman, who had isolated himself and his family from the local community. In this dense, dark play, Southman learns, "We are here—all of us—to die. Nothing more than that."

Whiting's next play, *Marching Song*, appeared in 1954. Describing it as formally austere and antitheatrical, Whiting used the figure of General Rupert Forster, who was guilty of war crimes involving the slaughter of children, to present images of death and violence, underscoring the nihilistic forces operating in the universe. Whiting wrote only one more full-length stage play in the 1950's, a withdrawal directly resulting from negative reactions to his work. He did, however, write many screenplays.

In 1960 Whiting was invited to write *The Devils*, an adaptation of Aldous Huxley's book *The Devils of Loudun* (1952). Successfully performed in 1961, the play explored the diabolic possession of a group of nuns through the influence of a charismatic priest named Grandier, who was horribly tortured. Another of Whiting's self-destructive characters, he was a tragic figure, flawed by his refusal to accept responsibility for his actions. Epic in style, the play achieved its effects through a relentless series of visual and verbal grotesqueries, stressing that "the purpose of man [is] loneliness and death."

Whiting's death of cancer on June 16, 1963, abruptly ended his reestablished dramatic career. Other plays discovered among his papers and performed posthumously include *Conditions of Agreement* and *No More A-Roving*, both written in 1946.

All Whiting's best plays, the editor Simon Trussler has suggested, are "most readily understood as parables and paradigms of human behavior." Whiting was concerned with exploring the human soul in its abstracted, self-destructive preoccupation with the processes of dying. At the center of his plays stand tormented men who are caught in webs of unmotivated cruelty. In their isolation, they radiate hatred toward others and especially toward themselves. Southman, in *Saint's Day*, and Forster, in *Marching Song*, commit suicide; Grandier, in *The Devils*, provokes others to torture him to death. The structures of Whiting's plays are marked by density, austerity, and ambiguity; the tone is dark and pessimistic. Whiting characteristically uses potent and provocative stage pictures to frame the words of the text, as in the opening scene of *The Devils*, in which a corpse hangs from the gallows and a sewer worker labors in his pit.

During his lifetime, Whiting's plays were neither popular nor the subject of much literary criticism. He allied himself with the tradition of the intellectual elite, writing plays that were obscure and difficult even for a discriminating audience. Embedded within his theater were structural and thematic references and allusions that were often part of a private mythology. In his recurrent concern with the nature of violence and the limits of personal responsibility, Whiting anticipated the work of later writers. In his use of Brechtian techniques in *The Devils*, he paved the way for further experimentations in the theater. Whiting's contributions to the development of British theater were significant, although they have been underestimated. In 1965 the Arts Council of Great Britain instituted the John Whiting Award, an annual stipend given to younger British dramatists whose work is only beginning to be known.

Lori Hall Burghardt

Bibliography

Demastes, William W., and Katherine Kelly, eds. *British Playwrights, 1956-1995: A Research and Production Sourcebook*. Westport, Conn.: Greenwood Press, 1996. An essay on Whiting discusses his life and works plus provides an assessment of the playwright's career. Includes bibliography.

Goodall, Jane. "*The Devils* and Its Sources: Modern Perspectives on the Loudun Possession." In *Drama and Philosophy*, edited by James Redmond. New York: Cambridge University Press, 1990. The essay shows how Whiting shifts the emphasis from Grandier's villainy to his inner struggle. It also compares the play with Henry de Montherlant's *Port-Royal* (pr., pb. 1954; English translation, 1962) and Jean Genet's *Le Balcon* (pb. 1956; *The Balcony*, 1957).

_______. "Musicality and Meaning in the Dialogue of *Saint's Day*." *Modern Drama* 29 (December, 1986): 567-579. This essay defends the play against the early charges of abstruseness by demonstrating its underlying logic. It seeks to show the dramatic elements of this logic in terms of the search for revelation. Looks particularly at the play's dialogue.

Robinson, Gabrielle. *A Private Mythology: The Manuscripts and Plays of John Whiting*. Cranbury, N.J.: Associated University Press, 1988. Robinson examines myth as it is manifested in the works of Whiting. Includes bibliography and index.

Salmon, Eric. *The Dark Journey: John Whiting as Dramatist*. London: Barrie and Jenkins, 1979. An account of Whiting's complete oeuvre. It traces in particular Whiting's obsession "with the innate tendency of the sensitive towards self-destruction." Includes appendices, a bibliography, and an index.

Walt Whitman

American poet

Born: West Hills, New York; May 31, 1819
Died: Camden, New Jersey; March 26, 1892
Identity: Gay or bisexual

POETRY: *Leaves of Grass*, 1855, 1856, 1860, 1867, 1871, 1876, 1881-1882, 1889, 1891-1892; *Drum-Taps*, 1865; *Sequel to Drum-Taps*, 1865-1866; *Passage to India*, 1871; *After All, Not to Create Only*, 1871; *As a Strong Bird on Pinions Free*, 1872; *Two Rivulets*, 1876; *November Boughs*, 1888; *Good-bye My Fancy*, 1891; *Complete Poetry and Selected Prose*, 1959 (James E. Miller, editor).

LONG FICTION: *Franklin Evans*, 1842.

SHORT FICTION: *The Half-Breed, and Other Stories*, 1927.

NONFICTION: *Democratic Vistas*, 1871; *Memoranda During the War*, 1875-1876; *Specimen Days and Collect*, 1882-1883; *Complete Prose Works*, 1892; *Calamus*, 1897 (letters; Richard M. Bucke, editor); *The Wound Dresser*, 1898 (Bucke, editor); *Letters Written by Walt Whitman to His Mother, 1866-1872*, 1902 (Thomas B. Harned, editor); *An American Primer*, 1904; *Walt Whitman's Diary in Canada*, 1904 (William S. Kennedy, editor); *The Letters of Anne Gilchrist and Walt Whitman*, 1918 (Harned, editor).

MISCELLANEOUS: *The Collected Writings of Walt Whitman*, 1961-1984 (22 volumes).

Walter Whitman was born at West Hills, near Huntington, Long Island, May 31, 1819, the second child of Walter Whitman and Louisa Van Velsor, of English and Dutch descent. The father, a farmer and carpenter, had difficulty supporting his large family, which grew to nine children, though one died in infancy. In 1823 he moved to Brooklyn, where Walt, his only son ever to show marked ability, received a meager public school education, learned the printing trade, became a journalist, and finally became a poet.

After teaching school on Long Island and starting and abandoning a newspaper, the *Long Islander*, Walt Whitman worked as a printer in New York City and at twenty-three edited a daily paper, the New York *Aurora*. Returning to Brooklyn in 1845, he worked on the Long Island *Star* and for two years edited the Brooklyn *Eagle*, from which he was dismissed because of his editorial defense of the "free soil" faction of the Democratic Party. For three months in 1848 he was employed on the New Orleans *Crescent* but again returned to Brooklyn and for a few months edited a free soil paper called the *Freeman*. Thereafter for five years he built and sold houses and dabbled in real estate. He did not edit another paper until 1857, when he took charge of the Brooklyn *Times* for approximately two years.

While employed as printer, journalist, and editor, Whitman

published sentimental poems and stories in newspapers and magazines, but he first became a serious poet when he printed at his own expense the first edition of *Leaves of Grass* in 1855. The book's transcendental theme of seeking life experiences in nature was acclaimed by Ralph Waldo Emerson and a few others but was mostly ignored or denounced as unpoetic because the lines did not rhyme or scan, or as indecent because of the frank language. Undaunted, the poet brought out a second edition in 1856 and a third in 1860. The latter was published by Thayer and Eldridge in Boston, but the outbreak of the Civil War bankrupted this firm, and Whitman did not have another commercial publisher until 1881.

He participated in the war by ministering to the wounded, writing accounts for the New York and Brooklyn newspapers, and composing his *Drum-Taps* poems, which he printed in 1865. Whitman spent long hours in the hospitals helping the wounded veterans. He visited them regularly, comforting the sick and the dying and writing long letters for them to their worried and bereaved families. After the assassination of President Abraham Lincoln, Whitman wrote what were to become his two best-known poems, "O Captain! My Captain!" and "When Lilacs Last in the Dooryard Bloom'd," which he included in an annex to the second issue of *Drum-Taps*. From 1865 until 1873, when he suffered a paralytic stroke, he was employed as a government clerk in Washington. His mother having died in 1873, for several years he lived with his brother George in Camden, New Jersey, a "battered, wrecked old man." Although partially disabled for the remainder of his life, he recovered sufficiently to make some trips—several to New York, one as far west as Denver in 1879, and another to Canada the following year.

In 1881 James Osgood, a respected Boston publisher, issued another edition of *Leaves of Grass* but stopped distribution after the poet refused to withdraw several lines (for a new printing) which had provoked the threat of criminal prosecution. Whitman secured new publishers in Philadelphia, first Rees Welsh and Company, then David McKay, who thereafter remained his publisher during his lifetime. In 1882 McKay published *Specimen Days and Collect*, a volume of prose containing sketches of the poet's early life, experiences in the hospitals, and old-age diary notes. *November Boughs*, 1888, also contained some prose and an important literary apologia, "A Backward Glance o'er Travel'd Roads." With the income from the 1881 edition of *Leaves of Grass* Whitman was able to buy a small house for himself in Camden, on Mickle Street, which soon began to be visited by many prominent writers and artists from England, where Whitman's reputation was greater than in his own country. At the time of his death in Camden, March 26, 1892, he was one of the best-known poets in the United States, partly because of the publicity resulting from the accusations made against the Boston edition of 1881 and partly because he had relentlessly publicized himself. Consequently, the metropolitan newspapers gave many columns of space to his death, and it was mentioned in many European papers. However, Whitman was not generally accepted by the literary critics and historians in his own country for another quarter century. By the mid-twentieth century, however, he was almost universally regarded as the greatest poet the United States had produced. *Leaves of Grass* has been translated in whole or in part into most of the languages of the world. Successful complete translations have been published in France, Germany, Spain, Italy, and Japan. *Leaves of Grass* is an acknowledged masterpiece in world literature.

In its growth and structure *Leaves of Grass* is probably unique in literary history. Between 1855 and 1892 Whitman used the same title for nine editions of his collected poems, no two alike, and several dramatically different in size, content, and arrangement. Not only did the poet constantly revise and augment his poems, but he also altered titles, divided or combined poems, dropped some, and constantly shifted their relative positions in the book until 1881, when he solidified the order, thereafter merely annexing new poems. A posthumous tenth edition, published in 1897, contains the final annex, "Old Age Echoes," comprising poems first collected by the literary executors. On his deathbed the poet declared the 1892 edition to be definitive, but critics and biographers have often found earlier editions to be more interesting, more revealing, and even of higher literary merit—especially the first (1855) and third (1860).

Whitman is credited with inventing a new metrical style of poetry called free verse that is based on the transcendental idea of organicism in literature. This revolutionary mid-nineteenth century theory was promoted by writers such as Samuel Taylor Coleridge and Emerson, who urged literary artists to create their works according to the patterns of growth and development present in the natural world.

Considerable controversy has arisen over the sexual imagery of two groups of poems first assembled in 1860 and titled "Enfans d'Adam" (later "Children of Adam") and "Calamus." Theoretically, the former group treats procreative or sexual love, the latter friendship or "manly love." Earlier critics objected to the realism of "Children of Adam"; later critics have been more intrigued with the eroticism of "Calamus." The "Calamus" poems have stirred much speculation about Whitman's sexual orientation. Although the poet usually refuted implications of his homosexuality, his correspondence reveals the fond attachments he sought with young men. Two of Whitman's most intense relationships were with the streetcar conductor Peter Doyle, whom he met in Washington, D.C., in 1865, and Harry Stafford, the young friend he knew later when he moved to Camden, New Jersey.

Whitman wanted to be known as the spokesman of democracy—in many countries he has become a symbol of American democracy—but his poems have survived as poems rather than as repositories of ideas. Whitman's most characteristic poem is "Song of Myself." Though uneven, it contains some of the finest lyrical passages in the whole range of American poetry.

Angelo Costanzo

Bibliography

Allen, Gay Wilson. *The Solitary Singer: A Critical Biography of Walt Whitman*. Rev. ed. New York: New York University Press, 1967. A careful, scholarly biography based on extensive archival sources, including manuscripts and letters, that attempts to treat Whitman's life in terms of the poet's work.

Asselineau, Roger. *The Evolution of Walt Whitman*. Expanded ed. Iowa City: University of Iowa Press, 1999. Asselineau writes with authority on a vast range of topics that define both Whitman the man and Whitman the mythical personage.

Gold, Arthur, ed. *Walt Whitman: A Collection of Criticism.* New York: McGraw Hill, 1974. Concentrates on academic criticism, on the poet's creative process, his literary reputation, his revisions of *Leaves of Grass*, and his vision of the United States in *Democratic Vistas.* A detailed chronology and a select, annotated bibliography make this collection a useful volume.

Kaplan, Justin. *Walt Whitman: A Life.* New York: Simon & Schuster, 1980. An elegant, deeply imagined biography that focuses on both Whitman and his times. Kaplan provides the fullest, most sensitive account of the poet's career, taking a chronological approach but managing to pinpoint and to highlight the most important phases of his subject's life.

Miller, James E., Jr. *Walt Whitman.* Rev. ed. Boston: Twayne, 1990. Miller concentrates on the development and structure of *Leaves of Grass*, its democratic "poetics," the major poems within it, "recurring images," "language and wit," and the "bardic voice." The first chapter and chronology provide a factual and analytical discussion of Whitman's biography, and Miller assesses the new criticism of the poet that has appeared since the original publication of his book in 1962. Includes bibliography.

Pearce, Roy Harvey, ed. *Whitman: A Collection of Critical Essays.* Englewood Cliffs, N.J.: Prentice-Hall, 1962. A comprehensive collection of criticism, including commentary by Ezra Pound and D. H. Lawrence, three articles on the structure of *Leaves of Grass*, and additional discussion of the poet's style and other works. Contains a chronology of important dates, an introductory overview of the critical literature on Whitman, and a bibliography.

Reynolds, David S., ed. *A Historical Guide to Walt Whitman.* New York: Oxford University Press, 2000. Combines contemporary cultural studies and historical scholarship to illuminate Whitman's diverse contexts. The essays explore dimensions of Whitman's dynamic relationship to working-class politics, race and slavery, sexual mores, the visual arts, and the idea of democracy.

Woodress, James, ed. *Critical Essays on Walt Whitman.* Boston: G. K. Hall, 1983. Divided into reviews and early reactions, essays and other forms of criticism, with an introduction surveying the history of Whitman criticism. This collection provides a good history of Whitman's place in American culture and an informative, if highly selective, view of scholarly treatments of his work. Contains an index.

Zweig, Paul. *Walt Whitman: The Making of a Poet.* New York: Basic Books, 1984. This volume is not a chronological biography but rather a biographical and critical meditation on Whitman's development as a poet. Zweig explores how the "drab" journalist of the 1840's transformed himself into a major poet.

John Greenleaf Whittier

American poet

Born: Haverhill, Massachusetts; December 17, 1807
Died: Hampton Falls, New Hampshire; September 7, 1892

POETRY: *Legends of New-England*, 1831; *Moll Pitcher*, 1832; *Mogg Megone*, 1836; *Poems Written During the Progress of the Abolition Question in the United States*, 1837; *Poems*, 1838; *Lays of My Home, and Other Poems*, 1843; *Voices of Freedom*, 1846; *Poems*, 1849; *Songs of Labor, and Other Poems*, 1850; *The Chapel of the Hermits, and Other Poems*, 1853; *The Panorama, and Other Poems*, 1856; *The Sycamores*, 1857; *The Poetical Works of John Greenleaf Whittier*, 1857, 1869, 1880, 1894; *Home Ballads and Poems*, 1860; *In War Time*, 1863; *Snow-Bound: A Winter Idyl*, 1866; *The Tent on the Beach, and Other Poems*, 1867; *Maud Muller*, 1869; *Among the Hills, and Other Poems*, 1869; *Ballads of New England*, 1869; *Miriam, and Other Poems*, 1871; *The Pennsylvania Pilgrim, and Other Poems*, 1872; *Hazel-Blossoms*, 1875; *Mabel Martin*, 1876; *Favorite Poems*, 1877; *The Vision of Echard, and Other Poems*, 1878; *The King's Missive, and Other Poems*, 1881; *The Bay of Seven Islands, and Other Poems*, 1883; *Saint Gregory's Guest, and Recent Poems*, 1886; *At Sundown*, 1890.

LONG FICTION: *Narrative of James Williams: An American Slave*, 1838; *Leaves from Margaret Smith's Journal*, 1849.

NONFICTION: *Justice and Expediency: Or, Slavery Considered with a View to Its Rightful and Effectual Remedy, Abolition*, 1833; *The Supernaturalism of New England*, 1847; *Old Portraits and Modern Sketches*, 1850; *Literary Recreations and Miscellanies*, 1854; *Whittier on Writers and Writing: The Uncollected Critical Writings of John Greenleaf Whittier*, 1950 (Edwin H. Cady and Harry Hayden Clark, editors); *The Letters of John Greenleaf Whittier*, 1975 (John B. Pickard, editor).

EDITED TEXTS: *The Journal of John Woolman*, 1871; *Child Life*, 1872; *Child Life in Prose*, 1874; *Songs of Three Centuries*, 1876.

MISCELLANEOUS: *Prose Works of John Greenleaf Whittier*, 1866; *The Writings of John Greenleaf Whittier*, 1888-1889.

Time and geography link John Greenleaf Whittier (HWIHT-ee-ur) with such American literary figures as Ralph Waldo Emerson, Henry Wadsworth Longfellow, James Russell Lowell, and Oliver Wendell Holmes—the so-called New England Group. Whittier's New England, however, was never the same as theirs; he stands apart from them in background, schooling, and the general direction of his writing talents. To begin with, he did not share their Puritan heritage—Whittier was a Quaker, derived from Quaker stock. Nor did he inherit a ticket of admission to the cultural benefits that nineteenth century Cambridge, Concord, and Boston were able to provide. Instead, "the American Burns" was born to the rugged labors and simple pleasures of rural life and to such limited educational opportunities as were open to a Massachusetts farm lad.

Whittier was born near Haverhill, Massachusetts, on December 17, 1807. His birthplace was the plain colonial homestead that he later made famous in *Snow-Bound*, and his boyhood environment, though not poverty-stricken, provided no luxury or special incentives to a literary career. Whittier's formal education was confined to winter sessions of a district school and two terms at Haverhill Academy. It was the village schoolmaster, Joshua Coffin, who introduced him to the poetry of Robert Burns, a powerful source of inspiration to the imaginative boy.

Whittier's early poems appeared chiefly in local newspapers, one of which was published by William Lloyd Garrison. When he was about twenty-one, Whittier left home to embark on a career of itinerant journalism which led him to Boston, back to Haverhill, then to Hartford and Philadelphia. In 1833 he attended an antislavery convention in Philadelphia, thus launching abolitionist efforts so zealous as to engage his best strength for the next thirty years. The end of the Civil War, however, freed him to endeavors less didactic, and in 1866 the success of *Snow-Bound* gave him not only important literary recognition but also the beginnings of financial security. As the poet of rural New England and as a voice of calm and sincere religious faith, he became increasingly popular. His seventieth and eightieth birthdays were widely celebrated. He died at Hampton Falls, New Hampshire, on September 7, 1892, at the age of eighty-five.

Whittier's reputation today rests on poems which, at their best, express the very heart of rural New England. His literary reputation has suffered a marked decline, and the reasons are easily discernable. For one thing, most of Whittier's antislavery poems have not survived the cause in which they were written. For another, the author's work, despite its sincerity and intensity, often suffers from limitations of range and craftsmanship. Finally, his poetry is direct, simple, and emotional, qualities to which modern criticism tends to turn a deaf ear. Interesting also is the now almost-forgotten *Leaves from Margaret Smith's Journal*, a fictitious but accurate account of colonial life.

Nevertheless, *Snow-Bound* alone is enough to place posterity in debt to Whittier. The simplicity and dignity of family affection, the sharply etched view of a winterbound farmhouse, and the recaptured charm of a lost way of life—in these features no other American poem displays a greater, or perhaps even equal, degree of felicity.

Bibliography

Grant, David. "'The Unequal Sovereigns of a Slaveholding Land': The North as Subject in Whittier's 'The Panorama.'" *Criticism* 38, no. 4 (Fall, 1996): 521-549. Whittier's "The Panorama" discusses the interdependence of the two ideals exploited by the Republicans and Democrats: sovereignty and Union. The poem places the slave system at the root of the threats to the North.

Hollander, John, ed. *American Poetry: The Nineteenth Century.* New York: Library of America, 1993. Contains a biographical sketch of Whittier and a year-by-year chronology of poets and poetry.

Kribbs, Jayne K., comp. *Critical Essays on John Greenleaf Whittier.* Boston: G. K. Hall, 1980. Kribbs's extended introduction locates four periods of the poet's writing career and suggests in conclusion that the central question about Whittier is not how great, but how minor a figure he is in American literature. All the essays are written by respected scholars. Contains a bibliography and an index.

Leary, Lewis Gaston. *John Greenleaf Whittier.* New York: Twayne, 1961. Although this introductory study looks at Whittier's life and art, the poetry discussion is more useful than the biographical section, which contains some errors and no new information. Leary discusses the poet's limitations, especially as a critic. Includes bibliography.

Miller, Lewis H. "The Supernaturalism of *Snow Bound.*" *New England Quarterly* 53 (1980): 291-307. A good reading of how Whittier broke through his usually plain style to create an impressive rhythm, tone, and syntax in his striking creation of a bleak landscape and snow-bound universe.

Pickard, John B. *John Greenleaf Whittier: An Introduction and Interpretation.* New York: Barnes & Noble Books, 1961. The book begins with a biographical summary; the last seven chapters are a critical guide to Whittier's work.

Wagenknecht, Edward. *John Greenleaf Whittier: A Portrait in Paradox.* New York: Oxford University Press, 1967. Wagenknecht arranges his facts and anecdotes topically rather than chronologically. The result is a vibrant and energetic portrait of Whittier that displays the richness of his inner and outer life. The thesis of this book is that many facets of Whittier's life seem paradoxical to one another. Includes bibliography.

Warren, Robert Penn. *John Greenleaf Whittier's Poetry: An Appraisal and a Selection.* Minneapolis: University of Minnesota Press, 1971. Warren discusses "Snow-Bound," "Telling the Bees," "Ichabod," "To My Old Schoolmaster," and other poems addressing themes of childhood and nostalgia, as well as a controversial Freudian view of the poet's development. Includes thirty-six poems by Whittier.

Woodwell, R. H. *John Greenleaf Whittier: A Biography.* Haverhill, Mass.: Trustees of the John Greenleaf Whittier Homestead, 1985. This biography, based on years of research, is encyclopedic but has a very good index. Woodwell's 636 pages are not highly readable, but he includes a useful review of Whittier's criticism.

Benjamin Lee Whorf

American linguist

Born: Winthrop, Massachusetts; April 24, 1897
Died: Wethersfield, Connecticut; July 26, 1941

NONFICTION: "An Aztec Account of the Period of the Toltec Decline," 1928; "A Central Mexican Inscription Combining Mexican and Maya Day Signs," 1932; "The Phonetic Value of Certain Characters in Maya Writing," 1933; "The Punctual and Segmentative Aspects of Verbs in Hopi," 1936; "Some Verbal Categories of Hopi," 1938; "Science and Linguistics," 1940; "Linguistics as an Exact Science," 1940; "The Relation of Habitual Thought and Behavior to Language," 1941; "Languages and Logic," 1941; "Language, Mind, and Reality," 1942; *Language, Thought, and Reality: Selected Writings*, 1956.

When he died in 1941, the work of Benjamin Lee Whorf (hwawrf) was little known outside a limited circle of linguists, but his reputation as a powerful and influential thinker has since grown considerably. Born into an unusually eclectic and artistic suburban Boston household, he lived virtually all of his adult life in central Connecticut. Like his fellow Hartford-area resident Wallace Stevens, Whorf pursued a highly successful career in the insurance field at the same time that he pursued other, more literary interests. He has become best known for his development of the theory of linguistic relativity, the idea that the basic structural qualities of a given group's language largely determine the fundamental character of that society.

Educated in Winthrop public schools, Whorf graduated from the Massachusetts Institute of Technology (MIT) with a bachelor of science degree in chemical engineering in the fall of 1918. Early the following year, he accepted a position as a trainee with the Hartford Fire Insurance Company. In the new field of fire prevention engineering, he advanced rapidly from special agent to assistant secretary, the position he held at the time of his death.

An interest in fundamentalist religion seems to have driven his study of language. In the early 1920's, after he had married and established residence in the Hartford area, he began to teach himself Hebrew so that he could better understand biblical tradition. His interest in the qualities of a language that might influence the cultures using it soon led him to study other languages, including Mayan and Aztec.

As he advanced in the insurance business, so his "hobby" of linguistic analysis prospered. His first published article, "An Aztec Account of the Period of the Toltec Decline," attracted considerable attention among linguists and students of indigenous American cultures. From this early work emerged developing statements on the derivation of some languages from a limited number of stems, or from a slightly larger group of morphemes (the smallest individual units of meaning in a language). Whorf more firmly established his growing reputation as a brilliant translator of hieroglyphs with published work on the Mayan civilization. His developing fascination with the puzzles of Aztec and Mayan culture was partially satisfied in 1930, when he won funding from the Social Sciences Research Council to travel to central Mexico and spend time in areas where the inhabitants still used a language and observed other cultural practices very close to the ancient Aztec language and traditions.

Following the period of his fellowship, during which he pursued anthropological and architectural as well as cultural and linguistic researches, Whorf worked diligently at organizing and arranging his data. In 1931 the renowned linguist Edward Sapir accepted an appointment at Yale University; Whorf immediately enrolled in order to study American Indian linguistics under Sapir. Sapir's study *Language* (1921) emphasized the tremendous potential inherent in language as social determinant and in grammar as the basis of poetry. In some of his work Sapir was following the lead of Franz Boas, the pioneering American anthropologist linguist whose *Handbook of American Indian Languages* (1911) was the first American work to demonstrate how language patterns—most important, grammatical patterns—that underlie a culture might actually determine much of that culture. Such study of interrelations among language, thought, and culture provided the basis of the theory of linguistic relativity and led to its being called the "Sapir-Whorf hypothesis" or the "Whorfian hypothesis." When Whorf's fascination with Native American ethnography was tempered by the stabilizing influence of Sapir's disciplined linguistic precision, he began to do his greatest work.

From 1935 to his death, Whorf worked feverishly at publishing his ideas. Articles on the Hopi demonstrate how the Hopi's unique grammar underlies a highly unusual conception of the universe. He shows how the Hopi are concerned largely with space, while Indo-European languages emphasize temporal concerns. From observing how such an orientation can be detected in the organization of the different societies, Whorf draws conclusions on the psychological potential of sounds and grammars. His article "The Relation of Habitual Thought and Behavior to Language," written in 1939 and published in 1941, offers his most developed statement of how the syntax, grammar, and characteristic thought construction of a language determine the way that its speakers conceive of the universe in which they exist. Though he was suffering from lung cancer the last two years of his life, he worked until his death at expanding his statements regarding linguistic relativity into a book, the projected title of which—*Language, Thought, and Reality*—was used for a collection of his works published posthumously.

Peter Valenti

Bibliography

Clarke, Mark A., et al. "Linguistic Relativity and Sex/Gender Studies: Epistemological and Methodological Considerations." *Language Learning* 34 (1984). A study that brings to bear later theoretical schools.

Farb, Peter. "How Do I Know You Mean What You Mean?" *Horizon* 10 (1968). A general introduction.

Kaye, Alan S. "Schools of Linguistics: Competition and Evolution." *Studies in Language* 10 (1986). Places linguistic relativity in relation to other linguistic theories.

Lee, Penny. *The Whorf Theory Complex: A Critical Reconstruction.* Philadelphia: J. Benjamins, 1996. A volume in the Amsterdam Studies in the Theory and History of Linguistic Science.

Schultz, Emily A. *Dialogue at the Margins: Whorf, Bakhtin, and Linguistic Relativity.* Madison: University of Wisconsin Press, 1990. Schultz, an anthropologist, reinterprets Whorf's work in relation to that of Russian theorist Mikhail Bakhtin.

Sherzer, Joel. "A Discourse-Centered Approach to Language and Culture." *American Anthropologist* 89 (1987). A useful later study. Considers Whorf's ideas in relation to contemporary discourse theory.

Whorf, Benjamin Lee. *Language, Thought, and Reality.* Edited by John B. Carroll. 1956. Reprint. Cambridge, Mass.: MIT Press, 1967. Includes critical and biographical introductions and, in addition to Whorf's major essays, publishes for the first time many of Whorf's other writings from various stages of his career.

George J. Whyte-Melville

British novelist

Born: Near St. Andrews, Scotland; June 19, 1821
Died: Berkshire, England; December 5, 1878

LONG FICTION: *Digby Grand*, 1853; *Tilbury Nogo*, 1854; *Kate Coventry*, 1856; *The Interpreter*, 1858; *Holmby House*, 1859; *Market Harborough*, 1861; *The Queen's Maries*, 1862; *The Gladiators*, 1863; *Cerise*, 1866; *The White Rose*, 1868; *Sarchedon*, 1871; *Satanella*, 1872; *Uncle John*, 1874; *Katerfelto*, 1875.

George John Whyte-Melville was born near St. Andrews, Scotland, June 19, 1821, into society, his father being a landowner in Scotland and his mother a daughter of the duke of Leeds. As a boy Whyte-Melville attended Eton, the famous English public school, and at the age of seventeen he became a commissioned officer in the Ninety-third Highlanders Regiment. After seven years with that regiment he transferred to the Coldstream Guards and retired from the British army at the age of twenty-seven with the rank of captain. When the Crimean War broke out in 1853, Whyte-Melville volunteered his services to the government and went on active duty with the rank of major. He served with units of Turkish irregular cavalry. During his service in the Crimean War he wrote some poetry, and a portion of it was published. After the war he returned to civilian life to continue writing and hunting, his favorite sport.

The novels of Whyte-Melville fall easily into two categories: sporting novels, for which he is best known, and historical romances. As a wealthy man of property and a retired officer, Whyte-Melville was completely familiar with the society he depicted in his sporting novels. He wrote from first-hand knowledge of fashionable, military, and sporting people. His novels about fox hunting had a particular appeal for British sportsmen, for they were authentically written, with a great deal of attention to detail. They are also filled with action. The best-known of the sporting novels is *Market Harborough*, a picaresque account of a series of fox-hunting episodes with considerable realistic description of life among the people in rural England and London society who follow the hounds. Other novels in this category are *Digby Grand*, *Tilbury Nogo*, and *Kate Coventry.* One interesting sidelight to these novels is that horses are often important characters.

Whyte-Melville's later fiction is largely in the field of historical romance. In 1858 he published *The Interpreter*, a novel based on the Crimean War and relating the activities of a beautiful female spy. *Holmby House* is a novel about the English Civil War of the seventeenth century, with an interesting depiction of Oliver Cromwell. In *Cerise* the author moved from backgrounds he knew well to write a novel about France and the court of Louis XIV. In *The Gladiators* and *Sarchedon* appear the times and deeds of exotic countries, the former being laid in Rome and Palestine and the latter depicting Egypt and Assyria under the rule of Semiramis. Perhaps the best of Whyte-Melville's historical novels is *Katerfelto*, the story of a famous horse of eighteenth century England.

Whyte-Melville did not write to earn money, and most of his income from his books was spent in charitable activity, especially among the poor people who were hangers-on about stables. Of his personal life little is known except that it was not happy with respect to marriage. Whyte-Melville met his death in the hunting field in White Horse Vale, Berkshire, on December 5, 1878, when one of his favorite horses stumbled and fell while at a gallop, throwing his rider and killing him instantly.

Bibliography

Baker, Ernest A. *History of the English Novel.* Vol. 7. New York: Barnes & Noble Books, 1936.

Drinkwater, John, ed. *The Eighteen-sixties: Essays by Fellows of the Royal Society of Literature.* Cambridge, England: Cambridge University Press, 1932.

Melville, Lewis. "G. J. Whyte-Melville." In *Victorian Novelists.* 1906. Reprint. Folcroft, Pa.: Folcroft Press, 1970.

John Edgar Wideman

American novelist and short-story writer

Born: Washington, D.C.; June 14, 1941
Identity: African American

LONG FICTION: *A Glance Away*, 1967; *Hurry Home*, 1970; *The Lynchers*, 1973; *Hiding Place*, 1981; *Sent for You Yesterday*, 1983; *The Homewood Trilogy*, 1985 (includes *Damballah*, *Hiding Place*, and *Sent for You Yesterday*); *Reuben*, 1987; *Philadelphia Fire*, 1990; *The Cattle Killing*, 1996; *Two Cities*, 1998.

SHORT FICTION: *Damballah*, 1981; *Fever: Twelve Stories*, 1989; *All Stories Are True*, 1992 *The Stories of John Edgar Wideman*, 1992.

NONFICTION: *Brothers and Keepers*, 1984; *Fatheralong: A Meditation on Fathers and Sons, Race and Society*, 1994; *Conversations with John Edgar Wideman*, 1998 (Bonnie TuSmith, editor); *Hoop Roots*, 2001; *The Island: Martinique*, 2003.

EDITED TEXTS: *My Soul Has Grown Deep: Classics of Early African-American Literature*, 2001; *Twenty: The Best of the Drue Heinz Literature Prize*, 2001.

John Edgar Wideman's literary achievements since the publication of his first novel, *A Glance Away*, provide compelling evidence of the diverse cultural and creative influences operating upon the imagination. Having grown up in the black community of Homewood in Pittsburgh, Pennsylvania, Wideman began his odyssey away from those roots—a central theme of his early writing—when in 1959 he was awarded a Benjamin Franklin scholarship to the University of Pennsylvania, where he became a Phi Beta Kappa scholar and distinguished himself in both creative writing and intercollegiate basketball. His assimilation into the world of academe continued when, as a Rhodes Scholar, he attended New College, Oxford, from 1963 to 1966 and studied British literature, particularly the eighteenth century novel, which fed his interest in the possibilities of contemporary narrative form.

Wideman received a Kent Fellowship to the Iowa Writers' Workshop at the University of Iowa in 1966. After 1967 he served on the faculties of several universities, including the University of Pennsylvania, the University of Wyoming, and the University of Massachusetts at Amherst, where he was named Distinguished Professor in 2001. As a novice teacher of African American studies at the University of Pennsylvania, he immersed himself for the first time in the literary tradition of black American writers, an experience he claims "absolutely transformed" his subsequent creative endeavors.

Wideman's prose experiments over the course of his career serve as a primer of modern aesthetic concerns. His early works, *A Glance Away*, *Hurry Home*, and *The Lynchers*, reveal modernist preoccupations with myth and ritual, fractured narrative, surrealism, and polyphonic voicings. Like James Joyce and William Faulkner before him, he mapped the landscape of familial history along with his own memories, translating their literal specificity into universal dramas of the human condition in the late twentieth century. Yet Wideman also demonstrates a postmodern skepticism about narrative's traditional promises of coherence and truth, his work increasingly collapsing distinctions between autobiography and fiction to produce self-conscious linguistic meditations on the ways in which the creative impulse impersonates and interrogates lived experience, efforts as likely to fail as to succeed in the quest for illumination. Postmodernism's embrace of incoherence and its assault on the fictions of selfhood enable Wideman to convey the jarringly irreconcilable paradoxes of racism as they most tellingly surface in the fractured psyches of contemporary black males.

Many of Wideman's fictional techniques express his belief in the accessibility of a collective racial memory transcending temporal and spatial divisions through the sustaining energies provided by family, community, or culture. He exposes the inner dynamics propelling his characters' lives and articulates that mystery through the creation of a chorus of distinct but overlapping voices energetically capturing the immediacies of vernacular speech. Wideman's efforts to fuse a novelistic whole from seemingly disparate narrative strands in such works as the PEN/Faulkner Award-winning *Sent for You Yesterday* or *Reuben* rest in part upon a similar theoretical supposition that from fragmentation the imagination can generate potentially healing linkages and echoes, an activity always bathed in postmodernist suspicion that the cloudiness of human vision isolates one completely from real communion with others.

Wideman achieved tremendous critical acclaim for *The Homewood Trilogy*, which consists of *Damballah* and two novels, *Hiding Place* and *Sent for You Yesterday.* Set in the Homewood of his youth, Wideman's imaginative return to his cultural past is a journey through which he explores the intricate and mysterious interweavings of history, memory, and tradition. *Damballah* and *Hiding Place*, published concurrently, offer fictive meditations on the multigenerational past of a black family as it recapitulates the social history of Homewood itself. *Sent for You Yesterday*, the culminating work in the series, draws its title from a blues song and itself becomes a "blues" rendering of Homewood's history as it has been mythically sustained in the collective memory of the community and particularized in the integrative imagination of the narrator.

With the publication of *Brothers and Keepers* Wideman made explicit the links between his biography and the fictional plottings of his previous work, particularly *The Homewood Trilogy.* In *Brothers and Keepers* Wideman steps out from behind the mask of fiction to write a painfully analytic and introspective first-person account of his relationship with Robby (his brother, Robert Wideman), a former drug addict and petty criminal then serving a life sentence in prison. Although nonfiction, the book employs a familiar array of Wideman's literary devices: a sophisticated alternation of voices shifting between formal English and street colloquialism, a dislocated chronology and colliding narrative forms, metafictional foregrounding, and a dissection of the creative process itself. The themes that dominate Wideman's fiction also operate in this text, particularly his meditations on the power of family and community to support the individual, and the countervailing pressures working to erode the cultural health of the black community and the faith of even its most resilient members.

In *Fatheralong*, a second memoir published a decade later, Wideman continues that meditation. In the course of his attempt to invoke a new relationship with his father, Edgar, the text becomes a study of his own paternal grief over his son, serving a life sentence in Arizona following the 1988 murder of another teenager. Wideman uses the rupture of family to further disrupt orthodox distinctions between the worlds within and without his texts. In the PEN/Faulkner Award-winning *Philadelphia Fire*, for example, the narrative moves between two independent frames of reference, one belonging to a disaffected writer determined to locate a child seen running from the catastrophic 1985 police siege of the MOVE community in Philadelphia, the other belonging to a writerly consciousness identified as Mr. Wideman, who is trying to break through the literal and figurative walls closing him off from his prison inmate son. The urgency in Wideman's work after the early 1980's reflects the haunting personal dimension of his investigations into the mysteries of human character and his hunger for the restorative possibilities of imagination and art. In 1993 his extraordinary talents led to his being awarded a MacArthur Foundation grant.

Barbara Kitt Seidman

Bibliography

Auger, Philip. *Native Sons in No Man's Land: Rewriting Afro-American Manhood in the Novels of Baldwin, Walker, Wideman, and Gaines*. New York: Garland, 2000. Analyzes the representation of masculinity in Wideman's works.

Byerman, Keith Eldon. *John Edgar Wideman: A Study of the Short Fiction*. New York: Twayne, 1998. A critical look at Wideman's short fiction, including interview material. Includes a bibliography and an index.

Coleman, James W. *Blackness and Modernism: The Literary Career of John Edgar Wideman*. Jackson: University Press of Mississippi, 1989. Contends that Wideman's fiction has evolved from a modernist emphasis on alienation and despair to a postmodernist portrayal of black communities that are strong and sustaining. Coleman evaluates the fiction for its fantasy, surrealism, magic, ritual, folklore, and mainstream influences.

Dubey, Madhu. "Literature and Urban Crisis: John Edgar Wideman's *Philadelphia Fire*." *African American Review* 32 (Winter, 1998): 579-595. Dubey examines *Philadelphia Fire* in relation to its implicit critique of urban renewal and its attenuating glorification of consumption and excess, legitimation of law and order, and the resulting dispossession, displacement, and segregation of the city's inhabitants.

Gysin, Fritz. "John Edgar Wideman: 'Fever.'" In *The African-American Short Story: 1970 to 1990*, edited by Wolfgang Karrer and Barbara Puschmann-Nalenz. Trier, Germany: Wissenschaftlicher Verlag, 1993. A detailed discussion of the title story of Wideman's 1989 collection. Provides historical background for the 1793 Philadelphia yellow fever epidemic and the part African American citizens played in fighting the epidemic.

Mbalia, Doreatha D. *John Edgar Wideman: Reclaiming the African Personality*. London: Associated University Presses, 1995. Examines the African influences on Wideman's work. Includes bibliographical references and an index.

Rushdy, Ashraf. "Fraternal Blues: John Edgar Wideman's Homewood Trilogy." *Contemporary Literature* 32, no. 3 (Fall, 1991): 312-345. Rushdy begins by suggesting that the narrator of the trilogy utilizes three modes of narrating which are depicted in the three texts, respectively: letters, stories, and "the blues." He argues that the narrative voice gains an understanding of self when it finds a "blues voice."

Wilson, Matthew. "The Circles of History in John Edgar Wideman's *The Homewood Trilogy*." *CLA Journal* 33 (March, 1990): 239-259. Examines interconnections among individual family histories, events from American enslavement, and the histories of the Fon and Kongo cultures. A central theme of the trilogy is that black Americans resist annihilation and vanquish the oppressive acts of whites by telling their own stories and exposing their authentic histories.

Rudy Wiebe

Canadian novelist

Born: Fairholme, Saskatchewan, Canada; October 4, 1934

LONG FICTION: *Peace Shall Destroy Many*, 1962; *First and Vital Candle*, 1966; *The Blue Mountains of China*, 1970; *The Temptations of Big Bear*, 1973; *The Scorched-Wood People*, 1977; *The Mad Trapper*, 1980; *My Lovely Enemy*, 1983; *A Discovery of Strangers*, 1994; *Sweeter than All the World*, 2001.

SHORT FICTION: *Where Is the Voice Coming From?*, 1974; *Alberta: A Celebration*, 1979; *The Angel of the Tar Sands, and Other Stories*, 1982.

DRAMA: *Far as the Eye Can See*, pr., pb. 1977.

NONFICTION: *A Voice in the Land: Essays by and About Rudy Wiebe*, 1981; *Playing Dead: A Contemplation Concerning the Arctic*, 1989; *Stolen Life: The Journey of a Cree Woman*, 1998 (with Yvonne Johnson).

CHILDREN'S/YOUNG ADULT LITERATURE: *Chinook Christmas*, 1992.

EDITED TEXTS: *The Story-Makers: A Selection of Modern Short Stories*, 1980; *West of Fiction*, 1983 (with Leah Flater and Aritha van Herk); *War in the West: Voices of the 1985 Rebellion*, 1985 (with Bob Beal).

MISCELLANEOUS: *River of Stone: Fictions and Memories*, 1995.

Rudy Wiebe (WEE-bee) was born in 1934 on his family's farm in a small Mennonite community in Fairholme, Saskatchewan; his parents were émigrés from the Soviet Union. Wiebe began writing seriously during his undergraduate years at the University of Alberta (1953-1956) and took an M.A. in creative writing from that institution in 1960. He has held various teaching posts since that time, including one at Goshen College, Indiana (1963-1967), but in 1967 he began teaching full-time as a professor of creative writing at the University of Alberta, where he remained until his retirement in 1992.

It is Wiebe's work as a novelist that has given him his fine reputation in his native land, though he has also carved out a formidable career as a short-story writer, playwright, and editor/critic. He has candidly described himself as "one who tries to explore the world that I know, the land and people of Western Canada, from my particular worldview: a radical Jesus-oriented Christianity." To perform this function, Wiebe has characteristically chosen experimental modes of narration, particularly the use of multiple, omniscient narrators, whose compelling voices establish the theme that the struggle for personal identity is resolvable only through wrestling with one's family and cultural past. As Wiebe explains, "I believe fiction must be precisely, peculiarly rooted in a particular place, in particular people." His first language was Low German, and this cultural background—coupled with his devout Mennonite faith—forms the thematic landscape in which his early fiction is constructed. He has thus come to be widely praised as one of Canada's most innovative "Prairie" writers.

The characters in Wiebe's first three novels share the common plight of being "strangers in a strange land," a religious remnant fighting for their faith and family identity in a modern world gone mad. Mennonite Christianity, evolving from the radical Anabaptist tradition, is a fiercely independent faith that demands of its practitioners a separation from the world—it compelled them to leave their native land, customs, and language in search of a country where they could live out their faith. Wiebe's first novel, *Peace Shall Destroy Many*, the title of which alludes to the Book of Daniel, is an ironic juxtaposition of two men's wartime legalism and arrogance: the arrogant militarism of Adolf Hitler and the arrogant pacifism of Deacon Block, a Western Canadian Mennonite. Welcomed by critics for its evocation of time and place but equally criticized for its overt moralizing, this novel served notice that a new, yet unharnessed narrative power had emerged in Canadian letters. *First and Vital Candle* and *The Blue Mountains of China* both extend and display Wiebe's unique narrative powers, again focusing on the theme of living out the Christian vision of society and culture when the signs, symbols, and very language of Christianity are seen as defunct and irrelevant. The former novel contains powerful evocations and celebrations of American Indian and Eskimo life, filtered through the consciousness of Abe Ross, a man in search of his lost faith. In *The Blue Mountains of China* Wiebe experiments further with his quasi-epic mode of narration. The novel has no conventional plot; each chapter is a somewhat self-contained and idiosyncratic account of the events, relationships, and inner thoughts of five principal characters, all Mennonites searching for the "land God had given them for their very own, to which they were called." Wiebe's epigraph to *The Blue Mountains of China* perhaps serves as a sardonic reminder of the common thread running through all of his novels: "They are still trying to find [this land], and it isn't anywhere on earth."

Native Western Canadians—the American Indians and Eskimos of Manitoba, Saskatchewan, and parts farther north—often populate Wiebe's fiction because they represent spiritual values markedly different from those of the world that has displaced them. The otherness and isolation characteristic of the radical Mennonite Christian community that Wiebe has attempted to chronicle are often mirrored in these non-Christian characters as well, who are themselves outcasts and wayfarers when measured against the mind-set of their times. That is certainly the case with Wiebe's next novel, perhaps his most important, *The Temptations of Big Bear*, for which he received the Canadian Governor General's Literary Award in 1973. Here Wiebe fictionalizes the life and times of the great Prairie Indian chief Big Bear, who suffers, along with his tribe, the fate of all those who attempt to fight against the treacheries of the modern world, and the ethnocentrism of its leaders and social planners. Wiebe's 1977 novel *The Scorched-Wood People* investigates the historical particulars surrounding the subjugation of the Metis, a proud people of mixed French and Indian descent. In a radical indictment of the prevailing Scottish and English Canadian politics, Wiebe depicts the Metis as a people better equipped to rule their land because of their close connection with their heritage. In contrast, white Canada is seen as thoroughly cut off from its own Christian heritage, as a consequence of which it has been guilty of cultural imperialism on a vast scale.

The two novels published in the 1980's marked a departure. *The Mad Trapper* features a spine-tingling chase between the Royal Canadian Mounted Police and a wordless, solitary fugitive across the deadly Richardson Mountains. It is a first-rate adventure story but does not have the depth of his earlier works. *My Lovely Enemy* in 1983, on the other hand, suffered from excessive symbolism as it probes the ironic contraries between flesh and spirit, between dogma and truth.

In 1994 Wiebe enlarged his growing international reputation when he received his second Governor General's Award for *A Discovery of Strangers*. It is the epic story of John Franklin's first expedition to the Arctic in 1820, a story of bravery and treachery, of love and death. The ignorance and arrogance of the English explorers stand in ironic contrast to the patience and wisdom of the Indians on whom their survival depends. *Sweeter than All the World* is an even more epic tale, beginning with the persecution of the original Mennonites in the seventeenth century Netherlands and tracing the fortunes of their descendants down to World War II. Wiebe chose historical figures as the central characters of his novel, up to the final narrator, Adam Wiebe, born in 1935 Saskatchewan.

Wiebe's fiction often employs a variety of narrative techniques, multiple voices, and radical shifts in point of view and time. He shares with such fellow Canadian writers as Alice Munro and Robertson Davies a keen eye for the distinctiveness of Canadian life and landscape and remains one of North America's most eloquent and gifted fiction writers, focusing his attention especially on the life and meaning of the disfranchised indigenous peoples of North America.

Bruce L. Edwards
Henry J. Baron

Bibliography

Beck, Ervin. "Postcolonial Complexity in the Writings of Rudy Wiebe." *Modern Fiction Studies* 47 (Winter, 2001). Critiques Wiebe's religious agenda and his depiction of indigenous peoples.

Bilan, R. P. "Wiebe and Religious Struggle." *Canadian Literature* 77 (Summer, 1978). Particularly insightful in its analysis of Wiebe's religious worldview and the way it informs his fiction.

Keith, W. J. *Epic Fiction: The Art of Rudy Wiebe*. Edmonton: University of Alberta Press, 1981. Somewhat dated but good book-length critical work.

Manbridge, Francis. "Wiebe's Sense of Community." *Canadian Literature* 77 (Summer, 1978). Deals with the broader thematic issues in Wiebe's fiction.

Solecki, Sam. "Giant Fictions and Large Meanings: The Novels of Rudy Wiebe." *Canadian Forum* 60 (March, 1981). Deals with the broader thematic issues in Wiebe's fiction.

Toorn, Penny van. "Dialogizing the Scriptures: A Bakhtinian Reading of the Novels of Rudy Wiebe." *Literature & Theology* 9 (December, 1995). Particularly insightful in its analysis of Wiebe's religious worldview and the way it informs his fiction.

_______. *Rudy Wiebe and the Historicity of the Word*. Edmonton: University of Alberta Press, 1995. A critical study.

Weisman, Adam Paul. "Reading Multiculturalism in the United States and Canada: The Anthological Versus the Cognitive." *University of Toronto Quarterly* 69 (Summer, 2000). Compares Wiebe's *The Temptations of Big Bear* with Mark Twain's *Adventures of Huckleberry Finn* (1884) in an analysis of the different meanings of "multiculturalism" in the United States and Canada.

Whaley, Susan. *Rudy Wiebe and His Works*. 1983. Reprint. Toronto: University of Toronto Press, 1987. Somewhat dated but good book-length critical work.

Elie Wiesel

Romanian-born American novelist, memoirist, and biographer

Born: Sighet, Transylvania, Romania; September 30, 1928
Identity: Jewish

LONG FICTION: *L'Aube*, 1960 (novella; *Dawn*, 1961); *Le Jour*, 1961 (novella; *The Accident*, 1962); *La Ville de la chance*, 1962 (*The Town Beyond the Wall*, 1964); *Les Portes de la forêt*, 1964 (*The Gates of the Forest*, 1966); *Le Mendiant de Jérusalem*, 1968 (*A Beggar in Jerusalem*, 1970); *Le Serment de Kolvillàg*, 1973 (*The Oath*, 1973); *Le Testament d'un poète juif assassiné*, 1980 (*The Testament*, 1981); *Le Cinquième Fils*, 1983 (*The Fifth Son*, 1985); *Le Crépuscule, au loin*, 1987 (*Twilight*, 1988); *L'Oublié*, 1989 (*The Forgotten*, 1992); *Les Juges*, 1999 (*The Judges*, 2002).

SHORT FICTION: *Le Chant des Morts*, 1966 (essays and short stories; *Legends of Our Time*, 1968); *Entre deux soleils*, 1970 (essays and short stories; *One Generation After*, 1970); *Un Juif aujourd'hui*, 1977 (essays and short stories; *A Jew Today*, 1978).

DRAMA: *Zalmen: Ou, La Folie de Dieu*, pb. 1968 (*Zalmen: Or, The Madness of God*, 1974); *Le Procès de Shamgorod tel qu'il se déroula le 25 février 1649*, pb. 1979 (*The Trial of God: As It Was Held on February 25, 1649, in Shamgorod*, 1979).

NONFICTION: *Un di Velt hot geshvign*, 1956 (in Yiddish), 1958 (in French as *La Nuit*; *Night*, 1960); *Les Juifs du silence*, 1966 (travel sketch; *The Jews of Silence*, 1966); *Discours d'Oslo*, 1987; *Le mal et l'exil: Recontre avec Élie Wiesel*, 1988 (*Evil and Exile*, 1990); *From the Kingdom of Memory: Reminiscences*, 1990; *A Journey of Faith*, 1990 (with John Cardinal O'Connor); *Tous les fleuves vont à la mer*, 1994 (memoir; *All Rivers Run to the Sea*, 1995); *Et la mer n'est pas remplie*, 1996 (*And the Sea Is Never Full: Memoirs*, 1999); *Le Mal et l'exil: Dix ans après*, 1999; *Conversations with Elie Wiesel*, 2001 (Thomas J. Vinciguerra, editor); *After the Darkness: Reflections on the Holocaust*, 2002; *Elie Wiesel: Conversations*, 2002 (Robert Franciosi, editor).

MISCELLANEOUS: *Célébration hassidique*, 1972-1981 (2 volumes; biographical sketches and stories; volume 1 *Souls on Fire*, 1972; volume 2 *Somewhere a Master: Further Hasidic Portraits and Legends*, 1982); *Ani Maamin: Un Chant perdu et retrouvé*, 1973 (cantata; *Ani*

Maamin: A Song Lost and Found Again, 1973); *Célébration biblique*, 1975 (biographical sketches and stories; *Messengers of God: Biblical Portraits and Legends*, 1976); *Four Hasidic Masters and Their Struggle Against Melancholy*, 1978 (biographical sketches and stories); *Images from the Bible*, 1980 (biographical sketches and stories); *Five Biblical Portraits*, 1981 (biographical sketches and stories); *Paroles d'étranger*, 1982 (biographical sketches and stories); *Somewhere a Master*, 1982 (biographical sketches and stories); *The Six Days of Destruction: Meditations Towards Hope*, 1988 (with Albert H. Friedlander); *Silences et mémoire d'hommes: Essais, histoires, dialogues*, 1989; *Célébration talmudique: Portraits et légendes*, 1991; *Sages and Dreamers: Biblical, Talmudic, and Hasidic Portraits and Legends*, 1991; *Célébration prophétique: Portraits et légendes*, 1998; *Celebrating Elie Wiesel: Stories, Essays, Reflections*, 1998 (Alan Rosen, editor).

CHILDREN'S/YOUNG ADULT LITERATURE: *King Solomon and His Magic Ring*, 1999.

Eliezer (Elie) Wiesel (vee-ZEHL) received his early education completely within Jewish tradition; he attended a religious primary school (*heder*) and then went to a local *yeshiva* for Torah and talmudic studies. In 1944, at the age of fifteen, he was interned in several German concentration camps, where his parents and his younger sister all perished. Upon his release from Buchenwald in April, 1945, he went to France as a displaced person. Within three years, after working as a choir director and Bible teacher, he was able to begin university studies at the Sorbonne, where he majored in philosophy, literature, and psychology.

Wiesel first worked in journalism. As a writer for French newspapers covering Israel's 1948 war for independence and related Middle Eastern events, he traveled extensively. These travels eventually brought him to the United States in 1956. In the same year Wiesel published his first literary work, a massive autobiographical account of his experience of the Holocaust, *Un di Velt hot geshvign* (and the world remained silent). From this work, written in Yiddish and published in Argentina, Wiesel quarried the book that made him famous: *Night*, a brief but unforgettable Holocaust memoir, written in French and soon widely translated.

Because of visa complications Wiesel was unable to return to France. After applying for immigrant status in the United States, he served as United Nations correspondent for a New York Yiddish newspaper. At the same time he was working on his first novel, which appeared first in French, then in English translation. Over the next few years he published a novel almost every year. He became an American citizen in 1963, and by 1964 he had gained sufficient recognition as an author to abandon his salaried work as a journalist. For the next few years, until his first academic appointment, he was able to earn a living through his writing and lecturing. An important experience that affected both his work as a novelist and as a lecturer occurred in 1965 when he visited the Soviet Union. There he observed conditions of Jewish life under the Soviet regime, a subject that became the focus of a series of articles published in 1966 under the title *The Jews of Silence*. This work was followed by another novel, *A Beggar in Jerusalem*, based on Wiesel's impressions of Israel's experience of the 1967 Arab-Israeli Six-Day War. The book, originally published in French, earned the author the Prix Médicis.

In 1969 Wiesel married Marion Erster Rose, a concentration-camp survivor, who soon contributed directly to her husband's literary pursuits by translating his works into English. By this date Wiesel had completed his first drama, *Zalmen*, which had to wait six years before being performed for the first time in Washington, D.C. In 1970 another autobiographical work reflecting on the experience of the Holocaust, *One Generation After*, gained international recognition and prepared the way for Wiesel's first academic appointment, in 1972, to a distinguished professorship of Jewish studies at the City College of New York. From this point, and without interrupting his active career as a writer, Wiesel was involved in a number of academic and humanitarian public-service posts. In 1976 he was appointed to a special chair in the humanities at Boston University, a position he maintained while lecturing (in 1982-1983) at Yale University. Wiesel was named by President Jimmy Carter to chair the President's Special Commission on the Holocaust in 1979, but he resigned from this post to protest President Ronald Reagan's 1986 visit to the German military cemetery in Bitburg.

Increasingly, recognition was extended to Wiesel as a writer driven by an intense dedication to the cause of world peace. This recognition came first in the form of the Belgian International Peace Prize, which was awarded to Wiesel in 1983. In quick succession after this, Wiesel received special awards from French president François Mitterrand and American president Reagan (1984). The crowning recognition was the award in 1986 of the Nobel Peace Prize, which he dedicated to all the remaining survivors of the Holocaust.

Afterward, Wiesel continued to speak out in behalf of the downtrodden and disinherited, and he continued to produce both fiction and nonfiction. In *The Forgotten* he reprised the important themes of memory, remembrance, and mental and psychological forgetting, all of which are themes of earlier works as well. In 1994 he published *All Rivers Run to the Sea*, the first volume of his memoirs.

Byron D. Cannon
Pierre L. Horn

Bibliography

Berenbaum, Michael. *Elie Wiesel: God, the Holocaust, and the Children of Israel*. West Orange, N.J.: Behrman House, 1994. This reprint of *The Vision of the Void*, Berenbaum's thoughtful 1979 study of Elie Wiesel, emphasizes Wiesel's insights about Jewish tradition.

Bloom, Harold, ed. *Elie Wiesel's "Night."* New York: Chelsea House, 2001. A collection of critical essays representing the spectrum of response to Wiesel's memoir.

Cargas, Harry James. *Conversations with Elie Wiesel*. South Bend, Ind.: Justice Books, 1992. An updated and expanded edition of Cargas's 1976 interviews with Wiesel, this important book features Wiesel speaking not only about the Holocaust but also about his audience, craft, and mission as a witness and writer.

Estess, Ted L. *Elie Wiesel*. New York: Frederick Ungar, 1980. Despite its brevity, this general introduction is well argued and often insightful.

Horowitz, Sara. *Voicing the Void: Muteness and Memory in Holocaust Fiction*. Albany: State University of New York Press, 1997. Contains a helpful discussion of Wiesel's emphasis on the importance of memory.

Kolbert, Jack. *The Worlds of Elie Wiesel: An Overview of His Career and His Major Themes*. Snelinsgrove, Pa.: Susquehanna University Press, 2001. A useful starting point for Wiesel's work. Combines biography with literary and philosophical analysis.

Mass, Wendy, ed. *Readings on "Night."* New York: Greenhaven Press, 2000. Includes biographical chapters, a summary of the plot and characters of Wiesel's book, and discussion of major themes, the author's art, relationships in the novel, literary interpretation, and the legacy of the book.

Patterson, David. *The Shriek of Silence: A Phenomenology of the Holocaust Novel*. Lexington: University Press of Kentucky, 1992. Patterson's book explores the distinctive ways in which Wiesel wrestles with the theme of silence as a feature of the Holocaust and its aftermath.

Rittner, Carol, ed. *Elie Wiesel: Between Memory and Hope*. New York: New York University Press, 1990. A balanced collection of provocative essays, written by scholars from different disciplines.

Rosen, Alan, ed. *Celebrating Elie Wiesel: Stories, Essays, Reflections*. Notre Dame, Ind.: University of Notre Dame Press, 1998. Distinguished scholars reflect on the ethical and religious dimensions of Wiesel's essays and novels.

Rosenfeld, Alvin H., and Irving Greenberg, eds. *Confronting the Holocaust: The Impact of Elie Wiesel*. Bloomington: Indiana University Press, 1978. Including "Why I Write," a significant essay by Wiesel, this volume contains a balanced collection of worthwhile essays written by scholars from varied disciplines.

Sibelman, Simon P. *Silence in the Novels of Elie Wiesel*. New York: St. Martin's Press, 1995. This study of a dominant theme in Wiesel is thorough, intelligent, and stimulating.

Stern, Ellen Norman. *Elie Wiesel: Witness for Life*. New York: Ktav, 1982. A fine and useful biography that deals more with the man than with his writings.

Marianne Wiggins

American novelist and short-story writer

Born: Lancaster, Pennsylvania; November 8, 1947

LONG FICTION: *Babe*, 1975; *Went South*, 1980; *Separate Checks*, 1984; *John Dollar*, 1989; *Eveless Eden*, 1995; *Almost Heaven*, 1998; *Evidence of Things Unseen*, 2003.

SHORT FICTION: *Herself in Love, and Other Stories*, 1987; *Learning Urdu*, 1990; *Bet They'll Miss Us When We're Gone*, 1991.

Of Scottish and Greek ancestry, Marianne Wiggins was born to John Wiggins and Mary Klonis. Her father was a grocer and preacher. She married Brian Porzak, a film distributor, on June 6, 1965, but divorced him in 1970. They had a daughter, Lara Porzak. Wiggins's second marriage, to the Indian-born British writer Salman Rushdie on January 23, 1988, led to a few years of fame and controversy, not because of the marriage itself but for the religious edict issued by Iran's Ayatollah Khomeini condemning Rushdie to death. Rushdie and Wiggins's marriage ended in 1992.

Wiggins worked as a stockbroker in the early 1970's. Before being known for marrying Rushdie, she had begun writing. Her first book, *Babe*, concerns a single mother raising a child and the challenges of single motherhood. This novel reflected Wiggins's personal experience after her divorce, having to work and raise her daughter, Lara. Her debut was not widely reviewed.

After the novel's publication, she and Lara lived in Martha's Vineyard, where Wiggins wrote her next two novels, *Went South* and *Separate Checks*, and a collection of short stories titled *Herself in Love*. All of these deal with modern-day single women, mothers in love, and divorce. Again, some of the core issues of these works are reminiscent of Wiggins's life circumstances. While the second novel did not receive much notice, the third book, *Separate Checks*, gained her considerable attention and critical acclaim.

Before experiencing the controversy surrounding Rushdie, Wiggins lived through her own cultural turmoil during her childhood in the United States. Growing up in Lancaster, Pennsylvania, she had a conservative and religious father who preached in a Protestant church (founded by her grandfather) every Sunday. At age nine, she was baptized into the Greek Orthodox religion of her mother. Her father later committed suicide. Wiggins harbored an aversion to all organized religion throughout her adulthood; these cultural concerns prevail in some of her works, in which organized religion is sometimes depicted as evil.

Wiggins moved to England and, about five years later, married Rushdie. After they had been married a year, the publication of Rushdie's controversial book *The Satanic Verses* (1989) caused the Ayatollah Khomeini of Iran to issue a fatwa to his Shiite followers. This decree offered a reward of more than one million dollars for Rushdie's death. The death sentence was imposed because Rushdie's book was deemed offensive, blasphemous, and irreverent to Islam and to the world's Muslim community. Wiggins and Rushdie were thereafter forced to live under the protection of the British government.

Wiggins was hardly mentioned in public statements at the many rallies in support of her husband. While the international attention made Rushdie and his book even more famous, Wiggins's identity was somewhat subordinated during her husband's debacle. As an author with feminist concerns, she decided that she had to continue her writing career, even without Rushdie by her side. After five months of residing underground and changing locations at a moment's notice, Wiggins left hiding and went to live apart from her husband. A book tour to promote the publication of her novel *John Dollar* took her to the United States.

John Dollar is set against the backdrop of Burma (now Myanmar) in the early twentieth century, at the time of British colonial rule. Lost love, the failure of American imperialism, cannibalism, and savagery figure in this novel, and the protagonist, John Dollar, is reminiscent of those in works by Daniel Defoe and William Golding. Wiggins promoted *John Dollar*, which was more widely reviewed than her previous books, and also worked on a number of new books and short-story collections. Although she received critical acclaim for the novel and her literary career was beginning to regain its momentum, life and marriage were strained for Wiggins. One short story, "Croeso I Gymru" in the collection *Bet They'll Miss Us When We're Gone*, was based on her experience living in hiding with Rushdie. The short story deals with restraint, constricted actions, secrecy, fear of discovery, and the rarity of privacy. Though fictional, the story reveals a great part of what life was like while living in hiding with her husband. After she came out of hiding, Wiggins became much more interested and concerned with world and political events and their ramifications.

Despite Khomeini's death in June, 1989, Rushdie's death sentence remained in place until the Iranian government ended the fatwa in 1998. Wiggins and Rushdie's marriage, strained by the fatwa, had ended in 1992. Wiggins continued to produce works. Her sixth novel, *Almost Heaven*, deals with breakneck love, loss, the millennial United States, and two people drawn to each other in an erotic frenzy. The narrator of the novel is named Holden and is often compared to the protagonist of the same name in J. D. Salinger's *The Catcher in the Rye* (1951). Though the book met mixed reviews, it was a fair success.

In many of her works, Wiggins is concerned with snapshots of human relationships. With her skill as a storyteller and creative energy to make impossible events and story lines into believable plots, Wiggins has had her share of success as a writer. There is increasing literary attention paid to her body of works, which is becoming important to American literature.

H. N. Nguyen

Bibliography

Boon, Jo-Ellen Lipman, and Alvin K. Benson. "Marianne Wiggins." In *Critical Survey of Short Fiction*, edited by Charles E. May. 2d rev. ed. Pasadena, Calif.: Salem Press, 2001. A thorough overview of Wiggins's life and career, emphasizing her short stories.

Pfalzgraf, Taryn Benchow, ed. *American Women Writers: A Critical Reference from Colonial Times to the Present*. Vol. 4. Boston: St. James Press, 2000. Overview article discussing the themes in Wiggins's writing.

Tyler, Anne. Review of *John Dollar*, by Marianne Wiggins. *The New Republic* 200, no. 13 (March 27, 1989): 35-36. A highly favorable review by a noted novelist.

Richard Wilbur

American poet

Born: New York, New York; March 1, 1921

POETRY: *The Beautiful Changes, and Other Poems*, 1947; *Ceremony, and Other Poems*, 1950; *Things of This World*, 1956; *Poems, 1943-1956*, 1957; *Advice to a Prophet, and Other Poems*, 1961; *Loudmouse*, 1963 (juvenile); *The Poems of Richard Wilbur*, 1963; *Walking to Sleep: New Poems and Translations*, 1969; *Digging for China*, 1970; *Opposites*, 1973 (juvenile); *The Mind-Reader: New Poems*, 1976; *Seven Poems*, 1981; *New and Collected Poems*, 1988; *More Opposites*, 1991 (juvenile); *Runaway Opposites*, 1995 (juvenile); *The Disappearing Alphabet*, 1998 (juvenile); *Mayflies: New Poems*, 2000.

DRAMA: *Candide: A Comic Operetta*, pr. 1956 (lyrics; book by Lillian Hellman, music by Leonard Bernstein).

TRANSLATIONS: *The Misanthrope*, 1955 (of Molière); *Tartuffe*, 1963 (of Molière); *The School for Wives*, 1971 (of Molière); *The Learned Ladies*, 1978 (of Molière); *Andromache*, 1982 (of Jean Racine); *Four Comedies*, 1982 (of Molière); *Phaedra*, 1986 (of Racine); *The School for Husbands*, 1991 (of Molière); *The Imaginary Cuckold: Or, Sgarnarelle*, 1993 (of Molière); *Amphitryon*, 1995 (of Molière); *The Bungler*, 2000 (of Molière); *Don Juan*, 2001 (of Molière); *The Suitors*, 2001 (of Racine).

NONFICTION: *Responses, Prose Pieces: 1953-1976*, 1976, expanded 2000; *On My Own Work*, 1983; *Conversations with Richard Wilbur*, 1990 (William Butts, editor); *The Catbird's Song: Prose Pieces, 1963-1995*, 1997.

EDITED TEXTS: *A Bestiary*, 1955; *Modern America and Modern British Poetry*, 1955 (with Louis Untermeyer and Karl Shapiro); *Poe: Complete Poems*, 1959; *Shakespeare: Poems*, 1966 (with Alfred Harbage); *The Narrative Poems and Poems of Doubtful Authenticity*, 1974.

Richard Purdy Wilbur, the son of Lawrence Lazear Wilbur, an artist, and Helen Ruth Purdy Wilbur, was born in New York City but spent many early years in a rural area near North Caldwell, New Jersey. He has asserted that this country experience accounts for his earlier nature poetry. He wrote his first poem, "That's When the Nightingales Wake," at the age of eight. After graduating from Montclair High School, he attended Amherst College, where he edited the college newspaper and considered a career in journalism. He graduated in 1942 and that same year married Charlotte Ward, with whom he had four children, Ellen, Christopher, Nathan, and Aaron.

He wrote poetry from a young age, but it was the experience of the war that turned him toward writing as a serious endeavor. From 1943 to 1945 he served as an enlisted man in Europe at some of the major fronts. After the war he returned to school, and in 1947 he received an M.A. in English at Harvard University, where he remained as a junior fellow until 1950. In 1947 and 1950 his first two books of poems, *The Beautiful Changes* and *Ceremony*, appeared. In 1950, committed to an academic career, he became an assistant professor of English at Harvard, an unusual post for one without a doctorate. He took time out in 1952 to visit Mexico on a grant from the Guggenheim Foundation. During this time he won the Harriet Monroe and the Oscar Blumenthal prizes from *Poetry* magazine, and in 1954 he won the three-thousand-dollar Prix de Rome from the American Academy of Arts and Sciences. His scholarly work was centered on Edgar Allan Poe, whose complete poems he edited.

In 1955 Wilbur was made an associate professor of English at Wellesley College, where he taught for two years. In that same year his translation of Molière's *The Misanthrope* was published and produced in Cambridge, Massachusetts, at the Poet's Theatre; the following year it was staged at the Theatre East Off-Broadway. *A Bestiary* (an anthology) was published at this time; later came *The Pelican from a Bestiary of 1120*, a privately printed 1963 translation of a poem by Philippe de Thuan.

In 1957 he was awarded a Pulitzer Prize and a National Book Award for *Things of This World*. The same year he was appointed professor of English at Wesleyan University in Middletown, Connecticut. He won the Boston Festival Award in 1959, and in 1960 received a Ford Fellowship and was awarded an honorary L.H.D. degree by Sarah Lawrence College. He became vice president of the National Institute of Arts and Letters in 1959. In September, 1961, the year of his fourth book of poems, *Advice to a Prophet*, he traveled to Russia as an American literary specialist for the State Department. In 1977 he left Wellesley to become writer-in-residence at Smith College, a position he held until 1986.

During this time a paperback release, *The Poems of Richard Wilbur*, came out, as did *Walking to Sleep*, *The Mind-Reader: New Poems*, and *New Poems*. In 1989 a collection of poems from all his books was published under the title *New and Collected Poems*, which won him a second Pulitzer Prize in poetry as well as many other awards and nominations. From 1987 to 1988 he was the Poet Laureate of the United States.

Most of Wilbur's publications in the 1990's, following his laureateship, were of juvenile poetry. However, in 2000 he published *Mayflies*, a collection of his adult work composed throughout the previous decade. In addition to new poems that show his continuing formalist style, the book includes translations of poems by Dante and Molière.

Wilbur also continued producing fine translations of classical French drama. He translated Molière's *Tartuffe* in 1963, for which he was the co-recipient of the Bollingen Prize, and *The School for Wives* in 1971, *The Learned Ladies* in 1978, and *School for Husbands* in 1992. He also translated two plays by Racine and wrote or rewrote most of the lyrics for *Candide* by Leonard Bernstein.

Robert W. Peckham

Bibliography

Bixler, Frances. *Richard Wilbur: A Reference Guide*. Boston: G. K. Hall, 1991. A useful bibliographical guide to Wilbur's work and its criticism.

Cummins, Paul F. *Richard Wilbur: A Critical Essay*. Grand Rapids, Mich.: Wm. B. Eerdmans, 1971. Defends Wilbur's poetry against the charge of passionless elegance; argues that the poet uses rhyme and meter skillfully to enhance tone and meaning. A largely thematic study. Includes a primary and a secondary bibliography (both of which, naturally, are dated), but no index.

Edgecombe, Rodney Stenning. *A Reader's Guide to the Poetry of Richard Wilbur*. Tuscaloosa: University of Alabama Press, 1995. Edgecombe provides some worthwhile insights into Wilbur's poems up to those included in *New and Collected Poems* (1988). He provides a brief but penetrating introduction, as well as an extensive bibliography and a serviceable index.

Hill, Donald L. *Richard Wilbur*. New York: Twayne, 1967. The biographical chronology extends only through 1964. Devotes a chapter each to *The Beautiful Changes*, *Ceremony*, *Things of This World*, and *Advice to a Prophet*, with both thematic and technical discussions. A final chapter looks at Wilbur's prose writings and evaluates his place among twentieth century poets. Notes, a bibliography, and an index are included.

Hougen, John B. *Ecstasy Within Discipline: The Poetry of Richard Wilbur*. Atlanta: Scholar's Press, 1995. The author's chief concerns are theological. Hougen provides some useful insights into the formal aspects of Wilbur's writing.

Michelson, Bruce. *Wilbur's Poetry: Music in a Scattering Time*. Amherst: University of Massachusetts Press, 1991. In this first comprehensive study of Wilbur's poetry since that late 1960's, Michelson attempts to counter the widespread opinion that Wilbur is a bland poet. Michelson's close readings of the major poems contradict and dispel much that has been written critically about the poet.

Salinger, Wendy, ed. *Richard Wilbur's Creation*. Ann Arbor: University of Michigan Press, 1983. A rich collection featuring, in part 1, many previously published reviews of Wilbur's chief works through 1976; contributors include such luminaries as Louise Bogan, Randall Jarrell, Donald Hall, and John Ciardi. The second half presents more comprehensive critical essays on various aspects of the poet's themes and craft. Valuable for its scope and for the quality of its writing.

Oscar Wilde

Irish playwright, novelist, and poet

Born: Dublin, Ireland; October 16, 1854
Died: Paris, France; November 30, 1900
Identity: Gay or bisexual

DRAMA: *Vera: Or, The Nihilists*, pb. 1880; *The Duchess of Padua*, pb. 1883; *Lady Windermere's Fan*, pr. 1892; *Salomé*, pb. 1893 (in French), pb. 1894 (in English); *A Woman of No Importance*, pr. 1893; *An Ideal Husband*, pr. 1895; *The Importance of Being Earnest: A Trivial Comedy for Serious People*, pr. 1895; *A Florentine Tragedy*, pb. 1906 (one act; completed by T. Sturge More); *La Sainte Courtisane*, pb. 1908.

LONG FICTION: *The Picture of Dorian Gray*, 1890 (serial), 1891 (expanded).

SHORT FICTION: "The Canterville Ghost," 1887; *The Happy Prince, and Other Tales*, 1888; *A House of Pomegranates*, 1891; *Lord Arthur Savile's Crime, and Other Stories*, 1891.

POETRY: *Ravenna*, 1878; *Poems*, 1881; *Poems in Prose*, 1894; *The Sphinx*, 1894; *The Ballad of Reading Gaol*, 1898.

NONFICTION: *Intentions*, 1891; *De Profundis*, 1905; *The Letters of Oscar Wilde*, 1962 (Rupert Hart-Davis, editor); *The Complete Letters of Oscar Wilde*, 2000 (Merlin Holland and Hart-Davis, editors).

MISCELLANEOUS: *Works*, 1908; *Complete Works of Oscar Wilde*, 1948 (Vyvyan Holland, editor); *Plays, Prose Writings, and Poems*, 1960.

Oscar Fingal O'Flahertie Wills Wilde was born the second son of Sir William Robert Wills Wilde, surgeon oculist in ordinary to the Queen, and Jane Francesca Elgee Wilde, known as the Irish revolutionary author "Speranza." Early noted for his casual brilliance, Wilde won prizes at the Portora Royal School in Enniskillen, and later in Trinity College, Dublin, where the Reverend John Mahaffy encouraged Wilde's passion for Hellenic culture. Having studied under two famous masters, John Ruskin and Walter Pater, Wilde achieved recognition at Magdalen College, Oxford, for taking double firsts in classics examinations and for winning the Newdigate Prize for the poem "Ravenna" in 1878.

Famous for his peacock feathers, sunflowers, dados, blue china, long hair, velveteen breeches, and later his green carnations, Wilde first distinguished himself with the public as the leader of London's art-for-art's-sake school of aesthetics. He and his cohorts were lampooned in cartoons, novels, and comic opera, but he remained a sought-after conversationalist. Everyone eagerly followed his outrageous affectations, witty sayings, and paradoxes; and no one ever heard him utter an oath or an off-color remark.

When Gilbert and Sullivan's *Patience* (1881), a spoof of aestheticism, was to tour North America, Richard D'Oyly Carte engaged Wilde for a lecture series to promote American interest in the operetta. Then, following a stint in Paris, where he mingled with the artistic elite and wrote the quasi-Elizabethan tragedy *The Duchess of Padua*, Wilde returned to the United States to see *Vera*, his political romance set in revolutionary Russia, open and close after one week on the boards. He went back to Great Britain to lecture on *Impressions of America* and there rekindled his acquaintance with Constance Mary Lloyd, the daughter of a prominent Irish barrister, whom he married in 1884 and with whom he had two sons, Cyril and Vyvyan. In 1886 Wilde met Robert Ross, the unfailing friend who most aided Wilde after his release from prison and who, after Wilde's death, fought to protect his corpus and resurrect his name. From 1887 to 1889 Wilde edited *The Lady's World* magazine—changing the title to *The Woman's World*—and began the eight-year period that saw his most significant work appear.

The first version of *The Picture of Dorian Gray* appeared in *Lippincott's Monthly Magazine* in 1890 to a flurry of outrage. Expanded and balanced, the second version, Wilde's only novel, fully works through the human implications of the conflict between the aesthetics of Ruskin and Pater (represented by the artist Basil Hallward and the writer Lord Henry Wotton) as they vie for influence over Dorian.

The year 1891 witnessed the production in New York of *The Duchess of Padua* (under the title *Guido Ferranti*), the publication in England of several volumes of new and collected works, the writing of *Lady Windermere's Fan*, and the composition in France (in French) of *Salomé*, the Symbolist jewel that Richard Strauss later transformed into an opera. In that year also occurred the fateful encounter with Lord Alfred Douglas ("Bosie") that ensnared Wilde in the cycle of dependency and abuse he so heartrendingly detailed to Bosie in his letter from prison, a severely edited version of which was first published in 1905 as *De Profundis*. Four years later this relationship led the Marquess of Queensbury (Douglas's father) to address Wilde publicly as a "sodomite," bringing about, at Douglas's instigation, Wilde's suit against Queensbury for libel and the ensuing countersuit that earned Wilde two years' hard labor in Wandsworth and Reading prisons.

Happily for Wilde and for generations of theatrical audiences, those intervening four years provided Wilde scope to create his four social comedies, the works (outside of *The Picture of Dorian Gray* and Wilde's eminently quotable epigrams) for which he remains most widely remembered. Each of these plays achieved astounding success on the London stage, furnishing Wilde both with a well-deserved respite from debt and with the opportunity playfully to deconstruct Victorian ideology, perhaps the true reason behind his incarceration.

After his release from prison, Wilde took the name Sebastian Melmoth from the 1820 gothic novel *Melmoth the Wanderer*, written by his maternal great-granduncle, the Reverend Charles Maturin. Though personally always light-hearted, Wilde lived out his last sad years on the Continent, grievously estranged from his wife and children, at the insistence of the Lloyds, and always short of funds, though Constance increased his allowance after he published *The Ballad of Reading Gaol*, called by William Butler Yeats the strongest poem of the century. Following an operation for encephalitis arising from an ear injury sustained in prison, Wilde died at the Hôtel d'Alsace after embracing the Catholicism to which he had long aspired. Originally buried in Bagneux Cemetery, his remains were moved in 1909 to Père Lachaise, where they lie beneath a tomb sculpted by Sir Jacob Epstein.

Wilde's talents were, in his own time, acknowledged by George Bernard Shaw, Frank Harris, James McNeill Whistler, and, of course, Wilde himself. One has only to read his gemlike fairy tales or his letter to the *Daily Chronicle* (1897), urging the state to reconsider its policy of incarcerating young children under the same hideous conditions as hardened criminals, to recognize the depth of love for humanity that hides behind what often passes in both Wilde's work and behavior for mere sparkling frivolity. Perhaps the true brilliance of his last and best-loved play, *The Importance of Being Earnest*, lies in its visionary conception of a genial and benevolent society unencumbered by hypocritical moral earnestness or snobbish self-importance.

David B. Arnett

Bibliography

Beckson, Karl E. *The Oscar Wilde Encyclopedia*. New York: AMS Press, 1998. At nearly five hundred pages, a compendium of useful information on Wilde and his times.

Belford, Barbara. *Oscar Wilde: A Certain Genius*. New York: Random House, 2000. An examination of Wilde's life with a somewhat revisionist view of Wilde's post-prison years.

Calloway, Stephen, and David Colvin. *Oscar Wilde: An Exquisite Life*. New York: Welcome Rain, 1997. A brief, heavily illustrated presentation of Wilde's life.

Cohen, Philip K. *The Moral Vision of Oscar Wilde*. Rutherford, N.J.: Fairleigh Dickinson University Press, 1978. Examines Wilde's writings as unified by his moral development through dialectical contraries of Old and New Testament codes. Contains illustrations, a select bibliography, and an index.

Ellmann, Richard. *Oscar Wilde*. New York: Alfred A. Knopf, 1988. A biography of Wilde, drawing much insight from Wilde's published works. The book is extensively documented and footnoted and makes use of many of Wilde's writings and recorded conversations. Includes bibliography and appendices.

Eriksen, Donald H. *Oscar Wilde*. Boston: Twayne, 1977. This small volume is a useful corrective to studies of Wilde that see him and his work as anomalies of literature and history. After a brief chapter on Wilde's life and times, Eriksen assesses his poetry, fiction, essays, and drama. A chronology, notes and references, an annotated bibliography, and an index supplement the text.

Gagnier, Regenia A. *Idylls of the Marketplace: Oscar Wilde and the Victorian Public*. Stanford, Calif.: Stanford University Press, 1986. This study attempts to reach an understanding of Wilde by focusing less on his life and work and more on the relation of his work to his audiences. Leaning heavily on contemporary critical theory, it connects Wilde, Friedrich Engels, and Fyodor Dostoevski in ways that some may find more confusing than illuminating, but Gagnier's readings of the works are generally insightful and persuasive. Includes bibliography and index.

Harris, Frank. *Oscar Wilde*. Reprint. New York: Carrol and Graf, 1997. A biography written by one of Wilde's dedicated friends. Although hardly an objective work, Harris's book, written in the first person, provides details and insights about Wilde's life that many books do not.

Kohl, Norbert. *Oscar Wilde: The Works of a Conformist Rebel*. Translated by David Henry Wilson. Cambridge, England: Cambridge University Press, 1989. Interprets Wilde's works mainly through textual analysis, although it includes discussions of the society in which Wilde lived and to which he responded. Kohl argues that Wilde was not the imitator he is often accused of being but a creative adapter of the literary traditions he inherited. Supplemented by detailed notes, a lengthy bibliography, and an index.

McCormack, Jerusha Hull. *The Man Who Was Dorian Gray*. New York: St. Martin's Press, 2000. John Gray, the supposed model for Wilde's most famous character, is profiled in this examination of the life of a decadent poet turned priest. Although not focused on the poetry, this work reveals much about early twentieth century literary society and the emerging gay culture.

Pearce, Joseph. *The Unmasking of Oscar Wilde*. London: HarperCollins, 2000. Pearce avoids lingering on the actions that brought Wilde notoriety and instead explores Wilde's emotional and spiritual search. Along with a discussion of *The Ballad of Reading Gaol* and the posthumously published *De Profundis*, Pearce also traces Wilde's fascination with Catholicism.

Raby, Peter. *Oscar Wilde*. Cambridge, England: Cambridge University Press, 1988. Includes biographical information because, Raby argues, it is most useful to see Wilde as indivisible from his works. The 1881 collection of poems, he says, makes it clear that Wilde's artistic purpose was a life's work. Includes chronology, notes, a bibliography, and an index.

Small, Ian. *Oscar Wilde: A Recent Research—A Supplement to "Oscar Wilde Revalued."* Greensboro, N.C.: ELT Press, 2000. A follow-up to Small's earlier work on Wilde that surveys previously unknown biographical and critical materials. Includes bibliography.

Varty, Anne. *A Preface to Oscar Wilde: Preface Books*. New York: Longman, 1998. An introduction to the life and works, particularly the period from 1890 to 1895. Some discussion of earlier work provides a view of some of the motivating forces behind his output. Also offers a chapter on his circle. Includes index.

Wilde, Oscar. *The Complete Letters of Oscar Wilde*. Edited by Merlin Holland and Rupert Hart-Davis. New York: Henry Holt, 2000. A collection of correspondence including previously unpublished letters that unveil the full extent of Wilde's genius in an intimate exploration of his life and thoughts. Includes bibliographical references and indexes.

Laura Ingalls Wilder

American novelist

Born: Pepin, Wisconsin; February 7, 1867
Died: Mansfield, Missouri; February 10, 1957

CHILDREN'S/YOUNG ADULT LITERATURE: *Little House in the Big Woods*, 1932; *Farmer Boy*, 1933; *Little House on the Prairie*, 1935; *On the Banks of Plum Creek*, 1937; *By the Shores of Silver Lake*, 1939; *The Long Winter*, 1940; *Little Town on the Prairie*, 1941; *These Happy Golden Years*, 1943; *The First Four Years*, 1971.

NONFICTION: *On the Way Home: The Diary of a Trip from South Dakota to Mansfield, Missouri, in 1894*, 1962; *West from Home: Letters of Laura Ingalls Wilder, San Francisco, 1915*, 1974; *A Little House Sampler*, 1988 (with Rose Wilder Lane); *Little House in the Ozarks: The Rediscovered Writings*, 1991; *Laura Ingalls Wilder: A Family Collection*, 1993.

Best known for her award-winning and much-beloved "Little House" series, Laura Ingalls Wilder did not start writing these autobiographical stories based on her childhood until she was in her sixties. Born Laura Elizabeth Ingalls, Wilder spent the first twelve years of her life on the move with her family via covered wagon as the American frontier expanded westward. Her books are noted for their vivid and detailed descriptions of the spartan pioneer lifestyle as well as their depiction of a close-knit family subsisting on the American frontier of the late nineteenth century.

When Wilder was only a year old, she moved with her parents and older sister Mary from Wisconsin to Missouri. They stayed there a year before moving on to Kansas, in Indian Territory, where Wilder's sister Carrie was born. This area was the site of Wilder's third book, *Little House on the Prairie*. In 1871, the family returned to their former homestead in Wisconsin. Wilder combined her two stays in Wisconsin for her first book in the series, *Little House in the Big Woods*. From the very first book, Laura emerges as a spunky, energetic, bright child, her beloved Pa's "little half-pint," who, over the course of the series, matures into a very capable young woman.

The Ingalls family again sold their homestead and headed west in 1874 to Walnut Grove, Minnesota, the setting of *On the Banks of Plum Creek*. There, in 1875, their fourth child, Charles, was born, only to die the next year. Unfortunately, a grasshopper plague spoiled their crops. In 1876, the family "back-trailed" to Burr Oak, Iowa, where they helped run a hotel. In 1877, Wilder's youngest sister, Grace, was born. Later that year, her family returned to Walnut Grove, where, in 1879, Mary became ill and was rendered blind. Wilder would later credit her descriptive powers as a writer to her duty to Mary to serve as her "eyes."

In 1879, the family made their final move—to the Dakota Territory. *By the Shores of Silver Lake* covers this move to the town of De Smet, South Dakota, of which the Ingallses were a founding family. *The Long Winter* tells of the devastating winter of 1880-1881, when the family, and the rest of the town, nearly starved to death; *Little Town on the Prairie* describes Wilder's adolescence. *These Happy Golden Years* chronicles her first teaching job at age fifteen and her courtship by and marriage to Almanzo Wilder, whose childhood she recounted in *Farmer Boy*. Throughout, although these stories describe numerous battles with diseases such as malaria and scarlet fever, countless crop failures, and near-poverty, they also bring to life Wilder's cherished memories of her happy family life with her kind and hard-working parents, and her close kinship with her sister Mary.

The final book in the series, *The First Four Years*, was published posthumously and is significantly bleaker in tone. It tells of the Wilders' first four years of marriage. In 1886, they had a baby girl, Rose. In 1888, both Laura and Almanzo contracted diphtheria, as a result of which Almanzo became partially paralyzed. The next year, they had a son who died when twelve days old. Then their house burned down. Although this is the point at which Wilder's series ends, the family's adventures continued. After a failed attempt to settle in Florida, the Wilders set out for Mansfield, Missouri, in 1894. This trip is described in Wilder's diary, which was published posthumously. There they purchased Rocky Ridge Farm, where the Wilders lived for the rest of their lives.

Wilder began her writing career in 1911 with articles on farm life for the Missouri *Ruralist*. Nevertheless, it was the Wilders' daughter who was the first to make her mark as a writer, and by 1915 was a journalist with the San Francisco *Bulletin*. Wilder was coached in her writing by Rose, who encouraged her to write for higher-paying magazines. In 1930, when Wilder sat down to write her autobiography, her desire was to record for posterity her childhood growing up on the American frontier. Yet the books are not strictly autobiographical, as Wilder omitted certain events that she believed were not suitable for children and refashioned others. With Rose's help as editor and her connections with publishers, Wilder saw her first book published in 1932, when she was sixty-five years old. She spent the next eleven years completing her multivolume work.

Wilder's Little House books became immediately popular, winning numerous awards. Among them, *On the Banks of Plum Creek*, *By the Shores of Silver Lake*, *The Long Winter*, *Little Town on the Prairie*, and *These Happy Golden Years* were named Newbery Honor Books, and the Laura Ingalls Wilder Award was created in her honor in 1954 to be presented to outstanding authors of children's books. The series found renewed popularity in the 1970's when it was adapted for the successful television series *Little House on the Prairie* (1974-1982).

C. K. Breckenridge

Bibliography

Anderson, William. *Laura Ingalls Wilder: A Biography.* New York: HarperCollins, 1992. A comprehensive biography by a noted Wilder historian.

Miller, Dwight M. *Laura Ingalls Wilder and the American Frontier: Five Perspectives.* Lanham, Md.: University Press of America, 2002. A collection of essays resulting from a symposium on Wilder.

Miller, John E. *Becoming Laura Ingalls Wilder: The Woman Behind the Legend.* Columbia: University of Missouri Press, 1998. A thorough biography that looks at Wilder's life between the years captured in her novels and her apotheosis as a beloved children's writer.

Romines, Ann. *Constructing the Little House: Gender, Culture, and Laura Ingalls Wilder.* Amherst: University of Massachusetts Press, 1997. A feminist analysis of Wilder's works.

Wolf, Virginia L. *Little House on the Prairie: A Reader's Companion.* New York: Twayne, 1996. Examines the Little House books thematically.

Zochert, Donald. *Laura: The Life of Laura Ingalls Wilder.* Chicago: Contemporary Books, 1976. A full-length biography.

Thornton Wilder

American playwright and novelist

Born: Madison, Wisconsin; April 17, 1897
Died: Hamden, Connecticut; December 7, 1975

DRAMA: *The Trumpet Shall Sound*, pb. 1920; *The Angel That Troubled the Waters, and Other Plays*, pb. 1928 (includes 16 plays); *The Happy Journey to Trenton and Camden*, pr., pb. 1931 (one act); *The Long Christmas Dinner*, pr., pb. 1931 (one act; as libretto in German, 1961; translation and music by Paul Hindemith); *The Long Christmas Dinner, and Other Plays in One Act*, pb. 1931 (includes *Queens of France*, *Pullman Car Hiawatha*, *Love and How to Cure It*, *Such Things Only Happen in Books*, and *The Happy Journey to Trenton and Camden*); *Lucrece*, pr. 1932 (adaptation of André Obey's *Le Viol de Lucrèce*); *A Doll's House*, pr. 1937 (adaptation of Henrik Ibsen's play); *The Merchant of Yonkers*, pr. 1938 (adaptation of Johann Nestroy's *Einen Jux will er sich machen*); *Our Town*, pr., pb. 1938; *The Skin of Our Teeth*, pr., pb. 1942; *Our Century*, pr., pb. 1947; *The Matchmaker*, pr. 1954 (revision of *The Merchant of Yonkers*); *A Life in the Sun*, pr. 1955 (commonly known as *The Alcestiad*; act 4 pb. as *The Drunken Sisters*); *Plays for Bleecker Street*, pr. 1962 (3 one-acts: *Someone from Assissi*; *Infancy*, pb. 1961; and *Childhood*, pb. 1960); *The Collected Short Plays of Thornton Wilder*, pb. 1997-1998 (2 volumes).

LONG FICTION: *The Cabala*, 1926; *The Bridge of San Luis Rey*, 1927; *The Woman of Andros*, 1930; *Heaven's My Destination*, 1934; *The Ides of March*, 1948; *The Eighth Day*, 1967; *Theophilus North*, 1973.

SCREENPLAYS: *Our Town*, 1940 (with Frank Craven and Harry Chantlee); *Shadow of a Doubt*, 1943 (with Sally Benson and Alma Revelle).

NONFICTION: *The Intent of the Artist*, 1941; *American Characteristics, and Other Essays*, 1979; *The Journals of Thornton Wilder, 1939-1961*, 1985.

TRANSLATION: *The Victors*, 1948 (of Jean-Paul Sartre's play *Morts sans sépulture*).

The winner of three Pulitzer Prizes, Thornton Niven Wilder was one of twentieth century America's leading playwrights and novelists. Born on April 17, 1897, in Madison, Wisconsin, he was the son of Amos Parker Wilder, editor of the *Wisconsin State Journal*, and Isabella Thornton Niven Wilder. Though his father disapproved of writers, all five Wilder children—Amos, Charlotte, Isabel, Janet Frances, and Thornton—became authors. His father's peripatetic career, ranging from Madison to Hong Kong to New Haven, Connecticut, guaranteed Wilder a sophisticated upbringing. After attending high school in Chefoo, China, and Ojai and Berkeley, California, Wilder went to Oberlin College for two years, and then received his bachelor's degree in 1920 from Yale University. During World War I, Wilder was a corporal in the Coast Artillery Corps. His education continued with a year in Rome at the American Academy, where he collected material for his first published novel, *The Cabala*, originally entitled "Memoirs of a Roman Student," a description of aristocratic life in contemporary Italy. The receipt of a master's degree in French from Princeton University in 1926 completed Wilder's education.

From 1921 to 1928, Wilder was housemaster and French teacher at the Lawrenceville School in New Jersey. Torn between teaching and writing, Wilder submitted a play, *The Trumpet Shall Sound*, to the American Laboratory Theatre in 1926. Most critics were less than enthusiastic, *The New York Times* reviewer calling it "a rather murky evening." Resigned to being an educator, Wilder nevertheless was working on the novel that would change his life, *The Bridge of San Luis Rey.* Set in colonial Peru, it pioneered a new type of fiction, one in which diverse characters are arbitrarily brought together by an accident, in this case, the collapse of an ancient bridge. Exploring the philosophical themes of fate and freedom, this novel not only caught the popular imagination but also won for Wilder his first Pulitzer Prize.

Resigning his post at Lawrenceville in 1928, Wilder turned his attention to full-time writing. His novel *The Woman of Andros*, set in pre-Christian Greece, explores the questions, "How does one live?" and "What does one do first?" Wilder was fond of taking philosophical themes from the Bible or the classics (both ancient and modern) and then developing them with a new twist. Having become a celebrity, Wilder made "walking tours of Europe" with prizefighter Gene Tunney and lecture tours of America to garner material for future works. *The Long Christmas Dinner* was Wilder's experiment with a play that would have a minimum of props, no curtain, and maximum attention to plot and personality. Travels in the heartland prompted Wilder to move to the Midwest.

From 1930 to 1936, Wilder was a lecturer in literature at the University of Chicago, where "boy wonder" Robert M. Hutchins was stressing a program in the humanities centered on a core course of "great books." Wilder was to be resident six months annually, teaching a large course on literature and a small seminar on writing, the remainder of the year to be free for writing. The Chicago years were mingled glory and tragedy. Lionized by North Shore society, Wilder was often shunned by more scholarly members of the university community. In 1930 he was stunned by Michael Gold's accusation, in the essay, "Wilder: Prophet of the Genteel Christ," in *The New Republic*, that he avoided topics of social relevance. The next novel, *Heaven's My Destination*, became a Book-of-the-Month Club selection.

Wilder believed the theater was "the greatest of all art forms" and "the most immediate way in which a human being can share with another the sense of what it is to be a human being." That conviction and economic circumstance led him to settle permanently in New Haven in 1937 and to turn his attention once more to drama. It was a wise decision. His play *Our Town* won for him his second Pulitzer Prize. Set in New Hampshire at the start of the twentieth century, *Our Town* explores "ordinary lives," finding in them "extraordinary meaning." Perhaps Wilder's most widely known work, *Our Town* experimented with simplicity of stage set and complexity of theme.

In World War II, Wilder served in the Air Force Intelligence Corps, seeing action in Italy and rising to the rank of major. Profoundly disturbed by this crisis in Western civilization, Wilder wrote the play for which he won his third Pulitzer Prize, *The Skin of Our Teeth*, which opened in New York's Plymouth Theatre on November 18, 1942. An "allegorical comedy of man's struggle for human survival," it was both praised as "the best pure theater" of the 1940's and panned as "a philosophy class conducted in a monkey house." Traumatic for Wilder was the accusation, made by Joseph Campbell and Henry Robinson, that his play was plagiarized from James Joyce's novel *Finnegans Wake* (1939). Once more Wilder was vindicated but deeply shaken.

Wilder toured Latin America, lectured in postwar Europe, and was visiting professor at a number of institutions, including Harvard University. *Our Century*, a play in three brief vignettes, appeared in 1947, followed the next year by his novel *The Ides of March*, a study in identity featuring Julius Caesar. In 1955 Wilder revised an earlier play, *The Merchant of Yonkers*, producing it as *The Matchmaker*. The play had previously failed; now it proved popular. Reworked again as the popular musical *Hello, Dolly!* (1964), starring Carol Channing, it gave Wilder even more exposure.

A time of "summing up" began. Wilder's novel *The Eighth Day* explores the dilemma of humankind's struggle against benevolent and malevolent forces. A mystery set in the Midwest, its theme is that humankind is yet young, that the eighth day of creation is at hand, and that "there are no Golden Ages and no Dark Ages," but rather the "oceanlike monotony of the generations of men under the alternations of fair and foul weather." This work won the National Book Award and prepared the way for Wilder's finale, the novel *Theophilus North*. The main character often mirrors Wilder's own personality and career. Torn by many contradictory dimensions and aspirations, the hero finds unity in his "desire to be a lover." Favorably received, the novel was Wilder's own obituary, for "the kindly grandad of American letters" died at Hamden, Connecticut, on December 7, 1975.

The recipient of honorary degrees from Harvard University, the University of Zurich, and other colleges, as well as the Legion of Honor and the Order of Merit (West Germany and Peru, respectively), and many other distinctions, Wilder is assured his place in American and world literature. Perceiving him as "sophisticated and urbane," critics commented on Wilder's "consecration to perfection," his "commitment to the classics," and his "passion for absolute excellence." A lifelong Congregationalist, always a teacher, whether in the classroom or in the theater, Wilder embodied the humanist ideals of the classical tradition and reinterpreted them in the light of twentieth century realities.

C. George Fry

Bibliography

Blank, Martin, ed. *Critical Essays on Thornton Wilder.* New York: G. K. Hall, 1996. A solid collection of criticism on Wilder. Includes bibliographical references and an index.

Blank, Martin, Dalma Hunyadi Brunauer, and David Garrett Izzo, eds. *Thornton Wilder: New Essays*. West Cornwall, Conn.: Locust Hill Press, 1999. A contemporary look at Wilder and his oeuvre.

Burbank, Rex J. *Thornton Wilder.* 2d ed. Boston: Twayne, 1978. In this updated version of the 1962 edition, Burbank traces the history of critical controversy surrounding Wilder's work, offers insights into his methods of fictional and dramatic composition, and assesses his work's relative merits. Chronology, bibliography.

Castronovo, David. *Thornton Wilder.* New York: Ungar, 1986. A useful introductory study of Wilder's works, both novels and plays, including chronology, notes, and bibliography.

Goldstein, Malcolm. *The Art of Thornton Wilder.* Lincoln: University of Nebraska Press, 1965. An early and still useful introduction to Wilder's novels and plays. A short biographical sketch is followed by an in-depth look at his work through the one-act play *Childhood* (1962). Includes bibliographical notes and an index.

Goldstone, Richard H. *Thornton Wilder: An Intimate Portrait.* New York: Saturday Review Press, 1975. An intimate portrait of Wilder by a close friend who had written previous studies on the subject, had access to personal documents, and interviewed family and friends. Includes notes, a selected bibliography, and an index.

Harrison, Gilbert A. *The Enthusiast: A Life of Thornton Wilder.* New York: Ticknor and Fields, 1983. A chatty biographical study of Wilder by a biographer who was provided access to Wilder's notes, letters, and photographs. Harrison successfully recreates Wilder's life and the influences, both good and bad, that shaped him.

Lifton, Paul. *"Vast Encyclopedia": The Theatre of Thornton Wilder.* Westport, Conn.: Greenwood Publishing, 1995. A critical overview of Wilder's drama.

Simon, Linda. *Thornton Wilder: His World.* Garden City, N.Y.: Doubleday, 1979. A solid biographical study of Wilder that includes examinations of his published works and photographs, notes, a bibliography, and an index.

Walsh, Claudette. *Thornton Wilder: A Reference Guide, 1926-1990.* New York: G. K. Hall, 1993. A complete guide to Wilder and his works. Includes bibliographical references and an index.

Wilder, Amos Niven. *Thornton Wilder and His Public.* Philadelphia: Fortress Press, 1980. A short critical study of Wilder by his older brother, who offers an inside family look at the writer. A supplement includes Wilder's "Culture in a Democracy" address and a selected German bibliography.

C. K. Williams

American poet

Born: Newark, New Jersey; November 4, 1936

POETRY: *A Day for Anne Frank*, 1968; *Lies*, 1969; *I Am the Bitter Name*, 1972; *The Sensuous President*, 1972; *With Ignorance*, 1977; *Tar*, 1983; *Flesh and Blood*, 1987; *Poems, 1963-1983*, 1988; *A Dream of Mind*, 1992; *Selected Poems*, 1994; *New and Selected Poems*, 1995; *The Vigil*, 1997; *Repair*, 1999; *Love About Love*, 2001.

TRANSLATIONS: *Women of Trachis*, 1978 (of Sophocles' play *Trachinai*; with Gregory Dickerson); *The Lark, the Thrush, the Starling*, 1983 (of Issa's poetry); *The Bacchae*, 1985 (of Euripides' play *Bakchai*; with H. Golder); *The Bacchae of Euripides: A New Version*, 1990; *Canvas*, 1991 (of Adam Zagajewski's poetry; with Renata Gorczynski and Benjamin Ivry); *Selected Poems*, 1994 (of Francis Ponge; with John Montague and Margaret Guiton).

EDITED TEXTS: *Selected and Last Poems*, 1989 (of Paul Zweig); *The Essential Hopkins*, 1993 (Gerard Manley Hopkins's poetry).

NONFICTION: *Poetry and Consciousness*, 1998; *Misgivings: My Mother, My Father, Myself*, 2000.

Born November 4, 1936, in Newark, New Jersey, the son of Paul B. and Dossie (née Kasdin) Williams, Charles Kenneth Williams was educated at Bucknell University and at the University of Pennsylvania, where he was graduated with a B.A. in 1959. In 1965, he married Sarah Jones; they had a daughter, Jessica Anne, who figures in Williams's personal poems. At the Pennsylvania Hospital in Philadelphia, he founded a program of poetry therapy and was a group therapist for disturbed adolescents.

A Day for Anne Frank led to the publication of two volumes of poetry in 1969 and 1972 that established Williams as a protest poet of the Richard Nixon era. He was a visiting professor at Franklin and Marshall College in 1977 and at the University of California at Irvine in 1978 before becoming professor of English at George Mason University. In addition, he has taught creative writing at various workshops and colleges, including Boston University, Columbia University, and University of California at Berkeley.

A Guggenheim Fellowship in 1974 resulted in *With Ignorance*, the first book in his new style. In 1975, Williams married Catherine Mauger, a jeweler, with whom he had a son. Williams was awarded the Bernard F. Conner Prize for the long poem by *The Paris Review* in 1983; the National Book Critics Circle Award in 1987; the Morton Dauwen Zabel prize in 1989; the Lila Wallace Reader's Digest Writers' award in 1993; and the Harriet Monroe Prize from *Poetry* magazine, also in 1993. In 2000 he won the Pulitzer Prize in poetry for *Repair.*

William H. Green

Bibliography

Bawer, Bruce. Review of *Tar*, by C. K. Williams. *Poetry* 144 (September, 1984): 353-355. Praises *Tar* for its portraiture, citing "Waking Jed" and "The Color of Time" as the best of the collection. Compares Williams to Walt Whitman, but says the former has more warmth and intensity of feeling. Argues that *Tar* is a reminder not only of "what poetry is all about, but what life is all about." An appreciative review.

Coles, Robert. Review of *With Ignorance*, by C. K. Williams. *The American Poetry Review* 8 (July/August, 1979): 12-13. Likens Williams to Søren Kierkegaard because both stay in the world while "groping for inner truth." Coles says Williams has achieved in these poems a "humble intelligence" and considers the task in these poems as a journey fraught with challenges.

Howard, Richard. Review of *The Vigil*, by C. K. Williams. *Boston Review*, Summer, 1997. Although Howard has serious and well-expressed reservations about the formal imposition of an extremely long line, he allows himself to admire those poems and passages in which Williams's technique works effectively. Howard praises Williams's successes in rendering "immediacy of sensation."

Jarman, Mark. *The Secret of Poetry.* Ashland, Ore.: Story Line Press, 2001. The chapter "The Pragmatic Imagination and the Secret of Poetry" compares Williams with Charles Wright and Philip Levine.

Phillips, Brian. "Plainly, but with Flair." *New Republic*, September 18, 2000, 42-45. Phillips reviews both *Repair* and the memoir *Misgivings*. He objects to Williams's habit of moralizing and of glossing the beginning of a poem at the end. Williams forces the reader away from direct experience toward a preferred comprehension. This habit undermines his great descriptive powers. Phillips also notes the tension between Williams's colloquial diction and his erudite range of references.

Riding, Alan. "American Bard in Paris Stokes Poetic Home Fires." *The New York Times*, October 4, 2000, p. E4. This flavorful piece of biographical journalism treats Williams's relationship with Paris as well as the patterns of his writing and teaching careers.

Santos, Sherod. *A Poetry of Two Minds*. Athens: University of Georgia Press, 2000. In a comparison of mid-career poems by Williams and Charles Wright, Santos examines parallel aesthetic experimentation and the determination to overcome despair through art.

Charles Williams

English novelist, poet, and critic

Born: London, England; September 20, 1886
Died: Oxford, England; May 15, 1945

LONG FICTION: *War in Heaven*, 1930; *Many Dimensions*, 1931; *The Place of the Lion*, 1931; *The Greater Trumps*, 1932; *Shadows of Ecstasy*, 1933; *Descent into Hell*, 1937; *All Hallows' Eve*, 1945; *Flecker of Dean Close*, 1946.

DRAMA: *A Myth of Shakespeare*, pb. 1928; *Three Plays*, pb. 1931; *Thomas Cranmer of Canterbury*, pb. 1936; *Judgement at Chelmsford*, pb. 1939; *The House of the Octopus*, pb. 1945; *Seed of Adam, and Other Plays*, pb. 1948; *Collected Plays*, pb. 1963.

POETRY: *The Silver Stair*, 1912; *Poems of Conformity*, 1917; *Divorce*, 1920; *Windows of Night*, 1924; *Heroes and Kings*, 1930-1931; *Taliessin Through Logres*, 1938; *The Region of the Summer Stars*, 1944; *Arthurian Torso*, 1948.

NONFICTION: *Poetry at Present*, 1930 (criticism); *The English Poetic Mind*, 1932 (criticism); *Reason and Beauty in the Poetic Mind*, 1933 (criticism); *Bacon*, 1933; *James I*, 1934; *Rochester*, 1935; *The Rite of the Passion*, 1936 (philosophy); *He Came Down from Heaven*, 1938 (philosophy); *The Descent of the Dove*, 1939 (philosophy); *Religion and Love in Dante*, 1941 (criticism); *Witchcraft*, 1941 (philosophy); *The Forgiveness of Sins*, 1942 (philosophy); *The Figure of Beatrice*, 1943 (criticism); *The Image of the City, and Other Essays*, 1958; *To Michal from Serge: Letters from Charles Williams to His Wife, Florence, 1939-1945*, 2002 (Roma A. King, Jr., editor).

Charles Williams was the son of Walter Williams, a foreign correspondence clerk who also wrote poetry under the name Stansby. Charles was educated at St. Albans School and had two years at the University of London before he was forced to end his formal studies to earn his living. During years in a publishing job he continued his studies, however, and without acquiring any formal degrees he became a profound literary scholar, historian, theologian, poet, and novelist. Throughout his career as an editor with Oxford University Press he taught, lectured, and wrote prolifically. In 1917 he married Florence Conway, and they had one son. He lived all his life in London, except for a few years during World War II when his publishing firm was evacuated to Oxford. There he joined the Inklings, a literary group that included C. S. Lewis and J. R. R. Tolkien. After his death in 1945 the tributes of these and other literary friends such as W. H. Auden, T. S. Eliot, and Dorothy Sayers brought him wider recognition than he had had during his lifetime.

Williams's literary career developed gradually, with four volumes of poems published between 1912 and 1924. His first play, *A Myth of Shakespeare*, was published in 1928. During the next decade he published eighteen books covering the entire range of his varied but closely related interests. In his three critical works he explored the religious basis of the creative imagination: *Poetry at Present*, *The English Poetic Mind*, and *Reason and Beauty in the Poetic Mind*. His historical studies were concerned with the relationship between the individual and the pattern of history: *Bacon*, *James I*, and *Rochester*. The depth of his thought as an original but profoundly orthodox Anglican was revealed in two religious books, *The Rite of the Passion* and *He Came Down from Heaven*. He also maintained a predominantly religious emphasis in the plays. His religious conviction was combined with an interest in witchcraft and the occult, which formed the basis of a remarkable series of novels, including *War in Heaven, Many Dimensions, The Place of the Lion, The Greater Trumps, Shadows of Ecstasy*, and *Descent into Hell*. Described by critics as supernatural thrillers, these novels employ a realistic contemporary English setting as the background for the eternal conflict between good and evil, revealing both the mystic and the sensuous facets of Williams's personality.

In 1938 Williams published his first verse collection since 1924, *Taliessin Through Logres*, a series of brilliant but difficult poems based on Arthurian legends. His historical, poetic, and religious interests became focused on two of the greatest myths of European culture: the English legend of the king and the Italian poet's legend of the beloved lady. Williams's two books about Dante, *Religion and Love in Dante* and *The Figure of Beatrice*, are among the most stimulating interpretations of Dante in English. He further explored his passionate interest in the supernatural in the three religious and philosophical studies *The Descent of the Dove, Witchcraft*, and *The Forgiveness of Sins*. In 1944 he published the second volume of Arthurian poems, *The Region of the Summer Stars*. He also continued to write plays with a historical background and religious theme: *Judgement at Chelmsford*, *The House of the Octopus*, and *Seed of Adam, and Other Plays* (published posthumously). The novel *All Hallows' Eve* was published shortly before his death in 1945, and *Flecker of Dean Close* in 1946.

Williams's death came at a time when he was thought to have been at the height of his literary power. He left behind a large body of material that he had intended to use in both poetic and critical interpretations of the Arthurian myth, which had increasingly absorbed him during the war years. C. S. Lewis edited and enlarged upon this material in a volume called *Arthurian Torso*. Williams's Arthurian studies during the war were in no sense escapist. He saw England's role in the conflict as part of a pattern in history that had been foreshadowed in the Arthurian cycle. The company of the Grail knights on their quest was to Williams not merely a poetic image but a spiritual reality. To Williams, all of creation was unified in God across all time and space; this idea permeates all his works subtly or overtly, no matter what the genre or the subject. The wide range of his interests and considerable scope of his literary powers were all concentrated, in Eliot's phrase, "to apprehend the point of intersection of the timeless with time."

Bernadette Lynn Bosky

Bibliography

Carpenter, Humphrey. *The Inklings*. Boston: Houghton Mifflin, 1978. Discusses Williams along with other writers.

Cavaliero, Glen. *Charles Williams: Poet of Theology*. Grand Rapids, Mich.: Wm. B. Eerdmans, 1983. Useful general study of Williams.

Fredrick, Candice, and Sam McBride. *Women Among the Inklings: Gender, C. S. Lewis, J. R. R. Tolkien, and Charles Williams*. Westport, Conn.: Greenwood Press, 2001. A study of the attitudes toward women among the Inklings, both in their relationships with the women in their lives and in their depictions of women in fiction.

Hadfield, Alice Mary. *Charles Williams*. New York: Oxford University Press, 1982. Useful general study of Williams.

Hillegas, Mark R., ed. *Shadows of Imagination: The Fantasies of C. S. Lewis, J. R. R. Tolkien, and Charles Williams*. Carbondale: University of Illinois Press, 1969. Discusses Williams along with other writers.

Howard, Thomas. *The Novels of Charles Williams*. New York: Oxford University Press, 1983. Elementary but helpful.

Huttar, Charles, and Peter Schakal, eds. *The Rhetoric of Vision: Essays on Charles Williams*. Lewisberg, Pa.: Bucknell University Press, 1996. A collection of essays on Williams's works.

King, Roma A., Jr. *The Pattern in the Web: The Mythical Poetry of Charles Williams*. Kent, Ohio: Kent State University Press, 1990. Williams's poetry receives attention.

Sibley, Agnes Marie. *Charles Williams*. Boston: Twayne, 1982. An introductory literary biography, including criticism and bibliography.

Spencer, Kathleen. *Charles Williams*. San Bernardino, Calif.: Borgo Press, 1986. An excellent introduction to Williams.

Weeks, Dennis L. *Steps Toward Salvation: An Examination of Coinherence and Substitution in the Seven Novels of Charles Williams*. New York: P. Lang, 1991. A study of the religious philosophy espoused in Williams's fiction.

Emlyn Williams

Welsh playwright

Born: Mostyn, Wales; November 26, 1905
Died: London, England; September 25, 1987

DRAMA: *Vigil*, pr. 1925, pb. 1954 (one act); *Full Moon*, pr. 1927; *Glamour*, pr. 1928; *A Murder Has Been Arranged*, pr., pb. 1930; *Port Said*, pr. 1931, revised pr. 1933 (as *Vessels Departing*); *The Late Christopher Bean*, pr., pb. 1933 (adaptation of Sidney Howard's play); *Spring 1600*, pr. 1934, revised pr. 1945; *Night Must Fall*, pr., pb. 1935; *He Was Born Gay: A Romance*, pr., pb. 1937; *The Corn Is Green*, pr., pb. 1938; *The Light of Heart*, pr., pb. 1940; *The Morning Star*, pr. 1941, pb. 1942; *A Month in the Country*, pr. 1943 (adaptation of Ivan Turgenev's play); *Pen Don*, pr. 1943; *The Druid's Rest*, pr., pb. 1944; *The Wind of Heaven*, pr., pb. 1945; *Thinking Aloud: A Dramatic Sketch*, pr. 1945, pb. 1946; *Trespass: A Ghost Story*, pr., pb. 1947; *Accolade*, pr. 1950, pb. 1951; *Someone Waiting*, pr. 1953, pb. 1954; *Beth*, pr. 1958, pb. 1959; *The Collected Plays*, pb. 1961; *The Master Builder*, pr. 1964 (adaptation of Henrik Ibsen's play); *Cuckoo*, pb. 1986.

LONG FICTION: *Headlong*, 1980; *Dr. Crippen's Diary: An Invention*, 1987.

SCREENPLAYS: *Friday the Thirteenth*, 1933 (with G. H. Moresby-White and Sidney Gilliat); *Evergreen*, 1934 (with Marjorie Gaffney); *The Man Who Knew Too Much*, 1934 (with A. R. Rawlinson and Edwin Greenwood); *The Divine Spark*, 1935 (with Richard Benson); *Broken Blossoms*, 1936; *The Citadel*, 1938 (with Frank Wead, Ian Dalrymple, Elizabeth Hill, and John Van Druten; based on A. J. Cronin's novel); *This England*, 1941 (with Bridget Boland and Rawlinson); *Major Barbara*, 1941 (based on George Bernard Shaw's play); *The Last Days of Dolwyn*, 1949; *Ivanhoe*, 1952 (based on Sir Walter Scott's novel).

TELEPLAYS: *A Month in the Country*, 1947; *Every Picture Tells a Story*, 1949; *In Town Tonight*, 1954; *A Blue Movie of My Own True Love*, 1968; *The Power of Dawn*, 1976.

RADIO PLAYS: *Pepper and Sand*, 1947; *Emlyn*, 1974 (adaptation of his autobiography).

NONFICTION: *George: An Early Autobiography*, 1961; *Beyond Belief: A Chronicle of Murder and Its Detection*, 1967; *Emlyn: An Early Autobiography, 1927-1935*, 1973.

Playwright, actor, and director George Emlyn Williams was born to a working-class Welsh family; he never heard English spoken until he attended Holywell County School at age ten. Yet his talent as a linguist changed his life when Grace Cooke, a London social worker, recognized his extraordinary ability and helped him win a scholarship to Saint Julien's in Switzerland and then to Christ Church College, Oxford, from which he received his degree in 1927.

Williams became involved in Oxford University Drama Society productions, first acting and then writing a one-act play, *Vigil*, produced with the playwright in the lead. Even this initial effort presaged some of the characteristics of Williams's best work: the Welsh background, the fascination with murder, and the roles that he created for himself.

In 1927, *Full Moon*, his first full-length play, was staged. During the next several years, while acting in London in productions of plays by Luigi Pirandello, Émile Zola, Sean O'Casey, and others, Williams found time to write his first important drama, *A Murder Has Been Arranged*. The most noteworthy element is the main character, Maurice Mullins, a bright, attractive young man who misuses his charm for a nefarious end, the murder of his uncle.

Williams's next few efforts were not successful, although his adaptation of *The Late Christopher Bean* (changed from its New England setting to an English one) received excellent reviews, primarily as the result of Dame Edith Evans's appearance as Guenny, a Welsh maid. During these years, the playwright continued to act in London and New York and did several film roles as well. In 1935 *Night Must Fall* established Williams as a major dramatist.

In the introduction to *The Collected Plays*, Williams remarked, "There was only one living playwright sufficiently interested in my acting to write a part which only I could play. Me!" Because *Night Must Fall* begins with the Lord Chief Justice's declaration that the "prisoner is to be hanged by the neck until dead," the audience, aware of the outcome, can concentrate on the dazzling performance of the psychopathic killer created and played by Williams.

Dan, a pageboy at a resort in Essex, uses his affair with Mrs. Bramson's maid, Dora, as an excuse to move into the Bramson cottage, where he soon works his wiles on the elderly hypochondriac. Mrs. Bramson's niece, Olivia, suspects that he is "acting," and when the decapitated body of a female guest missing from the hotel is found in the woods nearby, the strange sealed hatbox belonging to Dan takes on more than casual significance. Strangely fascinated, Olivia almost saves Dan, although he has murdered her aunt and threatened her. When Inspector Belsize interrupts Dan's final act—setting the cottage on fire to cover his crimes—the psychopath feels compelled to confess with much bravado, promising to "give 'em their money's worth at the trial." Williams's fascination with murder and psychopathic murderers makes *Night Must Fall* a seminal example of the genre.

In 1938 Williams's wife, Molly, suggested that he write a play about the teacher who changed his life; he did so in *The Corn Is Green*. Grace Cooke became Miss Moffat, a woman determined to run a school for Welsh miners and their children. She discovers Morgan Evans (played by the playwright), an exceptional fifteen-year-old, and grooms him for admission to Oxford. The young man succeeds, but all is nearly lost when a single encounter with the sluttish Bessie Watty results in a child. In a somewhat improbable denouement, Miss Moffat decides to adopt the baby so that Morgan is free to go on with his life. Yet because the major characters come out of Williams's own life experiences, both the teacher and the young Welshman are believable. When *The Corn Is Green* was staged in New York with Ethel Barrymore as the teacher, it won the New York Drama Critics Circle Award for the Best Foreign Play of 1941.

Williams played more than fifty roles on stages in London, Stratford, and on various tours from 1927 through 1950, and many of these plays were also directed by the actor. Additionally, from 1932 through 1955, he acted in more than twenty films.

Williams scored his greatest triumph in 1952 with his one-man show in which he impersonated Charles Dickens—complete with Victorian costume, props, and makeup—reading from Dickens's works, just as the novelist had done a century earlier. After successfully appearing in England, Europe, North America, and South Africa with this tour de force, the actor began a series of public readings from the works of his fellow Welshman Dylan Thomas. These performances, wrote the eminent theater critic, Walter Kerr, "communicated a kind of lyric fire that our regulation plays have long denied us." In 1962 Williams was made a Commander of the Order of the British Empire.

Edythe M. McGovern

Bibliography

Brantley, Ben. "A Killer Just Loaded with Charm." Review of *Night Must Fall*, by Emlyn Williams. *The New York Times*, March 9, 1999, p. 1. This favorable review of a 1999 staging of *Night Must Fall* by the Tony Randall's National Actors Theater remarks on how well the play works more than sixty years after its premiere. The discussion of the production and the plot sheds light on Williams's well-known work.

Dale-Jones, Don. *Emlyn Williams*. Cardiff: University of Wales Press, 1979. This monograph focuses on how Williams's Welsh background, including his studies in psychology and foreign literatures, determined his interest in the theater and influenced his plays. A thorough study of Williams. Bibliography.

Findlater, Richard. *Emlyn Williams*. New York: Macmillan, 1956. A copiously illustrated biography that covers every facet of Williams's life and career.

Harding, James. *Emlyn Williams: A Life*. 1993. Reprint. Cardiff: Welsh Academic Press, 2002. This biography of Williams looks at his life and works. Provides a listing of his works, bibliography, and index.

Stephens, John Russell. *Emlyn Williams: The Making of a Dramatist*. Chester Springs, Pa.: DuFour Editions, 2000. Stephens's biography traces the development of Williams as a dramatist and examines his works. Bibliography and index.

Whitford-Roberts, Edward. *The Emlyn Williams Country*. Foreword by Emlyn Williams. Penarth, Wales: Penarth Times, 1963. This study attempts a further understanding of the Welsh content—characters, settings, atmosphere, and ethical principles—of Williams's plays. It includes a map of Flintshire and photographs of places that might have fueled the playwright's imagination and people who might have encouraged his career.

John A. Williams

American novelist

Born: Jackson, Mississippi; December 5, 1925
Pseudonym: J. Dennis Gregory
Identity: African American

LONG FICTION: *The Angry Ones*, 1960 (also known as *One for New York*); *Night Song*, 1961; *Sissie*, 1963; *The Man Who Cried I Am*, 1967; *Sons of Darkness, Sons of Light: A Novel of Some Probability*, 1969; *Captain Blackman*, 1972; *Mothersill and the Foxes*, 1975; *The Junior Bachelor Society*, 1976; *!Click Song*, 1982; *The Berhama Account*, 1985; *Jacob's Ladder*, 1987; *Clifford's Blues*, 1998.

NONFICTION: *Africa: Her History, Lands and People*, 1962; *The Protectors: The Heroic Story of the Narcotics Agents, Citizens, and Officials in Their Unending, Unsung Battles Against Organized Crime in America and Abroad*, 1964 (as J. Dennis Gregory with Harry J. Ansliger); *This Is My Country Too*, 1965; *The Most Native of Sons: A Biography of Richard Wright*, 1970; *The King God Didn't Save: Reflections on the Life and Death of Martin Luther King, Jr.*, 1970; *Flashbacks: A Twenty-Year Diary of Article Writing*, 1973; *If I Stop I'll Die: The Comedy and Tragedy of Richard Pryor*, 1991; *Way B(l)ack Then and Now: A Street Guide to African Americans in Paris*, 1992 (with Michel Fabre).

POETRY: *Safari West: Poems*, 1998.

DRAMA: *Last Flight from Ambo Ber*, pr. 1981; *Vanqui*, pr. 1999 (libretto).

EDITED TEXTS: *The Angry Black*, 1962; *Beyond the Angry Black*, 1966; *Amistad 1*, 1970 (with Charles F. Harris); *Amistad 2*, 1971 (with Harris); *The McGraw-Hill Introduction to Literature*, 1985 (with Gilbert H. Muller); *Bridges: Literature Across Cultures*, 1994 (Gilbert H. Muller, author).

John Alfred Williams is one of the most important African American writers of the twentieth century. The son of a laborer, John Henry Williams, and a domestic, Ola Jones Williams, Williams spent his boyhood in Syracuse and describes it as an urban idyll in which various racial and ethnic groups were crowded into one area. In April, 1943, he left high school and joined the U.S. Navy. It was a formative experience since he came into contact for the first time with organized racism. The treatment of African Americans by whites in the military became a touchstone for Williams, and he alludes to it in many of his later novels, even though his first attempt to write a book on those experiences never came to fruition. After being discharged from the navy in 1946, Williams began completing his education. He finished high school, attended Morris Brown College for a short time, and graduated from Syracuse University in 1950. A degree in journalism, however, did not provide immediate employment on newspapers, magazines, or in public relations. Instead, he worked in a steel mill and a supermarket and as an insurance agent. The problems that Williams and other black writers have had with publishers is a major theme in his novels. He kept writing all this time in the face of rejection and deception, and finally a novel was accepted by a publisher.

Williams's first novel, *The Angry Ones*, deals primarily with the difficulties of an educated and articulate black man in a white world. It is an early novel with a simple reversal structure; Williams avoided this structure and easy optimism in his later novels. Williams wrote two other early novels, *Sissie* and *Night Song*, but the breakthrough into his middle period came with the addition of historical contexts in *The Man Who Cried I Am. The Man Who Cried I Am* is an excellent though pessimistic novel in which the protagonist and another black writer are killed because they learned of a conspiracy to kill or relocate blacks. It is Williams's first investigation of where power is located and how it works against blacks. *Sons of Darkness, Sons of Light* continues Williams's investigation of a black man in a world in which the centers of power are controlled by whites; however, the historical vision has become more immediate and the race war that was contemplated by the repressive power structure in *The Man Who Cried I Am* has become a reality. *Captain Blackman* is also a novel deeply connected with history, but the perspective has been expanded. In the beginning of the novel Captain Blackman is in a firefight in Vietnam; suddenly, the time frame shifts, and he is a black man caught up in the events of the American Revolution. Williams traces his actions in all the wars that America fights; in each case, his contribution is ignored by those he has fought for and his condition is not improved.

Mothersill and the Foxes explores a new aspect of myths dealing with blacks: sex. Williams attacks the ludicrousness of these myths, which are another side of racism. *The Junior Bachelor Society* also confronts racial conflict, but the context is not war or politics but sports. *!Click Song* is a long autobiographical novel in which a black writer struggles with a white establishment. It contrasts the treatment given to a black writer and a Jewish one. The black writer meets nothing but opposition while the white writer is supported by the establishment, even to the point of critical approval of his novel about black people. It is more hopeful in using personal relationships as a focus, however, and it moves away from Williams's genocidal vision of the fate of blacks in America. *Sissie* is an unusual novel in Williams's canon: It is the one novel that is set entirely in a black world. This world is nurturing and loving, although it is filled with conflict. *Night Song* is also unusual since it deals not with the usual isolated black man but with a jazz musician who is modeled after a historical figure, Charlie Parker.

The most important element in Williams's fiction is the struggle of blacks against the conscious and unconscious racism of a white society. Williams not only dramatizes the social and psychological problems engendered by racism but also places that struggle in a historical perspective and context. Williams often shows the positive black contribution to their country's wars, economy, arts, and other areas that are wiped out, ignored, or hidden. He shows that the American Dream remains hollow for blacks oppressed by overt and hidden sources of power. Williams is in the tradition of Richard Wright and Ralph Ellison in exposing white myths of black life and people. He takes the conflicts of black and white that these writers present and carries them more than a few steps further into an analysis of the use and abuse of power in America. Williams does not give political answers to the problems he presents but takes the necessary step to make blacks and whites aware of the world they live in, who runs it, and how they run it. With that knowledge, and the demystification of myths about blacks, some kind of beginning might be made. It may only be between a black man and a white woman, as in *!Click Song*, but Williams shows how to begin.

James Sullivan

Bibliography

Cash, Earl A. *John A. Williams: The Evolution of a Black Writer.* New York: Third Press, 1975. This text is the first book-length study of Williams's works, covering the nonfiction and the novels through *Captain Blackman.*

Fleming, Robert. "John A, Williams." *Black Issues Book Review* 4 (July/August, 2002): 46-49. A profile of Williams and his work.

Gayle, Addison, Jr. *The Way of the New World: The Black Novel in America.* Garden City, N.Y.: Doubleday, 1975. Gayle addresses the shift from protest to history in *The Man Who Cried I Am* and *Captain Blackman.*

Muller, Gilbert H. *John A. Williams.* Boston: Twayne, 1984. Containing a chronology and thematic approach, this study is a comprehensive treatment of Williams's life and work through *!Click Song.*

Nadel, Alan. "My Country Too: Time, Place, and Afro-American Identity in the Work of John Williams." *Obsidian II: Black Literature in Review* 2, no. 3 (1987): 25-41. This article examines selected nonfiction and fiction, showing political orientation and modernist patterns.

Ramsey, Priscilla R. "John A. Williams: The Black American Narrative and the City." In *The City in African-American Literature*, edited by Yoshinobu Hakutani and Robert Butler. Madison, N.J.: Fairleigh Dickinson University Press, 1995. Focusing on urban realities, this study offers an overview of selected Williams novels.

Reilly, John M. "Thinking History in *The Man Who Cried I Am.*" *Black American Literature Forum* 21, nos. 1/2 (1987): 25-42. Reilly considers Williams's novel in relation to naturalism and history.

Ro, Sigmund. "Toward the Post-Protest Novel: The Fiction of John A. Williams." In *Rage and Celebration: Essays on Contemporary Afro-American Writing.* Atlantic Highlands, N.J.: Humanities Press, 1984. This essay argues that Williams's novels develop from protest fiction to novelistic treatments of 1960's racial issues.

Smith, Virginia W. "Sorcery, Double-Consciousness, and Warring Souls: An Intertextual Reading of *Middle Passage* and *Captain Blackman.*" *African American Review* 30 (Winter, 1996): 659-674. Smith asserts that Charles Johnson's *Middle Passage* was influenced by *Captain Blackman.* She points out a number of similar themes between the novels, such as war and interracial and intraracial conflict.

Tal, Kali. "'That Just Kills Me.'" *Social Text* 20 (Summer, 2002): 65-92. Discusses *Sons of Darkness, Sons of Light* in a study of militant black futurist novels.

Sherley Anne Williams

American novelist and poet

Born: Bakersfield, California; August 25, 1944
Died: San Diego, California; July 6, 1999
Identity: African American

LONG FICTION: *Dessa Rose*, 1986.
POETRY: *The Peacock Poems*, 1975; *Some One Sweet Angel Chile*, 1982.
CHILDREN'S/YOUNG ADULT LITERATURE: *Working Cotton*, 1992; *Girls Together*, 1999.
NONFICTION: *Give Birth to Brightness: A Thematic Study in Neo-Black Literature*, 1972.

The poet, critic, and novelist Sherley Anne Williams was one of the talented African American writers who emerged on the post-Civil Rights movement literary scene. Born to Lena and Jessee Winston Williams, hardworking farm laborers in the San Joaquin Valley, Williams experienced a childhood marked by loss: Her father died of tuberculosis when she was seven, and her mother died when Sherley was sixteen.

Williams attended California State University at Fresno, where, in 1966, she received her bachelor of arts degree. A student of literature, Williams began writing her own fiction during her college years. Viewing writing as a means of communicating, she wrote with publication as her goal, one she soon achieved: The *Massachusetts Review* published her first short story in 1967. "Tell Martha Not to Moan" was inspired by Williams's desire to write about lower-income black women, largely absent from literature. This drive to communicate the significance of black women, to give them a voice in literature, forms a common thread throughout Williams's writing.

As she started her writing career, Williams continued to pursue the education necessary for her career as a teacher. From 1966 to 1967 she studied at Howard University. In 1972 she completed her master's degree in English at Brown University. During her years of graduate study Williams wrote her first critical study of African American literature. In *Give Birth to Brightness: A Thematic Study in Neo-Black Literature* Williams defines a contemporary black aesthetic, one that represents black life as culturally rich on its own terms, and not merely in terms of its relationship to white culture. Analyzing the role of the hero in Amiri Baraka's *Dutchman* (pr., pb. 1964) and *The Slave* (pr., pb. 1964), James Baldwin's *Blues for Mister Charlie* (pr., pb. 1964), and Ernest Gaines's *Of Love and Dust* (1967), Williams concludes that the black hero must be rooted in black culture, community, and folklore.

While studying and writing, Williams was also gaining teaching experience as a community educator at Federal City College in Washington, D.C. After finishing her master's degree, she returned to California State University at Fresno, her alma mater, to teach English. In 1975 she moved to the University of California at San Diego.

Though talented in fiction and criticism, it was Williams's poetry that first brought her national attention. *The Peacock Poems*, published in 1975, was nominated for a National Book Award in poetry. This collection combines poetry, lyrical prose narratives, and the blues tradition in a highly autobiographical work. Poems about Williams's son frame the collection: "Say Hello to John" describes his birth, and "I See My Life" describes his movement from child to mature individual. Between these poems, Williams's lyrical blues poetry renders a woman's suffering and pain and the transcendent healing the blues makes possible.

Published in 1982, *Some One Sweet Angel Chile* extends Williams's poetic exploration of the blues tradition. Drawing upon nineteenth century slave narratives, part 1, "Letters from a New England Negro," describes the experiences of the fictional Hannah, a freeborn woman of color, as she teaches freed slaves in the South. Part 2, "Regular Reefer," focuses on an actual historical figure, blues singer Bessie Smith. The poems in this section use blues rhythms and language to chronicle events from Smith's life. Parts 3 and 4, "The Songs of the Grown" and "The Iconography of Childhood," also draw upon the blues. Throughout *Some One Sweet Angel Chile*, Williams uses poetry to recover and give voice to the history of black women and to re-create imaginatively histories that have been lost.

In *Dessa Rose*, published in 1986, Williams chose the novel as her vehicle for recovering the history of black women. In the author's note she explains that her title character and plot are based on historical incidents. One, from Angela Davis's "Reflections on the Black Woman's Role in the Community of Slaves" (1971), involved a pregnant black woman who led an uprising among a group of slaves. The second, from Herbert Aptheker's *American Negro Slave Revolts* (1969), concerned a white woman who assisted runaway slaves. In Williams's novel these historical figures join forces to subvert the forces of sexism and racism; their collaboration makes it possible for Dessa Rose to journey from slavery to freedom, from silence to literacy, and from isolation to community. She becomes the sort of hero that Williams celebrates in *Give Birth to Brightness*, one rooted in an African American community and folklore tradition. *Dessa Rose* was named a notable book by *The New York Times*.

In her author's note to *Dessa Rose* Williams observes, "Afro-Americans, having survived by word of mouth—and made of that process a high art—remain at the mercy of literature and writing; often, these have betrayed us." Throughout her literary career, Williams sought to correct that betrayal and to restore to the American literary tradition the voices and stories of African American women.

Suzan Harrison

Bibliography

Basu, Biman. "Hybrid Embodiment and an Ethics of Masochism: Nella Laren's *Passing* and Sherley Anne Williams's *Dessa Rose*." *African American Studies* 36, no. 3 (Fall, 2002). Explores the increasing interrogation of racial and cultural boundaries and proliferation of images of hybridity in Williams's novel.

Carby, Hazel. "Ideologies of Black Folk: The Historical Novel of Slavery." In *Slavery and the Literary Imagination*, edited by Deborah McDowell and Arnold Rampersad. Baltimore: The Johns Hopkins University Press, 1989. Excellent article that examines *Dessa Rose*'s treatment of history.

Davis, Mary Kemp. "Everybody Knows Her Name: The Recovery of the Past in *Dessa Rose*." *Callaloo* 12, no. 3 (Summer, 1989). Excellent article that examines the novel's treatment of history.

Goldman, Anne. "'I Made the Ink': (Literary) Production and the Reproduction in *Dessa Rose* and *Beloved*." *Feminist Studies* 16, no. 2 (Summer, 1990). Explores women's issues.

Henderson, Mae Gwendolyn. "Speaking in Tongues: Dialogics, Dialectics, and the Black Woman Writer's Literary Tradition." In *Reading Black, Reading Feminist*, edited by Henry Louis Gates, Jr. New York: Meridian, 1990. Explores women's issues.

Henderson, Stephen. *Understanding the New Black Poetry*. New York: Morrow, 1973. Mentions Williams's work.

Rushdy, Ashraf H. A. "Reading Mammy: The Subject of Relation in Sherley Anne Williams's *Dessa Rose*." *African American Review* 27, no. 3 (Fall, 1997). Looks at Williams's depiction of communicative interactions among African Americans and her literary style.

Tate, Claudia. *Black Women Writers at Work*. New York: Continuum, 1983. Includes an interview with Williams about her poetry.

Tennessee Williams
(Thomas Lanier Williams)

American playwright

Born: Columbus, Mississippi; March 26, 1911
Died: New York, New York; February 25, 1983
Identity: Gay or bisexual

DRAMA: *Fugitive Kind*, pr. 1937; *Spring Storm*, wr. 1937, pr., pb. 1999; *Not About Nightingales*, wr. 1939, pr., pb. 1998; *Battle of Angels*, pr. 1940; *This Property Is Condemned*, pb. 1941 (one act); *I Rise in Flame, Cried the Phoenix*, wr. 1941, pb. 1951 (one act); *The Lady of Larkspur Lotion*, pb. 1942 (one act); *The Glass Menagerie*, pr. 1944; *Twenty-seven Wagons Full of Cotton*, pb. 1945 (one act); *You Touched Me*, pr. 1945 (with Donald Windham); *Summer and Smoke*, pr. 1947; *A Streetcar Named Desire*, pr., pb. 1947; *American Blues*, pb. 1948 (collection); *Five Short Plays*, pb. 1948; *The Long Stay Cut Short: Or, The Unsatisfactory Supper*, pb. 1948 (one act); *The Rose Tattoo*, pr. 1950; *Camino Real*, pr., pb. 1953; *Cat on a Hot Tin Roof*, pr., pb. 1955; *Orpheus Descending*, pr. 1957 (revision of *Battle of Angels*); *Suddenly Last Summer*, pr., pb. 1958; *The Enemy: Time*, pb. 1959; *Sweet Bird of Youth*, pr., pb. 1959 (based on *The Enemy: Time*); *Period of Adjustment*, pr. 1959; *The Night of the Iguana*, pr., pb. 1961; *The Milk Train Doesn't Stop Here Anymore*, pr. 1963, revised pb. 1976; *The Eccentricities of a Nightingale*, pr., pb. 1964 (revision of *Summer and Smoke*); *Slapstick Tragedy: "The Mutilated" and "The Gnädiges Fräulein,"* pr. 1966 (one acts); *The Two-Character Play*, pr. 1967; *The Seven Descents of Myrtle*, pr., pb. 1968 (as *Kingdom of Earth*); *In the Bar of a Tokyo Hotel*, pr. 1969; *Confessional*, pb. 1970; *Dragon Country*, pb. 1970 (collection); *The Theatre of Tennessee Williams*, pb. 1971-1981 (7 volumes); *Out Cry*, pr. 1971 (revision of *The Two-Character Play*); *Small Craft Warnings*, pr., pb. 1972 (revision of *Confessional*); *Vieux Carré*, pr. 1977; *A Lovely Sunday for Creve Coeur*, pr. 1979; *Clothes for a Summer Hotel*, pr. 1980; *A House Not Meant to Stand*, pr. 1981; *Something Cloudy, Something Clear*, pr. 1981.

LONG FICTION: *The Roman Spring of Mrs. Stone*, 1950; *Moise and the World of Reason*, 1975.

SHORT FICTION: *One Arm, and Other Stories*, 1948; *Hard Candy: A Book of Stories*, 1954; *The Knightly Quest: A Novella and Four Short Stories*, 1967; *Eight Mortal Ladies Possessed: A Book of Stories*, 1974; *Collected Stories*, 1985.

SCREENPLAYS: *The Glass Menagerie*, 1950 (with Peter Berneis); *A Streetcar Named Desire*, 1951 (with Oscar Saul); *The Rose Tattoo*, 1955 (with Hal Kanter); *Baby Doll*, 1956; *The Fugitive Kind*, 1960 (with Meade Roberts; based on *Orpheus Descending*); *Suddenly Last Summer*, 1960 (with Gore Vidal); *Stopped Rocking, and Other Screenplays*, 1984.

POETRY: *In the Winter of Cities*, 1956; *Androgyne, Mon Amour*, 1977; *The Collected Poems of Tennessee Williams*, 2002.

NONFICTION: *Memoirs*, 1975; *Where I Love: Selected Essays*, 1978; *Five O'Clock Angel: Letters of Tennessee Williams to Maria St. Just, 1948-1982*, 1990; *The Selected Letters of Tennessee Williams, 1920-1945*, 2000.

Tennessee Williams is considered one of the greatest American playwrights, ranking alongside Eugene O'Neill and Arthur Miller. He was born Thomas Lanier Williams, the son of Cornelius Coffin Williams, a traveling salesman, and Edwina Dakin Williams, a minister's daughter. Williams, his mother, and his older sister, Rose, lived with Williams's maternal grandparents until his father was transferred to his firm's main office in St. Louis in 1918. The move was shattering to both Williams and his sister, and it was almost certainly at least partially responsible for Williams's emotional instability and for his sister's retreat from reality—which resulted in a prefrontal lobotomy and institutionalization. *The Glass Menagerie* is an autobiographical representation of two days in the St. Louis years after the children were grown, but it omits the children's father and their younger brother.

Unable to bear life at home, Williams began his lifelong wanderings, though he also attended college at the University of Missouri and Washington University and finally completed a degree at the University of Iowa. He presently attracted the attention of an important literary agent, Audrey Wood, received grants, and, after having written one-act plays, poetry, and short stories, had his first full-length play, *Battle of Angels*, produced in Boston in 1940, where it failed. His first successful play was *The Glass Menagerie*, first produced in Chicago in 1944, where it attracted attention and praise from the critics; after several months it was moved to New York, where it had great success.

Williams's 1947 play *A Streetcar Named Desire* is still considered his greatest, and it won for him his first Pulitzer Prize. Its central character, Blanche Dubois, is one of the best remembered and most vividly characterized in modern drama. The daughter of an aristocratic southern family which has gone downhill for generations and finally lost all of its wealth and its estate, she has become a prostitute, and, after losing her job as a teacher, spends months with her sister and brother-in-law in a New Orleans slum, finally being taken to an insane asylum.

Williams's other most important plays include *Summer and Smoke*, *Camino Real* (though a failure on Broadway), *Cat on a Hot Tin Roof* (for which he won his second Pulitzer), and *The Night of the Iguana*. He continued to write plays after *The Night of the Iguana*, but none had the quality of his earlier plays.

As Williams's *Memoirs* makes clear, he was very frankly homosexual, and over the years he had many companions. Several of his plays (including, in the play's background, *Cat on a Hot Tin Roof*) contain homosexual characters. He continued traveling widely all of his life, his most frequent stopping places being New Orleans, New York, Rome, and Key West, where he owned a home. He died in a New York hotel from choking on a medicine bottle cap.

Williams's more important plays are usually set in the South, either in Mississippi or in New Orleans, the only notable exceptions being *The Glass Menagerie* (St. Louis), *Camino Real* (a mythical Central America), and *The Night of the Iguana* (Mexico). His plays frequently center on three character types: the "gentleman caller" (actually called that in *The Glass Menagerie*), usually a young man, whether "gentleman" or not, who "calls upon" a young woman; a frequently but not invariably innocent and vulnerable young woman; and a usually tougher and more experienced older woman. The pattern is obvious in both *The Glass Menagerie* and *A Streetcar Named Desire*, though in the latter play the tougher woman, Stella, is younger than her vulnerable sister, Blanche, and the gentleman caller, Mitch, is not the most important male character in the play. In *Cat on a Hot Tin Roof*, there is only the tough young woman, whose husband is ironically the opposite of a gentleman caller in that his fear of being homosexual (probably unfounded) has led him to ignore his wife sexually and has led his wife desperately (and perhaps successfully at play's end) to lure, or force, him back.

Williams's best plays are also notable for their use of impressionistic sound and lighting effects: the music from a nearby tavern in *The Glass Menagerie*; the roar of trains passing in *A Streetcar Named Desire*; the spotlight in *The Glass Menagerie*, centering on the seriously upset Laura while her mother and brother quarrel; and Blanche's covering of the naked ceiling light bulb with a shade in her sister's apartment in *A Streetcar Named Desire*. The earlier playwright who was the principal influence on Williams is Anton Chekhov, who is also noted for his impressionism and for presenting characters such as Blanche (and perhaps Amanda in *The Glass Menagerie*), characters who have fallen from the level of significant aristocracy. Yet Williams is also noted for his use of extreme violence, which relates him to the American, and more particularly southern, gothic style, exemplified in the violence in some of the novels of William Faulkner. Examples of such violence in Williams's work include cannibalism in the background of *Suddenly Last Summer* and imminent castration in *Sweet Bird of Youth*.

All Williams's major plays fit the impressionistic, and in general realistic, pattern, except *Camino Real*, which is expressionistic, dealing with both real and fictional characters in a mythical Central America. In that play, people struggle with their inability to give life meaning and their inability to love; a few characters who succeed in overcoming their problems manage to escape. Two of the plays in Williams's major period are comedies: *The Rose Tattoo*, a successful play about a Sicilian woman on the Mississippi coast who is seriously disturbed by the loss of her husband in an accident and who finally finds a man to take his place, and the lightweight and insignificant *Period of Adjustment*.

Jacob H. Adler

Bibliography

Bloom, Harold, ed. *Tennessee Williams*. New York: Chelsea House, 1987. This collection of critical essays carries an introduction by Bloom that places Williams in the dramatic canon of American drama and within the psychological company of Hart Crane and Arthur Rimbaud. Authors in this collection take traditional thematic and historical approaches, noting Williams's "grotesques," his morality, his irony, his work in the "middle years," and the mythical qualities in his situations and characters.

Crandall, George W. *Tennessee Williams: A Descriptive Bibliography*. Pittsburgh: University of Pittsburgh Press, 1995. An important bibliographical source.

Kolin, Philip, ed. *Tennessee Williams: A Guide to Research and Performance*. Westport, Conn.: Greenwood Press, 1998. A helpful collection of twenty-three essays devoted to individual plays except the last three, which are devoted to Williams's fiction, poetry, and films respectively. Contains three indexes that allow the reader easily to locate specific information.

Leverich, Lyle. *Tom: The Unknown Tennessee Williams*. New York: Crown, 1995. Traces Williams's life for the first thirty-three years. Draws on previously unpublished letters, journals, and notebooks. Discusses Williams's focus on how society has a destructive influence on sensitive people and his efforts to change drama into an unrealistic form.

Martin, Robert A., ed. *Critical Essays on Tennessee Williams*. New York: G. K. Hall, 1997. An excellent, accessible collection of criticism of Williams's works.

Pagan, Nicholas. *Rethinking Literary Biography: A Postmodern Approach to Tennessee Williams*. Rutherford, N.J.: Fairleigh Dickinson University Press, 1993. Discusses the symbolism of Williams's characters in relation to his life.

Rader, Dotson. *Tennessee: Cry of the Heart*. Garden City, N.Y.: Doubleday, 1985. A chatty biography that, while it does not have the virtue of notes or a scholarly biography, does have the appeal of a firsthand, fascinating account, filled with gossip and inside information, to be taken for what it is worth.

Roudané, Matthew C., ed. *The Cambridge Companion to Tennessee Williams*. Cambridge, England: Cambridge University Press, 1997. Contains copious amounts of information on Williams and his works.

Spoto, Donald. *The Kindness of Strangers: The Life of Tennessee Williams*. 1985. Reprint. New York: DaCapo Press, 1998. Spoto's lively chronicle details Williams's encounters with such diverse influences as the Group Theatre, Frieda and D. H. Lawrence, Senator Joseph R. McCarthy, Fidel Castro, Hollywood stars, and the homosexual and drug subcultures of Key West. Forty-two pages of notes, bibliography, and index make this study a valuable resource for further scholarship.

Thompson, Judith. *Tennessee Williams' Plays: Memory, Myth, and Symbol*. New York: P. Lang, 2002. A Jungian analysis of Williams's plays, focusing on the manifestation of archetypes in his work.

Tischler, Nancy Marie Patterson. *Student Companion to Tennessee Williams*. Westport, Conn.: Greenwood Press, 2000. A well-known Williams scholar brings together the playwright's biography and critical assessments of his works to provide students with a thorough introduction and appreciation of Williams's achievements.

Williams, Dakin, and Shepherd Mead. *Tennessee Williams: An Intimate Biography*. New York: Arbor House, 1983. One of the more bizarre duos in biographical writing, Williams (Tennessee's brother) and Mead (Tennessee's childhood friend) produce a credible biography in a highly readable, well-indexed work. Their account of the playwright also helps to capture his almost schizophrenic nature. A solid index and extensive research assist the serious scholar and general reader.

Windham, Donald. *As if*. . . Verona, Italy: D. Windham, 1985. This reminiscence of Williams's one-time friend portrays the writer as a man of bizarre contradictions and reveals in telling vignettes the downward spiral of his self-destructive lifestyle.

Woodhouse, Reed. *Unlimited Embrace: A Canon of Gay Fiction, 1945-1995*. Amherst: University of Massachusetts Press, 1998. Includes a chapter on Williams's gay short stories; claims the most astonishing thing about the stories is their lack of special pleading, that while they are not graphic, they are not apologetic for their homosexuality. Provides an extended analysis of the story "Hard Candy."

William Carlos Williams

American poet

Born: Rutherford, New Jersey; September 17, 1883
Died: Rutherford, New Jersey; March 4, 1963

POETRY: *Poems*, 1909; *The Tempers*, 1913; *Al Que Quiere!*, 1917; *Kora in Hell: Improvisations*, 1920; *Sour Grapes*, 1921; *Spring and All*, 1923; *Collected Poems, 1921-1931*, 1934; *An Early Martyr, and Other Poems*, 1935; *Adam & Eve & The City*, 1936; *The Complete Collected Poems of William Carlos Williams, 1906-1938*, 1938; *The Broken Span*, 1941; *The Wedge*, 1944; *Paterson*, 1946-1958; *The Clouds*, 1948; *Selected Poems*, 1949; *Collected Later Poems*, 1950, 1963; *Collected Earlier Poems*, 1951; *The Desert Music, and Other Poems*, 1954; *Journey to Love*, 1955; *Pictures from Brueghel*, 1962; *Selected Poems*, 1985; *The Collected Poems of William Carlos Williams: Volume I, 1909-1939*, 1986; *The Collected Poems of William Carlos Williams: Volume II, 1939-1962*, 1988.

LONG FICTION: *The Great American Novel*, 1923; *A Voyage to Pagany*, 1928; *White Mule*, 1937; *In the Money*, 1940; *The Build-up*, 1952.

SHORT FICTION: *The Knife of the Times, and Other Stories*, 1932; *Life Along the Passaic River*, 1938; *Make Light of It: Collected Stories*, 1950; *The Farmers' Daughters: The Collected Stories of William Carlos Williams*, 1961; *The Doctor Stories*, 1984.

DRAMA: *Many Loves, and Other Plays*, pb. 1961.

NONFICTION: *In the American Grain*, 1925; *A Novelette, and Other Prose*, 1932; *The Autobiography of William Carlos Williams*, 1951; *Selected Essays of William Carlos Williams*, 1954; *The Selected Letters of William Carlos Williams*, 1957; *The Embodiment of Knowledge*,

1974; *A Recognizable Image*, 1978; *William Carlos Williams, John Sanford: A Correspondence*, 1984; *William Carlos Williams and James Laughlin: Selected Letters*, 1989; *Pound/Williams: Selected Letters of Ezra Pound and William Carlos Williams*, 1996 (Hugh Witemeyer, editor).

TRANSLATIONS: *Last Nights of Paris*, 1929 (of Philippe Soupault; with Raquel Hélène Williams); *A Dog and the Fever*, 1954 (of Francisco de Quevedo; with Raquel Hélène Williams).

MISCELLANEOUS: *The Descent of Winter*, 1928 (includes poetry, prose, and anecdotes); *Imaginations*, 1970 (includes poetry, fiction, and nonfiction).

William Carlos Williams was a major American modernist poet to whom recognition came late in his career, and who influenced many subsequent poets in their search for a contemporary voice and form. Williams was born in Rutherford, New Jersey, on September 17, 1883, to a mother born in Puerto Rico and an English father. Both parents figure in a number of Williams's poems. In 1902 Williams began the study of medicine at the University of Pennsylvania and while a student formed important friendships with Ezra Pound and the painter Charles Demuth. In 1910 Williams began his forty-year medical practice in Rutherford, marrying Florence Herman in 1912.

Williams's first book of poems, entitled *Poems* and privately printed by a local stationer, was replete with the kind of archaic poetic diction and romantic longing typical of much American magazine poetry at the time. (In later years, Williams refused to allow the book to be reprinted.) As a result of Pound's directive that he become more aware of avant-garde work in music, painting, prose, and poetry, Williams's next book, *The Tempers*, reflected Pound's pre-Imagist manner—a variety of verse forms, short monologues, and medieval and Latinate allusions. Williams responded with enthusiasm to the Imagist manifestos of 1912 and 1913, and much of his subsequent poetry reflects the Imagist emphasis upon concrete presentation, concision, and avoidance of conventional rhythms. Williams developed these principles in his own way, arguing that the new conditions of America itself and the primitive state of its literature demanded eschewing European literary conventions and traditions, and developing an American poetics of international standard, yet expressive of the American language and landscape. *Al Que Quiere!* reflects Williams's working out of these and associated strategies, his developing an aesthetic that insists upon the ultimately creative reward of despair and destruction, and the importance of passionately engaging the object world of the native landscape with a kind of preconscious energy that breaks the conventions of perceptual habit. The 1920's volumes *Sour Grapes*, *Spring and All*, and *The Descent of Winter* (the latter two works can be found in the collection *Imaginations*) bring these concerns to fruition.

After 1913, Williams formed friendships with a number of important writers and painters working in and around New York, including Marsden Hartley, Wallace Stevens, and Charles Sheeler. He saw his hopes for native expression confirmed by the arrival in New York of such major modernist figures as Marcel Duchamp and Francis Picabia at the time of World War I. He was doubly disappointed in the early 1920's by the exodus of these figures and many American artists to Paris and by the success of T. S. Eliot's *The Waste Land* (1922). Both events signified to Williams the triumph of the international school of modernism against which he had spiritedly set himself in the 1918 "Prologue" to his *Kora in Hell*.

Williams labored on his writing for the next twenty years, largely unrecognized except by readers of the short-lived small magazines that printed experimental American work. What some critics consider Williams's finest book, the prose and poetry sequence *Spring and All*, was printed in Paris in an edition of only three hundred and not reprinted in full until 1970, seven years after his death. The sequential format suggesting multiple but loosely linked relationships among the twenty-seven poems and interspersed prose illustrates Williams's inventiveness on the levels of individual poems and overall formal structure. This book contains the famous "The Red Wheelbarrow," later printed by Williams as a separate poem, and often anthologized as the quintessential Imagist expression.

In the 1930's, Williams's work took a more overtly political turn, although he had always shared the view of Pound and Eliot that the work of the poet was central to the health and potential of a civilization and that the state of a culture was reflected in its response to its serious artists. These concerns form a central theme of *Paterson*, his long poem initially conceived and published in four books (1946 to 1951; Williams added a fifth book in 1958). The past and present of this New Jersey city are examined in a collagelike mix of poetry and prose—including newspaper accounts, histories, and letters Williams himself received while writing the work—to dramatize the lack of creative response to the rich potential of the landscape. The theme is an extension of that in Williams's book of historical essays, *In the American Grain*. Paterson's once-famous falls serves as a central motif representing the unrealized promise of native language and expression, its insistent and ever-present roar ignored amid the scenes of exploitation, sterile love affairs, and mindless escapism documented throughout the poem.

In 1951 Williams suffered the first of a series of strokes that forced him to retire from medicine and, gradually, came to affect his vision and typing ability. Williams's restricted life, and his severe depression of 1952 to 1953, color the tone and subject matter of the poems in *The Desert Music* and *Journey to Love*. These poems are written in the three-step line Williams had initially used in part of the second volume of *Paterson*, and many of his critical statements of the 1950's are concerned with his concepts of the "variable foot" and "the American idiom" behind this development in his poetics. Essentially, both concepts are restatements of his career-long concern with a nonliterary language to treat the local American scene and a rejection of the conventional rhythms and forms of English poetry. Nevertheless, the descending three-step line proves an ideal structural and visual form for these more meditative poems, many of which delve into memory to discover formerly unrealized significance. Williams's major achievement of these years is generally considered "Asphodel, That Greeny Flower"—a poem of reconciliation to Florence Williams, considered by W. H. Auden "one of the most beautiful love poems in the language."

Never one to rest in any one mode, for his final book of poems, *Pictures from Brueghel*, Williams returned to the more concentrated, pictorial strategies of his early career. The book was awarded the Pulitzer Prize in poetry shortly after the poet's death.

In the 1950's, Williams became an important figure for poets seeking an alternative to the neoclassical poetics of T. S. Eliot and his followers, and such figures as Robert Lowell, Allen Ginsberg, and Denise Levertov acknowledged a large debt to his example. Since that decade, too, Williams's career-long achievement has gradually come to be more and more fully recognized. Although still not accorded the status of Eliot and Stevens by some critics of modernism, on the whole these two—along with Williams and Pound—are considered the four major figures of American modernist poetry.

Christopher MacGowan

Bibliography

Axelrod, Steven Gould, and Helen Deese, eds. *Critical Essays on William Carlos Williams*. New York: G. K. Hall, 1995. A solid collection of essays.

Beck, John. *Writing the Radical Center: William Carlos Williams, John Dewey, and American Cultural Politics*. Albany: State University of New York Press, 2001. Analyzes Williams's political convictions as reflected in his writings, and compares them with those of philosopher John Dewey.

Bremen, Brian A. *William Carlos Williams and the Diagnostics of Culture*. New York: Oxford University Press, 1993. An examination of the development of Williams's poetry, focused on his fascination with the effects of poetry and prose, and his friendship with Kenneth Burke. Looks at how the methodological empiricism in Williams's poetic strategy is tied to his medical practice.

Fisher-Wirth, Ann W. *William Carlos Williams and Autobiography: The Woods of His Own Nature*. University Park: Pennsylvania State University Press, 1989. Considers the autobiographical aspects of certain works by Williams. Adds new insight into Williams's conception of the self and its relationship to the world. Supplemented by thorough notes and an index.

Gish, Robert. *William Carlos Williams: A Study of the Short Fiction*. Boston: Twayne, 1989. A very fine single-volume study of Williams's substantial contributions to the short story and the essay.

Laughlin, James. *Remembering William Carlos Williams*. New York: New Directions, 1995. The founder of the publishing firm New Directions excerpts his *Byways* verse memoir of the many poets he has published over the years, capturing both humorous and poignant memories of poet-physician Williams.

Lenhart, Gary, ed. *The Teachers and Writers Guide to William Carlos Williams*. New York: Teachers & Writers Collaborative, 1998. Offers more than a dozen practical and innovative essays on using Williams's work to inspire writing by students and adults, including the use of both his classics and his neglected later poems.

Lowney, John. *The American Avant-Garde Tradition: William Carlos Williams, Postmodern Poetry, and the Politics of Cultural Memory*. Lewisburg, Pa.: Bucknell University Press, 1997. A good examination of postmodernism and Williams's poetry and literature.

Mariani, Paul. *William Carlos Williams: A New World Naked*. 1981. Reprint. New York: W. W. Norton, 1990. Essential reading; a thorough and insightful biography.

Vendler, Helen, ed. *Voices and Visions: The Poet in America*. New York: Random House, 1987. A well-written introduction to the American literary modernists. Includes a substantial chapter on Williams. This book is tied to the Public Broadcasting Service television series of the same name.

Whitaker, Thomas R. *William Carlos Williams*. Boston: Twayne, 1989. This work provides a useful key to Williams's writing. The primary focus of Whitaker's study is the works themselves and not Williams's biographical or literary history. Includes a chronology, a selected bibliography, and an index.

David Williamson

Australian playwright and screenwriter

Born: Melbourne, Australia; February 24, 1942

DRAMA: *The Coming of Stork*, pr. 1970, pb. 1974; *The Removalists*, pr. 1971; *Don's Party*, pr. 1971; *Jugglers Three*, pr. 1972; *What If You Died Tomorrow*, pr. 1973; *The Department*, pr. 1974; *A Handful of Friends*, pr., pb. 1976; *The Club*, pr. 1977 (in U.S. as *Players*); *Travelling North*, pr. 1979; *Celluloid Heroes*, pr. 1980; *The Perfectionist*, pr. 1982; *Sons of Cain*, pr. 1985; *Collected Plays*, pb. 1986 (includes *The Coming of Stork, The Removalists, Don's Party, Jugglers Three*, and *What If You Died Tomorrow*); *Emerald City*, pr., pb. 1987; *Top Silk*, pr., pb. 1989; *Siren*, pr. 1990; *Money and Friends*, pr., pb. 1992; *Brilliant Lies*, pr., pb. 1993; *Sanctuary*, pr., pb. 1994; *Dead White Males*, pr., pb. 1995; *Heretic: Based on the Life of Derek Freeman*, pr., pb. 1996; *After the Ball*, pr., pb. 1997; *Third World Blues*, pr., pb. 1997 (revision of *Jugglers Three*); *Corporate Vibes*, pr., pb. 1999; *Face to Face*, pr., pb. 1999; *The Great Man*, pr., pb. 2000; *Up for Grabs*, pr., pb. 2000; *Soulmates*, pr. 2002.

SCREENPLAYS: *Stork*, 1971 (adaptation of *The Coming of Stork*); *Petersen*, 1974; *The Removalists*, 1974 (adaptation of his play); *Don's Party*, 1976 (adaptation of his play); *Eliza Frazer*, 1976; *The Club*, 1980 (adaptation of his play); *Gallipoli*, 1981; *Partners*, 1981; *The Year of Living Dangerously*, 1982 (with C. J. Koch and Peter Weir; adaptation of Koch's novel); *Pharlap*, 1984; *Travelling North*, 1986 (adaptation of his play); *Emerald City*, 1988 (adaptation of his play); *Sanctuary*, 1995 (adaptation of his play); *Brilliant Lies*, 1997 (adaptation of his play).

TELEPLAYS: *The Department*, 1980; *The Last Bastion*, 1984 (miniseries; with Denis Whitburn); *The Club*, 1986; *The Four-Minute Mile*, 1988 (miniseries); *Princess Kate*, 1988 (miniseries); *The Perfectionist*, 1995; *Dogs Head Bay*, 1999.

NONFICTION: "*The Removalists:* A Conjunction of Limitations," 1974 (in *Meanjin*); "The Australian Image," 1981 (in *Counterpoint*); "Men, Women, and Human Nature," 1996 (in *Double Take*).

David Keith Williamson once described himself as "bourgeois . . . the product of a middle-class environment." However, the world he now knows as an internationally acclaimed playwright and screenwriter has taken him far afield from his provincial background. Born in 1942, Williamson spent his early years in a Melbourne suburb and his adolescence in a country town where his father worked in a bank. Williamson graduated from Monash University, Melbourne, with a degree in mechanical engineering. After a year at the General Motors plant, he started teaching in the engineering department of Melbourne's Swinburne College of Technology.

Even as he was pursuing a scientific education, however, he had devoted time and energy to writing and producing college revues. At that point he found the idea of becoming a writer appealing, but his "bourgeois" side kept him in the safe field of engineering. While lecturing at the technical college, he also studied psychology at the University of Melbourne and eventually began teaching the subject at Swinburne. He continued to write, and in 1968 he saw his first full-length play on stage; this work, *The Indecent Exposure of Anthony East*, has not been published.

In 1970, *The Coming of Stork* was produced in Melbourne. In 1971 two more plays, *The Removalists* and *Don's Party*, were produced in Melbourne and later in London. *The Removalists*, an absurdist drama concerned with gratuitous violence, remains one of Williamson's most durable works.

The enthusiastic reception of these plays set Williamson on his way to becoming Australia's premier dramatist, one who would help change the course of the Australian theater. Long dependent on world (mainly British and American) drama, Australians generally ignored plays by their own writers. Such is no longer the case, and Williamson played an important role in this theatrical revolution.

Williamson and his first wife, Carol Cranby, were divorced in 1972. Two years later he married Kristin Green, a journalist, and they moved from Melbourne to Sydney, the more sophisticated and internationally oriented of the two cities. Overcoming the temptation of many successful Australian writers to migrate to New York or London, Williamson remained in Australia, where he continues to be active in numerous organizations that fund and promote the arts. A modest, unassuming man, he carries his success lightly and epitomizes the professional writer entirely devoted to his craft. The popularity of his work, both in Australia and abroad, has engendered criticism from some of his fellow playwrights, who have accused him of selling out to mainstream audiences and turning away from the alternative theater that served him so well at the beginning of his career.

Whatever the case, Williamson's plays speak boldly to Australians, in particular to the urban middle class, which makes up the largest part of Australia's inhabitants. Each play resonates with "Australianness": the language drawn from the vernacular, the theme focusing on a local concern, and the milieu, exact in its representation. Critics have pointed out that the plays reflect the social, cultural, and political changes in Australia during Williamson's career. Yet a drama like *The Club*, about behind-the-scenes maneuvering in a Melbourne professional sports team, played successfully in London and on Broadway. A keen observer of the human condition, Williamson writes about the world he knows, primarily that of Sydney, a teeming city perched on the edge of a vast, empty continent. At the same time, however, he has caught an elusive universality in his work. *Travelling North*, for example, examines the circumstances of aging, hardly an exclusive Australian plight. Both as a play and as a film (the screenplay by Williamson), *Travelling North*, like all of his work, transcends its locale.

Williamson's most widely known screenplay, *Gallipoli*, focuses on the role of Australia in World War I, when its soldiers met senseless deaths defending the indefensible. He also collaborated in adapting *The Year of Living Dangerously*—a novel written by fellow Australian C. J. Koch—for the screen; the film was directed by another countryman, Peter Weir. Williamson has been involved as well in television projects for both Australian and international networks. One noteworthy series, *The Last Bastion*, was written in collaboration with Denis Whitburn. This historical account depicts Australia's dangerous predicament during World War II, when Great Britain deserted its colony. Born in the midst of the war in 1942, when Japanese invasion of Australia seemed likely, Williamson might well have wondered as he re-created the events what course his life would have taken had things unfolded differently. For that matter, had the self-professed "bourgeois" Williamson continued in his engineering or teaching career, both his life and the condition of the Australian theater would be far different—and far less rich.

Robert L. Ross

Bibliography

Carroll, Dennis. "David Williamson." In *Australian Contemporary Drama, 1909-1982*. New York: Peter Lang, 1985. Focuses on Williamson's depiction of the "ocker"—the stereotypical Australian male proud to be a colonial bumpkin—loud, rude, uncouth, uncultured, and generally obnoxious. A limited discussion.

Fitzpatrick, Peter. "Styles of Love: New Directions in David Williamson." In *Contemporary Australian Drama*, edited by Peter Holloway. Rev. ed. Sydney: Currency Press, 1987. In addition to discussing Williamson's early plays, the article explores the playwright's reputation and the criticism that his work is repetitious and slick, charges made against him all through his career.

_______. *Williamson*. North Ryde, Australia: Methuen Australia, 1987. Describes Williamson as a "storyteller to the tribe" and "a shaper of cultural images." Uses this approach to analyze the plays to *The Perfectionist*, focusing on their handling of "ockerism," meaningful human relationships, and public institutions. The appendices provide a chronology of Williamson's career and a survey of the plays in performance. Select bibliography.

Kiernan, Brian. *David Williamson: A Writer's Career.* Melbourne, Australia: Heinemann, 1990. Rev. ed. Paddington, Australia: Currency Press, 1996. Called a "critical biography," this comprehensive study chronicles Williamson's personal life along with his development as a writer. Discusses each of the plays, providing background on productions as well as interpretation. Provides extensive information on Williamson's film and television career. Bibliographical materials. Most complete work on Williamson.

_______. "David Williamson: Satiric Comedies." In *International Literature in English: Essays on the Major Writers*, edited by Robert Ross. New York: Garland Press, 1991. Contains a biographical sketch, an essay on the plays through 1989, a primary bibliography, and an annotated secondary bibliography. Kiernan argues that while the plays are highly "accessible" on any level, they exceed both satire and comedy to combine those forms into an original drama with a rare "human dimension."

Montesano, A. P. "A Dangerous Life." *American Film* 13 (November, 1988): 8. Examines "A Dangerous Life," the documentary about the fall of the Ferdinand Marcos regime, and compares it to Williamson's screenplay, *The Year of Living Dangerously*.

Zuber-Skerritt, Ortrun, ed. *David Williamson*. Amsterdam: Rodopi, 1988. Offers excerpts from selected talks and articles by, and interviews with, Williamson. Provides an extensive bibliography of newspaper and magazine articles as well as international reviews.

Henry Williamson

English novelist

Born: Brockley, near Lewisham, England; December 1, 1895
Died: London, England; August 13, 1977

LONG FICTION: *The Beautiful Years*, 1921; *Dandelion Days*, 1922; *The Dream of Fair Women*, 1924; *The Pathway*, 1928 (the 4 previous volumes known collectively as *The Flax of Dreams*, 1936); *Tarka the Otter*, 1927; *The Star-Born*, 1933; *Salar the Salmon*, 1935; *The Phasian Bird*, 1948; *The Dark Lantern*, 1951; *Donkey Boy*, 1952; *Young Phillip Madison*, 1953; *How Dear Is Life*, 1954; *A Fox Under My Cloak*, 1955; *The Golden Virgin*, 1957; *Love and the Loveless*, 1958; *A Test to Destruction*, 1960; *The Innocent Moon*, 1961; *It Was the Nightingale*, 1962; *The Power of the Dead*, 1963; *The Phoenix Generation*, 1965; *A Solitary War*, 1966; *Lucifer Before Sunrise*, 1967; *The Gale of the World*, 1969 (the 15 previous volumes known collectively as *A Chronicle of Ancient Sunlight*); *The Scandaroon*, 1972.

SHORT FICTION: *The Old Stag*, 1926; *Tales of Moorland and Estuary*, 1953; *The Henry Williamson Animal Saga*, 1960; *Collected Nature Stories*, 1970, 1995.

NONFICTION: *The Story of a Norfolk Farm*, 1941; *Life in a Devon Village*, 1945; *Tales of a Devon Village*, 1945; *A Clear Water Stream*, 1958; *Spring Days in Devon, and Other Broadcasts*, 1992; *Pen and Plough: Further Broadcasts*, 1993.

EDITED TEXTS: *Anthology of Modern Nature Writing*, 1936; *Richard Jefferies: Selections from His Work*, 1937.

Henry Williamson's lonely childhood was spent in a Bedfordshire house that had belonged to his family for more than four centuries. During his formative years he read and admired the writings of Richard Jefferies, who thus provided the inspiration for his later work. When World War I began Williamson enlisted; he was then nineteen. He served throughout the war in Flanders, where some of the bitterest fighting occurred and casualties were appalling. He returned to civilian life with gray hair and shattered nerves in 1920. Completely unable to cope with the hectic pettiness of the life around him, he attempted to earn a living as a reporter for the *Weekly Dispatch*, but he was forced to give up the position. He then tried to eke out an existence on his pension, which provided the meager income of forty pounds a year; this was supplemented by small sums received for nature articles that he contributed weekly to the *Daily Express*. He slept in haystacks in the nearby countryside or under trees on the Thames embankment. He was depressed and morbid, and he contemplated suicide. He had almost reached the end of his tether when he decided to abandon his impossible urban existence. He walked to Devonshire and settled down in a cottage at Exmoor to complete his first novel. As time passed, he found it possible to earn a living with his pen, and he found contentment in his rural surroundings. His work was admired by such famous writers as Walter de la Mare, Arnold Bennett, Thomas Hardy, and T. E. Lawrence. His nature novel *Tarka the Otter* won the Hawthornden Prize in 1927 and brought him widespread recognition; it has remained a modern nature classic. Two of his later books, *Salar the Salmon* and *The Phasian Bird*, the story of a pheasant, are considered equally significant.

Although Williamson was a prolific and successful writer, much of his work has not been issued in the United States. Nevertheless, he is widely regarded as one of the most gifted of nature writers; his novels reveal the lives of wild creatures from their own viewpoints, as evoked by a mind of deep insight and understanding. His somber prose transmits, faithfully, the eternal struggle of living things to survive and with it a deep awareness of the transitory fragility of life.

In his later years, he returned to the themes of his first series of novels, known collectively as *The Flax of Dreams*, which concerns an idealistic young officer who seeks to understand the causes of war. In *A Chronicle of Ancient Sunlight*, a vast, autobiographical series of fifteen novels, he updates his themes into the 1950's and reaches a happier conclusion. His accounts of rural life in Devon and Norfolk have also retained some of their popularity.

David Barratt

Bibliography

Caron, Sue. *A Glimpse of the Ancient Sunlight: Memories of Williamson*. Wirral, England: Aylesford, 1986.

Cook, Don. "The Great War and Its Effect on Henry Williamson." *Contemporary Review* 244 (June, 1984).

Farson, Daniel. *Henry Williamson: A Portrait*. London: Robinson, 1986.

Fullager, Brian. "Henry Williamson and the Battle of the Somme." *T. E. Lawrence Newsletter* 2, no. 9 (November, 1991).

Lamplugh, Lois. *The Shadowed Man: Williamson, 1895-1977*. Swimbridge, Devon, England: Wellspring, 1990.

Williamson, Anne. *Henry Williamson: Tarka and the Last Romantic*. Stroud, Gloucestershire, England: Alan Sutton, 1995.

_______. *A Patriot's Progress: Henry Williamson and the First World War*. Stroud, Gloucestershire, England: Sutton, 1998.

Ellen Willis

American essayist

Born: New York, New York; December 14, 1941
Identity: Jewish

NONFICTION: *Beginning to See the Light: Pieces of a Decade*, 1981 (also known as *Beginning to See the Light: Sex, Hope, and Rock and Roll*); *No More Nice Girls: Countercultural Essays*, 1992; *Don't Think, Smile! Notes on a Decade of Denial*, 1999.

The writings of Ellen Jane Willis trace the history of some of the leading social and political questions from the 1960's through the 1990's: popular music and culture, social and political revolution, feminism, and civil liberties. A continuing theme in her writing is the tension between individual freedom and the liberation of oppressed groups, with an attempt to maximize both wherever possible. This approach has placed her squarely on the anticensorship side of the feminist debate over whether pornography or censorship is the greater problem, and she is probably best known for her writings on this question.

Willis was born in 1941. She often mentions in her essays how unusual she felt, growing up as the daughter of a liberal Jewish police officer. After graduation from Barnard College in 1962 and two years of graduate study at Berkeley, she began writing rock criticism.

Her early writings view rock and roll as a liberating, sexually energizing force, with such figures as Bob Dylan and the Who as heroes. But by the late 1960's, she had become more aware of the sexism and commercialism behind the music, and her writing, as in "Cultural Revolution Saved from Drowning," an account of the Woodstock festival, reflects an effort to include this awareness without losing sight of the liberating power of the music.

In general her writing became more political, and specifically feminist, in the late 1960's. With Shulamith Firestone, she started the Redstockings, one of the most influential of the feminist groups of that time. She saw her approach at that time as an attempt to apply the class analysis of the Left to women as a class, while remaining concerned with the cultural oppression of both sexes that forced everyone into overly constrained roles.

Her essays in the 1970's showed the range of her concerns. On one hand, she sought sexual freedom for women and men alike, exploring the range of sexual possibilities in "Classical and Baroque Sex in Everyday Life" (1979). On the other, she was aware of the dangers of this approach, particularly to women, and in "The Trial of Arline Hunt" (1979), she reported on the case of a woman who was raped by a man she had met in a singles bar. Hunt brought the case to trial, but she had to watch as her assailant was acquitted—the jury apparently believing that any woman who stepped outside the bounds of traditional double-standard roles was "fair game." One can see the beginning of Willis's role in the feminist censorship debate in her essay "Hard to Swallow: *Deep Throat*," in which she expresses her revulsion at the pornographic film while making clear that she could find liberation and even arousal in an equally explicit film that would better reflect women's concerns. These essays were collected, along with thoughts on such subjects as Herbert Marcuse, abortion rights, and "The Myth of the Powerful Jew," in *Beginning to See the Light*.

In the 1980's, Willis continued to write on a broad variety of topics—cultural, sexual, and political. Her articles, collected in *No More Nice Girls*, show this range. In the ironically titled "Escape from New York," she describes a bus tour of the United States, visiting old friends and meeting the inhabitants of the heartland, and finally expresses her relief at returning to New York City. "Exile on Main Street: What the Pollard Case Means to Jews" (1987), returns to the question of the relationship of the Jews to the radical Left and to the United States in general, in the light of the first person convicted of spying on the United States for Israel. "Putting Women Back in the Abortion Debate" (1985), looks at the missing element in many discussions of fetuses and their status. "In Defense of Offense: Salman Rushdie's Religious Problem" (1989), excoriates the sort of "pluralism" which emphasizes the rights of small groups to oppress their own members.

The 1980's were a time of cultural fragmentation, much of it in the name of "identity politics"; one consequence was the division of women and feminists along the same lines of class, race, and sexual orientation that were dividing the country as a whole. Much of Willis's energy was devoted to healing such rifts in the women's movement. In "Sisters Under the Skin" (1982), she attempted to address the concerns of black feminists such as Michelle Wallace, Gloria Joseph, and Bell Hooks. "Radical Feminism and Feminist Radicalism" (1984), traces the history of feminism since the 1960's.

The issue in which Willis is most notably involved is that of feminist sexuality, as discussed in a major essay, specifically rewritten for *No More Nice Girls:* "Toward a Feminist Sexual Revolution." In 1982 Willis and other feminists of similar viewpoint organized a conference on feminism and sexuality at Barnard College. A group of antipornography feminists picketed the conference and persuaded the college to confiscate conference materials on the grounds that they encouraged pornography, if they were not themselves pornographic. Willis insists that the placement of pornography at the center of the feminist worldview comes from a traditionalist view of sexuality which it shares with right-wing conservatism: Male sexuality is demandingly genital, while proper women see sex only in terms of nurturance, and hence must be protected from the bestial lusts of the male. Willis's eloquent feminism, incorporating insights from other liberal and radical approaches, makes her an important social critic.

Arthur D. Hlavaty

Bibliography

Aronowitz, Stanley. *Roll over Beethoven: The Return of Cultural Strife*. Hanover, N.H.: Wesleyan University Press, 1993. Aronowitz's novel and cogently argued thesis is that Willis and other rock critics of the 1960's were inventing a cultural studies approach similar to the one that had developed in Great Britain since World War II. He uses Willis as a prime example of these writers' abilities to find meaningful aesthetic and social values in pop culture.

Featherstone, Liza. "The Joy of Sex." *The Nation*, October 4, 1993, pp. 360-363. Reviews *No More Nice Girls*.

Levinson, Nan. "Unconventional Wisdom." *The Women's Review of Books* 17 (October, 1999): 1-3. Reviews *Don't Think, Smile!*

Scialabba, George. "Entrapments of Modernity." *Dissent* 46 (Fall, 1999): 101-105. Thorough review of *Don't Think, Smile!* also offers a good overview of Willis's career and thought.

A. N. Wilson

English novelist and critic

Born: Stone, Staffordshire, England; October 27, 1950

LONG FICTION: *The Sweets of Pimlico*, 1977; *Unguarded Hours*, 1978; *Kindly Light*, 1979; *The Healing Art*, 1980; *Who Was Oswald Fish?*, 1981; *Wise Virgin*, 1982; *Scandal*, 1983; *Gentlemen in England*, 1985; *Love Unknown*, 1986; *Incline Our Hearts*, 1988; *A Bottle in the Smoke*, 1990; *Daughters of Albion*, 1991; *The Vicar of Sorrows*, 1993; *Hearing Voices*, 1995; *A Watch in the Night: Being the Conclusion of the Lampitt Chronicles*, 1996; *Dream Children*, 1998.

NONFICTION: *The Laird of Abbotsford: A View of Sir Walter Scott*, 1980; *The Life of John Milton*, 1983; *Hilaire Belloc*, 1984; *How Can We Know?*, 1985; *Pen Friends from Porlock*, 1988; *Tolstoy*, 1988; *Eminent Victorians*, 1989; *C. S. Lewis*, 1990; *Jesus*, 1992; *The Rise and Fall of the House of Windsor*, 1993; *Paul: The Mind of the Apostle*, 1997; *God's Funeral: The Decline of Faith in Western Civilization*, 1999.

CHILDREN'S/YOUNG ADULT LITERATURE: *Stray*, 1987; *The Tabitha Stories*, 1988; *Hazel the Guinea Pig*, 1989.

EDITED TEXTS: *The Faber Book of Church and Clergy*, 1992; *The Faber Book of London*, 1993.

The British have had a long and distinguished line of satirical novelists intent upon putting society in its place. It began almost as soon as the novel in the works of Henry Fielding in the eighteenth century, continues in the works of Tobias Smollett, and was carried on in the novels of Charles Dickens. This tradition reached its most elegant expression in the early twentieth century with Evelyn Waugh, who has been succeeded first by Kingsley Amis and second by Andrew Norman Wilson. Wilson carries on the tradition within a much wider career as scholar, essayist, social critic, and sometime religious commentator.

Wilson's wittily jaundiced eye for the middle to the upper classes of Britain is consistent with his own social background. He was educated at the lower-school level at one of the great English public schools, Rugby School, and went on from there to New College, Oxford. He was a prizewinning student and has had a career as an academic at Oxford University. He has also been rewarded for his literary work, winning the John Llewelyn Rhys Memorial Prize in 1978 for *The Sweets of Pimlico* and in 1980 for *The Laird of Abbotsford*, the Somerset Maugham Award and the Arts Council National Book Award in 1981 for *The Healing Art*, the W. H. Smith Annual Literary Award in 1983 for *Wise Virgin*, and the Whitbread Prize for Best Biography for *Tolstoy*. Wilson is a fellow of the Royal Society of Literature. He is married and has two daughters.

Wilson is also a public personality, partly because of his further career as a journalist, writing for the quality press of England. He has had a long association with *The Spectator*, the conservative weekly journal of political comment, literary review, and social attack, often of a scurrilously witty stamp. Indeed, it is necessary to understand a peculiar mark of social satire in that it is not necessarily confined to writing of a liberal or leftish bent and can often be at its best in the hands of writers who espouse old social structures and old social values. Jonathan Swift was not a liberal, but he was devastatingly sensitive to the excesses of his society. Wilson, if less powerful than Swift, has strong inclinations to looking upon society as debased and sloppy in its political leanings to the left, but he is also aware of how badly responsible aspects of conservative power misuse their opportunities. A novel such as *The Healing Art* exposes, with mordant wittiness, the slipshod irresponsibilities of the medical profession, and *Scandal* looks balefully at the immodest and often stupid behavior of politicians.

Wilson has never been simply one kind of novelist. The early novel *The Sweets of Pimlico* is hardly satiric at all although it deals with upper-middle-class social life in the center of London. It has a kind of offbeat comic zaniness about it which might have been taken as the beginning of an exclusively comic career, and his two religious novels, *Unguarded Hours* and *Kindly Light* (which ought to be read as one), if touched with a scrupulously detailed awareness of the shambles of modern Christianity, are so cheerfully forgiving that the satire might well be missed without too much damage. Wilson also uses black comedy as in *Wise Virgin*, in which an irascible blind scholar gets what he deserves for being an emotional thug, but in *The Healing Art* that inclination to run a sick joke into the ground is distinctly unpleasant and upsetting. What is always a pleasure is the way in which he brings his enthusiasms into his art. His deep affection for Anglicanism as it used to be, his general concern for the failing Christian church can produce a sensitive, sensible discussion in *How Can We Know?* or can be made an integral part of his deliberately old-fashioned fake Victorian work, *Gentlemen in England*, which is a fond re-creation of London life in the 1870's, historically accurate and stylistically as bloated as a Victorian sofa.

Scandal and *Love Unknown* have that easy, sophisticated capacity to scent out the fools and villains of the English class system, but his 1988 novel, *Incline Our Hearts*, setting out to look like a satire on the misery which the affluent English impose on their children by sending them away to school, turns into a tale of *Doppelgänger* intrigue in which the narrator begins to explore the nature of his real personality. Wilson returned to this set of characters, with more emotional development, in *A Bottle in the Smoke*, *Daughters of Albion*, *Hearing Voices*, and *A Watch in the Night*, a series he terms the Lampitt Chronicles. The focal character, Julian Ramsey, makes his way through prep school, public school, the National Service, and ultimately becomes an actor over a time span reaching from the 1930's to the early twenty-first century. Wilson's other novels of this period, *Dream Children* and *The Vicar of Sorrows*, are more intensively serious. The first deals with pedophilia, portraying the sexual relationship of an adult philosopher and a prepubescent girl, while the second deals with the crisis of faith faced by a married Anglican clergyman after his mother dies and he falls in love with a New Age traveller.

Wilson is also a critic but not a pedant. His essays on literature and his critical biographies fall into a civilized area between the popular works of oversimplification and the barbarisms of academic footnoting and hairsplitting. His conservatism reveals itself as a generous civility tempered by a sense that he would not suffer fools gladly. He would, however, address them with gentlemanly fastidiousness and style.

Charles Pullen

Bibliography

Atlas, James. "'A Busy, Busy Wasp.'" *The New York Times Magazine*, October 18, 1992, pp. 34-40. A profile presaging Wilson's *Jesus*.

CSL: The Bulletin of the New York C. S. Lewis Society 10, no. 8/9 (June/July, 1990): 1-16. Introduction is by Jerry L. Daniel, and articles are by John Fitzpatrick, George Sayer, and Eugene McGovern. The entire issue is devoted to reviews of Wilson's 1990 biography of C. S. Lewis, which are mostly unfavorable because of disagreement with his biographical approach and speculative interpretation.

Landrum, David W. "Is There Life After Jesus? Spiritual Perception in A. N. Wilson's *The Vicar of Sorrows*." *Christianity and Literature* 44 (Spring/Summer, 1995): 359-368. A discussion of Wilson's first novel after he declared his unbelief in Christianity. Wilson deals much more seriously here with the problem of evil and other difficult religious questions than in his other fiction.

Weales, Gerald. "Jesus Who?" *The Gettysburg Review* 6, no. 4 (Autumn, 1993): 688-696. A comparison of Gore Vidal's treatment of Christ in his novel *Live from Golgotha* (1992) to Wilson's treatment of Christ in *Jesus*.

Weinberg, Jacob. "A. N. Wilson: Prolific to a Fault." *Newsweek* 112 (September 13, 1988): 75. A short but well-written essay, interspersed with comments by Wilson, on his novels and biographies. Also concerns Wilson as a "Young Fogey," a term used to describe young members of the Conservative party in England.

Wolfe, Gregory. "Off Center, on Target." *Chronicles* 10, no. 10 (1986): 35-36. Wolfe's essay concerns Wilson's affinities with Evelyn Waugh, particularly in terms of their style and in their perspectives on Western Christianity. Sees Wilson as in the tradition of P. G. Wodehouse, who epitomized the light comic novel, but in Wilson's hands that novel becomes a vehicle for satire and social criticism.

Angus Wilson

English novelist and short-story writer

Born: Bexhill, East Sussex, England; August 11, 1913
Died: Bury St. Edmunds, Suffolk, England; June 1, 1991

LONG FICTION: *Hemlock and After*, 1952; *Anglo-Saxon Attitudes*, 1956; *The Middle Age of Mrs. Eliot*, 1958; *The Old Men at the Zoo*, 1961; *Late Call*, 1964; *No Laughing Matter*, 1967; *As If by Magic*, 1973; *Setting the World on Fire*, 1980.

SHORT FICTION: *The Wrong Set, and Other Stories*, 1949; *Such Darling Dodos, and Other Stories*, 1950; *A Bit off the Map, and Other Stories*, 1957; *Death Dance: Twenty-five Stories*, 1969.

DRAMA: *The Mulberry Bush*, pr., pb. 1956.

NONFICTION: *Émile Zola: An Introductory Study of His Novels*, 1952; *For Whom the Cloche Tolls: A Scrapbook of the Twenties*, 1953 (with Philippe Jullian); *The Wild Garden: Or, Speaking of Writing*, 1963; *Tempo: The Impact of Television on the Arts*, 1964; *The World of Charles Dickens*, 1970; *The Strange Ride of Rudyard Kipling*, 1977; *Diversity and Depth in Fiction: Selected Critical Writings of Angus Wilson*, 1983 (Kerry McSweeney, editor); *Reflections in a Writer's Eye: Travel Pieces*, 1986.

Angus Frank Johnstone Wilson was born on the south coast of England in the small resort town of Bexhill, not far from Brighton. He was the last child of William and Maude Johnstone-Wilson. His father was a Londoner but descended from a wealthy Scottish family; his mother came from South Africa. The youngest of six brothers, the next oldest being thirteen years his senior, Angus was reared in adult company and was a lonely, highly imaginative, and even more highly strung youngster. Childhood has always loomed large in his fiction, but it was not until *Setting the World on Fire* that Wilson wrote a novel that approached a *Bildungsroman*; it is a story about two brothers growing up in postwar England. Though his heroes are not typically teenagers or young men, his work is very concerned with young people both in his short fiction and in novels such as *No Laughing Matter* and *As If by Magic*.

Although the elder Johnstone-Wilsons had once been affluent, the postwar period saw them, like many others, fallen on harder times. Their shabby genteel existence colored Angus's earliest years as the family moved from hotel to hotel, often only a step or two ahead of their creditors. If his mother does not appear directly in his fiction, his father often does, especially in the early stories, as a kind of raffish old sport—for example, in the character of Mr. Gorringe in "A Story of Historical Interest" or Trevor in "The Wrong Set." Wilson's sympathies with women other than his mother, whom he dearly loved, appear otherwise in extended portraits, such as those of Meg Eliot in *The Middle Age of Mrs. Eliot* and Sylvia Calvert in *Late Call*. Both of these women confront the bleak emptiness in their lives after being widowed, each in a different way and each successfully when she is finally able to face the loneliness that Wilson views as an essential part of the human condition.

For years before and after World War II, Wilson worked in the British Museum's Department of Printed Books, eventually becoming assistant superintendent of the Reading Room. He wrote his first short story, "Raspberry Jam," in his thirties. Before long he attained literary prominence, first as a short-story writer, then as a novelist. His first novel, *Hemlock and After*, is the story of a man in middle age who faces—and fails—an important crisis in his life. Soon Wilson would face a midlife crisis of his own: As his writing took more and more of his time and he found himself increasingly committed to it, he finally decided to give up his job at the museum, and the pension that went with it, for the much less secure career of a professional writer. The decision came when he realized that he would have to devote more time to the production of his play *The Mulberry Bush* and to writing his second novel than his job at the Reading Room afforded or than his few weeks' annual holiday provided. Thus, with a scant few hundred pounds in the bank, he left to embark on his writing full-time.

What Meg Eliot and Sylvia Calvert achieve through courage in the face of loneliness and deprivation is precisely what Bernard Sands in *Hemlock and After* fails to do and what Gerald Middleton in *Anglo-Saxon Attitudes* accomplishes only after a long period of dry despair and failure. This achievement lies at the heart of Wilson's humanism, an attitude and conviction that has often linked him with humanists such as E. M. Forster, despite important and telling differences between them. Wilson was a much greater activist, both in his life and in his fiction, than Forster was, as evidenced by the character Alexandra Grant in *As If by Magic* and in Wilson's vigorous participation in Amnesty International, the Royal Literary Fund, the National Book League, and the National Arts Council.

Wilson has also been compared with Charles Dickens, a writer he loved throughout his life and whose critical reputation he did much to restore in the twentieth century. In addition to books on Dickens, Rudyard Kipling, and Émile Zola, Wilson wrote incisive and perceptive essays on literature, collected in *Diversity and Depth in Fiction* in 1983. When he was a professor at the University of East Anglia in the 1960's and 1970's, his curriculum included Dickens and Fyodor Dostoevski, another writer he greatly admired. *The Wild Garden* clearly shows his love for both reading and writing, as well as offering insights into some of the images and ideas in his fiction.

In addition to Wilson's humanist concerns, his fiction reflects a great interest in the form and technique of the contemporary novel. *No Laughing Matter* is a tour de force and perhaps his masterpiece. In it, he utilizes a variety of fictional techniques rivaled only by James Joyce in *Ulysses* (1922). Wilson never stopped experimenting with the form as well as the content of his novels, and critics were often been puzzled by what came next. For example, his futuristic *The Old Men at the Zoo* was a radical departure from *The Middle Age of Mrs. Eliot*, the Jamesian novel that immediately preceded it. He developed the interior monologue to a hitherto unrealized flexibility and precision, and his acute ear for different voices and accents earned for him the soubriquet of mime (he actually was an excellent mimic). The cinematic opening of *No Laughing Matter* is difficult reading at first, but thereafter the playlets interspersed throughout the novel lend a liveliness and immediacy few fictions in the twentieth century had attained.

His last two novels, *As If by Magic*, 1973, and *Setting the World on Fire*, 1980, were more experimental than their predecessors and attracted less critical and popular attention. Wilson died in 1991, out of fashion and remembered, if at all, for his early stories and novels.

Jay L. Halio
Arthur D. Hlavaty

Bibliography

Brooke, Allen. "The Mimetic Brilliance of Angus Wilson." *New Criterion* 15 (October, 1996): 28-37. In this biographical essay, Brooke describes Wilson's childhood and youth, his early literary career, his homosexual relationship with Tony Garrett, his disillusionment with communism, and his declining final years.

Conradi, Peter. *Angus Wilson*. Plymouth, England: Northcote House, 1997. A very fine introduction to Wilson's work, including a biographical outline, a section on his stories, chapters on his major novels, notes, and a very useful annotated bibliography.

Drabble, Margaret. *Angus Wilson: A Biography*. New York: St. Martin's Press, 1995. Written by a fine novelist and biographer, this book is a sympathetic, well-researched, and astute guide to Wilson's life and work. Includes notes and bibliography.

Gardner, Averil. *Angus Wilson*. Boston: Twayne, 1985. The first full-length study of Wilson published in the United States, representing a well-rounded introduction to Wilson's fiction. Includes a biographical sketch and analyses of Wilson's stories and novels through 1980. Contains a useful annotated bibliography of secondary sources.

Halio, Jay L. *Angus Wilson*. Edinburgh: Oliver and Boyd, 1964. The first full-length study of Wilson, this slender volume covers Wilson's writing through *The Wild Garden*. After a biographical sketch, Halio examines Wilson's fiction in chronological order. Concludes with a chapter on Wilson's literary criticism.

_______, ed. *Critical Essays on Angus Wilson*. Boston: G. K. Hall, 1985. Includes an overview of Wilson's writings, several reviews of his work, three interviews with the author, and fourteen essays that offer a diverse study of Wilson's individual works as well as his career as a whole. The selected bibliography draws readers' attention to further resources.

Mackay, Marina. "Mr. Wilson and Mrs. Woolf: A Camp Reconstruction of Bloomsbury." *Journal of Modern Literature* 23 (Summer, 1999): 95-110. An overview of Wilson's career and works.

Stape, J. H., and Anne N. Thomas. *Angus Wilson: A Bibliography, 1947-1987*. London: Mansell, 1988. This thorough and indispensable resource includes a foreword by Wilson and a useful chronology of his life. Part 1 is a bibliography of works by Wilson, including books, articles, translations of his works, and interviews. Part 2 is a bibliography of works about Wilson.

August Wilson

American playwright

Born: Pittsburgh, Pennsylvania; April 27, 1945
Identity: African American

DRAMA: *Ma Rainey's Black Bottom*, pr. 1984; *Fences*, pr., pb. 1985; *Joe Turner's Come and Gone*, pr. 1986; *The Piano Lesson*, pr. 1987; *Two Trains Running*, pr. 1990; *Three Plays*, pb. 1991; *Seven Guitars*, pr. 1995; *Jitney*, pr. 2000; *King Hedley II*, pr. 2001.

TELEPLAY: *The Piano Lesson*, 1995 (adaptation of his play).

NONFICTION: *The Ground on Which I Stand*, 2000.

August Wilson's long-range project—a cycle of ten plays about the African American experience, one taking place in each decade of the twentieth century—is to chronicle the struggle of the black family to reconcile its necessary integration into white society with its desire (and, Wilson would say, need) to retain its heritage. Himself a child of mixed parentage, he was born in 1945 in Pittsburgh's Hill District to a German baker and Daisy Wilson, a black displaced North Carolinian. Reared by his mother and his black stepfather, David Bedford, Wilson dropped out of high school at the age of fifteen, preferring to educate himself in the public library, where he read all the works he found on a shelf marked "Negro," including novels and essays by Richard Wright, Langston Hughes, Ralph Ellison, and others, as well as the work of such poets as Dylan Thomas, John Berryman, Carl Sandburg, Robert Frost, and Amiri Baraka.

Wilson's sensitivity to the problems of black America shows the influence of the Black Power movement of the late 1960's, and he refers to himself as a Black Nationalist. With his longtime friend Rob Penny, Wilson cofounded the company Black Horizon on the Hill Theatre. Wilson was, however, a poet first, and he began publishing in black literary journals as early as 1971. His connection with Penumbra, a black theater in St. Paul, brought Wilson to Minnesota in 1978, where he lived until moving to Seattle in 1990.

Perhaps the most influential person in Wilson's playwriting life was Lloyd Richards, who, as director of the National Playwrights Conference at the O'Neill Center in Waterford, Connecticut, first encouraged Wilson to pursue a life of writing for the stage and staged his plays throughout the 1990's. After working on *Ma Rainey's Black Bottom* in the staged reading process at the conference in 1982, Richards brought the play to Yale Repertory Theater for a 1984 production that subsequently appeared on Broadway. This collaboration was followed by work at the conference on Fences, which later opened at Yale and followed *Ma Rainey's Black Bottom* to Broadway. There *Fences* was, in 1987, awarded the Pulitzer Prize, which was later also awarded to *The Piano Lesson*.

Ma Rainey's Black Bottom, representing the decade of the 1920's, is the story of a piquant jazz singer and her fellow musicians caught in a compromise between financial survival and purity of art. Like all Wilson's plays, it dramatizes the conflict of all blacks to retain their identity against the forces of assimilation. *Fences*, which takes place in the 1950's, treats its protagonist, Troy Maxson, as an archetypal breadwinner in the black family, imperfect and human, fighting his son's attempts to gain freedom from the cycle of hopelessness in which Troy himself is trapped. Brent Staples, a black writer, once remarked about Maxson's generation, "Our fathers had by circumstances become nearly impossible to love." The Maxson role, which has been compared in thematic power to that of Willy Loman in Arthur Miller's *Death of a Salesman* (pr., pb. 1949), was played by James Earl Jones in Richards's production. *Joe Turner's Come and Gone* dramatizes the transition of a freed slave from his "ownership" by Joe Turner to his struggles to find his wife in a Pittsburgh slum community; the action of the play takes place in 1911. *The Piano Lesson* also takes place in Pittsburgh, this time in 1936, and concerns two family members arguing about selling the family heirloom, a bloodstained piano that represents their cultural past. The piano represents past sufferings but also opportunity for the present members of the family, who must decide whether to sell their past for a brighter future. Like all the plays in this series, it received its development at the National Playwrights Conference and its premiere performance at the Yale Repertory Theater.

Two Trains Running, set in 1969, focuses on death and entitlements. Hambone demands the ham to which he is entitled, and Memphis insists that he receive the full price for his restaurant. The characters refuse to be manipulated by the white-dominated culture.

The value of Wilson's contribution to the stage literature of black America lies in his clear vision of the importance of retaining the distinct black heritage that gives life and dignity to the individual, rather than subsuming that "blackness" in attempts to integrate or assimilate the individual into a white world. His work is far from mere agitprop or political pamphleteering. The broad appeal of his work, which has earned for him a wide audience and every important literary award (including Guggenheim and Rockefeller fellowships to continue his work), lies in his humanity, in the grace of his characterization, and in his uncanny ability to find the cadences of ghetto speech, rendering into poetry what has long been considered substandard English. The structure of his plays drives the plots and character development forward with great force, drawing the audience into the world of the play with seamless craftsmanship.

The accuracy of his vision is attributable only to his talent and his sensitivity to the suffering of the people around whom he grew up. Critics have treated Wilson's body of work with considerable respect and seriousness, comparing him favorably to Alex Haley as a chronicler of the black experience and citing his early successes as indicative of a long and fruitful career. Observers of regional theaters have noted the process by which Wilson's texts are refined in not-for-profit theater productions before venturing onto the Broadway stage, a process that may well serve as a model for other promising playwrights.

Thomas J. Taylor
Eric Sterling

Bibliography

Bigsby, C. W. E. *Modern American Drama, 1945-1990*. Cambridge, England: Cambridge University Press, 1992. The author interviewed Wilson for pertinent biographical data and includes some in-depth analysis of the first four plays.

Birdwell, Christine. "Death as a Fastball on the Outside Corner: *Fences'* Troy Maxson and the American Dream." *Aethlon* 8 (1990). Information and critical discussion.

Bogumil, Mary L. *Understanding August Wilson*. Columbia: University of South Carolina Press, 1999. Bogumil provides readers with a comprehensive view of the thematic structure of Wilson's plays, the placement of his plays within the context of American drama, and the distinctively African American experiences and traditions that Wilson dramatizes.

Brustein, Robert. *Reimagining American Theatre*. New York: Hill and Wang, 1991. Brustein, critic and former artistic director of the Yale Repertory Theatre before Lloyd Richards, is one of the few negative voices criticizing Wilson's drama. He finds particular fault with the mechanisms and symbols of *The Piano Lesson* and hopes that Wilson will work to develop the poetic rather than historical aspects of his talent.

Elkins, Marilyn, ed. *August Wilson: A Casebook*. New York: Garland, 1994. The essays investigate such thematic, artistic, and ideological concerns as Wilson's use of the South and the black human body as metaphors; his collaboration with Lloyd Richards; the influences of the blues and other writers on his work; his creative method; and his treatment of African American family life.

Herrington, Joan. *I Ain't Sorry for Nothin' I Done: August Wilson's Process of Playwriting*. New York: Limelight Editions, 1998. Herrington traces the roots of Wilson's drama to visual artists such as Romare Bearden and to the jazz musicians who inspire and energize him as a dramatist. She goes on to analyze his process of playwriting—how he brings his experiences and his ideas to stage life—by comparing successive drafts of his first three major plays.

Hill, Holly. "Black Theatre into the Mainstream." In *Contemporary American Theatre*, edited by Bruce King. New York: St. Martin's Press, 1991. Hill's analysis of the plays sets them in the context of their period.

Nadel, Alan. *May All Your Fences Have Gates*. Iowa City: University of Iowa Press, 1994. Nadel deals individually with five major plays and also addresses issues crucial to Wilson's canon: the role of history, the relationship of African ritual to African American drama, gender relations in the African American community, music and cultural identity, the influence of Romare Beardern's collages, and the politics of drama.

Theater 9 (Summer/Fall, 1988). This special issue includes the script of *The Piano Lesson* with an earlier version of the ending, production photographs, and two informative essays. The articles "Wrestling Against History" and "The Songs of a Marked Man" explore Wilson's themes, especially the importance of myths and superstitions.

Wolfe, Peter. *August Wilson*. London: Macmillan, 1999. A comprehensive analysis of Wilson's theater. Wolfe sees the dramatist as exploding stereotypes of the ghetto poor, through his juxtapositions of the ordinary and the African American surreal, which evoke anger, affection, and sometimes hope.

Edmund Wilson

American critic

Born: Red Bank, New Jersey; May 8, 1895
Died: Talcottville, New York; June 12, 1972

NONFICTION: *Axel's Castle: A Study in the Imaginative Literature of 1870-1930*, 1931; *The American Jitters: A Year of the Slump*, 1932; *Travels in Two Democracies*, 1936; *The Triple Thinkers: Ten Essays on Literature*, 1938; *To the Finland Station: A Study in the Writing and Acting of History*, 1940; *The Boys in the Back Room: Notes on California Novelists*, 1941; *The Wound and the Bow: Seven Studies in Literature*, 1941; *Europe Without Baedeker: Sketches Among the Ruins of Italy, Greece, and England*, 1947; *Classics and Commercials: A Literary Chronicle of the Forties*, 1950; *The Shores of Light: A Literary Chronicle of the Twenties and Thirties*, 1952; *Eight Essays*, 1954; *The Scrolls from the Dead Sea*, 1955 (revised as *The Dead Sea Scrolls, 1947-1969*, 1969); *A Piece of My Mind: Reflections at Sixty*, 1956 (literary criticism); *Red, Black, Blond, and Olive: Studies in Four Civilizations: Zuñi, Haiti, Soviet Russia, Israel*, 1956; *The American Earthquake: A Documentary of the Twenties and Thirties*, 1958; *Apologies to the Iroquois*, 1960; *Patriotic Gore: Studies in the Literature of the American Civil War*, 1962; *The Cold War and the Income Tax: A Protest*, 1963; *The Bit Between My Teeth: A Literary Chronicle of 1950-1965*, 1965; *O Canada: An American's Notes on Canadian Culture*, 1965; *A Prelude: Landscapes, Characters, and Conversations from the Earlier Years of My Life*, 1967 (literary criticism); *The Fruits of the MLA*, 1968; *Upstate: Records and Recollections of Northern New York*, 1971; *A Window on Russia: For the Use of Foreign Readers*, 1972; *The Twenties: From Notebooks and Diaries of the Period*, 1975; *Letters on Literature and Politics, 1912-1972*, 1977; *The Nabokov-Wilson Letters, 1940-1971*, 1979, revised and expanded as *Dear Bunny, Dear Volodya: The Nabokov-Wilson Letters, 1940-1971*, 2001; *The Thirties: From Notebooks and Diaries of the Period*, 1980; *The Forties: From Notebooks and Diaries of the Period*, 1983; *The Portable Edmund Wilson*, 1983, revised and expanded as *The Edmund Wilson Reader*, 1997; *The Fifties: From Notebooks and Diaries of the Period*, 1986; *The Sixties: The Last Journal, 1960-1972*, 1993 (Lewis M. Dabney, editor); *From the Uncollected Edmund Wilson*, 1995; *Edmund Wilson: The Man in Letters*, 2002 (David Castronovo and Janet Groth, editors).

LONG FICTION: *I Thought of Daisy*, 1929; *Memoirs of Hecate County*, 1946; *"Galahad" and "I Thought of Daisy,"* 1957; *The Higher Jazz*, 1998 (Neale Reinitz, editor).

DRAMA: *Discordant Encounters: Plays and Dialogues*, pb. 1926; *This Room and This Gin and These Sandwiches*, pb. 1937; *The Little Blue Light*, pb. 1950; *Five Plays*, pb. 1954; *The Duke of Palermo, and Other Plays, with an Open Letter to Mike Nichols*, pb. 1969.

POETRY: *Note-Books of Night*, 1942; *Three Reliques of Ancient Western Poetry Collected by Edmund Wilson from the Ruins*, 1951; *Night Thoughts*, 1961.

EDITED TEXTS: *The Last Tycoon: An Unfinished Novel by F. Scott Fitzgerald, Together with "The Great Gatsby" and Selected Stories*, 1941; *The Shock of Recognition: The Development of Literature in the United States Recorded by the Men Who Made It*, 1943; *The Crack-Up: With Other Uncollected Pieces, Note-Books, and Unpublished Letters*, 1945 (by F. Scott Fitzgerald); *The Collected Essays of John Peale Bishop*, 1948; *Peasants, and Other Stories*, 1956 (by Anton Chekhov).

Edmund Wilson was an authentic man of letters, a rarity in the twentieth century. Primarily known as a literary critic, he was also a novelist, poet, playwright, historian, and social critic. Wilson was the son of a distinguished New Jersey attorney, a somewhat distant man who inculcated in his only son the virtues of decency and honor. The young man attended Hill School and Princeton University, where he became a close friend and adviser of the novelist F. Scott Fitzgerald and the poet John Peale Bishop. After service in France during World War I, Wilson began a career as a writer and editor for various journals published in New York, including *Vanity Fair, The New Republic*, and, eventually, *The New Yorker.* The latter association began in 1943 and continued until his death.

Wilson was already a well-known critic when he published his book-length study of literary modernism, *Axel's Castle*. The first such study to treat the Symbolist and Freudian elements in literature as significant and coherent, *Axel's Castle* was an eloquent defense of such writers as James Joyce and Gertrude Stein as well as a clear exposition of their methods and achievements. During the same period of time, Wilson caused something of a scandal with his novel, *I Thought of Daisy.* Based loosely on the character of Wilson's great early love, the poet Edna St. Vincent Millay, *I Thought of Daisy* chronicles the life and loves of what in the Roaring Twenties was called a flapper, a young woman who goes from one man to another in search of enjoyment with little regard for the future or for the consequences of her actions. The novel shared with his later work of fiction *Memoirs of Hecate County* a frankness about sex regarded as shocking at the time of its publication.

Wilson was not particularly interested in theories of criticism. He had been taught by his famed Princeton teacher Christian Gauss that literature, like all art, is the product of particular times and places, and that it is a critic's job to explain literary works in terms of their relationship to the times that produced them. Wilson therefore regarded his interest in the ideas and the history of his time and of earlier times as essential aspects of his work. In the early 1930's, he traveled widely in the United States, looking for the manifestations of the Great Depression. This search led to his book *The American Jitters*. His interest in modern psychological theory led to the critical study *The Wound and the Bow*, which argues that every writer's works are profoundly influenced by some wound or trauma suffered in the past.

Wilson made his reputation as a defender of the new literature of his own time, but later in his career he became much more interested in history and in earlier writing. Never committed to any political party or theory, he became fascinated by Marxism during the 1930's, an interest that took the form of research into the history of the development of socialism from Karl Marx and the French and German socialists of the nineteenth century down to the beginning of the Russian Revolution. The result was *To the Finland Station*. During the 1940's and 1950's, he took an interest in the discoveries of the ancient Qumran scrolls of the Essene sect and traveled to Israel to see them and discuss them with specialists, a project that led to his controversial study *The Dead Sea Scrolls*. Wilson's major interest, however, was always in his own country and its history. He spent years studying the literature and history of the Civil War, a project that led eventually to the book many other critics regard as his finest work, *Patriotic Gore*. This work examines some lesser-known writers who showed, in Wilson's view, aspects of the United States' past which history had neglected; it included writers such as Oliver Wendell Holmes, Harold Frederic, Mary Chesnut, and Thomas Wentworth Higginson. It was Wilson's conclusion that the war was fought for cynical reasons having to do with power and that Abraham Lincoln was far from the hero history has made him out to be.

Wilson was amazingly prolific. In addition to writing books on specific subjects, he was a regular reviewer for different journals, and his reviews were collected in such volumes as *Classics and Commercials*, *The Shores of Light*, and *The Bit Between My Teeth.* Some of these reviews later led to more extended studies. The collections contain an inclusive history of Wilson's view of literature from the early 1920's until 1970. Leon Edel, after Wilson's death, edited the journals Wilson had kept for most of his adult life, *The Twenties*, *The Thirties*, *The Forties*, and *The Fifties*. These chronicled the somewhat tangled details of Wilson's personal life, including his four marriages. *Upstate* concerns his experiences in Talcottville, New York, and the surrounding area, where he lived during the summers of his later years, in an old stone house inherited from his mother's family.

Everything Wilson wrote, however intimate or remote the subject matter, is couched in his characteristic prose: His style was somewhat formal, but it was lucid, precise, and often exciting. He tended to be magisterial in his judgments, as if the conclusions he reached were inarguable. Because he was human, he sometimes erred, especially in his judgments of poetry. He was, nevertheless, a careful and exact observer of his own time, and his comments on the literature and history of the middle years of the twentieth century are a substantial and fascinating record of a time of radical change as seen through the eyes of an observer who is very much a part of his own times. Wilson saw those times with a clear eye. He thought and wrote about them interestingly and well.

John M. Muste

Bibliography

Castronovo, David. *Edmund Wilson.* New York: F. Ungar, 1984. A thorough study of Wilson's work, emphasizing his criticism.

Costa, Richard Hauer. *Edmund Wilson: Our Neighbor from Talcottville.* Syracuse, N.Y.: Syracuse University Press, 1980. Gives insights into the warmth and capacity for friendship of a man often regarded as frighteningly brusque.

Dabney, Lewis. "Edmund Wilson and *The Wound and the Bow.*"

The Sewanee Review 91 (Winter, 1983). Examines Wilson's critical study of writers and writing.

_______, ed. *Edmund Wilson: Centennial Reflections*. Princeton, N.J.: Mercantile Library of New York in association with Princeton University Press, 1997. A collection of papers originally presented at two symposia held at the Mercantile Library of New York. Includes index.

Douglas, George H. *Edmund Wilson's America*. Lexington: University Press of Kentucky, 1983. Focuses attention on the author's view of the relations between the American past and his own time.

Frank, Charles. *Edmund Wilson*. New York: Twayne, 1970. Concentrates on Wilson's fiction.

Groth, Janet. *Edmund Wilson: A Critic for Our Time*. Athens: Ohio University Press, 1989. Focuses on Wilson's criticism.

Meyers, Jeffrey. *Edmund Wilson*. Boston: Houghton Mifflin, 1995. A full-length biography.

Wain, John, ed. *Edmund Wilson: The Man and His Work*. New York: New York University Press, 1978. A collection of essays about the personal and professional sides of Wilson; it includes biographical essays by Alfred Kazin and Angus Wilson and critical articles by Larzer Ziff and John Wain.

Edward O. Wilson

American entomologist, ethologist, and ecologist

Born: Birmingham, Alabama; June 10, 1929

NONFICTION: *The Theory of Island Biogeography*, 1967 (with Robert H. MacArthur); *A Primer of Population Biology*, 1971 (with William H. Bossert); *The Insect Societies*, 1971; *Sociobiology: The New Synthesis*, 1975; *On Human Nature*, 1978; *Biophilia*, 1984; *The Ants*, 1990 (with Bert Hölldobler); *The Diversity of Life*, 1992; *Journey to the Ants: A Story of Scientific Exploration*, 1994 (with Hölldobler); *Naturalist*, 1994; *In Search of Nature*, 1996; *Consilience: The Unity of Knowledge*, 1998; *The Future of Life*, 2002.

EDITED TEXTS: *Ecology, Evolution, and Population Biology: Readings from "Scientific American,"* 1974; *Biodiversity*, 1988; *The Biophilia Hypothesis*, 1993 (with Stephen R. Kellert); *The Best American Science and Nature Writing 2001*, 2001.

Edward Osborne Wilson, Jr., began his career studying ants and other social insects. He went on to develop the theory of sociobiology, which established a genetic basis for behavior in all animals, including humans. His advocacy for the preservation of endangered species and ecosystems spurred conservationist efforts worldwide.

"Most children have a bug period, and I never grew out of mine," Wilson wrote in his autobiography, *Naturalist*. As a small, shy boy, he developed a love of nature while roaming the woods and beaches of Alabama and Florida and frequenting the Museum of Natural History and the National Zoo in Washington, D.C. His loss of vision in one eye following a fishing accident led him to focus his scientific inquiries on creatures small enough to be observed at close range.

Following his graduation from high school in Decatur, Alabama, he entered the University of Alabama at Tuscaloosa. There, he completed a B.S. in biology in 1949 and an M.S. in biology in 1950. He received his Ph.D. in biology from Harvard University in 1955. He became assistant professor at Harvard in 1956 and full professor in 1964. He served as curator in entomology of the Harvard Museum of Comparative Zoology from 1973 to 1997, when he was named honorary curator. In 1994, he became Pellegrino University Professor and was awarded emeritus status in 1997. Throughout his career at Harvard, he lived in Lexington, Massachusetts, with his wife, Renee. The couple had one daughter, Catherine.

In the 1950's, Wilson conducted field research in Cuba, Mexico, and several islands of the South Pacific. In collaboration with Robert MacArthur, Wilson developed and published *The Theory of Island Biogeography*, today regarded as a classic ecological work. In 1953, Wilson began investigating chemical communication in ants. He documented the trail-laying behavior of fire ants as they foraged between the nest and a food source. He found that a substance produced in the insect's Dufour's gland acts as a pheromone (a substance made by one organism that influences the behavior of another). He extended his study of chemical communication in ants with German entomologist Bert Hölldobler. Their book, *The Ants*, was widely read by nonscientists and praised by critics for its clarity and lyrical appeal. It earned for the pair a Pulitzer Prize in 1991.

Wilson was influenced by British evolutionary biologist William Hamilton and his kin selection hypothesis. Behaviors that promote survival not of the individual, but of its *genes*, lead to a selective advantage in the evolution of a species, Hamilton argued: the closer the kinship, the larger the fraction of genes held in common. Wilson used this principle to explain altruistic behaviors (such as the apparently self-sacrificing labor of nonreproducing worker ants) and as evidence of a biological basis for behavior in all animals.

The resulting book, *Sociobiology: The New Synthesis*, provoked public and academic controversy. In the book's final chapter, Wilson suggested a genetic basis for human behavior, an idea deemed politically incorrect at the time. Accused of racism and sexism, Wilson had water dumped on his head at a meeting of the American Association for the Advancement of Science. Despite the controversy, President Jimmy Carter awarded Wilson the National Medal of Science, the highest scientific honor in the United States, in 1977. Wilson's next book, *On Human Nature*, advocated the scientific study of human behavior, with the ultimate goal of integrating the natural and social sciences and the humanities. Praised as a sophisticated and humane work, the book won a Pulitzer Prize in 1979.

Wilson, alarmed by what he saw as humans' destruction of habitats critical to the survival of native flora and fauna, became a tireless and influential advocate for environmental preservation. In *Biophilia*, he maintained that humans are genetically predisposed to derive spiritual (as well as material) sustenance from nature. In *The Diversity of Life*, he argued that people are obligated to conserve ecosystems. In *The Future of Life*, he advocated human population control and habitat protection to forestall the mass extinction of species. In *Consilience*, Wilson contended that the world is orderly and will ultimately be explained by a small number of natural laws. He suggested that humans, soon to escape the forces of natural selection, would ultimately be free to choose the destiny of their species.

Wilson received numerous honors, including the William Procter Prize for Scientific Achievement of Sigma Xi, the Scientific Research Society; the Eminent Ecologist Award of the Ecological Society of America; and the Distinguished Service Award of the American Institute of Biological Sciences. In 1994 he received the Award for Public Understanding of Science and Technology from the American Association for the Advancement of Science. In 1990 he won the Crafoord Prize, the top honor bestowed by the Royal Swedish Academy of Science for achievements in fields not covered by the Nobel Prize. The depth of Wilson's research, the breadth of his thought, and the clarity and passion of his writing place him among the greatest scientists and science writers of all time.

Faith Hickman Brynie

Bibliography

Carpenter, Betsy. "Living with Nature: E. O. Wilson Argues That Species Extinction Threatens the Human Spirit." *U.S. News and World Report* 113 (November 30, 1992): 60. Wilson asserts that natural environments and a diversity of species are essential to human psychological and spiritual well-being.

Horgan, John. "Revisiting Old Battlefields." *Scientific American* 270 (April, 1994): 36. An overview of Wilson's life and work in evolutionary biology, philosophy, and environmental science.

Joyce, Christopher. "Return to the Ants." *New Scientist* 130 (May 11, 1991): 55. A short biography and an interview with Wilson.

Lessem, Don. "Dr. Ant." *International Wildlife* 21 (January/February, 1991): 30. A personal profile of Wilson as an entomologist.

Lueders, Edward, ed. *Writing Natural History: Dialogues with Authors*. Salt Lake City: University of Utah Press, 1989. A conversation with Wilson (and other authors) about science writing.

Reed, Susan. "E. O. Wilson: The Famed Biologist Says Saving Other Species Is the Only Way to Save Ourselves." *People Weekly* 40 (October 11, 1993): 123. An analysis of controversy and environmental activism in Wilson's career.

Ethel Wilson

Canadian novelist and short-story writer

Born: Port Elizabeth, South Africa; January 20, 1888
Died: Vancouver, British Columbia, Canada; December 22, 1980

LONG FICTION: *Hetty Dorval*, 1947; *The Innocent Traveller*, 1949; *The Equations of Love*, 1952; *Lilly's Story*, 1953; *Swamp Angel*, 1954; *Love and Salt Water*, 1956.
SHORT FICTION: *Mrs. Golightly, and Other Stories*, 1961.
MISCELLANEOUS: *Ethel Wilson: Stories, Essays, and Letters*, 1987 (David Stouck, editor).

Ethel Davis Bryant Wilson was born in Port Elizabeth, South Africa, on January 20, 1888, to Robert William Bryant and Lila (Malkin) Bryant. Her mother died when she was only two, and her father took her to Staffordshire, England, to be reared by her maternal grandmother and successive aunts and uncles. Her family members were involved in a number of literary activities, including reading, journalism, and translation, and were acquainted with Matthew Arnold and Arnold Bennett. This literary atmosphere no doubt stimulated her interest in letters, and the literary allusions and quotations in her works demonstrate a comprehensive familiarity with the English tradition. Her father died when she was ten, and she went to Vancouver, British Columbia, to join her grandmother, who had moved there. Many of these family and early personal experiences are recounted in *The Innocent Traveller*, the semibiographical novel based on the life of her aunt.

In Vancouver, Wilson attended Miss Gordon's School, but she was sent to Trinity Hall School in Southport, England, for her secondary education. In 1907, she graduated from Vancouver Normal

School with a Second Class Teacher's Certificate. Between 1907 and 1920, she taught in Vancouver elementary schools.

On January 4, 1921, Wilson married Wallace Wilson. Their marriage was a happy one, marked by much traveling in Canada, Europe, and around the Mediterranean, and the successful development of both their careers. Her husband became a respected physician; he studied internal medicine in Vienna in 1930, represented Canada at the British Medical Association's convention in 1938 and at the World Health Organization in Paris in 1947, and was president of the Canadian Medical Association in 1946 and 1947. The relationship between the Wilsons may have provided details for the happy marriages and the deepening love relationships in *Hetty Dorval*, *Lilly's Story*, and *Love and Salt Water*. The love of travel is also obvious in her work; travel is healing, broadening, and sensitizing to her characters, and Wilson's ability to describe the essential atmosphere of various locales is one of her strongest attributes.

Wilson published her first short story in 1937, at the age of forty-nine, and another in 1939 before her career was interrupted by World War II. Although her husband was in the Canadian army, and although Wilson herself served by editing a Red Cross magazine between 1940 and 1945, she made little use of wartime experiences in her novels, except tangentially in *The Innocent Traveller* and *Love and Salt Water*. Only the short story "We Have to Sit Opposite" deals specifically with wartime problems.

It is likely that Wilson's career in writing was encouraged by ill health. She was a victim of arthritis, which by 1956 had become so severe that she could not walk around in London, an experience she described in her essay "To Keep the Memory of So Worthy a Friend." She wrote, "One of the advantages of being lame is that one can sit and think. . . . And so I often think and think." In her last three novels, several major characters suffer handicaps, either physical or psychological, which affect their relationships with others in various ways and which must be transcended. No doubt her own disability enabled her to interpret this theme sympathetically.

The late 1940's and the 1950's were Wilson's most productive years; all of her novels and most of her short stories and essays were written or published during that period. At the peak of her success, after the publication of *Swamp Angel*, she received three awards: an honorary doctorate from the University of British Columbia in 1955, a special medal from the Canada Council in 1961 for contributions to Canadian literature, and the Lorne Pierce Gold Medal from the Royal Society of Canada in 1964. Dr. Wilson died in 1966, and Ethel Wilson lived in retirement in Vancouver until her death in 1980.

Perhaps because Wilson did not attempt to follow literary trends, and perhaps also because she began publishing relatively late in life, her works did not have a dramatic effect on Canadian letters. She was publishing out of her generation, and her realism and understatement seemed somewhat old-fashioned to those authors who were following naturalistic trends. Still, she was influential in raising the quality of the art in Canada and in quietly introducing the theme of women "finding themselves" well before the theme became popular among feminists. Her heroines are not necessarily strong or aggressive, but they mature, meet the vicissitudes of their lives with determination and ingenuity, and for the most part succeed in small but important ways. Wilson's treatment of this theme and her impeccable craftsmanship contributed significantly to the maturing of the novel in Canada.

Carol I. Croxton

Bibliography

Bhelande, Anjali. *Self Beyond Self: Ethel Wilson and Indian Philosophical Thought*. Mumbaim, India: S.N.D.T. Women's University, Bharatiya Vidya Bhavan, 1996. Examines the Indic influences on Wilson and her philosophy.

McAlpine, Mary. *The Other Side of Silence: A Life of Ethel Wilson*. Madeira Park, British Columbia: Harbour Publishing, 1989. The first biography.

McMullan, Lorraine, ed. *The Ethel Wilson Symposium*. Ottowa: University of Ottowa Press, 1982. Papers presented at a conference held April 24-26, 1981, at the University of Ottawa, Canada. McMullan's introduction is especially useful.

McPherson, Hugo. "Fiction: 1940-1960." In *Literary History of Canada: Canadian Literature in English*, edited by Carl Frederick Klinck. 2d ed. Vol. 2. Toronto: University of Toronto Press, 1976. Wilson's fiction is discussed in the context of a supposed "search for identity" thought to infuse Canadian literature's development in the mid-twentieth century. McPherson notes a contrary individuality in Wilson's writing that transcends her failure at times to reconcile her creative impulses as both "artist and sibyl."

Mitchell, Beverley. "Ethel Wilson." In *Canadian Writers and Their Works: Fiction Series*, edited by Robert Lecker, Jack David, and Ellen Quigley. Vol. 6. Toronto: ECW Press, 1985. Wilson's life and complete works are thoroughly examined. An exhaustive bibliography follows Mitchell's straightforward, readable analysis, making this study a must for Wilson readers.

Pacey, Desmond. *Ethel Wilson*. New York: Twayne, 1967. This thorough, readable overview of Wilson's long and short fiction is not deeply analytical, but it does consider Wilson's lightly ironic vision and her valuable contribution to Canadian literature despite her relatively short publishing history. Despite its age, the book still contains some useful insights. A selected bibliography and an index are included.

Woodcock, George. "Innocence and Solitude: The Fictions of Ethel Wilson." In *Modern Times*. Vol. 3. in *The Canadian Novel*, edited by John Moss. Toronto: NC Press, 1982. Woodcock discusses Wilson's originality and vision as they are expressed in her novels and novellas.

________. "On Ethel Wilson." In *The World of Canadian Writing: Critiques and Recollections*. Vancouver, British Columbia: Douglas and McIntyre, 1980. Slightly revised since its 1974 publication, this reflective personal essay enumerates the strengths of Wilson's personality and her unique works. This volume contains an index of the names of authors mentioned or treated in the book.

Harriet E. Wilson

American novelist

Born: New Hampshire or Virginia; 1808 or c. 1827-1828
Died: Boston(?); c. 1870
Identity: African American

LONG FICTION: *Our Nig: Or, Sketches from the Life of a Free Black, in a Two-Story White House, North. Showing That Slavery's Shadow Falls Even There*, 1859.

The vast majority of what is known about Harriet E. Adams Wilson has been gleaned from her sole published work, *Our Nig*, an autobiographical novel. The chronology of events therein suggests that Harriet was born in approximately 1827-1828, given that Frado (pseudonym in the novel for Harriet) is described as gaining at age eighteen her freedom from the family to whom she was an indentured servant/slave, and that she then lived another ten or fifteen years before the publication of her story in 1859.

Our Nig shows that Harriet's first eighteen years were difficult. Born to a white mother and a black father, at age six she was abandoned at the home of the well-to-do Bellmonts (a fictitious name in the novel). Harriet never again saw her parents, who left to escape destitution. At the mercy of strangers, she was assigned an attic cubicle as bedroom and was made into a house servant. Although Harriet was treated well by the male and two female members of the Bellmont family, Mrs. Bellmont and her daughter Mary saw to it that she was overworked (assigned farm chores and dishwashing duties immediately) and received little food and only ten minutes in which to eat while standing. She was also regularly beaten, often with her mouth propped open with a wooden block. Allowed to attend school for three years, she was frequently ridiculed as the only black child (in the nineteenth century United States mulattoes were unquestioningly considered to be "Negroes").

Still, Harriet often found refuge in the quarters of Mr. Bellmont's sister, also a member of the household. Jack and James, two of the Bellmont sons, also provided her some protection, James even commanding that Harriet eat at the table rather than standing. Harriet also found solace in religion, to which she was introduced by Mr. Bellmont's sister, whom Harriet often accompanied to evening church meetings—although she was not allowed to accompany the family to church in the daytime, merely to drive them there and bring them home afterward.

Nonetheless, the beatings by Mrs. Bellmont (the "tyrant" and "plague") continued. At one point, Harriet dared to respond to a command to work by saying "I am sick," at which Mrs. Bellmont "suddenly inflicted a blow which lay the tottering girl prostrate on the floor. Excited by so much indulgence of a dangerous passion, she seemed left to unrestrained malice; and snatching a towel, stuffed the mouth of the sufferer, and beat her cruelly."

Thus, after James's death and Jack's departure, Harriet decided to leave the Bellmonts immediately upon reaching age eighteen, the age at which she concluded her servitude. However, she was repeatedly ill in subsequent years due to the prior abuse, and was further victimized by an alleged former slave who, after marrying her and fathering her child, left her, never to return. Harriet was reduced to the expedient of writing about her ghastly experiences in order to earn money for herself and her child. Her son died soon after the novel was published, and she moved to Boston, where the last Boston Directory listing for her appeared in 1863. Virtually nothing is known about the remainder of her life.

Although she produced only one literary work, and despite virtually all knowledge of that novel being lost until Henry Louis Gates, Jr., unearthed it in the early 1980's, Harriet E. Wilson is a very important author for a number of reasons. One is that *Our Nig* is the first novel by an African American woman, antedating the earliest previously known such work by some thirty-five years. Gates himself has stated that Wilson "invented her own plot structure" and "in this important way . . . inaugurates the Afro-American literary tradition in a manner more fundamental than did . . . the two black Americans who published complete novels before her." Also, authors such as Ralph Ellison and Alice Walker have testified to the novel's enormous significance, Walker stating that it presents "heretofore unexamined experience, a whole new layer of time and existence in American life and literature."

Such uniqueness helps to explain the novel's quick disappearance in 1859, too. As an indictment of northern slavery, the book was ignored by most abolitionists (despite the abolitionist publisher), and its frank, positive presentation of the interracial marriage of Harriet's mother and father doubtless also contributed to the quick demise. Likely even greater reason for the novel's poor distribution (it was only one small printing in 1859) and poor reception is the fact that the it broadly indicts the American capitalistic system, in its delineation of economic power and lack thereof, as the defining cruelty, not just of slavery, but also of class-based life among white Americans. Harriet's mother is driven to an interracial marriage by the sexual exploitation of an economically privileged white male, and only the black man's kindness prevents her starvation. Similarly, the callousness of Mrs. Bellmont is explicitly tied to her avariciousness and social condescension, evident in her attempt to force one daughter to marry for money only, as well as her attempt to disrupt Jack's marriage to a working-class woman.

Such a portrait of economic-based cruelty in America at a depth beyond antislavery polemics, particularly by a mixed-race woman whose acerbic wit powerfully satirizes the status quo, doubtless won the novel few admirers among its primarily middle-class, white, northern readership. Further, its unique combination of autobiographical details and sentimental novelistic conventions probably confused many readers. Since its unearthing in 1983, however, Wilson's autobiographical novel has been deservedly recognized as a tremendously important literary achievement.

John L. Grigsby

Bibliography

Breau, Elizabeth. "Identifying Satire: *Our Nig*." *Callaloo* 16, no. 2 (Spring, 1993). This formalistic essay contends that Gates understates the novel's satiric richness and overstates its sentimental imitativeness.

Ernets, John. "Economics of Identity: Harriet E. Wilson's *Our Nig*." *PMLA* 109, no. 3 (May, 1994). This Marxist analysis examines economic exploitation and empowerment in the novel.

Gardner, Eric. "'This Attempt of Their Sister': Harriet Wilson's *Our Nig* from Printer to Reader." *New England Quarterly* 66, no. 2 (June, 1993). This reader-response analysis analyzes the novel's readers to explain the book's lack of popularity at the time it appeared.

Paratofiorito, Ellen. "'To Demand Your Sympathy and Your Aid': *Our Nig* and the Problem of No Audience." *Journal of American and Comparative Cultures* 24, no. 1/2 (2001). An analysis of the contemporary reception of *Our Nig*.

West, Elizabeth J. "Reworking the Conversion Narrative: Race and Christianity in *Our Nig*." MELUS 24, no. 2 (1999). Analyzes the role of Christianity in determining Wilson's depictions of womanhood and domesticity.

White, Barbara A. "*Our Nig* and the She-Devil: New Information About Harriet Wilson and the 'Bellmont' Family," *American Literature* 65, no. 1 (March, 1993). Biographical essay, which identifies the "Bellmonts" as the Nehemiah Hayward family.

Lanford Wilson

American playwright

Born: Lebanon, Missouri; April 13, 1937

DRAMA: *So Long at the Fair*, pr. 1963 (one act); *Home Free!*, pr. 1964 (one act); *The Madness of Lady Bright*, pr. 1964 (one act); *No Trespassing*, pr. 1964 (one act); *Balm in Gilead*, pr., pb. 1965; *Days Ahead: A Monologue*, pr. 1965 (one scene); *Ludlow Fair*, pr., pb. 1965 (one act); *The Sand Castle*, pr. 1965 (one act); *Sex Is Between Two People*, pr. 1965 (one scene); *This Is the Rill Speaking*, pr. 1965 (one act); *The Rimers of Eldritch*, pr. 1966; *Wandering: A Turn*, pr. 1966 (one scene); *Untitled Play*, pr. 1967 (one act; music by Al Carmines); *The Gingham Dog*, pr. 1968; *The Great Nebula in Orion*, pr. 1970 (one act); *Lemon Sky*, pr., pb. 1970; *Serenading Louie*, pr. 1970; *Sextet (Yes)*, pb. 1970 (one scene); *Stoop: A Turn*, pb. 1970; *Ikke, Ikke, Nye, Nye, Nye*, pr. 1971; *Summer and Smoke*, pr. 1971 (libretto; adaptation of Tennessee Williams's play; music by Lee Hoiby); *The Family Continues*, pr. 1972 (one act); *The Hot l Baltimore*, pr., pb. 1973; *Victory on Mrs. Dandywine's Island*, pb. 1973 (one act); *The Mound Builders*, pr. 1975; *Brontosaurus*, pr. 1977 (one act); *Fifth of July*, pr., pb. 1978; *Talley's Folly*, pr., pb. 1979 (one act); *A Tale Told*, pr. 1981 (pb. as *Talley and Son*, 1986); *Thymus Vulgaris*, pr., pb. 1982 (one act); *Angels Fall*, pr., pb. 1982; *Balm in Gilead, and Other Plays*, pb. 1985; *Say deKooning*, pr. 1985; *Sa-Hurt?*, pr. 1986; *A Betrothal*, pr., pb. 1986 (one act); *Burn This*, pr., pb. 1987; *Dying Breed*, pr. 1987; *Hall of North American Forests*, pr. 1987; *A Poster of the Cosmos*, pr. 1987 (one act); *Abstinence: A Turn*, pb. 1989 (one scene); *The Moonshot Tape*, pr., pb. 1990; *Eukiah*, pr., pb. 1992; *Redwood Curtain*, pr. 1992; *Twenty-one Short Plays*, pb. 1993; *Collected Works*, pb. 1996-1999 (3 volumes; Vol. 1, *Collected Plays, 1965-1970*; Vol. 2, *Collected Works, 1970-1983*; Vol. 3, *The Talley Trilogy*); *Day*, pr., pb. 1996 (one act); *A Sense of Place: Or, Virgil Is Still the Frogboy*, pr. 1997; *Sympathetic Music*, pr. 1997; *Book of Days*, pr. 1998; *Rain Dance*, pr. 2000.

TRANSLATION: *Three Sisters*, 1984 (of Anton Chekhov's play *Tri sestry*).

TELEPLAYS: *One Arm*, 1970; *The Migrants*, 1973 (with Tennessee Williams); *Taxi!*, 1978; *Sam Found Out: A Triple Play*, 1988; *Lemon Sky*, 1988; *Burn This*, 1992; *Talley's Folly*, 1992.

Lanford Eugene Wilson, a model of the playwrights of the generation bred and nurtured in the fertile Off-Off-Broadway lofts and churches of the 1960's, may be the most prolific American writer for the stage since Eugene O'Neill. His Pulitzer Prize-winning *Talley's Folly* takes him about halfway through his lifelong chronicling of the fictitious Talley family and its richly variegated American environment.

Wilson was affected by the early divorce of his parents. After spending his childhood with his mother and stepfather in Springfield and Ozark, Missouri, he moved to San Diego, where his reacquaintance with his father (after thirteen years), however imperfect, served as the basis for his examination of his life through drama in the creative years that followed, culminating in the anguished, autobiographical *Lemon Sky*. Gradually working his way eastward, Wilson found himself in New York at the moment of the birth of Off-Off-Broadway theater, which welcomed his idiosyncratic dramatic voice.

Three New York theaters were integral to Wilson's growth as an artist and person during those formative years. The Caffé Cino, operated with great daring and foresight by Joe Cino, staged Wilson's first effort, *So Long at the Fair*, and some other one-act plays, including *This Is the Rill Speaking*, *Wandering*, and *The Madness of Lady Bright*, which won an Obie for its star, Neil Flanagan. Ellen Stewart's equally daring and innovative La Mama Experimental Theatre Club staged some of Wilson's longer works; *Balm in Gilead* and *The Rimers of Eldritch* demonstrate Wilson's multicharacter scene study approach to depicting whole slices of American culture in decay, a layering technique refined in subsequent work such as *The Hot l Baltimore*.

The third theater to influence Wilson's work was the Circle Repertory Company, which he cofounded in 1969 with Tanya Berezin, Rob Thierkield, and Marshall Mason, who had directed Wilson's play *The Sand Castle* at Café La Mama in 1965. This relationship continued: As playwright in residence at the Circle Repertory, Wilson created, developed, and directed more than a dozen plays, many of which moved on to Broadway and won awards and honors.

Wilson's mature output has centered on the continuing saga of the Talley family, in some respects intensely autobiographical but also, more important, a metaphorical construction that dramatizes the best and worst of the American family tradition. *Fifth of July*, a rambling front-porch drama with kaleidoscopic focus, was followed by *Talley's Folly*, a thirty-year step backward to examine in closer detail the odd love of two characters, Matt Friedman and Sally Talley (who appears as a mature aunt in the first play). *A Tale Told* takes place at the same moment, but in the main house on the hill above the boathouse where Matt and Sally are declaring their love. Wilson's *Angels Fall* examines other themes (nuclear devastation), but *Talley and Son*, a rewriting of *A Tale Told*, brought the family back to the Circle Repertory Company in 1985. In the same year a brilliant revival of *Lemon Sky*, directed by Mary B. Robinson, was performed to rave reviews at the Second Stage Theatre. *Burn This*, opening on Broadway in 1987, returns to an urban setting to tell a story of postmodern nonlove non-triangles. By contrast *Redwood Curtain* takes place in the redwood forest of northwest California. In this, his eighteenth full-length play, Wilson looks at the United States as it approaches the twenty-first century. He shows a country not yet recovered from the Vietnam War and threatened by the fragmentation of families and by the greed of corporate giants.

Critics have seen in Wilson's themes and techniques a complex but dramatically exciting vision of the American family situation, the traditions of former generations implanted on the next, in conflict with a world changing more rapidly in its external indifference than in the basically unchanging human interrelationships that make up the private lives of the family members. His plays take place in two essential environments: the family setting, in which ties to former and future generations (represented by impending and dissolving marriages) are reinforced; and hard-edged urban settings peopled with failures and those isolated from their families but forming alliances among themselves for security and hope. His predilection for seedy hotel lobbies and all-night restaurants as settings has invited comparison with William Saroyan and Eugene O'Neill; the roving, unfocused plots, stripping away the layers of complex family relationships with slowly revealed exposition and attention to details of characterization, show the influence of Anton Chekhov, Henrik Ibsen, and Lillian Hellman; the sense of isolation, especially in the shorter works, owes something to Eugene Ionesco, an early influence for Wilson; the "poetic realism" of his language (sometimes referred to as "lyric realism" by spokespersons of the Circle Repertory Company) is reminiscent of Tennessee Williams. In form, as in theme, subject, and style, Wilson's works are varied. With the same seeming ease he turns out lavish, melodramatic stage plays like *Redwood Curtain*, simple monologues like *Moonshot and Cosmos*, and television versions of his own work, as in *Lemon Sky*.

As early as 1975 Wilson began to be called a young genius. His subsequent successes, not only on Broadway and at Circle Rep but also in the regional theaters throughout the United States, ensured his high reputation among future critics and audiences. With David Mamet, Sam Shepard, and Arthur Kopit, he belongs to the generation of playwrights whose voices began to be heard during the Vietnam War, a kind of American absurdist school, nurtured by both Off-Off-Broadway and the regional theater movement.

Thomas J. Taylor
Rosemary M. Canfield Reisman

Bibliography

Barnett, Gene A. *Lanford Wilson*. Boston: Twayne, 1987. The most valuable general study of Wilson. This book carries chapters on all the major plays through *Talley and Son*. It also includes a family genealogy and a family chronology for the entire Talley clan.

Bode, Walter. "Lanford Wilson." In *Contemporary Dramatists*, edited by D. L. Kirkpatrick. 4th ed. Chicago: St. James Press, 1988. Bode's brief article contains a complete primary bibliography through *Burn This*. The analysis that follows discusses Wilson's work as it relates to the conflict between the traditional values of the past and the "insidious pressures of modern life."

Bryer, Jackson R. *Lanford Wilson: A Casebook*. New York: Garland, 1994. This collection includes ten critical articles, covering plays through *Burn This*. Also includes an introduction and chronology, and two interviews with Wilson.

Busby, Mark. *Lanford Wilson*. Boise, Idaho: Boise State University, 1987. Busby's brief monograph focuses on how Wilson's own family history influenced his dramatic themes of longing for the past and conflict between generations. Literary influences, including Franz Kafka, and the influence of Wilson's early theater-going experiences, are also explored.

Dean, Anne M. *Discovery and Invention: The Urban Plays of Lanford Wilson*. Rutherford, Md.: Fairleigh Dickinson University Press, 1995. Written with the cooperation of Wilson, Marshall Mason, and other members of the Circle Repertory Company, this passionately affirming book examines Wilson's themes and the use of realistic yet poetic language, particularly in *Balm in Gilead*, *Hot l Baltimore*, and *Burn This*.

Herman, William. "Down and Out in Lebanon and New York: Lanford Wilson." In *Understanding Contemporary American Drama*. Columbia: University of South Carolina Press, 1987.

Herman's chapter includes explications of Wilson's major plays. He praises Wilson for the "delicate poetic language at the heart of his style" and for his "epic encompassment of American experience and mythologies."

Robertson, C. Warren. "Lanford Wilson." In *American Playwrights Since 1945*, edited by Philip C. Kolin. New York: Greenwood Press, 1989. An accessible reference to primary and secondary sources through 1987. Robertson provides a complete primary bibliography of Wilson's works and brief discussions entitled "Assessment of Wilson's Reputation" and "Production History." The article also includes an informative survey of secondary sources and a complete secondary bibliography.

Robert Wilson

American playwright

Born: Waco, Texas; October 4, 1941

DRAMA: *Dance Event*, pr. 1965; *Solo Performance*, pr. 1966; *Theater Activity*, pr. 1967; *Spaceman*, pr. 1967 (with Ralph Hilton); *ByrdwoMAN*, pr. 1968; *The King of Spain*, pr. 1969; *The Life and Times of Sigmund Freud*, pr. 1969; *Deafman Glance*, pr. 1970; *Program Prologue Now, Overture for a Deafman*, pr. 1971; *Overture*, pr. 1972; *Ka Mountain, GUARDenia Terrace: a story about a family and some people changing*, pr. 1972; *king lyre and the lady in the wasteland*, pr. 1973; *The Life and Times of Joseph Stalin*, pr. 1973; *DiaLOG/A MAD MAN A MAD GIANT A MAD DOG A MAD URGE A MAD FACE*, pr. 1974; *The Life and Times of Dave Clark*, pr. 1974; *Prologue to a Letter for Queen Victoria*, pr. 1974; *A Letter for Queen Victoria*, pr. 1974 (with Christopher Knowles); *To Street*, pr. 1975; *$ Value of Man*, pr. 1975; *DiaLOG*, pr. 1975 (with Knowles); *Einstein on the Beach*, pr., pb. 1976 (music by Philip Glass); *I Was Sitting on My Patio This Guy Appeared I Thought I Was Hallucinating*, pr. 1977; *Prologue to the Fourth Act of Deafman Glance*, pr. 1978; *DiaLOG/NETWORK*, pr. 1978; *Death Destruction and Detroit*, pr. 1979; *DiaLOG/Curious George*, pr. 1979; *Edison*, pr. 1979; *Medea*, pr. 1981; *The Golden Windows*, pr. 1982; *the CIVIL warS: a tree is best measured when it is down*, partial pr. 1983 and 1984 (includes *Knee Plays*); *Alcestis*, pr. 1985 (based on Euripides' play); *Knee Plays*, pr. 1986; *Parzifal*, pr. 1987 (with Tankred Dorst and Knowles); *Cosmopolitan Greetings*, pr. 1988; *The Forest*, pr. 1988; *The Black Rider: The Casting of the Magic Bullets*, pr. 1990 (with Tom Waits and William S. Burroughs); *When We Dead Awaken*, pr. 1991 (adaptation of Henrik Ibsen's play *Naar vi døde vaagner*); *Lohengrin*, pr. 1991, revised pr. 1998 (adaptation of Richard Wagner's opera); *Alice*, pr. 1992 (with Tom Waits, Kathleen Brennan, and Paul Schmidt; adaptation of Lewis Carroll's *Alice's Adventures in Wonderland*); *Dr. Faustus Lights the Lights*, pr. 1992 (adaptation of Gertrude Stein's story); *Hamlet: A Monologue*, pr. 1995; *The Magic Flute*, pr. 1995; *Time Rocker*, pr. 1996 (with Lou Reed and Darryl Pinckney); *A Dream Play*, pr. 1998 (adaptation of August Strindberg's play *Ett drømspel*); *Das Rheingold*, pr. 2000 (adaptation of Wagner's opera); *POEtry*, pr. 2000 (with Reed); *Woyzeck*, pr. 2000 (with Waits and Brennan; adaptation of Georg Büchner's play); *Siegfried*, pr. 2001; *Doctor Caligari*, pr. 2002; *Osud*, pr. 2002.

Robert Wilson has blazed a diverse and unusual artistic trail, becoming known as one of the most prolific experimental theater artists of the twentieth century. His long and highly visual theater pieces could hardly be classified as conventional plays, but they are vivid theatrical endeavors comparable only with the works of experimental dramatists such as England's Peter Brook, Poland's Jerzy Grotowski, and a handful of others. Wilson's works combine dance, drama, and poetry to create highly stylized productions such as *the CIVIL warS* (which was nominated for the Pulitzer Prize) and *Ka Mountain, GUARDenia Terrace* (unusual combinations of upper- and lowercase letters are common in Wilson titles), the latter a 168-hour event in which cast and audience trekked up a mountain after a prologue delivered by Wilson's eighty-five-year-old grandmother.

Wilson was born Robert M. Wilson to D. M. and Loree Velma Wilson on October 4, 1941 in Waco, Texas. His early childhood was filled with amateur theatrics, mostly plays and skits that he wrote and performed in the garage. Some of these early playlets were nonverbal: Wilson was already an experimenter of sorts, trying to find a form that would accommodate his speech difficulties (he had a marked stammer). Some of his early professional work was in creating ways for autistic and brain-damaged children and chronically ill adults to express themselves.

The stammer went away when he was approximately seventeen, and Wilson enrolled in the University of Texas as a business administration major. He became increasingly interested in his work with brain-damaged children, and in his painting, and subsequently left Texas for the highly regarded Pratt Institute for arts in Brooklyn, New York. He taught movement to students there, and later used some of the students in his productions. (In general, early Wilson productions featured casts largely made up of amateurs; a deaf student named Raymond Andrews and an autistic student named Christopher Knowles were early collaborators.)

Receiving his M.F.A. degree in 1965 from Pratt Institute, Wilson began his work in earnest. He founded the Byrd Hoffman studios in New York City (which later became the Byrd Hoffman

Foundation), designed sets and costumes, and created performance pieces at Byrd Hoffman and other avant-garde spaces. In 1964 he created a dance performance for the New York World's Fair.

Suffering a nervous breakdown in 1966, Wilson spent some time in a mental institution. Overcoming some of the frustration that led to his hospitalization, he returned to his unusual work, creating a slow-motion "dance" for patients in iron lungs in 1967. In 1969 he created his first truly large-scale work, *The King of Spain*, which featured everything from a stereotypical Black Mammy to a number of animal legs hanging from the ceiling. Some of these same characters and images populated other of his early endeavors, such as *The Life and Times of Sigmund Freud*.

Having made little or no money for many years, Wilson was taken by surprise when his production *Deafman Glance* (later incorporated into *The Life and Times of Joseph Stalin*) was a financial success. He was given a large gift by the French government to stage the major piece *Einstein on the Beach*, and he became a favorite of European theatrical intellectuals. (The gift did not go far enough, however, and Wilson was in debt after the end of the production's tour.) The European tour of *Einstein on the Beach* occurred in 1976, and the production opened at the Metropolitan Opera House in New York that fall. Wilson's apparently disconnected visual images sparked comparisons with the work of painter René Magritte and to the early twentieth century Dadaists, whose reconstruction of reality was the basis of Surrealism. Wilson might also be compared with French poet and dramatist Guillaume Apollinaire, whose 1917 play *Les Mamelles de Tirésias* (*The Breasts of Tiresius*, 1961) contains similarly strange and disconnected images. In *Einstein on the Beach* Wilson was able to explore his interest in the scientist as destroyer and the role of the innocent in popular culture. He collaborated on the piece with the renowned composer Philip Glass.

Wilson went on to create sensational and whimsical sets and lighting for opera and theater, and he continued to create his strange images for his own hybrid productions such as *The Life and Times of Joseph Stalin*, which juxtaposes a line of apes holding apples and a woman in eighteenth century dress whose parasol is aflame. He directed highly respected opera and dance productions, won numerous awards (both in the United States and internationally), created furniture, and oversaw the formation of the Byrd Hoffman Foundation. In the 1990's and 2000's, Wilson began a series of adaptations of classic works including *Alice*, *Hamlet: A Monologue*, *Das Rheingold*, and *Woyzeck*.

While many critics see Wilson as a visionary pioneer, others have dismissed him as a painter of three-dimensional pictures with no unifying voice. "The fact is," said Wilson in an interview, "I don't really understand my own stuff. Artists very seldom understand what they are doing. My work is a mystery to me, and I feel that words only confuse people about my work." With that, perhaps, Wilson does answer the questions about the meaning of his work. He was a young boy unable to communicate verbally, and he learned to communicate visually. As he told *The New York Times*, "I don't wish to mystify people. It's best not to say anything at all."

Kirby Tepper

Bibliography

Bigsby, C. W. E. *Beyond Broadway*. Vol. 3 in *A Critical Introduction to Twentieth Century American Drama*. Cambridge, England: Cambridge University Press, 1985. A full chapter on Wilson covers his life, his early work with speech-impaired individuals, and his association with the Byrd Hoffman School of Byrds, and describes *Ka Mountain, GUARDenia Terrace, $ Value of Man*, and other stage pieces. Behind his work, Bigsby says, "there lies a romantic conviction about continuity, a touching faith about the possibility of communication and the essentially holistic nature of experience."

Byrne, David. "*The Forest:* A Preview of the Next Wilson-Byrne Collaboration." Interview by Laurence Shyer. *Theater* 19 (Summer/Fall, 1988): 6-11. This interview with David Byrne discusses the nature of his collaboration with Wilson and contains many indirect Wilson quotations. Much on Wilson's forming a Berlin company in the fall of 1987 to make this Gilgamesh version (*The Forest*). Includes a seven-act breakdown of images in photographs and text.

Croyden, Margaret. *Lunatics, Lovers, and Poets: The Contemporary Experimental Theatre*. New York: McGraw-Hill, 1974. A description of the Byrd Hoffman School of Byrds, its "aesthetic of the Beautiful," and Wilson's experiences with brain-damaged children who "responded to dance and movement therapy." Much of the theatre of silence is wordless, Croyden notes, "and in some of his later workshop pieces, where words are uttered, the effect is that of silence nonetheless." Deals at length with *Deafman Glance*.

Deak, Frantisek. "Robert Wilson." In *The New Theatre: Performance Documentation*, edited by Michael Kirby. New York: New York University Press, 1974. A reprint of an article originally appearing in *The Drama Review* (June, 1974), unique in its fully illustrated (with photographs by Carl Paler) white-on-black pages. Gives a strong impression of the performance itself, in an act-by-act visual description accompanied by striking production shots.

Holmberg, Arthur. *The Theatre of Robert Wilson*. New York: Cambridge University Press, 1997. Holmberg, who was associated with Robert Wilson at the American Repertory Theatre and beyond, examines Wilson's vast production corpus and organizes his material thematically. His explication serves as an invaluable tool for anyone interested in Wilson, novice and scholar alike.

Quadri, Franco, Franco Bertoni, and Robert Stearns. *Robert Wilson*. New York: Rizzoli, 1998. A coffee-table book in the traditional sense of size and photographs, this book is enhanced by its critical essays and its detailed chronology of Wilson's work.

Shyer, Laurence. *Robert Wilson and His Collaborators*. New York: Theatre Communications Group, 1989. The most complete and authoritative record of Wilson's busy artistic life and his relationships with his collaborators (arranged by artistic specialty). This indispensable volume is illustrated with photographs and drawings of most of Wilson's productions and is complemented by a strong chronology (with comments by contemporaries) and a select bibliography.

Zurbrugg, Nicholas. "Post-Modernism and the Multi-Media Sensibility: Heiner Muller's *Hamletmachine* and the Art of Robert Wilson." *Modern Drama* 31 (September, 1988): 439-453. Zurbrugg finds that "Wilson's aesthetic seems to hover somewhere between [Samuel] Beckett's and [John] Cage's antithetical explorations of form, ambiguity, chance and rule." Offers a strong discussion of Wilson's collaboration with the East German playwright and follows this article by Arthur Holmberg's "conversation" with Wilson and Heiner Müller.

Yvor Winters

American poet and critic

Born: Chicago, Illinois; October 17, 1900
Died: Palo Alto, California; January 25, 1968

POETRY: *The Immobile Wind*, 1921; *The Magpie's Shadow*, 1922; *The Bare Hills*, 1927; *The Proof*, 1930; *The Journey, and Other Poems*, 1931; *Before Disaster*, 1934; *Poems*, 1940; *The Giant Weapon*, 1943; *To the Holy Spirit*, 1947; *Collected Poems*, 1952, 1960; *Early Poems of Yvor Winters, 1920-1928*, 1966; *The Collected Poems of Yvor Winters*, 1978; *The Uncollected Poems of Yvor Winters, 1919-1928*, 1997 (R. L. Barth, editor); *The Uncollected Poems of Yvor Winters, 1929-1957*, 1997 (Barth, editor).

SHORT FICTION: "The Brink of Darkness," 1932, revised 1947.

NONFICTION: *Primitivism and Decadence: A Study of American Experimental Poetry*, 1937; *Maule's Curse: Seven Studies in the History of American Obscurantism*, 1938; *The Anatomy of Nonsense*, 1943; *Edwin Arlington Robinson*, 1946; *In Defense of Reason*, 1947; *The Function of Criticism: Problems and Exercises*, 1957; *On Modern Poets*, 1957; *The Poetry of W. B. Yeats*, 1960; *Forms of Discovery: Critical and Historical Essays on the Forms of the Short Poem in English*, 1967; *Uncollected Essays and Reviews*, 1973 (Francis Murphy, editor); *Hart Crane and Yvor Winters: Their Literary Correspondence*, 1978; *The Selected Letters of Yvor Winters*, 2000 (R. L. Barth, editor).

EDITED TEXTS: *Twelve Poets of the Pacific*, 1937; *Selected Poems*, 1948 (of Elizabeth Daryush); *Poets of the Pacific*, 1949 (second series).

Arthur Yvor Winters was a poet, literary critic, college professor, and breeder of airedale terriers. Born in Chicago, as a child he also lived in California and Oregon, returning with his family to Illinois in 1913. Although his parents hoped Winters would be a doctor, they underwrote his efforts to earn degrees in languages and literature. Winters's dedication to writing poetry and to the study of literature began when he was a high school student in Chicago, where he read *Poetry*, a leading monthly publication specializing in new American verse, and corresponded with its editor, Harriet Monroe.

In 1917 Winters entered the University of Chicago, but he was forced to withdraw in 1918 after he was diagnosed with tuberculosis. He left the Midwest for New Mexico, where he resided in a sanatorium from 1918 to 1922. During this time, he read widely and began writing poetry. Monroe accepted his first efforts in 1920 for *Poetry*. The next year, Winters published his first book of verse, *The Immobile Wind*, a collection of nineteen poems on the observation of nature. In his earliest work, it is possible to detect Winters's preoccupations with formal techniques of verse composition, his interests in the power of evocative language, and his ability to compose poems with strong images. His second book of verse, *The Magpie's Shadow*, was published in 1922.

With his health improved, Winters enrolled at the University of Colorado, where he earned B.A. and M.A. degrees in Romance languages. In 1925 he was hired by the University of Idaho as an instructor of languages, and he remained there until 1927. He married the writer Janet Lewis in 1926; in 1927, he published a third book of poems, *The Bare Hills*, again drawn from his observations of the natural world, especially the landscape of New Mexico.

Winters enrolled at Stanford University in 1927 to study for his doctoral degree. In 1928 he was appointed a lecturer. While teaching, Winters continued to write and study poetry, publishing in 1930 *The Proof*, a significant work in his canon. Divided into three sections, the book features free-verse poetry, Winters's first published sonnet sequence, and a thematic section on loss. In *The Proof*, Winters demonstrated how powerful traditional forms of poetry could be in expressing current ideas, observations, and emotions. His fifth book, *The Journey, and Other Poems*, furthered Winters's explorations of such themes as wisdom, being, time, the seasons, and human actions and their consequences. By 1934 Winters had earned his Ph.D.; his thesis was indicative of his research and verse writing at this time: "A Study of the Post-Romantic Reaction to Lyrical Verse, and Incidentally in Certain Other Forms." He published another book of poetry, *Before Disaster*, which contains some of his better-known work, including "To My Infant Daughter" and "By the Road to the Sunnyvale Air-Base."

From 1934 to 1966, Winters was a professor at Stanford. He published two more collections of poetry in 1940 and 1952. The first, called simply *Poems*, contains verse written between 1939 and 1940; it was printed by Winters at his Gyroscope Press in Los Altos, California. The second, *Collected Poems*, was published in 1952 by Alan Swallow Press of Denver.

Simultaneous with his verse writing, Winters was a student of literature and of literary criticism. Between 1937 and 1967, he published six books reflecting his theories of literature and verse composition. As a critic, Winters showed great range, commenting on a diverse group of writers including Emily Dickinson, Henry James, T. S. Eliot, Robert Frost, and Hart Crane.

Forms of Discovery, Winters's major critical book, is noteworthy as an example of his ability to define his positions and to support them with strong examples. In this work, he divides poetry into two main groups: one located in English poetry before 1700 and the other in American poetry written after 1830. To illustrate his claims, Winters lists and analyzes many individual poems, and he argues that verse should be ranked and judged according to the quality of the formal elements: tone, style, logic, rhythm, and word choice, especially as these make the meaning of a composition clear to the reader. Winters's insistence on these quantitative aspects of verse made him unpopular as a literary critic, as poetry is often written without formal structure. Winters, though, was concerned with the effect the poem had on the reader rather than with the poet's objectives in writing the piece. Winters's reading and appreciation of the theological writings of St. Thomas Aquinas was the greatest influence on his critical method, and Winters addressed the moral effect of poetry's form, content, and meaning in the scope of his entire critical work.

Winters also translated French and Spanish verse for magazine publications; wrote book reviews and literary articles, many of which are collected in *Uncollected Essays and Reviews*; operated his own printing press; published a short-lived magazine, *The Gyroscope* (1929-1930); wrote studies of the poets Edwin Arlington Robinson and William Butler Yeats; and edited the poetry of Elizabeth Daryush for publication in 1948. He died of cancer on January 25, 1968. In 1993 his letters were released from the terms of his will and became available for scholarly use and publication.

Beverly Schneller

Bibliography

Gelpi, Albert. "Yvor Winters and Robinson Jeffers." In *A Coherent Splendor.* Cambridge, England: Cambridge University Press, 1987. Gelpi notes that Winters's early poems belie his critical precepts. They display the strong influence of Ezra Pound and William Carlos Williams, despite Winters's furious anti-Romantic denigration of both poets in his criticism. Winters strongly identified with the California landscape, as can be seen in *The Magpie's Shadow.*

Gunn, Thom. "On a Drying Hill." In *The Occasions of Poetry.* San Francisco: North Point Press, 1985. Gunn was a student of Winters at Stanford University. He describes Winters's strong personality and his efforts to convert his students to his critical principles. Foremost among these was the rejection of Romantic poetry.

Kaye, Howard. "The Post-symbolist Poetry of Yvor Winters," *The Southern Review* 7, no. 1 (Winter, 1971): 176-197. Winters's poetry strongly evokes landscape. His ability to portray the external world in a precise manner was remarkable. In Kaye's view, Winters counts as one of the great twentieth century poets. His stress upon rationality and control reflects a fear of being overwhelmed by death and strong emotion. Winters's struggle with his emotions is a leitmotif of his poetry. He attempted to extirpate his own Romantic tendencies.

Rexroth, Kenneth. *American Poetry in the Twentieth Century.* New York: Herder, 1971. Rexroth contends that Winters was the true exile of his generation of writers. Most of his friends went to Paris, but health problems forced Winters to live in a dry climate. His move to Northern California kept him isolated, and his criticism became cranky and cliquish. He was an important poet who created an original variant of neoclassicism.

Wellek, René. "Yvor Winters." In *A History of Modern Criticism: American Criticism, 1900-1950.* Vol. 6. New Haven, Conn.: Yale University Press, 1986. Wellek gives a careful summary of the principles that underlie Winters's poetry and criticism. A poem should express a moral judgment. The judgment, based on absolute moral values, is ideally incapable of being paraphrased. Winters deprecated the expression of emotion not under the strict dominance of reason.

Winters, Yvor. *The Selected Letters of Yvor Winters.* Edited by R. L. Barth. Athens: Ohio University Press, 2000. Selected correspondence offering insights into the life of a brilliant man, erudite writer, and lofty poet. Includes bibliographical references and indexes.

Jeanette Winterson

English novelist

Born: Manchester, England; August 27, 1959
Identity: Gay or bisexual

LONG FICTION: *Oranges Are Not the Only Fruit*, 1985; *Boating for Beginners*, 1985; *The Passion*, 1987; *Sexing the Cherry*, 1989; *Written on the Body*, 1993; *Art and Lies: A Piece for Three Voices and a Bawd*, 1994; *Gut Symmetries*, 1997; *The PowerBook*, 2000.
SHORT FICTION: *The World and Other Places*, 1998.
NONFICTION: *Fit for the Future: The Guide for Women Who Want to Live Well*, 1986; *Art Objects: Essays on Ecstasy and Effrontery*, 1995.
EDITED TEXT: *Passion Fruit: Romantic Fiction with a Twist*, 1986.

In a brief amount of time the British writer Jeanette Winterson established a special place for herself in the literary community. Published in fourteen languages, her work early began to meet with popular and critical succes. After receiving a degree in English from Oxford University, she set out to look for editorial jobs but met with no success. At an interview for one such job, she began telling her interviewer stories about her life. The prospective employer encouraged her to write them down, and the result was her first novel, *Oranges Are Not the Only Fruit.*

Winterson herself remains elusive as to the exact details of her own life, but she refers to *Oranges Are Not the Only Fruit* as "semi-autobiographical." The novel details a childhood spent in a Pentecostal community with a domineering and strictly religious mother. Throughout her youth, the protagonist, aptly named "Jeanette," nurtured her skills as a preacher and a potential missionary. However, Jeanette leaves the church and is kicked out of her home when both the congregation she had considered her extended family and her mother reject her upon discovering she is a lesbian. The novel won the prestigious Whitbread First Novel Award and was later made into a miniseries for the British Broadcasting Corporation.

Oranges Are Not the Only Fruit established Winterson as a witty commentator on accepted social standards. Even she expresses surprise that her novels, which question social perspectives that view heterosexuality and religion as undeniable "truths," could be so popular. Using an unconventional novel structure characterized by a collage of reinterpreted fairy tales, parables, and other metaphorical narratives that interrupt the central story, Winterson unveils a social reality rooted in spiritual hypocrisy and, ultimately, patriarchy.

Boating for Beginners, a comical retelling of the story of Noah and the ark with a contemporary consciousness, displays Winterson's ability to use humor to explore hypocrisy in faith. Her third novel, *The Passion*, won the 1987 John Llewellyn Rhys Prize for fiction, receiving international acclaim for its unique fusion of the historical and the fantastic. Narrated alternately by Henri, who worships his employer, Napoleon, and the cross-dresser Villanelle, an inhabitant of Venice with webbed feet that allow her to walk on water, the novel examines the Napoleonic era through a magical eye that entwines literal and figurative images in its telling of history.

After *The Passion*, critics classified Winterson as a novelist of the "magic realism" genre. Her styled use of fantastic imagery makes the figurative appear to be fact in the context of her stories. *Sexing the Cherry* provides the best example of Winterson's success with these methods. The story of a mother, the Dog Woman, and her son Jordan occurs during the Protestant Reformation. The images throughout distort common perceptions of gender by depicting a grotesque female character who carries out acts of cartoonish violence, and by providing a feminist interpretation of what really happens in fairy tales. The novel's very structure then confuses common perceptions of time by making a transgressive leap into a contemporary time that seems to run parallel to the period already familiar in the main story. A winner of the E. M. Forster Award from the Academy of Arts and Letters, *Sexing the Cherry* earned recognition as a "postmodern" novel, a label that was the source of both its sharpest criticism and its highest praise.

In the 1990's Winterson began to earn a reputation as an eccentric. At around the same time, there seemed to be a marked shift in her stylistic approach to writing. A didactic, though lyrical, language replaced the magic realism and fantasy that characterized much of the wit and thematic substance in her previous novels. *Written on the Body* continues Winterson's explorations into sexual identity but distinguishes this theme only by a conspicuous failure to mention the narrator's gender. The narrator's seduction of and eventual parting from a wealthy married woman stricken with leukemia mirrors the controversy enveloping Winterson at that time, as she made public her own affair with the wealthy wife of a well-known British businessman.

Winterson's next book, *Art and Lies*, is considered a dense work because of its epicurean language, symbolic imagery, slim plot, and ethereal characterizations of the three narrators: Handel, Picasso, and Sappho. Through their voices Winterson explores how definitions of "art" oversimplify its true meaning in the complicated context of individual lives. The "gut" in *Gut Symmetries* refers to the physicist's Holy Grail, the Grand Unification Theory, and tells of the interrelationships between two physicists, a male who has an affair with a female, and the male physicist's wife, who also has an affair with the female physicist. Winterson uses physics theory as a metaphor for love throughout the book, narrated from the perspectives of all three participants. *The PowerBook* moves into cyberspace, with a narrator who is a virtual storyteller named Ali—or sometimes Alix—whose stories open windows—and Windows—into life.

Winterson also periodically published a few short stories. "Psalms" and "Only the Best for the Lord" appeared in 1985 and 1986, respectively, and "The World and Other Places" and "The Lives of Saints" in 1990 and 1993. A collection, *The World and Other Places*, appeared in 1998. Through all her writing, Jeanette Winterson remains known as an innovative and often controversial writer who tackles the written word without fear and styles it within an often unique and innovative story.

Kari Olivadotti

Bibliography

Allen, Carolyn. *Following Djuna: Women Lovers and the Erotics of Loss*. Bloomington: Indiana University Press, 1996. Winterson is covered in this study of the influence of Djuna Barnes.

Gilmore, Leigh. *The Limits of Autobiography: Trauma and Testimony*. Ithaca, N.Y.: Cornell University Press, 2001. Contains an essay on the "anatomy of absence" in *Written on the Body.*

Grice, Helena, and Tim Woods, eds. *"I'm Telling You Stories": Jeanette Winterson and the Politics of Reading*. Atlanta: Rodopi, 1998. A collection of nine essays, many of a very dense theoretical nature. The essays by Lynne Pearce and by the editors, however, are good introductory studies.

Harris, Andrea. *Other Sexes: Rewriting Difference from Woolf to Winterson*. Albany: State University of New York Press, 2000. A study of the representation of lesbianism and "alternate" sexuality in Virginia Woolf, Marianne Hauser, Djuna Barnes, and Winterson.

Pressler, Christopher. *So Far So Linear: Responses to the Work of Jeanette Winterson.* Nottingham, England: Pauper's Press, 2000. A study of the critical reception of Winterson's work.

Reynolds, Margaret, and Jonathan Noakes. *Jeanette Winterson.* New York: Vintage, 2003. A reader's guide to four of Winterson's novels, *Oranges Are Not the Only Fruit, The Passion, Sexing the Cherry,* and *The PowerBook.*

Owen Wister

American novelist

Born: Philadelphia, Pennsylvania; July 14, 1860
Died: North Kingstown, Rhode Island; July 21, 1938

LONG FICTION: *The Dragon of Wantley,* 1892; *The Virginian,* 1902; *Lady Baltimore,* 1906.

SHORT FICTION: *Red Men and White,* 1895; *Lin McLean,* 1897; *The Jimmyjohn Boss, and Other Stories,* 1900; *Philosophy 4,* 1903; *When West Was West,* 1928.

NONFICTION: *Ulysses S. Grant,* 1900; *The Seven Ages of Washington,* 1907; *Roosevelt: The Story of a Friendship, 1880-1919,* 1930.

MISCELLANEOUS: *Romney, and Other New Works About Philadelphia,* wr. 1912-1914, pb. 2001 (essays and unfinished novel; James A. Butler, editor).

Owen Wister, born in Philadelphia, Pennsylvania, on July 14, 1860, began his career with a serious interest in music and only later became interested in writing. After being educated in private schools in the United States and abroad, he attended Harvard University, where he was graduated with highest honors in music in 1882. He then spent two years abroad, studying composition in Paris until ill health forced his return to the United States. Following a period as a bank employee in New York City, he suffered a nervous breakdown and traveled to Wyoming to recuperate in the healthful atmosphere of a Western cattle ranch. He associated with the large cattle barons who were then engaged in a struggle with smaller ranchers that culminated in the Johnson County Range War of 1892. What Wister saw and heard formed the background for his novel *The Virginian.* From 1885 to 1888 he attended the Harvard Law School. After graduation he was admitted to the bar and practiced law in Philadelphia.

His growing fondness for the West led Wister to make other trips to Wyoming during the early 1890's, and he incorporated incidents and experiences into short stories that won immediate recognition. Two short stories based on Western life, "Hank's Woman" (1891) and "How Lin McLean Went West" (1891), published in *Harper's Magazine,* were his first literary works to attract a wide audience. Such volumes as *Red Men and White* and *The Jimmyjohn Boss, and Other Stories* followed. In the meantime, Wister married Mary Channing, of Philadelphia, in 1898.

Wister's only well-known novel, *The Virginian,* achieved a high degree of popular success when it appeared in 1902. Drawing on Wister's experiences in Wyoming, it combined the confrontation of good and evil on the range with a classic love story. The book became the basis for several movies and helped establish the "western" as a distinct field in American literature. Wister dedicated the book to his close friend Theodore Roosevelt, another outdoorsman and lover of the West. Frederic Remington, the famous painter of life in the West, illustrated an edition of *The Virginian.* Wister continued to write, and he explored other themes than the West, but his other works were never widely accepted. *Philosophy 4,* for example, was a story about life at Harvard University, with limited appeal to general readers. *Lady Baltimore* was his one venture in the field of historical romance.

In the years after World War I, Wister wrote little. His last book was *Roosevelt: The Story of a Friendship, 1880-1919.* He died of a cerebral hemorrhage at North Kingstown, Rhode Island, on July 21, 1938.

Lewis L. Gould

Bibliography

Cobbs, John L. *Owen Wister.* Boston: Twayne, 1984. Makes a strong case for Wister's importance as a writer and contains an informative survey of his work.

Estleman, Loren D. *The Wister Trace: Classic Novels of the American Frontier.* New York: Jameson Books, 1987. Discusses frontier or Western fiction as a genre.

Etulain, Richard W. *Owen Wister.* Boise, Idaho: Boise State College, 1973. Offers a good, brief analysis of Wister's career as a western writer.

Payne, Darwin. *Owen Wister: Chronicler of the West, Gentleman of the East.* Dallas: Southern Methodist University Press, 1985. A good biography of Wister, which draws on the large collection of Wister's papers at the Library of Congress.

White, G. Edward. *The Eastern Establishment and the Western Experience: The West of Frederic Remington, Theodore Roosevelt, and Owen Wister.* 1968. Reprint. Austin: University of Texas Press, 1989. Excellent on Wister's days in the West and the influence of that experience on *The Virginian* and his other writings about the region.

George Wither

English poet

Born: Bentworth, Hampshire, England; June 11, 1588
Died: London, England; May 2, 1667

POETRY: *Abuses Stript, and Whipt*, 1613; *Fidelia*, 1615; *The Shepheards Hunting*, 1615; *Wither's Motto: nec habeo, nec careo, nec curo*, 1621; *Faire-Virtue, the Mistresse of Phil'arete*, 1622; *Juvenilia*, 1622; *The Hymnes and Songs of the Church*, 1623; *Britain's Remembrancer*, 1628; *A Collection of Emblemes, Ancient and Moderne*, 1635; *Haleluiah: Or, Britans Second Remembrancer*, 1641; *The Poetry of George Wither*, 1902.

George Wither was the son of a Hampshire gentleman. He was sent to Oxford in 1603, where he apparently did not do well. Two years later, at the age of seventeen, he left the university without graduating and went to London, where he entered one of the Inns of Chancery to study law. He was eventually introduced at court. In 1612 and 1613, respectively, he wrote an elegy on the death of Prince Henry and a poem celebrating the marriage of Princess Elizabeth. In 1613 he also published his collection of satires, *Abuses Stript, and Whipt*, in which, among other unwise things, he insulted the lord chancellor. The poet was imprisoned for a few months but was released at the intercession of Princess Elizabeth.

While in prison, Wither continued to write. After his release he was admitted to Lincoln's Inn (1615); the same year he published *Fidelia*, the book containing his best-known lyric, "Shall I, wasting in despair." By 1621 he was again writing satire, publishing *Wither's Motto*, a biting poem that is said to have quickly sold thirty thousand copies and which again landed him in jail with charges of libel. He was soon released without trial, however, and in 1622 he published *Faire-Virtue, the Mistresse of Phil'arete*, his best single volume of poetry. This book was a watershed in Wither's career; it ended what he later called his juvenilia.

Most of the rest of his writing is religious in character. Wither had begun as a moderate in religion and politics, but he became increasingly Puritan. He published a book of hymns in 1623. In 1628, after witnessing the London plague of 1625, he published *Britain's Remembrancer*, in which he described what he saw and prophesied disaster for England. In 1641 Wither's best book of religious poems, *Haleluiah: Or, Britans Second Remembrancer*, was published in Holland.

In 1639 the poet served as a captain of horse in King Charles I's expedition against the Scottish Covenanters, but at the outbreak of the civil war he sided with Parliament and sold his estate to raise a troop of cavalry. During the war he was once captured by the Royalist forces and threatened with execution. He was saved, it is said, by the intervention of the Royalist poet Sir John Denham. Denham purportedly begged Wither's life on the grounds that, as long as Wither was alive, Denham could not be called the worst poet in England.

Before the end of the civil war, Wither was promoted to the rank of major; he was present at the siege of Gloucester (1643) and the battle of Naseby (1645), though because of legal troubles he had been deprived of command in 1643. During the years of Oliver Cromwell's administration the poet experienced various financial troubles and also managed to lose Cromwell's favor by, claimed Wither, "declaring unto him those truths which he was not willing to hear of." After the restoration of Charles II in 1660, the poet was imprisoned for three years. He died at the age of seventy-eight in London.

Victoria Gaydosik

Bibliography

Bush, Douglas. *English Literature in the Earlier Seventeenth Century*. 2d ed. Oxford, England: Clarendon Press, 1966. A summary of Wither's accomplishments.

Hensley, Charles Stanley. *The Later Career of George Wither*. Paris: Mouton, 1969. Studies Wither's Puritanism.

Hunter, Williams Bridges, Jr., ed. *The English Spenserians: The Poetry of Giles Fletcher, George Wither, Michael Drayton, Phineas Fletcher, and Henry More*. Salt Lake City: University of Utah Press, 1977. An overview of Wither's historical context.

Jonas, Leah. *The Divine Science: The Aesthetic of Some Representative Seventeenth-Century Poets*. New York: Columbia University Press, 1940. Devotes one chapter to Wither.

Norbrook, David. "Levelling Poetry: George Wither and the English Revolution." *English Literary Renaissance* 21 (Spring, 1991). Studies Wither's religious and political writings.

Stanisław Ignacy Witkiewicz

Polish playwright

Born: Warsaw, Poland; February 24, 1885
Died: Jeziory, Poland (now in Ukraine); September 18, 1939

DRAMA: *Mister Price: Czyli, Bzik tropikalny*, wr. 1920, pr. 1926 (*Mr. Price: Or, Tropical Madness*, 1972); *Oni*, wr. 1920, pb. 1962 (*They*, 1968); *Straszliwy wychowawca*, wr. 1920, pr., pb. 1935; *Pragmatyści*, pb. 1920 (*The Pragmatists*, 1971); *Tumor Mózgowicz*, pr., pb. 1921 (*Tumor Brainiowicz*, 1980); *Metafizyka dwugłowego cielęcia*, wr. 1921, pr. 1928 (*Metaphysics of a Two-Headed Calf*, 1972); *Gyubal Wahazar: Czyli, Na przełęczach bezsensu*, wr. 1921, pb. 1962 (*Gyubal Wahazar: Or, Along the Cliffs of the Absurd*, 1971); *Bezimienne dzieło*, wr. 1921, pb. 1962 (*The Anonymous Work*, 1974); *Kurka wodna*, pr. 1922 (*The Water Hen*, 1968); *Nowe wyzwolenie*, pb. 1922; *Nadobnisie i koczkodany: Czyli, Zielon pigułka*, wr. 1922, pb. 1962 (*Dainty Shapes and Hairy Apes: Or, The Green Pill*, 1980); *W małym dworku*, pr. 1923 (*Country House*, 1997); *Mątwa: Czyli, Hyrkaniczny światopogląd*, pb. 1923 (*The Cuttlefish: Or, The Hyrcanian World View*, 1970); *Szalona lokomotywa*, wr. 1923, pb. 1962 (*The Crazy Locomotive*, 1968); *Matka*, wr. 1924, pb. 1962 (*The Mother*, 1968); *Wariat i zakonnica: Czyli, Nie ma złego, co by na jeszcze gorsze nie wyszło*, pr. 1924 (*The Madman and the Nun: Or, There Is Nothing Bad Which Could Not Turn into Something Worse*, 1966); *Jan Maciej Karol Wścieklica*, pr. 1925; *Sonata Belzebuba: Czyli, Prawdziwe zdarzenie w Mordowarze*, pb. 1938 (*The Beelzebub Sonata: Or, What Really Happened at Mordowar*, 1980); *Szewcy*, pb. 1948 (*The Shoemakers*, 1968).

LONG FICTION: *Pożegnanie jesieni*, 1927; *Nienasycenie*, 1930 (*Insatiability: A Novel in Two Parts*, 1977); *Jedyne wyjście*, 1968; *622 upadki Bunga: Czyli, Demoniczna kobieta*, 1972.

NONFICTION: *Nowe formy w malarstwie i wynikające stąd nieporozumienia*, 1919; *Szkice estetyczne*, 1922; *Teatr: Wstęp do teorii czystej formy w teatrze*, 1923; *Nikotyna, alkohol, kokaina, peyotl, morfina, eter, + dodatek*, 1932; *Pojęcia i twierdzenia implikowane przez pojęcie istnienia*, 1935; *Niemyte dusze: Studia obyczajowe i społeczne*, 1975; *Witkacy, malarz*, 1985 (*Witkacy, the Painter*, 1987); *Przeciw nicości: fotografie Stanisława Ignacego Witkiewicza*, 1986.

Stanisław Ignacy Witkiewicz (VIHT-kah-vihts) was a talented and important writer and dramatist who also left his mark in painting, dramatic and aesthetic theory, and philosophy. He was born on February 24, 1885, in Warsaw, as the only child of the noted painter and art critic Stanisław Witkiewicz. Taking his son's education under his own aegis, Stanisław Witkiewicz secured the best private instructors for his child and supervised his schooling at home. The future artist passed his maturity exam in 1901. Upon completion of his secondary studies, Witkiewicz set off for Germany and Italy for practical experience in painting. He also painted in Cracow and Zakopane. Accepted into the prestigious Cracovian Akademia Sztuk Pięknych (Academy of Fine Arts), he attended lectures there only for a short while, against his father's wishes. Witkiewicz soon began to write creatively. The years from 1910 to 1911 saw the composition of his first mature literary work, the novel *622 upadki Bunga* (the 622 downfalls of Bunga), which, however, was not published until after the author's death.

Somehow tangled up in the unusual circumstances of his fiancé's suicide, in 1914 Witkiewicz left Poland for Australia in the company of his friend, sociologist Bronisław Malinowski. The outbreak of World War I, however, in this same year prompted the young artist to enlist in the Russian army, in search of the novelty of wartime experiences and military life. According to many, he served with bravery. The Bolshevik Revolution of 1917 exerted a great influence on Witkiewicz. Those close to the artist report that the dramatist and painter often referred to his fear of the Communist regime in the Soviet Union and considered Soviet iconoclasm a grave threat to European culture.

Witkiewicz published his views on graphic technique in two critical volumes of aesthetics published in 1919 and 1922 respectively: *Nowe formy w malarstwie i wynikające stąd nieporozumienia* (new forms in painting) and *Szkice estetyczne* (aesthetic sketches). The complete and definitive bound collection of Witkiewicz's artwork (with many color plates) is *Witkacy, the Painter*, published in 1985. Witkacy was Witkiewicz's pseudonym. The first period of Witkiewicz's literary career occurred during the *Młoda Polska* (young Poland) period, a time of great change in Polish artistic spheres. For a long time, Witkiewicz was unable to define and stabilize his manner and style of thought, which was, for this particular period, quite shocking to the large number of Polish literati and theatergoers. The first few years of the 1920's saw the beginning of Witkiewicz's career as a playwright, which was to bring him his greatest fame. Between the years 1919 and 1923, the artist created a large number of his thirty dramatic works, among which are *They*, *Country House*, and *The Water Hen*. His later *The Shoemakers*, though, became his best-known drama.

In his theoretical tract *Teatr*, Witkiewicz laid out his dramatic aesthetic, which he called "pure form." Similar to his theories of graphic art, Witkiewicz's theatrical aesthetic is based on the premise that, in drama, it is not content but form which is all-important. Pondering the course of Western aesthetics, Witkiewicz noted the decline and, as he saw it, disappearance of religion and metaphysics as aids to humankind's struggle with the eternal question of life. Only art remained to humankind in its last hour of culture, before the eventual triumph of the leveling philosophy of totalitarianism would put an end to Western culture by "replacing metaphysics with ethics" and herding the questioning individual into the happy mass of the unthinking, animally satisfied collective. According to

Witkiewicz, the modern artist is to abandon logic and mix the most varied elements into his or her work in order to create an artistic whole of satisfying formal completeness, without regard to the particular logical associations of the elements which go into the play's makeup.

As for prose, Witkiewicz did not see the novel as an art form but rather as an arena for polemic and philosophizing. As well as *622 upadki Bunga*, written in 1910-1911, Witkacy wrote several other novels, among which the most notable are the antiutopian *Pożegnanie jesieni* (farewell to autumn) and *Insatiability*. This latter work, reputedly his best novelistic endeavor, deals with the problem which agonized him for the majority of his mature life: the undermining of Western civilization's cultural heritage by the insidious suffocation of the individual soul in a dully satisfying stagnation. Caught in the pincers of the totalitarian onslaught that propelled Poland into World War II and fearing that the dreaded hour of the death of culture had come round, Witkiewicz committed suicide on September 18, 1939, in a forest in eastern Poland.

Charles Kraszewski

Bibliography

Brandes, Philip. "A Wild Blend of Wit and the Macabre Fills *Madman and the Nun*." Review of *The Madman and the Nun*, by Stanisław Ignacy Witkiewicz. *Los Angeles Times*, April 2, 1999, p. 26. This review of a 1999 performance of *The Madman and the Nun* by the Buffalo Nights Theatre Company in Santa Monica, California, sheds some light on this absurdist play.

Esslin, Martin. *The Theatre of the Absurd*. 3d ed. New York: Penguin Books, 1991. The latest edition of a classic work on the Theater of the Absurd. Includes references to Witkiewicz. Includes bibliography and index.

Gerould, Daniel, ed. *Witkacy: Stanisław Ignacy Witkiewicz as an Imaginative Writer.* Seattle: University of Washington Press, 1981. Translator Gerould provides a biography of Witkiewicz that examines both his life and his writings. Includes bibliography and index.

Kiebuzinska, Christine Olga. *Revolutionaries in the Theater: Meyerhold, Brecht, and Witkiewicz*. Ann Arbor: University of Michigan Research Press, 1988. A study of experimental theater, particularly the works of Witkiewicz, Bertolt Brecht, and V. E. Meierkhold. Includes bibliography and index.

Witkiewicz, Stanisław Ignacy. *Witkacy, Metaphysical Portraits: Photographs by Stanisław Ignacy Witkiewicz*. Leipzig, Germany: Connewitzer Verlag, 1997. This bilingual book contains essays along with selected photographs by Witkiewicz from an exhibition held in 1997 and 1998. The essays provide insight into his philosophy. Includes bibliography.

Ludwig Wittgenstein

Austrian philosopher

Born: Vienna, Austro-Hungarian Empire (now in Austria); April 26, 1889
Died: Cambridge, England; April 29, 1951
Identity: Gay or bisexual

NONFICTION: "Logisch-philosophische Abhandlung," 1921 (best known by the bilingual German and English edition title of *Tractatus Logico-Philosophicus*, 1922, 1961); *Philosophische Untersuchungen/Philosophical Investigations*, 1953 (bilingual German and English edition); *Remarks on the Foundations of Mathematics*, 1956 (bilingual German and English edition); *The Blue and Brown Books*, 1958; *Philosophische Bemerkungen*, 1964 (*Philosophical Remarks*, 1975); *Lectures and Conversations on Aesthetics, Psychology, and Religious Belief*, 1966; *Zettel*, 1967 (bilingual German and English edition); *Philosophische Grammatik*, 1969 (*Philosophical Grammar*, 1974); *Über Gewißheit/On Certainty*, 1969 (bilingual German and English edition); *Vermischte Bemerkungen*, 1977 (*Culture and Value*, 1980); *Remarks on the Philosophy of Psychology*, 1980; *Last Writings on the Philosophy of Psychology*, 1982-1992 (2 volumes; bilingual German and English edition).

Ludwig Josef Johann Wittgenstein (VIHT-guhn-stin) has been a controversial figure in philosophy, but he is second only to Bertrand Russell among philosophers of the twentieth century. Though his academic career was spent largely in England, he was born in Vienna to a wealthy and talented family, originally Jewish but for two generations Christian. He was at first educated by tutors but in 1903 was sent to a *Realschule*, or technical school, at Linz. The choice of a nonclassical school indicates that his father considered his son suited to a career such as engineering; in fact, he did study engineering in Berlin and, after 1908, in Manchester, where he also interested himself in aeronautics. (He was to put his technical knowledge to good use during World War I and later practiced briefly as an architect.) His interests, however, shifted to mathematics and philosophy, and on the advice of the distinguished philosopher Gottlob Frege, a professor at the University of Jena, he went to the University of Cambridge to study under Bertrand Russell. Russell was at first puzzled by the young man but before long thought that he should abandon the field of logic to Wittgenstein, who combined abject feelings of unworthiness with an arrogant aggressiveness on professional subjects.

In early 1914 Wittgenstein was staying in an isolated hut in Norway, but when World War I broke out he returned to Austria and immediately volunteered for active service. He proved to be a loyal, brave, and capable soldier and officer, who ended the war in an Italian prisoner-of-war camp. His period of active service was far from being an intellectual vacuum. In part as a result of reading such authors as Leo Tolstoy, he developed a mystical bent that annoyed Russell when they were reunited. Throughout the war he carried with him notebooks in which he recorded his philosophical reflections; these eventually became his first major work, *Tractatus Logico-Philosophicus*, which was published in 1922.

There followed a fallow period in Wittgenstein's career. His feelings of unworthiness (verging on the suicidal) led him to consider a religious life; eventually he chose instead to become an elementary schoolteacher in rural Austria. It was at this time, too, that he renounced his claims to his inheritance from his father and gave away much of what he did inherit. Wittgenstein pursued his teaching with great dedication, but ultimately he was drawn back to philosophy. In the late 1920's he was associated with the logical positivists of the Vienna Circle, a group with which he has sometimes been mistakenly identified. In 1929 he returned to the University of Cambridge and was, on the basis of the *Tractatus Logico-Philosophicus*, granted a Ph.D. and elected to a research fellowship at Trinity College.

At this point began the most fruitful period of Wittgenstein's life. His brilliant if eccentric teaching soon made him famous. Furthermore, he began multiplying the manuscripts that would be published after his death. In 1939 he was elected to the professorship of philosophy at Cambridge upon the retirement of G. E. Moore. When World War II broke out, Wittgenstein, who had by then become a British subject, faithfully served in the war as a medical orderly. After the war he returned to his professorship but resigned in 1947. After a retreat in rural Ireland and a pleasant trip to the United States, where he stayed with a former student, Norman Malcolm, he fell ill with cancer and died on April 29, 1951.

Given his complexity, his obscurity, and his frequent changes of opinion, it is no simple matter to give a short summary of Wittgenstein's doctrine. Some critics have seen a paradoxical combination of change and continuity in Wittgenstein, a contrast and yet a resemblance between the doctrine of his early work and his more mature work of the 1930's; the link is a preoccupation with language. In the *Tractatus Logico-Philosophicus*, under the influence of Frege and Russell, Wittgenstein dreamed of a rigorously logical system of propositions that would picture in their logical structure the structure of the world; his aim was to eliminate from the language any logical flaws that would interfere with the picture. In his later work language has a different, one might say a social, function; it is a tool that human beings use in their "language games," which obey rules as various and flexible as those of athletic games. The meaning of a word is defined not by its correspondence to something outside itself but by its "use" in the game. Of course this theory would sound more convincing if expounded with Wittgenstein's overwhelming personality in his barren upstairs rooms at Cambridge.

John C. Sherwood

Bibliography

Edmonds, David, and John Eidenow. *Wittgenstein's Poker.* New York: Ecco Press, 2001. Starting with a ten-minute confrontation between Wittgenstein and fellow philosopher Karl Popper in 1946, the authors present a wide-ranging exploration of the philosophies of the two men and the biographical contexts that produced the altercation.

Fann, K. T., ed. *Ludwig Wittgenstein: The Man and His Philosophy.* New York: Dell, 1967. A collection of articles by friends, students, and scholars of Ludwig Wittgenstein. Included are articles on Wittgenstein as a person, a teacher, and a philosopher, and treatments of various aspects of Wittgenstein's philosophical work.

Hacker, P. M. S. *Wittgenstein.* New York: Routledge, 1999. An excellent biographical introduction to the thoughts of the philosopher, clearly presented and requiring no special background. Bibliography.

________. *Wittgenstein's Place in Twentieth-Century Analytic Philosophy.* Oxford, England: Blackwell, 1996. A monumental work by a leading authority of Wittgenstein. This book thoroughly treats philosophical history before, during, and after the time of Wittgenstein.

Hallett, Garth L. *Essentialism: A Wittgensteinian Critique.* Albany: State University of New York Press, 1991. Strictly speaking, this book is an application of Wittgenstein's later thought rather than an introduction to it, but Hallett is so faithful to Wittgenstein's philosophy that the book is in fact a good guide to a correct understanding of it.

Hodges, Michael, and John Lachs. *Thinking in the Ruins: Wittgenstein and Santayana on Contingency.* Nashville: Vanderbilt University Press, 2000. A comparison of the two quite different philosophers.

Janik, Allan, and Stephen Toulmin. *Wittgenstein's Vienna.* New York: Simon and Schuster, 1973. An illustrated survey showing the many connections between Wittgenstein's philosophical development and twentieth century movements in architecture, literature, music, psychoanalysis, and other fields, in the setting of late nineteenth century Viennese culture.

Klaage, James, ed. *Wittgenstein: Philosophy and Biography.* New York: Cambridge University Press, 2001. Essays examine the interrelationship between Wittgenstein's life and his philosophy.

McGinn, Marie. *Wittgenstein and the "Philosophical Investigations."* New York: Routledge, 1997. A very useful and well-written introductory guide to Wittgenstein's *Philosophical Investigations.*

Malcolm, Norman. *Ludwig Wittgenstein: A Memoir.* 2d ed. 1984. Reprint. New York: Oxford University Press, 2001. This book, written by Wittgenstein's most prominent American philosophical student, is a gem. Malcolm allows the reader to see the force of Wittgenstein's personality as well as his particular way of practicing philosophy. The second edition includes numerous letters that Wittgenstein wrote to Malcolm.

Monk, Ray. *Ludwig Wittgenstein: The Duty of Genius.* New York: Free Press, 1990. This is the definitive biography of Wittgenstein. It is thorough and detailed, examining Wittgenstein's private life as well as his philosophy.

Pitcher, George, ed. *Wittgenstein: The "Philosophical Investigations."* Garden City, N.Y.: Doubleday, 1966. Although many of the articles in this collection are rather technical, the book's first article is a general account of the historical context of Wittgenstein's philosophy. This is followed by several articles that are book reviews of his *Philosophical Investigations*.

Sluga, Hans, and David G. Stern, eds. *The Cambridge Companion to Wittgenstein*. Cambridge, England: Cambridge University Press, 1996. Some of the articles in this collection are rather narrowly focused, but the first two contain general introductions to Wittgenstein's life, his work, and his critical approach to philosophy.

Stroll, Avrum. *Moore and Wittgenstein on Certainty*. New York: Oxford University Press, 1994. This volume looks at the relationship between these two philosophers, particularly Wittgenstein's critical stance on G. E. Moore's views on certainty based on common sense.

P. G. Wodehouse

English novelist, short-story writer, and lyricist

Born: Guildford, Surrey, England; October 15, 1881
Died: Southampton, Long Island, New York; February 14, 1975

LONG FICTION: *The Pothunters*, 1902; *A Prefect's Uncle*, 1903; *The Gold Bat*, 1904; *The Head of Kay's*, 1905; *Love Among the Chickens*, 1906; *Not George Washington*, 1907 (with Herbert Westbrook); *The White Feather*, 1907; *Mike: A Public School Story*, 1909 (also known as *Enter Psmith*, *Mike at Wrykyn*, and *Mike and Psmith*); *The Swoop: How Clarence Saved England*, 1909; *Psmith in the City: A Sequel to "Mike,"* 1910; *A Gentleman of Leisure*, 1910 (also known as *The Intrusion of Jimmy*); *The Prince and Betty*, 1912; *The Little Nugget*, 1913; *Something Fresh*, 1915 (also known as *Something New*); *Psmith Journalist*, 1915 (revision of *The Prince and Betty*); *Uneasy Money*, 1916; *Piccadilly Jim*, 1917; *Their Mutual Child*, 1919 (also known as *The Coming of Bill*); *A Damsel in Distress*, 1919; *The Little Warrior*, 1920 (also known as *Jill the Reckless*); *Indiscretions of Archie*, 1921; *The Girl on the Boat*, 1922 (also known as *Three Men and a Maid*); *The Adventures of Sally*, 1922 (also known as *Mostly Sally*); *The Inimitable Jeeves*, 1923 (also known as *Jeeves*); *Leave It to Psmith*, 1923; *Bill the Conqueror: His Invasion of England in the Springtime*, 1924; *Sam the Sudden*, 1925 (also known as *Sam in the Suburbs*); *The Small Bachelor*, 1927; *Money for Nothing*, 1928; *Summer Lightning*, 1929 (also known as *Fish Preferred and Fish Deferred*); *Very Good, Jeeves*, 1930; *Big Money*, 1931; *If I Were You*, 1931; *Doctor Sally*, 1932; *Hot Water*, 1932; *Heavy Weather*, 1933; *Thank You, Jeeves*, 1934; *Right Ho, Jeeves*, 1934 (also known as *Brinkley Manor: A Novel About Jeeves*); *Trouble down at Tudsleigh*, 1935; *The Luck of the Bodkins*, 1935; *Laughing Gas*, 1936; *Summer Moonshine*, 1937; *The Code of the Woosters*, 1938; *Uncle Fred in the Springtime*, 1939; *Quick Service*, 1940; *Money in the Bank*, 1942; *Joy in the Morning*, 1946; *Full Moon*, 1947; *Spring Fever*, 1948; *Uncle Dynamite*, 1948; *The Mating Season*, 1949; *The Old Reliable*, 1951; *Barmy in Wonderland*, 1952 (pb. in U.S. as *Angel Cake*); *Pigs Have Wings*, 1952; *Ring for Jeeves*, 1953 (also known as *The Return of Jeeves*); *Jeeves and the Feudal Spirit*, 1954 (also known as *Bertie Wooster Sees It Through*); *French Leave*, 1956; *Something Fishy*, 1957 (also known as *The Butler Did It*); *Cocktail Time*, 1958; *Jeeves in the Offing*, 1960 (also known as *How Right You Are, Jeeves*); *Ice in the Bedroom*, 1961; *Service with a Smile*, 1961; *Stiff Upper Lip, Jeeves*, 1963; *Biffen's Millions*, 1964 (also known as *Frozen Assets*); *Galahad at Blandings*, 1965 (also known as *The Brinkmanship of Galahad Threepwood: A Blandings Castle Novel*); *Company for Henry*, 1967 (also known as *The Purloined Paperweight*); *Do Butlers Burgle Banks?*, 1968; *A Pelican at Blandings*, 1969 (also known as *No Nudes Is Good Nudes*); *The Girl in Blue*, 1970; *Jeeves and the Tie That Binds*, 1971 (also known as *Much Obliged, Jeeves*); *Pearls, Girls, and Monty Bodkin*, 1972 (also known as *The Plot That Thickened*); *Bachelors Anonymous*, 1973; *The Cat-Nappers: A Jeeves and Bertie Story*, 1974 (also known as *Aunts Aren't Gentlemen*); *Sunset at Blandings*, 1977.

SHORT FICTION: *Tales of St. Austin's*, 1903; *The Man Upstairs, and Other Stories*, 1914; *The Man with Two Left Feet, and Other Stories*, 1917; *My Man Jeeves*, 1919; *The Clicking of Cuthbert*, 1922 (also known as *Golf Without Tears*); *Ukridge*, 1924 (also known as *He Rather Enjoyed It*); *Carry on, Jeeves!*, 1925; *The Heart of a Goof*, 1926 (also known as *Divots*); *Meet Mr. Mulliner*, 1927; *Mr. Mulliner Speaking*, 1929; *Jeeves Omnibus*, 1931 (revised as *The World of Jeeves*, 1967); *Mulliner Nights*, 1933; *Blandings Castle and Elsewhere*, 1935 (also known as *Blandings Castle*); *Mulliner Omnibus*, 1935 (revised as *The World of Mr. Mulliner*, 1972); *Young Men in Spats*, 1936; *Lord Emsworth and Others*, 1937 (also known as *The Crime Wave at Blandings*); *Dudley Is Back to Normal*, 1940; *Eggs, Beans, and Crumpets*, 1940; *Nothing Serious*, 1950; *Selected Stories*, 1958; *A Few Quick Ones*, 1959; *Plum Pie*, 1966; *The Golf Omnibus: Thirty-one Golfing Short Stories*, 1973; *The World of Psmith*, 1974.

DRAMA: *A Gentleman of Leisure*, pr. 1911 (with John Stapleton); *Oh, Lady! Lady!*, pr. 1918; *The Play's the Thing*, pr. 1926 (adaptation of Ferenc Molnár); *Good Morning, Bill*, pr. 1927 (adaptation of László Fodor); *A Damsel in Distress*, pr. 1928 (with Ian Hay); *Baa, Baa*

Black Sheep, pr. 1929 (with Hay); *Candlelight*, pr. 1929 (adaptation of Siegfried Geyer); *Leave It to Psmith*, pr. 1930 (adaptation of his novel; with Hay); *Anything Goes*, pr. 1934 (with Guy Bolton and others); *Carry On, Jeeves*, pb. 1956 (adaptation with Bolton).

NONFICTION: *William Tell Told Again*, 1904 (with additional fictional material); *Louder and Funnier*, 1932; *Bring on the Girls: The Improbable Story of Our Life in Musical Comedy, with Pictures to Prove It*, 1953 (with Guy Bolton); *Performing Flea: A Self-Portrait in Letters*, 1953 (revised as *Author! Author!*, 1962; W. Townend, editor); *America, I Like You*, 1956 (revised as *Over Seventy: An Autobiography with Digressions*, 1957).

EDITED TEXTS: *A Century of Humour*, 1934; *The Best of Modern Humor*, 1952 (with Scott Meredith); *The Week-End Book of Humor*, 1952 (with Meredith); *A Carnival of Modern Humor*, 1967 (with Meredith).

Pelham Grenville Wodehouse (WOOD-hows) is a name that conjures up the most lighthearted and sunniest of comic worlds described by a master stylist of the English language. Born on October 15, 1881, in Guildford, England, he was the third son of a British civil servant serving in Hong Kong. To give their children an English education, his parents sent them to England; there they attended various boarding schools and visited relatives during the summer holidays. Wodehouse's upbringing explains the relative scarcity of parental figures and the corresponding preponderance of aunts in his most popular works, especially in those featuring Bertie Wooster and Jeeves. Bertie is firmly ruled by the strength of will of his female relatives, whether as likable as Aunt Dahlia or as terrifying as Aunt Agatha—both characters based on Wodehouse's own aunts, undoubtedly an affectionate tribute to these important figures from his childhood.

Wodehouse, who early acquired the lifelong nickname "Plum," claimed that he started writing stories when he was five years old. His father, however, wanted his son to have a more secure future and obtained a position for Wodehouse as a clerk in the Hong Kong and Shanghai Bank. To please his father, Wodehouse remained with the bank for two years, all the while writing short pieces for magazines. Then he landed a much more congenial job writing a column for a newspaper, the *Globe*, and in 1902 became a full-time writer. In 1904 he was asked to write lyrics for a new play, and thereupon launched on another long career, as a lyricist.

Wodehouse traveled to the United States a few times and was particularly impressed with the possibilities there in 1909, when he sold two short stories on the day he arrived. On his third visit, in 1914, he met and married Ethel Rowley, an Englishwoman. Writing under a number of pen names, Wodehouse became a theater critic for *Vanity Fair*. Over the years, with Jerome Kern and Guy Bolton, Wodehouse was part of a legendary trio that produced several successful Broadway shows. In his literary biography of Wodehouse, Benny Green argues that Wodehouse's contribution to fifty-two dramatic works over a period of fifty years and his collaboration with other Broadway greats, such as Cole Porter, Florenz Ziegfeld, and George and Ira Gershwin, helped shape Wodehouse's prose fiction.

A tragic incident that reveals the nature, appeal, and, for some critics, the problem with Wodehouse as a writer occurred during World War II. Wodehouse was already established as a master comic stylist and had created the major characters who would continue to be the mainstay of his work: Psmith, who first appeared in the schoolboy stories and later as an adult; Ukridge, an impoverished but creative zany; Mulliner, the narrator of Hollywood stories; two elderly earls—the bouncy and youthful Lord Ickenham and the dreamy but dedicated pig breeder Lord Emsworth; the dim-witted young men of the Drones Club; and the most famous Drone Club member, Bertie Wooster, and his stupendously well-read and intelligent personal valet, Jeeves. Wodehouse, who by all accounts was an extremely good-natured, innocent, and apolitical man, found himself a prisoner of the Germans during the occupation of France, where he and his wife were living at the time. He agreed to a request from some American companies to tape broadcasts to his concerned fans in the United States. Wodehouse described his unpleasant experiences in the humorous style so peculiarly his own, ridiculing the Germans and making light of his own miseries. He was branded a traitor by those who never heard the broadcasts but assumed that his agreeing to do them at all was suspect. While those who heard or read the broadcasts stoutly defended him, the storm of protest hurt Wodehouse. Though completely cleared of any charges, Wodehouse moved to the United States permanently in 1947, where he continued to write in much the same fashion as before the war.

The unworldly innocence apparent in this incident characterizes Wodehouse's work. As Richard J. Voorhees notes, Wodehouse was born in the Victorian Age, came to manhood in the Edwardian, and continued to write, until the age of ninety-three, as if he still lived in that earlier time. His enduring appeal lies not only in the fantasy world he created but also in his careful and imaginative use of the full resources of the English language.

Shakuntala Jayaswal

Bibliography

Green, Benny. *P. G. Wodehouse: A Literary Biography.* New York: Rutledge Press, 1981. This very useful study, arranged chronologically, traces the connections between Wodehouse's personal experiences and his fictional creations. Illustrations, a chronology, notes, a bibliography, and an index are included.

Hall, Robert A., Jr. *The Comic Style of P. G. Wodehouse*. Hamden, Conn.: Archon Books, 1974. Provides a discussion of three types of Wodehouse's stories, including school tales and juvenilia, romances and farces, and the various sagas. The analysis of Wodehouse's narrative techniques and linguistic characteristics is indispensable for anyone interested in understanding his style. Contains an index and a bibliography.

Phelps, Barry. *P. G. Wodehouse: Man and Myth*. London: Constable, 1992. In this sympathetic biography, Phelps provides an unusual number of useful appendices, including a Wodehouse chronology, family tree, and bibliography.

Sproat, Iain. *Wodehouse at War.* New Haven, Conn.: Ticknor & Fields, 1981. This volume is necessary to those studying the sad war events that clouded Wodehouse's life and to those interested in exploring the individual psychology that produced such comic delight. Sproat, a politician as well as a fan, vindicates Wodehouse in the infamous Nazi broadcasts, which are reprinted here. Includes appendices of documents in the case.

Usborne, Richard. *After Hours with P. G. Wodehouse.* London: Hutchinson, 1991. A collection of entertaining pieces on Wodehouse's life and death, written somewhat in the spirit of Wodehouse himself.

_______. *Wodehouse at Work to the End.* 1961. Rev. ed. London: Barrie and Jenkins, 1976. Includes individual chapters on Wodehouse's major series characters, helpful appendices of lists of his books, plays, and films, and an index. For the diehard fan, each chapter is followed by a brief section called "Images," with humorous quotations from the works. The introduction refers to other secondary sources.

Voorhees, Richard J. *P. G. Wodehouse.* New York: Twayne, 1966. An excellent introductory volume on Wodehouse, with chapters on his life, his public school stories, his early novels, the development of his romantic and comic novels, a description of the Wodehouse world, and a discussion of the place of that world in British literature. A chronology, notes and references, and a bibliography of primary and secondary sources are provided.

Wodehouse, P. G. *Yours, Plum: The Letters of P. G. Wodehouse.* New York: James H. Heineman, 1993. Mainly addressed to a small group of close friends and Wodehouse's stepdaughter Leonora, the letters cover all aspects of Wodehouse's life and career. The long section in which he discusses his writing gives fascinating insight into an author at work

Larry Woiwode

American novelist

Born: Carrington, North Dakota; October 30, 1941

LONG FICTION: *What I'm Going to Do, I Think*, 1969; *Beyond the Bedroom Wall: A Family Album*, 1975; *Poppa John*, 1981; *Born Brothers*, 1988; *Indian Affairs*, 1992.

SHORT FICTION: *The Neumiller Stories*, 1989; *Silent Passengers: Stories*, 1993.

POETRY: *Poetry North: Five North Dakota Poets*, 1970 (with Richard Lyons, Thomas McGrath, John R. Milton, and Antony Oldknow); *Even Tide*, 1977.

NONFICTION: *Acts*, 1993; *Aristocrat of the West: The Story of Harold Schafer*, 2000; *What I Think I Did: A Season of Survival in Two Acts*, 2000.

Larry Alfred Woiwode (WI-wood-ee) grew up in Sykeston, North Dakota, a predominantly German settlement in a rugged, often forbidding, terrain. It is this area that was probably the source of the author's appreciation of the effect of nature upon the individual. When he was ten years old, Woiwode and his family moved to Manito, Illinois, another evocatively Midwestern environment that fostered his descriptive powers. He attended the University of Illinois intermittently between 1960 and 1964 but failed to complete his B.A. After leaving with an associate of arts degree in rhetoric he married Carol Ann Patterson in 1965 and moved to New York, where he supported his family with freelance writing, publishing in *The New Yorker* and other periodicals while he worked on two novels simultaneously.

Woiwode's first novel, *What I'm Going to Do, I Think*, appeared in 1969 and won the William Faulkner Foundation Award as the most notable first novel of 1969; it brought him immediate and favorable critical attention. An absorbing study of two newlyweds, the title accentuates the protagonists' self-doubt and indecision as each contemplates the responsibility of couples and parents in an age lacking a transcendent faith in an all-wise, benevolent God. As an intense, psychological study of two troubled individuals, *What I'm Going to Do, I Think* stands in marked contrast to Woiwode's later work in both narrative strategy and characterization, but it shares with all Woiwode's output a commitment to portraying the value of "walking by faith, not by sight" in human relationships, of trusting one's parents, spouse, and children to help one navigate through a hostile world.

Woiwode's second novel, *Beyond the Bedroom Wall*, is an expansive, comic novel that reads as a discontinuous montage of events, images, and personality. Published in 1975, but actually begun earlier than his first published novel, *Beyond the Bedroom Wall* is an engaging homage to the seemingly evaporating nuclear and extended families of mid-twentieth century America. True to its subtitle, *A Family Album*, Woiwode parades before the reader sixty-three different characters before the beginning of chapter 3. Critics have remarked upon the sentimental, "old-fashioned" quality Woiwode achieves in this family chronicle and his eloquent evocation of once-embraced, now-lamented values—values that often cannot bear scrutiny "beyond the bedroom wall," beyond the support of a nurturing family intimacy. The critic and novelist John Gardner placed Woiwode in the company of some of literature's great epic novelists—among them Charles Dickens and Fyodor Dostoevski—for his rejection of fashionable pessimism and his affirmation of seeking one's dreams without sacrificing family life.

Woiwode's eye for the details of daily life enables him to move through four generations, creating an authentic and vividly realized family history.

In the 1970's, while working on a book of poems and a third novel, Woiwode held teaching posts at various colleges, including the University of Wisconsin at Madison and Wheaton College in Illinois. The collection of poems, *Even Tide*, which appeared in 1977, received modest but positive critical reception for its informal, conversational quality and its diversity of concrete religious imagery. *Poppa John*, published in 1981, is more a novella than a novel and was judged by most critics as less successful because its title character, a soap-opera actor summarily dismissed and out of a job at Christmastime, is never fully realized; *Poppa John* contains some of Woiwode's most lyrical scenes, however.

After 1983 Woiwode served as a faculty member at the State University of New York at Binghamton and completed work on another novel. In *Born Brothers*, published in 1988, Woiwode returns to the characters introduced in his most successful work, *Beyond the Bedroom Wall*, the Neumiller family. In some ways a sequel, *Born Brothers* chronicles the lives of Charles and Jerome Neumiller and their sometimes stormy sibling rivalry, this time with middle brother Charles himself as narrator rather than younger brother Tim. Here Woiwode has revitalized the relationship between memory and imagination that he evoked in the earlier narrative, frankly exhorting the reader to regard remembrance of what was as a healthier and more healing endeavor than fantasizing about what might be.

Woiwode continues to mine these elements in subsequent novels and short stories. The collection *The Neumiller Stories*, makes use of unpublished and reworked chapters of *Beyond The Bedroom Wall*, expanding the life of Charles Neumiller and others. *Indian Affairs*, continues with the lives of the two main characters in his first novel, *What I'm Going to Do, I Think*, this time probing deeply especially into both Chris Van Eenanam's Native American roots and the spiritual awakening he undergoes. The collection of short stories *Silent Passengers* shows Woiwode at his lyrical best. A new turn in his output came with his book *Acts*, 1993, a study of the Acts of the Apostles from a writerly perspective. Much biographical insight into Woiwode's writing and religious commitments can be found here; even more appears in his 2000 memoir, *What I Think I Did*.

Understanding Woiwode's writing involves recognizing the essentially religious character of his narratives and their thematic structure. Woiwode rejects the notion that there can be legitimate novels of "ideas" that do not devolve into mere propaganda; he chooses to handle this problem not by creating characters who spout philosophical soliloquies but by creating authentically ordinary characters who settle comfortably into the mundane world that is life.

As a novelist Woiwode stands apart from most of his contemporaries in refusing to drown his characters in the angst-ridden excesses that became conventional in the late twentieth century American novel. His characters are not helpless victims of their times but participants in them. The characters in Woiwode's *Beyond the Bedroom Wall* and *Born Brothers* recognize that the answers to life's dilemmas are found in securing trust in personal friendships and family relationships. Woiwode's willingness to reaffirm these traditional values and to point toward a transcendent moral order grounded in biblical faith makes him unusual in his time.

Bruce L. Edwards
William Jenkins

Bibliography

Chappell, F. "American Gothic." *National Review*, March 24, 1989, 45-46. A favorable review of *Born Brothers* that explores the book's American roots.

Connaughton, Michael E. "Larry Woiwode." In *American Novelists Since World War II, Second Series*. Vol. 6 in *Dictionary of Literary Biography*, edited by James E. Kibler, Jr. Detroit: Gale Research, 1980. An assessment of Woiwode's gift for regional fiction that explores the themes and narrative style of his first two novels.

Flower, Dean. Review of *The Neumiller Stories*, by Larry Woiwode. *The Hudson Review* 43 (Summer, 1990): 311. Flower's extensive and perceptive review of Woiwode's stories examines the early stories, their alterations in novel form, and their "ungathering," revising, and "unrevising" in *The Neumiller Stories*.

Freise, Kathy. "Home Again on the Prairie." *North Dakota Horizons* 23 (Summer, 1993): 19-23. Details Woiwode's connections with the state and its role in his books dealing with the Neumiller family.

Gardner, John. Review of *Beyond the Bedroom Wall*, by Larry Woiwode. *The New York Times Book Review* 125 (September 28, 1975): 1-2. An enthusiastic review of what most critics believe is Woiwode's best novel; Gardner's plaudits won a wide audience for Woiwode beyond the small circle of intellectuals who had hailed his first novel.

Moritz, Charles. *Current Biography Yearbook*. New York: H. W. Wilson, 1989. The essay on Woiwode traces his life and literary work and reviews critical responses to his novels. Particularly helpful, since it identifies and evaluates the available secondary sources. Includes a bibliography.

Pesetsky, Bette. Review of *Born Brothers*, by Larry Woiwode. *The New York Times Book Review* 93 (August 4, 1988): 13-14. An affirmative evaluation of Woiwode's narrative mode and a defense of the novel's difficult thematic structure.

Scheick, William J. "Memory in Larry Woiwode's Novels." *North Dakota Quarterly* 53, no. 3 (1985): 29-40. Scheick discusses the importance of memory in *What I'm Going to Do, I Think*, *Beyond the Bedroom Wall*, and *Poppa John*. He identifies two types of memories, those that make a character feel guilt and long for death and those that develop a sense of connection to one's family. The ability to order these allows Woiwode's characters to achieve a balance between them.

Siconolfi, Michael T. Review of *The Neumiller Stories*, by Larry Woiwode. *America* 163 (December 1, 1990): 434-435. In this lengthy, informative review, Siconolfi discusses the reworkings of stories as they become parts of novels and then resurface as the short stories in this collection.

Christa Wolf

German novelist

Born: Landsberg an der Warthe, Germany (now Gorzów Wielkopolski, Poland); March 18, 1929

LONG FICTION: *Der geteilte Himmel: Erzählung*, 1963 (*Divided Heaven: A Novel of Germany Today*, 1965); *Nachdenken über Christa T.*, 1968 (*The Quest for Christa T.*, 1970); *Kindheitsmuster*, 1976 (*A Model Childhood*, 1980; also known as *Patterns of Childhood*, 1984); *Kein Ort: Nirgends*, 1979 (*No Place on Earth*, 1982); *Kassandra: Erzählung*, 1983 (*Cassandra: A Novel and Four Essays*, 1984); *Störfall: Nachrichten eines Tages*, 1987 (*Accident: A Day's News*, 1989); *Sommerstück*, 1989; *Was Bleibt: Erzählung*, 1990 (novella; *What Remains*, 1993); *Medea: Stimmen*, 1996 (*Medea: A Modern Retelling*, 1998); *Leibhaftig*, 2002.

SHORT FICTION: *Moskauer Novelle*, 1961; *Unter den Linden: Drei unwahrscheinliche Geschichten*, 1974; *Gesammelte Erzählungen*, 1980 (*What Remains, and Other Stories*, 1993); .

SCREENPLAYS: *Der geteilte Himmel*, 1964 (adaptation of her novel; with Gerhard Wolf); *Fräulein Schmetterling*, 1966 (with Wolf); *Till Eulenspiegel*, 1972 (with Gerhard Wolf).

NONFICTION: *Lesen und Schreiben: Aufsätze und Betrachtungen*, 1971 (*The Reader and the Writer: Essays, Sketches, Memories*, 1977); *Fortgesetzter Versuch: Aufsätze, Gespräche, Essays*, 1979; *Lesen und Schreiben: Neue Sammlung*, 1980; *Die Dimension des Autors: Essays und Aufsätze, Reden, und Gespräche, 1959-1985*, 1987 (partial translations as *The Fourth Dimension: Interviews with Christa Wolf*, 1988 and *The Author's Dimension: Selected Essays*, 1993); *Ansprachen*, 1988; *Sei gegrüsst und lebe: Eine Freundshaft in Briefen, 1964-1973*, 1993: *Auf dem Weg nach Tabou: Texte, 1990-1994*, 1994 (*Parting from Phantoms: Selected Writings, 1990-1994*, 1997); *Monsieur, wir finden uns wieder: Briefe, 1968-1984*, 1995.

Christa Wolf (vawlf) is one of the most prominent novelists of the former East Germany. Born in the eastern part of Germany in what would later become Gorzów Wielkopolski, Poland, she joined the German Socialist Party at the age of twenty and was a student of German literature at the Universities of Jena and Leipzig from 1949 to 1953. Wolf married in 1951; she gave birth to a daughter in the following year and to a second daughter in 1956. She worked as a literary critic until 1959, then began living as an independent writer in East Berlin in 1962. She received numerous prestigious literary honors in both German nations. Wolf resigned from the Socialist Party in 1989 and later spoke out against reunification with West Germany. After the publication of *What Remains* in 1990, she was attacked by West German critics for loyalty to the Socialist party despite earlier East German attacks on her work.

Wolf's writings are a creative and refreshing turn from the East German literature of the 1950's, which was by and large dominated by the style of socialist realism, a programmatic literature dictated by the political and social goals of socialist society. Literary works were expected to provide positive models of behavior for the socialist individual—self-sacrifice for the group's goals, for example—and any problematic themes, such as alienation within socialist society, were to be avoided. Wolf's works began to examine difficult and even embarrassing issues of socialist society.

Wolf's first major novel, *Divided Heaven*, suggests her commitment to the East German nation and its socialist program. Despite its somewhat immature, even trivial plot, the painful decision of the novel's heroine, Rita, not to follow her lover to West Germany but to remain in the East with the factory workers' brigade that she has come to know and trust exemplifies the kind of inner conflict that plagues some of Wolf's later characters: a deeply felt commitment to the goals of the socialist country in which she believes, versus a personal need for individual fulfillment. This theme is continued in the innovatively written *The Quest for Christa T.*, in which the narrator seeks to reconstruct from letters, notes, and personal memories the inner life of her recently deceased friend, the schoolteacher Christa T. The latter was a dedicated member of her society who believed in—but at times also honestly doubted the possibility of—the practical implementation of the socialist ideals of the equality and perfectibility of humankind. She was at the same time a staunch and romantic individualist who had her own wishes and desires in life. This dilemma—personal self-sacrifice for the good of the community versus the existential need for self-realization—seems to undermine Christa T.'s life and health and she succumbs to a fatal disease. Both these novels provoked a controversial reaction in East Germany, in response to the often explicit critique leveled at this socialist society, especially in its early years.

In the novel *A Model Childhood* Wolf continues her examination of East German society, namely its coming to terms with the country's fascist past during the Nazi period. It is a strongly autobiographical novel that draws on Wolf's own childhood years in National Socialist (Nazi) Germany. She suggests that many of the attitudes and stereotypes of this time have continued. The lyrical story *No Place on Earth* depicts a fictional meeting between two brilliant but tragic eighteenth century German Romantic writers, Heinrich von Kleist and Karoline von Günderode, who represent male and female attitudes in the society and literary culture of that era. Wolf's narrative technique makes use of extensive quotations from these and other authors of the German Romantic period. These two characters illustrate, in part, the fundamental alienation of the writer-intellectual within society and the essential differences as well as complementary aspects between man and woman. The work also expresses a utopian wish for the equality and harmonious integration of conflicting social as well as gender relationships. In this text Wolf's themes become more explicitly feminist as well as universalist.

Cassandra utilizes the figure of the prophetess and seer from the legendary Greek story of the siege of Troy in an exploration of both feminist and antiwar concerns. Within the decidedly patriarchal context of the Trojan War (fought over the possession of a woman), Cassandra—Priam's daughter who was cursed by Apollo because she refused his love and who was killed by the invading Greeks—represents, to a degree, the fate of all women in history: to be manipulated by others (usually men). The novel, which is structured as a long monologue by Cassandra, seeks to lay open to rational discussion the patriarchal assumptions that distort the writing of history and promote the oppression of all peoples by equating aggression and possessiveness with visions of nature and the divine. These views also provoked controversy and heated debate within the East German society. Wolf returned to similar themes in her unexpectedly sympathetic and feminist retelling of the story of the Thracian sorceress Medea in her novel of the same name.

The "accident" of Wolf's next novel, *Accident: A Day's News*, refers to the April 26, 1986, meltdown of the Chernobyl nuclear reactor in the Ukraine. The narrator, a middle-aged East German writer, must simultaneously deal with the meltdown and its implications and the brain surgery that her brother is undergoing in a distant hospital. Wolf asks what it means to be human in an increasingly technologically-driven society.

The novella *What Remains*, first written in 1979, revised in 1989, and published in 1990, is the apparently autobiographical account of Wolf's surveillance by the East German government. Upon its publication she was condemned for not having published it earlier and for what was perceived as an attempt to claim status as a victim of the socialist government she had previously supported.

In addition to fiction Wolf has also written literary criticism and essays.

Thomas F. Barry
Elisabeth Anne Leonard

Bibliography

Drees, Harjo. *A Comprehensive Interpretation of the Life and Work of Christa Wolf, Twentieth Century German Writer.* Lewiston, N.Y.: Edwin Mellen Press, 2002. An ambitious study of Wolf and her work, making links between her fiction and her life.

Finney, Gail. *Christa Wolf.* New York: Twayne, 1999. A thorough introduction and overview of Wolf's life and works.

Fries, Marilyn Sibley, ed. *Responses to Christa Wolf: Critical Essays.* Detroit: Wayne State University Press, 1989. Twenty-one excellent essays in English. Conference proceedings of the special session on Christa Wolf at the 1982 Modern Language Association of America convention. Contains a list of secondary articles and books and review articles on each of Wolf's books.

Love, Myra N. *Christa Wolf: Literature and the Conscience of History.* New York: Peter Lang, 1991. Deals with the main works up to *Cassandra* from different theoretical points of view. Presupposes familiarity with all the works.

Resch, Margit. *Understanding Christa Wolf: Returning Home to a Foreign Land.* Columbia: University of South Carolina Press, 1997. Separate sections clearly identified in the table of contents provide good analyses of all the major works up to 1990. Contains a useful chronology, a list of selected articles in English, and an annotated bibliography of critical works.

Rossbacher, Brigitte. *Illusions of Progress: Christa Wolf and the Critique of Science in GDR Women's Literature.* New York: P. Lang, 2000. Shows how considerations of gender are implicated in the critique of scientific-technological progress expressed by East German women writers, particularly Wolf

Smith, Colin E. *Tradition, Art, and Society: Christa Wolf's Prose.* Essen, Germany: Die blaue Eule Verlag, 1987. Provides lists that cannot be found elsewhere: the seven books edited by Wolf between 1959 and 1985, her many reviews, essays, and articles from 1952 to 1985, and conversations and interviews from 1959 to 1984. Secondary literature is conveniently subdivided into the literature on specific works. Each chapter deals with a single work.

Wallace, Ian, ed. *Christa Wolf in Perspective.* Atlanta: Rodopi, 1994. Eleven of the thirteen essays are in English. They deal with individual works, with Wolf's politics, and with themes and imagery. Written after Wolf came under attack from Western journalists.

George C. Wolfe

American playwright, director, actor, and producer

Born: Frankfort, Kentucky; September 23, 1954
Identity: African American

DRAMA: *Up for Grabs*, pr. 1975; *Block Party*, pr. 1977; *Tribal Rites*, pr. 1978; *Back Alley Tales*, pr. 1978; *Paradise*, pr. 1985 (libretto and lyrics; music by Robert Forrest); *The Colored Museum*, pr. 1986 (libretto and lyrics); *Queenie Pie*, pr. 1986 (libretto; music by Duke Ellington); *Urban Blight*, pr. 1988 (with others); *Spunk: Three Tales*, pr. 1990 (adaptation of Zora Neale Hurston's short stories "Story in Harlem Slang," "Sweat," and "The Gilded Six Bits"; music by Chic Street Man); *Blackout*, pr. 1991; *Jelly's Last Jam*, pr. 1991 (libretto; lyrics by Susan Birkenhead; music by Jelly Roll Morton and Luther Henderson); *The Wild Party*, pr. 2000 (libretto with Michael John LaChiusa; music and lyrics by LaChiusa); *Minimum Wage*, pr. 2001.

TELEPLAY: *Hunger Chic*, 1989.

George Costella Wolfe is an eminent playwright, producer, actor, and director in American theater. Born in Frankfort, Kentucky, and raised with three siblings (the youngest died in infancy), Wolfe's father, Costella, a government state worker, and mother, Anna, a high school teacher and principal of an all-black school, provided him with the support and encouragement that he needed to succeed. After moving to an integrated neighborhood, his experiences of being one of few black students in school caused him to withdraw; he turned to books and other solitary activities.

On a visit to New York City when he was thirteen, Wolfe saw a production of *Hello Dolly* starring Pearl Bailey and developed a love of the theater. As a result, he started directing plays at Frankfort High School when he returned home. After graduating, he attended Kentucky State College and later transferred to Pomona College in Claremont, California, where he continued to work in theater, first as an actor and later as a director. Wolfe received a B.A. 1976 from Pomona College. In Los Angeles, he wrote, directed, and acted in plays, working as a playwright and director at the Los Angeles Inner City Cultural Center; he left California because he discovered that success could only be made in movies and television, not theater. In 1979 Wolfe returned to New York City, enrolled as a graduate student in musical theater at New York University and continued to write, act, and direct. He received an M.A. degree in 1983.

Dissatisfied with plays by and about African Americans that he directed because they only focused on hardships that blacks suffered, Wolfe began writing his own plays. Wolfe's first effort, *Up for Grabs*, a comedy satire, was produced in 1975 when he was an undergraduate at Pomona College. It won the regional festival at the American Theater Festival. In 1977 he won the same award for *Block Party*, his second play. From 1978 to 1979, his plays *Tribal Rites* and *Back Alley Tales* were produced by the Inner City Cultural Center in Los Angeles. In New York City, where Wolfe taught at City College of New York and at the Richard Allen Center for Cultural Arts, he continued his education as a graduate student in the musical theater program at New York University and graduated with an M.F.A. degree in dramatic writing. Although his first plays did not win a wide audience, a major reception greeted his next production, *The Colored Museum*, a satire on black people and culture that exploded black cultural myths and challenged some of African Americans' most cherished icons and plays, including Lorraine Hansberry's *A Raisin in the Sun* (pr., pb. 1959) and Eldridge Cleaver's *Soul on Ice* (1968). When the play opened at the Shakespeare Festival Public Theater, it was a critical success and provided him other opportunities as an administrator and director. More important, the play established Wolfe as a master of social analysis and as an astute stage manager. A series of critically acclaimed plays followed over the next seven years: *Paradise*, *Queenie Pie* (libretto), *Hunger Chic*, *Spunk*, *Blackout*, and *Jelly's Last Jam*, a box-office success and the pinnacle of his theater experience. The play premiered in Los Angeles in 1991 and in 1992 then moved to Broadway, where Gregory Hines starred. A tribute to Jelly Roll Morton, an African American jazz musician and composer, it emphasizes the role of suffering and community in the creation of jazz. Critic Thulani Davis argued that the play was misogynistic and trivialized black struggle.

In 1989 Wolfe creatively adapted Zora Neale Hurston's three short stories: "Story in Harlem Slang," "Sweat," and "The Gilded Six Bits," as *Spunk*, which was produced in New York City in 1990 with music by Chic Street Man Theater Group, choreography by Hope Clarke, sets by Loy Arcenas, lights by Don Holder, and costumes by Toni-Leslie James. He also directed an adaptation of Bertolt Brecht's *The Caucasian Chalk Circle* (1965) in 1990, written by Thulani Davis.

As artistic director of the New York Shakespeare Festival, Wolfe also continues to produce. He received the season's major assignment in 1993: Pulitzer Prize winner Tony Kushner's *Angels in America* (1991), a two-part epic drama based on gay culture in the United States, acquired immunodeficiency syndrome (AIDS), and politics. That same year Wolfe directed part one of the drama *Millennium Approaches*, which earned him a Tony Award. Opening in the spring of 1993 to highly enthusiastic reviews, the play received the Pulitzer Prize, won five Drama Desk Awards, the New York Drama Critics Circle Award, and four Tony Awards, including best director. He had numerous projects as administrator: overseeing the Shakespeare Festival's four-million-dollar annual budget, restructuring the organization's staff, and developing new plans and programs for the future. The second part of *Millennuim Approaches: Angels in America*, subtitled *Perestroika*, opened on Broadway in November, 1993, to critical acclaim.

The success of Wolfe's plays underscores the fluency of his stage management. In spring, 1994, he directed *Twilight Los Angeles*, a one-woman show by Anna Deavere Smith about racial tensions that resulted from black motorist Rodney King's violent arrest, which ultimately sparked riots in Los Angeles. Having been awarded a Tony as best director for *Angels in America: Millennium Approaches*, Wolfe was nominated for the same award for part 2 of *Angels in America: Perestroika*. Other awards included the Elizabeth Hull-Kate Warriner Award of the Dramatists' Guild in 1986 for *The Colored Museum*; an Obie Award in 1990 for *Spunk:* Antoinette Perry Award nominations, best book of a musical and best director of a musical, both in 1992, for *Jelly's Last Jam*; Tony Award, best director of a play in 1994, for *Angels in America: Millennium Approaches*; and an Antoinette Perry Award nomination for book of a musical, 2000, for *The Wild Party*.

Jacquelyn L. Jackson

Bibliography

"George C. Wolfe." In *Contemporary Black Biography*. Vol. 6. Detroit: Gale, 1994. An in-depth profile of Wolfe's life and career achievements.

"George C. Wolfe." In *Contemporary Dramatists*. 6th ed. Detroit: St. James Press, 1999. A concise summary of the dramatist's work, with a bibliography and a critical essay.

Wolfe, George C. "'I Just Want to Keep Telling Stories': An Interview with George C. Wolfe." Interview by Charles H. Rowell. *Callaloo* 16, no. 3 (Summer, 1993). A chronicle of Wolfe's career to 1993. This issue also contains "George C. Wolfe: A Brief Biography," by John Keene.

Thomas Wolfe

American novelist and short-story writer

Born: Asheville, North Carolina; October 3, 1900
Died: Baltimore, Maryland; September 15, 1938

LONG FICTION: *Look Homeward, Angel*, 1929; *Of Time and the River*, 1935; *The Web and the Rock*, 1939; *You Can't Go Home Again*, 1940; *The Short Novels of Thomas Wolfe*, 1961 (C. Hugh Holman, editor).

SHORT FICTION: *From Death to Morning*, 1935; *The Hills Beyond*, 1941; *The Complete Short Stories of Thomas Wolfe*, 1987.

DRAMA: *Welcome to Our City*, pr. 1923 (pb. only in Germany as *Willkommen in Altamont*, 1962); *The Mountains*, pb. 1940; *Mannerhouse*, pb. 1948.

POETRY: *The Face of a Nation: Poetical Passages from the Writings of Thomas Wolfe*, 1939; *A Stone, a Leaf, a Door: Poems by Thomas Wolfe*, 1945.

NONFICTION: *The Story of a Novel*, 1936; *Thomas Wolfe's Letters to His Mother*, 1943 (John Skally Terry, editor); *The Portable Thomas Wolfe*, 1946 (Maxwell Geisman, editor); *The Letters of Thomas Wolfe*, 1956 (Elizabeth Nowell, editor); *The Notebooks of Thomas Wolfe*, 1970 (Richard S. Kennedy and Paschal Reeves, editors); *The Thomas Wolfe Reader*, 1982 (Cottugh Holman, editor); *Beyond Love and Loyalty: The Letters of Thomas Wolfe and Elizabeth Nowell*, 1983 (Kennedy, editor); *My Other Loneliness: Letters of Thomas Wolfe and Aline Bernstein*, 1983 (Suzanne Stutman, editor); *To Loot My Life Clean: The Thomas Wolfe-Maxwell Perkins Correspondence*, 2000 (Matthew J. Bruccoli and Park Bucker, editors).

Thomas Clayton Wolfe was born October 3, 1900, in Asheville, North Carolina. He was the youngest child in the family. His father, W. O. Wolfe, was a stonecutter who had been born in central Pennsylvania and who went south to live soon after the Civil War. His mother was Julia Westall, of Asheville. Wolfe was educated in public schools until he was twelve, when he was entered at the North State School. Attending school there until graduation in 1916, he then entered the University of North Carolina, which he attended from 1916 to 1920.

Wolfe's stay at Chapel Hill was maturing and exciting; he stood well in his classes, became interested in the Carolina Playmakers, and wrote plays of his own in which he acted. He became one of the most popular and outstanding figures on the campus. Encouraged by Professor Frederick H. Koch of the Playmakers, Wolfe decided to do graduate work at Harvard University in George Pierce Baker's 47 Dramatic Workshop and to make playwriting his career.

He remained three years at Harvard, two of them as a student, taking his M.A. degree in 1922 and hoping to have one of his plays produced on Broadway. During his years at Harvard, his father died, and Wolfe accepted a teaching appointment as instructor in English at New York University. He began teaching in February, 1924.

In September of 1925 Wolfe met Aline Bernstein and found the direction he needed for his career. Nineteen years Wolfe's senior, she was a married woman and the mother of two grown children. A set designer with some knowledge of the theater, she quickly realized that Wolfe's talent did not lie in playwriting but in the novel. As their friendship developed into a love affair, she invited him to join her in Manchester, England, where she was working on a play. Freed from his teaching duties and encouraged by Bernstein, Wolfe completed an outline for his first novel in two weeks.

In August Bernstein went home to America, but she generously agreed to finance Wolfe's stay in England through the remainder of the year. When he returned to New York City in December of 1926, he moved into an apartment that Bernstein had rented for him. He continued to work on his book until July, when he and Bernstein went again to Europe. After they returned, Wolfe resumed his teaching, but Bernstein still helped him financially and continued to do so until after he had completed *Look Homeward, Angel* in March of 1928. The novel was placed by Madeline Boyd with Maxwell Perkins, managing editor of Scribner's, and published in 1929.

The book was generally well received; only at home in North Carolina were the reactions antagonistic. The turmoil occasioned by *Look Homeward, Angel* in his hometown hurt Wolfe; he was naïvely surprised that his novel should be so patently recognized for what it was—a very thinly disguised autobiography—and he avoided a return to Asheville until the year before his death.

Recognition came somewhat slowly for Wolfe. In 1930, Sinclair Lewis, in his address of acceptance of the Nobel Prize in Literature, paid Wolfe tribute on the basis of his only book, *Look Homeward, Angel*, and prophesied a great future for the younger novelist. In the meantime Wolfe was working on a second novel, a continuation of the story of Eugene Gant that was published in 1935 as *Of Time and the River*. Although equally autobiographical, *Of Time and the River* stirred no animosities in Asheville; the scenes of the book were removed to Boston, New York, and Europe. In the summer of 1935 Wolfe was invited to speak at a writers' conference at Boulder, Colorado, where he delivered a series of lectures. An account of the writer's craft, they were published the following year as *The Story of a Novel*.

By 1937 Wolfe, smarting from criticism suggesting too much dependence on his editor Maxwell Perkins, had decided to change publishers. He signed a contract with Harper and Brothers and began delivering his work in progress, an account of the life of a young man very much like Thomas Wolfe and Eugene Gant of *Look Homeward, Angel*. This year also marked a triumphant return to Asheville, where he was forgiven and hailed as a favorite son.

In the spring of 1938 Wolfe was invited to lecture at Purdue University. From there he started on a trip to the West, stopping at Denver and making a great sweep through the national park country. In Seattle he was ill with a cold, locally diagnosed as pneumonia; he was moved to a hospital, and his brother Fred was called West to attend him. When his condition grew worse, Fred Wolfe was joined by his sister, Mabel Wheaton. Consulting physicians suspected a brain tumor and believed that an operation was indicated. The family conference determined that any operation should be done at Johns Hopkins, in Baltimore, and there Wolfe was brought in August. The operation revealed multiple tuberculosis of the brain. Wolfe never came out of the coma that followed the operation, and he died in Baltimore on September 15, 1938, less than a month before his thirty-eighth birthday. His body was taken to Asheville for burial; only in death could the wanderer "go home again."

Wolfe's third and fourth novels, *The Web and the Rock* and *You Can't Go Home Again*, were readied for posthumous publication by Edward C. Aswell, Wolfe's editor and personal friend at Harper. The novels added to Wolfe's stature and brought his fictional work to a reasonable conclusion. In 1941 *The Hills Beyond* appeared (another series of short stories and sketches), as did "The Hills Beyond," a fragmentary and incomplete novel introducing some of the Gant-Webber family members of an earlier time in the Carolina mountains. *Mannerhouse*, a play first written by Wolfe during his stay at Harvard, appeared in published form in 1948.

Even before his death Thomas Wolfe was becoming a legend. Everything about him seemed larger than life—not only his physical appearance but also his compulsion to record every detail of his personal quest for identity. His capacity for recalling and rendering all of life's experiences almost obviated the need for a biographer. More important, Wolfe's attempt to understand and define his own isolation led to more understanding of the human condition.

James D. Bryant, Sr.

Bibliography

Bassett, John Earl. *Thomas Wolfe: An Annotated Critical Bibliography.* Lanham, Md.: Scarecrow Press, 1996. A helpful tool for the student of Wolfe. Indexed.

Bloom, Harold, ed. *Thomas Wolfe*. New York: Chelsea House, 2000. A compendium of critical essays on Wolfe's oeuvre. Introduction, chronology, and bibliography.

Donald, David Herbert. *Look Homeward: A Life of Thomas Wolfe.* 1987. Reprint. Cambridge, Mass.: Harvard University Press, 2003. Donald's fine late biography stresses Wolfe's accomplishment as a social historian and his novels as "a barometer of American culture." Like others, Donald admits the presence of much bad writing but confesses to responding enthusiastically to the good. Makes full use of Wolfe's letters to his mistress, Aline Bernstein.

Evans, Elizabeth. *Thomas Wolfe.* New York: Frederick Ungar, 1984. Provides an excellent shorter introduction to Wolfe for both the beginning and the advanced student. Economical and accurate, it is keyed clearly to Wolfe scholarship and is rich in unpretentious literary allusion. Though Evans is cautious in her admiration of Wolfe's fiction, she is appreciative of it as well. Contains a chronology and a good short bibliography.

Field, Leslie A., ed. *Thomas Wolfe: Three Decades of Criticism.* New York: New York University Press, 1968. This collection contains landmark essays by many of the most important critics in the field of Wolfe criticism; revealed are the central issues and the range of critical response provoked by Wolfe's work, from its first publication through the mid-1960's.

Idol, John Lane. *Literary Masters: Thomas Wolfe.* Detroit: Gale, 2001. A thorough study guide to Wolfe's fiction.

Johnston, Carol Ingalls. *Of Time and the Artist: Thomas Wolfe, His Novels, and the Critics*. Columbia, S.C.: Camden House, 1996. Looks at Wolfe's autobiographical fiction and the critical response to it.

Kennedy, Richard S. *The Window of Memory.* Chapel Hill: University of North Carolina Press, 1962. Remains indispensable to the study of Wolfe; objective, scholarly, and analytic, it melds the work and the man into an artistic synthesis. Particularly valuable as a study of the creative process.

McElderry, Bruce R. *Thomas Wolfe.* New York: Twayne, 1964. An excellent basic introduction to Wolfe's life and work, McElderry's study provides lucid analysis well supported by standard critical opinion. Contains a useful chronology and annotated select bibliographies of primary and secondary sources.

Phillipson, John S., ed. *Critical Essays on Thomas Wolfe.* Boston: G. K. Hall, 1986. Essays on each of Wolfe's major novels, stories, and plays as well as overviews of his career. Includes an introduction but no bibliography.

Rubin, Louis D., Jr., ed. *Thomas Wolfe: A Collection of Critical Essays*. Englewood Cliffs, N.J.: Prentice-Hall, 1973. A collection, with an introduction by Rubin, of a dozen stimulating essays by a variety of critics, scholars, and writers ranging from the impressionistic—a mode Wolfe inevitably inspires—to the scholarly. Contains the notorious Bernard De Voto review (1936) of *The Story of a Novel* entitled "Genius Is Not Enough."

Tom Wolfe

American journalist and novelist

Born: Richmond, Virginia; March 2, 1931

NONFICTION: *The Kandy-Kolored Tangerine-Flake Streamline Baby*, 1965; *The Pump House Gang*, 1968; *The Electric Kool-Aid Acid Test*, 1968; *Radical Chic and Mau-Mauing the Flak Catchers*, 1970; *The New Journalism*, 1973; *The Painted Word*, 1975; *Mauve Gloves and Madmen, Clutter and Vine, and Other Stories, Sketches, and Essays*, 1976; *The Right Stuff*, 1979; *In Our Time*, 1980; *From Bauhaus to Our House*, 1981; *The Purple Decades: A Reader*, 1982; *Hooking Up*, 2000.
LONG FICTION: *The Bonfire of the Vanities*, 1987; *A Man in Full*, 1998.

Thomas Kennerly Wolfe, Jr., is a prominent and popular writer of fiction and social commentary. He was born in Richmond, Virginia, on March 2, 1931, the son of Thomas Kennerly and Helen (Hughes) Wolfe. He received a bachelor's degree from Washington and Lee University (1951) and a Ph.D. in American studies from Yale University (1957). In 1978 he married Sheila Berger, art director of *Harper's Magazine*. While Wolfe was establishing himself as a writer of satirical essays on contemporary American culture, he worked as a reporter for various newspapers and magazines, beginning in the late 1950's with the *Springfield Union* and continuing in the 1960's with *The Washington Post*, *New York Herald Tribune*, *New York* Sunday magazine, and *New York World Journal Tribune*. Wolfe has served as a contributing editor for *New York* and *Esquire* magazines and contributing artist for *Harper's Magazine*. As an artist, he has exhibited in one-man shows and illustrated many of his own works.

With the exception of an occasional short story, Wolfe wrote no fiction until *The Bonfire of the Vanities*. Until then, he was known for his witty and incisive social commentaries, written in a style characterized as "new journalism," a term associated with Wolfe since the publication in *Esquire* of "The Kandy-Kolored Tangerine-Flake Streamline Baby." New journalism is a blend of journalistic objectivity and fictional subjectivity, written in a colloquial style, often with the reporter intruding into the narrative. *The Kandy-Kolored Tangerine-Flake Streamline Baby*, a collection of twenty-two essays including the celebrated *Esquire* piece, was published in 1965. It was followed in 1968 by *The Pump House Gang* and *The Electric Kool-Aid Acid Test*, the latter an account of Ken Kesey and his "Merry Pranksters," a group of counterculture hippies dedicated to the drug LSD and the pursuit of the psychedelic experience. Wolfe achieved notoriety in 1970 with *Radical Chic and Mau-Mauing the Flak Catchers*, two long essays satirizing contemporary liberal sacred cows. Of the two, "Radical Chic" created the greatest furor because it ridiculed the so-called beautiful people of elite culture who catered to revolutionary Black Panthers.

What impressed most critics about "Radical Chic" was Wolfe's thorough reporting and his total detachment. Although his style calls attention to his presence in the midst of what he observes, Wolfe lets the participants speak for—and thus incriminate—themselves. It was these same qualities that infuriated the targets of two later books, *The Painted Word*, an exposé of the world of contemporary art, and *From Bauhaus to Our House*, an attack on the patronizing socialist ideology that begat modern architecture. Insiders in both art and architecture accused Wolfe of ignorance and philistinism; others praised Wolfe for his painstaking research and persuasive logic. Critics were generally in agreement, however, on the virtues of *The Right Stuff*, Wolfe's tribute to heroism as exhibited by the first American astronaut team.

Wolfe's first novel, *The Bonfire of the Vanities*, first appeared in serialized form in *Rolling Stone*. It was written in installments, recalling nineteenth century serial novels by Charles Dickens and others who saw the beginnings of their works published before they knew what the endings would be. The revised book version remained for more than a year on *The New York Times* best-seller list. Wolfe's theme—the existence of class distinctions in a supposedly egalitarian society—is so thoroughly explored in the novel that Wolfe has been compared with Dickens and Honoré de Balzac. His second novel, *A Man in Full*, leaves Wolfe's usual New York stomping grounds for Atlanta, Georgia, but again he depicts the upward and downward social trajectories of his characters as they struggle for power. Like *Bonfire of the Vanities*, *A Man in Full* was a critical and commercial success.

Wolfe's critics fall into two general camps: those who distrust the new journalism and those who deplore what they see as his neoconservatism. The former say that Wolfe blurs the traditional distinction between fiction and nonfiction to the detriment of both; the latter claim that Wolfe started out as a liberal critic of American society only to turn reactionary. His humor goes far toward explaining his appeal, yet Wolfe's real talent lies in the invigorating energy of his style. Indeed, his admirers contend that he has breathed new life into both the fiction and nonfiction.

Thomas Whissen
Richard A. Hill

Bibliography

Bloom, Harold, ed. *Tom Wolfe*. New York: Chelsea House, 2001. Part of Bloom's Modern Critical Views series, this book collects important critical responses to Wolfe's work, as well as providing a thorough introduction by Bloom himself.

McKeen, William. *Tom Wolfe*. New York: Twayne, 1995. Provides students and general readers with an introduction to Wolfe's life and career. Especially good in discussing Wolfe's career as a practicing journalist, including his articles, such as his piece on *The New Yorker* which so outraged traditionalists.

Ragan, Brian Abel. *Tom Wolfe: A Critical Companion*. Westport, Conn.: Greenwood Press, 2002. Intended as a guide for students, this book contains a biographical chapter, a contextual chapter introducing the concept of "new journalism" and Wolfe's role in it, and then analyses each of his major works.

Salamon, Julie. *The Devil's Candy: "The Bonfire of the Vanities" Goes to Hollywood.* Boston: Houghton Mifflin, 1991. Although primarily about the making of the film version of Wolfe's novel, this study helps the reader better understand and appreciate the many artistic nuances and insights in Wolfe's carefully layered work, which were lost in its translation to the big screen.

Shomette, Doug, ed. *The Critical Response to Tom Wolfe.* Westport, Conn.: Greenwood Press, 1992. Contains a variety of critical responses to Wolfe's writings over the years, with a section devoted to the early responses and criticisms of *The Bonfire of the Vanities.*

Tobias Wolff

American short-story writer and memoirist

Born: Birmingham, Alabama; June 19, 1945

SHORT FICTION: *In the Garden of the North American Martyrs*, 1981; *Back in the World*, 1985; *The Stories of Tobias Wolff*, 1988; *The Night in Question*, 1996.

LONG FICTION: *Ugly Rumours*, 1975; *The Barracks Thief*, 1984.

NONFICTION: *This Boy's Life*, 1989; *In Pharaoh's Army: Memories of the Lost War*, 1994.

EDITED TEXTS: *Matters of Life and Death: New American Stories*, 1983; *The Vintage Book of Contemporary American Short Stories*, 1994; *The Best American Short Stories, 1994*, 1994; *Best New American Voices, 2000*, 2000; *Writers Harvest 3*, 2000.

Tobias Jonathan Ansell Wolff is one of the most highly respected writers of short fiction to have achieved prominence in the 1980's. He was born in Birmingham, Alabama, on June 19, 1945, the son of Arthur and Rosemary (Loftus) Wolff, and grew up in the state of Washington, where he and his mother had moved some six years after his parents' divorce in 1951. Wolff left his home in rural Washington to attend preparatory school at the Hill School in Pennsylvania but failed to graduate from that institution. After enlisting in the U.S. Army, Special Forces, serving from 1964 to 1968, during which time he served in Vietnam, Wolff earned a bachelor's degree from Oxford University in 1972 and a master's degree from Oxford in 1975. He spent the 1975-1976 academic year at Stanford University, having won a Wallace Stegner Fellowship in creative writing. He earned a master's degree from Stanford in 1978, the same year in which he received his first National Endowment for the Arts Fellowship. Like many other contemporary writers, Wolff has supported himself by teaching. He has served on the faculties of Stanford University, Goddard College, Arizona State University, and Syracuse University and has been a reporter for *The Washington Post.* Wolff published his first collection of stories, *In the Garden of the North American Martyrs*, in 1981. The book received exceptional reviews, and the following year it earned for Wolff the St. Lawrence Award for Fiction. In the stories' range of characters, situations, and literary techniques, this collection revealed Wolff to be a writer not merely of promise but of manifest achievement as well.

Wolff's second book, the novella *The Barracks Thief*, confirmed his narrative gifts. Originally a novel-length manuscript, it was subjected to intense revision that eliminated inessential characters as well as unnecessary passages of exposition and that introduced greater complexity of narrative technique—including Wolff's startling yet successful shifts from third-person to first-person points of view. Widely admired by reviewers, *The Barracks Thief* won the PEN/Faulkner Award in 1985 as the best work of fiction published during the preceding year. The year 1985 also saw the publication of Wolff's second collection of stories, *Back in the World.* Frequently set in either California or the Pacific Northwest, all the stories in this volume use third-person points of view that tend to distance the reader from the characters. Although this collection did not generate as enthusiastic a response from reviewers as did Wolff's first two books, it continued to develop a number of his characteristic themes and situations.

Since the publication of *Back in the World*, Wolff has also published *The Barracks Thief, and Selected Stories*, a volume that reprints six of the twelve stories from his first collection, *The Night in Question*, another short-story collection, and *This Boy's Life*, an autobiographical memoir that appeared in 1989. In vivid, often humorous, sometimes painful scenes, Wolff's memoir recounts his experiences from age ten through enrollment at Hill School. With utter candor, he records the duplicity with which he created an assortment of identities for himself and describes the difficult relationship he had with his stepfather. Among the book's major strengths are its honesty, its hopefulness amid disillusionment, and its repudiation of self-pity.

This Boy's Life was made into a film starring Robert De Niro. Although Wolff disliked the film's gratuitous sex scene, he had little other criticism, stating that the film reinvented him the way he had reinvented himself from memories. *In Pharoah's Army*, a memoir of Wolff's Vietnam years, received mixed reviews. A few considered it pale compared with *This Boy's Life*, but most critics hailed *In Pharoah's Army* as an unflinching depiction of a young man's struggle to come to terms with himself. Nonetheless, the book was a National Book Award finalist and a nominee for the *Los Angeles Times* Book Award for biography.

In an essay on the fiction of Paul Bowles, Wolff describes the characters of Bowles's novel *The Sheltering Sky* (1949) as "refugees of a sort peculiar to our age: affluent drifters dispossessed spiritually rather than materially." The same might be said of many of Wolff's characters. Against what Wolff calls, in the same essay, "that voice in each of us that sings the delight of not being responsible, of refusing the labor of choice by which we create ourselves," Wolff seeks to bring his characters into the realm of responsibility, where questions of good and evil, justice and injustice, are central. His stories—written in a style marked by clarity, grace, and an unpretentious metaphorical richness—take their place in the tradition of realism, not among the metafictions of Donald Barthelme, Robert Coover, and John Barth.

Some of Wolff's fiction assumes the shape of moral parable, as in the title story of his first collection and in "The Rich Brother," the concluding story in *Back in the World*, with its fablelike opening and its affirmation of the responsibilities that brotherhood imposes. Other stories, such as "Next Door" and "The Liar," the opening and closing pieces in his first book, culminate in visionary glimpses of a world that impinges on ordinary reality but rarely coincides with it, a world of tranquillity, love, and compassion. Yet despite the clear ethical concerns of his stories, Wolff often complicates the moral judgments of his readers. In *The Barracks Thief*, for example, the novella's shifting narrative perspectives enlist the readers' sympathy for Lewis, the thief. In "Coming Attractions," a teenage girl who makes a practice of shoplifting and who keeps whatever lost belongings she finds in the movie theater where she works, is shown, at story's end, struggling selflessly to raise a bicycle from a swimming pool so that she can give it to her younger brother. Such unanticipated acts of generosity occur regularly in Wolff's fiction, suggesting the mysterious depths of human motivation and the regenerative potential of people's capacity for change. Although Wolff's characters are frequently flawed, directionless human beings, Wolff presents many of them in situations in which they discover unsuspected or obscured dimensions of themselves, as does the protagonist of "The Other Miller." Wolff's stories, grounded in their author's belief that "storytelling is one of the sustaining arts," thus serve to evoke moral and spiritual alternatives to the spiritlessness of so much of contemporary life. They affirm the possibilities of renewal. Wolff's themes of human frailty, possible regeneration, and moral imperatives reflect a Christian perspective, a vision that haunts rather than pervades his work.

John Lang
Mary Hanford Bruce

Bibliography

Challener, Daniel D. *Stories of Resilience in Childhood: The Narratives of Maya Angelou, Maxine Hong Kingston, Richard Rodriguez, John Edgar Wideman, and Tobias Wolff*. New York: Garland, 1997. Compares the poverty-stricken childhoods of several notable writers, analyzing what led them to overcome early hardship and go on to literary greatness. Includes a bibliography and index.

Desmond, John F. "Catholicism in Contemporary American Fiction." *America* 170, no. 17 (1994): 7-11. Notes Wolff's Christian ethos and comments on his use of liars and lying as means of exploring the manipulation of reality in his fiction.

Hannah, James. *Tobias Wolff: A Study of the Short Fiction*. New York: Twayne, 1996. A good critical study of the short fiction of Wolff.

Kelly, Colm L. "Affirming the Indeterminable: Deconstruction, Sociology, and Tobias Wolff's 'Say Yes.'" *Mosaic* 32 (March, 1999): 149-166. In response to sociological approaches to literature, argues that stories like Wolff's are polysemous and therefore not reducible to any single interpretation, providing a deconstructive reading of the story.

Prose, Francine. "The Brothers Wolff." *The New York Times Magazine*, February 5, 1989, 22. Prose's fine article introduces the writing of the Wolff brothers, Geoffrey and Tobias. Traces how they grew up apart but became inseparable, even bearing striking resemblances to each other. The article also provides background on their parents, particularly their father.

Wolfram von Eschenbach

German poet

Born: Probably Eschenbach bei Ansbach, Franconia (now in Germany); c. 1170
Died: Probably Eschenbach bei Ansbach, Franconia (now in Germany); c. 1217

POETRY: *Lieder*, c. 1200; *Parzival*, c. 1200-1210 (English translation, 1894); *Willehalm*, c. 1212-1217 (English translation, 1977); *Titurel*, c. 1217 (*Schionatulander and Sigune*, 1960).

Few facts are known about Wolfram von Eschenbach (VAWL-frahm vawn EHSH-uhn-bahk), the strongest of the thirteenth century epic poets writing in Middle High German. Probably born in Eschenbach bei Ansbach, Franconia (now in Germany), about 1170, he was a member of a noble Bavarian family, apparently impoverished, as he says jestingly in his poetry. Many scholars claim that he was a younger son. He served powerful overlords, like the counts of Wertheim and the landgrave Hermann of Thuringia. His feats of sword and spear are subjects for his boasting rather than for his poetry. He mentions being unlettered, yet the French *chanson de geste* known as *La Bataille d'Aliscans* was his source for *Willehalm*, and French originals inspired much of his other poetry. His own work is characterized by acute observation, deep psychology, broad toleration, and sense of humor.

The greatest of his poems is *Parzival*, a romance of twenty-five thousand lines believed to have been composed between 1200 and 1210. Its popularity is proved by the fifteen complete manuscripts of the work still in existence. Wolfram accredited it to the troubadour Kyot le Provençal, who has never been identified. Its praise of noble marriage and its high moral tone may derive from the personality of the author. Wolfram was admired by all as a deeply religious man; in fact, one contemporary wrote a poem selecting him as the champion of Christianity against an evil enchanter. *Willehalm* deals also with a noble knight remarkable for his chivalrous treatment of the Saracens. This work, unfinished at Wolfram's death, was continued by Ulrich von Turkheim (fl. 1235-1250) and Ulrich von dem Türlin (fl. 1261-1270). *Titurel*, a third romance left only in fragments, was completed by one Albrecht about 1260.

When the landgrave died in 1216, Wolfram apparently left Wartburg Castle and returned to his native town, where he died about 1217. He was reportedly buried in the Church of Our Lady in Eschenbach, but the location of his grave has never been determined.

With the rise of German nationalism in the nineteenth century, Wolfram became a cultural icon. In his opera *Tannhäuser* (1845) Richard Wagner dramatized the famous, though probably apocryphal, story of a singing contest between Wolfram and his contemporary Tannhäuser, and he based the libretto of his last opera, *Parsifal* (1882), on Wolfram's text.

Thomas Willard

Bibliography

Green, Dennis H. *The Art of Recognition in Wolfram's "Parzival."* New York: Cambridge University Press, 1982.

Hanlin, Todd C. "Wolfram von Eschenbach." In *Critical Survey of Poetry*, edited by Philip K. Jason. 2d rev. ed. Pasadena, Calif.: Salem Press, 2003.

Hasty, Will, ed. *A Companion to Wolfram's "Parzival."* Columbia: Camden House, 1999.

Hutchins, Eileen. *Parzival: An Introduction*. London: Temple Lodge, 1979.

Jones, Martin, and Timothy McFarland, eds. *Wolfram's "Willehalm": Fifteen Essays*. New York: Camden House, 2001.

Poag, James F. *Wolfram von Eschenbach*. New York: Twayne, 1972.

Sivertson, Randal. *Loyalty and Riches in Wolfram's "Parzifal."* New York: P. Lang, 1999.

Mary Wollstonecraft

English critic and philosopher

Born: London, England; April 27, 1759
Died: London, England; September 10, 1797

NONFICTION: *Thoughts on the Education of Daughters, with Reflections on Female Conduct in the More Important Duties of Life*, 1787; *Original Stories from Real Life: With Conversations Calculated to Regulate the Affections and Form the Mind to Truth and Goodness*, 1788; *The Female Reader: Or, Miscellaneous Pieces in Prose and Verse, Selected from the Best Writers, and Disposed Under Proper Heads: For the Improvement of Young Women*, 1789; *A Vindication of the Rights of Men, in a Letter to the Right Honourable Edmund Burke*, 1790; *A Vindication of the Rights of Woman, with Strictures on Political and Moral Subjects*, 1792; *An Historical and Moral View of the Origin and Progress of the French Revolution*, 1794; *Letters Written During a Short Residence in Sweden, Norway, and Denmark*, 1796.

LONG FICTION: *Mary: A Fiction*, 1788; *The Wrongs of Woman: Or, Maria*, incomplete posthumous pb. 1798.

The pioneer feminist Mary Wollstonecraft (WOOL-stuhn-kraft) endured a long eclipse of her literary and personal reputation until the emergence of the twentieth century feminist movement and the publication of a biography of this radical writer by Ralph Wardle (1951). Wollstonecraft was the second child and first daughter of the seven children of Edward and Elizabeth Dickson Wollstonecraft. Her childhood and adolescence were marred by her father's improvidence and brutality and her mother's indifference. Her early life was punctuated by several moves, particularly to Beverly in Yorkshire, where she attended a day school. On the family's return to London, she found refuge with the family of her friend Fanny Blood.

In 1778, repelled by her family life, she became a paid companion to a widow, Mrs. Dawson, in Bath, but she was forced to return home to nurse her ailing mother, who died in 1782. Wollstonecraft thereupon moved into the Blood household until it became necessary to rescue her sister Eliza from an unsuccessful marriage; Eliza left her husband and baby daughter to join Mary and Fanny Blood in establishing a school for young ladies, first in Islington and then in Newington Green. Soon after Fanny left to marry and live in Portugal. Mary traveled to Lisbon to assist Fanny during childbirth, but both Fanny and her child died, and a dispirited Mary returned to England to face the problem of supporting herself after the school had to be closed. Her first published book, *Thoughts on the Education of Daughters*, excited little attention, but Wollstonecraft won a friend in its publisher, Joseph Johnson. She accepted a post as a governess to the children of Lord Kingsborough in Ireland, but although she was a favorite with the children, she was dismissed. She returned to London with a completed novel, *Mary: A Fiction*, a strongly autobiographical work with a feminist perspective. The book was not financially successful but steered the development of the novel toward the inclusion of independently minded heroines.

Wollstonecraft next turned to her publisher for employment and taught herself French, German, Dutch, and Italian to equip herself for translating work. She translated and "adapted" such works as Jacques Necker's *Of the Importance of Religious Opinions* and Mme de Cambon's *Young Grandison*. Wollstonecraft became a frequent contributor to Johnson's newly launched *Analytic Review*, providing reviews and acting as an assistant editor; she also became acquainted with the Johnson circle, meeting the poet-painter William Blake, the radical pamphleteer Thomas Paine, the philosopher William Godwin, and the Swiss writer and painter Henry Fuseli, with whom she became obsessed.

In response to Edmund Burke's *Reflections on the Revolution in France* (1790), Wollstonecraft wrote *A Vindication of the Rights of Men, in a Letter to the Right Honourable Edmund Burke*, her views on the issues of human rights and social justice, in which she declared that women must be regarded as rational beings and not as frail objects of homage. The work, only one of the many replies to Burke, was a success and established women as significant political theorists. In 1792 she published her *Vindication of the Rights of Woman*, an original statement based on her own experience and reflection. After an emotional crisis that severed her tie to Fuseli, she left for France in December of 1792 to observe conditions there. Among her new friends was an American, Gilbert Imlay, with whom she began an affair; to protect her from danger if France went to war with Britain, he registered her as his wife at the American Embassy in Paris. Their daughter Fanny was born on May 14, 1794; that same year Wollstonecraft published *An Historical and Moral View of the Origin and Progress of the French Revolution*, in which she expressed criticism of the direction taken by the revolutionaries.

She returned to London with her daughter, Fanny, but rebuffed by Imlay, who had taken a new mistress, she attempted suicide in May of 1795. During a subsequent but only temporary reconciliation with Imlay, she undertook a mission for him to Scandinavia and published *Letters Written During a Short Residence in Sweden, Norway, and Denmark*. A second suicide attempt followed when she and Imlay failed to reestablish their relationship. Charmed, however, by a mind that resembled her own, she renewed her acquaintance with William Godwin, and the two became lovers by the autumn of 1796. Mary became pregnant shortly after, and on March 29, 1797, they married. Their daughter, Mary (later Mary Shelley), was born on August 30. Eleven days later, Wollstonecraft died of septicemia. Godwin published her works, some still fragments, posthumously.

Elizabeth Nelson

Bibliography

Conger, Syndy McMillen. *Mary Wollstonecraft and the Language of Sensibility*. Rutherford, N.J.: Fairleigh Dickinson University Press, 1994. A scholarly, well-documented assessment of Wollstonecraft's change in attitudes toward the language of emotions and feeling, from uncritical acceptance to critical rejection to a mature reacceptance and adaptation of it to new contexts, including feminism and political revolution. A corrective to standard twentieth century interpretations of Wollstonecraft that focus on the emphasis on reason during her middle years.

Falco, Maria J., ed. *Feminist Interpretations of Mary Wollstonecraft*. University Park: Pennsylvania State University Press, 1996. A collection of twelve essays on a variety of political issues. Contains two essays that compare the thought of Rousseau and Wollstonecraft, as well as essays dealing with liberalism, slavery, the evolution of women's rights since the time of Wollstonecraft, and the changing reactions to Wollstonecraft since her death.

Ferguson, Moira, and Janet M. Todd. *Mary Wollstonecraft*. Boston: Twayne, 1984. A volume in the Twayne authors series providing concise, scholarly, and well-documented accounts of both Wollstonecraft's life and her literary career. Includes an assessment of her ideas, style, and influence. Stresses her professional achievements more than her personal experience.

Flexner, Eleanor. *Mary Wollstonecraft: A Biography*. New York: Coward-McCann, 1972. Concentrates on Wollstonecraft's early life, associating her childhood disappointments and hardships with later behavior patterns, especially her relationships with and attitudes toward both parents. Emphasizes Edward Wollstonecraft's financial situation and its effect on his daughter. Well documented.

Jump, Harriet Devine, ed. *Mary Wollstonecraft and the Critics, 1790-2001*. 2 vols. New York: Routledge, 2003. A hefty (1200-page) collection of essays on Wollstonecraft's writings, from reviews of her books published in the 1790's to contemporary feminist critiques.

Kramnik, Miriam Brody. Introduction to *A Vindication of the Rights of Woman*. New York: Penguin Books, 1975. This lengthy introduction to Wollstonecraft's most famous work surveys her life and literary contributions. It discusses her within the framework of the history of feminism and compares her approach with the piecemeal efforts of nineteenth century feminists. Rather uncritical of Wollstonecraft's literary shortcomings.

Lorch, Jennifer. *Mary Wollstonecraft: The Making of a Radical Feminist*. New York: Berg, 1990. A concise account of Wollstonecraft's life, focusing on her relationships and her development as a feminist thinker. Stresses her personal experiences more than her professional achievements. Included is an analysis of her relevance to twentieth century feminism. Good documentation.

Poovey, Mary. *The Proper Lady and the Woman Writer: Ideology as Style in the Writings of Mary Wollstonecraft, Mary Shelley, and Jane Austen*. Chicago: University of Chicago Press, 1984. Describes Wollstonecraft from the vantage point of eighteenth century British bourgeois ideology, juxtaposing her to the prevailing cultural model of the middle-class married female. Shows how Wollstonecraft both rebelled against this unfulfilling state and became enmeshed in it. Sharp critiques of Wollstonecraft's reasoning and her style.

Todd, Janet. *Mary Wollstonecraft: A Revolutionary Life*. New York: Columbia University Press, 2000. A close examination of the life and work of the radical eighteenth century author and the mother of modern feminism.

Jade Snow Wong

American memoirist

Born: San Francisco, California; January 21, 1922
Identity: Chinese American

NONFICTION: *Fifth Chinese Daughter*, 1950; *No Chinese Stranger*, 1975.

A pioneering voice in Asian American literature, Jade Snow Wong was born to a large family of Chinese immigrants in San Francisco in 1922. As described in her first autobiography, *Fifth Chinese Daughter*, she grew up in a large building that served as her family's home and its sewing factory, which specialized in denim overalls. She attended American public schools and excelled there, twice skipping a grade and graduating from high school with honors at the age of sixteen. By attending Chinese school in the evenings and receiving private lessons from her father, she also became familiar with Chinese customs, language, and culture. By her own account, her father was the strongest influence on her life: In many ways traditionally Chinese, insisting on firm discipline and his absolute authority in the home, he was also an iconoclast of sorts, a devout Christian convert who stayed in America because he admired its more enlightened attitude toward women.

Striving to reconcile her American and Chinese values, Wong gradually asserted her own independence, insisting on the right to see her own friends whenever she wanted, resisting pressure for an early marriage, and resolving to go to college even without her parents' financial support. Unable to afford the University of California, she attended San Francisco Junior College for two years; then, after a friend arranged a meeting with the president of Mills College, she was offered a job and scholarship that enabled her to attend that college and graduate in 1942. While she majored in economics and sociology, an art class in her senior year inspired a lasting interest in making pottery and ceramics. After working as a secretary during World War II, she decided on a career as a potter and writer. Opening a small pottery business, where she worked in a storefront window, she was quickly successful: Her products sold well, received national awards, and were exhibited in prominent galleries. She also published two magazine articles about her family, which led to an offer from Harper and Row to write her autobiography. Right before it was published in 1950, she married Woody Ong, an old family friend.

Fifth Chinese Daughter proved a spectacular success, both in the United States and abroad, for two reasons: Its careful descriptions of foods, rituals, and decorations subtly evoked the characteristics of Chinese life, and its narrative dramatically conveyed the struggle of a young woman to harmonize two disparate cultural influences. Because of the book's popularity, Wong and her husband were sent by the U.S. State Department in 1953 on a speaking tour of several Asian countries. In Hong Kong she met some of her family's relatives, and elsewhere in Asia she became aware of the different problems faced by Chinese immigrants in other countries. Surprisingly, despite her obvious talents and growing reputation, she did not pursue a career as a writer; instead, she continued to maintain and expand her pottery business, and in 1957, she and her husband also launched a travel agency, personally leading tourists on extended visits to Asian countries. Her time was also occupied by a traditional Chinese family life, as she chose to accept her husband's authority and personally raised their four children. For a long time, her only writing took the form of occasional magazine articles and a column in *The San Francisco Examiner*.

In 1972, after President Richard Nixon's diplomatic initiatives, Wong and her husband were finally able to visit mainland China, a stimulating experience that reaffirmed her enduring connections to both Chinese and American culture. She soon published a second autobiography, *No Chinese Stranger*, which described her life in the 1950's and 1960's before focusing on her trip to China. This book was not as popular as its predecessor, perhaps because it was not infused with the personal and cultural tensions that made *Fifth Chinese Daughter* so involving; instead, it was more like a well-written travel book. For a while, Wong again enjoyed a high public profile: In 1976 she returned to Mills College to receive an honorary doctorate in humane letters; she served from 1975 to 1981 as a member of the California Council for the Humanities, and from 1978 to 1981 she was the director of the Chinese Culture Center. Following her husband's death in 1985 she became less visible, though she continued to lead annual tours to China and wrote a new introduction for the 1989 edition of *Fifth Chinese Daughter.*

Wong's firm commitment to Chinese traditions may make her seem old-fashioned to modern Asian Americans, but she must be credited for her remarkable achievements in an era of few opportunities for both women and Asian Americans, and for her willingness to examine both Chinese and American culture critically.

Gary Westfahl

Bibliography

Blinde, Patricia Lin. "The Icicle in the Desert: Perspective and Form in the Works of Two Chinese-American Women Writers." *The Journal of the Society for the Study of the Multi-Ethnic Literature of the United States* 6, no. 3 (1979). Compares Wong to Maxine Hong Kingston.

Chin, Frank. "Come All Ye Asian-American Masters of the Real and the Fake." In *The Big Aiiieeeee! An Anthology of Chinese American and Japanese American Literature*, edited by Jeffery Paul Chan et al. New York: Meridian, 1991. Chin argues that Wong breaks with a proper Chinese literature in two ways: She chooses Christian Chinese as models rather than Chinese who remain with their ancestral religion, and she portrays Chinese men as either lifeless or inconsequential.

Kim, Elaine. *Asian American Literature: An Introduction to the Writings and Their Social Context*. Philadelphia: Temple University Press, 1982. Kim finds Wong's very reticence about certain aspects of Chinese life admirable. Wong does not play up the Christianity or Americanization of her heroine. Kim does find the protagonists of *Fifth Chinese Daughter* manipulative, for by the end she is acting "Chinese" for Caucasians and "Caucasian" for Chinese.

Ling, Amy. *Between Worlds: Women Writers of Chinese Ancestry.* New York: Pergamon Press, 1990. Wong is one of several writers discussed.

Shawn Hsu Wong

American novelist, editor, and critic

Born: Oakland, California; 1949
Identity: Chinese American

LONG FICTION: *Homebase*, 1979; *American Knees*, 1995.
DRAMA: *Dope*, pr. 1985 (with Louise DiLenge).
POETRY: "Chinese Invented the Damn Buffalo!," 1973; "Kicking Lego Blocks," 1978; "Lapis," 1983.
NONFICTION: "Shootout in the Streets of Chinese America," 1973; "Anybody in the Place Speak Good English?," 1976; "Asian American Literary History: A Bridge to the Heroic Tradition," 1991; "The Real vs. the Fake," 1991.
EDITED TEXTS: *Aiiieeeee! An Anthology of Asian American Writers*, 1974 (with Frank Chin); *Yardbird Reader*, 1975; *Calafia: An Anthology of California Poets*, 1979 (with Ishmael Reed and Al Young); *The Big Aiiieeeee! An Anthology of Chinese American and Japanese American Literature*, 1991 (with Jeffery Paul Chan); *The Before Columbus Foundation Fiction Anthology: Selections from the American Book Awards 1980-1990*, 1992 (with others); *The Before Columbus Foundation Poetry Anthology: Selections from the American Book Awards 1980-1990*, 1992 (with Reed and Kathryn Trueblood); *The Literary Mosaic: An Anthology of Asian American Literature*, 1995; *Asian American Literature: A Brief Introduction and Anthology*, 1996.

In the middle of the 1970's Shawn Wong made two major decisions; to begin the Before Columbus Foundation and to remove himself from his California roots and form his future along the misty shores of Puget Sound, near the University of Washington. The Before Columbus Foundation, a group cofounded by Wong to develop multicultural literature, grew with the guidance and care of its lettered professionals. Wong and his group would later publish two anthologies, *The Before Columbus Foundation Fiction Anthology* and *The Before Columbus Foundation Poetry Anthology*. These publications honored the authors who had won the American Book Awards held by the Foundation beginning in 1980. Wong's Foundation was a success; his reputation for boldness and creativity grew.

He sympathized with the Asian American youth in the San Francisco Bay area (the locale of Wong's youth) who were searching for an identity. Wong grew intensely aware of his need to learn of his past to affirm his future. He attended San Francisco State University after graduating from high school across the bay in Berkeley. After two inspirational years, he returned to the Berkeley campus of the University of California to attain his B.A. in English. Three years later, in 1974, he earned his master's degree in creative writing from San Francisco State University. The same year, he published the anthology of Asian American literature *Aiiieeeee!*, coedited with Frank Chin; the cover caricature of a screaming yellow man, the stereotypical Asian, offered Wong an icon for Asian American silence. Wong's followed his first anthology with another, *The Big Aiiieeeee!*, despite criticism that the book was a political weapon against the Asian writers who sold out with fake stories, manufactured cultural misrepresentations, and fairy tales. With several anthologies to his editorial credit, Wong has been highly influential in publicizing and promoting writing by artists—not only Asian American—who might otherwise be overlooked, as well as honoring established icons of American literature such as Allen Ginsberg.

Wong began his own writing career editing a monthly Methodist church newsletter while in college. He taught creative writing, became an assistant stage manager, directed Frank Chin's *The Chickencoop Chinaman* (pr. 1972), and developed an interest in race cars. He began lecturing on media stereotyping of Asian American identity; Wong's intellectual approach to the Chinese American and Japanese American social position gave him unique control of his media and audience.

In 1979, Wong began publishing his own work as well as that of others. *Homebase* was only the third Chinese American novel to be published in the United States, preceded by Diana Chang's *The Frontiers of Love* (1956) and Louis Chu's *Eat a Bowl of Tea* (1961). *Homebase*, written just as Wong had settled in Seattle, defines the American homebase of four generations of a Chinese American family. In his continuing attempt to define the ethnic American experience, the author educates his readers about the subtle stereotypes presented in the media. *Homebase* portrays the episodic life of Rainsford Chan as he comes of age in the 1950's, removed from his past by a society that does not recognize his past, his culture, or his values.

In Wong's next novel, *American Knees*, children taunt a boy, wanting to know if he is Chinese, Japanese, or "American knees." The author begs the reader to view and accept the cultural image of a new Asian man. Wong explores cultural dilemmas of identity, tradition, and even philosophy—the ironies of ethnic existence in a foreign world. The protagonist, Raymond Ding, is a Chinese American whose insistence on finding some kind of authentic Asian identity in his romantic partners inevitably sabotages the relationships as one partner or the other becomes obsessed with which one is the more "authentically" Asian.

In 1984, Wong began teaching in the American Ethnic Studies program at the University of Washington, where he has also taught creative writing and served as the chair of the English department. His steadfast mission is to expose cultural stereotypes, to develop creative outlets for expressing multicultural voices, and to assimilate Asian American identities into the American culture without losing the thrill of the homeland.

Craig Gilbert

Bibliography

Brown, Bill. "How to Do Things with Things (a Toy Story)." *Critical Inquiry* 24 (Summer, 1998). Discusses the representation of the material object world in *Homebase*.

Hsu, Ruth. "The Mythic West and the Discourse of Nation in Shawn Wong's *Homebase*." *Passages* 2, no. 2 (2000). Discusses regionalism, the marginalized position of minority groups, and the ideology of national myths in Wong's novel.

Kim, Elaine. *Asian American Literature: An Introduction to the Writings and Their Social Context*. Philadelphia: Temple University Press, 1982. Discusses Wong's writings and influence as an editor.

Lee, A. Robert. "Afro-America, the Before Columbus Foundation, and the Literary Multiculturalization of America." *Journal of American Studies* 28 (December, 1994). An extensive review of the Before Columbus Foundation anthologies analyzes their impact on the field of multicultural literary studies.

Wong, Sau-ling Cynthia. *Reading Asian American Literature: From Necessity to Extravagance*. Princeton, N.J.: Princeton University Press, 1993. Discusses Wong's writings.

Virginia Woolf

English novelist and critic

Born: London, England; January 25, 1882
Died: Rodmell, Sussex, England; March 28, 1941
Identity: Gay or bisexual

LONG FICTION: *Melymbrosia*, wr. 1912, pb. 1982, revised 2002 (early version of *The Voyage Out*; Louise DeSalvo, editor); *The Voyage Out*, 1915; *Night and Day*, 1919; *Jacob's Room*, 1922; *Mrs. Dalloway*, 1925; *To the Lighthouse*, 1927; *Orlando: A Biography*, 1928; *The Waves*, 1931; *Flush: A Biography*, 1933; *The Years*, 1937; *Between the Acts*, 1941.

SHORT FICTION: *Two Stories*, 1917 (one by Leonard Woolf); *Kew Gardens*, 1919; *The Mark on the Wall*, 1921; *Monday or Tuesday*, 1921; *A Haunted House, and Other Short Stories*, 1943; *Mrs. Dalloway's Party*, 1973 (Stella McNichol, editor); *The Complete Shorter Fiction of Virginia Woolf*, 1985.

NONFICTION: *The Common Reader: First Series*, 1925; *A Room of One's Own*, 1929; *The Common Reader: Second Series*, 1932; *Three Guineas*, 1938; *Roger Fry: A Biography*, 1940; *The Death of the Moth, and Other Essays*, 1942; *The Moment, and Other Essays*, 1947; *The Captain's Death Bed, and Other Essays*, 1950; *A Writer's Diary*, 1953; *Letters: Virginia Woolf and Lytton Strachey*, 1956; *Granite and Rainbow*, 1958; *Contemporary Writers*, 1965; *Collected Essays, Volumes 1-2*, 1966; *Collected Essays, Volumes 3-4*, 1967; *The London Scene: Five Essays*, 1975; *The Flight of the Mind: The Letters of Virginia Woolf, Vol. I, 1888-1912*, 1975 (pb. in U.S. as *The Letters of*

Virginia Woolf, Vol. I: 1888-1912, 1975; Nigel Nicolson, editor); *The Question of Things Happening: The Letters of Virginia Woolf, Vol. II, 1912-1922*, 1976 (pb. in U.S. as *The Letters of Virginia Woolf, Vol. II: 1912-1922*, 1976; Nicolson, editor); *Moments of Being*, 1976 (Jeanne Schulkind, editor); *Books and Portraits*, 1977; *The Diary of Virginia Woolf*, 1977-1984 (5 volumes; Anne Olivier Bell, editor); *A Change of Perspective: The Letters of Virginia Woolf, Vol. III, 1923-1928*, 1977 (pb. in U.S. as *The Letters of Virginia Woolf, Vol. III: 1923-1928*, 1978; Nicolson, editor); *A Reflection of the Other Person: The Letters of Virginia Woolf, Vol. IV, 1929-1931*, 1978 (pb. in U.S. as *The Letters of Virginia Woolf, Vol. IV: 1929-1931*, 1979; Nicolson, editor); *The Sickle Side of the Moon: The Letters of Virginia Woolf, Vol. V, 1932-1935*, 1979 (pb. in U.S. as *The Letters of Virginia Woolf, Vol. V: 1932-1935*, 1979; Nicolson, editor); *Leave the Letters Til We're Dead: The Letters of Virginia Woolf, Vol. VI, 1936-1941*, 1980 (Nicolson, editor); *The Essays of Virginia Woolf*, 1987-1994 (4 volumes).

The preeminent literary figure of the Bloomsbury circle, Adeline Virginia Stephen Woolf is an important modern experimental writer. The second daughter of Leslie Stephen (knighted in 1902) and his second wife, Julia Prinsep Duckworth Stephen, she was born in Kensington, London, on January 25, 1882. Even as a child she exhibited the two traits that would characterize her life: a highly creative imagination and keen intelligence, coupled with extreme nervousness that resulted in breakdowns under stress. Because of this nervousness she did not attend school, but her father, one of London's leading literati, gave her free rein to use his library at Hyde Park Gate. The family spent its summers at Tallant House, St. Ives, on the Cornish coast, the setting for *To the Lighthouse*. At the suggestion of Violet Dickinson, Woolf began sending samples of her writing to Margaret Lyttleton, editor of the women's pages for the weekly *The Guardian*; her first article, a review of William Dean Howells's *The Son of Royal Langbrith* (1904), appeared in that periodical on December 14, 1904. Even after she became an established writer she continued to review, especially for *The Times Literary Supplement*; some of these pieces developed into essays such as those collected in *The Common Reader*.

The year 1904 not only marked the launching of Woolf's literary career but also witnessed the beginning of the Bloomsbury circle. Following the death of their father in February of that year, Virginia, her sister Vanessa, and her brother Adrian set up house in Gordon Square. Their home became a gathering place for many of their brother Thoby Stephen's Cambridge University friends, among them Roger Fry, John Maynard Keynes, Lytton Strachey, Clive Bell, whom Vanessa would marry, and Leonard Sidney Woolf, who married Virginia in 1912. Woolf's first novel, *The Voyage Out*, appeared in 1915; it and *Night and Day*, published four years later, are conventional. With *Jacob's Room*, however, she began to experiment; she was free to try out new techniques because in 1917 she and her husband had established the Hogarth Press. Intended initially as a hobby, it became an important conduit for modern writers, including T. S. Eliot and Katherine Mansfield (whom the Woolfs met because of the press), Sigmund Freud, Harold Laski, Robert Graves, and E. M. Forster.

Over the next two decades, a steady stream of work flowed from Woolf's pen: six more novels; biographies of Roger Fry and Elizabeth Barrett Browning's dog, Flush; two volumes of *The Common Reader*; and numerous short stories, essays, and letters. Writing was a relief, but it was also a struggle, against both the blank page and mental breakdown. Overwhelmed by the Blitz and fears for her Jewish husband's life in the event of a Nazi conquest of England, Woolf committed suicide on March 28, 1941. As this event so tragically demonstrates, Woolf was not oblivious to the great world events of her time. War intrudes into *Jacob's Room*, *Mrs. Dalloway*, and *Between the Acts*, and feminism into *The Years*, but Woolf's concern is largely with the intimate and the interior. As early as 1919, in her essay "Modern Fiction," she attacked the Edwardians as "materialists" for their emphasis on external reality. As much as Ezra Pound and the Imagists in poetry, she adhered to the creed, "Make it new!" She urged writers to "look within," to focus on the psychological state of their characters.

Hence, in the tradition of Samuel Richardson and Jane Austen, she concentrates on the small but revealing action—or inaction. A look can charge the air and make everyone in the room twitch. Like the Victorians, she is a realist, but for her reality is, as she states in *A Room of One's Own*, "now . . . in a dusty road, now in a scrap of newspaper in the street, now in a daffodil in the sun." In Woolf's fiction, children, artists, women, and those who reject outworn beliefs and conventions can perceive that reality. Even for them, though, the luminous moment cannot last, for evil and stupidity can easily overwhelm goodness and intelligence. Thus, in *Between the Acts*, the child George enjoys a perfect moment of happiness as he holds a flower. Then he is bowled over by his grandfather and an Afghan hound.

Woolf treats a small world of artists, scholars, intellectuals—the people she knew from Bloomsbury—but within that world she confronts all the important issues: love and hate, freedom and bondage, solitude and society. Her novels, like her criticism, focus on the small detail, the seemingly insignificant element that can illuminate a character and, indeed, the world. Dismissed or ignored by many critics during the mid-twentieth century, Woolf has since that time gained recognition as one of the principal innovators in modern literature. Her experimental fiction helped to liberate the novel from the tyranny of plot, encouraging other writers to follow her in the exploration of consciousness. Woolf's works have been translated into more than fifty languages; three journals are devoted to analyzing her life and works; and virtually every available scrap of her writing, even the reading notes she made for her book reviews, has been published. Woolf commented that her father gave her only one piece of advice about writing—to say clearly, in the fewest words possible, precisely what she meant. Among scholars and lay readers alike, the consensus is that she mastered this lesson well.

Joseph Rosenblum

Bibliography

Abel, Elizabeth. *Virginia Woolf and the Fictions of Psychoanalysis*. Chicago: University of Chicago Press, 1989. With a focus upon symbolism and stylistic devices, this book comprehensively delineates the psychoanalytic connections between Woolf's fiction and Sigmund Freud's and Melanie Klein's theories. Sometimes difficult to follow, however, given Abel's reliance on excellent but extensive endnotes.

Baldwin, Dean R. *Virginia Woolf: A Study of the Short Fiction*. Boston: Twayne, 1989. Baldwin's lucid parallels between Woolf's life experiences and her innovative short-story techniques contribute significantly to an understanding of both the author and her creative process. The book also presents the opportunity for a comparative critical study by furnishing a collection of additional points of view in the final section. A chronology, a bibliography, and an index supplement the work.

Barrett, Eileen, and Patricia Cramer, eds. *Virginia Woolf: Lesbian Readings*. New York: New York University Press, 1997. This collection of conference papers features two essays on Woolf's stories: one on Katherine Mansfield's presence in Woolf's story "Moments of Being," and one that compares lesbian modernism in the stories of Woolf with lesbian modernism in the stories of Gertrude Stein.

Dalsimer, Katherine. *Virginia Woolf: Becoming a Writer.* New York: Yale University Press, 2002. Woolf has long been associated with psychoanalysis as the first English-language publisher of Sigmund Freud. Dalsimer, a psychoanalyst herself, analyzes Woolf's writings in all genres to uncover the psychology that underlies her literary persona.

Dick, Susan, ed. Introduction to *The Complete Shorter Fiction of Virginia Woolf.* 2d ed. San Diego, Calif.: Harcourt Brace Jovanovich, 1989. Along with classification of stories into traditional ones and fictional reveries, with affinities in works of nineteenth century writers such as Thomas De Quincey and Anton Chekhov, invaluable notes are given on historical, literary, and cultural allusions, as well as textual problems, for every story.

Dowling, David. *Mrs. Dalloway: Mapping Streams of Consciousness*. Boston: Twayne, 1991. Divided into sections on literary and historical context and interpretations of the novel. Dowling explores the world of Bloomsbury, war, and modernism; the critical reception of the novel and how it was composed; Woolf's style, theory of fiction, handling of stream of consciousness, structure, characters, and themes. Includes a chronology and concordance to the novel.

Goldman, Jane. *The Feminist Aesthetics of Virginia Woolf: Modernism, Post-Impressionism, and the Politics of the Visual*. New York: Cambridge University Press, 2001. A feminist reading of Woolf's works that focuses on the influence of literary and artistic modernism and places her in her historical and cultural context.

Heilbrun, Carolyn G. *Women's Lives: The View from the Threshold*. Toronto: University of Toronto Press, 1999. This volume discusses George Eliot, Woolf, Willa Cather, and Harriet Beecher Stowe. Focuses on the female view and feminism in literature.

King, James. *Virginia Woolf.* New York: W. W. Norton, 1995. A literary biography that relates Woolf's life to her work. Shows how the chief sources of her writing were her life, her family, and her friends.

Lee, Hermione. *Virginia Woolf.* New York: Knopf, 1997. The most complete biography of Woolf so far, drawing on the latest scholarship and on primary sources. Includes family tree, notes, and bibliography.

Marder, Herbert. *The Measure of Life: Virginia Woolf's Last Years*. Ithaca, N.Y.: Cornell University Press, 2000. An examination of the life and work of Woolf during her final, suicide haunted decade.

Reid, Panthea. *Art and Affection: A Life of Virginia Woolf.* New York: Oxford University Press, 1996. Drawing on the wealth of material available about Woolf and her circle, Reid reexamines the writer's personal relationships and literary theories.

Roe, Sue, and Susan Sellers, eds. *The Cambridge Companion to Virginia Woolf.* New York: Cambridge University Press, 2000. A landmark collection of essays by leading scholars that addresses the full range of Woolf's intellectual perspectives—literary, artistic, philosophical and political.

Dorothy Wordsworth

English memoirist

Born: Cockermouth, Cumberland, England; December 25, 1771
Died: Rydal Mount, Cumberland, England; January 25, 1855

NONFICTION: *The Alfoxden Journal*, 1798; *Journal of a Visit to Hamburg and of a Journey from Hamburg to Goslar*, 1798; *The Grasmere Journals*, 1800-1803; *Recollections of a Tour Made in Scotland*, 1803; *Excursion of the Banks of Ullswater*, 1805; *Excursion up Scawfell Pike*, 1818; *Journal of a Tour on the Continent*, 1820; *Journal of My Second Tour in Scotland*, 1822; *Journal of a Tour in the Isle of Man*, 1828; *Letters of William and Dorothy Wordsworth*, 1935-1939 (6 volumes; Ernest de Selincourt, editor).

Dorothy Wordsworth was the only sister of William Wordsworth, the English Romantic poet. She was separated from her brothers at the age of six, upon the death of her mother. While living at Halifax with her mother's cousin, Elizabeth Threlkeld, she attended a day school, except for one six-month stay at a boarding school. In 1787 young Dorothy went to live with her maternal grandparents, her education at an end. Life with her grandparents was unhappy, especially as they made her four brothers unwelcome as visitors. The following year, her maternal uncle, the Reverend William Cookson, married and took his niece into his household until 1794. In 1795, through a legacy and the loan of a house, Wordsworth was finally able to live with her older brother William. From that time to his death in 1850 she was seldom separated from him, living amicably in his household even after he was married.

In 1798, while Dorothy and William were living at Alfoxden to be near Samuel Taylor Coleridge, Dorothy began the first of her journals, from which both Coleridge and her brother drew descriptions for some of their poems in *Lyrical Ballads*. This practice continued for William; often in later years he depended upon his sister's descriptions of people and natural scenes to furnish him with poetic material. She wrote her journals for her own pleasure and her brother William's, none of the journals being published until after her death, although she did allow some of the manuscripts to circulate among their friends. Living in his home and acting as a second mother to his children, Dorothy was a constant companion to her brother, except for her brief periods of travel and visiting with friends.

This happy existence was shattered when she was stricken by illness in April, 1829. She was not expected to live, but she recovered. However, she no longer had sufficient vitality for the activities she loved: walking, mountain climbing, traveling, and writing her journals. Her mind began to fail, and she became like an excitable young child. She died five years after her brother's death at Rydal Mount, where she and William had lived for more than half a century.

Michael J. Hofstetter

Bibliography

Alexander, Meena. *Women in Romanticism: Mary Wollstonecraft, Dorothy Wordsworth, and Mary Shelley*. Savage, Md.: Barnes & Noble Books, 1989.

Ellis, Amanda M. *Rebels and Conservatives: Dorothy and William Wordsworth and Their Circle*. Bloomington: Indiana University Press, 1967.

Gittings, Robert. *Dorothy Wordsworth*. Oxford, England: Clarendon Press, 1985.

Hughes-Hallett, Penelope. *Home at Grasmere: The Wordsworths and the Lakes*. London: Collins & Brown, 1993.

Levin, Susan M. *Dorothy Wordsworth and Romanticism*. New Brunswick, N.J.: Rutgers University Press, 1987.

Polowetzky, Michael. *Prominent Sisters: Mary Lamb, Dorothy Wordsworth, and Sarah Disraeli*. Westport, Conn.: Praeger, 1996.

Thomas, Annabel. *Dorothy Wordsworth: On a Wander by Ourselves*. London: New Millennium, 1997.

Worthen, John. *The Gang: Coleridge, the Hutchinsons, and the Wordsworths in 1802*. New Haven, Conn.: Yale University Press, 2001.

William Wordsworth

English poet

Born: Cockermouth, Cumberland, England; April 7, 1770
Died: Rydal Mount, Cumberland, England; April 23, 1850

POETRY: *An Evening Walk*, 1793; *Descriptive Sketches*, 1793; *Lyrical Ballads*, 1798 (with Samuel Taylor Coleridge); *Lyrical Ballads, with Other Poems*, 1800 (with Coleridge, includes preface); *Poems in Two Volumes*, 1807; *The Excursion*, 1814; *Poems*, 1815; *The White Doe of Rylstone*, 1815; *Peter Bell*, 1819; *The Waggoner*, 1819; *The River Duddon*, 1820; *Ecclesiastical Sketches*, 1822; *Poems Chiefly of Early and Late Years*, 1842; *The Prelude: Or, The Growth of a Poet's Mind*, 1850; *Poetical Works*, 1940-1949 (5 volumes; Ernest de Selincourt and Helen Darbishire, editors).

NONFICTION: *The Prose Works of William Wordsworth*, 1876; *Letters of William and Dorothy Wordsworth*, 1935-1939 (6 volumes; Ernest de Selincourt, editor).

Comparing William Wordsworth with other great English poets was once a parlor game for critics. Matthew Arnold places him below only William Shakespeare and John Milton; others, ranging less widely, are content to call him the greatest of the Romantic poets. Incontestably, Wordsworth stands supreme among English nature poets, and the stamp of his influence so strongly marks the brief period of nineteenth century Romanticism that some have called it the age of Wordsworth.

The second son of a lower-middle-class family, Wordsworth was born April 7, 1770, at Cockermouth in the Lake District of Cumberland. When he was eight, his mother died; the loss of his father, five years later, made him dependent upon his uncles for an education. School at Hawkshead was followed by matriculation at Cambridge University, where he entered St. John's College in 1787. He interrupted his career there in 1790 to take a summer tour of Switzerland, France, and Italy; in 1791, after receiving his degree, he returned to France, ostensibly to learn the language.

Much besides language, however, quickly absorbed Wordsworth's attention. The years 1791 to 1792 found him developing two passions, one for Annette Vallon and the other for the French Revolution. Both were probably sincere, while they lasted, but both were soon to suffer from a change of heart. Wordsworth's daughter Anne Caroline was born to Annette Vallon while he was still in France; for reasons that have never become clear, he acknowledged the child without marrying the mother. Wordsworth's other passion, the Revolution, stirred him deeply and left an indelible impression. His enthusiasm waned chiefly because of its growing excesses and because of the accession of Napoleon. Even so, the philosophy he acquired from Michel Beaupuy and his fellow revolutionists was an important factor in making Wordsworth the great poetic spokesman for that element as yet relatively voiceless—the "common man."

Back in England, Wordsworth briefly found congeniality in the circle of young freethinkers surrounding William Godwin. Godwin, future father-in-law of Percy Bysshe Shelley, was a radical philosopher and the author of *An Enquiry Concerning Political Justice and Its Influence on General Virtue and Happiness* (1793). Like Wordsworth, he was an ardent disciple of Jean-Jacques Rousseau, a fact which helps to explain his temporary hold on the young man's attention. In 1795, however, a fortunate legacy enabled Wordsworth to settle at Racedown with his devoted and talented sister Dorothy. There occurred a brush with fate which was to change the lives of two men: In meeting Samuel Taylor Coleridge, Wordsworth formed the most significant connection of his career. Mutual intellectual stimulation and constant companionship were its immediate dividends. When Coleridge moved into Somersetshire in 1797, the Wordsworths followed. The next year the two men published jointly a small volume which would become a milestone of English literature.

The initial reception of the 1798 edition of *Lyrical Ballads* gave no clue as to the status it would achieve in the future. Most of the collection's contents came from the industrious Wordsworth, including "Tintern Abbey" and a group of shorter, balladlike compositions celebrating and exalting nature and the ordinary person. In his single contribution, "The Rime of the Ancient Mariner," Coleridge, on the other hand, had the task of making the supernatural seem ordinary.

Scorned by some critics and ignored by others, *Lyrical Ballads* survived its initial reception sufficiently well to justify a second printing in 1800. Though this edition contained some interesting new poems, its most significant feature was Wordsworth's long preface, which amounted to a literary declaration of independence, breaking completely with neoclassical theory. Reflecting strongly the continuing influence of Rousseau, this credo stated formally the ideals of sincerity, democracy, reverence for nature, and adherence to simple, natural diction—to all of which Wordsworth and Coleridge had vowed allegiance.

With *Lyrical Ballads* as its starting point, most of Wordsworth's great poetry was compressed into the quarter century between 1798 and 1823. Many of his celebrated short poems, such as the Lucy poems and "The Solitary Reaper," illustrate the simplicity advocated in his preface. Still, he could successfully depart from his principles when he felt the need, employing more elevated diction in his sonnets as well as in such longer poems as "Tintern Abbey" and *The Prelude*.

Valued by descriptive linguists for revealing the cultural and aesthetic milieu of the late eighteenth and early nineteenth centuries, debated by New Historians and dialogic critics, and analyzed by literary critics of various persuasions, Wordsworth's poetry is as timely now as it was in his own day. His reverence for nature, his concern with ordinary human beings, and his belief in the power of transcendence all speak to the present time—whenever that present time happens to be. Wordsworth speaks to commonalities, to those concerns that all civilizations share. If any change in regard for Wordsworth's work is worthy of note, it would have to be the critical regard of some works previously considered aesthetically inferior, such as "The Idiot Boy."

Unfortunately, although both Wordsworth and Coleridge profited from their collaboration on *Lyrical Ballads*—which was followed by productive careers for them both in which they earned respect for their theories as well as for their poetry—their friendship did not endure. In 1803 a misunderstanding arose during a tour of Scotland, leading to a breach between the two men which was never fully mended.

In 1802 Wordsworth married his childhood friend Mary Hutchinson, the inspiration for "She Was a Phantom of Delight." As he grew older, Wordsworth became more and more conservative in matters of religion and politics. From the government, which had once been the object of his youthful censure, he now received employment, being appointed, in 1813, distributor of stamps in Westmorland County. In 1843 he was appointed poet laureate, succeeding Robert Southey. Wordsworth died at Rydal Mount on April 23, 1850, and was buried in Grasmere churchyard. A monument erected in his honor stands in Westminster Abbey.

Barbara A. Heavilin

Bibliography

Bloom, Harold, ed. *William Wordsworth*. New York: Chelsea House, 1985. This collection of eleven previously published critical essays includes some of the most advanced and influential work on Wordsworth. Bloom's introduction is a lively and persuasive overview.

Bromwich, David. *Disowned by Memory: Wordsworth's Poetry of the 1790's*. Chicago: University of Chicago Press, 1998. Bromwich connects the accidents of Wordsworth's life with the originality of his works, tracking the impulses that turned him to poetry after the death of his parents and during his years as an enthusiastic disciple of the French Revolution.

Gill, Stephen. *William Wordsworth: A Life*. New York: Oxford University Press, 1989. This first biography of Wordsworth since 1965 makes full use of information that came to light after that time, including the 1977 discovery of Wordsworth's family letters as well as more recent research on his boyhood in Hawkshead and his radical period in London.

Jacobus, Mary. *Tradition and Experiment in Wordsworth's "Lyrical Ballads," 1798*. Oxford, England: Clarendon Press, 1976. One of the most important studies of *Lyrical Ballads*. Jacobus argues that Wordsworth's strength lay in his ability to assimilate the literary traditions of the past with his own radical innovations. She explores the eighteenth century philosophical and literary background, Wordsworth's relationship with Samuel Taylor Coleridge, and contemporary ballads and magazine verse.

Lindenberger, Herbert. *On Wordsworth's "Prelude."* Princeton, N.J.: Princeton University Press, 1963. One of the best and most accessible of the many books on Wordsworth's masterpiece. It consists of thirteen essays, each of which approaches the poem in a different way.

Liu, Yü. *Poetics and Politics: The Revolutions of Wordsworth*. New York: P. Lang, 1999. Liu focuses on the poetry of Wordsworth in the late 1790's and the early 1800's. In the context of Wordsworth's crisis of belief, this study shows how his poetic innovations constituted his daring revaluation of his political commitment.

Mahoney, John L. *William Wordsworth: A Poetic Life*. New York: Fordham University Press, 1997. A biographical study using key and representative writings of Wordsworth to examine his literary achievements as well as his life. Written for the college-level student. Includes bibliographical references and index.

Noyes, Russell. *William Wordsworth*. New York: Twayne, 1971. Several short introductory studies of Wordsworth exist, and this is one of the best. Noyes possesses a deep understanding of Wordsworth, and his elegant prose gets to the heart of the poetry. The book is arranged chronologically to show Wordsworth's development, and Noyes integrates biographical information with literary analysis. Includes chronology and bibliography.

Worthen, John. *The Gang: Coleridge, the Hutchinsons, and the Wordsworths in 1802*. New Haven, Conn.: Yale University Press, 2001. Worthen describes the relationships among Samuel Taylor Coleridge and his wife Sarah, William Wordsworth and his sister Dorothy, and the Hutchinson sisters, Mary and Sara.

Herman Wouk

American novelist, playwright, and screenwriter

Born: New York, New York; May 27, 1915
Identity: Jewish

LONG FICTION: *Aurora Dawn*, 1947; *The City Boy*, 1948; *The Caine Mutiny*, 1951; *Marjorie Morningstar*, 1955; *Slattery's Hurricane*, 1956; *Youngblood Hawke*, 1962; *Don't Stop the Carnival*, 1965; *The Lomokome Papers*, 1968; *The Winds of War*, 1971; *War and Remembrance*, 1978; *Inside, Outside*, 1985; *The Hope*, 1993; *The Glory*, 1994.

DRAMA: *The Traitor*, pr., pb. 1949; *The Caine Mutiny Court-Martial*, pr., pb. 1954; *Nature's Way*, pr. 1957; *Don't Stop the Carnival*, pr. 1998 (adaptation of his novel; musical, with Jimmy Buffett).

SCREENPLAY: *Slattery's Hurricane*, 1949 (with Richard Murphy).

TELEPLAYS: *The Winds of War*, 1983; *War and Remembrance*, 1988.

NONFICTION: *This Is My God*, 1959, 1973; *The Will to Live On: This Is Our Heritage*, 2000.

Herman Wouk (wohk) is one of the few twentieth century American novelists who creates fiction that is both enjoyable entertainment and serious literature. He was born to Abraham Isaac and Esther Levine Wouk, both Russian Jewish immigrants. His father started his life in the United States as a poor laborer and gradually built a successful chain of laundries. Wouk has incorporated many specific experiences of his youth, such as living in a family constantly beset by business worries, into several of his novels. His grandfather, an Orthodox rabbi, instilled in him a lifelong devotion to Judaism. After attending Townsend Harris Hall in the Bronx from 1927 to 1930, Wouk at the age of nineteen graduated with honors from Columbia University, where he majored in comparative literature and philosophy. While in college he was editor of the college humor magazine, *Columbia Jester*, and wrote two of the popular annual variety shows. The philosopher Irwin Edman was Wouk's mentor at Columbia; his conservative humanist outlook was a major influence on Wouk's thinking.

In 1935 Wouk took his first professional position, as a radio comedy writer. In 1941 he began writing scripts to promote the sale of United States war bonds, but his radio career ended when he enlisted in the U.S. Navy in 1942. In 1943, while serving as deck officer aboard a destroyer/minesweeper, Wouk began writing his first novel, *Aurora Dawn*, which he completed in May, 1946. Earlier, in December, 1945, he was married to Betty Sarah Brown, who converted to Judaism. The Wouks had three children, Abraham Isaac (who died in 1951 at the age of five), Nathaniel, and Joseph.

Aurora Dawn is a satirical look at the business of radio and advertising, written in the stylized manner of eighteenth century novels such as Henry Fielding's *Tom Jones* (1749). It was chosen as a Book-of-the-Month Club selection, but Wouk was more widely acknowledged after the appearance of his second novel, *The City Boy*, the humorous, poignant story of the fat eleven-year-old Jewish boy Herbie Bookbinder. *The City Boy* was favorably compared with Mark Twain's *The Adventures of Tom Sawyer* (1876) as a universal tale of maturation. It also foreshadows Wouk's later concern with the experience of Jews in America.

Wouk next turned to drama with *The Traitor*, which opened on Broadway in April, 1949. The theme of an atom bomb scientist's decision to divulge secrets to the enemy seemed to parallel the contemporaneous Klaus Fuchs spy case, and the play was not a great success. In 1951 Wouk published what is generally considered his greatest novel, *The Caine Mutiny*, which won a Pulitzer Prize. The book was so well-received that Wouk later turned it into a play, *The Caine Mutiny Court-Martial*, and a film of the book was produced in 1954.

Wouk's novels *Marjorie Morningstar* and *Youngblood Hawke* were also made into films. *Marjorie Morningstar* portrays the attempts of a young Jewish woman in New York to become an actress. As in most of Wouk's novels, social commentary is gently integrated into a complex plot with endearing characters. *Youngblood Hawke* is the story of a talented southern novelist, perhaps modeled on Thomas Wolfe, who is destroyed by the stresses of fame. Between *Marjorie Morningstar* and *Youngblood Hawke* Wouk produced his third play, *Nature's Way*, and wrote *This Is My God*, an informative discussion of Jewish beliefs, customs, and traditions with interesting biographical highlights.

From 1962 to 1969 Wouk was a member of the board of trustees for the College of the Virgin Islands, an experience that provided much of the background material for his next novel, *Don't Stop the Carnival*, a dark comedy that he turned into a musical in 1998. Wouk's next work, *The Lomokome Papers*, is a science-fiction fable that was published only in paperback.

The Winds of War and *War and Remembrance*, an epic two-part novel which Wouk researched for twelve years, is a panorama of the world at war from 1939 to 1945; many consider this work Wouk's masterpiece. Using multiple points of view, the author weaves military history and human nature into a story that rivals Leo Tolstoy's *War and Peace* (1865-1869) for narrative power.

Wouk's *Inside, Outside* is a semiautobiographical rebuttal of the work of Jewish writers who in Wouk's opinion reject their heritage and portray the Jewish American experience as grotesque. Completing the large-scale project that Wouk had begun in 1962 with research for *Winds of War* are the two novels *The Hope* and *The Glory*, which constitute a fictionalized history of Israel between 1948 and 1988. Wouk uses several fictional families interwoven with historical personages and events to chronicle Israel's second birth and survival. Wouk completed *The Glory* at the age of seventy-nine and, as he says in the afterword, "turn[ed] with a lightened spirit to fresh beckoning tasks." With this work he demonstrated that he remained a major presence in American literature.

Thomas C. Schunk
Richard A. Hill

Bibliography

Beichman, Arnold. *Herman Wouk: The Novelist as Social Historian*. New Brunswick, N.J.: Transaction Books, 1984. A lifelong friend of Wouk, Beichman offers a strident defense of the novelist against those who fault him for both his conservative political stance and his decision to stress narrative and action over complex characterization.

Darby, William. *Necessary American Fictions: Popular Literature of the 1950's*. Bowling Green, Ohio: Bowling Green State University Press, 1987. Examines *The Caine Mutiny* as a mirror of 1950's popular values.

Gerard, Philip. "The Great American War Novels." *World and I* 10 (June, 1995): 54-63. Gerard notes that World War II was "the last public event that defined a generation of novelists." In this essay, he looks at the works of many of them, including Wouk's *The Caine Mutiny*.

Mazzeno, Laurence W. *Herman Wouk*. New York: Twayne, 1994. Offers a brief biographical sketch and analyses of the major novels through *Inside, Outside*. The book contains excerpts from hundreds of reviews of Wouk's fiction, providing a sense of the contemporary reaction to each of Wouk's major works.

Shapiro, Edward S. "The Jew as Patriot: Herman Wouk and American Jewish Identity." *American Jewish History* 84 (December, 1996): 333-351. Shapiro provides a retrospective review of Wouk's career, arguing persuasively that Wouk is concerned principally with defining American Jewish identity.

Shatzky, Joel, and Michael Taub, eds. *Contemporary Jewish-American Novelists: A Bio-critical Sourcebook*. Westport, Conn.: Greenwood Press, 1997. Includes an entry on Wouk's life, major works, and themes, with an overview of his critical reception and a bibliography of primary and secondary sources.

Charles Wright

American poet

Born: Pickwick Dam, Hardin County, Tennessee; August 25, 1935

POETRY: *The Dream Animal*, 1968; *The Grave of the Right Hand*, 1970; *The Venice Notebook*, 1971; *Hard Freight*, 1973; *Bloodlines*, 1975; *China Trace*, 1977; *The Southern Cross*, 1981; *Country Music: Selected Early Poems*, 1982, 2d ed. 1991; *The Other Side of the River*, 1984; *A Journal of the Year of the Ox*, 1988; *Zone Journals*, 1988; *Xiona*, 1990; *The World of the Ten Thousand Things: Poems, 1980-1990*, 1990; *Chickamauga*, 1995; *Black Zodiac*, 1997; *Appalachia*, 1998; *Negative Blue: Selected Later Poems*, 2000; *A Short History of the Shadow*, 2002.
TRANSLATIONS: *The Storm and Other Poems*, 1978 (of Eugene Montale); *Orphic Songs*, 1984 (of Dino Campana).
NONFICTION: *Halflife: Improvisations and Interviews 1977-1987*, 1988; *Quarter Notes: Improvisations and Interviews*, 1995.

Charles Penzel Wright, Jr., one of the most inventive and consistently interesting American poets of the last half of the twentieth century, was born in the small town of Pickwick Dam in Hardin County, Tennessee, in 1935. He attended Davidson College, from which he received a B.A. in history in 1957. He later described his college experience as "wasted years"; he had no vocation to be a poet at the time and had not read much poetry in college. After graduating from Davidson, he spent three years in Army Intelligence, most of them in Italy. There he read Ezra Pound and began to think of becoming a poet. Pound was living during those years nearby in Rapallo, but Wright was too shy to introduce himself to the great but disgraced founder of modernism. Nevertheless, Pound's work, particularly the imagery of his early poems remained a great influence on Wright's poetry.

After leaving the Army, Wright enrolled at the University of Iowa's distinguished Writers' Workshop, from which he received an M.F.A. in 1963. At Iowa, he studied under Donald Justice and Paul Engle; he speaks with warmth of Justice as a superb poet and teacher. In 1966 he began teaching at the University of California at Irvine. For a time he lived in Laguna Beach, California, a seaside resort about which he has written some sardonic poems; he subsequently became a professor at the University of Virginia at Charlottesville. He has been the recipient of a number of awards, including a Guggenheim Fellowship, an Edgar Allan Poe Award from the Academy of American Poets, and a Fulbright grant.

In one of his essays, Wright has cited two quite different figures as important influences: A. P. Carter, the head of the famous group of country musicians the Carter Family, and Emily Dickinson. His own poetry is a curious mixture of rural language, humor, and esoteric philosophical concerns. Wright has described his method as the "metaphysical quotidian" in which philosophical speculation is rooted in the particulars of a landscape. Wright's first significant book of poems, *The Grave of the Right Hand*, includes a number of prose poems that are meditations on nature; many of these are set in Italy, a region to which he has continually returned in his work. (He has also translated volumes by the Italian poets Eugene Montale and Dino Campana, and he has acknowledged the influence of Montale's "hermetic" method on his own work.) The poems in his next important book, *Hard Freight*, pay homage to a number of his poetic mentors, including Pound and Arthur Rimbaud. However, the volume's last poem, "Clinchfield Station," examines Wright's Southern roots. His background is even more evident in *Bloodlines*, which contains a number of elegies, including one on his father entitled "Hardin County." The book also contains a sequence of short poems called "Tattoos," each of which is related to a specific event in Wright's life.

China Trace is a very different sort of book; the poems are very short and are structured around central images. One poem, "Reply Chi' Ki'ang," makes the connection with Chinese poetry clear. The greatest influence, however, seems to be Pound's free renderings of original Chinese poems. Throughout the volume, Wright focuses on imagery as structure in a manner quite unlike his usual meditations on landscape. *The Southern Cross* is interesting for its four "Self Portraits." Wright does not always speak in his own voice, even though he uses an "I" as a poetic speaker, and these poems are as far removed from confessional poetry as possible; one critic has described the speaker as a "transcendental I." There is also an extensive poem on the painter Paul Cézanne that suggests yet another structural influence on Wright's poems. *Country Music: Selected Early Poems*, which received the American Book Award, demonstrates Wright's range as well as a growth in style and structure. The volume enables readers to trace Wright's development from the tentative early poems to those that display his assured voice and style. *The World of the Ten Thousand Things: Poems, 1980-1990* is an impressive collection of a decade of Wright's work; one critic has described the book as an extended metaphysical search. Yet one of Wright's finest books is, perhaps, *Chickamauga*, in which his interest in the nature of reality finds full expression. Wright plays with the idea of presence and absence in many of the poems, although the philosophic discussion is rooted in specific imagery—which, as always, serves him as a starting place. His next collection, *Black Zodiac*, won the Pulitzer Prize in poetry and the National Book Critics Circle Award.

James Sullivan

Bibliography

Andrews, Tom, ed. *The Point Where All Things Meet: Essays on Charles Wright*. Oberlin, Ohio: Field Editions, 1995. These twenty-seven essays make clear that Wright is one of a handful of poets around whom American poetry has been centered in the last quarter of the twentieth century. Contributors include David Kalstone, Helen Vendler, Calvin Bedient, David Walker, J. D. McClatchy, and Bonnie Costello.

Costello, Bonnie. "Charles Wright, Giogio Morandi, and the Metaphysics of the Line." *Mosaic* 35, no. 1 (March, 2002): 149-171. Traces the influence of Italian modernist painter Morandi on Wright's visual presentation of his poetry.

McClatchy, J. D. *White Paper: On Contemporary American Poetry.* New York: Columbia University Press, 1989. McClatchy draws upon an interview he conducted with Wright to explicate Wright's major poem "The Southern Cross." He prepares for this explication with an informative overview of Wright's development as a poet and the primary characteristics of his style. McClatchy writes intelligibly and with discernment, covering a lot of ground in seventeen pages.

McCorkle, James. "Things That Lock Our Wrists to the Past: Self-Portraiture and Autobiography in Charles Wright's Poetry." In *The Still Performance: Writing, Self, and Interconnection in Five Postmodern American Poets.* Charlottesville: University Press of Virginia, 1989. This long, dense, deconstructionist essay examines the relationship between self-portraiture and language in Wright's poetry. It analyzes the books through *The Other Side of the River.*

Santos, Sherod. "A Solving Emptiness: C. K. Williams and Charles Wright." In *A Poetry of Two Minds.* Athens: University of Georgia Press, 2000. A comparison of mid-career poems by both poets, Santos examines parallel aesthetic experimentation and the shared determination to overcome despair through art.

Stitt, Peter. "Charles Wright: Resurrecting the Baroque." In *Uncertainty and Plenitude: Five Contemporary Poets.* Iowa City: University of Iowa Press, 1997. Stitt demonstrates an affinity between Wright's style and concerns and those of the British Metaphysical poets of the early seventeenth century. Wright's poems, despite narrative elements, are meditative and circular. Stitt gives "Lost Bodies" a close reading. He also notes Wright's avoidance of politics and contemporary events.

Upton, Lee. *The Muse of Abandonment: Origin, Identity, Mastery, in Five American Poets.* London: Associated University Presses, 1998. A critical study of five poets, including Wright, dealing with sociological issues in their work. Includes bibliographical references and an index.

James Wright

American poet

Born: Martins Ferry, Ohio; December 13, 1927
Died: New York, New York; March 25, 1980

POETRY: *The Green Wall*, 1957; *Saint Judas*, 1959; *The Branch Will Not Break*, 1963; *Shall We Gather at the River*, 1968; *Collected Poems*, 1971; *Two Citizens*, 1973; *Moments of the Italian Summer*, 1976; *To a Blossoming Pear Tree*, 1977; *This Journey*, 1982; *Above the River: The Complete Poems*, 1990.

NONFICTION: *Collected Prose*, 1983.

TRANSLATIONS: *Twenty Poems of George Trakl*, 1961 (with Robert Bly); *Twenty Poems*, 1962 (of César Vallejo; with Bly and John Knoepfle); *The Rider on the White Horse, and Selected Stories*, 1964 (of Theodor Storm); *Twenty Poems of Pablo Neruda*, 1967 (with Bly); *Poems*, 1970 (of Hermann Hesse); *Wandering*, 1972 (of Hesse; with Franz Wright).

James Arlington Wright is one of the most significant poetic voices reacting to what has been called the "high modernist" American poetry of the early twentieth century, represented by T. S. Eliot, Ezra Pound, and others. His early break from this type of highly formal poetry was associated with the "deep image" school of Robert Bly but soon outgrew such categories. Wright was born in Martins Ferry, Ohio, an industrial town on the upper Ohio River, in 1927, fourteen months before the stock market crash that precipitated the Great Depression of the 1930's. The insecurities of an industrial town during the Depression haunt his poetry, and the Ohio Valley, with its paradoxical conflux of natural beauty and industrial ugliness, remained prominent in his imagery, even in his poetry written in Europe.

Despite this emphasis on his Ohio home in his writing, Wright's early years were marked by his keen desire to get away from it. Upon graduation in 1946, he enlisted in the Army and served a tour in Japan. After completing military service, Wright entered Kenyon College in 1948. His senior year, 1952, was filled with milestones: He married his high school sweetheart, Liberty Kardules; had his first poem published in the *Western Review*; won the Robert Frost Poetry Prize; and received a Fulbright scholarship to the University of Vienna. His first son, Franz, was born in Vienna.

Returning to the United States, Wright began graduate study in English literature at the University of Washington in the fall of 1953. In 1957, his first book of poetry, *The Green Wall*, was published in the Yale Younger Poets series, a prestigious venue for which the competition is sharp. Further distinction was given the volume via its foreword by the eminent modernist poet W. H. Auden. The verse of *The Green Wall* is very much like that of the modernist poetry of the first half of the twentieth century: rhythmically freer than earlier verse forms, yet retaining the measured cadence of blank verse. Many sections of "Sappho," one of the best poems in the book, can be scanned as iambic pentameter. "A Gesture by a Lady with an Assumed Name" is in iambic pentameter quatrains of alternating rhyme—the type of formal structure most of his contemporaries were rejecting.

In 1957 Wright began teaching at the University of Minnesota, where he began his association with Robert Bly a year later. His next collection of poems, *Saint Judas*, little reflects the association, but the one after that, *The Branch Will Not Break*, represents a significant shift in style. In fact, it has been widely recognized as a watershed work for modern American poetry in general. With Bly, Wright had been studying the surrealistic, highly subjective poetry of the Peruvian César Vallejo and the Chilean Pablo Neruda. Wright's translations of these two poets' works, in collaboration with Bly, infused his own poetry with what South American critics had called Vallejo's "personalist" style, consciously rejecting the studied objectivity of high modernism, though maintaining the modernist tendency to develop a poem by images.

Wright spent much of the next five years on the move. His first marriage had ended in divorce in 1962. In 1964 he taught at Macalester College in St. Paul, Minnesota. The following year he won a Guggenheim Fellowship which allowed him to travel to California, back to his home state of Ohio, and to New York, where he began teaching at Hunter College in 1966. In 1967 he married Edith Anne Runk in New York.

Wright's next collection of poems, *Shall We Gather at the River*, offered more of the newer style of poetry seen in his previous book and contained what would become some of his most anthologized poems. He confirmed his own importance as a major American poet by gathering all of his previous poems, as well as thirty-three new ones, in *Collected Poems*, which won the Pulitzer Prize in poetry.

The 1970's were marked by travel in Europe (in 1972 and, with a second Guggenheim, in 1978) and by increased recognition for his work. During this time he also experienced significant personal loss, the death of his father in 1973 and that of his mother in 1974, which precipitated a nervous collapse. In his poetry volumes *Two Citizens*, *Moments of the Italian Summer*, and *To a Blossoming Pear Tree*, he continued developing his deep symbolist mode. Unable to shake a sore throat that he first noticed at the end of his last trip to Europe in the autumn of 1979, Wright was diagnosed with cancer of the tongue in December. He died the following March, having already completed his last volume of poems, *This Journey*.

John R. Holmes

Bibliography

Dougherty, David. *James Wright*. Boston: Twayne, 1987. This essential book provides the reader with a historical study of Wright's development as a craftsman, thereby allowing the individual to judge the poet's historical importance. In addition, the book suggests—and examines—the intended unity in each of Wright's books and provides readers with insightful readings of key Wright texts.

_______. *The Poetry of James Wright*. Tuscaloosa: University of Alabama Press, 1991. Critical interpretation of selected works by Wright. Includes bibliographical references and index.

Roberson, William. *James Wright: An Annotated Bibliography*. Lanham, Md.: Scarecrow Press, 1995. Good resource for locating articles and other publications by and about Wright.

Smith, Dave. *The Pure Clear Word: Essays on the Poetry of James Wright*. Urbana: University of Illinois Press, 1982. Attempts to determine the degree to which Wright confessed the truth and to which he fabricated reality in his work. The essays include W. H. Auden's foreword to "The Green War," Robert Bly's "The Work of James Wright," and others that cover a variety of topics from Wright's personal life to his poetry. Contains a bibliography.

Stein, Kevin. *James Wright: The Poetry of a Grown Man*. Athens: Ohio University Press, 1989. An academic study that traces the growth of the entire body of Wright's work. The poems are examined to show that his stylistic changes are frequently more apparent than actual, that he experienced an ongoing personal and artistic evolution, and that the transition of his themes from despair to hope is the result of his gradual acceptance of the natural world.

Jay Wright

American poet

Born: Albuquerque, New Mexico; May 25, 1935
Identity: African American, American Indian (Cherokee)

POETRY: *Death as History*, 1967; *The Homecoming Singer*, 1971; *Soothsayers and Omens*, 1976; *Dimensions of History*, 1976; *The Double Invention of Komo*, 1980; *Explications/Interpretations*, 1984; *Elaine's Book*, 1986; *Selected Poems of Jay Wright*, 1987; *Boleros*, 1991; *Transfigurations: Collected Poems*, 2000.

Jay Wright was born in 1935 in Albuquerque, New Mexico, to Leona Dailey, a Virginian of black and Native American ancestry. His father, George Murphy, a light-complexioned African American construction worker, jitney driver, and handyman who later adopted the name of Mercer Murphy Wright, claimed both Cherokee and Irish descent. Wright remained with his mother until the age of three, when Leona gave the boy to Frankie Faucett and his wife Daisy, a black Albuquerque couple known for taking in children. Daisy Faucett was as religious as her husband was proud and generous, and Wright's intense early exposure to the African American church was attributable to her. Mercer Wright, in the meantime, had relocated to California. It was not until his son was in his early teens that he went to live with his father, and later his stepmother Billie, in San Pedro. During his high school years in San Pedro, Wright began to play baseball. In the early 1950's, he worked as a minor-league catcher for the San Diego Padres, the Fresno Cardinals, and the Mexicali Aguilars; he also learned to play the bass. In 1954, he joined the Army, and he served in the medical corps until 1957. He was stationed in Germany for most of that time, which gave him the opportunity to travel throughout Europe.

A year after his return to the United States, Wright enrolled in the University of California at Berkeley under the G.I. Bill. At Berkeley, he devised his own major in comparative literature and was graduated after only three years. Before deciding to continue his literary studies, Wright considered studying theology, and he spent a semester at Union Theological Seminary in New York on a Rockefeller grant. He left Union for Rutgers University in 1962. In 1964, Wright interrupted his graduate studies to spend a year teaching English and medieval history at the Butler Institute in Guadalajara, Mexico. He returned to Rutgers in 1965. During the next three years, Wright completed all the requirements for his doctoral degree except the dissertation. While at Rutgers, Wright lived and worked part-time in Harlem, where he came into contact with a number of other young African American writers, among them Henry Dumas, Larry Neal, and LeRoi Jones (who later changed his name to Amiri Baraka).

In 1968, Wright married Lois Silber, who joined him during his second and longest sojourn in Mexico. The couple lived briefly in Guadalajara and then moved to Jalapa, where they maintained a residence until the autumn of 1971. Many of Wright's poems recall these and other Mexican settings. Wright returned to the United States from time to time, spending brief periods as a writer-in-residence at Tougaloo and Talladega Colleges and at Texas Southern University, as well as several months as a Hodder Fellow at Princeton University. In early 1971, the Wrights departed for Scotland. During Wright's two-year tenure as Joseph Compton Creative Writing Fellow at Dundee University, they lived in Penicuik, outside Edinburgh. Upon their return to the United States in 1973, the Wrights moved first to Warren and then to Piermont, New Hampshire.

Wright has traveled extensively throughout Europe, the United States, Central and South America, and Canada. In 1988, he was part of a group of writers who visited the People's Republic of China under the auspices of the University of California at Los Angeles. Since 1975, he has taught at Yale University, at the universities of Utah, Kentucky, and North Carolina at Chapel Hill, and at Dartmouth College.

Wright's poetic vision is unique in its cross-cultural approach to African American spiritual and intellectual history. He has been called one of the most original and powerful voices in contemporary American poetry. Though critical acclaim of his work has been slow in coming, he has received a number of prestigious awards: an Ingram Merrill Foundation Award and a Guggenheim Fellowship in 1974; an American Academy and Institute of Arts and Letters Literature Award in 1981; an Oscar Williams and Gene Derwood Writing Award in 1985; and a MacArthur Fellowship in 1986.

Vera M. Kutzinski

Bibliography

Callaloo 6 (Fall, 1983). This special issue includes an excellent interview in which Wright outlines the theories behind his poetry. It also contains a general introduction to Wright's poetry by Robert B. Stepto, a rather superficial assessment of his early poetry by Gerald Barrax, and detailed commentary by Vera M. Kutzinski on the Benjamin Banneker poems.

Clifford, James. *The Predicament of Culture: Twentieth-Century Ethnography, Literature, and Art.* Cambridge, Mass.: Harvard University Press, 1988. This critical look at the rise of modern anthropology and its entwinement with literature is useful background reading for some of Wright's main sources, notably Marcel Griaule and his team. Equally relevant are Clifford's comments on the West's representation of other cultures and the negotiation of cultural differences.

Harris, Wilson. *The Womb of Space: The Cross-Cultural Imagination.* Westport, Conn.: Greenwood Press, 1983. While this study includes a brief discussion of *The Double Invention of Komo*, it is valuable primarily for its conceptualization of the literary dynamics of "the cross-cultural imagination." Though Wright's debt is to Harris's earlier writings, this book summarizes the main concepts and ideas that have guided Harris's thinking since the beginning of his career.

Kutzinski, Vera M. *Against the American Grain: Myth and History in William Carlos Williams, Jay Wright, and Nicolás Guillén.* Baltimore: The Johns Hopkins University Press, 1987. The second part of this book, "The Black Limbo: Jay Wright's Mythology of Writing," provides the fullest available commentary on Wright's poetry. Focusing on *Dimension of History* and its historical and theoretical sources, it places Wright's cross-cultural poetics within the context of the diverse cultural and literary histories of the Americas.

Okpewho, Isidore. "Prodigal's Progress: Jay Wright's Focal Center." *MELUS* 23, no. 3 (Fall, 1998): 187-209. Wright's search for a satisfactory cultural identity through the successive volumes of his poetry is examined. Wright's movement from the autobiographical to the scholarly to a poetic self-creation through ritual and religion is traced.

Stepto, Robert B. "After Modernism, After Hibernation: Michael Harper, Robert Hayden, and Jay Wright." In *Chant of Saints: A Gathering of Afro-American Literature, Arts, and Scholarship,* edited by Michael S. Harper and Robert B. Stepto. Urbana: University of Illinois Press, 1979. This article concentrates on portions of *Dimensions of History*. It is useful for situating Wright's poetry within the "call-and-response" structures of an African American literary tradition whose central concern, according to Stepto, is with "freedom and literacy."

Welburn, Ron. "Jay Wright's Poetics: An Appreciation." *MELUS* 18, no. 3 (Fall, 1993): 51. The historical and metaphysical codes that add energy to Wright's poetry are examined. In spite of his relative obscurity, Wright deserves appreciation for his creative intellect.

Richard Wright

American novelist, short-story writer, and memoirist

Born: Natchez, Mississippi; September 4, 1908
Died: Paris, France; November 28, 1960
Identity: African American

LONG FICTION: *Native Son*, 1940; *The Outsider*, 1953; *Savage Holiday*, 1954; *The Long Dream*, 1958; *Lawd Today*, 1963.
SHORT FICTION: *Uncle Tom's Children: Four Novellas*, 1938 (expanded as *Uncle Tom's Children: Five Long Stories*, 1938); *Eight Men*, 1961.
DRAMA: *Native Son: The Biography of a Young American*, pr. 1941 (with Paul Green).
POETRY: *Haiku: This Other World*, 1998 (Yoshinobu Hakutani and Robert L. Tener, editors).
NONFICTION: *Twelve Million Black Voices: A Folk History of the Negro in the United States*, 1941 (photographs by Edwin Rosskam); *Black Boy: A Record of Childhood and Youth*, 1945; *Black Power: A Record of Reactions in a Land of Pathos*, 1954; *The Color Curtain*, 1956; *Pagan Spain*, 1957; *White Man, Listen!*, 1957; *American Hunger*, 1977; *Richard Wright Reader*, 1978 (Ellen Wright and Michel Fabre, editors); *Conversations with Richard Wright*, 1993 (Keneth Kinnamon and Fabre, editors).
MISCELLANEOUS: *Works*, 1991 (2 volumes).

Richard Nathaniel Wright's literary reputation has been largely determined by the political and racial concerns of his fiction. From the time he published *Native Son* until his death, he was viewed primarily as the literary spokesman for black radicalism. It has only been since the 1970's that critics have begun to examine his writing in a broader perspective. Born on September 4, 1908, to Ella and Nathan Wright on a farm near Natchez, Mississippi, Richard had a difficult childhood of economic deprivation, familial disruption, and frequent relocations. The family was living in Memphis when his father abandoned them in 1914. His mother's poverty and increasing illness made it necessary to rely on relatives and to move frequently. For a short time, Wright and his younger brother were placed in an orphanage. For the remainder of his youth, the family traveled between Elaine, Arkansas; West Helena, Arkansas; Greenwood, Mississippi; and Jackson, Mississippi.

Wright received the bulk of his formal education at Smith-Robinson High School in Jackson, from which he graduated as valedictorian in 1925. While in high school, he wrote "The Voodoo of Hell's Half Acre," a story that was published in the *Southern Register*, a local black newspaper. After graduation, he worked in Memphis and began an intensive period of reading H. L. Mencken, Sinclair Lewis, and Theodore Dreiser. In 1927 he traveled to Chicago. There he worked at a variety of jobs, but in 1931 he was forced to go on relief. He continued writing and sold the story "Superstition" to *Abbott's Monthly Magazine*. He subsequently found work at Michael Reese Hospital, the South Side Boys' Club, and the Illinois Federal Writers' Project. In 1932 he began attending meetings of the John Reed Club, a communist literary society. That connection led him to publish numerous crudely didactic poems in leftist journals. In 1933 Wright officially joined the Communist Party. It was not long, though, before the cynicism of the communist movement, particularly its decision to eliminate the literary aspects of the John Reed Club, angered Wright.

Despite his arguments with the Communist Party in Chicago, Wright was named Harlem editor of the *Daily Worker* and moved to New York in 1937. During his last two years in Chicago, he had begun to publish the stories that first brought him national attention. His first novel, which was posthumously published as *Lawd Today*, was rejected, but winning first prize in *Story* magazine's fiction contest made it easier for him to find a publisher for *Uncle Tom's Children*. *Uncle Tom's Children*, in turn, helped Wright get a Guggenheim Fellowship. With this financial support, he was able to finish *Native Son*, and that sensational novel became the first best-seller written by a black author. In *Native Son*, Wright consciously eliminated the sentimentality that had made *Uncle Tom's Children* too easy for liberal white readers. In Bigger Thomas, he created one of the least attractive protagonists in American literature, an uncompromising portrait of black anger and frustration.

Buoyed by the success of his novel, Wright entered an artistically active period during which he collaborated with Paul Green on a dramatic version of *Native Son*, collaborated with photographer Edwin Rosskam on *Twelve Million Black Voices*, a pictorial history of black Americans, and began work on another novel, the final section of which was published as "The Man Who Lived Underground." He also worked on his autobiography, the first part of which was published in 1945 as *Black Boy*. Some critics consider this powerful retelling of his early years Wright's best work. Disappointed by the continued racism of American society after World War II, Wright emigrated to France in 1947. The influence of Jean-Paul Sartre and other existentialists is evident in *The Outsider*, which Wright published in 1953. During the 1950's he published three books of political commentary based on his travels and lectured on contemporary issues. His last two novels, *Savage Holiday* and *The Long Dream*, were critical failures. He died of a heart attack in 1960, and unsubstantiated rumors that his death was directly or indirectly caused by agents of the United States government have become a persistent part of his legend.

Wright introduced white America to an assertive black literature and encouraged a generation of black authors that followed his lead. *Native Son* and several of his short stories are considered masterpieces of social realism, and *Black Boy* is one of the most influential American autobiographies. Critics have become more appreciative of Wright's existential novel, *The Outsider*, but most agree that his most important work was behind him when he left the United States.

Carl Brucker

Bibliography

Baldwin, James. *The Price of the Ticket: Collected Nonfiction, 1948-1985*. New York: St. Martin's Press/Marek, 1985. The essays "Everybody's Protest Novel" and "Alas, Poor Richard" provide important and provocative insights into Wright and his art.

Bloom, Harold, ed. *Richard Wright*. New York: Chelsea House, 1987. Essays on various aspects of Wright's work and career, with an introduction by Bloom.

Butler, Robert. *"Native Son": The Emergence of a New Black Hero*. Boston: Twayne, 1991. An accessible critical look at the seminal novel. Includes bibliographical references and index.

Fabre, Michel. *The Unfinished Quest of Richard Wright*. Translated by Isabel Barzun. New York: William Morrow, 1973. An important and authoritative biography of Wright.

Felgar, Robert. *Richard Wright*. Boston: Twayne, 1980. A general biographical and critical source.

Hakutani, Yoshinobu. *Richard Wright and Racial Discourse*. Columbia: University of Missouri Press, 1996. Chapters on *Lawd Today, Uncle Tom's Children, Native Son, The Outsider*, and *Black Boy* as well as discussions of later fiction, black power, and Wright's handling of sexuality. Includes an introduction and a bibliography.

Kinnamon, Keneth, ed. *Critical Essays on Richard Wright's "Native Son."* New York: Twayne, 1997. Divided into sections of reviews, reprinted essays, and new essays. Includes discussions of Wright's handling of race, voice, tone, novelistic structure, the city, and literary influences. Includes an index but no bibliography.

_______. *A Richard Wright Bibliography: Fifty Years of Criticism and Commentary: 1933-1982*. Westport, Conn.: Greenwood Press, 1988. A mammoth annotated bibliography (one of the largest annotated bibliographies ever assembled on an American writer), which traces the history of Wright criticism. This bibliography is invaluable as a research tool.

Rand, William E. "The Structure of the Outsider in the Short Fiction of Richard Wright and F. Scott Fitzgerald." *CLA Journal* 40 (December, 1996): 230-245. Compares theme, imagery, and form of Fitzgerald's "The Diamond as Big as the Ritz" with Wright's "The Man Who Lived Underground" in terms of the treatment of the outsider.

Walker, Margaret. *Richard Wright: Daemonic Genius*. New York: Warner, 1988. A critically acclaimed study of Wright's life and work written by a friend and fellow novelist. Not a replacement for Michel Fabre's biography but written with the benefit of several more years of scholarship on issues that include the medical controversy over Wright's death. Includes a bibliographic essay.

Sarah E. Wright

American novelist and poet

Born: Wetipquin, Maryland; December 9, 1928
Identity: African American

LONG FICTION: *This Child's Gonna Live*, 1969.
POETRY: *Give Me a Child*, 1955 (with Lucy Smith).
CHILDREN'S/YOUNG ADULT LITERATURE: *A. Philip Randolph: Integration in the Workplace*, 1990 (biography).

Sarah Elizabeth Wright was born in the town of Wetipquin on Maryland's Eastern Shore, the birthplace of abolitionists Harriet Tubman and Frederick Douglass. The pride and heroics of these cultural icons live on in Wright's books. In "An Appreciation," the afterword to the 1986 edition of Wright's acclaimed novel *This Child's Gonna Live*, author John Oliver Killens, who was Wright's mentor, identifies a similarity of faith and humanistic struggle between Wright's commitment to encouraging humankind and that of the historical models of African American struggle.

Wright's father, Willis Charles, was an oysterman, barber,

farmer, and musician. Her mother, the former Mary Amelia Moore, was a homemaker, barber, farmworker, and factory worker. Wright married Joseph G. Kaye, a composer, and had two children, Michael and Shelley. She attended Howard University (1945-1949) and the former Cheyney State Teachers College (1950-1952). In addition to being a writer, she worked as a teacher, a bookkeeper, and an office manager.

Wright had a rich history of artistic organization. She was a member of the Authors Guild, the Authors League of America, International PEN, and the International Women's Writing Guild. She served as vice president of the Harlem Writers Guild and as president of Pen & Brush, Inc. (1992-1993), the oldest professional organization of women in the United States. Wright put these experiences together to develop a career as a certified poetry therapist. She has also been active as a lecturer, teacher, and panelist on forums for radio and television talk shows, community centers, and schools.

Wright began writing in the third grade, and during her college years at Howard University she received encouragement from Sterling A. Brown, Langston Hughes, and Owen Dodson. She is best known as a novelist, although her first published work, *Give Me a Child*, with Lucy Smith, is an illustrated book of poems aimed at making poetry accessible to the general public. Her best-known and most frequently anthologized poem, "To Some Millions Who Survive Joseph Mander, Sr.," was first published in *Give Me a Child*. The poem reflects an actual incident in which an African American man drowned while attempting to save a white person. In the poem, Wright urges readers to embrace Mander's humanism and compassion.

Although Wright has published few works, she is critically acclaimed. *This Child's Gonna Live* was selected as one of the most important books of 1969 by *The New York Times*, and the novel was celebrated in 1994, on its silver anniversary, for being continuously in print since 1969. Some readers cite *This Child's Gonna Live* as one of the most painful novels they have ever read. The story of Mariah Upshur and her family struggling during the Depression is a dramatic saga of despair. The trials of the Upshur family—thematically centered on Mariah's resolve to save her children from hopelessness—reflect the realities of early twentieth century poverty and racism. Wright does not attempt to spare readers from understanding the tragedy.

Her later works include *A. Philip Randolph: Integration in the Workplace*, a young adult book published as part of a series on the history of the Civil Rights movement. Wright announced that she was working on a sequel to her first novel.

Christel N. Temple

Bibliography

Campbell, Jennifer. "'It's a Time in the Land': Gendering Black Power and Sarah E. Wright's Place in the Tradition of Black Women's Writing." *African American Review* 31, no. 2 (1997): 211-222. This article is a critical treatment of gender and black nationalism in Wright's *This Child's Gonna Live*.

Harris, Trudier. "Three Black Women Writers and Humanism: A Folk Perspective." In *Black Literature and Humanism*, edited by R. Baxter. Lexington: University Press of Kentucky, 1981. This study of how three black women writers address small-town community values, achievements, and survival strategies compares Wright's *This Child's Gonna Live*, Alice Walker's *The Third Life of Grange Copeland* (1970), and Paule Marshall's *The Chosen Place, the Timeless People* (1969).

Houston, Helen. R. "Sarah Elizabeth Wright." In *Oxford Companion to African American Literature*, edited by William L. Andrews, Frances Smith Foster, and Trudier Harris. New York: Oxford University Press, 1997. This essay offers contemporary biographical data on Wright, highlighting her works and her contemporaries.

White, Linda. "Sarah Elizabeth Wright." In *Contemporary African American Novelists: A Bio-bibliographical Critical Sourcebook*. Westport, Conn.: Greenwood Press, 1999. Wright has not penned an autobiography, so this essay is one of the lengthier biographical treatments available on the author with an exhaustive bibliography.

Wu Chengen

Chinese novelist

Born: Huainan (now in Jiangsu Province), China; c. 1500
Died: Huainan (now in Jiangsu Province), China; c. 1582

LONG FICTION: *Xiyou ji*, pb. 1592 (also known as *Hsi-yu chi*; partial translation as *Monkey*, 1942; *The Journey to the West*, 1977-1983).

Few facts have been preserved concerning the life of Wu Chengen (wew chuhng-uhn). It is known that he was a native of Huainan, in Jiangsu Province, a town approximately one hundred miles north of Nanjing; that he began to write when he retired from the post of district magistrate; and that he was a friend of one of the leading figures of the revival of classical literature that took place during his lifetime. A handful of his poems can be found in Ming Dynasty anthologies.

However, to Wu Chengen is attributed the authorship of one of the most popular and enduring works of the Chinese tradition, *The Journey to the West*, first published anonymously at least ten years after his death. The local history of Huainan, compiled in 1625, does indeed treat Wu Chengen's authorship of the novel as established fact. Moreover, throughout the years, his reputation both as a connoisseur of popular tales of the supernatural and as a masterful creator of humorous stories, reinforced the belief that he had composed *The Journey to the West*.

In any case, many works entitled *The Journey to the West*—stories in the oral tradition, religious treatises, even dramatic performances—circulated long before Wu Chengen was born. The Buddhist priest Hsuan Tsang (602-664) first employed the title for his autobiographical account of the seventeen-year journey from China to India and back that he undertook in order to bring Buddhist scriptures to China. Hsuan Tsang relates the difficulties of his pilgrimage, his life as a student of Buddhism in India, and finally his triumphant journey home to the Tang court. Through the years his story became embroidered with tales of the supernatural, with animal fables and folklore, and with Buddhist miracles from the popular tradition, until it was transformed into the tale of a courageous priest, beset by monsters and demons, who overcomes evil with the forces of good that are placed at his command by Lord Buddha.

Wu Chengen reshaped this diverse material into a novel of one hundred chapters informed not only by rich humor but also by a profound religious allegory of the nature of self-cultivation. His novel begins not with the story of the human pilgrim Hsuan Tsang but with that of a magic monkey.

Monkey (known in China as Sun Wu Kong, or "enlightened about emptiness," after the monastic name he adopts later in the novel) is a creature born from a stone egg nourished by Heaven and Earth, who rules over an idyllic kingdom of monkeys in the Water Curtain Cave on the Mountain of Flowers and Fruit. The first seven chapters relate how Monkey, spurred by the awareness of his own mortality, leaves his terrestrial paradise and obtains supernatural powers, which he in turn abuses by wreaking havoc in Heaven and, among other alarming misdeeds, feasting on the peaches of immortality. Powerful gods, including the Daoist sage Laozi, try to annihilate him, but the best that can be done—and this only with the help of Buddha—is to imprison him beneath the Mountain of the Five Elements.

Chapters 8 through 12 relate how, after the passing of five hundred years, Buddha announces his intention of imparting the scriptures to China, and the bodhisattva Guanyin contacts the pilgrim Hsuan Tsang and enlists the support of his sidekick-disciples Sandy, Pigsy, and the powerful and mischievous Monkey, all of whom are performing some kind of penance for past misdeeds.

Eighty-one adventures ensue (chapters 13-97), consisting largely of captures and releases of the pilgrims by a colorful variety of ogres, demons, animal spirits, and demigods. All is not what it seems in the narrative: Although the human pilgrim Hsuan Tsang is in charge, it is often the irrepressible energy, boundless courage, and comic detachment displayed by Monkey that advances the pilgrims on their way. Often, too, it is the cunning, gluttony, greed, and selfishness of Pigsy, on one hand—or the petulance, fearfulness, and nervous attachment to the world of phenomena of the somewhat literal-minded Hsuan Tsang, on the other—that get them into trouble.

As though to underline the paradoxes that underlie their pilgrimage, in the last two chapters the pilgrims must travel by a bottomless boat to receive wordless scriptures. The humor and allegory of the work are embodied in the extent to which Monkey all along has known what the others must learn by trial and error and instruction: the identity of form and emptiness taught by the Heart Sutra, for example (one of the scriptures originally brought to China by Hsuan Tsang), in which the search for enlightenment is itself a form of illusion; or the teaching of Ming Dynasty syncretism that the Three Teachings of Daoism, Buddhism, and Confucianism form an essential unity. "It's all one to me," says Monkey, unintentionally revealing one of the novel's major teachings. At the end of the novel the pilgrims are carried back to the capital of Xi'an on divine winds, and each is rewarded with his heart's desire.

Bruce M. Wilson

Bibliography

Dudbridge, Glen. *The "Hsi-yu chi": A Study of Antecedents to the Sixteenth-Century Chinese Novel*. Cambridge, England: Cambridge University Press, 1970. Includes bibliography.

Hsia, C. T. *The Classic Chinese Novel*. Ithaca, N.Y.: Cornell University East Asia Program, 1996. Provides informative critical introduction to *The Journey to the West*.

Jenner, William J. F., trans. *The Journey to the West*, by Wu Chengen. 3 vols. Hong Kong: Commercial Press, 1994. Includes an extensive scholarly introduction and notes that address the allegorical significance of the novel.

Liu Ts'un-yan. *Wu Ch'eng-en: His Life and Career.* Leiden, the Netherlands: E. J. Brill, 1967. Biography of the writer to whom *The Journey to the West* is attributed.

Plaks, Andrew H. *The Four Masterworks of the Ming Novel*. Princeton, N.J.: Princeton University Press, 1987. Provides informative critical introduction to the work.

Waley, Arthur, trans. *Monkey*. 1942. Reprint. New York: Grove Press, 1984. A lively, much-loved translation. Waley, however, translates only about a fourth of the original text, omitting many of the trials undergone by the pilgrims during their journey. See Antony C. Yu and William J. F. Jenner for complete translations.

Wang, Jing. *The Story of Stone: Intertextuality, Ancient Chinese Stone Lore, and the Stone Symbolism in "Dream of the Red Chamber," "Water Margin," and "The Journey to the West."* Durham, N.C.: Duke University Press, 1992. Compares masterworks of Chinese literature.

Yu, Anthony C., trans. *Journey to the West*, by Wu Chengen. 4 vols. Chicago: University of Chicago Press, 1977-1983. A complete translation.

Sir Thomas Wyatt

English poet

Born: Allington, near Maidstone, Kent, England; 1503
Died: Sherborne, Dorset, England; October, 1542

POETRY: *The Courte of Venus*, c. 1539 (includes 3 to 10 Wyatt poems); *Certayne Psalmes Chosen Out of the Psalter of David*, 1549; *Songes and Sonettes*, 1557 (known as *Tottel's Miscellany*, Richard Tottel, editor; includes 90 to 97 Wyatt poems); *Collected Poems of Sir Thomas Wyatt*, 1949 (Kenneth Muir, editor); *Sir Thomas Wyatt and His Circle: Unpublished Poems*, 1961 (Muir, editor); *Collected Poems*, 1975 (Joost Daalder, editor).
TRANSLATION: *Plutarckes Boke of the Quyete of Mynde*, 1528 (of Plutarch).

Throughout the Renaissance, the European noble was expected to be a creditable poet as well as a capable soldier and diplomat, so much of the best poetry of sixteenth century England was written by members of high-ranking families who contributed to their country's development. Sir Thomas Wyatt (WI-uht) and Henry Howard, earl of Surrey, who inaugurated the golden age of English poetry with their adoption of the verse forms and subject matter of French and Italian works, fall into the long line of courtier poets who wrote sonnets, songs, and satires for their own and their friends' satisfaction.

Wyatt composed his poems during intervals in a busy, if checkered, career as a public official. The son of Sir Henry Wyatt, a minor noble, he was born in 1503 at Allington Castle in Kent. He went to St. John's College, Cambridge, when he was thirteen, and was made master of arts in 1520. In that year he married Elizabeth, daughter of Lord Cobham, and began to serve as a court official. In 1526 he traveled to France as a courier for the English ambassador. His mission to Italy in the following year was probably more significant for his poetic development; it gave him an opportunity to become familiar with the works of the Italian poets who greatly influenced his writing, among them Petrarch and Pietro Aretino. During the course of his Italian mission Wyatt was captured by Spanish troops, but he escaped before his ransom was paid. For the next four years he served as marshal of Calais, re turning to England in 1532 as commissioner of the peace in Essex.

Wyatt was imprisoned in May, 1536, probably because of a quarrel with the powerful duke of Suffolk, although there has been considerable speculation about his involvement with Queen Anne Boleyn, who was executed that same year. There is a strong tradition, supported by some evidence, that Anne was Wyatt's mistress before her marriage to Henry VIII, and several of his poems have been interpreted as references to his love for her. These lines, translated from a sonnet by Petrarch, are often quoted: "*Noli me tangere*, for Caesar's I am;/ And wild for to hold, though I seem tame."

Wyatt remained in prison only briefly; then, after a few months at his father's home, he was appointed ambassador to Spain, faced with the unenviable task of placating the Emperor Charles V, nephew of Henry VIII's divorced queen, Catherine of Aragon. The last years of Wyatt's life proved turbulent, marked by the execution of his friend Thomas Cromwell, Henry's capable minister who fell from royal favor and was convicted of treason in 1540, and by the enmity of Thomas Bonner, bishop of London, who had Wyatt brought to trial on charges of treason in 1541. Wyatt spoke brilliantly in his own defense and received a full pardon. He was made both a member of Parliament and a vice admiral, but before he could enjoy his new positions, he died of a fever contracted as he was traveling to the coast to greet the Spanish ambassador.

Wyatt did not publish any poems during his lifetime because he was a noble; during his era, the publication of one's own poems was not considered genteel. His poems, however, circulated at court. Some appeared for the first time in print in Richard Tottel's *Songes and Sonettes* (1557), also known as *Tottel's Miscellany*. The meter in Wyatt's poetry is sometimes irregular, and Tottel made some revisions before printing the noble's poems in his collection. Henry Howard, earl of Surrey, also wrote poems that appear in *Tottel's Miscellany*; the poetry of these contemporaries is often compared. Surrey's, modern scholars agree, is smoother. Wyatt was nonetheless an important Renaissance poet, an innovator who introduced Petrarchan sonnets and conceits to England and whose verse contains passion. Wyatt wrote primarily of love—love scorned or betrayed—in poems such as "They Flee from Me" and "The Long Love That in My Thought Doth Harbor." He also wrote an important satirical poem titled "Mine Own John Poins," an autobiographical piece apparently written in 1536 during his banishment from court.

A poem by Wyatt's young friend and disciple, the earl of Surrey, pays tribute to his intelligence, his integrity, and his faith: "Wyatt resteth here, that quick could never rest;/ Whose heavenly gifts increaséd by disdain,/ And virtue sank the deeper in his breast;/ Such profit he by envy could obtain."

Eric Sterling

Bibliography

Estrin, Barbara L. *Laura: Uncovering Gender and Genre in Wyatt, Donne, and Marvell*. Durham, N.C.: Duke University Press, 1994. A study acknowledging the tyranny to women that most Petrarchan poems impose. Includes bibliographical references and index.

Foley, Stephen Merriam. *Sir Thomas Wyatt*. Boston: Twayne, 1990. Examines the meaning of Wyatt's poetry and, more important, how he came to write in such pioneering forms in Tudor England.

Harrier, Richard. *The Canon of Sir Thomas Wyatt's Poetry*. Cambridge, Mass.: Harvard University Press, 1975. This study attempts to establish the canon of Wyatt's poetry. Harrier analyzes the history and physical characteristics of Wyatt's manuscripts and scrutinizes them in the context of the poet's complete output of work.

Heale, Elizabeth. *Wyatt, Surrey, and Early Tudor Poetry.* New York: Longman, 1998. An indispensable resource containing critical interpretation of the works of two early English sonneteers. Includes bibliographical references and index.

Jentoft, Clyde W. *Sir Thomas Wyatt and Henry Howard, Earl of Surrey: A Reference Guide.* Boston: G. K. Hall, 1980. An invaluable book for the student of Wyatt. Contains annotated information from books, magazines, studies, and monographs as well as introductions and commentaries from important editions of Wyatt's work and sections about him that appeared in other scholarly works.

Ross, Diane M. *Self-Revelation and Self-Protection in Wyatt's Lyric Poetry.* New York: Garland, 1988. This book examines how Wyatt's attempts to express his themes relate to the lyric genre. Ross accomplishes this primarily by contrasting Wyatt's work to other Renaissance lyric poetry.

Thomson, Patricia, ed. *Wyatt: The Critical Heritage.* Boston: Routledge & Kegan Paul, 1975. The critical tradition of Wyatt's poetry is presented in sixteen commentaries on his work ranging from an unsigned 1527 preface to *Plutarckes Boke of the Quyete of Mynde*, to C. S. Lewis's comments written in 1954. Includes an informative introduction to this material.

William Wycherley

English playwright

Born: Clive(?), near Shrewsbury, Shropshire, England; May 28, 1641(?)
Died: London, England; December 31, 1715

DRAMA: *Love in a Wood: Or, St. James's Park*, pr. 1671; *The Gentleman Dancing-Master*, pr. 1672 (adaptation of Pedro Calderón de la Barca's play *El maestro de danzar*); *The Country Wife*, pr., pb. 1675; *The Plain-Dealer*, pr. 1676; *Complete Plays*, pb. 1967.
POETRY: *Miscellany Poems: As Satyrs, Epistles, Love-Verses, Songs, Sonnets, Etc.*, 1704.

William Wycherley (WIHCH-ur-lee) was born of an old family near Shrewsbury, Shropshire, probably in 1641. When he was about fifteen years of age, he was sent to France, where he frequented refined circles, notably the salon of the duchess de Montausier. Also while in France, Wycherley became a Catholic. Returning to England in 1660, just prior to the Restoration of King Charles II to the throne, he spent a short time at Queen's College, Oxford, from which he went to the Inner Temple in London. In London he soon found a place in the pleasure-loving society of the town, rejoicing after eighteen years of enforced Puritan virtue, and he gravitated toward the theater, the most notable social entertainment of the day.

In 1671 his first play, *Love in a Wood*, gained him the intimacy of one of the king's mistresses, the duchess of Cleveland, through whose influence he secured in 1672 a commission in a foot regiment. His acquaintance with the duchess brought him into favor with the king, which favor, however, he lost in 1679 due to a brief and unfortunate marriage to the countess of Drogheda. The marriage led to Wycherley's banishment from the court and temporary retirement from the theater. He shortly found himself in debt and, consequently, in Fleet Prison. He was released in 1686 by the proceeds of a benefit performance of his last play, *The Plain-Dealer.*

After 1704 he formed a friendship with young Alexander Pope, who revised many of Wycherley's later verses. Eleven days before his death, Wycherley married a young woman named Elizabeth Jackson—for the purpose, it is said, of keeping a nephew he despised from receiving any inheritance.

Wycherley, with four plays to his credit, stands next after Sir George Etherege, with three plays, as the innovator of modern English comedy. Etherege transcribed life, but he lacked philosophy; life was to him a frivolous game, and to become emotionally engrossed in it was perhaps slightly vulgar. Wycherley, on the other hand, while he partook of Etherege's cynicism, felt not aloof amusement but more than a little resentment. There is bitterness, even malice, in Wycherley's satire.

In typical Restoration fashion, to Wycherley the greatest sin is foolishness. For instance, in *Love in a Wood*, Alderman Gripe, a hypocritical Puritan, ultimately marries a wench; Dapperwit, a fop, gets Gripe's daughter for his wife but does not get her fortune, which he was really after. Wycherley's third play, *The Country Wife*, is an extremely realistic picture of cuckold-gulling, the great aristocratic pastime of the day. Horner, recently returned from France, pretends impotence in order better to practice his formidable art of despoiling chastity. His chief success is to win the favor of Margery, the country wife of the superannuated sensualist, Pinchwife. Without subtlety, but certainly with power, Wycherley makes his spectators partisans in condemning selfishness, pretentiousness, and hypocrisy.

The Country Wife is nowadays considered Wycherley's best play, but in his own day *The Plain-Dealer* was considered his finest achievement; it is still more commonly included in anthologies. The same theme of exposing pretension and hypocrisy is present in this play as in *The Country Wife*. Manly, the plain dealer, has been robbed and wronged by his mistress, Olivia, and his closest friend, Vernish. Wycherley's attack on selfishness and treachery in the persons of Vernish and Olivia is open and savage. Indeed, the play is not at all typical of the Restoration, being hardly funny, hardly even amusing.

Paul Varner

Bibliography

Markley, Robert. *Two Edg'd Weapons: Style and Dialogue in the Comedies of Etherege, Wycherley, and Congreve*. New York: Oxford University Press, 1988. This study is concerned with the comic style and language of Sir George Etherege, Wycherley, and William Congreve as the rewriting or adaptation of systems of theatrical signification in predecessors, as the reflection of particular cultural codes of speech and behavior that would be accessible to their audience, and as a comment on the culture of which they and their audience were a part. Includes bibliography.

Marshall, W. Gerald. *A Great Stage of Fools: Theatricality and Madness in the Plays of William Wycherley*. New York: AMS Press, 1993. Marshall examines the concept of mental illness as it appears in the works of Wycherley. Includes bibliography and index.

Thompson, James. *Language in Wycherley's Plays: Seventeenth-Century Language Theory and Drama*. University: University of Alabama Press, 1984. Thompson discusses how Wycherley used language in his dramas and relates his usage to the broader context. Includes bibliography and index.

Vance, John A. *William Wycherley and the Comedy of Fear*. Newark, N.J.: University of Delaware Press, 2000. An analysis of Wycherley and his works with the focus on his treatment of fear. Includes bibliography and index.

Young, Douglas M. *The Feminist Voices in Restoration Comedy: The Virtuous Women in the Play-Worlds of Etherege, Wycherley, and Congreve*. Lanham, Md.: University Press of America, 1997. A study of feminism and women in the works of Wycherley, George Etherege, and William Congreve. Includes bibliography and index.

Elinor Wylie

American poet and novelist

Born: Somerville, New Jersey; September 7, 1885
Died: New York, New York; December 16, 1928

POETRY: *Nets to Catch the Wind*, 1921; *Black Armour*, 1923; *Trivial Breath*, 1928; *Angels and Earthly Creatures*, 1928; *Last Poems*, 1943.
LONG FICTION: *Jennifer Lorn: A Sedate Extravaganza*, 1923; *The Venetian Glass Nephew*, 1925; *The Orphan Angel*, 1926; *Mr. Hodge and Mr. Hazard*, 1928.

A woman of mercurial temperament and a dedicated artist in both poetry and prose, Elinor Wylie (WI-lee) emerged as one of the "new traditionalists" of American literature in the 1920's. In a space of eight years, she wrote four books of poems and four novels in which her tragic vision of life is portrayed in fantasy and satire. Dead at forty-three, she had achieved recognition as an eloquent and picturesque writer whose work revealed the frustrations of a woman oppressed by society's dictates.

Born Elinor Morton Hoyt in Somerville, New Jersey, on September 7, 1885, she was the oldest child of Henry Martyn and Anne (McMichael) Hoyt, both descended from old Pennsylvania families distinguished in society and public affairs. Her education was as fashionably correct as her family background. She attended private schools in Bryn Mawr and Washington, where her father, appointed to the post of assistant attorney general of the United States in 1897, became solicitor general in 1903. During her schooldays her interests were divided between art and poetry, the latter chiefly through her discovery of Percy Bysshe Shelley. Following her social debut and a brief, unhappy love affair, she married Philip Hichborn in 1905. For the next five years she lived the life of a fashionable young matron according to the standards of Philadelphia and Washington society. In 1910, to the surprise of family and friends, she abandoned her husband and small son and eloped with a married man, Horace Wylie, a cultivated scholarly man fifteen years her senior. Two years later Hichborn committed suicide. The elopement created a scandal kept alive by gossip and the press for years; it was even noted in the headline of her obituary.

When Horace Wylie found it impossible to obtain a divorce, the couple went to England and lived there under an assumed name. *Incidental Numbers*, Wylie's first book of poems, was privately printed in London in 1912. Published anonymously, for presentation only, it holds only occasional promise of her mature powers as a poet. Unable to remain in England under wartime conditions, she and Wylie returned to Boston in 1916. His divorce having been granted, they were married the next year. After several years of restless travel from Maine to Georgia, Horace Wylie secured a minor government post, and they returned to Washington in 1919. Cut off from most of her former friends, Elinor Wylie became one of a literary group that included William Rose Benét and Sinclair Lewis, and with their encouragement she continued to write poetry. In 1921 she left Washington to make her home in New York.

She came late to the literary scene but with the manner of one whom no disastrous circumstance could subdue. The disillusionment Wylie felt when reality never quite measured up to her ideals resulted in poignant and often eccentric descriptive poetry. *Nets to Catch the Wind*, published in 1921, was awarded the Julia Ellsworth Ford Prize by the Poetry Society of America. To those who knew her best, she remained a person of contradictions. Although frequently overcome by life's fragility, she never relinquished her quest for the ideal existence. She could be remote and proud (the "iced chalk" to which one critic compared her), but she was also mirthful and gracious, and her speech, like her writing, crackled with the wit and vigor of her mind. She had become a figure of literary legend when, having divorced Horace Wylie, she married William Rose Benét in 1923 and in the same year published both her second book of poems and a successful first novel.

Although Shelley was her lifelong passion, to the extent that she often identified herself with him, he was by no means the only influence on her work. In *Nets to Catch the Wind* and *Black Armour* there is evidence of the tradition of John Donne and William Blake, poets who found an approach to spiritual truth in a disembodied ecstasy of thought and emotion. Wylie's erudition and wit are plain in the sharpened epithet, the aristocratic scorn, the language framing stark abstractions, a delight in subtleties of thought, and an imagery of symbolic birds and beasts. On the whole, the poems in these books are songs of experience, with much bitterness in the singing. *Trivial Breath* is a more uneven collection, divided as it is between lyrics of personal experience and payment of her literary debts. But there is little of the "overfine" in the elegiac moods which pervade *Angels and Earthly Creatures*. Most of these poems were written in England during the summer of 1928, when some presentiment of death seemed to have given Wylie a final certainty of vision and language. The desire for escape is less persistent, the note of resignation less profound. Instead, there is exultant affirmation of love and faith transcending all fears of death in the magnificent sonnet sequence, "One Person." These poems, her most passionate revelation of the woman and the poet, are in the great tradition.

Her novels are like much of her poetry, exquisite and erudite. *Jennifer Lorn*, for example, is set against a droll background blending sophisticated elegance with simple manners. It is a satire on the twin themes of magnificence and folly, reflected in the ambitions of an eighteenth century empire builder and the attitude of a heroine unmoved by the bustle of all practical affairs until death frees her at last from a husband who bores her and a world that intrudes upon her romantic dreaming. The artifice of *The Venetian Glass Nephew* seems on the surface as brittle as its spun-glass hero, but it contains deeper meanings as life is defeated by art in the story of a heroine willing to be transformed into a cold, decorative porcelain figure just to please her glass husband.

The Orphan Angel is a picaresque romance in which Shelley is miraculously rescued off Viareggio and brought to the United States aboard a Yankee ship. *Mr. Hodge and Mr. Hazard* is a more personal fable, in many ways Wylie's best. The disillusioned poet who returns to England in the twilight of the Romantic period is not Shelley, as many readers have supposed, but any artist who survives into a later period than his or her own. The summer idyll of the old poet ends in a fiasco of stale cream buns and an epigram; the whole is an ironic allegory of the poet's tragedy and the world's indifference.

Wylie was not to share her hero's fate. In England, where she spent the summer of 1928, she fell while visiting a country house and suffered a painful but temporary back injury. In October a mild stroke left one side of her face partly paralyzed. She returned to New York early in December of that year. On December 16 she had arranged the poems in *Angels and Earthly Creatures* for the printer and was sitting reading in the Benét apartment when she had a second stroke and died before her husband could summon assistance.

Sandra C. McClain

Bibliography

Benét, William Rose. *The Prose and Poetry of Elinor Wylie*. 1934. Reprint. Folcroft, Pa.: Folcroft Press, 1969. Transcript of Benét's lecture.

Farr, Judith. *The Life and Art of Elinor Wylie*. Baton Rouge: Louisiana State University Press, 1983. A substantial critical and biographical study.

Gray, Thomas. *Elinor Wylie*. New York: Twayne, 1969. Early study that provides basic information and rather unsympathetic criticism.

Hilt, Kathryn. "Elinor Wylie: A Bibliography." *Bulletin of Bibliography* 42 (1985). An excellent, thorough bibliography.

Olson, Stanley. *Elinor Wylie: A Life Apart*. New York: Dial Press, 1979. Biography studies Wylie's life and works.

Johann Rudolf Wyss

Swiss novelist

Born: Bern, Switzerland; March 4, 1782
Died: Bern, Switzerland; March 21, 1830

LONG FICTION: *Der schweizerische Robinson*, 1812-1827 (*The Swiss Family Robinson*, 1814, 1818, 1820).
EDITED TEXTS: *Reise im Berner Oberland*, 1808; *Die Alpenrose*, 1811-1830 (15 volumes); *Idyllen, Volkssagen, Legenden, und Erzählungen aus der Schweiz*, 1815-1822.

Johann Rudolf Wyss (vees), who is usually credited as the author of *The Swiss Family Robinson*, was born in Bern, Switzerland, on March 4, 1782. He studied at several German universities and in 1806 became a professor of philosophy at the University of Bern, where he also served as the chief librarian. In his native Switzerland he became known as a collector and editor of Swiss folklore, publishing such volumes as *Idyllen, Volkssagen, Legenden, und Erzählungen aus der Schweiz* (idylls, folktales, legends, and stories from the Swiss), *Reise im Berner Oberland* (travels in the Bernese uplands), and the fifteen-volume *Die Alpenrose*, an almanac. He was also the author of the Swiss national anthem.

Johann Rudolf Wyss did not apparently actually compose *The Swiss Family Robinson* but only wrote it down in revised form and saw to its publication. The story, obviously in partial imitation of Daniel Defoe's *Robinson Crusoe* (1719), was originally conceived by Wyss's father, Johann David Wyss (1743-1818), for the enjoyment of his sons. Of the father, who was a chaplain in the Swiss army, little is known, except that he was born in 1743, became a chaplain, served in Italy, and died in 1818.

The history of *The Swiss Family Robinson* is an interesting one. Apparently Pastor Wyss committed his story to writing before his son revised the manuscript and had it published at Zurich, Switzerland, under the title *Der schweizerische Robinson: Oder, Der schiffbrüchige Schweizerprediger und seine Familie, ein lehrreiches Buch für Kinder und Kinderfreunde zu Stadt und Land* (the Swiss family Robinson: or, the shipwrecked Swiss preacher and his family, an instructional book for children and their friends in city and country). The first known English translation was by William Godwin, British philosopher, reformer, and novelist, a short time after the Zurich edition appeared. A Frenchwoman, Baroness de Montolieu, with Johann Rudolf Wyss's approval, enlarged the story, translated it into French, and published it in 1824. Two years later the original publisher in Zurich brought out a new German edition that incorporated the baroness's additions. Wyss died in Bern on March 21, 1830.

The first English translation of the enlarged story was made in 1868, by Mrs. H. B. Paull, who also translated Grimms' fairy tales. Most later editions have followed Baroness de Montolieu's edition. The book has been immensely popular in the United States and Europe with generations of children.

Bibliography

Allen, Francis H. "News for Bibliophiles." *The Nation* 95, no. 2462 (September 5, 1912): 210-211.

Becker, May Lamberton. Introduction to *The Swiss Family Robinson*, by Johann Rudolf Wyss. Cleveland: World Publishing, 1947.

Bosworth, Allan R. Introduction to *The Swiss Family Robinson*, by Johann Rudolf Wyss. New York: Harper & Row, 1966.

Glaenzer, R. B. "The Swiss Family Robinson." *Bookman* 34 (1911).

Howells, William Dean. Introduction to *The Swiss Family Robinson*, by Johann Rudolf Wyss. New York: Harper & Brothers, 1909.

Wyss, Robert L. "The Real Swiss Wysses." *Life*, no. 26 (December 27, 1954): 63-64.

Xenophon

Greek historian and essayist

Born: Athens, Greece; c. 431 B.C.E.
Died: Corinth, Greece; c. 354 B.C.E.

NONFICTION: *Logos eis Agēsilaon Basilea* (*Agesilaus*, 1832); *Kyrou anabasis* (*Anabasis*, 1623; also known as *Expedition of Cyrus* and *The March Up Country*); *Apologia Sōkratous* (*Apology of Socrates*, 1762); *Kynēgetikos* (also known as *Cynegeticus*; *On Hunting*, 1832); *Poroi* (*On Ways and Means*, 1832); *Ellēnika* (also known as *Hellenica*; *History of the Affairs of Greece*, 1685); *Hipparchikos* (*On the Cavalry General*, 1832); *Peri hippikēs* (*The Art of Riding*, 1584); *Apomnēmoneumata* (*Xenophon's Memorable Things of Socrates*, 1712; also known as *Memorabilia of Socrates*); *Oikonomikos* (*Xenophon's Treatise of Household*, 1532); *Lakedaimoniōn politeia* (*Polity of the Lacedaemonians*, 1832; also known as *Constitution of Sparta*); *Hierōn ē tyrannikos* (*Hiero*, 1713; also known as *On Tyranny*); *Symposion* (*Symposium*, 1710; also known as *The Banquet of Xenophon*).
LONG FICTION: *Kyrou paideia* (*The Cyropaedia: Or, Education of Cyrus*, 1560-1567).
MISCELLANEOUS: *The Whole Works*, 1832.

Born in Athens about 431 B.C.E., Xenophon (ZEHN-uh-fuhn), son of Gryllus of the Attic deme Erchia, belonged to a well-to-do family and was a disciple of Socrates, though not a member of his intimate circle. He grew up at a time of oligarchic revolution in Athens, and he probably left Athens in 401 B.C.E. because of political precariousness. That same year, he joined in an adventurous expedition to overthrow the king of Persia. He then spent a few years in Asia Minor with mercenary troops under Spartan command. Exiled from Athens around 399, he eventually settled in the Peloponnese, where he lived with his two sons and wife, Philesia, as a country gentleman on an estate granted him by the Spartans at Scillus near Olympia. He lost this estate around 371 when the Eleans recovered Scillus from the Spartans. In 368 the decree of exile was rescinded, after Athens entered into an alliance with Sparta. Thereafter he occasionally visited Athens and sent his sons to serve in the Athenian cavalry. In 366-365 Athenians were expelled from Corinth, so Xenophon returned to Athens permanently. He died about 354 B.C.E. while on a visit to Corinth.

It is as a writer that Xenophon is best known. He wrote history, romance, and essays of practical and moral import. His most famous work is the *Anabasis*, an account of the expedition of ten thousand mercenaries hired by Cyrus, the younger brother of King Artaxerxes, to win for himself the throne of Persia. Though Cyrus's army defeated the king's, Cyrus was killed. The Greek generals having been treacherously captured and slain, Xenophon found himself in command of the hazardous retreat of the mercenaries to Trebizond on the Black Sea. After making contact with the Spartan general Thibron, Xenophon turned the mercenaries over to him and remained in Asia with the Spartans for some years. The *Anabasis* is a thrilling adventure story, written in good, if somewhat uninspired, Greek.

In the *History of the Affairs of Greece* Xenophon completed the unfinished *History of the Peloponnesian War* of Thucydides and continued the history of Greek war and politics down to the battle of Mantinea in 362 B.C.E. The work is inferior to that of Thucydides both in style and in historical understanding, but it is a primary source for the history of the period it covers.

Association with Socrates supplied the material and motive for several works: The *Memorabilia of Socrates* is a defense of Socrates, with illustrative anecdotes and many short dialogues between Socrates and his friends, usually on moral questions. Xenophon lacked Plato's interest in speculative philosophy. The *Apology of Socrates* purports to explain why Socrates did not defend himself any better than he did. The *Symposium* consists of an imagined dinner party conversation at the house of Callias, with some serious philosophizing by Socrates. In general these works portray a more matter-of-fact Socrates than the protagonist of Plato's dialogues but one probably no nearer the historical truth. Another dialogue, *Xenophon's Treatise of Household*, between Socrates and Critobulos, sets forth Xenophon's views on the management of an estate. It reflects the life at Scillus and is a valuable document for the economy of the period.

A work of a different sort, *The Cyropaedia* is a romanticized account of the youth and education of Cyrus the Great of Persia. It is intended to lay down the ideals of education for political leadership. It is unfavorably remarked on by Plato in the *Republic*

(c. 388-368 B.C.E.). Xenophon's political interests were also expressed in the laudatory *Constitution of Sparta* and in *On Tyranny*. The latter is a dialogue between the king of Syracuse and the poet Simonides, dealing with the relative happiness of the despot and the private citizen and with the question of how a despot should rule in order to win the affection of his people.

Four technical treatises were also written by Xenophon: *On the Cavalry General*, on the duties of a cavalry commander; *The Art of Riding* (or *On Horsemanship*), an authoritative manual, the first of its kind to come down to us from antiquity; *On Ways and Means*, suggestions for improving the finances of Athens; and *On Hunting*, a treatise that includes, oddly enough, an attack on the Sophists. Xenophon was a man of affairs, with intelligence and wide interests, who wrote plainly and with a taste for platitude. His works reflect the attitudes of a Greek gentleman of his time.

Alan Cottrell

Bibliography

Dillery, John. *Xenophon and the History of His Times*. New York: Routledge, 1995. A treatment of Xenophon's historical writing in context.

Nadon, Christopher. *Xenophon's Prince: Republic and Empire in the "Cyropaedia."* Berkeley: University of California Press, 2001. Discusses the *Cyropaedia* as political theory.

O'Sullivan, James N. *Xenophon of Ephesus: His Compositional Technique and the Birth of the Novel*. New York: W. de Gruyter, 1995. Includes texts in ancient Greek as well as bibliographical references and indexes.

Pomeroy, Sarah B. *Xenophon "Oeconomicus": A Social and Historical Commentary*. New York: Oxford University Press, 1994. Includes Greek text with English translation and commentary.

Schmeling, Gareth L. *Xenophon of Ephesus*. Boston: Twayne, 1980. A solid, basic biography.

Strauss, Leo. *On Tyranny: Including the Strauss-Kojève Correspondence*. Rev. and expanded ed. Chicago: University of Chicago Press, 2000. This postscript to Strauss's *Xeonphon's Socratic Discourse* also addresses political thought.

_______. *Xenophon's Socratic Discourse: An Interpretation of the Oeconomicus*. 1970. Reprint. South Bend, Ind.: St. Augustine's Press, 1998. A famous essay on political thought.

Xiao Hong
(Zhang Naiying)

Chinese novelist and short-story writer

Born: Hulan County, Heilongjiang Province, China; 1911
Died: Hong Kong; January 22, 1942

LONG FICTION: *Shengi chang*, 1935 (*The Field of Life and Death*, 1979); *Ma Bole*, 1940; *Hulanhe zhuan*, 1941 (*Tales of Hulan River*, 1979).
SHORT FICTION: *Bashe*, 1933 (with Xiao Jun); *Qiao*, 1936; *Niuche shang*, 1937; *Kuangye li di hukan*, 1946; *Selected Stories of Xiao Hong*, 1982.
NONFICTION: *Shangshi jie*, 1936 (*Market Street*, 1986); *Huiyi Lu Xun xiansheng*, 1940.

Xiao Hong (zhow hong) is one of the best writers in modern Chinese literature. She was born Zhang Naiying into a wealthy landowning family in 1911. Her mother died when she was nine; her father, a miser, became the archetype of the cruel oppressor in her fiction, but her grandfather taught her classical poems and the meaning of love. Her childhood, as captured in *Tales of Hulan River*, was cloistered and troubled but not without moments of joy. Her coming-of-age was adventurous, reflecting the spirit of the new woman in the early twentieth century. To escape an arranged marriage at the age of nineteen, she fled to Harbin and cohabited with a local teacher. After she was expelled from school, she traveled with the teacher to Beijing, only to discover that he already had a wife. Pregnant and destitute, she went back to Harbin alone and was stranded in a hotel. Out of desperation, she wrote to a Harbin newspaper for help. Xiao Jun, a contributor to the paper, came to her rescue.

Xiao Hong's literary career started with her cohabitation with Xiao Jun. In August, 1933, they self-published *Bashe*, a joint anthology of stories and prose. In 1934 they went to Shandong and stayed there for six months before traveling on to Shanghai. In Shandong, Xiao Jun wrote *Village in August*, and Xiao Hong wrote *The Field of Life and Death*. Both novels, first published in Shanghai, became overnight sensations in China. Although both writers chronicled rural life in northeast China during the Japanese occupation, Xiao Jun's style is masculine and propagandistic, whereas Xiao Hong's style is feminine and naturalistic. Xiao Hong, particularly, portrays the mute suffering of rural women in the cycle of monotonous life and death. She gradually unfolds the disruptions of that monotony caused by the Japanese invasion and the creation of a meaning in life with increasing anti-Japanese consciousness among the peasants.

In 1935 Xiao Hong wrote *Market Street*, an imaginative re-creation of her life with Xiao Jun during their final years in Harbin. Apart from her vivid description of psychological distortions caused by constant hunger, Xiao Hong poked at Xiao Jun for his self-centered male chauvinism. In Shanghai, Xiao Jun's condescending protectiveness and intellectual disdain toward her became unbearable, and in the summer of 1936 she traveled alone to Japan. Xiao Hong was physically and emotionally frail. Fortunately, she had developed an intimate relationship with Lu Xun and his family. The death of Lu Xun in October of that year threw her into utter loneliness and isolation; however, she did not stop writing. Her *Huiyi Lu Xun xiansheng* (remembrance of Lu Xun), an intensely personal and honest account, established a model for modern memorial narrative.

Her three best-known stories, "The Bridge," "The Hands," and "On the Oxcart," fully demonstrate her mastery of storytelling. "The Bridge," through musical refrains, recaptures the tragic fate of a poor Chinese woman who is forced to be a nanny for a rich man's child. "Hands" is her most artistic achievement in structure and characterization. "On the Oxcart" skillfully uses the first-person narrator as a sympathetic listener to indict the evils of war. Xiao Hong also used short story as preliminary exploration to longer fiction. "The Family Outsider" was later incorporated into her famous novel *Tales of Hulan River*, a lyrical account of the author's hometown narrated by an innocent girl. "Flight from Danger," a caricature of a sham revolutionary, was developed into *Ma Bole*, a comic novel that bears the influence of Lu Xun and Lao She in probing the diseased psychology of a Chinese man.

Although Xiao Hong was not overtly a feminist, she was inwardly resistant and softly stubborn, traits revealed in her writing. She left Xiao Jun and became common-law wife of Duanmu Hongliang in 1938, but in their relationship she again suffered from male selfishness. In 1940 they fled to Hong Kong. During the Japanese attack of Hong Kong in December 1940, Xiao Hong entered Queen Mary's Hospital, where she died of a throat infection on January 22, 1942.

Unlike another Chinese woman writer, Ding Ling, Xiao Hong seldom focuses her writing on gender issues. Although *Tales of Hulan River* and *Market Street* reveal her feminist consciousness, her writings are preoccupied with victimized women, peasant suffering, and the Chinese character during national crisis. Largely because of Xiao Hong's broad perspective, Lu Xun remarked in 1936 that she was "the most promising of our women writers, and shows possibilities of becoming as much in advance of Miss Ding Ling as the latter was in succeeding Miss Bing Xin."

The preeminent feature of Xiao Hong's writing is a distinctively female style. Her writing is different not only from that of male writers such as Xiao Jun but also from that of Shen Congwen, the leading lyrical stylist of her time. Her style is fluid and breath-borne; it can be best compared with that of the Brazilian Clarice Lispector.

Qingyun Wu

Bibliography

Binji, Luo. "A Brief Biography of Xiao Hong." *Chinese Literature*, no. 11 (November, 1980). Gives a short biographical sketch.

Goldblatt, Howard. *Hsiao Hung*. Boston: Twayne, 1976. Gives a reliable study of Xiao Hong's life and works. Includes chronology and a selected bibliography.

Ziyun, Li. "Women's Consciousness and Women's Writing." In *Engendering China: Women, Culture, and the State*, edited by Christina K. Gilmartin. Cambridge, Mass.: Harvard University Press, 1994. Discusses Xiao Hong in the context of other modern Chinese women writers.

Agustín Yáñez

Mexican novelist

Born: Guadalajara, Mexico; May 4, 1904
Died: Mexico City, Mexico; January 17, 1980

LONG FICTION: *Archipiélago de mujeres*, 1943 (novella); *Pasión y convalecencia*, 1943; *Al filo del agua*, 1947 (*The Edge of the Storm*, 1963); *La tierra pródiga*, 1960; *Las tierras flacas*, 1962 (*The Lean Lands*, 1968).
SHORT FICTION: *Espejismo de Juchitán*, 1940; *Esta es mala suerte*, 1945.
NONFICTION: *Genio y figuras de Guadalajara*, 1940; *Flor de juegos antiguos*, 1942; *Fray Bartolomé de las Casas, el conquistador conquistado*, 1942 (biography); *El contenido social de la literatura iberoamericana*, 1944; *Alfonso Gutierrez Hermosillo y algunos amigos*, 1945 (biography); *Yahualica*, 1946; *Don Justo Sierra, su vida, sus ideas y su obra*, 1950 (biography).

Even as a child and adolescent, Agustín Yáñez (yah-NYAYS) had what he later called a "rigorous critical sense" as well as a "sentimental temperament" so intense that it "could not but manifest itself, even exaggeratedly, and ended in coloring his life absolutely." The characteristics of seriousness, austerity, and preoccupation with artistic form shaped all his literary work.

Yáñez associated himself with other young writers of Guadalajara and founded a literary journal, *Bandera de Provincias* (provincial banner), the establishment of which was a national event. He received his law degree in Guadalajara and later moved to Mexico City, where he devoted himself to university teaching and writing and held several important public offices.

According to the aesthetic creed of Yáñez, the ideal of art is form. For him, the idea of literary form follows a movement inward, a theory of composition initiated by means of living the reality and then reliving it in the literary work until one completes it in the appropriate verbal form. "I never write—least of all when writing novels—with the intention of sustaining a premeditated thesis, committed to predetermined conclusions." After intuiting a form, he would develop it until it took on consistency; it was then necessary that he follow it, striving not to falsify characters, situations, and atmosphere.

Yáñez as a writer was very conscious and cognizant of his function. His style is elaborate, reflective, grave, and refined. His knowledge of contemporary philosophy, of the Spanish classics, and of the resources of the modern novel infuses his work. Almost all of Yáñez's works have reminiscence as a common ingredient. On the occasion of the commemoration of the fourth centennial of the founding of Guadalajara, he wrote two books: *Flor de juegos antiguos*, lyrical memories of his childhood and of the games of his province, and *Genio y figuras de Guadalajara*, in which he presents a brief description of this city in 1930 and character studies of its principal citizens throughout its history. In 1943 he published *Archipiélago de mujeres*, a collection of seven stories, each one called by the name of a woman who represents a step on the author's "ladder of adolescence": music, revelation, desire, beauty, folly, death, and love.

In *The Edge of the Storm* (the literal translation of the title is "to the edge of the water"), Yáñez produced his best novel and, according to many critics, one of the finest Mexican novels of the mid-twentieth century. In a prose that is dense, unhackneyed, and subtle, he presents the life of a typical pueblo of Jalisco. In the routine and monotony of everyday life, passion and religion are the two stimuli of these provincial small-town people. The dramas of conscience brought about by the conflicts of flesh and spirit are analyzed with subtle introspection.

Two other books complete his trilogy of novels about Jalisco, his native land—*La tierra pródiga* (the lavish land) and *The Lean Lands*. During the time he held the office of governor of Jalisco, he had the opportunity to obtain firsthand knowledge of the inhabitants of its coastal region. From this contact, *La tierra pródiga* was born as a portrait of the struggle between barbarism and civilization that results in humankind's finally overcoming nature. In *The Lean Lands* he re-creates the atmosphere of *The Edge of the Storm*, namely, the secluded, traditional life of small towns, with arid lands and a people unfazed by the appearance of technology.

Yáñez's studies of Mexican literature are well regarded. Particularly outstanding are those devoted to the chronicles of the Spanish conquest of Mexico and to the native myths of the pre-Hispanic epoch. Yáñez contributed to the modernization of the Mexican novel, and he is considered a forerunner of the Spanish American narratives of the 1960's that achieved world acclaim.

Emil Volek

Bibliography

Brushwood, John S. "The Lyric Style of Agustín Yáñez." *Symposium* 26 (1972). Discusses *Al filo del agua.*

Durand, Frank. "The Apocalyptic Vision of *Al filo del agua.*" *Symposium* 25 (1971). Aspects of *Al filo del agua* are examined.

Harris, Christopher. *The Novels of Agustín Yáñez: A Critical Portrait of Mexico in the Twentieth Century.* Lewiston, N.Y.: E. Mellen Press, 2000. Argues that the novelist of the Mexican Revolution, who was also a member of the government, was dedicated to economic development, eradication of corruption, and freedom of artistic expression.

Longo, Teresa. "Renewing the Creation of Myth: An Analysis of Rhythm and Image in the 'Acto preparatorio' of Yáñez's *Al filo del agua.*" *Confluencia* 4, no. 1 (Fall, 1988). Structure and myth in this novel are reconsidered.

Merrell, Floyd. "Structure and Restructuration in *Al filo del agua.*" *Chasqui* 17, no. 1 (May, 1988). Discusses structure and myth in this novel.

Sommers, Joseph. "Genesis of the Storm: Agustín Yáñez." In *After the Storm: Landmarks of the Modern Mexican Novel.* Albuquerque: University of New Mexico Press, 1968. An excellent point of departure for a study of Yáñez.

William Butler Yeats

Irish poet and playwright

Born: Sandymount, near Dublin, Ireland; June 13, 1865
Died: Cap Martin, France; January 28, 1939

POETRY: *Mosada: A Dramatic Poem*, 1886; *Crossways*, 1889; *The Wanderings of Oisin, and Other Poems*, 1889; *The Countess Kathleen, and Various Legends and Lyrics*, 1892; *The Rose*, 1893; *The Wind Among the Reeds*, 1899; *In the Seven Woods*, 1903; *The Poetical Works of William B. Yeats*, 1906, 1907 (2 volumes); *The Green Helmet, and Other Poems*, 1910; *Responsibilities*, 1914; *Responsibilities, and Other Poems*, 1916; *The Wild Swans at Coole*, 1917, 1919; *Michael Robartes and the Dancer*, 1920; *The Tower*, 1928; *Words for Music Perhaps, and Other Poems*, 1932; *The Winding Stair, and Other Poems*, 1933; *The Collected Poems of W. B. Yeats*, 1933, 1950; *The King of the Great Clock Tower*, 1934; *A Full Moon in March*, 1935; *Last Poems and Plays*, 1940; *The Poems of W. B. Yeats*, 1949 (2 volumes); *The Collected Poems of W. B. Yeats*, 1956; *The Variorum Edition of the Poems of W. B. Yeats*, 1957 (P. Allt and R. K. Alspach, editors); *The Poems*, 1983; *The Poems: A New Edition*, 1984.

SHORT FICTION: *John Sherman and Dhoya*, 1891, 1969; *The Celtic Twilight*, 1893; *The Secret Rose*, 1897; *The Tables of Law; The Adoration of the Magi*, 1897; *Stories of Red Hanrahan*, 1904; *Mythologies*, 1959.

DRAMA: *The Countess Cathleen*, pb. 1892; *The Land of Heart's Desire*, pr., pb. 1894; *Cathleen ni Houlihan*, pr., pb. 1902; *The Pot of Broth*, pr. 1902 (with Lady Augusta Gregory); *The Hour-Glass*, pr. 1903, revised pr. 1912; *The King's Threshold*, pr., pb. 1903 (with Lady Gregory); *On Baile's Strand*, pr. 1904; *Deirdre*, pr. 1906 (with Lady Gregory); *The Shadowy Waters*, pr. 1906; *The Unicorn from the Stars*, pr. 1907 (with Lady Gregory); *The Golden Helmet*, pr., pb. 1908; *The Green Helmet*, pr., pb. 1910; *At the Hawk's Well*, pr. 1916; *The Player Queen*, pr. 1919; *The Only Jealousy of Emer*, pb. 1919; *The Dreaming of the Bones*, pb. 1919; *Calvary*, pb. 1921; *Four Plays for Dancers*, pb. 1921 (includes *Calvary, At the Hawk's Well, The Dreaming of the Bones*, and *The Only Jealousy of Emer*); *The Cat and the Moon*, pb. 1924; *The Resurrection*, pb. 1927; *The Words upon the Window-Pane*, pr. 1930; *The Collected Plays of W. B. Yeats*, pb. 1934, 1952; *The King of the Great Clock Tower*, pr., pb. 1934; *A Full Moon in March*, pr. 1934; *The Herne's Egg*, pb. 1938; *Purgatory*, pr. 1938; *The Death of Cuchulain*, pb. 1939; *Variorum Edition of the Plays of W. B. Yeats*, pb. 1966 (Russell K. Alspach, editor).

NONFICTION: *Ideas of Good and Evil*, 1903; *The Cutting of an Agate*, 1912; *Per Amica Silentia Lunae*, 1918; *Essays*, 1924; *A Vision*, 1925, 1937; *Autobiographies*, 1926, 1955; *A Packet for Ezra Pound*, 1929; *Essays, 1931-1936*, 1937; *The Autobiography of William Butler Yeats*, 1938; *On the Boiler*, 1939; *If I Were Four and Twenty*, 1940; *The Letters of W. B. Yeats*, 1954; *The Senate Speeches of W. B. Yeats*, 1960 (Donald R. Pearce, editor); *Essays and Introductions*, 1961; *Explorations*, 1962; *Ah, Sweet Dancer: W. B. Yeats, Margot Ruddock, A Correspondence*, 1970 (Roger McHugh, editor); *Uncollected Prose by W. B. Yeats*, 1970, 1976 (2 volumes); *Memoirs*, 1972; *The Collected Letters of William Butler Yeats: Volume I, 1865-1895*, 1986.

MISCELLANEOUS: *The Collected Works in Verse and Prose of William Butler Yeats*, 1908.

William Butler Yeats (yayts) was the son of John Butler Yeats, an artist of considerable merit who had given up a moderately lucrative law practice in order to devote himself to painting. His mother was a frail, beautiful woman who nurtured in her son a deep love for the "west country" of Ireland that was to last all his life. His early childhood and later vacations were spent there, among the green hills and lakes of Sligo which were to become, in such poems as "The Lake Isle of Innisfree," a symbol of his imaginative escape from the disappointments and unpleasant realities of life.

Much of Yeats's early life was spent in London, but he and his family spent the years from 1880 to 1887 in Dublin. This time was to have a lasting effect on the impressionable young poet. Stimulated by his father, who loved to read aloud, Yeats discovered William Shakespeare, the Romantic poets, and the pre-Raphaelites, explored popular works on Eastern mysticism, became interested in Irish myths and folklore, and, perhaps most important, met the poets and intellectuals of the Irish literary revival, many of whom were to remain lifelong friends. During the period he made several attempts at poetic drama, but the plays were highly imitative and hopelessly cluttered with magic islands and timid shepherds. Back in London, Yeats embarked on a serious study of Irish folk tales in the British Museum and published his first major poem, *The Wanderings of Oisin*, in 1889. Although the poem is superficially reminiscent of those of Edmund Spenser, Percy Bysshe Shelley, and Yeats's friend William Morris, the Gaelic theme and unorthodox rhythms are characteristic of Yeats's quest for a fresh tradition and an individual style.

There is, however, little that is imitative in poetic plays such as *The Countess Cathleen* and *The Land of Heart's Desire*, or in the lyrics that accompanied the former. The continued use of Irish themes evident in these volumes is indicative of an important and complex aspect of Yeats's early development. In common with the other writers of the nationalistic Irish literary revival, he wished to create a literature that was purely Irish in tone and subject matter. As part of the same general movement, he strove to reawaken in his people a sense of the glory and significance of Ireland's historical and legendary past. Furthermore, the remoteness of these Celtic themes was consistent with Yeats's aesthetic theory, later repudiated in part, of the separation of art from life. Finally, Irish folklore offered an answer to his search for a personal and individual mythology, for he found there a treasury of symbols hitherto unused in English poetry. Yeats's tendency to make mythical figures into private symbols was encouraged by his contacts with such symbolist poets as Arthur Symons and Stéphane Mallarmé, and by his undisciplined but enthusiastic dabbling in such esoteric subjects as "hermetic" philosophy, astrology, and spiritualism. *The Secret Rose* and *The Wind Among the Reeds* are representative of Yeats's work at this time, and while the clues to the meaning of the poems in these volumes are not always readily accessible to the uninitiated reader, they reveal a major step forward in terms of artistic skill and emotional maturity.

In spite of Yeats's theoretic dissociation from contemporary Irish life and politics, he could not escape his environment, particularly because he was in love, and was to be for two decades, with the beautiful and fiery actress and nationalist Maud Gonne. In 1899 he and Isabella Augusta, Lady Gregory, founded the Irish National Theatre Society, which presently became the famous Abbey Theatre of Dublin. During the first decade of the twentieth century, working alongside Lady Gregory and John Millington Synge, Yeats wrote several plays for the Abbey, the best of which are the patriotic propaganda piece *Cathleen ni Houlihan* and the tragedy *Deirdre*. In the poetry of this period, too, Yeats reacted against what he considered the sentimentality and divorce from reality of his earlier work. As the legendary past became less important, in order to rescue his imagination from abstractions and bring it closer to actuality, he pressed everything into his poetry: the theater, patriotism, and contemporary controversies.

The Green Helmet characteristically shows a tremendous advance in precision of imagery and syntax as well as an increased use of personal and contemporary themes. Yet along with the substitution of a hard, dry manner and lively, homely detail for the dreamy vagueness of the early poetry, the symbolism that he was evolving becomes more and more esoteric and obscure. In 1917, having had proposals of marriage rejected by both Maud Gonne and her daughter Iseult, Yeats precipitously married Georgie Hyde-Lees. The marriage was on the whole a success; one of its curious by-products was their joint experiment in spiritualism and "automatic writing," begun by Hyde-Lees as a game to distract Yeats from personal worries. From the renewed interest in the occult and the mystical that arose out of these investigations, Yeats developed a system of symbols by means of which he hoped to express his philosophy of life and art. This symbolism, which Yeats discusses in detail in *A Vision*, privately printed in 1925, is extremely complex; but while it provided the poet with a device that gave unity to his ideas on history, art, and human experience, its difficulties need not be a barrier to an understanding of his poems. It is probably enough for the average reader to recognize in the gyre, or ascending spiral, and the phases of the moon, Yeats's theories regarding the cyclical natures of both human nature and history.

For the aging Yeats, this concept of the cyclical character of history was in a sense his defense against time. The poems of his later years are dominated by the figure of the poet, withdrawn from the "blood and mire" of life into the eternal realm of art, smiling with "tragic joy" at the cycles of life and death, creation and destruction, which mark human existence. However, Yeats could not, either in his life or in his art, consistently maintain this withdrawal. In 1923 he was made a senator of the new Irish Free State, a post he entered into with enthusiasm, if not always tact. Some of Yeats's last poems, such as the "Crazy Jane" group, are a harsh, almost bitter glorification of the physical and even the sensual. As he says in "The Circus Animal's Desertion" from *Last Poems and Plays*, he "Must lie down where all the ladders start,/ In the foul rag-and-bone shop of the heart."

The period after 1923, when Yeats was awarded the Nobel Prize in Literature, saw the production of some of his best and most exciting poetry. In 1939, his mind still alert and active, Yeats died on the French Riviera. No sparse biographical outline can adequately characterize the complex personality of Yeats. He was fascinated by strange and supernatural phenomena but scorned the wonders of modern science. He was by nature inclined toward mysticism but found little that attracted him in Christianity. He was an ardent patriot who dissociated himself as far as possible from the revolutionary course his country was following; he was a disciple of the doctrine of the separation of life from art. His poetry had its basis in his own quick response to life and was indeed a criticism of life. Yeats was aware of the contradictions in his nature and in life, and throughout his career he sought a philosophical and artistic system that would resolve the conflict between his vision of what art should be and the recognition of what life is. Yeats is not always an easy poet to read, but his compact, intellectually intense, and supremely lyrical poetry deserves the careful attention it demands.

Bibliography

Aldritt, Keith. *W. B. Yeats: The Man and the Milieu*. New York: Clarkson Potter, 1997. Discusses Yeats's life and times.

Bloom, Harold. *Yeats*. New York: Oxford University Press, 1970. The emphasis is on Yeats's Romanticism. The poet is seen as the English Romantic poetry's heir. The prosodic, aesthetic, and imaginative implications of the inheritance are the subject of much intense and sophisticated discussion.

Brown, Terence. *The Life of W. B. Yeats: A Critical Biography*. Malden, Mass.: Blackwell, 1999. Brown's book is very much a critical biography, attending more to Yeats's art than to his life, with relatively little frolicking around in the poet's boudoir. Still, Brown conveys the texture of Yeats's life, selecting just the right details from what is now a copious historical record.

Donoghue, Denis. *Yeats*. London: Fontana, 1971. A good brief survey of the subject. Yeats's life, works, and thoughts are clearly presented in their many complex interrelations. The study's unifying argument is the author's conception of Yeats's understanding of, and identification with, power. Contains chronology and bibliography.

Ellmann, Richard. *Yeats: The Man and the Masks*. New York: Macmillan, 1948. Rev. ed. New York: W. W. Norton, 1979. The classic study, written by the leading Yeats scholar less than a decade after Yeats's death, when many of his friends were alive, including Yeats's wife. Uses voluminous papers from Yeats's Dublin house.

Fleming, Deborah. *"A Man Who Does Not Exist": The Irish Peasant in the Work of W. B. Yeats and J. M. Synge*. Ann Arbor: University of Michigan Press, 1995. Discusses Yeats's transforming Irish folklore into art and thus helping establish a new sense of cultural identity in Ireland. Examines Yeats as a postcolonial writer and his belief that peasant culture was a repository of ancient wisdom.

Fletcher, Ian. *W. B. Yeats and His Contemporaries*. New York: St. Martin's Press, 1987. Places the Anglo-Irish Protestant Yeats firmly in his time and illuminates his work in the context of contemporary writers. The volume includes new essays and revised work on Yeats and the visual arts and the resurgence in the 1890's of the political and religious movement central to Yeats's career as a poet, dramatist, critic, and nationalist leader.

Foster, R. F. *W. B. Yeats: A Life*. New York: Oxford University Press, 1997. An excellent guide to Yeats and his work.

Holdridge, Jefferson. *Those Mingled Seas: The Poetry of W. B. Yeats, The Beautiful and the Sublime*. Dublin: University College Dublin Press, 2000. A study of Yeats's poetry that focuses on the source of the power of Yeats's mysticism.

Jeffares, A. N. *A New Commentary on the Poems of W. B. Yeats*. 2d ed. London: Macmillan, 1984. The contents of Yeats's *The Collected Poems* are comprehensively annotated. Dates of composition are supplied, difficult allusions clarified, links to other works by Yeats made. An indispensable students' guide. Includes an appendix, suggestions for further reading, and a bibliography.

_______. *W. B. Yeats: A New Biography*. New York: Farrar, Straus and Giroux, 1989. A definitive biography of Yeats.

Raine, Kathleen. *W. B. Yeats and the Learning of the Imagination*. Ipswich, Mass.: Golgonooza Press, 1999. Raine argues that by his "learning of the Imagination" Yeats was not only a great poet but also a great imaginative mind. His work marks a cultural watershed; whereas English poetry up to and including T. S. Eliot drew upon European civilisation, Yeats additionally drew upon world culture: Irish mythology, Arabic, Japanese, Indian wisdom, and much besides.

Laurence Yep

American novelist

Born: San Francisco, California; June 14, 1948
Identity: Chinese American

CHILDREN'S/YOUNG ADULT LITERATURE: *Sweetwater*, 1973; *Dragonwings*, 1975; *Child of the Owl*, 1977; *Sea Glass*, 1979; *Dragon of the Lost Sea*, 1982; *Kind Hearts and Gentle Monsters*, 1982; *The Mark Twain Murders*, 1982; *Liar, Liar*, 1983; *The Tom Sawyer Fires*, 1984; *Serpent's Children*, 1984; *Dragon Steel*, 1985; *Mountain Light*, 1985; *The Curse of the Squirrel*, 1987; *The Rainbow People*, 1989 (folktales); *When the Bomb Dropped: The Story of Hiroshima*, 1990 (nonfiction); *Dragon Cauldron*, 1991; *The Lost Garden*, 1991 (autobiography); *The Star Fisher*, 1991; *Tongues of Jade*, 1991 (folktales); *Dragon War*, 1992; *The Butterfly Boy*, 1993; *Dragon's Gate*, 1993; *The Ghost Fox*, 1994; *Later, Gator*, 1995; *Hiroshima*, 1995 (novella); *Tree of Dreams: Ten Tales from the Garden of Night*, 1995; *Ribbons*, 1996; *The Khan's Daughter: A Mongolian Folktale*, 1997; *The Case of the Lion Dance*, 1998; *The Cook's Family*, 1998; *The Imp That Ate My Homework*, 1998; *The Amah*, 1999; *The Case of the Firecrackers*, 1999; *Cockroach Cooties*, 2000; *Dream Soul*, 2000; *The Journal of Wong Ming-Chung: A Chinese Miner*, 2000; *The Magic Paintbrush*, 2000; *Angelfish*, 2001; *Lady of Chi'iao Kuo: Warrior of the South*, 2001; *Spring Pearl: The Last Flower*, 2002; *When the Circus Came to Town*, 2002; *The Tiger's Apprentice*, 2003; *The Traitor: Golden Mountain Chronicles, 1885*, 2003.

LONG FICTION: *Seademons*, 1977; *Shadow Lord: A Star Trek Novel*, 1985; *Monster Makers, Inc.*, 1986.
DRAMA: *Dragonwings*, pb. 1993 (adaptation of his novel).
EDITED TEXT: *American Dragons: Twenty-five Asian American Voices*, 1993.

A major writer of children's literature, Laurence Michael Yep was born and grew up in San Francisco, living on the upper floor of his Chinese American parents' grocery store. His uneventful childhood, recounted in *The Lost Garden*, later provided material for novels such as *Child of the Owl* and *Sea Glass*. Two turning points in his adolescence were his discovery of science fiction and having a high school English teacher who inspired him to become a writer. While studying journalism at Marquette University, he published a science-fiction story, "The Selchey Kids" (1968), anthologized in Donald A. Wollheim and Terry Carr's *World's Best Science Fiction: 1969* (1969). Its protagonist—a survivor of the flooding of California who discovers that he was created by an experimental combination of human and dolphin genes—imaginatively foreshadows the focus of several later novels involving young Chinese Americans troubled because they are not fully Chinese, not fully American, but a combination of the two.

Yep continued his education, earning a B.A. from the University of California at Santa Cruz in 1970 and a Ph.D. in English from the State University of New York, Buffalo, in 1975. Encouraged by his future wife and then-editor Joanne Ryder, he wrote a children's science-fiction novel, *Sweetwater*, in 1973. Though he later wrote three more science-fiction novels for adults—*Seademons*, a *Star Trek* novel (*Shadow Lord*, 1985), and *Monster Makers, Inc.*—the direction of Yep's career was set by his second, more successful, children's novel, *Dragonwings*. In the early 1900's, a Chinese boy goes to San Francisco to live with his father, who works at a laundry but believes the message of a dream that he is really a dragon in human form. Possessing a natural aptitude for mechanical work, he abandons his career in order to build an airplane that he eventually completes and flies. *Dragonwings*, which won a Newbery Honor Book Award, may be Yep's most striking achievement, effectively mingling Chinese folklore with a captivating portrait of an energetic visionary. After briefly teaching at two colleges, Yep became a full-time writer and soon published two more children's novels, *Child of the Owl* and *Sea Glass*, involving modern Chinese American teenagers who learn about their heritage from elderly relatives; the latter won the 1979 Commonwealth Club Award.

In the 1980's, Yep moved beyond individual novels to launch three multivolume series, the least noteworthy being two mystery stories featuring Mark Twain, *The Mark Twain Murders* (1982) and *The Tom Sawyer Fires* (1984). More impressive is the Shimmer and Thorn fantasy series (*Dragon of the Lost Sea*, *Dragon Cauldron*, *Dragon Steel*, and *Dragon War*) about an irascible dragon, Shimmer, who teams up with a brash boy named Thorn to defeat the enemies of her dragon kingdom and restore the stolen sea that was once their home. A third series, The Serpent's Children, describes the experiences of nineteenth century Chinese immigrants. The first novel, *Serpent's Children*, takes place in China and is related by Cassia Young, the spirited daughter of a rebel whose brother, Foxfire, moves to America to restore the family fortunes. The second, *Mountain Light*, is the story of Squeaky, a young man from a neighboring village who meets and falls in love with Cassia during a rebellion and later follows Foxfire to America, where his friend Tiny is killed. The third, *Dragon's Gate*, also a Newbery Honor Book Award winner, is narrated by Tiny's son Otter, who accidentally kills an official and flees to America, where he joins Foxfire and Squeaky in the dangerous work of building a transcontinental railroad through snowy mountains. While Yep's earlier novels displayed a certain gentleness, these are distinguished by a stark, brutal realism. *Dragonwings* and *Child of the Owl* are loosely connected to this series.

As he approached his fortieth birthday, Yep began moving in several new directions. He returned to teaching, in 1987-1988 at the University of California at Berkeley and in 1990 as a writer-in-residence at the University of California at Santa Barbara. He published a play, *Dragonwings*, based on his novel; three collections of Chinese folktales, of which *Tongues of Jade* is the most effective; several picture books for younger children based on Chinese folktales, such as the evocative *The Butterfly Boy*; an autobiography; and the nonfictional *When the Bomb Dropped: The Story of Hiroshima*, which later inspired a novella for children, *Hiroshima*. He also edited a literary anthology, *American Dragons: Twenty-five Asian American Voices*. In addition to these efforts to demonstrate his versatility, Yep continued to produce realistic children's novels about Chinese American immigrants, such as *The Star Fisher*, which have consistently been his best-received works.

Gary Westfahl

Bibliography

Davis, Rocio C. "Metanarrative in Ethnic Autobiography for Children: Laurence Yep's *The Lost Garden* and Judith Ortiz Cofer's *Silent Dancing*." *MELUS* 27 (Summer, 2002): 139-156. Proposes that language, immigrant histories, family and location exist in a relation of dynamic interdependent parts for metanarrative in ethnic autobiographies for children.

Fisher, Leona W. "Focalizing the Unfamiliar: Laurence Yep's Child in a Strange Land." *MELUS* 27 (Summer, 2002): 157-177. Discusses issues of memory, subjectivity, genre, and ideology in Yep's work.

Johnson-Feelings, Dianne. *Presenting Laurence Yep*. New York: Twayne, 1995. Provides biographical information about this Chinese American award-winning author and presents critical essays of his works for young adults. A good overall source for comparing and contrasting Yep's works.

Frank Yerby

American novelist

Born: Augusta, Georgia; September 5, 1916
Died: Madrid, Spain; November 29, 1991
Identity: African American

LONG FICTION: *The Foxes of Harrow*, 1946; *The Vixens*, 1947; *The Golden Hawk*, 1948; *Pride's Castle*, 1949; *Floodtide*, 1950; *A Woman Called Fancy*, 1951; *The Saracen Blade*, 1952; *The Devil's Laughter*, 1953; *Benton's Row*, 1954; *Bride of Liberty*, 1954; *The Treasure of Pleasant Valley*, 1955; *Captain Rebel*, 1956; *Fairoaks*, 1957; *The Serpent and the Staff*, 1958; *Jarrett's Jade*, 1959; *Gillian*, 1960; *The Garfield Honor*, 1961; *Griffin's Way*, 1962; *The Old Gods Laugh: A Modern Romance*, 1964; *An Odor of Sanctity*, 1965; *Goat Song*, 1968; *Judas, My Brother*, 1968; *Speak Now: A Modern Novel*, 1969; *The Dahomean: An Historical Novel*, 1971 (pb. in England as *The Man from Dahomey*, 1971); *The Girl from Storyville*, 1972; *The Voyage Unplanned*, 1974; *Tobias and the Angel*, 1975; *A Rose for Ana Maria*, 1976; *Hail the Conquering Hero*, 1978; *A Darkness at Ingraham's Crest*, 1979; *Western*, 1982; *Devilseed*, 1984; *McKenzie's Hundred*, 1985.
SHORT FICTION: "Health Card," 1944.

Frank Garvin Yerby, the son of Rufus Gavin, a black, half-Indian postal clerk, and his Scotch-Irish wife, Wilhelmina Smythe Yerby, was born and reared in Augusta, Georgia. After high school Yerby earned an A.B. from Paine College in 1937, and an M.A. from Fisk one year later; in 1939 he began graduate studies at the University of Chicago. Financial problems forced Yerby out of graduate school, and he, along with Richard Wright, Margaret Walker, and Langston Hughes, briefly worked for the Federal Writers' Project in the Chicago area.

That same year, in 1939, Yerby secured a position as an English instructor with Florida Agricultural and Mechanical College in Tallahassee. During 1940 to 1941 he taught English at Southern University and at A & M College in Baton Rouge, Louisiana. In 1941 he married Flora Helen Claire Williams and left the teaching profession, claiming that colleges had a "stifling" atmosphere and were "Uncle Tom factories." He and his wife, with whom he eventually had one son and three daughters, moved to Dearborn, Michigan, where Yerby worked as a lab technician with Ford Motor Company until 1944. During 1944 to 1945 he was chief inspector at Magnaflux with Ranger (Fairchild) Aircraft in Jamaica, New York.

In 1944 Yerby published the short story "Health Card" in *Harper's* and was awarded the O. Henry Memorial Award for "best first short story." It was a bitter story about racial injustice, the last fiction he would publish with such a theme until *The Dahomean*, a novel set in nineteenth century black Africa. In 1945 Yerby became a full-time writer. One year later his *The Foxes of Harrow* became a best-seller.

From 1946 through 1964 Yerby published one book a year. Of the first ten, all but one were among the top ten best-sellers of the year, which put Yerby in the elite list of top commercial American novelists. Novels that sell well on the commercial market do not generally receive critical acclaim, however, and critics' refusal to accord Yerby's novels respect was two-pronged: Black reviewers faulted his novels for "abandoning" his race in using white protagonists. Others faulted him for stereotypical characters and plots and for writing purple prose. Yerby responded to such criticism by pointing to his racially mixed parentage, asserting that, "I simply insist on remaining a member of the human race." In a 1959 essay he also wrote that he had a "houseful of rejection slips" for works about "ill-treated factory workers, or people who suffered because of their religions or the color of their skins." He contended that this led him to the "awesome conclusion" that such was not the proper ground for novelists. He recounts that he had thereupon begun systematic research to discover what combination of content, plot, character, and theme created "universal" fiction. Deciding that classics are yesterday's best-sellers, he opted to write novels that would reach his readers; he called them "costume" novels.

After his divorce from his first wife, Yerby in 1956 married Blanca Call-Perez, who managed his professional affairs. There was much to manage: Not only was Yerby a prolific writer, he was also an impeccable researcher and noted for historical detail in his fiction. Through research, he came to be a proficient reader in eight languages. Before his death his works had sold 55 million copies in eighty-two countries and had been translated into twenty-three languages. Throughout his successful life Yerby, with his mixed racial heritage, felt he really did not belong anywhere. His fiction illustrates his research, his realism, and, through his protagonists, this sense of being an outsider. Yerby was a political independent and belonged to no church, though he considered himself a Christian. In 1955 he became an expatriate, settling, finally, in Spain, where he died.

In *The Voyage Unplanned* the protagonist and authorial narrator John Farrow, a self-isolated, middle-aged man, says, "I belong nowhere. I am alien—a stranger," and when he returns to peacetime Europe he recounts scenes from his Office of Strategic Services (OSS) days during World War II in flashbacks. Yerby depicts the Nazis' torture of Jews, having, in his preface, translated the account of a woman who suffered—and survived—the same experiences as does Yerby's heroine. The simplicity of her words sets the tone of the novel, which rivals the stark profundity of *The Dahomean*, a novel about Nyasanu, an African chieftain, and his culture. This work, a rite-of-passage story dealing with friendship, family, and betrayal, was judged by many critics to be profound in its simplicity.

Yerby's simplicity is a mark of realism. The critic John Crowe Ransom contends that irony, a mark of realism, is the way people live with their realization that the ideal and the real do not match. Each of Frank Yerby's fictions provides compelling depictions of reality, yet, simultaneously, all of his works uplift readers through characters who, fully aware of ugly reality, which they have endured, choose to give credence to aspects of dreams.

Jo Culbertson Davis

Bibliography

Bone, Robert A. *The Negro Novel in America*. Rev. ed. New Haven, Conn.: Yale University Press, 1965. A general survey of black novels. Bone dismisses Yerby as the "prince of pulpsters."

Glasrud, Bruce. "'The Fishes and the Poet's Hands': Frank Yerby, a Black Author in White America." *Journal of American and Comparative Cultures* 23 (Winter, 2000): 15-21. A profile of Yerby that compares his lack of scholarly attention to the situation of Chester Himes.

Hemenway, Robert, ed. *The Black Novelist*. Columbus, Ohio: Merrill, 1970. Darwin Turner comments on Yerby's "painful groping for meaning" behind a "soap-opera façade."

Klotman, Phyllis. "A Harrowing Experience: Frank Yerby's First Novel to Film." *College Language Association Journal* 31 (December, 1987): 210-222. Focuses on the changes made to Yerby's story when *The Foxes of Harrow* was adapted to the screen.

Yevgeny Yevtushenko

Russian poet

Born: Stantsiya Zima, Siberia, Soviet Union (now in Russia); July 18, 1933

POETRY: *Razvedchicki gryadushchego*, 1952; *Tretii sneg*, 1955; *Stantsiya Zima*, 1956 (*Zima Junction*, 1962); *Shossye entuziastov*, 1956; *Obeshchaniy*, 1957; *Luk i lira*, 1959; *Stikhi raznykh let*, 1959; *Yabloko*, 1960; *Nezhnost*, 1962; *Vzmakh ruki*, 1962; *Selected Poetry*, 1963; *Bratskaya GES*, 1965 (*Bratsk Station, and Other New Poems*, 1966); *The Poetry of Yevgeny Yevtushenko, 1953-1965*, 1965; *Kachka*, 1966; *Yevtushenko: Poems*, 1966; *Poems Chosen by the Author*, 1967; *Idut belye snegi*, 1969; *Stolen Apples*, 1971; *Doroga Nomer Odin*, 1972; *Poyushchaya dambra*, 1972; *Otsovskiy slukh*, 1975; *From Desire to Desire*, 1976; *Ivanovskiye sitsi*, 1976; *V Polniy Rost*, 1977; *Golub' v Sant'iago*, 1978 (novel in verse; *A Dove in Santiago*, 1983); *Tyazholive zemli*, 1978; *The Face Behind the Face*, 1979; *Ivan the Terrible and Ivan the Fool*, 1979; *Invisible Threads*, 1981 (poems and photographs); *Ty na planete ne odin*, 1981; *The Poetry of Yevgeny Yevtushenko*, 1981; *Grazhdane, poslushaite menia*, 1989; *Early Poems*, 1989; *Stikhotvoreniya i poemy*, 1990; *The Collected Poems, 1952-1990*, 1991; *Pre-Morning: A New Book of Poetry in English and Russian*, 1995.

LONG FICTION: *Yagodnye mesta*, 1981 (*Wild Berries*, 1984); *Don't Die Before You're Dead*, 1995.

DRAMA: *Pod kozhey statuey sbobody*, pr. 1972.

NONFICTION: *Primechaniya k avtobiografii*, 1963 (*A Precocious Autobiography*, 1963); *Talant est' chudo nesluchainoe: Kniga statei*, 1980.

Yevgeny Alexandrovich Yevtushenko (yehv-tew-SHEHNG-koh) is considered, with Andrey Voznesensky, among the best representatives of the generation of Russian poets after Stalin's death. He was born at Zima Station, a small Siberian junction near Lake Baika. His ancestors had been deported from Ukraine for political reasons. He spent his childhood surrounded by beautiful Siberian nature but also amid political uncertainty: Both of his grandfathers were purged in the late 1930's. After World War II his mother took him to Moscow, where he began to write poetry and almost became a professional soccer player. He published his first poem in 1949, then entered the Gorky Literary Institute in Moscow and, after publishing his first collection of poems, *Razvedchicki gryadushchego* (prospectors of the future), in 1952, decided to devote his life to literature.

Emotionally charged poems and audacity made him a leader of the poets of his generation, who questioned everything, even the results of the revolution. From the beginning Yevtushenko believed that, in line with the age-old tradition of poets' role in Russian society, he was bringing something new to Russian poetry. In the first line of "Prologue," 1953, he declares "I am different," speaking not only for himself but for his entire generation. His early poems are characterized by yearning for freedom and rebellion against restrictions, love and respect for nature, faith in people and love for one's land, a strong belief in oneself, and loyalty to the original aims of the revolution. A strong lyrical bent and readiness for poetic experiments complete his early poetic portrait.

At the height of the campaign against Stalin in the late 1950's and early 1960's Yevtushenko wrote several rebellious poems. The best of these, and the one that became best known, is "Babii Yar," a poem about a ravine in Ukraine where thousands of Jews were killed by the Nazis. Yevtushenko bemoans the fact that there is no monument to these innocent victims, indirectly accusing the authorities of anti-Semitism, for the Russian people, "international to the core," are not guilty of this oversight. In "The Heirs of Stalin" and "The Dead Hand" he warns that many heirs to Stalin are still around and that his hand still holds the people in its grip. What saves these poems from being merely political manifestos is Yevtushenko's reliance on strong emotions and dramatics and his use of striking metaphors and similes.

Another audacious work, *A Precocious Autobiography*, published in 1963 in Paris without the permission of Soviet authorities, reveals much about the poet's early life and thinking, as well as being a commentary on Soviet society. At first Yevtushenko considered Communism the best political system, though he was not blind to its shortcomings, as demonstrated most vividly during Stalin's funeral. The only way to reconcile his faith in Communism with crimes committed in its name (the murder of his grandfathers, for example) was for him to cling to an idealistic faith in the innate goodness of the Communist ideas. Although Yevtushenko initially refrains from examining the basic premises of the system, he expresses the belief that his country has been in a spiritual revolution since Stalin's death in 1953, searching for the truth and fighting against lies, the abuse of power, and the exploitation of humankind. Aside from its literary merits as a lively and heartfelt narrative, *A Precocious Autobiography* remains a document of the spiritual and political awakening of an entire nation, especially its poets and intellectuals, from a decades-long dream.

As the political climate in the Soviet Union changed in the mid-1960's, Yevtushenko began to experience difficulties with the authorities. He was publicly chastised and even exiled for a short while in the Caucasus, yet he was able to return. When he was allowed to publish again he softened his attacks but remained firm in his opposition to censorship.

As he matured Yevtushenko turned to wider themes and concerns. He remained politically active, as evidenced in poems such as "Zima Station" and "Conversations with an American Writer," but this attitude had as its price that Yevtushenko has often been labeled a topical poet who lent his talent to prosaic social and political causes of the day. It cannot be denied that his political activism contributed heavily to his popularity in the Soviet Union and abroad. Yevtushenko himself resents being labeled as a political or topical poet, pointing out his faith in the integrity of poets, who, though interested in social issues, should express themselves artistically and pursue aesthetic goals.

In the 1980's Yevtushenko became even more involved in politics and supported democratic reforms. He also wrote film scenarios, directed and acted in movies, though still claiming poetry as his main avocation. His forays into long fiction have not been considered successful. *Wild Berries* and *Don't Die Before You're Dead* suffer from the fact that, being foremost a poet, he has not mastered novelistic technique. His collection of essays, *Talant est' chudo nesluchainoe*, along with many articles, reflects his ongoing fascination with social and political matters. However, his main contribution to Russian and world literature remains his poetry.

Vasa D. Mihailovich

Bibliography

Brown, Deming. *The Last Years of Soviet Russian Literature: Prose Fiction, 1975-1991*. New York: Cambridge University Press, 1993. History and criticism of late Soviet era Russian literature. Includes bibliographical references and index.

_______. *Soviet Russian Literature Since Stalin*. New York: Cambridge University Press, 1978. A historical and critical study of Russian literature. Includes bibliographic references and an index.

Brown, Edward J. *Russian Literature Since the Revolution*. Rev. ed. Cambridge, Mass.: Harvard University Press, 1982. A survey and critical analysis of Soviet literature. Includes bibliographic references.

The Economist. "Past, Implacable." 306, no. 7535 (January 30, 1988): 75-76. Draws parallels between Yevtushenko's poetic themes and glasnost, concentrating on "Bukharin's Widow" and "Monuments Not Yet Erected."

Hingley, Ronald. *Russian Writers and Soviet Society, 1917-1978*. New York: Random House, 1979. A history of Russian literature of the Soviet era. Includes a bibliography and index.

Slonim, Mark. *Soviet Russian Literature*. 2d ed. New York: Oxford University Press, 1977. A historical and critical study of Russian literature.

Vanden Heuvel, Katrina. "Yevtushenko Feels a Fresh Wind Blowing." *Progressive* 24 (April, 1987): 24-31. Addresses Yevtushenko's views on Russian politics, poetry's public service, glasnost, and relations with the West.

Anzia Yezierska

American novelist and short-story writer

Born: Plinsk, Russian Poland (now in Poland); 1880(?)
Died: Ontario, California; November 21, 1970
Identity: Jewish

LONG FICTION: *Salome of the Tenements*, 1923; *Bread Givers: A Struggle Between a Father of the Old World and a Daughter of the New*, 1925; *Arrogant Beggar*, 1927; *All I Could Never Be*, 1932.

SHORT FICTION: *Hungry Hearts*, 1920; *Children of Loneliness: Stories of Immigrant Life in America*, 1923; *The Open Cage: An Anzia Yezierska Collection*, 1979; *How I Found America*, 1991.

MISCELLANEOUS: *Red Ribbon on a White Horse*, 1950.

Anzia Yezierska (yih-ZYIHR-skuh), novelist and short-story writer, is generally acclaimed as a founding mother of Jewish American immigrant literature and Jewish feminism. Born into poverty in Russian Poland, Yezierska immigrated with her parents in the 1890's to the Jewish ghetto on the lower East Side of New York. The daughter of a Talmudic scholar, Yezierska helped support the family with various menial tasks in sweatshops, laundries, and private homes. She was determined to move up in the world, however, and attended night school to learn English. A scholarship enabled her to graduate from Columbia University Teachers College with certification in domestic science.

Yezierska's first marriage in 1910 was annulled almost immediately. Married to Arnold Levitas the following year, she insisted on a religious rather than a legally binding civil ceremony. A daughter, Louise, was born ten months later. Yezierska soon quit the marriage, but unable to support herself and a child, she returned Louise to her father, maintaining close contact with her throughout life.

While struggling to support herself through substitute teaching, Yezierska published her first story, "The Free Vacation House," in 1915. The story centers on the humiliating effects of charity on the poor. When Yezierska showed it and other writings to John Dewey, with whom she was romantically involved for a short period, 1917 to 1918, he encouraged her to give up teaching and pursue writing. Yezierska heeded Dewey's advice and enjoyed almost immediate success. In 1919 the anthologist Edward O'Brien selected "The Fat of the Land" as the best short story of the year. The main character, Hannah Breinah, is an immigrant who spends her life chasing the American Dream, only to find that wealth, once attained, does not bring the happiness she anticipated.

The publisher Houghton Mifflin offered Yezierska a contract for her first collection of short stories, *Hungry Hearts*, and its publication in 1920 led to wide critical acclaim but limited sales. Always a self-promoter, Yezierska marched into the office of Frank Crane, a columnist for the Hearst newspapers, and provided him with an embellished version of her rise to authorship despite little education or knowledge of writing. Crane's subsequent story helped bring Yezierska widespread recognition, increased sales, and ten thousand dollars from Samuel Goldwyn for the film rights to the book.

In *Hungry Hearts* Yezierska effectively records the immigrant's longing for acceptance in American society. She focuses primarily on the struggle of a woman to achieve independence in the face of a patriarchal society, orthodox religious beliefs, and economic difficulties. Her style is often unpolished and effusive, but it is honest and direct and reflects an excellent ear for immigrant dialect.

In her first novel, *Salome of the Tenements*, Yezierska continued her depiction of the Jewish immigrant experience and was even more financially successful. She was suddenly the embodiment of the American Dream, the Cinderella from the sweatshop. Critical reception of the novel was mixed, however, and publication that same year (1923) of a collection of highly uneven stories titled *Children of Loneliness* produced mostly negative reactions from critics who had begun to tire of her obsessive repetition of theme and sentimental excesses.

Yezierska's subsequent autobiographical novel, *Bread Givers*, was better received and is still generally regarded as her best work. The subtitle, *A Struggle Between a Father of the Old World and a Daughter of the New*, emphasizes the theme, but the novel ends ambiguously with the heroine, Sara Smolinsky, apparently becoming a dutiful daughter after all. Yezierska's next two novels, *Arrogant Beggar* and *All I Could Never Be*, also center on the immigrant experience. Although they are clearly inferior as literary works, the latter is interesting for its fictional account of her relationship with Dewey.

Yezierska's fame vanished as rapidly as it came, and once again she struggled for economic survival, working on the Works Progress Administration's Writers' Project during the Great Depression. She spent much of her time during the late 1930's and the 1940's writing and trying to find a publisher for her autobiography *Red Ribbon on a White Horse*. W. H. Auden's agreement to write an introduction was undoubtedly influential in persuading Scribner's to publish the work. Although Yezierska presented the work as autobiography, the mixture of fiction and autobiography makes it similar in content and form to her earlier autobiographical fiction. It received favorable reviews and continues to elicit praise but did not sell well.

Yezierska spent the last two decades of her life writing reviews and other short pieces. In her fiction she continued to write about the struggle of the underprivileged or mistreated female. Her last story, "Take Up Your Bed and Walk," published a year before her death, deals with the problems of aging.

Less than a decade after her death, the forgotten Yezierska was rediscovered. Doctoral candidates began studying her life and work; feminist and ethnic critics lauded her contributions; and biographies, critical studies, and reprints of her work made Yezierska again accessible to the general public. She is now highly regarded as a major chronicler of Jewish immigrant life in the early twentieth century United States.

Verbie Lovorn Prevost

Bibliography

Ferraro, Thomas J. "'Working Ourselves Up' in America: Anzia Yezierska's *Bread Givers*." *South Atlantic Quarterly* 89 (Summer, 1990). Provides a perceptive evaluation of Yezierska's most significant novel.

Henriksen, Louise Levitas. *Anzia Yezierska: A Writer's Life*. New Brunswick, N.J.: Rutgers University Press, 1988. Henriksen attempts to distinguish truth from myth in her mother's life.

Konzett, Delia. *Ethnic Modernisms: Anzia Yezierska, Zora Neale Hurston, Jean Rhys, and the Aesthetics of Dislocation*. New York: Palgrave Macmillan, 2002. Includes bibliographical references and an index.

Rosen, Norma. *John and Anzia: An American Romance*. Syracuse, N.Y.: Syracuse University Press, 1997. Focuses on a brief but highly influential relationship in Yezierska's life.

Schoen, Carol B. *Anzia Yezierska*. Boston: Twayne, 1982. The first full-length study is valuable for its summary and evaluation of all of Yezierska's major works.

Zierler, Wendy. "The Rebirth of Anzia Yezierska." *Judaism* 42 (Fall, 1993). Analyzes Yezierska's meteoric rise to fame, fall from popularity, and subsequent reclamation.

Jose Yglesias

American novelist

Born: Tampa, Florida; November 29, 1919
Died: New York, New York; November 7, 1995
Identity: Cuban American

LONG FICTION: *A Wake in Ybor City*, 1963; *An Orderly Life*, 1968; *The Truth About Them*, 1971; *Double, Double*, 1974; *The Kill Price*, 1976; *Home Again*, 1987; *Tristan and the Hispanics*, 1989; *Break-In*, 1996; *The Old Gents*, 1996.
SHORT FICTION: *The Guns in the Closet*, 1996.
DRAMA: *Chattahoochee*, pr. 1989; *The Dictatorship of the Proletariat*, pr. 1989; *You Don't Remember?*, pr. 1989; *New York 1937*, pr. 1990.
NONFICTION: *The Goodbye Land*, 1967; *In the Fist of the Revolution: Life in a Cuban Country Town*, 1968; *Down There*, 1970; *The Franco Years*, 1977.
TRANSLATIONS: *Island of Women*, 1962 (of Juan Goytisolo); *Sands of Torremolinos*, 1962 (of Goytisolo); *Villa Milo*, 1962 (of Xavier Domingo); *The Party's Over*, 1966 (of Goytisolo).

Jose Yglesias (eeg-LAY-see-uhs) is best known for being a prolific writer whose works are often about individual lives and hardship in Cuba and in Latin American countries affected by revolutions. Of Cuban and Spanish descent, Yglesias was born to Jose and Georgia Milian Yglesias in Tampa, Florida. He worked as a stock clerk and a dishwasher when he moved to New York City at age seventeen. Yglesias then served in the U.S. Navy from 1942 to 1945 during World War II; he received a naval citation of merit. After the war, he attended Black Mountain College in 1946. He married Helen Basine, a novelist, on August 19, 1950. Yglesias held numerous jobs during his lifetime, from assembly line worker to film critic, from assistant to a vice president of a pharmaceutical company to Regents Lecturer at the University of California at Santa Barbara in 1973.

Yglesias's birthplace greatly influenced his literary concern and career. He was born in the section of Tampa called Ybor City. Until Ybor City, a cigar-making town, was founded by V. Martinez Ybor in 1885, there were not many Latinos in Tampa. As Ybor City and its economy grew, Cubans and other Latinos arrived and brought their own cultural activities and vibrant traditions. These aspects of life in Ybor City served as inspiration and material for Yglesias's plays and books. According to him, these events must be documented so that the history and cultural richness of that part of America will not be forgotten.

Descriptions of Ybor City and its history can be found in the pages of Yglesias's first novel, *A Wake in Ybor City*. The novel is a colorful and interesting depiction of Cuban immigrants in the Latin section of Tampa on the eve of the Cuban Revolution in 1958. The story deals with family dynamics, class envy, sexual intrigues, and cultural assimilation, along with machismo and matriarchal powers in conflict. This novel started his prolific writing career, in which he would move back and forth between fiction and nonfiction.

Being of Cuban and Spanish ancestry also greatly influenced Yglesias's second book, *The Goodbye Land*. The laborious energy required—as well as personal desire—to travel to the mountainside village of Galacia, Spain, in 1964 in order to trace his father's birth and death there proved to be worthwhile; the book was a great success and was praised by many critics for its authenticity as a travel narrative.

Many of Yglesias's books since *The Goodbye Land* deal with personal statements and individuality amid the revolutionary experience. His nonfiction work *In the Fist of the Revolution* addresses individual lives and hopes amid political and social problems in the town of Miyari, Cuba. *The Franco Years* depicts the living conditions of the author's Spanish acquaintances under the Fascist regime of dictator Francisco Franco, who died in Spain in 1976. (Yglesias was in Spain at the time.) Again, many critics agreed that these two books demonstrate authentic social reporting because the author, while in Cuba and Spain interviewing people, experienced their hardships and turmoil. That authenticity reflects the critical talent and genuine objectivity of Yglesias, who went against the mainstream literary fashion of political and social analysis and moralizing.

Yglesias's talent and honesty in his literary desire to present emotions, aspirations, and disappointments unique to Latino émigrés in the United States led to success and critical acclaim in his novels as well as nonfiction works. His persistent interest in individual lives, the immigrant experience, and cultural assimilation can be seen in novels such as *The Kill Price*, *Home Again*, and *Tristan and the Hispanics*.

Mainly known for writing novels, nonfiction, and translation, Yglesias was also a talented dramatist. He wrote only four plays, three of which—*Chattahoochee*, *The Dictatorship of the Proletariat*, and *You Don't Remember?*—form a trilogy set in Ybor City in 1912, 1920, and 1989, respectively. The fourth play, *New York 1937*, is an autobiographical comedy involving cigar making and the Great Depression, set in Manhattan's Washington Heights. In his plays, Yglesias's creative drive and imagination brings his characters to life upon the stage.

In addition to his efforts as novelist and dramatist, Yglesias contributed major articles for prestigious literary magazines, newspapers, and other periodicals. He was the patriarch of a literary family, which included his former wife and his son Rafael, also a novelist and screenwriter. Yglesias died of cancer in 1995. His body of work places him as one of the pioneers of modern American and Latino literature.

H. N. Nguyen

Bibliography

Baskin, Leonard. "Jose Yglesias." *Tampa Review* 13 (1996). This article examines Yglesias, the literary influence of his work, and his overall literary life.

"Jose Yglesias." In *Contemporary Novelists*. 6th ed. Detroit: St. James Press, 1996. This reference article provides an overview of Yglesias's significant work and highlights a few of his books.

Al Young

American novelist and poet

Born: Ocean Springs, Mississippi; May 31, 1939
Identity: African American

LONG FICTION: *Snakes*, 1970; *Who Is Angelina?*, 1975; *Sitting Pretty*, 1976; *Ask Me Now*, 1980; *Seduction by Light*, 1988.

POETRY: *Dancing*, 1969; *The Song Turning Back into Itself*, 1971; *Geography of the Near Past*, 1976; *The Blues Don't Change: New and Selected Poems*, 1982; *Heaven: Collected Poems, 1956-1990*, 1992; *Conjugal Visits, and Other Poems in Verse and Prose*, 1996; *The Sound of Dreams Remembered: Poems, 1990-2000*, 2001.

NONFICTION: *Bodies and Soul: Musical Memoirs*, 1981; *Kinds of Blue: Musical Memoirs*, 1984; *Things Ain't What They Used to Be: Musical Memoirs*, 1987; *Mingus/Mingus: Two Memoirs*, 1989 (with Janet Coleman); *Drowning in the Sea of Love: Musical Memoirs*, 1995.

EDITED TEXTS: *Changing All Those Changes*, 1976 (of James P. Girard); *Zeppelin Coming Down*, 1976 (of William Lawson); *Yardbird Lives!*, 1978 (with Ishmael Reed); *Calafia: An Anthology of California Poets*, 1979 (with Reed and Shawn Hsu Wong); *Quilt*, 1981-1986 (with Reed; 5 volumes); *African American Literature: A Brief Introduction and Anthology*, 1996.

Albert James Young was born in Mississippi in 1939 to Albert James, an auto worker and a musician, and his wife. The family lived in rural Mississippi until 1946, when they moved to Detroit, but even after that Young often spent summers in the South. That area consequently exerted a strong influence on his development. After attending the University of Michigan from 1957 to 1961 he moved to the San Francisco area. Later he attended Stanford University and the University of California at Berkeley, and he received a bachelor's degree in Spanish from Berkeley in 1969. He married in 1963 and had one son.

Among the many jobs Al Young assumed during his early life was that of professional musician; in fact, he considers himself as much a musician as a writer, and his participation in and enjoyment of that other means of artistic expression informs and is often the subject of his written work. As he explains in his three volumes of "musical memories" (*Bodies and Soul*, *Kinds of Blue*, and *Things Ain't What They Used to Be*), music became a means of understanding life even before he began to play music. Young's first book, *Dancing*, is a volume of poems that seem to demand oral expression. The work's title is a further clue to Young's view that music helps people to understand and express themselves. Those who hear the music can no longer remain the same, so they dance, helping to complete the statement made by the music as they "analyze" it with their physical responses.

Young's first novel, *Snakes*, is an "education" novel about MC, a young black adolescent from Detroit who resembles Young himself and who, with his band, writes and performs a song, "Snakes," that is a local hit. The band dissolves and the euphoria dissipates, but the young hero wants to continue his musical career and sets out on a bus for New York, leaving behind the grandmother who had raised him lovingly after the deaths of his parents. This novel includes that important theme in Young's oeuvre, close family ties and both the warmth and the restrictions that develop from them, as well as the technique of using a first-person narrator who speaks with the vocabulary and rhythms, the music, of the streets.

Young's interest in the lives of adolescents did not end with *Snakes*. From 1961 to 1965 he was an instructor and linguistic consultant with the Neighborhood Youth Corps Writing Workshops in San Francisco, and from 1968 to 1969 he was a writing instructor at the Teenage Workshop of the San Francisco Museum of Art. He also served as a lecturer in creative writing at Stanford University, 1969 to 1976.

Other honors Young has received for his writing include a Wallace Stegner Creative Writing Fellowship at Stanford (1966-1967), National Arts Council Awards for Poetry and Editing (1968 and 1969), a Guggenheim Fellowship (1974), and a National Endowment for the Arts Fellowship (1979). Young used his Guggenheim Fellowship year to finish his second novel, *Who Is Angelina?* which, as the title indicates, retains the same subject as *Snakes*, a young person's search for identity. Angelina Green is also from Detroit, but better off than MC. Her discoveries about herself and her family reveal Young's increasing interest in spirituality, a concern that reaches full flowering in *Seduction by Light*.

In 1972 Al Young wrote a screenplay adaptation of Dick Gregory's 1964 autobiography, *Nigger*, but no film ever resulted from this project. Young has written a number of other screenplays that have not been filmed and a novel, *Sitting Pretty*, which was planned as a later film vehicle for Bill Cosby but also was never produced. Some of Young's work has been used by film producers, but he has not been credited. He has been more successful in his efforts with small literary magazines. He founded and edited *Loveletter* (1966-1968), and with fellow novelist and poet Ishmael Reed he founded and edited *Yardbird Reader* (1972) and a number of anthologies from that journal; he is also a contributing editor of *Changes*, *Umoja*, and *Calafia*, all "little magazines." He continued to live in the Bay Area and pursue his writing projects, some of which, like his memoir of the bassist Charles Mingus, *Mingus/Mingus*, also involve his interest in jazz. He has won numerous awards for his work, including the PEN/Library of Congress Award for Short Fiction in 1991 and the PEN/USA Award for Best Non-Fiction Book of the Year in 1996 for *Drowning in the Sea of Love*. In 2002 he received the American Book Award for *The Sound of Dreams Remembered*.

The free-form quality of the jazz that Al Young loves to play and hear is an effective model for his poetry and musical memoirs, but it has been considered a detriment in the novels, in which the plot tends to be a weak element. In traditional terms, the novels start nowhere and go nowhere. Some critics have pointed out that Young is writing a different kind of novel. In his works, changes that happen to the characters are not as important as changes that happen to the reader who lives with the characters for a time and delights in the sounds of their voices and the movement of their dances.

Jim Baird

Bibliography

Bell, Bernard W. *The Afro-American Novel and Its Tradition*. Amherst: University of Massachusetts Press, 1987. Bell compares Young's *Snakes* to 1960's novels by Gordon Parks, Kristin Hunter, Rosa Gunn, Barry Beckham, and Louise Meriwether.

Broughton, Irv. *The Writer's Mind: Interviews with American Authors*. Vol. 3. Fayetteville: University of Arkansas Press, 1990. Contains a rare and enlightening interview with Young in which he explains his poetic philosophy. This source is widely available and is useful to undergraduate as well as graduate students. A good overview.

Draper, James P. *Black Literature Criticism: Excerpts from Criticism of the Most Significant Works of Black Authors over the Past Two Hundred Years*. Detroit: Gale Research, 1997. Contains a fifteen-page chapter on Young that includes criticism, interviews from 1976 to 1989, a short biography, and a bibliography.

Johnson, Charles. *Being and Race: Black Writers Since 1970*. Bloomington: Indiana University Press, 1988. Contains a thorough discussion of the common background of black American writers plus lengthy discussions of female and male viewpoint-writing, with philosophical references and a preface which establishes the text's postmodernist critical approach.

Lee, Don. "About Al Young." *Ploughshares* 19, no. 1 (Spring, 1993): 219. A short profile of Young's life as poet and screenwriter.

Ostendorf, Berndt. *Black Literature in White America*. Totowa, N.J.: Barnes and Noble Books, 1982. Considers black writers' roots and the influence of music on their lives and art as both expression and performance. While the references to Young are brief and pertain to his poetry, the musical context of this presentation will be useful for those researching Young's concern for music in American culture and literature.

Schultz, Elizabeth. "Search for 'Soul Space': A Study of Al Young's *Who Is Angelina?* and the Dimensions of Freedom." In *The Afro-American Novel Since 1960*, edited by Peter Bruck and Wolfgang Karrer. Amsterdam: Gruner, 1982. Young's novel was written in 1975, a time when few fiction works by African Americans were being published. Schultz analyzes his work in terms of the quest for expression, especially when the speaker is out of the mainstream.

Edward Young

English critic and poet

Born: Upham, Hampshire, England; July 3, 1683 (baptized)
Died: Welwyn, Hertfordshire, England; April 5, 1765

NONFICTION: *A Vindication of Providence: Or, A True Estimate of Human Life*, 1728; *An Apology for Princes: Or, The Reverence Due to Government*, 1729; *The Centaur Not Fabulous: In Six Letters to a Friend on the Life in Vogue*, 1755; *An Argument Drawn from the Circumstances of Christ's Death for the Truth of His Religion*, 1758; *Conjectures on Original Composition in a Letter to the Author of Sir Charles Grandison*, 1759 (better known as *Conjectures on Original Composition*).

DRAMA: *Busiris, King of Egypt*, pr., pb. 1719; *The Revenge*, pr., pb. 1721; *The Brothers*, wr. 1724, pr., pb. 1753.

POETRY: *An Epistle to the Right Honourable the Lord Landsdowne*, 1713; *A Poem on the Last Day*, 1713; *The Force of Religion: Or, Vanquished Love, a Poem, in Two Books*, 1714; *On the Late Queen's Death, and His Majesty's Accession to the Throne*, 1714; *A Paraphrase on Part of the Book of Job*, 1719; *A Letter to Mr. Tickell Occasioned by the Death of Joseph Addison*, 1719; *The Instalment to the Right Honourable Sir Robert Walpole, Knight of the Most Noble Order of the Garter*, 1726; *Cynthio*, 1727; *Love of Fame, the Universal Passion: In Seven Characteristical Satires*, 1728 (verse satires); *Ocean: An Ode Occasion'd by His Majesty's Late Royal Encouragement of the Sea-Service*, 1728; *Imperium Pelagi: A Naval Lyrick, Written in Imitation of Pindar's Spirit*, 1730; *Two Epistles to Mr. Pope, Concerning the Authors of the Age*, 1730; *The Foreign Address: Or, The Best Argument for Peace*, 1735; *The Poetical Works of the Reverend Edward Young*, 1741; *The Complaint: Or, Night Thoughts on Life, Death, and Immortality*, 1742-1746 (commonly known as *Night-Thoughts*); *Resignation: In Two Parts, and Postscript*, 1762.

MISCELLANEOUS: *The Complete Works, Poetry and Prose, of the Rev. Edward Young*, 1854.

The poet, critic, and dramatist Edward Young was born at Upham, near Winchester, probably in early July, 1683, the son of Edward Young, rector of Upham and fellow of Winchester. Young probably deserved the comment of Alexander Pope, that he had spent "a foolish youth, the sport of peers and poets." He very likely was not then the pious man of religion and morality that he later became.

Young graduated from Oxford as a bachelor of civil law on April 23, 1714, and as a doctor of civil law on June 10, 1719. Thereafter he capitalized on his friendships and acquaintances as he attempted to make his way in the world and gain admittance to literary circles. He wrote many and various "literary" works on many and various subjects, from literature to politics, some of which he later regretted.

Although he wrote two successful blank verse tragedies, *Busiris, King of Egypt* and *The Brothers*, Young is remembered primarily for his long blank verse meditation on death, *The Complaint: Or, Night Thoughts on Life, Death, and Immortality*. This work went through hundreds of reprints, editions, and translations during the following centuries, and it was illustrated by William Blake. By the early 1740's Young had become wealthy and, although he continued to write, his creative powers had weakened. He eventually sank into melancholy and irritability.

Paul Varner

Bibliography

Forester, Harold. *Edward Young: The Poet of "The Night Thoughts," 1683-1765*. New York: Erskin, 1986. Containing a wealth of information, this biography provides a thorough investigation of Young's career and his position within eighteenth century British culture.

Morris, David B. *The Religious Sublime: Christian Poetry and Critical Tradition in Eighteenth Century England*. Lexington: University Press of Kentucky, 1972. Morris's study provides a particularly useful reading of *Night-Thoughts* and positions Young's work within the context of eighteenth century religious controversies.

Nussbaum, Felicity. *The Brink of All We Hate: English Satires on Women, 1660-1750*. Lexington: University Press of Kentucky, 1984. Nussbaum provides a cogent discussion of Young's frequently overlooked satire, *Love of Fame, the Universal Passion*.

Patey, Douglas Lane. "Art and Integrity: Concepts of Self in Alexander Pope and Edward Young." *Modern Philology* 83, no. 4 (1986): 364-378. Patey's essay examines the relationship between Alexander Pope's *An Essay on Man* and *Night-Thoughts*.

St. John Bliss, Isabel. *Edward Young*. New York: Twayne, 1969. This older study still provides an excellent starting point for readers of Young's poetry.

Wanko, Cheryl L. "The Making of a Minor Poet: Edward Young and Literary Taxonomy." *English Studies* 72, no. 4 (1991): 355-367. Wanko argues convincingly that Young's reputation suffered throughout the twentieth century because of "our system of literary taxonomy." She demonstrates how eighteenth and nineteenth century appraisals of Young's work made him appear to be a literary anomaly.

Marguerite Young

American novelist, poet, and historian

Born: Indianapolis, Indiana; August 26, 1908
Died: Indianapolis, Indiana; November 17, 1995

LONG FICTION: *Miss MacIntosh, My Darling*, 1965.

SHORT FICTION: *Below the City*, 1975.

POETRY: *Prismatic Ground*, 1937; *Moderate Fable*, 1944.

NONFICTION: *Angel in the Forest: A Fairy Tale of Two Utopias*, 1945; *Nothing but the Truth*, 1993; *Harp Song for a Radical: The Life and Times of Eugene Victor Debs*, 1999.

MISCELLANEOUS: *Inviting the Muses: Stories, Essays, Reviews*, 1994.

From early childhood, Marguerite Vivian Young believed she was destined to be a writer. She was right: Her long career was devoted to writing, as author, editor, and teacher. While she published few books during her lifetime, the sheer mass of two of them clearly illustrates her passion for writing. Although many now agree that Young's books were received less enthusiastically than they deserved, they nonetheless earned for her a respected position within the body of twentieth century American writers.

Young's parents divorced when she was three, an event both disruptive and momentous in her life. Marguerite and her younger sister were then raised by their maternal grandmother but remained in contact with their parents and stepparents. Their grandmother helped instill in young Marguerite a love of literature and the desire to express herself creatively. With her grandmother's support and encouragement, Young read well and widely as a child and young adult, feasting on the works of William Makepeace Thackeray, George Eliot, Charles Dickens, Honoré de Balzac, and other classic English and French writers. After a stroke altered her mental state, Young's grandmother sometimes spoke delusively about angels and other such creatures, a recurrent theme throughout some of Young's later works.

With an English and French major and a criminology minor, Young earned a B.A. from Butler University in Indianapolis in 1930. She helped edit the university's poetry publication (*The Cocoon*) and literary magazine (*The Tower*). Shortly after graduation, she experienced her first published success with the inclusion of four poems in Chicago's *Poetry: A Magazine of Verse*. After earning her M.A. from the University of Chicago in 1936 with a focus on epic, Elizabethan, and Jacobean literature, Young did some postgraduate work at the University of Iowa but never completed the degree. Returning to Indianapolis after a brief period of living in Kentucky, she accepted a position teaching high school English in her hometown.

The year 1937 saw the publication of Young's first volume of poetry, *Prismatic Ground*; it was also the year she began her fascination with a topic that would fuel her third book. During a visit with her mother and stepfather to New Harmony, Indiana, Young developed an interest in the area's utopian societies of the early 1800's. Dividing her time between Indianapolis and New Harmony, Young spent the following seven years learning and writing about these societies, in particular those of the Rappites and Owenites. Originally composing a series of folk ballads on the subject, she later revised them as blank verse. After a final revision to prose form, this work eventually became her third published book, *Angel in the Forest*.

By 1942, Young was keeping busy as an English lecturer at the University of Iowa, a Ph.D. candidate, a high school teacher, and a teacher at the Indiana Writers' Conference (Indiana University), all the while continuing her writing. When, in 1943, she submitted *Moderate Fable*, her second volume of poetry, and *Angel in the Forest*, both were accepted for publication. With those successes and with her increasing status in the American literary community, Young felt compelled to relocate from the Midwest to New York's Greenwich Village. This move was partially funded by a fellowship from the American Association of University Women. Around this time, a noticeable shift occurred in Young's writing, with a new focus on fiction rather than poetry. While writing and publishing several short stories, she also continued working on her novel. In 1945 Young submitted a draft of what would eventually become her epic 1,198-page *Miss MacIntosh, My Darling*, and she was extended a contract for that novel. However, the book's completion took a long, agonizingly slow path before its publication in 1965.

New York life brought Young into proximity with other notable authors: In 1945, she and Henry Miller coedited *The Conscientious Objector*, and for two summer seasons (1946 and 1947), she lived at Yaddo, an artists' community in Saratoga Springs, New York, where she enjoyed the company of such literary figures as Robert Lowell, Theodore Roethke, Carson McCullers, and Truman Capote. Young was one of the editors of the short-lived *The Tiger's Eye* and a frequent contributor to many other periodicals, in addition to her teaching. Following a 1952 to 1954 extended visit to Europe, she returned to the United States, teaching three years at the University of Iowa Writers' Workshop, gaining widespread respect as a creative writing teacher and influencing countless students and future writers, among them John Gardner. Returning to New York City, Young taught at various colleges and universities throughout the rest of her years and received numerous prestigious awards and honors. Her relationship with her students was warm and inviting, and classes often extended into long, late-night discussions at local pubs and coffeehouses.

After taking nearly twenty years to write her first novel, Young began her next book, a biography of Indiana poet James Whitcomb Riley. Her research into Riley's friendship with American labor organizer and socialist leader Eugene V. Debs, however, led her to shift her topic from Riley to Debs. Twenty-five years in the writing, *Harp Song for a Radical: The Life and Times of Eugene Victor Debs* was published posthumously, the enormous 2,500-page first volume (prior to editing) of an intended three-volume work. Shortly after signing the biography's publication contract, a frail and ill Young moved once more to Indianapolis, where she lived with a niece until her death on November 17, 1995, at age eighty-seven. Young's writing style, with its profound symbolism, mythical imagery, and poetic syntax, along with her unwavering lifelong dedication to the teaching of writing, has secured her place among contemporary American writers.

Cherie Castillo

Bibliography

Eichenlaub, Constance. "Marguerite Young." *Review of Contemporary Fiction* 20, no. 2 (Summer, 2000): 121-148. Extensive overview of Young's life, education, career, and writing.

Kellner, Bruce. "Miss Young, My Darling: A Memoir." *Review of Contemporary Fiction* 20, no. 2 (Summer, 2000): 149-164. Biographical memoir. Kellner, a former student of Young, includes personal remembrances of conversations with the author.

Shaviro, Steven. "Lost Chords and Interrupted Births: Marguerite Young's Exorbitant Vision." *Critique* 31, no. 3 (Spring, 1990): 213-222. Discussion of *Miss MacIntosh, My Darling* and its refusal to comply with rules of modernism or postmodernism.

Stark Young

American novelist and critic

Born: Como, Mississippi; October 11, 1881
Died: New York, New York; January 6, 1963

LONG FICTION: *Heaven Trees*, 1926; *The Torches Flare*, 1928; *River House*, 1929; *So Red the Rose*, 1934.
SHORT FICTION: *The Street of the Islands*, 1930; *Feliciana*, 1935.
DRAMA: *Guenevere*, pb. 1906; *Addio, Madretta, and Other Plays*, pb. 1912; *The Queen of Sheba*, pb. 1922; *The Colonnade*, pb. 1924; *The Saint*, pb. 1925.
POETRY: *The Blind Man at the Window*, 1906.
NONFICTION: *The Flower in Drama*, 1923 (criticism); *The Three Fountains*, 1924 (travel); *Glamour*, 1925 (theatrical criticism); *Encaustics*, 1926 (essays and sketches); *Theatre Practice*, 1926; *The Theatre*, 1927; *Immortal Shadows*, 1948 (theatrical criticism); *The Pavilion*, 1951 (reminiscence).

Stark Young, known chiefly as the author of *So Red the Rose* and often ranked as a minor figure among the Southern Agrarians, was born in Mississippi in 1881. When a typhoid epidemic closed the preparatory school he was attending, he was allowed to enter the University of Mississippi at the age of fourteen. After graduating in 1901 he continued his studies at Columbia University, from which he received his master's degree in English in 1902.

His first career was in the classroom. After a short period of teaching in a military school for boys he became an instructor in English at the University of Mississippi in 1904. Three years later he joined the faculty of the University of Texas, where he taught until 1915, when he became professor of English at Amherst College. In 1921 he resigned to become a member of the editorial staff of the *New Republic*, a position he held until 1947, except for one year (1924-1925) when he served as drama critic of *The New York Times*. Concurrently he was an associate editor of *Theatre Arts Monthly* from 1921 to 1940. His close association with the theater resulted in five books of drama criticism, the plays he wrote in both prose and verse, translations, and the direction of several productions, including that of Henri-René Lenormand's *The Failures* and Eugene O'Neill's *Welded*, on Broadway.

Young's most sustained work was in the novel. *So Red the Rose*, one of the earliest and most popular of the Civil War novels, achieves scope and depth because the writer has dramatized against a factual historical background the symbolic conflict between opposing forces of tradition and disintegration implicit in southern life and character. This novel and Young's earlier ones—*Heaven Trees*, a nostalgic re-creation of plantation life in antebellum days, and *The Torches Flare* and *River House*, which deal with later periods of the regional experience—make up, in effect, four panels of a dramatic and somberly realized social and moral history of the South. Young also declared his local loyalties in an essay in *I'll Take My Stand: The South and the Agrarian Tradition*, written for a symposium by "Twelve Southerners" and published in 1930.

Noel Schraufnagel

Bibliography

Bentley, Eric. "Stark Young." *Theater* 14, no. 1 (Winter, 1982).
Harder, Kelsie B. "Dialect Duplicity in Stark Young's *So Red the Rose*." *Mississippi Folklore Register* 16, no. 2 (Fall, 1982).
Miller, J. W. "Stark Young, Chekhov, and the Method of Indirect Action." *Georgia Review* 18 (1964).
Pilkington, John. *Stark Young*. Boston: Twayne, 1985.
Sommers, John J. "The Critic as Playwright: A Study of Stark Young's *The Saint*." *Modern Drama* 7 (February, 1965).
The Southern Quarterly: A Journal of the Arts in the South 24, no. 4 (Summer, 1986).
Young, Stark. *Stark Young, a Life in the Arts: Letters, 1900-1962*. Edited by John Pilkington. Baton Rouge: Louisiana State University Press, 1975.

Marguerite Yourcenar
(Marguerite de Crayencour)

Belgian-born American novelist

Born: Brussels, Belgium; June 8, 1903
Died: Northeast Harbor, Maine; December 17, 1987

LONG FICTION: *Alexis: Ou, Le Traité du vain combat*, 1929 (*Alexis*, 1984); *La Nouvelle Eurydice*, 1931; *Denier du rêve*, 1934 (*A Coin in Nine Hands*, 1982); *Le Coup de grâce*, 1939 (*Coup de Grâce*, 1957); *Mémoires d'Hadrien*, 1951 (*Memoirs of Hadrian*, 1954; also known as

Hadrian's Memoirs); *L'Œuvre au noir*, 1968 (*The Abyss*, 1976; also known as *Zeno of Bruges*, 1994); *Anna, Soror . . .* , 1981; *Comme l'eau qui coule*, 1982 (3 novellas; includes *Anna, Soror . . .* , *Un Homme obscur*, and *Une Belle Matinée*; *Two Lives and a Dream*, 1987).

SHORT FICTION: *La Mort conduit l'attelage*, 1934; *Nouvelles orientales*, 1938 (*Oriental Tales*, 1985); *"Conte bleu," "Le Premier soir," "Maléfice,"* 1993 (*A Blue Tale, and Other Stories*, 1995).

DRAMA: *Électre: Ou, La Chute des masques*, pb. 1954 (*Electra: Or, The Fall of the Masks*, 1984); *Rendre à César*, pb. 1961 (*Render unto Caesar*, 1984); *Le Mystère d'Alceste*, pb. 1963; *Qui n'a pas son Minotaure?*, pb. 1963 (*To Each His Minotaur*, 1984); *Théâtre*, pb. 1971 (partial translation as *Plays*, 1984).

POETRY: *Le Jardin des chimères*, 1921; *Les Dieux ne sont pas morts*, 1922; *Feux*, 1936 (*Fires*, 1981); *Les Charités d'Alcippe, et autres poèmes*, 1956 (*The Alms of Alcippe*, 1982).

NONFICTION: *Pindare*, 1932; *Les Songes et les sorts*, 1938 (*Dreams and Destinies*, 1999); *Sous bénéfice d'inventaire*, 1962 (*The Dark Brain of Piranesi, and Other Essays*, 1984); *Souvenirs pieux*, 1974 (*Dear Departed*, 1991); *Archives du Nord*, 1977 (*How Many Years*, 1995); *Les Yeux ouverts: Entretiens avec Matthieu Galey*, 1980 (*With Open Eyes: Conversations with Matthieu Galey*, 1984); *Mishima: Ou, La Vision du vide*, 1980 (*Mishima: A Vision of the Void*, 1986); *Le Temps, ce grand sculpteur*, 1983 (*That Mighty Sculptor, Time*, 1988); *La Voix des choses*, 1987; *Quoi? L'Éternité*, 1988; *Le Labyrinthe du monde*, 1990 (autobiography; includes *Souvenirs pieux*, *Archives du Nord*, and *Quoi? L'Éternité*).

TRANSLATIONS: *Les Vagues*, 1937 (of Virginia Woolf's novel *The Waves*); *Ce que savait Maisie*, 1947 (of Henry James's novel *What Maisie Knew*); *Présentation critique de Constantin Cavafy*, 1958 (of Cavafy's poetry); *Fleuve profond, sombre rivière: Les Negro Spirituals*, 1964 (of spirituals); *Présentation critique d'Hortense Flexner*, 1969 (of Flexner's poetry); *La Couronne et la lyre*, 1979 (selection of Greek poetry); *Le Coin des "Amen,"* 1983 (of James Baldwin's play *The Amen Corner*); *Blues et gospels*, 1984 (of American songs).

MISCELLANEOUS: *Œuvres romanesques*, 1982.

The first woman to be elected to the French Academy, Marguerite Yourcenar (yewr-suh-nahr) was one of the most original writers of post-World War II France. She was born in Brussels, Belgium, on June 8, 1903, the only daughter of aristocratic and wealthy parents, Michel and Fernande de Crayencour. Several days after her birth, her mother died of puerperal fever and peritonitis; Marguerite was raised then by a series of nurses and maids, as she and her father moved from Belgium to northern France to Paris. Her father, as she lovingly and admiringly portrays him in her autobiographical *Archives du Nord* (northern archives), was an adventurous and unconventional man who loved the cosmopolitan excitement of European casino and spa towns. Well-read in literature, he revealed to his daughter the beauty of French, English, Latin, and Greek masterpieces, while private tutors taught her the other school subjects. She was thus able to pass the *baccalauréat* examinations in 1919.

Two years later, at age eighteen, she published *Le Jardin des chimères* (the garden of chimeras) at her father's expense, under the pen name Marguerite Yourcenar (an incomplete anagram of her surname), followed the next year by another work of poetry, *Les Dieux ne sont pas morts* (the gods are not dead). The publication in 1929 of her novel *Alexis* not only saw the first favorable reviews but also was followed in quick succession by other novels and short stories, mostly written in the confessional letter-monologue genre. These involve psychological studies of men in conflict with their sexuality, with life and art, and with love.

In 1939 Yourcenar, who had come to the United States on a lecture tour, could not return to Nazi-occupied Europe. At the recommendation of the English poet Stephen Spender, she was able to secure a part-time instructorship in French and art history at Sarah Lawrence College in Bronxville, New York (a position she held until 1950), while she contributed articles and poems to émigré periodicals. At the end of the war, she decided to remain in the United States and became an American citizen in 1947, at the same time officially changing her name to Marguerite Yourcenar. In 1950 she moved to Mount Desert Island, off the coast of Maine, with Grace Frick, her longtime friend and cotranslator.

The first work to be a critical and popular success was the 1951 prizewinning *Memoirs of Hadrian*, the fictional first-person narrative of the great Roman emperor. In an altogether different style, the dark and brooding *The Abyss*, published in 1968 and translated into eighteen languages, received the coveted Prix Fémina and finally brought Yourcenar fame and recognition. It was made into a film by André Delvaux in 1988. In between had appeared essays, plays, and translations, including an anthology of Negro spirituals titled *Fleuve profond, sombre rivière* (wide, deep, troubled water)—to be followed in 1984 by *Blues et gospels* (blues and gospels).

In recognition of her literary contributions, Yourcenar was awarded honorary degrees from such prestigious institutions as Harvard University, elected to the Belgian Royal Academy (1970), honored with numerous prizes, decorated with the rank of officer (promoted later to commander) in the prestigious French Légion d'Honneur. On March 6, 1980, by a vote of twenty to twelve, she became an "Immortal" member of the French Academy, thereby breaking an all-male tradition dating back to 1635. Despite increasingly severe pulmonary illnesses, she continued to write, mainly essays, short stories, translations, and critical studies. She died at her Maine home on December 17, 1987.

During a 1968 interview with the noted French author Françoise Mallet-Joris, Yourcenar declared, "I believe in the nobility of refusal." Indeed, all of her protagonists rebel against moral or cultural limits and engage in deviant behavior or radical thought, but they often find themselves unable to resolve the conflicts between society's demands and their passions. Yourcenar is recognized for the loftiness of her thought, the breadth of her culture, and the humanity of her creations, and her works continue to enjoy great popularity.

Pierre L. Horn

Bibliography

Farrell, C. Frederick, and Edith R. Farrell. *Marguerite Yourcenar in Counterpoint*. Lanham, Md.: University Press of America, 1983. An introductory study of Yourcenar's novels and essays, with a biographical note, chronology, and bibliography.

Frederick, Patricia E. *Mythic Symbolism and Cultural Anthropology in Three Early Works of Marguerite Yourcenar: "Nouvelles orientales," "Le Coup de grâce," "Comme l'eau qui Coule."* Lewiston: Edwin Mellen Press, 1995. Concentrates mainly on Yourcenar's short fiction, but the introduction and conclusion contain valuable insights into all of her writing. Includes notes and bibliography.

Horn, Pierre. *Marguerite Yourcenar.* Boston: Twayne, 1985. A reliable introductory study, with a biographical chapter, two chapters on *Memoirs of Hadrian*, a chapter on autobiographical works, and another on writing in other genres. Includes chronology, notes, and an annotated bibliography.

Howard, Joan E. *From Violence to Vision: Sacrifice in the Works of Marguerite Yourcenar.* Carbondale: Southern Illinois University Press, 1992. Contains chapters on all the major fictional works, with notes and bibliography.

Savignau, Josyane. *Marguerite Yourcenar: Inventing a Life*. Translated by John E. Howard. Chicago: University of Chicago Press, 1993. A reliable and well annotated biography which also examines the significance of her contributions to literature. Includes family tree, notes, and bibliography.

Shurr, Georgia Hooks. *Marguerite Yourcenar: A Reader's Guide*. Lanham, Md.: University Press of America, 1987. Two chapters on Yourcenar's experimental fiction, her fictional studies of politics, a chapter on *Memoirs of Hadrian*, and a chapter on women in Yourcenar's fiction. Includes a chronology, notes, a bibliography of books and articles about Yourcenar, and a bibliography of Yourcenar's works in English translation.

Yevgeny Zamyatin

Russian novelist

Born: Lebedyan, Russia; February 1, 1884
Died: Paris, France; March 10, 1937

LONG FICTION: *Uyezdnoye*, 1913 (novella; *A Provincial Tale*, 1966); *Na kulichkakh*, 1914 (novella; *A Godforsaken Hole*, 1988); *Ostrovityane*, 1918 (novella; *The Islanders*, 1972); *My*, wr. 1920-1921, 1927 (corrupt text), 1952 (*We*, 1924); *Bich bozhy*, 1939.
SHORT FICTION: *Bol'shim detyam skazki*, 1922; *Nechestivye rasskazy*, 1927; *Povesti i rasskazy*, 1963; *The Dragon: Fifteen Stories*, 1966.
DRAMA: *Ogni Svyatogo Dominika*, wr. 1920, pb. 1922 (*The Fires of Saint Dominic*, 1971); *Blokha*, pr. 1925 (*The Flea*, 1971); *Obshchestvo pochetnikh zvonarei*, pr. 1925 (*The Society of Honorary Bell Ringers*, 1971); *Attila*, wr. 1925-1927, pb. 1950 (English translation, 1971); *Afrikanskiy gost*, wr. 1929-1930, pb. 1963 (*The African Guest*, 1971); *Five Plays*, pb. 1971.
SCREENPLAY: *Les Bas-fonds*, 1936 (*The Lower Depths*, 1937; adaptation of Maxim Gorky's novel *Na dne*).
NONFICTION: *Gerbert Uells*, 1922 (*H. G. Wells*, 1970); *Kak my pishem: Teoria literatury*, 1930; *Litsa*, 1955 (*A Soviet Heretic*, 1970).
MISCELLANEOUS: *Sobranie sochinenii*, 1929 (collected works); *Sochineniia*, 1970-1972.

Yevgeny Ivanovich Zamyatin (zuhm-YAHT-yihn) was an important Russian satirist, one of the formulators of the dystopian genre, and a masterful essayist, dramatist, and writer of short fiction. He was born on February 1, 1884, in Lebedyan, Tambov Province, in the central farmland of Russia. His family belonged to the educated middle class, his father being a priest and teacher in the local school and his mother a pianist. Zamyatin was educated from 1893 to 1902 locally and at Voronezh. In 1902 he commenced the study of naval engineering at the St. Petersburg Polytechnic Institute, spending his summers touring Russia and the Middle East.

As a result of a certain innate rebelliousness, Zamyatin early became a Bolshevik, was briefly imprisoned in 1905, and was several times exiled from St. Petersburg. He completed his studies in 1908, accepting a lectureship at the Institute in Naval Architecture. During World War I, he spent some eighteen months in England but returned during the Revolution. He had long before ceased to be a Bolshevik but sympathized with the cause. After witnessing massive impoverishment and government brutality, however, he frequently satirized the state. He was most overtly critical of authoritarian regimes in the dystopian novel *We*, his masterpiece.

Throughout his career, Zamyatin continued to lecture at the institute. He produced innumerable stories, fables, sketches, and essays, and served on the editorial boards of several publishing houses and journals, editing the works of such authors as H. G. Wells, O. Henry, and Jack London. He was a creative and influential author and lecturer, guiding the Serapion Brotherhood, a group of young writers in the early 1920's intent upon experimentation in fiction and freedom of self-expression.

Indeed, Zamyatin himself was independent by nature. Most of his writing was experimental and satiric. He frequently used the sharp, jagged imagery of the expressionists, together with touches of caricature and the grotesque. His work was usually tragic and, more often, satiric—filled with irony and literary parody. He commenced early, about 1908, to write short tales and fables, later moving to the novella and the longer story in the 1920's. In this later period, he also wrote essays and a number of plays. Because of Communist pressures, however, much of his work was never published or performed, and most stories appeared individually in journals only. He remained throughout fiercely autonomous as a writer, even once asserting that major authors are outsiders.

Accordingly, his work was increasingly criticized by party-liners. The formation of a strong writers' union in 1929 was accompanied by more censorship. Many writers were refused publication, silenced, arrested; a number committed suicide. Amazingly, Zamyatin, after writing a candid letter to Joseph Stalin in 1931, was permitted with his wife to emigrate. Settling in Paris, he remained there until his death in 1937, a gentlemanly outsider. Of his demise, no notice was taken by the Soviet press, and his name was not included in major Soviet volumes on modern Russian literature.

Typical of his early stories is the novella *A Provincial Tale*. Filled with slang and dialect, it depicts life in provincial Russia in gloomy terms. From the outset, Zamyatin published numerous shorter pieces and fables as well as stories and tales. Most reveal a cruel world, wrought with impressionistic, almost nightmarish imagery. At its best, life is tragic; in a lengthy later tale, "Yola" (1928;

the yawl), a romantic fisherman in the North has saved for years to purchase his own fishing yawl. No sooner has he obtained it than a squall sinks man and boat together.

A persistent theme is revealed in the satiric story about England, *The Islanders*, which examines bourgeois philistinism. In it, Vicar Dooley seeks to institute a means of effecting "compulsory" salvation. In "Rasskaz o samon glavnom" (1923; "A Story About the Most Important Thing"), an ardent Bolshevik, Dorda, is ominously portrayed as nothing more than a revolver in a black metallic holster. Zamyatin understood how easily people can sacrifice their humanity, becoming subhuman. He told the tale of Attila the Hun three times: as a story (1924), as a play (1927), and in an unfinished novel, *Bich Bozhy* (the scourge of God), which he was still writing when he died.

His masterpiece is his one completed novel, *We*. Here is his most powerful literary conception—a dystopian novel set in the Superstate's future, when all people have become mere numbers, reduced to slavery and adulation of nation and leader. A small group of subversives yearns to overturn the mechanized, lifeless dictatorship, but even they become somewhat mechanical, shedding their humanity while rigidly pursuing their goals. At the close, the rebels have breached some of the walls of the Superstate, although their revolution has been stalled. In order to keep citizens docile, the leaders lobotomize them, reducing them to robots; however, rebels always tend to rise against such tyranny. One of Zamyatin's guiding principles maintained that humankind incessantly required fresh revolutions to offset entropy.

This last theory did much to antagonize the Communists. For that reason, Zamyatin became a voice unwanted and often unheard, a prophet unwelcome in the Soviet Union. However, his influence and creative zest have endured. Originally confined and prevented from addressing much of an audience, Zamyatin has, with every decade, widened his sphere of influence. He acquired his largest audience long after his demise.

John R. Clark

Bibliography

Billington, Rachel. "Two Russians." *Financial Times*, January 5, 1985, p. 18. This discussion of Zamyatin's *Islanders* notes that the anti-British story helped to make Zamyatin's name in Russia.

Brown, Edward J. "Zamjatin and English Literature." In *American Contributions to the Fifth International Congress of Slavists*. Vol. 2. The Hague: Mouton, 1965. Discusses Zamyatin's interest in, and debt to, English literature stemming from his two-year stay in England before and during World War I.

Collins, Christopher. *Evgenij Zamjatin: An Interpretive Study*. The Hague, the Netherlands: Mouton, 1973. In this ambitious study, Collins advances a rather complex interpretation of Zamyatin, mostly of *We*, on the basis of Carl Gustav Jung's idea of the conscious, unconscious, and individualism.

Cooke, Brett. *Human Nature in Utopia: Zamyatin's "We."* Evanston, Ill.: Northwestern University Press, 2002 .From the series titled Studies in Russian Literature and Theory. Includes index and bibliography.

Kern, Gary, ed. *Zamyatin's "We": A Collection of Critical Essays*. Ann Arbor, Mich.: Ardis, 1988. A collection of essays on Zamyatin's magnum opus, *We*, covering the Soviet view, mythic criticism, aesthetics, and influences and comparisons. It includes one of the best essays on the subject, Edward J. Brown's "*Brave New World*, *1984*, and *We:* An Essay on Anti-Utopia."

Mihailovich, Vasa D. "Critics on Evgeny Zamyatin." *Papers on Language and Literature* 10 (1974): 317-334. A useful survey of all facets of criticism of Zamyatin's opus, in all languages, through 1973. Good for gaining the introductory knowledge of Zamyatin.

Quinn-Judge, Paul. "Moscow's Brave New World: Novelist Zamyatin Revisited." *The Christian Science Monitor*, April 4, 1988, p. 8. A brief biographical background to accompany a story about the publication of Zamyatin's antitotalitarian novel *We* in Moscow.

Richard, D. J. *Zamyatin: A Soviet Heretic*. London: Hillary House, 1962. A brief overview of the main stages and issues in Zamyatin's life and works. An excellent, though truncated, presentation of a very complex writer.

Russell, Robert. *Zamiatin's "We."* London: Bristol Classical Press, 2000. Critical study of Zamyatin's masterpiece includes bibliography and index.

Shane, Alex M. *The Life and Works of Evgenij Zamjatin*. Berkeley: University of California Press, 1968. A comprehensive work on Zamyatin in English, covering, exhaustively but pertinently, his life and the most important features of his works, including short fiction. Shane analyzes chronologically Zamyatin's works, in a scholarly but not dry fashion, and reaches his own conclusions. Contains bibliography.

"Soviets to Publish *We*." *The New York Times*, June 25, 1987, p. C25. An article on the Soviet decision to publish *We*, the long-banned antitotalitarian novel.

Israel Zangwill

English novelist

Born: London, England; February 14, 1864
Died: Midhurst, West Sussex, England; August 1, 1926
Identity: Jewish

LONG FICTION: *The Premier and the Painter*, 1888 (with Louis Cowen, as J. Freeman Bell); *The Big Bow Mystery: The Perfect Crime*, 1892; *Children of the Ghetto: Being Pictures of a Peculiar People*, 1892; *The Master*, 1895; *The People's Saviour*, 1898; *The Mantle of Elijah*, 1900; *Jinny the Carrier: A Folk Comedy of Rural England*, 1919.

SHORT FICTION: *The Bachelors' Club*, 1891; *The Old Maids' Club*, 1892; *Ghetto Tragedies*, 1893; *Merely Mary Ann*, 1893; *The King of Schnorrers: Grotesques and Fantasies*, 1894; *Dreamers of the Ghetto*, 1898; *The Celibate's Club: Being the United Stories of the Bachelors' Club and the Old Maids' Club*, 1898; *The Grey Wig: Stories and Novelettes*, 1903; *Ghetto Comedies*, 1907.

DRAMA: *The Great Demonstration*, pr. 1892; *Aladdin at Sea*, pr. 1893; *The Lady Journalist*, pr. 1893; *Six Persons*, pr. 1893; *Threepenny Bits*, pr. 1895; *Children of the Ghetto*, pr. 1899 (adaptation of his novel); *The Moment of Death*, pr. 1900; *The Revolted Daughter*, pr. 1901; *Merely Mary Ann*, pr., pb. 1903 (adaptation of his short story); *The Serio-Comic Governess*, pr., pb. 1904; *Nurse Marjorie*, pr., pb. 1906; *The Melting-Pot*, pr., pb. 1909; *The War God*, pr., pb. 1911; *The Next Religion*, pr., pb. 1912; *Plaster Saints*, pr., pb. 1914; *The Moment Before*, pr. 1916; *Too Much Money*, pr. 1918; *The Cockpit*, pr., pb. 1921; *The Forcing House: Or, The Cockpit Continued*, pb. 1922; *We Moderns*, pr. 1923; *The King of Schnorrers*, pr. 1925 (adaptation of his novella).

POETRY: *The Ballad of Moses*, 1892; *Blind Children*, 1903.

NONFICTION: *Motza Kleis*, 1882 (anonymously with Louis Cowen); *"A Doll's House" Repaired*, 1891 (with Eleanor Marx Aveling); *Hebrew, Jew, Israelite*, 1892; *The Position of Judaism*, 1895; *Without Prejudice*, 1896; *Dreamers of the Ghetto*, 1898; *The People's Saviour*, 1898; *The East African Question: Zionism and England's Offer*, 1904; *What Is the ITO?*, 1905; *A Land of Refuge*, 1907; *Talked Out!*, 1907; *One and One Are Two*, 1907; *Old Fogeys and Old Bogeys*, 1909; *The Lock on the Ladies*, 1909; *Report on the Purpose of Jewish Settlement in Cyrenaica*, 1909; *Be Fruitful and Multiply*, 1909; *Italian Fantasies*, 1910; *Sword and Spirit*, 1910; *The Hitertos*, 1912; *The Problem of the Jewish Race*, 1912; *Report on the Jewish Settlement in Angora*, 1913; *The War and the Women*, 1915; *The War for the World*, 1916; *The Principle of Nationalities*, 1917; *The Service of the Synagogue*, 1917 (with Nina Davis Salaman and Elsie Davis); *Chosen Peoples: The Hebraic Ideal Versus the Teutonic*, 1918; *Hands off Russia*, 1919; *The Jewish Pogroms in the Ukraine*, 1919 (with others); *The Voice of Jerusalem*, 1920; *Watchman, What of the Night?*, 1923; *Is the Ku Klux Klan Constructive or Destructive? A Debate Between Imperial Wizard Evans, Israel Zangwill, and Others*, 1924; *Now and Forever: A Conversation with Mr. Israel Zangwill on the Jew and the Future*, 1925 (with Samuel Roth); *Our Own*, 1926; *Speeches, Articles, and Letters*, 1937; *Zangwill in the Melting-Pot: Selections*, n.d.

TRANSLATION: *Selected Religious Poems of Ibn Gabirol, Solomon ben Judah, Known as Avicebron, 1020?-1070?*, 1923.

Israel Zangwill, born in London on February 14, 1864, was one of the outstanding Jewish authors and leaders of his time. His family, Russian Jews, had fled Russia and settled in England before his birth. A graduate of the Jews' Free School in London, he remained at the school as a teacher in order to finance his studies at London University, which he attended at the same time he was teaching. Despite the rigor of this dual program, Zangwill graduated from the university with highest honors. After graduation he left teaching for a career in journalism. He founded and edited *Ariel, the London Puck*, and he wrote for various other London periodicals.

His critical fame began with the publication of *Children of the Ghetto*, the first of his novels of Jewish life. At the time the novel attracted considerable attention largely because of its subject matter, and Zangwill has been credited with the prevention of anti-Jewish legislation by Parliament through its publication. Other novels about Jewish people followed, including *The Master* and *The Mantle of Elijah*. *Dreamers of the Ghetto* is a series of essays on such notable Jewish thinkers and leaders as Baruch Spinoza, Heinrich Heine, and Benjamin Disraeli.

Although he won fame as—and will probably be remembered as—a novelist interpreting Jews and Jewish life, Zangwill wished to excel as a dramatist rather than as a writer of fiction. Some of his most popular plays were dramatizations of his fiction that had been published earlier, such as *Merely Mary Ann*, his most popular comedy, and *Children of the Ghetto*. Zangwill's plays were produced in Jewish communities everywhere, in both Yiddish and English, and he tried for more than a decade to be the great dramatist of the Yiddish theater. Later critics have not been kind to his plays, and even the dramatist admitted that they were less successful artistically than they were popular. In addition to being a writer, Zangwill was an influential Jewish leader and a popular lecturer whose work in the cause of twentieth century Zionism was of considerable historical importance.

Zangwill is also remembered for two other reasons. First, his detective novel, a police procedural titled *The Big Bow Mystery*, is considered the first full-length treatment of the "locked room" type of story (in which a murder victim is discovered in a room that it seems impossible for the perpetrator to have entered) in detective literature. Second, his play *The Melting-Pot* popularized the notion of the United States as a crucible, or melting pot, in which the new identity of "real Americans" would emerge from the combination of many European immigrant cultures. Its optimistic, romanticized view of the melting away of differences and hatreds was appreciated by many, including President Theodore Roosevelt, who reportedly declared, "That's a great play, Mr. Zangwill," after its Broadway opening.

Irene Struthers

Bibliography

Adams, Elise Bonita. *Israel Zangwill.* New York: Twayne, 1971.
Baraitser, Marion. *The Crystal Den.* London: Oberon Books, 2002.
Chametzky, Jules. "Beyond Melting Pots, Cultural Pluralism, Ethnicity." *MELUS* 16, no. 4 (Winter, 1989): 3.
Kahn-Paycha, Danièle. *Popular Jewish Literature and Its Role in the Making of an Identity.* Lewiston, N.Y.: E. Mellen Press, 2000.
Rochelson, Meri-Jane. "Language, Gender, and Ethnic Anxiety in Zangwill's *Children of the Ghetto.*" *English Literature in Transition* 31, no. 4 (1988).
Shumsky, Neil Larry. "Zangwill's *The Melting Pot:* Ethnic Tensions on Stage." *American Quarterly* 27 (1975).
Udelson, Joseph H. *Dreamer of the Ghetto: The Life and Works of Israel Zangwill.* New York: Columbia University Press, 1990.

Stefan Żeromski

Polish novelist

Born: Strawczyn, near Kielce, Poland, Russian Empire; November 1, 1864
Died: Warsaw, Poland; November 20, 1925

LONG FICTION: *Syzyfowe Prace*, 1897; *Ludzie bezdomni*, 1900; *Popioły*, 1904 (*Ashes*, 1928); *Wierna rzeka*, 1912 (*The Faithful River*, 1943); *Wiatr od morza*, 1922; *Przedwiośnie*, 1925; *Puszcza jodłowa*, 1925.
SHORT FICTION: *Rozdziobią nas kruki, wrony*, 1895; *Opowiadania*, 1895; *Utwory powieścowe*, 1898.
DRAMA: *Róża*, pr. 1909; *Uciekła mi przepióreczka*, pr. 1924.

Stefan Żeromski (zheh-RAWM-skee) was born near Kielce in Russian Poland, November 1, 1864, of an impoverished noble family. Throughout his life he chafed under this czarist domination, and his short stories frequently take as their subject the resistance of Polish secret organizations. Żeromski was even more directly involved. In 1905, during the revolt against Russia, he was imprisoned; later he went into semi-voluntary exile in France and Austrian Galicia, where he remained until the end of World War I.

Żeromski wrote plays and poetry, but his claim to greatness stems from his novels. Most famous of these is *Ashes*, which has been called the *War and Peace* of Poland. Although his great lyrical descriptive vein is not so evident in this work as it is in *Wiatr od morza* (the wind from the sea), *Ashes* possesses the scope and richness of characterization to make it an authentic masterpiece.

There is a dark pessimism to Żeromski's writing that is characteristic of the Polish positivist school; perhaps it was this quality—as well as his extreme nationalism—that prevented him from winning the Nobel Prize in Literature. During his career he contributed many characters to the Polish national consciousness, and for that he was honored by his fellow Poles. He died in Warsaw on November 20, 1925.

Irene Struthers

Bibliography

Borowy, W. "Żeromski." *Slavonic Review* 14 (1936).
Kuk, Zenon. "Depiction of Fictional Characters in *War and Peace* and *Ashes.*" *The Polish Review* 25, no. 2 (1980).
_______. "The Napoleonic Era in Tolstoy's *War and Peace* and Żeromski's *Ashes:* Realities and Legends." *University of Hartford Studies in Literature* 11 (1979).
_______. "Tolstoy's *War and Peace* and Żeromski's *Ashes* as Historical Novels." *Folio: Essays on Foreign Languages and Literature* 14 (December, 1982).
Lechon, Jan. "Stefan Żeromski." *Harvard Slavic Studies* 2 (1954).

Zhang Jie

Chinese novelist and short-story writer

Born: Beijing, China; April 27, 1937

LONG FICTION: *Chenzhong de chibang*, 1981 (*Leaden Wings*, 1987; better known as *Heavy Wings*, 1989); *Zhi you yi ge taiyang*, 1988.
SHORT FICTION: *Ai, shi buneng wangji de*, 1979 (*Love Must Not Be Forgotten*, 1986); *Fangzhou*, 1983; *Zai nei lu cao dishang*, 1983; *Zum lu*, 1985; *Zhang Jie chi*, 1986; *As Long as Nothing Happens, Nothing Will*, 1988; *Yige zhongguo nuren zai Ouzhou*, 1989; *You Are a Friend of My Soul*, 1990; *Shi jie shang zui teng wo de na ge ren qu le*, 1994.
NONFICTION: *Fang mei sanji*, 1982; *Zongshi nanwang*, 1990.

Zhang Jie (jong jay) is the best-known contemporary Chinese woman writer. Her first novel, *Heavy Wings*, won the Mao Dun National Award for Novels in 1985 (an award granted once every three years); it has been translated and published in Germany, France, Sweden, Finland, Norway, Denmark, Holland, Great Britain, United States, Spain, Brazil, and Russia. Since 1978, she has published numerous stories and won various prizes. Two collections of her stories, *Love Must Not Be Forgotten* and *As Long as Nothing Happens, Nothing Will*, are widely studied in European and American college classrooms. *As Long as Nothing Happens, Nothing Will* won the Italian Malaparte Literary Prize, an honor also accorded such well-known Western writers as Anthony Burgess and Saul Bellow.

Zhang was born in 1937. During World War II, her father left the family, and her mother, a teacher, brought her up in a village in Liaoning Province. From childhood she showed a strong interest in music and literature. After graduating from the People's University of Beijing in 1960, she was assigned to one of the industrial ministries. Her novella *Heavy Wings* and short story "Today's Agenda" benefit from her acquaintance with industrial management and bureaucracy. Later Zhang transferred to the Beijing Film Studio, where she wrote film scripts. She started to write fiction at the age of forty, near the end of the Cultural Revolution, and in 1978 her story "The Music of the Forest" won a prize as one of the best short stories of the year. In 1979 she won another national short-story award for "Who Lives a Better Life"; "Love Must Not Be Forgotten" also became a widely read and controversial story. In 1985 she reached the climax of her literary career by winning the Mao Dun National Novel Award for *Heavy Wings* and the National Novella Award for *Emerald*, which appeard in *Love Must Not Be Forgotten*. Zhang actively participates in international creative activities. She has visited West Germany and America and was a visiting professor at Wesleyan University from 1989 to 1990. Zhang has been a council member of the Chinese Writers' Association and the vice chair of Beijing Association of Writers.

Zhang is known as a tough woman. She took part in many political movements and joined the Chinese Communist Party at an early age. Although she mercilessly dissects the causes of China's backwardness, which she attributes to feudal ideology as well as to the corruption of the Communist Party, she firmly defends the socialist system as best suited to China. Despite her support for socialism and genuine Marxism, however, she is often criticized inside China for her liberal tendencies. She proudly admits that she loves to read Western novels, particularly those of the eighteenth and nineteenth centuries. Like Dai Houying, Wang Anyi, and other contemporary Chinese writers, she believes that the humanism in classical Western literature is something Chinese people should learn. She has been influenced by Western Romanticism as well as by social critical realism; she stresses love and sacrifice, conscience and responsibility in all her writings.

Zhang is also a pioneering feminist writer. She has one daughter, and she has been divorced twice because she could not tolerate men who attempted to dominate her. As a result of her bitter experiences of discrimination against women, especially divorced and unmarried ones, Zhang attacks male supremacy and patriarchal ideology in the Chinese social structure as well as in the consciousness and subconsciousness of every man. She staunchly insists on a woman's right to remain single and free from sexual harassment and political discrimination. Like early feminist writers in the West, however, she regards denial of sexuality as necessary to achieve female autonomy.

Zhang writes on a number of themes with various characters. From national political and economic reform to individual daily problems; from unmarried girls' idealistic pursuits to divorced women's struggles against alienation; and from doctors' housing problems to an intellectual's vicissitudes, she writes in a vigorous, fresh, and romantic style. Her work has received considerable critical acclaim both in China and abroad. As a feminist writer, she has forged a distinctive style that blends utopian idealism with social reality in her exploration of women's problems concerning love, marriage, and career. As a social critic, she exposes China's hidden corruption and stubborn bureaucracy and vehemently champions democratic reform through literary means. For her integrated concern for women and society, Zhang can be compared with such Western writers as Doris Lessing, Marge Piercy, and Ursula Le Guin.

Qingyun Wu

Bibliography

Bailey, Alison. "Travelling Together: Narrative Technique in Zhang Jie's *The Ark*." In *Modern Chinese Women Writers: Critical Appraisals*, edited by Michael S. Duke. Armonk, N.Y.: M. E. Sharpe, 1989. Bailey analyzes Zhang's narrative technique according to Western theories and compares her "narrated monologue" with European writers of the nineteenth century.

Chen, Xiaomei. "Reading Mother's Tale—Reconstructing Women's Space in Amy Tan and Zhang Jie." *Chinese Literature: Essays, Articles, Reviews* 16 (1994). Analyzes the central roles of mother/daughter bonding in Zhang's work.

Dillard, Annie. *Encounters with Chinese Writers*. Middletown, Conn.: Wesleyan University Press, 1984. Dillard's chapter on Zhang contrasts her reception by Chinese and American audiences.

Hsu, Vivian Ling. "Contemporary Chinese Women's Lives as Reflected in Recent Literature." *Journal of the Chinese Teachers' Association* 23, no. 3 (1988). Hsu analyzes several of Zhang's stories about women. She particularly notes the two women's realization of their enslaved status in relation to the man whom they love in *Emerald*.

Liu, Lydia H. "Invention and Intervention: The Female Tradition in Modern Chinese Literature." In *Gender Politics in Modern China: Writing and Feminism*, edited by Tani E. Barlow. Durham, N.C.: Duke University Press, 1993. Discusses female subjectivity in Zhang's fiction.

Louie, Kam. *Between Fact and Fiction*. Sydney, Australia: Wild Peony, 1989. In chapter 5, "Love Stories: The Meaning of Love and Marriage in China, 1978-1981," Louie treats Zhang's story "Love Must Not Be Forgotten" as a social commentary against the background of China's present problems concerning love and marriage.

Yichin Shen. "Womanhood and Sexual Relations in Contemporary Chinese Fiction by Male and Female Authors: A Comparative Analysis." *Feminist Issues* 12 (Spring, 1992). Compares Zhang's novella *The Ark*, found in *Love Must Not Be Forgotten*, with novels by Gu Hua and Zhang Xianling.

Paul Zindel

American playwright and novelist

Born: Staten Island, New York; May 15, 1936
Died: New York, New York; March 27, 2003

DRAMA: *Dimensions of Peacocks*, pr. 1959; *Euthanasia and the Endless Hearts*, pr. 1960; *A Dream of Swallows*, pr. 1964; *The Effect of Gamma Rays on Man-in-the-Moon Marigolds*, pr. 1965; *And Miss Reardon Drinks a Little*, pr. 1967; *The Secret Affairs of Mildred Wild*, pr. 1972; *The Ladies Should Be in Bed*, pb. 1973; *Ladies at the Alamo*, pr. 1975; *A Destiny with Half Moon Street*, pr. 1983; *Amulets Against the Dragon Forces*, pr., pb. 1989; *Every Seventeen Minutes the Crowd Goes Crazy!*, pr. 1995.

LONG FICTION: *When a Darkness Falls*, 1984.

SCREENPLAYS: *Up the Sandbox*, 1972; *Mame*, 1974; *Runaway Train*, 1983; *Maria's Lovers*, 1984.

TELEPLAYS: *Let Me Hear You Whisper*, 1966; *Alice in Wonderland*, 1985 (adaptation of Lewis Carroll's novel *Alice's Adventures in Wonderland*); *A Connecticut Yankee in King Arthur's Court*, 1989 (adaptation of Mark Twain's novel).

CHILDREN'S/YOUNG ADULT LITERATURE: *The Pigman*, 1968; *My Darling, My Hamburger*, 1969; *I Never Loved Your Mind*, 1970; *I Love My Mother*, 1975; *Pardon Me, You're Stepping on My Eyeball!*, 1976; *Confessions of a Teenage Baboon*, 1977; *The Undertaker's Gone Bananas*, 1978; *A Star for the Latecomer*, 1980 (with Bonnie Zindel); *The Pigman's Legacy*, 1980; *The Girl Who Wanted a Boy*, 1981; *To Take a Dare*, 1982 (with Crescent Dragonwagon); *Harry and Hortense at Hormone High*, 1984; *The Amazing and Death-Defying Diary of Eugene Dingman*, 1987; *A Begonia for Miss Applebaum*, 1989; *The Pigman and Me*, 1992 (autobiography); *Attack of the Killer Fishsticks*, 1993; *David and Della*, 1993; *Fifth Grade Safari*, 1993; *Fright Party*, 1993; *Loch*, 1994; *The One Hundred Percent Laugh Riot*, 1994; *The Doom Stone*, 1995; *Raptor*, 1998; *Reef of Death*, 1998; *Rats*, 1999; *The Gadget*, 2001; *Night of the Bat*, 2001.

Paul Zindel (zihn-DEHL), a prizewinning young adult author and playwright, is known for his realistic, if sometimes bizarre, presentation of issues and situations appealing to contemporary adolescent readers. According to Zindel, these stories were based on his personal experiences as a teenager and a high school teacher. As a child, Zindel never really knew his father, but his hardworking mother juggled a variety of jobs in order to provide for Zindel and his older sister. Although the family moved frequently, Zindel found that each neighborhood offered a new background for his imaginative pursuits.

While still in high school, Zindel contracted tuberculosis and spent a year and a half in a sanatorium, the only teenager in a sterile world filled with adults. This experience, in addition to his exposure to the private nursing patients cared for by Zindel's mother, shaped the development of fictional medical incidents that occur in some of his works. From this isolated and lonely time, Zindel developed the voice of an alienated narrator which even reluctant readers have found appealing.

While his major at Wagner College was chemistry (in which he was awarded a B.S. in 1958 and an M.S. in 1959), Zindel also took classes in creative writing; playwright Edward Albee was one of his instructors. After a brief period serving as a technical writer for a chemical company, Zindel spent ten years working as a high school chemistry teacher, writing fiction in his spare time. Wagner College later awarded him an honorary doctorate for his achievements in literature.

Zindel's literary success began with the production of his play *The Effect of Gamma Rays on Man-in-the-Moon Marigolds*, the story of a tormented family of outcasts. After its initial run in Houston in 1965, the play opened Off-Broadway in 1970 and on Broadway in 1971, winning numerous awards, including the Pulitzer Prize in drama that same year. The play caught the attention of editor Charlotte Zolotow, who encouraged Zindel to write for teenagers. *The Pigman*, his first young adult novel, earned immediate critical and popular acclaim. The story, which features two alienated teenagers who exploit an elderly man, was named by the American Library Association as one of the Best Books for Young Adults in 1975.

The next year, Zindel published *My Darling, My Hamburger*, an honest and realistic look at the sensitive personal issues faced by members of his adolescent audience; it was subsequently selected as an Outstanding Children's Book of the Year (1969) by *The New York Times*. The books that followed established Zindel's appeal for the disaffected underdog, each of which was listed as *The New*

York Times Outstanding Children's Book of the Year in the year of their publication: *I Never Loved Your Mind*; *Pardon Me, You're Stepping on My Eyeball!*; *The Undertaker's Gone Bananas*; and *The Pigman's Legacy*.

Zindel's other awards of note included the selection of several of his works as the Best Young Adult Book by the American Library Association in their years of publication, including *The Effect of Gamma Rays on Man-in-the-Moon Marigolds* and the young adult novels *Pardon Me, You're Stepping on My Eyeball!*; *Confessions of a Teenage Baboon*; and *The Pigman's Legacy*.

Zindel's later works appealed to a slightly younger group of readers. In 1993, *Attack of the Killer Fishsticks* introduced the Wacky Facts Lunch Bunch, a group of fifth graders and their bully rivals. In addition, Zindel explored themes ranging from adventure to horror. In *Raptor*, *Loch*, and *Reef of Death*, Zindel's characters encounter literal monsters as well as dysfunctional adults. Both *Loch* and *The Doom Stone*, another book of horror by Zindel, were chosen as Recommended Books for Reluctant Young Adult Readers by the American Library Association. Zindel married Bonnie Hildebrand in 1973; they had two children, David and Elizabeth. Zindel died of cancer in March, 2003, at the age of sixty-six.

Kathleen M. Bartlett

Bibliography

Dace, Tish. "Paul Zindel: Overview." In *Contemporary Dramatists*, edited by K. A. Berney. 5th ed. Detroit: St James Press, 1993. Discusses characters, plot, and themes of *The Effect of Gamma Rays on Man-in-the-Moon Marigolds*, Zindel's best-known play.

Haley, Beverly A., and Kenneth L. Donelson. "Pigs and Hamburger, Cadavers and Gamma Rays: Paul Zindel's Adolescents." *Elementary English* 51, no. 7 (October, 1974): 940-945. Provides social analysis of the values embodied by Zindel's character development.

Oliver, Edith. "Why the Lady Is a Tramp." *The New Yorker* 46, no. 9 (April 18, 1970): 82, 87-88. Reprinted in *Drama for Students*, volume 12. Reviews the 1970 performance of *The Effects of Gamma Rays on Man-in-the-Moon Marigolds* directed by Melvin Bernhardt.

Strickland, Ruth L. "Paul Zindel." In *Twentieth Century American Dramatists*, edited by John MacNicholas. Vol. 7 in *Dictionary of Literary Biography*. Detroit: Gale, 1981. Includes discussion of Zindel's primary themes.

Zindel, Paul. Interview by Audrey Eaglen. *Top of the News* 34, no. 2 (Winter, 1978): 178-185. Includes a discussion of Zindel's early influences.

Émile Zola

French novelist

Born: Paris, France; April 2, 1840
Died: Paris, France; September 28, 1902

LONG FICTION: *La Confession de Claude*, 1865 (*Claude's Confession*, 1882); *Le Vœu d'une morte*, 1866 (*A Dead Woman's Wish*, 1902); *Les Mystères de Marseille*, 1867 (*The Flower Girls of Marseilles*, 1888; also known as *The Mysteries of Marseilles*, 1895); *Thérèse Raquin*, 1867 (English translation, 1881); *Madeleine Férat*, 1868 (English translation, 1880); *La Fortune des Rougon*, 1871 (*The Rougon-Macquart Family*, 1879; also known as *The Fortune of the Rougons*, 1886); *La Curée*, 1872 (*The Rush for the Spoil*, 1886; also known as *The Kill*, 1895); *Le Ventre de Paris*, 1873 (*The Markets of Paris*, 1879; also known as *Savage Paris*, 1955); *La Conquête de Plassans*, 1874 (*The Conquest of Plassans*, 1887; also known as *A Priest in the House*, 1957); *La Faute de l'abbé Mouret*, 1875 (*Albine: Or, The Abbé's Temptation*, 1882; also known as *Abbé Mouret's Transgression*, 1886); *Son Excellence Eugène Rougon*, 1876 (*Clorinda: Or, The Rise and Reign of His Excellency Eugène Rougon*, 1880; also known as *His Excellency*, 1897); *L'Assommoir*, 1877 (English translation, 1879; also known as *The Dram-Shop*, 1897); *Une Page d'amour*, 1878 (*Hélène: A Love Episode*, 1878, also known as *A Love Affair*, 1957); *Nana*, 1880 (English translation, 1880); *Pot-Bouille*, 1882 (*Piping Hot*, 1924); *Au bonheur des dames*, 1883 (*The Bonheur des Dames*, 1883; also known as *The Ladies' Paradise*, 1883); *La Joie de vivre*, 1884 (*Life's Joys*, 1884; also known as *Zest for Life*, 1955); *Germinal*, 1885 (English translation, 1885); *L'Œuvre*, 1886 (*His Masterpiece*, 1886; also known as *The Masterpiece*, 1946); *La Terre*, 1887 (*The Soil*, 1888; also known as *Earth*, 1954); *Le Rêve*, 1888 (*The Dream*, 1888); *La Bête humaine*, 1890 (*Human Brutes*, 1890; also known as *The Human Beast*, 1891); *L'Argent*, 1891 (*Money*, 1891); *La Débâcle*, 1892 (*The Downfall*, 1892); *Le Docteur Pascal*, 1893 (*Doctor Pascal*, 1893; previous 20 novels [*La Fortune des Rougon* through *Docteur Pascal*] collectively known as *Les Rougon-Macquart* [*The Rougon-Macquart Novels*]); *Lourdes*, 1894 (English translation, 1894); *Rome*, 1896 (English translation, 1896); *Paris*, 1898 (English translation, 1897, 1898; previous 3 novels collectively known as *Les Trois Villes*); *Fécondité*, 1899 (*Fruitfulness*, 1900); *Travail*, 1901 (*Work*, 1901); *Vérité*, 1903 (*Truth*, 1903; previous 3 novels collectively known as *Les Quatre Evangiles*).

SHORT FICTION: *Contes à Ninon*, 1864 (*Stories for Ninon*, 1895); *Esquisses parisiennes*, 1866; *Nouveaux Contes à Ninon*, 1874; *Le Capitaine Burle*, 1882 (*A Soldier's Honor, and Other Stories*, 1888); *Naïs Micoulin*, 1884; *Contes et nouvelles*, 1928; *Madame Sourdis*, 1929.

DRAMA: *Madeleine*, wr. 1865, pb. 1878; *Thérèse Raquin*, pr., pb. 1873 (adaptation of his novel; English translation, 1947); *Les Héritiers Rabourdin*, pr., pb. 1874 (*The Rabourdin Heirs*, 1893); *Le Bouton de rose*, pr., pb. 1878; *Théâtre*, pb. 1878; *Renée*, pr., pb. 1887 (adaptation of his novel *La Curée*); *Lazare*, wr. 1893, pb. 1921 (libretto; music by Alfred Bruneau); *Violaine la chevelue*, wr. 1897, pb. 1921; *L'Ouragan*, pr., pb. 1901 (libretto; music by Bruneau); *Sylvanire: Ou, Paris en amour*, wr. 1902, pb. 1921 (libretto; music by Robert Le Grand); *L'Enfant-Roi*, pr. 1905 (libretto; music by Bruneau); *Poèmes lyriques*, pb. 1921.

POETRY: *L'Amoureuse Comédie*, wr. 1860 (in *Œuvres complètes*).

NONFICTION: *Mes haines*, 1866 (*My Hates*, 1893); *Le Roman expérimental*, 1880 (*The Experimental Novel*, 1893); *Documents littéraires*, 1881; *Le Naturalisme au théâtre*, 1881 (*Naturalism on the Stage*, 1893); *Nos auteurs dramatiques*, 1881; *Les Romanciers naturalistes*, 1881 (*The Naturalist Novel*, 1964); *Une Campagne*, 1882; *The Experimental Novel, and Other Essays*, 1893 (includes *The Experimental Novel* and *Naturalism on the Stage*, better known as *Naturalism in the Theater*); *Nouvell Campagne*, 1897; *La Vérité en marche*, 1901.

MISCELLANEOUS: *Œuvres complètes*, 1966-1968 (15 volumes).

Émile Zola (ZOH-luh) was probably the most important and controversial French novelist of the late nineteenth century. The son of an engineer of mixed Greek and Italian ancestry who died when his son was only seven, Zola was educated at Aix and returned to Paris in 1858 to start his career as a writer. He worked as a critic, then in 1867 also began to write novels. In 1871 he published *The Rougon-Macquart Family*, the first volume of twenty in a series called the "Rougon-Macquart Novels," which deals with the history of a family under the Second Empire. The first of these novels attracted little attention, but with the publication of *L'Assommoir*, a merciless study of the effects of alcohol, Zola was recognized as being among the foremost French writers of a brilliant literary period.

In the Rougon-Macquart series it was Zola's intention to study, with scientific precision and detachment, the fortunes of the various branches of a typical French family of his time. He wished to show, in the vast and complicated web of relationships he created, how the members of the family were affected by their combined heredity and environment. This approach was a reaction against the Romanticism of the generation of Victor Hugo and Alexandre Dumas, *père*, and meant an advance beyond anything that realism had as yet accomplished in fiction. The explanation of his method is set forth in his essay *The Experimental Novel*. The literary school he established has been given the name of naturalism.

The naturalists claimed that they descended from Stendhal, through Honoré de Balzac and Gustave Flaubert, all of whom minutely dissected the personality of individuals and the society in which they found themselves, thus presenting a picture of the contemporary world as it actually is. The naturalists, however, went considerably further. Literature, according to them, must be scientific in its approach, not imaginative; and in this attitude they were echoing the mechanistic statements of mid-nineteenth century science. Human beings, according to this point of view, are merely animals among other animals, the products of heredity and environment that can be studied almost as in a laboratory. When transferred to literature, this theory, as the naturalists contended, meant that novelists should invent nothing but should observe facts and collect data as scientists do. If the observations are complete, if the facts are all gathered, then the behavior and even the final end of the individual can be predicted with scientific accuracy. The plot of the novel will be as inevitable as the solution to a problem in mathematics.

The scientific spirit in which Zola approached his gigantic task is shown by his submitting to his publisher a detailed outline of ten of the projected novels. The subtitle of the series, "The natural and social history of a family under the Second Empire," gives the impression that he was studying his characters as an entomologist might study a colony of ants. He was painstaking in preparing his material; if he wished to introduce minor characters engaged in a particular trade, he was capable of spending weeks at the task of mastering the technical jargon peculiar to that trade. He took voluminous notes so that his details might be correct. It is not surprising that it took him twenty-five years to complete the series.

Although Zola tried to include all strata of society, the volumes by which he is best known deal with the lower—at times the lowest—classes. It is in this picture of the brutalized, almost animalistic existence of the poor that his uncompromising realism was strongest. The details aroused protest even in France; in England there was a cry of outrage from the few readers who became familiar with his work.

In the course of studying the fortunes of a particular family, Zola also gave an analysis of the Second Empire, a glittering, ornate facade with very little back of it. The hollowness of this society is best shown in *Nana*, a picture of the corruption of Paris even among the rich. Nana, risen from the position of a simple prostitute to that of a *grande cocotte*, destroys those men who are convinced that no amount of money spent on her could be too great. She is the epitome of the vast luxury and vice of Paris, and the novel ends with the terrible irony of the dead Nana, abandoned by everyone, while outside in the streets the crowds are shouting "To Berlin!"; the scene is a prelude to the downfall that is to follow.

Near the end of his life Zola became involved in a cause that brought him an international recognition far beyond his fame as an author: the Dreyfus case that split France at that time. In 1898, having become convinced that the French army officer Alfred Dreyfus was the innocent victim of a government plot, Zola published his famous letter that began "J'accuse" (I accuse), in which he attacked the general staff and French officialdom for persecuting Dreyfus. He was tried twice for libel and had to flee to England, returning to Paris only after a general amnesty had been proclaimed. He died under mysterious circumstances in his home in Paris.

Zola's influence on the twentieth century novel cannot be overemphasized. It was his work, along with that of his French imitators, that helped shatter Victorian reticence in English literature; after that, novelists were free to deal truthfully with their subjects.

Jeffrey L. Buller

Bibliography

Baguley, David, ed. *Critical Essays on Émile Zola*. Boston: G. K. Hall, 1986. In a lengthy introductory essay, Baguley surveys the range of reaction to Zola's work. The volume reprints eighteen essays, starting with an 1868 review of *Thérèse Raquin* titled "Putrid Literature." The volume also includes a list of works by Zola and a bibliography of works about him for readers of English.

Berg, William J., and Laurey K. Martin. *Émile Zola Revisited*. New York: Twayne, 1992. Focusing on *The Rougon-Macquart Family*, this book employs textual analysis rather than biography to analyze each of the twenty volumes in Zola's most widely known series. Berg and Martin use Zola's literary-scientific principles to organize their study.

Brown, Frederick. *Zola: A Life*. New York: Farrar, Straus and Giroux, 1995. A detailed and extensive biography of Zola that discusses his fiction and the intellectual life of France, of which he was an important part. Shows how Zola's naturalism was developed out of the intellectual and political ferment of his time. Argues that Zola's naturalism was a highly studied and artificial approach to reality.

Hemmings, F. W. J. *The Life and Times of Émile Zola*. New York: Scribner's, 1977. Hemmings is particularly good at describing how the cross-fertilization between naturalism in literature and Impressionism in art manifested itself in Zola's works.

Johnson, Roger, Jr. "Looking and Screening in Zola's *Vierge au cirage*." *Studies in Short Fiction* 29 (Winter, 1992): 19-25. Discusses the device of the beholder in Zola's tale; asserts that in the story "looking" is both a central narrative event and a recurring motif.

Nelson, Brian. *Zola and the Bourgeoisie*. New York: Macmillan, 1983. Illuminates the specific aspects of Zola's writing that demonstrate the nineteenth century's class structure and the results of the burgeoning bourgeoisie that had replaced the aristocracy and had come to hold the bulk of the country's wealth. Explores how the bourgeoisie vilified the artist who uncovered the base side of that class's nature through his social vision.

Newton, Ruth, and Naomi Lebowitz. *The Impossible Romance: Dickens, Manzoni, Zola, and James*. Columbia: University of Missouri Press, 1990. Discusses the impact of religious sensibility on literary form and ideology in Zola's fiction.

Richardson, Joanna. *Zola*. New York: St. Martin's Press, 1978. This short, well-written biography moves along at a fast pace and does a fine job of relating the details of Zola's life while maintaining a strong narrative line. A postscript relates what happened to the other major players in the writer's life after he was gone. Decidedly nonacademic, Richardson's biography nonetheless includes a substantial selected bibliography of works by and about Zola written in French and English.

Schom, Alan. *Émile Zola*. London: Queen Anne Press, 1987. This eleven-year research effort considers Zola the journalist, the novelist, and the man himself and his values. Places Zola in the context of the artist as crusader against nineteenth century France and its societal ills. Includes photographs, illustrations, and a select bibliography.

Walker, Philip D. *Zola*. London: Routledge & Kegan Paul, 1985. A biography drawn from this professor of French literature's own studies, as well as those of many other critics, historians, and biographers. With a select bibliography.

José Zorrilla y Moral

Spanish playwright and poet

Born: Valladolid, Spain; February 21, 1817
Died: Madrid, Spain; January 23, 1893

DRAMA: *Juan Dándolo*, pb. 1830 (with Antonio García Gutiérrez); *Vivir loco y morir más*, pb. 1837; *Más vale llegar a tiempo que rondar un año*, pb. 1839; *Cada cual con su razón*, pr. 1839; *Ganar perdiendo*, pb. 1839 (adaptation of Lope de Vega Carpio's play *La noche de San Juan*); *Lealtad de una mujer: O, Aventuras de una noche*, pr., pb. 1840; *El zapatero y el rey*, pr., pb. 1840 (part 1); *Apoteosis de don Pedro Calderón de la Barca*, pb. 1840 (verse drama); *El zapatero y el rey*, pr., pb. 1842 (part 2); *El eco del torrente*, pr., pb. 1842; *Los dos virreyes*, pr., pb. 1842 (adaptation of Pietro Angelo Fiorentino's novel *El virrey de Nápoles*); *Un año y un día*, pr., pb. 1842; *Sancho García*, pr., pb. 1842; *El caballo del rey don Sancho*, pr., pb. 1843; *El puñal del godo*, pr., pb. 1843 (*Dagger of the Goth*, 1929); *Sofronia*, pr., pb. 1843; *La mejor razón, la espada*, pb. 1843 (adaptation of Augustín Moreto y Cabaña's play *Las travesuras de Pantoja*); *El molino de Guadalajara*, pr., pb. 1843; *La oliva y el laurel*, pr., pb. 1843; *Don Juan Tenorio*, pr., pb. 1844 (English translation, 1944); *La copa de marfil*, pr., pb. 1844; *El alcalde Ronquillo: O, El diablo en Valladolid*, pr., pb. 1845; *El rey loco*, pr., pb. 1847; *La reina y los favoritos*, pr., pb. 1847; *La calentura*, pr., pb. 1847 (part 2 of *El Puñal del godo*); *El excomulgado*, pr., pb. 1848; *Traidor, inconfeso y mártir*, pr., pb. 1849; *El cuento de las flores*, pr., pb. 1864; *El encapuchado*, pr. 1866; *Pilatos*, pr., pb. 1877; *Don Juan Tenorio*, pr. 1877 (operatic version; music by Nicolás Manent).

POETRY: *Poesías de don José Zorrilla*, 1837-1839 (6 volumes); *Cantos del trovador*, 1840-1841 (3 volumes); *Vigilias del estío*, 1842; *Flores perdidas*, 1843; *Recuerdos y fantasías*, 1844; *La azucena silvestre*, 1845; *El desafío del diablo*, 1845; *Un testigo de bronce*, 1845; *María*, 1850; *Un cuento de amores*, 1850 (with José Heriberto García de Quevedo); *Granada*, 1852 (2 volumes); *Al-Hamar, el Nazarita, rey de Granada*, 1853; *La flor de los recuerdos*, 1855-1859 (2 volumes); *El drama del alma*, 1867; *La leyenda del Cid*, 1882; *¡Granada mía!*, 1885; *Gnomos y mujeres*, 1886; *El cantar del romero*, 1886; *¡A escape y al vuelo!*, 1888; *De Murcia al cielo*, 1888; *Mi última breca*, 1888.
NONFICTION: *Recuerdos del tiempo viejo*, 1880-1883 (3 volumes).
MISCELLANEOUS: *Obras de Don José Zorrilla*, 1847; *Obras completas*, 1943 (2 volumes).

José Zorrilla y Moral (zawr-REE-yah ee moh-RAHL) is representative of Spanish Romanticism not only in his writing but in his life. As a young man he was, despite parental opposition, lured from the study of law by his love for poetry. His marriage to a woman of whom his father disapproved widened the breach, and as a bohemian, he frequently lived in poverty. He was able, however, to visit France in 1846 to meet the leading poets of Paris and later to travel to Mexico at the request of Emperor Maximilian to direct the National Theater. He lived in Mexico from 1855 until 1866.

He became famous in 1837, when as a gaunt youth he leaped into the grave of the suicide Mariano José de Larra, a poet and journalist who wrote under the name Figaro, and read emotional verses about the loneliness of a poet and the sacredness of his mission. This act initiated fifty years of literary production. He became a member of the Royal Academy in 1848. His lyrical and dramatic poetry was characterized by themes of mystery, melancholy, and religion against a background of wild nature. Old legends provided him with themes, and he wrapped himself in the splendor of his country's past.

Zorrilla was also the author of about twenty original dramas, all written with speed and facility and many patterned on the cape-and-sword dramas of the Golden Age. His mastery of many verse forms established him as one of Spain's leading poets, and in 1881, appropriately in Granada, he was proclaimed poet laureate of Spain. *Don Juan Tenorio* brought him his highest fame, though he called it "the greatest nonsense ever written." In spite of its exaggerations, melodramatic improbability, and technical flaws, the drama expresses the spirit of Spanish Romanticism and is performed throughout the Spanish-speaking world on the first of November for the Day of the Dead. A good performance of it is an artistic delight. Many like to believe that the play dramatizes fundamental eternal truths and that the characters personify the inner duality of the earthy and spiritual elements inherent in human nature. Zorilla's Don Juan, the archetypal Romantic hero, is saved by the pure love of his Inés.

Charlene E. Suscavage

Bibliography

Arias, Judith H. "The Devil at Heaven's Door: Metaphysical Desire in *Don Juan Tenorio*." *Hispanic Review* 61, no. 1 (Winter, 1993): 15. A discussion of the boundary between the real and the fictional in *Don Juan Tenorio*.

Cardwell, Richard A., and Ricardo Landeira, eds. *José de Zorrilla: Centennial Readings*. Nottingham, England: University of Nottingham, 1993. These essays honoring the one-hundred-year anniversary of Zorrilla y Moral's death discuss his life and works. Includes bibliographical references.

Schurlknight, Donald E. *Spanish Romanticism in Context: Of Subversion, Contradiction, and Politics: Espronceda, Larra, Rivas, Zorrilla*. Lanham, Md.: University Press of America, 1998. A study of the role of politics in Spanish Romanticism that examines the works of Zorrilla y Moral, José de Espronceda, Mariano José de Larra, and Angel de Saavedra (Rivas). Includes bibliography and index.

Ter Horst, Robert. "Epic Descent: The Filiations of Don Juan." *MLN* 111, no. 2 (March, 1996): 255. The author compares and contrasts Zorrilla y Moral's *Don Juan Tenorio* with Tirso de Molina's *El burlador de Sevilla* (1630).

Louis Zukofsky

American poet

Born: New York, New York; January 23, 1904
Died: Port Jefferson, New York; May 12, 1978

POETRY: *Fifty-five Poems*, 1941; *Anew*, 1946; *Barely and Widely*, 1958; *I's (Pronounced "Eyes")*, 1963; *After I's*, 1964; *All: The Collected Short Poems, 1923-1958*, 1965; *All: The Collected Short Poems, 1956-1964*, 1965; *Little*, 1970; *All: The Collected Short Poems, 1923-1964*, 1971; *"A,"* 1978, 1993; *Eighty Flowers*, 1978; *Complete Short Poetry*, 1991.
TRANSLATION: *Catullus*, 1969 (with Celia Zukofsky; of Gaius Valerius Catullus)
LONG FICTION: *Ferdinand, Including "It Was,"* 1968; *Little, for Careenagers*, 1970; *Collected Fiction*, 1990.
DRAMA: *Arise, Arise*, pb. 1962 (magazine), pr. 1965.

NONFICTION: *Le Style Apollinaire*, 1934 (with René Taupin); *A Test of Poetry*, 1948; *Five Statements for Poetry*, 1958; *Bottom: On Shakespeare*, 1963; *Prepositions: The Collected Critical Essays of Louis Zukofsky*, 1967, expanded 1981 (revised as *Prepositions +: The Collected Critical Essays*, 2000); *Autobiography*, 1970 (text, with poems set to music by Celia Zukofsky); *Pound/Zukofsky: Selected Letters of Ezra Pound and Louis Zukofsky*, 1987 (Barry Ahearn, editor).
EDITED TEXT: *An "Objectivists" Anthology*, 1932.

Although Louis Zukofsky (zew-KAHF-skee) has been called the consummate poet's poet and even one of the greatest American poets born in the twentieth century, his challenging and innovative poetry has received little attention from either the popular or the academic world. Zukofsky pioneered the Objectivist movement in the 1930's, wrote an inventive poetry that emphasized the music of verse, and contributed various innovations to the epic tradition in his lengthy poem *"A,"* which represents a lifelong endeavor.

The son of immigrant Russian Jews who spoke only Yiddish, Zukofsky was born in the lower East Side of New York City. He learned English and succeeded in school, and at the age of fifteen he enrolled in Columbia University, earning an M.A. in English by the time he was twenty. While at Columbia, Zukofsky began to write poetry and to read such poets as T. S. Eliot, Ezra Pound, and H. D.

In 1926 Zukofsky wrote his first significant work, *Poem Beginning "The,"* a text clearly influenced by T. S. Eliot's *The Waste Land* (1922). He sent the poem to Ezra Pound, who published it in his 1928 spring issue of *Exile*. As he did for a number of talented writers, Pound acted as a mentor to the young poet. It was on his urging that Zukofsky met the American poet William Carlos Williams in 1928, the beginning of a lifelong friendship in which each commented upon and supported the other's work.

In 1928 Zukofsky also began writing his long poem *"A,"* a work that was a lifelong undertaking and eventually consisted of twenty-four movements drawing from art, economics, and Zukofsky's personal life. Zukofsky has stated that part of his purpose in writing his epic included the desire to incorporate "historic and contemporary particulars" in his poem and to transfer the form of the fugue to poetry. Over almost fifty years Zukofsky used his autobiographic epic to enact aesthetic theories concerning language's musicality and its materiality—that is, the ways that words themselves not only represent ideas but also act as physical objects in his poems.

In the 1930's Harriet Monroe, the editor of *Poetry*, invited Zukofsky to guest-edit an issue. For this issue Zukofsky gathered together such writers as William Carlos Williams, Carl Rakosi, Charles Reznikoff, and George Oppen—most of whom later came to be identified as Objectivists. Although Zukofsky disliked the idea of "isms" and later disclaimed that he had inaugurated any movement, he participated in a number of joint projects with members of the group—including collaborating on *An "Objectivists" Anthology* and founding To Publishers and the Objectivist Press. Moreover, Zukofsky the theoretician also articulated some of the aesthetic assumptions that the group shared in his essay "Sincerity and Objectification." Later Zukofsky claimed that the objectivist was simply a craftsman who put words together in an object and a poet who was interested in "living with things as they exist."

In many ways the 1930's were Zukofsky's most socially active years—in both senses of the word "social." During these Depression-era years he wrote some of his most politically committed poetry, including such works as "Mantis" and *"A,"* which demonstrated his interest in the philosophy of Karl Marx. Although Zukofsky and Pound were quite close in the early 1930's—Zukofsky even visited Pound in Italy—they became estranged as the decade closed because of their political differences, heightened by Pound's increasing commitment to fascism and anti-Semitism.

During this decade Zukofsky also met and married his wife Celia Thaew, an accomplished pianist. They shared a love for music, and their son Paul, born in 1943, proved to be a gifted violinist. Although Zukofsky worked at various times as a teacher, editor, and technical writer, his lifelong commitment was primarily to his family and to his poetry.

In the second half of his life Zukofsky became increasingly reclusive, and his personal and poetic interests focused increasingly on his family. This may have resulted above all from Zukofsky's conviction that he had not been granted sufficient recognition. In the 1960's and 1970's, however, he won awards from such institutions as the National Endowment for the Arts and was able to publish not only his poetry but also his criticism, his translation *Catullus*, and his drama *Arise, Arise*—a work actually written in 1936. He died in 1978, while *"A"* was being prepared for publication. Although Zukofsky never achieved the renown he desired, some critics have predicted that his poetry will eventually become more widely acknowledged as a significant part of twentieth century literature.

Sandra K. Stanley

Bibliography

Ahearn, Barry. *Zukofsky's "A": An Introduction*. Berkeley: University of California Press, 1983. Zukofsky once said that a poet writes only one poem for his whole life. He began the eight-hundred-page poem *"A"* in 1928, when he was twenty-four years old, and did not finish it until 1974, when he was seventy. Ahearn gives the student a framework to understand Zukofsky's magnum opus. Includes bibliographical references and indexes.

Leggott, Michele J. *Reading Zukofsky's "Eighty Flowers."* Baltimore: The Johns Hopkins University Press, 1989. Leggott attempts to explain Zukofsky's rare work, written the last four years of his life. Zukofsky wanted to condense the sense of his lifetime of poetry into a last book. Leggott offers a plausible interpretation for *Eighty Flowers* and thus explains the entire philosophy of Zukofsky's writing.

Penberthy, Jenny Lynn. "Lorine Niedecker and Louis Zukofsky: Her Poems and Letters." *Dissertation Abstracts International* 47 (October, 1986): 1326A. Zukofsky corresponded with Objectivist poet Lorine Niedecker for forty years, and his ideas substantially influenced her work. She even wrote some collage poems incorporating quotations from his letters to her.

Pound, Ezra. *Pound/Zukofsky: Selected Letters of Ezra Pound and Louis Zukofsky.* Edited by Barry Ahearn. New York: New Directions, 1987. Zukofsky considered Pound to be the greatest twentieth century poet writing in English. Therefore, he wrote to Pound more than he wrote to anyone else, in part to glean some words of literary wisdom. The two men met only three times, yet Zukofsky considered Pound to be his literary father.

Stanley, Sandra Kumamoto. *Louis Zukofsky and the Transformation of a Modern American Poetics.* Berkeley: University of California Press, 1994. Stanley argues that Zukofky's works serve as a crucial link between American modernism and postmodernism. Stanley explains how Zukofsky emphasized the materiality of language and describes his legacy to contemporary poets.

Terrell, Carroll Franklin. *Louis Zukofsky: Man and Poet.* Orono: National Poetry Foundation, University of Maine at Orono, 1979. Zukofsky essentially lived the history of twentieth century American poetry. This is the essential Zukofsky biography. It was written shortly after the poet's death in 1978, at the age of seventy-four. Contains a bibliography and an index.

Arnold Zweig

German novelist, short-story writer, and playwright

Born: Gross-Glogau, Prussia (now Głogów, Poland); November 10, 1887
Died: Berlin, East Germany; November 26, 1968
Identity: Jewish

LONG FICTION: *Die Novellen um Claudia*, 1912 (*Claudia*, 1930); *Der Streit um den Sergeanten Grischa*, 1927 (*The Case of Sergeant Grischa*, 1928); *Junge Frau von 1914*, 1931 (*Young Woman of 1914*, 1932); *De Vriendt kehrt heim*, 1932 (*De Vriendt Goes Home*, 1933); *Erziehung vor Verdun*, 1935 (*Education Before Verdun*, 1936); *Einsetzung eines Königs*, 1937 (*The Crowning of a King*, 1938); *Versunkene Tage*, 1938; *Das Beil von Wandsbek*, 1946 (*The Axe of Wandsbek*, 1947); *Die Feuerpause*, 1954; *Die Zeit ist reif*, 1957 (*The Time Is Ripe*, 1962); *Traum ist teuer*, 1962.

SHORT FICTION: *Aufzeichnungen über eine Familie Klopfer*, 1911; *Die Bestie*, 1914; *Geschichtenbuch*, 1916; *Bennarone*, 1918; *Drei Erzählungen*, 1920; *Gerufene Schatten*, 1923; *Söhne: Das zweite Geschichtenbuch*, 1923; *Frühe Fährten*, 1925; *Regenbogen: Erzählungen*, 1925; *Der Spiegel des grossen Kaisers*, 1926; *Knaben und Männer*, 1931; *Mädchen und Frauen*, 1931; *Spielzeug der Zeit*, 1933 (*Playthings of Time*, 1935); *Stufen: Fünf Erzählungen*, 1949; *Über den Nebeln*, 1950; *Der Elfenbeinfächer*, 1952; *Westlandsaga: Erzählung*, 1952; *Der Regenbogen*, 1955; *A Bit of Blood, and Other Stories*, 1959.

DRAMA: *Abigail und Nabal: Tragödie in drei Akten*, pr., pb. 1913, revised pb. 1920; *Ritualmord in Ungarn: Jüdische Tragödie in fünf Aufzügen*, pr., pb. 1914, revised pb. 1918 (as *Die Sendung Semaels*); *Die Lucilla*, wr. 1921; *Die Umkehr des Abtrünnigen*, pb. 1925; *Das Spiel vom Sergeanten Grischa*, pb. 1929; *Die Aufrichtung der Menorah: Entwurf einer Pantomime*, pb. 1930; *Laubheu und keine Bleibe: Schicksalscomödie*, pb. 1930; *Bonaparte in Jaffa: Historisches Schauspiel*, pb. 1949; *Soldatenspiele: Drei dramatische Historien*, pb. 1956.

POETRY: *Der englishche Garten*, 1910; *Entrückung und Aufruhr*, 1920; *Fünf Romanzen*, 1958.

NONFICTION: *Das ostjüdische Antlitz*, 1920; *Das neue Kanaan*, 1925; *Lessing-Kleist-Büchner*, 1925; *Caliban: Oder, Politik und Leidenschaft*, 1927; *Juden auf der deutschen Bühne*, 1928; *Herkunft und Zukunft: Zwei Essays zum Schicksal eines Volkes*, 1929; *Bilanz der deutschen Judenheit*, 1934 (*Insulted and Exiled: The Truth About the German Jews*, 1937); *Der Früchtekorb*, 1956; *Literatur und Theater*, 1959; *Über Schriftsteller*, 1967; *Sigmund Freud-Arnold Zweig: Briefwechsel*, 1968 (*The Letters of Sigmund Freud and Arnold Zweig*, 1970).

Arnold Zweig (tsvihk) was born into a Jewish middle-class family in 1887. His father, Adolf Zweig, was a saddler and grocer; his mother was Bianca von Spandow. He was educated at the technical school in Kattowitz, Upper Silesia, and then at several German universities, including Breslau, Munich, Berlin, Göttingen, Rostock, and Tübingen, where he studied philosophy and languages and developed an interest in psychology, history, and the arts.

Arnold Zweig had planned to be a teacher, but during his education he began to devote considerable time to writing; his earliest short stories date from 1909. His first novel, a series of episodes unified by a central character, Claudia, appeared in 1912. Traces of his careful, ironic style are apparent in that early work, an experimental book in which he portrayed the sufferings and growth of a sensitive, upper-class woman as she strives, while married to a shy professor, to free herself from her inhibitions and release her natural forces. Zweig's interest in the psychology of the individual continued to govern most of his work.

During World War I he was a private in a labor battalion in France and Serbia, and from 1917 to the armistice he worked in the press section of the German army at the eastern front. He had already attracted some attention with his short stories and plays. *Abigail und Nabal* was presented in 1913, and *Ritualmord in Ungarn*, written in 1914; it was revised and produced four years later as *Die Sendung Semaels* by Max Reinhardt in Berlin. After a successful tour in Germany and Austria, the play received the Kleist Prize in 1915.

After the war Zweig lived in Bavaria. His war novel *The Case of Sergeant Grischa*, which appeared after Adolf Hitler's putsch of 1923, compelled him to leave his home in Starnberg. The novel is a powerful story about a Russian sergeant who falls victim to the power of the Prussian war machine. As a study of war and the individual, the book ranks as Zweig's best and has won a place as one of the outstanding war novels in modern literature. It demonstrates Zweig's progress from a concern with the problems of young intellectuals to an absorption in the inner lives of persons confronting situations in which their entire systems of values are upset.

The books of the Grischa cycle, which also includes *Young Woman of 1914*, *Education Before Verdun*, and *The Crowning of a King*, are characterized by pacifism, antinationalism, and opposition to German imperial philosophy. After the Nazis forced Zweig to leave Berlin in 1933 he traveled across Europe and settled in Palestine, where he became closely identified with the Zionist movement. At that time a serious eye disease forced him to dictate his books, including *Education Before Verdun*, the manuscript of which was destroyed when he left Berlin. Many of Zweig's essays and some of his novels and plays show his concern for the Zionist cause; *De Vriendt Goes Home*, set in Palestine and centering on the Jewish problem, expresses growing aversion to Zionist nationalism.

Increasing conversion to Marxism brought him to East Berlin in 1948, where he remained for the rest of his life. There he won prizes and other honors from the Communist government and served as president of the East German Academy of Letters. His communism and rejection of Israeli nationalism coincided with a marked loss of appreciation of him and his work on the part of American scholars and the public.

Ralph L. Langenheim, Jr.

Bibliography

Feuchtwanger, Lion. "*The Case of Sergeant Grischa*: Germany's First Great War Novel." Chicago Tribune, December 1, 1928, sec. 2, p. 21. An insightful review by a noted German novelist.

Fishman, Solomon. "The War Novels of Arnold Zweig." *Sewanee Review* 49, no. 4 (October/December, 1941): 433-451. An overview of Zweig's war novels published before 1941. Provides the best place for the general reader to begin further study.

Freud, Sigmund, and Arnold Zweig. *The Letters of Sigmund Freud and Arnold Zweig*. Edited by Ernst L. Freud. New York: Harcourt, Brace & World, 1970. An informative source.

Kahn, Lothar. "Arnold Zweig: From Zionism to Marxism." In *Mirrors of the Jewish Mind: A Gallery of Portraits of European Jewish Writers of Our Time*. New York: T. Yoseloff, 1968. Analyzes Zweig's philosophic evolution and his impact.

Salamon, George. *Arnold Zweig*. New York: Twayne, 1975. A comprehensive treatment of Zweig's works in English. The bulk of the book explores Zweig's war novels. An excellent overview for the general reader. Also contains biographical information on Zweig and a brief bibliography.

White, Ray Lewis. *Arnold Zweig in the U.S.A.* New York: Peter Lang, 1986. Reprints many American reviews of English translations of Zweig's works and evaluates his changing reputation in the United States.

Cyclopedia
of
WORLD AUTHORS

TIME LINE

early eighth century B.C.E.	Homer, 1533
700 B.C.E.	Hesiod, 1481
630 B.C.E.	Sappho, 2750
620 B.C.E.	Aesop, 26
571 B.C.E.	Anacreon, 93
551 B.C.E.	Confucius, 673
525 B.C.E.	Aeschylus, 24
518 B.C.E.	Pindar, 2483
500 B.C.E.	Vālmīki, 3175
496 B.C.E.	Sophocles, 2932
485 B.C.E.	Euripides, 989
484 B.C.E.	Herodotus, 1475
470 B.C.E.	Socrates, 2921
459 B.C.E.	Thucydides, 3095
450 B.C.E.	Aristophanes, 126
431 B.C.E.	Xenophon, 3400
427 B.C.E.	Plato, 2497
384 B.C.E.	Aristotle, 128 Demosthenes, 805
342 B.C.E.	Menander, 2163
308 B.C.E.	Theocritus, 3079
305 B.C.E.	Callimachus, 512
254 B.C.E.	Plautus, 2500
second century B.C.E.	Bion, 312
190 B.C.E.	Terence, 3073
175 B.C.E.	Moschus, 2259
140 B.C.E.	Meleager, 2160
106 B.C.E.	Cicero, 624
100 B.C.E.	Caesar, Julius, 501 Kālidāsa, 1693 Sudraka, 3026
98 B.C.E.	Lucretius, 1989
85 B.C.E.	Catullus, 562
70 B.C.E.	Vergil, 3191
65 B.C.E.	Horace, 1542
59 B.C.E.	Livy, 1946
57 B.C.E.	Propertius, Sextus, 2552
43 B.C.E.	Ovid, 2407
4 B.C.E.	Seneca the Younger, 2815
early to mid-first century C.E.	Longinus, 1960
20 C.E.	Petronius, 2471
34 C.E.	Persius, 2468
38 C.E.	Martial, 2123
39 C.E.	Lucan, 1985
45 C.E.	Statius, 2963
46 C.E.	Plutarch, 2502
55 C.E.	Epictetus, 975
56 C.E.	Tacitus, 3047
60 C.E.	Juvenal, 1688
61 C.E.	Pliny the Younger, 2501
69 C.E.	Suetonius, 3027
120 C.E.	Lucian, 1989
121 C.E.	Marcus Aurelius, 2105
124 C.E.	Apuleius, Lucius, 119
third century C.E.	Longus, 1964
213	Longinus, Cassius, 1962
354	Augustine, Saint, 166
480	Boethius, 340
701	Li Bo, 1930 Wang Wei, 3243
712	Du Fu, 880
825	Ariwara no Narihira, 129
978	Murasaki Shikibu, 2280
1048	Omar Khayyám, 2383
1079	Abelard, Peter, 4
1100	Geoffrey of Monmouth, 1183
1150	Chrétien de Troyes, 612 Marie de France, 2108
1160	Hartmann von Aue, 1411
1170	Wolfram von Eschenbach, 3375
1178	Snorri Sturluson, 2917
1200	Layamon, 1866
1210	Gottfried von Strassburg, 1269
1215	Guillaume de Lorris, 1327
1224	Thomas Aquinas, 3087
1240	Jean de Meung, 1327
1254	Polo, Marco, 2512
1265	Dante, 755
1290	Shi Naian, 2853
1303	Gao Ming, 1150
1304	Petrarch, 2470

TIME LINE

Year	Author
1584	Beaumont, Francis, 250
1585	Rowley, William, 2691
1586	Ford, John, 1058
1588	Hobbes, Thomas, 1514 Wither, George, 3360
1590	Bradford, William, 388 Brome, Richard, 417
1591	Herrick, Robert, 1477
1593	Herbert, George, 1467 Walton, Izaak, 3241
1594	Carew, Thomas, 533
1596	Descartes, René, 814 Shirley, James, 2855
1600	Calderón de la Barca, Pedro, 505
1605	Browne, Sir Thomas, 441
1606	Corneille, Pierre, 698 Davenant, Sir William, 763 Waller, Edmund, 3234
1607	Scudéry, Madeleine de, 2803
1608	Fuller, Thomas, 1124 Milton, John, 2203
1609	Clarendon, Edward Hyde, earl of, 631 Suckling, Sir John, 3022
1612	Bradstreet, Anne, 392 Butler, Samuel (1612-1680), 486 Crashaw, Richard, 720
1613	La Rochefoucauld, François, 1849
1618	Cowley, Abraham, 711 Lovelace, Richard, 1974
1619	Cyrano de Bergerac, 744
1620	Evelyn, John, 992
1621	Grimmelshausen, Hans Jakob Christoffel von, 1319 La Fontaine, Jean de, 1823 Marvell, Andrew, 2129
1622	Molière, 2220 Vaughan, Henry, 3184
1623	Pascal, Blaise, 2431
1626	Aubrey, John, 157 Sévigné, Madame de, 2821
1628	Bunyan, John, 468
1631	Dryden, John, 878
1632	Locke, John, 1949 Spinoza, Baruch, 2950
1633	Pepys, Samuel, 2457
1634	La Fayette, Madame de, 1822
1635	Etherege, Sir George, 986
1636	Boileau-Despréaux, Nicolas, 345
1637	Traherne, Thomas, 3122
1639	Racine, Jean, 2579
1640	Behn, Aphra, 266 Pu Songling, 2558
1641	Wycherley, William, 3396
1642	Ihara Saikaku, 1598
1643	Newton, Sir Isaac, 2315
1644	Matsuo Bashō, 2141
1645	Taylor, Edward, 3062
1647	Rochester, John Wilmot, earl of, 2657
1648	Cruz, Sor Juana Inés de la, 734
1652	Otway, Thomas, 2405
1653	Chikamatsu Monzaemon, 604
1660	Defoe, Daniel, 785
1663	Mather, Cotton, 2137
1664	Prior, Matthew, 2547 Vanbrugh, Sir John, 3176
1667	Swift, Jonathan, 3040
1668	Lesage, Alain-René, 1898
1670	Congreve, William, 675
1671	Cibber, Colley, 623
1672	Addison, Joseph, 20 Steele, Sir Richard, 2965
1674	Crébillon, Prosper Jolyot de, 722
1677	Farquhar, George, 999
1683	Young, Edward, 3414
1685	Berkeley, George, 293 Gay, John, 1176
1688	Marivaux, 2109 Pope, Alexander, 2518 Swedenborg, Emanuel, 3035
1689	Montesquieu, Charles-Louis de Secondat, 2231 Richardson, Samuel, 2629
1694	Chesterfield, Philip Dormer Stanhope, Lord, 601 Voltaire, 3212
1697	Prévost, Abbé, 2541
1700	Thomson, James, 3092
1703	Brooke, Henry, 423 Edwards, Jonathan, 928
1706	Franklin, Benjamin, 1081
1707	Fielding, Henry, 1021 Goldoni, Carlo, 1242
1709	Johnson, Samuel, 1661

1783	Irving, Washington, 1610 Stendhal, 2979
1784	Hunt, Leigh, 1581 Morier, James Justinian, 2249
1785	De Quincey, Thomas, 806 Grimm, Jacob, 1317 Manzoni, Alessandro, 2101 Peacock, Thomas Love, 2448
1786	Crockett, David, 729 Grimm, Wilhelm, 1317 Haydon, Benjamin Robert, 1426
1787	Mitford, Mary Russell, 2216
1788	Byron, George Gordon, Lord, 495 Eichendorff, Joseph von, 937 Ingoldsby, Thomas, 1602 Schopenhauer, Arthur, 2784
1789	Cooper, James Fenimore, 691 Scott, Michael, 2799
1790	Lamartine, Alphonse de, 1831 Longstreet, Augustus Baldwin, 1963
1791	Grillparzer, Franz, 1315
1792	Eckermann, Johann Peter, 920 Marryat, Frederick, 2119 Shelley, Percy Bysshe, 2843
1793	Clare, John, 630
1794	Bryant, William Cullen, 446 Carleton, William, 536
1795	Carlyle, Thomas, 537 Keats, John, 1713 Kennedy, John Pendleton, 1732 Thompson, Daniel Pierce, 3087
1796	Prescott, William Hickling, 2539
1797	Heine, Heinrich, 1446 Horton, George Moses, 1551 Lover, Samuel, 1974 Shelley, Mary Wollstonecraft, 2842 Vigny, Alfred de, 3197
1798	Leopardi, Giacomo, 1894
1799	Balzac, Honoré de, 193 Pushkin, Alexander, 2562
1800	Macaulay, Thomas Babington, 2001 Vörösmarty, Mihály, 3217
1801	Newman, John Henry, 2314
1802	Dumas, Alexandre, *père*, 891 Hugo, Victor, 1574 Lönnrot, Elias, 1964
1803	Beddoes, Thomas Lovell, 261 Borrow, George Henry, 364 Bulwer-Lytton, Edward, 465 Emerson, Ralph Waldo, 963 Griffin, Gerald, 1313 Heredia, José María de, 1471 Mérimée, Prosper, 2170 Surtees, Robert Smith, 3031
1804	Disraeli, Benjamin, 834 Hawthorne, Nathaniel, 1422 Mörike, Eduard, 2250 Sainte-Beuve, Charles-Augustinp, 2727 Sand, George, 2742 Sue, Eugène, 3026
1805	Ainsworth, William Harrison, 34 Andersen, Hans Christian, 96 Stifter, Adalbert, 2989 Tocqueville, Alexis de, 3101
1806	Bird, Robert Montgomery, 314 Browning, Elizabeth Barrett, 442 Lever, Charles James, 1908 Mill, John Stuart, 2185 Simms, William Gilmore, 2878
1807	Longfellow, Henry Wadsworth, 1959 Whittier, John Greenleaf, 3309
1808	Nerval, Gérard de, 2312 Wilson, Harriet E., 3351
1809	Darwin, Charles, 760 FitzGerald, Edward, 1031 Gogol, Nikolai, 1235 Holmes, Oliver Wendell, 1531 Lincoln, Abraham, 1932 Poe, Edgar Allan, 2505 Tennyson, Alfred, Lord, 3071
1810	Fuller, Margaret, 1120 Gaskell, Elizabeth, 1170 Musset, Alfred de, 2288
1811	Gautier, Théophile, 1174 Stowe, Harriet Beecher, 3006 Thackeray, William Makepeace, 3077
1812	Browning, Robert, 443 Conscience, Hendrik, 684 Delany, Martin Robison, 794 Dickens, Charles, 822 Goncharov, Ivan, 1248 Lear, Edward, 1869
1813	Büchner, Georg, 450 Hebbel, Friedrich, 1435 Jacobs, Harriet, 1620 Kierkegaard, Søren, 1745 Maquet, Auguste, 2103

1814	Brown, William Wells, 439 Le Fanu, Joseph Sheridan, 1882 Lermontov, Mikhail, 1895 Reade, Charles, 2597
1815	Dana, Richard Henry, Jr., 750 Stanton, Elizabeth Cady, 2960 Trollope, Anthony, 3135
1816	Brontë, Charlotte, 420 Freytag, Gustav, 1099
1817	Douglass, Frederick, 863 Mommsen, Theodor, 2225 Storm, Theodor, 3002 Thoreau, Henry David, 3093 Zorrilla y Moral, José, 3428
1818	Brontë, Emily, 422 Marx, Karl, 2130 Turgenev, Ivan, 3143
1819	Eliot, George, 945 Fontane, Theodor, 1049 Keller, Gottfried, 1717 Kingsley, Charles, 1756 Lowell, James Russell, 1977 Melville, Herman, 2161 Mowatt, Anna Cora, 2262 Ruskin, John, 2702 Whitman, Walt, 3307
1820	Anthony, Susan B., 115 Boucicault, Dion, 368 Brontë, Anne, 419 Engels, Friedrich, 970 Fromentin, Eugène, 1107 Multatuli, 2274
1821	Baudelaire, Charles, 238 Dostoevski, Fyodor, 855 Flaubert, Gustave, 1038 Nekrasov, Nikolai, 2308 Tuckerman, Frederick Goddard, 3141 Whyte-Melville, George J., 3312
1822	Arnold, Matthew, 133 Goncourt, Edmond de, 1249 Hale, Edward Everett, 1354 Hughes, Thomas, 1572 Murger, Henri, 2283
1823	Chesnut, Mary Boykin, 599 Parkman, Francis, 2427
1824	Collins, Wilkie, 663 Dumas, Alexandre, *fils*, 890 Valera, Juan, 3171
1825	Blackmore, R. D., 321 Harper, Frances Ellen Watkins, 1393 Huxley, Thomas Henry, 1590 Jókai, Mór, 1666
1826	De Forest, John William, 787 Gage, Matilda Joslyn, 1133 Mulock, Dinah Maria, 2273
1827	Coster, Charles de, 706 Trowbridge, John Townsend, 3136 Wallace, Lewis, 3232
1828	About, Edmond François, 5 Ibsen, Henrik, 1595 Meredith, George, 2165 O'Brien, Fitz-James, 2352 Rossetti, Dante Gabriel, 2681 Rydberg, Viktor, 2708 Taine, Hippolyte-Adolphe, 3049 Tolstoy, Leo, 3108 Verne, Jules, 3194
1829	Mitchell, Silas Weir, 2213 Robertson, Thomas William, 2651 Warner, Charles Dudley, 3246
1830	Cooke, John Esten, 688 Dickinson, Emily, 825 Goncourt, Jules de, 1249 Heyse, Paul, 1485 Kingsley, Henry, 1757 Mistral, Frédéric, 2208 Rossetti, Christina, 2680
1831	Davis, Rebecca Harding, 775 Leskov, Nikolai, 1899 Nievo, Ippolito, 2329 Raabe, Wilhelm, 2575
1832	Alcott, Louisa May, 50 Bjørnson, Bjørnstjerne, 319 Carroll, Lewis, 542 Echegaray y Eizaguirre, José, 919 Gaboriau, Émile, 1127
1833	Alarcón, Pedro Antonio de, 46 Lie, Jonas, 1931 Pereda, José María de, 2460
1834	Altamirano, Ignacio Manuel, 75 Du Maurier, George, 896 Halévy, Ludovic, 1358 Hernández, José, 1473 Morris, William, 2251 Shorthouse, Joseph Henry, 2860 Stockton, Frank R., 2991
1835	Butler, Samuel (1835-1902), 487 Carducci, Giosuè, 532 Twain, Mark, 3150

1836	Aldrich, Thomas Bailey, 54 Bécquer, Gustavo Adolfo, 260 Gilbert, W. S., 1198 Harte, Bret, 1408
1837	Eggleston, Edward, 931 Grimké, Charlotte L. Forten, 1316 Howells, William Dean, 1562 Swinburne, Algernon Charles, 3042
1838	Adams, Henry, 14 Bryce, James Bryce, Viscount, 448 Muir, John, 2268 Tourgée, Albion Winegar, 3117
1839	De Morgan, William, 804 Herne, James A., 1474 Machado de Assis, Joaquim Maria, 2032 Ouida, 2406 Pater, Walter, 2437 Sully Prudhomme, 3028
1840	Daudet, Alphonse, 762 Hardy, Thomas, 1386 Sumner, William Graham, 3029 Verga, Giovanni, 3189 Zola, Émile, 3426
1841	Hudson, W. H., 1566
1842	Bierce, Ambrose, 310 Fogazzaro, Antonio, 1047 James, William, 1631 Lanier, Sidney, 1843 Mallarmé, Stéphane, 2079
1843	Doughty, Charles Montagu, 857 James, Henry, 1626 Pérez Galdós, Benito, 2465
1844	Cable, George Washington, 498 France, Anatole, 1077 Hopkins, Gerard Manley, 1539 Nietzsche, Friedrich, 2328 Russell, W. Clark, 2706 Verlaine, Paul, 3192
1845	Corbière, Tristan, 696 Eça de Queiróz, José Maria de, 918 Spitteler, Carl, 2952
1846	De Amicis, Edmondo, 784 Eucken, Rudolf Christoph, 988 Sienkiewicz, Henryk, 2867 Westcott, Edward Noyes, 3296
1847	Jacobsen, Jens Peter, 1622 Mikszáth, Kálmán, 2184 Stoker, Bram, 2993
1848	Harris, Joel Chandler, 1397 Huysmans, Joris-Karl, 1591
1849	Gosse, Edmund, 1267 Henley, William Ernest, 1463 Jewett, Sarah Orne, 1646 Strindberg, August, 3011
1850	Bellamy, Edward, 270 Hearn, Lafcadio, 1431 Loti, Pierre, 1970 Maupassant, Guy de, 2146 Stevenson, Robert Louis, 2987 Vazov, Ivan, 3185
1851	Chopin, Kate, 610 Harper, Ida A. Husted, 1394 Jones, Henry Arthur, 1671 Ward, Mary Augusta, 3244
1852	Bourget, Paul, 370 Freeman, Mary E. Wilkins, 1093 Gregory, Lady Augusta, 1309 Moore, George, 2236 Peretz, Isaac Leib, 2463
1853	Howe, Edgar Watson, 1557 Page, Thomas Nelson, 2416
1854	Frazer, Sir James George, 1088 Rimbaud, Arthur, 2639 Wilde, Oscar, 3321
1855	Pinero, Arthur Wing, 2484 Schreiner, Olive, 2785
1856	Baum, L. Frank, 240 Frederic, Harold, 1090 Freud, Sigmund, 1098 Haggard, H. Rider, 1350 Shaw, George Bernard, 2836 Washington, Booker T., 3253
1857	Bullen, Frank T., 463 Conrad, Joseph, 680 Gissing, George, 1216 Gjellerup, Karl, 1217 Liu E, 1943 Pontoppidan, Henrik, 2516 Saussure, Ferdinand de, 2766 Sudermann, Hermann, 3024 Veblen, Thorstein, 3186
1858	Boas, Franz, 337 Chesnutt, Charles Waddell, 600 Durkheim, Émile, 909 Gourmont, Rémy de, 1272 Lagerlöf, Selma, 1827
1859	Aleichem, Sholom, 57 Bergson, Henri, 292 Dewey, John, 817 Doyle, Arthur Conan, 868 Grahame, Kenneth, 1278

Huizinga, Johan, 1576
Powys, John Cowper, 2535
Russell, Bertrand, 2705

1873

Azuela, Mariano, 174
Barbusse, Henri, 205
Cather, Willa, 560
Colette, 657
De la Mare, Walter, 791
Ford, Ford Madox, 1056
Glasgow, Ellen, 1218
Jarry, Alfred, 1635
Jensen, Johannes V., 1644
Onions, Oliver, 2392
Péguy, Charles-Pierre, 2454
Richardson, Dorothy, 2626
Tomlinson, H. M., 3112
Wassermann, Jakob, 3255

1874

Beard, Charles A., 244
Berdyayev, Nikolay, 288
Chesterton, G. K., 602
Churchill, Sir Winston (1874-1965), 620
Day, Clarence, Jr., 778
Frost, Robert, 1108
Gale, Zona, 1139
Hofmannsthal, Hugo von, 1520
Kraus, Karl, 1803
Lowell, Amy, 1975
Martínez Sierra, María, 2126
Maugham, W. Somerset, 2144
Montgomery, L. M., 2232
Stein, Gertrude, 2972

1875

Buchan, John, 449
Burroughs, Edgar Rice, 478
Dunbar-Nelson, Alice, 900
Futrelle, Jacques, 1126
Jung, Carl Gustav, 1684
Machado, Antonio, 2029
Mann, Thomas, 2093
Powys, T. F., 2537
Reid, Forrest, 2605
Rilke, Rainer Maria, 2637
Sánchez, Florencio, 2736
Schweitzer, Albert, 2795

1876

Anderson, Sherwood, 102
Beard, Mary R., 245
Duun, Olav, 915
Glaspell, Susan, 1220
London, Jack, 1956
Mofolo, Thomas, 2219
Rölvaag, O. E., 2665
Trevelyan, George Macaulay, 3129

1877

Beach, Rex, 243
Douglas, Lloyd C., 860
Granville-Barker, Harley, 1281
Hesse, Hermann, 1482

1878

Artsybashev, Mikhail, 142
Bowers, Claude G., 373
Coppard, A. E., 694
Crothers, Rachel, 732
Döblin, Alfred, 837
Dunsany, Lord, 904
Masefield, John, 2132
Molnár, Ferenc, 2222
Ramuz, Charles-Ferdinand, 2587
Sandburg, Carl, 2743
Sinclair, Upton, 2887
Walser, Robert, 3239

1879

Cabell, James Branch, 497
De la Roche, Mazo, 797
Fisher, Dorothy Canfield, 1027
Forster, E. M., 1065
Franklin, Miles, 1083
Grove, Frederick Philip, 1322
Hutchinson, A. S. M., 1586
Klee, Paul, 1778
Lindsay, Vachel, 1935
Singmaster, Elsie, 2892
Stevens, Wallace, 2986

1880

Apollinaire, Guillaume, 116
Asch, Sholem, 145
Bely, Andrey, 274
Blok, Aleksandr, 329
Hall, Radclyffe, 1363
Hémon, Louis, 1459
Hergesheimer, Joseph, 1471
Keller, Helen, 1718
Mencken, H. L., 2164
Musil, Robert, 2287
O'Casey, Sean, 2357
Stephens, James, 2981
Strachey, Lytton, 3007
Van Vechten, Carl, 3181
Yezierska, Anzia, 3410

1881

Colum, Padraic, 667
Jiménez, Juan Ramón, 1650
Lu Xun, 1983
Macaulay, Rose, 1999
McFee, William, 2023
Martin du Gard, Roger, 2124
Martínez Sierra, Gregorio, 2126
Neihardt, John G., 2306
Roberts, Elizabeth Madox, 2648
Teilhard de Chardin, Pierre, 3070
Webb, Mary, 3264

	Steinbeck, John, 2974
	Thurman, Wallace, 3097
	Waters, Frank, 3258
	West, Jessamyn, 3290
1903	Caldwell, Erskine, 507
	Callaghan, Morley, 510
	Connolly, Cyril, 679
	Cozzens, James Gould, 715
	Cullen, Countée, 737
	Duggan, Alfred, 889
	Edmonds, Walter D., 926
	Horgan, Paul, 1543
	Jackson, Charles, 1616
	Luce, Clare Boothe, 1987
	Mallea, Eduardo, 2081
	Niedecker, Lorine, 2326
	Nin, Anaïs, 2331
	O'Connor, Frank, 2361
	Orwell, George, 2401
	Paton, Alan, 2437
	Queneau, Raymond, 2572
	Rakosi, Carl, 2583
	Sargeson, Frank, 2754
	Simenon, Georges, 2874
	Stone, Irving, 2994
	Waugh, Evelyn, 3262
	West, Nathanael, 3292
	Yourcenar, Marguerite, 3417
1904	Birney, Earle, 315
	Campbell, Joseph, 519
	Carpentier, Alejo, 538
	Day Lewis, Cecil, 781
	Eberhart, Richard, 917
	Farrell, James T., 1001
	Gombrowicz, Witold, 1247
	Greene, Graham, 1302
	Hart, Moss, 1406
	Isherwood, Christopher, 1612
	Kavanagh, Patrick, 1704
	McNickle, D'Arcy, 2057
	Martinson, Harry, 2128
	Neruda, Pablo, 2310
	Perelman, S. J., 2461
	Singer, Isaac Bashevis, 2889
	Skinner, B. F., 2897
	Yáñez, Agustín, 3403
	Zukofsky, Louis, 3429
1905	Bates, H. E., 235
	Canetti, Elias, 524
	Enchi, Fumiko, 967
	Galarza, Ernesto, 1137
	Green, Henry, 1296
	Hellman, Lillian, 1454
	Koestler, Arthur, 1786
	Kunitz, Stanley, 1812
	O'Hara, John, 2371
	Patrick, John, 2438
	Powell, Anthony, 2529
	Rand, Ayn, 2587
	Renault, Mary, 2607
	Rexroth, Kenneth, 2610
	Sartre, Jean-Paul, 2761
	Schary, Dore, 2772
	Sholokhov, Mikhail, 2859
	Snow, C. P., 2918
	Trilling, Lionel, 3133
	Trumbo, Dalton, 3137
	Warner, Rex, 3248
	Warren, Robert Penn, 3251
	Williams, Emlyn, 3328
1906	Arendt, Hannah, 123
	Beckett, Samuel, 255
	Betjeman, John, 305
	Bonhoeffer, Dietrich, 356
	Buzzati, Dino, 489
	Carr, John Dickson, 540
	Empson, William, 965
	Icaza, Jorge, 1597
	Lindbergh, Anne Morrow, 1934
	Llewellyn, Richard, 1946
	Narayan, R. K., 2297
	Odets, Clifford, 2364
	Roth, Henry, 2685
	Senghor, Léopold, 2817
	Shostakovich, Dmitri, 2861
	Still, James, 2990
	White, T. H., 3303
1907	Auden, W. H., 161
	Barzun, Jacques, 231
	Carson, Rachel, 546
	Chase, Mary Coyle, 585
	Du Maurier, Daphne, 895
	Eiseley, Loren, 938
	Ekelöf, Gunnar, 939
	Eliade, Mircea, 943
	Fry, Christopher, 1110
	Godden, Rumer, 1225
	Grekova, I., 1310
	Heinlein, Robert A., 1449
	Hope, A. D., 1537
	MacLennan, Hugh, 2046
	MacNeice, Louis, 2055
	Michener, James A., 2181
	Moravia, Alberto, 2244
	Schaefer, Jack, 2771
	Shalamov, Varlam, 2830
	Stuart, Jesse, 3016

Hayden, Robert, 1424
Inge, William, 1601
Nims, John Frederick, 2330
Olsen, Tillie, 2380
Pym, Barbara, 2566
Rukeyser, Muriel, 2698
Schwartz, Delmore, 2792
Shapiro, Karl, 2835
Shaw, Irwin, 2838
Simon, Claude, 2879
Thomas, Lewis, 3085
Weidman, Jerome, 3269
Wilson, Angus, 3343

1914 Berryman, John, 303
Bioy Casares, Adolfo, 313
Burroughs, William S., 480
Cortázar, Julio, 702
Dodson, Owen, 842
Duras, Marguerite, 907
Ellison, Ralph, 956
Gibson, William (playwright), 1191
Hersey, John, 1479
Hillesum, Etty, 1503
Hrabal, Bohumil, 1564
Jarrell, Randall, 1634
Lockridge, Ross, Jr., 1951
Malamud, Bernard, 2075
Mauriac, Claude, 2149
Mitchell, W. O., 2214
Paz, Octavio, 2446
Randall, Dudley, 2589
Reed, Henry, 2602
Schulberg, Budd, 2786
Stafford, William, 2957
Thomas, Dylan, 3082

1915 Barthes, Roland, 230
Bellow, Saul, 272
Chu, Louis, 616
Fermor, Patrick Leigh, 1012
Gonzalez, N. V. M., 1252
Goyen, William, 1273
Holiday, Billie, 1527
Kantor, Tadeusz, 1697
Kazin, Alfred, 1712
Lawrence, Jerome, 1860
Lewis, Alun, 1917
Macdonald, Ross, 2017
Merton, Thomas, 2175
Miller, Arthur, 2188
Stafford, Jean, 2955
Walker, Margaret, 3229
Welch, Denton, 3274
Wouk, Herman, 3385

1916 Anderson, Jessica, 97
Bassani, Giorgio, 234
Cela, Camilo José, 565
Childress, Alice, 605
Ciardi, John, 621
Dahl, Roald, 746
Fielding, Gabriel, 1018
Foote, Horton, 1051
Foote, Shelby, 1053
Ginzburg, Natalia, 1207
Hardwick, Elizabeth, 1385
Hébert, Anne, 1436
Herriot, James, 1478
Hildesheimer, Wolfgang, 1496
Jacobs, Jane, 1621
McGrath, Thomas, 2026
Merriam, Eve, 2172
Murray, Albert, 2284
Oldenbourg, Zoé, 2375
Percy, Walker, 2458
Weiss, Peter, 3272
Yerby, Frank, 3408

1917 Anderson, Robert, 100
Auchincloss, Louis, 159
Böll, Heinrich, 350
Bowles, Jane, 374
Brooks, Gwendolyn, 428
Burgess, Anthony, 470
Clarke, Arthur C., 635
Davis, Ossie, 774
Gironella, José María, 1215
Lowell, Robert, 1978
McCullers, Carson, 2009
Metcalf, Paul, 2179
Powers, J. F., 2532
Roa Bastos, Augusto, 2645
Schlesinger, Arthur M., Jr., 2779
Taylor, Peter, 3066
Whiting, John, 3306

1918 Arreola, Juan José, 139
Elliott, George P., 951
Lee, Robert E., 1880
L'Engle, Madeleine, 1888
Morante, Elsa, 2242
O'Connor, Edwin, 2358
Rosenfeld, Isaac, 2677
Rulfo, Juan, 2699
Settle, Mary Lee, 2820
Solzhenitsyn, Aleksandr, 2924
Spark, Muriel, 2941
Spillane, Mickey, 2949
Sturgeon, Theodore, 3018
Swarthout, Glendon, 3034

Dumitriu, Petru, 897
Frame, Janet, 1075
Gass, William H., 1171
Herbert, Zbigniew, 1469
Kirkwood, James, 1772
Lambert, Gavin, 1835
Lins, Osman, 1938
Markandaya, Kamala, 2110
Miller, Isabel, 2192
Mueller, Lisel, 2267
Škvorecký, Josef, 2899
Tournier, Michel, 3119
Uris, Leon, 3166
Villarreal, José Antonio, 3198

1925 Aldiss, Brian W., 53
Astley, Thea, 151
Baker, Russell, 186
Booth, Philip, 360
Buckley, William F., Jr., 455
Cardenal, Ernesto, 530
Castaneda, Carlos, 556
Cormier, Robert, 697
Fanon, Frantz, 997
Gilroy, Frank D., 1204
Hawkes, John, 1419
Hillerman, Tony, 1501
Jones, Madison, 1674
Justice, Donald, 1686
Kizer, Carolyn, 1776
Kumin, Maxine, 1808
La Guma, Alex, 1829
Leonard, Elmore, 1890
Lispector, Clarice, 1941
Malcolm X, 2077
Mishima, Yukio, 2206
O'Connor, Flannery, 2359
Salter, James, 2734
Sinyavsky, Andrei, 2893
Spicer, Jack, 2948
Strugatsky, Arkady, 3015
Styron, William, 3019
Trifonov, Yuri, 3132
Tuohy, Frank, 3142
Vidal, Gore, 3195
Wain, John, 3221
Williams, John A., 3330

1926 Adams, Alice, 11
Ammons, A. R., 91
Berger, John, 289
Bly, Robert, 336
Buechner, Frederick, 457
Butor, Michel, 488
Creeley, Robert, 722
Donleavy, J. P., 844
Fo, Dario, 1045
Foucault, Michel, 1069
Fowles, John, 1071
Geertz, Clifford, 1177
Ginsberg, Allen, 1205
Heath, Roy A. K., 1434
Heilbrun, Carolyn Gold, 1445
Kirkpatrick, Jeane, 1770
Knowles, John, 1783
Konwicki, Tadeusz, 1793
Kops, Bernard, 1798
Laurence, Margaret, 1851
Lee, Harper, 1878
Leonard, Hugh, 1891
Lurie, Alison, 1994
Matheson, Richard, 2138
Merrill, James, 2174
O'Hara, Frank, 2370
Reaney, James, 2599
Shaffer, Anthony, 2825
Shaffer, Peter, 2826
Snodgrass, W. D., 2915
Wallant, Edward Lewis, 3233

1927 Abbey, Edward, 1
Ashbery, John, 146
Benet, Juan, 279
Coulette, Henri, 707
Davenport, Guy, 764
Grass, Günter, 1283
Herlihy, James Leo, 1472
Jhabvala, Ruth Prawer, 1648
Kahn, Roger, 1692
King, Coretta Scott, 1750
Kinnell, Galway, 1762
Lamming, George, 1836
Ludlum, Robert, 1990
Matthiessen, Peter, 2142
Merwin, W. S., 2177
Miller, Jean Baker, 2194
Nichols, Peter, 2323
Simon, Neil, 2881
Tomlinson, Charles, 3110
Walser, Martin, 3237
Wright, James, 3388

1928 Albee, Edward, 48
Angelou, Maya, 110
Brookner, Anita, 426
Chomsky, Noam, 608
Daly, Mary, 749
Dick, Philip K., 820
Fuentes, Carlos, 1115
García Márquez, Gabriel, 1156
Gardam, Jane, 1158
Guy, Rosa, 1338

1939
Allen, Paula Gunn, 68
Armah, Ayi Kwei, 131
Atwood, Margaret, 156
Ayckbourn, Alan, 172
Bambara, Toni Cade, 195
Banner, Lois W., 200
Bateson, Mary Catherine, 237
Bidart, Frank, 308
Breytenbach, Breyten, 406
Brown, Rosellen, 436
Chase-Riboud, Barbara, 586
Delaney, Shelagh, 793
Drabble, Margaret, 872
Fuller, Charles, 1118
Greer, Germaine, 1306
Haskell, Molly, 1414
Heaney, Seamus, 1429
Heat-Moon, William Least, 1433
Horovitz, Israel, 1548
McGuane, Thomas, 2028
McNally, Terrence, 2053
Oz, Amos, 2412
Paulsen, Gary, 2442
Taylor, Sheila Ortiz, 3068
Young, Al, 3413

1940
Banks, Russell, 198
Brodsky, Joseph, 416
Carter, Angela, 547
Chatwin, Bruce, 589
Chernin, Kim, 597
Chesler, Phyllis, 598
Chin, Frank, 606
Coetzee, J. M., 649
Galeano, Eduardo, 1141
Gao Xingjian, 1151
Herr, Michael, 1476
Heyen, William, 1484
Ingalls, Rachel, 1600
Kingston, Maxine Hong, 1760
Mason, Bobbie Ann, 2133
Medoff, Mark, 2157
Mitchell, Juliet, 2211
Mukherjee, Bharati, 2269
Nichols, John, 2322
Patterson, Orlando, 2440
Pinsky, Robert, 2488
Plante, David, 2494
Rabe, David, 2576
Sainz, Gustavo, 2728
Stack, Carol B., 2953
Toth, Susan Allen, 3116
Valdez, Luis Miguel, 3168
Villaseñor, Victor, 3199
Welch, James, 3275

1941
Bynum, Caroline Walker, 492
Collins, Billy, 662
Dante, Nicholas, 757
Dovlatov, Sergei, 866
Ehrenreich, Barbara, 934
Ephron, Nora, 973
Fox-Genovese, Elizabeth, 1074
Gould, Stephen Jay, 1270
Gray, Spalding, 1293
Jackson, George, 1617
Kristeva, Julia, 1805
Ortiz, Simon, 2397
Rice, Anne, 2620
Showalter, Elaine C., 2862
Theroux, Paul, 3080
Tyler, Anne, 3152
Wideman, John Edgar, 3313
Willis, Ellen, 3340
Wilson, Robert, 3354
Woiwode, Larry, 3366

1942
Allende, Isabel, 72
Asante, Molefi K., 143
Brenton, Howard, 402
Brito, Aristeo, 410
Crichton, Michael, 726
Delany, Samuel R., 796
Dorfman, Ariel, 849
Garner, Helen, 1164
Hacker, Marilyn, 1345
Handke, Peter, 1378
Hannah, Barry, 1382
Hawking, Stephen, 1421
Hill, Susan, 1500
Hospital, Janette Turner, 1553
Irving, John, 1608
Jong, Erica, 1676
Keillor, Garrison, 1715
Madhubuti, Haki R., 2065
Olds, Sharon, 2376
Rose, Phyllis, 2676
Smith, Dave, 2909
Smith, Martin Cruz, 2911
Voigt, Cynthia, 3208
Williamson, David, 3337

1943
Arenas, Reinaldo, 121
Auerbach, Nina, 164
Barker, Pat, 210
Barthelme, Frederick, 228
Carey, Peter, 535
Cheever, Susan, 594
Erickson, Carolly, 981
Galati, Frank, 1138
Gallagher, Tess, 1142
Giovanni, Nikki, 1210

Davis, Thulani, 777
Durang, Christopher, 906
Follett, Ken, 1048
Gordon, Mary, 1263
Hagedorn, Jessica, 1349
Johnson, Denis, 1655
Jones, Gayl, 1669
Kincaid, Jamaica, 1748
Pielmeier, John, 2478
Robison, Mary, 2656
Smiley, Jane, 2905
Swift, Graham, 3038
Turow, Scott, 3147
Wong, Shawn Hsu, 3379

1950 Alvarez, Julia, 77
Bradley, David, 389
Campbell, Bebe Moore, 518
Carson, Anne, 545
Esquivel, Laura, 985
Forché, Carolyn, 1055
Gates, Henry Louis, Jr., 1173
Ludwig, Ken, 1992
Mo, Timothy, 2218
Naylor, Gloria, 2303
Sayles, John, 2769
Sedgwick, Eve Kosofsky, 2806
Wasserstein, Wendy, 3256
Wilson, A. N., 3341

1951 Diamant, Anita, 819
Edson, Margaret, 927
Frazier, Ian, 1089
Gotanda, Philip Kan, 1268
Graham, Jorie, 1277
Harjo, Joy, 1391
Hempel, Amy, 1460
Hijuelos, Oscar, 1495
Hongo, Garrett Kaoru, 1534
Lucas, Craig, 1986
McMillan, Terry, 2050
Muldoon, Paul, 2271
Tolstaya, Tatyana, 3106
Vogel, Paula, 3207

1952 Adams, Douglas, 13
Baca, Jimmy Santiago, 178
Cunningham, Michael, 743
Dove, Rita, 864
Fulton, Alice, 1124
Henley, Beth, 1461
Hoffman, Alice, 1518
Hooks, Bell, 1535
Lesser, Wendy, 1901
Mistry, Rohinton, 2210
Mosley, Walter, 2260
Mura, David, 2279
Nye, Naomi Shihab, 2344
Ortiz Cofer, Judith, 2398
Phillips, Jayne Anne, 2476
Ríos, Alberto, 2640
Seth, Vikram, 2818
Shapiro, Alan, 2834
Soto, Gary, 2935
Tally, Ted, 3051
Tan, Amy, 3052

1953 Bhutto, Benazir, 307
Bogosian, Eric, 343
Boswell, Robert, 367
Castillo, Ana, 559
Chamoiseau, Patrick, 578
Collier, Michael, 660
Lee, Andrea, 1876
McDermott, Alice, 2013
Machado, Eduardo, 2031
Pinckney, Darryl, 2482
Schine, Cathleen, 2775
West, Cornel, 3289

1954 Cervantes, Lorna Dee, 572
Cisneros, Sandra, 625
Erdrich, Louise, 979
Fierstein, Harvey, 1023
Gaitskill, Mary, 1136
Ishiguro, Kazuo, 1614
Margulies, Donald, 2107
Moss, Thylias, 2261
Viramontes, Helena María, 3201
Wolfe, George C., 3369

1955 Cloud, Darrah, 646
Grisham, John, 1320
Kingsolver, Barbara, 1758
McInerney, Jay, 2036
Otto, Whitney, 2404
Song, Cathy, 2929

1956 Cary, Lorene, 552
Drury, Tom, 876
Everett, Percival, 993
Jen, Gish, 1643
Jin, Ha, 1651
Kadohata, Cynthia, 1689
Kushner, Tony, 1814
McKnight, Reginald, 2041
Ng, Fae Myenne, 2318

1957 Baker, Nicholson, 184
Espada, Martín, 984
Hamilton, Jane, 1367
Hornby, Nick, 1546
Hwang, David Henry, 1592

GEOGRAPHY AND IDENTITY INDEX

LIST OF CATEGORIES

ENGLAND

AUTHOR INDEX